DEBORAH LIEDER KIESEY
PRESIDING BISHOP

2014

WEST MICHIGAN CONFERENCE

OF

THE UNITED METHODIST CHURCH

FORTY - SIXTH SESSION

Calvin College

Grand Rapids, Michigan

June 11 – 14, 2014

Bishop Deborah Lieder Kiesey, Presiding Bishop
Greg Buchner, Annual Conference Secretary

OFFICIAL MINUTES & RECORDS

VOLUME 2

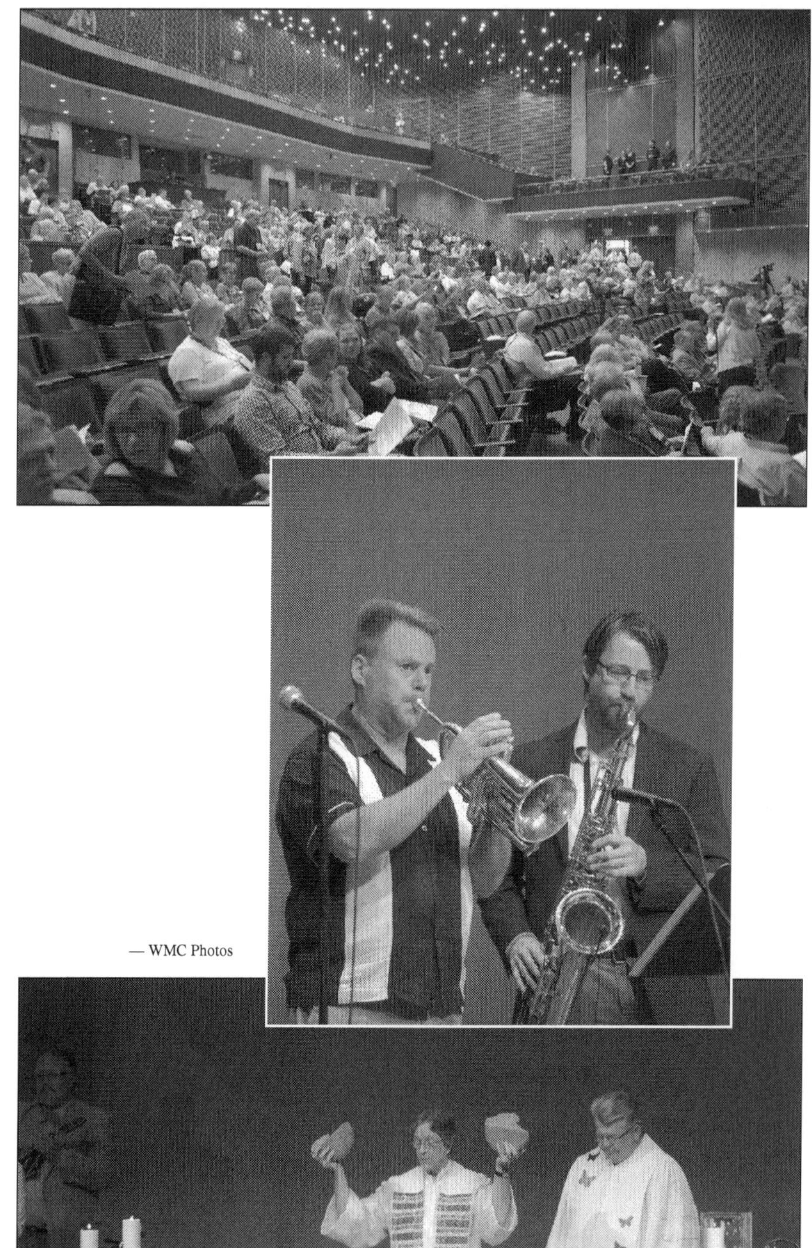

— WMC Photos

TABLE OF CONTENTS

I. OFFICERS OF THE CONFERENCE

RESIDENT BISHOP
Deborah Lieder Kiesey
Michigan Area, United Methodist Church
1011 Northcrest Road, Lansing, MI 48906
Phone: 517-347-4030 Fax: 517-347-4003
Email: bishop@miareaumc.org

EXECUTIVE ADMINISTRATIVE ASSISTANT TO THE BISHOP
Deana Nelson
Email: dnelson@miareaumc.org

CLERGY ASSISTANT TO THE BISHOP
Rev. William D. Dobbs
Email: bdobbs@miareaumc.org

EXECUTIVE ADMIN. ASSISTANT TO CLERGY ASSISTANT TO THE BISHOP
Jennifer Weaver
Email: jweaver@miareaumc.org

ACCOUNTS RECEIVABLE AND DATABASE MANAGER
Stuart Hallgren
Email: shallgren@miareaumc.org

MICHIGAN AREA COMMUNICATIONS
Mark Doyal, Director of Communications mark@miareaumc.org
Jim Searls, Web Administrator jim@miareaumc.org
Kay DeMoss, Senior Writer for Area Online Publications kay@miareaumc.org
Valerie Celestin-Mossman, MIConnect Editor valerie@miareaumc.org

DISTRICT SUPERINTENDENTS

ALBION: **Tamara S. Williams** dstamara@albiondistrict.org
Administrative Assistant: **Sarah Gillette** office@albiondistrict.org
600 E. Michigan Ave., Albion 49224-1849
Phone: 517-629-8150; Fax: 517-629-8230

GRAND RAPIDS: **William E. Haggard** billh5955@comcast.net
Administrative Assistant: **Elizabeth M. Bode** GRdistrict@wmcumc.org
11 Fuller, SE, PO Box 6247, Grand Rapids 49516-6247
Phone: 616-459-4503; Toll Free: 888-217-1905; Fax: 616-459-0242

GRAND TRAVERSE: **Anita K. Hahn** glue4evr@yahoo.com
Administrative Assistant: **Jill Haney** gtdistrictoffice@tcchrist.com
1249 Three Mile Rd., Traverse City 49696-8307
Phone: 231-947-5281; Fax: 231-947-0181

HEARTLAND: **David F. Hills** dsdave@umcheartland.org
Administrative Assistant: **Melanie Zalewski** office@umcheartland.org
1400 S. Washington St., Mt. Pleasant 48858-4268
Phone: 989-773-5140; Fax: 989-775-6599

KALAMAZOO: **John W. Boley** john@kazoodistumc.org
Administrative Assistant: **Mandana Nordbrock** mandana@kazoodistumc.org
810 Rankin Ave., Suite B, Kalamazoo 49006-5644
Phone: 269-372-7525; (800) 596-0739; Fax: 269-372-7644

LANSING: **Kennetha J. Bigham-Tsai** lansingds@miareaumc.org
Administrative Assistant: **Sus'ann Busley** lansingdistrict@miareaumc.org
2111 University Park Dr., Suite 500, Okemos 48864-6907
Phone: 517-347-4173; Fax: 517-347-4798

CONFERENCE SECRETARY
Greg Buchner
7296 9 Mile Rd., Mecosta 49332
Phone: 989 621-7782; Email: pastorgreg.ncd@gmail.com

JOURNAL EDITOR
Don Hiler
3123 Waterford NE, Grand Rapids 49505-3244
Phone: 616-363-6130; Email: dchiler@sbcglobal.net

ASSISTANT SECRETARIES
Jon VanDop — Head Teller
Joe DeLany — Ministry of Legislation
Blair Cutler — Ministry of Scribes (Minutes)

CONFERENCE TREASURER
Prospero Tumonong
P.O. Box 6247, Grand Rapids 49516-6247
Phone: 616-459-4503; Fax: 616-459-0191; Email: treas@wmcumc.org

CONFERENCE STATISTICIAN
Thomas Fox
1626 Lake Dr., Apt 189, Haslett 48840
Phone: (269) 921-5812; Email: preacher1947@yahoo.com

ASSISTANT STATISTICIAN
Ron Iris
Email: Ludroniris@aol.com

CONFERENCE CHANCELLOR
Andrew Vorbrich
151 S. Rose Street Ste 900, Kalamazoo 49007-4719
Phone: 269-381-8844; Email: AVorbrich@LennonMiller.com

CONFERENCE LAY LEADER
Anne Soles
PO Box 467, Pentwater 49449
Phone: 231-869-7651; Email: annesoles@charter.net

FACILITATOR

Laura Witkowski, 11 Fuller SE, PO Box 6247, Grand Rapids 49516-6247
Phone: 616-459-4503; Email: lauraw@wmcumc.org

DISASTER RESPONSE COORDINATOR

II. CONFERENCE OFFICE STAFF

Note: Names of Laypersons are **underlined**

11 Fuller SE, PO Box 6247, Grand Rapids 49516-6247
TELEPHONE 616-459-4503
TOLL FREE: 1-888-217-1905 FAX: 616-459-0191

DIRECTOR OF CONNECTIONAL MINISTRIES

Benton R. Heisler Benton@wmcumc.org

DIRECTOR OF NEW CHURCH DEVELOPMENT & CONGREGATIONAL TRANSFORMATION

Gary G. Step garys@wmcumc.org

ASSOCIATE DIRECTOR OF DISCIPLESHIP

Iris Naomi García naomi@wmcumc.org

EXECUTIVE DIRECTOR OF CAMPING MINISTRIES

George H. Ayoub georgea@ wmcumc.org

ADMINISTRATIVE STAFF

Laura Witkowski, Connectional Ministries Office Administrator lauraw@wmcumc.org
Kathy Hippensteel kathy@wmcumc.org
Pamela Stewart pstewart@wmcumc.org
Kiri Salazar reception@wmcumc.org
Scherry vanHartesveldt reception@wmcumc.org

CONFERENCE TREASURER'S OFFICE

Prospero Tumonong, Treasurer treas@wmcumc.org
John Kosten johnk@wmcumc.org
Russ Geske rgeske@wmcumc.org
Ann Buck abuck@wmcumc.org

UNITED METHODIST FOUNDATION OF MICHIGAN

David Bell President and Executive Director david@umfmichigan.org
840 W. Grand River Ave.,
Brighton, MI 48116 Phone: 888-451-1929

Wayne Barrett Senior Executive wayne@umfmichigan.org

Jeff Regan Senior Director of Stewardship jeff@umfmichigan.org

Marian Coles Operations Manager marian@umfmichigan.org

Kay Yoder Director of Accounting Services, MI Area Loan Fund kay@umfmichigan.org

III. CAMPS, COLLEGES, WESLEY FOUNDATIONS AND OTHER INSTITUTIONS

UNITED METHODIST CAMPS:

Albright Park: Dennis Dull, Director albright.campground@yahoo.com
3156 – 190th Avenue, Reed City 49677 231-832-9094
www.albrightpark.org Fax: 231-832-3856

Crystal Springs: Dan Stuglik, Director crystal@locallink.net
33774 Crystal Springs Street, Dowagiac 49047 269-683-8918
www.crystalspringscamp.com Fax: 269-782-7167

Lake Louise: David Gladstone, Executive Director lakelouise@lakelouisecommunity.org
11037 Thumb Lake Road, Boyne Falls 49713 231-549-2728
www.lakelouisecommunity.org Fax: 231-549-2729

Lake Michigan: Nick Delaney, Director lakemichigancamp@gmail.com
5807 N. Ridge Road, Pentwater 49449 231-869-5317
www.LakeMichiganCamp.org Fax: 231-869-4890

Lakeview: Debra Steed, Director lakeview.campground@yahoo.com
5300 Cutler Road, Lakeview 48850 800-985-2267
www.lakeviewcamp.org Fax: 989-352-6038

Wesley Woods: Kenneth Brown, Director Ken@wesleywoodscamp.com
1700 Clear Lake, Dowling 49050 888-992-2267
www.wesleywoodscamp.com Fax: 616-721-8291

UNITED METHODIST-RELATED COLLEGES

Adrian College: Christopher Momany, Chaplain cmomany@adrian.edu
Valade Hall 133, 110 S. Madison St., Adrian 49221
www.adrian.edu 517-265-5161, ext. 4211

Albion College: Daniel McQuown, Chaplain DMcQuown@albion.edu
Ferguson Hall 103, 611 E. Porter St., Albion 49224 517-629-0492
www.albion.edu

WESLEY FOUNDATIONS

Central Michigan University

Charles Farnum director@cmuwesley.net
1400 S. Washington, Mt. Pleasant 48858 989-400-7214
www.cmuwesley.org

Ferris State University

Devon Herrell fsuwesleyhouse@gmail.com
Wesley House, 628 S. Warren, Big Rapids 49307 231-796-8315
www.ferrismi.wesley.org

Grand Valley State University

Greg Lawton
Wesley Fellowship @ GVSU wesleygv@mail.gvsu.edu
4539 Luce St., Jennison 49428 616-805-5407
www.gvwesley.org

Kalamazoo

Lisa Batten lisa.m.batten@wmich.edu
2101 Wilbur, Kalamazoo 49006-5610 269-344-4076
www.wmu.miwesley.org

Michigan State University

Bill Chu wmwchu@gmail.com
1118 S. Harrison Rd., East Lansing 48823 517-332-0861
www.MSUwesley.org

HEALTH AND WELFARE INSTITUTIONS

Bronson Health Care Group

Bob Persenaire persenar@bronsonhg.org
Pastoral Care Dept. Box 48
Bronson Methodist Hospital
601 John Street, Kalamazoo 49007 269-341-6171
www.bronsonhealth.com

Clark Retirement Community:

Timothy T. Tuthill, Director of Life Enrichment timt@clarkretirement.org
1551 Franklin SE, Grand Rapids 49506-3331 616-452-1568
www.clarkretirement.org

United Methodist Community House:

Richard Clanton, Chief Executive Officer rclanton@umchousegr.org
904 Sheldon SE, Grand Rapids 49507 616-452-3226
www.umchousegr.org

—WMC Photos

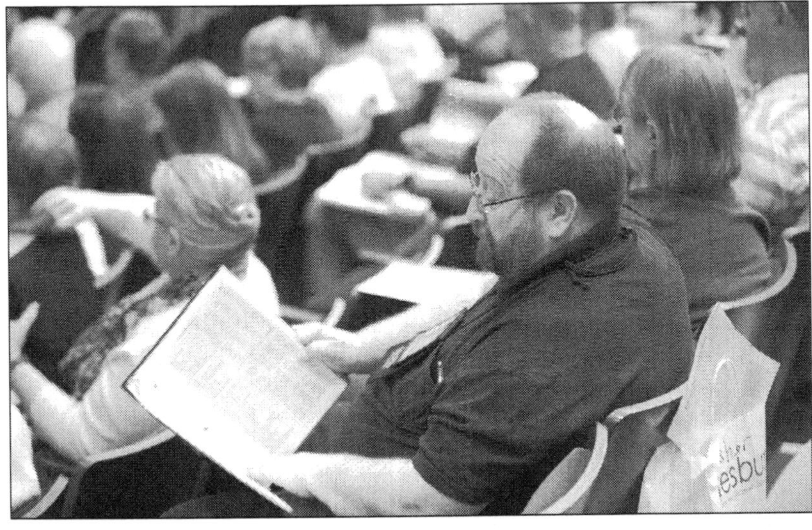

IV. WEST MICHIGAN CONFERENCE ORGANIZATIONS AND RELATED PERSONNEL

-- Date following name indicates year of election.
-- **Boldfaced** to show CNC nominations.
-- Names of laypersons are underlined.
-- Parentheses ( ) indicate elected by action of Annual Conference in 2014.
-- Two asterisks ** by name indicate chairperson.

ACRONYMS

AC: Annual Conference
CLT: Conference Leadership Team
CCOYM: Conference Council on Youth Ministries
CFA: Council on Finance and Administration
CNC: Conference Nominating Committee
COSROW: Commission on the Status and Role of Women
IWC: Area Indian Workers Conference
NCJ: North Central Jurisdiction
RELC: Racial Ethnic Local Church Committee
UMC: United Methodist Church
UMW: United Methodist Women
UMM: United Methodist Men

A. STANDING COMMITTEES

COMMITTEE ON AGENDA

Conference Facilitator: Laura Witkowski
Chairperson, Rules of Order Committee: Judy Coffey
Chairperson, Annual Conference Program Committee: **Nichea Ver Veer Guy
Chairperson, Committee on Reference: Anne Soles
Representatives, Conference Worship Committee: Jennifer Browne, Julie Liske
Director of Connectional Ministries: Benton R. Heisler

COMMITTEE ON JOURNAL

Members-at-Large (6) *(2 clergy; 2 laywomen; 2 laymen)*:
Sus'ann Busley 11 **(Robert Eckert 14)** **Merna Francis 09**
(Virginia Heller 14) ****Mandana Nordbrock 09** **Joyce Showerman 13**

COMMITTEE ON MEMOIRS

Merna Francis 13 ****Edrye Maurer 10** **Carrie Morton 13**

ANNUAL CONFERENCE PROGRAM COMMITTEE

The Bishop: Deborah L. Kiesey
Clergy Assistant to the Bishop: William D. Dobbs
District Superintendent selected by the Cabinet: David Hills
Host Pastor: Julie Liske
Conference Secretary: Gregory L. Buchner
Conference Lay Leader or Associate Conference Lay Leader: Anne Soles 12
Conference United Methodist Women President: Jenny Kroeze
Conference United Methodist Men President: _ _ _ _ _ _ _ _
Conference Council on Youth Ministries representative: Joel Fitzgerald
Director of Connectional Ministries: Benton R. Heisler
Director of Communications: Mark Doyal
Rules of Order Chair: Judy Coffey
Conference Facilitator: Laura Witkowski
Representative of Host Institution: _ _ _ _ _ _ _ _ _
Worship Representatives: Jennifer Browne 13, Julie Liske 14
Child Care Representative: Mary Jo DeLany 99
Board of Ordained Ministry representative: _ _ _ _ _ _ _ _

Members at Large:

Sharon Burkart 13 | ****Nichea Ver Veer Guy 11** | **(Devon Herrell 14)**
(Pigeon Hundley 14) | **Andrew Stange 13** | **David Wiltse 08**

Physical Limitations Representative *(selected by Cmte on Disability)*: Darryl Miller 14

COMMITTEE ON REFERENCE

Conference Lay Leader or Associate Conference Lay Leader: **Anne Soles
Chair, Annual Conference Program Committee: Nichea Ver Veer Guy
Conference Facilitator: Laura Witkowski
Director of Connectional Ministries: Benton R. Heisler
Conference Secretary: Gregory L. Buchner
Chair, Rules of Order Committee: Judy Coffey

COMMITTEE ON RULES OF ORDER

Members at Large (9) *(elected annually)*:

(Judy Coffey)** | **(Joel Fitzgerald)** | **(Bill Johnson)**
(David Lundquist) | **(Valerie DeLany 14)** | **(Mark Thompson)**
(Donald Williams) | **(Larry Zomer)** | **(Herb Vanderbilt)**

Ex-Officio:
Conference Facilitator: Laura Witkowski
Director of Connectional Ministries: Benton R. Heisler
District Superintendent *(for information only)*: Tamara Williams

B. CONFERENCE MINISTRIES

1. LEADERSHIP TEAM

	Position	Person	Gender	Clergy/ /Lay	Race	District
VOTING: Twelve to fourteen Voting Members, at least one of whom shall be a voting member of the Commission on Religion and Race (¶643.5):						
1.	Lay Leader	Anne Soles	Female	Lay	Caucasian	GT
2.	DCM	Benton Heisler	Male	Clergy	Caucasian	GR
3.	DS	David Hills	Male	Clergy	Caucasian	HT
4.	CFA	Susan Cobb	Female	Lay	Caucasian	GR
5.	At Large '08	**Rick Blunt**	Male	Clergy	Caucasian	GR
6.	At Large '08	**Bo Rin Cho***	Male	Clergy	Asian	LN
7.	At Large '09	**(Cori Cypret)**	Female	Clergy	Caucasian	GR
8.	At Large '09	**(Zach McNees)**	Male	Lay	Caucasian	HT
9.	At Large '10	**Andy Croel**	Male	Clergy	Caucasian	HT
10.	At Large '10	****Len Schoenherr**	Male	Clergy	Caucasian	AL
11	At Large '11	**(Dan Colthorp)**	Male	Lay	Caucasian	KZ
12.	At Large '13	**Chris Lane**	Male	Clergy	Caucasian	GT
13.	Bishop	Bishop Kiesey	Female	Clergy	Caucasian	NA
14.	Communications	Mark Doyal	Male	Lay	Caucasian	LN
15.	Treasurer	Pros Tumonong	Male	Lay	Asian	GR
16.	At Large (annual)	(Caleb Williams)	Male	Lay	Caucasian	KZ
17.	At Large (annual)	Patti Harpole	Female	Clergy	Caucasian	KZ
18.	Any person residing within the bounds of the annual conference with membership on the Connectional Table:	Kennetha Bigham-Tsai	Female	Clergy	African-American	LN

* Representing Religion and Race

CONFERENCE PERSONNEL

2. AGENCIES AMENABLE TO THE LEADERSHIP TEAM: CONFERENCE MINISTRIES

BOARD OF CHRISTIAN CAMPING

MEMBERS AT LARGE:

(_ _ _ _ _ _ _ _ 14)
(**Glen Kinder 14)
(_ _ _ _ _ _ _ _ 14)
Phil Hammond 12
(Tom McComb 14)
John Ward 12
(Michelle Hills 14)
Bill Polzin 11
(_ _ _ _ _ _ _ _ 14)

EX-OFFICIO *(voice but without vote)*:
Conference Staff: George Ayoub
District Superintendent *(for information only)*: Anita Hahn

BOARD OF CHURCH AND SOCIETY

MEMBERS AT LARGE (15):

(Emily Beachy 14)
(Kristin Harrison 14)
(David Knapp 14)
Bob Roth 12
Carol Voigts 13
Thom Davenport 07
Constance Heffelfinger 10
Clarice McKenzie 12
(Veroneze Strader 14)
Karen Wheat 11
John Fisher 11
Vern Jones 10
****Amee Paparella 13**
(Mark Thompson 14)
(_ _ _ _ _ _ _ _ 14)

EX-OFFICIO (VOICE AND VOTE):
Mission Coordinator of Social Action, Conference United Methodist Women: Joyce Mitchell 12
Conference Council on Youth Ministries Representative: _ _ _ _ _ _ _ _ _
Chairperson of Homeless Ministries *(CNC nomination)*: _ _ _ _ _ _ _ _
Conference Peace With Justice Coordinator: Ellen Brubaker
District Superintendent *(for information only)*: John Boley

CONFERENCE COUNCIL ON YOUTH MINISTRIES

YOUTH REPRESENTATIVES
ALBION DISTRICT: Sarah Gerke
GRAND RAPIDS DISTRICT: Valerie DeLany 13
GRAND TRAVERSE DISTRICT: Liam Wieringa
HEARTLAND DISTRICT: _ _ _ _ _ _ _ _
KALAMAZOO DISTRICT: _ _ _ _ _ _
LANSING DISTRICT: Rachel Krahulik

Conference Administrator: Joy Mills
Annual Conference Liaison: Joel Fitzgerald
Meeting Coordinator: Jorge Costales
Adult Workers With Youth Coordinator: John Scott
Conference Staff: Naomi García
District Superintendent: Tamara Williams

OLDER ADULT MINISTRIES COMMITTEE

CONFERENCE COORDINATOR: Laurie Dahlman 12
DISTRICT COORDINATORS:
ALBION: _ _ _ _ _ _ _ _
HEARTLAND: _ _ _ _ _ _ _ _
GRAND RAPIDS: Tim Tuthill 12
GRAND TRAVERSE: Betty Riggs 12
KALAMAZOO: Sarah McCall 12
LANSING: David Dekker
MEMBERS-AT-LARGE:
Wendy Clark
Lorraine Lancaster
Dave Meister
Gordon Schleicher
Clark Retirement Community: Anna Clifford
Representative, NCJ Committee on Older Adult Ministries:

BOARD OF EVANGELISM

District Secretaries of Evangelism:

Albion: Ed Ross 11
Grand Traverse: _ _ _ _ _ _ _ _
Heartland: Jon VanDop 10
Kalamazoo: David Meister 11
Grand Rapids: N/A _ _ _ _ _ _ _ _
Lansing: _ _ _ _ _ _ _ _

Members at Large (7):

Nelson Hall 10
(Patti Haas 14)
Chuck Hill 09
Bridget Huyck 13
David Rhodes 12
****Jon VanDop 13**
(_ _ _ _ _ _ _ _ _ 14)

Ex-Officio (voice and vote):

General Church Agency: _ _ _ _ _ _ _ _ _ _
Conference Council on Youth Ministries Representative: _ _ _ _ _ _ _ _ _

Ex-Officio (voice Only):

Regional Director of the Foundation for Evangelism: _ _ _ _ _ _ _ _

District Superintendent *(for information only)*: Anita Hahn

BOARD OF GLOBAL MINISTRIES

Members at Large (10):

Dwayne Bagley 13
Patricia Catellier 13
Julia Deemer 08
(Julie Elmore 14)
Jane Hoekwater 12
(Ruth Jones 14)
(Waltha Leavitt 14)
Vipin Singh 07
(Delberta Troutman 10)**
(Sandra Vandenbrink 14)

District Mission Secretaries (6)

Albion: John Williams 06
Grand Traverse: Mike Simon 14
Heartland: Kathy Shepard 11
Kalamazoo: _ _ _ _ _ _ _ _
Grand Rapids: Laure Mieskowski 14
Lansing: _ _ _ _ _ _ _ _ _

Conference Secretary of Global Ministries *(nominated by the Bishop)*: _ _ _ _ _ _ _ _
Conference UMCOR/Hunger Coordinator *(CNC nomination)*: **Robert Freysinger 13**
Conference Coordinator of Cooperative Ministries: Jodie Flessner 13
Mission Coordinator of Education & Interpretation, Conference United Methodist Women: Shirley Chappell
Coordinator of Bible Distribution: _ _ _ _ _ _ _ _ _
United Methodist Women Board of Directors: Nichea Ver Veer Guy 08
Conference Council on Youth Ministries Representative: _ _ _ _ _ _ _ _ _
District Superintendent *(for information only)*: Anita Hahn
Volunteer in Mission Coordinator *(CNC nomination)*: **(Gordon Schleicher 14)**
Chairperson of Hispanic Ministry: Stacy Mabus Caballero 11
Refugee and Immigration Ministries Coordinator: Shirley Freeman 12
Health and Welfare Ministries Coordinator: Wendy Clark 06
Urban Network Representative: Billie Dalton 14
Town and Country Representative: Linda Burton-Collier

BOARD OF HIGHER EDUCATION AND CAMPUS MINISTRY

Members at Large (12):

(Len Brown 14)
(_ _ _ _ _ _ _ _ 14)
(Mark Johnson 14)
(Sami Marasigan 14)
James McCartney 12
Zach Oaster 11
(_ _ _ _ _ _ _ _ 14)
Steven Snyder 11
Lyne Stull-Lipps 13
****Jeffrey Williams 13**
Christina Yalda 12
(_ _ _ _ _ _ _ _ 14)

Ex-Officio (voice and vote):

Chairperson or Representative of Wesley Foundation Boards of Directors:

Central Michigan University: Curt Jensen
Ferris State University: Dan Adsmond
Grand Valley State University: Manzel Berlin
Michigan State University: Bill Donohue
Western Michigan University: Blair Cutler

Chairperson or Representative from Albion College:
Chairperson or Representative from Adrian College:
Chairperson or representative of Wesley Fellowship at Grand Valley State University: ________
College student (1) *(selected by each local Wesley Foundation Board and church-related college)*:
Albion College: student
Adrian College: student
Central Michigan University: student
Ferris State University: student
Western Michigan University: student
Grand Valley State University: student
General Board of Higher Education and Ministry: _______
Conference Council on Youth Ministries Representative: _______
District Superintendent *(for information only)*: Tamara Williams

COMMISSION ON RELIGION AND RACE

RACIAL/ETHNIC PERSONS (8):

African American (4):	**(Lisa Gorman 14)**	**(Loretta Lee 14)**
	Shirley McKinney 13	**(Marshall Murphy 14)**
Native American (2):	**Scott Manning 07**	**Betty McBride 13**
Hispanic American (1):	**(Nohemi Ramirez 13)**	
Asian American (1):	**Bo Rin Cho 12**	

MEMBERS AT LARGE (4):

****Mike Johnson 13**	**Jane Knapp 11**	**E. Jeanne Koughn 13**
Vipin Singh 13		

NOTE: Out of all the above members each district shall be represented.
General Commission Member *(if any)*:
Conference Council on Youth Ministries Representative: _________
District Superintendent *(for information only)*: Kennetha Bigham-Tsai

COMMISSION ON THE STATUS AND ROLE OF WOMEN

MEMBERS AT LARGE (11) *(majority of whom shall be women; the chairperson shall be a woman)*:

Lou-Ellen Briggs 08	**Sue Emmons 13**	**Nancy Ham 12**
Julie Hane 13	**Daniel Hofmann 13**	**Judy Krchmar 11**
****Amy Latimer 09**	**Kathryn Strouse 11**	**(Mary Lou Vinson 13)**
Sue Yoder 08	**(________ 14)**	

Mission Coordinator of Membership Nurture and Outreach, Conference United Methodist Women (1): Sue Emmons 10
General Commission Member *(if not in members-at-large)*: _________
Conference Council on Youth Ministries Representative: ________, ________
District Superintendent *(for information only)*: Tamara Williams

COMMITTEE ON DISABILITY CONCERNS

Members-at-Large (10):

Mark Babb 10	**Carol Bunn 07**	**(Jean Christie 14)**
****John Huizing 07**	**Julie Lester 11**	**Darryl Miller 09**
Gayla Phillips 10	**(Richard Smith 14)**	**R. John Thompson 13**
Marjory Timmerman 13		

DISASTER RESPONSE TEAM

Conference Disaster Response Coordinator *(appointed by the Bishop)*: ________

District Coordinators (6) *(selected by district conferences)*:

ALBION: ________	GRAND TRAVERSE: Bob Freysinger 14
HEARTLAND: ________	KALAMAZOO: ________
GRAND RAPIDS: David Salisbury 07	LANSING: Bruce Wheaton 14

Volunteer In Mission Coordinator: Gordon Schleicher 14
Board of Global Ministries Representative: __________
District Superintendent *(for information only)*: Bill Haggard
Director of Communications: Mark Doyal

COMMITTEE ON HISPANIC / LATINO MINISTRIES

MEMBERS-AT-LARGE (10):

Tamara Brubaker 11
Randy Hansen 12
(Ivelisse Tiburcio 14)
(_________ 14)
****Stacy Caballero 11**
Jennifer Jue 13
Lea Tobar 11
Patsy Coffman 11
Ingrid Portillo 11
(_________ 14)

CO-OPTED MEMBERS *(maximum of 4; may be asked to fill the following positions such as but not limited to)*:
Training Coordinator: Nohemi Ramirez
Grant Application Coordinator:
Immigration Advisor:
EX-OFFICIO:
District Superintendent: Bill Haggard
Conference Treasurer: Prospero Tumonong
Director of Connectional Ministries: Benton Heisler
Staff employed by the Conference Leadership Team and assigned to the Committee on Hispanic/Latino Ministry: Sonya Luna

NEW CHURCH ESTABLISHMENT AND DEVELOPMENT COMMITTEE

MEMBERS-AT-LARGE (12) *(3 of these shall have been in the first 10 years of a new church start)*:

****Tom Arthur 10**
(Matt Bistayi 14)
James Lambrix 12
(Scott Otis 14)
Lisa Batten 13
Jay Brooks 12
(Heather Molner 14)
Matthew Stoll 13
Jean Bina 10
Kathryn Brooks 12
Ken Nash 12
Paul Thomas 13

Conference Council on Youth Ministries Representative: _________
Director of New Church Development and Congregational Transformation: Gary G. Step
District Superintendent *(for information only)*: Bill Haggard

COMMITTEE ON PRISON MINISTRY AND RESTORATIVE JUSTICE CONCERNS

MEMBERS-AT-LARGE (9) *(including at least 1 from each district)*:

Victor Asbury 10
Dennis O'Neill 10
John Waite 13
Dennis Hoag 12
Gary Peterson 11
(Beverley Williams 14)
****Richard Moore 10**
James Stilwell 10
(________ 14)

Conference Council on Youth Ministries Representative: _________
Conference Adjunct Staff for Prison and Restorative Justice Ministries: ________
District Superintendent *(for information only)*: Bill Haggard

RACIAL ETHNIC LOCAL CHURCH COMMITTEE

MEMBERS-AT-LARGE (11) *(nominated by CNC)*:

Barbara Brechting 07
Mary Lou Fassett 08
Mildred Mallard 11
(Enrique Ramirez 14)
Carolyn Davis 08
(Paul Hane 14)
Daniel Nuygen 13
Molly Tate 13
Daniel Davis 10
(Jane Lippert 14)**
Simmie Proctor 07

Conference Council on Youth Ministries Representative: _________
District Superintendent *(for information only)*: Kennetha Bigham-Tsai

CONFERENCE PERSONNEL

MICHIGAN AREA INDIAN WORKERS CONFERENCE

Executive Committee:
Chairperson: Norm Pigeon
Vice-Chairperson: _ _ _ _ _ _ _ _
Secretary: Valerie Maidens
treasurer: Valerie Maidens
West Michigan Conference Representative: _ _ _ _ _ _ _ _
Detroit Conference Representative: Carmen Misener
Youth Representative: _ _ _ _ _ _ _ _ _

Members-at-Large *(2 persons elected by each Native American United Methodist congregation; the pastor may be a delegate or alternate, as determined by the church):*

West Michigan Conference
Bradley Indian Mission UMC
Chippewa Indian UMC
Salem Indian Mission UMC
Greensky Hill Indian Mission UMC
Kewadin Indian Mission UMC
Northport Indian Mission UMC
PaWaTing MaGedwin Kikaajik (Native American Elders Program)

Detroit Conference
Oscoda UMC
Saganing Native American Mission UMC
Zeba Indian Mission UMC

Ex-Officio *(voice but not vote; on because of category)*:
Bishop: Deborah L. Kiesey
Cabinet: Anita Hahn
Director of Connectional Ministries: Benton Heisler

UMCOR / HUNGER COMMITTEE

Chairperson *(CNC nomination)*: ****Robert Freysinger 13**
Haiti Task Force representative: Dave Morton
Conference Disaster Response Coordinator: _ _ _ _ _ _ _ _ _
Members-at-Large *(8 or less) (named by the committee)*:
Wayne Disegna
Linda Tafolla
Nichea Ver Veer Guy
Nicki Holland
Melodye Surgeon Rider
Michelle Wisdom-Long
District Superintendent *(for information only)*: John Boley

3. AGENCIES AMENABLE TO THE LEADERSHIP TEAM: COMMUNICATIONS AND RECORDS MINISTRIES

COMMISSION ON COMMUNICATIONS

Members-at-Large (7):
****Carole Armstrong 11**
(Robert Huisingh 14)
John Warnock 10
Joseph DeLany 10
(Heidi Rawson 14)
Shelia Huis 12
Ken Vanderlaan 13

District Representatives:
Albion: Heidi Rawson 10
Heartland: Paul Thomas 14
Grand Rapids: John Warnock 07
Grand Traverse: Melody Olin 13
Kalamazoo: Burke Webb 13
Lansing: Shelia Huis 13

Ex-Officio (voice and vote):
Conference Council on Youth Ministries Representative: _ _ _ _ _ _ _ _ _
Ex-Officio (voice but without vote):
Any Conference Staff persons employed in communications or media tasks:
Michigan Area Director of Communications: Mark Doyal
Michigan Area Web Administrator: Jim Searls
Annual Conference Media: Andrew Stange
District Superintendent *(for information only)*: Kennetha Bigham-Tsai

COMMISSION ON ARCHIVES AND HISTORY

MEMBERS-AT-LARGE (7):

Lois Baumer 09
Betty Uithoven 10
(_ _ _ _ _ _ _ _ _ 14)
Lee Greenawalt 13
****Melanie Young 12**
Don Hiler 11
(Inge Kyler 14)

HISTORIAN: Dan Yakes
ARCHIVAL CONSULTANT: Lawrence Hall
EX-OFFICO (WITH VOICE AND VOTE):
Archivist: Nicole Garrett
Conference Council on Youth Ministries representative: _ _ _ _ _ _ _ _ _

4. AGENCIES AMENABLE TO THE LEADERSHIP TEAM: DISTRICT & LOCAL CHURCH MINISTRIES

DISTRICT COUNCILS ON MINISTRIES OR THE EQUIVALENT

Each district shall select/elect its own manner of organization as a District Council on Ministries to accomplish program ministries within the several districts. One person from each district shall be designated to work with those from other districts as needed.

COOPERATIVE MINISTRY COMMITTEE (CMC)

MEMBERS-AT-LARGE: ***(5 to 9 members) (At least one half the CMC shall be members or pastors of a church which is: part of a cooperative parish; on a multi-point charge; or a part-time appointment.)***

Mark Baker 13
****Jodie Flessner 13**
Molly Tate 13
Kim DeLong 13
Betty Kusterer 13
Jeremy Wicks 13
Bryce Feighner 13

District Superintendent: Kennetha Bigham-Tsai

C. FINANCE AND PROPERTY MINISTRIES

CONFERENCE COUNCIL ON FINANCE AND ADMINISTRATION

MEMBERS-AT-LARGE (15) *(majority of 15 to be laity; 5 from congregations of less than 200 members (elect their own chair):*

Kathleen Anderson 09
(Roger Bradshaw 14)
****Susan Cobb 10**
(_ _ _ _ _ _ _ _ 14)
Russell McReynolds 09
Brad Bartelmay 12
Pat Bromberek 13
(_ _ _ _ _ _ _ _ 14)
Susan MacGregor 08
Patrick Tiedt 08
Jim Bosserd 13
(Arnold Burke 14)
Nolan Hudson 07
Georgia Marsh 09
Molly Williams 13

EX-OFFICIO (VOICE BUT WITHOUT VOTE):
Bishop: Deborah L. Kiesey
Clergy Assistant to the Bishop: William D. Dobbs
Conference Treasurer: Prospero Tumonong
Director of Connectional Ministries: Benton R. Heisler
United Methodist Foundation of Michigan Director: David S. Bell
District Superintendent: John Boley
Conference Council on Youth Ministries Representative: _ _ _ _ _ _ _ _
General Council on Finance and Administration Member:

TRUSTEES OF WEST MICHIGAN CONFERENCE

MEMBERS-AT-LARGE (12): *(elect their own chair)*

(David Apol 14)
Lyle Ball 11
****William Gehman 08**
John Scott 11
James Baker 12
Michael Belt 11
James LeBaron 13
(Deborah Skinner 14)
Mark Baker 12
David Bloss 11
Cliff Radtke 09
(Carolin Spragg 14)

District Superintendent *(for information only)*: Kennetha Bigham-Tsai
Conference Treasurer: Prospero Tumonong
Conference Director of Connectional Ministries: Benton R. Heisler

CONFERENCE PERSONNEL

BOARD OF PENSION AND HEALTH BENEFITS

MEMBERS-AT-LARGE (12):

Wendy Clark 11 **David Dekker 08** **Deborah Fennel 10**
****Louis Grettenberger 09** **Joe Huston 12** **Norm Kohns 11**
Jennifer Loding 10 **(Kenneth Norton 14)** **Kelly Potes 13**
Eric Simmons 13 **Walt Urick 12** **(_ _ _ _ _ _ _ _ _ 14)**

General Board of Pensions: Patricia Gilleran
District Superintendent *(for information only)*: David Hills
Conference Treasurer: Prospero Tumonong
Advisor (Voice but no vote): Sue Graybill

COMMISSION ON EQUITABLE COMPENSATION

MEMBERS-AT-LARGE (12) *(equal number of laypersons and clergy; at least 3 racial/ethnic representatives; 1 layperson and 1 clergypeson from congregations of fewer than 200 members)*:

(Andy Baek 14) **Don Buege 12** **Bill Chu 13**
(Rob Cook 14) **DeAnn Dobbs 12** **Bill Dye 13**
(Jerry Hagans 14) **Patti Kozminski 11** ****Nancy Patera 08**
Connie Swinger 10 **Geraldine Wright 11** **(_ _ _ _ _ _ _ _ _ 14)**

EX-OFFICIO (VOICE AND VOTE):
District Superintendent: Anita Hahn
EX-OFFICIO (VOICE BUT WITHOUT VOTE):
Treasurer or Assistant: Russ Geske

D. HUMAN RESOURCES MINISTRIES

ABUSE PREVENTION TEAM

Paula Damkoehler 12 **Laura Foreback 13** **Benita Fyan 08**
Meg Goerke 13 **(_ _ _ _ _ _ _ _ 14)** ****Nona Spackman 06**

Conference Staff: Naomi García

COMMITTEE ON EPISCOPACY

Conference Lay Leader or Associate Conference Lay Leader: Anne Soles 12
Members at Large (7) *(4 of 10 shall be clergy; representation of racial/ethnic persons included)*:

(Gordon Barry 14) **Jennifer Browne 08** **Koom Cho 13**
Tom Clement 11 **Jay Hook 10** **Mary Jo Nye 11**
Jody Pratt 09

Selected by the Bishop (2):
(_ _ _ _ _ _ _ _ _ 14) (_ _ _ _ _ _ _ _ _ 14)
Ex-Officio - Members of Jurisdictional Committee on Episcopacy:
Laurie Dahlman Laurie Haller

BOARD OF LAITY

MEMBERS-AT-LARGE (2) *(1 shall be a clergyperson)*:
(_ _ _ _ _ _ _ _ _ 14) **(_ _ _ _ _ _ _ _ _ 14)**
Conference United Methodist Women representative: Phyllis Jackson 12
Conference United Methodist Men representative: _ _ _ _ _ _ _ _
Coordinator of Scouting: Keith Anderson 10
Conference Council on Youth Ministries representative: _ _ _ _ _ _ _ _ _
Conference Director of Lay Servant Ministries: **Jody Pratt 13**
District Lay Leaders:
ALBION: Max Waagner 11
HEARTLAND: Ned Weller 14
GRAND RAPIDS: Helen Reid 12
GRAND TRAVERSE: Denny Olin 14

KALAMAZOO: Wynne Hurlbut 13
LANSING: Deb Fennell 11
Conference Lay Leader *(chairperson)*: **Anne Soles 12
Associate Conference Lay Leader: ________
District Superintendent *(for information only)*: Tamara Williams

CONFERENCE AND DISTRICT DIRECTORS OF LAY SERVANT MINISTRIES

CONFERENCE DIRECTOR: **Jody Pratt 13**

ALBION: Victoria Fisher, Tresa Tulley-Yates
HEARTLAND: David Hanna 14
GRAND RAPIDS: Jody Pratt
GRAND TRAVERSE: Julie Lawhead
KALAMAZOO: Patrick McCrevan 14
LANSING: ________

BOARD OF ORDAINED MINISTRY

(Nominated by the Bishop) (term up to 3 quadrennium/12 years)

CLERGY:

Susan Babb 11	(________ 14)	(________ 14)
Martin Culver 08	Thomas Davenport 12	Mark Erbes 12
Jodie Flessner 11	Diane Gordon 11	Lyle Heaton 12
Mary Ivanov 08	Deborah Johnson 10	Jane Ellen Johnson 08
Margaret Jones 12	Jennifer Jue 11	E. Jeanne Koughn 12
Kathy Kursch 12		James Mitchum 12
Wade Panse 09*^	Dean Prentiss 08	Jeff Reese 11+
James Richie 08	Carolyn Spragg 08	**Sherri Swanson 12
Ronald Brooks 13	Kim DeLong 13	DeAnn Dobbs 13
Harris Hoekwater 13	Robert Hundley 13	William Johnson 13

LAITY:

Laurie Dahlman 12	Annete Erbes 11	Claire Hills 13
Allen Horstman 09	Phyllis Jackson 10	Steve Lett 11
Gerry Tibbits 13	(________ 14)	(________ 14)

EX-OFFICIO (VOICE AND VOTE) ¶635:1a
Chairperson of Board of Elders: J. Lynn Pier-Fitzgerald 13
Chairperson of Board of Deacons: Greg Lawton 13
Chairperson of John Wesley Assoc.: Jeremy Wicks 14+
Cabinet Representative: William Haggard 14
General Board of Higher Education and Ministry member:

** denotes Chairperson of Board
* denotes Chairperson of Conference Relations Committee
\+ denotes Licensed Local Pastor
^ denotes Retired Clergyperson

CABINET

BISHOP: **Deborah L. Kiesey
CLERGY ASSISTANT TO THE BISHOP: William D. Dobbs

DISTRICT SUPERINTENDENTS:
ALBION DISTRICT: Tamara S. Williams
HEARTLAND DISTRICT: David F. Hills
GRAND RAPIDS DISTRICT: William E. Haggard
GRAND TRAVERSE DISTRICT: Anita K. Hahn
KALAMAZOO DISTRICT: John W. Boley
LANSING DISTRICT: Kennetha J. Bigham-Tsai

FULL CABINET *(includes the above plus the following)*
Director of Connectional Ministries: Benton R. Heisler
Director of New Church Development and Congregational Transformation: Gary G. Step
Director of Communications: Mark Doyal
Conference Treasurer: Prospero Tumonong
Conference Lay Leader: Anne Soles

COMMITTEE ON LEADERSHIP DEVELOPMENT

Intentionally left blank as the Conference Leadership Team reviews this function and fulfills in alternative ways.

MEMBERS-AT-LARGE (8) *(nominated by the Cabinet)*:

(**_________ 13) (_________ 13) (_________ 13)
(_________ 13) (_________ 13) (_________ 13)
(_________ 13) (_________ 13)

Youth representative *(named by CCOYM)*:

CONFERENCE NOMINATING COMMITTEE (CNC)

MEMBERS-AT-LARGE (12) *(nominated by the Cabinet)*:

(Lisa Batten 14) (Barb Brechting 14) Melissa Claxton 11
Laurie Dahlman 08 Virginia Heller 10 (Minette Himes 14)
Harris Hoekwater 11 (Simmie Proctor 14) Don Spachman 13
Herb Vanderbilt 13 **Glenn Wagner 13 Ellen Zienert 10

EX-OFFICIO (VOICE AND VOTE):

President, United Methodist Women: Jenny Kroeze
President, United Methodist Men: _______
Conference Secretary: Gregory L. Buchner
Conference Lay Leader or Associate Conference Lay Leader: Anne Soles, ________
Youth (3) *(named by CCOYM)*: ________, ________, ________
Volunteer Adult Worker with Youth *(named by CCOYM)*: _________

EX-OFFICIO (VOICE BUT WITHOUT VOTE):

Director of Connectional Ministries: Benton R. Heisler

CONFERENCE PERSONNEL COMMITTEE

MEMBERS-AT-LARGE (9):

Eric Beck 09 **(Sandra Douglas 14)** **Virginia Heller 13**
Joan Hook 11 **Kathy Keating 13** **Georgia Marsh 10**
(Max Waagner 14) **(James White 14)** ****Ellen Zienert 10**

EX-OFFICIO (WITH VOICE AND VOTE):

Bishop or Clergy Assistant to the Bishop: Deborah L. Kiesey, William D. Dobbs
Director of Connectional Ministries: Benton R. Heisler
District Superintendent: William Haggard

JOINT COMMITTEE ON INCAPACITY

(¶ 652 in *2008 Book of Discipline)*

Representative from Board of Pensions: _________, _________
Representative from Board of Ministry: ________
Cabinet Representative: John Boley

E. OTHER CONFERENCE ORGANIZATIONAL UNITS

TRUSTEES OF MICHIGAN AREA ENDOWMENT LOAN FUND AND MISSIONS AND CHURCH EXTENSION TRUST FUND

[TENURE: Bylaw terms are limited to 9 years.]

Sheila Aleshire 07 **Nancy Craig 10** **George Fleming 10**
(David Lundquist 14) **(Pete Shelby 14)** **Marsha Wilcox 08**

Church Extension Staff Person: David S. Bell
President: Wayne C. Barrett

AREA HISTORICAL SOCIETY

Chairperson of West Michigan Commission on Archives and History: Melanie Young 12
Elected by Commission on Archives and History:
David Crawford 10 Ken Gackler 08 Dan Yakes 08 Merna Francis 08

EX-OFFICIO (VOICE AND VOTE):
Archivist: Nicole Garrett

TRUSTEES OF CLARK RETIREMENT COMMUNITY

(Reported only, election is by Clark, as per change in Clark by-laws.)

MEMBERS-AT-LARGE (7): *[TENURE: Bylaw terms are limited to 9 years.]*

**Charles Burpee 08 Mark Erbes 09 (Robert Gillette 13)
David Gombert 11 Marcia Haas 08 Karen Lott 12

TRUSTEES OF ALBION COLLEGE

[TENURE: Bylaw terms are limited to 12 years.]

[Stephen MG Charnley 07] [_________]

Area Bishop: Deborah L. Kiesey

[ ] Indicate names submitted for election of two by College in coordination with Board of Higher Education and Campus Ministry.

TRUSTEES OF ADRIAN COLLEGE

[TENURE: Bylaw terms are limited to 9 years.]

[Linda Depta 00*] Bonnie S. Garbrecht 08 Russell McReynolds 06

Area Bishop: Deborah L. Kiesey

[ ] Indicate names submitted for election of two by College in coordination with Board of Higher Education and Campus Ministry.

* Term extended by request of the Trustees of Adrian College.

METHODIST CHILDREN'S HOME SOCIETY DIRECTORS

[TENURE: Bylaw terms are limited to 10 years.]

William Amundsen 08 David Bennett 11 [Steve Lyon 11]
[Steve Dosca 00*] Steven Lett 07 Ruth Whaley 10

[ ] Names submitted for election of two by Children's Home.

* Term extended by decision of Directors

TRUSTEES OF LAKE LOUISE ASSOCIATION

[TENURE: Bylaw terms are limited to 9 years. Elect their own chair.]

(Dan Brubaker 14) (Lisa Carr 14) **Phil Friedrick 10
Inge Whittemore 09

Emeritus:

MICHIGAN INTERFAITH COUNCIL ON ALCOHOL PROBLEMS REPRESENTATIVES

William Amundsen Richard Braun Patti Cook
Ken Hoffman Robert Kersten George Lewis
John L. Moore Vernon K. Smith Mike Tobias
Executive Director: Linda Keefe

TRUSTEE OF METHODIST THEOLOGICAL SCHOOL IN OHIO (MTSO)

Jim Gysel 11

TRUSTEES OF BRONSON HEALTHCARE GROUP

2008 Floyd Parks

UNITED METHODIST FOUNDATION OF MICHIGAN

Directors (12) *(6 from each Conference, elected by the Foundation)*:

Class of 2015	**Class of 2016**	**Class of 2014**
**Joy Barrett (D) (11)	Lauren Frey (D) (11)	Ransom Leppink (WM) (12)
Roger Colby (D) (13)	Gary Glanville (D) (14)	Joe Perez (D) (12)
Karen Thompson (WM) (13)	Gary Haller (WM) (12)	Ed Ross (WM) (12)
Sue Woodard (WM) (11)	David Nellist (WM) (14)	Joy Stair (D) (12)

Ex-Officio (without vote):
President & Executive Director: David S. Bell
Senior Executive: Wayne C. Barrett
Resident Bishop: Deborah L. Kiesey
Detroit Conference Treasurer: David Dobbs
West Michigan Conference Treasurer: Prospero Tumonong

ADMINISTRATIVE REVIEW COMMITTEE

Gerald Hagans 12	William Johnson 12	Molly Turner 12
Reserves:	Ellen Brubaker 12	Richard Erickson 12

MISSION PERSONNEL COMMITTEE

(Appointed by the Bishop)

MEMBERS-AT-LARGE (4):

**Lynn & Kay DeMoss 09	Susan Hansen 01
Deborah Miller 02	Mike Tupper 11

General Board of Global Ministries member:
Conference Secretary of Global Ministries: _ _ _ _ _ _ _ _
United Methodist Women President: Jenny Kroeze
Haiti Task Force representative: Dave Morton

COMMITTEE ON GENERAL CONFERENCE PETITIONS

(committee was added per 2014AC legislation; names were approved by Conference Nominating Committee)

MEMBERS-AT-LARGE (8) (4 lay, 4 clergy):

(Kennetha Bigham-Tsai 14)	**(Laurie Dahlman 14)**	**(Deb Fennell 14)**
(Laurie Haller 14)	**(Benton Heisler 14)**	**(Mary Ivanov 14)**
(David Lundquist 14)	**(Ryan Minier 14)**	

OFFICERS OF THE CONFERENCE

CHANCELLOR
Andrew Vorbrich 10
CONFERENCE LAY LEADER
Anne Soles 12
ASSOCIATE LAY LEADER
(_ _ _ _ _ _ _ 14)
DIRECTOR OF COMMUNICATIONS
Mark Doyal 09

FACILITATOR
(Laura Witkowski 11)
CONFERENCE TREASURER
(Nominated by CFA) Prospero Tumonong 96
DIRECTOR OF CONNECTIONAL MINISTRIES
Benton R. Heisler 09

CONFERENCE SECRETARY

Secretary: **Greg Buchner 13**
Assistants to the Secretary (appointed annually):
Head Teller - Jon Van Dop
Head of Legislation - Joe DeLany
Head of Scribes - Blair Cutler
Journal Editor - Don Hiler

STATISTICIANS

Statistician: **Tom Fox 10**
Assistant to the Statistician (appointed annually):
(Ron Iris)

CONFERENCE PERSONNEL

F. DISTRICT COMMITTEES

DISTRICT BOARDS OF CHURCH LOCATION AND BUILDING

(Nominated by D.S. - elected annually by Annual Conference)

Albion District --
Mark Crawford 05
Rob Hughes 10
Larry Rizor 89
Jeff Hart 10
**Martin Overheiser 08
(Robert Stover 14)
Elaine Rice 10

Heartland District --
**Jim Baker 07
(Terri Bentley 14)
Melvin Houck 13
(Mark Baker 14)
Tom Bentley 12
Steve Pung 04
Lyle Ball 03
David Hills 10
Randall Roose 05

Grand Rapids District --
**David Apol 09
Roger Howard 04
Sue Norton 06
Dennis Bekken 12
Steve Meredith 09
Dave Turner 11
Luann Hoffman 13
Larry Nichols 12

Grand Traverse District:
Eugene Baughan 11
**Madeleine Mathieu 81
Tom Bowman 02
Lyle Matteson 11
William Maguire 03
Walter Urick 06

Kalamazoo District --
William Breyfogle 07
**Ron Hansen 05
Jeff Reese 09
Jay Brown 13
(Wynne Hurlbut 14)
Jo Slager 12
Gene Lewis 10

Lansing District --
Norm Austin 06
Jim LeBaron 06
(Lynne Stull-Lipps 14)
Mark Baker 06
(Paul Powers 14)
(Keith Treman 14)
(Tom Burchman 14)
(Jeanne Randels 14)

DISTRICT COMMITTEES ON DISTRICT SUPERINTENDENCY

(* Denotes District Superintendent's Appointment)

Albion District --
District Lay Leader: Max Waagner 11
Members at Large:
(Peggy Baker 14)
(Sarah Gerke 14)
Karen Scheetz 12
(Greg Wolfe 14)
Jane Case 13
Donna Gause 13
Ethan Stout 12
**Steven Young 11
Melany Chalker 13
Shirley McKinney 13
Max Waagner 11

Heartland District --
District Lay Leader: Ned Weller 14
Members at Large:
Linda Andersen 13 | Jane Duffey 13
Waltha Gaye Leavitt 12 | Anne Riegler 10 | Cindi Scheiern 13

Grand Rapids District --
District Lay Leader: Helen Reid 12
Members at Large:
Bill Bills 09 | Terri Cummins 12 | Marcia Elders 10
Joe Kohley 10 | **Aileen Leipprandt 09 | (Sami Marasigan 14)
Bill Rocker 13 | Jerry Selleck 12 | Jayne Thomas 10

Grand Traverse District --
District Lay Leader: Denny Olin 14
Members at Large:
(Peggy Boltz 14) | Al Bouda 12 | Tom Carey 12
Brian Highway 12 | Carl Litchfield 11 | Valerie Maidens 05
**Cheryl Peterson 12 | Ken Tabor 13

Kalamazoo District --
District Lay Leader: Wynne Hurlbut 13
Members at Large:
(Sheila Baker 13) | Lisa Coe 13 | Earl Collier 12
David Haase 11 | Tracey Hatch 08 | **Barry Petrucci 07
Wayne Price 08 | Ellen Rowe 13 | Deb Search-Willoughby 13
Burke Webb 11

Lansing District --
District Lay Leader: Deb Fennell 11
Members at Large:
**Bryce Feighner 08 | Deb Fennell 11
Jerry Granger 08 | Russell McReynolds 10
Marilyn Rothert 11 | Joyce Showerman 06 | Molly Turner 12

DISTRICT COMMITTEES ON ORDAINED MINISTRY

(Nominated by D.S., approved by Annual Conference)

Albion District --
Ordained Ministry Representative: _ _ _ _ _ _ _ _
District Superintendent: Tamara Williams 09
Pat Brook 10 | Judy Fuller 13 | Richard Kelley 03
Bruce Kintigh 09 | **Glenn Litchfield 13 | Edrye Maurer 10
David Morton 86 | Len Schoenherr 09 | Barb Vallieu 10
(Jessica Walsworth 14)

Heartland District --
Ordained Ministry Representative: Kimberly DeLong 13
District Superintendent: David Hills 10
(Terri Bentley 14) | Kara Lynne Burns 13 | Kimberly DeLong 13
(Charlie Farnum 14) | (Diane Gordon 14) | Rebecca Morrison 12
(Randall Roose 14) | Ned Weller 11 | Larry Wyman 13

Grand Rapids District --
Ordained Ministry Representative: _ _ _ _ _ _ _ _
District Superintendent: Bill Haggard 12
Jane Bosserd 13 | Barb Brechting 13 | Dan Davis 11
Bill Johnson 13 | John Morse 13 | **Tom Pier-Fitzgerald 07
Mark Thompson 09

Grand Traverse District --
Ordained Ministry Representative: James Mitchum 14
District Superintendent: Anita Hahn 11
Tom Ball 08 | (Jim Boehm 14) | Greg Culver 11

Barbara Fay 11
Charlene Heim 09
Debie Horn 12
Denny Olin 14
(James Mitchum 14)
Richard Morrison 13
**Dale Ostema 96
(Jen Smith 13)

Kalamazoo District --
Ordained Ministry Representative: Thom Davenport 14
District Superintendent: John Boley 14
(Gordon Barry 14)
(William Foust 14)
(Wayne Hurlbut 13)
James Kraus, Jr 14
(Leslie Lynch 14)
Rob McPherson 10
(Heather Molner 14)
Cliff Radtke 13
(Cyndi Trobeck 14)
Cara Weiler 13
Karen Wheat 12

Lansing District --
Ordained Ministry Representative: Jane Ellen Johnson 08, Lyle Heaton 13
District Superintendent: Kennetha Bigham-Tsai 13
Carole Armstrong 05
**Dwayne Bagley 10
Nancy Powers 13
Marty DeBow 07
Kathy Dobie 07
Lyle Heaton 10
Joseph Huston 12
Lonnie Lowery 08
Jane Ellen Johnson 07
Eric Simmons 12
Kathleen Smith 11
Colleen Treman 10

CONFERENCE PERSONNEL

REPORT SUBMITTED BY CONFERENCE NOMINATING COMMITTEE

Glenn Wagner, Chair
Melissa Claxton
Laurie Dahlman
Mary Lou Fassett
Virginia Heller
Harris Hoekwater
Don Spachman
Mark Thompson
Herb Vanderbilt
Ellen Zienert

G. WESLEY FOUNDATION BOARDS

CENTRAL MICHIGAN UNIVERSITY WESLEY FOUNDATION BOARD

Director: Charles Farnum, 1400 S Washington St, Mt Pleasant 48858, (989) 545-1761
Heartland District Superintendent: David Hills
Chair Conference BHEM: Jeff Williams
Student E-Board President: Kaitlyn Buzalski
Student E-Board Treasurer: Sean Griffin
Members at Large:
Jan Huffman
Curt Jensen (chair)
Meaghan McCollow
Katrina Piatek-Jimenez
Linda Wicander
Dianne Young
Bill Zehnder

FERRIS STATE UNIVERSITY WESLEY FOUNDATION BOARD

Director: Devon Herrell, 628 S. Warren, Big Rapids, MI 49307, (231) 796-8315
Board of Directors:
Dan Adsmond (06)
Christy Baker (05)
Lyle Ball (13)
Timothy Brotherton (10)
Jeff Jennings (13)
Ed Milan (13)
Beck Morrison (13)
Cathy Woolen (13)
Officers of Board:
President:
Vice-President: Dan Adsmond (06)
Secretary: Denise Jennings (13)
Treasurer: Karen Thompson (13)

KALAMAZOO WESLEY FOUNDATION BOARD

Director: Lisa Batten, 2101 Wilbur, Kalamazoo, MI 49006, (269) 344-4076
Representatives at Large:
2015 Sheila Baker
Tracy Farnsworth
Alex Lueth
2016 Tom Lundquist
Don Weaver
Paul VanWestrienen

2017 Gail Secord Deb Lindstrom Blair Cutler
2018 Larry Oppliger Jill Murphy Derek Andre Jerry Ditto

Wesley Foundation Students:
Paul Reissman, Sarah Goodenow

Ex-Officio Membership:
Wesley Foundation Director: Lisa Batten
Kalamazoo District Superintendent: John Boley
Senior Pastor, Kalamazoo First: Stephen Charnley
Associate Pastor, Kalamazoo First: Julie Kline
United Methodist Women, Kalamazoo First: Barb van Westrienen
Bishop Deborah L. Kiesey

Officers: July 1, 2013 - June 30, 2014
President: Sheila Baker
Vice-President: Gail Secord
Secretary: Jill Murphy
Treasurer: Tracy Farnsworth

MICHIGAN STATE UNIVERSITY WESLEY FOUNDATION

Director: William Chu, 1118 S. Harrison Rd., East Lansing, MI 48823, (517) 332-0861
Officers of Wesley Foundation Board of Directors:
Chair: Bill Donohue
Development: Lynn Stull-Lipps
Finance: Grovenor (Kip) Grimes
Personnel: Stephanie Sundhimer, Tom Fox
Building: Rick Erickson, Darby Harris
RSO President: Kaitlyn Szczypka
Representative of Lansing District UMW: Rhonda Crackel
Ex-Officio:
District Superintendent: Kennetha Bigham-Tsai
University UMC Pastor *(only 1)*: Jennie Browne

WESLEY FELLOWSHIP AT GRAND VALLEY STATE UNIVERSITY

Director: Gregory W. Lawton, 4539 Luce St., Jenison, MI 49428
Board of Trustees
2014 Cassie Trapp (Student President) Zach Oaster (Treasurer)
2015 Suzeanne Benet (Advisor)
2016 Manzel Berlin (Chair) Bob Kleinhans Don Graham
2017 Kinnith Gibbs

H. OFFICERS OF CONFERENCE ORGANIZATIONS AND ASSOCIATIONS

2014-2015 BOARD OF ORDAINED MINISTRY EXECUTIVE COMMITTEE

***Chairperson**
Sherri L. Swanson Three Oaks UMC, 2 Sycamore St E, Three Oaks 49128-1146 (269) 756-2053
***Conference Relations (Changes in Clergy Status)**
Wade S. Panse 1218 Riverwood Terrace, St Joseph 49085-2118 (269) 982-2920
***Registrar Full Membership (Elder's & Deacon's Orders; Ordination)**
Dean N. Prentiss Wesley Park UMC, 1150 32nd St SW, Wyoming 49509-2875 (616) 534-4411
***Registrar Provisional Membership (Elder's & Deacon's Orders; Commissioning)**
Kathleen S. Kursch Shepherd UMC, PO Box 309, Shepherd 48883-0309 (989) 828-5866
***Registrar Local Pastors and Associate Members**
Martin H. Culver 511 Landsdowne Ave, Portage 49001-0559 (269) 615-1360
***Registrar Certified Candidates, DCOM, Certification, Diaconal**
Lyle D. Heaton Christ UMC, 517 W Jolly Rd, Lansing 48910-6609 (517) 394-2727

***Support and Development Chair**
Jeffrey L. Reese Hope UMC, PO Box 624 Edwardsburg 49112-0624 (269) 663-5321
***Enlistment and Mentoring Chair**
Jane Ellen Johnson Grace UMC, 1900 Boston Blvd, Lansing 48910-2493 (517) 482-5750
***Secretary**
Carolin S. Spragg 1063 Gale Rd, Eaton Rapids 48827-9107 (269) 598-0266
***Treasurer/Loan Officer**
Diane L. Gordon First UMC, 400 S Main St, Mt Pleasant 48858-2598 (989) 773-6934
***Order of Elders Chair**
Lynn Pier-Fitzgerald First UMC, 57 W 10th St, Holland 49423-3197 (616) 396-5205
***Order of Deacons Chair**
Gregory W. Lawton Wesley Fellowship at GVSU, 4539 Luce St, Jenison 49428-9527 (616) 895-2235
***John Wesley Association Chair**
Jeremy J. Wicks 1956 N M 52, Stockbridge 49285-9625 (517) 851-7853
***Cabinet Representative**
William E. Haggard UMC WMC Grand Rapids District Office, 11 Fuller SE, Grand Rapids 49506 (616) 459-4503
***Laity Representative**
Laurie Dahlman 1228 Southern Ave, Kalamazoo 49001-4339 (269) 343-1490
***Annual Conference Ordination Service Coordinator**
Deborah M. Johnson 2849 110th Ave, Tustin 49688-8626 (231) 825-2580

CONFERENCE PERSONNEL

OTHER IMPORTANT BOARD OF ORDAINED MINISTRY CONTACTS

Counseling Funds
Jeffrey L. Reese Hope UMC, PO Box 624 Edwardsburg 49112-0624 (269) 663-5321
Continuing Education, Grants, Renewal Leaves, Sabbatical Leaves, Spiritual Formation Retreats
Allen Horstman 1750 Outer Dr W, Traverse City 49685-8832 (231) 946-9314
Mentoring Groups for Commissioned Candidates
Mary Ivanov Lake Harbor UMC, 4861 Henry St, North Shores 49441-5436 (231) 798-2181
Specialized Ministries
Susan J. Babb First UMC, 275 W Michigan Ave, Jackson 49201-2283 (517) 787-6460

JOHN WESLEY ASSOCIATION

Chair: Jeremy Wicks
Vice-Chair: --------
Secretary/Treasurer: Jon Pohl
Cabinet Representative: Tamara Williams

UNITED METHODIST MEN CONFERENCE EXECUTIVE COMMITTEE

President: [contact Mike Bremer until new president elected]
Vice-President:
Secretary:
Treasurer: John Huizing
Resident Bishop (honorary president): Bishop Deborah L. Kiesey
Conference Lay Leader or representative: Anne Soles
Prayer Advocate: --------
Hunger Advocate: --------
Albion District President: --------
Heartland District President: Mark Hann

Grand Rapids District President: _ _ _ _ _ _ _ _
Grand Traverse District President: John Huizing
Kalamazoo District President:
Lansing District President: _ _ _ _ _ _ _ _
North Central Jurisdiction President: Lee Donley
Cabinet representative: William Haggard

UNITED METHODIST WOMEN CONFERENCE EXECUTIVE COMMITTEE

President: Jenny Kroeze
Vice-President: Phyllis Jackson
Secretary: Linda Luce
Treasurer: Julia Paradine Rice
Secretary of Program Resources: Clara VanderLaan
Communications Coord/Highlights Editor: Dorie Litchfield
Spiritual Growth Coord: Simmie Proctor
Education and Interpretation Coord: Shirley Chappell
Social Action Coord: Joyce Mitchell
Membership Nurture and Outreach Coord: Sue Emmons
Committee on Nominations Chair: Meredith Richter
Nominations Members: Sue Franklin, Linda Darrow, Beth Mitchell, Bonnie Worley

Albion District President: Donna Smith
Grand Rapids District President: Connie Swinger
Grand Traverse District President: Julie Gasco
Heartland District President: Christy Baker
Kalamazoo District President: Adele Paxson
Lansing District President: Joyce Plumhoff
United Methodist Women Board of Directors: Nichea Ver Veer Guy
NCJ President: Ruth Whaley
Bishop: Deborah L. Kiesey
Cabinet Representative: Anita Hahn

I. WEST MICHIGAN CABINET SERVICE OPPORTUNITIES

2014 – 2015

Appointive Cabinet

President of the Cabinet .... Bishop Deborah L. Kiesey
Dean of the Cabinet .... David Hills
Secretary of the Cabinet .... Anita Hahn
Secretary of Audit/Strings .... Bill Haggard
Secretary of Inquiries .... Kennetha Bigham-Tsai
Secretary of Technology and Prayer Concerns .... Tamara Williams

Cabinet Representatives on Conference-wide Organizations

David Hills

*Conference Leadership Team
*AC Program Committee
*Board of Pensions and Health Benefits

Kennetha Bigham-Tsai

*Conference Leadership Team
*Communications Commission
*WMC Trustees
Racial Ethnic Local Church Committee
Religion and Race Commission
MI Area School for Pastoral Ministry
Cooperative Ministries Committee

Anita Hahn
*Equitable Compensation Commission
*Board of Christian Camping
Board of Global Ministries
Indian Workers Conference
Board of Evangelism
United Methodist Women

Bill Haggard
*Ordained Ministry
*New Church Establishment and Development
*Personnel Committee
Prison Ministries and Concerns Committee
Hispanic/Latino Ministries Committee
Disaster Response Team
United Methodist Men

John Boley
*Council on Finance & Administration
*Joint Committee on Incapacity
Board of Church and Society
UMCOR/Hunger Committee

Tamara Williams
*New Pastor Orientation
*Conference Council on Youth Ministries
*Higher Education and Campus Ministry
Rules of Order Committee
John Wesley Association
Board of Laity / Lay Ministries
Status and Role of Women Commission

*denotes committees of primary importance for DS attendance

Last updated June 14, 2014

—WMC Photos

J. GENERAL AND JURISDICTIONAL CONFERENCE PERSONNEL

(Elected in 2014)

(CLERGY) (LAY)

2016 DELEGATES TO GENERAL CONFERENCE

Laurie Haller **(248) 646-1200**
Birmingham First UMC
1589 West Maple
Birmingham, MI 48009

Nichea VerVeer Guy **(616) 451-7058**
125 Baynton NE
Grand Rapids, MI 49503

2016 DELEGATES TO JURISDICTIONAL CONFERENCE

(also Reserve Delegates to General Confernce)

Kennetha Bigham-Tsai **(517) 347-4173**
Lansing District Office
2111 University Park Dr. Ste 500
Okemos, MI 48864-8907

Laurie Dahlman **(269) 343-1490**
1228 Southern
Kalamazoo, MI 49001

2016 DELEGATE ALTERNATES

(in order of election - Costs Covered by Conference)

Benton Heisler **(616) 459-4503**
United Methodist Center
11 Fuller Ave SE, PO Box 6247
Grand Rapids, MI 49506-1633

Laura Witkowski **(616) 459-4503**
United Methodist Center
11 Fuller Ave SE, PO Box 6247
Grand Rapids, MI 49506-1633

John Boley **(269) 372-7525**
Kalamazoo District Office
810 Rankin Ave, Ste. B
Kalamazoo, MI 49006

Anne Soles **(231) 869-7651**
217 Old State Road, PO Box 467
Pentwater, MI 49449

REMAINING NAMES IN FINAL BALLOT ELECTED ORDER

(Rule 33.G)

Mary Ivanov

Valerie Celestin-Mossman
Simmie Proctor

—WMC Photos

K. LAY MEMBERS TO ANNUAL CONFERENCE

ALBION DISTRICT

Albion First – Sally Ammerman *sallya@spindlegrinding.com*
826 Jupiter, P O Box 128, Albion 49224 .... (517) 629-9334
Augusta Fellowship – Phyllis Gary *phyllisgary01@att.net*
15 Westwood Dr, Springfield 49037 .... (269) 760-0681
BC Baseline / Bellevue UMCs
BC Baseline – Chriss Leatherman *leathermanmc@gmail.com*
23069 Struin Rd., Battle Creek 49017 .... (269) 963-3883
BC Birchwood / Trinity UMCs
Battle Creek Trinity – Paula Kintigh 17102 11 Mile Rd, Battle Creek 49014 .... (269) 223-7245
BC Chapel Hill – Linda Autterson *lindabautt@sbcglobal.net*
243 S 21st St, Battle Creek 49015 .... (269) 965-5968
BC Christ – Debra Fryman *debrafryman@yahoo.com*
221 Glendale Ave, Battle Creek 49017 .... (269) 965-0973
BC Convis Union – Brenda Gerke *bren8708@aol.com*
291 W. Burnham, Battle Creek 49015 .... (269) 966-8875
BC First – Terry Smith *terrence50@comcast.net* 1088 S 24th St, Battle Creek 49015 .... (269) 963-3646
BC Maple – Richard Strader *dstrader40@yahoo.com* 178 Feld, Battle Creek 49037 .... (269) 963-6830
BC Sonoma / Battle Creek Newton UMCs
Battle Creek Newton – Sue Ratliff *ratcellars@gmail.com*
6577 K Drive S, Burlington 49029 .... (269) 979-9171
BC Washington Heights – Shirley McKinney *smckmsw@aol.com*
112 Bowen Ave, Battle Creek 49037 .... (269) 964-6884
Bronson – Virginia Wilber 1249 Round Lake Rd., Burr Oak 49030 .... (269) 489-2909
Camden / Montgomery / Stokes Chapel UMCs
Montgomery – Jim Reese 7721 Topinabee Dr, Montgomery 49255 .... (517) 296-4348
Montgomery – Linda Shiffler *lshiffler@pipedreamsart.com*
105 E Wales St, Camden 49232 .... (517) 368-5222
Stokes Chapel – Linda Shiffler PO Box 202, Camden 49232 .... (517) 368-5222
Center Park – Ruth Moyer 53822 Stevens Lane, Three Rivers 49093 .... (269) 273-8924
Centreville – Michelle Brokaw 60890 Anthony Dr., Centreville 49032
Coldwater – Sally Brayton *greg@gbrayton.com* 147 S Sunset Dr, Coldwater 49036 .... (517) 278-8489
Concord – Earl Miller 6236 Horton Rd, Jackson 49201 .... (517) 563-8441
Constantine / White Pigeon UMCs
Constantine – Mary Ann Grile *griletma@msn.com* 925 Canaris, Constantine 49042 .... (269) 435-7245
White Pigeon – Hazel Klaiber 69483 S River Rd, White Pigeon 49099-6948 .... (269) 483-9030
Delton Faith – Dolores Mohn 10295 Brickyard Rd, Delton 49046 .... (269) 623-2601
Frontier – Alice Britton *alice.britton34@gmail.com* 3651 Skuse, Osseo 49266 .... (517) 357-4342
Galesburg – Susan Jefferson *gamasu@hotmail.com*
60 Center, PO Box 301, Galesburg 49053 .... (269) 665-9338
Girard – Stephanie Avra *momaspanky@hotmail.com* 138 N Ray Quincy Rd, Quincy 49082 .. (517) 652-4837
Grass Lake – Calvin Holser *holserc@yahoo.com* 723 Church St, Grass Lake 49240 .... (517) 522-4206
Hillsdale First – Marla Bowen *bowen.hillsdalefirstumc@gmail.com*
405 W Fayette Street, Hillsdale 49242 .... (517) 439-4698
Jackson Brookside – Wendell Collver 6656 Ackerson Lake Rd, Jackson 49201 .... (517) 764-5453
Jackson Calvary / Zion UMC
Jackson Calvary – Florence Silvernail 3832 Perrine Rd., Rives Junction 49277 .... (517) 569-3715
Jackson Zion – Marge Clute *maclute@netzero.net*
11000 Cooper Rd, Pleasant Lake 49272 .... (517) 769-2525
Jackson First – Terri Reynolds *joughrey@gmail.com* 703 S Webster St, Jackson 49203 .... (517) 784-7507
Jackson First – Pamela Waagner *pdw0437@aol.com* 928 Sunburst Rd, Jackson 49203 .... (517) 787-2924
Jackson Trinity / Parma UMCs
Jackson Trinity – Elaine Eicher *elaineeicher@gmail.com* 11182 Baker Road, Jerome 49249

Jonesville / Allen UMCs
Allen – Julie Albright 214 Murphy St, Jonesville 49250 ....(517) 849-2300
Jonesville – Mike Potts *mpotts@hillsdale-isd.org*
1803 Grays Lake Rd, Jonesville 49250-9764 ....(517) 750-3803
Lee Center – Connie Lack *lackcv@yahoo.com* 22386 24 Mile Rd, Olivet 49076 ....(517) 857-3447
Litchfield / Quincy UMCs
Litchfield – Tom Beckner *becknertm@qcnet.net* 9220 Homer Rd, Litchfield 49252 ....(517) 542-3705
Marengo – Harold Oswald 221 Chapel Hill Dr N, Battle Creek 49015 ....(269) 962-2858
Marshall – John Seppanen *jseppanen313@gmail.com*
141 Shadowood Lane, Battle Creek 49014 ....(269) 965-4931
Napoleon – Linda Babcock ....(517) 536-4855
North Adams / Jerome UMCs
North Adams – Jim Swider *judyswider@frontier.com* 3285 Zona Dr, Osseo 49266 ....(517) 523-3931
Pope – Mike McDonald *mmcdonald@voyager.net* 12353 Clinton, Onondaga 49264 ....(517) 569-2211
Reading – Norma Smith *normasmith30@yahoo.com*
8840 Quackenbush Rd, Reading 49274 ....(517) 283-2726
Sturgis – Marcia Harrington *shorty209@charter.net* 209 Merryview, Sturgis 49091 ....(269) 651-4047
Three Rivers First / Mendon UMCs
Mendon – Janet Babcock *jaybee361@msn.com* PO Box 207, Mendon 49072 ....(269) 496-7713
Three Rivers Ninth Street / Schoolcraft Pleasant Valley UMCs
Schoolcraft Pleasant Valley – Jane Johnson 8057 W. V. Ave, Schoolcraft 49087 ....(269) 679-2022
Three Rivers Ninth Street – Connie Luegge *cdlteach2@yahoo.com* 10658 M 216, Marcellus 49067
Union City / Athens UMCs
Athens – Sandra Belmore *sanbel01@sbcglobal.net* 65 Jennings Rd, Battle Creek 49015.(269) 965-1930

GRAND RAPIDS DISTRICT

Alto / Bowne Center UMCs
Alto – Lois Heffron *heffrl@cablespeed.com* 6724 Beechwood Dr, Saranac 48881 ....(616) 868-6257
Bowne Center – Richard Hawkins Sr. 3839 Eckert Rd, Freeport 49325-9736
Byron Center – James Brown *junkyarddog01@att.net*
5387 Canal SW, Wyoming 49418 ....(616) 531-6595
Caledonia – Joan Pierce *jpierce3817@charter.net*
10089 Crossroads Circle, Caledonia 49316 ....(616) 826-3817
Carlisle – Gary Zinger *garyzinger@gmail.com*
6559 Burlingame SW, Byron Center 49315 ....(616) 890-2744
Cedar Springs – Carolyn Davis *cadadavis@charter.net*
16655 Simmons, Cedar Springs 49319 ....(616) 696-1939
Coopersville – Lynn Swart *lynn.swart@gmail.com* 523 Spring St, Coopersville 49404 ....(616) 970-0812
Courtland-Oakfield – Diane Harvey *biglouii@att.net* 7641 9 Mile Rd, Rockford 49341 ....(616) 874-3205
East Nelson – Linda Harry *jane8529@sbcglobal.net*
8555 Mowry, PO Box 124, Sand Lake 49343 ....(616) 636-8779
Fremont – Karen Barnes *barneskw@yahoo.com* 2010 S Baldwin Ave, Fremont 49412 ....(231) 924-4594
Georgetown – Doug Barry *douglas-barry@comcast.net* 7658 Teakwood, Jenison 49428 ....(616) 457-4734
Grand Haven Church of the Dunes – Donald Reis *donreis@hotmail.com*
13213 Hidden Creek Drive, Grand Haven 49417 ....(616) 607-2099
Grand Rapids Aldersgate – Sheila Bennett *sblynn1949@comcast.net*
3835 Fuller Avenue NE, Grand Rapids 49525-2250 ....(616) 364-0269
Grand Rapids Cornerstone – Marcus Schmidt *marcusschmidt@rocketmail.com*
Grand Rapids Cornerstone – Ken Watkins *archconcepts@sbcglobal.net*
7087 Summit Hill Ct., Caledonia 49316 ....(616) 656-2858
Grand Rapids Faith – Carol Smith *whitecat1024@comcast.net*
4320 Royal Glen Dr NE, Comstock Park 49321-9191 ....(616) 647-2155
Grand Rapids First – Nagnon Diarrassouba *diarrasn@gvsu.edu*
1844 Wilmont Dr SE, Grand Rapids 49508-6592 ....(616) 827-8389
Grand Rapids First – Carol Ann Youells *gryouells@gmail.com*
740 Clark Crossings S.E., Grand Rapids 49506 ....(616) 243-3759

Grand Rapids Northlawn – Pat Whyatt *patwhyatt@yahoo.com*
1647 Bradford St. NE, Grand Rapids 49503 ....(616) 460-0480
Grand Rapids St Paul's – Roni McNeil *cmacroni@comcast.net*
3043 Rich Ct., SE, Grand Rapids 49508 ....(616) 245-0703
Grand Rapids South – Shirley Meyers *djmeyers37@chartermi.net* 824 Edge Creek Dr, Wayland 49348
Grand Rapids Trinity – Joy Murphy *joymurphygr@gmail.com*
2515 Union SE, Grand Rapids 49507 ....(616) 245-5546
Grand Rapids Trinity – Molly Woodworth *molly.woodworth@shos.com*
409 Hoover St NE, Grand Rapids 49505 ....(616) 706-2593
Grandville – Edward McDaniels 1765 Jackson, Hudsonville 49426
HESPERIA / FERRY UMCs
Ferry – Randy Ackley *raackley@live.com* 515 E South Ave, Hesperia 49421 ....(231) 854-0075
Hesperia – Randy Ackley *ackleyclan@live.com* 515 E South Ave, Hesperia 49421 ....(231) 854-0075
Holland First – Sarah DeLany 3648 New Holland St., Hudsonville 49426 ....(616) 797-0244
Holton – Rosemary Johnson *rinellar@comcast.net* 2275 Duff Rd, Twin Lake 49457 ....(231) 828-5551
Kent City Chapel Hill – Colleen Moerdyk *cmfish@i2k.com*
1347 16 Mile Rd NW, Kent City 49330 ....(616) 887-7843
Leighton – Keith Pratt *prattman.com@hotmail.com* 56 Nancy SE, Kentwood 49548 ....(616) 406-3809
Lowell – Bunny Rice *riceladies@att.net* 310 King St, Lowell 49331 ....(616) 897-0314
Marne – Tom Strack *Lovemy71GS@charter.net* 1340 Franklin, Marne 49435 ....(616) 677-3461
MARTIN / SHELBYVILLE UMCs
Martin – Luesettie Phelps *luephelps@gmail.com*
1064 Wedgewood Dr, Plainwell 49080 ....(269) 204-6047
MIDDLEVILLE / SNOW UMCs
Middleville – Sue Rietman *middlevilleumc@gmail.com* 15 Market St, Middleville 49333
Snow – Ted Johnson *tlj818@sbcglobal.net* 818 Sarasota SE, Grand Rapids 49546 ....(616) 940-0094
Montague – Ann Erler 10624 Lost Valley, Montague 49437 ....(231) 893-3424
Muskegon Central – Richard Swanson *rswanson1238@comcast.net*
1731 Sheridan Road, Muskegon 49445 ....(231) 744-5419
Muskegon Hts Temple – Dan Long *sclong42@verizon.net*
1729 Winchester, Muskegon 49441 ....(231) 963-3546
Muskegon Lake Harbor – Ron Benkert *rbenkert@charter.net*
17 Ronda, Nunica 49448 ....(616) 846-9829
MUSKEGON LAKESIDE / CRESTWOOD UMCs
Muskegon Crestwood – Jim McCormick *jaymar.mccormick@gmail.com*
681 Carlton, Muskegon 49442 ....(231) 773-5460
Muskegon Wolf Lake – Nita Smith *njsmith26@frontier.com*
1482 S. Hilton Park Rd., Muskegon 49442 ....(231) 788-5122
Newaygo – Harriet Kiper 5545 South Cyprss, Newaygo 49337 ....(231) 652-6416
North Muskegon Community – Doug Wood *dwood1952@gmail.com*
3969 Dame Road, Whithall 49461 ....(231) 894-9677
Parmelee – Patricia Cooper *patricia_cooper@att.net*
Ravenna – Pat Goodrich P.O. Box 56, Ravenna 49451 ....(231) 853-2480
Rockford – Alex Terranova *acterra@att.net* 144 Oak St, Rockford 49341 ....(616) 866-2284
SALEM / BRADLEY INDIAN MISSIONS
Bradley Indian Mission – D.K. Sprague *DKSprague@mbpi.org*
1624 Parker Ave., Wayland 49348 ....(616) 795-1246
Saugatuck – Carol Huyser 5756 Old Allegan Rd, Hamilton 49419 ....(269) 751-5986
Shelby – Denise Schuitema *dmschuit@hotmail.com* 6967 W Buchanan Rd, Shelby 49455 ....(231) 286-5277
Sitka – Robin Zerlaut *headbellyacre@aol.com* 10360 Dickinson Rd, Holton 49425 ....(231) 821-2998
Sparta – Vickie Hammond *victoria5349@att.net*
1415 Richmond NW, Grand Rapids 49504 ....(616) 453-7636
Twin Lake – Bobbie Springer *bobbiespringer1@comcast.net*
3220 First St, PO Box 351, Twin Lake 49457 ....(231) 828-4203
Wayland – Gwen Meisenbach *gharnish6320@charter.net*
107 Apollo Place, Wayland 49348 ....(269) 792-6320
White Cloud – Richard Long *longrp@msn.com* 866 E. 8th St., White Cloud 49349 ....(231) 689-6757

WHITEHALL / CLAYBANKS UMC
Claybanks – Edith Bogart *ebphleb@peoplepc.com*
8160 Flower Creek Rd, Montague 49437 ....(231) 894-8766
Wyoming Park – June Harrington *harringtonjune@yahoo.com*
2217 Clarion SW, Wyoming 49509 ....(616) 532-6237
Wyoming Wesley Park – Cindy Lang *dougcindy.lang@comcast.net* 1150 32nd St SW, Wyoming 49509
South Wyoming – Luann Hoffman *luannh663@sbcglobal.net*
4136 Honeyvale SW, Grandville 49418 ....(616) 531-5360

GRAND TRAVERSE DISTRICT

ALDEN / CENTRAL LAKE UMCs
Central Lake – Gary Sage PO Box 607, Central Lake 49622 ....(231) 544-6314
BALDWIN COVENANT COMMUNITY / LUTHER UMCs
Luther – Lois Langenburg *llangenburg@hotmail.com* 15 W Runway Dr, Luther 49656...(231) 429-4194
Luther – Karen Neiger *kneiger63@yahoo.com* PO Box 99, Luther 49656....................(231) 797-5261
BARNARD / E JORDAN / NORWOOD UMCs
East Jordan – Linda Chase *windyridge@torchlake.com*
01420 LaLonde Rd., East Jordan 49727-8626 ....(231) 350-6917
BEAR LAKE / ARCADIA UMCs
Arcadia – Betty Hull *bettyhull65@gmail.com*
3269 Lake Street, P.O. Box 52, Arcadia 49613 ....(231) 889-5555
Bear Lake – Joanne Schroeder *Adventureland1@mac.com*
12241 Maple St, PO Box 424, Bear Lake 49614 ....(231) 864-2314
Bellaire Community – Bob Ayala PO Box 583, Bellaire 49615 ....(231) 533-8973
BOYNE CITY / BOYNE FALLS UMCs
Boyne City – Helen Deming *gramma_49712@yahoo.com*
208 N. Lake St., Boyne City 49712 ....(231) 582-6278
BRETHREN EPWORTH / GRANT UMCs
Brethren Epworth – Walt Briggs 13537 Yates Rd, Copemish 49626 ....(231) 409-4774
Grant – Jeff Kretzschmer 2094 Lakes Dr., Interlochen 49643 ....(231) 276-9832
Cadillac – Joan Deer *jjdeer44@gmail.com* 1009 1st Ave., Cadillac 49601 ....(231) 775-4208
Charlevoix – Gail Seidel *jgac@nmo.net* 04316 Marion Center Rd, Charlevoix 49720 ....(231) 547-2181
CRYSTAL VALLEY / WALKERVILLE UMCs
Crystal Valley – Michael Mayse 9015 N 120th Ave, Hart 49420 ....(231) 873-4144
Walkerville – Carol Abe *cabe1@frontier.com* 1884 W Tyler Rd, Hart 49420 ....(231) 873-4397
Empire – Carolyn Pelky 8424 Indian Hill Rd, Honor 49640 ....(231) 325-5712
EPSILON / NEW HOPE UMCs
Epsilon – John Engler 570 South Creek Road, Petoskey 49770 ....(231) 347-2457
FIFE LAKE-BOARDMANS PARISH
East Boardman – Debora Sieting *dsieting@forestarea.k12.mi.us*
5661 Quarter Line Rd SW, South Boardman 49680-9745 ....(231) 369-2966
Fife Lake – Debora Sieting *debalynn57@yahoo.com*
5661 Quarterline Rd SW, South Boardman 49680
FRANKFORT / ELBERTA UMCs
Elberta – Joyce Gatrell *joyceg911@yahoo.com* POB 382, Elberta 49628 ....(231) 352-4076
Frankfort – Trudi Hook *Trudihook@charter.net* PO Box 122, Beulah 49617
Grawn – Deb Nickerson *nickerson@centurytel.net* 1745 N Thompsonville, Beulah 49617.....(231) 325-2657
Greensky Hill – Carol Tunison *ctuni@charter.net*
309 Mason St, Charlevoix 49720 ....(231) 547-5009
HARBOR SPRINGS / ALANSON UMCs
Alanson – Juris Brants *brantsj@yahoo.com* PO Box 127, Alanson 49706 ....(231) 548-1215
Hart – Maureen Huizing *huizingathart@charter.net* 40 N. Plum St., Hart 49420 ....(231) 873-0418
Indian River – Mark Fielder *marksuefielder@aol.com*
2010 Mac-A-Vista, Indian River 49749 ....(231) 238-4751

Kalkaska – Jeanine Roe *roesritz@triton.net* 4940 Sands Park NE, Kalkaska 49646................(231) 258-5473
Keswick – Kristin Harrison 7071 S. Center Highway, Traverse City 49684
KEWADIN / NORTHPORT INDIAN MISSIONS
Kewadin Indian Mission – Phyllis John *vjmaidens@yahoo.com*
13735 Indian Rd, Kewadin 49648 ....(231) 264-0527
Northport Indian Mission – Charlene John *vjmaidens@yahoo.com*
9465 N. Carlson Rd., Northport 49670
Kingsley – Diane Walton PO Box 142, Kingsley 49649 ....(231) 263-7436
Lake Ann – Shelly Vandermeulen *vanderdogs@charter.net*
20860 Red Oak Dr., Lake Ann 49650................(231) 275-2488
Lake City – Jane Tinsley *jharecol@hotmail.com* 1269 S Audrey Ln, Lake City 49651...........(231) 839-2885
Leland – Joan Hook *jwhook1@centurytel.net*
2230 W Nemeskal Rd, Maple City 49664................(231) 228-6250
Ludington St Paul – Dick Stearns 4720 Hawley Rd., Ludington 49431 ....(231) 843-1703
Ludington United – Wayne Disegna *wdisegna@frontier.com*
6647 W. Jackson Rd., Ludington 49431 ....(231) 843-6841
MANCELONA / ALBA UMCs
Alba – Ellen Whitehead 7197 Crescent Dr, Mancelona 49659
Mancelona – Ellen Whitehead *twinlakede@gmail.com*
7197 Crescent Dr., Mancelona 49659................(231) 668-8852
Manistee – Betty Riggs *bjriggs699@chartermi.net* 699 Harbor Dr, Manistee 49660 ....(231) 723-2414
Manton – Cheryl Peterson *peterson_cheryl@prodigy.net*
515 W. Main St., PO Box 93, Manton 49663-0093 ....(231) 824-3119
MARION / CADILLAC SOUTH UMCs
Marion – Sondra Baughan *jim.mort@sbcglobal.net*
11750 W. Long Lk Rd., Marion 49665................(231) 743-6272
Mears – Marc DeMaat *susan@acsmi.us* 9468 W. Sandy Dr., Mears 49436 ....(231) 873-5945
MESICK / HARRIETTA UMCs
Harrietta – Vlasta Bovee 8195 Wedeln Tr, Cadillac 49601 ....(231) 862-3842
Mesick – Dorothy Casaday 3180 N. 17 Rd., Mesick 49668 ....(231) 885-1747
Old Mission Peninsula – Marge Long *margelong@chartermi.net*
139 Mathison, Traverse City 49686................(231) 941-8657
Pentwater Centenary – Susan MacGregor *jsmac1@frontier.com*
PO Box 914, Pentwater 49449................(231) 869-4364
Petoskey – Judy Brummeler *jrae38@charter.net* 1477 Kilborn Dr., Petoskey 49770...............(231) 347-8995
PINE RIVER PARISH: LEROY / ASHTON UMCs
Pine River Parish: LeRoy – Mike Ramsey 10297 7 Mile Rd., Evart 49631
Scottville – Linda Starr 411 N. Gaylord, Ludington 49431................(231) 845-6530
Traverse Bay – Judy Care 3182 S. Candace Lane, Lake Leelanau 49653................(231) 256-9163
Traverse City Central – Sarah Bye *sarah@tccentralumc.org*
3863 Sandia Place, Traverse City 49684 ....(231) 645-1002
Traverse City Central – Allen Horstman *ahhorstman@hotmail.com*
1750 Outer Drive West, Traverse City 49685................(231) 946-9314
Traverse City Christ – Cam Williams *cam422@hotmail.com*
188 Peach Tree Drive, Traverse City 49696 ....(231) 947-2414
Williamsburg – Douglas Bronkema *doug@dougbronkema.com*
128 E Fourth St, Elk Rapids 49629 ....(231) 944-8751

HEARTLAND DISTRICT

Alma – Gary Shirely *garyshirely@yahoo.com* 1325 Euclid, Alma 48801 ....(989) 576-0896
Amble – Delores "Dee" Barringer *deeb@pathwaynet.com*
20564 One Mile, PO Box 193, Morley 49336 ....(231) 856-7091
ASHLEY / BANNISTER / GREENBUSH UMCs
Ashley – Karen Follett 5386 Garfield Road, Ashley 48806 ....(989) 847-4804
Bannister – Doris Edgar *mapled1@juno.com* 3244 S Bagley Road, Ithaca 48847.............(989) 875-3083

AVONDALE / NORTH EVART UMCs
North Evart – Peggy Meyer 8927 80th Ave, Evart 49631 ....(231) 734-5975
Big Rapids First – David Rhodes *davidmrhodes24@hotmail.com*
Lot A-3, 606 Bjornson, Big Rapids 49307 ....(231) 796-4185
Breckenridge – Ray Rohn *karensue952@yahoo.com* 619 Cedar St, Breckenridge 48615 ....(989) 842-5503
BROOKS CORNERS / BARRYTON FAITH / SEARS UMCs
Barryton Faith – Patrick Tiedt *patiedt@hotmail.com* 9859 River Rd, Evart 49631 ....(231) 734-2932
Brooks Corners – Shari Schmidt *sschmidt@netonecom.net*
11743 23 Mile Road, Evart 49631 ....(231) 734-6520
CHASE-BARTON / GRANT CENTER UMCs
Grant Center – James Maxfield 19463 160th Avenue, Big Rapids 49307-9377 ....(231) 796-8088
Clare – Colleen Bremer *d_cbremer@hotmail.com* 1421 Woodlawn, Clare 48617 ....(989) 386-4096
Clare – Janet Thomas 6500 Woodridge, Lake 48632
Edmore Faith – Cindi Scheiern *Cindi216@hotmail.com*
509 W. Home Street, PO Box 559, Edmore 48829-0559 ....(989) 427-3863
Evart – Ken White 12996 Hersey Rd, Hersey 49639 ....(231) 832-5991
FENWICK / PALO / VICKERYVILLE UMCs
Fenwick – Louise Belyou *fenwickumc@cmsinter.net*
175 E Fenwick Road, Fenwick 48834 ....(989) 248-3349
Greenville First – Jim VanderLaan *vanfam84@yahoo.com*
500 W Grove St, Greenville 48838-1718 ....(616) 754-5389
HARRISON: THE GATHERING / WAGARVILLE UMCs
Harrison: The Gathering – John Mostiller *johnjgm6@gmail.com*
550 Ridge Rd, Harrison 48625 ....(989) 539-8582
Heritage – Rogena Brinks *rbrinks@live.com* 8661 Huron, Howard City 49329 ....(231) 937-7537
Hersey – Jesse Tatum *jessie.tatum@genmills.com* 3693 170th Ave., Hersey 49639 ....(231) 832-3931
Ionia Easton – Timothy Tindall *ttindall11@gmail.com* 13290 Vergennes St, Lowell 49331-9687
Ionia First – Beverly Brown *larrybev@outlook.com* 119 E Main Street, Ionia 48846 ....(616) 527-4654
IONIA PARISH: LEVALLEY / BERLIN CENTER
Berlin Center – Carol Braun 2730 Cylde Road, Ionia 48846 ....(616) 527-0034
LeValley – Carol Braun *levalleybc@gmail.com* 2730 Clyde Road, Ionia 48846 ....(616) 527-0034
LeValley – Judy Huynh *judyhuynh@hughes.net* 2101 Clarksville Rd, Portland 48875 ....(616) 374-4764
Ionia Zion – Vicky Burrows *vickylburrows@gmail.com* 2732 Woods Rd, Ionia 48846 ....(616) 527-0367
ITHACA / BEEBE UMCs
Ithaca – Roger Silverthorn *rogersilverthorn@charter.net* 475 Webster St, Ithaca 48847 ...(989) 875-4821
Lincoln Road – Dan Throop *danthroop@hotmail.com*
9480 W Lincoln Road, Riverdale 48877 ....(989) 463-1276
Mecosta New Hope – Dan Houts *danlwf@yahoo.com*
8338 W. Ridge Blvd., Canadian Lakes 49346 ....(231) 972-8944
Mt Pleasant First – George Aultman *georgeaultman@yahoo.com*
1235 South Crawford Road, Mt. Pleasant 48858 ....(989) 773-3846
MT PLEASANT TRINITY / COUNTRYSIDE / LEATON UMCs
Leaton – Dale Haton 5028 W. River Rd., Mount Pleasant 48858
New Life – Barbara Ray *grambjr@yahoo.com* 12346 Cutler Rd., Lakeview 48850
Ovid: United Church – Janell Kebler *kebler@msu.edu* 2156 N. Hollister, Ovid 48866 ....(989) 834-1420
POMPEII / PERRINTON / MIDDLETON / NORTH STAR UMCs
Middleton – William Troub 3491 W. Garfirld Rd., Perrinton 48871 ....(989) 236-5023
North Star – William Troub 3491 W. Garfield Rd., Perrinton 48871 ....(989) 236-5023
Perrinton – William Troub 402 N. Arnold, Perrinton 48871 ....(989) 236-5023
Pompeii – William (Bill) Troub *bcetroub@yahoo.com* ....(989) 236-5023
Reed City – Bonnie Dalman *bbdalman@aol.com*
1800 N Ironwood Dr, Apache Junction AZ 85220-1912 ....(231) 832-5493
Rosebush – Lori Thompson *thompsongl08@att.net* 4101 N Mission St, Rosebush 48878 ....(989) 433-0154
St Johns First – Amy Latimer *latimer.amy@gmail.com*
305 N. Prospect St., St Johns 48879 ....(989) 224-2293
St Johns Pilgrim – Dennis Pennock *penfamdr@yahoo.com*
2261 W Pratt Rd, DeWitt 48820 ....(517) 281-6719

LAY MEMBERS

St Louis First – Stan McMann *finnlynn@charter.net* 319 w. Washington, St. Louis 48880
SAND LAKE / SOUTH ENSLEY UMCS
South Ensley – John Rau *raushill@charter.net*
17900 Simmons Ave, Sand Lake 49343 ....(616) 696-1863
Shepardsville – William Hartman *bchartman2@gmail.com*
7998 E. Walker Rd., Ovid 48866 ....(989) 834-5831
Shepherd – Linda Miller 8963 Riverview, Shepherd 48883 ....(989) 828-5504
Stanwood Northland – Cindy Smith *csmith.advancetitle@gmail.com*
10693 Otahnagon, Stanwood 49346 ....(231) 796-5619
THIRD AVENUE / PARIS / RODNEY UMCS
Paris – Laura Dix *Laura_Dix@ferris.edu*
17110 Youngs Lake Rd, Big Rapids 49307-9004 ....(231) 592-5717
TURK LAKE / BELDING UMCS
Belding – Jennifer Schumaker *jennifer.schumaker@gmail.com*
733 Merrick Street, Belding 48809 ....(616) 794-0003
Turk Lake – Gary Kluzak 472 Burgess Lk. Drive, Greenville 48838 ....(616) 754-8257
Weidman – Jean Holland *Jean.M.H.90@gmail.com*
4350 W. Beal City Rd., Weidman 48893 ....(989) 644-5578

KALAMAZOO DISTRICT

Allegan – Hanford Brink *brinkha@Hotmail.com* 2532 30th. Street, Allegan 49010 ....(269) 673-6031
Bangor Simpson – Marty Maurer *angeldaisy71@hotmail.com*
212 Randolph St, Bangor 49013-1441 ....(269) 427-8340
BERRIEN SPRINGS / HINCHMAN / ORONOKO UMCS
Berrien Springs – Joyce Lindt 10324 US 31, Berrien Springs 49103 ....(269) 473-2311
Bloomingdale – Rhonda Griffin *Rgalegriffin@gmail.com*
205 W. Howard Street, Grand Junction 49056 ....(269) 870-1404
Buchanan Faith – Wayne Wilcox 2415 S Redbud Tr, Niles 49120 ....(269) 695-9049
BURNIPS / MONTEREY CENTER UMCS
Burnips – Eric Buckleitner 4280 30th Street, P.O. Box 34, Burnips 49314 ....(616) 896-7799
Burnips – Matt Frank 2888 130th, Dorr 49010
Monterey Center – Matt Frank 2888 130th, Dorr 49010
Casco – William Warren *bwarren14@gmail.com* 1059 68th St, South Haven 49090 ....(269) 227-3916
Cassopolis – Dawn Atkinson *dawnatkinson@comcast.net*
61148 Cass Rd, Cassopolis 49031 ....(269) 445-2789
Coloma – Darleen Rowe *rrowedar@aol.com* 5586 Wendzel Dr., Coloma 49038
Dowagiac First – Kathy Hall *rkhall5@juno.com* 25615 Marcellus Hwy., Dowagiac 49047
Edwardsburg Hope – Martha Bartels *mbartels@aol.com*
68459 Scott St, Edwardsburg 49112 ....(269) 699-5304
FENNVILLE / PEARL UMCS
Fennville – David Babbitt *fenumc@frontier.com* 6464 119th Ave, Fennville 49408 ....(269) 543-4272
Pearl – David Babbitt 6464 119th Ave., Fennville 49408 ....(269) 543-4272
GALIEN / OLIVE BRANCH UMCS
Galien – Mary Kutemeier *kutemeier.1@att.net* 1823 Ontario Rd, Niles 49120 ....(269) 362-1837
GANGES / GLENN UMCS
Ganges – Marcia A. Tucker *friar.tuck2009@live.com* 6948 Colver, Fennville 49408 ....(269) 857-4797
GOBLES / KENDALL UMCS
Gobles – Cheryl Rumery *milllake@frontier.com* 35686 Mill Lake Rd, Gobles 49055 ....(269) 628-4894
Gull Lake – Theresa Meinert *tmeinert121@charter.net* 9156 Weathervane Trail, Galesburg 49053
Hartford – Kari Unrath *kunrath1@yahoo.com* 62525 Red Arrow Highway, Hartford 49057
HOPKINS / SOUTH MONTEREY UMCS
Hopkins – Alys Edgell *aedgell@triton.net* 2146 Parker Dr, Wayland 49348 ....(269) 795-2069
Kalamazoo First – Carol Hodges *carolhodges.kalamazoo@gmail.com*
222 N Kalamazoo Mall Apt 320, Kalamazoo 49007-3894 ....(269) 342-6647
Kalamazoo First – Molly Williams *Molly.Williams@wmich.edu*
2716 N 9th St, Kalamazoo 49009 ....(269) 375-4867

Kalamazoo Milwood – Ruth Breyfogle *rbreyfogle@sbcglobal.net*
157 Fairview, Kalamazoo 49001 ....(269) 349-1258
Kalamazoo Sunnyside – Tonya Murphy *murphy.tonya@gmail.com*
1152 Mount Royal Dr, Kalamazoo 49009
Kalamazoo Sunnyside – Jeremy Orr *jeremyforr@gmail.com* 3100 Staten Ave Apt 2, Lansing 48910
Kalamazoo Westwood – Sally Mahieu *Smahieu42@aol.com*
1433 Barney Road, Kalamazoo 49004 ....(269) 349-4562
Lacota – Joy Dee 04903 County Rd 687, South Haven 49090....(269) 637-4565
Lakeside – Beverly Lawton *bevlawton@csinet.net*
8000 Warren Woods Rd. #79, Three Oaks 49128....(269) 469-8468
Lakeside – A. Thomas Smith *atsmith@semperdomino.com* PO Box 234, Lakeside 49116 ....(269) 369-2738
Lawrence – Susan McGowan
Lawton St Paul's – Cathy Ditto 753 72nd Ave, Lawton 49065 ....(269) 624-6735
LifeSpring – John Brooks *johnboytravel@gmail.com*
4429 Willow Point Lane, Kalamazoo 49004-3743....(269) 226-9756
MARCELLUS / WAKELEE UMCs
Marcellus – Burke Webb *bawebbfoot@juno.com* PO Box 579, Marcellus 49067
Wakelee – Charles Goodrich *cegoodrich36@gmail.com*
Niles Wesley – Janet Smiedendorf *jjsmied1@aol.com* 515 Archer, St Joseph 49085....(269) 983-4713
Oshtemo – Betty Houghton 5747 Wood Valley Road, Kalamazoo 49009....(269) 375-6953
Otsego – Donna Church *zaidos@sbcglobal.net* 1294 Hill Road, Otsego 49078....(269) 694-6492
Parchment – Kay O'Boyle *roboyle@ocba.com*
2736 Burlington Drive, Hickory Corners 49060 ....(269) 671-5625
Paw Paw – Connor Bailey *4-connor@comcast.net* ....(269) 312-3153
Plainwell First – Gail Hill *kittygran@mei.net* 11126 E. Shore Dr., Delton 49046....(269) 623-8066
Pokagon – Jeff VanLue *jtvanlue@netzero.net* 2267 Warren Rd, Niles 49120....(269) 684-7254
Portage Chapel Hill – Daryl Perkins *darylperkins@yahoo.com*
1935 Bloomfield, Kalamazoo 49001 ....(269) 373-5793
Portage Chapel Hill – Jenaba Waggy Apt. 1B, 993 Richmond Ct, Kalamazoo 49009 ....(317) 534-7248
PORTAGE PRAIRIE / ARDEN UMCs
Portage Prairie – Sharon Harris *siharris1@comcast.net* 1320 South St., Niles 49120....(269) 683-9523
Portage Prairie – RuthAnne Vite *ppumcs@aol.com* 2750 S. Redbud Tr, Niles 49120 ....(269) 695-7772
Riverside – Candy Evett 4391 Greenwood, Benton Harbor 49022 ....(269) 849-0469
St Joseph First – Michael Dumke *mike@tagliafirm.com*
2535 Old Lakeshore Rd., St. Joseph 49085....(269) 983-0439
St Joseph First – Keith Foote *kgfoote@aep.com* 2882 Oak St., Stevensville 49127....(269) 556-0686
Schoolcraft – Martha Reeves *theweaver@charter.net*
9837 Pine View Drive, Portage 49002....(269) 324-5546
SCOTTDALE / BRIDGMAN FAITH UMCs
Bridgman Faith – Dawn Oldenburg *zambonidrvr1218@aol.com*
9862 Vineyard St, Bridgman 49106-8313 ....(269) 465-3514
Scottdale – Dawn Oldenburg *zambonidrvr1218@aol.com*
9862 Vineyard St, Bridgman 49106-8313 ....(269) 465-3514
SILVER CREEK / KEELER UMCs
Keeler – Betty Kusterer 68060 Territorial Rd, Watervilet 49098 ....(269) 463-3336
Sodus Chapel Hill – Margie Krieger *mkkrieger@att.net*
1115 S M 140, Benton Harbor 49022-9412 ....(269) 944-1755
South Haven – Mary Blashill *mary_blashill@yahoo.com* 07909 M 43, South Haven 49090..(269) 639-9675
Stevensville – Lona Vogie *jlvogie@sbcglobal.net* 3372 W Valley View Dr, St. Joseph 49127.(269) 428-1765
Three Oaks – Alexis Renbarger *alexisren@sbcglobal.net* 407 Cherry St, Three Oaks 49128..(269) 756-5611
Townline – Aaron Leedy *aaron_leedy@yahoo.com* 53 Derek Dr, Paw Paw 49079....(269) 998-9041
Trowbridge – Sandra Davidson *motor_home@ymail.com* 38467 6th Ave, Gobles 49055....(269) 217-1127
Vicksburg – Rachel Freeman *relfmuw@sbcglobal.net* 303 S Main St, Vicksburg 49097....(269) 649-3537
Water's Edge – Devinnie Wysocki *dwysocki@nbas.org*
120 S. Clinton, New Buffalo 49117....(269) 469-2145

LANSING DISTRICT

BATH / GUNNISONVILLE UMCs
Bath – Johanna Balzer *rjbalzer.1@gmail.com* 3450 Clark Road, Bath 48808....................(517) 484-3273
Gunnisonville – Johanna Balzer *rjbalzer.1@gmail.com* 3450 Clark Rd, Bath 48808.........(517) 484-3273
Brookfield Eaton – Janice Hisler *ilv@vcconsulting.com* 9280 Brookfield Rd, Charlotte 48813
Charlotte Lawrence Avenue – Patricia Snyder *dpsnyder807@peoplepc.com*
807 S Sheldon, Charlotte 48813 ....(517) 543-5646
Country Chapel – Andrew Hovanec *ahovanec@mei.net*
13220 Banfield Rd, Battle Creek 49017....................(269) 721-8123
Dansville – Scott Clarke *etapa@msu.edu* 2088 E Dansville Rd, Dansville 48819..................(517) 623-6381
Delta Mills – Priscilla Lane 215 N Canal Rd Lot 188, Lansing 48917
DeWitt Redeemer – Paul Blankenship *office@dewittredeemer.org*
11494 W River Dr, Dewitt 48820 ....(517) 669-7383
DIMONDALE / GROVENBURG UMCs
Dimondale – Tonie Lokker *tonielokker@gmail.com*
Grovenburg – Robin Towsley 6473 McCue Rd, Holt 48842-8610....................(517) 646-0664
Peoples Church – Amy Buttery *amynrob@yahoo.com* 2979 Whistlewood Way, Lansing 48911
East Lansing University – Barbara Burke 922 Huntingto Road, East Lansing 48823 ....(517) 332-6274
East Lansing University – Sara Cardinal *kidsnyouthstuff@gmail.com*
Eaton Rapids First – Alice Botti *Bottiw1@juno.com* 6120 S Clinton Tr, Eaton Rapids 48827(517) 663-3423
Grand Ledge First – David Peake *Peakegl@aol.com* 9205 S Hartel Rd, Grand Ledge 48837.(517) 627-7023
Gresham – Tom Raymond *cindylouraymond@hotmail.com*
6315 Mulliken Rd, Charlotte 48813-8812....................(517) 541-0865
Hastings First – Larry Hensley *hens4th06@gmail.com* 220 Penny Ave, Hastings 49058
Hastings Hope – Jim Frederick 4857 Hathaway Ct, Hastings 49058....................(269) 948-1979
Holt – Dennis Kelley *mrgolfbowl@sbcglobal.net* 1220 Prospect, Lansing 48912
Kalamo – Lee Everett *cherieeverett@yahoo.com* 489 S Pease Rd, #R2, Vermontville 49096
Lake Odessa Central – John Gentner *ajgentner@ATT.net* 545 Lake Dr, Lake Odessa 48849..(616) 374-7126
Lake Odessa Lakewood – Fran Courser *franola@centurytel.net*
258 Washington, PO Box 179, Sunfield 48890....................(517) 566-8682
Lansing Asbury – Dave Mongson *web22ncj@sbcglobal.net* 9011 Summit Ct, Ypsilanti 48197-6029
Lansing Central – Patricia Bell *porcbell@comcast.net* 2500 Clifton Ave, Lansing 48910.......(517) 482-4098
Lansing Faith & South Lansing Ministries – Nicole Proctor-Kanyama *proctorn@msu.edu*
824 Nipp Ave, Lansing 48915....................(517) 367-8287
Lansing First – David Baur *dbaur@provide.net* 5105 Deanna Dr, Lansing 48917..................(517) 321-3070
Lansing Grace – Pat Spellman *pspellm@comcast.net* 2747 Granger Dr, Lansing 48917.........(517) 322-0103
Lansing Korean – Eun Il Lee 3539 Stagecoach, Okemos 48864....................(517) 349-4459
Lansing Mt Hope – Judy Lott *ronandjudylott@comcast.net*
2512 Arbor Forest Dr, Lansing 48910-3865....................(517) 882-8150
Lansing Mt Hope – Ron Lott *ronandjudylott@comcast.net*
2512 Arbor Forest Dr, Lansing 48910-3865....................(517) 882-5180
Lansing Sycamore Creek – Mark Aupperlee *m_aupperlee@hotmail.com*
5127 Aurelius Road Ste D, Lansing 48911
Lansing Trinity – Barbara Beachy *babeachy@comcast.net*
230 E Knight St, Eaton Rapids 48827....................(517) 441-9456
LESLIE / FELT PLAINS UMCs
Leslie – Esther Jackson *jacksonfarm@fnwusers.com*
560 E. Kinneville Road, Leslie 49251....................(517) 589-9625
Mason First – Glenn Darling *gadarling40@gmail.com* 1111 Barnes Rd, Mason 48854 ....(517) 676-2154
Millville – Don Tippin *dtippin@yahoo.com*
320 W Elizabeth St., Stockbridge 49285-9791....................(517) 740-8723
Okemos Community Church – Jim White *jwhite@whiteschneider.com*
2410 Emerald Lake Dr, East Lansing 48823....................(517) 336-7785
PERRY / SHAFTSBURG UMCs
Perry – Janice Luft 1138 Ellsworth Rd., Perry 48872....................(517) 625-3643
Shaftsburg – Rosalie Young PO Box 42, Shaftsburg 48882....................(517) 675-5345
Pleasant Lake – Eleanor Smith 1220 E Territorial Rd, Rives Junction 49277 ....(517) 589-9297

Portland – Carol McLane *camclane@wowway.com* 327 S East St, Portland 48875................(517) 647-6192
Potterville – Kathy Dobie *gddkld@aol.com* 15248 Jones Rd, Eagle 48822-9606....................(517) 627-1351
Quimby – Robert Lowell *bobnrita0082@sbcglobal.net*
2025 Nashville Rd, Hastings 49058..(269) 945-9342
Robbins – Dan Ellsworth *dan@ellsworthlink.net* 1089 S Michigan Rd, Eaton Rapids 48827.(517) 663-1343
Sunfield – Gerald Gilbert *tellergilbertj@gmail.com*
2443 E Tupper Lake Rd, Lake Odessa 48849 ....(517) 566-8566
Wacousta – Jackie Salisbury *jagbury1@aol.com*
8950 W. Herbison Rd., Eagle 48822...(517) 626-6193
Waterloo First – Veronica Hackworth *veronicahackworth1966@gmail.com* ....(517) 937-2358
Waterloo First – Nancy Hughes *emhughes366@gmail.com*
16849 Waterloo Rd, Chelsea 48118...(734) 475-2980
Waterloo Village – Nancy Hughes *emhughes366@gmail.com*
16849 Waterloo Rd, Chelsea 48118...(734) 475-2980
Webberville – Douglas Elzerman *delzerman@cablespeed.com*
3786 E Grand River Ave, Williamston 48895...(517) 202-2037
Welcome Corners / Freeport / Peace UMCs
Freeport – Arlene Stanton *revsolsen@hotmail.com* 3813 Baldwin Rd, Hastings 49058....(269) 948-8816
Peace – Arlene Stanton
Welcome Corners – Arlene Stanton
Wheatfield – Neva Curtis 1409 S Zimmer Rd, Williamston 48895..(517) 655-1484

LAY MEMBERS

ALBION DISTRICT EQUALIZATION LAY MEMBERS

Robin Burdick *grandmawho55@hotmail.com*
12326 E Chicago Rd, PO Box 252, Somerset Center 49282 ....(517) 688-9506
Beverly Clark *beverlyjclark@frontier.com* PO Box 355, Hanover 49241 ....(517) 563-8966
Elaine Eicher *elaineeicher@gmail.com* 11182 Baker Road, Jerome 49249
Larry Embury *bralembury@myfrontiermail.com*
1855 Sarossy Lake Rd, PO Box 86, Grass Lake 49240...(517) 206-2952
Victoria Fisher *cyto49@yahoo.com* 201 McKee St, Sturgis 49091...(269) 651-8496
Christine Friedel *chensell@peoplepc.com* 54351 Parkville Rd, Mendon 49072.......................(269) 535-1032
Sarah Gerke *sarahgerke48@yahoo.com* 291 W Burnham St, Battle Creek 49015...................(269) 966-8875
Kathy Holser *kholser@yahoo.com* 723 Church St., Grass Lake 49240 ....(517) 522-8665
Cydney Idsinga *cydinga@gmail.com* 992 Marshall Rd, Coldwater 49036...............................(517) 279-0123
Dorie Litchfield *creator.dorie@gmail.com* 331 Prairie Dr, Climax 49034 ....(269) 746-8728
Connie Luegge *cdlteach2@yahoo.com* 10658 M 216, Marcellus 49067
Alexander (Sandy) Miller *sandymthepreacherman@juno.com*
61616 Filmore Rd, Sturgis 49091-9318...(269) 467-7134
Carrie Morton *dove1010@yahoo.com* 4285 E Kirby Rd, Battle Creek 49017 ....(269) 964-7098
Esther Puckett *puckettesther@yahoo.com* 10445 Folks Rd, Hanover 49241 ....(517) 936-5835
Heidi Rawson *heidithelibrarian@yahoo.com* 200 E. Garfield Lot 230, Coldwater 49036.......(517) 617-9922
Gary Selbee *gasalase@yahoo.com* 4787 Capital Ave SW, Battle Creek 49015 ....(269) 979-4629
Donna Smith *smithd42f@gmail.com* 304 Beckett Park, Battle Creek 49015...........................(269) 565-0958
Shelly Snow *snow.robert@sbcglobal.net* 483 Greenbriar Place, Jonesville 49283.................(517) 849-5066
Pamela Stilwell *sjimstilwell@yahoo.com* 700 Ninth St, Three Rivers 49093 ....(269) 858-3541
Veroneze Strader *verstrader@yahoo.com* 178 Feld Drive, Battle Creek 49037 ....(269) 963-6830
Marjorie Suggs *mwondermiss@aol.com* 32 Convis St, Battle Creek 49017............................(269) 965-5946
Shelley Szekely *bisho2sa@hotmail.com* 113 E Cherry St, Reading 49274 ....(269) 753-4231
Arlene Thompson *thompsonarlene6@aol.com* 1134 Orchard Dr, Three Rivers 49093............(269) 273-2829
John Williams *jwilliams@albion.edu* 803 S Superior St Apt 301, Albion 49224 ....(517) 629-6768

GRAND RAPIDS DISTRICT EQUALIZATION LAY MEMBERS

Elizabeth Batten *battene@mail.gvsu.edu* GVSU Wesley, 4539 Luce Street, Jenison 49428
Barbara Brechting *bbrechting@aol.com* 5092 Southglow Ct SE, Kentwood 49508................(616) 261-4814
Elena Brubaker *elena.brubaker@yahoo.com* 523 Lincoln Lk, Lowell 49331-1358 ....(616) 897-6357
Wendy Clark *gracewac@gmail.com* 4250 Summerwind Ave NE, Grand Rapids 49525..........(616) 363-8500

Daniel Davis *cadadavis@charter.net* 16655 Simmons, Cedar Springs 49319 ....(616) 696-1939
Chad Decker *chadm01007@gmail.com* 2813 84th St. SE, Caledonia 49316 ....(616) 698-0045
Annette Erbes *annettee@grandrapidsfumc.org* 1322 Clayton Ave, Muskegon 49441 ....(231) 780-3951
Mary Lou Fassett *mlfassett2@yahoo.com*
1551 Franklin SE Apt 2028, Grand Rapids 49506 ....(616) 285-4795
Thomas Fifer *thomas.fifer@gmail.com* 2011 Bedford St #3, Durham 27707 ....(616) 560-3914
Beverly Gassdorf *bev.gassdorf@sbcglobal.net*
2500 Breton Woods Apt #1037, Kentwood 49512 ....(616) 455-2657
Gary Gassdorf *gary.gassdorf@sbcglobal.net*
2500 Breton Woods Apt #1037, Kentwood 49512 ....(616) 455-2657
Kinnith Gibbs *gibbskinnith@yahoo.com* 2603 Falcon Pointe Dr. NW, Grand Rapids 49534
Pat Hiler *ijpathiler@sbcglobal.net* 3123 Waterford NE, Grand Rapids 49505 ....(616) 363-6130
Carol Hollebeek *oldhippy32@yahoo.com* 1538 44th St SW Apt 4, Wyoming 49509-4361
Joseph Jennings *dfafumc@att.net* 3072 Ramshore Dr., Fremont 49412-1717 ....(231) 519-2127
Sue Norton *campnorton@aol.com* 3937 Illinois SW, Wyoming 49509 ....(616) 538-6126
Zach Oaster *zoaster@gmail.com* 4455 13 Mile Rd NE, Rockford 49341 ....(616) 856-2204
Carrie Otis *carrie.otis@crosswindcc.org* 4380 Tracy Trail, Dorr 49323 ....(616) 681-0283
James Searls Jr *jrs@macatawa.org* 53 East Central, Zeeland 49464 ....(616) 772-4306
Julie Spurlin-Hane *juliespurlinhane@yahoo.com* 231 E South Ave, Hesperia 49421 ....(231) 854-6132
Amelia Stine *astine95@yahoo.com* 9560 Catalpa, Newaygo 49337 ....(231) 225-1011
Connie Swinger *connieswinger@att.net* 255 Brown SW, Grand Rapids 49507 ....(616) 452-3532
Lea Tobar *flt62@hotmail.com* 2430 Highridge Ln SE, Grand Rapids 49546-7536 ....(616) 940-0406
John Warnock *john_warnock@prodigy.net* 1830 Linson Ct SE, Grand Rapids 49546 ....(616) 942-8445
Sandy Williams *wms.sandy@gmail.com* 526 Forest View Ct., Hudsonville 49426 ....(616) 669-9086
Stephanie Wiltse *wiltse@iserv.net* 1046 San Juan SE, Grand Rapids 49506 ....(616) 243-3729
Paula C Wright *wright.paulac@gmail.com* 1141 Northlawn NE, Grand Rapids 49505 ....(616) 361-2321

GRAND TRAVERSE DISTRICT EQUALIZATION LAY MEMBERS

Kendra Baty *baty_08@hotmail.com* 515 W Main Street, PO Box 93, Manton 49663 ....(231) 824-3119
Irene Carboneau *istarr@lear.com* 390 S. Long Lake Rd., Traverse City 49684
Randie Clawson *randie.clawson@yahoo.com* 384 Lind Dr., Traverse City 49696 ....(231) 929-7808
Deborah Cole *deb.cole@petoskeyumc.org* 394 Hillview Dr, Petoskey 49770 ....(231) 348-3460
Lois Edson *loedson312@gmail.com* 4249 Ramblewood Drive, Traverse City 49684
Eric Falker *eric.irumc@gmail.com* 6113 Pine Trace Rd, Indian River 49749
Andrew Hahn *Hibyeakh@gmail.com* 4505 Stone Ridge Ct, Traverse City 49684 ....(231) 421-8397
Dave Hamman *dbhamman@charter.net* 701 W Tinkham Ave, Ludington 49431 ....(231) 845-0174
Jill Haney *gtdistrictoffice@tcchrist.com* 9150 E 22 Rd, Manton 49663 ....(231) 824-6541
Neil Haney *neil_h_haney2@yahoo.com* 9150 E 22 Rd., Manton 49663 ....(231) 824-6541
Everett Harpole *everett.harpole@icloud.com* 5954 Berry Lane, Indian River 49749 ....(269) 806-2816
Richard Hartrick *dick758@aol.com* 4790 Old Point Ridge, East Jordan 49727 ....(231) 536-2271
Jeanette Hayes *greenacres@avci.net* 6542 Hollyglen Dr., Elmira 49730 ....(231) 585-6922
Jay Hook *jwhook1@centurytel.net* 2230 W Nemeskal Rd, Maple City 49664 ....(231) 228-6250
Julie Lawhead *juleslawhead@yahoo.com* 1117 Mill Rd., Kingsley 49649 ....(231) 342-2487
Nancy LeValley *nblvly@charter.net* 2961 Crescent Shores Dr, Traverse City 49684 ....(231) 929-3155
Sandra Mallory *sandy.mallory2@gmail.com* 5171 Revnell Rd., Beulah 49617 ....(231) 882-0440
Linda Matchett *lindamatchett@hotmail.com* 01362 Matchett Rd., Charlevoix 49720
Joyce Mitchell *joycemitchell56@gmail.com* 124 Boyd St, Fife Lake 49633 ....(231) 879-5330
Jim Myers *thejimster51@gmail.com* 592 1/2 E. Main St., Harbor Springs 49740 ....(231) 838-8041
Denny Olin *dennyolin@gmail.com* 14432 Peninsula Dr, Traverse City 49686 ....(231) 223-4141
Richard Roberts *onchristthesolidrockistandd@gmail.com*
2415 E Michigan St, Free Soil 49411 ....(231) 233-8954
Marian Saur *hugsmarian@charter.net* 5133 Vinton Rd., Williamsburg 49690 ....(231) 267-5242
Kathi Schrock *katrsc@centurylink.net* 7037 E. Houghton Lake Rd., Merritt 49667 ....(231) 328-2039
Jennifer Smith *jenn4smith13@yahoo.com* 133 N. Park St., Lake City 49651
Mary Beth Stark *serenityridge61@yahoo.com* 11649 E 14 1/2 Road, Manton 49663 ....(231) 824-3294
Troy Trombley *lynn.k1057@sbcglobal.net* 2141 Stronach Road, Manistee 49660 ....(231) 723-0667
Richard Tunison *ctuni@charter.net* 309 Mason Street, Charlevoix 49720 ....(231) 547-5009

Michael Windover *mjw888@charter.net* 11612 N Long Lake Rd, Traverse City 49685..........(231) 275-7483
Robert Wirgau *rwirgau@freeway.net* 917 W. Sheridan, Petoskey 49770..................................(231) 347-5463
Susan Wirgau *onthebay@chartermi.net* 917 W. Sheridan, Petoskey 49770..............................(231) 347-5463

HEARTLAND DISTRICT EQUALIZATION LAY MEMBERS

Linda Andersen *lka83038@hotmail.com* 8741 Six Lakes Rd, Six Lakes 48886......................(989) 365-3307
Christy Baker *christy3256@yahoo.com* 605 W. Edgerton St., Howard City 49329................(231) 648-6126
Mark Baker *mfbaker@peoplepc.com* 1006 Hampshire Dr, St Johns 48879-2404...................(989) 224-2415
Tom Bentley *tlbxtwo@yahoo.com* 116 N East St, St Louis 48880-1721..................................(989) 593-2621
Kaylee Blackwell *kayleelblackwell@yahoo.com* 323 Bankson St., St. Louis 48880................(989) 388-6191
Larry W Collins *wmlaco@charter.net* 1413 E Gaylord St, Mt Pleasant 48858-3626..............(989) 773-0994
Terrie Eisenmann *terrieblue41@gmail.com* 9720 Beckley Road, Blanchard 49310................(989) 561-2578
Kendall Farnum *kendall_farnum@yahoo.com* 1160 Glen Ave, Mt Pleasant 48858.................(989) 854-0343
Susan Franklin *Lsfbflat@gmail.com* 2392 Fern Ct, Farwell 48622..(989) 588-6378
Sean Griffin *mrmuse12@yahoo.com* 488 E. Stoneridge Dr., Plainwell 49080.........................(269) 685-5589
Keegan Hartman *keegan.hartman@gmail.com* 319 S Jeffrey Ave, Ithaca 48847......................(989) 875-8264
Kathryn Heaton *k.heaton@live.com* 8727 Sheridan St., Montague 49437
Claire Hills *cbhills@gmail.com* 3510 Mineral Springs Trail, Mt Pleasant 48858.....................(989) 317-0081
John Holland *sewerlurker@yahoo.com* 4350 W Beal City Rd, Weidman 48893.....................(989) 644-5578
Zachary McNees *zach@mtpfumc.org* 413 N Fancher Apt 3, Mt. Pleasant 48858
Clara Molby *molby@ispmgt.com* 11984 E. McBride Rd., Riverdale 48877
Russell Morgan *fatpastor@cmsinter.net* 8135 Mill St, PO Box 366, Winn 48896...................(989) 824-0653
Tiffany Newsom *tiffany_loved@yahoo.com* 226 S State St, PO Box 183, Pewamo 48873-0183
Kirk Perry *kbperry@chartermi.net* 906 E. Evergreen, Greenville 48838.................................(616) 754-6045
Ray Rohn *karensue952@yahoo.com* 619 Cedar Street, Breckenridge 48615...........................(989) 842-5503
Kathy Shepard *kshepard@edzone.net* 7575 S Leaton Rd, Shepherd 48883-9303....................(989) 828-6486
John Skinner *johnskinner43@hotmail.com* 418 S Elizabeth, Mt Pleasant 48858.....................(989) 773-4340
Kathryn Strouse *katjoy98@yahoo.com* 220 N Main, PO Box 84, North Star 48862................(989) 875-2894
Meredith VanderHill *cedirector@cmsinter.net* 1820 S. Crawford St. F1, Mount Pleasant 48858
Alene Ward *ward8170@yahoo.com* 775 S Coventry Ave, Owosso 48867...............................(517) 449-7145
Ned Weller *nedweller@yahoo.com* 95 Meadow Lane, Ithaca 48847-1846
Lois White *loiswhite1215@gmail.com* 12996 Hersey Rd., Hersey 49639...............................(231) 832-5991
Dennis Wissinger *dowraw@charter.net* 2797 Lone Pine, Farwell 48622.................................(989) 386-8900

KALAMAZOO DISTRICT EQUALIZATION LAY MEMBERS

Jeff Anson *jeffanson@gmail.com* 1821 Humphrey Street, Kalamazoo 49048..........................(269) 345-4559
Lisa Coe *church_ladi@yahoo.com* 4104 Waterview Dr, Vicksburg 49097...............................(269) 649-0602
Earl Collier *earlcollier2574@gmail.com* 2574 127th Ave, Allegan 49010..............................(269) 793-7340
Annette Crandall *acrand@btc-bci.com* 57219 Corwin Road, PO Box 622, Lawrence 49064 .(269) 655-5181
Fred Douglas *dugkazoo@att.net* 5138 Old Colony, Portage 49024..(269) 373-6838
Jason Harpole *PastorJHarpole@gmail.com* 205 Amos Ave, Portage 49002............................(269) 388-8312
Joey Jacobson *joseph.b.jacobson@wmich.edu*
John Mahan *jemamahan@yahoo.com* 403 Walnut Woods Ct., Plainwell 49080.....................(269) 685-6142
Sarah Mannschreck *sarah.m.mannschreck@wmich.edu*..(248) 990-4385
Scott Marsh *smarsh3386@gmail.com* 336 S. Kendall Apt. 34, Kalamazoo 49008
Patrick McCrevan *patrickmccrevan@gmail.com* 5772 Scottdale Rd, St. Joseph 49085...........(269) 556-9592
Natalie McDermont *natzmcdrmnt@gmail.com* 52333 Ackley Terrace, Paw Paw 49079..........(269) 657-4506
Adele Paxson *adelepax@charter.net* 1332 Royce Ave, Kalamazoo 49001..............................(269) 343-2903
Reba Peterson *rebapeterson@netzero.net* 687 W Fennville St, Fennville 49408.....................(269) 561-2537
John Pickron *john707@charter.net* 1104 Barton St., Otsego 49078..(269) 692-2197
James Robertson *jc.robertson@ymail.com* 55130 County Rd 384, Grand Junction 49056......(269) 434-6499
Karen Saddler *wesleycampaignmanager@gmail.com* 4381 Foxfire Trail, Portage 49024
Deborah Search-Willoughby *dsearchwillo@charter.net*
1410 Turwill Lane, Kalamazoo 49006..(269) 349-9311
Molly Shaffer *orcf@aol.com* 33053 Crystal Springs St, Dowagiac 49047..............................(269) 684-6347
Cindy Thiele *cindahthiele@gmail.com* 319 River Street, Allegan 49010................................(269) 673-4514

Delberta Troutman *dtroutman1@comcast.net* 108 Austin Dr, Hartford 49057 ....(269) 308-3011
Amber Walker *amber.wlkr@gmail.com* 3130 Stonebridge Ct Apt 10, Portage 49024..............(269) 321-0538
Pam Walker *walkerpjane@gmail.com* 5016 N Watervliet Rd, PO Box 22, Watervliet 49098..(269) 277-0232
Burke Webb *bawebbfoot@juno.com* PO Box 579, Marcellus 49067
Caleb Williams *caleb.b.williams@gmail.com* 7146 Oakland Dr., Portage 49024......................(231) 313-9005
Jackie Witt *witt5685@frontier.com* 4569 Donna Dr, Bridgman 49106 ....(269) 465-3296

LANSING DISTRICT EQUALIZATION LAY MEMBERS

Richard Ahti *richardahti@gmail.com* 4461 Oaklawn Dr, Okemos 48864 ....(517) 349-1314
Mark Baker *mfbaker@peoplepc.com* 1006 Hampshire Dr, St Johns 48879-2404 ....(989) 224-2415
Jerry Bukoski *jerry.bukoski@gmail.com* 1069 S Ionia Rd, Vermontville 49096.......................(517) 588-8415
Jodi Cartwright *jodikelley5@gmail.com* 3948 Windy Heights, Okemos 48864-3589
Brian Crackel *crackelb@msu.edu* Wesley Foundation @ MSU, 1118 S Harrison Rd, East Lansing 48823
Keeley Davenport *keeleydavenport@gmail.com* 1227 Grand Ave, Kalamazoo 49006
David Dekker *youfoundation@youfoundation.org* 3209 Hillgate Cir, Lansing 48912 ....(517) 324-4968
Nancy Ham *nancymham@gmail.com* 1917 Maple Shade Dr, Williamston 48895 ....(517) 655-2754
Julia Humenik *jrh15@albion.edu* 118 W Henry St, Charlotte 48813-1809.............................(517) 543-0579
Matt Kreh *matt@oasislansing.org* 501 E. Mt. Hope Ave, Lansing 48910
Jim LeBaron *jlebaronllc@aol.com* 13401 Peacock Rd, Laingsburg 48848-9296....................(517) 641-8042
Lonnie Lowery *LonnieDLowery@yahoo.com* 4618 Manitou Dr, Okemos 48864 ....(517) 381-1322
Chris Mathis *Chris@msuwesley.org* 2227 Meadowlawn Dr, Holt 48842
James McCartney *jemllc.cpa@gmail.com* 1414 Safire Ct, East Lansing 48823.......................(517) 574-5262
Kim Metzer *kim@dewittredeemer.org* 13543 Turner Rd, DeWitt 48820 ....(517) 256-0646
Christine Pease *peasechris@yahoo.com* 340 Pleasant St, Charlotte 48813-1626....................(517) 543-5618
Paul Powers *powers.paul@att.net* P O Box 142, Perry 48872 ....(517) 635-3444
Nicole Proctor-Kanyama *proctorn@msu.edu* 824 Nipp Ave, Lansing 48915 ....(517) 367-8287
Andy Sass *to4cc2me@comcast.net* 216 Harrison St, Grand Ledge 48837 ....(517) 627-0452
Timothy Trommater *tim.trommater@gmail.com* 717 N Jordan Ave, Liberal 67901-2911
Keeton Tsai 6137 Horizon Dr, East Lansing 48823
Kelly Wasnich *kelly.wasnich@gmail.com* 401 E Ash St, Mason 48854...................................(517) 515-1827
Toinette Wicks *Wicks6@yahoo.com* 1956 N M 52, Stockbridge 49285-9625 ....(517) 623-6594

CONFERENCE EQUALIZATION LAY MEMBERS

Kathy Anderson *kathyanderson47@charter.net* 12127 Edgerton Dr, Cedar Springs 49319.....(616) 696-1589
Keith Anderson *k.w.anderson@sbcglobal.net* 775 133rd Ave, Wayland 49348 ....(269) 792-9338
Carole Armstrong *armstr15@gmail.com* 1216 Downer Ave, Lansing 48912-4432.................(517) 485-9813
Jim Bosserd *jbosserd@choiceone.com* 3631 13 Mile Rd NW, Sparta 49345 ....(616) 887-7805
Sharon Burkart *sharonannburkart@gmail.com* 1517 S Broadway St, Hastings 49058............(269) 660-8881
Sus'ann Busley *lansingdistrict@miareaumc.org* 555 S Williamston Rd, Dansville 48819......(517) 623-6239
Stacy Caballero *maestrastacy@aol.com* 141 Kimball Ave, Battle Creek 49014-5829 ....(269) 965-0285
Jane Case *janecase@comcast.net* 113 West, PO Box 146, Napoleon 49261............................(517) 536-8781
Susan Cobb *scobb@charter.net* 9092 Deer Point Dr, Newaygo 49337
Judy Coffey *jcoffeyumc@yahoo.com* 128 Forest Lawn Dr, Cadillac 49601-9734 ....(231) 775-6095
Blair Cutler *blair.r.cutler@wmich.edu* 623 Darby Lane, Kalamazoo 49006
Laurie Dahlman *milwoodumc@sbcglobal.net* 1228 Southern Ave, Kalamazoo 49001 ....(269) 343-1490
Joseph DeLany *jhdelany@gmail.com* 3648 New Holland St., Hudsonville 49426...................(616) 797-0244
Mary-Jo DeLany *maryjo.delany@gmail.com*
3648 New Holland St., Hudsonville 49426 ....(616) 797-0244
Mark Doyal *mark@miareaumc.org* 525 University Dr, East Lansing 48823-3046 ....(517) 333-4203
Cheyenne Farr *cfarr15@live.com* 3181 Hill Rd NW, Rapid City 49676 ....(231) 534-3190
Deborah Fennell *dfennell@dartenergy.com* 3409 Rolfe Rd, Mason 48854-9749.....................(517) 676-1887
Daphna Flegal *dflegal@umpublishing.org* 610 Burgundy Dr, Madison, TN 37115-3502........(615) 885-6621
Margaret Foster 660 Lake Dr, Altamonte Springs, NC 32701-5412
Merna Francis *mernfran@aol.com* 2924 N 33rd St, Galesburg 49053 ....(269) 665-9430
Naomi Garcia *naomi@wmcumc.org* 11 Fuller Ave SE, PO Box 6247, Grand Rapids 49516-6247
William Gehman *w.gehman@earthlink.net* 4471 Foxtail Circle, Grand Ledge 48837 ....(517) 626-6716

Nichea Ver Veer Guy *orangecelt00@aol.com* 125 Baynton NE, Grand Rapids 49503 ....(616) 451-7058
Sarah Hercula *shercula@gmail.com* 118 S Mayhew, New Buffalo 49117
Donald Hiler *dchiler@sbcglobal.net* 3123 Waterford NE, Grand Rapids 49505 ....(616) 363-6130
Helene Hill *helenerhill@bellsouth.net* 266 Merrimon Ave Apt D, Asheville, NC 28801 ....(705) 255-8065
Katie Hiscock *khiscock@umc-kzo.org* 1389 Concord Place Dr. Apt.1C, Kalamazoo 49009
Nolan Hudson *shonohs@hotmail.com* 6355 Bivens Rd, Nashville 49073 ....(517) 852-1821
John Huizing *john@hartumc.org* 40 N. Plum Street, Hart 49420 ....(231) 873-0418
Wynne Hurlbut *wynne_hurlbut@frontier.com* 36146 Cherry St, Gobles 49055 ....(269) 628-2944
Jenna Johnson *jenna.k.johnson@wmich.edu*
Michael Johnson *mjohnson3@yahoo.com* 84 E Kingman, Battle Creek 49014 ....(269) 962-6401
Glen Kinder *glen.kinder@gmail.com* 640 Dart Road, Mason 48854 ....(517) 676-5552
Jenny Kroeze *jenk@ncats.net* 640 Seminole Dr, Fremont 49412 ....(231) 924-4814
Steven Lett *slett@wlklaw.com* 9417 W Scenic Lake Dr, Laingsburg 48848-9749
C David Lundquist *dlundquist@ameritech.net* 5920 Wood Valley Rd, Kalamazoo 49009 ......(269) 352-0582
Georgia Marsh *georgiamarsh212@gmail.com* 212 Chauncey Court, Marshall 49068 ....(269) 781-2501
Cameron McDermont *cammcdermont@gmail.com*
52333 Ackley Terrace, Paw Paw 49079 ....(269) 657-4506
Michael McDonald *m_mcdonald@charter.net* 10843 Talon Ct, Traverse City 49686 ....(231) 935-3759
Joy Mills *millsjoy@ymail.com* 1014 Barton Street, Otsego 49078 ....(269) 929-4954
Ryan Minier *ryan.minier@gmail.com*
2551 W Springfield Ave Apt 11, Champagne IL 61821 ....(231) 832-9566
Valerie Mossman-Celestin *valeriemcelestin@gmail.com*
300 Alten Ave NE, Grand Rapids 49503 ....(616) 459-6604
Mandana Nordbrock *office@kazoodistumc.org* 431 Timber Ridge Dr, Kalamazoo 49006.......(269) 720-6152
Kristina Person *persont@michigan.gov* 10832 Cooper Rd, Pleasant Lake 49272 ....(517) 769-3012
Norm Pigeon *vjmaidens@yahoo.com* 1854 Schanz Rd, Allegan 49010 ....(269) 793-7769
Jody Pratt *prattgji@hughes.net* 2984 5th St, Shelbyville 49344 ....(269) 792-0481
Simmie Proctor *simmiepr@hotmail.com* 73486 8th Ave, South Haven 49090 ....(269) 637-6053
Helen Reid *mysticmethodist1954@yahoo.com* 3839 Alger Ave, White Cloud 49349 ....(231) 689-0344
Paul Reissmann *paul.c.reissmann@gmail.com* 810 Rankin Ave, Kalamazoo 49006
Judi Ryan *judith-ryan@sbcglobal.net* 5417 Newcastle Dr SE, Grand Rapids 49508 ....(616) 455-1825
Joyce Showerman *jshowerman@fumer.org* 600 S Main St, Eaton Rapids 48827 ....(517) 663-5284
Allegra Smith *unfaded@gmail.com* 29740 Pine Tree Dr, New Hudson 48165
Anne Soles *annesoles@charter.net* 217 Old State Rd, PO Box 467, Pentwater 49449 ....(231) 869-7651
Nona Spackman *nspackman12@gmail.com* 3806 Cornice Falls Dr Apt 6, Holt 48842 ....(517) 694-8346
Madeline Stagner *justmadinicole@gmail.com* 74 Orchard Pl, Battle Creek 49017 ....(269) 963-5711
Andrew Stange *andrew.stange@gmail.com* 118 S Mayhew St, New Buffalo 49117
Sue Stickle *ssti775872@aol.com* 10970 Dutch Settlement Rd, Marcellus 49067-9457 ....(269) 646-9425
Patrick Tiedt *patiedt@hotmail.com* 9859 River Road, Evart 49631 ....(231) 734-2932
Prospero Tumonong *treas@wmcumc.org* 6247 Meadowlark Dr NE, Rockford 49341 ....(616) 866-5410
Bill Vert *w.vert@comcast.net* 5670 Loftwood Dr. SE, Kentwood 49508 ....(616) 455-0091
Andrew Vorbrich *AVorbrich@LennonMiller.com* 1914 Waite Ave, Kalamazoo 49008 ....(269) 343-1906
Max Waagner *Max.Waagner@dawnfoods.com* 928 Sunburst Rd, Jackson 49203 ....(517) 787-2924
Patricia Watson *pattywatson@grar.com*
REMAX Sunquest, 6255 28th St SE, Grand Rapids 49546 ....(616) 813-6506
Donald Williams *wms.don@gmail.com* 5226 Forest View Court, Hudsonville 49426 ....(616) 669-9086
Molly Williams *Molly.Williams@wmich.edu* 2716 N 9th St, Kalamazoo 49009 ....(269) 375-4867
David Wiltse *dmwiltse@att.net* 7056 Northland Drive NE, Rockford 49341-8838 ....(616) 866-1051
Laura Witkowski *lauraw@wmcumc.org* 1164 Treeway Dr NW, Sparta 49345
Larry Wyman Sr. *lwyman@toast.net* 480 Witbeck Dr, Clare 48617-9721 ....(989) 386-3123
Lynda Zeller *lyndazeller@comcast.net* 2314 E Libbie Dr, Lansing 48917 ....(616) 706-2017
Larry Zomer *Larry.zomer@gmail.com* 23450 2 Mile Rd, Reed City 49667 ....(231) 832-4563

L EQUALIZATION OF LAY and CLERGY MEMBERSHIP

Under Rule 8

(Calculations for the 2014 Annual Conference)

	Clergy	Lay
Total Clergy Members (Rule 8, B)	**554**	
(2013 Annual Conference Disciplinary Question #57a, p67)		

Pastoral Charges Entitled to Elect Professing Lay Members (Rule 8, C, 2a)

	Lay
Total Pastoral Charges on the Six Districts	**308**
Additional Laity for Co-Pastor, Associate Pastors and Appointed Ordained Deacons	**13**

Albion	**Grand Rapids**	**Grand Traverse**
Jackson First-2	Grand Rapids Cornerstone	Traverse City Central
	Grand Rapids First	
	Grand Rapids Trinity	
	Holland First	
	Muskegon Central	
Heartland	**Kalamazoo**	**Lansing**
	Kalamazoo Sunnyside	East Lansing University
	Kalamazoo Westwood	Lansing Mt. Hope
	St. Joseph First	

Lay Members described in the Constitution ¶32 Article I & Discipline ¶602.4 (Rule 8, C, 2b)

	Lay
Diaconal Ministers:	**4**
Jane Case; Daphna Flegal; Margaret Foster; Helene Hill	
Active Deaconesses: **Valerie Mossman-Celestin**	**1**
Home Missioners under episcopal appointment within Conference: *none*	**0**
Conference President, United Methodist Women: **Jenny Kroeze**	**1**
Conference President, United Methodist Men: *(presently unfilled)*	**0**
Conference Lay Leader: **Anne Soles**	**1**
District Lay Leaders:	**6**
Albion: **Max Waagner** Grand Rapids: **Helen Reid** Grand Traverse: **Mike McDonald**	
Heartland: **Larry Wyman, Sr.** Kalamazoo: **Wynne Hurlbut** Lansing: **Deb Fennell**	
Conference Director of Lay Servant Ministries *(in ¶32 only)* **Jody Pratt**	**1**
Conference Secretaries of Global Ministries: *(in ¶32 only)* Lynn DeMoss; Kay DeMoss	**0**
President or equivalent-Young Adult Organization: Rebecca Wieringa	**0**
President, Conference Youth Organization: *(No Current Youth President)*	**0**
One (1) young person between the ages of 12-17 from each District	**6**
One (1) young person between the ages of 18-30 from each District	**6**
Chair of Annual Conference College Student Organization *(in ¶602.4 only) none*	**0**
Total provided in Constitution and Discipline	**26**
	347

Number of additional Lay Members needed for equalization: (564-347 = 207)

Additional Lay Members (Rule 8, C, 3c)

		Lay
1.	Members of General and Jurisdictional boards, councils, and standing commissions or their divisions, departments, committees, units and other sub-groups residing within Conference:	**1**
	Connectional Table: Kennetha Bigham-Tsai	
	Global Ministries, Women's Division: **Nichea VerVeer Guy**	
	NCJ Missions Council: *Valerie Mossman-Celestin; John Boley	
2.	Lay Chairpersons of Conference Boards:	**2**
3.	Global Ministries: **Lynda Zeller**	
	Lay Ministries: *Anne Soles	
	Trustees: **William Gehman**	
4.	Conference Treasurer: **Pros Tumonong**	**1**
5.	Conference Facilitator: **Laura Witkowski**	**1**
6.	Lay members of the following agencies:	
•	Conference Leadership Team	**3**
	*Anne Soles; **Sue Cobb; Glen Kinder; Mark Doyal;** *Pros Tumonong	
•	Council on Finance and Administration	**9**
	Kathleen Anderson; Jim Bosserd; *Sue Cobb; **Nolan Hudson; David Lundquist;** **Susan MacGregor; **Georgia Marsh; Patrick Tiedt; Bill Vert; Patricia Watson; Molly Williams**; *Pros Tumonong	
•	Conference Program Committee	**6**
	*Anne Soles; *Jenny Kroeze; **Judy Coffey**; *Laura Witkowski; **Mary Jo DeLany**; *Nichea VerVeer Guy; **Sue Stickle; Andrew Stange; David Wiltse**; **Sharon Burkat**	
•	Rules of Order Committee	**2**
	*Judy Coffey; *David Lundquist; **Don Williams;**	

Larry Zomer; *Laura Witkowski;
- Committee on Journal 4
  Sus'ann Busley; Merna Francis; Mandana Nordbrock; Joyce Showerman; *Max Waagner

7. Lay chairpersons of District Council on Ministries or equivalent 1
   Albion: **Kristina Person** Heartland: Kim DeLong
   Grand Rapids: Rick Blunt Kalamazoo: Buff Coe
   Grand Traverse: Jean Smith Lansing: Kennetha Bigham-Tsai
8. Conference Missionary Secretary: Lynn DeMoss; Kay DeMoss 0
9. Conference Secretary and all Lay Assistant Secretaries: 5
   Greg Buchner; **Dan Brook; Blair Cutler; Joe DeLany; Sarah Hercula; Allegra Smith;** *Andrew Stange; Jennifer Wheeler
10. Conference Statistician: Tom Fox 0
11. Conference Chancellor: **Andrew Vorbrich** 1
12. Director of Communications: *Mark Doyal 0
13. Lay Directors of WMC Campus Ministries: (currently vacant) 0
14. Lay chairpersons/coordinator of these Conference agencies: 8
    Abuse Prevention Team: **Nona Spackman**
    Archives and History: Melanie Young
    Christian Unity and Interreligious Concerns: Paul Hane
    Communications: **Carole Armstrong**
    Disability Concerns: **John Huizing**
    Disaster Response Team: Jeremy Wicks
    Episcopacy (Vice-Chair if Chair is not a member of WMC): *(*Jody Pratt)*
    Equitable Compensation: Nancy Patera
    Hispanic/Latino Committee: **Stacy Caballero**
    Michigan Area Indian Workers Conference: **Norm Pigeon**
    New Church Establishment and Development: Tom Arthur
    Nominations: Glenn Wagner
    Leadership Development: *none*
    Older Adult Ministries: **Laurie Dahlman**
    Personnel: Ellen Zienert
    Prison Ministries and Restorative Justice Concerns: Richard Moore
    Racial/Ethnic Local Church: Geri Litchfield
    Religion and Race: **Mike Johnson**
    Scouting: **Keith Anderson**
    Status and Role of Women: **Amy Latimer
    UMCOR/Hunger: Robert Freysinger
15. Lay General and Jurisdictional Conference delegates and reserves elected for the last General and Jurisdictional Conference: 3
    *Laurie Dahlman; *NicheaVerVeer Guy; *Valerie Mossman-Celestin;
    Steven Lett; Ryan Minier; Simmie Proctor; *Patrick Tiedt
16. Lay Conference Ministry Consultant: **I. Naomi Garcia** 1
17. Associate Conference Lay Leader: *Max Waagner **0**
18. Conference Youth Ministries Coordinator: **Joy Mills** 1
19. Conference Journal Editor: **Don Hiler** 1

Total provided by Rule 8, C, 3c (Items 1-18) **50**

Lay Members to be Elected by the Districts: (Rule 8, C, 3e) **157**

Albion: 25	Grand Rapids: 27	Grand Traverse: 27
Heartland: 26	Kalamazoo: 27	Lansing: 25

Totals: CLERGY: **554** LAY: **554**

Also, each District is to elect two (2) alternates PLUS one (1) young person between the ages of 12-17, and one young person between the ages of 18-30 and one (1) reserve member for the age group of 12-17 and one (1) reserve member for the age group of 18-30. (The young person age 12-17 may be elected by either the District Conference or the District Youth Council.)

Names in Bold are lay equalization members
* Denotes already included in a previous category
** Denotes Lay Member from their Local Church – not counted again as lay member for equalization

EQUALIZATION

THE UNITED METHODIST CHURCH
THE BUSINESS OF THE ANNUAL CONFERENCE

The Minutes of the West Michigan Annual Conference
Held in Calvin College, Grand Rapids, Michigan
From (date) June 11, 2014, through June 14, 2014
Bishop Deborah Lieder Kiesey, Presiding
Date When Organized 1968; Number of This Session Forty-sixth

PART I ORGANIZATION AND GENERAL BUSINESS

1. Who are elected for the quadrennium (¶¶603.7, 619)?

Secretary? **Gregory L. Buchner**
Mailing Address: 7296 9 Mile Road, Mecosta, MI 49332
Telephone: 231-972-2838
Email: pastorgreg.ncd@gmail.com

Statistician? **Thomas Fox**
Mailing Address: 1626 Lake Drive, Apt 189, Haslett, MI 48840
Telephone: 269-921-5812
Email: preacher1947@yahoo.com

Treasurer? **Prospero Tumonong**
Mailing Address: 11 Fuller SE, PO Box 6247, Grand Rapids, MI 49516-6247
Telephone: 616-459-4503
Email: treas@wmcumc.org

2. Is the Annual Conference incorporated (¶603.1)? Yes

3. Bonding and auditing:
What officers handling funds of the conference have been bonded, and in what amounts (¶¶618, 2511)?

Name	Position	Amount Bonded
Mr. Prospero Tumonong	Conference Treasurer	$1,000,000.00

Have the books of said officers or persons been audited (¶¶617, 2511)? (See report, page 446 of Journal.)

4. What agencies have been appointed or elected?
   a) Who have been elected chairpersons for the mandated structures listed?

Structure	Chairperson	Mailing Address	Phone No.	Email
Council on Finance and Administration (¶611)	Susan Cobb	9092 Deer Point Drive, Newaygo, MI 49337	616-784-4445	scobb@charter.net
Board of Ordained Ministry (¶635)	Sherri Swanson	19603 Oak Drive, New Buffalo, MI 49117	269-756-2053	toumc@att.net
Board of Pensions (¶639)	Lou Grettenberger	1960 Skyview Dr., Sparta, MI 49345	616-887-8255	pastorlou@chartermi.net
Board of Trustees of the Annual Conference (¶2512)	William Gehman	4471 Foxtail Circle, Grand Ledge, MI 48837	517 - 626-6716	w.gehman@earthlink.net
Committee on Episcopacy (¶637)	Genie Bank	6651 Lakeshore Rd, Lexington, MI 48450	810-359-7281	geniebank@gmail.com
Administrative Review Committee (¶636)	William Johnson	4390 Summer Lane NE, Grand Rapids, MI 49525	616-361-0024	bjinside@gmail.com

b) Indicate the name of the agency (or agencies) and the chairperson(s) in your annual conference which is (are) responsible for the functions related to each of the following general church agencies (¶610.1):

General Agency	Conference Agency	Chairperson	Mailing Address	Phone Number	Email
General Board of Church and Society	Board of Church and Society	Amee Paparella	9590 Looking Glass Brook Dr., Grand Ledge, MI 48837	517-626-6623	pastor@ wacoustaumc.org
General Board of Discipleship	Associate Director of Discipleship	Naomi Garcia	11 Fuller Ave SE, PO Box 6247, Grand Rapids, MI 49516-6247	616-459-4503	naomi@wmcumc. org
General Board of Global Ministries	Board of Global Ministries	Delberta Troutman	108 Austin Dr, Hartford, MI 49057	269-308-3011	dtroutman1@ comcast.net
Higher Education and Campus Ministry	Board of Higher Education and Campus Ministry	Jeff Williams	220 Church Street, Wayland, MI 49348	269-792-2208	jeffwrev@gmail. com
General Commission on Archives and History	Commission on Archives and History	Melanie Young	124 S. Rutledge, Pentwater, MI 49449	231-869-5900	msyoung14760@ gmail.com
General Commission on Religion and Race	Commission on Religion and Race	Michael Johnson	84 E. Kingman, Battle Creek, MI 49014	269-962-6401	mjohnson3@ yahoo.com
General Commission on the Status and Role of Women	Commission on the Status and Role of Women	Amy Latimer	305 North Prospect, St. Johns, MI 48879	989-224-2293	latimer.amy@ gmail.com
United Methodist Communications	Commission on Communications	Carole Armstrong	1216 Downer, Lansing, MI 48912	517-485-9813	armstr15@gmail. com

c) Indicate the conference agencies and chairpersons which have responsibilities for the following functions:

General Agency	Name of Agency	Chairperson	Mailing Address	Phone	Email
Criminal Justice and Mercy Ministries (¶657)?	Prison Ministries and Restorative Justice Committee	Richard Moore	PO Box 410, 121 West North, Hastings, MI 49058	269-945-4995	rmoore@ choiceonemail.com
Disability Concerns (¶653)?	Committee on Disability Concerns	John Huizing	40 N. Plum St., Hart, MI 49420	231-873-0418	john@hartumc.org
Equitable Compensation (¶625)?	Commission on Equitable Compensation	Nancy Patera	4290 Summer Creek Drive, Dorr, MI 49323	616) 896-8410	nancypatera@mac. com

Laity (¶631)?	Board of Lay Ministries	Anne Soles	PO Box 467, 217 Old State Rd., Pentwater, MI 49449	231-869-4059	annesoles@charter.net
Native American Ministry (¶654)?	Indian Workers Conference	Norm Pigeon	1854 Schanz Rd., Allegan, MI 49010	269-672-5255	vjmaidens@yahoo.com
Small Membership Church (¶645)?	Town and Country Committee	Linda J. Burton-Collier	2574 127th Ave, Allegan, MI 49010	269-793-7340	lindaburtoncollier@gmail.com

d) Indicate the president or equivalent for the following organizations.

Organization	Name of Agency	Chairperson	Mailing Address	Phone	Email
Conference United Methodist Women (¶647)	Conference United Methodist Women	Jenny Kroeze	640 Seminole Dr., Fremont, MI 49412	888-544-5388	jenk@ncats.net
Conference United Methodist Men (¶648)	Conference United Methodist Men	–	–	–	–
Conference Council on Youth Ministry (¶649)	Youth Ministries	Naomi Garcia	11 Fuller Ave SE, PO Box 6247, Grand Rapids, MI 49516-6247	616-459-4503	naomi@wmcumc.org
Conference Council on Young Adult Ministry (¶650)?	Young Adult Ministry	Rebecca Wieringa	3818 Melody Lane, Hart, MI 49420	231-873-3516	pastorbecca7@gmail.com

e) Have persons been elected for the following district boards and committees? Answer yes or no.
(1) District Boards of Church Location & Building (¶2518)? Yes
(2) Committees on District Superintendency (¶669)? Yes
(3) District Committees on Ordained Ministry (¶666)? Yes

f) What other councils, boards, commissions, or committees have been appointed or elected in the annual conference?

Structure	Chairperson	Mailing Address	Phone	Email
Leadership Team	Leonard Schoenherr	4500 Mountain Ash Lane, Kalamazoo, MI 49004	269-665-7952	schoenherrien@gmail.com
Abuse Prevention Team	Nona Spackman	3806 Cornice Falls Dr., Apt. 6, Holt, MI 48842	517-321-8100	nspackman12@gmail.com
Board of Christian Camping	Glen Kinder	640 Dart Road, Mason, MI 48854	517-676-5552	glen.kinder@gmail.com
Conference Disaster Response Team	–	–	–	–
Cooperative Ministry Committee	Jodie Flessner	260 Vine St., Caledonia, 49316	616-891-8669	pastor.jodie@caledoniaumc.org
Children's Ministries	Glenys Nellist	1507 Lenox Dr SE Grand Rapids, MI 49506	269-903-8549	daveglenys@msn.com
Older Adult Ministries	Laurie Dahlman	1228 Southern Ave., Kalamazoo, MI 49001	269-343-1490	laddmsu@att.net
Board of Evangelism	Jonathan Van Dop	119 E. Main St., Ionia, MI 48846	616-527-1860	uscgemt@yahoo.com

MI Area Haiti Task Force	David Morton	4285 E. Kirby Rd., Battle Creek, MI 49017	269-964-7098	RevMorton62@yahoo.com
Committee on Hispanic/Latino Ministries	Stacy Caballero	141 Kimball Ave., Battle Creek, MI 49014	269-965-0285	maestrastacy@aol.com
New Church Establishment and Development Committee	Tom Arthur	5058 Glendurgan Ct., Holt, MI 48842	517-394-6100	tomarthur@sycamorecreekchurch.org
Conference Personnel Committee	Ellen Zienert	1006 Hampshire Dr., St. Johns, MI 48879	989-224-6859	pastorellen@4wbi.net
Racial Ethnic Local Church Committee (RELC)	Jane Lippert	10160 E Pickwick Ct., Traverse City, MI 49684	231-946-5323	jane@traversebaychurch.org
UMCOR/Hunger Committee	Robert Freysinger	2301 Shawn Rd NW, Kalkaska, MI 49646	231-258-2820	pastorrjf913@yahoo.com
AC Program Committee	Nichea Ver Veer Guy	125 Baynton NE , Grand Rapids, MI 49503	616-456-7168	orangecelt00@aol.com
Agenda and Reference Committee	Anne Soles	PO Box 467, 217 Old State Rd., Pentwater, MI 49449	231-869-4059	annesoles@charter.net
Rules of Order Committee	Judy Coffey	128 Forest Lawn Dr, Cadillac, MI 49601	(231)775-6095	jcoffeyumc@yahoo.com
Committee on Memoirs	Derye Maurer	3639 Sweetgum Dr., Jackson, MI 49201	517-782-0543	edryemaurer@gmail.com
Conf Nominating Committee (CNC)	Glenn Wagner	633 Hillock Ct, Grand Haven, MI 49417	616-842-7980	pastorglenn@umcdunes.org
Area School for Pastoral Ministry	Melany Chalker	762 N Kalamazoo Ave, Marshall, MI 49068	269-781-5107	pastormelany@gmail.com
Clark Retirement Community Trustees	Charles Burpee	1621 Falcon Crest Dr, NE Grand Rapids, MI 49525-7012	616-752-2141	chuckburpee@comcast.net
Conference Director of Lay Servant Ministries	Jody Pratt	2984 5th St., Shelbyville, MI 49344	616-292-1220	prattgji@hughes.net
John Wesley Association	Jeremy Wicks	1956 N M52, Stockbridge, MI 49285-9625	517-655-4668 x6720	jeremy_wicks@yahoo.com
Trustees of Lake Louise Christian Community	Phillip Friedrick	2317 Marquard St., Muskegon, MI 49445	231-744-4491	pastorphil@communitychurchumc.org
MI Area Loan Fund Trustees	Charles Veenstra	41360 Fox Run, Novi, MI 48377	248-859-4626	ckveenstra@gmail.com
United Methodist Foundation of Michigan	Joy Barrett	128 Park Street, Chelsea, MI 48118	734-475-8119	jbarrett@chelseaumc.org
Volunteer in Mission Coordinator	Gordon Schleicher	1586 Hagadorn, Mason, MI 48854	517-833-4988	mschleicher@wowway.com

General Conference Petitions Committee	C David Lundquist	5920 Wood Valley Road, Kalamazoo, MI 49009	269-352-0582	dlundquist@ ameritech.net
Committee on Journal	Mandana Nordbrock	431 Timber Ridge Dr, Kalamazoo, MI 49006	269-372-7525	mandana@ kalamazoodist.org

5. Have the secretaries, treasurers, and statisticians kept and reported their respective data in accordance to the prescribed formats? (¶606.8)? Yes

6. What is the report of the statistician? (See report, page 477 of Journal.)

7. What is the report of the treasurer? (See report, page 148 & 477 of Journal.)

8. What are the reports of the district superintendents as to the status of the work within their districts? (See report, page 144 of Journal.)
9. What is the schedule of minimum base compensation for clergy for the ensuing year (¶¶342, 625.3)?

10. What amount has been apportioned to the pastoral charges within the conference to be raised for the support of the district superintendents for the ensuing year (¶614.1a)? $1,221,515 (District Superintendents Fund)

11. a) What amount has been apportioned to the pastoral charges within the conference to be raised for the support of the pension and benefit programs of the conference for the ensuing year (¶¶614.1d, 1507)? $35,000 (lines 4+5 of connectional ministry funds)
    b) What are the apportionments to this conference for the ensuing year?
       (1) For the World Service Fund? $842,439
       (2) For the Ministerial Education Fund? $289,219
       (3) For the Black College Fund? $115,372
       (4) For the Africa University Fund? $ 25,816
       (5) For the Episcopal Fund? $252,666
       (6) For the General Administration Fund? $101,687
       (7) For the Interdenominational Cooperation Fund? $ 22,630

12. What are the findings of the annual audit of the conference treasuries? (See report, page 446 of Journal)

13. Conference and district lay leaders (¶¶603.9, 659):
    a) Conference lay leader: Name: Anne Soles
       Mailing Address: PO Box 467, 217 Old State Rd., Pentwater, MI 49449
    b) Associate conference lay leaders: Max Waagner
    c) District and associate district lay leaders:
       ALBION: Max Waagner 11 — 928 Sunburst Rd, Jackson, MI, 49203
       HEARTLAND: Ned Weller 14 — 95 Meadow Lane, Ithaca, MI 48847
       GRAND RAPIDS: Helen Reid 12 — 3839 Alger Ave., White Cloud, MI 49349
       GRAND TRAVERSE: Denny Olin 14 — 14432 Peninsula Dr, Traverse City, MI 49686
       KALAMAZOO: Wynne Hurlbut 13 — 36146 Cherry St., Gobles, MI 49055
       LANSING: Deb Fennell 11 — 3409 Rolfe Rd, Mason, MI 48854

14. List local churches which have been:
    a) Organized or continued as New Church Starts or Mission Congregations (¶259,1-4, continue to list congregations here until listed in questions 14.c, d, or e)

Church Name	District	Mailing Address	Phone Number	Date Founded
Rivercrest Church	Grand Rapids	214 Spencer St NE, Grand Rapids MI 49505	(580) 559-1207	1-1-14
New Church Start	Lansing	None yet	None yet	7-1-14

   b) Satellite congregations (¶259.5-10, continue to list here until listed in questions 14.c, d, or e)

Church Name	District	Mailing Address	Phone Number	Date Launched
–	–	–	–	–

c) Chartered

Church Name	District	Mailing Address	Phone Number	Date Chartered
Valley UMC	Grand Rapids	5980 Lake Michigan Dr Allendale MI 49401	(269) 501-8602	9-22-13
–	–	–	–	–

d) Merged (¶¶2546, 2547)

(1) United Methodist with United Methodist

Name of First Church	Name of Second Church	Name of Merged Church	Date Merged
Osseo UMC	North Adams UMC	North Adams UMC	4-6-14

(2) Other mergers (indicate denomination)

Name of First Church	Name of Second Church	Name of Merged Church	Date Merged
–	–	–	–

e) Discontinued or abandoned (¶¶229, 341.2, 2549) (State which for each church listed.)

(1) New Church Start (¶259.2,3)

Church Name	District	Location	Date Closed
–	–	–	–

(2) Mission Congregation (¶259.1a)

Church Name	District	Location	Date Closed
–	–	–	–

(3) Satellite Congregation

Church Name	District	Location	Date Closed
–	–	–	–

(4) Chartered Local Church (¶259.5)

Church Name	District	Location	Date Closed
Parma UMC	Albion	Parma, MI	5-28-14
Waterloo First UMC	Lansing	Munith, MI	2-16-14

f) Relocated and to what address

Church Name	District	Mailing Address	Physical Location	Date Relocated
–	–	–	–	–

g) Changed name of church? (Example: "First" to "Trinity")

Former Name	New Name	Address	District
–	–	–	–

h) Transferred this year into this conference from other United Methodist conference(s) and with what membership (¶¶41, 260)?

Name	Membership	Sending Conference
–	–	–

BUSINESS OF THE A/C

i) What cooperative parishes in structured forms have been established? (¶206.b)

Parish Name	Charge Name	Church Name	District
Greenville First, Turk Lake/Belding Cooperative Parish	Greenville First UMC	Greenville First UMC	Heartland
Greenville First, Turk Lake/Belding Cooperative Parish	Turk Lake/Belding UMCs	Turk Lake UMC	Heartland
Greenville First, Turk Lake/Belding Cooperative Parish	Turk Lake/Belding UMCs	Belding UMC	Heartland
Barry-Eaton Cooperative Ministry	Gresham UMC	Gresham UMC	Lansing
Barry-Eaton Cooperative Ministry	Kalamo UMC	Kalamo UMC	Lansing
Barry-Eaton Cooperative Ministry	Nashville UMC	Nashville UMC	Lansing
Barry-Eaton Cooperative Ministry	Vermontville UMC	Vermontville UMC	Lansing
Barry-Eaton Cooperative Ministry	Woodland UMC	Woodland UMC	Lansing
Barry-Eaton Cooperative Ministry	Quimby UMC	Quimby UMC	Lansing
Barry-Eaton Cooperative Ministry	Sebewa Center UMC	Sebewa Center UMC	Lansing
Barry-Eaton Cooperative Ministry	Sunfield UMC	Sunfield UMC	Lansing
Barry-Eaton Cooperative Ministry	Mulliken UMC	Mulliken UMC	Lansing
M-52 Cooperative Ministry	Millville UMC	Millville UMC	Lansing
M-52 Cooperative Ministry	Dansville UMC	Dansville UMC	Lansing
M-52 Cooperative Ministry	New Church Start	New Church Start	Lansing
M-52 Cooperative Ministry	Webberville UMC	Webberville UMC	Lansing
M-52 Cooperative Ministry	Williamston Crossroads UMC	Williamston Crossroads UMC	Lansing

j) What other changes have taken place in the list of churches?
See charge re-aligments in #16.

15. Are there Ecumenical Shared Ministries in the conference? (¶208)

a) Federated church

Name	District	Other Denomination(s)
None	–	–

b) Union Church

Name	District	Other Denomination(s)
None	–	–

c) Merged Church

Name	District	Other Denomination(s)
None	–	–

d) Yoked Parish

Name	District	Other Denomination(s)
None	–	–

16. What changes have been made in district and charge lines?

Albion District:

Frontier became single-point charge 2014
Jackson Trinity became single-point charge 2014
Jonesville/Allen became single charges 2014

Grand Rapids District:
Claybanks realigned from Whitehall/Claybanks to Shelby/Claybanks 2014
Muskegon Crestwood realigned from Lakeside/Crestwood to Whitehall/Crestwood 2014
Muskegon Lakeside became a single-point charge 2014
Shelby became a two-point charge Shelby/Claybanks 2014
Whitehall realigned from Whitehall/Claybanks to Whitehall/Crestwood 2014

Grand Traverse District:
Boyne City/Boyne Falls/Horton Bay became a 3-point charge 2014
Brethren Epworth / Grant became single-point charges 2014
Epsilon/New Hope/Harbor Springs/Alanson became a 4-point charge 2014

Heartland District:
Elsie/Salem became a charge 5-1-14
Salem/Maple Rapids/Lowe charge re-aligned 5-1-14 to Maple Rapids/Lowe charge

Kalamazoo District:
Berrien Springs/Pokagon became a 2-point charge 2014
Ganges/Glenn became single-point charges 2014
Hinchman / Oronoko became 2-point charge 2014
LifeSpring/Lawton St. Paul's became 2-point charge 2014
Portage Prairie/Arden became single-point charges 2014

PART II PERTAINING TO ORDAINED AND LICENSED CLERGY

(Note: A ***(v)*** *notation following a question in this section signifies that the action or election requires a majority vote of the clergy session of the annual conference. If an action requires more than a simple majority, the notation* ***(v 2/3)*** *or* ***(v 3/4)*** *signifies that a two-thirds or three-fourths majority vote is required. Indicate credential of persons in Part II: FD, FE, PD, PE, and AM when requested.)*

17. Are all the clergy members of the conference blameless in their life and official administration (¶¶604.4, 605.6)? **Yes,** attested to be means of a signed statement from the District Superintendents that has been submitted to the Board of Ordained Ministry; and also signed by Bishop Deborah L. Kiesey. We, the bishop and superintendents, take very seriously the call to moral excellence in the lives of clergy. We gladly offer our signatures to answer this question, knowing that only by the grace of God can any of us be blameless in our life and official administration. Obviously, we make no judgment about the moral character of clergy who are involved in supervisory correction or administrative complaint process.

18. Who constitute:
    a) The Administrative Review Committee (¶636)? **(v)**

Three Clergy in Full Connection	Two Alternatives
Gerald F. Hagans, RE	**Ellen A. Brubaker, RE**
William C. Johnson, RE	**Richard R. Erickson, RE**
Molly C. Turner, RE	

    b) The Conference Relations Committee of the Board of Ordained Ministry (¶635.1d)?

Wade S. Panse, RE – Chair	**Laurie Dahlman, Laity**
Kimberly A. DeLong, FD	**Steven Lett, Laity**
Mark R. Erbes, FE	**William Russner, Laity**
Robert L. Hundley, FE	**Gerry Tibbits, Laity**
William C. Johnson, RE	
James P. Mitchum, FE	

19. Who are the certified candidates (¶ ¶ 310, 313, 314)
    a) Who are currently certified as candidates for ordained or licensed ministry?

Name	District	Date Certified
Julie E. Fairchild *(Seminary Student, GETS)*	Grand Rapids	2014
Alejandro D. Fernandez *(Licensed)*	Grand Rapids	2013
Thomas C. Fifer *(Seminary Student, Duke)*	Grand Rapids	2013
Ginny K. Mikita *(Seminary Student, GETS)*	Grand Rapids	2008
Daniel J. Wallington	Grand Rapids	2014

Caleb B. Williams *(M.Div., MSM, Boston Univ)*	Grand Rapids	2012
Eric M. Falker	Grand Traverse	2014
Gerald A. Erskine	Heartland	2014
Tiffany M. Newsom	Heartland	2014
Russell D. Morgan	Heartland	10-17-2013
Ryan L. Wenburg *(Seminary Student, Asbury)*	Heartland	2011
Daniel L. Barkholz	Kalamazoo	2013
William G. Bernhard	Kalamazoo	2012
John M. Brooks	Kalamazoo	04-29-2014
Sara L. Carlson *(Licensed)*	Kalamazoo	2012
Daniel R. Colthorp *(Seminary Student, GETS)*	Kalamazoo	2008
Katherine L. Fahey *(Seminary Student, GETS)*	Kalamazoo	2013
Everett L. Harpole *(5 COS)*	Kalamazoo	2009
Michele D. Childs *(M.Div., MTSO)*	Lansing	2011
Lauren K. Dennis-Bucholz *(Seminary Student, MTSO)*	Lansing	2014
Timothy W. Trommater *(Seminary Student, St Paul)*	Lansing	2014
Wendy S. Walz	Lansing	2009
Danielle M. Williams *(M.Div., GETS)*	Lansing	2011

BUSINESS OF THE A/C

b) Who have had their candidacy for ordained or licensed ministry accepted by a District Committee on Ordained Ministry in another annual conference? (Include name of accepting conference.)

Name	Receiving Conference	Date Originally Certified	Date Accepted by District in Other Conference
None	–	–	

c) Who have been discontinued as certified candidates for licensed or ordained ministry?

Name	District	Date Certified	Date Discontinued
Barbara L. Beachy *(Withdrew)*	Lansing	2007	10-28-2013
Stephen K. Kadwell	Kalamazoo	2002	08-12-2013
Richard J. Reineke	Grand Traverse	2010	06-13-2013

20. Who have completed the studies for the license as a local pastor, are approved, but are not now appointed? (¶315 —Indicate for each person the year the license was approved.):

Name	District	Year Last Licensed
Jack E. Balgenorth (Seminary Student, AMBS)	Kalamazoo	2013
Dale A. Hotelling (Completed COS *)	Grand Rapids	2012
Mona L. Kindel (8 COS)	Heartland	2013
Jeanne M. Laimon (12 COS)	Lansing	2013
Deborah Reid Miller (7 COS)	Grand Rapids	2003

21. Who are approved and appointed as: (Indicate for each person the first year the license was awarded. Indicate what progress each has made in the course of study or the name of the seminary in which they are enrolled. Indicate with an asterisk those who have completed the five year course of study or the M.Div. (¶319.4)? PLEASE NOTE: Persons on this list must receive an episcopal appointment. (**v**)

a) Full-time local pastors? (¶318.1)

Name	First Year License Awarded	Years Completed with Course of Study
ALBION		
Scott M. Bouldrey	2003	M.Div., MTSO *
Brian R. Bunch	1993	M.Div., Earlham *
Sueann K. Hagan	2003	M.Div., GETS *
Cydney M. Idsinga	2014	M.Div., Asbury *
Patricia A. Pebley	2012	M.Div., United
James W. Stilwell	2005	M.Div., GETS *
GRAND RAPIDS		
Carleton R. Black	2011	1 Yr, 4 COS
Jeffrey J. Bowman	1995	Completed COS *
Terri L. Cummins	2010	3 Yrs, 12 COS
Joel T. Fitzgerald	2012	M.Div., Vanderbilt *
Donald J. Graham	2001	Completed COS *
Kevin K. Guetschow	2010	2 3/4 Yrs, 11 COS
Paul E. Hane	2003	Completed COS *
Jan Marie Johnson (Chaplain)	2010	Student, Western Theology ¶344.1.b.
Sean K. Kidd	2014	Licensed
Mary K. Loring (Coord Pastoral Care)	2010	M.Div., MTSO, ¶344.1.b.
Daniel Q. Nguyen	2012	Licensed
Lawrence A. Nichols	1979	Completed COS *
Kellas D. Penny, III	2013	M.Div., Asbury *
Steven C. Place	2011	1/2 Yr, 2 COS
Anthony C. Shumaker	2002	Completed COS *
Edwin D. Snook	2002	Completed COS *
Mary A. Sweet	2011	M.Div., Candler *
GRAND TRAVERSE		
Peggy Ann Boltz	1995	Completed COS *
Thomas H. John, Sr.	1998	Retired ¶320.5, Completed COS *
Scott R. Loomis	2012	1 Yr, 4 COS
Michael R. Neihardt	2013	Licensed
Melody Lane Olin	2006	Completed COS *
Craig A. Pahl	2000	4 Yrs, 16 COS
Jon L. Pohl	2006	Completed COS *
Jeffrey J. Schrock	2000	M.Div., Asbury *
Todd W. Shafer	2010	2 1/2 Yrs, 10 COS
Michael J. Simon	2006	3 3/4 Yrs, 15 COS
Nathaniel R. Starkey	2013	Licensed
Colleen A. Wierman	2011	1 1/4 Yrs, 5 COS
Beverley J. Williams	2012	1 Yr, 4 COS

HEARTLAND		
Clifford L. Allen	2007	2 1/2 Yrs, 10 COS
Joseph L. Beavan	2010	2 Yrs, 8 COS
Terri L. Bentley	2002	Completed COS *
Connie R. Bongard	1992	Completed COS *
Paul A. Damkoehler	2008	M.Div., Asbury *
Mona J. Dye	2007	3 1/2 Yrs, 14 COS
Bryan K. Kilpatrick	2014	M.Div., GETS *
Charles "Ed" Edward Milam	2011	1 Yr, 4 COS
David Michael Palmer	2010	1 1/4 Yrs, 5 COS
Scott B. Smith	2013	M.Div., United
Paul W. Thomas	2013	1/4 Yr, 1 COS
KALAMAZOO		
Lisa M. Batten (Wesley Foundation)	2009	Seminary Student, GETS, ¶344.1.a.
Nelson L. Hall	1999	Completed COS *
Trevor J. McDermont	2009	2 Yrs, 8 COS
Wayne E. McKenney	1995	M.Div., AMBS *
John D. Messner	2008	Completed COS *
Mark E. Mitchell	1995	M.Div., AMBS *
Nancy J. Patera	2007	Completed COS *
Gary L. Peterson	2008	4 1/4 Yrs, 17 COS
Ralph A. Posnik, Jr.	2009	4 Yrs, 16 COS
David A. Price	2006	Completed COS *
Clifford L. Radtke	2006	Completed COS *
LANSING		
Richard J. Foster	2012	1/4 Yr, 1 COS
Clare Walter Huyck	2007	3 1/2 Yrs, 14 COS
Peggy A. Katzmark	2007	Completed COS *
Seok Nam Lim	2014	M.Div., Union-PSCE *
Jeremy J. Wicks	2011	1 Yr, 4 COS

b Part-time local pastors? (¶318.2) (Fraction of full-time in one-quarter increments)

Name	First Year License Awarded	Fraction of full time to be served	Years Completed with Course of Study
ALBION			
Martin H. Culver	1991	1/4 Time	Retired ¶320.5, Completed COS *
Marshall Murphy, Jr.	2011	3/4 Time	M.Div., GETS *
Timothy R. Puckett	2011	1/4 Time	M.Div., Asbury *
John M. Sterner, Jr.	2012	3/4 Time	Retired ¶346.2, Presbyterian
Cynthia L. Veilleux	2011	3/4 Time	Seminary Student, GETS
Jennifer J. Wheeler	11.09.2013	1/4 Time	Seminary Student, MTSO
GRAND RAPIDS			
Nancy L. Boelens	1996	2/4 Time	Retired ¶320.5, Completed COS *
Robert Eckert	2001	3/4 Time	4 Yrs, 16 COS

Michael J. Ramsey	2010	3/4 Time	1 1/2 Yrs, 6 COS
Sandra K. VandenBrink	1993	1/4 Time	Retired ¶320.5, M.Div., MTSO *
Herbert J. VanderBilt	2004	2/4 Time	3 3/4 Yrs, 15 COS
Ronald L. Worley	2004	1/4 Time	3 Yrs, 12 COS
GRAND TRAVERSE			
Dianne Doten Morrison	1996	1/4 Time	Completed COS *
Noreen S. Shafer	2013	3/4 Time	Licensed
HEARTLAND			
Lyle J. Ball	2010	2/4 Time	1 3/4 Yrs, 7 COS
William F. Dye	2003	3/4 Time	Completed COS *
Lemuel O. Granada	2002	1/4 Time	2 Yrs, 8 COS
Judith A. Hazle	2012	1/4 Time	1/4 Yr, 1 COS
Kathryn L. Leydorf-Keck	2007	3/4 Time	3 1/4 Yrs, 13 COS
Darryl L. Miller	2007	1/4 Time	Licensed
Anne W. Riegler	2009	3/4 Time	2 3/4 Yrs, 11 COS
KALAMAZOO			
Jeffrey O. Cummings	2013	3/4 Time	M.Div., Ashland *
Samuel C. Gordy	2012	1/4 Time	1/4 Yr, 1 COS
David L. Haase	2008	2/4 Time	4 1/4 Yrs, 17 COS
Jason E. Harpole	2014	1/4 Time	Licensed
Donna Jean Keyte	2003	2/4 Time	Completed COS *
George W. Lawton	1999	1/4 Time	Retired ¶320.5, Completed COS *
Michael A. Pinto	2007	1/4 Time	1/4 Yr, 1 COS
O'Ryan Rickard	2003	1/4 Time	Retired ¶320.5, M.Div., AMBS *
James C. Robertson	2014	1/4 Time	Licensed
Ronald D. Slager	2010	1/4 Time	1 Yr, 4 COS
LANSING			
Jerry J. Bukoski	2014	1/4 Time	Licensed
Daniel J.W. Phillips	2013	1/4 Time	Licensed
Irene L. Vittoz	2005	1/4 Time	Completed COS *
Kelly M. Wasnich	2014	2/4 Time	Seminary Student, GETS

c) Students from other annual conferences or denominations serving as local pastors and enrolled in a school of theology listed by the University Senate (¶318.3, ,4)?

Name	First Year License Awarded	Seminary	Home Conference
None	–	–	–

d) Students who have been certified as candidates in your annual conference and are serving as local pastors in another annual conference while enrolled in a school of theology listed by the University Senate (¶318.3)

Name	First Year License Awarded	Years Completed in Course of Study
None	–	–

BUSINESS OF THE A/C

e) Persons serving as local pastors while seeking readmission to conference membership (¶¶366.4, 367, 369.3)? (If not in this conference indicate name of conference where serving.)

Name	Years Completed in Course of Study
None	–

22. Who have been discontinued as local pastors (¶320.1)?

Name	Date discontinued
Dawn E. Laupp	08-26-2013
Mary Beth Rhine *(Withdrew)*	03-01-2014
Lawrence H. Wonsey	2014

23. Who have been reinstated as local pastors (¶320.4)?

Name	Years Completed in Course of Study
None	–

24. What ordained ministers or provisional members from other Annual Conferences or Methodist denominations are approved for appointment in the Annual Conference while retaining their conference or denominational membership (¶¶331.8, 346.1)? (List alphabetically; indicate Annual Conference or denomination where membership is held. Indicate credential.)

a) Annual Conferences

Name	Clergy Status	Home Conference
David G. Elmore	OE/FE	Alaska Pacific Northwest
Julie Y. Elmore	OE/FE	Alaska Pacific Northwest
Linda J. Farmer-Lewis	OE/FE	Wisconsin
Melody H. Johnson	OE/FE	Detroit
Mark D. Miller	OE/FE	Detroit
Rey Carlos Borja Mondragon	OE/FE	Detroit
Nohemi Ramirez	OE/FE	Rio Grande
Deborah S. Thomas	OE/FE	Detroit

b) Other Methodist Denominations

Name	Clergy Status	Denomination
Benjamin D. Hutchison (Bras)	OE	African Methodist Episcopal
David Nellist	OE	British Methodist
Hillary Thurston-Cox	OE	Free Methodist
Vaughn Thurston-Cox	OE	Free Methodist

25. What clergy in good standing in other Christian denominations have been approved to serve appointments or ecumenical ministries within the bounds of the Annual Conference while retaining their denominational affiliation (¶¶331.8, 346.2)? (v) (Designate with an asterisk those who have been accorded voting rights within the annual conference. Indicate credential.)

Name	Clergy Status	Denomination
Marcia L. Elders (2003, 3/4 Time)	OF	Reformed Church of America
Forest B. Nelson (2005, 3/4 Time)	OF	Presbyterian Church USA
Mack C. Strange (2007, Full-Time)	OF	Southern Baptist Church

26. Who are affiliate members:
(List alphabetically; indicate annual conference or denomination where membership is held.)
a) With vote (¶586.4 [**v**])?

Name	Member Conference/Denomination	First Year of Affiliation
None	–	–

b) Without vote (¶¶334.5, 344.4)? (**v 2/3**)

Name	Member Conference/Denomination	First Year of Affiliation
David S. Bell	East Ohio	2009
Carol B. Cooley	West Ohio	2000
William D. Dobbs	Detroit	2013
Charles R. Ellinwood	North Indiana	1999
Ronald Lewis Figgins Iris	Detroit	2014
P. Kay Welsch	Wisconsin	2013

NOTE: If your conference has admitted or ordained persons as a courtesy to another conference, list these persons in Question 40 only. If persons have been admitted or ordained by another annual conference as a courtesy to your conference, list these persons in Questions 27-39, whichever are appropriate, giving the date and name of the accommodating conference.

27. Who are elected as associate members? ¶322 (**v**) (List alphabetically-see note preceding Question 27):

Name
None

28. Who are elected as provisional members and what seminary are they attending, if in school? (under ¶¶322.4, 324, 325)
a) Provisional Deacons under the provisions of ¶¶ 324.4a, c or ¶324.5? (**v**)

Name	Seminary *(if in school)*
None	–

b) Provisional Elders under the provisions of ¶¶ 324.4a, b or ¶324.6 (**v**)); ¶ 322.4 (**v 3/4**)

Name	Seminary *(if in school)*
Stephen F. Lindeman (¶324.4.a)	–
Heather A. Molner (¶324.4.a)	–
Chad M. Parmalee (¶324.4.a)	–
Dennis B. Bromley (322.4)	–
John J. Conklin (322.4)	–
James C. Noggle (322.4)	–

29. Who are continued as provisional members, in what year were they admitted to provisional membership, and what seminary are they attending, if in school (¶326)?
a) In preparation for ordination as a deacon or elder? (¶326)

Name	Clergy Status (PD or PE)	Date	Seminary *(if in school)*
Emily K. Beachy	PE	2012	–
Martha S. Beals (LOA 2013)	PD	2009	–
Matthew J. Bistayi	PE	2007	–
James Thomas Boutell	PE	2010	–
Eric M. Burton-Krieger (Serving in TN)	PE	2012	–
Melissa J. Claxton	PE	2011	–

Martin T. Cobb	PE	2007	–
Cori Lynn Cypret	PE	2012	–
Nancy V. Fancher	PD	2013	–
Erin B. Fitzgerald	PE	2012	–
Kimberly A. Metzger (LOA 12/19/2011)	PE	2008	–
Cheryl A. Mulligan	PD	2012	–
Amee A. Paparella	PE	2009	–
Beth A. Reum	PE	2011	–
Linda (Lyne) K. Stull-Lipps	PE	2007	–

b) Provisional deacons who became provisional elders?

Name	**Original Year of Membership**
None	–

c) Provisional elders who became provisional deacons? (Indicate year)

Name	**Original Year of Membership**
None	–

d) Provisional members who transferred from other conferences or denominations? (¶347.1)

Name	**Clergy Status (PD or PE)**	**Original Year of Membership**	**Previous Conference or Denomination**
None	–	–	–

30. What ordained clergy, coming from other Christian denominations, have had their orders recognized (¶348): **(v)** A person's orders may be recognized when they are transferring their membership into your annual conference from another Christian denomination. A person who is listed in Q.30 must also be listed in either Q. 31 a or b, depending on the transfer status.

Name	**Clergy Status**	**Previous Denomination**
Gary L. Simmons	PE	M.Div., Southern Baptist

31. What ordained clergy have been received from other Christian denominations (¶347.3):
(List alphabetically—see note preceding Question 27):
a) As provisional members (¶347.3a,b)? **(v)**

Name	**Clergy Status (PD or PE)**	**Date Received**	**Former Denomination**
Gary L. Simmons	PE	2014	M.Div., Southern Baptist

b) As local pastors (¶347.3a)? **(v)**

Name	**Clergy Status (FL or PL)**	**Date Received**	**Former Denomination**
None	–	–	–

32. Who are elected as members in full connection? (List alphabetically-see note preceding Question 27. Anyone appearing on this question must also be listed somewhere in questions 33-34 or 36, unless the clergy's orders from another denomination were recognized on question 30 in a previous year.) (v 2/3):

a) Deacons

Name
Patricia L. Catellier

b) Elders

Name
Letisha M. Bowman
Catherine M. Christman
Patricia Ann Haas
Jonathan D. VanDop
Rebecca L. Wieringa

33. Who are ordained as deacons and what seminary awarded their degree? Or, if their master's degree is not from a seminary, at what seminary did they complete the basic graduate theological studies?: (List alphabetically-see note preceding Question 27)

a) After provisional membership (¶330)? **(v 2/3)**

Name	Seminary
Patricia L. Catellier	GETS

b) Transfer from elder? (¶309) **(v 2/3)**

Name	Seminary
None	–

34. Who are ordained as elders and what seminary awarded their degree?

a) After provisional membership? (¶335) **(v 2/3)**

Name	Seminary
Letisha M. Bowman	GETS and Western
Catherine M. Christman	MTSO
Patricia Ann Haas	AMBS
Jonathan D. VanDop	MTSO
Rebecca L. Wieringa	MTSO

b) Transfer from deacon? (¶309) **(v 2/3)**

Name	Seminary
None	–

35. What provisional members, previously discontinued, are readmitted (¶365)? **(v)**

Name	Clergy Status	Year Previously Discontinued
None	–	–

36. Who are readmitted (¶¶366-368 **[v]**, ¶369 **[v 2/3]**):

Name	Clergy Status	Previous Status
None	–	–

37. Who are returned to the effective relationship after voluntary retirement (¶358.7): **(v)**

Name	Clergy Status	Year Retired
None	–	–

38. Who have been received by transfer from other annual conferences of The United Methodist Church (¶¶347.1, 416.5, 635.2m)? (List alphabetically. Indicate credential. See note preceding Question 27.)

Name	Clergy Status	Previous Conference	Date of Transfer
George H. Ayoub	FE	Eastern Pennsylvania	03-01-2014

39. Who are transferred in from other Methodist denominations (¶347.2)? (List alphabetically. Indicate credential.)

Name	Clergy Status	Previous Methodist Denomination	Date of Transfer
None	–	–	–

40. Who have been ordained as a courtesy to other conferences, after election by the other conference? (See note preceding Question 27. Such courtesy elections or ordinations do not require transfer of conference membership.)

a) Deacons?

Name	Member Conference
None	–

b) Elders?

Name	Member Conference
None	–

41. Who have been transferred out to other annual conferences of The United Methodist Church (¶416.5)? (List alphabetically. Indicate credential. See note preceding Question 27.)

Name	Clergy Status	New Conference	Date of Transfer
Emilie Forward	AM	Rocky Mountain/Sunshine	07-01-2014
Jerome R. DeVine	FE	Detroit Conference	07-01-2014

42. Who are discontinued as provisional members (¶327)? (**v**).

a) By expiration of eight-year time limit (¶ 327)

Name	Clergy Status
None	–

b) By voluntary discontinuance (¶ 327.6) (**v**)

Name	Clergy Status
None	

c) By involuntary discontinuance (¶ 327.6) (**v**)

Name	Clergy Status
None	

d) By reaching Mandatory Retirement Age (¶ 327.7)

Name	Clergy Status
None	

43. Who are on location?

a) Who has been granted honorable location (¶359.1)?
(1) This year? (**v**)

Name	Clergy Status	Charge Conference Membership	Date Effective
None			

(2) Previously?

Name	Year Originally Granted	Charge Conference Membership	Year of Most Recent Report
Thomas A. Crossman	1991	St. Paul/St. Andrew, NY, NY	2009
Bruce W. Dempsey	1993	Montague UMC, Montague, MI	2014
C. David Hainer	1996	Riverside UMC, Moline, IL	2014
Michael Edward Long	1998	Traverse Bay, Traverse City, MI	2014
Terry L. MacArthur	06-15-1985	Chapel Hill UMC, Portage, MI	2014
Clinton McKinven-Copus	2007	Ludington United, Ludington, MI	2014
Allen C. Myers	1980	Trinity UMC, Grand Rapids, MI	2014
Michelle Wisdom-Long	2011	First UMC, Kalamazoo, MI	2014

b) Who on honorable location are appointed ad interim as local pastors? (¶359.2) (Indicate date and appointment.)

Name	Appointment	Year Originally Granted Location
None	–	–

c) Who has been placed on administrative location (¶360)?
(1) This year? (**v**)

Name	Date Effective	Charge Conference Membership
None	–	–

(2) Previously?

Name	Year Originally Placed	Charge Conference Membership	Year of Most Recent Report
Valerie M. Hill	1999	Greenville	–
Vinh Q. Tran	03.22.2005	–	–

44. Who have been granted the status of honorable location–retired (¶359.3):
a) This year? (**v**)

Name	Clergy Status	Year Honorable Location Originally Granted	Charge Conference Membership
None	–	–	–

b) Previously?

Name	Clergy Status	Year Honorable Location Originally Granted	Charge Conference Membership
Dwight M. Benner	FE	1988	First UMC Birmingham, MI
William D. Carr	FE	1993	Allegan UMC Allegan, MI

David L. Draggoo	FE	1986	Williamston UMC Williamston, MI
James E. Leach	FE	1972	Memorial UMC Lake Placid, FL
Laurie J. McKinven-Copus	FE	04-02-05	Ludington United Ludington, MI
Charles D. McNary	FE	1977	Bangor Simpson UMC Bangor, MI
Thurlan E. Meredith	FE	1993	Northlawn UMC Grand Rapids, MI
Edward F. Otto	FE	10-01-78	First UMC Chicago, IL
Paul K. Scheibner	FE	1983	Good Shepherd of the North Roscommon, MI
J. Chris Schroeder	FE	1998	Sunfield UMC Sunfield, MI
Wilbur L. Silvernail	FE	1971	Calvary UMC Jackson, MI
David E. Small	FE	1999	Nooksack Valley UMC Everson, WA
Dale D. Spoor	FE	10-01-1974	Central UMC Lansing, MI
Philip P. Steele	FE	1971	Milwood UMC Kalamazoo, MI
Robert E. Tomlinson	FE	1989	Chapel Hill UMC Battle Creek, MI
Bertram W. Vermeulen	FE	1984	Fremont UMC Fremont, MI
Robert W. Wellfare	FE	10-01-74	University Carillion Oveido, FL

45. Who have had their status as honorably located and their orders terminated (¶359.2)? (**v**)

Name	**Date Effective**	**Prior Clergy Status**
None	–	–

46. Who have had their conference membership terminated?

a) By withdrawal to unite with another denomination (¶361.1, .4)? (**v**)

Name	**Date Effective**	**Prior Clergy Status**
None	–	–

b) By withdrawal from the ordained ministerial office (¶361.2, .4)? (**v**)

Name	**Date Effective**	**Prior Clergy Status**
None	–	–

c) By withdrawal under complaints or charges (¶¶361.3, .4; 2719.2)?

Name	**Date Effective**	**Prior Clergy Status**
None	–	–

d) By termination of orders under recommendation of the Board of Ordained Ministry (¶354.12)? (v)

Name	Date Effective	Prior Clergy Status
None	–	–

e) By trial (¶2713)?

Name	Date Effective	Prior Clergy Status
None	–	–

47. Who have been suspended under the provisions of ¶363.1d, ¶2704.2c or ¶2711.3? (Give effective dates. Indicate credential.)

Name	Date Effective	Clergy Status
None	–	–

48. Deceased (List alphabetically in the spaces provided)
   a) What associate members have died during the year?
   Effective:

Name	Date of Birth	Date of Death
None	–	–

Retired:

Name	Date of Birth	Date of Death
Mary E. Curtis	07-25-1928	03-19-2014

b) What provisional members have died during the year? (Indicate credential.)
Effective:

Name	Date of Birth	Date of Death
None	–	–

Retired:

Name	Date of Birth	Date of Death
None	–	–

c) What elders have died during the year?
Effective:

Name	Date of Birth	Date of Death
None	–	–

Retired:

Name	Date of Birth	Date of Death
Richard L. Matson	09-09-1940	10-06-2013
Donald H. Merrill	10-06 1920	10-29-2013
Daniel E. Miles	05-01-1946	05-26-2014
Arthur C. Murphy, Jr.	01-11-1945	09-29-2013
Charles Richards	08-29-1935	02-26-2014
Charles McLean Shields	06-19-1936	11-25-2013
Carl W. Staser	09-11-1928	04-30-2014

d) What deacons have died during the year?
Effective:

Name	Date of Birth	Date of Death
None	–	–

Retired:

Name	Date of Birth	Date of Death
Janilyn McConnell	02-17-1933	07-14-2013

e) What local pastors have died during the year?
Active:

Name	Date of Birth	Date of Death
None	–	–

Retired:

Name	Date of Birth	Date of Death
Charlene "Char" A. Minger	11-12-1943	04-01-2014

49. What provisional or ordained members (elders and deacons) have received appointments in other Annual Conferences of The United Methodist Church while retaining their membership in this Annual Conference (¶¶331.8, 346.1)?

Name	Clergy Status	Conference Where Appointed	Appointment
Eric Burton-Krieger	PE	Tennessee/Nashville – Brentwood	07-01-2012
Catherine M. Christman	FE	Detroit/Saginaw Bay – Vassar First	07-01-2013
Cornelius "Neil" Davis, Jr.	FE	Detroit/Detroit Renaissance – Southfield Hope	07-01-2014
Dale A. Golden	FE	Florida/Southeast – Homestead	07-01-2014
Gary Haller	FE	Detroit/Detroit Renaissance – Birmingham First	07-01-2013
Laurie A. Haller	FE	Detroit/Detroit Renaissance – Birmingham First	07-01-2013
Jennifer J. Jue	FE	Detroit/Blue Water – Oxford	07-01-2014
Cynthia M. Parsons	FE	Detroit/Blue Water – Sebewaing Trinity	07-01-2014
William P. Sanders	RE	Detroit/Saginaw Bay – Fairgrove/ Watrousville	07-01-2013
Sandra Lee Spahr	RE	Rocky Mountain/Sunshine – Avondale	07-01-2012
Charles A. Williams	FE	Detroit/Marquette – Houghton Grace	07-01-2013

50. Who are the provisional, ordained members or associate members on leave of absence and for what number of years consecutively has each held this relation (¶354)? (Indicate credential. Record Charge Conference where membership is held.)

a) Voluntary?

(1) Personal, 5 years or less (¶354.2a 3) (**v**)

Name	Clergy Status	Date Effective		Charge Conference
Melanie J. Baker	FE	07-01-2013	1 Year	Lansing Grace
Martha S. Beals	PD	07-01-2013	1 Year	Grand Rapids First
Linda J. Burson	FE	07-01-2009	5 Years	Albion First
Robert M. Hughes	FE	07-13-2014	0 Year	Reading UMC
Gregory J. Martin	FE	07-01-2012	2 Years	East Lansing University
Kimberly A. Metzger	PE	12-19-2011	3 Years	Hastings First
Todd J. Query	FD	01-01-2014	0 Year	–

(2) Personal, more than 5 years (¶354.2a 3) (**v 2/3**)

Name	Clergy Status	Date Effective	Charge Conference
None	–	–	–

(3) Family, 5 years or less (¶354.2b 3) (**v**)

Name	Clergy Status	Date Effective		Charge Conference
Brian F. Rafferty	FE	07-01-2010	4 Years	Lansing: Mt Hope

(4) Family, more than 5 years (¶354.2b 3) (**v 2/3**)

Name	Clergy Status	Date Effective	Charge Conference
None	–	–	–

(5) Transitional (¶354.2c)

Name	Clergy Status	Date Effective	Charge Conference
None	–	–	–

b) Involuntary (¶ 355)? (**v 2/3**)

Name	Clergy Status	Date Effective	Charge Conference
None	–	–	–

51. Who are granted sabbatical leave (¶352)? (**v**)

Name	Clergy Status	Date Effective	Charge Conference
None	–	–	–

52. Who have been granted medical leave due to medical or disabling conditions (¶357)? (**v**)

Name	Clergy Status	Date Effective	Charge Conference
Randall R. Hansen	FE	07-01-2014	Montague
Constance L. Heffelfinger	FE	09-01-1995	Holland First
Timothy J. Miller	FE	01-01-2002	Grand Rapids Cornerstone
Sharyn K. Osmond	FL	10-01-2008	Farwell
Theresa "Little Eagle" Sayles	FE	04-15-2009	–

53. What members in full connection have been retired (¶358):
(**List** alphabetically. If retiring in the interim between conference sessions (¶358.2d), indicate the effective date of retirement.) (**Under ¶358.1, no vote required; under ¶358.2, v; under ¶358.3, v 2/3**)

Deacons

a) This year?

Name	**Date Effective**
None	

b) Previously?

Name	**Date Effective**
Dorothy M. Blakey	1999
Rae L. Franke	01-01-2004
Joyce Hanlon	2001
Janet A. Lee	2002
Pamela J. Mathieu	2012
Dorothy D. Mercer	03-01-03

Elders

a) This year?

Name	**Date Effective**
William M. Beachy	2014
Gary L. Bekofske	2014
Lawrence P. Brown	2014
Billie R. Dalton	09-01-2013
Daniel M. Duncan	2014
Deborah M. Johnson	07-08-2014
Karin K. Orr	2014
Susan M. Petro	2014
Jeanne M. Randels	01-01-2014
Richard M. Riley	2014
Roy G. Testolin	11-01-2013

b) Previously?

Name	**Date Effective**
1. Craig L. Adams	2010
2. Pegg Ainslie	1997
3. William J. Amundsen	2003
4. Francis F. Anderson	1991
5. J. Leon Andrews	1992
6. Wayne H. Babcock	01-01-2003
7. Dean I. Bailey	2002
8. Paul F. Bailey	05-01-2001
9. Theron E. Bailey	1994
10. James W. Barney	08-31-2005
11. Marilyn B. Barney	2008
12. Wayne C. Barrett	2011
13. Jack M. Bartholomew	1995

14. Kenneth W. Bensen	2003
15. Joseph J. Bistayi	2005
16. James W. Boehm	09-01-1998
17. Gilbert R. Boersma	10-31-2011
18. Keith A. Bovee	1994
19. Dianne M. Bowden	2013
20. J. Melvin Bricker	1995
21. Patricia L. Bromberek	2011
22. Dale D. Brown	1993
23. Ellen A. Brubaker	12-31-2001
24. Ray W. Burgess	2000
25. Dennis G. Buwalda	04-01-2008
26. John E. Cermak	1994
27. Victor D. Charnley	2013
28. David A. Cheyne	2005
29. William V. Clegg, Jr.	2011
30. Michael T. Conklin	2012
31. Kathryn M. Coombs	2002
32. Wilbur Courter	1998
33. David L. Crawford	1990
34. Reva H. Daniel	2005
35. Lynn A. DeMoss	1997
36. Isabell M. Deppe	2000 (Involuntary)
37. James A. Dibbet	2011
38. Vance M. Dimmick, Jr.	1992
39. William H. Doubblestein	2006
40. David L. Dryer	2006
41. Paula Jane Duffey	2005
42. Eldon K. Eldred	2003
43. Joe D. Elenbaas	2010
44. John W. Ellinger	2007
45. Richard R. Erickson	2006
46. Thomas J. Evans	2013
47. Elmer J. Faust	1990
48. Raymond D. Field	05-01-2003
49. Harold F. Filbrandt	1994
50. Frederick H. Fischer	1996
51. John W. Fisher	2013
52. David L. Flagel	2013
53. George W. Fleming	2002
54. Barbara J. Flory	2011
55. Carolyn Floyd	2008
56. James E. Fox	1995
57. Thomas P. Fox	2012

58. Lillian T. French	09-01-2010
59. Charles E. Fry	1989
60. Donald R. Fry	2008
61. Charles W. Fullmer	1997
62. Charles F. Garrod	1995
63. James C. Grant	06-23-1999
64. Ronald B. Grant	11-01-2012
65. Joseph M. Graybill	2011
66. George R. Grettenberger	1992
67. A. Ray Grienke	08-16-1999
68. James M. Gysel	2011
69. Gerald F. Hagans	09-01-2006
70. Susan J. Hagans	2006
71. Frederick G. Hamlin	1994
72. Joan K. Hamlin	1994
73. Claudette I. Haney	2005
74. Lloyd R. Hansen	1988
75. Ronald W. Hansen	2011
76. Carl L. Hausermann	2001
77. Geoffrey L. Hayes	2009
78. Stanley L. Hayes	1999
79. Leonard B. Haynes	1998
80. Keith W. Heifner	2006
81. William A. Hertel	2001
82. Robert L. Hinklin	2001
83. Lawrence E. Hodge	2000
84. Ronald A. Houk	1997
85. Laurence E. Hubley	06-01-2002
86. James R. Hulett	1998
87. Joseph D. Huston	2009
88. James L. Hynes	2000
89. Andrew Jackson	2006
90. Jerry L. Jaquish	2012
91. Curtis E. Jensen	2010
92. William C. Johnson	2012
93. David L. Johnston	2009
94. Margaret Zee Jones	06-24-2006
95. Robert E. Jones	2009
96. Emmett Kadwell, Jr.	2011
97. Ron L. Keller	1998
98. O. Jay Kendall	09-01-2012
99. Robert L. Kersten	1995
100. David G. Knapp	2009
101. Norman C. Kohns	2005

102. Jack G. Kraklan	1991
103. Richard Kuhn	1998
104. Sally J. LaFrance	10-01-2004
105. D. Keith Laidler	1997
106. Jung Kee Lee	02-28-2013
107. Ben B. Lester	2011
108. Eugene A. Lewis	2003
109. Kendall A. Lewis	1990
110. Kenneth A.O. Lindland	1987
111. David L. Litchfield	2006
112. Leicester R. Longden	2013
113. John D. Lover	2000
114. Paul E. Lowley	2000
115. Carole S. Lyman	2010
116. Frank W. Lyman Jr.	2010
117. Gary V. Lyons	1996
118. Charles William Martin	1989
119. Robert J. Mayo	06-30-2013
120. Paul D. Mazur	1990
121. Kenneth D. McCaw	2000
122. Allen D. McCreedy	2000
123. Sandra B. Hoffman McNary	2007
124. John W. McNaughton	2003
125. Russell F. McReynolds	2007
126. David L. Miles	1999
127. David H. Minger	2006
128. Daniel J. Minor	2001
129. John L. Moore	1995
130. Richard A. Morrison	2007
131. John D. Morse	2012
132. David L. Morton	2001
133. David B. Nelson	1998
134. R. Ivan Niswender	1994
135. Wade S. Panse	01-01-2012
136. Edward L. Passenger	1999
137. Paul E. Patterson	10.01.1990
138. William V. Payne	1996
139. Douglas L. Pedersen	2005
140. A. Edward Perkins	2006
141. Keith I. Pohl	12-31-1993
142. Gerald A. Pohly	1996
143. Robert L. Pumfery	1999
144. Blaine B. Rader	2004
145. Wayne G. Reece	2000

146. Kenneth C. Reeves	2006
147. Beatrice K. Robinson	2007
148. Marvin R. Rosa	1999
149. Edward C. Ross	2012
150. Larry W. Rubingh	2012
151. Donald A. Russell	1996
152. William P. Sanders	2003
153. Leonard R. Schoenherr	06-30-2013
154. Ward N. Scovel	03-01-1998
155. Richard A. Selleck	1996
156. Jane B. Shapley	1996
157. Larry R. Shrout	1998
158. Edward H. Slate	2012
159. Dennis E. Slattery	2012
160. Stephen C. Small	10-01-2004
161. Betty A. Smith	2004
162. Charles W. Smith	2011
163. Robert C. Smith	1983
164. Joseph L. Spackman	2013
165. Sandra Lee Spahr	2006
166. Gordon E. Spalenka	1993
167. Carolin S. Spragg	2013
168. Robert W. Stark	2008
169. Ethel Z. Stears	1999
170. Robert P. Stover	2012
171. Michael P. Streevy	2010
172. Verne Carl Summers	1992
173. Royal J. Synwolt	1991
174. Harold M. Taber	1980
175. Milton J. TenHave	1990
176. J. Todd Thompson	2010
177. John Ross Thompson	12-31-2010
178. R. John Thompson	2010
179. Ronald J. Thompson	1995
180. William J. Torrey	1993
181. Gerald L. Toshalis	2006
182. Raymond J. Townsend	2009
183. Arthur R. Turner	2006
184. Molly C. Turner	2012
185. Diane E. Vale	1990
186. Kenneth R. Vaught	1994
187. Oscar Ventura	2009
188. Douglas W. Vernon	2010
189. Donald Vuurens	10-16-1995

190. Lynn W. Wagner	09-01-2002
191. Lowell F. Walsworth	2002
192. Maurice E. Walworth, Jr.	2006
193. Glenn R. Wegner	2004
194. Gerald L. Welsh	1994
195. Robert L. Wessman	1999
196. Bobby Dale Whitlock	2009
197. Myron K. Williams	1994
198. Richard K. Williams	2001
199. Margaret Halls Wilson	11-01-2009
200. Richard D. Wilson	2008
201. Douglas E. Wingeier	2000
202. Gregory R. Wolfe	2013
203. David W. Yingling	1991
204. Richard A. Youells	1995
205. Lee F. Zachman	12-01-2010

54. What associate members have been retired (¶358):
(List alphabetically. If retiring in the interim between conference sessions (¶358.2d), indicate the effective date of retirement.) (**Under ¶358.1, no vote required; under ¶358.2, v; under ¶358.3, v 2/3**)

a) This year?

Name	**Date Effective**
Geraldine M. Litchfield	2014

b) Previously?

Name	**Date Effective**
Eugene L. Baughan	2002
Elaine M. Buker	1997
John T. Charter	1999
Jane A. Crabtree	07-16-2003
Jean Arthur Crabtree	03-31-1994
Stanley A. Finkbeiner	1996
Dale F. Jaquette	1992
Clyde E. Miller	1987
Bernard R. Randolph (Current Cane Holder)	1978
Randall E. Roose	1993
Howard Seaver	2012
Brian K. Sheen	2004
Wesley E. Smith	1996
Mary L. Soderholm	1998 (Involuntary)
Charles R. VanLente	2010
Nola R. Williams	01.01.2000

55. What provisional members have been previously retired (¶358, 2008 *Book of Discipline*)?
(*NOTE:* Provisional members who reach mandatory retirement age and have not retired by Jan. 1, 2013 shall be discontinued (¶ 327.7) and listed in Q. 42.)

Name	Date Effective
Carol Lynn Bourns	2007

56. Who have been recognized as retired local pastors (¶320.5):

a) This year?

Name	Date Effective
Sheila F. Baker	02.02.2014
Gayle Sue (Berntsen) Zaagman	2014
Linda J. Burton-Collier	2014
Roberta W. Cabot	2014
Richard A. Fritz	2014

b) Previously?

Name	Date Effective
1. Rex Bean	1987
2. Leo "Bud" Elwood Bennett	1993
3. Nancy L. Boelens	04-12-2009
4. David Gunnar Carlson	2010
5. Linda J. Carlson	2009
6. Paulette G. Cheyne	04-01-2008
7. Esther Cox	1988
8. Martin H. Culver	2011
9. Merlin Delo	1997
10. Judy K. Downing-Siglin	2001
11. Richard J. Duffey	2005
12. Edna M. Fleming	2011
13. Joyce F. Gackler	2012
14. Sandra J. Gastian	01-01-2011
15. Sue J. Gay	2007
16. Carl E. Greene	2011
17. Thomas H. John, Sr.	2012
18. J. Robert Keim	12-31-2011
19. Suzanne P. Kornowski	2011
20. George W. Lawton	2007
21. Vernon L. Michael	1987
22. Larry W. Nalett	08-09-2004
23. Judith A. Nielsen	2007
24. O'Ryan Rickard (¶327.7)	2013
25. John F. Ritter	11-01-2001
26. Carolyn A. Robinson-Fisher	2001

27. Connie E. Shatz	2012
28. Kathleen Smith	12-31-2012
29. John R. Sternaman	2002
30. Diane E. Stone	2010
31. Kenneth E. Tabor	2010
32. Sandra K. VandenBrink	2013
33. Donald R. Wendell	11-01-2009
34. Donald Woolum	2003
35. David L. Youngs	2006

57. What is the number of clergy members of the Annual Conference:
By appointment category and conference relationship?

NOTES:

(1) Where applicable, the question numbers on this report form corresponding to each category have been placed in parenthesis following the category title. Where these question numbers appear, the number reported in that category should agree with the number of names listed in the corresponding questions.

(2) For the three categories of Appointments to Extension Ministries, report as follows:
¶344.1a, c): the number of clergy members appointed within United Methodist connectional structures, including district superintendents, or to an ecumenical agency.
¶344.1b): the number of clergy members appointed to extension ministries, under endorsement by the Division of Chaplains and Related Ministries of the General Board of Higher Education and Ministry.
¶344.1d): the number of clergy members appointed to other valid ministries, confirmed by a two-thirds vote of the Annual Conference.

Note: Report those in extension ministry in one category only.
See the Discipline paragraphs indicated for more detailed description of these appointment categories.)
Note: Those approved to serve as a local pastor, but not currently under appointment, are not counted as clergy members of the conference.

(Chart for question #57 found on next page)

Categories	Deacons in Full Connection	Elders in Full Connection	Provisional Deacons	Provisional Elders	Associate Members & Affiliate Members With Vote	Full–time Local Pastors	Part–time Local Pastors
Pastors and deacons whose primary appointment is to a Local Church (¶¶331.1c, 339) (76, 78c)	3	128	2	17	5	59	30
Deacons (in full connection and provisional) serving Beyond the Local Church (¶331.1a, b) (78a,b)	9	XXXXX XXXXX XXXXX	0	XXXXX XXXXX XXXXX	XXXXX XXXXX XXXXX	XXXXX XXXXX XXXXX	XXXXX XXXXX XXXXX
Appointments to Extension Ministries (¶316.1; 344.1a, c) (77a)	XXXXX XXXXX XXXXX	17	XXXXX XXXXX XXXXX	0	0	1	0
Appointments to Extension Ministries (¶316.1; 344.1b) (77b)	XXXXX XXXXX XXXXX	8	XXXXX XXXXX XXXXX	0	0	2	0
Appointments to Extension Ministries (¶316.1; 344.1d) (77c)	XXXXX XXXXX XXXXX	3	XXXXX XXXXX XXXXX	0	2	0	0
Appointments to Attend School (¶331.3) (79)	1	0	0	0	0	XXXXX XXXXX	XXXXX XXXXX
Appointed to Other Annual Conferences (49)	0	8	0	1	0	XXXXX XXXXX	XXXXX XXXXX
On Leave of Absence (50a1, a2)	1	4	1	1	0	XXXXX XXXXX	XXXXX XXXXX
On Family Leave (50a3, a4)	0	1	0	0	0	XXXXX XXXXX	XXXXX XXXXX
On Sabbatical Leave (51)	0	0	0	0	0	XXXXX XXXXX	XXXXX XXXXX
On Medical Leave (52)	0	4	0	0	0	1	0
On Transitional Leave (50a5)	0	0	0	0	0	XXXXX XXXXX	XXXXX XXXXX
Retired (53, 54, 55)	6	216	0	1	17	XXXXX XXXXX	XXXXX XXXXX
Total Number, Clergy Members	20	389	3	20	24	63	30
Grand Total, All Conference Clergy Members	549						

Note: Information on clergy by race and gender in the annual conference is available through the General Council on Finance and Administration at www.gcfa.org.

PART III CERTIFICATION IN SPECIALIZED MINISTRY

Note: Indicate credential of persons in Part III: FD, FE, PD, PE, AM, FL, PL, and LM.

58. Who are the candidates in process for certification in specialized ministry?

Name	Clergy/Lay Status	Specialized Ministry
None	–	–

59. Who is certified in specialized ministry?
(List the areas of specialized ministry. Indicate by an asterisk those certified this year.)

Name	Clergy/Lay Status	Specialized Ministry
Mark R. Babb	FD	Music Ministry
Lisa M. Batten	FL	Spiritual Formation
M. Kay DeMoss	FD	Christian Education
Eric Falker	Laity	Youth Ministry
Daphna Lee Flegal	Diaconal Minister	Christian Education
I. Naomi Garcia	Laity	Christian Education
Sueann K. Hagan	FL	Spiritual Formation
Randall R. Hansen	FE	Spiritual Formation
Jennifer J. Jue	FE	Spiritual Formation
Janet A. Lee	RD	Music Ministry
Nancy LeValley	Laity	Spiritual Formation
Colleen T. Treman	FD	Christian Education

60. Who are transferred in as a certified person in specialized ministry?

Name	Clergy/Lay Status	Specialized Ministry	Sending Conference
None	–	–	–

61. Who are transferred out as a certified person in specialized ministry?

Name	Clergy/Lay Status	Specialized Ministry	Receiving Conference
None	–	–	–

62. Who have been removed as a certified person in specialized ministry?

Name	Clergy/Lay Status	Specialized Ministry
None	–	–

PART IV CERTIFIED LAY MINISTRY

(¶¶ 271, and 666.10 ***The Book of Discipline***)

63. Who are certified as lay ministers (¶ 271, and 666.10)? (List alphabetically, by district)

Name – (Certified/Re-Certified)	District
Lois Fennimore – 2011/2013/2014	Albion
Gary Zinger – 2014	Grand Rapids
Deborah Sue Cole – 2009/2011/2013	Grand Traverse
Nancy LeValley – 2011/2013	Grand Traverse

Donna Stone – 2009/2011/2013	Grand Traverse
Kara Lynne Burns – 2012	Heartland
Russell D. Morgan – 2009/2011/2013	Heartland
Caryl Snider – 2009	Kalamazoo

PART V DIACONAL MINISTERS

(Paragraph numbers in questions 65-72 refer to The 1992 ***Book of Discipline***)

64. Who constitute the Committee on Investigation (¶2703.3)? **(v)**

Name
None

65. Who are transferred in as diaconal ministers (¶312)?

Name	Previous Annual Conference	Date
None	–	–

66. Who are transferred out as diaconal ministers (¶312)?

Name	Previous Annual Conference	Date
None	–	–

67. Who have had their conference relationship as diaconal ministers terminated by Annual Conference action (¶313.3)? **(Under ¶313.3a, no vote; under ¶313.3b, v 2/3)**

Name	Date Effective
None	–

68. What diaconal ministers have died during the year?

a) Effective:

Name	Date of Birth	Date of Death
None	–	–

b) Retired:

Name	Date of Birth	Date of Death
None	–	–

69. What diaconal ministers have been granted leaves of absence under ¶313.1a, c, d) (disability, study/sabbatical, or personal leave): **(v)**

Name	Type of Leave	Date Originally Granted
None	–	–

70. What diaconal ministers have been granted an extended leave (¶313.1e):

Name	Date Originally Granted
None	–

71. Who have returned to active status from extended leave (¶313.1e)? **(v)**?

Name	Date Originally Granted
None	–

72. Who have taken the retired relationship to the Annual Conference as diaconal ministers (¶313.2): **(Under ¶313.2b, v 2/3)**

a) This year?

Name	Date Effective
None	–

b) Previously?

Name	**Date Effective**
Jane Case	2011
Margaret L. Foster	1999
Helene R. Hill	1986

PART VI APPOINTMENTS AND CONCLUDING BUSINESS

73. Who are approved for less than full-time service?

a) What associate members, provisional, or full elders are approved for appointment to less than full-time service, what is the total number of years for which such approval has been granted to each, and for what fraction of full-time service (in one-quarter increments) is approval granted (for purposes of equitable compensation claim and pension credit) ¶¶338.2, 342.2, 1506)? **(v 2/3, after 8 years v 3/4):**

Name	**Appointment**		**Fraction of Full-Time Service**
Jana Lynn Almeida – FE	07-01-2010	4 Years	3/4 Time
Charles D. Farnum – FE	01-01-2014	0 Year	1/4 Time
Bryce E. Feighner – FE	07-01-2007	7 Years	2/4 Time
Susan J. Trowbridge – FE	07-01-2014	0 Year	2/4 Time
Ryan B. Wieland – FE	01-01-2011	3 Years	3/4 Time

After Eight (8) Years (v3/4):

Name	**Appointment**		**Fraction of Full-Time Service**
Linda D. Stoddard – FE	07-01-2000	14 Years	1/4 Time

b) What deacons in full connection and provisional deacons are approved for appointment to less than full-time service (¶331.7)?

Name	**Appointment**		**Fraction of Full-Time Service**
Patricia L. Catellier – FD	07-01-2010	4 Years	2/4 Time
Kimberly A. DeLong – FD	07-01-2013	1 Year	2/4 Time
Mariel Kay DeMoss – FD	07-01-2013	1 Year	3/4 Time
Colleen T. Treman – FD	07-01-2008	6 Years	2/4 Time
Cara Beth Ann Weiler – FD	07-01-2009	4 Years	3/4 Time

74. Who have been appointed as interim pastors under the provisions of ¶338.3 since the last session of the annual conference, and for what period of time?

Name	**Appointment**	**Start Date**	**End Date**
None	–	–	–

75. What changes have been made in appointments since the last annual conference session? (**Attach** list. Include and identify Appointments Beyond the Local Church (Deacons) and Appointments to Extension Ministries (Elders). Give effective dates of all changes.)

76. What elders (full connection and provisional), associate members, and local pastors are appointed to ministry to the local church and where are they appointed for the ensuing year? (**Attach** a list.)

77. What elders (full connection and provisional), associate members, and local pastors are appointed to extension ministries for the ensuing year? (**Attach** a list)
    a) Within the connectional structures of United Methodism (¶344.1a, c)?
    b) To ministries endorsed by the Board of Higher Education and Ministry (344.1b)?
    c) To other valid ministries under the provisions of ¶344.1d? (**v 2/3**)
    Valerie Fons, FE, Bread and Water and L.A.U.N.C.H., Wisconsin Conference
    D. Kay Pratt, AM, President, PAPAS (Pastors and Priests Available for Service) Ministries, Methodist Church in the Caribbean and The Americas
    Merlin H. Pratt, AM, Minister of Port Antonio Methodist Circuit, Methodist Church of the Caribbean and Americas, Jamaica District
    Barbara L. Smith-Jang, FE, Pastoral Counselor, Taejon Christian International School Taejon South Korea

Alice Fleming Townley, FE, (¶345) Parish Associate, Okemos Presbyterian Church, Okemos, MI

78. Who are appointed as deacons (full connection and provisional) for the ensuing year? (**Attach** a list.)
    a) Through non-United Methodist agencies and settings beyond the local church (¶331.1a)?
    b) Through United Methodist Church-related agencies and schools within the connectional structures of The United Methodist Church (¶331.1b)?
    c) Within a local congregation, charge, or cooperative parish (¶331.1c)?

79. Who are appointed to attend school (¶416.6)?
    (List alphabetically all those whose prime appointment is to attend school.)

Name	Clergy Status	School
Christina L. Wright	FD	University of West Georgia

80. Where are the diaconal ministers appointed for the ensuing year (¶310) [**1992 Discipline**]? (**Attach** list)

81. What other personal notations should be made? (Include such matters as changes in pension credit (¶1506.5), corrections or additions to matters reported in the "Business of the Annual Conference" form in previous years, and legal name changes of clergy members and diaconal ministers.)
    - **Question # 19 a) Changed First Year License Awarded to 2003 for Scott M. Bouldrey.**
    - **Question # 19 b) Changed First Year License Awarded to 1996 for Nancy L. Boelens.**
    - **Question # 19 b) Changed First Year License Awarded to 1993 for Sandra K. VandenBrink.**
    - **Question # 48.c – Arthur C. Murphy, Jr. correct middle initial is "C."**
    - **Question # 48.d – Janilyn McConnell, please note, she passed away in 2013 (07.14.2013).**
    - **Question # 56 – Richard Muessig, did NOT complete Course of Study, his name was removed from the Retired Local Pastor Lists.**
    - **Question # 59 – Daphna Lee Flegal should have been listed as a Diaconal Minister in the past.**

82. Where and when shall the next Conference Session be held (¶603.2, 3)?
    Calvin College, Grand Rapids, Michigan, June 3-6, 2015

—WMC Photos

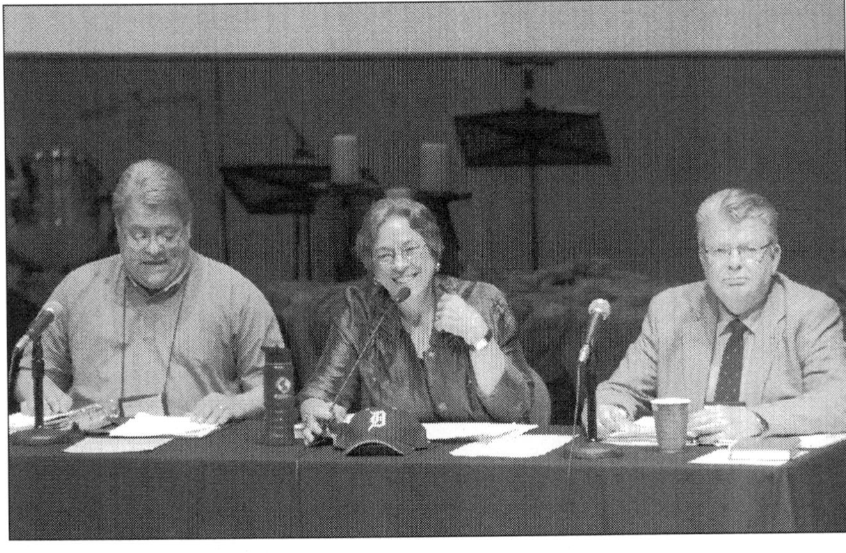

VI. DAILY PROCEEDINGS
of the West Michigan Annual Conference

FIRST DAY ~ CLERGY SESSION
Wednesday, June 11, 2014 1:30 PM

Bill Dobbs called the meeting to order on behalf of Bishop Kiesey.

Congregation sang And Are We Yet Alive.

Motion: Boley moved to allow Sus'ann Busley, Mark Doyal, Vicki Gibbs, and Deana Nelson, to be granted voice but no vote. Motion carried.

Motion: Boley moved for all those Provisional and Associate Members, Full and Part-Time Local Pastors and those on Honorable Locations be granted voice but no vote. Motion carried.

Boley gave special recognition for Bob Smith for attending his 74th Clergy Session.

Motion: Boley moved to allow Eric Mulanda to be granted voice but no vote. Motion carried.

Motion: Boley moved to allow Pat Gilleran from the General Board of Pension and Health Benefits to be granted voice but no vote. Motion carried.

Laurie Haller introduced Marcia McFee and invited all clergy members to participate in clergy choir.

Haller led Clergy Members in Come, Live in the Light.

McFee led Clergy Members in Alleluia.

Boley introduced the Chair of the Conference Board of Pension and Health Benefits. Lou Grettenberger presented a 5-minute video containing information about clergy health benefits and care plans. Grettenberger relayed information about current health care plans to the Clergy and encouraged Clergy to maintain healthy lifestyle behaviors.

Deb Johnson gave an overview of the Ordination Service and asked twelve local pastors to help at the Ordination Service taking place on Saturday, June 14.

Kennetha Bigham-Tsai from the Connectional Table informed Clergy of the current state of the Vital Church Initiative. 33% of congregations in the Conference are currently classified as vital. The Connectional Table is working to raise awareness about VCI within the Conference and the greater jurisdiction. The representative informed the Clergy of ongoing efforts of the Connectional Table.

Molly Turner asked Clergy Member to bring their church's pledge cards for Imagine No Malaria to the worship service this evening.

A video was played for information regarding the Michigan Area School for Pastoral Ministry.

Melany Chalker, the Dean for School for Pastoral Ministry in the West Michigan Conference spoke about hands-on, practical experiences requested from Clergy. Recreation for pastors at the school this year was also mentioned. As a reminder to Clergy, the ecumenical colleagues are encouraged to participate.

Tamara Williams presented the Cabinet Report. Williams discussed a history of the conference itineracy process in connection with the current itineracy decision-making process. This year, 17 retirements, 3 leaves of absences, and other special transitions resulted in 27 open churches in the conference. 14 moves were initiated due to lack of churches' ability to meet pastoral salary packages. 84 total moves took place this year. The cabinet has developed some creative ways to fill these moves; one of these ways has been shorter term appointments, a less preferable solution. There are currently 307 clergy serving appointments. More than half of current clergy members are nearing retirement age. An average of 4 new clergy are appointed each year in contrast with the annual average of 17 retirees. Appointments were barely filled this year. This time in the life of the conference will introduce new and challenging stresses to the itineracy process. Williams urged all clergy members to be understanding and willing to answer the appointments and movements which develop and are assigned in the approaching years.

Boley led clergy in a silent prayer.

Program Committee Guide Chair informed clergy of new event orders at Annual Conference this year. Chair referred to Judy Lyon of the Purple Shirts hosts on the Calvin College campus. The Purple Shirts are able to direct clergy to golf carts for campus transportation. New and improved access portals are available for clergy members with different physical needs. Water bottles will not be provided at this year's conference; clergy are encouraged to bring and refill their own water containers. Sign language interpreters will be present on the right side of the auditorium in the Fine Arts Center. The interpreters are available for any other meetings or sessions, including meals.

Sherri Swanson centered the Clergy in a call-and-response liturgy within the verses of the song Spirit of God.

Boley invited the Order of Deacons, Order of Elders and Chair of the John Wesley Association to the floor.

Motion: Jeremy Wicks was nominated to become chair of John Wesley Association. Motion carried.

The current Chair of the John Wesley Association, Mike Riegler, spoke about the role of the local pastor in church appointments and the importance of the roles that local pastors play.

The Order of the Deacons, Greg Lawton read 1 Corinthians 12 and spoke about the gifts God's people are awarded in order to serve the church. Members of the Order of Deacons were recognized. The Order of Deacons was celebrated for the ministry networks in which deacons participate -- Conference, jurisdiction, and world-wide.

The Order of Elders, Lynn Pier-Fitzgerald, talked about a model for holy conversations in the Conference and the church abroad, keeping them safe and loving. The speaker urged for common ground to be found in conversation.

Boley called for a 3-minute break to allow Clergy to stand.

Question 17 was brought to the floor. Boley asked for editions to be mentioned after the Clergy Session. Moral excellence is promoted as a striving goal of clergy by the Bishop and the Conference.

Prayer of Confession and Response were spoken.

The clergy sang Here I Am Lord.

Questions 19 and 20 were offered for information only.

Motion: Marty Culver presented Question 21. Question 21 carried.

Question 22 were offered for information only.

Question 24: Ordained Ministers from other Annual Conference were asked to stand.

Motion: Boley presented Question 25. Question 25 carried.

Motion: Wade Panse presented Question 26. Question carried.

Provisional Membership Registrar, Kathy Kursch asked David Hills and Steve Charnley to speak in support on behalf of Steve Lindeman.

Hills and Charnley presented a brief history of Lindeman's life and ministry.

Motion: Kursch moved to accept Steve Lindeman as a Provisional Elder. Motion carried.

Kursch invited Neil Davis and Doug Vernon to speak in support of Heather Molner.

Davis and Vernon presented a brief history of Heather Molner's life and ministry.

Motion: Kursch moved to accept Heather Molner as a Provisional Elder. Motion carried.

Kursch invited Scott Otis and Ed Ross to speak in support of Chad Parmalee. Otis and Ross presented a brief history on Paramlee's life and ministry.

Motion: Kursch moved to accept Chad Parmalee as a Provisional Elder. Motion carried.

Boley explained that the next three candidates have completed the necessary work in order to become Provisional Elders.

Kursch invited two speakers to speak in support on behalf of Dennis Bromley. Anita Hahn and Dick Riley presented a brief history on Bromley's life and ministry.

Motion: Kursch moved to accept Dennis B. Bromley as a Provisional Elder. Motion carried.

Kursch invited Hahn and Gary Step to speak in support of John Conklin. Hahn and Step presented a brief history on Conklin's life and ministry.

Motion: Kursch moved to accept John J. Conklin as Provisional Elder. Motion carried.

Kursch invited Laurie Haller and Brad Kalajainen to approach the floor and speak on behalf of James Noggle. Haller and Kalajainen presented a brief history on Noggle's life and ministry.

Motion: Kursch moved to accept James C. Noggle as a Provisional Elder. Motion carried.

Boley explained that Bromley and Noggle were already ordained and will not be part of the Ordination Service on Saturday, June 14, 2014.

Question 29 was presented for information only.

Kursch called Bob Hundley and Bill Beachy to speak in support of Gary Simmons, from the Southern Baptist denomination. Beachy and Hundley presented a brief history of Simmon's life and ministry.

Motion: Kursch moved to recieve Gary L. Simmons as a Provisional Elder. Motion carried.

Questions 32, 33, and 34 were brought to the floor.

Motion: Question 32a and 33a for Patricia Catellier. Question 32b and 33a carried.

Motion: Question 32b and 34a for Letisha Bowman. Question 32b and 34a carried.

Motion: Question 32b and 34a for Catherine Christman. Question 32b and 34a carried.

Motion: Question 32b and 34a for Patricia Ann Haas. Question 32b and 34a carried.

Motion: Question 32b and 34a for Jonathan Van Dop. Question 32b and 34a carried.

Motion: Question 32b and 34a for Rebecca Wieringa. Question 32b and 34a carried.

Question 38 was presented information only.

Clergy sang You Are Mine.

Question 43 and 44 were presented for information only.

Question 77 was brought to the floor.

Motion: Question 77 voted. Question 77 carried.

Questions 59, 63, 72, 41 and 49 were presented for information only.

Bob Roth offered information to correct the printed date of his appointment to the Wesley Foundation: The appointment was commenced in 2010, and the listed date is 2014. Bishop Kiesey indicated that Roth's information would be correct and he would be awarded all the necessary recognition.

Question 50 under Changes in Conference Relationship was presented for information only.

Motion: Question 50 a) (1) voted. Question 50 a) (1) carried.

Motion: Question 50 a) (3) on behalf of Brian Rafferty. Question 50 a) (3) carried.

Question 52 under Changes in Conference Relationship was present for information only.

The Clergy prayed and sang You Are Mine (verse 3 and 4).

Boley announced all retiring Clergy.

Question 53 Deacons b) under Transitions - Retirements was presented for information only.

Question 53 Elders a) under Transitions - Retirements was presented for information only.

Question 54 under Transitions - Retirements was brought to the floor.

Question 56 under Transitions - Retirements was brought to the floor.

Before the vote, Bishop Kiesey invited all present to recognize the service of all retiring Clergy members.

Motion: Move to recognize the retirement of clergy. Motion is carried.

Question 48: The Clergy are invited to recognize the Transitions to Eternal Life as all Clergy members who have passed away within the past year are named.

The Clergy were called to prayer by Bishop Kiesey.

Clergy sang We Are Called.

Question 18 under Concluding Business is for information only.

Motion: Question 18a for the Administrative Review Committee. Question 18a carried.

Question 18b is for information only.

Motion: Approve Question 73a under Concluding Business. Motion carried.

Motion: Presented Question 73b under Concluding Business. Motion carried.

Question 79 and 81 was presented for information only.

Motion: Accept the full report of the Board of Ordained Ministry. Motion carried.

The Clergy sang The Summons.

Closing Business officiated by Bishop Kiesey.

Clergy Session adjourned at 4:48 PM.

FIRST DAY ~ LAITY SESSION

Wednesday, June 11, 2014 1:30 PM

Anne Soles, Conference Lay Leader, introduced Bishop Kiesey who greeted the Laity.

Nichea Ver Veer Guy, Conference Program Committee Chairperson, thanked the Program Committee for their work throughout the year. Ver Veer Guy oriented laity to Calvin College and gave an overview of the services available at Annual Conference.

Soles introduced Ralph Zewinski, Assistant Lay Leader from the Detroit Annual Conference, who gave greetings and blessings from the Detroit Conference.

Soles spoke about Imagine No Malaria.

Laura Witkowski addressed the Laity and stated she is available for any assistance or questions with the Legislative Procedures or Committees.

Soles introduced the districts: Albion, Grand Rapids, Grand Traverse, Heartland, Kalamazoo and Lansing.

Jodie Flessner spoke about the benefits of working with other churches.

Soles asked for questions from the Laity.

Jody Pratt, Conference Director of Servant Ministries, discussed the different classes and certifications available to Laity.

Kendall Farnum, asked about the duties and responsibilities of a Lay Servant regarding certifications.

Soles introduced Lou Grettenberger, Chair of Conference Board of Pensions, who gave a presentation on Clergy Pensions. A video made by the General Board of Pensions was shown for information only. Grettenberger explained benefits and services provided to the clergy.

David Lundquist presented the lay candidates for General Conference: Nichea Ver Veer Guy, Laura Clark Witkowski, and Simmie Proctor. The delegates briefly introduced themselves to the Laity.

Soles introduced Bill Chu, Director of MSU Wesley Foundation, to speak about the legislative process. Chu welcomed questions from the Laity regarding the Legislative Committees. A concern was raised regarding the possibility of an item not being heard by the entire Conference. Chu gave alternatives for raising a legislative piece for the entire Conference should the legislation be ruled non-concurrence in the Legislative Committee.

Chu and Wesley Foundation students demonstrated the Legislative Process for the Laity.

Soles answered questions from the Laity.

Soles closed the Laity Session with prayer at 3:30 PM.

FIRST DAY ~ OPENING WORSHIP/MEMORIAL SERVICE

Wednesday, June 11, 2014 7:00 PM

Marcia McFee greeted the Conference and initiated the worship service at 7:05 PM.

McFee invoked the spirit through a "Gathering Chant" and invited the Conference to rise and join in singing.

The Conference sang For All the Saints.

A speaker read the passage "Living Memory" by Brian Andreas for the First Reading.

The band Gooder 'n Grits played Ashoken Farewell to invoke the Word in Music.

Four speakers read Ephesians 1:3-14 for the Second Reading.

Bishop Kiesey delivered her message on "Creative Courage," the Proclamation of the Word.

The Chamber Choir sang The Road Home by Stephen Paulus.

McFee led the Conference in The Lone Wild Bird.

The Conference remembered the lives of Clergy Members: Charles Cooley, Mary Curtis, Bruce Felkner, Richard Kidder, Richard Matson, Donald Merrill, John Miller, Jr., Char Minger, Arthur Murphy, Allen Rice II, Charles Richards, Charles Shields, Wayne Sparks and Carl Staser.

The Conference remembered the lives of Clergy Spouses: David Bourns, Dorothy Doten, June Entenman, Juanita Fischer, Marcile Garrod, Beatrice Horton, Helen Pratt, Joan Rickard, Alice Short, and Ruth Walkinshaw-Bowen.

The Conference remembered the life of a child of the parsonage: Timothy Dykema.

The Conference remembered the lives of laypersons Joy Crawford, Louise Thomas, and Mike Zalewski.

Bishop Kiesey led the Conference in prayer.

The musicians played an instrumental song during a slideshow of pictures celebrating the lives of the individuals memorialized this evening.

Bishop Kiesey initiated the Invitation to the Meal.

All present recited the Unison Confession.

McFee led the Conference in Come to the Table of Grace.

All present passed the Peace of Christ.

McFee led the Conference to resume singing Come to the Table of Grace as part of invoking the Sacrament of Holy Communion.

Bishop Kiesey blessed communion elements and completed the preparation of the table.

All present recited the Lord's Prayer.

McFee gave instructions for receiving communion to the Conference.

The Conference partook in communion while the band played As I Went Down to the River to Pray. The Chamber Choir sang Unclouded Day. McFee continued the music by leading the Conference in Fill My Cup, Lord.

Bishop Kiesey led the Conference in the prayer after communion.

Bill Dobbs gave the benediction.

McFee led the Conference in I'll Fly Away.

The worship service closed.

SECOND DAY ~ MORNING SESSION

Thursday, June 12, 2014 8:30 AM

Marcia McFee called the Conference to order by centering singing Alleluia.

Bishop Kiesey greeted the Conference and opened with prayer.

All present blessed the worship space.

McFee led the Conference in prayer and in singing And Are We Yet Alive.

Bishop Kiesey declared the 2014 West Michigan Annual Conference open.

Nichea Ver Veer Guy, Conference Program Committee Chair, welcomed the Conference to Calvin College as well as those attending from the Detroit Annual Conference.

Motion: Ver Veer Guy moved to set the limits of the floor to be set as all seated in the Lower Level of the Fine Arts Center and the middle areas on the balcony. All guests will be directed to sit on the sides of the balcony. Motion Carried.

Rick Blunt, Clergy, Lowell UMC, asked for clarification about sitting in the bar.

Motion: Ver Veer Guy moved that the Conference Administrative Assistant and the spouse of the Bishop, those with disabilities, and those assisting others to sit within the bar with no voice and no vote. Motion carried.

Motion: Benton Heisler, Director of Connectional Ministry, moved to accept Volume One of the Conference Journal. Motion carried.

Greg Buchner, Conference Secretary, offered greetings and regrets from absent members of the Conference.

Ver Veer Guy introduced Mary Halst, the chaplain of Calvin College. Halst addressed the Conference with information about surrounding areas of interest and reminded the Conference of the availability of Calvin Staff to assist on campus.

Julie Liske, Clergy of Grand Rapids Trinity and Executive Director of Grand Rapids Metropolitan Ministries, welcomed the Conference to the Grand Rapids area.

Sue Cobb, Chair of Council on Finance and Administration presented a slideshow explaining where funds are currently designated and the giving patterns from the past fifteen years. Bishop Kiesey was given a framed poster for financial giving with the World Church.

Glenn Wagner, Chair of the Nominations Committee, presented a slideshow celebrating the gifts and potential of the West Michigan Annual Conference as part of the global body of Christ. Wagner discussed the different Committees within the Conference. Wagner highlighted the following who have completed their service to the Conference Committee: Sheila Baker, John

Boley, Ellen Brubaker, Mike Conklin, Lynn and Kay DeMoss, Mary Lou Fassett, George House, Geri Litchfield, Paul Hane, Deb Johnson, Mike Johnson, Joy Mills, David Morton, Ethel Stears, Jeremy Wicks, Linda Zeller, Charles VanLente and Jeremy Williams. These individuals were presented with a Hebron Glass Bell.

Motion: Wagner moved that the Haiti Covenant be presented to the floor. Motion carried.

Motion: Heisler moved the Haiti Covenant to be presented to the Conference without a Legislative Committee. Motion carried.

Motion: Rev. David Morton moved to present Item #4. Motion carried.

Marco Depestre, Jr., the Secretary of the Haiti District Conference, addressed the Conference and thanked all present for their renewed commitment to efforts in Haiti.

Chair of the Rules of Order Committee, Judy Coffey, presented the report from the Rules of Order Committee, indicating changes to the Rules of Order this year.

Motion: Item #11 was presented to the Conference for vote. Motion carried.

Coffey invited David Lundquist to speak about the response petition Item #11-R. Lundquist gave rationale for Item #11-R.

Motion: Bishop Kiesey brought Item #11-R to the floor for vote.

Heisler clarified Item #11-R will be effective only if all attendees sign up for Annual Conference on time. Heisler spoke in opposition of the motion.

Motion: Bishop Kiesey led the vote on Item #11-R. Motion not carried.

Motion: Bishop Kiesey led the vote on Item #11. Motion carried.

Coffey presented Item #12 to the floor. Discussion was held. Bishop Kiesey clarified how the cards would be used to call on members to speak.

Motion: Bishop Kiesey moved to vote on Item #12. A standing vote was held and was inconclusive. The vote was counted. Item #12 carried.

Motion: Coffey presented Item #13 to the floor. Item #13 carried.

David Lundquist moved to amend Rule 23B(7)(b1) and (c) of the 2013 Journal by addition and deletion as follows:

1) All legislative items considered by Legislative Committees which received approval for concurrence with or without amendment by 90% of the Legislative Committee members present and voting shall be included in the Consent Calendar.

c. All recommendations for concurrent or concurrence by amendment by less than 90% of the Legislative Committee members present and voting, and all recommendations for concurrence with amendment, shall automatically be before the Conference for action. Abstentions shall be counted as present, but not voting, and shall not be counted in the computation of votes.

Anne Soles offered clarification regarding the Consent Calendar and the items placed on it.

Motion: Bishop Kiesey moved the amendment to Item #13. Motion carried.

Motion: Bishop Kiesey moved for the Rules of Order business to come to a vote. Motion carried.

Clarification was given about the expanse of the bar for voting purposes.

Nominations for General Conference Laity Candidates were received: Laurie Dahlman and Valerie Mossman-Celestin.

Ballot envelopes were passed out to all voting members. The Balloting Process for Clergy and Laity was explained. The list of Nominees was projected on the screen for the Conference.

The Order of the Day was called by Bishop Kiesey at 10:15 AM.

Marcia McFee greeted the group and initiated the session at 10:15 AM.

The audience sang Jesus, We Are Here and invited into prayer.

McFee introduced the "Creating Worship with Deep Soul" program. The group shared examples of "M-M-Good !" (Meaningful & Memorable) with their neighbors and reflected on why the example was memorable. McFee invited the audience to share their value(s) within worship. McFee presented the clip from the film, "Under the Tuscan Sun" and invited discussion on the clip and how elements from it can be attributed to worship.

McFee closed the workshop period.

The Genesis UMC band played an opening song.

Bishop Kiesey introduced Rev. DeAnn Dobbs who spoke on "Open Doors, Open Hearts and Open Minds".

McFee presented a short video clip.

The band led in two more songs, Praise to the Lord, the Almighty and All Creatures of Our God and King.

Rev. Sue Petro led in a Call to Worship

The band led in another song, Oh, How I Need You

McFee read Luke 13:33-34

Members performed Resistance: A Conversation

Dobbs gave her sermon

The band performed Brokenness Aside.

McFee led the Call and Response

Gathered Offering

Members performed Resistance: A Conversation

The band led in Amazing Grace/My Chains Are Gone.

Dobbs gave the benediction

The band closed with Build Your Kingdom Here.

Worship ended at 12:15 PM!

SECOND DAY ~ AFTERNOON SESSION

Thursday, June 12, 2014 3:30 PM

Bishop Kiesey called for a ballot to take place.

A ballot was taken.

Kiesey introduced Molly Turner who invited Katie Dawson to speak about the Imagine No Malaria Campaign and highlighted on Imaging a world without Malaria. Turner presented a gift to Dawson

As of June 12th, the amount of money raised toward the goal of $1.5 million for Imagine No Malaria was $802,704. Turner offered prayer over the riders for their trip from South Dakota to Ohio on the Ride For Change .

Kiesey introduced Jeremy Williams, Chair of Board of Christian Camping. Williams honored Naomi García for her service with Camping with three full scholarships. Williams recognized the new Chair of the Board of Christian Camping, Glen Kinder. Erin Fitzgerald, Devon Herrell, David Hills, and Anita Hahn gave testimonies of children who have benefited from their camp experiences and Williams emphasized the importance of camp in the lives of the youth. George Ayoub spoke about what efforts he and the board have made to improve the quality of camp and asked the lay group what they can do to improve. Ayoub also encouraged members of the lay group to send children to camp and help with camp scholarships. $24,320 had already been awarded in camp scholarship money. Ayoub also spoke about the importance of the presence of a Camp Booster in the church and presented that Wesley Woods received a $200,000 grant from the Granger Foundation, if Wesley Woods can raise $300,000.

Bishop Kiesey gave the result of the Ballot: Clergy: Total Ballots-173: Valid-170; 86 votes needed for election Laurie Haller: 89, Benton Heisler: 39, Kennetha Bigham-Tsai: 22, Mary Ivanov: 11, John Boley: 9. No election took place.

Laity Ballot: Total Ballots-355, Valid-340, 172 votes needed for election. Nichea VerVeer Guy: 123, Laurie Dahlman: 69, Laura Witkowski: 56, Anne Soles: 46, Simmie Proctor: 29, Valerie Mossman-Celestin: 20. No election took place.

Gary Step and García spoke about New Church Development and Vital Church Initiative, highlighting the outcomes of the initiative in the West Michigan Conference. Glenn Wagner, and Mona Dye shared their churches' experience with the Vital Church Initiative.

Kiesey introduced the Wesley Foundation Campus Directors. Charlie Farnum, Greg Lawton, Bill Chu, and Lisa Batten gave testimonies of Wesley Students emphasizing the importance of Wesley Campus Ministries to student life.

Kiesey gave the Second Ballot results:

Laity: Total Ballots: 354, Valid Ballots: 342; 172 votes needed for election, Nichea Ver Veer Guy: 189. Dahlman: 75, Witkowski: 32, Soles: 30, Proctor: 11, Mossman-Celestin: 5.

Clergy: Total Ballots: 167, Valid Ballots: 162; 82 votes needed for election Bigham-Tsai: 78, Heisler: 59, Ivanon: 14, Boley: 11.

Ver Veer Guy gave announcements and adjoined Conference at 5:30 PM.

SECOND DAY ~ MARKING SACRED TIME

Thursday, June 12, 2014 7:30 PM

John Boley led the Conference in a call-and-response.

John Boley led the Conference in I Surrender All (v. 1)

Marty Culver recognized all Local Pastors who have completed Licensing School: Jerry Bukoski, Ales Fernandez, Jason Harpole, Thoreau May, Daniel Phillips, James Robertson and Jennifer Wheeler.

Culver recognized Donna Keyte for completing her Course Study work and serving as a local Pastor.

Culver recognized Dennis Bromley, Jack Conklin, and James Noggle for completing their Advance Course of study.

Culver recognized Jerry Bukoski, Jason Harpole, Cydney Idsinga, Sean Kid, Bryan Kilpatrick, Seok Nam Lim, Daniel Phillips, James Robertson, Nathaniel Starkey, Kelly Wasnich, and Jennifer Wheeler.

Dean Prentiss recognized Bernard Randolph as the Conference Cane Holder and shared a brief history of Randolph's life and ministry.

Wade Panse recognized George Ayoub as a transferring member from the Eastern Pennsylvania Conference.

Kathy Kursch recognized Provisional Elders. Steve Lindeman, Heather Molner, Chad Parmalee and Associate Members, Dennis Bromley, Jack Conklin and Jim Noggle. Gary Simmons also was received as a Provisional Elder.

Dean Prentiss invited all Clergy who are to become ordained elders to approach the stage.

Letisha Bowman, Catherine Christman, Patricia Haas, Jonathan VanDop, Rebecca Wieringa, and Pat Catellier.

Bishop Kiesey asked the Historic Questions to all newly ordained elders in full connection.

The Conference sang I Surrender All (v. 3).

Speaker invited all retirees and their supporters to stand upon the calling of their name.

Speaker recognized William Beachy as a retiring clergy member.

Speaker led the Conference in the call-and-response to honor retirees.

Speaker recognized Sheila Baker as a retiring clergy member.

Speaker led the Conference in the call-and-response to honor retirees.

Speaker recognized Gary L. Bekofske as a retiring clergy member.

Speaker led the Conference in the call-and-response to honor retirees.

Speaker recognized Gayle S. Berntsen as a retiring clergy member.

Speaker led the Conference in the call-and-response to honor retirees.

Speaker recognized Lawrence P. Brown as a retiring clergy member.

Speaker led the Conference in the call-and-response to honor retirees.

Speaker recognized Billie R. Dalton as a retiring clergy member.

Speaker led the Conference in the call-and-response to honor retirees.

Speaker recognized Linda Burton-Collier as a retiring clergy member.

Speaker led the Conference in the call-and-response to honor retirees.

Speaker recognized Roberta W. Cabot as a retiring clergy member.

Speaker led the Conference in the call-and-response to honor retirees.

Speaker recognized Daniel M. Duncan as a retiring clergy member.

Speaker led the Conference in the call-and-response to honor retirees.

Speaker recognized Richard A. Fritz as a retiring clergy member.

Speaker led the Conference in the call-and-response to honor retirees.

Speaker recognized Deborah M. Johnson as a retiring clergy member.

Speaker led the Conference in the call-and-response to honor retirees.

Speaker recognized Geraldine M. Litchfield as a retiring clergy member.

Speaker led the Conference in the call-and-response to honor retirees.

Speaker recognized Karin K. Orr as a retiring clergy member.

Speaker led the Conference in the call-and-response to honor retirees.

Speaker recognized Susan M. Petro as a retiring clergy member.

Speaker led the Conference in the call-and-response to honor retirees.

Speaker recognized Jeanne M. Randels as a retiring clergy member.

Speaker led the Conference in the call-and-response to honor retirees.

Speaker recognized Roy G. Testolin as a retiring clergy member.

Speaker led the Conference in the call-and-response to honor retirees.

Speaker recognized Richard M. Riley as a retiring clergy member.

Speaker led the Conference in the call-and-response to honor retirees.

Speaker invited Riley to return to the floor on behalf of all retirees.

Speaker invited Bowman to return to the floor on the behalf of the newly ordained.

Bishop Kiesey begins the passing of the mantle.

Riley passed the mantel to Bowman, signifying the passing of ministry from one generation to the next.

The Conference joined in singing I Surrender All (v. 4).

Boley led the Conference in the Blessing of Dismissal.

The worship service closed.

THIRD DAY ~ MORNING DEVOTIONS

Friday, June 13, 2014 8:30 AM

The devotional time began when a representative from La Nueva Esperanza UMC greeted the Conference and led all present in opening prayer. The Conference sang opening praise songs in both Spanish and English. After the Conference was seated, speakers read a passage from Ephesians in both Spanish and English. The reflection message was about the empowerment Jesus granted to His Disciples in the beginning of the early church to gather together and be strong in one church body. The church is called to transformation by the voice of God. The speaker pointed out that although there is only one Hispanic church in the entire West Michigan Annual Conference, La Nueva Esperanza is part of the connected whole of the church through Christ. The speaker offered the question: How much are we willing to give to gather together across barriers of language and culture to be part of one church? After the reflection, the worship leader led the Conference in a centering prayer.

District Superintendent Bill Haggard approached the floor, greeted the Conference, and spoke about MissionInsite, an online tool available for measuring the demographic information of the communities surrounding every church. Haggard urged churches in communities with Hispanic and Latino populations to reach out to and embrace their Hispanic and Latino neighbors. The Director of Connectional Ministries thanked Stacy Mabus Caballero on behalf of the Committee on Hispanic/Latino Ministries' ability to bring $50,000 into the Annual Conference budget for the purpose of strengthening and enabling Hispanic and Latino outreach ministries. A speaker recognized individuals, including Sonya Luna, Michigan Area Director of Latino and Hispanic Ministeries, for their services in strengthening the connections between Hispanic-Latino communities and the West Michigan Conference.

A speaker presented a slideshow depicting the National Hispanic-Latino Ministry Logo and spoke of the mission and vision of Hispanic-Latino Ministries within the West Michigan Annual Conference. A video about the importance of Hispanic and Latino Ministries and the need for the church to embrace Hispanic and Latino Communities as part of the church was shared with the Conference. After the video, the report concluded.

THIRD DAY ~ MORNING SESSION

Friday, June 13, 2014 9:05 AM

Bishop Kiesey greeted the Conference at 9:05 AM

Kiesey gave the Second Ballot results from Thursday Afternoon.

Laity: Total Ballots: 354: Valid Ballots: 342; Nichea Ver Veer Guy: 189. Dahlman: 75, Witkowski: 32, Soles: 30, Proctor: 11, Mossman-Celestin: 5.

Clergy: Total Ballots: 167, Valid Ballots: 162. Bigham-Tsai: 78, Heisler: 59, Ivanov: 14, Boley: 11.

Bishop Kiesey explained what the ballot voting would represent and Conference Secretary Greg Buchner gave instructions for ballot voting. David Lundquist raised a question on electing the alternates for Jurisdictional Conference.

Greg Buchner directed all present to view the Consent Calendar. Buchner stated that any items desired to be removed from the calendar should be submitted to the Conference Secretary's office with the name and contact information of the person who wants the item removed. All suggestions must be submitted to the office by noon.

Paul Hane addressed the Bishop regarding the Consent Calendar Summary. Petition 17 and Petition 18 are incorrectly labeled. Petition 17 should be labeled Petition 18 and Petition 18 should be labeled Petition 19. Item information is correctly numbered after the Summary page.

Bishop Kiesey read Rule #33-F3b: Persons receiving votes beyond those elected to the Jurisdictional Conference shall be reserve delegrates.

Anne Soles, Conference Lay Leader, thanked all present on behalf of their efficient work in yesterday's Legislative Committees. Soles gave the Laity Report and elaborated with stories to illustrate her appreciation of the Conference's ability to work together and resolve issues. Soles commented on her perceptions of forming disciples for Christ by changing one heart at a time and emphasized the importance of working together.

Soles presented Item #3 and opened the floor for discussion.

Jeff Williams, Chair of the Board of Higher Education and Campus Ministry, addressed the floor. Williams opened by reading a passage from 1 Corinthians. Williams explained the role of the Board of Higher Education and Campus Ministry in preserving Wesley Foundations within the West Michigan Annual Conference and elaborated on the Board's support of Item #3. Williams provided information about the continual budget cuts which have been delivered to Wesley Foundations since 2000.

Ryan Minier spoke in favor of Item #3.

Kate Heaton, Len Schoenherr, Devon Herrell, Matt Weiler, Herb Griffin, Larry Edress and Kaylee Blackwell spoke in favor of Item #3.

Bill Haggard spoke against Item #3.

Herb Griffin stated that his Conference in Okinawa, Japan would donate $10,000 to Wesley Foundations this quarter.

Bishop Kiesey tabled the discussion of Item #3 due to time constraints.

Bishop Kiesey gave the Third Ballot results:.

Clergy: Total Ballots: 161, Valid Ballots: 157; 79 were needed for election of a Jurisdictional Delegate. Kennetha Bigham-Tsai was elected with 93 votes. The alternates are Benton Heisler with 54 votes, John Boley with 6 votes, and Mary Ivanov with 4 votes.

Bishop Kiesey gave the Third Ballot results:

Laity: Total Ballots: 359, Valid Ballots: 335; 168 needed for election. Dahlman had 132 votes, Witkowski had 99, Soles had 46, Mossman-Celestin had 35, and Proctor had 23.

Bishop Kiesey called for a Laity ballot vote.

Bishop Kiesey closed the Legislative Session.

THIRD DAY ~ AFTERNOON SESSION

Friday, June 13, 2014 1:30 PM

Bishop Kiesey called the Conference back into session through song at 1:31 PM.

Motion: Mandana Nordbrock, Chair of the Journal Committee, moved that the minutes from Wednesday, June 11 and Thursday, June 12 be approved as printed. Minutes are posted outside of the Conference Secretary's Office. Motion carried.

David Lundquist provided clarification on nominations and alternates to General and

Jurisdictional Conference. Bishop Kiesey stated the Conference would only pay for two of the alternates to attend these conferences.

Benton Heisler, Director of Connectional Ministries, gave the DCM Report. Heisler highlighted the work of the VCI and Conference Leadership Team. The Conference viewed a video demonstrating the work Cornerstone UMC has done with Campus Elementary School in Grand Rapids. Campus Elementary was about to close, but through the donations from Cornerstone UMC, the school has doubled its enrollment and is thriving. Heisler discussed the culture of giving and generosity that is apparent in the West Michigan Conference. A video from the Imagine No Malaria Campaign was shown and the Conference was encouraged to continue contributing to the Imagine No Malaria Campaign.

Anne Soles opened the floor to legislation. Item #3 was brought back to the floor for discussion.

One individual spoke against Item #3.

One individual spoke in favor of Item #3.

Motion: Mike Riegler moved to call the question. Motion carried.

Jeff Williams, Chair of the Board of Higher Education and Campus Ministry, gave a final statement in response to Item #3.

Item #3 carried.

Soles announced Items 1 and 5 had been lifted from the Consent Calendar.

Motion: Soles moved to approve Consent Calendar - Plan of Organization Petitions (Items 14, 15 and 16). Motion carried.

Motion: Soles moved to approve Consent Calendar - Petitions, passed during the Legislative Committees with at least 90% concurrence (Items 2, 7, 8, 9, 10, 18 and 19). Motion carried.

Ellen Brubaker, author of Item #1, offered rationale for Item #1.

Ryan Minier made a point of order.

Scott Manning, Keith Pratt and Don Tippin spoke against Item #1.

Trevor McDermont, Burke Webb, Nichea Ver Veer Guy and one other individual, spoke for the petition.

Motion: Neil Davis move to call the question. Motion carried.

Davis offered a prayer prior to voting on Item #1.

Item #1 carried.

Soles presented Item #5 for discussion. Ellen Brubaker, author of Item #5, offered rationale for Item #5.

DeAnn Dobbs asked a question of clarification.

One individual spoke against the petition.

Bob Lynch, Amee Paparella, Don Tippin and one other individual spoke for the petition.

Motion: Bishop Kiesey invited the Conference to vote on Item #5. Motion carried; Item #5 carried.

John Boley, Chair of the Board of Ordained Ministry gave a report. Boley explained the role of the Board of Ordained Ministry in the Conference. He explained the online policy on the conference website for the purpose of education. He also explained the necessity for new clergy and for relevance in the evolution of the occupation of the Board of Ordained Ministry.

Dean Prentiss introduced The Reverend Lynn Grimes Spirit Award and presented it to John Boley as the first recipient.

Lynn Pier-Fitzgerald, Chair of the Board of Elders and Human Sexuality Conversation

Task Force, presented the goals and the purpose of the Board of Elders and Human Sexuality Conversation Task Force.

Benton Heisler took the podium.

The Conference watched a Spirit Journey slideshow of photos.

Nichea Ver Veer Guy introduced Cokesbury. The Cokesbury representative greeted the Conference and gave a report on Cokesbury.

Ver Veer Guy gave announcements.

Bishop Kiesey issued a 10 minute break at 3:29 PM.

Conference Session resumed at 3:41 PM. Bishop Kiesey led the Conference in singing They Will Know We Are Christians By Our Love.

Sherri Swanson offered a prayer to the Conference.

Soles presented Item #6 to the Conference for discussion.

David Lundquist, author of Item #6, offered rationale for Item #6.

Mike Tupper spoke for the Item #6.

Motion: Lyne Stull-Lipps offered an amendment. Stull-Lipps spoke to the amendment.

Charlie Farnum spoke in favor of the amendment.

David Lundquist offered a Point of Order regarding the Amendment.

Item #6 was tabled for further discussion at a later time.

Bishop Kiesey ended the Business Session at 4:03 PM.

Tom Arthur and Gary Step, Director of New Church Start, discussed New Church starts. A video was shown highlighting Valley Church's success as a New Church Start. Another video was shown that described the different models for New Church starts. Plainfield UMC, now called Rivercrest, was presented as a church restart. Matt Bistayi offered a prayer for Kel and Leanne Penny, who were appointed to Rivercrest. Arthur talked about the Reach Summit and how Conference members can register.

Laurie Haller spoke about the Ubuntu Center at Africa University. Haller discussed how the education Africa University provides is creating leaders and making a difference in the lives of those who attend. A video was shown highlighting the services and impact of Africa University.

A video was shown about historically Black Colleges supported by the United Methodist Church.

Marcia McFee was introduced to the Conference. McFee led the Conference in an Alleluia chant. McFee presented the materials available in the Worship Design Studio. Two tools were presented: Imaginate and Integrity. McFee discussed the importance of looking at the overall goal of the worship experience. Using Anchor Images, Visual Metaphors, Framing and Threading or repeating themes, provides consistency and decreases monoton. Threshold moments are important to center and provide an spiritual journey. When no decisions are to be made, more people can be involved. However, when a decision needs to be made, less people need to be involved. McFee discussed the Design Process that is important for planning worship services. Mark Miller spoke about his experience with Worship Design Retreats. McFee closed the session through singing Alleluia at 5:31 PM.

Ver Veer Guy gave the announcements and Conference was dismissed until 7:00 PM.

THIRD DAY ~ WORSHIP SERVICE

Friday, June 13, 2014 7:00 PM

"The 127s" opened with Come Rain or Come Shine

Marcia McFee greeted the Conference and invited all to pass the peace together.

Bishop Kiesey introduced Anthony Hood from the Detroit Annual Conference.

McFee invited the Conference into worship with a prayer and by leading All Are Welcome with the band. 1 Corinthians 12:4-11 was read during this.

Lisa Batten invited the Holy Spirit into the space to set the attitude for the service.

McFee read "The House of Belonging" by David Whyte.

The band played You Are the Sunshine of My Life while a slideshow for Christian Camping played in the background.

Anthony Hood read 1 Corinthians 14:26, prayed upon the group that they may receive his words, and gave his sermon on a "Time for Inspection" emphasizing how the people of a Conference and a church must change and transform to be what God calls them to be.

Bill Dobbs invited the Conference to receive an offering for Youth Mission Trips. The band played God Bless the Child while the offering baskets were passed.

McFee asked the Conference to share with a neighbor what unique gifts they bring into ministry, and the gift that their Conferences bring to the world, and asked the Conference to name those gifts aloud. McFee and the Conference joined in a closing prayer and a closing hymn Gather Us In.

Hood gave the blessing and sent the Conference to go forth from the service while the band played a postlude.

THIRD DAY ~ FRIDAY EVENING LEGISLATION

Friday, June 13, 2014 8:15 PM

Bishop Kiesey called the session to order.

Bishop Kiesey invited the Conference to share in an opening meditation about gentle and holy debate behaviors.

Bishop Kiesey resumed the discussion about the Amendment to Item #6.

Larry Edris, Carl Black and Deb Johnson spoke against the Amendment to Item #6.

Motion: Tonya Murphy proposed an Amendment to the Amendment to Item #6. Motion carried.

Murphy gave rationale for her Amendment to the Amendment to Item #6.

Discussion on the Amendment to the Amendment was held.

Steven Lett asked for clarification on the meaning behind the capitalization of the term "Marriage Equality." David Lundquist, author of Item #6, gave clarification.

Kristin Harrison and Andy Baek spoke against the Amendment to the Amendment to Item #6.

Scott Manning, Molly Woodworth, Paul Reissmann and Benjamin David Hutchison spoke in favor of the Amendment to the Amendment to Item #6.

Heather Molner asked if Item #6 should be called at this time.

Motion: Pat Bromberek called the question on the Amendment to the Amendment to Item #6. Motion carried.

Murphy provided a final rationale to the Amendment to Item #6.

Bishop Kiesey reread the Amendment to Item #6 for further clarification.

Motion: The Conference voted to pass the Amendment to the Amendment to Item #6. Motion carried.

DeAnn Dobbs proposed an Amendment to Item #6 as Amended: decapitalize the words "Marriage Equality."

Bishop Kiesey invited the Conference to speak to the Amendment to Item #6 as Amended.

Lundquist spoke in favor of the Amendment to Item #6.

Motion: The Amendment to Item #6. Motion carried.

Bishop Kiesey called Item #6 to the floor.

Joey Jacobson, Don Tippin, Matt Weiler and Tim Trommater spoke in favor of Item #6.

Mike Riegler, spoke against Item #6.

Motion: Judy Coffey moved to called the question on Item #6. Motion carried.

Lundquist provided a final rationale to Item #6.

Ryan Minier led the Conference in prayer.

Item #6 carried.

Bishop Kiesey expressed her appreciation for the Conference's respectful tone during the debate process of Item #6.

Marcia McFee led the Conference in Spirit of the Living God.

Bishop Kiesey closed the session.

FOURTH DAY ~ MORNING DEVOTIONS

Saturday, June 14, 2014 8:30 AM

Marcia McFee welcomed the congregation and lead them in song: Peace is Flowing Like a River. McFee encouraged the congregation to turn to their neighbor and say something that they are hopeful for. While people were seated, the lights were dimmed and McFee lead the group again in song Where Heaven Touches Earth. A moment of silence and reflection was had after the song. A video presentation played reflecting the troubles that people face, and how they can turn to God in those troubles. McFee read a scripture passage while the piano played underneath and lead the congregation in song Take My Hand, Precious Lord and invited members to lift up names of those who need to take the hand of the Lord. McFee invited people to lift up the names of their churches and to let go of the things that they were clinging to in that moment.

McFee opened the teaching session and invited people to join in a "fireside chat" to talk about 3 important things that they remember from a worship service. McFee asked individuals from the congregation for examples of what they had just shared with their neighbors. McFee shared a story about a church she had an encounter with that had a conflict over worship and continued with her lesson on the Politics of Change. McFee spoke about the Primal Patterns of worship planning and service. The congregation sang Up From the Grave He Arose, and We Are Marching to describe one of the primal patterns. The congregation sang The Church's One Foundation to describe another primal pattern. The congregation sang Hallelujah and Sanctuary to describe another primal pattern. The congregation sang Jesus, Remember Me to describe the last primal pattern. McFee went over the reactions of worship which are theological, historical, sociological, and physiological. McFee went over what to do with the subjectivity of those reactions. McFee gave a blessing over the group.

Morning Session

Bishop Kiesey and the West Michigan Conference members thanked Marcia McFee for her time spend bringing worship and teaching to 2014 Conference.

Lynn DeMoss, Chair of the Conference Mission Personnel Committee, introduced three missionaries

John Daniel Gore spoke about his area of ministry and how to get involved

Paul Webster spoke about his missionary work in Zambia

Nichea Ver Veer Guy presented a Father's Day video.

Rachel Krahulik, Conference Council on Youth Ministries, presented the report and a video about the Conference Council on Youth Ministries.

FOURTH DAY ~ CORPORATE SESSION

Saturday, June 14, 2014 9:45 AM

Bill Gehman, Chair of Trustees for Conference opened the Corporate Session.

Motion: Kennetha Bigham-Tsai presented Item #CS-I. Motion carried.

Bigham-Tsai offered a prayer for Item #CS-I.

Motion: Tamara Williams moved to discontinue the Parma United Methodist Church effective May 28th, 2014. Motion carried.

Williams offered a prayer for the Parma United Methodist Church. Williams offered a hopeful message that other small churches in the conference are merging together at this time instead of discontinuing.

Gehman spoke about the progress of the Area Ministry Center and the development of a non-profit organization that is supporting this progress. Rob Long, Project Manager, gave a detailed presentation about the progress of the project for Area Ministry Center and invited the conference to the Area Open House Event in September. Gehman took questions from the group. Lou Grettenberger asked for clarification regarding why the Lansing District Office is not moving.

Johanna Balzer gave a welcome to the the people moving to the Lansing District

Gehman closed the Corporate Session and released people to break

FOURTH DAY ~ MID-MORNING SESSION

Saturday, June 14, 2014 10:30 AM

Conference sang Lord Listen to Your Children Praying.

Tamara Williams, Dean of the Cabinet and Albion District Superintendent, introduced Elbert Dulworth, Dean of Cabinet from the Detroit Annual Conference. Dulworth read John 3:2 and offered greetings from the Detroit Conference.

Neil Davis, Kalamazoo District Superintendent, shared a passage of scripture.

Williams presented the Cabinet Report. She commented on retiring clergy and the importance of recruitment. Williams then lead the conference in a prayer. Afterwards, she addressed grief in the church community and how it holds back ministry.

Dobbs presented the Conference Ministerial Appointment Document. Dobbs presented the Appointments into Extension Ministries with no changes. Bishop Kiesey fixed the Appointments into Extension Ministries. Tamara Williams presented Albion District for the fixing of appointments with the following change: Pacific North will be Pacific Northwest. Williams was appointed to Albion District and Bishop Kiesey fixed the Albion District Appointments. Bill Haggard presented the Grand Rapids District for the fixing of appointments with no changes. Haggard was appointed to Grand Rapids District and Bishop Kiesey fixed the Grand Rapids Appointments.

Anita Hahn presented Grand Traverse District for the fixing of appointment with the following changes: Colleen A. Wierman to Full Time appointment, Dennis Bromley as a Provisional Elder and John Conklin as a Provisional Elder. Hahn was appointed to Grand Traverse District and Bishop Kiesey fixed the Grand Traverse District Appointments. David Hills presented the Heartland District for the fixing of appointments with the following change: Michael Riegler as a Provisional Elder. Hills was appointed to Heartland District. Neil Davis presented the Kalamazoo District for the fixing of appointments with no changes. John Boley was appointed to Kalamazoo District. Kennetha Bigham-Tsai presented the Lansing District for the fixing of appointments with the following change: James Noggle as a Provisional Elder. Bigham-Tsai was appointed to the Lansing District.

A response was read by the Laity and Clergy.

Davis was recognized for his service as the Kalamazoo District Superintendent.

Glenn Wagner, Chair of the Conference Nominating Committee, gave the Nominations Report.

Sue Cobb, CF&A Chair, presented the 2015 West Michigan Conference Budget. The new total Budget will be $6,324,067. Ministry Shares rate will be 13.1%.

Motion: Jeremy Williams called the question. Motion carried.

Motion: 2015 West Michigan Conference Budget. Motion carried.

Bishop Kiesey thanked the Conference Program Committee, Conference Secretary, Clergy Assistant to the Bishop, and the American Sign Language Interpreters of the 2014 West Michigan Annual Conference.

Nichea Ver Veer Guy took the podium to make announcements.

Motion: Greg Buchner, Conference Secretary, moved the 2014 West Michigan Annual Conference adjourned following the Ordination Service at 1:30 PM. Motion carried.

FOURTH DAY ~ ORDINATION SERVICE

Saturday, June 14, 2014 1:30 PM

The Ordination Service began with Come Let Us Worship God, Hallelujah, and God of Grace and God of Glory while Clergy entered.

Bill Dobbs led the Conference in prayer and response.

Bishop Kiesey called the Conference to remember their baptism. The Conference was sprinkled with water while Spirit of the Living God was sang.

Dobbs introduced John Geaney, Ecumenical Representative.

John Boley presented those to be commissioned. Greg Lawton presented the individual to be ordained as Deacon. Dean Prentiss presented those to be ordained as elders.

Bishop Kiesey led the Conference in a response.

Bill Haggard read Acts 13:1-3 and Bishop Kiesey spoke led the General Examination of those being commissioned or ordained.

How Shall I Come Before the Lord was sang.

David Hills read "The Commissioning". Anita Hahn read "The Prayer of Commissioning".

Bishop Kiesey and Dobbs laid hands on and prayed over those being commissioned.

Halle Halle was sang.

Kennetha Bigham-Tsai read 1 John 3:1-3.

Bishop Kiesey gave a sermon titled "The Promise". Bishop Kiesey spoke about the different types of promises and about the call into ministry. Bishop Kiesey discussed the Latin meaning of the word promise and the challenges those in ministry will face. Bishop Kiesey closed her sermon with the song God is a River.

Dobbs invited the Conference to give during the Offering. Grace was played instrumentally during the Offertory.

The Servant Song was sang and the "Prayer of Thanksgiving".

Davis gave the Examination of the Deacon Candidate. Bishop Kiesey examined the Deacon Candidate. Patricia Catellier was called forward and Bishop Kiesey, the Cabinet and sponsors laid hands on Catellier while Bishop Kiesey prayed. Halle Halle was sang as Catellier was introduced.

The Clergy Choir sang We Are Called.

Tamara Williams gave the Examination of the Elders Candidate. Bishop Kiesey examined the Candidates with responses. Veni Sancte Spritus (Come, Holy Spirit) was sang. Lynn Pier-Fitzgerald prayed. Family and friends of each Candidate were asked to stand during the Ordination of that Candidate. Each Candidate was called forward and Bishop Kiesey, the Cabinet and sponsors laid hands on them as Bishop Kiesey prayed. New Elders were presented to the Conference and Halle, Halle was sung.

Jesu, Jesu was sang as Bishop Kiesey washed the newly ordained individuals feet.

The Sacrament of Holy Communion was given and Communion was given. The Conference participated singing.

Bishop Kiesey provided the Invitation to Ministry and Here I Am Lord and Spirit of the Living God was sung.

Bishop Kiesey and Catellier ended the service with a blessing.

Marching to Zion was sang as the Clergy filed out.

2014 West Michigan Conference was closed at 3:30 PM.

Deborah L. Kiesey,
Presiding Bishop

Greg Buchner,
Conference Secretary

CERTIFICATE OF ORDINATION AND COMMISSIONING

This is to certify that on Saturday, June 14, 2014,
at Calvin College in Grand Rapids, Michigan...

I commissioned as a provisional elder of The United Methodist Church:

Dennis B. Bromley, John C. Conklin, Stephen F. Lindeman, Heather Ann Molner, James C. Noggle, and Chad Michael Parmalee.

I ordained as a deacon of The United Methodist Church:

Patricia Louise Catellier.

I ordained as elders of The United Methodist Church:

Letisha May Bowman, Catherine Marie Christman, Patricia Ann Haas, Jonathan Dennis VanDop, and Rebecca Lee Farrester Wieringa.

Deborah L. Kiesey, Bishop
Michigan Area United Methodist Church

VII. APPOINTMENTS

A. Appointments by District

DM – Diaconal Minister
PD – Provisional Deacon
PM – Provisional Member
FD – Deacon in Full Connection
DP – Deacon from other denomination serving UM probation
OD – Deacon Member of Other Annual Conference
PE – Provisional Elder
FE – Elder in full connection
EP – Elder/full minister from other denomination serving UM probation
OE – Elder member of other annual conference

OF – Full member of other denomination
AF – Affiliated Member
AM – Associate Member
FL – Full Time Local Pastor
PL – Part Time Local Pastor
SP – Student Local Pastor
RA – Retired Associate Member
RE – Retired Full Member
RD – Retired Deacon
RP – Retired Provisional Member

RL – Retired Local Pastor
RLA – Retired Local Pastor Under Appointment
OR – Retired Member of Other Conference
HL – Honorable Location
HLOC – Honorable Location Other Conference
DSA – District Superintendent Assignment (name)
CLM – Certified Lay Minister
++ – Ad Interim Appointment
*Home address

ALBION DISTRICT

District Superintendent	Tamara S. Williams	FE6	600 E. Michigan Ave., Albion 49224-1849 DS Email: dstamara@albiondistrict.org	Office Phone: (517) 629-8105 Home Phone: (517) 629-6531
Administrative Assistant	Sarah Gillette		Office Email: office@albiondistrict.org	Fax: (517) 629-8230

CHARGE	PASTOR		ADDRESS	TELEPHONE CHURCH	HOME
Albion First	Jeremy PH Williams	FE6	600 E. Michigan, Albion 49224 *11184 29 Mile Rd, Albion 49224-9735	(517) 629-9425	(517) 629-6531
Allen	Eric Iden	DSA1	PO Box 103, 167 W Chicago Rd, Allen 49227 *300 Hanover St, Concord 49237	(517) 200-8416	(517) 945-2802
Augusta Fellowship	Jennifer J. Wheeler	PL2	PO Box 337, 103 N. Webster, Augusta 49012 *PO Box 137, Galesburg 49053-0137	(269) 731-4222	(231) 343-0388
Battle Creek Baseline	Peggy J. Baker	FE4	9617 E Baseline Rd, Battle Creek 49017	(269) 963-7710	(269) 763-3201
Bellevue			122 W. Capital Ave., Bellevue 49021 *523 Sherwood Rd, Bellevue 49021	(269) 763-9421	(269) 763-3201
Battle Creek Birchwood	Bruce R. Kintigh	FE5	3003 Gethings Rd., Battle Creek 49015	(269) 963-2084	(269) 223-7245
Battle Creek Trinity			10 W. Bidwell, Battle Creek 49015 *17102 11 Mile Rd, Battle Creek 49014	(269) 962-4900	(269) 223-7245
Battle Creek Chapel Hill	Chad M. Parmalee	PE2	157 Chapel Hill Drive, Battle Creek 49015-4631 *192 Brentwood Dr, Battle Creek 49015-4512	(269) 963-0231	(269) 589-9872
Battle Creek Christ	Scott M. Bouldrey	FL4	65 Bedford Road N, Battle Creek 49037 *15 Woodlawn Ave N, Battle Creek 49037-1539	(269) 965-3251	(269) 282-1490
Battle Creek Convis Union	Sueann K. Hagan	FL9	18990 12 Mile Rd, Battle Creek 49014-8496 *12040 N Drive North, Battle Creek 49014-8417	(269) 965-3787	(269) 964-2741

CHARGE	PASTOR		ADDRESS	CHURCH	HOME
Battle Creek First	Marshall Murphy	PL1	111 East Michigan Avenue, Battle Creek 49014-4012	(269) 963-5567	(269) 223-7949
			*26 W Roosevelt, Battle Creek 49037		
	Scott M. Bouldrey	FL1	111 East Michigan Avenue, Battle Creek 49014-4012	(269) 963-5567	(269) 282-1490
			*15 Woodlawn Ave N, Battle Creek 49037-1539		
Battle Creek Maple	Linda D. Stoddard	FE7	342 Capital Ave. NE, Battle Creek 49017	(269) 964-1252	(269) 965-1671
			*99 Mowerson Dr, Battle Creek 49017		
Battle Creek Sonoma	Sally Kay Harrington	DSA3	4790 Capital Ave SW, Battle Creek 49015	(269) 979-1000	(269) 917-2823
Battle Creek Newton			8804 F Drive South, Ceresco 49033	(269) 979-2779	(269) 917-2823
			*4495 B Drive South, Battle Creek 49015		
Battle Creek Washington Heights	Marshall Murphy	PL4	153 N. Wood St., Battle Creek 49037	(269) 968-8773	(269) 223-7949
			*26 W Roosevelt, Battle Creek 49037		
Bronson	Cynthia L. Veilleux	PL4	312 E. Chicago St., Bronson 49028	(517) 369-6555	(517) 858-1022
			*330 E Corey St, Bronson 49028-1504		
Camden	Frederick G. Cain	OR2	PO Box 155, 201 S Main St, Camden 49232	(517) 368-5406	(517) 797-5530
Montgomery			PO Box 155, 201 S Main St, Camden 49232	(517) 269-4232	(517) 797-5530
Stokes Chapel			PO Box 155, 201 S Main St, Camden 49232	(517) 368-5406	(517) 797-5530
			*PO Box 155, 201 S Main St, Camden 49232		
Center Park	Martin H. Culver	RLA4	18662 Moorepark Rd., Three Rivers 49093	(269) 279-9109	(269) 615-1360
			*511 Landsdowne Ave, Portage 49002		
Centreville	Emily K. Beachy	PE1	305 E Main Street, Centreville 49032	(269) 467-8645	(269) 467-7715
			*304 E Market St, Centreville 49032		
Climax	Glenn C. Litchfield	FE6	PO Box 125, 133 East Maple, Climax 49034-0125	(269) 746-4023	(269) 746-8728
Scotts			PO Box 112, 8458 Wallene, Scotts 49088	(269) 626-9757	(269) 746-8728
			*331 Prairie Dr, Climax 49034		
Coldwater	Steven R. Young	FE5	26 Marshall St, Coldwater 49036	(517) 279-8402	(517) 278-2854
			*20 Parsons Ct, Coldwater 49036		
Colon	John M. Sterner	PL3	PO Box 646, 224 N. Blackstone, Colon 49040	(269) 432-2783	(269) 432-3754
Burr Oak			PO Box 91, 105 S. Fourth St., Burr Oak 49030	(269) 489-2985	(269) 432-3754
			*PO Box 65, 403 Maple, Colon 49040		
Concord	David G. Elmore	OE2	PO Box 366, 119 S. Main St., Concord 49237	(517) 524-6156	(517) 524-6111
			*PO Box 392, 229 W Center St, Concord 49237		
Constantine	Scott E. Manning	FE6	285 White Pigeon St., Constantine 49042	(269) 435-8151	(269) 435-4885
White Pigeon			PO Box 518, White Pigeon 49099	(269) 483-9054	(269) 435-4885
			*265 White Pigeon St, Constantine 49042		

ALBION DISTRICT

CHARGE	PASTOR		ADDRESS	CHURCH	HOME
Delton Faith	Brian R. Bunch	FL3	PO Box 467, 503 S Grove, Delton 49046-0467	(269) 623-5400	(269) 623-5335
			*146 Bush St, Delton 49046-9798		
Frontier	[PASTOR TO BE SUPPLIED]		PO Box 120, Frontier 49239	(859) 421-8931	
Galesburg	Leonard R. Schoenherr	RE2	PO Box 518, 111 W Battle Creek St, Galesburg 49053	(269) 665-7952	(269) 903-2182
			*4500 Mountain Ash Lane, Kalamazoo 49004		
Girard	Cydney M. Idsinga	FL1	990 Marshall Rd., Coldwater 49036	(517) 279-9418	(517) 279-0123
			*992 Marshall Rd, Coldwater 49036		
Grass Lake	Dennis E. Slattery	RE3	449 E. Michigan Ave., Grass Lake 49240	(517) 522-8040	(517) 522-8135
			*659 Church St, Grass Lake 49240		
Griffith	David H. Minger	RE2	9537 S Clinton Trail, Eaton Rapids 48827	(517) 663-6262	(517) 256-5857
			*806 Emmaus Rd, Eaton Rapids 48827		
Hillsdale First	Patricia L. Brook	FE5	45 N. Manning, Hillsdale 49242	(517) 437-3681	(517) 437-2392
			*1079 Markris Dr, Hillsdale 49242		
Hillside	Patricia A. Pebley	FL1	6100 Folks Rd., Horton 49246	(517) 563-2835	(517) 563-8920
Somerset Center			PO Box 277, 12095 E. Chicago Rd., Somerset Center 49282	(517) 688-4330	(517) 563-8920
			*6094 Folks Rd, Horton 49246		
Homer	Robert P. Stover	RE3	PO Box 175, Homer 49245-0175	(517) 568-4001	(517) 568-1126
Lyon Lake			PO Box 175, Homer 49245-0175	(269) 789-0017	(517) 568-1126
			*105 E Adams St, Homer 49245		
Jackson Brookside	Ronald K. Brooks	FE2	4000 Francis, Jackson 49203	(517) 782-5167	(517) 782-2706
			*217 Mohawk, Jackson 49203		
Jackson Calvary	Edrye A. Eastman Maurer	FE5	925 Backus St, Jackson 49202	(517) 782-0543	(517) 962-2237
Jackson Zion			7498 Cooper Rd, Jackson 49201	(517) 769-2570	(517) 962-2237
			*3639 Sweetgum Dr, Jackson 49201-9029		
Jackson First	Eric S. Beck	FE3	275 W Michigan Ave, Jackson 49201	(517) 787-6460	(517) 962-2451
			*1734 Malvern Dr, Jackson 49203		
Associate	Susan J. Babb	FE11	275 W Michigan Ave, Jackson 49201	(517) 787-6460	(517) 783-3803
			*2440 Smiley Way, Jackson 49203		
Deacon	Mark R. Babb	FD5	275 W Michigan Ave, Jackson 49201	(517) 787-6460	(517) 783-3803
			*2440 Smiley Way, Jackson 49203-3625		
Jackson Trinity	Robert Q. Bailey	OR1	1508 Greenwood Ave, Jackson 49203-4048	(517) 782-7937	(517) 750-2821
			*PO Box 87, 375 Richard Street, Spring Arbor 49283		
Jonesville	Jennifer C. Ward	DSA1	203 Concord Rd., Jonesville 49250	(517) 849-9565	(269) 462-8225
			*161 Waterman Ave, Coldwater 49036		

CHARGE	PASTOR		ADDRESS	CHURCH	HOME
Lee Center	James M. Gysel	RE1	22392 24 Mile Road, Olivet 49076-9533		(269) 979-8192
			*3239 Nighthawk Lane, Battle Creek 49015		
Litchfield	Julie Yoder Elmore	OE2	PO Box 472, 160 Marshall St, Litchfield 49252-0472	(517) 542-3366	(517) 542-3775
Quincy			32 W. Chicago St., Quincy 49082	(517) 639-5035	(517) 542-3775
			*969 Adams St, Litchfield 49252-9779		
Marengo	Gerry Retzloff	DSA5	221 N. Chapel Hill Dr., Battle Creek 49015		(269) 660-0141
			*29 Wolfe, Battle Creek 49017		
Marshall	Melany A. Chalker	FE2	721 Old US 27N, Marshall 49068-9609	(269) 781-5107	(517) 403-8528
			*762 N Kalamazoo Ave, Marshall 49068-1071		
Napoleon	Gregory R. Wolfe	RE2	PO Box 337, Napoleon 49261	(517) 536-8609	(517) 536-4903
			*10014 Sunset Dr, Jackson 49201-9850		
North Adams	Timothy R. Puckett	PL1	PO Box 62, 228 E Main St, North Adams 49262	(517) 287-5190	(517) 936-5835
Jerome			8768 Jerome Rd N, Jerome 49249		(517) 936-5835
			*10445 Folks Rd, Hanover 49241-9777		
North Parma	Melissa J. Claxton	PE6	PO Box 25, Parma 49269	(517) 531-4619	(517) 531-4740
Springport			PO Box E, Springport 49284-1004	(517) 857-2777	(517) 531-4740
			*223 S Union, Parma 49269		
Nottawa	Alexander Miller	DSA12	PO Box 27, 25838 M-86, Nottawa 49075	(269) 467-7134	(269) 467-7134
			*61616 Filmore Rd. Sturgis 49091-9318		
Pope	Robert S. Moore-Jumonville	FE5	10401 Townley Rd, Springport 49284-0228	(517) 857-3655	(517) 524-6818
			*21 Dickens Street, Spring Arbor 49283		
Reading	[PASTOR TO BE SUPPLIED]		PO Box 457, 312 E Michigan St, Reading 49274	(517) 283-2443	
Sturgis	E. Jeanne Koughn	FE1	200 Pleasant Ave., Sturgis 49091	(269) 651-5990	(269) 651-6087
			*1332 Rolling Ridge Ln, Sturgis 49091		
Three Rivers First	Robert D. Nystrom	FE3	215 N. Main, Three Rivers 49093	(269) 278-4722	(269) 278-5565
Mendon			PO Box 308, Mendon 49072-0308	(269) 496-4295	(269) 278-5565
			*1101 Elm St, Three Rivers 49093		
Three Rivers Ninth Street	James W. Stilwell	FL6	700 Ninth St, Three Rivers 49093	(269) 273-2065	(269) 279-9267
Schoolcraft Pleasant Valley			PO Box 517, 9300 West XY Ave, Schoolcraft 49087-0517	(269) 679-5352	(269) 279-9267
			*700 9th St, Three Rivers 49093-1206		
Union City	Seung Ho (Andy) Baek	FE3	PO Box 95, Union City 49094-0095	(517) 741-7028	(517) 741-9041
Athens			PO Box 267, 123 Clark St, Athens 49011	(269) 729-9370	(517) 741-9041
			*635 Walnut Lane, Union City 49094		
West Mendon	Thoreau May	DSA2	22994 Portage Lake Road, Mendon 49072	(269) 496-7364	(269) 496-8070
			*52952 Lakehead Dr, Mendon 49072		

ALBION DISTRICT

NAME	POSITION / ADDRESS	OFFICE	HOME
APPOINTMENTS TO EXTENSION MINISTRIES LOCATED IN THE ALBION DISTRICT: *(further information at end of appointment section)*			
Mark Babb (FD)	Director of Music, Federated Church of Grass Lake 519 E Michigan Ave, Grass Lake 49240	(517) 522-4480	(517) 783-3803
	Associate Faculty, online instructor, University of Phoenix		
Robert Moore-Jumonville (FE)	Associate Professor of Religion, Spring Arbor University 106 East Main Street, Spring Arbor University, Spring Arbor 49283	(517) 750-6693	(517) 524-6818
Roy Testolin (RE)	Pastoral Counselor, Heritage Interfaith Counseling Center 9 Heritage Oak Lane Ste 3, Battle Creek 49015	(269) 979-5180	(269) 781-9257
Tamara Williams (FE)	District Superintendent, Albion District Office 600 E Michigan, Albion 49224	(517) 629-8150	(517) 629-6531

GRAND RAPIDS DISTRICT

District Superintendent	William E. Haggard	FE3	11 Fuller Ave, SE, Grand Rapids 49506 *Mail to:* PO Box 6247, Grand Rapids 49516-6247	Office Phone: (616) 459-4503 Home Phone: (616) 430-9964
Administrative Assistant	Elizabeth M. Bode		DS Email: bill5955@gmail.com; Office Email: grdistrict@wmcumc.org	Fax: (616) 459-0242

CHARGE	PASTOR		ADDRESS	TELEPHONE CHURCH	TELEPHONE HOME
Alto	Andrew Jackson	RE1	PO Box 122, 11365 64th St SE, Alto 49302	(616) 868-7306	(616) 878-1284
Bowne Center			3782 Murray Lake Ave, Lowell 49331 *978 Amber View Dr SW, Byron Center 49315-9740		(616) 878-1284
Byron Center	Lawrence A. Nichols	FL5	2490 Prescott SW, Byron Center 49315 *8650 Meadow Haven Dr SW, Byron Center 49315-9243	(616) 878-1618	(616) 878-9739
Caledonia	Jodie R. Flessner	FE3	250 Vine St, Caledonia 49316 *260 Vine St, Caledonia 49316	(616) 891-8669	(616) 891-8167
Carlisle	Michael J. Ramsey	PL5	1084 76th St SW, Byron Center 49315 *8649 Shore Way Dr, Byron Center 49315	(616) 878-1836	(616) 878-9165
Cedar Springs	Stephen Frederick Lindeman	PE1	PO Box K, 140 S Main St, Cedar Springs 49319 *128 E Muskegon St, Cedar Springs 49319	(616) 696-1140	(616) 263-9542
Coopersville	Cori Lynn Cypret	PE3	105 68th Ave N, Coopersville 49404-9704 *422 Harrison St., Coopersville 49404	(616) 997-9225	(616) 384-3210
Courtland-Oakfield	Robert W. Eckert	PL4	10295 Myers Lake Ave NE, Rockford 49341-9511 *9777 Myers Lake Ave NE, Rockford 49341-9508	(616) 866-4298	(616) 291-7093
CrossWind Community	Scott K. Otis	FE11	1683 142nd Avenue, Dorr 49323 *4380 Tracy Tr, Dorr 49323	(616) 681-0302	(616) 681-0302
East Nelson	Herbert J. VanderBilt	PL11	9024 18 Mile Rd NE, Cedar Springs 49319-9217 *2204 Gee Dr, Lowell 49331	(616) 696-0661	(616) 897-8642
Fremont	Martin T. Cobb	PE2	351 Butterfield St., Fremont 49412 *352 Butterfield, Fremont 49412	(231) 924-0030	(231) 924-2456
Georgetown	William C. Bills	FE8	2766 Baldwin St, Jenison 49428 *2032 Pinewood St, Jenison 49428	(616) 669-0730	(616) 719-3769
Grand Haven Church of the Dunes	Glenn M. Wagner	FE1	717 Sheldon Road, Grand Haven 49417-1860 *633 Hillock Ct, Grand Haven 49417	(616) 842-7980	(616) 842-3586
Grand Rapids Aldersgate	James E. Hodge	FE2	4301 Ambrose Avenue NE, Grand Rapids 49525-6122 *5160 Windcrest Ct SW, Wyoming 49418	(616) 363-3446	(616) 308-9925
Grand Rapids Cornerstone	Bradley P. Kalajainen	FE25	1675 84th St SE, Caledonia 49316 *7810 Golf Meadows Dr SE, Caledonia 49316-8462	(616) 698-3170	(616) 891-8443
Associate	Kenneth J. Nash	FE9	1675 84th St SE, Caledonia 49316 *6760 Airfield Ct SW, Byron Center 49315	(616) 698-3170	(616) 534-2074

GRAND RAPIDS DISTRICT

CHARGE	PASTOR		ADDRESS	CHURCH	HOME
Grand Rapids Faith	Mark E. Thompson	FE6	2600 Seventh St. NW, Grand Rapids 49504 *1018 Charlotte Ave NW, Grand Rapids 49504-3770	(616) 453-0693	(616) 453-4519
Grand Rapids First	Robert L. Hundley	FE2	227 Fulton St E, Grand Rapids 49503-3236 *3035 Grenada Dr SE, Grand Rapids 49546	(616) 451-2879	(616) 427-3749
Associate	Letisha M. Bowman	FE4	227 Fulton St E, Grand Rapids 49503-3236 *3358 Oak Hollow Dr SE, Grand Rapids 49546-2126	(616) 451-2879	(616) 260-2994
Grand Rapids Genesis	DeAnn J. Dobbs	FE1	1601 Galbraith Ave SE Ste 304, Grand Rapids 49546-6479 *832 Firwood Dr, Middleville 49333	(616) 974-0400	(616) 916-2684
Grand Rapids Iglesia Metodista Unida La Nueva Esperanza	Nohemi Vivas De Ramirez	OE2	1005 Evergreen St. SE, Grand Rapids 49507 *324 Griswold SE, Grand Rapids 49507	(616) 560-4207	(616) 248-1770
Grand Rapids Mosaic	Steven C. Place	FL4	4275 Shaffer Ave SE, Kentwood 49512 *5669 Bentbrook St SE, Kentwood 49508-6504	(616) 554-4969	(616) 281-2355
Grand Rapids Northlawn	Timothy B. Wright	FE2	1157 Northlawn NE, Grand Rapids 49505 *1141 Northlawn NE, Grand Rapids 49505	(616) 361-8503	(616) 361-2321
Deacon	Janice T. Lancaster	FD1	1157 Northlawn NE, Grand Rapids 49505 *4722 Westgate Dr, Comstock Park 49321	(616) 361-8503	(616) 784-5662
Grand Rapids Rivercrest Church	Kellas D. Penny III	FL1	214 Spencer NE, Grand Rapids 49505 *930 Elmdale, Grand Rapids 49525	(580) 559-1207	(616) 209-2828
Grand Rapids St Paul's	Erin B. Fitzgerald	PE3	3334 Breton Rd. SE, Grand Rapids 49512-2798 *2716 Byron Center Rd SW, Wyoming 49519	(616) 949-0880	(616) 510-7941
Grand Rapids South	Mack C. Strange	OF8	4500 S. Division Ave., Grand Rapids 49548 *5103 Marlowe SE, Grand Rapids 49508	(616) 534-8931	(616) 532-9226
Grand Rapids Trinity	David Nellist	OE5	1100 Lake Dr SE, Grand Rapids 49506-1538 *1507 Lenox Dr SE, Grand Rapids 49506	(616) 456-7168	(269) 903-8560
Associate	Julie Liske	FD5	1100 Lake Dr SE, Grand Rapids 49506-1538 *1857 Mayberry St SE, Grand Rapids 49508	(616) 456-7168	(616) 299-0115
Grand Rapids Vietnamese	Daniel Dung Nguyen	FL3	212 Bellevue St SE, Wyoming 49548 *497 Harp St. SE, Kentwood 49548	(616) 534-6262	(616) 288-3007
Grandville	Thomas M. Pier-Fitzgerald	FE10	3140 S Wilson, Grandville 49418 *83 West 18th St, Holland 49423	(616) 538-3070	(616) 393-6242
Hesperia Ferry	Paul E. Hane	FL4	187 E. South Ave., Hesperia 49421 187 E. South Ave., Hesperia 49421 *231 E South Ave, Hesperia 49421-9105	(231) 854-5345 (231) 854-5345	(231) 854-6132 (231) 854-6132
Holland First	J. Lynn Pier-Fitzgerald	FE10	57 West 10th St, Holland 49423 *83 West 18th St, Holland 49423	(616) 396-5205	(616) 393-6242
Holton	Gerald L. Selleck	FE9	9530 Holton-Duck Lake Rd., Holton 49425 *P.O. Box 39, 8670 Ward St, Holton 49425	(231) 821-2323	(231) 821-0374
Kent City Chapel Hill	Kevin K. Guetschow	FL5	14591 Fruit Ridge Ave NW, Kent City 49330 *14555 Fruit Ridge Ave, Kent City 49330-9751	(616) 675-7184	(616) 675-7241

CHARGE	PASTOR		ADDRESS	CHURCH	HOME
Leighton	David L. McBride	FE9	4180 Second St, Caledonia 49316-9627 *4180 Second St, Caledonia 49316	(616) 891-8028	(616) 891-1646
Lowell	James Bradley Brillhart	FE1	621 E Main St, Lowell 49331 *640 Shepard Dr, Lowell 49331	(616) 897-5936	(616) 897-8267
Deacon	Cheryl A. Mulligan	PD1	621 E Main St, Lowell 49331 *3170 Buttrick Ave SE, Ada 49301-9216	(616) 897-5936	(616) 340-7995
Marne	James Thomas Boutell	PE5	PO Box 85, 14861 Washington, Marne 49435 *14861 Washington St, Marne 49435	(616) 677-3957	(616) 677-3991
Martin Shelbyville	Sean K. Kidd	FL1	PO Box 154, 969 E. Allegan, Martin 49070 PO Box 154, Martin 49070 *PO Box 86, 948 Lee St, Martin 49070	(269) 672-7097 (269) 672-5927	(269) 672-4132 (269) 672-4132
Middleville Snow	Anthony C. Shumaker	FL3	PO Box 400, 111 Church St, Middleville 49333 3189 Snow Ave. SE, Lowell 49331 *1497 120th Ave, Hopkins 49328-9626	(269) 795-9266 (616) 897-9863	(269) 650-5112 (269) 650-5112
Montague	Mary S. Brown	FE1	8555 Cook St, Montague 49437 *5181 Hancock St, Montague 49437	(231) 894-5789	(231) 357-4506
Muskegon Central	Mark D. Miller	OE2	1011 Second Street, Muskegon 49440 *1707 Ritter Dr, Norton Shores 49441	(231) 722-6545	(231) 766-8989
Deacon	Mariel Kay DeMoss	FD10	1011 Second Street, Muskegon 49440 *2006 Mills Ave, North Muskegon 49445	(231) 722-6545	(231) 744-0336
Muskegon Hts Temple	Jeffrey J. Bowman	FL3	2500 Jefferson, Muskegon Heights 49444 *1205 Yorkshire Dr, Muskegon 49441-5358	(231) 733-1065	(231) 798-9309
Muskegon Lake Harbor	Mary Letta-Bement Ivanov	FE1	4861 Henry St, Muskegon 49441-4536 *1322 Clayton Ave, Muskegon 49441	(231) 798-2181	(231) 798-3951
Muskegon Lakeside	Donald J. Graham	FL1	2160 Crozier Ave, Muskegon 49441 *3951 Grand Haven Rd, Norton Shores 49441	(231) 759-7850	(269) 503-0354
Muskegon Unity	Ronald L. Worley	PL1	1600 North Getty St, Muskegon 49445 *PO Box 254, 76 W Muskegon St NW, Kent City 49330	(231) 744-1972	(616) 485-4441
Muskegon Wolf Lake	Bobby Dale Whitlock	RE4	370 Vista Terrace, Muskegon 49442 *4512 S Quarterline, Muskegon 49444	(231) 788-3663	(231) 457-4705
Newaygo	Kathleen Groff	OR4	PO Box 366, 101 W. State Road, Newaygo 49337 *PO Box 366, 104 State Rd, Newaygo 49337	(231) 652-6581	(231) 652-5272
North Muskegon Community	Phillip J. Friedrick	FE3	1614 Ruddiman, North Muskegon 49445 *2317 Marquard St, Muskegon 49445	(231) 744-4491	(231) 744-1443
Parmelee	William V. Clegg Jr	RE3	PO Box 237, 9266 W Parmelee Rd, Middleville 49333 *4593 N Camrose Court, Wyoming 49519	(269) 795-8816	(616) 366-2486
Ravenna	Carleton R. Black	FL4	PO Box 191, 12348 Stafford St, Ravenna 49451 *3482 Lo Al Dr, Ravenna 49451-9405	(231) 853-6688	(231) 853-6111

GRAND RAPIDS DISTRICT

CHARGE	PASTOR		ADDRESS	CHURCH	HOME
Rockford	Kenneth J. Bremer	FE1	159 Maple St, Rockford 49341	(616) 866-9515	(616) 884-3051
			*6821 Homestead Dr NE, Rockford 49341		
Salem Indian Mission	Nancy L. Boelens	RLA2	3644 28th St, Hopkins 49328		(616) 914-9300
Bradley Indian Mission			695 128th Ave, Shelbyville 49344		(616) 914-9300
			*1875 Parkcrest Dr. S.W., Apt 2, Wyoming 49519		
Director, Senior Meals Program	Sandra Kay VandenBrink	RLA2	*3933 Kerri Ct, Holland 49424		(616) 738-9030
Saugatuck	Emmett H. Kadwell Jr	RE4	PO Box 647, 250 Mason St., Saugatuck 49453	(269) 857-2295	(231) 912-0806
			*2794 6th St, Shelbyville 49344		
Shelby	Terri L. Cummins	FL5	68 E. Third St., Shelby 49455	(231) 861-2020	(231) 861-4331
Claybanks			117 S Division, Whitehall 49461		(231) 861-4331
			*89 E 4th St, Shelby 49455-1137		
Sitka	Gerald F. Hagans	RE6	9606 S. Dickinson Rd., Holton 49425	(231) 755-1767	(231) 755-1767
			*1249 Lakeshore Dr #305, Muskegon 49441		
South Wyoming	Marcia L. Elders	OF12	2730 56th St SW, Wyoming 49418	(616) 532-0131	(616) 292-6712
			*3246 Wayburn Ave SW, Grandville 49418-1913		
Sparta	Louis W. Grettenberger	FE6	54 E. Division St., Sparta 49345	(616) 887-8255	(616) 887-0783
			*1960 Skyview Dr, Sparta 49345		
Twin Lake	John D. Morse	RE2	PO Box 352, 5940 S Main St, Twin Lake 49457-0352	(231) 828-4083	(616) 844-0841
			*14879 Cross Lane, Spring Lake 49456		
Valley	Matthew J. Bistayi	PE6	5980 Lake Michigan Dr Ste B, Allendale 49401	(269) 501-8602	(616) 892-6240
			*10811 Lance Ave, Allendale 49401		
Vergennes	Matthew T. Stoll	FE5	10411 Bailey Dr. NE, Lowell 49331	(616) 897-6141	(616) 987-1887
			*110 Tia Trail, Lowell 49331		
Wayland	Jeffrey C. Williams	FE1	200 Church St., Wayland 49348	(269) 792-2208	(269) 944-9231
			*220 Church St, Wayland 49348		
White Cloud	Edwin D. Snook	FL3	PO Box 188, 1125 Newell St., White Cloud 49349	(231) 689-5911	(231) 689-6774
			*718 E Pine Hill Ave, White Cloud 49349-9146		
Whitehall	Mary A. Sweet	FL1	117 S. Division, Whitehall 49461	(231) 893-2315	(231) 881-7367
Crestwood			1220 Creston, Muskegon 49442	(231) 773-9696	(231) 881-7367
			*1220 Creston, Muskegon 49442		
Wesley Park	Dean N. Prentiss	FE4	1150 32nd St SW, Wyoming 49509	(616) 534-4411	(616) 514-7124
			*2664 Borglum Avenue NE, Grand Rapids 49505		
Wyoming Park	Joel T. Fitzgerald	FL3	2244 Porter St. SW, Wyoming 49519	(616) 532-7624	(616) 848-9759
			*2716 Byron Center Ave SW, Wyoming 49519-2118		

NAME	POSITION ADDRESS	OFFICE	HOME
APPOINTMENTS TO EXTENSION MINISTRIES LOCATED IN THE GRANDRAPIDS DISTRICT: *(further information at end of appointment section)*			
George Ayoub (FE)	Interim Executive Director of Camping Ministries, West Michigan Conference - United Methodist Church PO Box 6247, 11 Fuller Ave SE, Grand Rapids 49516-6247	(616) 459-4503	(989) 224-2608
David Bell (AF) *(East Ohio Conference)*	President and Executive Director, United Methodist Foundation of Michigan 840 W Grand River Ave, Brighton 48116	(810) 534-3001	
Janet Carter (FD)	Chaplain, Pine Rest Christian Mental Health Services 300 68th St SE, Grand Rapids 49508	(616) 281-6363 ext.2117	(616) 260-9604
Mariel Kay DeMoss (FD)	Senior Writer & Content Editor, MI Area Communications Team	(231) 670-5921	(231) 744-0336
William Haggard (FE)	District Superintendent, Grand Rapids District Office PO Box 6247, Grand Rapids 49516-6247	(616) 459-4503	(616) 430-9964
Benton Heisler (FE)	Director of Connectional Ministries, West Michigan Conference – United Methodist Church PO Box 6247, 11 Fuller Ave SE, Grand Rapids 49516-6247	(616) 459-4503	(616) 974-9152
Jan Johnson (FL)	Chaplain, Mercy Health Partners PO Box 358, 1500 E Sherman Blvd, Muskegon 49443	(231) 672-3629	(231) 343-8268
Melody Johnson (OE) *(Detroit Conference)*	Chaplain, Porter Hills Presbyterian Retirement Community 4450 Cascade Rd SE Ste 200, Grand Rapids 49546-8330	(616) 949-4975	(616) 949-8185
Nathaniel Johnson (SY)	Pediatrics/NICU Chaplain, Helen DeVos Children's Hospital & Spectrum Health United Hospital 100 Michigan Street NE, Grand Rapids 49503	(616) 391-3147	(616) 682-1210
Janice Lancaster (FD)	Clinical Nurse, Emmanuel Hospice of Grand Rapids 2161 Leonard St NW, Grand Rapids 49504	(616) 719-0919	(616) 784-5662
Gregory Lawton (FD)	Director, Wesley Fellowship at Grand Valley State University 4539 Luce St., Wesley Fellowship @ GVSU, Jenison 49428	(616) 805-5407	(616) 805-5407
Julie Liske (FD)	Executive Director, United Methodist Metropolitan Ministry of Greater Grand Rapids 1100 Lake Drive SE, Grand Rapids 49506	(616) 456-7133	(616) 299-0115
Mary Loring (FL)	Coordinator of Pastoral Care, Clark Retirement Community 1551 Franklin SE, Grand Rapids 49506-3331	(616) 452-1568	(616) 363-0480
Cheryl Mulligan (PD)	Respiratory Therapist, Helen DeVos Pediatric Pulmonary Clinic 35 Michigan St NE Ste 3003, Grand Rapids 49503	(616) 267-2200	(616) 340-7995
Gary Step (FE)	Director of New Church Development and Congregational Transformation, West Michigan Conference – United Methodist Church PO Box 6247, 11 Fuller Ave SE, Grand Rapids 49516-6247	(616) 459-4503	(231) 420-2676
Timothy Tuthill (FE)	Director of Life Enrichment, Clark Retirement Community 1551 Franklin SE, Grand Rapids 49506-3331	(616) 452-1568	(616) 635-2669

GRAND TRAVERSE DISTRICT

GRAND TRAVERSE DISTRICT

District Superintendent	Anita K. Hahn	FE4	1249 Three Mile Rd. S, Traverse City 49696-8307	Office Phone: (231) 947-5281
			Email: glue4evr@yahoo.com	Home Phone: (231) 421-8397
Administrative Assistant	Jill Haney		Office: gtdistrictoffice@tcchrist.com	Fax: (231) 947-0181

CHARGE	PASTOR		ADDRESS	TELEPHONE CHURCH	TELEPHONE HOME
Alden	Daniel W. Biteman	FE5	PO Box 130, 9015 Helena, Alden 49612-0130	(231) 331-4132	(231) 331-6762
Central Lake			PO Box 213, Central Lake 49622		(231) 331-6762
			*PO Box 157, 9022 Franklin, Alden 49612-0157		
Baldwin Covenant Community	James A. Richie	FE3	PO Box 250, 5330 S M-37, Baldwin 49304	(231) 745-3232	(231) 745-2522
Luther			PO Box 175, 315 State St, Luther 49656	(231) 797-0073	(231) 745-2522
			*2386 W 44th St, Baldwin 49304		
Barnard	Craig A. Pahl	FL1	PO Box 878, East Jordan 49727-0878	(231) 547-5269	(231) 536-7596
East Jordan			PO Box 878, East Jordan 49727-0878	(231) 536-2161	(231) 536-7596
Norwood			PO Box 878, East Jordan 49727-0878		(231) 536-7596
			*PO Box 238, 305 Esterly, East Jordan 49727		
Bear Lake	Jane D. Logston	FE1	PO Box 157, 7861 Main St, Bear Lake 49614-0157	(231) 864-3680	(231) 970-2048
Arcadia			PO Box 72, 3378 Division, Arcadia 49613	(231) 864-3680	(231) 970-2048
			*PO Box 157, 12318 Smith St, Bear Lake 49614-0157		
Bellaire Community	Peggy Ann Boltz	FL2	PO Box 235, 401 N Bridge St, Bellaire 49615-0235	(231) 533-8133	(231) 267-3133
			*111 W Antrim St, Bellaire 49615-9594		
Boyne City	Michael Neihardt	FL2	324 S. Park St., Boyne City 49712	(231) 582-9776	(231) 258-6180
Boyne Falls			324 S Park St, Boyne City 49712	(231) 582-9776	(231) 258-6180
Horton Bay			4961 Boyne City Rd, Boyne City 49712-9217	(231) 582-9262	(231) 258-6180
			*2347 Shawn Rd., Kalkaska 49646		
Brethren Epworth	Judy Coffey	DSA1	PO Box 177, 3939 High Bridge Rd, Brethren 49619	(231) 477-5486	(231) 775-6095
			*128 Forest Lawn Dr, Cadillac 49601-9734		
Cadillac	Thomas E. Ball	FE8	PO Box 37, 1020 E. Division St., Cadillac 49601	(231) 775-5362	(231) 775-1851
			*114 Barbara St, Cadillac 49601		
Charlevoix	Gregory P. Culver	FE5	104 State St, Charlevoix 49720	(231) 547-2654	(231) 547-5168
			*1206 State St, Charlevoix 49720		
Crystal Valley	Ronald Lewis Figgins Iris	OR2	PO Box 125, Walkerville 49459	(231) 873-5422	(231) 843-8352
Walkerville			PO Box 125, Walkerville 49459	(231) 873-4236	(231) 843-8352
			*2774 W Victory Dr, Ludington 49431		

CHARGE	PASTOR		ADDRESS	CHURCH	HOME
Empire	Russell K. Logston	FE1	PO Box 261, 10050 W. Michigan St., Empire 49630	(231) 326-5510	(231) 326-6098
			*PO Box 261, 10205 Aylsworth Rd, Empire 49630		
Epsilon	Vaughn Thurston-Cox	OE5	8251 E. Mitchell Rd., Petoskey 49770	(231) 347-6608	(231) 347-5382
New Hope of Emmett County			PO Box 72, 4516 N US 31, Levering 49755	(231) 537-2000	(231) 347-5382
Harbor Springs			343 East Main St., Harbor Springs 49740	(231) 526-2414	(231) 347-5382
Alanson			343 E Main St, Harbor Springs 49740	(231) 548-5709	(231) 347-5382
			*8204 E Mitchell Rd, Petoskey 49770-8831		
Associate	Hillary Thurston-Cox	OE1	8251 E. Mitchell Rd., Petoskey 49770	(231) 347-6608	(231) 347-5382
			*8204 E Mitchell Rd, Petoskey 49770-8831		
Fife Lake-Boardmans Parish:					
East Boardman	Donald L. Buege	FE1	PO Box 69, South Boardman 49680	(231) 879-5330	(231) 879-5330
Fife Lake			PO Box 69, Fife Lake 49633	(231) 879-4270	(231) 879-5330
South Boardman			PO Box 112, 5488 Dagle St, South Boardman 49680	(231) 879-5330	(231) 879-5330
			*124 Boyd St, Fife Lake 49633		
Frankfort	Barbara Fay	AM5	PO Box 1010, 537 Crystal Ave, Frankfort 49635	(231) 352-7427	(231) 352-4724
Elberta			PO Box 405, Elberta 49628	(231) 352-4311	(231) 352-4724
			*320 Maple Street, Frankfort 49635		
Free Soil	Richard D. Roberts	DSA2	PO Box 71, Freesoil 49411		(231) 233-8954
Fountain			PO Box 173, Fountain 49410	(231) 690-4591	(231) 233-8954
			*2415 E Michigan St, Free Soil 49411		
Grant	Colleen A. Wierman	FL4	PO Box 454, Interlochen 49643	(231) 269-3981	(231) 263-4145
			*8658 Hency Rd, Kingsley 49649		
Grawn	Colleen A. Wierman	FL1	1260 S West Silver Lake Rd, Traverse City 49685	(231) 943-8353	(231) 263-4145
			*8658 Hency Rd, Kingsley 49649		
Greensky Hill	Jonathan D. Mays	DSA2	8484 Green Sky Hill Rd, Charlevoix 49720-9686	(231) 547-2028	(231) 459-8067
			*409 Prospect St, Charlevoix 49720		
Hart	Rebecca L. Wieringa	FE4	308 S. State St., Hart 49420	(231) 873-3516	(231) 873-4766
			*3818 Melody Lane, Hart 49420		
Indian River	Patricia A. Harpole	AM1	PO Box 457, Indian River 49749	(231) 238-7764	(269) 806-2814
			*5954 Berry Lane, Indian River 49749		
Kalkaska	Robert J. Freysinger	FE2	2525 Beebe Rd, Kalkaska 49646	(231) 258-2820	(231) 258-5995
			*2301 Shawn Rd NW, Kalkaska 49646		
Keswick	Patricia Ann Haas	FE4	3376 S Center Hwy, Suttons Bay 49682	(231) 271-3755	(231) 271-4117
			*3400 S. Center Hwy, Suttons Bay 49682		
Kewadin	Eugene L. Baughan	RA6	PO Box 277, Kewadin 49648	(231) 264-9640	(231) 943-0354
			*400 Heartland Dr, Traverse City 49684		

GRAND TRAVERSE DISTRICT

CHARGE	PASTOR		ADDRESS	CHURCH	HOME
Kewadin Indian Mission	Thomas H. John Sr	RLA10	PO Box 227, Kewadin 49648	(231) 632-4920	(231) 264-0527
Northport Indian Mission			PO Box 401, Northport 49670	(231) 941-2360	(231) 264-0527
			*13735 Indian Rd, Kewadin 49648		
Kingsley	Carl Q. Litchfield	FE2	PO Box 395, 113 Blair Street, Kingsley 49649	(231) 263-5278	(231) 263-5999
			*PO Box 337, 449 N. Brownson St., Kingsley 49649		
Associate	Colleen A. Wierman	FL1	PO Box 395, 113 Blair Street, Kingsley 49649	(231) 263-5278	(231) 263-4145
			*8658 Hency Rd, Kingsley 49649		
Lake Ann	Michael J. Simon	FL2	6583 First St, Lake Ann 49650	(231) 275-7236	(231) 349-1914
			*6596 First St, Lake Ann 49650-9549		
Lake City	Jean M. Smith	AM5	PO Box - Drawer P, Lake City 49651	(231) 839-2123	(231) 839-7542
			*133 N Park St, Lake City 49651		
Leland	Daniel B. Hofmann	FE1	PO Box 602, 106 N 4th St, Leland 49654	(231) 256-9161	(231) 994-2159
			*PO Box 1134, 4840 Golfview Dr, Leland 49654-1134		
Ludington St Paul	Jon L. Pohl	FL4	3212 W. Kinney Rd., Ludington 49431	(231) 843-3275	(231) 843-8470
			*3257 W Kinney Rd, Ludington 49431-9780		
Ludington United	Dennis B. Bromley	PE2	5810 Bryant Road, Ludington 49431-1504	(231) 843-8340	(231) 425-4386
			*914 Seminole, Ludington 49431		
Mancelona	Todd W. Shafer	FL5	PO Box 301, Mancelona 49659	(231) 587-8461	(231) 587-9446
Alba			PO Box 301, Mancelona 49659	(231) 587-8461	(231) 587-9446
			*406 Sunnyside St, Mancelona 49659		
Manistee	David A. Selleck	FE3	387 First St, Manistee 49660	(231) 723-6219	(231) 723-3304
			*819 Elm Street, Manistee 49660		
Manton	Noreen S. Shafer	PL2	PO Box B, Manton 49663-0902	(231) 824-3593	(231) 587-9446
			*406 Sunnyside St, Mancelona 49659-9771		
Marion	James J. Mort	FE8	PO Box C, 216 W Main St, Marion 49665	(231) 743-2834	(231) 743-0062
Cadillac South Community			PO Box C, Marion 49665	(231) 775-3067	(231) 743-0062
			*205 Flemming St, Marion 49665		
Mears	Kenneth D. Vanderlaan	DSA22	PO Box 100, 1990 N. Joy St., Mears 49436	(231) 873-0875	(231) 742-0152
			*5763 W 9th St, Mears 49436-9569		
Mesick	Beverley J. Williams	FL3	PO Box 337, Mesick 49668	(231) 885-1699	(231) 885-1179
Harrietta			PO Box 13, 116 N. Davis Street, Harrietta 49638	(231) 389-0267	(231) 885-1179
			*3851 N 15 Rd, Mesick 49668-9757		
NE Missaukee Parish:					
Merritt-Butterfield	Jeffrey J. Schrock	FL3	428 S Merritt Rd, Merritt 49667	(231) 328-4598	(231) 328-2039
Moorestown-Stittsville			4509 E Moorestown Rd, Lake City 49651	(231) 328-4598	(231) 328-2039
			*7037 E Houghton Lake Rd, Merritt 49667-9786		

CHARGE	PASTOR		ADDRESS	CHURCH	HOME
Old Mission Peninsula	Melody Lane Olin	FL5	16426 Center Rd, Traverse City 49686-9775	(231) 223-4393	(231) 223-4141
			*14432 Peninsula Dr, Traverse City 49686		
Pentwater Centenary	Melanie S. Young	FE1	PO Box 111, 82 S Hancock, Pentwater 49449	(231) 869-5900	(231) 869-6881
			*124 S Rutledge St, Pentwater 49449		
Petoskey	James P. Mitchum	FE18	1804 E. Mitchell Road, Petoskey 49770-9686	(231) 347-2733	(231) 374-4747
			*900 Jennings, Petoskey 49770		
Pine River Parish:					
LeRoy	Scott R. Loomis	FL3	PO Box 38, LeRoy 49655-0038	(231) 768-4972	(231) 768-4512
Ashton			PO Box 38, LeRoy 49655-0038	(231) 832-8347	(231) 768-4512
			*PO Box 234, 400 W Gilbert St, LeRoy 49655-0234		
Scottville	John J. Conklin	PE6	114 W State St, Scottville 49454	(231) 757-3567	(231) 757-4781
			*301 W Maple Ave, Scottville 49454		
Traverse Bay	Jane R. Lippert	FE6	1200 Ramsdell St., Traverse City 49684-1451	(231) 946-5323	(231) 947-5594
			*10160 E Pickwick Ct, Traverse City 49684		
Traverse City Central	Dale P. Ostema	FE8	222 Cass St., Traverse City 49684	(231) 946-5191	(231) 933-4026
			*1713 Indian Woods Dr, Traverse City 49686		
Associate	M. Christopher Lane	FE6	222 Cass St., Traverse City 49684	(231) 946-5191	(231) 947-5594
			*10160 E Pickwick Ct, Traverse City 49684		
Traverse City Christ	Dianne Doten Morrison	PL4	1249 Three Mile Rd. S, Traverse City 49696	(231) 946-3048	(231) 944-5704
			*7750 S West Bayshore Dr, Traverse City 49684		
Williamsburg	Nathaniel R. Starkey	FL1	PO Box 40, Williamsburg 49690	(231) 267-5792	(586) 229-5767
			*8401 Crisp Rd, Williamsburg 49690		

NAME	POSITION ADDRESS	OFFICE	HOME
APPOINTMENTS TO EXTENSION MINISTRIES LOCATED IN THE GRAND TRAVERSE DISTRICT: *(further information at end of appointment section)*			
Anita Hahn (FE)	District Superintendent, Grand Traverse District Office 1249 Three Mile Rd S, Traverse City 49696	(231) 947-5281	(231) 421-8397
Kathryn Steen (FE)	Lead Hospital Chaplain, Munson Medical Center 1105 Sixth Street, Traverse City 49684	(231) 935-7163	(231) 421-5138

HEARTLAND DISTRICT

District Superintendent	David F. Hills	FE5	1400 S. Washington St., Suite A, Mt. Pleasant 48858-4268 DS Email: dsdave@umcheartland.org Office Email: office@umcheartland.org	Office Phone: (989) 773-5140 Home Phone: (989) 317-0081 Fax: (989) 775-6599
Administrative Assistant	Melanie Zalewski			

CHARGE	PASTOR		ADDRESS	TELEPHONE CHURCH	HOME
Alma	Deborah S. Thomas	OE2	501 Gratiot Ave, Alma 48801	(989) 463-4305	(989) 463-1485
			*627 Woodworth Ave, Alma 48801		
Amble	Anne W. Riegler	PL6	PO Box 392, Howard City 49329		(231) 631-0573
			*320 S Maple St, Edmore 48829-7300		
Ashley	Mona J. Dye	FL4	PO Box 7, Ashley 48806	(989) 862-4392	(989) 847-2305
Bannister			103 Hanvey St., Bannister 48807	(989) 862-4392	(989) 847-2305
Greenbush			PO Box 7, Ashley 48806	(989) 429-1892	(989) 847-2305
			*PO Box 7, 307 N Farr St, Ashley 48806		
Avondale	[PASTOR TO BE SUPPLIED]		P.O. Box 388, Evart 49631		
North Evart			8927 80th Avenue, c/o Elden Meyer, Evart 49631		
Big Rapids First	Rebecca K. Morrison	FE4	304 Elm Street, Big Rapids 49307	(231) 796-7771	(231) 796-5311
			*14080 Wildwood Dr, Big Rapids 49307-8782		
Blanchard-Pine River	Russell D. Morgan	CLM1	7655 W. Blanchard Rd., Blanchard 49310	(989) 561-2864	(989) 824-0653
Christian Community of Fellowship:					
Coomer			7655 W. Blanchard Rd., Blanchard 49310	(989) 561-5250	(989) 824-0653
Winn			8187 S. Winn Road, Mt. Pleasant 48858	(989) 866-2417	(989) 824-0653
			*PO Box 366, 8135 Mill St, Winn 48896		
Breckenridge	Paul W. Thomas	FL2	PO Box 248, Breckenridge 48615	(989) 842-3632	(989) 463-1485
			*627 Woodworth Ave, Alma 48801-1746		
Brooks Corners	Bryan Kelly Kilpatrick	FL1	5951 30th Avenue, Sears 49679	(231) 734-2733	(231) 734-2733
Barryton Faith			5951 30th Ave., Sears 48679	(989) 382-5431	(231) 734-2733
Sears			5951 30th Avenue, Sears 49679	(231) 734-2733	(231) 734-2733
			*5951 30th Ave, Sears 49679		
Carson City	Charles Edward Milam	FL1	PO Box 298, 119 E Elm Street, Carson City 48811	(989) 584-3797	(989) 584-3366
			*121 S Abbott St, Carson City 48811		
Chase-Barton	Lyle J. Ball	PL5	PO Box 104, 6957 S Depot Street, Chase 49623	(231) 832-5069	(231) 972-7335
Grant Center			15260 21 Mile Road, Big Rapids 49307	(231) 796-8006	(231) 972-7335
			*6874 5 Mile Rd, Blanchard 49310-9474		

CHARGE	PASTOR		ADDRESS	CHURCH	HOME
Clare	John G. Kasper	FE2	105 E. Seventh Street, Clare 48617	(989) 386-2591	(989) 386-7683
			*714 S Rainbow Dr, Clare 48617		
Edmore Faith	Michael A. Riegler	AM4	833 S First Street, Edmore 48829	(989) 427-5575	
			*320 S Maple St, Edmore 48829		
Elsie	Donald R. Ferris-McCann	FE2	PO Box 189, Elsie 48831-0189	(989) 862-5239	(989) 862-5780
Salem			2307 W Maple Rapids Rd, St. Johns 48879		(989) 862-5780
			*156 W Main St, Elsie 48831		
Evart	Melodye Surgeon-Rider	FE3	PO Box 425, Evart 49631	(231) 734-2130	(231) 734-2003
			*8543 Seven Mile Rd, Evart 49631		
Farwell	Connie R. Bongard	FL8	PO Box 709, 281 E. Ohio Street, Farwell 48622	(989) 588-2931	(989) 588-9620
			*551 N Superior St, Farwell 48622		
Fenwick	Gerald Erskine	DSA1	PO Box 241, Sheridan 48884	(989) 291-5547	(989) 682-4779
Palo			PO Box 241, Sheridan 48884	(989) 291-5547	(989) 682-4779
Vickeryville			PO Box 241, Sheridan 48884	(989) 291-5547	(989) 682-4779
			*10963 Sundog Trail, Perrinton 48871		
Greenville First, Turk Lake/Belding Cooperative Parish:					
Greenville First	Donald E. Spachman	FE1	204 W. Cass Street, Greenville 48838	(616) 754-8532	(616) 712-6024
Turk Lake			8900 W. Colby Road, Greenville 48838	(616) 754-3718	(616) 712-6024
Belding			301 South Pleasant, Belding 48809	(616) 794-1244	(616) 712-6024
			*405 W Grant St, Greenville 48838		
Deacon	Kimberly A. DeLong	FD3	204 W. Cass Street, Greenville 48838	(616) 754-8532	(616) 866-3191
			*4934 Brownstone Dr NE, Rockford 49341		
Harrison: The Gathering / Wagarville, Detroit Conf.					
	Vincent John Nader	DSA1	426 N. First St. Suite 106, PO Box 904, Harrison 48625	(989) 539-1445	(248) 914-3221
			*714 Foell Court, Gladwin 48624		
Heritage	Stephan Weinberger	FE1	19931 W. Kendaville Rd, Pierson 49339	(231) 937-4310	(231) 937-4748
			*18985 W Coral Rd, Howard City 49329		
Hersey	Lemuel O. Granada	PL3	PO Box 85, 200 W. Second Street, Hersey 49639	(231) 832-5168	(231) 723-2763
			*351 2nd St, Manistee 49660-1747		
Ionia Easton	Donna Jean Sperry	DSA1	4970 Potters Rd, Ionia 48846	(616) 527-6529	(586) 255-6228
			*230 Churchill St., Ionia 48846		
Ionia First	Jonathan D. VanDop	FE1	105 E. Main Street, Ionia 48846	(616) 527-1860	(616) 527-4654
			*119 E Main St, Ionia 48846		

HEARTLAND DISTRICT

CHARGE	PASTOR		ADDRESS	CHURCH	HOME
Ionia Parish:					
LeValley	Raymond R. Sundell	FE3	4018 Kelsey Highway, Ionia 48846	(616) 527-1480	(616) 527-9656
Berlin Center			4018 Kelsey Hwy, Ionia 48846	(616) 527-1480	(616) 527-9656
			*1461 E David Hwy, Ionia 48846-9674		
Ionia Zion	Clifford L. Allen	FL8	423 W. Washington Street, Ionia 48846	(616) 527-1910	(616) 527-2025
			*620 N Rich St, Ionia 48846		
Ithaca	Cynthia S.L. Greene	FE5	327 E. Center Street, Ithaca 48847	(989) 875-4313	(989) 875-3086
Beebe			327 E. Center Street, Ithaca 48847		(989) 875-3086
			*601 N Union St, Ithaca 48847		
Lincoln Road	Jana Lynn Almeida	FE5	PO Box 100, 9479 W. Lincoln Rd, Riverdale 48877	(989) 463-5704	(989) 466-2979
			*9437 W Lincoln Rd, Riverdale 48877		
Lyons-Muir Church	Forest Bertran Nelson	OF10	1074 Olmstead Road, Muir 48860	(989) 855-2247	(616) 891-8918
			*1074 Olmstead Road, Muir 48860		
Maple Rapids	Kathryn L. Leydorf-Keck	PL8	330 Maple St, Maple Rapids 48853	(989) 224-8811	(517) 282-4446
Lowe			5485 W Lowe Rd, St. Johns 48879	(989) 224-8811	(517) 282-4446
			*10886 S Woodbridge Rd, Bannister 48807		
Mecosta New Hope	Gregory L. Buchner	FE2	7296 9 Mile Road, Mecosta 49332-9722	(231) 972-2838	(989) 967-8801
			*3955 9 Mile Rd, Remus 49340		
Mt Pleasant Chippewa Indian	Owen L. White-Pigeon	DSA21	3490 S. Leaton, Mt Pleasant 48858		(989) 772-5521
			*3490 S Leaton Rd, Mt Pleasant 48858		
Mt Pleasant First	Diane Gordon	FE2	400 S. Main Street, Mount Pleasant 48858	(989) 773-6934	(231) 457-3744
			*1109 Glenwood Dr, Mt. Pleasant 48858		
Mt Pleasant Trinity	David Michael Palmer	FL5	202 S Elizabeth Street, Mt Pleasant 48858	(989) 772-5690	(989) 772-3725
Countryside			202 S. Elizabeth Street, Mt Pleasant 48858	(989) 773-0359	(989) 772-3725
Leaton			6890 E Beal City Road, Mt Pleasant 48858	(989) 773-3838	(989) 772-3725
			*250 S Crawford Rd, Mt Pleasant 48858-9053		
New Life	John A. Scott	FE4	6584 M 46, Six Lakes 48886	(989) 352-7788	(989) 352-6728
			*8544 M 46, Lakeview 48850		
Ovid: United Church	Paul A. Damkoehler	FL2	PO Box 106, 131 West Front Street, Ovid 48866	(989) 834-5958	(989) 307-5104
			*141 W Front St, Ovid 48866-9601		
Pompeii	William F. Dye	PL3	PO Box 125, Pompeii 48874	(989) 838-4159	(989) 847-2305
Perrinton			PO Box 125, Pompeii 48874	(989) 236-5398	(989) 847-2305
Middleton			PO Box 125, Pompeii 48874		(989) 847-2305
North Star			PO Box 125, Pompeii 48874		(989) 847-2305
			*PO Box 7, 307 N Farr St, Ashley 48806		

CHARGE	PASTOR		ADDRESS	CHURCH	HOME
Reed City	Kathryn S. Cadarette	FE4	503 S. Chestnut, Reed City 49677	(231) 832-9441	(231) 675-2172
			*219 S State St, Reed City 49677		
Rosebush	Joseph L. Beavan	FL1	PO Box 187, 3805 School Street, Rosebush 48878-0187	(989) 433-2957	(989) 433-5509
			*3272 E Weidman Rd, Rosebush 48878		
St Johns First	Ellen K. Zienert	FE3	200 E. State Street, St. Johns 48879	(989) 224-6859	(989) 224-2415
			*1006 Hampshire Dr, St. Johns 48879-2404		
St Johns Pilgrim	Andrew L. Croel	FE1	2965 W Parks Road, St. Johns 48879	(989) 224-6865	(989) 224-4423
			*2917 W Parks Rd, St. Johns 48879		
St Louis First	Terri L. Bentley	FL7	116 S. Franklin Street, St. Louis 48880	(989) 681-3320	(989) 681-2486
			*116 N East St, St Louis 48880-1721		
Sand Lake	Darryl L. Miller	PL8	PO Box 97, Sand Lake 49343	(616) 636-5673	(616) 696-4057
South Ensley			PO Box 97, Sand Lake 49343	(616) 636-5659	(616) 696-4057
			*1568 Solon, Cedar Springs 49319-9438		
Shepardsville	Judith A. Hazle	PL3	6990 East Winfield Road, Ovid 48866	(989) 834-5104	(989) 224-4260
			*1795 W Centerline Rd, St Johns 48879-9275		
Shepherd	Kathleen S. Kursch	FE8	PO Box 309, 107 W Wright Ave, Shepherd 48883	(989) 828-5866	(989) 828-5700
			*175 North Dr, Shepherd 48883		
Stanwood Northland	Gary D. Bondarenko	FE1	PO Box 26, 6842 Northland Dr., Stanwood 49346-0026	(231) 629-4590	(231) 823-2514
			*18835 Fillmore Rd, Stanwood 49346		
Third Avenue	David Cadarette	DSA1	226 N Third Ave, Big Rapids 49307	(231) 796-4157	(231) 675-1624
Paris			226 N Third Ave, Big Rapids 49307	(231) 796-4157	(231) 675-1624
Rodney			PO Box 14, Rodney 49342	(231) 796-4157	(231) 675-1624
			*219 S State St, Reed City 49677		
Weidman	Scott B. Smith	FL2	PO Box 98, 3200 N. Woodruff Rd., Weidman 48893	(989) 644-3148	(989) 644-3441
			*5765 Lindy Ln, Weidman 48893-7726		

HEARTLAND DISTRICT

NAME	POSITION / ADDRESS	OFFICE	HOME
APPOINTMENTS TO EXTENSION MINISTRIES LOCATED IN THE HEARTLAND DISTRICT: *(further information at end of appointment section)*			
Charles Farnum (FE)	Director, Wesley Foundation - Central Michigan University 1400 S Washington St, Mt Pleasant 48858	(989) 545-1761	(989) 545-1761
Devon Herrell (FE)	Director, Wesley Foundation - Ferris State University 628 S Warren Ave, Big Rapids 49307	(231) 796-8315	(231) 649-2302
David Hills (FE)	District Superintendent, Heartland District Office 1400 S Washington Street Ste A, Mt. Pleasant 48858	(989) 773-5140	(989) 317-0081

KALAMAZOO DISTRICT

District Superintendent — John W. Boley — FE1 — 810 Rankin Ave, Suite B, Kalamazoo 49006-5644
DS Email: john@kazoodistumc.org
Office Phone: (269) 372-7525, (800) 596-0739
Home Phone: (269) 216-3012
Fax: (269) 372-7644

Administrative Assistant — Mandana Nordbrock — Office Email: mandana@kazoodistumc.org

CHARGE	PASTOR		ADDRESS	TELEPHONE CHURCH	TELEPHONE HOME
Allegan	Robert K. Lynch	FE3	409 Trowbridge St., Allegan 49010	(269) 673-4236	(269) 673-2512
			*1310 South M 40, Allegan 49010		
Almena	Donna Jean Keyte	PL9	27503 County Rd 375, Paw Paw 49079	(269) 668-2811	(269) 329-1560
			*7632 Sandyridge St, Portage 49024-5028		
Arden	O'Ryan Rickard	RLA6	6891 M 139, Berrien Springs 49103	(269) 429-4931	(269) 235-1700
			*6148 Avon St, Portage 49024		
Bangor Simpson	Thomas A. Davenport	FE8	507 Joy St., Bangor 49013-1123	(269) 427-7725	(269) 353-9711
			*1227 Grand Ave, Kalamazoo 49006-3254		
Berrien Springs	Brenda E. Gordon	FE1	310 West Mars, Berrien Springs 49103	(269) 471-7220	(231) 631-1055
Pokagon			31393 Kansas St, Dowagiac 49047-9708	(269) 683-8515	(231) 631-1055
			*10 S 10th St, Niles 49120		
Bloomingdale	Carol A. Newman	DSA3	PO Box 9, Bloomingdale 49026	(269) 521-3323	(269) 628-2414
			*20584 Meadow Dr, Gobles 49055		
Breedsville	Jason E. Harpole	PL1	PO Box 21, 113 W Main Street, Breedsville 49027	(269) 359-1077	(269) 388-8312
			*205 Amos Ave, Portage 49002		
Buchanan Faith	Edward H. Slate	RE3	728 North Detroit Street, Buchanan 49107	(269) 695-3261	(269) 262-0011
			*1358 Honeysuckle Ln, Niles 49120		
Buchanan First	Rob A. McPherson	FE9	132 S. Oak Street, Buchanan 49107	(269) 695-3282	(269) 695-3896
			*304 Pontiac Court, Buchanan 49107-1273		
Burnips	Nancy J. Patera	FL1	PO Box 30, Burnips 49314	(616) 896-8410	(616) 371-7051
Monterey Center			PO Box 30, Burnips 49314	(616) 896-8410	(616) 371-7051
			*4290 Summer Creek Dr, Dorr 49323		
Casco	David W. Meister	FE9	880 66th Street, South Haven 49090	(269) 227-3328	(269) 227-3914
			*870 66th St, South Haven 49090		
Cassopolis	Benjamin David Hutchison	OE2	PO Box 175, 209 South Rowland Street, Cassopolis 49031-0175	(269) 445-3107	(269) 569-1586
			*61165 Quinnesec Road, Cassopolis 49031		

KALAMAZOO DISTRICT

CHARGE	PASTOR		ADDRESS	CHURCH	HOME
Coloma	Ronald D. VanLente	FE4	PO Box 670, 144 South Church St, Coloma 49038	(269) 468-6062	(269) 468-4905
			*331 Tannery Dr, Coloma 49038		
Associate	David L. Haase	PL1	PO Box 670, 144 South Church St, Coloma 49038	(269) 468-6062	(269) 463-3536
			*211 W Saint Joseph St, Watervliet 49098-9214		
Dowagiac First	David A. Price	FL2	PO Box 393, 326 N Lowe, Dowagiac 49047	(269) 782-5167	(269) 782-2444
			*504 Sunnyside Dr, Dowagiac 49047-1162		
Edwardsburg Hope	Jeffrey L. Reese	FE18	PO Box 624, 69941 Elkhart Rd., Edwardsburg 49112	(269) 663-5321	(269) 358-6115
			*PO Box 444, Edwardsburg 49112		
Fennville	Gary L. Peterson	FL7	PO Box 407, 5849 124th Ave, Fennville 49408	(269) 561-5048	(269) 561-2537
Pearl			PO Box 407, Fennville 49408	(269) 561-5048	(269) 561-2537
			*687 W Fennville St, Fennville 49408-8404		
Galien	Jeffrey O. Cummings	PL2	PO Box 266, 208 N. Cleveland Ave., Galien 49113	(269) 545-2275	(269) 545-8074
Olive Branch			PO Box 266, Galien 49113	(269) 545-2275	(269) 545-8074
			*201 N Cleveland Ave, Galien 49113		
Ganges	Marcia A. Tucker	DSA1	PO Box 511, 2218 68th Street, Fennville 49408	(269) 543-3581	(269) 857-4797
			*6948 Colver, Fennville 49408		
Glenn	Harold F. Filbrandt	RE1	PO Box 46, Glenn 49416	(269) 227-3930	(269) 637-3087
			*77020 County Road 380, South Haven 49090		
Gobles	Nelson L. Hall	FL2	PO Box 57, 210 E. Exchange St., Gobles 49055	(269) 628-2263	(269) 628-9126
Kendall			PO Box 57, Gobles 49055	(269) 628-2263	(269) 628-9126
			*31880 Jefferson Ave, Gobles 49055-9659		
Gull Lake	Mona K. Joslyn	FE5	8640 Gull Rd, Richland 49083	(269) 629-5137	(269) 731-5829
			*13091 M 89, Augusta 49012		
Hartford	Rey Carlos Borja Mondragon	OE1	425 East Main Street, Hartford 49057	(269) 621-4103	(734) 645-8991
			*143 Paras Hill Dr, Hartford 49057		
Hinchman	Linda R. Gordon	OR1	8154 Church St, Berrien Springs 49103	(269) 471-5492	(269) 815-6094
Oronoko			8154 Church St, Berrien Springs 49103	(269) 471-5492	(269) 815-6094
			*116 S Detroit St, Buchanan 49107		
Hopkins	Dominic A. Tommy	FE1	PO Box 356, Hopkins 49328	(269) 793-7323	(616) 534-7626
South Monterey			PO Box 356, Hopkins 49328	(269) 793-7323	(616) 534-7626
			*3226 Badger Ave SW, Wyoming 49509		
Kalamazoo First	Stephen MG Charnley	FE1	212 South Park Street, Kalamazoo 49007	(269) 381-6340	(269) 312-8633
			*471 W South St #403, Kalamazoo 49007		
Kalamazoo Milwood	Heather A. Molner	PE2	3919 Portage Road, Kalamazoo 49001	(269) 381-6720	(269) 459-6237
			*6830 Cypress St, Portage 49024-3208		

CHARGE	PASTOR		ADDRESS	CHURCH	HOME
Kalamazoo Stockbridge Avenue	Ronald D. Slager	PL5	1009 E Stockbridge Ave, Kalamazoo 49001 *6481 East S Ave, Scotts 49088	(269) 385-8919	(269) 327-8291
Kalamazoo Sunnyside	John Matthew Weiler	FE6	2800 Gull Road, Kalamazoo 49048-1384 *3279 Cardinal Hills Trail, Kalamazoo 49004	(269) 349-3047	(269) 762-5591
Deacon	Cara Beth Ann Weiler	FD6	2800 Gull Road, Kalamazoo 49048-1384 *3279 Cardinal Hills Trail, Kalamazoo 49004	(269) 349-3047	(269) 323-9279
Kalamazoo Westwood	Wayne A. Price	FE8	538 Nichols Road, Kalamazoo 49006-2994 *1003 Greenway Terrace, Kalamazoo 49006-2616	(269) 344-7165	(269) 762-4787
Deacon	Sandra V. Douglas	FD4	538 Nichols Road, Kalamazoo 49006-2994 *2021 March St, Kalamazoo 49001-3957	(269) 344-7165	(269) 369-8803
Lacota	Michael A. Pinto	PL8	PO Box 7, 01160 CR 681, Lacota 49063 *2321 Tamarack, Kalamazoo 49006-1426	(269) 253-4382	(269) 342-2747
Lakeside	George W. Lawton	RLA8	PO Box 402, Union Pier 49129 *8000 Warren Woods Rd #79, Three Oaks 49128-8519	(269) 469-8468	(269) 469-8468
Lawrence	Clifford L. Radtke	FL9	PO Box 276, 122 S Exchange St, Lawrence 49064 *115 E James St, Lawrence 49064-9415	(269) 674-8381	(269) 674-8386
LifeSpring Lawton St Paul's	Wayne E. McKenney	FL1	1560 S 8th Street, Oshtemo 49009 PO Box 456, 63855 N. M-40, Lawton 49065	(269) 353-1303 (269) 624-1050	
Marcellus Wakelee	John D. Messner	FL7	PO Box 396, 197 W Main St, Marcellus 49067 15921 Dutch Settlement, Marcellus 49067-9530 *224 Davis St, Marcellus 49067	(269) 646-5801 (269) 646-2049	(269) 646-7791 (269) 646-7791
Morris Chapel	Robert L. Snodgrass, II	DSA1	1730 Holiday, Niles 49120-8007 *16270 Lewis Rd, Vandalia 49095	(269) 684-5194	(574) 261-5139
Niles Grace	Anthony J. Tomasino	DSA11	501 Grant Street, Niles 49120-2955 *2729 Congress St, Niles 49120	(269) 683-8770	(269) 684-3454
Niles Wesley	Cathi M. Huvaere	FE3	302 Cedar Street, Niles 49120 *1502 Broadway, Niles 49120	(269) 683-7250	(616) 550-2570
Northwest	Samuel C. Gordy	PL2	3140 N 3rd Street, Kalamazoo 49009 *35795 Riverview Dr, Paw Paw 49079-9670	(269) 290-1312	(269) 657-6410
Oshtemo	John W. Fisher	RE2	PO Box 12, 6574 Stadium Dr, Oshtemo 49077-0012 *3506 East Shore Dr, Portage 49002	(269) 375-5656	(269) 327-3277
Otsego	Joseph D. Shaler	FE14	PO Box 443, 223 E. Allegan St., Otsego 49078-0443 *411 Walden Dr, Otsego 49078-9652	(269) 694-2939	(269) 806-9087
Parchment	Michael J. Tupper	FE4	225 Glendale Blvd, Parchment 49004 *45554 West Street, Lawrence 49064	(269) 344-0125	(269) 303-3743

KALAMAZOO DISTRICT

CHARGE	PASTOR		ADDRESS	CHURCH	HOME
Paw Paw	Trevor J. McDermont	FL2	420 W. Michigan Ave., Paw Paw 49079	(269) 657-7727	(269) 657-4506
			*52333 Ackley Terrace, Paw Paw 49079-9567		
Plainwell First	Kathy E. Brown	FE5	PO Box 85, 200 Park St., Plainwell 49080	(269) 685-5113	(269) 312-1378
			*714 E Gun River Dr, Plainwell 49080		
Portage Chapel Hill	Barry T. Petrucci	FE14	7028 Oakland Dr., Portage 49024	(269) 327-6643	(269) 276-0482
			*5300 Bronson Blvd, Portage 49024		
Portage First	Gregory B. Wood	FE17	8740 S Westnedge Ave, Portage 49002	(269) 327-6761	(269) 327-0410
			*8731 Newhouse, Portage 49024		
Portage Prairie	Ralph A. Posnik Jr	FL1	2450 Orange Road, Niles 49120	(269) 695-6708	(269) 695-9822
			*3310 Chicago Rd, Niles 49120		
Riverside	David L. Haase	PL1	PO Box 152, Riverside 49084	(269) 849-1131	(269) 463-3536
			*211 W Saint Joseph St, Watervliet 49098-9214		
St Joseph First	Harris J. Hoekwater	FE3	2950 Lakeview Ave., St. Joseph 49085	(269) 983-3929	(269) 235-9156
			*4921 S Roosevelt Rd, Stevensville 49127		
Deacon	James W. Kraus Jr	FD14	2950 Lakeview Ave., St. Joseph 49085	(269) 983-3929	(269) 983-5798
			*2820 Willa Dr, St Joseph 49085-2555		
Schoolcraft	Karen S. Wheat	FE5	PO Box 336, 342 N Grand Ave, Schoolcraft 49087	(269) 679-4845	(269) 679-4501
			*318 Willow Ct, Schoolcraft 49087		
Scottdale	Terrill Schneider	AM15	4276 Scottdale Rd., St. Joseph 49085-9366	(269) 429-7270	(269) 556-9869
Bridgman Faith			PO Box 414, 9156 Red Arrow Hwy, Bridgman 49106	(269) 465-3696	(269) 556-9869
			*4276 Scottdale Rd, St Joseph 49085-9366		
Silver Creek	Beth A. Reum	PE2	31994 Middle Crossing Rd, Dowagiac 49047	(269) 782-7061	(269) 782-2828
Keeler			31994 Middle Crossing Rd, Dowagiac 49047	(269) 782-7061	(269) 782-2828
			*53441 Garrett Rd, Dowagiac 49047		
Sodus Chapel Hill	Mark E. Mitchell	FL1	4071 Naomi Road, Sodus 49126	(269) 927-3454	(269) 925-4528
			*4033 Naomi Rd, Sodus 49126		
South Haven	Virginia L. Heller	FE1	429 Michigan, South Haven 49090-1333	(269) 637-2502	(269) 637-4803
			*12320 76th St, South Haven 49090		
Stevensville	B. Gordon Barry	FE12	5506 Ridge Rd., Stevensville 49127	(269) 429-5911	(269) 429-5749
			*5846 Ponderosa Dr, Stevensville 49127		
Three Oaks	Sherri L. Swanson	FE16	2 East Sycamore Street, Three Oaks 49128	(269) 756-2053	(269) 469-4488
			*19603 Oak Dr, New Buffalo 49117		
Townline	James C. Robertson	PL1	41470 24th Ave., Bloomingdale 49026	(269) 521-4559	(269) 434-6499
			*55130 County Rd 384, Grand Junction 49056		
Trowbridge	John L. Moore	RE1	355 26th Street, Otsego 49078-9621	(269) 673-5502	(269) 327-1243
			*2924 Vanderbilt Ave, Portage 49024		

CHARGE	PASTOR		ADDRESS	CHURCH	HOME
Vicksburg	Bufford W. Coe	FE15	217 S. Main Street, Vicksburg 49097 *4104 Waterview Dr, Vicksburg 49097	(269) 649-2343	(269) 649-0602
Water's Edge	Bradley S. Bartelmay	FE15	24 S. Whittaker, New Buffalo 49117 *19603 Oak Dr, New Buffalo 49117	(269) 469-1250	(269) 469-4488

NAME	POSITION ADDRESS	OFFICE	HOME

APPOINTMENTS TO EXTENSION MINISTRIES LOCATED IN THE KALAMAZOO DISTRICT:
(further information at end of appointment section)

NAME	POSITION / ADDRESS	OFFICE	HOME
Lisa Batten (FL)	Director, Wesley Foundation of Kalamazoo 2101 Wilbur Ave, Kalamazoo 49006	(269) 344-4076	(269) 496-7033
John Boley (FE)	District Superintendent, Kalamazoo District Office 810 Rankin Ave Ste B, Kalamazoo 49006	(269) 372-7525	(269) 216-3012
Patricia Catellier (FD)	Chaplain, Borgess Medical Center 1521 Gull Road, Kalamazoo 49048	(269) 226-7000	(269) 382-0708
Sandra Douglas (FD)	Representative Payee, Guardian Finance and Advocacy Services 420 E Alcott St, Kalamazoo 49001	(269) 344-0688 ext.465	(269) 369-8803
Cara Weiler (FD)	Social Worker, Southwest Michigan Childen's Trauma Assessment Center 1000 Oakland Drive, Unified Clinics – WMU, Kalamazoo 49008	(269) 387-7073	(269) 323-9279

LANSING DISTRICT

District Superintendent	Kennetha J. Bigham-Tsai	FE2	2111 University Park Dr, Suite 500, Okemos 48864-6907 Email: lansingds@miareaumc.org	Office Phone: (517) 347-4173 Home Phone: (517) 281-5035 Fax: (517) 347-4798
Administrative Assistant	Sus'ann M. Busley			

CHARGE	PASTOR		ADDRESS	TELEPHONE CHURCH	TELEPHONE HOME
Barry-Eaton Cooperative Ministry:					
Gresham	Bryce E. Feighner	FE2	4800 Lamie Highway, Charlotte 48813	(517) 652-1580	(517) 541-9605
			*220 N Chester Rd, Charlotte 48813-9547		
Kalamo	Daniel J.W. Phillips	PL2	PO Box 374, Vermontville 49096-0374	(810) 986-0240	(810) 986-0240
			*947 Sever Dr, East Lansing 48823		
Nashville	Gary L. Simmons	PE2	PO Box 370, Nashville 49073-0370	(517) 852-2043	(517) 622-2286
Vermontville	Gary L. Simmons	PE2	PO Box 186, Vermontville 49096-0186	(517) 726-0526	(517) 622-2286
Woodland	Gary L. Simmons	PE4	203 N Main St, Woodland 48897-9638	(269) 367-4061	(517) 622-2286
			*1137 DeGroff St, Grand Ledge 48837-2150		
Quimby	Jerry J. Bukoski	PL1	PO Box 63, Hastings 49058	(269) 945-9392	(517) 588-8415
			*1069 S Ionia Rd, Vermontville 49096-8576		
Sebewa Center	[PASTOR TO BE SUPPLIED]		PO Box 25, Sunfield 48890-0025		
Sunfield	Clare Walter Huyck	FL3	227 Logan St, Sunfield 48890	(517) 566-8448	(517) 566-2066
Mulliken	Clare Walter Huyck	FL2	400 Charlotte St, Mulliken 48861-9772	(517) 649-8382	(517) 566-2066
			*235 Dunham St, Sunfield 48890-9772		
M-52 Cooperative Ministry:					
Millville	Jeremy J. Wicks	FL2	1932 N M-52, Stockbridge 49285-9625	(517) 851-7853	(517) 623-6594
Dansville	Jeremy J. Wicks	FL4	PO Box 175, Dansville 48819-0175	(517) 851-7853	(517) 623-6594
New Church Start	Jeremy J. Wicks	FL1			(517) 623-6594
			*1956 N M 52, Stockbridge 49285-9625		
Webberville	Richard J. Foster	FL2	4215 E Holt Rd, Webberville 48892-8208	(517) 521-3631	(517) 521-3434
Williamston Crossroads	Richard J. Foster	FL3	5491 N Zimmer Rd, Williamston 48895-9181	(517) 655-1466	(517) 521-3434
			*120 E Beech St, Webberville 48892-9702		
Bath	Mark G. Johnson	FE8	PO Box 308, Bath 48808-0308	(517) 641-6551	(517) 898-6960
Gunnisonville			2031 E Clark Rd, Bath 48808-9413	(517) 482-7987	(517) 898-6960
			*13505 Webster Rd, Bath 48808		
Brookfield Eaton	Irene L. Vittoz	PL10	PO Box 430, 7681 Brookfield, Charlotte 48813-0430	(517) 543-4225	(517) 543-5361
			*5503 Long Hwy, Eaton Rapids 48827-9016		

CHARGE	PASTOR		ADDRESS	CHURCH	HOME
Charlotte Lawrence Avenue	Gary S. Wales	FE2	PO Box 36, Charlotte 48813-0036 *1072 N Stonehill Dr, Charlotte 48813	(517) 543-4670	(517) 231-6775
Country Chapel	Ryan B. Wieland	FE4	PO Box 26, Dowling 49050-0026 *3400 Lacey Rd, Dowling 49050	(269) 721-8077	(269) 758-3400
Delta Mills	Joseph L. Spackman	RE2	6809 Delta River Dr, Lansing 48906-9002 *3806 Cornice Falls Dr Apt 6, Holt 48842	(517) 321-8100	(517) 694-8346
DeWitt Redeemer	Rodney J. Kalajainen	FE27	13980 Schavey Rd, DeWitt 48820-9013 *2155 Longwoods Dr, DeWitt 48820	(517) 669-3430	(517) 669-9140
Dimondale Grovenburg	Joseph D. Huston	RE6	PO Box 387, Dimondale 48821-0387 1368 Grovenburg Rd, Holt 48842-8628 *6747 Creyts Rd, Dimondale 48821	(517) 646-0641 (517) 694-7683	(517) 646-6530 (517) 646-6530
Peoples Church	Andrew Pomerville		200 W Grand River Ave, East Lansing 48823-4212	(517) 332-5073	
East Lansing University	Jennifer Browne	FE4	1120 S Harrison Rd, East Lansing 48823-5201 *3343 Glasgow Drive, Lansing 48911	(517) 351-7030	(517) 898-4575
Associate	William W. Chu	FE4	1120 S Harrison Rd, East Lansing 48823-5201 *733 Orchard Dr, Williamston 48895	(517) 351-7030	(517) 992-5038
Eaton Rapids First	Martin M. DeBow	FE1	600 S Main St, Eaton Rapids 48827-1426 *702 State St, Eaton Rapids 48823	(517) 663-3524	(517) 663-8256
Grand Ledge First	Cynthia A. Skutar	FE2	411 Harrison St, Grand Ledge 48837-1575 *912 E Scott St, Grand Ledge 48837	(517) 627-3256	(517) 627-7347
Hastings First	Mark R. Payne	FE1	209 W Green St, Hastings 49058-2229 *935 N Taffee Dr, Hastings 49058	(269) 945-9574	(269) 945-2343
Hastings Hope	Richard D. Moore	FE15	PO Box 410, Hastings 49058-0410 *121 W North St, Hastings 49058	(269) 945-4995	(269) 945-3397
Holt	Mark R. Erbes	FE1	PO Box 168, Holt 48842-0168 *1951 Heatherton Dr, Holt 48842	(517) 694-8168	(517) 649-8277
Lake Odessa Central	Karen J. Sorden	FE3	PO Box 485, Lake Odessa 48849-0485 *455 Sixth Ave, Lake Odessa 48849	(616) 374-8861	(616) 374-8294
Lake Odessa Lakewood	James C. Noggle	PE2	10265 E Brown Rd, Lake Odessa 48849-9207 *10290 N Polk Ave, Harrison 48625	(269) 367-4800	(269) 367-4161
Lansing Asbury	Bo Rin Cho	FE1	2200 Lake Lansing Rd, Lansing 48912-3614 *2412 Post Oak Ln, Lansing 48912	(517) 484-5794	(517) 484-3306
Lansing Central	Linda J. Farmer-Lewis	OE2	215 N Capitol Ave, Lansing 48933-1372 *14 Hidden Ridge Trail, Jackson 49203	(517) 485-9477	(517) 783-9003

LANSING DISTRICT

CHARGE	PASTOR		ADDRESS	CHURCH	HOME
Lansing Christ	Lyle D. Heaton	FE2	517 W Jolly Rd, Lansing 48910-6609 *4747 W Stoll Rd, Lansing 48906-9384	(517) 394-2727	(517) 580-5058
Lansing Faith & South Lansing Ministries	Russell F. McReynolds	RE7	4301 S Waverly Rd, Lansing 48911-2560 *1721 Dover Place, Lansing 48910-1146	(517) 882-0661	(517) 483-2727
Lansing First	Lori J. Sykes	FE3	3827 Delta River Dr, Lansing 48906-3477 *3727 Delta River Dr, Lansing 48906-3476	(517) 321-5187	(517) 721-1676
Lansing Grace	Jane Ellen Johnson	FE8	1900 Boston Blvd, Lansing 48910-2456 *2915 S Cambridge Rd, Lansing 48911	(517) 482-5750	(517) 484-0227
Lansing Korean	Seok Nam Lim	FL1	2400 E Lake Lansing Rd, East Lansing 48823-9712	(517) 333-3633	(517) 669-1275
Lansing Mt Hope	Robert B. Cook	FE3	501 E Mt Hope Ave, Lansing 48910-9136 *1707 Woodside Dr, East Lansing 48823	(517) 482-1549	(517) 449-4826
Deacon	Colleen T. Treman	FD7	501 E Mt Hope Ave, Lansing 48910-9136 *309 Grape St, Portland 48875-1134	(517) 482-1549	(517) 647-6460
Lansing Sycamore Creek	Thomas F. Arthur	FE6	5127 Aurelius Rd Ste D, Lansing 48911 *5058 Glendurgan Ct, Holt 48842-9438	(517) 394-6100	(517) 889-5540
Lansing Trinity	Steven J. Buck	OR1	7533 W St Joe Hwy, Lansing 48917-9647 *4100 Mountain Glade Apt 5, Holt 48842	(517) 627-8388	(810) 444-7089
Leslie Felt Plains	Kelly M. Wasnich	PL1	401 S Main St, Leslie 49251-9402 401 S Main St, Leslie 49251-9402 *401 E Ash St, Mason 48854	(517) 589-9211	(517) 604-6157 (517) 604-6157
Mason First	Dwayne E. Bagley	FE6	201 E Ash St, Mason 48854-1775 *616 Hall Blvd, Mason 48854-1704	(517) 676-9449	(517) 244-0456
Munith	Susan J. Trowbridge	FE1	PO Box 189, Munith 49259-0189 *PO Box 151, 329 S Main, Vermontville 49096-0151	(517) 596-2441	(517) 726-0541
Okemos Community Church	Richard W. Blunt	FE1	PO Box 680, Okemos 48805-0680 *2441 S Wild Blossom Ct, East Lansing 48823-7203	(517) 349-4220	(517) 721-1301
Perry Shaftsburg	Nancy G. Powers	FE3	PO Box 15, Perry 48872-0015 PO Box 161, Shaftsburg 48882-0161 *PO Box 142, 121 S Madison St, Perry 48872	(517) 675-1567	(517) 625-3444 (517) 625-3444
Pleasant Lake	Christine L. Pease	DSA1	PO Box 83, 4815 E Territorial Rd, Pleasant Lake 49272 *340 Pleasant St, Charlotte 48813		(517) 543-5618
Portland	Keith R. Treman	FE7	310 E Bridge St, Portland 48875-1439 *309 Grape St, Portland 48875-1134	(517) 647-4649	(517) 647-6460

CHARGE	PASTOR		ADDRESS	CHURCH	HOME
Potterville	Linda K. Stull-Lipps	PE4	PO Box 458, Potterville 48876-0458	(517) 645-7701	(517) 645-4526
			*4115 Scenic View Ct, Potterville 48876-8600		
Robbins	Peggy A. Katzmark	FL1	6419 Bunker Rd, Eaton Rapids 48827-9108	(517) 663-5226	(517) 663-8417
			*827 S Waverly Rd, Eaton Rapids 48827		
Stockbridge	Susan J. Trowbridge	FE1	219 E Elizabeth St, Stockbridge 49285-9666	(517) 851-7676	(517) 726-0541
			*PO Box 151, 329 S Main, Vermontville 49096-0151		
Wacousta	Amee A. Paparella	PE2	9180 Herbison Rd, Eagle 48822-9718	(517) 626-6623	(517) 862-2599
			*9590 Looking Glass Brook Dr, Grand Ledge 48837		
Waterloo Village	Edward C. Ross	RE2	8110 Washington St, Grass Lake 49240-9241	(734) 475-1171	(517) 750-3987
			*5976 McCain Rd, Jackson 49201-9329		
Welcome Corners	Susan D. Olsen	FE9	3185 N M-43 Hwy, Hastings 49058-7944	(269) 945-2654	(616) 765-3838
Freeport			PO Box 142, Freeport 49325-0142	(616) 765-5316	(616) 765-3838
Peace			6043 E M-79 Hwy, Nashville 49073	(517) 852-1993	(616) 765-3838
			*175 Cherry St, Freeport 49325		
Wheatfield	Richard J. Ahti	DSA1	520 E Holt Rd, Williamston 48895-9463	(517) 851-7853	(517) 349-1314
			*4461 Oaklawn Dr, Okemos 48864-2921		
Williamston	Julie A. Greyerbiehl	FE4	211 S Putnam St, Williamston 48895-1309	(517) 655-2430	(517) 992-5038
			*733 Orchard Dr, Williamston 48895		

LANSING DISTRICT

NAME	POSITION / ADDRESS	OFFICE	HOME
APPOINTMENTS TO EXTENSION MINISTRIES LOCATED IN THE LANSING DISTRICT: *(further information at end of appointment section)*			
Kennetha Bigham-Tsai (FE)	District Superintendent, Lansing District Office 2111 University Park Dr Ste 500, Okemos 48864-6907	(517) 347-4173	
William Chu (FE)	Director, Wesley Foundation - Michigan State University 1118 S. Harrison, East Lansing 48823	(517) 332-0861	(517) 992-5038
William Dobbs (AF) *(Detroit Conference)*	Clergy Assistant to the Bishop, Michigan Area Episcopal Office 1011 Northcrest Road, MI Area Episcopal Office, Lansing 48906	(517) 347-4030	(517) 898-9791
Alice Townley (FE)	Parish Associate, Okemos Presbyterian Church 2258 Bennett Rd, Okemos 48823	(517) 507-5117	(517) 324-5432

MEMBERS OF THE W. MICHIGAN ANNUAL CONFERENCE APPOINTED TO OTHER CONFERENCES

(Paragraph 346.1, *Book of Discipline*)

CHARGE	PASTOR ADDRESS	OFFICE	HOME
DETROIT CONFERENCE			
Catherine Christman (FE)	Pastor, Vassar First UMC 139 North Main St, Vassar 48768	(989) 823-8811	(989) 823-2131
Cornelius Davis Jr (FE)	Pastor, Southfield Hope UMC 26275 Northwestern Hwy, Southfield 48076	(248) 356-1020	
Gary Haller (FE)	Pastor, Birmingham: First UMC 1589 W Maple, Birmingham 48009	(248) 646-1200	(248) 258-0903
Laurie Haller (FE)	Pastor, Birmingham: First UMC 1589 W Maple, Birmingham 48009	(248) 646-1200	(248) 258-0903
Jennifer Jue (FE)	Pastor, Oxford UMC 21 E Burdick St, Oxford 48371	(248) 628-1289	(248) 628-1022
Cynthia Parsons (FE)	Pastor, Sebewaing Trinity UMC 513 Washington, Sebewaing 48759	(989) 883-3350	(989) 883-2350
William Sanders (RE)	Pastor, Fairgrove/Watrousville UMCs PO Box 10, 5116 W Center, Fairgrove 48733	(989) 683-6564	(989) 674-2421
Charles Williams (FE)	Pastor, Houghton: Grace UMC 201 Isle Royle, Houghton 49931	(906) 482-2780	(906) 482-1751
FLORIDA CONFERENCE			
Dale A. Golden (FE)	Pastor, Homestead UMC 622 N Krome Ave, Homestead, FL 33030	(305) 248-4770	(989) 330-1932
ROCKY MOUNTAIN CONFERENCE			
Sandra Spahr (RE)	Pastor, Monte Vista / Bowen UMCs 215 Washington Street, Monte Vista, CO 81144	(719) 852-2853	(719) 568-5858
TENNESSEE CONFERENCE			
Eric Burton-Krieger (PE)	Assoc. Pastor, Brentwood UMC 309 Franklin Rd, Brentwood, TN 37027	(615) 373-3663	

B. 2014 APPOINTMENTS TO EXTENSION MINISTRIES

Appointments within the Connectional Structures of United Methodism

(¶344.1a, *The Book of Discipline 2012*)

Annuity Credit

Ayoub, George H., Executive Camp Director - West Michigan Conference — Annual Conference
Charge Conference: ________________
PO Box 6247, 11 Fuller Ave SE, Grand Rapids, MI 49516-6247, (616) 459-4503, Fax: (616) 459-0191

Batten, Lisa, Director - Wesley Foundation of Kalamazoo — Agency Served
Charge Conference: ________________
Wesley Foundation of Kalamazoo, 2101 Wilbur Ave, Kalamazoo, MI 49006, (269) 344-4076, Fax: (269) 344-8697

Bigham-Tsai, Kennetha J., Lansing District Superintendent — Annual Conference
Charge Conference: ________________
2111 University Park Dr. Suite 500, Okemos, MI 48864-6907, (517) 347-4173, Fax: (517) 347-4798

Boley, John W., Kalamazoo District Superintendent — Annual Conference
Charge Conference: ________________
810 Rankin Ave Ste B, Kalamazoo, MI 49006, (269) 372-7525, Fax: (269) 372-7644

Chu, William, Director - Wesley Foundation - Michigan State University — Agency Served
Charge Conference: ________________
1118 S. Harrison, East Lansing, MI 48823, (517) 332-0861

Farnum, Charles D., Director - Wesley Foundation - Central Michigan University — Agency Served
Charge Conference: Mt. Pleasant: First UMC
1160 Glen Avenue, Mt Pleasant, MI 48858, (989) 545-1761

Haggard, William E., Grand Rapids District Superintendent — Annual Conference
Charge Conference: ________________
PO Box 6247, Grand Rapids, MI 49516-6247, (616) 459-4503, Fax: (616) 459-0242

Hahn, Anita K., Grand Traverse District Superintendent — Annual Conference
Charge Conference: ________________
1249 Three Mile Rd S, Traverse City, MI 49696, (231) 947-5281, Fax: (231) 947-0181

Heisler, Benton R., Director of Connectional Ministries, West Michigan Conference — Annual Conference
Charge Conference: Cornerstone UMC Church
PO Box 6247, 11 Fuller Ave SE, Grand Rapids, MI 49516-6247, (616) 459-4503, Fax: (616) 459-0191

Herrell, Devon R., Director - Wesley Foundation - Ferris State University — Agency Served
Charge Conference: ________________
628 S Warren Avenue, Big Rapids, MI 49307, (231) 796-8315

Hills, David F., Heartland District Superintendent — Annual Conference
Charge Conference: ________________
1400 S Washington Street Ste A, Mt. Pleasant, MI 48858, (989) 773-5140, Fax: (989) 775-6599

Momany, Christopher P., Chaplain/Director of Church Relations, Adrian College — Agency Served
Charge Conference: Adrian First C.C.
110 S Madison St, Adrian College Valade Hall 133, Adrian, MI 49221-2575, (517) 265-5161 ext4211

Moore, Joy J., Associate Dean of African-American Church Studies and Assistant Professor of Preaching, Fuller Theological Seminary, — Agency Served
Charge Conference: Lansing: Trinity UMC
135 N. Oakland Ave., Pasadena, CA 91182, 626-584-5599

Powers, Jon R., Chaplain, Ohio Wesleyan University — Agency Served
Charge Conference: Grand Rapids: Trinity UMC
40 Rowland Ave, Delaware, OH 43015, (614) 368-3082

Roth Jr., Robert H., Director, Wesley Foundation, University of Michigan — Agency Served
*Charge Conference:*____________________
120 S State Street, c/o First UMC, Ann Arbor, MI 48104, (734) 662-4536

Step, Gary G., Director of New Church Development and Congregational Transformation, West Michigan Conference — Annual Conference
*Charge Conference:*____________________
PO Box 6247, 11 Fuller Ave SE, Grand Rapids, MI 49516-6247, (616) 459-4503, Fax: (616) 459-0191

Tuthill, Timothy T., Director of Life Enrichment, Clark Retirement Community — Agency Served
Charge Conference: East Lansing: University C.C.
1551 Franklin SE, Grand Rapids, MI 49506-3331, (616) 452-1568

Williams, Tamara S., Albion District Superintendent — Annual Conference
Charge Conference: ____________________
600 E Michigan, Albion, MI 49224, (517) 629-8150, Fax: (517) 629-8230

Appointments from Other Conferences

(¶346.1, 2 *The Book of Discipline 2012*)

EAST OHIO ANNUAL CONFERENCE

Bell, David, President and Executive Director, United Methodist Foundation of Michigan, — Agency Served
Charge Conference: Brighton: First UMC (Detroit Conference)
840 W Grand River Ave, Brighton, MI 48116, (810) 534-3001

DETROIT ANNUAL CONFERENCE

Dobbs, William D., Clergy Assistant to the Bishop, Michigan Area Episcopal Office — Annual Conference
Charge Conference: ____________________
1011 Northcrest Road, Lansing, MI 48906, (517) 347-4030, Fax: (517) 347-4003

Johnson, Melody H., Chaplain, Porter Hills Presbyterian Retirement Community — Agency Served
Charge Conference: Birmingham: First UMC, (Detroit Conference)
4450 Cascade Rd SE Ste 200, Grand Rapids, MI 49546-8330, (616) 949-4975

Appointments to Extension Ministries

(¶344.1b, c, ¶331.1 *The Book of Discipline 2012*)

Carter, Janet S., Deacon, Lead Chaplain, Pine Rest Christian Mental Health Services — Agency Served
Charge Conference: Grand Rapids: First UMC
669 Braeside Dr., Byron Center, MI 49315, w-(616) 281-6363 ext. 2117

Catellier, Patricia L., Deacon, Chaplain - Borgess Medical Center, Kalamazoo and Portage Chapel Hill UMC - *Charge Conference: Portage: Chapel Hill UMC* — Agency Served
Borgess - 1521 Gull Road, Kalamazoo, MI 49048, (269)226-7000

DeMoss, Mariel Kay, Deacon, Senior Writer and Content Editor, MI Area United Methodist Church and Ministry Coach at Muskegon Central UMC — Annual Conference
Charge Conference: Muskegon Central UMC
2006 Mills Ave, North Muskegon, MI 49445, c-(231) 670-5921, h-(231)744-0336

Griffin Jr., Herbert L., Regimental Chaplain, US Navy — Agency Served
Charge Conference: Battle Creek: Washington Heights UMC
1st Marine Regiment, 1st Marine Division, ATTN: Regimental Chaplain, Camp Pendleton, CA 92055

Johnson, Jan Marie, Chaplain, Mercy Health Partners — Agency Served
Charge Conference: Montague UMC
PO Box 358, 1500 E Sherman Blvd, Muskegon, MI 49443, (231) 672-3629

Johnson, Nathaniel, Chaplain, Helen DeVos Children's Hospital & Spectrum Health United Hospital, Grand Rapids, MI - *Charge Conference: Vergennes UMC* — Agency Served
2821 Boynton Ave, NE, Ada, MI 49301, (616) 710-9703

Kendall, Jayme L., Chaplain, United States Air Force — Agency Served
Charge Conference: ____________________
5103 Stormy Hills, San Antonio, TX 78247 w-(210)916-6296/h-(505)319-7873

Lancaster, Janice T., Deacon, Clinical Nurse, Emmanuel Hospice of Grand Rapids and Associate Pastor of Congregational Care - Grand Rapids: Northlawn UMC. — Agency Served
Charge Conference: ____________________
1157 Northlawn NE, Grand Rapids, MI 49505, (616) 361-8503

Lawton, Gregory W., Deacon, Director of Campus Ministry, Grand Valley State University, *Charge Conference: South Wyoming UMC* — Agency Served
4539 Luce St., Wesley Fellowship @ GVSU, Jenison, MI 49428, (616) 895-2235

Liske, Julie, Deacon, Executive Director, United Methodist Metropolitan Ministry of Greater Grand Rapids, *Charge Conference: Grand Rapids: First UMC* — Agency Served
1100 Lake Drive SE, Grand Rapids, MI 49506, (616) 456-7133

Loring, Mary, Coordinator of Pastoral Care, Clark Retirement Community, Grand Rapids, MI *Charge Conference:* ____________________ — Agency Served
1551 Franklin SE, Grand Rapids, MI 49506 (616) 452-1568

McCoy, J. Patrick, Director of Chaplaincy, Dartmouth-Hitchcock Medical Center — Agency Served
Charge Conference: Three Rivers: First UMC
32 Sargent Street, Norwich, VT 05055 (802) 649-3736

Minger, Stacy R., Assistant Professor of Preaching, Asbury Theological Seminary — Agency Served
Charge Conference: Girard UMC
204 N Lexington Ave, Wilmore, KY 40390, (859) 858-2000

Moore-Jumonville, Robert S., Associate Professor of Religion, Spring Arbor University - *Charge Conference: Jackson: First UMC* — Agency Served
106 E. Main St., Spring Arbor University, Spring Arbor, MI 49283, (517)750-6693

Mulligan, Cheryl A., Respiratory Therapist, Helen DeVos Pediatric Pulmonary Clinic & Lowell UMC *Charge Conference:* ____________________ — Agency Served
621 East Main Street, Lowell, MI 49331, (616)897-5936

Schlimm, Matthew R., Associate Professor of Old Testament, University of Dubuque Theological Seminary, *Charge Conference: Westwood UMC (Kalamazoo)* — Agency Served
2000 University Ave, Dubuque, IA 52001, (563) 589-3101

Steen, Kathryn M., Lead Hospital Chaplain, Munson Medical Center — Agency Served
Charge Conference: Traverse City: Central UMC
951 Hammond Place S., Traverse City, MI 49686, (231)499-3652-h, (231)935-7163-w

Testolin, Roy G., Pastoral Counselor, Heritage Interfaith Counseling Center — Agency Served
Charge Conference: Battle Creek: First UMC
9 Heritage Oak Lane Ste 3, Battle Creek, MI 49015, (269) 979-5180

Weiler, Cara, Deacon - Social Worker, Southwest Michigan Children's Trauma Assessment Center, *Charge Conference: Kalamazoo: Sunnyside UMC* — Agency Served
Unified Clinics – WMU, 1000 Oakland Drive, Kalamazoo, MI 49008, (269) 387-7073, Fax: (269) 387-7050

Appointments to Other Valid Ministries

(¶344.1d, 331.6 *The Book of Discipline 2012*)

Babb, Mark R., Deacon, ½ Associate Faculty, University of Phoenix, and ¼ Director of Music, Federated Church of Grass Lake; and ¼ Spiritual Formation Consultant, Jackson First UMC. — Agency Served
Charge Conference: Jackson: First UMC
Federated Church, 519 East Michigan Ave, Grass Lake, MI 49240, (517)522-4480

Douglas, Sandra V., Deacon, Representative Payee, Guardian Finance and Advocacy Services - *Charge Conference: Westwood UMC* — Agency Served
420 E Alcott St, Kalamazoo, MI 49001, (269) 344-0688 ext.465, Fax: (269) 344-3030

Fons, Valerie, Bread and Water, LLC and L.A.U.N.C.H. (Wisconsin) — Agency Served
Charge Conference: (Wisconsin Conference)
1275 Main Rd, Washington Island, WI 54246, (920) 847-2400

Pratt, D. Kay, Vice-President of PAPA'S (Pastors and Priests Available for Service) Ministries and Methodist Resources Development Officer — Agency Served
Charge Conference: (Methodist Church of the Caribbean and Americas)
1857 South County Road 50 W, Brownstown, Indiana 47220 h-(876) 993-2680, w-(876)505-8256

Pratt, Merlin H., MPresident of PAPA's (Pastors and Priests Available for Service) Ministries and Methodist Resources Development Officer — Agency Served
Charge Conference: (Methodist Church of the Caribbean and Americas)
1857 South County Road 50 W, Brownstown, Indiana 47220 h-(876) 993-2680, w-(876)505-8256

Smith-Jang, Barbara L., Pastoral Counselor, Taejon Christian International School — Agency Served
Charge Conference: East Lansing: University UMC
210-1 O-Jung Dong Daedeok-Gu, Daejeon, Republic of Korea 306-819, (042) 829-7029

Townley, Alice Fleming, Associate for Parish Life, The Presbyterian Church of Okemos — Agency Served
Charge Conference: East Lansing: University UMC (¶345 Book of Discipline 2008)
1035 Prescott Drive, East Lansing, MI 48823, (517) 324-5432

Appointments to Attend School
(¶326.1, 3 *The Book of Discipline 2012*)

Wright, Christina L., Deacon, University of West Georgia
717 Burns Road #3114, Carrollton, GA 30177 (617)875-6955

C. 2013 SALARIES OF PERSONS WITH APPOINTMENTS TO EXTENSION MINISTRIES

Appointments within the Connectional Structures of United Methodism
(¶344.1a, ¶331.1b; ¶316 *The Book of Discipline 2012*)

	Salary	Travel	Housing & Utilities	Health Insurance	Other
Ayoub, George H.	69,919	8500	20,000	16,980	-
Batten, Lisa	35,120	-	10,000	-	-
Bigham-Tsai, Kennetha J.	77,688	-	20,000	3,000	-
Chu, William	35,460	-	-	823	-
Farnum, Charles D.	16,000	-	-	-	-
Haggard, William E.	77,688	6,000	20,000	3,000	-
Hahn, Anita K.	77,688	-	-	16,980	-
Heisler, Benton R.	75,736	10,000	-	16,980	-
Herrell, Devon R.	53,321	-	-	16,980	-
Hills, David F.	77,688	-	-	16,980	-
Momany, Christopher P.	61,000	-	-	-	-
Moore, Joy J.	-	-	-	-	-
Powers, Jon R.	-	-	-	-	-
Roth Jr., Robert H.	-	-	-	-	-
Step, Gary G.	69,919	-	20,000	16,980	-
Tuthill, Timothy T.	-	-	-	-	-
Williams Tamara S.	77,688	-	-	833	-

Appointments from Other Conferences
(¶344.1, *The Book of Discipline 2012*)

Bell, David	–	–	–	–	–
Dobbs, William D.	–	–	–	–	–
Johnson, Melody H.	–	–	–	–	–

Appointments to Extension Ministries
(¶344.1b, c and ¶331.1 *The Book of Discipline 2012*)

Catellier, Patricia L.	(19.75/17.00 per hr/hour)	–	–	–	–
Carter, Janet S.	45,000	–	–	–	–
DeMoss, Mariel K.	33,000/13,500	–	–	–	–
Griffin Jr, Herbert L	–	–	–	–	–
Johnson, Jan Marie	–	–	–	–	–
Johnson, Nathaniel	50,300	–	–	–	–
Kendall, Jayme L.	74,880	–	17,028	–	–
Lancaster, Janice T.	NUMC:unpaid	–	–	–	–
Lawton, Gregory	42,243	2,300	9,000	–	1,500
Liske, Julie	32,380	–	10,000	–	–
Loring, Mary	35,014	–	–	–	–
McCoy, J Patrick	107,000	Voucher	–	–	–
Minger, Stacy R	–	–	–	–	–
Moore-Jumonville, R.S.	–	–	–	–	–
Mulligan, Cheryl A.	–	–	–	–	–
Schlimm, Matthew	67,372	750	–	–	–
Steen, Karthyrn M.	47,690	–	–	–	–
Testolin, Roy G	–	–	–	–	–
Weiler, Cara	–	–	–	–	–

Appointments to Other Valid Ministries
(¶344.1d, ¶331.4 *The Book of Discipline 2012*)

Babb, Mark R	–	–	–	–	–
Douglas, Sandra	–	–	–	–	–
Fons, Valerie A	–	–	–	–	–
Pratt, Kay D	(all expenses	paid by	agency)	–	–
Pratt, Merlin H	(all expenses	paid by	agency)	–	–
Smith-Jang, Barbara L	–	–	–	–	–
Townley, Alice Fleming	7,596	1,000	30,404	–	1,500

Appointments to Attend School
(¶326, 1,3 *The Book of Discipline 2012*)

Wright, Christina	–	–	–	–	–

VIII. REPORTS

A. DIRECTOR OF CONNECTIONAL MINISTRIES REPORT

The past few years I have composed this speech as a thank you list, program descriptions, facts, and figures. You can read those details on the hand-out or in the Volume I Report.

I begin with a deep word of appreciation to my wife Linda. Her personal witness of daily sacrificial living and compassionate care giving touches my soul, and as my best friend, she inspires my heart.

You and I are supported week in and out by your excellent Connectional Ministries Staff. They are Laura, Pam, Kathy, Kiri, Scherry, George, Gary, Naomi, Mark, Kay, Jim and Valerie. This team helps keep you all connected in a wide variety of ways. Please show them your appreciation.

I received my first "pay check" from Mr. Kiboloski. He was our next door neighbor. I had mowed his lawn while he was on vacation for 2 weeks = $3. (It was the 1960's). My dad helped me set up Passbook bank account. It was my first lesson in keeping track of numbers and the importance of having a goal. For me, that goal was a basketball backboard & hoop.

Purpose of Saving = Opportunity

- John & Charles Wesley – "Earn all you can; Save all you can; Give all you can"
- The early Methodists in England established hospitals, orphanages, and Sunday School. All were a result of this discipleship model.

Resources we save can become opportunities to help or hoard.

The Conference Leadership Team has committed some resources from Conference reserves, (money saved), to fund the Executive Director of Camping position in 2014. The CLT is counting on you to approve a Conference budget that will partially fund this executive director position in 2015 and 2016, so that, this ministry that reaches almost 2,000 children through site camping, and more than 10,000 others through family camps and retreats, will become as vibrant and effective as we believe is its potential.

The CLT guiding vision is for the Conference to help equip and connect congregations so that they can truly be "**vital and fruitful,**" and be as the Discipline states, "the most significant arena for making disciples and transforming the world." As you know all too well these significant arenas have slipped a bit in their capacity to grow. The numbers tell the story.

Eighteen years ago, our General Conference 1996 Delegation included ten persons. This year we elect, based on our numbers, we will send Nichea and Laurie, two persons instead of the ten. The CLT has taken a variety of direct actions to help equip congregations to grow. You have seen this photo of the white board in Laura's office as she tracks the 22 VCI consultations taking place this past spring.

Since we began with the first Vital Church Initiative pilot 3 years ago, more than 70 larger and smaller congregations have engaged this process that is geared toward continuous learning, peer-mentoring, transformation and fruitfulness. More than 100 clergy and laity have been trained for leadership roles in the Vital Church Initiative. More than 3,000 laity have been engaged in this process.

You heard the testimony of Mona Dye, pastor of Bannister UMC on the Heartland District. It was one of the first smaller church consultations. They now report; "Community persons are now actively engaged in new opportunities. We are in a whole new economic place. It's the same people with same income who are now inspired to contribute to ministry and complete the necessary facilities improvements that were part of the prescriptions."

Prescriptions often include encouragement to improve:

1. **Vision/Mission**:
2. **Outreach**:
3. **Spiritual formation**: discipleship process, guest welcoming
4. **Stewardship of financial and property resources**
5. **Building Issues:** Nursery, signage, clutter, curb appeal, neglected maintenance, (Please plant a flower and trim the grass. Make it look like someone is there and there is life!)
6. **Communications:**
7. **Worship excellence**

Vitality in our conference can be seen in other contexts:

Last year you gave, in a one-time offering, almost $6,000 toward Spirit Journey, an emerging ministry among Native American young people in the Northport area. Easter Sunday the Northport UMC was standing room only. Why? Many of the adults were in church for their first time ever. They came to hear their children sing.

Your generosity is helping to make disciples and transform the world.

Watch this brief video testimony of how Cornerstone UMC has helped transform the world of some school children in Grand Rapids. The relationship first began when they gave 200 coats to the school. Likely the story has been and/or could be repeated across the conference.

Releasing our gifts into the flow of God's power is an act of trusting God to provide for us and multiply those gifts all at the same time. The CFA report noted what could be done if tithing was more common across all our households. The Ministry Share rate would be 10% and the Conference would have $11,000,000 in resources with which to do ministry.

So let me share a little bit about giving.

Manna was a resource the Israelites trusted God to provide and they gathered it daily.

Ex. 16:4-5 "The people are to go out each day and gather enough for that day. On the sixth day they are to prepare what they bring in and that is to be twice as much as they gathered on the other day." Why, so that they could rest on the Sabbath.

Exodus 16: 16-20 "Some of them paid no attention to Moses; They kept part of the manna until morning, but it was full of maggots and began to smell."

Gather & keep more than is necessary and it rots!

How many times have you forgotten you had something stored away, only to discover it later and find it unusable?

Habit of Giving: Yields Perspective

- People of Israel crossed the Jordan River. Left behind the wilderness and entered a land of plenty.
- Deut. 8:17 was a reminder to keep God's commandments "Lest we forget that not by our power and might have we acquired this wealth."
- Habit of giving reinforces the perspective that that all we have belongs to God
- A habit of giving to God is a way of establishing a priority of gratitude.
- It's like a constant stream of thank you notes.

Giving Habits take on many forms.

A vivid childhood memory for me was placing my parent's envelope in the plate.

The key to the file cabinet where my savings passbook was stored was in the church envelope box.

Earning, saving, & giving was modeled over and over in my family of origin.

Earning saving and giving is part of the West MI Conference DNA. It is who we are and what we do.

Text giving, on-line auto-payments, writing checks, placing cash in the offering are all acts of faith.

Giving of first fruits, whether in plenty or want; healthy or sick; employed or lay aside for the moment, we trust God to provide, no matter what our circumstances. 45 years ago, I was just entering middle school. My father had a surgery that also required six weeks of radiation treatment. That long term illness for my dad led to a major employment change that severely limited our household income as I entered high school and my sister was in college. I saw my parents model an incredible trust in God.

I didn't have a baseball glove as I tried out for the team. Pete Plumb's baseball mitt was bought with $10 of my profits from my three jobs: lawn mowing, a paper route and work on a sod farm. Well I made the team and was assigned to first base when I wasn't pitching. There was no extra money for a new first basemen's mitt. This small mitt wasn't going to work. I remember the awkward embarrassment of telling my coach. A week later he called me in and said, "Hey Heisler. This is for you." He threw a new first basemen's mitt my way. Let me tell you of the joy I experienced because of somebody else's generosity.

$10 simply bought a baseball mitt. Today that $10 can save a life thru Imagine No Malaria.

All our West MI congregations regularly celebrate generosity and the joy that is found thru giving and receiving.

Joy of Giving = an experience within

Your generosity has provided more than $50,000 toward our Committee on Hispanic/ Latino Ministry through the conference and districts' budget, the New Church Development and Congregational Transformation Committee and special gifts from the Wesley Campus Ministries. This amount has been matched with $50,000 over the next 3 years from the National Hispanic Plan. These are our General Church Ministry Shares returning to us. Sonya Luna, our Area Director of Hispanic Latino Ministries, is part of the fruit of this act of generosity and our area-wide sharing of staff resources.

Look at these pictures of people putting gifts in action.

Last year, Cornerstone's Kenya Team went to a village in need of clean water. The village had been told by people in the past that they'd get water, but no one ever has fulfilled this promise. Zoe Waters will be installing a solar pumping system on an existing, hand dug well to reduce the long lines of people waiting to collect water for their daily needs. This solar pumping system will be installed to help provide water for the thousands of refugees and native people living in and traveling through the area.

There is a man in Kenya whose name is Gilbert. He is a water well driller that Zoe Waters has used to drill some of the wells. His 34 year old wife died this past winter from Malaria, a preventable, treatable and beatable disease. Our action or inaction has life giving consequences.

Here is Tracy Bowers, Dir. Of Cornerstone Outreach, distributing the solar powered bibles in native Kenyan language called "treasures." The gift of God's word in a person's own language, changes everything, a new generation is inspired. We can estimate that almost 150,000 people will have been exposed to the Bible through this solar bible distribution. That is nearly the equivalent of all the United Methodists in MI. We are helping save lives from Malaria and we are proclaiming the Word of Life found in Scripture.

There is a song that speaks to my spirit each time I wonder if I am making a difference.

Sing: "Sometimes I feel discouraged, and think my works in vain, but then the Holy Spirit, revives my soul again. There is a balm in Gilead, to make the wounded whole. There is a balm in Gilead to heal the sin sick soul."

When you serve faithfully, give generously and unite around life giving ministry, West MI, you are a Balm in Gilead!

Blessing of Giving results in the legacy of being a difference maker

Genesis 12:2 God said to Abraham (and speaks to us) "You will be blessed to be a blessing."

Our working together with the Detroit Conference has allowed us to multiply our gifts, make a difference and be a blessing in multiple areas:

- Communications,
- Camping Ministries,
- Hispanic/Latino Ministry,
- Vital Church Initiative,
- New Church Development,
- Wesley Campus Ministry
- Commission on Religion and Race Cross Cultural Training,
- Area Human Sexuality Dialogue Task Force,
- 2014 Annual Conference Worship & Keynote teaching
- Planning for a shared 2016 Annual Conference Session.

Other area collaboration conversations have included the:

- Conference Leadership Teams,
- Boards of Pension and Health Care Benefits,
- Area Appointive Cabinet and Ministry Team.
- The complete list of ministries we are sharing with the Detroit Conference is in your handout. Other groups are planning joint conversations.

Your Conference leaders continue to pray and discern about any "next steps" for greater MI Area unity toward which the Spirit of God may move us. We continue to discover ways that we have been blessed to be a blessing and often that blessing comes as we collaborate closely. Another example of our shared blessing is our Area INM goal. Thank you Molly turner for your excellent leadership!

My friends Ralph and Kathy were missionaries in Africa. A late evening worship service exposed them and their 2 sons to the **killer in the dark known as Malaria**. They were fortunate enough to have the medicine to treat this disease that was transmitted by the **simple bite of a mosquito**. This child, Domingus Antoinic, was not as fortunate. He died of malaria, just 20 minutes after this photo was taken by an aid worker delivering supplies.

Because as United Methodists we have demonstrated that **we care**, those persons most at risk for this disease **have cared about what we know**. Working with the local leaders across the continent of sub-Saharan African, not only have we been able to distribute nets, healthcare and prevention techniques, but persons have been receptive to hear the Gospel. **Tribal chiefs** responded in one predominantly Muslim region in Sierra Leon by coming to the United Methodists bishop. They said, “You cared for our bodies. Please help **care for our souls**.” New congregations have been created in this region.

Somebody’s generosity in the small town of 400 where I went to high school provided me with a baseball mitt.

Linda and I have made a 3 year pledge to INM that will help give 400 others a healthy life.

Our MI Area UM congregations have crossed the $800,000 mark and done excellent generous work toward this $1.5 million goal. That amount will save 150,000 lives. We still have a way to go. Some of you may be able to give five and six figure gifts toward our goal, or you know someone who may be willing. Molly Turner and I look forward to hearing from you.

My friends we are saving lives, we are not playing games! Sometimes it feels like a game. We have long debates over rules or money, or structure, or approving the writing letters to congress that then are not sent. Too often we have given a minimum amount of time & energy to “How is it with your soul?” or asking one another, “How will you help the soul of another connect with Christ?” It sometimes feels like we are playing games.

But Jesus was clear in Luke 19:10; “I came to seek and save the lost.” At times we aren’t even willing to admit we are lost, let alone name that someone else may need the transforming power of the grace of God and ours is the only voice they might ever hear!

Each time I see this child’s photo, I wonder what she is praying. Perhaps our actions, our decisions, our gifts, God’s ministry thru us will be the answer to this child’s prayer. **Surely God wants us to be her answer and there is no turning back.**

Please sing with me… I have decided to follow Jesus. I have decided to follow Jesus. I have decided to follow Jesus, no turning back, no turning back.

Rev. Benton R. Heisler
Director of Connectional Ministries

REPORTS

B. DISTRICT SUPERINTENDENTS’ REPORT

Good morning, Church!

During his Board of Ordained Ministry report, John Boley said that he didn’t want to “steal my thunder” based on what he heard me report to the Clergy Session on Wednesday afternoon. He didn’t know that I wasn’t going to bring it up today. But that caused me to reflect and decide after all that I would quickly share the same numbers with you here today, so the laity can hear them as well. There are currently some 307 clergy serving in appointments in the West Michigan Conference. 31 of these are already retired. Of the 276 who aren’t yet retired, 172 are age 55 and over—which means that *over the next ten years, more than half of the clergy currently serving in appointments will reach retirement age*. The average number of retirements will be 17 per year over the next ten years—which is exactly how many clergy retired this year. But only 4 new clergy joined this year by completing seminary or Course of Study. We *barely* found pastoral leadership for all the churches this year. The crisis is already here. You need to know this.

Now to my “report”:

What I am about to say is largely framed in terms of the Local Church, because that’s mostly who we are. But I hope what I’m about to say has a wider application. If your context for ministry is not a local church, please substitute YOUR MINISTRY every time I mention a local church or a congregation. Wesley

Foundations, Camps, Community Ministries, whatever. OK?

I invite you to pray with me:

Lord. You have our hearts. You are our life. You meet each of us right where we are in our journey of faith, accepting us as is, and inviting us to follow you to a new place. So help us in these moments to set down our burdens and baggage, so that our hands and our minds and our hearts will be free to hold onto whatever you place within us. And help us to remember that really, this is not about us—we already have new life with you and in you. This is really about those who still don't know you, and all that you want to bring to life within them.

Speak, Lord. Your servants are listening.

You know, don't you, that the Church (with a "Capital C") is NOT going to die?

You know, don't you, that the good news message of Jesus Christ will not be silenced?

You know, don't you, that the presence of the Lord with us, and the power of God's Holy Spirit moving and working among us will not be stopped?

Certainly, the Church—the Body of Christ, the community of believers, the communion of saints—will change. In the future, the Church may or may not be like the Church we are part of today. But it WILL live. We serve the God of creation and RE-creation. We hold dear the promises in the Scripture which proclaim that Christ overcomes death with resurrection and new life. When we belong to God, there is ALWAYS a future!

So let me ask you again, my brothers and sisters in Christ: YOU KNOW, DON'T YOU, THAT THE CHURCH OF JESUS CHRIST IS NOT GOING TO DIE?

God wins! Christ wins! Perfect love and grace and healing and NEW LIFE WIN! Amen!

Now let's talk about the church with a "small c"—the congregation. There's something I want to name for us today—something we don't like. What I want to name is GRIEF. As a people called United Methodist in the West Michigan Conference, we are GRIEVING. We are grieving our LOSS. Even in those places where spiritual growth is happening, where discipleship is developing, where worship is uplifting, where mission and outreach are making a profound impact…there is still a sense of LOSS. GRIEF is still present. Beloved members and friends have grown old and died; others are no longer with us because their health limits them; others in our church family had to find a job in another state and POOF they were gone. And then of course there are our children. We raised them in the faith and in the church, but something happened; so many of them grew up, moved away, and stopped going to church—ANY church. They tell us they don't need organized religion to believe in God. But the harder truth is that some of our children don't believe in God at all. Which means our grand-children aren't being raised in the faith. Some of our grandchildren have no CONCEPT of God, much less a relationship with God. We are reminded of ALL OF THIS LOSS every time we go to church, because it's always right there in front of us: Fewer people in the pews. Fewer visitors. Decreased giving. More frequent reports about financial troubles. Harder still, there are fewer laity who are physically able to be involved. How many hundreds of times have I heard the stories that begin with "we used to…" We used to raise money through church dinners.... We used to have an active youth group… We used to have a huge Sunday School full of kids.... We used to have several UMW circles—now there's only one. Lots of people used to show up and spruce up the place when we had church work days…now we're lucky if two or three do. Friends and stranger used to respect and admire our church—now they seem to pity us, if they even know about us at all.

I could go on and on, couldn't I? SO MUCH HAS CHANGED. SO MUCH HAS BEEN LOST. IT HURTS! WE ARE GRIEVING.

I know that there are always exceptions. There are some congregations in our connection that are strong and growing. Praise the Lord! There are also some congregations among us who are discovering how to turn things around. Halleluiah! And yet, even the strongest congregations are still touched by loss and grief. Every choice we make means that another choice has NOT been made—and there are always some among us who grieve the loss of that choice *not* made. In addition, regardless of how much or how little our own local church is struggling, we all grieve together the loss of the presence and influence of the Church in our society. The church used to matter; the church used to be relevant; that's been lost, too. My husband Jeremy and I were recently in a small Michigan tourist town; we were looking over a very cute new placemat in a local restaurant that showed a hand-drawn map of the town. It eventually dawned on us that this map, drawn by a local resident, DIDN'T SHOW A SINGLE CHURCH. Every restaurant, yes. Every boat rental. Every park. Every school and Laundromat and gift shop. But not one church—and there are at least five different congregations in the heart of that town. We looked closely, and realized that the map treated churches in the same way it did houses—just a square with no special markings. Jeremy and I probably shouldn't have been shocked, but we were. The church is so irrelevant now that it doesn't make the map in a tourist town. That would have been unheard of 60, 40, 20, even 10 years ago, right? AND WE GRIEVE. WE ALL GRIEVE.

There is a natural reaction to deep grief which is common to most human beings. When faced with loss, WE HOLD ON TIGHTLY TO WHAT REMAINS. When I was in middle school, the little sister of one of my best friends died. Years later, I inadvertently discovered that the little sister's bedroom was still preserved exactly as it was on the day she died. I completely understand what that family did. When faced with loss, WE HOLD ON TIGHTLY TO WHAT REMAINS. Even Mary Magdalene tried to do so on Easter morning at the tomb!

So many of us, and so many of the people in our congregations, are smack-dab in the midst of that natural response to grief and loss. We're HOLDING ON to what remains, afraid of losing any more. Let me make sure you understand: I'm not talking about prayerfully, thoughtfully, intentionally carrying forward those things that will help our church fulfill its mission. That's fine. That's great. I'm talking about NOT EVEN CONSIDERING that there might be a worthwhile alternative. I'm talking about a response borne out of pain and fear that leads to a HIGHLY NEGATIVE VIEW OF CHANGE. We're hurting. We're scared. We don't know what to do. So we CLING to what we still have: The same traditions. The same leaders. The same worship service. The same hymns. The same committees meeting on the same night in the same space. And sometimes these honestly do give us a measure of comfort. But the downward trajectory continues. Our fear and grief ramp up, until sooner or later, someone in our church—maybe even one of us—says:

"All I want is for this church to stay open long enough that I can have my funeral here."

Now I'M GRIEVING. How did we reach this point where we church-folk actually say and mean such things? How did we come to believe that Christ created the church to serve US, instead of so that we can serve him? I am convinced that OUR UNADDRESSED GRIEF is directly in the way of our ability to truly MAKE DISCIPLES—because when we grieve, we hold on tight; when we hold on tight, nothing changes; and when nothing changes, we lose our ability to reach and impact people with the Gospel in the EVER CHANGING WORLD AROUND US.

There are far too many congregations that just don't get this. But in every one of them, there are people—literally maybe only one, but usually more—who DO. And chances are really good that those people who "get it", who recognize that God is calling their congregation to GET UN-STUCK—are YOU, the Lay Members and the Clergy Members of Annual Conference. So I want to thank you for being here these past few days, and I want to encourage you to keep on trying to engage your congregation back home with the things you've learned or re-learned here at conference. Because friends, with the help of God WE HAVE TO TURN THIS AROUND!!! NOW! But how? How do we break out of this downward cycle?

I have some ideas!

First, let's start by ACKNOWLEDGING OUR GRIEF. Let's name and claim this painful truth that we HAVE experienced and CONTINUE TO experience great loss as the Church. Let's admit that in our grief we've sometimes held on too tightly to aspects of our church that really only comfort US. Let's ask God to help us learn how to LIVE WITH our grief, so that we won't have to be STUCK and PARALYZED by it. I believe that congregations who learn how to do this will have a BLESSED future. *They are the congregations that will carry the Good News of Jesus Christ forward.*

Second, let's acknowledge that most of the loss we have experienced was actually beyond our control to stop. This may be a new thought for you, so let me tell you why I'm saying this. I learned a vital fact this past year. Statistically, the decline in church membership in the UMC in the USA is DIRECTLY ATTRIBUTABLE to the DECREASE IN THE NUMBER OF CHILDREN we had. You know that our country had a huge baby boom in the years following the end of WWII. At the same time, there was a rise in both prosperity and education. Statistics show that whenever there is a rise in prosperity or a rise in education levels, there is a corresponding decrease in the number of children born. That's exactly what happened to us, and a number of other denominations too. WE HAD FEWER BABIES! And they in turn had fewer babies. Know what this implies? It implies that back in the hey-day—that very hey-day that we're grieving the loss of—when pews were full, and Sunday school classes overflowed with children, and everything seemed to be on the rise.... *THE PRIMARY WAY WE MADE DISCIPLES WAS BY HAVING CHILDREN, AND RAISING THEM IN THE CHURCH.*

It worked! For a while. And then it didn't work anymore.

We had fewer kids. They went away to college. More and more of them didn't come back home to stay. Here in Michigan, it's been even worse. We are the ONLY state that lost population between the census of 2000 and the census of 2010. So please, please, stop beating yourselves up! Because after five years of being a DS, and interacting with thousands of people in local churches, *I am convinced that we really never were taught HOW TO MAKE DISCIPLES beyond our own children and grandchildren and family members in the first place.* We may have been taught how to invite people to church, which is great, but it's not the same as inviting people to know and follow Jesus. Again, I know that there are always exceptions. But I suspect that most of us NEVER LEARNED HOW to make disciples. For some strange reason, we were taught that the PREACHER was going to take care of that! So we weren't taught how to share our faith story with those who aren't Christian. We didn't learn how to pray with and for those who aren't Christian. We rarely saw others invite people outside of their own family members into a relationship with Jesus Christ

IT WAS A PERFECT STORM FOR DECLINE. And we were just happily bobbing along, not fully realizing what was happening around us. So let's stop blaming ourselves and each other so much. It happened. We can't change it. We can only go forward.

Friends, the best way that I know to go forward is to CHANGE OUR FOCUS. We don't need change for the sake of change, or change as a gimmick. But we do need to CHANGE OUR FOCUS. As individuals, as congregations, we need to look OUTWARD. We need to be MISSIONAL. GRIEF has caused us to spend a great deal of our time and energy focusing inward, on ourselves. It's well past time to look out—out at the amazing community of people living right beyond the church's doors. I'm no church guru, but as a DS I have a constant balcony-view of all kinds of churches. The churches in our Conference that are most fruitful RIGHT NOW in helping others connect with Christ have STOPPED looking at their own belly-buttons, STOPPED allowing the walls of the church building to INSULATE them from the community around them, and are ENGAGING WITH THOSE "OTHERS" in wonderful new ways. As Jesus used to say, those fruitful churches are learning how to BE NEIGHBORS. I just recently heard of a 95 year old man who, every time someone new moves in or visits his church, he invites that person or that family over to his house for a banana-split party. And then he also invites some of the friendliest people from his church so they can build relationships over a banana-split. I understand he is very "fruitful" in this approach! Outward focused. Missional. I recently visited a church that took its women's study group out of the church building, into the community, to a local coffee shop. And then—heaven help us!—they switched to some very edgy books that are awesome for fruitful conversations... Conversations between women from the church and women NOT from a church. Outward focused. Missional. Your local church, your Wesley Foundation, your ministry, has been planted by God in a completely unique, one-of-a-kind mission field: YOUR NEIGHBORHOOD. Your community. Discover it! Get to know it! Get to know the people who live there! Build relationships. Respond to needs. Be Jesus Christ to them. Introduce them to him. Welcome them into HIS love and grace. *Stop focusing so desperately on what to do to save your local church. Focus instead on loving God's people around you with the mind-blowing love of Jesus Christ. Then see what God does next.*

Then, take a field trip. *If you remember nothing else of what I've said, remember this. Take a field trip and visit a church that is spiritually healthy and growing in discipleship and disciple-making.* See and experience what's happening. Listen to the pastor and people as they tell you about the journey God has been taking them on. Here is a *partial* list of some that the Cabinet recommends you take your field trip to: Brethren; Centreville; Cornerstone; Grass Lake; Greenville First; Mason; Middleville; Sunnyside; St. John's Pilgrim; Sycamore Creek; Traverse Bay; Water's Edge. There are others. Go, visit, learn. They've clearly got some things figured out, and we would all be blessed to learn from them.

And last but not least, CONSIDER WHEN WOULD BE AN OPPORTUNE TIME FOR YOUR CONGREGATION TO ENGAGE IN VCI—THE VITAL CHURCH INITIATIVE. It's not a program for a quick and easy fix. It's a PROCESS. It requires a hefty commitment of time, energy, learning, creativity, and teamwork on the part of both clergy and laity. But it's one of the best things I've seen come down the pike in a long time! I think it's awesome! And the process can be done by any church of any size or location. Talk to your DS, Gary Step or Naomi Garcia if you'd like to know more.

All of this is to say, DON'T GIVE UP. There is abundant hope for those who are willing to grieve, let go, be missional in focus, learn from others, and embrace change when that is where the Lord is leading. Jesus is LEADING—we are FOLLOWING. If he's leading, it means he's MOVING. He's GOING SOMEWHERE. He says to us, "Come on, get up, let's go!" There is a time to sit at his feet, to listen and to learn—a time that feels safe and comfortable. But it doesn't last long. Before we know it, Jesus is up and out the door! Are we up and out the door after him?

In closing, I'm going to ask again those questions I asked earlier:

You know, don't you, that the Church (with a Capital C) is NOT going to die?

You know, don't you, that the good news message of Jesus Christ will not be silenced?

You know, don't you, that the presence of the Lord with us, and the power of God's Holy Spirit moving and working among us will not be stopped?

When we belong to God, there is ALWAYS a future!

God wins! Christ wins! Perfect love and grace and healing and NEW LIFE WIN! Amen!

Rev. Tamara Williams
Albion District Superintendent

C. TREASURER and BENEFITS OFFICER REPORT

This most generous God who gives seed to the farmer that becomes bread for your meals is more than extravagant with you. He gives you something you can give away, which grows into full-formed lives, robust in God, wealthy in every way, so that you can be generous in every way... Yes, you will be enriched so that you can give even more generously. And when we take your gifts to those who need them, they will break out in thanksgiving to God.

2 Corinthians 9:10-11, The Message

Our connectional giving is about people working together to accomplish something bigger than ourselves. In so doing, we effect change around the world, all in the name of Jesus Christ.

The UMCGiving reports, "The impact of 13 million United Methodists in 136 countries is phenomenal. Together we are witnessing to the love that Jesus Christ has for a hurting world and are transforming lives and communities in his name.

"Together, United Methodists do remarkable ministry around the world. We care for survivors recovering from earthquakes and storms; we invest, long term, in vulnerable communities; we implement the most effective solutions to diseases like malaria; we equip the next generation to lead the church and society. In all of this, we share the good news of Jesus Christ. Through UMC giving, we're prepared to respond to crises, develop innovative solutions to challenges facing communities, advocate for justice and peace and so much more."

So, **Thank You**, West Michigan churches for your generous support of our shared mission and ministry. Your generous contribution enabled the Council on Finance and Administration (CFA) to pay 100% of our apportioned support to the global mission and ministry of The United Methodist Church which is phenomenal, indeed. United Methodist churches, large and small in the United States contributed almost $200 million in 2013. Of that amount we contributed $3,116,967.

From the offering plate to the world. Through our connectional system, your giving in the offering plate reaches many places to bring healing and renewed hope to many people you will never meet. Based on compilation of the 2013 Table II reports, our West Michigan churches provided $71 million to support various ministries. On the average, for every dollar given: 89 cents are spent to undergird the local church program and operation including the outreach and mission directed by the church; 11 cents go to the Conference Treasurer of which 6 cents go to Ministry Shares, 2 cents to the Six-Lanes projects designated by the church, another 2 cents go to pay the apportioned general funds allocated to the conference and I cent goes to the district conference ministries.

Beyond the dollars, our churches served 264,745 persons in community ministries and 16,855 children in VBS. 407 participated in 65 VIM teams and 6,444 went to serve in mission team projects. Our churches served about 265,000 persons in community ministries of justice and mercy and education like day care. More than 1,300 youth attended our conference camps and about 200 students participated in our college campus ministries.

CONFERENCE AND DISTRICT MINISTRY SHARES RECEIPTS		12/31/11	12/31/12	12/31/13
CONFERENCE	Ministry Shares & District Funds Paid	$6,219,893	$6,267,114	$6,376,785
	% Paid	85.1%	86.3%	84.5%
	Special Giving	$1,487,123	$1,380,352	$1,313,466
ALBION	Remittances Year To Date	$809,364	$798,167	$860,773
	% Paid	86.2%	88.6%	87.8%
	Special Giving	$145,273	$140,765	$145,846
HEARTLAND	Remittances Year To Date	$746,739	$763,798	$707,015
	% Paid	90.4%	89.6%	81.9%
	Special Giving	$158,557	$147,875	$151,600
GRAND	Remittances Year To Date	$1,798,355	$1,859,502	$1,882,400
RAPIDS	% Paid	93.9%	95.6%	92.2%
	Special Giving	$443,378	$450,411	$372,921
GRAND	Remittances Year To Date	$812,061	$799,746	$825,705
TRAVERSE	% Paid	85.7%	83.5%	82.0%
	Special Giving	$203,349	$163,241	$166,035
KALAMAZOO	Remittances Year To Date	$1,000,986	$924,915	$989,888
	% Paid	76.9%	72.9%	76.9%
	Special Giving	$266,379	$242,486	$255,334
LANSING	Remittances Year To Date	$1,052,388	$1,120,986	$1,111,004
	% Paid	76.2%	83.9%	81.0%
	Special Giving	$270,187	$235,574	$221,730

SPECIAL GIVING	12/31/11	12/31/12	12/31/13
1. Imagine No Malaria			$76,896
2. Camp Endowment Campaign	$720	$1,543	285
3. Christian Education Sunday Offering	5,259	3,884	4,111
4. Racial Ethnic Local Church Sunday Offering	4,363	6,804	5,724
5. Human Relations Day Offering	15,192	14,002	13,983
6. Rural Life Sunday	4,962	4,091	5,047
7. Peace With Justice Sunday	12,711	12,756	10,798
8. Camp Sunday	7,858	5,877	7,675
9. Native American Ministry Sunday	12,922	14,150	17,246
10. Golden Cross Sunday Offering	5,614	5,338	5,353
11. United Methodist Student Day Offering	10,154	7,915	9,061
12. World Communion Offering	17,335	17,808	18,887
13. One Great Hour of Sharing	72,687	77,190	71,208
14. Africa University Endowment Fund	3,046	142	487
15. World Missionary Support	174,584	137,073	139,581
16. World Mission Projects	148,692	183,436	208,629
17. United Methodist Children's Fund	1,048	0	1,010

19. National Missions		60,001	51,186	47,132
20. Appalachia Service Project		0	0	0
21. U.M.C.O.R.		685,359	558,275	596,494
22. Ethnic Ministries		22,635	19,013	26,402
23. Conference Ministries		218,298	267,683	138,154
24. Other Benevolences		3,683	-7,815	-90,698
Giving Summary	Special Giving	$1,487,123	$1,380,351	$1,313,465
	District Funds	$491,506	$507,432	$512,070
	Conference Ministry Shares	***$5,741,225***	***$5,759,683***	***$5,864,716***
	TOTAL RECEIPTS	$7,707,016	$7,647,466	$7,690,251
	Conference Budget	$6,159,550	$5,951,495	$6,085,389
	% of Conference Budget Received	***93.2%***	***96.8%***	***96.4%***

Conference Ministry Shares Expenditures

Praise God for the provision that is given to administer God's grace in various forms (1Pe 4:10).

Superintendency and Ministerial Support	$ 1,615,673	28%
Conference Program Ministries	$ 1,458,474	25%
New Church Development	$ 313,317	5%
Conference and Area Administration	$ 786,929	13%
World Service and General Church Apportionments	$ 1,686,199	29%
Total	$ 5,860,592	100%

Conference Property: The Conference property and equipment was valued at $2.4 million net of depreciation with acquisition cost of $5.6 million. The Board of Trustees holds the deeds of all Conference real property. The Conference Board of Christian Camping operates the five camp sites (Albright, Crystal Springs, Lakeview, Lake Michigan and Wesley Woods). Other conference real property directly managed by the Board includes five parsonages (in Lansing, Kalamazoo, Grand Rapids, Traverse City and Mt. Pleasant), the Conference Center in Grand Rapids, and the bishop's residence in DeWitt Township which is jointly owned with the Detroit Conference. The bishop's residence in DeWitt was made ready for the new episcopal area leader, Bishop Deb Kiesey. Several repairs and updates on the property were done for about $20,000. This sum was provided by the Area Capital Fund which is jointly owned with the Detroit Annual Conference. The Area Capital Fund was left over from the sale of the bishop's residence in Southfield after Bishop Ott completed his term in 2004.

The Lansing District parsonage was sold on September 18, 2013 for $205,000 and the net proceeds of $188,000 were invested in the UM Foundation of Michigan. The Trustees investments had a balance of $355,969 designated for conference parsonage capital fund.

Pension and Health Care: The 2012 General Conference approved significant changes in the Clergy pension program called the Clergy Retirement Security Plan. These changes are found in the Board of Pension and Health Benefits report in Volume 1 of the Conference Journal. Another significant mandate under paragraph 1506.8 of the 2012 Book of Discipline requires the annual conference to develop, adopt and implement a formal funding plan for all its benefit obligations. The Funding Plan was approved by the Conference of Pension and Health Benefits and received a favorable opinion from the General Board of Pension and Health. Following is the West Michigan 2015 Comprehensive Benefit Funding Plan Summary.

West Michigan Annual Conference

2015 Comprehensive Benefit Funding Plan Summary

The 2012 *Book of Discipline* ¶ 1506.6 requires that each annual conference develop, adopt and implement a formal comprehensive funding plan for funding all of its benefit obligations. The funding plan shall be submitted annually to the General Board of Pension and Health benefits for review and be approved annually by the annual conference Board of Pension and Health Benefits. Following the receipt and inclusion of a favorable written opinion from the General Board of Pension and Health Benefits (GBOPHB), this summary document which is only a portion of the information contained in the actual signed funding plan is hereby published in the Conference Journal as part of the Conference Treasurer and Benefits Officer's Report. As such, it might not contain all the information required for a comprehensive view of the benefit obligations of the conference. You may request the full contents of the 2015 comprehensive benefit funding plan from your conference benefit office.

Following is the summary of the Comprehensive Benefit Funding Plan (CBFP) that received a favorable written opinion from GBOPHB for the 2015 conference benefit obligations:

Clergy Retirement Security Program (CRSP) Defined Benefit (DB) and Defined Benefit Contribution (DC)

Plan Overview: The Clergy Retirement Security Program (CRSP) is an Internal Revenue Code section 403(b) retirement program providing lifetime income and account flexibility designed for those who serve as clergy of The United Methodist Church. The plan is designed to provide participants with one portion of their overall retirement portfolio. CRSP replaced the Ministerial Pension Plan (MPP) effective January 1, 2007, which replaced the Pre-82 for service rendered prior to January 1, 1982

CRSP consists of both a defined benefit (DB) plan, which provides a monthly benefit at retirement based upon years of credited service to the Church, and a defined contribution (DC) plan, which provides a retirement account balance established and funded by annual conferences. The Clergy Retirement Security Program (CRSP-DB) annuities total liability as of January 1, 2013 is $923.7 million, while total plan assets are $978.5 million resulting in a current plan funded ratio of 106%. The West Michigan Conference portion of the liability is 1.43% and the 2015 contribution is $1,381,701. The conference anticipates that the amount will be funded by: Direct Billing. Additionally, General Conference 2012 approved a change to CRSP that provides each annual conference the discretion to determine whether to cover three-quarter and/or half-time clergy. The West Michigan Annual Conference has elected to cover clergy serving 50%+ under CRSP effective January 1, 2015.

Effective January 1, 2014 CRSP-DC plan was reduced from a 3% to a 2% of plan compensation non-matching contribution. Clergy will have the opportunity to earn up to an additional 1% CRSP DC contribution by contributing at least 1% of their plan compensation to UMPIP, therefore if a participant contributes at least 1% of plan compensation to UMPIP, the individual will receive a contribution of 3%, which is unchanged from 2013 and prior. The 2013 CRSP-DC contribution was $480,800 and was funded by: Direct bill to churches. It is anticipated that increases for future years will average 3.00%, due to: CAC trend but fewer may be eligible. Less than half-time will not qualify in CRSP.

Ministerial Pension Plan (MPP)

Plan Overview: The Ministerial Pension Plan (MPP) provides clergy with a pension for their years of ministry with The United Methodist Church from 1982 through 2006. MPP is an Internal Revenue Code section 403(b) retirement plan. Effective January 1, 2014, exactly 65% of the account balance must be annuitized when it is to be distributed. The remainder may be rolled over to UMPIP, another qualified plan or IRA, or paid in a lump sum.

The Ministerial Pension Plan (MPP) annuities total liability as of January 1, 2013 is $2.7 billion, while total plan assets are $3.0 billion resulting in a current plan funded ratio of 109% and no required contribution for 2015. The West Michigan Conference's portion of the total liability is 1.50%. Future MPP annuitants have a total account balance of $4.4 billion and the West Michigan Conference's portion of that balance is $62.68 million or 1.43% of the total.

Pre-1982 Plan

Plan Overview: Supplement One to the Clergy Retirement Security Program (CRSP), also known as the Pre-82 Plan, provides clergy with a pension for their years of ministry with The United Methodist Church prior to 1982. The Pre-82 Plan was replaced by MPP effective January 1, 1982. When participants enter a Retired relationship with your Conference, and does not terminate, the minimum benefit payable to them is based on two factors: 1) years of Service with pension credit and 2) Conference pension rate. Years of Service with pension credit are approved by each Conference on the recommendation of the Conference Board of Pensions in accordance with plan provisions and *The Book of Discipline*. The pension rate, also called the past service rate PSR), is the dollar amount chosen by the Conference as the amount payable for each approved year of Service with pension credit. Typically, the pension rate changes from year to year. The number of years of Service with pension credit is multiplied by the PSR, and the product is the minimum annual benefit payable to those eligible for Pre-82 Plan benefits. In certain situations the benefit received from the Pre-82 plan, may vary based on the applicability of what is referred to as Defined Benefit Service Money (DBSM), which is the defined contribution feature of the Pre-1982 Plan. At the time that a participant retires, the DBSM account is converted to a life based benefit. At that point the participants benefit is the greater of the PSR benefit or DBSM benefit. As the conference increases the PSR, the participants benefit is recalculated; however the DBSM based benefit does not change.

The 2015 Past Service Rate (PSR) recommended to the West Michigan Annual Conference will be $726.00 representing no increase from the 2014 rate. The conference expects future increases to be approximately 2.00%, which is based on increases not to exceed 2%. The contingent annuitant percentage is recommended to remain at the 85% level.

Based on the final actuarial valuations from the General Board of Pensions and Health Benefits as of January 1, 2013 for 2015, the portion of the Pre-82 liability attributable to the West Michigan Conference and funded status is, as of 1/1/2013, as follows:

Funding Plan Liability $40,521,511
Assets in the Plan $43,940,289
Funded status .... $3,418,778 represented by a 108% funded ratio

(Defined benefit plan liabilities (Pre-82, MPP and CRSP-DB) continue until the last benefit is paid to participants and their surviving spouses irrespective of the funding level of the plan. That is, even if the assets in the plan are larger than the liabilities in the plan, the conference still has a liability (obligation) with the plan.)

Active Health Benefit Program

Plan Overview: The West Michigan Conference offers a Self-Insured program to the active participants. During the 2013 year, the total cost of the program was $4,310,493 and was funded by Salary paying units (churches and conference) pay 85% and participants pay 15%. The projected average increase for future years is expected to be 5%, due to: medical inflation.

Post-Retirement Medical Benefit Program (PRM)

Plan Overview: The West Michigan Conference post-retiree medical plan (PRM) currently offered to eligible retirees and their dependents. The PRM is a supplement to Medicare Part B with $1,000 Deductible Rider with United American Insurance Company and Pharmacy benefit with Express Script.

The current annual cost is anticipated to be $1,082,748 with the funding sources to be: Incoming money provided by churches and participants contributing at least 30% of cost per person. On a longer term basis the West Michigan Conference intends to arrive at a contribution of 50-50 ratio between churches and participants. Additionally, churches are billed $1,500 annually per FTE clergy appointment. To effectively manage the PRM program, actuarial study of post-retirement medical liability is done at least every 2 years.

Based on the most recent PRM valuation dated Planned by: 4/15/2014, following is the funded position of the post-retiree medical benefits:

Accumulated Post Retirement Obligation (APBO) or net conference cost $14,266,000
Expected Post Retirement Obligation (EPBO) or net conference cost $15,924,000
Service Cost (SC) or net conference cost $202,000
Assets designated for PRM $9,500,000

These values are based on 6% long term discount rate, 6% long-term expected return, and a current increase trend of 7% decreasing to 5% by 2016.

Comprehensive Protection Plan (CPP)

Plan Overview: The Comprehensive Protection Plan (CPP) provides death, long-term disability and other welfare benefits for eligible clergy of The United Methodist Church and their families and is an Internal Revenue Code 414(e) "church plan" funded by plan sponsor insurance premiums. Generally, you are eligible to participate in CPP if your conference or salary-paying unit sponsors the plan and you satisfy the eligibility requirements which include full-time episcopal appointment and plan compensation equal to or greater than 60% of the Denominational Average Compensation or the Conference Average Compensation whichever is less. The West Michigan Annual Conference has elected to make CPP-eligible clergy, who are appointed at least 50%, have mandatory participation.

Currently (for 2013) the West Michigan Conference has a required contribution to the Comprehensive Protection Plan of $444,610, which is anticipated to be funded by direct bill to churches. The anticipated average increase in future years is expected to be 3.00% per year due to: CAC average trend.

United Methodist Personal Investment Plan (UMPIP) for Lay and Clergy

Plan Overview: The United Methodist Personal Investment Plan (UMPIP) is an Internal Revenue Code section 403(b) defined contribution retirement savings plan for clergy and lay employees of The United Methodist Church and affiliated organizations. Participants may make before-tax and/or after-tax contributions through payroll deductions. Participant contributions, contributions your plan sponsor may make on the participants behalf and investment earnings comprise the individual's retirement account balance.

Conference office lay employees working an average of 30 hours per week or more are eligible upon employment for a pension contribution of 9% of salary. Lay employees are encouraged to contribute personal funds toward their retirement through payroll deductions to the UMPIP. The estimated contribution for the West Michigan Conference is anticipated to be $89,680 and funded through the conference budget.

Conclusion:

The 2015 Comprehensive Benefit Funding Plan and the above outlined Summary document incorporates to the best of our understanding , the West Michigan Conference's obligations and funding requirements of the benefits provided to the Clergy and Laity of the West Michigan Conference.

General Board of Pension and Health Benefits

Opinion on West Michigan 2015 Comprehensive Benefit Funding Plan

This Funding Plan meets the standards for a Pre-82 funding plan as established by the General Board, and the requirements for a favorable opinion of a Funding Plan.

Note: The statement above and any written opinion provided by the General Board do not imply any representation as to the ability or probability of the applicable Conference to fulfill the obligations included in the Funding Plan.

General Board of Pension and Health Benefits

Glenview, Illinois

I am blessed to serve along the various agencies to advance the mission and ministry of the Conference and The United Methodist Church. Without the support and diligence of my associates in the Treasurer's Office, this ministry would not be possible. I acknowledge with gratitude the dedication and diligence of Russ Geske, John Kosten and Ann Buck. And to the members of the CFA, the Board of Pension and Health Benefits, and the Board of Trustees, a big thank you for your invaluable counsel and support.

Pros Tumonong
Conference Treasurer and Benefits Officer

D. BOARD OF MINISTRIES REPORT

Well friends, it has been a privilege to serve on the Board of Ordained Ministry for the last eight years and to serve as chair for the last three. Many of you have asked me in the hall what the board of ordained ministry does as much of it is behind the scenes, so a little bit of education is in order.

The Board of Ordained Ministry is responsible for the credentialing of clergy. This means it supervises the entire candidacy process. And this includes the credentialing of local pastors with the help of the District Committees on Ministry, all deacons, associate members, elders and clergy with specialized ministry certificates. The Board is responsible for monitoring and facilitating all changes in conference relationships, such as leaves of absence and honorable locations, and for the support and development of clergy, for enlistment and mentoring, and for supervising the candidacy process. It is a huge job, one for which all of us on the Board feel inadequate, and yet the members of the Board generally love our work and count it a privilege to serve on the Board.

The Board works closely with the Bishop and Cabinet on many of matters of concern and interest for our collective live in the church, but also maintains a checks and balances relationship with the, the Board being responsible for credentialing, and the Bishop and Cabinet being responsible for supervision and appointment making. This is usually a healthy division of labor.

This year, we are receiving into membership seven provisional members: Steve Lindeman, Heather Molner and Chad Parmalee who interviewed with the Board in March; Gary Simmons who is ordained in another denomination and is seeking membership and recognition of his orders in the West Michigan Conference, and three individuals, Jack Conklin, Jim Noggle and Dennis Bromley, who are long time Associate members who are now provisional members on their way to full membership. These individuals were voted into provisional membership at the clergy session and 4 of them will be commissioned at the Ordination Service.

In addition, we have five individuals who were voted into full membership at the clergy session and will be ordained as Elders at the ordination service; Letisha Bowman, Cathy Christman, Patty Haas, Jon Van Dop, and Rebecca Wieringa. These individuals have been in this process for many years, from being inquiring candidates, through seminary and provisional membership, and now as full member elders. Congratulations to all of these individuals moving forward in new ways to serve Christ.

Throughout the year, the Board of Ordained Ministry works on a variety of matters to improve our life together and help us serve the church more effectively. I would like to highlight just a few of the important things on the Board's plate.

First, I want to reiterate that last year we adopted an online policy due to the changing nature of education in our world. This policy is on the Conference website. For local pastors, in accordance with the Discipline, up to ½ of Course of Study may be taken online. For those going to seminary, we are abiding by the decision of the University Senate last year, up to 2/3 of seminary education can be taken online. And for those who need United Methodist courses in history, doctrine and polity, those can now be taken online through the General Board of Higher Education and Ministry.

Second, as you know, a few years ago, the Board and Cabinet adopted a document on clergy effectiveness. I would remind all clergy and local churches that this effectiveness document is in place and accessible and can easily be tapped for both evaluation and improvement. Ways to implement that and keep it in front of us are always being looked at. This year you can expect some new Charge Conference documents that more closely connect the evaluation forms with the effectiveness document. This is a step in the right direction.

A major task of the Board and Cabinet together over the next years will be the enlistment and recruiting of clergy. Due to our demographics and the upcoming retirement of many of our clergy, we are facing a clergy shortage. As the Bishop has mentioned, everyone has the job of recruiting clergy. And this is confession time for the Board—we have been a bit complacent in recruiting since for many years it has always just worked out—the number of people coming in has matched the number of people going out. But we are entering into a new time and the Board has received its wake-up call to be stronger in its recruiting efforts.

Finally, I want to thank those who have served in this important work. Would the members of the Board please stand. If you serve on or have ever served on a District Committee on Ministry, please stand. You are the most important people in this process and you receive the least amount of recognition or thanks.

At Clergy Session we elected Jeremy Wicks as the new Chair of the John Wesley Association.

This year we have several Board Members who are rotating off: Myself, Sharon Purdy, Julie Liske, Mike Reigler and Jack Conklin. Thank you for your service.

And I am very pleased to inform you that the new chair of the Board will be Sherri Swanson.

And now I'd like to introduce Lynn Pier-Fitzgeralds, Chair of the Order of Elders.

John Boley
Chair, Board of Ministry

E. CONFERENCE LAY LEADERS' REPORT

Traditional and Impossible are two words that describe a "Lay Report". Traditional in that this job has been tackled by many before me. Giving thanks for the year—which we do—and carving up the praise—which we do a lot of in this space.

At the same time "Impossible" is the word. There are so many members of the laity, each unique. It is impossible to see the all of the large things, let alone the small things at work in our congregations and our lives. How do you measure the underground current of activities and changes? Some people track numbers. Some people take samples or stories. Impossible to know all things.

My friends in the DNR complimented Oceana County on the velocity of its ground water. Not Tahquamenon Falls, not Lake Michigan with a northwest wind. No, ground water, living water that keeps us vital. This morning I'd like to talk about this underground current in our church.

So water! Verses from John's gospel and two songs come to mind: The scripture is John 7, Jesus asked for water from the well. He was human and thirsty and asked for that very basic thing—water.

And then he offered water, living water…and that is the captivating part of the story. Peter, Paul and Mary lifted up the old song: Jesus met the woman at the well. "And he told her everything she'd ever done." And Jesus knows every thing—clergy and lay---we've ever done. Talk about transparency! That would be an interesting report!

There is a second song—you might remember it from camp, a silly circular song going back campfires and bus rides "There's a hole in the bucket". Dear Lisa, Dear Lisa…with what shall I mend it Dear Georgie, Dear Georgie? (She was a little whiny as you recall) with straw then dear Lisa. If the straw is too long? Then cut it, deal Lisa. With a knife dear Lisa. But my knife is too dull, dear Georgie. Then whet it, Lisa! But stone is too dry. Then wet it. Lisa. What shall I wet it, Georgie? With water, Lisa. But I have a hole in my bucket!

And that might be a report from our part of the world.

Tip O'Neil told fellow legislators that "all politics is local"

We are finding out in the church that all disciples are local. If you are going to make disciples for the transformation of the world, it is local. This is the time of the local church. And it is a time when a local church can reach around the world. And some do! And it is time to be reaching out in our communities. Turning hearts and minds, teaching, tending, caring, helping, building, correcting—are all individual actions. Actions of individuals. Making disciples one heart at a time.

It is as if we are with Jesus at that well in Samaria. Hot, dry, dusty, no holds barred. "And he told her everything she'd ever done". A time for honesty, not pomposity.

On this June day in 2014, our congregations are at that well
Some people are thirsty
Some are ladling water
And some are standing back

Some are thirsty for living water
Some are ladling living water
And some are standing back

Some are thirsty for living water—and don't know it. They are dehydrated, dried up
Some are ladling living water—by the teaspoon, by the pint, the quart, the fire hose.
Some are standing back, hesitating, a little frightened.

And some churches need new points on their wells.

As the camp song goes, there's a hole in the bucket. We are not perfect. That's our report.

BUT—there is hope…not for perfection…but for a better bucket.

We are fixing that leaking bucket

Vital Church Initiative is really a plumbing repair program

REPORTS

Reorganizing the camp program or Higher Ed or youth ministries—revitalizing is a source of living water

Cooperative parishes—another plumbing program—let the water flow

Local churches reaching out to Africa, Syria, Lithuania, urban neighborhoods, planning, Justice for our Neighbors, Hispanic Ministries. Social media, church in a diner, free stores…reaching out to extend the lines from the well.

No one likes to see the plumber coming…expense, mess, change. Change is hard. I thought this copper piping would last forever!

We've been grumpy, short tempered, "my way or the high-way" at times. The Changes coming through the church, (Capital C) the churches, through families and communities produce a lot of pressure. Anyone who has been through Vital Church Initiative can attest to that.

At least we know our bucket is leaking and we know that Jesus said "carry water to the world". As practical people living in the world to be transformed, we are working on it.

That's our lay report. We are a connectional system. We are Jesus bucket brigade. We are not the living water but we steward that water and carry that water and share that water from the well that is our father. The H hole requires a W Whole.

Praise be to God.

Anne Soles
West Michigan Conference Lay Leader

—WMC Photos

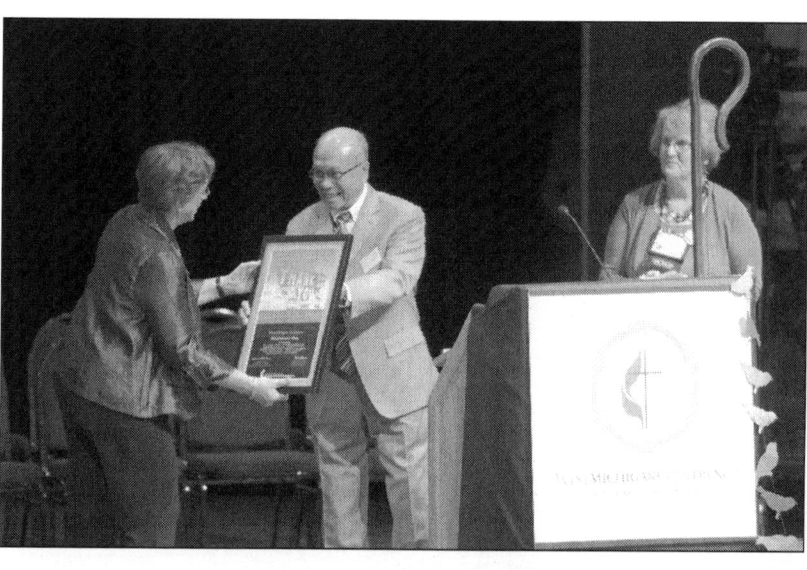

IX. LEGISLATION

A. LEGISLATIVE ACTION INDEX

ANNUAL CONFERENCE PETITIONS				
ITEM #	PAGE	SUBJECT	ACTION	COMMITTEE/ PERSON IMPLEMENTATION
1	201	Divestment	Passed	Finance & Administration and Pension, Health & Benefits
1.R	306	Divestment: Substitution	Accepted by Committee	–
2	201	Finance And Accounting	Passed	Finance & Administration
3	202	Funding Formula for Higher Ed. & Campus Min.	Passed With Amendment	Finance & Administration
3-R	306	Response: AMENDMENT funding – Board of Higher Ed	Passed By Committee	–
4	203	Renewed Covenant Rel. Eglise Meth d'Haiti/ Mich Area UMC	Passed	Global Ministries
5	204	Immigrant Reform	Passed	Church & Society
6	204	Support for Ministry to All Persons	Passed With Amendment	Church & Society, local churches
6-R1	307	Response: AMENDMENT 1 Support for All Persons	Passed	–
6-R2	307	Response to Pet 6 AMENDMENT 2 Support for all Persons	Passed	–
7	205	Minimum Salary Support for 2015	Passed	Equitable Compensation.
8	207	Guidelines for Equitable Comp. Support	Passed	Equitable Compensation, Dist. Superintendents
9	207	Ministers' Reserve Pension Fund (MRPF) Pre-82 Past Service Rate	Passed	Pension, Health, & Benefits
10	207	Annual Policy Recommendations for 2015	Passed	Finance & Administration, local churches
11	209	Rules of Order Amendment to Various Rules	Passed	Rules of Order
11-R	308	Response to Pet 11: AMENDMENT Amendment various rules	Failed	–
12	211	Rules of Order - Rules 26 & 29 Amendments	Passed	Rules of Order
13	211	Rules of Order - New Rule 36: Addition of Committee on Gen Conf. Pet.	Passed	Rules of Order

ITEM #	PAGE	SUBJECT	ACTION	IMPLEMENTATION
14	213	Plan of Org: CLT Purpose and Relationship – Amendment	Passed	Rules of Order
15	213	Plan of Org: Reassigning Duties of Board of Discipleship	Passed	Rules of Order
16	214	Plan of Org: CLT Chair Selected by Nomination Committee Amendments	Passed	Rules of Order
16-R	308	Response to Pet 16 SUBSTITUTION	Passed by Committee	–
17	214	West Mich Budget Recommendations for 2015	Passed	Finance & Administration and Conference Leadership Team
17	302	West Mich Budget Recommendations for 2015 UPDATED	–	Finance & Administration and Conference Leadership Team
18	305	Kalamazoo Wesley Foundation Loan	Passed	Finance & Administration
19	305	BCC Special Conference Wide Financial Appeal	Passed	Finance & Administration and Conference Leadership Team and local churches
CS-I	309	Discontinuation of Waterloo First UMC	Passed	District Superintendents
CS-2	0	Discontinue Parma UMC	Passed	District Superintendents
CS-3		Osseo UMC Merged with North Adams UMC	No Action – Information Only	District Superintendents

B. ANNUAL CONFERENCE PETITIONS
LEGISLATIVE ITEMS THAT PASSED

ITEM #1
SUBJECT: **Divestment.**
RESULT: **PASSED (as amended)**

MOTION: **The West Michigan Conference of The United Methodist Church calls on the leadership of the governments of the United States, Israel and Palestine to reject all acts of aggression and violence, to respect the equality and dignity of the region's people, and to forge solutions based on the principles of non-violence, international law, and human rights.**

ACTION: The Conference Finance Administration (CFA), Conference Board of Pension and Health Benefits (CBOPHB), and Conference Board of Trustees shall direct their Investment Managers, which include the United Methodist Foundation of Michigan and the General Board of Pension and Health Benefits, to review and research companies within their respective investment portfolios that attain material benefit from the occupation of Palestine, so that the respective conference agencies will be informed accordingly. Their finding shall be included each year in their reports to the West Michigan Annual Conference in Volume 1 of the Conference Journal.

Rev. Lou Grettenberger, Chair, on behalf of the
Board of Pension and Health Benefits
West Michigan Conference

ITEM #2
SUBJECT: **Finance and Accounting.** *(See page 180 of the 2013 Conference Journal Vol. 2)*
RESULT: **PASSED (as amended)**

MOTION: **Amend Finance and Accounting Policy of the Annual Conference by deleting paragraphs 10 and 12, inserting a new paragraph 10, and editing paragraph 11 as follows:**

10. It is the responsibility of the Council on Finance and Administration to receive, consider, report, and make recommendations to the annual conference regarding the following prior to final decision by the annual conference:
  (a) any proposal to raise capital funds for any purpose;
  (b) funding considerations related to any proposal that may come before the conference;
  (c) any requests to conduct a special conference-wide financial appeal, whether by special collections, campaigns, or otherwise in the local churches of the conference.

11. Request for conference funding of projects, programs, or agencies located within a district shall be presented for information to the District Council on Ministries or equivalent ministries before being presented to a conference program board, the Conference Leadership Team, or the Council on Finance and Administration. The funding request shall include:
  [1] the amount to be requested from the conference,
  [2] the total budget projected, including anticipated income and estimated expenditures, and
  [3] a separate listing of United Methodist sources of income anticipated or to be solicited.

Exceptions to this are the conference-related institutions of Adrian and Albion colleges, Bronson Methodist Hospital, campus ministries, Methodist Children's Home, Clark Retirement Community, and state-wide interdenominational bodies which may continue to make requests directly to the related conference agency board. These provisions shall apply to emergency askings as well as to annual budget requests.

Susan Cobb, President
Council on Finance and Administration

ITEM #3
SUBJECT: **Funding Formula for the Board of Higher Education and Campus Ministry.**
RESULT: **PASSED (as amended)**

MOTION: **The Conference Budget proposed by the Council on Finance and Administration, shall contain a line item for the Board of Higher Education and Campus Ministry equal to at least 5.2 times the "Estimated Basic Expense of a Minimum Salary Elder with Parsonage, Health Care, Pension, Travel, and Professional Expenses" of the current year, as determined by the conference "Guidelines on Basic Pastoral Related Expenses."**
Reflecting this 5.2 formula, the 2015 Budget amount for the Board of Higher Education and Campus Ministry shall be set to $360,000.

West Michigan Conference Board of Higher Education
and Campus Ministries, Jeff Williams, Chair

ITEM #4

SUBJECT: **Renewed Covenant Relationship Between Eglise Methodiste d'Haiti / Michigan Area United Methodist Church.**

RESULT: **PASSED**

MOTION: **The Conference Board of Global Ministries and the Michigan Area Haiti Task Force recommend the renewal of the 1996 Haiti Covenant Relationship with the following document.**

Eglise Methodiste d'Haiti / Michigan Area United Methodist Church Covenant Relationship 2014

Be it resolved that the West Michigan Annual Conference of The United Methodist Church enter into a revised Covenant Relationship with Eglise Methodiste d'Haiti District of The Methodist Church of the Caribbean and the Americas as described in the following document; and

Be it further resolved that this covenant relationship be in cooperation with the West Michigan Annual Conference of The United Methodist Church, thus re-authorizing the Michigan Area Covenant with the Eglise Methodiste d'Haiti District of The Methodist Church of the Caribbean and the Americas.

In thankful recognition and faithful allegiance to the call of the Holy Spirit who equips and enables the church community to be in ministry and mission together, we join in partnership for the advancement of Christ, and we respond in faith and love reaching beyond our geographic boundaries in mutual servanthood. The Eglise Methodiste d'Haiti of The Methodist Church of the Caribbean and the Americas and the Michigan Area of The United Methodist Church join together our gifts and graces in shared vision of ministry.

We will partner together for the advancement of Jesus Christ and jointly commit ourselves to:

1. Pray for each other on a regular and recurring basis;
2. Work together in a supporting and mutual relationship as the pastors, people, congregations; circuits; and districts;
3. Help the people in the District and the conferences to learn about each other, including our history and cultures our blessings and challenges, our faith and life;
4. Encourage church–to–church, and pastor-to-pastor relationships for mutual learning, support and growth;
5. Exchange information and establish processes to evaluate the various projects and their socioeconomic impact through joint partnership teams and establish a means for effective and regular communication among the leaders of both the District and the conferences;
6. Develop procedures that will assist in timely, accountable, and transparent transfer of funds for us in implementing the projects and ministries made possible through this covenant;
7. Exchange leadership between the District and the conferences to interpret the work and mission and to generate understanding and support;
8. Actively promote the understanding and sharing of the joint resources of the District and conferences with emphasis on the 50/50 sharing in planning, resourcing, and carrying out our joint ministries;
9. Promote the Advance Specials relating to the Haiti District, especially the Haiti Hot Lunch Program;
10. Encourage participation in the United Methodist Volunteers in Mission

(UMVIM) program;

11. Report, each year, to our governing bodies regarding the projects and ministries being implemented through this covenant relationship;
12. Advocate FOR the People of Haiti for peace, justice, hope, and the redemption and transformation of the world;
13. Cooperate and coordinate with other agencies, organizations, programs and projects who share these and similar goals, especially UMCOR, UMVIM, the General Board of Global Ministries, and other conferences and churches;

A program for the training of lay ministers strengthening their faith and enabling them to support the Christian families is needed. This program will assist in strengthening the faithful and especially promote the evangelical expansion of the Church. In addition, this program will strengthen the lay ministers and equip them to support and encourage people in their faith, and;

This Covenant replaces in its entirety the Covenant Relationship between the Haiti District of The Methodist Church of the Caribbean and the Americas adopted in June, 1996.

The Rev. Gesner Paul, President, Eglise Methodiste d'Haiti District of The Methodist Church of the Caribbean and the Americas
Bishop Deborah Kiesey, Resident Bishop of The Michigan Area of The United Methodist Church
The Rev. Donald D. Gotham, Chair, Board of Global Ministries of the Detroit Annual Conference
Lynda Zeller, Chair, Board of Global Ministries of the West Michigan Annual Conference

RATIONALE: In 1996, under the leadership of the late Rev. Paul Doherty, the Michigan Area Haiti Task Force facilitated a covenant between the Boards of Global Ministries of the Detroit and West Michigan annual conferences and the Eglise Methodiste d'Haiti District of The Methodist Church of the Caribbean and the Americas.

Over these past 18 years we have grown in our love for the people and church leadership in Haiti. Leadership has changed in both our conferences and in the Haitian church. As Volunteer in Mission teams have gone and returned, and we have responded to the aftermath of hurricanes and earthquakes, and working with the leadership of the Haitian church, and being led by the Holy Spirit, representatives of both conferences came together to draft a new covenant. It was affirmed by the Eglise Methodiste d'Haiti in January 2014 at their annual meeting and is now before us for ratification.
(It should be noted for clarification, the "District" is the way the Eglise Methodiste d'Haiti refers to itself as a part of The Methodist Church of the Caribbean and the Americas, and should not be confused with our conference "districts".)

Lynda Zeller, Chair, West Michigan Conference Board of Global Ministries
David Morton, Co-Chair, Michigan Area Haiti Task Force

ITEM #5
SUBJECT: **Immigration Reform.**
RESULT: **PASSED (as amended)**

MOTION: **The West Michigan Conference urges our federal legislators to continue to work diligently toward a pathway to citizenship for the 11 million undocumented immigrants living and/or working in the United States.**

West Michigan Conference Board of Church and Society
Ellen A. Brubaker, Chair

ITEM #6
SUBJECT: **Support for Ministry to All Persons.**
RESULT: **PASSED (as amended)**

MOTION: **That the West Michigan Annual Conference adopt the following resolution:**

Whereas, the United Methodist Social Principles (2012) states:

"We implore families and churches not to reject or condemn lesbian and gay members and friends. We commit ourselves to be in ministry for and with all persons."

Whereas, consistent with this core principle of The United Methodist Church, at its 2013 session our annual conference adopted a resolution called Welcoming All Persons Into Local Church Community which said:
"The West Michigan Conference encourages all congregations to welcome into their congregational community gay, lesbian, bisexual and transgendered individuals and couples, welcoming them into full participation. We encourage pastors to provide care to all individuals and couples, regardless of their sexual orientation. We encourage our churches to make this openness known in as many ways as possible."

Whereas, in response to these statements in the Social Principles and last year's conference resolution as well as living out the understanding of their call, over 1200 clergy across the church, including upwards of 100 in our annual conference, have borne witness to a call for "An Act of Biblical Obedience," declaring their willingness to perform marriages between prepared same-sex couples in the normal course of their pastoral duties.

Now therefore, we encourage all United Methodists within our annual conference and beyond, lay and clergy, in accordance with our membership vows to "resist evil, injustice, and oppression in whatever forms they present themselves," by supporting spiritually, emotionally and prayerfully the issue of marriage equality and the clergy and local congregations who faithfully minister to all persons, courageously risking any consequences for their living fully into the duty of performing marriages for all people.

The West Michigan Conference desires a cessation of church trials for conducting ceremonies which celebrate homosexual unions or performing same-sex wedding ceremonies and instead recommend we continue a process of theological, spiritual, and ecclesiastical conversation.

Further, we ask that members of the West Michigan Annual Conference hold our divided denomination in prayer out of our love for the unity of Christ's church.

David Lundquist, Deb Search Willoughby, Jim Willoughby, and Molly Williams, lay members, Kalamazoo First UMC
Ellen Brubaker, John Ross Thompson, Joe Bistayi, Ed Perkins, and Susan Hagans, clergy retired
George Bob, lay member, Grand Rapids First UMC
Gerald Hagans, clergy/pastor, Sitka UMC
Georgia Marsh, lay member, Marshall UMC
Douglas Vernon, clergy/pastor, Lawton St. Paul's UMC
Mark Thompson, clergy/pastor, Grand Rapids Faith UMC
Jim Searls, lay member, Holland First UMC
Zach and Lindsay Oaster, lay members, Georgetown UMC
Barry Petrucci, clergy/pastor, Portage: Chapel Hill UMC
Veroneze and Dick Strader, lay members, Battle Creek Maple UMC
Ryan Minier, lay member, Kalamazoo Wesley Foundation

ITEM #7
SUBJECT: **Minimum Salary Support for 2015.**
RESULT: **PASSED (as amended)**

MOTION: **The Commission on Equitable Compensation recommends the following Minimum Salary Schedule be adopted for 2015.**

In addition, churches and ministries shall budget a minimum of $1,500 for professional expenses and continuing education, exclusive of mileage reimbursements, for each full time clergy person under appointment. In cases of less than full time appointment, it is recommended that the budgeted amount be prorated in accordance with the appointment (i.e., ½ Time = $750, etc.)

2015 Minimum Salary Schedule

	Full Time Local Pastor		**Associate Member**	
	2014	**2015**	**2014**	**2015**
Year 1	**33,767**	**34,105**	*	*
Year 2	**34,106**	**34,447**	*	*
Year 3	**34,444**	**34,788**	*	*
Year 4	**34,781**	**35,129**	*	*
Year 5	**35,120**	**35,471**	**36,704**	**37,071**
Year 6	**35,458**	**35,813**	**37,068**	**37,439**
Year 7	**35,795**	**36,153**	**37,433**	**37,807**
Year 8	**36,134**	**36,495**	**37,802**	**38,180**
Year 9	**36,473**	**36,838**	**38,174**	**38,556**
Year 10	**36,810**	**37,178**	**39,419**	**39,813**
YOS	**372**		**398**	

	Provisional Member		Full Member	
	2014	2015	2014	2015
Year 1	37,682	38,059	**	**
Year 2	38,058	38,439	**	**
Year 3	38,435	38,819	40,208	40,610
Year 4	38,812	39,200	40,618	41,024
Year 5	39,187	39,579	41,025	41,435
Year 6	39,564	39,960	41,434	41,844
Year 7	39,941	40,340	41,796	42,214
Year 8	40,318	40,721	42,243	42,665
Year 9	40,694	41,101	42,651	43,078
Year 10	41,071	41,482	43,058	43,489
YOS	415		435	

$200 shall be added to the Minimum for a 2-Point Charge
$350 shall be added to the Minimum for a 3-Point Charge

In accordance with ¶625.3 of the 2012 31 Book of Discipline, the Minimum Salary Schedule reflects the mandatory minimum cash salary which pastors shall be paid based on their status and years of service. While not mandatory, local congregations are strongly encouraged to give consideration to paying pastors with more than 10 years of service an additional 1% of the tenth year minimum for each additional year of service they have completed. As examples: A Full Member with 15 years of service must be paid a minimum of $43,489, but the congregation is encouraged to consider paying an additional $2,175 (5 x $435), for a total of $45,664 based on 5 additional years service. A Local Pastor with 20 years of service must be paid a minimum $37,178, but the congregation is encouraged to consider paying an additional $3,720 (10 x $372), for a total of $40,898 based on 10 additional years service.

Counting Years of Service To Determine Minimum Compensation
Pastors serving under appointment full or part time will have years of service counted equally for the purpose of moving through the salary schedule. Pastors serving more than six months under appointment in a year will be credited with a full year's service for the purpose of moving through the salary schedule. Pastors serving six months or less under appointment in a year will remain in the year of the salary schedule they are in. When an additional full year of service is completed, pastors will move to the next year in the salary schedule. For salary schedule purposes, years of service are carried over equally from one category to another as clergy status changes.

Nancy Patera, Chair, Commission on Equitable Compensation of the West Michigan Annual Conference

ITEM #8
SUBJECT: **Guidelines for Equitable Compensation Support.**
RESULT: **PASSED**

MOTION: **The Commission on Equitable Compensation moves the Conference Guidelines for Equitable Compensation Support for 2015.**
Guidelines for Equitable Compensation Support

1. Local congregations shall conduct an annual stewardship campaign. Congregations receiving Equitable Compensation support are expected to participate in ongoing stewardship education and planning through programs such as the Stewardship Academy offered through the United Methodist Foundation of Michigan and the Vital Church Initiative (VCI).
2. Local congregations receiving Equitable Compensation grants shall annually counsel with the district superintendent concerning levels of pastoral support.
3. Churches should be grouped, where feasible, in a denominational or ecumenical grouping so as to provide an average attendance of at least 134 under the care of one pastor.
4. Multi-church charges that become single-point charges will not be eligible for financial assistance from the Commission unless the church seeking assistance has an average attendance of at least 134.
5. Local congregations requesting equitable compensation support shall voucher pastors' travel and business expenses according to the guidelines of the Council on Finance and Administration.
6. Local congregations may receive Equitable Compensation support for up to three consecutive years, reducing the original grant amount by 30% each year. Equitable Compensation funds shall not be used to fund more than the conference minimum salary.
7. Congregations receiving Equitable Compensation shall pay Ministry Shares in full.
8. Churches receiving or applying for Equitable Compensation that have planned or are planning to enter into building or remodeling projects that require permission of the District Board of Church Location and Building, or which exceed 10% of the total annual budget of the local congregation, shall not proceed with proposed projects and/or related capital campaigns until such time as a plan for ending Equitable Compensation support has been presented and approved by the Commission on Equitable Compensation and the district superintendent. Exceptions to this guideline shall be given greater consideration when proposed projects are related to building accessibility.
9. Exceptions to these guidelines may be considered upon recommendation of the Bishop and the Cabinet.

– Approved by Annual Conference 1984, Revised 1993, 2002, 2007, 2009, 2010, 2011, 2012.

Nancy Patera, Chair, Commission on Equitable Compensation of the West Michigan Annual Conference

ITEM #9
SUBJECT: **Ministers' Reserve Pension Fund (MRPF) – Pre-82 Past Service Rate.**
RESULT: **PASSED**

MOTION: **The Past Service Rate (PSR) in 2015 for clergy service before 1982 shall be $726 for every year of service. The surviving spouse benefit shall remain at 85 percent.**

Louis Grettenberger, Chair, Board of Pension and Health Benefits of the West Michigan Annual Conference

ITEM #10
SUBJECT: Annual Policy Recommendations for 2015.
RESULT: PASSED

MOTION: **The following shall be the policy recommendation for 2015:**

A. Special Sundays: The following Special Sundays will be observed with offerings in compliance with the action of the 2012 General Conference:

	2014	**2015**
Human Relations Day	January 19	January 18
One Great Hour of Sharing	March 30	March 15
Native American Ministry Sunday	May 4	April 19
*Peace with Justice Sunday	*June 15	*May 31
World Communion Sunday	October 5	October 4
United Methodist Student Sunday	November 30	November 29
World Aids Day	December 7	December 6
These Sundays will be observed with offerings:		
Racial Ethnic Local Church Sunday	February 2	February 1
Golden Cross Sunday	May 4	May 3
United Methodist Volunteer in Mission Awareness	June 1	June 7
Rural Life Sunday	August 24	August 23
Christian Education Sunday	September 7	September 6
Disability Awareness Sunday	October 26	October 25

**Camp Sunday*
**or on a date to be determined by the local church*

B. Youth Ministries: From the Ministry Shares $2.00 per youth member will be allocated for the YOUTH SERVICE FUND. 70% is to be used by the conference youth program and 30% by the general church youth program. A ministry share of 0.15% shall be authorized to continue to partially fund the staffing of Conference Young People and Camping Staff Support and camping ministries.

C. The Council on Finance and Administration is authorized to establish a line of credit with the depository bank in the amount it determines appropriate to meet the needs of the conference.

D. The auditor of record of the Conference Treasurer shall be a firm of certified public accountants, to be determined by the Council on Finance and Administration.

E. Furnishings allowance according to IRS regulations shall be allowed for the district superintendents and conference clergy staff persons as payroll withholding within their approved salary. A similar provision is available for local church pastors in an amount determined by the charge conference.

F. District superintendents and other clergy on the conference staff shall be allowed to designate the amount of their individual housing allowance within the approved salary and housing allowance in accordance with IRS regulations.

West Michigan Conference Council on Finance and Administration
Susan Cobb, President / Pros Tumonong, Treasurer

ITEM #11
SUBJECT: **"Rules of Order," Amendments to Various Rules.**
RESULT: **PASSED**

MOTION: **We move to amend the Conference Rules of Order by addition or substitution (bold) and deletion (strikethrough) as follows:**

1. Amend Rule 1B1b as follows:
   b. The word "Discipline" with the first letter capitalized shall mean the current version of The Book of Discipline of The United Methodist Church.
2. Amend Rule 1D1 by addition of a new subparagraph "d" as follows:
   d. The Committee may make any necessary changes to the Rules of Order to reflect the most recent provisions and paragraph numbers in The Book of Discipline.
3. Amend Rule 4A2 by deletion and addition as follows:
   2. The term of office shall begin on January 1 of the year following election and continue for four years.
4. Amend Rule 8B to reflect current disciplinary references as follows:
   B. CLERGY MEMBERS:
   Clergy members of the Conference are as defined in ¶602.1 of the Discipline.
   [The clergy membership of an annual conference (¶370) shall consist of deacons and elders in full connection (¶333), probationary members (¶327), associate members, affiliate members (¶¶344.4, 586.4), and local pastors under full-time and part-time appointment to a pastoral charge (¶317), (see also ¶32).]
5. Amend Rule 8C as follows:
   I. Amend Rule 8, C, 2a as follows:
      2. Lay Members of the Annual Conference are:
         a. Professing lay members elected by each charge of the conference.
      Those elected by the pastoral charges reported in the Disciplinary Question "What is the number of Pastoral Charges?" in the previous year's Journal. (#58a – 2012 Journal);
   II. Amend Rule 8, C, 3a by deleting the parenthetical reference (#59a-2012 Journal, p. 70).
   III. Amend Rule 8, C, 3c, 6) by deleting the words "council on ministries" and inserting in their place the words "leadership team".

IV. Amend Rule 8, C, 3c, 13) by addition between "Religion and Race" and "Status and Role of Women" the word "Scouting" as follows:
   13) Chairperson/coordinator of these other conference agencies, committees and groups:
   - Religion and Race
   - Scouting
   - Status and Role of Women

V. Amend Rule 8, C, 3c, 15) by deletion and substitution as follows:
   15) Conference Ministry Consultants Program Staff

VI. Amend Rule 8, C, 3c by addition of a new item 18 as follows:
   18) Conference Journal Editor

6. Am 1 end Rule 9 by deleting items 3 a-e and 4 and adding item 2 l-p as follows:
   l. The Chairperson of the Committee on Rules of Order
   m. The Conference Facilitator
   n. A representative designated by the host institution
   o. A representative from the Committee on Disability Concerns
   p. Six (6) members at large, one of whom shall be less than 30 years of age at the time of election. Three of the six shall be lay persons nominated by the Conference Committee on Nominations and elected by the Conference.

7. Amend Rule 12 as follows:
   I. Amend Rule 12A by deleting the word "created" and substituting the word "submitted".
   II. Amend Rule 12 D by:
      a. Adding the bold and underlined words "Response Petitions" at the beginning of item "2";
      b. Moving current item "3" to become the last sentence of item "2" with the last four words to read as follows: "…the Conference session convenes."; and
      c. Renumbering current item "4" as item "3".

8. Amend Rule 15 by addition of the following last sentence:
   All vote counts shall be conducted by recognizing those eligible to vote on the question.

9. Amend Rule 21 by deleting current item "A" and re-lettering the remaining three items.

10. Amend Rule 32B4 adding the words "council or charge conference" after the word "church" and deleting the words "administrative board".

11. Amend Rule 33F as follows:
   I. Amend the last sentence of Rule 33F2 to read as follows:
      On the seventh ballot, the vote-getters in order of votes received shall be elected to complete the election of Jurisdictional Conference delegates and reserve delegates.;
   II. Amend Rule 33F3b by deletion of the word "above" in the first sentence.; and
   III. Amend the first part of Rule 33F4 before the comma by deletion and addition as follows:
      If there is a tie on any ballot which results in the election of a any delegate or reserve delegate,…
      These amendments to Rule 33F shall become effective upon adoption.

12. Renumber present Rule 36 as Rule 37 and amend as follows:

    Rule 37 Statement of Effect

    The Rules of Order approved by the Conference in its most recent session in June 2013 shall supersede all previous Rules of the West Michigan Conference.

West Michigan Conference Committee on Rules of Order, Judy Coffey, Chair

ITEM #12
SUBJECT: **"Rules of Order," Rules 26 and 29: Amendments.**
RESULT: **PASSED**

MOTION: **We move to amend the Conference Rules of Order by addition or substitution (bold) and deletion (strikethrough) as follows:**

1. Amend the first sentence of Rule 26A1 as follows:
    1. A conference member who desires to speak or present any matter to the conference shall raise the card provided while seated within the bar and wait to be recognized by the presiding bishop. When recognized, she/he shall proceed to the nearest microphone and first announce her/his name and local church or other conference relationship. Unless rising for a point of order or parliamentary inquiry, the member shall not speak until given the floor. or debate shall stand from within the limits of the floor and move to the nearest microphone to await recognition by the President.
    2. Amend Rule 29 by deleting the words "a show of hands" and substituting the words "raising the card provided" in the first sentence.

West Michigan Conference Committee on Rules of Order, Judy Coffey, Chair

ITEM #13
SUBJECT: **"Rules of Order," a new Rule 36: Addition of Committee on General Conference Petitions.**
RESULT: **PASSED**

MOTION: **We move to amend the Conference Rules of Order by addition (bold) as follows:**

Delete present Rule 1C3c and add a new Rule 36 as follows:

RULE 36 PETITIONS TO GENERAL CONFERENCE

A. Committee on General Conference Petitions
    1) At the Annual Conference session two years prior to the next General Conference the Conference Nominating Committee shall nominate and the Conference shall elect a Committee on General Conference Petitions consisting of four (4) lay persons and four (4) clergy who have an interest in or knowledge of and experience in the general church and include:
        a) One lay and one clergy delegate to a General Conference.
        b) One member serving or having served on a General Agency.

c) One member of the Committee on Rules of Order
d) The Director of Connectional Ministries

2) No member of 1 the Committee may serve in more than one of the above categories.
3) The Director of Connectional Ministries shall convene the organizing meeting of the Committee at which it shall elect such leadership as it determines.
4) The Committee's term shall be for two years, ending at the conclusion of the annual conference at which General Conference petitions are considered.

B. Duties and Responsibilities
1) The Committee shall solicit petitions to General Conference from United Methodist organizations, churches, clergy and laypersons within theWest Michigan Conference.
2) The Committee may also develop its own recommendations in the form of a petition to the General Conference.
3) Any other annual conference petitions pertaining to General Conference matters shall be considered by this committee.
4) When considering and developing petitions to the General Conference, it is recommended that the Committee consult with other persons, such as former General and Jurisdictional Conference delegates, persons knowledgeable about the general church (i.e. general agency members, staff, etc.) and others with experience and expertise who can assist them in their work.

C. Reporting to and Action by the Annual Conference
1) General Conference petitions shall be considered at the Annual Conference session the year prior to General Conference.
2) The Committee shall prepare a report on General Conference petitions together with its recommendation for concurrence, concurrence with amendment or non-concurrence on each petition. This report shall be included in the pre-conference materials.
3) Each petition considered by the conference may be debated and may be amended.
4) The Conference shall vote on all petitions recommended by the Committee for concurrence or concurrence with amendment. All petitions recommended by the Committee for non-concurrence shall not be considered unless 20% of the members of the Conference present and voting request consideration.
5) Prior to annual conference the Committee shall inform each petitioner of its recommendation on her/his/their petition and following annual conference advise the petitioner of the conference action on her/his/their petition.

D. Forwarding Petitions to General Conference
1) By the deadline established by the General Conference Secretary, the Annual Conference Secretary shall forward all petitions approved by the Annual Conference to the General Conference in accordance with The Book of Discipline and related procedures.

West Michigan Conference Committee on Rules of Order,
Judy Coffey, Chair

ITEM #14
SUBJECT: **"Plan of Organization": CLT Purpose and Relationship – Amendment.**
RESULT: **PASSED**

MOTION: **I move to amend the Conference Leadership Team section of the "Plan of Organization" in the 2013 Conference Journal (pages 222-225) as follows:**

Conference Leadership Team
Page 222

1 Purpose: The Conference Leadership Team (Leadership Team) shall act on behalf of the Annual Conference between sessions in order to give general direction, guidance, and ensure the alignment of the resources, structure and ministries in support of the mission, vision and strategic goals of the Conference.

Page 225

7) Relationships:

b) The Leadership Team, subject to their accountability to the Annual Conference and as limited or granted by the DISCIPLINE, has the authority to approve or deny the continuation of funding for programs in the Conference.

9) Narrative Summary of Conference Leadership Team
The Leadership Team is a body designed to replace the former Council on Ministries. It shall act on behalf of the Annual Conference between sessions in order to give general direction, guidance, and alignment of resources in support of the mission and vision of the Conference.

Replace strikethrough with: "It shall give general direction, guidance, and ensure the alignment of the resources, structure and ministries in support of the mission, vision and strategic goals of the Conference."

Benton R. Heisler, on behalf of the Conference Leadership Team

ITEM #15
SUBJECT: **"Plan of Organization": Reassigning the Duties of the Board of Discipleship – Amendment.**
RESULT: **PASSED**

MOTION: **I move to amend the "Plan of Organization" as follows:**

Delete the Board of Discipleship section in the "Plan of Organization" from the 2013 Journal (page 229, letter c, and as it appears in the various lists in the "Plan of Organization.")

ADD to the Conference Leadership section of the "Plan of Organization" in the 2013 Journal (on page 224):
Responsibilities:

6. k) Be the equivalent structure to provide the functions and maintain the connectional relationships for the discipleship functions of the conference as outlined in ¶630 with the exception of Camping and Evangelism which shall have their own structure.

Benton R. Heisler, on behalf of the Conference Leadership Team

ITEM #16
SUBJECT: **"Plan of Organization": CLT Chairperson Selected by Nominations Committee**
RESULT: **PASSED (with amendment)**

MOTION: **We move that Item #16 "CLT Chairperson Selected by Nominations Committee Amendment" be amended by substitution with the following:**

- The chairperson of the CLT shall be nominated by the Conference Committee on Nominations in consultation with the Bishop from the members at large on the Conference Leadership Team (CLT).
- The Director of Connectional Ministries (DCM) shall be a member but not chairperson of Conference Leadership Team (CLT) with voice and vote.
- The Rules of Order Committee in consultation with the Conference Secretary and Director of Connectional Ministries shall make the necessary editorial and substantive changes to the Plan of Organization so that this conference action would be reflected in the Plan of Organization.

Anne Soles, Vice Chair of CLT
of the West Michigan Annual Conference

ITEM #17
SUBJECT: **West Michigan Budget Recommendation for 2015 – UPDATED.**
RESULT: **PASSED (as amended)**

MOTION: **The Council on Finance and Administration recommends the following:**

1. As a result of 2014 Annual Conference action, the amount of $6,324,067 shall be the Conference budget for 2015. The Ministry Share rate will be 13.1%.
2. The World Service and Conference Benevolence budget will be distributed as follows: 34% to World Service and 66% to Conference Benevolence.
3. The salary of district superintendents, conference director of connectional ministries and conference treasurer shall be $78,410, increase of 0.93% based on the formula approved by Annual Conference in 2011; and, their housing allowance shall remain at $20,000.
4. Support staff wages adjustment of 1.75% using a rate increase of 0.25% above inflation rate of 1.5%

Revenue Assumptions:
Table III Income of All Churches X Percentage Rate X Projected Pay-in Rate = Ministry Shares Revenue
$55,498,611 x 12.8% x 87% = $6,180,325
Plus $55,498,611 x 0.15% x 87% = $72,426
MINISTRY SHARES REVENUE = $6,252,751

2015 West Michigan Conference Budget

	2013 *Actual*	2013 *Approved*	2014 *Approved*	2015 *Proposed*
Base Income from Table III			**55,018,096**	**55,498,611**
Percentage Rate			**12.80%**	**13.10%**
Pay-in Rate			**87.0%**	**86.0%**
Anticipated Revenue	**$5,810,714**	**$6,038,215**	**$6,126,815**	**$6,252,474**

LEGISLATION

Plus: Young People and Camping Staff (0.15% in 2015)				
	$45,757	**$47,174**	**$47,866**	**$71,593**
Total Anticipated Revenue	**$5,856,471**	**$6,085,389**	**$6,174,681**	**$6,324,067**
Expenditures Budget				
A. Connectional Ministry				
DS Salary	$74,490	$75,736	$77,688	$78,410
1. District Superintendents Fund				
Salaries	$454,416	$454,416	$466,128	$470,463
New Pastor Orientation	476	500	500	500
Continuing Education	7,794	9,000	9,000	9,000
Health Care Plan	82,675	109,310	101,009	117,322
Workers Comp Insurance	1,753	1,400	1,400	2,100
Pension Support	85,603	85,203	87,399	88,212
Travel Expense & Intro Meetings	88,268	62,441	70,000	70,000
BOM and Fall Retreat	913	1,000	1,500	1,500
New Superintendent Transition Fund	0	2,000	2,000	2,000
Renewal Leave	0	2,000	2,000	2,000
Contingency	774	5,000	–	–
	$722,672	$732,270	$740,936	$763,097
2. District Office Expense				
Albion	$67,202	$64,346	$67,038	$69,283
Heartland	66,374	63,946	66,638	68,517
Grand Rapids	63,510	64,776	67,468	69,347
Grand Traverse	64,264	65,346	68,038	69,917
Kalamazoo	65,412	64,766	67,458	69,337
Lansing	47,864	66,306	56,498	58,377
District Office Rentals	59,436	64,049	59,186	53,640
Misc. Exp/Office Equipment	included above	10,228	16,228	included above
Total District Office Expense	**$434,062**	**$463,763**	**$468,552**	**$458,418**
Total District Superintendents Fund	**$1,156,734**	**$1,196,033**	**$1,209,488**	**$1,221,515**
3. Episcopal Fund	$248,299	$248,299	$251,363	$252,666
4. Equitable Compensation Fund	155,787	180,000	200,000	185,000
5. Health Care Program	47,741	50,000	50,000	30,000
6. Ministerial Pension & Insurance Reserve	4,738	5,000	5,000	5,000
7. Bd. Of Ordained Min/Min Enhancement	55,075	57,500	57,500	57,500
8. Clergy Advocacy	0	2,500	2,500	2,500
9. Moving Expense Fund	190,608	165,000	180,000	190,000
10. Clergy Transition Fund	–	–	–	–
11. Abuse Prevention Team	252	500	500	500
12. Contingency Fund	4,738	5,000	5,000	–
Connectional Ministry Funds	**$1,863,972**	**$1,909,832**	**$1,961,351**	**$1,944,681**
B. Administrative Funds				
1. General Church Apportionments				
Interdenominational Cooperation	**$22,995**	**$22,995**	**$23,102**	**$22,630**
General Administration	**103,392**	**$103,392**	**103,887**	**101,687**
Total General Apportionments	**$126,387**	**$126,387**	**$126,989**	**$124,317**
2. Jurisdictional Conference	16,931	16,000	16,000	16,000
3. Michigan Area Administration				
Area Expense Fund	$49,117	$48,232	$37,751	$42,787

Area Assistant To Bishop's Office	104,322	124,844	110,833	98,402
Area Episcopal Committee	800	800	800	800
Area Communications	–	–	–	123,514
Area Parsonage Committee	3,358	3,500	3,500	3,500
Total Area Administration	$157,597	$177,376	$152,884	$269,003
4. Conference Administration				
Commission on Archives and History	$18,570	$15,000	$15,000	$17,500
Conference Properties	155,292	163,200	170,000	170,000
Program Committee	374	5,000	5,000	5,000
Secretary Expenses	22,763	32,000	16,200	25,000
Statistician Expenses	0	0	500	500
Victim's Fund	0	0	–	–
Legal Contingencies-Conf Chancellor	14,513	6,000	7,000	12,000
At Large Lay Members Expense	50,172	42,000	43,000	50,000
5. Council on Finance & Administration				
Treasurer's Office	$234,208	$245,800	$261,000	$266,000
Auditing Expense	20,390	22,000	$22,000	$22,000
CFA Meeting Expenses	1,529	1,200	$1,200	$1,500
Administrative Services	44,362	40,000	$42,000	$42,000
Total CF&A	$300,489	$309,000	$326,200	$331,500
Conference Committees	180	500	$500	$500
Nomination & Leadership Development	1,028	2,500	$4,000	$2,500
Total Conference Administration	**$563,381**	**$575,200**	**$587,400**	**$614,500**
6. Administration Contingency Fund	4,720	5,000	$5,000	–
7. Conference Budget Reserve	44,300	33,112	$40,000	$11,500
8. Camps Deficit Reduction		20,000	$20,000	$20,000
Total Administrative Funds	**$913,316**	**$953,075**	**$948,273**	**$1,055,320**
C. World Service & Converence Benevolences				
1. World Service	**$856,829**	**$856,829**	**$860,836**	**$842,439**
2. Conference Benevolence Programs				
Commission on Christian Unity	–	500	500	500
Commission on Religion & Race	1,960	5,000	500	500
COSROW	–	500	500	500
Board of Christian Camping	169,854	175,000	175,000	298,500
Board of Church & Society	3,886	5,000	500	500
Board of Discipleship	437	3,000	500	–
Conference Council on Youth Ministry (CCYM)	1,063	5,000	5,000	5,000
Board of Global Ministries	266,410	274,500	260,000	255,000
Racial/Ethnic Local Church	80,541	90,000	90,000	85,000
Higher Ed. & Campus Ministry	298,100	299,500	308,000	360,000
Communications Commission	65,317	85,000	100,000	43,000
Connnectional Ministries Office	542,703	606,000	618,000	543,000
Board of Lay Ministries	2,259	3,000	3,000	3,000
Conference Personnel Committee	1,291	1,000	1,000	1,000
Board of Evangelism	198	5,000	500	500
United Methodist Men	–	1,000	500	500
Hunger Committee	–	1,500	500	500
Prison Ministry	–	5,000	500	500
Indian Workers Conference	1,480	2,000	500	500
Disability Concerns Committee	962	1,000	500	500

Vital Church Initiative	9,609	10,000	35,000	35,000
Hispanic/Latino Committee	2,795	8,500	12,000	55,000
CLT Pooled Ministry Fund	–	–	25,000	25,000
Cooperative Ministry Fund	–	–	1,000	500
CLT Contingency	9,609	10,000	6,500	-
Total Conference Benevolences	**$1,458,474**	**$1,597,000**	**$1,645,000**	**$1,714,000**
WORLD SVC & CONF BENEVOLENCE	**$2,315,303**	**$2,453,829**	**$2,505,836**	**$2,556,439**
D. New Church Development	$313,317	$330,400	$330,400	$335,000
E. Ministerial Education Fund	294,163	294,163	295,538	289,219
F. Black Colleges Fund	117,333	117,333	117,882	115,372
G. Africa University Fund	26,257	26,257	26,380	25,816
TOTAL CONFERENCE BUDGET	**$5,843,661**	**$6,084,889**	**$6,185,660**	**$6,321,847**
Excess Revenue Over Expenditure	$12,810	$500	($10,979)	$2,220
Budget Increase/(Decrease) vs. Last Year		241,228	$100,771	$136,187
Percent Increase/(Decrease) vs. Last Year		4.13%	1.66%	2.20%

Susan Cobb, President
Council on Finance and Administration

ITEM #18
SUBJECT: **Kalamazoo Wesley Foundation Loan.**
RESULT: **PASSED**

MOTION:

1. **In accordance with Conference Policy PPR#4 Item 9, the Council on Finance and Administration (CFA) recommends that the West Michigan Annual Conference approve the request of the Kalamazoo Wesley Foundation to borrow funds from a financial institution for the construction of its Student Ministry Center at Western Michigan University.**

2. **The Council on Finance and Administration recommends that the 2014 Annual Conference guarantee the Kalamazoo Wesley Foundation (Wesley) construction loan for its Student Ministry Center up to an amount of $350,000, provided that:**

    a. Wesley will furnish evidence that:
        1) The building cost based on an appraisal will be at least $1,200,000.
        2) The construction loan amount will be $1,000,000.
        3) The loan term will be 3 years with interest-only payments.
        4) The loan will be secured by the Student Ministry Center land and building.

    b. The Conference guarantee will terminate when the construction loan balance due reaches $400,000.

    c. n consideration of the West Michigan Annual Conference guaranteeing Wesley's loan as outline above, Wesley will give the annual conference or appropriate conference body a second mortgage on their property or another secondary secured position and other assurances regarding their performance in paying their construction loan in order to provide the West Michigan Annual Conference with security in the event of Wesley's default on its construction loan.

3. The CFA Executive Committee, in consultation with the Conference Chancellor and the Conference Board of Trustees, is authorized to act after the 2014 Annual Conference upon all necessary actions required to complete the loan guarantee, agreements with Wesley, and other matters, including review of all terms and documents, authorizations for signing documents and other requirements.

Susan Cobb, President, Council on Finance and Administration
of the West Michigan Conference

ITEM #19
SUBJECT: **BCC Special Conference-wide Financial Appeal.**
RESULT: **PASSED**

MOTION: **In accordance with Discipline ¶613.2 (c), the Council on Finance and Administration (CFA) recommends that the West Michigan Annual Conference authorize the Board of Christian Camping (BCC) to engage in a special conference-wide financial appeal with the following directives:**

1. The campaign will be conducted over the timeframe of July, 2014, through 2016.
2. Proceeds from the campaign will be directed toward the following:
   a. The Camp Scholarship Fund – a $100,000 goal.
   b. Transitional steps toward three full-time site director positions – $250,000 goal.
   c. Fund development expenses for this campaign and local camp-specific campaigns – $100,000 goal.
   d. Proceeds raised beyond the $450,000 will be invested in the current Camp Endowment Fund.

Susan Cobb, President, Council on Finance and Administration
of the West Michigan Conference

LEGISLATIVE ITEMS FROM THE FLOOR THAT PASSED

ITEM #A
SUBJECT: **Legislative Committees and the Consent Calendar – Amend Rule 23B (7)(b1)**
RESULT: **PASSED**

MOTION: **I move to amend Rule 23B(7)(b1) and (c) on page 260 of the 2013 Conference Journal by addition and deletion as follows:**

1) All legislative items considered by Legislative Committees which received approval for concurrence with or without amendment by 90% of the Legislative Committee members present and voting shall be included in the Consent Calendar.
   c. All recommendations for concurrence or concurrence by amendment by less than 90% of the Legislative Committee members present and voting ,and all recommendations for concurrence with amendment shall be counted as present, but not voting, and shall not be counted in the computation of votes.

David Lundquist
First United Methodist Church of Kalamazoo

LEGISLATION

CORPORATE SESSION LEGISLATION

ITEM #CS-I
SUBJECT: Discontinuation of Waterloo First United Methodist Church.
RESULT: PASSED

MOTION: In accordance with paragraph 2549.2a of the Book of Discipline, the West Michigan Conference Cabinet moves that the West Michigan Annual Conference declare the Waterloo First United Methodist Church (located at 11990 Territorial Rd, Munith, MI 49259) discontinued effective February 16, 2014.

Kennetha Bigham-Tsai, Lansing District Superintendent of the West Michigan Annual Conference

ITEM #CS-II
SUBJECT: Motion To Be Approved by the West Michigan Annual Conference Corporate Session in Regard to the Discontinuation of Parma United Methodist Church.
RESULT: PASSED

MOTION: In accordance with paragraph 2549.2a of the Book of Discipline, the West Michigan Conference declares the Parma United Methodist Church located at 100 East Main Street, Parma, Michigan, 49269, discontinued effective May 28, 2014.

Tamara Williams, Albion District Superintendent of the West Michigan Annual Conference

C. POLICIES, PROCEDURES AND RULES OF THE ANNUAL CONFERENCE

EXPLANATORY NOTE:

At the Thirty-first Session of the Annual Conference, June 2-6, 1999, Conference amended Rule 23.B.7.b.3 of the Rules of Order, by adding the following: "Conference Policies, Procedures, and Rules regarding financial matters need to be considered by Legislative Committees and come before the Annual Conference only if they are changed." The items listed below are the aforesaid policies, procedures and rules, and are designated with the initials "PPR", followed by a number.

Addresses for the Six Lanes projects plus full bios, country profiles and recent newsletters are available by checking the Conference Mission Web Site at www.westmichiganconference.org.

PPR #1 Advance Specials 2013-2014

This is the list of Advance Specials that the Conference Board of Global Ministries recommends for local church support in the next two years.

Lane 1 – Missionary Salary Support

Robert Amundsen #773978 – Pastor of Thousand Sticks UMC, Red Bird Mission
Delbert Groves #12150Z – Director of Spiritual Growth at the New Life Center in Zambia
Sandy Groves #12151Z – Coordinator of ministries for women & children at New Life Center
Jeff Hoover #07989Z – Professor at University of Katanga, DR Congo
Ellen Hoover #07990Z – Director of TESOL (The English Speaking School of Lubumbashi)
Dieudonne Karihano #3019569 – Agriculturist in Mozambique
Elma Jocson #13980Z – Surgeon waiting for re-assignment within the UMC medical health system
Darlene Logston #3021516 – US-2 serving Primavera Foundation in Tucson, AZ
Sonya Luna #3019618 – Hispanic Plan Missionary serving the Michigan Area
Valerie Mossman-Celestin #3020490 – Deaconess serving Haitian Artisans for Peace International
Nkemba Ndjungu #12910Z – Director UM Initiative in Cameroon
Mbwizu Ndjungu #12909Z – Director UM Initiative in Cameroon
Stephanie Plotas #3021848 – US2 from Battle Creek doing refugee ministry in Tucson AZ
Kelly Schaefer #3021506 – Mission Intern for Servant Hill Community in Wisconsin
Helen Sheperd #11810Z – Hospice nurse at United Methodist Center in Mongolia
Mark Smallwood #773728/Covenant 822 – Teacher at Red Bird School, Kentucky
Rebecca Smallwood #773728/Covenant 822 – Teacher at Red Bird School, Kentucky
Ut To #14175Z – Leader of the United Methodist Initiative in Vietnam
Karen Vo-To #14174Z – Leaders of the United Methodist Initiative in Vietnam
Paul Webster #11865Z – Agricultural specialist serving in Mujila Falls, Zambia

Lane 2 – Global Projects

AFRICA...

CAMEROON

Cameroon Initiative #00344A (served by Nkemba & Mbwizu Ndjungu)

DEMOCRATIC REPUBLIC OF CONGO

Katanga Methodist University #14433A (served by Jeff & Ellen Hoover)
Mulungwishi Seminary Scholarships #05773A
English Speaking School of Lubumbashi #10337A (served by Ellen Hoover)

LIBERIA

Bishop Judith Craig's Children's Village #11820A
Ganta Hospital #15080N

ZAMBIA

Lord's Mountain Orphanage (formerly Front Porch Orphans) #14420T
Bwafwano Care Project in Kitwe #3021211
Kafakumba Pastors' School #11438A
Mujila Falls Ag Project #15016A (served by Paul Webster)
New Life Center (Uzima Mupya) #15057A (served by Delbert & Sandy Groves)

ZIMBABWE

Babyfold at Old Mutare Hospital #11713T
Emergency Fund for Africa University Students #3020619

ASIA...

CHINA

Amity Printing Press #11422A

MONGOLIA

Mongolia Initiative #00209A (served by Helen Sheperd)

VIETNAM

Vietnam Initiative #14932A (served by Ut To & Karen Vo To)

EASTERN EUROPE...

RUSSIA

Russia Initiative #11510A

LATIN AMERICA/CARIBBEAN...

BOLIVIA

Urban Santa Cruz Children's Ministry #12320A

JAMAICA

PAPA's Ministries (Pastors and Priest Available for Service) #3021286

SPECIAL OFFERING...

World Communion Sunday – Fund #5820

Lane 3 – National Projects

GENERAL PROJECTS IN THE UNITED STATES:

A Child #123456
National Hispanic Plan #3021217
NOMADS #982658
North Central UMVIM #901375

REGIONAL PROJECTS IN THE UNITED STATES:

APPALACHIA

Appalachia Service Project #982050

KENTUCKY

Henderson Settlement #773365
Red Bird Mission #773726
Red Bird Missionary Conference #773978 (served by Amundsen)
Red Bird School #773728 (served by Smallwoods)

NEW MEXICO

McCurdy Ministries -#581479

SPECIAL OFFERINGS:

Human Relations Day – Fund #5807
Peace with Justice Sunday – Fund #5809
United Methodist Student Day – Fund #5816

Lane 4 – UMCOR/Hunger

GLOBAL PROJECTS

Bread for the World #982325
Church World Service Tools of Hope-Blankets #982810
Church World Service CROP #982380
ECHO (Education Concerns Hunger Organization) #982447
Heifer Project International #982530
Heifer Fill the Ark #982418
International Disaster Response Fund #982450
Imagine No Malaria #3021190
Prosthesis Program #982580
Material Resources #901440
Medicine Box #982630
Water and Sanitation #3020600
World Hunger/Poverty Mission Emphasis #982920

REGIONAL PROJECTS

ASIA

Aghanistan Emergency #602225

CARIBBEAN/HAITI

Brakeman-Smith Scholarship Fund #515-11
HAPI (Haitian Artisans for Peace International) #3020490-Project
Haiti School Hot Lunch Program #418790
Haiti Solar Ovens #418812
Grace Children's Hospital #418520
School, Health, Sewing and Layette Kits

UNITED STATES

Food Resource Bank #982493
National Disaster Response Fund #901670
Society of St. Andrew (Potato Project) #801600
Sager-Brown UMCOR Depot #901515

SPECIAL OFFERING

One Great Hour of Sharing – Fund #5822

Lane 5 – Racial-Ethnic Churches

AFRICAN AMERICAN CHURCHES

Battle Creek Washington Heights UMC

ASIAN AMERICAN CHURCHES

Grand Rapids Vietnamese UMC
Lansing Korean UMC

HISPANIC CHURCH

Grand Rapids La Nueva Esperanza

NATIVE AMERICAN CHURCHES

Bradley Indian Mission of the UMC
Charlevoix Greensky Hill Indian Church
Kewadin Indian Mission
Mt. Pleasant Chippewa Indian Church
Northport Indian Mission
Salem Indian Mission of the UMC
Indian Workers Conference

MULTI-ETHNIC CHURCHES

Lansing Faith UMC

SPECIAL OFFERINGS

Native American Ministries Sunday – Fund #5813

RELC Sunday – Fund #5806

Lane 6 – Local Projects

COMMUNITY DEVELOPMENT

Battle Creek: Washington Heights Community Ministries, Benton Harbor: Lighthouse Ministries (formerly Harbor Harvest), Grand Rapids: GRASP (Grand Rapids Area Service Project)

Grand Rapids: Martin Luther King Academy

Grand Rapids: Justice for our Neighbors (JFON)

Grand Rapids: La Nueva Outreach Ministries

Grand Rapids: North End Community Ministry (NECM)

Grand Rapids: South End Community Outreach Ministry (SECOM), Grand Rapids: Trinity UMC Community Ministries, Grand Rapids: United Methodist Community House, Grand Rapids: United Methodist Metropolitan Ministry, Holton: Holton Community Center, Kalkaska: Kalkaska Area Interfaith Resources, Laingsburg: Looking Glass Community Services (LGCS)

Lansing: Open Door Ministry

Lansing: South Lansing Ministries

Missaukee Area Cooperative Ministries/Lake City UMC and others, Muskegon: Pathfinders Muskegon Heights: Mission for Area People (M.A.P.)

HEALTH AND WELFARE

Detroit: Methodist Children's Home Society, Children's Village

Grand Rapids: Clark Retirement Community

Grand Rapids: PaWaTing MaGedWin Senior Meals

Holland: PET Holland, manufacturing child-size Personal Energy Transports

Kalamazoo: Bronson Methodist Hospital

OUTREACH TO COLLEGE STUDENTS

Central Michigan University Wesley Foundation

Ferris State University Wesley Foundation

Michigan State University Wesley Foundation

Grand Valley Wesley Fellowship

Western Michigan University Wesley Foundation

UNITED METHODIST CAMPS

Conference Camps: Albright, Crystal Springs, Lake Michigan, Lakeview, and Wesley Woods

Lake Louise Christian Community and Camp

Scholarships for Ethnic Youth…Fund #6910

Camp Scholarships…Fund #7480

Camp New Day Scholarships…Fund #7482

ADDITIONAL POSSIBILITIES FOR GIVING

Conference Youth Council Mission Trip to HAPI in Mizak, Haiti 2013 Habitat for Humanity… all West Michigan affiliates Michigan Interfaith Council on Alcohol Problems (MICAP)

West Michigan Centers for Peace and Justice

Creative Peace Movement (Central District)

Peace with Justice Community (Grand Rapids District)

Swords into Plowshares Peace Center (Grand Traverse District)

Swords into Plowshares Peace Center (Kalamazoo District)

Shalom Center for Justice and Peace (Lansing District)

SPECIAL OFFERINGS

Camp Sunday #5812
Christian Education Sunday #5442
Golden Cross Sunday #5814
Rural Life Sunday #5808
Volunteer in Mission Awareness Sunday #5850

PPR #2 Local Church

1. All churches shall submit payments on Ministry Shares and other giving to the Conference Treasurer on a monthly basis.
2. All contributions, whether apportioned or unapportioned, for Michigan Area agencies and institutions, and for all benevolent causes of The United Methodist Church, shall be sent to the Conference Treasurer for distribution.
3. Every church shall assume responsibility for adequate travel reimbursement for its pastor or pastors in its annual budget. Following are guidelines to help a local church administer its travel allowance for pastors:
   a. Each pastor shall keep an accurate record of the number of miles traveled on church business.
   b. The payment for mileage driven in any given year shall be by voucher at the maximum rate allowed by the Internal Revenue Service for that year. Other travel expenses, including room and board at Annual Conference up to Conference rates, shall be at cost.
4. Every church shall assume responsibility to provide in its annual budget for health family rate insurance through the conference group policy for its pastor or pastors. If such provision is not necessary because coverage is provided by some other source (pastor's spouse), half the savings benefit will remain with the church.
5. Effective dates for salary and Clergy Retirement Security Plan/Comprehensive Protection Plan (CRSP/CPP) payments for Ministerial Appointment changes:
   a. The salary shall be paid through June 30 when an appointment change is made at the session of the Annual Conference. Salary payments for mid-year appointments will coincide with the effective date of the appointment.
   b. Payment on CRSP/CPP billing from the General Board of Pension and Health Benefits shall be made for the entire month of June for those appointment changes made during the session of Annual Conference. CRSP/CPP payments for mid-year appointments with an effective date of the first of the month shall be made for the previous month for the outgoing pastor and for the current month for the incoming pastor. Payments for appointment changes effective the 15th of a month shall be made for half of the current month for the out-going pastor and half of the current month for the in-coming pastor.

PPR #3 Conference and District Travel Expenses Reimbursement

1. All conference and district travel and dependent care expenses shall be by voucher only.
2. Conference personnel who draw travel allowances by voucher shall receive reimbursement equivalent to the Federal IRS allowance for business mileage.
3. All others drawing travel expenses from conference funds shall receive reimbursement equivalent to the Federal IRS allowance for volunteer mileage for car and travel, and $.02 per mile per passenger up to five people.
4. The travel expense of authorized representatives of conference agencies attending meetings convened by conference agencies drawing their full budget from the conference shall be paid by the agency that calls the meeting.
5. The travel expense of authorized conference representatives attending meetings convened by non-United Methodist agencies within the state of Michigan shall be paid by the conference, as provided in item 2, to the extent the expenses are not borne by the convening agency.
6. It is expected that all pastors and local church staff will be reimbursed from their local church travel expense account; therefore, reimbursement checks from the Conference Treasurer shall be

payable to the local church. Other reimbursable costs may include approved lodging, tolls, parking and telephone, if the organizational unit has budgeted for them.

7. Reimbursement cost necessary for dependents (children, sick or elderly) may be included in the administrative budget of any organization for members attending board, commission or committee meetings. The amount reimbursed shall not exceed $20.00 per day per member.

PPR #4 Finance and Accounting

1. All agencies and institutions outside the Conference central treasury that are receiving money in the total amount of $5,000 or more within a year from the West Michigan Conference shall file a copy of their annual audit report, a financial review by an independent CPA, or other financial statements approved by the Conference Treasurer with the Conference Treasurer's Office.
2. Depositories for the funds of Central Treasury are as follows:

Eaton Rapids:	Consumers Professional Credit Union
Grand Rapids:	Fifth Third Bank
	Merrill Lynch, Pierce, Fenner & Smith
	Macatawa Bank

3. The books of Central Treasury shall be audited annually by a CPA.
4. There shall be no carrying forward of budgeted funds from one year to the next by any agency or board of the Conference without approval of the Council on Finance and Administration. The following exceptions have been approved:
   a. The Conference Properties budget of the Conference Board of Trustees may accumulate unexpended funds in order to establish a maximum reserve fund of $25,000 for property maintenance.
   b. The Board of Christian Camping is permitted to establish an insurance Deductible Reserve Fund not to exceed $5,000. The funding of this reserve account will come from the Camp Board budget.
   c. The Equitable Salary Commission may accumulate up to an amount of $10,000 in a Temporary Disability Fund.
   d. The Treasurer's office may set aside up to $7,500 annually for the purchase of computer hardware and systems.
   e. The New Church Development Commission may accumulate annually its unexpended funds up to the rate of Apportionments received in that year.
   f. The Connectional Ministry Section, the Administrative Funds Section and the World Service and Conference Benevolences Section of the Conference Budget may accumulate apportioned or unspent funds in a Contingency Fund account from year to year up to a maximum of 10% of the amount budgeted in the current year.
5. Before the beginning of the year, the Council on Finance and Administration will determine if it will be necessary to restrict spending for the following year. If the spending restriction requires reducing salary levels, the salary changes will be implemented effective January 1 after consultation with and approval of the Conference Council on Ministries and the Cabinet. If there are no restrictions, the Conference Treasurer will distribute the actual amount received for each organizational unit of the Conference on a monthly basis. During the first six months of the fiscal year, the Conference Treasurer will honor vouchers presented for expenditures up to 70 percent of the approved budget for that board or agency. At the end of the six-month period, the Conference Council on Finance and Administration will review the Ministry Shares receipts and the disbursements made to determine if it will be necessary to restrict spending for the balance of the year. If a restriction is found to be necessary and if that restriction involves reducing salary levels, the changes will be implemented after consultation with and approval of the Conference Council on Ministries and the Cabinet. The Conference Council on Finance and Administration will advise all organizational units of the budget reduction through the Conference Treasurer. The World Service Apportionments will be paid at 100% of the amount budgeted, and all other General Church Apportionments will be paid at least equal to the ratio of actual receipts.

6. After consultation with and approval of affected boards and agencies, and the Cabinet, the Conference Council on Finance and Administration may re-designate the use of certain funds to meet the short-term needs of conference boards and agencies.
7. All interest earned on General Funds carried in Central Treasury shall be accumulated in a General Funds Interest Account. (This does not include funds in Central Treasury which are being held for specific purposes and have been designated as Interest Earning Funds by the Council.) At the end of each fiscal year, this General Interest Account shall be transferred and accumulated in the Conference Contingency Fund to be administered by the Council on Finance and Administration.
8. The Conference Contingency account may accumulate funds from interest earnings and budgeted Apportionments not to exceed an amount equal to one month's operating expenditures of the Conference. This would be 1/12 of the Conference budget.
9. Guidelines for the borrowing of money from financial institutions to fund capital expenditures of certain organizational units of the West Michigan Conference:
   a. Requests to borrow $75,000 or less will be acted upon by the Council on Finance and Administration. Requests to borrow more than $75,000 will be automatically referred to the next session of the Annual Conference with recommendation.
   b. Emergency or unexpected borrowing needs will also be referred to the Council on Finance and Administration, which may act on behalf of the Annual Conference.
   c. The Chairperson and the Secretary of both the Council on Finance and Administration and the organizational unit seeking the funds will sign the promissory note and/or other documents required by the lending institution. If the loan is to be secured by a mortgage, the signature of the authorized officers of the corporation holding title to the property will also be required.

   NOTE: To the extent not prohibited by *The Book of Discipline*, the organizational units governed by the foregoing policy shall be all Councils, Boards and Commissions of the Conference and District; all Divisions, Sections, Committees and similar sub-groups of the foregoing; all Wesley Foundations; the Conference Equitable Salary Commission; the United Methodist Foundation of the West Michigan Conference; all District Boards of Trustees, District Boards of Missions, United Methodist Unions and City Missionary Societies.
10. Prior to any request for action by the Annual Conference on a proposal which will require funding by the Annual Conference, such proposal shall be submitted to the Council on Finance and Administration for its recommendation to the Annual Conference.
11. Request for Conference funding of projects, programs, or agencies located within a District shall be presented for information to the District Council on Ministries before being presented to a Conference program board, the Conference Council on Ministries, or the Council on Finance and Administration. The funding request shall include:

   [1] The amount to be requested from the Conference,

   [2] The total budget projected, including anticipated income and estimated expenditures, and

   [3] A separate listing of United Methodist sources of income anticipated or to be solicited.

   Exceptions to this are the Conference related institutions of Adrian and Albion colleges, Bronson Methodist Hospital, campus ministries, Methodist Children's Home, Clark Retirement Community, the Michigan Christian Advocate, and state-wide interdenominational bodies which may continue to make requests directly to the related Conference board. These provisions shall apply to emergency askings as well as to annual budget requests.
12. Any requests for a Conference-wide Capital Funds Crusade shall be presented to the Council on Finance and Administration for recommendation to the Annual Conference. Upon recommendation of the Annual Conference, the proposal shall be presented to the Charge Conferences for information and study only and returned to the next session of the Annual Conference for final action.

PPR #5 Conference Conflict of Interest Policy

West Michigan Annual Conference officials, employees and/or members of the various boards and commissions of the Conference shall not, during their term of service, receive any compensation or have any financial interest in any contract, or in any firm or corporation which provides goods or services (excluding publicly held companies where the official, employee, or member owns less than 1% of the voting stock thereof) or in any contract for the supply of goods or services, or the procurement of furnishings or equipment, interest in any construction project of the Conference, site procurement by the Conference, or any other business matter whatsoever, unless approved in advance by the official's or employee's immediate supervisor or the board or commission upon which the member participates, after full disclosure of the conflict including the amount of compensation and/or benefit the official, employee or member will receive.

The term official, employee or member of the board or commission shall include the officials, employee's or member's immediate family. Immediate family shall be defined as any person residing with the official, employee or member and their mother, father, and/or sons or daughters.

PPR #6 Moving Expense Code West Michigan Conference – UMC

A. Eligible Persons and Moves

1. All pastors under Active appointment within the West Michigan Conference structure are eligible to receive moving expense benefits. This will include local church pastors, district superintendents, staff members of conference or district councils, boards, and agencies, treasurers, bishop's assistants, superintendents or directors of parish development, conference-approved evangelists, and campus ministers.
2. Seminary students and pastors from outside the West Michigan Conference who are accepting appointment in the conference are eligible for moving expense benefits as provided in this code up to a limit of 750 miles.
3. The conference will pay for one retirement move for pastors who have retired or plan to retire from Episcopal appointment in the conference. The designation of a retirement move must be declared in writing before the moving expense is incurred. A move within the state of Michigan shall be paid in accordance with the provisions of this code. A move outside the state shall be paid up to a limit of 500 miles beyond the state border.
   Pastors called out of retirement and assigned to a charge will be granted an additional retirement move.
4. A disability move or the move of the surviving spouse of an eligible pastor shall be paid in accordance with the policy for retiring pastors. The conference shall pay for the move, out of the parsonage or other approved housing to another residence in the event of an eligible pastor's death, in accordance with the policy for retiring pastors.
5. When a separation or pending divorce action makes a move advisable, the spouse of a pastor is entitled to reimbursement for one move. Benefits are the same as those available to a surviving spouse of a deceased pastor.
6. Moves within a charge from one parsonage to another are the responsibility of the local charge unless ordered by the Cabinet.
7. Pastors not eligible for moving expense benefits include those:
   a. Under appointment outside the structure of the Conference
   b. On sabbatical, leave of absence or location
   c. Who no longer have membership in the Annual Conference?

B. Policy for Moves

1. Interstate Moves – For interstate moves, 2 or 3 estimates should be obtained before choosing a moving company to get the lowest rate available.
2. Local Zone Moves (8 miles outside of corporate limits) – Local zone moves are not regulated, as are other moves within the state. Therefore, 2 or 3 estimates should be obtained to get the lowest rate available.

3. Family Travel – Family travel for pastors covered by this policy will be paid upon request, for one car, at the conference rate, except the first 100 miles, plus tolls. If used and receipts presented, one overnight lodging will be paid for moves in excess of 350 miles.
4. Expenses covered by this code:
   a. Normal state tariff provision for loading, transporting and unloading of household goods up to a maximum weight of 20,000 pounds, including professional books and equipment. Hand written weight certificates will not be accepted.
   b. Up to $125 will be paid by the conference to cover needed packing materials, including wardrobes and dish packs.
   c. One extra pickup and one extra delivery.
   d. Reasonable charges for necessary handling of special items such as a piano or freezer.
   e. Standard liability insurance of 60 cents per pound which is furnished by the moving company, at no extra charge, under basic tariff provisions.
      NOTE: *It is now required that the householder sign a release statement on the Bill of Landing on the day of the move to release the shipment to a value of 60 cents per pound per article. Failure to do this will allow the moving company to charge a premium for insurance to cover the shipment at a value of up to $1.50 per pound.*
   f. Where there are medically recognized physical limitations, up to $1,000 additional shall be allowed for packing.
   g. Storage charges are the responsibility of the local church if the parsonage is not ready for occupancy. The conference will pay only to the place of storage.
5. Expenses NOT covered by this code:
   a. Moving of items other than normal household goods and books, such as boats, trailers, autos, building materials, firewood, fishing shanties, dog houses, etc.
   b. Packing and/or unpacking services, except as noted in 4.f.
   c. Full value insurance beyond standard liability insurance provided by the moving company.
   d. Charges for waiting time, extra labor, connecting and disconnecting appliances.

C. Miscellaneous Policies

1. No moving company shall employ a pastor or an immediate member of his/her family to solicit business at any time for the purpose of receiving a commission or other consideration.
2. No company shall be allowed to establish an office at the seat of the conference for the purpose of soliciting business.
3. Each pastor is advised to request a copy of his/her inventory sheet from the mover at the time of loading and that it be signed by both the pastor and the moving company.
4. Pastors may want to check with their moving company or home insurance company and request an All-Risk policy that would cover all damages in the moving of their household goods from one residence to another.

D. Administration

1. The Conference Treasurer shall administer the Moving Expense Fund.
2. Pastors anticipating a move shall consult with the Conference Treasurer's office to review the guidelines of this code.
3. The pastor shall be responsible for contacting a moving company and for scheduling the loading and unloading of household goods.
4. A written estimate of the Cost of Moving Services shall be made by the moving company and a copy shall be sent to the Conference Treasurer's office in advance of the move.
5. A letter of authorization shall be sent from the Conference Treasurer's office to the moving company with a copy to the pastor.
6. Billing for the cost of moving expenses covered by this code shall be made directly to the Conference Treasurer's office. Moving expenses not covered by this code shall be billed directly to the pastor.
7. Provision for payment of any unusual expenses which are not defined by this code shall be arranged through consultation with the Conference Treasurer prior to the move.

8. Requests for exception to the provisions of this code shall be made to the Conference Treasurer in advance of the move. The treasurer shall review and decide on each exception after consultation with the Cabinet and/or CFA, as necessary.

PPR #7 Ministry Shares Formula

The West Michigan Annual Conference adopted the following Ministry Share (apportionments) effective January 1, 2005.

Ministry Shares Formula

The projected income of the West Michigan Annual Conference will be based on a Proportional Giving Model built upon the Biblical principle of "tithing." Our Ministry Shares formula will be based on each congregation sharing a *Base Percentage Rate* of the *Actual Receipts* each local church as the basic conference budget. Special Needs funding may be added when necessary.

Definitions

a. *Actual Receipts* is the total annual income of the local church excluding receipts for capital fund campaign approved by the District Committee on Church Building and Location. Actual Receipts are funds that are to be used exclusively in support of the annual operating and benevolence budgets and do not include funds used for capital improvements and acquisitions. These funds include:
   1. Payment of pledges or other commitments toward the annual operating and benevolence budgets of the church.
   2. Receipts from constituents or members who did not pledge or amounts given beyond the amount pledged.
   3. Receipts from unidentified givers (for example, loose currency in the offering plate).
   4. Interest earned on funds on deposit or investments and used for the general operating or benevolence causes of the church.
   5. Proceeds from sale of church assets designated for the general operating or benevolence budget only.
   6. Proceeds from rental or fees.
   7. Fund raisers for operational and benevolent causes. Exceptions maybe granted by CFA upon request by the pastor for funds raised for special causes like UMCOR, VIM, Youth Mission trips, etc.
   8. Amounts received from undesignated grants and contract sources used to fund church programs.
   9. In-kind donations recorded in church financial statements.
   10. Donations of property, memorials and bequests designated for church operating and benevolence expenses. Bequests and endowments designated for other designated causes are excluded.

   Note: A local church may request a determination from CFA whether or not certain funds received are to be included as "Actual Receipts" before January 15.

b. *Base Percentage Rate* is ten percent of the annual local church receipts. For 2005 only, the increase or decrease of ministry shares will be capped at 20%. The percentage figure will be reviewed annually and recommended by the Council on Finance and Administration to the Annual Conference churches for adoption, with a 60% vote of members present and voting required to change from the 10% base rate.

c. *Special needs* - Additional connectional giving opportunities may be recommended by CFA to the Annual Conference for special needs or strategic planning emphasis, such as capital funds, new church development, pension plans, or health care, etc. Additional percentage giving opportunities will be presented for churches to pledge their partnership and financial support.

Methodology

a. Annually, by February 1, each Local Church Treasurer shall submit to the Conference Treasurer, as part of the year end reports, the church's *Actual Receipts* information, using a Table III form.

b. The compilation of Actual Receipts information from all the churches will provide an objective basis for the Council on Finance and Administration to prepare its Ministry Shares recommendation to the Annual Conference. (For example, 2005 Ministry Shares based on 2003 data.). The Ministry Shares recommendation includes the Base Percentage Rate, any Special Needs and the Conference Budget.

c. Within thirty days after approval of the Ministry Shares recommendation by annual conference, the local church shall submit to the Conference Treasurer a pledge adopted by its administrative council stating the amount of its Ministry Shares based on the approved Base Percentage Rate, any Special Needs and its reported Actual Receipts. If the Conference Treasurer finds a variance between the pledge amount submitted by the church and the expected Ministry Shares amount, he/she shall bring it to the respective church for resolution and if necessary to CFA and Cabinet for final resolution within thirty days.

d. By August 15, the Conference Treasurer shall provide the churches their respective Ministry Shares statement showing the distribution of funds based on the ratio of each fund in the approved conference budget.

e. A congregation in financial distress shall be provided consultation assistance by other churches or advisors within the district or conference staff upon request from the local church with the recommendation of the District Superintendent. Written documentation of the financial issues and the projected solution will be filed with the Council on Finance and Administration through the office of the District Superintendent.

f. As a regular practice, it is recommended that local church treasurers remit at least 10% of their actual receipts or one-twelfth of their annual ministry shares to the conference treasurer monthly.

PPR # 8 District Superintendent Salary Formula

The salary of district superintendents shall be recommended by the Council on Finance and Administration annually by taking into consideration factors such as:

- The conference average compensation
- The consumer price index or inflation rate
- The salary of the top 10 highest paid pastors
- The salary of district superintendents across the denomination
- The salary of district superintendents in the Detroit Conference
- Such other factors that are deemed appropriate under the circumstances.

PPR #9 Tax Relief for Retired Pastors and Pastors on Disability (Ministers of the Gospel)

1. An amount equal to 100% of the pension payments received by a retired pastor, or 100% of the disability benefit payments received by a pastor on disability, during any given year may be and is hereby designated as a rental/housing allowance respectively for each retired or disabled ordained or licensed pastor of The United Methodist Church who is or was a member of the West Michigan Conference at the time of his or her retirement or disability.
2. This rental/housing allowance shall apply to each ordained or licensed pastor who has been granted the retired relation or placed on disability leave by the West Michigan Conference and whose name and relationship to the conference is recorded in the Journal of the West Michigan Conference and in other appropriate records maintained by the conference.
3. The pension or disability payment to which this rental/housing allowance applies shall be the pension or disability payment resulting from all service of such retired or ordained or licensed pastor on disability, from all employment by any local church, Annual Conference, General Agency, or institution of The United Methodist Church or of any former denomination that is now a part of The United Methodist Church, or from any other employer who employed the pastor

to perform services related to the ministry and who elected to make contributions to the pension or benefit funds of The United Methodist Church for such retired pastor's pension or benefits of pastors on disability.

NOTE: The rental/housing allowance which may be excluded from a pastor's gross income is limited to the lesser of [a] the amount of the rental/housing allowance designated the Conference (total pension or disability benefits received), [b] the amount actually expended by the retired or pastor on disability to provide his or her housing, or [c] the legally-determined fair rental value of the housing. The cost of all utilities may also be excluded over and above all other housing costs. This provision does not apply to the surviving spouse unless said spouse is also a retired or ordained minister on disability.

PPR #10 Health Care - Premium Rates

That the Conference Board of Pension and Health Benefits be authorized to establish the annual premium rates for all participants in accordance with the amounts required to provide for the anticipated needs and within the amount provided in the Conference budgets for 2011 AND 2012 and to evaluate and implement improvement in benefits of the existing plans as opportunity may arise.

PPR #11 Special Sundays

A. Special Sundays: The following Special Sundays will be observed with offerings in compliance with the action of the 2008 General Conference:

	2014	**2015**
Human Relations Day	Jan 19	Jan 18
One Great Hour of Sharing	March 30	March 15
Native American Ministry Sunday	May 4	April 19
Peace with Justice Sunday*	*June 15	*May 31
World Communion Sunday	Oct 5	Oct 4
United Methodist Student Sunday	Nov 30	Nov 29
**or on a date to be determined by the local church*		
World Aids Day	Dec 7	Dec 6
These Sundays will be observed with offerings:		
Racial Ethnic Local Church Sunday	Feb 2	Feb 1
Golden Cross Sunday	May 4	May 3
United Methodist Volunteer in Mission Awareness	June 1	Jun 7
Rural Life Sunday	Aug 24	Aug 23
Christian Education Sunday	Sept 7	Sept 6
Disability Awareness Sunday (no offering)	Oct 26	Oct 25
Camp Sunday*		
**To be determined by the individual church*		

B. Youth Ministries: From the Ministry Shares $2.00 per youth member will be allocated for the YOUTH SERVICE FUND. 70% is to be used by the conference youth program and 30% by the general church youth program. A mission share of $50,000 shall be authorized to continue to partially fund the staffing of conference and camping ministries.

C. The line of credit, which has been established with Macatawa Bank, shall be continued up to a limit of $300,000.

D. The auditor of record of the Conference Treasurer shall be a firm of certified public accountants, to be determined by the Council on Finance and Administration.

E. Furnishings allowance according to IRS regulations shall be allowed for the District Superintendents and Conference clergy staff persons as payroll withholding within their approved salary. A similar provision is available for local church pastors in an amount determined by the charge conference.

F. District superintendents and other clergy on conference staff shall be allowed to designate the amount of their individual housing allowance within the approved salary and housing allowance in accordance with IRS regulations.

PPR #12 Abuse Prevention Policy
Entrusted to our care: Adults with special needs, children, and youth
Abuse Prevention Policy of the West Michigan Conference of the United Methodist Church

Preamble

Through baptism we renounce the spiritual forces of wickedness and reject the evil powers of this world. We will surround all God's children with a community of love and forgiveness that they may grow in their trust of God. The faith community lays the foundation for them to grow to be true disciples who walk in the way that leads to life. The occurrence of abuse or neglect within the household of God breaks this covenant. Sadly, abuse remains a reality in today's society both outside and within the church. The West Michigan Conference accepts its biblical and moral responsibility to address this issue. Therefore, this policy is intended to provide for the safety and health of adults with special needs, children and youth during conference-related functions, events or activities.

Abuse and neglect cannot be tolerated or allowed to continue. Our adults with special needs, children and youth must be protected. Too often a victim continues to be abused and/or a perpetrator continues the offensive behavior because it goes unreported. The perpetrator is unlikely to report his/her conduct, and adults with special needs, children or youth often do not report it because of fear or a variety of other reasons. Therefore, it is everyone's moral obligation to report all known and suspected cases of abuse or neglect. The reporting of abuse or neglect must be handled delicately and appropriately while protecting the rights of confidentiality and privacy of all the involved parties.

This document hereafter shall be referred to as the Abuse Prevention Policy or, simply, this Policy.

The goals of this Policy include:

1. protecting our adults with special needs, children and youth from abuse and neglect;
2. protecting our care providers from false accusations of abuse; and
3. protecting the vitality of our ministries.

To reach these goals, the Conference has adopted and implemented this Policy. This Policy is intended to supplement and not replace the continuing need of our Conference to minister to the spiritual and emotional needs of both the victims and perpetrators of abuse. All camp ministry functions, events and activities shall be in compliance with this Policy and the State of Michigan Family Independence Agency Camp Licensing Rules and Regulations for Children and Adult Foster Care Camps.

[The definitions of terms used in this Policy may be found at the end of this document.]

Section I: Care Provider Selection

A. Minimum Requirements

1. All persons working directly with adults with special needs, children, and/or youth shall before the function, event or activity,
    a. be 16 years of age
    b. complete a Care Provider Application
    c. Provide written references
    d. Submit written permission and pertinent information for a criminal record check to be pursued with local, county, state and/or federal law enforcement agencies.
    All applications and related documents shall be held confidential and kept by the event director. Persons will be allowed to work at a given event only with a clear background/crime report, and with the approval of the event director and/or the

sponsoring agency's chairperson. A clear report does not guarantee the privilege to work at a function, event or activity.

2. All potential care providers will complete the Care Provider Application prior to the function, event or activity. Training will be provided by the Abuse Prevention Team or its designee. [See Section II: Care Provider Training and Education.]

B. Policy Statement

The West Michigan Conference of The United Methodist Church is responsible for doing all it can to make every conference-related function, event or activity a nurturing environment and safe from potential harm. The West Michigan Conference embraces its calling to provide functions, activities and events which are spiritually and developmentally appropriate and free from abuse.

Careful screening is one step to prevent abuse. Screening calls for a careful review of all information (through interviews, written information, personal contacts, and reference checks) in search of persons who can provide a safe and nurturing environment with adequate supervision.

All applicants shall satisfactorily complete the screening process required in this Policy before being permitted to work with or provide any services involving any adults with special needs, children, or youth. Anyone who does not satisfactorily complete the required screening process shall NOT be permitted to work with or provide any services involving any adults with special needs, children, or youth.

C. Screening Documents

1. Application: The applicant must complete and sign an Application for Care Provider Certification using a form approved by the Abuse Prevention Team. The application shall include an affidavit.
2. Reference Check: The event director or designee shall confirm references regarding the suitability of the applicant to work with adults with special needs, children and youth.
3. Background check: No less than one background check shall be pursued for each applicant. Thc background checks may come from one of the agencies listed below. The processing of the application, references and criminal background checks shall be the responsibility of the event director. The applicant shall not be held responsible for the financial cost of such checks. A criminal record check of the applicant shall be obtained from the appropriate law enforcement agencies located in any state in which the applicant has resided for a period of at least one year within the last15 years while being at least 18 years of age. These law enforcement agencies may include and are not be limited to the Michigan State Police, Michigan State Bureau of Investigation, Michigan Division of Motor Vehicles, the State of Michigan Family Independence Agency, and /or the Federal Bureau of Investigation.
4. Six-Month Rule: The applicant shall be a member of and/or participant in a ministry setting for a period of at least six months prior to application.
5. Personal Interview: The applicant must be personally interviewed by the event director designee.
6. Approval: The applicant must satisfactorily complete the screening process.
7. Consent by Parent or Guardian: When provided for in this Policy the care provider shall have the written consent of the parent or guardian for each adult with special needs, child, or youth for whom he/she will be providing care services. This consent shall be on a form approved by the Abuse Prevention Team.
8. Other: The applicant shall submit to any other legal screening requested by the event director or designee.

D. Qualifications

1. No one shall be permitted to serve as a care provider who, in the belief of the leader, sponsoring agency or the event director or designee, may represent a potential threat of committing abuse or violating any of this Policy.
2. No one shall serve as a care provider if she/he is known to have been previously convicted of, or pled guilty or no contest to, any crime arising out of any act or conduct involving sexual abuse, or any act or conduct which is of a sexual, molesting, seductive, or criminally

deviant nature, whether or not such conduct involved a child. This includes, but is not limited to, crimes involving pedophilic behavior (molestation of a pre-adolescent child), incest, rape, assaults involving adults with special needs, children, or youth, murder, kidnapping, pornography, and the physical abuse of an adult with special needs, child, or youth. This qualifying rule shall be applicable no matter how long ago the crime occurred.

3. No one shall serve as a care provider who has had a verdict rendered against him or her in any civil action arising out of any personal act or conduct related to sexual abuse of an adult with special needs, child, or youth. This qualifying rule shall apply no matter how long ago the civil verdict was rendered.
4. No one shall serve as a care provider who has acknowledged or admitted that she/he has participated as a perpetrator in any previous act of sexual abuse of an adult with special needs, child, or youth. This qualifying rule shall apply no matter how long ago or whether a civil or criminal verdict was rendered.

E. **Screening Procedures**

1. The event director or designee shall be responsible for receiving, reviewing, confirming and processing all applications and related documents.
2. The event director or designee shall document the results of all interviews and reference checks of applicants.
3. After all the screening documents and information have been obtained, the event director or designee shall make a determination as to whether the applicant is qualified to serve as a care provider. This determination shall be able to appeal to the sponsoring agency who shall give written notification to the applicant of its decision in a timely manner.
4. All documents and records obtained from applicants not approved to serve as a care provider shall be returned to the applicant. All related documents not received directly from that applicant shall be destroyed.
5. The event director shall submit to the Abuse Prevention Team the names of applicants who did not satisfactorily complete the screening process. The list shall include the dates of the screening process, the name of the group sponsoring the related function, event or activity, and the name of the person who conducted the screening. Upon request, the Abuse Prevention Team will confirm if the name of a particular potential care giver appears on this list. This list shall not be distributed.
6. As the status of a care provider changes, she/he must satisfactorily complete any additional screening requirements that may be appropriate as provided above under "Screening Requirements".
7. Any care provider who fails to meet any of the qualifications of this Policy may at any time have her or his certification revoked by the Abuse Prevention Team.
8. An applicant may request that his or her screening be handled exclusively and confidentially by the West Michigan Conference connectional staff person assigned to the ministries of the sponsoring agency. In such cases, all the duties and responsibilities in the screening process assigned to the event director or designee may be performed by the staff person. The staff person shall give written notification to the event director or designee of the applicant's final status in the screening process.

F. **Confidentiality**

1. Except as otherwise provided herein, all documents and information obtained on all care providers shall remain confidential.
2. No Consent by Parent or Guardian, or any file containing such Consents shall be confidential. All such Consents and files shall be a public record, accessible to anyone in the Conference.
3. Notwithstanding the above, all documents and information obtained during the screening process may be disclosed when it is reasonably necessary in the context of any criminal or civil litigation involving the care provider or the Conference. In addition, a care provider's records, documents, files, and information may be disclosed with the written consent, or at the written direction or request of that care provider.

Section II: Care Provider Training and Education

A. The Abuse Prevention Team shall be responsible for training care providers for certification.

B. The Abuse Prevention Team shall be responsible for training those responsible for implementing this Policy.

C. Care providers shall complete Abuse Prevention training and education for Certification.

D. The Abuse Prevention training and education for Certification shall be designed to create and raise awareness of and sensitivity to the issues of abuse. The Abuse Prevention Certification shall include a knowledge, understanding, familiarity, and agreement to implement the Abuse Prevention Policy of the Conference. This training and education shall include how to avoid incidents and the appearance of abuse as portions of the strategy to prevent false accusations.

E. The Abuse Prevention Certification training and education shall be provided regularly. Abuse Prevention Certification shall be valid for three years.

F. The Abuse Prevention Team shall be responsible for maintaining a current list of all certified care providers. This list may reflect any restrictions or limitations on the services to be provided by each care provider, i.e., only for senior high youth, junior high youth, or nursery. This list shall be a public record and accessible to anyone in the Conference.

Section III: Care Provider Supervision

A. General Statement

Proper supervision of certified care providers is necessary to avoid creating the opportunity for both actual abuse and false accusations of abuse to occur. Proper supervision includes providing care providers with Abuse Prevention Certification. Supervision during the care providers' performance of their responsibilities shall give special attention to high-risk settings such as nurseries, restrooms, and overnights.

B. General Rules and Procedures

1. Adequate Staffing
   a. All Conference-related functions, activities, and events involving adults with special needs, children and youth shall be staffed to meet the standards of this Policy. The portion of the function, activity, or event which involves care providers as defined in this Policy shall be canceled when staffing required by this Policy is not provided.
   b. Providing staffing shall be the responsibility of the event director of the Conference-related function, activity or event.
   c. Certified care providers shall supervise participants as outlined in this policy.
   d. Certified care providers shall assist and support each other in implementing this Policy. This includes reminders to avoid conduct that may give the appearance of inappropriate behavior.
2. Two Certified Care Providers Rule
   c. At least two (2) certified care providers, one of which must be an adult, shall be present at each Conference-related function, activity, or event involving adults with special needs, children and youth.
   d. The two certified care providers rule in the preceding paragraph maybe waived in the following situations:
      1) The certified care provider is an adult and there are at least three (3) children over 12 years of age present;
      2) Cabin or tent sleeping during a function, event or activity in which there is only one adult care provider and there are at least three (3) adults with special needs, children or youth present;
      3) One (1) certified care provider remains while the other certified care provider temporarily leaves the area or room for a medical, family, or other reasonable necessity, i.e., escorting an adult with special needs, child, youth to the restroom;

4) One (1) adult certified care provider remains when the other certified care provider has to leave for an unexpected medical, family, or other reasonable necessity;
5) A certified care provider is taking an adult with special needs, child, or youth to or from a Conference-related function, activity, or event;
6) A certified care provider temporarily remains with an adult with special needs, child, or youth while waiting for others to arrive at, or while the adult with special needs, child, or youth is waiting to leave, a Conference-related function, activity, or event; or
7) One (1) adult certified care provider is acceptable when a parent or guardian for each of participating adult with special needs, child, or youth signs a Consent of Parent or Guardian, using a form approved by the Abuse Prevention Team.

3. An identification procedure shall be used so that each adult with special needs, child, or youth is released only to a properly identified and pre-authorized person.

C. Additional Nursery Procedures

No one other than those receiving care in the nursery, their parents or guardians, approved certified care providers, and the adults with special needs, children or youth of the servicing certified care providers shall remain in the nursery.

D. Additional Overnight Procedures

1. Only in exceptional circumstances with Abuse Prevention Team advance approval and a signed "Affidavit of Non-Certified Care Provider" in advance of the conference-related function, activity or event may an adult without West Michigan Conference care provider certification be present on any overnight with adults with special needs, children or youth only.
2. No males shall sleep in the same sleeping area as an unrelated female adult with special needs, child or youth.
3. No females shall sleep in the same sleeping area as an unrelated male adult with special needs, child or youth.

Section IV: Policy for Reporting Suspected Abuse or Neglect Involving Adults with Special Needs or Children or Youth

A. Persons Required to Report

1. All Care Providers and conference employees who have reasonable cause to suspect abuse or neglect of an adult with special needs, child or youth shall report all known and suspected cases of abuse or neglect which (1) occur on the Conference premises, (2) occur at a Conference-related function, activity, or event, or (3) are disclosed during Conference-related function, activity or event. All other persons may report known and suspected cases of abuse or neglect in accordance with this Policy and the laws of The State of Michigan.
2. If any adult with special needs, child or youth arrives at a conference-related function, activity or event with signs of abuse or neglect, the event director shall immediately implement this Policy's reporting procedures.
3. The reporting requirements in this Policy are the minimum requirements. This Policy does not preclude anyone from reporting a known or suspected case of abuse or neglect to others for the protection of an adult with special needs, child or youth. Unless such protection requires otherwise, however, confidentiality of the information reported or received shall be respected to protect the rights and interest of the victim, the alleged perpetrator, and their families.
4. Under Michigan law anyone reporting in good faith a known or suspected case of abuse or neglect to the Children's Protective Services or the Adult Protective Services is immune from civil or criminal liability which might otherwise be incurred thereby.

B. Reporting Procedures

1. The care provider shall immediately report the known or suspected abuse or neglect to the event director.

2. If suspected or alleged perpetrator is on premises he or she is to be isolated from the program and have no contact with adults with special needs, children, or youth.
3. Within 24 hours, the event director shall telephone an oral report to the Children's Protective Services or Adult Protective Services in the county of the function, activity or event. This oral report shall be made in conjunction with the person having made the observations or received the disclosure. The following information will probably be required in the oral report.
   a. Name, age and gender of the alleged victim and other family members
   b. Address, phone number and/or directions to the alleged victim's home
   c. Parents' place(s) of employment
   d. Description of the suspected abuse
   e. Current condition of the alleged victim.
4. Within 72 hours, the event director, with the person initiating there port, shall submit a completed State of Michigan "Report of Known or Suspected Child Abuse or Neglect" to Children's Protective Services or its equivalent to Adult Protective Services in accordance with the directions given at the time of the oral report.
5. The event director and the entire staff of the Conference-related function, event, activity or program shall cooperate with Children's Protective Services or Adult Protective Services in its subsequent investigations.
6. Following contact with local Children's Protective Services or Adult Protective Services the event director shall inform:
   a. The chairperson of the group sponsoring the Conference-related function, activity or event.
   b. The conference staff person assigned to the ministries of the sponsoring group. The staff person shall inform the Council Director, the Bishop and the District Superintendent of the sponsoring District.
   c. The facility director, manager or host church clergy person.
7. Notification of a parent or legal guardian of the alleged victim of abuse or neglect which occurred prior to the Conference-related function, activity or event shall be determined by Children's Protective Services or Adult Protective Services. When it is determined that a parent or legal guardian shall be notified, the event director shall call the parent or legal guardian informing her/him of what has been observed, and what steps have been taken in response to those observations. Unless otherwise instructed by Children's Protective Services or Adult Protective Services, the event director shall follow the parent's or legal guardian's wishes regarding the continued participation of the involved adult with special needs, child or youth.
8. As much as possible, the event director and all others shall keep matters of the known or suspected abuse or neglect completely confidential. The incident is not to be discussed with persons other than those involved in the reporting.

C. Reporting When the Alleged Perpetrator is the Care Provider or Conference Employee

When the event director becomes aware of or receives a report of alleged abuse or neglect by a care provider or Conference employee, or the care provider is the known or suspected perpetrator, the event director or the person who received the disclosure or the one witnessing the abuse or neglect shall report the abuse or neglect:

1. If suspected or alleged perpetrator is on premises he or she is to be isolated from the program and have no contact with adults with special needs, children, or youth.
2. Within 24 hours to Children's Protective Services or Adult Protective Services by oral report.
3. To the chairperson of the sponsoring group of the function, event, activity or program.
4. To the Conference staff person assigned to the ministries of the sponsoring group. The staff person shall inform the Council Director and the Bishop. For functions, events, activities or programs sponsored by a West Michigan District group, the corresponding District Superintendent.

5. To the facility director, manager or host church clergy person.
6. Within 72 hours, by a completed State of Michigan "Report of Known or Suspected Child Abuse or Neglect" to Children's Protective Services or its equivalent to Adult Protective Services in accordance with the directions given at the time of the oral report.

D. Reporting When the Alleged Perpetrator is the Event Director

When anyone at a Conference-related function, activity or event becomes aware of or receives a report of alleged abuse or neglect by the event director, she/he shall:

1. If suspected or alleged perpetrator is on premises he or she is to be isolated from the program and have no contact with adults with special needs, children, or youth.
2. Within 24 hours make an oral report to Children's Protective Services.
3. The chairperson of the sponsoring group shall inform:
   a. The Conference staff person responsible for the ministries of the sponsoring group. The staff person shall inform the Council Director and the Bishop. For functions, events, activities or programs sponsored by a West Michigan District group, the staff person shall inform the corresponding District Superintendent.
   b. The facility director or host church clergy person.
4. Within 72 hours, the chairperson of the sponsoring group, with the person initiating the report, shall submit a completed State of Michigan "Report of Known or Suspected Child Abuse or Neglect" to Children's Protective Services or its equivalent to Adult Protective Services in accordance with the directions given at the time of the oral report.

E. Reporting When the Alleged Perpetrator is a Michigan Area Clergy Person or Diaconal Minister

1. If suspected or alleged perpetrator is on premises he or she is to be isolated from the program and have no contact with adults with special needs, children, or youth.
2. The event director shall:
   a. Within 24 hours, make an oral report to Children's Protective Services or Adult Protective Services.
   b. Inform the Conference staff person assigned to the ministries of the sponsoring group. The staff person shall inform the Council Director and the Bishop. For functions, events, activities or programs sponsored by a West Michigan District group, the staff person shall inform the corresponding District Superintendent. This District Superintendent shall inform the respective supervising District Superintendent.
   c. Inform the facility director, manager or host church clergy person.
   d. Within 72 hours, the event director, with the person initiating the report, shall submit a completed State of Michigan "Report of Known or Suspected Child Abuse or Neglect" to Children's Protective Services or its equivalent to Adult Protective Services in accordance with the directions given at the time of the oral report.
3. The Michigan Area Clergy Sexual Misconduct Policy shall be implemented for Michigan Area clergy persons or diaconal ministers. For cases involving United Methodist clergy from outside the Michigan Area the respective supervising bishop shall be informed. For cases involving non-United Methodist clergy, the respective supervising judicatory authority shall be informed.

F. Reporting When the Alleged Perpetrator is Another Adult with Special Needs, Child or Youth

1. If suspected or alleged perpetrator is on premises he or she is to be isolated from the program and have no contact with adults with special needs, children, or youth.
2. When the event director becomes aware of or receives a report of alleged abuse or neglect by another adult with special needs, child or youth, she/he shall, within 24 hours, make an oral report to the local law enforcement agency and follow that agency's instructions.
3. The event director shall inform:
   a. The conference staff person assigned to the ministries of the sponsoring group. The staff person shall inform the Council Director, the Bishop and the corresponding District Superintendent for functions, activities or events sponsored by a West Michigan District.
   b. The facility director or manager.

c. The parents or guardians of both parties unless instructed otherwise by the local enforcement agency.

G. **Reporting All Other Suspected Cases of Abuse or Neglect**

In all other cases of suspected abuse or neglect, the event director and the conference staff person assigned to the ministries of the sponsoring group shall be immediately notified, and the reporting procedures referenced above shall be implemented.

Section V: Follow-Up Procedures After Reports of Known or Suspected Abuse or Neglect

A. **General Goals and Objectives**

After reporting procedures have been implemented, the following goals and objectives as prioritized below shall be addressed:

1. Protection for the alleged victim and other adults with special needs, children and youth from any continued exposure to abuse or neglect.
2. Care for the spiritual, emotional, and physical well-being of the alleged victim and the alleged perpetrator.
3. Respect and preservation of the legal rights of both the alleged victim and the alleged perpetrator.
4. Safeguarding the privacy of all parties involved.
5. Care for the spiritual and emotional well-being of the Conference.
6. Protection of the legal and financial interests of the Conference.

B. **Investigation**

1. Conference employees and volunteers shall not conduct any investigation of reports or accusations of abuse or neglect.
2. Following the guidance of an attorney representing the Conference, the Conference shall cooperate in any proper investigations by the Children's Protective Services, Adult Protective Services, law enforcement agency, liability insurer, and the parties involved.

C. **Response Procedures**

When the alleged abuse or neglect involves (1) a conference or district employee as the alleged perpetrator, (2) an abuse occurring on Conference premises, or (3) an adult with special needs, child or youth participating in any Conference-related function, activity, event, or program, the following procedures shall be observed: [For alleged abuse or neglect involving Michigan Area United Methodist clergy persons or diaconal ministers see item 8 in this section.]

1. The status of the accused care provider (if applicable) shall be immediately suspended, and he or she shall not be permitted to continue providing any services for adults with special needs, youth or children in any Conference-related function, activity, event, or program. Certification may be re-instated only after satisfactory completion of the screening qualifications set forth in this Policy.
2. The Bishop or designee shall appoint a contact person to handle, oversee, and/or represent the Conference in all communications with the Children's Protective Services, Adult Protective Services, law enforcement agencies, attorneys, and investigators.
3. The Bishop of designee shall give written notice to the liability insurance carrier for the Conference.
4. If the alleged perpetrator is an employee of the Conference, the Conference Personnel Committee may discharge or place the employee on a leave of absence pending the completion of any investigations by the Children's Protective Services, Adult Protective Services, any responding law enforcement agencies, and/or the completion on any legal proceedings. A leave of absence may be with or without pay, at the discretion of the Conference Personnel Committee. The employee may be reinstated after a leave of absence or discharge, only if approved by the Abuse Prevention Team following satisfactory completion of the screening qualifications set forth in this Policy.
5. The Bishop or designee shall be the spokesperson solely authorized to respond to the media and general public. The designee may or may not be the same person appointed in item 2 of this section.

6. When appropriate the bishop shall inform the Conference of the situation and how the Conference is responding to it.
7. Everyone involved in the response shall document her/his activities and all communications regarding the suspected abuse or neglect.
8. When the alleged perpetrator is a Michigan Area United Methodist clergy person, The Michigan Area Clergy Sexual Misconduct Policy shall be implemented.

D. Response to the Victim(s) and the Accused

1. Pastoral care shall be extended to the victim, the accused and their families.
2. The Conference shall continue to express and share its Christian care, love and support for, both, the victim and the accused, as well as their families. It will be a difficult time for all parties involved and may be when they need the love and support of their Conference family the most. Although the practice of abuse, neglect, or the making of false accusations is not to be condoned, we will continue to acknowledge that God's grace is available to all. All persons are valued human beings created in God's image.

Section VI: Revisions

A. This policy shall be reviewed annually by the Abuse Prevention Team.

B. The Abuse Prevention Team may temporarily adjust this Policy between sessions of the Annual Conference as needed in consultation with the Council Director or designated Conference staff person. Annual Conference approval is necessary to make these revisions permanent.

1. Proposed revisions shall be submitted in writing to the members of the Abuse Prevention Team at least 15 days prior to the consideration of said proposed changes by the Abuse Prevention Team.
2. Revisions shall be effective 120 days after Abuse Prevention Team action unless otherwise specified by the Abuse Prevention Team action.
3. All Conference-related groups shall be informed of the revision(s)within 30 days of the decision giving them 90 days notice.

Section VII: Implementation

This policy shall be effective June 1, 2000 for all Conference-related functions, events or activities.

Definitions

For this Policy, the following definitions will apply.

"Abuse" means harm or threatened harm to the health or welfare of an adult with special needs, child, or youth by any person responsible for the health or welfare of an adult with special needs, child, or youth that occurs through non-accidental physical or mental injury; sexual abuse, sexual exploitation, or maltreatment [State of Michigan Compiled Laws Act No. 238, Public Acts of 1975, Sections 722.622.2(c)]; sexual harassment, sexual contact, sexual molestation, disseminating, exhibiting, or displaying sexually explicit material.

"Abuse Prevention Certification" refers to the training and education of Abuse Prevention Certified care providers.

"Abuse Prevention Team" means all persons, individually and collectively, who are appointed by the Conference to serve on a committee or task force for the purpose of training care providers and those responsible for implementing this Policy.

"Adult" means a person at least 18 years of age.

"Adult Protective Services" refers to the Adults Protective Services Division of the Family Independence Agency in the State of Michigan which guards the safety and welfare of persons in Michigan over the age of 18 years.

"Adult with special needs" refers to persons overt he age of 18 years of age who are mentally or physically impaired (e.g., mental illness or disability) or incapacitated (e.g., drugged or unconscious).

"Applicant" means a person who is applying to be approved as a care provider.

"Appropriate" means conduct that one could reasonably assume would be acceptable and permissible by the child's parent or guardian.

"Child" or *"Children"* or *"Youth"* refers to a person under 18 years of age [State of Michigan Compiled Laws Act No. 238, Public Acts of 1975, Sections 722.622.2(b)].

"Care provider" means anyone (including employees, volunteers, lay and clergy) charged with supervising adults with special needs, children, and youth during a Conference-related function, event or activity. A certified care provider has completed the Abuse Prevention Certification.

"Child neglect" means harm or threatened harm to the health or welfare of an adult with special needs, child, or youth by a parent, legal guardian, or any other person responsible for the health or welfare of an adult with special needs, child, or youth that occurs through either of the following:

a. negligent treatment, including the failure to provide adequate food, clothing, shelter, health care, and protection from abuse; or

b. placing an adult with special needs, child, or youth at an unreasonable risk to the health or welfare of an adult with special needs, child, or youth by failure of the parent, legal guardian, or any other person responsible for the health or welfare of an adult with special needs, child, or youth to intervene to eliminate that risk when that person is able to do so, and has, or should have, knowledge of the risk. [State of Michigan Compiled Laws Act No. 238, Public Acts of 1975, Sections 722.622.2.(d)].

"Child Protective Services" refers to the Children's Protective Services Division of the Family Independence Agency in the State of Michigan which guards the safety and welfare of children in Michigan under the age of 18 years.

"Church" means the local congregation.

"Conference" means the West Michigan Conference of The United Methodist Church.

"Conference-related" means any function, event or activity sponsored by, planned and/or implemented by persons representing the Conference, any of its districts or other connectional body beyond the local congregation and within the Conference. This definition includes all camp ministry functions, events and activities.

"District Superintendent" means the acting District Superintendent of the respective District of the West Michigan Conference of The United Methodist Church or her/his designee.

"Employee" means any individual receiving a wage, salary or other compensation from the West Michigan Conference for services rendered beyond and not necessarily related to the specific Conference-related function, event or activity, including all full-time and part-time employees.

"Event director" refers to the person over seeing all personnel and programming at a Conference-related function, event or activity.

"Event site" means the location of a Conference-related function, event or activity. This does not exclusively apply to a United Methodist facility.

"Leader" means anyone directly responsible for supervising and overseeing the specific Conference- related function, event or activity.

"Parent or Guardian" means any parent, step-parent, foster parent, grandparent, or appointed guardian who has the general responsibility for the health, education, or welfare of a child, youth or adult with special needs.

"Sexual abuse" means engaging in any sexual contact or sexual penetration with a child, the sexual exploitation of an adult with special needs, child, or youth, the sexual harassment of an adult with special needs child, or youth, the sexual molestation of an adult with special needs, child, or youth, and/or disseminating, exhibiting, or displaying sexually explicit material to an adult with special needs, child, or youth, regardless of whether such conduct is with or without the knowledge or consent of the adult with special needs, child, or youth *[State of Michigan Compiled Laws Act No. 238, Public Acts of 1975, Sections 722.622.2(k)].* In general, sexual abuse of an adult with special needs, child, or youth includes any form of sexual conduct in which a victim is being used for the sexual stimulation of the perpetrator. It may be violent or nonviolent. It includes sexual behaviors involving touching, such as fondling, as well as oral, genital and anal penetration, intercourse, and rape. It also includes sexual behavior that does not involve touching, such as sexually suggestive comments, obscene phone calls, exhibitionism, displaying

pornographic materials, and allowing adult with special needs, children, or youth to witness sexual activity. It includes any conduct that involves adults with special needs, children, youth in sexual behaviors for which they are not personally, socially, emotionally, or developmentally ready.

"Sexual contact" means the intentional touching of the intimate parts or the clothing covering the immediate area of the intimate parts of a child, youth or adult with special needs.

"Sexual exploitation" means allowing, permitting, or encouraging an adult with special needs, child, or youth to engage in prostitution or in the photographing, filming, creating electronic or computer generated images or any other form of depicting an adult with special needs, child, or youth engaged in actual or suggestive sexual conduct. *[State of Michigan Compiled Laws Act No. 238, Public Acts of 1975, Sections 722.622.2(l)].*

"Sexual harassment" means any unwanted sexual advance or demand, either verbal or physical, which is perceived by the recipient as demeaning, intimidating or coercive. ***[See*** The Book of Resolutions of The United Methodist Church 1996, *p. 482]*

"Sexual penetration" means sexual intercourse or any other intrusion, however slight, of any part of one's body, or of any object, into any intimate part of the body of an adult with special needs, child, or youth.

"Sexually explicit material" means any printed, electronic or computer generated matter, picture, sculpture, or sound recording which can reasonably be construed as being produced for the purpose of stimulating sexual excitement, arousal, or gratification.

"Shall, Should, and May" were carefully chosen terms used in this Policy, given recognition to their different meanings. *"Shall"* is to be considered mandatory, *"may"* is to be considered permissive, and *"should"* is to be considered a term of strong encouragement.

"Volunteer" means any person receiving no salary, wages or other compensation for providing any services, care, guidance, assistance, or supervision for any adult with special needs, child, or youth in a Conference-related function, event or activity.

"Youth" [See "child"]

PPR #13 Covenant of Clergy Sexual Ethics
A Policy of the West Michigan Annual Conference

Statement of Covenant

God has called us, through the grace of Jesus Christ, into covenant with God and one another. This covenant is intended by God to be a means of reconciliation, justice, faith, hope, and love. We live out this covenant in the Church. This covenant implies that there are standards to which clergy are expected to adhere and assumes that each clergy person seeks to live according to these high standards. "Ordination and membership in an Annual Conference in The United Methodist Church is a sacred trust" (*The Book of Discipline of The United Methodist Church, 2000,* ¶359.1). Sexual misconduct/sexual abuse/sexual harassment of any kind is sinful behavior against God and one another. Not only does such behavior violate a person's integrity but it also constitutes an unjust use of status and power which breaks this sacred trust. Therefore all clergy are expected to exercise the most compassionate judgment and to live out the highest ethical standards regarding the role of human sexuality in all interpersonal relationships.

Preamble

This policy is intended to assist the ministry of the Church by stating expected standards of behavior and by defining inappropriate sexual conduct by clergy. It is further intended to provide guidance so that when incidents of sexual misconduct/sexual abuse/sexual harassment are alleged, the complainant and the respondent may experience grace, justice, and reconciliation. Grace means unconditional love, but it does not mean escaping the consequences of inappropriate actions.

This policy is provided to the lay and clergy members of the West Michigan Annual Conference with the hope that it can assist us in creating and maintaining healthy relationships of integrity and safety for the sake of our common ministry to the people of God in the name of Jesus Christ.

Theological Reflections

Scripture teaches that male and female are created in the image of God, and are of equal value in Christ. From the beginning God intended that all people live out this equality in relationship with one another. Jesus was sent into this world that all persons might experience whole relationships with God and each other.

The Book of Discipline of The United Methodist Church-2000 (¶161.G) states: "We recognize that sexuality is God's good gift to all persons. We believe persons may be fully human only when that gift is acknowledged and affirmed by themselves, the Church, and society. We call all persons to the disciplined, responsible fulfillment of themselves, others, and society in the stewardship of this gift."

I. Definitions

A. Clergy – The term "clergy" as used in this policy includes all ordained, commissioned, licensed, and consecrated persons serving in the West Michigan Annual Conference, including those serving in extension ministries, on leave, honorable location, retired, and those lay people assigned to pastoral ministry in a local church by a District Superintendent.

B. Sexual Misconduct and Sexual Abuse[1] – The terms sexual misconduct and sexual abuse as used in this policy include sexual contact or inappropriate sexual behavior (not limited to sexual intercourse) by the clergy with an adult or minor parishioner, client, church staff person, or colleague, abusing their vulnerability, regardless of by whom it was initiated.

C. Sexual Harassment[1] – The term sexual harassment as used in this policy applies to conduct by the clergy with an adult or minor parishioner, client, church staff person, or colleague, abusing their vulnerability, regardless of by whom it was initiated and is defined as follows: "*Sexual Harassment* – We believe human sexuality is God's good gift. One abuse of this good gift is sexual harassment. We define sexual harassment as any unwanted sexual comment, advance, or demand, either verbal or physical, that is reasonably perceived by the recipient as demeaning, intimidating, or coercive. Sexual harassment must be understood as an exploitation of a power relationship rather than as an exclusively sexual issue. Sexual harassment includes, but is not limited to, the creation of a hostile or abusive working environment resulting from discrimination on the basis of gender.

Contrary to the nurturing community, sexual harassment creates improper, coercive, and abusive conditions wherever it occurs in society. Sexual harassment undermines the social goal of equal opportunity and the climate of mutual respect between men and women. Unwanted sexual attention is wrong and discriminatory. Sexual harassment interferes with the moral mission of the Church" (*The Book of Discipline of The United Methodist Church-2000,* ¶161.I).

D. These definitions in I. B. and I. C. above are also applicable in the context of ministries in which there are not "parishioners," but there is a community which acknowledges the authority of the clergy as a spiritual leader, such as, but not limited to, appointments to extension ministries, honorable locations, leaves, or retirements.

---

[1]Sexual misconduct, sexual harassment, and sexual abuse are chargeable offenses in *The Book of Discipline of The United Methodist Church-2000 (¶2702).*

II. Standards for Clergy Conduct

A. Clergy related to the Annual Conference are accountable for the ways they respond to persons who ask assistance and/or over whom they have authority. A violation of clergy relationship, clergy responsibility, and clergy authority is abusive and unethical and could result in the discontinuance of ordained, commissioned, licensed, consecrated status or assignment.

B. Clergy have the responsibility for developing healthy and ethical relationships with other persons. Married clergy have made a vow to nurture and maintain a faithful marital relationship. Single clergy must maintain appropriate sexual conduct in dating relationships as understood in our Christian teaching.

C. Personal integrity and mature professional conduct are a part of every clergy relationship. Such standards prohibit any sexual misconduct/sexual abuse/sexual harassment with a parishioner or client entrusted to his/her sacred care.

III. Expectations

A. Clergy often relate to persons who are fragile and vulnerable, and therefore, clergy must exercise special care:
1. To maintain psychological, emotional, and spiritual health;
2. To be properly and adequately prepared and educated, including continuing education, in order to provide appropriate help for those in their care;
3. To seek counsel, advice, and supervision.

B. Clergy self-discipline requires self-awareness and a standard of ethics which is implied and described in the vows of ordination and consecration.

C. All those within the clergy covenant of the Church are encouraged to discern when particular support, therapy, or other assistance should be sought for clergy colleagues.

IV. Misunderstandings and False Accusations – Fear often surrounds the issues of misunderstandings and false accusations. Certain words and behaviors may be heard, seen, and felt in a different way by one person than by another person. False accusations may sometimes be made. It is understood, therefore, that all care will be taken by those involved in the investigation to determine the validity of a complaint and the appropriate response.

V. Retaliation – It is important to protect persons who truthfully disclose such misconduct. Retaliation against those persons by anyone is prohibited.

VI. Confidentiality and the Responsibility for Reporting Clergy Sexual Misconduct – Clergy sexual misconduct/sexual abuse/sexual harassment places an unfair and unavoidable burden on the victim of such conduct. Truth-telling may be risky and painful and may also stir up strong feelings of fear and anger for all involved. Even so, truth-telling has the power to release both offenders and victims from the secrecy, denial, and guilt that result from sexual misconduct/sexual abuse/sexual harassment.

The Church is a place for healing and justice; therefore, it must recognize, prevent, and stop sexual misconduct/sexual abuse/sexual harassment. All clergy and laity bear sacred responsibility to become informed of appropriate standards of conduct and to address alleged sexual misconduct/sexual abuse/sexual harassment. Clergy and laity alike bear responsibility for confronting one another with knowledge of sexual misconduct/sexual abuse/sexual harassment.

When the covenant of the clergy has been broken by instances of sexual misconduct/sexual abuse/sexual harassment pain and disruption occur. Sexual misconduct/sexual abuse/sexual harassment creates many victims: those directly involved, spouses, families, congregations, and their surrounding communities. In those moments the Church is called to bring about healing, reconciliation, and restoration of all parties. This may include encouragement and support of an aggrieved person, care for one committing the offense, and initiation of complaint procedures as outlined in *The Book of Discipline of The United Methodist Church 2000* (¶359).

VII. Procedure – If you have experienced sexual misconduct/sexual abuse/sexual harassment you may contact the office of a District Superintendent or the Bishop. These addresses and phone numbers are available in any local United Methodist Church.

The Book of Discipline of The United Methodist Church-2000 will be followed in response to complaints which are initiated. Every complaint will be taken seriously and treated with integrity and confidentiality.

VIII. Final Notes – If any provision of this policy is in conflict with *The Book of Discipline of The United Methodist Church, The Book of Discipline of The United Methodist Church* shall prevail. Such conflict shall not be grounds for invalidating the entire policy.

Copies of this document are available from the Conference and District Offices.

PPR #14 Conference Policy for the Health Insurance Program

I. ELIGIBILITY: There are two classes of eligibility under the Group Health Insurance Program, (or The Program, defined as follows:

A. Mandatory Class: Upon enrollment, participants under the Mandatory Class with their spouse, domestic partner and dependents shall be covered automatically during active appointment to and after retirement from a local church or employment in the Conference, unless they waive participation. Waiver of participation by persons in the Mandatory Class is allowed only if coverage for the participant is obtained through the employer of the participant's spouse, or domestic partner.

B. Optional Class: Persons under the Optional Class have the option to request coverage for themselves, their spouse, domestic partner and dependents within 90 days from date of the qualifying event, e.g., employment in a Conference agency or local church, divorce or leave status. If they choose not to participate and then later change their mind, they may enroll only during the open enrollment period. In all cases, it is required that the salary paying unit or the participant remits the premium monthly to the Conference Treasurer.

II. DOCUMENTATION: The Cabinet shall provide the Conference Treasurer with information of appointment, termination, or change of appointment status of Clergy persons in accordance with the guidelines for The Program. This set of information is contained in the Appointment Change Report of the respective district superintendent. Information for Lay persons shall be provided by the employing agency.

III. MANDATORY CLASS. Persons under the Mandatory Class are:

A. All Clergy persons who are appointed half-time or more by the bishop in local churches or Conference Agencies in the West Michigan Conference.

B. All full-time lay employees (minimum 30 hours per week) of the Conference.

C. Clergy persons on Incapacity Leave status who are qualified to receive CPP benefits.

D. Lay employees on Disability Leave who are qualified to receive Workers Compensation Insurance benefits.

E. Clergy on Retired status whose appointment of at least ten years immediately prior to retirement was within The United Methodist Church structure within the Michigan Episcopal Area; however, exemption may be granted by the Board of Pension and Health Benefits upon request by the Cabinet to facilitate clergy appointments. This rule will be effective for those with appointment dates on July 1, 2003 and later.

F. Surviving spouse and eligible dependents of deceased participants in the Mandatory Class.

IV. OPTIONAL CLASS. Premiums for this class of persons during active employment and after retirement are the responsibility of the participant or the employing agency and not of the Conference. Persons under the Optional Class are:

A. Full-time employees (minimum 30 hours per week) of a local church during active employment or after retirement.

B. Clergy granted voluntary leave of absence or sabbatical.

C. District Superintendent Appointees with the recommendation of the Cabinet

D. Spouse divorced from a participating clergy of a lay employee for a maximum duration of two years subject to termination upon remarriage or coverage elsewhere, and subject to the provisions of the court decree.

E. Retired clergy who are not receiving pension benefits or retired Conference lay employees who are less than 62 years old.

V. DEFINITIONS:

A. Eligible Dependents are dependents of the participant as of the date of retirement or disability leave, who are not permanent residents outside of the U.S.A. They are:

1. Spouse, or domestic partner of the participant The definition of domestic partner will be determined by the insurance carrier.
2. Unmarried children under 19 years of age.
3. Unmarried children 19 to 25 years of age who are registered students in regular full-time attendance in school, provided they are principally dependent upon the participant for support and maintenance.
4. Surviving spouse and/or eligible dependent children of deceased participant.
5. Handicapped children regardless of age who are qualified dependents under the law but excluding their spouse, domestic partner or children.

B. Retired participant means a clergy person who has been placed on a retired relationship by the West Michigan Conference, or a lay employee who retired from employment in the West Michigan Conference.

C. Clergy on Incapacity Leave means a clergy person who has been placed on incapacity leave status and receives CPP benefits from the General Board of Pension and Health Benefits.

D. Clergy on Leave of Absence or Sabbatical means clergy who has been placed on any of this status by action of the Conference Board of Ordained Ministry.

E. Ineligible Classes: The following persons shall not be eligible to participate in The Program.

1. Clergy members of the Conference who are employed outside the West Michigan Conference structure.
2. New spouse, new domestic partner and new dependents of a participant after the participant's retirement or being placed on disability leave.
3. Children who are no longer deemed dependents because of age.
4. Married children.

VI. EFFECTIVE DATE OF INSURANCE. The health insurance of persons in the Mandatory Class are effective on the first of the month following the date of the initial appointment of clergy persons or of the employment of lay persons in the Conference upon enrollment.

VII. TERMINATION OF INSURANCE.

A. Clergy or Lay Participants

1. Appointment or employment terminates for any reason, except retirement or incapacity leave.
2. The Program is terminated
3. Required payment is not made after the 60-days grace period.
4. Death

B. Dependent

1. Person no longer meets the definition of a Dependent
2. Required payment is not made after the 60-days grace period.
3. Participant requests termination of a dependent's coverage

VIII PREMIUM BILLING AND CONTRIBUTION. Insurance premium billing and contribution shall be determined as follows:

A. Mandatory Class.

1. The premium contribution of a Charge for each clergy participant in the Program shall be a Blended Rate which is a portion of the Composite Rate. The formula for calculating the Composite Rate consists of dividing the total cost of the Program for the following year by the number of participants enrolled as of July 1 of the current year.

2. The premium contribution of participants is the applicable percentage of the composite rate based on the participant's compensation and the approved sliding scale, as follows:

$20,000 and less	=	5% of composite rate
$20,001 to $25,000	=	6% of composite rate
$25,001 to $30,000	=	7% of composite rate
$30,001 to $35,000	=	8% of composite rate
$35,001 to $40,000	=	9% of composite rate
$40,001 to $45,000	=	10% of composite rate
$45,001 to $50,000	=	12% of composite rate
$50,001 to $55,000	=	13% of composite rate
$55,001 to $60,000	=	14% of composite rate
$60,001 and greater	=	15% of composite rate

3. A charge whose pastor's participation in the Program has been waived because of the spouse's or domestic partner's coverage in another plan will be billed $100 each month.

B. Optional Class
 1. The salary paying unit that is responsible for paying the premium shall pay monthly the actual cost of the premium as determined by the Board.
 2. If there is no salary paying unit responsible, the participant shall pay the actual premium cost as determined by the Board.

C. Subject to Payment of 10% Minimum Premium Contribution, premium billings of Retired Clergy, Clergy on Incapacity Leave Status and Retired Conference Lay Employees shall be determined as follows:
 1. Premiums for retired clergy who have attained age 65 years and 20 years of service to the church or 35 years of service to the church regardless of age, and eligible dependents, shall be paid by the Conference at the rate of 5% for every year up to 20 years of full-time service, subject to the preceding rule under

III. E. Less than full-time service shall earn pro-rata credit.
 2. Retirees not qualified to be in the Medicare supplemental program because of age (i.e. less than 65 years old), will pay the applicable premium percentage based on the rate of the active plan.
 3. Clergy on Incapacity Leave Status who were actively participating in the Program at the time of being placed on incapacity leave status with Cumulative Protection Plan (CPP) benefits, and their eligible dependents shall be provided coverage under the Program at the expense of the Conference. If such clergy remain on incapacity leave until retirement, they shall be eligible for the benefits as provided in the preceding paragraph (VIII.C.1) and the years on incapacity leave shall be counted as years of service.
 4. Premiums for Retired Conference Lay employees who have attained age 65 years and eligible dependents, shall be paid by the Conference at the rate of 5% for every year up to 20 years of full-time service to the church, provided that they shall have served in the Conference for the 10 years immediately preceding retirement.
 5. Conference Program coverage shall be Secondary and Medicare Primary. Persons under Medicare primary coverage are required to enroll in Medicare Parts A and B at their own expense.
 6. All retired participants in the Mandatory Class are required to contribute a minimum 10% of the retiree program cost as determined by the Board.

IX. PREMIUM COLLECTION
 A. In order to avail themselves of tax exemption benefits, participants in the active plan must complete a Flexible Spending Account enrollment form which authorizes the withholding of premium contribution.

B. Local churches shall be required to remit monthly to the Conference Treasurer the total of the blended rate and the amount of the participant's premium contribution as billed.

C. Likewise, Conference lay employees shall be required to pay their premium contribution and the Conference Treasurer is authorized to withhold the amount from payroll based on the completed Flexible Spending Account enrollment form.

D. Failure to remit premium payments for participants within the 60 days grace period from the due date shall result in termination of coverage, unless prior arrangements have been made with the Conference Treasurer.

E. The Conference Board of Pension and Health Benefits shall be authorized to arrange with the General Board of Pension and Health Benefits the monthly withholding from pension benefits of retired participants the amount of premium contribution required from each retired participant.

F. In the event of financial distress on the part of a mandatory participant, a Medical Benevolence grant may be requested according to the procedures and guidelines established by the Conference Board of Pension and Health Benefits. The application form shall be furnished by the Conference Treasurer upon request.

X. PLAN ADMINISTRATION

A. The Conference Board of Pension and Health Benefits is the designated plan administrator and fiduciary. The Plan is centrally administered through the Office of the Conference Treasurer who acts as the Conference Benefits Officer. The administration of The Program shall be governed by this policy and the Board is granted the authority:

1. To set benefit levels, premium rates, participant premium contributions and Plan funding arrangement including prudent Stop Loss insurance and reserve funding in order to keep The Plan financially sound. The board shall make an annual report on The State of the Plan at Annual Conference and, to the extent practicable, will seek input from the Annual Conference of administrative matters that affect Plan participants.
2. To retain consultants, retain or consult with actuaries and contract third party administrators and to select health care networks and providers of Stop Loss insurance coverage.
3. To invest funds through its Investment Committee in accordance with the social principles in The Book of Discipline.
4. To interpret Plan provisions through the Conference Treasurer whose interpretation in writing will be considered final unless appealed to the board which has the final authority to decide any issue under the Plan.

B. The Conference Board of Pensions and Health Benefits is amenable to the Annual Conference which has the final authority to amend, suspend or terminate The Program in whole or in part in an Annual Conference session or special session called for the purpose, provided that any proposal that may affect The Program shall be referred to the board for study, and evaluation before any Annual Conference action is taken.

PPR #15 Conference Plan for Disaster Response

This plan outlines the roles and responsibilities of those involved in disaster response in the West Michigan Conference, as well as processes to ensure the seamless flow of information and assistance to those affected by disaster. Local churches wishing to create a LOCAL CHURCH DISASTER RESPONSE plan should contact the Conference Office or visit the Disaster Response / Local Church Resources section of the West Michigan Conference website.

INTRODUCTION

A disaster is any specific event, natural or man-made, which results in overwhelming physical, economic and/or emotional damage to a community. It is in these settings that the Church has both the opportunity and the responsibility to reach out in meaningful ways with the love and hope of Jesus Christ. To ensure timeliness, avoid redundancy and provide an effective and appropriate response, the church must be ready, at all levels, when disaster strikes. This means planning and preparation *before* disaster strikes. With this in mind the West Michigan Annual Conference of The United Methodist Church has organized a structure and guidelines to facilitate the ability of the local church to be in ministry to persons in need as a result of a disaster. This plan establishes guidelines for responding to disasters within the West Michigan Annual Conference.

Purpose

- To provide immediate relief for acute human need and to respond to the suffering of persons in our communities caused by natural or man-made disaster.
- To resource and equip local United Methodist churches and districts as they assist their communities and individuals to prepare, respond to and recover from disaster.
- To assist and train District and local church disaster response coordinators to address emerging and ongoing issues related to disaster relief.
- To work cooperatively with the appropriate Conference units, ecumenical bodies, and interdenominational agencies in the identification of, advocacy for, and assistance with ministries for disaster response.
- To work cooperatively with United Methodist Communications in promotion of the One Great Hour of Sharing offering.

> *"I tell you the truth, whatever you did for one of the least of these friends of mine, you did for me."*
> Matthew 25:40 (modified)

Scope

In the event of a disaster, resources available to the local church (i.e., volunteers, money, expertise, etc.) are sometimes limited or may not match the need. This is where the connectional system of The United Methodist Church can provide support and resources to the local church to respond effectively and appropriately. The following individuals and teams are typically active in disaster response in the West Michigan, depending on the nature, size and location of the disaster:

- Local Church Disaster Coordinators and local volunteers
- District Disaster Response Coordinators
- Conference Disaster Response Coordinator
- Conference Emergency Preparedness Committee
- Bishop, District Superintendents and extended Cabinet members

Visibility

The visible presence of The United Methodist Church is essential in any type of disaster regardless of the scope. Specific responses by agents of the Annual Conference are essential for the on-going well-being of God's people. These responses deal in three areas of life: spiritual, emotional and physical.

- **Spiritual response**: Addresses the issues of seeing how God's presence is available in the midst of suffering, despair and grief. The Church's primary task is to be present in the midst of suffering and to act as an agent of reconciliation. It is the responsibility of the Church to remind people that God really does care and to urge troubled hearts to trust God in times of stress and disaster.
- **Emotional response**: Must address the problems of loneliness, shock, disbelief, delayed grief and a multitude of related emotions that accompany those disasters that affect the lives of people. Pastors should seek specialized training to better equip them for meeting the needs of their people under such trying times. The individual districts and the Annual Conference should be leading the way in providing such training and making it desirable for all pastors and other interested persons to attend.
- **Physical response**: Will be more immediately seen and needed but is no more important than the spiritual and emotional responses to the people. The physical response must address itself to physical needs that are immediate as well as long term: scope of physical loss, finances, facilities and an unending list of needs that are unseen and are unique to a particular situation.

Whom Do We Help?

We help all persons in need regardless of race, creed, religious affiliation, gender, etc. The love of Jesus Christ knows no limits.

Who Does What When?

This question is the one to which the majority of this plan addresses itself. In answering the question of "Who Does What When?" the concept of "TURF" must be set aside. "Who is in charge?" is not the primary concern because the plan is in charge of the situation and we all function under its guidance. Laity, local church pastors, Disaster Response Coordinators, District Superintendents, Conference staff persons, Bishops, all must work together to achieve the common goal of reaching out to and helping God's people in the name of Christian love.

BEFORE DISASTER STRIKES

Every local church in the West Michigan Annual Conference shall develop a disaster response plan for themselves, unique to their particular locale, circumstances and resources, which "dove-tails" into the Conference plan. For assistance in this, please contact the Conference Office.

Conference, District and Local Church Disaster Response Coordinators and Organizations will benefit by learning about disaster response needs and resources available in their particular areas. This will be accomplished best as they:

- Evaluate their disaster response capabilities.
- Develop a relationship with their county emergency management organization.
- Develop plans and protocols to assist local congregations in responding to communities following a disaster.
- Prepare their facilities.
- Train congregation members / staff.
- Secure supplies.

WHEN DISASTER STRIKES

It is to be remembered that the first response in a disaster is through the Emergency Management Division of the Michigan State Police. The next line of response is by the American Red Cross and/or the Salvation Army. These groups are responsible for the immediate needs of a disaster including rescue, mitigating the results of the disaster, providing food, shelter and other physical needs. We must be careful not to interfere with the services that they are mandated to provide.

1. The Local Church Disaster Response Coordinator is the point person in the local situation. He/she reports to the District Disaster Response Coordinator and the District Superintendent. Assessment needs to be done as soon as possible.
2. The District Disaster Response Coordinator is the point person for coordinating all relief efforts within the District. He/she maintains contact with the local church pastor(s), Local Church DRC, the District Superintendent, and the Conference Disaster Response Coordinator, and makes his/her assessment of the situation as needed.
3. The District Superintendent makes contact with the local church(es) and pastor(s), assimilates reports and forwards them to the Conference level, works with the District Disaster Response Coordinator and provides oversight and support.
4. The Bishop provides pastoral oversight through the Cabinet. An on-site visit within seventy-two (72) hours is highly recommended.
5. The Conference Disaster Response Coordinator coordinates relief efforts within the Conference and calls the Emergency Preparedness Committee together within seventy-two (72) hours to receive reports and coordinate action plans.

   While needs assessments are immediately necessary, our response depends on what agencies such as the American Red Cross, the Salvation Army, State and Federal agencies are doing. We need not and should not, duplicate their work. We need to respond to those who are left out of the system, meet the needs that the other agencies cannot, and to build on what they have done.

ORGANIZATION

The Conference Plan for Disaster Response defines the responsibilities of the local church, the District and the Conference. It also includes an overall plan of ministry towards those who are affected by a disaster.

Conference Emergency Preparedness Committee

- The Conference Disaster Response Team (CDRT) is that committee of the West Michigan Conference charged with the responsibility of responding to disaster(s) in the Conference. The membership (with voice and vote) consists of:
  - Conference Disaster Response Coordinator
  - District Disaster Response Coordinators or Representative
  - Conference Volunteer in Mission Coordinator
  - Conference Director of Communications
  - Representative from the Board of Global Ministries
  - Cabinet Representative
- The CDRT may be activated to meet the needs of a disaster by:
  - Bishop or Bishop's designee
  - Director of Connectional Ministries
  - Conference Disaster Response Coordinator
  - Affected district's Disaster Response Coordinator / Superintendent
- Upon such activation of the CDRT, the following persons shall automatically become ex-officio members with voice and vote:
  - Bishop or Bishop's designee
  - Director of Connectional Ministries
  - District Superintendent(s) of the affected area
  - Conference Treasurer or Assistant Treasurer.
- The CDRT shall coordinate the Conference response, establish policies, procedures, and funding guidelines, plan for the disbursement of funding, and arrange for evaluation and an accountability report.
- In cooperation with District Disaster Teams, assist districts and local churches in the preparation of disaster ministry plans.
- Provide training opportunities and resources in all phases of disasters including, but not limited to:
  - Early Response Teams (ERT)
  - Connecting Neighbors (Local Church Disaster Planning)
  - Spiritual and Emotional Care (Care Team)
  - Case Management
  - Volunteer Management
- Work collaboratively with other conferences of The United Methodist Church, The United Methodist Committee on Relief (UMCOR) and other organizations active in disaster as appropriate.
- Create and implement a system for tracking, coordinating and deploying trained disaster response volunteers within and outside of the West Michigan Annual Conference.
- Collaborate with District Disaster Teams for location of supply depots and distribution and collection sites.

Conference Disaster Response Coordinator

- Support the Conference Emergency Preparedness Committee in carrying out the plan. Responsibilities include administrative oversight and implementation of the plan, policies and funding procedures.
- Shall see to the provision of reports, materials, and secretarial services to facilitate the implementation of the plan.

- Coordinate disaster response / disaster ministry / preparedness training opportunities throughout the Conference.
- Assign and deploy Early Response Teams as needed / requested.

Office of the Bishop

Leadership by the resident Bishop is extremely important. For many, a bishop's appearance at the disaster site symbolizes the "awesome presence" of Christ and the commitment of his Church to relief of suffering. ***Don't dismiss or minimize the value of "symbols" to people in need. The Bishop's role as the symbol of a caring church cannot be filled by anyone else!*** Communities receiving a visit are grateful that their pain was important enough for the Bishop to be present with them. Communities not receiving a visit won't forget the slight. Unfortunately, District Superintendents and other well-intentioned staff members often try to "protect" a Bishop's time by wrongly advising that it isn't necessary for him or her to go to the disaster area. This protection does much damage to the Conference in the long run. A disaster is a tragedy, and the Conference cannot conduct "business as usual." *(Don't delay too long. A visit long after the crisis gives the impression that the Bishop couldn't be bothered enough to drop everything and come when people needed it.)*

- The Bishop, the Clergy Assistant to the Bishop, or the Conference Director of Connectional Ministries shall serve as the official liaison with the General Church and contact the United Methodist Committee On Relief (UMCOR) and arrange for an on-site visit by an UMCOR Disaster Response Coordinator, if necessary.
- In consultation with a representative of the CDRT and the Conference Treasurer, shall make a request to UMCOR for relief funds, if needed.
- The Bishop, or his/her designee, in consultation with the Conference Committee on Communications, shall become the official spokesperson and information officer. Said spokesperson and information officer will contact the appropriate Conference media outlets.
- Offer pastoral care and oversight either directly or through the Cabinet.

District Superintendent

The District Superintendent (DS) is responsible for oversight and supervision of churches and local pastors in the District where they serve. Therefore, in the event of a disaster affecting their District, it is imperative that the District Superintendents are kept informed so that they, in turn, can inform the Bishop as well as minister to those in their care. Including the DS on the District Disaster Team facilitates communication and ensures that the DS has input into the response effort.

- Contact and coordinate response with the District Disaster Response Coordinator (DDRC).
- Coordinate the compiling of needs assessment for the area or District.
- Develop a disaster plan for the District, in consultation with the District DRC.
- Provide support and guidance for the pastors involved.
- Contact all churches and pastors involved in the disaster as soon as possible. If contact is by telephone, a personal contact should be made within twenty-four (24) hours.
- Physically survey damage within twenty-four (24) to forty-eight (48) hours.
- If the DS is not functional an active DS or a former DS will be assigned by the Bishop to the affected area. This Superintendent will assume responsibilities for the District in consultation with the presiding DS and will function as long as necessary.
- If the disaster affects more than one-quarter (1/4) of the churches, an active DS or a former DS will be assigned by the Bishop to the affected area. This Superintendent will team with the presiding DS and will function as long as necessary.
- Will work out of the District office, if operational. If not operational, the District Superintendent and DDRC will determine an appropriate location, preferably an operational church close to the disaster area.

District Disaster Response Coordinator

The District Disaster Response Coordinator (DDRC) is the point of contact for coordinating disaster response and disaster-related efforts at the District level. The DDRC is a partner and advocate for the local churches in their District as it relates to disaster issues as well as liaison to the District office and the Conference Emergency Preparedness Team.

- Assume primary responsibility for implementing the Conference plan in his/her District.
- He/she will operate out of the nearest operational local church.
- He/she will coordinate relief efforts in the area: Who, What, When, Where, How.
- If DDRC is unable to function, the DDRC from the closest unaffected District will function in his/her place.
- Develop a District Disaster Team that includes your District Superintendent.
- In concert with the Conference and your District Disaster Team, develop a District Disaster Response Plan.
- Work with local churches and extension ministries to assist them in the preparation of their disaster ministry plans.
- Cooperate and coordinate with the District Superintendent, local church pastor(s), and laity on relief efforts.
- Participate in and build relationships with agencies active in disaster response in your District (*VOAD, COAD, LTRO, EOC, interfaith organizations, etc.) If you are unable to participate yourself, select a representative from the District team so that The United Methodist Church continues to be recognized, at all levels, as a valuable partner in the disaster response community.
- Identify locations for supply depots, identify and inventory available equipment, update forms and procedures as necessary. Collaborate with other District Disaster Teams for location of supply depots, distribution sites, etc…
- If not contacted by the local church(s) or the District Superintendent within twenty-four (24) hours of the disaster, he/she shall initiate contact.
- Serve as a member of the Conference Emergency Preparedness Committee.

Local Church

The point of contact at the community level for all United Methodist assistance in a disaster is the local United Methodist church. However, the local church is not expected to respond alone or in a vacuum. There are many resources available to assist the church. By working with a local church disaster team, the District Disaster Coordinator and the Conference Emergency Preparedness Committee, many of the necessary connections are easily made.

The Local Church Disaster Coordinator is the point person for ensuring fulfillment of the roles and responsibilities of the local church. See page 12 for more information.

The responsibilities of the Local Church include but are not limited to:

- Work with the pastor or designated church leadership to identify a Local Church Disaster Response Coordinator and recruit a disaster response team. If the pastor is not part of the team, ensure that the team includes a process for keeping the pastor informed and updated regarding activities before, during and after a disaster.
- Develop a local church plan that includes:
  - Caring for people
  - Caring for church facilities
  - Caring for community
  - Caring for others in the Conference and beyond
- The pastor and the Board of Trustees should annually review insurance coverage and make an annual inventory of church property and contents and provide a safe repository of valuable records.
- Communicate with the DDRC regularly to ensure knowledge of the church plans in the event of a disaster. This should include any plans the church has to partner with other organizations, such as the American Red Cross as a shelter, the county as a point of distribution, etc.

- Send a copy of the plan to the DDRC / District office, as well as the CDRC / Conference office.
- Encourage those with special needs to register with the county (most counties have plans to evacuate special needs persons).
- Know where the District depot(s) is located. Does the church have a plan to contribute to the depot regularly?
- Keep strict and separate accounting of disaster funding and document all expenditures and receipts of money.
- Annually receive UMCOR's One Great Hour of Sharing offering.

If a church wishes to become a shelter or work as a service center during a disaster, a written agreement between the American Red Cross and the local church is required. If the church contracts with the Red Cross, a signed copy of this agreement is to be sent to the Conference Office. With an agreement, the American Red Cross covers the liability and damage that might occur in relation to operating the shelter and also provides staff to run the operation.

Pastor

The point of contact at the community level for all United Methodist assistance in a disaster is the ßvacuum. There are many resources available to assist the church. By working with a local church disaster team, the District Disaster Coordinator and the Conference Emergency Preparedness Committee, many of the necessary connections are easily made.

- Work with church leadership to identify a Local Church Disaster Response Coordinator and recruit a disaster response team.
- Primarily function as spiritual caregiver to his/her local church. In the event that the local church does not have a LCDRC, the pastor would serve as point person for ensuring fulfillment of the roles and responsibilities of the local church.
- Provide a general needs assessment within twelve hours to the District Superintendent. *
- Provide a specific needs assessment within twenty-four (24) to forty-eight (48) hours including names and needs and submit them to the District Superintendent. *
- If the pastor is not functional, the church Lay Leader, Chairperson of the Trustees or other specifically named individual will become the primary contact person and assume responsibility for said needs assessment.
- Work out of the local church office, if operational. If not operational will work out of the parsonage. If that is not operational, it should be assumed that the local church is unable to provide any type of meaningful leadership. The District Superintendent should then immediately assign another qualified person to go into the charge to serve in pastoral ministry.

  * *unless he/she has specified someone else.*

Local Church Disaster Response Coordinator

It is important for the coordinator to know that this task is a team effort! By working with the District Coordinator, the Conference Coordinator, the pastor, lay leader, and church officials, many of the connections can be easily made. There are resources available in all of these areas. The Local Church Response Coordinator is the point person when a disaster strikes and should quickly team with the pastor and District Disaster Response Coordinator.

- Work with the pastor and Trustees in developing a disaster response plan.
- Develop a Disaster Response Committee to help the pastor and Trustees to make an assessment of special needs populations within the community (i.e., the elderly, poor, unemployed, immigrants, disabled, shut-ins, children, etc.), persons often most vulnerable in a disaster.
- Compile a list of persons willing to volunteer to implement the Disaster Plan (i.e., help serve food, do cleanups, provide transportation, child care, reconstruction, organize support groups, etc.).
- Keep church plans updated and apprise the congregation of those plans.

- Communicate with the District Disaster Coordinator and inform him/her of the scope of the church plans and the church's availability to help in a disaster that might occur outside of their local community.
- Encourage the church's participation in One Great Hour of Sharing and other special advances for the purpose of disaster relief.
- Establish communication with the District Disaster Coordinator and maintain a list of phone numbers to be used to connect with the appropriate Conference Disaster Response Team members.
- Develop contacts with local relief agencies (County Emergency Management, American Red Cross, Salvation Army, Faith Based Groups, etc.) through participation in the local VOAD (Volunteer Organizations Active in Disasters). If there is no local VOAD, it would be wise to talk with the Conference Disaster Coordinator about either helping set up a local VOAD or working with some other local group. As a Conference we encourage working with the VOAD if at all possible. (VOAD – Volunteer Organizations Active in Disasters).
- Become familiar with existing community service agencies. (Do they have a plan to help the needy in a disaster as an extension of their normal services?)
- Develop an Assessment Team and allow Conference Trainers to teach this team how to effectively do assessment work following a disaster.

FUNDING IN DISASTER RESPONSE

Policies and Procedures Related to Funds

Financial Limitations

- UMCOR money is to provide immediate relief of acute human need.
- UMCOR money cannot be used to repair or rebuild disaster-damaged church property.
- General Appeal money can only be used for its designated purpose.
- No money will be given to survivors. All disbursal of funds will be made to approved vendors.
- Annual Conference money will be used for needs designated by the **Emergency Preparedness Committee.**
- Conference money must be used first before General Appeal and UMCOR money can be used.
- All UMCOR money not used must be returned to UMCOR at time of close out.

Resources Available From UMCOR

- $10,000 will be sent to the Conference Treasurer as soon as the Bishop makes the request for UMCOR assistance. This is start-up money for disaster relief.
- UMCOR money can be requested for any additional amount over the original $10,000. Detailed budgets need to accompany the request. Requests for more than $100,000 need the approval of the entire UMCOR Board of Directors which meets only periodically.
- Upon invitation UMCOR personnel will assist the Conference and the Conference Disaster Response Coordinator following a disaster.
- Equipment such as generators, pressure washers, ice coolers for bulk ice, etc. can be requested. UMCOR takes care of transporting the equipment to the scene at no cost to the Conference.
- Flood Buckets and Health Kits are available through Sager Brown at no cost to the Conference.

General Information

- All West Michigan Annual Conference churches will be encouraged to participate in the special Sunday offering set aside for One Great Hour of Sharing. Funds will go to the United Methodist Committee on Relief.
- Churches will also be encouraged to donate moneys for disaster-response needs before and after a disaster. Unless specified, the moneys collected will be placed in a Conference Disaster-Response Fund and administered by the Conference Treasurer.

- Large disasters may generate significant amounts of donated money from within and outside the Conference, most of it arriving during the first one or two months following the event. In such cases, the Conference Treasurer will assign an accounting number for these designated funds.
- The Conference Treasurer will keep a record of expenditures based on purpose of expense (i.e., materials/furnishings, utilities, contractor services, etc.), and not according to districts or disasters. District Disaster Coordinators requesting funds are expected to keep a record of moneys spent on a disaster response under their leadership and make the necessary report.
- Request for money from the Disaster-Response Fund will follow rules governing check requisition as set forth by the Conference.
- Because of the nature of disasters, funds must be distributed during the relief phase in a timely manner. Paper trails and good accounting are essential for all transactions, but quickly launching disaster operations requires considerable flexibility in disbursing money. In most instances, once-a week disbursements work well.
- The Conference Treasurer is not responsible for spending decisions for a disaster.
- Church funds are needed most during the Recovery Phase, long after contributions have dwindled or stopped completely. For this reason, it is necessary to let government and other agencies spend their money during the Relief Phase while church funds are conserved. Special circumstances may make it necessary to provide small amounts of emergency assistance to a few survivors during the Relief Phase. Any assistance should be based on documented need, and pre-set equal amounts should not be provided to survivors. Assistance should wait until case management is in place to set priorities for genuine needs, before most funds are dispensed.
- As soon as possible following a disaster, the Conference Disaster Response Coordinator will use the network of the Conference and District leadership to notify congregations of the need for money. The Bishop will make the decision to request moneys for the disaster response. A Conference mailing to congregations, e-mail to pastor, and the Conference Web site may be used to inform churches of the disaster and ask that an offering be taken during two Sundays following the disaster. Congregations will be asked to help while the news is fresh. Any delay may cause members to assume the church is not involved in the response, and they will donate to other agencies.
- It is important to vigorously generate local funds for local disasters. UMCOR expects a conference to spend conference-generated funds first—before denominational money is used.

UMCOR Funding Guidelines

Part I - Relief Phase

- **Request for funds must come from the Bishop's office with the assistance of the Conference Disaster Response Coordinator.**
  - To meet immediate emergency needs—food, clothing, and shelter.
  - To begin set-up of response organization.
  - To assist local churches with added burdens caused by the response needs.
  - Relief Phase request may not exceed $10,000 per disaster incident.

Part II - Recovery Phase

- **Request for UMCOR grants must be accompanied by a preliminary budget and come from the Bishop's office. Assistance and format for this procedure can come from the Conference Disaster Response Coordinator.**
  - To provide direct assistance to clients.
  - To pay salary of conference-hired staff for recovery organization.
  - To help set up the disaster-recovery organization.
  - To cover administrative costs; which will be less than 20 percent of total request
  - Funds may not be used to repair church owned property unless specified in funding request.

APPENDIX A

Management of Volunteers

The role of volunteers is to assist people in the devastated area to rebuild their lives, often through rebuilding damaged structures. This work should be done so as to reduce the trauma and chaos of the situation as much as possible. The primary concern should be the survivor! The Conference Disaster Response Coordinator, or designee, in conjunction with the Conference UM-VIM Coordinator, makes all management and deployment decisions for volunteers (including Early Response Teams).

Volunteers should / must:

- Be Safe Sanctuary Certified by the Conference. This is ***required*** for all ERT members.
- Be willing to listen and assist survivors in obtaining a range of disaster-related services.
- Be ready and willing to go when their skills are needed and their team can be accommodated.
- Be caring, understanding, sensitive, and nonjudgmental.
- Be willing to do the tasks assigned.
- Know and understand the disaster stages and timelines.
- Contact the UM-VIM Coordinator, Early Response Coordinator or the designated contact in devastated areas to see when and how they can offer assistance.
- Check in with local coordinator / authorities for task assignments.
- Communicate so adequate time is available to prepare work assignments for skills of volunteers and the time they have to serve.
- Leave for the affected area with all sleeping and other personal needs for housing, gasoline and food.
- Only work on projects assigned by the appropriate coordinator (Unauthorized repairs can prevent owners from receiving insurance payments or federal assistance).
- Relief Phase Volunteers must be ERT-certified.
- Be Flexible.

Volunteer teams should:

- Be led by a trained UM-VIM / ERT team leader.
- Not go unprepared, unannounced or uninvited!
- Appoint a leader or liaison to coordinate with local response group.
- Plan on providing needed materials for rebuilding or cleanup.
- (ERT's) provide own transportation, food, lodging and first aid.
- Set aside time for sharing group experiences, rest, and worship.

Remember: Volunteers are guests and servants!

Early Response Teams (ERTs)

An Early Response Team is a specialized, trained and certified collection of volunteers that comes self-contained into an area, if and when requested.

The **purpose** of an Early Response Team is to provide a caring Christian presence in the aftermath of a disaster.

The **tasks** of an ERT are:

- Take steps to prevent further damage to a family's personal property (stabilize). Such steps may include tarping, debris removal, chainsaw work, and cleaning out flooded homes.
- To be part of a caring ministry of listeners who will help the survivors begin to heal.

Early Response Teams **DO NOT**:

- Make permanent repairs or begin rebuilding. To do so before insurance and government assessments are done and permission to proceed is given may reduce or eliminate any assistance from those sources. Such action can become a liability issue for team members, churches, and the Conference if teams are thought to hinder or duplicate a person's access to benefits.

- Arrive in a disaster area without an invitation from the Conference Disaster Response Coordinator.
- Out-of-conference teams DO NOT come in until invited by the North Central Jurisdiction UM-VIM Office or the affected conferences DRC.
- Come in unless they are trained, certified and recognized by the Conference, UMCOR and the UM-VIM Jurisdiction Office.
- Make promises to the survivors.

Connecting Neighbors – Local Church Preparedness

Disaster Response is an effective ministry by which we become instruments of God's healing and hope. By becoming the hands and feet of Christ, we share in a commitment to the spiritual, emotional and physical needs of people in a time of crisis. Local churches are in a unique position to be a positive force in response to disasters. While local church plans can not lessen the impact of a disaster, a well thought out and followed plan can help mitigate the emotional and spiritual impact. At the 2008 UMCOR Academy, Connecting Neighbors, Conference personnel were equipped to return to their respective conferences and share information for developing local church disaster response ministries. Part of this training is working with local churches to develop a written disaster response plan.

UM-VIM and Disaster Recovery Teams

Rebuilding and permanent repairs will be done by UM-VIM Disaster Recovery Teams and others who will work during the Recovery Phase.

These teams go in under the direction of the Conference UM-VIM Coordinator. Once the Recovery office is set up, the volunteer teams will work through the recovery office.

Donated Goods

- Do not solicit donations for clothing! Refer all such donations to the Seventh-day Adventists and/or the Salvation Army.
- Never send supplies unannounced or unexpected.
- In-kind (noncash) donations will be received based on specific needs or otherwise redirected to other agencies.
- Location for collection/distribution of donated goods will be determined by local coordinator based on available space and specific needs.
- Materials or financial assistance should be distributed through the direction of the local response unit.
- Cash donations are recommended and should be sent to the local church. Funds collected are for disaster relief. Some suggestions for use of excess funds:
  - Forward funds to the Conference Treasurer designated for the West Michigan Annual Conference Disaster Response Fund.
  - Use for local church disaster response ministry or missions trips.
  - Forward funds to UMCOR or apply to One Great Hour of Sharing offering.

Repair of Damaged Church Property

Unless specifically given for that purpose, money from the United Methodist Committee on Relief cannot be used for repairing churches. Under certain conditions, the District may seek to help churches raise money to repair churches damaged in a disaster. The Conference takes seriously the mandate that church-owned properties have adequate insurance, including flood coverage *(which requires a separate policy)*. The task of rebuilding or repairs will rest with each church and its trustees.

When Disaster Strikes – Checklist

Local Church Response Disaster Coordinator *and* Pastor	☐ Assesses general situation and physical needs of people and area and forwards initial assessment to the District Superintendent and the District Disaster Response Coordinator. ☐ Establishes contact with the local Emergency Management Team as soon as possible. ☐ Provides specific needs assignments within 24 hours. ☐ Begins seeking response to needs, general and specific. ☐ Coordinates relief efforts on a local basis.
District Superintendent	☐ Contacts pastor(s) involved and the District Disaster Response Coordinator as soon as possible. ☐ Receives report of pastor(s). ☐ Conducts on-site visit within 24 hours.
District Disaster Response Coordinator	☐ Conducts an on-site visit with the District Superintendent. ☐ Coordinates relief efforts for the District. ☐ Contacts the Conference Disaster Response Coordinator.
Conference Disaster Response Coordinator	☐ Conducts an on-site visit with the Bishop. ☐ Coordinates relief efforts, in cooperation with DDRC's.on a conference level. ☐ Works in consultation with the Bishop to coordinate communication efforts.
Conference Emergency Preparedness Committee	☐ Meets within 72 hours of the disaster. ☐ Receives reports, requests funds and dispenses funds as necessary and available.
Bishop	☐ Provides press information. ☐ Visits area(s) within 72 hours. ☐ Contacts District Superintendents. ☐ Requests funds from UMCOR, if needed.

X. MEMOIRS

A. Associates Members

1. Active

None

2. Retired

MARY CURTIS Born July 25, 1928. Died March 19, 2014.
Served Nashville Parish 1984; Sand Lake/South Ensley 1989; Comstock 1991; Retired 1998.

Mary was the mother of one son, Richard Curtis, whose wife is named Linda. Mary had two grandchildren: Corporal Ryan Curtis (Samantha) and granddaughter Kelly Curtis. Mary will be sadly missed by many.

B. Provisional Members

1. Active

None

2. Retired

None

C. Members in Full Connection

1. Active

None

2. Retired

RICHARD MATSON Born September 9, 1940. Died October 6, 2013.
Served Silver Creek 1963; Jonesville/Moscow Plains 1966; Cadillac: Selma St.-South Community 1968; Bear Lake Circuit Oct. 15, 1969; Whitehall/Claybanks 1971; Kalamazoo: Oakwood March 1, 1975; Harbor Springs Alanson 1979; Stockbridge 1987; Reed City 1990; Ovid 1993; Alden/Central Lake 1995; Retired 2003.
Richard Dingman was born September 9, 1940. He was adopted by Arthur and Beatrice Matson in 1942. He was an English major and enjoyed dramas. He wrote several dramas, directed dramas, and acted in them. Richard wrote and acted in "The Last Seder," an original re-enactment of the Last Supper. In the pastoral ministry, Richard served churches in the West Michigan Conference for 40 years and one year in the Kentucky Conference.

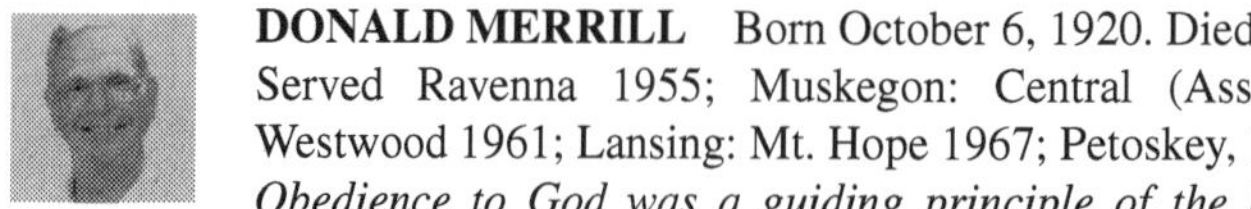

DONALD MERRILL Born October 6, 1920. Died October 29, 2013.
Served Ravenna 1955; Muskegon: Central (Assoc.) 1959; Kalamazoo: Westwood 1961; Lansing: Mt. Hope 1967; Petoskey, 1975; Retired 1986.

Obedience to God was a guiding principle of the life and ministry of Rev. Donald Merrill. In the last third of his life he steadfastly witnessed that his life would not have been as richly blessed if he had stayed in his very successful business career. As a current pastor in one of his early congregations said just last year, "I am still seeing today a harvest of the fruits of his ministry." Those of us who knew and loved him can honestly say we see that in our own lives almost every day.

DANIEL E. MILES Born May 1, 1946. Died May 26, 2014.
Served Concord 1969; East Lansing Chapel Hill/Gunnisonville Jan 1, 1972; Alden/Central Lake 1974; Honorable Location Dec 1, 1976 (Charge Conf: Saginaw State Street); Retired 2006

ARTHUR MURPHY Born January 11, 1945. Died September 29, 2013. Served Brandywine Trinity, 1987; Barryton/Chippewa Lake 1991; Bear Lake/Arcadia 1993; Colon 1999; Retired 2007.

CHARLES RICHARDS Born August 29, 1935. Died February 26, 2014. Served Bronson/Snow Prairie 1972; Bronson 1975; Kalamazoo: Stockbridge Avenue 1977; Lake Odessa: Central 1986; Coldwater 1989; Retired 1998.

Dad was genuine and had a wonderful way of reaching out and touching others that modeled Jesus' way of respecting the value of each individual child of God. He brought out the best in people, making sure they got the credit. He was humble, but never tired of telling others of the blessings God had given him. With a positive outlook, and in spite of challenges that might have worn down another, he trusted in God's goodness, grace and love, always looking forward to what God had in store for us and everyone he touched.

CHARLES SHIELDS Born June 19, 1936. Died November 25, 2013. Served Elk Rapids/Kewadin 1988; Battle Creek: Sonoma/Newton 1993; Galesburg 1995; Kalamazoo: Oakwood/Oshtemo 1997; Lake Odessa: Central 2000; Lincoln Road 2000; Retired 2002.

CARL STASER Born April 28, 1928. Died April 30, 2014. Served Lansing: Maple Grove 1956; Jonesville 1958; Frankfort/Elberta 1961; East Lansing: People's Church (Assoc.) 1964; Leave of absence 1978; Horton Bay 1979; Ovid 1980; Middleville/Parmelee Oct. 16, 1983; East Lansing: Chapel Hill/Gunnisonville 1988; Retired 1991.

Carl's happiest memory in the ministry was working with his wife Teddy to organize and lead a program for the care of children of migrant farm workers during the cherry harvests in 1963 and 1964 in Frankfort, MI. They teamed the Methodist and the Roman Catholic churches to care for up to 203 children per day, ages three months to ten years. Carl also helped organize and was the first secretary of the United Methodist North Central Jurisdiction Town and Country Association. A gregarious communicator, Carl wrote the "Religion in County Living" column for the "Michigan Farmer" magazine (twice a month), circulation 90,000, and had a daily radio talk show called "The Community Lives on WCSR" in Hillsdale, MI, for two years.

D. Deacons in Full Connection

1. Active

None

2. Retired

JANILYN McCONNELL Born February 17, 1933. Died July-14, 2013. Served in the following appointment in the West Michigan Conference as Deacon, Kewadin 1998; Retired 2003.

E. Local Pastors

1. Active

None

2. Retired

CHAR MINGER Born November 12, 1943. Died April 1, 2014.
Served Center Eaton/Brookfield (DSA) 1991; Center Eaton/ Brookfield (PTLP) Aug 1, 1991; Center Eaton/Brookfield (FTLP) Jan 1, 1994; Brookfield (PTLP) Dec 1, 1994; Galien/Olive Branch 1995; Kingsley 1999; Retired 2008; then served Griffith (RLA 1/4) 2009-2013.

Char enjoyed serving in ministry beyond the local church. She was an active member of the Emmaus Community, frequently serving on two and three Walks a year. Each year she and her husband, Dave, served in mission for a week at Henderson Settlement. The mission trip to Brazil and Bolivia with members of the West Michigan Annual Conference stood out as a high point of her ministry experience. Another highlight was traveling to Israel in 2000 with Dave, daughter, Stacy, and many dear friends.

F. Diaconal Ministers

None

G. Clergy in good standing from another denomination.

None

H. Other Clergy

CHARLES (CHUCK) F. COOLEY
Born June 27, 1918 • Died March 21, 2014

FRANK A. COZADD
Born May 17, 1927 • Died June 28, 2014

EDWARD L. DUNCAN
Died June 7, 2014

BRUCE FELKER
Born November 24, 1936 • Died September 17, 2013

RICHARD KIDDER
Born February 2, 1919 • Died August 14, 2013

WAYNE SPARKS
Born October 9, 1936 • Died May 19, 2013

I. Missionaries

None

J. Missionaries Spouses

None

K. Deaconesses

None

L. Certified Candidate for Ordination

None

M. Clergy Spouses

DAVID BOURNS Husband of Carol Bourns
Born March 8, 1940 • Died October 14, 2013

DOROTHY (DOTTIE) DOTEN Widow of Donn Doten
Born October 26, 1917 • Died August 16, 2013

JUNE ENTENMAN Wife of Ronald Entenman
Born June 1, 1934 • Died March 1, 2014

JUANITA FISCHER Wife of Fred Fischer
Born August 4, 1934 • Died January 20, 2014

MARCILE GARROD Wife of Charles Garrod
Born July 15, 1930 • Died September 7, 2013

BEATRICE (BEA) HORTON Wife of Robert Horton
Born April, 1929 • Died October 18, 2013

MARYLIN WESTON HUBLEY wife of Laurence (Larry) Hubley
Born November 17, 1942 • Died July 21, 2014.

MERRY ANN NADER Wife of Vince Nader
Born November 7, 1955 • Died May 22, 2014.

HELEN PRATT Widow of Ralph Pratt
Born July 3, 1925 • Died November 1, 2013

JOAN RICKARD Wife of O'Ryan Rickard
Born December 26, 1946 • Died November 8, 2013

ALICE SHORT Widow of Sidney Short
Born August 8, 1939 • Died November 17, 2013

RUTH WALKINSHAW-BOWEN Widow of Milford Bowen
Born August 3, 1905 • Died January 25, 2014

N. Child of the Parsonage

TIMOTHY DYKEMA Son of Nancy Boelens
Born March 23, 1969 • Died November 1, 2013

O. Diaconal Ministers' Spouses

None

P. Lay Persons *(Professionally Related to the Conference)*

JOY CRAWFORD Wife of Don Crawford, former Lakeview Camp manager
Born April 12, 1942 • Died September 27, 2013

LOUISE THOMAS Conference Older Adult Coordinator for many years
Born March 31, 1926 • Died October 13, 2013

MIKE ZALEWSKI Husband of Heartland District Administrative Assistant Melanie Zalewski
Born August 30, 1974 • Died November 18, 2013

XI. ROLL OF THE DEAD

For Roll of Deceased prior to July 20, 1938, consult Minutes of 1938 and before
For Roll of Deceased prior to June 12, 1967, consult Minutes of 1967 and before
For Roll of Deceased prior to April 7, 1977, consult Minutes of 1977 and before
For Roll of Deceased prior to June 2, 1986, consult Minutes of 1986 and before
For Roll of Deceased prior to July 1, 1994, consult Minutes of 1994 and before
For Roll of Deceased proir to July 1, 2005, consult Minutes of 2005 and before

Name	Date of Death	Place of Death	Age	Entered Reg. Ministry	Joined West Mich. Conference
Gordon Showers	October 23, 2005	Grand Rapids, MI	96	1940	1940
Ralph P. Witmer	January 3, 2006	Concord, MI	94	1934	1941
Paul Frederick	May 20, 2006	New Baltimore, MI	70	1958	1990
Phillip L. Brown	May 25, 2006	Columbus, OH	72	1953	1958
Marvin Zimmerman	August 20, 2006	Mason, MI	87	1960	1958
George O. Hartmann	August 24, 2006	Portage, MI	81	1954	1950
Timothy Boal	October 31, 2006	Grand Rapids, MI	59	1985	1978
Paul F. Albery	November 16, 2006	Chelsea, MI	90	1943	1941
Robert H. Jongeward, Sr.	Jan. 19, 2007	Deltona, FL	90	1942	1939
James W. Burgess	March 4, 2007	St. Louis, MI	88	1984	1981
William Foldesi	April 7, 2007	Mt. Pleasant, MI	55	(LP)	(LP)
William P. Myers, Jr.	April 15, 2007	Battle Creek, MI	61	(OF)	(OF)
Willard Gilroy	April 18, 2007	Battle Creek, MI	77	1960	1954
Harold L. Mann	May 4, 2007	Grand Rapids, MI	84	1957	1952
C. Robert Carson	July 17, 2007	Penney Farms, FL	101	1957	1958
William A. Blanding II	July 29, 2007	Clearwater, FL	101	1925	1925
Linda H. Hollies	August 18, 2007	Arizona	64	1996	1996
James H. Meines	November 3, 2007	Wyoming, MI	68	–	–
George C. Elliott	December 21, 2007	Fremont, MI	90	1939	1939
Laurence R. Grubaugh	Feb. 19, 2008	Hartford, MI	82	1959	1959
Theodore F. Cole	March 4, 2008	Chesterfield, MO	84	1959	1959
Thomas Peters	April 23, 2008	Potterville, MI	77	1958	1960
Richard A. Tester	April 29, 2008	Arizona	69		
Walter J. Rothfuss	April 30, 2008	Bridgman, MI	72	1961	1962
Kenneth W. Karlzen	June 14, 2008	–	72	1966	1966
H. James Birdsall	June 19, 2008	Grand Rapids, MI	95	–	–
Orin Daniels	July 28, 2008	–	–	–	–
Leon E. Dayringer	August 31, 2008	Apache Junction, AZ	83	1950	1967
Ronald M. Fassett	November 1, 2008	Grand Rapids, MI	75	1959	1959
D. Michael Maurer	November 10, 2008	East Jordan, MI	66	(FL)	(FL)
Sidney A. Short	January 16, 2009	Auburn, IN	81	1951	1951
John F. Sorensen	February 7, 2009	Grand Rapids, MI	85	1962	1962
Curtis W. Strader	March 11, 2009	St. Petersburg, FL	83	1954	1980
Arlo D. Vandlen	June 7, 2009	Comstock Park, MI	88	–	–
Robert Emory Betts	August 8, 2009	Eaton Rapids, MI	84	–	1951
Jesse Schwoebell	August 10, 2009	Plainwell, MI	76	–	–
Laurence Dekema	September 24, 2009	Plainwell, MI	89	–	–
James L. Breithaupt	October 9, 2009	Sears, MI	58	–	–
Russell M. Garrigus	December 16, 2009	Manistee, MI	77	–	–
Patricia A.Skinner	February 16, 2010	Mason, MI	73	–	–
John Buker	March 12, 2010	Pensacola, FL	78	–	1977
Lloyd A. Phillips	May 1, 2010	Niles, MI	82	–	1951
D. Hubert Lowes	May 25, 2010	Mattawan, MI	79	–	1963

Name	Date of Death	Place of Death	Age	Entered Reg. Ministry	Joined West Mich. Conference
Harry R. Johnson	June 6, 2010	Santee, CA	68	–	1979
Bernard W. Griner	1/2/2010	Interlochen, MI	95	–	–
R. Paul Doherty	7/26/2010	Rockford, MI	72	–	–
Howard A. Lyman	10/24/2010	Marshall, MI	90	1945	1945
David Yoh	12/8/2010	Holland, MI	–	1953	1953
Donald D. McLellan	12/12/2010	Harrisville, MI	85	–	–
Joseph Sprague, Sr.	6/1/2011	Wayland, MI	87	–	–
Frank S. Frick	6/19/2011	Quincy, MI	73	–	–
Bernard Fetty	1/30/2012	Scottville, MI	93	–	–
Doris L. Lyons	7/11/2011	Midland, MI	80	–	–
Harold R. Simon, Sr.	7/30/2011	Belding, MI	82	–	–
Carol Fetty (nee Cotton)	9/26/2011	Sccottville, MI	88	–	–
John L. Francis	2/20/2012	Grand Rapids, MI	84	–	–
John Myette	5/5/2012	Traverse City, MI	86	–	–
Lewis Arthur "Bud" Buchner	5/21/2012	Ovid, MI	66	–	–
Birt Beers	5/27/2012	Grand Haven, MI	82	–	–
Luella Mae Showers	6/30/2012	Grand Rapids, MI	70	–	–
Marshall R. Collins	7/18/2012	Northport, MI	82	–	–
H. Forest Crum	7/29/2012	Grand Rapids, MI	90	–	–
Gladstone L. Brown	8/2/2012	Alliance, OH	94	–	–
Carlos Page	8/9/2012	Tucson, AZ	88	–	–
Philip Jaquish	8/29/2012	Traverse City, MI	89	–	–
Edward L. Mohr	9/11/2012	Gobles, MI	64	–	–
Hoover Rupert	10/4/2012	Gaithersburg, MD	94	–	–
George W. Chaffee	10/14/2012	Grand Rapids, MI	93	–	–
Albert Frevert	12/1/2012	Mt. Pleasant, MI	86	–	–
Ward D. Pierce	12/2/2012	Three Rivers, MI	82	–	–
Eugene B. Moore	12/14/2012	Kalamazoo, MI	74	–	–
Garth D. Smith	1/20/2013	Logansport, IN	95	–	–
Lynn E. Grimes	1/20/2013	Grand Ledge, MI	69	–	–
Charles D. Grauer	4/3/2013	DeWitt, MI	68	–	–
Lloyd R. Van Lente	4/13/2013	Grand Rapids, MI	95	–	–
John Miller Moore, Jr	5/19/2013	Clio, MI	95	–	–
Allen B. Rice, II	6/16/2013	Sun City, AZ	89	–	–
Janilyn McConnell	7/14/2013	Traverse City, MI	80	–	–
Arthur C. Murphy	9/29/2013	Ocala, FL	68	–	–
Richard L. Matson	10/6/2013	Kentwood, MI	73	–	–
Don Merrill	10/29/2013	Grand Rapids, MI	93	–	–
Charles McLean Shields	11/25/2013	Rockford, MI	77	–	–
Charles Richards	02/26/2014	Bronson, MI	78	–	–
Mary Ellen Curtis	3/19/2014	Grass Lake, MI	85	–	–
Charlene A. Minger	04/01/2014	Eaton Rapids, MI	70	–	–
Carl W. Staser	4/30/2014	Penney Farms, FL	85	–	–
Daniel E. Miles	5/26/2014	Howell, MI	68	–	–
Richard M. Young	6/7/2014	Athens, MI	82	–	–

XII. HISTORICAL SESSIONS OF THE ANNUAL CONFERENCE

For information regarding previous sessions of the former Conferences of Evangelical United Brethren Church, refer to the Journal of the 107th Annual Session of the Michigan Conference (EUB) Pages 25 and 26 dated May 20-23, 1968.

For the Listing of previous Sessions of the West Michigan Annual Conference of the Methodist Church, please refer to the Journal of the West Michigan Annual Conference of the United Methodist Church Pages 240-241, dated June 12-15, 1974. (Note: Session no. 28 in 1996 refers to the 28th session of the United Methodist Church, as formed with the merger of the Methodist and EUB churches in 1968.)

No.	Date Began	Place	Bishop	Secretary
133	June 4, 1968	Albion, MI	Dwight E. Loder	H. A. Kirchenbauer
134	June 18, 1969	Albion, MI	Dwight E. Loder	H. A. Kirchenbauer
135	June 18, 1970	Albion, MI	Dwight E. Loder	H. A. Kirchenbauer
136	June 17, 1971	Albion, MI	Dwight E. Loder	H. A. Kirchenbauer
137	June 14, 1972	Albion, MI	Dwight E. Loder	L. R. Taylor
138	June 13, 1973	Albion, MI	Dwight E. Loder	L. R. Taylor
139	June 12, 1974	Albion, MI	Dwight E. Loder	L. R. Taylor
140	June 11, 1975	Albion, MI	Dwight E. Loder	L. R. Taylor
141	June 9, 1976	Albion, MI	Dwight E. Loder	L. R. Taylor
142	June 2, 1977	Albion, MI	Edsel A. Ammons	L. R. Taylor
143	June 14, 1978	Albion, MI	Edsel A. Ammons	E. K. Eldred
144	June 13, 1979	Albion, MI	Thomas M. Pryor	E. K. Eldred
145	June 11, 1980	Albion, MI	Edsel A. Ammons	E. K. Eldred
146	June 10, 1981	Albion, MI	James S. Thomas	E. K. Eldred
147	June 9, 1982	Albion, MI	Edsel A. Ammons	E. K. Eldred
148	May 31, 1983	Albion, MI	Edsel A. Ammons	Paul E. Patterson
149	May 29, 1984	Albion, MI	Edsel A. Ammons	Paul E. Patterson
150	June 11, 1985	Albion, MI	Judith Craig	Paul E. Patterson
151	June 10, 1986	Albion, MI	Judith Craig	Paul E. Patterson
152	June 9, 1987	Albion, MI	Judith Craig	Paul E. Patterson
153	June 14, 1988	Albion, MI	Judith Craig	Ronald B. Grant
154	June 13, 1989	Albion, MI	Judith Craig	Ronald B. Grant
155	June 12, 1990	Albion, MI	Judith Craig	Ronald B. Grant
156	June 11, 1991	Albion, MI	Judith Craig	Ronald B. Grant
157	June 9, 1992	Albion, MI	Judith Craig	John H. Hice
158	June 15, 1993	Albion, MI	Donald A. Ott	John H. Hice
159	June 14, 1994	Albion, MI	Donald A. Ott	John H. Hice
160	June 13, 1995	Albion, MI	Donald A. Ott	John H. Hice
28	June 11, 1996	Albion, MI	Donald A. Ott	Gail L. Friedrick
29	June 10, 1997	Albion, MI	Donald A. Ott	Gail L. Friedrick
30	June 8, 1998	Grand Rapids, MI	Donald A. Ott	Gail L. Friedrick
31	June 2, 1999	Grand Rapids, MI	Donald A. Ott	William C. Johnson
32	June 1, 2000	Grand Rapids, MI	Donald A. Ott	William C. Johnson
33	May 31, 2001	Grand Rapids, MI	Linda Lee	William C. Johnson
34	May 31, 2002	Grand Rapids, MI	Linda Lee	William C. Johnson
35	June 6, 2003	Grand Rapids, MI	Linda Lee	William C. Johnson
36	June 3, 2004	Grand Rapids, MI	Linda Lee	William C. Johnson
37	June 2, 2005	Grand Rapids, MI	Jonathan D. Keaton	Kathryn S. Cadarette
38	June 1, 2006	Grand Rapids, MI	Jonathan D. Keaton	Kathryn S. Cadarette
39	May 31, 2007	Grand Rapids, MI	Jonathan D. Keaton	Laura B. Clark
40	June 5, 2008	Grand Rapids, MI	Jonathan D. Keaton	Laura B. Witkowski
41	June 4, 2009	Grand Rapids, MI	Jonathan D. Keaton	Laura B. Witkowski
42	June 3, 2010	Grand Rapids. MI	Jonathan D. Keaton	William W. Chu
43	June 1, 2011	Grand Rapids, MI	Jonathan D. Keaton	William W. Chu
44	June 6, 2012	Grand Rapids, MI	Jonathan D. Keaton	William W. Chu
45	May 29, 2013	Grand Rapids, MI	Deborah L. Kiesey	Greg Buchner
46	June 11, 2013	Grand Rapids, MI	Deborah L. Kiesey	Greg Buchner

XIII. PLAN OF ORGANIZATION

Structure of the West Michigan Conference (effective July 1, 2014)

OUTLINE

I. INTRODUCTION
- A. Preamble to the Plan of Organization
- B. The West Michigan Conference Vision Statement
- C. Goal and Strategies
- D. Core Values and Beliefs
- E. Organizational Principles
- F. Definitions
- G. General Provisions
- H. Changes in the Plan or Organization

II. DISTRICT
- A. District Conference
- B. District Council on Ministries

III. ANNUAL CONFERENCE
- A. Standing Committees
- B. Conference Ministries
  - 1. Organization
  - 2. Meetings
  - 3. Responsibilities
  - 4. Conference Organizational Units:
    - a. Director of Connectional Ministries
    - b. Director of Communications
    - c. Conference Leadership Team
      - 1) Purpose
      - 2) Accountability
      - 3) Membership on the Conference Leadership Team
      - 4) Organization
      - 5) Meetings
      - 6) Responsibilities
      - 7) Relationships
      - 8) Conference Program Staff
      - 9) Narrative Summary
      - 10) Implementation
    - d. Agencies amenable to the Conference Leadership Team [If no "*" = amenable to the Annual Conference directly]
      - 1) Conference Ministries
        - a) Board of Christian Camping*
        - b) Board of Church and Society*
        - c) Board of Evangelism*
        - d) Board of Global Ministries*
        - e) Board of Higher Education and Campus Ministry*
        - f) Commission on Religion and Race*
        - g) Commission on the Status & Role of Women*

h) Committee on Cooperative Ministry*
i) Committee on Disability Concerns*
j) Committee on Disaster Response Team*
k) Committee on Hispanic/Latino Ministries*
l) Committee on New Church Establishment and Development*
m) Committee on Prison Ministry*
n) Committee on Racial/Ethnic Local Church*
o) Conference Council on Youth Ministries*
p) Michigan Area Haiti Task Force*
q) Michigan Area Indian Workers Conference*
r) UMCOR/Hunger Committee*
s) United Methodist Men*
t) United Methodist Women

2) <u>Communications and Records Ministries</u>
a) Communications Commission*
b) Commission on Archives and History*

3) <u>District and Local Church Ministries</u> (District Councils on Ministries or the equivalent)

e. <u>Finance and Property Ministries</u>
1) Council on Finance and Administration
2) Board of Trustees
3) Board of Pension and Health Benefits
4) Committee on Equitable Compensation

f. <u>Human Resources Ministries</u>
1) Abuse Prevention Team*
2) Area Committee on Episcopacy
3) Board of Lay Ministries*
4) Board of Ordained Ministry
5) Cabinet
6) Committee on Leadership Development
7) Conference Nominating Committee
8) Conference Personnel Committee
9) Joint Committee on Incapacity

g. <u>Other Conference Organizational Units</u>
1) Units With Conference Fiscal and Governing Control
2) Units Under Annual Conference Fiscal Control
3) Units Under Conference Governing Control
4) Units With Annual Conference Affiliation
5) Units With Annual Conference Representative Affiliation

I. <u>INTRODUCTION</u>

A. Preamble to the **<u>PLAN OF ORGANIZATION</u>:**

"The purpose of the Annual Conference is to make disciples for Jesus Christ by equipping its local churches for ministry and by providing a connection for ministry beyond the local church; all to the glory of God." ¶601, 2008 The Book of Discipline of The United Methodist Church.

The faithful Church remains open to what God is doing in the world. The Church aligns its organizations and practices with a vision of authentic Christian mission. In the spirit of Jesus Christ, disciples – corporately and individually – act boldly and creatively to reflect God's light to the world, to call persons to learn Christ's servant ways and to participate in God's purposes. Throughout history, when the Body of Christ has been open to God's new creation and willing to journey toward God's promise, the Holy Spirit has breathed vitality into its forms and blessed its ministry.

The radical nature of change today calls for continually rethinking both personal practices and connectional patterns. By God's grace we can create new paradigms more appropriate to the needs of our present day. The Conference must be grounded in mutual accountability and interdependency to live out its common vision for mission and ministry. As members offer diverse ideas and concerns, each person learns and grows through this interaction with one another. Thus, United Methodism continues to be grounded in the conciliatory principles of conferencing and connection.

This Plan of Organization of the West Michigan Conference establishes a structure that is flexible and responsive to the changing world in the 21st century while being faithful to the Conference's vision and mission. The WMC seeks to support and provide resources to the ministries of local congregations and provide for Conference organizational units that cannot be accomplished by local congregations.

B. THE WEST MICHIGAN CONFERENCE VISION STATEMENT:
"A living connection of disciples of Jesus Christ transforming the world through vital and fruitful congregations."

C. Goals and strategies
The following goals and strategies express specific ways by which the West Michigan Conference seeks to live out its vision:

1. Vitality and fruitfulness will be improved as we:
   - Create a culture where discipleship means more than membership
   - Create and nurture congregations that are seeking and reaching persons of all ages, genders, orientations, classes, religions, races, ethnicities, special needs, marital status and cultures.
   - Encourage the constant development and transformation of both lay and clergy leaders
   - Intentionally develop new congregations, new worship services, and new satellite locations for congregations
2. Discipleship will be fostered through congregations who:
   - Change lives through effective, engaging and inviting worship
   - Empower and equip people to call others into a new relationship with Christ
   - Teach and model effective Christ-like service as a way of life
   - Pray for healing and wholeness, both inward and beyond
   - Encourage people to identify and respond to a call of ministry and service
3. Transformation will take place as we create and nurture congregations who strive to:
   - Identify and engage the needs of their communities
   - Respond to ministries beyond the local church and throughout our United Methodist connection with both money and service
   - Work for justice so that all persons experience the peace of Christ
   - Risk change to move forward in mission and ministry

D. Core Values and Beliefs
This plan of organization is undergirded by the following core values and beliefs that are held by the West Michigan Conference:

A biblically based and spiritually centered culture, marked by:

- Ongoing Biblical Study – We continually seek and discern God's will for us through scripture. Through scripture "our faith is born and nourished, our understanding deepened, and the possibilities for transforming the world become apparent to us... Wesley believed that the living core of the Christian faith was revealed in Scripture, illumined by tradition, vivified in personal experience, and confirmed by reason."(¶104, 2008 The Book of Discipline of The United Methodist Church)
- Effective Communication – We will share with each other and the world the promise of new life that is found in Jesus Christ. The outward expression of our faith is contagious and transparent and desires to inform and to equip others who are spiritually lost and

seek Christ. The outcome for every Christian is to see the whole world as the people of God. We affirm the Great Commission. (Mathew 28:19-20)

- Flexibility and Responsiveness – We will intentionally and effectively respond to changing or new situations with passion and creativity. We expect an attitude of openness to the leading of the Holy Spirit in all matters, and responsiveness to the needs of all persons.
- Inclusiveness and Openness – Our practices will work toward inclusiveness with regard to ages, genders, orientations, classes, religions, races, ethnicities, special needs, marital status and cultures in all places and circumstances.

Faithfulness to our Wesleyan tradition of personal and social holiness, marked by:

- Accountability to a Common Vision and Mission – All conference, district, and local church organizations, boards, agencies and staff will be held accountable to align themselves with the vision and mission of the Conference.
- Discipleship – We will help people/churches strengthen their relationship with Christ through study, learning, growing and maturing in a faith that is real and a community that is alive and vital for this day and time. It affirms the talents and gifts given through the leading of the Holy Spirit and each person's place of service as their lives are transformed.
- Evangelism – We will focus on proclaiming the gospel and seeking, welcoming and gathering persons into the body of Christ. (¶122, 2008 The Book of Discipline of The United Methodist Church)
- Social justice – We desire a just world, and will be agents of healing. We reject all systems, structures and attitudes that divide. We pursue those things that will lead us to love our neighbor as ourselves as we "…do justice, love kindness and walk humbly with God (Micah 6:8)."

A connectional organization, marked by:

- Congregational Development – We will focus on starting new churches and revitalizing existing congregations.
- Leadership Development – We will provide for the ongoing preparation and development of lay and clergy leaders to carry out the ministry of the Church.
- Maintaining Connectionalism – The United Methodist connectional principle, born out of our historical tradition, biblical roots, and shared theological identity, is the basic form of our polity, the way in which we carry out God's mission as a people. Connectionalism is a network of interdependent relationships among persons and groups throughout the life of the whole Church. (¶112.3, 1992 The Book of Discipline of The United Methodist Church & ¶131, 2008 The Book of Discipline of The United Methodist Church)
- Ministry Focused on Local Congregations – We will offer support and resources for local congregations as they each offer evangelistic, nurture and witness responsibilities for their members and the surrounding area, and a missional outreach to the local and global community. (¶204, 2008 The Book of Discipline of The United Methodist Church)
- Faithful Stewardship – We take responsibility for the good care of resources entrusted to us such as: the talent, time and gifts of local churches and their constituents; the effective use, definition of and deployment of staff whether paid or volunteer; and the accumulation and distribution of resources facilitating the ministry of the local church, the Annual Conference and the wider connection.

E. Organizational Principles

The agencies of the West Michigan Conference will be more effective by being functional rather than representative. This structure is team-based rather than committee-based. Each member has a specific role.

The organizational principles of the councils, boards, commissions and committees (referred to as agencies) of the West Michigan Conference are that each agency will:

1. Fulfill its responsibilities in a manner consistent with achieving the vision, strategies and goals of the Annual Conference;
2. Organize itself around its functions, and have members chosen on the basis of functional need and passion for the area of the agency's work;
3. Adhere to the membership and organizational requirements in The Book of Discipline of The United Methodist Church;
4. Allow district conferences and district nominating committees to design their own organizational structures;
5. Recommend that The Conference Nominating Committee seek to achieve in all its nominations, the goal of 1/3 laymen, 1/3 laywomen, and 1/3 clergy with racial/ethnic representation in each organizational unit;
6. Emphasize the importance of nominating persons who expect to serve on a unit for at least four years. Although elections are annual, continuity of leadership is important, especially in smaller units.
7. Encourage the representation of youth and young adults on all organizational units of the Church and to affirm them as vital members of the Church of today.

F. DEFINITIONS:

- "Ad hoc" for the purpose of the particular end at hand.
- "Agency" a term to describe the various boards, councils, commissions, committees, divisions, or other units constituted. See ¶610 & 701, 2008 DISCIPLINE for fuller definition.
- "At-large" without regard to geography, specific responsibilities, or any other classification.
- "Board" one of the eight (8) program units of the Conference (Christian Camping, Church and Society, Evangelism, Global Ministries, Higher Education and Campus Ministry, Board of Laity, Ordained Ministry [program only]) each responsible to the Conference Leadership Team and having direct relationship with similar General Church agencies as well; The Board of Trustees, and the Board of Pension and Health Benefits each responsible to the Conference and having direct relationship with similar General Church agencies.
- "Conference" Hereafter the word Conference shall mean The West Michigan Conference of The United Methodist Church.
- "Conference Staff" Director of Connectional Ministries, Conference Treasurer/Administrator, Director of Communications, and such other program and/or administrative employees.
- "Co-opt" – to choose or elect as a member for a particular task or purpose.
- "DISCIPLINE" the word "DISCIPLINE" shall mean The Book of Discipline of The United Methodist Church as revised each quadrennium.
- "Matrix management style" coordinated system which works with intentional interweaving of operations and cooperation of organizational units to achieve an agreed upon end.
- "Ministry Team" employed leaders of the Annual Conference comprising the Bishop, Clergy Assistant to the Bishop, the District Superintendents, the Director of Connectional Ministries, Director of Communications, the Conference Treasurer/Administrator (all of the aforementioned comprise the Full Cabinet), the Conference Program Staff and the Director of the United Methodist Foundation.
- "Organizational Unit" an officially established council, board, commission, division, committee, task force, council, section of the Conference. This term means the same as "agency".
- "Task force" a small group selected to work for a designated time not to exceed two years on a designated assignment, then to be dissolved when the task is completed. Membership on a task force may come from anywhere, i.e., is not restricted to membership on the parent group. Persons who have membership on other organizational units may serve on a Task Force, if they choose. In the formation of the task force, attention should be given to inclusiveness (laity, clergy, gender, race and age.)
- "Exofficio" members on an organizational unit because of office or position with voice and vote unless otherwise stated.

G. General Provisions:

1. Membership eligibility. Only members of The United Methodist Church shall be eligible for membership on an organizational unit task forces excepted unless permitted otherwise by the DISCIPLINE, Conference, or this Plan of Organization.
2. Conflict of interest. No person receiving compensation from a Conference unit shall be eligible to be an officer on an organizational unit from which he/she would receive compensation, unless required by the DISCIPLINE, this Plan of Organization, or the expressed intention of this Conference. Care shall be given to avoid, as much as possible, appearance of conflict of interest of persons serving on organizational units who at the same time work with congregations or other bodies who receive funding from the Conference. No member of an organizational unit shall vote on any matters pertaining to Conference or District funding for any congregation or agency by which he/she is employed.
3. District Superintendency. The District Superintendents shall not be eligible for membership on any organizational unit of the Conference except as required by the DISCIPLINE or the expressed intention of this Conference.
   a. Superintendents shall serve as voting members of the respective District Councils on Ministries or the equivalent, and the several District Committees, etc. that exist.
   b. One District Superintendent shall serve as a voting member of the Conference Leadership Team as described herein.
   c. One District Superintendent shall be named by the Bishop to serve as a member
      1) without vote on
         i. The Council on Finance and Administration,
      2) and with vote on
         i. The Commission on Equitable Salaries,
         ii. The Personnel Committee.
         iii. The Board of Ordained Ministry
   d. For communication purposes District Superintendents may receive mailings and maintain contact with chairpersons of other organizational units but they shall not be expected to attend meetings of those units. Any person serving on a Conference organizational unit who is appointed to the Cabinet shall end such service at the Annual Conference when the appointment commences, or at least by the next Annual Conference if it is a midyear appointment. Nothing in these provisions shall be interpreted as preventing a District Superintendent from serving on any Jurisdictional or General Church agency, nor a Board of Trustees (or other governing body) of any group whose essential membership is not selected by this Conference.
4. Tenure. No person elected by the Annual Conference shall serve for more than eight (8) consecutive years from the date of his/her election on any organizational unit, or predecessor unit. Following any service of eight (8) years, there shall be a period of at least two (2) years before re-election to the same unit is possible. Persons elected shall serve until their successors are elected or appointed, even if this extends for a brief period the limit of their eight (8) year tenure.

   Exceptions to the rule of tenure are:
   a. the Board of Ordained Ministry who are elected and serve, in accordance with the current provisions of THE BOOK OF DISCIPLINE;
   b. The Rules of Order Committee and the Conference Facilitator who are elected annually;
   c. Those units listed under Article III., Section C.4.E. Other Conference Organizational Units. On these agencies, their election procedures, tenure, etc. shall take precedence.
5. Membership Restriction. A person shall not serve simultaneously as a member of more than one board. A Chair of any Conference board shall not serve on another Conference agency unless as an ex-officio member; exceptions could occur for missional reasons or when specific expertise is required by an agency. No person shall be elected to serve on an organizational unit in more than one capacity. However, for a limited time, persons who offer a specific missional value may serve in an advisory capacity without vote on

an organizational unit to which they have not been elected. If a person serving on a Conference unit is elected to serve on a Jurisdictional or General Conference agency that is different than the one they presently serve in the Conference, that person may relinquish membership on the former Annual Conference unit and shall become a member of the Annual Conference unit that corresponds to the one served on a general church level.

6. Vacancies. In the event of a membership vacancy on any organizational unit, the chairperson of such unit shall be entitled to select a person to fill that vacancy for no longer than the current Conference year. Consultation with the Conference Nominating Committee chairperson will occur as this is done, and consideration of other general provisions will be kept in mind. The appropriate nominating body will then in due process act to fill the position that was vacated. Any person selected to fill a vacancy shall be eligible for nomination and election at the ensuing Annual Conference subject to the tenure rules. In the case of the Board of Ordained Ministry, if the remaining tenure of that vacancy was two years or less for a quadrennium, that time shall not apply to the tenure rule.

7. Chairpersons and Membership. Elections of Chairpersons and selection of members of Conference organizational units.
   Chairpersons and members of organizational units named herein, shall be nominated by the Conference Nominating Committee and elected by the Annual Conference.
   a. Exceptions to this process are:
      1) Members and Chairs of Board of Ordained Ministry, Joint Committee on Review, and The Conference Nominating Committee who are nominated by the Bishop/Cabinet and
      2) Chairpersons of Conference Council on Finance and Administration, Board of Trustees, Board of Pension and Health Benefits, Board of Ordained Ministry, the Area Committee on Episcopacy, the Rules of Order Committee. These Chairpersons shall be elected by their respective organizations.
   b. The following process shall be used:
      1) Organizational units under this process shall be all area and conference boards, commissions, committees, the Conference Leadership Team, the Council on Finance and Administration, Conference Trustees (see above exception),
      2) Organizational units may suggest to the Conference Nominating Committee persons to be considered for nomination as members and chairperson on said unit.
      3) Not later than March 15 in any year when a new Chairperson is to be selected, (or immediately in the event of a vacancy), a unit may advise the Conference Nominating Committee of one or more persons it would place in nomination for such office;
      4) The respective organizational units shall nominate and elect, following the Annual Conference election of their chairperson, such other officers as they deem helpful for doing their business. Such elections will occur at any regular or called meeting for such purpose keeping in mind that presently elected officers continue until their successors are duly elected.
      5) While election of chairpersons and other officers may happen at any time, there is a historic process that such elections shall normally occur at the Annual Conference of the year when General Conference convenes. Potentially this would provide training for new leaders, normally occurring after Jurisdictional conferences.
      6) Each organizational unit will be intentional in seeking a balance of 1/3 laymen, 1/3 laywomen, and 1/3 clergy and to be representative of age and racial/ethnic persons. The Conference Nominating Committee has the task of seeking these balances.
      7) Any positions that are nominated by the Conference Nominating Committee and elected by the Annual Conference and are still open at the close of the Conference shall be filled by the Committee on Nominations in consultation as necessary

with the Bishop, the Cabinet and/or the organizational unit affected. Any person selected to fill such an opening shall be eligible for nomination and election at the ensuing Annual Conference subject to tenure rules.

8) Executive Committees. Unless otherwise prohibited by the DISCIPLINE, the Annual Conference, or this Plan or Organization, a duly elected executive committee of any organizational unit is authorized to act between meetings on behalf of such unit to implement or effectuate policies and/or actions of the organizational unit.

H. Changes in the Plan of Organization

This Plan of Organization shall always be changed so as to conform to DISCIPLINE.

1. By submission of a Petition to the Conference as provided for in the Rules of Order, or a Response Petition according to the same aforementioned process;
2. Petitions for a change in this Plan or Organization shall be referred, first, to the Rules of Order Committee for its comment and recommendation in writing; and, second, to the Annual Conference for its action as it is reported to the Conference.
3. When two thirds (2/3) of the members of the Conference present and voting, vote in favor of the amendment or change this Plan shall be so amended or changed.

II. DISTRICT

A. District Conference

There shall be a District Conference on each District in the Annual Conference.

1. It shall meet at the time and place specified by the District Superintendent with at least fourteen (14) days public notice
2. Membership of the District Conference shall be:
   a. The following persons from each local church on the District: all pastors; lay leader; president of the United Methodist Women; president of the United Methodist Men; chairperson of the Council on Ministries and/or Administrative Council; chairperson of the Finance Committee; church school superintendent; chairpersons of the Missions and Evangelism Work Areas; chairperson of the Trustees; chairperson of the Pastor Parish Relations Committee or Staff Parish Relations Committee; Lay Member(s) of the Annual Conference elected by the congregations of the District; and lay members of Annual Conference elected by District Conference.
   b. All members of the District Council on Ministries of the District (see Section B following).
3. In addition to such items as shall be determined by the District Conference, Council on Ministries, and/or the Superintendent as being necessarily a part of its order of business and rules of order, there shall be the following: The District Conference shall be held prior to March 10th. At this meeting the District Conference shall place on its agenda these items:
   a. Annually each District Conference, if requested by the Conference Nominating Committee, shall elect those persons requested to serve organizational units.
   b. Annually each District Conference shall elect the members of its District Council on Ministries (See Section B following). These shall be elected upon the nominations offered by the District Nominating Committee, providing that at no time shall nominations from the floor of the District Conference be denied. Vacancies shall be filled by the Nominating Committee subject to election at the next meeting of the District Conference.
   c. The adoption of any goals or priorities of programming may be forwarded to the Conference Leadership Team for coordination into the Conference program and possible funding.
   d. Any special requests for Conference and/or District finances must be coordinated with both the Conference Leadership Team and the Conference Council on Finance and Administration for the inclusion with the total financial projections within the Annual Conference.

4. Other meetings of the District Conference may be held during the year at the call of the District Superintendent, the Bishop, or one third of the District Council on Ministries, upon notice to the churches of at least fourteen days.

B. <u>District Council on Ministries or the equivalent:</u>

1. The District Council on Ministries, or the equivalent, shall be the basic unit of connectional organization for District programming. The authority of the District Council, or the equivalent, is limited only by the provisions of The DISCIPLINE, actions of the Annual Conference, and other parts of this Plan of Organization.
2. Each District shall develop those ministries it shall choose to undergird the ministries of the congregations within the District, and those given to it by the Annual Conference.
3. Each District through its nominating process and District Conference shall select the structure which shall best serve that District in order to accomplish those ministries it chooses and are given to it by the Annual Conference.
4. Membership and Organization:
   a. The following may be members of the District Council on Ministries, or the equivalent:
      1) The District Superintendent
      2) District UMCOR/Hunger Coordinator
      3) District Lay Leader (District Board of Laity)
      4) District Lay Members at large of the Annual Conference
      5) District President of the United Methodist Women
      6) District President of the United Methodist Men
      7) District President of the United Methodist Youth
      8) District Secretary of Global Ministries
      9) District Disaster Response Coordinator
      10) Members of the following groups on the District or persons fulfilling these responsibilities
         a) Finance & Property
            1. Board of Church Location & Building
            2. Church Extension (New Church Development) Committee
            3. Finance
         b) District & Local Church committees and organizations recognized by The United Methodist Church.
         c) Human Resources
            1. Ordained Ministry
            2. District Superintendency Committee
            3. Leadership Development
            4. Nominating Committee
            5. Funding of the District Councils on Ministries or the equivalent.
            6. A District, in order to fulfill the responsibilities above, must have control over allocation and use of funds for program purposes in that District. Such funds shall be made available as follows:
               a. Through regular Annual Conference budgetary processes there may be appropriated from Annual Conference sources to each District Council on Ministries, or the equivalent, an annual operations sum.
               b. The Conference Leadership Team shall determine annually what programs requested by the Annual Conference are appropriately district related. They may provide funds to the respective District Council on Ministries or the equivalent, to enable these programs. This statement shall be made at the earliest feasible date to assist the District Councils on Ministries or the equivalent, in their ministries.
               c. District Councils on Ministries or the equivalent, may have the option of submitting program and funding requests for

ministries on that District to the Conference Leadership Team for coordination, acceptance and implementation. Any funding requested of Conference monies, shall have been approved by the (1) District Conference, and (2) thereafter by the Annual Conference, including review by the Council on Finance and Administration, for continuation year after year.

III. ANNUAL CONFERENCE

A. Standing Committees

The following shall be the Standing Committees of the Session of the Annual Conference: Agenda, Journal, Memoirs, Program, Reference Committee, and Rules of Order. Membership on the aforementioned shall be as provided for by The Rules of Order. As provided for in the Book of Discipline of The United Methodist Church there shall be the Joint Review Committee.

B. Conference Ministries:

Organizational units of our Conference are grouped with others doing similar kinds of tasks and will function with a matrix style. We designate three such foci of tasks:

- Conference Leadership Team: program, direction and guidance oversight tasks of the Conference;
- Finance and Property Ministries: administrative tasks of the Conference; and,
- Human Resources Ministries: personnel recruitment, support and guidance tasks of the Conference.

1. Organization

The following organizational units shall have membership as designated. Unless specified otherwise, all members shall be nominated by The Committee on Nominations and elected by the Annual Conference in accordance with provisions of this Plan of Organization.

a. Chairpersons of each organizational unit (except the Chairpersons of Conference Leadership Team, Conference Board of Lay Ministries, Conference Council on Finance and Administration, Conference Board of Pension and Health Benefits, Conference Board of Ordained Ministry, and the Area Committee on Episcopacy), shall be nominated by in accordance with provisions of this Plan of Organization, and then elected by the Annual Conference. If a vacancy of Chairperson occurs between sessions of the Conference, The Committee on Nominations may select a Chairperson Pro Tem (using I., D., 7. B.) to serve until regularly elected by the Conference.

b. Each organizational unit will itself elect a vice chairperson, secretary, and such other officers as it shall determine are needed following the election of the chairperson.

c. Each organizational unit shall determine its own internal organization with reference to standing committees such as a Nominating Committee, etc., subject to the DISCIPLINE. Chairpersons of standing committees and task forces shall be selected from the membership of the agency, unless a non-agency member is approved in advance by the agency chairperson.

d. Each organizational unit shall have the authority to enlist nonmembers of that agency in any of their subgroups and/or task forces.

e. In order to provide continuity of leadership, a duly elected chairperson or other officer may continue on that agency, at the discretion of the organizational unit, until the expiration of that person's tenure even though the originating membership category (District representative, General Conference Board member, etc.) may change during that person's tenure as an officer.

2. Meetings

a. Each organizational unit shall meet at least once annually, and may meet more often to accomplish its work on call of its executive committee or chairperson. Meetings are to be scheduled and when possible published in the Conference calendar of meetings.

b. A special meeting of the organizational unit may be called by the chairperson, one third of its membership, or the Bishop upon ten (10) days notice.

3. Responsibilities
   a. To determine the unit's goals, priorities and work in light of the goals and priorities adopted by the Annual Conference and transmitted through the Conference Leadership Team and/or the Conference Staff.
   b. To develop, plan and implement programs in response to and on the basis of needs and requests of the districts and of local congregations as well as the General Conference. It is understood that:
      1) The District Councils on Ministries or the equivalent are responsible for ascertaining and communicating to the Conference organizational units the needs of the districts and of local churches along with program and administrative suggestions where possible;
      2) Local churches, or any local church member, may communicate directly with Conference organizational units;
      3) The organizational units may communicate (and promote) the need for program and/or administrative emphases to the District Councils on Ministries or the equivalent, and in such cases the organizational unit shall develop and implement program activities in cooperation with the District Councils on Ministries or the equivalent;
      4) The organizational units shall seek, wherever feasible, the cooperation of the District Councils on Ministries or the equivalent, in the promotion of specific projects and/or pilot testing programs.
   c. To provide, wherever possible, resources of any kind upon request of District Councils on Ministries or the equivalent, or of local churches.
   d. To fulfill the responsibilities outlined by the DISCIPLINE, and requested by the Annual Conference.
   e. To be the connecting link between the Annual Conference and the corresponding agencies of the General Church.
4. Conference Organizational Units
   a. Director of Connectional Ministries:
      1) Purpose: There shall be a Director of Connectional Ministries (DCM) who shall be the administrator and coordinator of the organization and ministry of the West Michigan Conference, as defined by the DISCIPLINE and outlined here.
      2) Accountability:
         The Director of Connectional Ministries shall be:
         - chosen and approved by the Bishop and by the Personnel Committee.
         - guided by the Conference Leadership Team and is accountable to the Bishop and the Personnel Committee.
      3) Responsibilities:
         The Director of Connectional Ministries shall:
         - Interpret the vision and mission of the Conference;
         - Ensure alignment of the total resources of the Conference to its vision
         - Link administrative and program ministries;
         - Supervise Conference staff and link full-time and part-time Conference staff, with an emphasis on enhancing the ministry of local congregations;
         - Coordinate the ministry of the Conference Leadership Team and provide linkage among the various entities of the Conference;
         - Serve, in consultation with the Bishop and the Director of Communications, as the Conference communicator to public media and other entities within and beyond the Conference;
         - Promote area, jurisdictional and general church ministry;
         - Serve as a member of the Cabinet;
         - Fulfill any other duties given by the DISCIPLINE to a DCM or equivalent position.

- Serve as a primary information source for congregational and Conference leaders.
- Be a member with voice but not vote of the Council on Finance and Administration, its Executive Committee and the Conference Board of Trustees.
- Not have the responsibilities of property management and those duties mandated by the DISCIPLINE to the Conference Treasurer.

b. Director of Communications

1) Purpose: Build, coordinate and improve the communications ministries of The United Methodist Church within the West Michigan Conference as it carries out the mission of making and empowering disciples of Jesus Christ for the transformation of the world.

2) Accountability: This person is chosen by the Bishop in consultation with the DCM and the Personnel Committee. This position is accountable to the Bishop, the DCM and is a member of the Full Cabinet; the Director of Connectional Ministries is the primary supervisor.

3) Responsibilities:

- Assist the Director of Connectional Ministries in his/her responsibilities as a communication linkage with the General Boards and Agencies.
- Coordinate, in collaboration with the Area Office, crisis communication strategies and develop related training opportunities for local churches and Conference leadership.
- Oversee the maintenance and facilitation of a Conference wide data base system, including the oversight of the Conference web site.
- Be responsible for the oversight and proper use of copyright permissions and/or restriction.
- Provide oversight/coordination of information technology (IT) support services for Conference and District Offices

c. Conference Leadership Team

1) Purpose: The Conference Leadership Team shall give general direction, guidance, and ensure the alignment of the resources, structure and ministries in support of the mission, vision and strategic goals of the Conference.

2) Accountability: The Conference Leadership Team is a council with governing responsibilities that shall be accountable to, and annually file a written report with, the Annual Conference. It shall request funding through the Conference Council on Finance and Administration. Minutes will be available in a timely fashion.

3) Membership:

a) Twelve - Fourteen Voting Members, at least one of whom shall be a voting member of the Commission on Religion and Race (¶643.5):

1. Conference Lay Leader
2. Director of Connectional Ministries
3. A District Superintendent assigned for a term of no less than two but not more than three years (A District Superintendent chosen by the Bishop may attend in the absence of the assigned District Superintendent.)
4. President of the Conference Council on Finance and Administration
5. Eight (8) Members-at-large
6. Two additional members at-large: the Director of Connectional Ministries (DCM), in consultation with the Committee on Nominations & the Commission on Religion and Race may select two additional members at-large, to ensure inclusiveness,

diversity, District representation, lay and clergy balance (¶608.6). These persons, if the DCM so chooses to act, will serve one year terms, and may be appointed annually for up to eight years

b) Other members with voice, but no vote:
1. Area Bishop (or in the Bishop's absence, the Clergy Assistant to the Bishop)
2. Director of Communications
3. The Conference Treasurer
4. Any person residing within the bounds of the Annual Conference with membership on the Connectional Table [The Book of Discipline of the UMC-2008. (901 ¶)]

c) Characteristics
Members at-large of the Leadership Team shall be nominated by the Conference Committee on Nominations, with input from the Conference's and Districts' Leadership Teams, based on their ability to:
- Think in terms of the future.
- Deal with the abstract.
- Deal with qualitative ideas.
- Give up a desire to make short term concrete decisions.
- Give up desire to be involved in day-to-day operations of the boards and agencies.
- Be involved in regular monitoring of one's self and the Leadership Team's performance.
- Think in terms of working for the Annual Conference and its connections rather than for a particular agency of the Annual Conference.

d) Criteria for the eight–ten members-at-large:
- They shall not be chairpersons or employees of Conference boards or agencies.
- They shall be elected for four-year terms in four classes of two persons each and are eligible for a second four year term.
- Members at-large who are laity shall be considered members of the Annual Conference in accordance with Rule 8. C, of the Conference Rules of Order, "Equalization of Lay and Clergy Members,"
- At least one of them shall be the age of 30 or under at the time of their election.
- All Districts shall have at least one voting member among the eight to ten members at-large

4) <u>Organization:</u>
a) The Director of Connectional Ministries (DCM) shall be a member, with voice and vote, but not the chairperson of the Conference Leadership Team.
b) The chairperson of the Conference Leadership Team shall be nominated by the Conference Committee on Nominations in consultation with the Bishop from the Conference Leadership Team members-at-large.
c) Another member-at-large of the Conference Leadership Team shall be elected by the Conference Leadership Team to serve as vice-chair. If the Conference Leadership Team Chairperson is a clergy person, the vice-chair shall be a lay person. If the Conference Leadership Team chairperson is a layperson, then a clergy member shall serve as vice-chair.
d) A recording secretary shall be appointed by the Director of Connectional Ministries for each meeting. This person shall not be a member of the Conference Leadership Team and shall not have voice or vote.

5) Meetings: The team shall meet at least every three months. A quorum of seven (7) voting members is required to take necessary actions. Meetings may be held in electronic forms. The bishop, the DCM or Conference lay leader may call special meetings as necessary to respond to the ministry needs of the Conference. Members of the team shall meet the minimum attendance requirement of being present at two-thirds (66 percent) of leadership team meetings. Failure to meet the minimum attendance requirement may result in being declared ineligible to serve as a member of the Leadership Team by a majority vote of the Leadership Team present and voting at a duly called meeting.

6) Responsibilities: In addition to the above stated Purpose, the Leadership Team shall:
   a) Design a process for implementing the action strategies of the West Michigan Conference.
   b) Annually convene the leaders of the Conference's and Districts' boards and agencies to test the current Conference vision, develop vision/strategic plans necessary for future changes for the Conference and provide an opportunity for training and collaboration.
   c) Recommend priorities to the Annual Conference on a quadrennial basis
   d) Hold the various boards and agencies accountable to the boards' and agencies' respective processes of visioning, planning, implementation, funding and evaluation, in accordance with the 2008 DISCIPLINE ¶610: "How are we intentionally reaching new people for Jesus Christ through our ministries?"; and "How are we helping new people grow and mature as disciples of Jesus Christ through our ministries and areas of responsibility?"
   e) Facilitate communication between the boards or agencies as they focus spiritual, human, and fiscal resources to accomplish mission and ministry goals.
   f) Ensure effective communication to and from local churches through the District and Conference agencies.
   g) Appoint Task Forces as needed.
   h) Recommend to the Annual Conference timely changes in the internal structure of the Leadership Team, and any of its organizational units;
   i) Compile and recommend an overall budget for the program boards and agencies to the Council on Finance and Administration.
   j) Invite input as necessary from other Conference leaders.
   k) Be the equivalent structure to provide the functions and maintain the connectional relationships for the discipleship functions of the conference as outlined in ¶630 (of *The United Methodist Book of Discipline*) with the exception of Camping and Evangelism which shall have their own structure.

7) Relationships:
   a) The Leadership Team has a responsibility for making sure that every board and agency is focused on work that relates directly to local congregations of the Conference and the fulfillment of these stated purposes. (¶201 of The Book of Discipline of the UMC – 2008 states; "The local church provides the most significant arena through which disciple-making occurs." ¶601 identifies the purpose of the Annual Conference as "equipping its local churches for ministry and providing a connection for ministry beyond the local church...")
   b) The Leadership Team may be invited to meet with the Full Cabinet in accordance with the provisions of ¶429.4 of The Book of Discipline of the UMC – 2008; "the Cabinet is charged with the oversight of the spiritual and temporal affairs of a conference, to be executed in regularized consultation

and cooperation with other councils and service agencies of the conference."

c) The Leadership Team shall make recommendations to the Conference Council on Finance and Administration based on ministry priorities and measurable outcomes as they work collaboratively on developing and submitting a comprehensive budget to the Annual Conference.

8) Conference Program Staff:
There may be employed Conference Program Staff as determined by the Leadership Team. The Conference Program Staff would resource and enable the Conference vision through local congregations and Conference programs. Individual job descriptions shall be proposed by the DCM in consultation with the Personnel Committee, and the Conference Program Staff, as guided by the priorities and annual program of the Conference. These job descriptions shall be confirmed by the Personnel Committee. Conference Program Staff shall be supervised by and accountable to the Director of Connectional Ministries.

9) Narrative Summary of Conference Leadership Team
The Leadership Team is a body designed to replace the Council on Ministries. It shall give general direction, guidance, and ensure the alignment of the resources, structure and ministries in support of the mission, vision and strategic goals of the Conference. It shall focus on the three strategies and goals of the Conference vision: Fruitfulness, Discipleship, and Transformation.
Its primary guiding questions shall be:

- Are we creating and nurturing dynamic and fruitful congregations who make disciples of Jesus Christ for the transformation of the world?
- What are the results that help us determine whether we are accomplishing our mission/ministry?
- What shall we do to more effectively accomplish our goals and strategies of Fruitfulness, Discipleship and Transformation?

The Leadership Team is intended to be a body that will consistently represent the interests of the Conference and its connection (local and general church). It is not to function as though its primary role and responsibility is to represent staff, or the boards and agencies of the Conference. The Leadership Team is a servant of the Annual Conference and its connections and is guided by the Conference's vision, mission, goals and strategies, core values, and beliefs.

The Leadership Team is to act with cohesive integrity, serving as one. It is to speak as a body for the Conference and its connections between sessions of the Annual Conference. It does not speak individually, except where mandated by the DISCIPLINE, for the Conference and its connections. The Leadership Team is to speak with authority when it passes official motions at a properly called meeting.

The Leadership Team must give careful attention to the principles of sound delegation, to increase the likelihood that boards and agencies will successfully carry out their responsibilities. Boards and agencies will be accountable to the Leadership Team for the achievement of results that fulfill vision, mission, goals and strategies, core values, and beliefs of the Conference and its connections.

The Leadership Team will focus on consistency, expectations, clarity and results. It will provide clear measureable expectations regarding performance and results, interpret those expectations to agencies with clarity and hold them accountable for results.

10) Implementation
The Plan of Organization of the Conference is to be amended so that the boards and agencies are organized following a primary template of: 1. Accountability; 2.

Purpose; 3. Membership; 4. Organization; 5. Meetings; 6. Responsibilities Where this information is missing, the Leadership Team is expected to work with the particular board or agency to complete this information and return those details to the next Annual Conference for action.

d. Agencies amenable to the Leadership Team

To facilitate their ministries, organizational units are grouped with others doing similar kinds of tasks and will function with a matrix style. We designate three such focuses of tasks: 1) Conference Ministries: ministries having major impact upon and support of the ministries congregations do collectively as a Conference; 2) Communications and Records Ministries: ministries of public relations, communication and promotion, and historical record keeping to help all know and share the programs of the Conference, districts and congregations; 3) District and Local Church Ministries: support, enablement, and cooperation with ministries essentially carried out for, with, on behalf of, and in local congregations, clusters of congregations, and districts.

Organizational units relating to each of these three focuses (Conference Ministries, Communications and Records Ministries, and District and Local Church Ministries) have their own several identities and will organize and function as outlined below. Those relating to the grouping of Conference Ministries are not required to meet with each other in the development of their work, but they may meet (as whole units, executive committees, or chairpersons) if they desire, to coordinate programming. Chairpersons of units or Conference Staff may initiate such meetings. Units will operate similarly under the focuses of Communications and Records Ministries, and District and Local Church Ministries.

1) Conference Ministries: ministries having a major impact upon and support of the ministries congregations do collectively as a Conference. There shall be the following organizational units:

a. Board of Christian Camping
b. Board of Church and Society
c. Board of Evangelism
d. Board of Global Ministries
e. Board of Higher Education and Campus Ministry
f. Commission on Religion and Race
g. Commission on the Status & Role of Women
h. Committee on Cooperative Ministry
i. Committee on Disability Concerns
j. Committee on Disaster Response Team
k. Committee on Hispanic/Latino Ministries
l. Committee on New Church Establishment and Development
m. Committee on Prison Ministry
n. Committee on Racial/Ethnic Local Church
o. Conference Council on Youth Ministries
p. Michigan Area Haiti Task Force
q. Michigan Area Indian Workers Conference
r. UMCOR/Hunger Committee
s. United Methodist Men
t. United Methodist Women

DESCRIPTIONS:

a. Board of Christian Camping

1) Accountability:

a) The Board shall be accountable to the Conference Leadership Team in matters of program and budget and shall annually file a written report with the Annual Conference.

b) The Executive Director reports to the Board of Christian Camping, which holds the executive director responsible for operating within the boundaries of board

PLAN OF ORGANIZATION

policy, and for the achievement of measurable goals. The executive director may be a Conference Program Staff person assigned to the role.

c) Each site director reports directly to the executive director.

d) Each site has a site committee that assists the site director.

e) All sites use the Conference Treasurer's office to manage payments received and due.

2) Purpose: We are outdoor ministries, making disciples of Jesus Christ.

3) Membership:

The board will provide a proposed slate of nominees in consultation with and to the Conference Nominating Committee for approval and for inclusion in the conference nominations report. Term limits and renewals shall be in accord with *The Book of Discipline ofThe United Methodist Church* and the Rules of Order of the West Michigan Conference. Membership of the board is as follows:

a) a chair;

b) a strategic planning coordinator;

c) a fiscal officer, who provides leadership for the board in financial goal- setting and evaluation, including projections and budget setting, accounting policy development, and who assists in communicating board financial processes and goals to staff;

d) a development coordinator, who organizes and manages fundraising projects;

e) a development director, who provides leadership, training and guidance in capital fund development for the many needs of the sites and their programs;

f) a recruitment training coordinator, who provides leadership for promotion training for site committees, site promotion task forces, district camping promoters, local church camping ministry boosters and volunteer deans;

g) a properties coordinator, who provides leadership in the management of properties, and who works with the directors and the executive director to identify needs and objectives for property maintenance and improvement;

h) a vice-chair, who will be designated from the above members (b-i);

i) a representative of the Appointive Cabinet;

j) at least one youth member;

k) other members as needed.

4) Organization: The organizational goal of the board is to approximate a governance model by 2017.

5) Meetings: The Board meets at least four times annually.

6) Responsibilities:

a) Of the camping ministry

1. Growth of the ministry. Any site should not fail to grow in ministry in at least 4 of any 5 years.

2. Net revenue maintenance. Any site should not fail to produce a net revenue of not less than 3% in at least 4 of any 5 years.

3. Policy. All camping ministry components shall comply with conference policies and State regulations. Further, the BCC shall provide policies under which all camping programs will be operated and all sites owned by the West Michigan Conference will be maintained and utilized. The BCC is a program agency of the conference, directly accountable to the Conference Leadership Team (CLT).

4. Promote awareness of camping, and registration for events, throughout the conference, in individual churches, and beyond to the public at large.

5. Ensure that leaders, servant workers, funding, training, and vision are available for the success of the whole camping ministry.

b) Of the Board

1. Communicate with the executive director, including receiving reports and input, and giving directives in terms of both policy and ad hoc decisions; a

significant tool in this communication in the BCC Handbook, which is continually edited and updated.

2. Communicate with other conference leadership on behalf of camping ministries, including CFA, CLT, Trustees, Communications, Treasurer and Cabinet;
3. Design an annual ministry plan, which reflects a four or five year ministry plan, and which includes goals for each site with regard to programming balance, attendance, revenue, and budget; and present this plan annually to a gathering of representatives of site committees, district promoters, the executive director, and site directors In time for each part of the plan to be implemented.
    a. a broad outline of programming goals
    b. a specific outline of major maintenance and facility improvement tasks for each site, as part of an ongoing facilities plan;
    c. an annual budget for both revenue and expenses, both operating and capital.
4. At least annually, host a gathering to include all site committee members, district coordinators, and site directors, for the purpose of gathering input and sharing ministry objectives.

b. Board of Church and Society:
    1) Accountability: The Board shall be accountable to the Conference Leadership Team in matters of program and budget and shall annually file a written report with the Annual Conference.
    2) Purpose:
    3) Membership:
        a) Fifteen (15) members at large;
        b) Ex-officio (voice and vote): one youth representative elected by the Conference Council on Youth Ministries; the mission coordinator for the Christian social involvement of the Conference United Methodist Women; any member of a related General Church agency.
        c) The Conference Chairperson of Homeless Ministries to be nominated by CONALD.
        d) One representative from each District as nominated by the district nominating committee.
    4) Organization:
    5) Meetings:
    6) Responsibilities:

c. Board of Evangelism
    1) Accountability: The Board shall be accountable to the Conference Leadership Team in matters of program and budget and shall annually file a written report with the Annual Conference.
    2) Purpose: To lead the congregations and agencies of our Conference in evangelism ministries.
    3) Membership
        a) Seven (7) members at large, one of whom shall be a representative to the Board of Discipleship.
        b) One person named by each of the six Districts to represent evangelism ministries.
        c) Ex-officio (voice and vote): the Director of Connectional Ministries; any member of a related General Church agency.
        d) Ex-officio (voice and vote) two youth representatives elected by the Conference Council on Youth Ministries.
    4) Organization:
    5) Meetings:
    6) Responsibilities:

d. Board of Global Ministries:
   1) Accountability: The Board shall be accountable to the Conference Leadership Team in matters of program and budget and shall annually file a written report with the Annual Conference.
   2) Purpose: This Board shall program for ministry as described in the DISCIPLINE.
   3) Membership:
      a) Ten (10) members at large;
      b) The Conference Secretary of Global Ministries who shall be nominated by the Bishop and elected by the Annual Conference;
      c) The Chairperson of the Conference UMCOR/Hunger Committee;
      d) The Conference United Methodist Women's coordinator of global concerns;
      e) Any member of a related General Church Agency;
      f) Volunteer in Mission Coordinator who shall be nominated by CONALD and elected by the Annual Conference;
      g) The Missions Secretary from each of the six (6) Districts;
      h) The Conference Coordinator of Cooperative Ministries;
      i) Coordinator of Bible Distribution Ministries;
      k) Coordinator of Refugee Ministries;
      l) Chairperson of the Hispanic Ministry Plan;
      m) Ex-officio (voice and vote) one youth representative as elected by the Conference Council on Youth Ministries.
      n) Health and Welfare Ministries representative
   4) Organization:
   5) Meetings:
   6) Responsibilities:

e. Board of Higher Education & Campus Ministry:
   1) Accountability: The Board shall be accountable to the Conference Leadership Team in matters of program and budget and shall annually file a written report with the Annual Conference.
   2) Purpose:
   3) Membership:
      a) Twelve (12) members at large;
      b) Ex-officio (voice and vote): one student and the chairperson, or representative, selected by each local Wesley Foundation Board and church- related college, and Grand Valley Student Fellowship.
      c) Ex-officio (voice and vote): any member of a related General Church agency.
      d) Ex-officio (voice and vote) two youth representatives elected by the Conference Council on Youth Ministries.
   4) Organization:
   5) Meetings:
   6) Responsibilities:

f. Commission on Religion and Race:
   1) Accountability: The Commission shall be accountable to the Conference Leadership Team in matters of program and budget and shall annually file a written report with the Annual Conference.
   2) Purpose:
   3) Membership:
      a) Eight (8) racial/ethnic persons including four African Americans, two Native Americans, one Hispanic American, one Asian American;
      b) Four (4) other members atlarge; any member of a related General Church Agency if not in the above membership;
      c) Out of all the above members each District shall be represented;
      d) Ex-officio (voice and vote) two youth representatives elected by the Conference Council on Youth Ministries.

4) Organization:
5) Meetings:
6) Responsibilities:

g. Commission on the Status & Role of Women:
1) Accountability: The Commission shall be accountable to the Conference Leadership Team in matters of program and budget and shall annually file a written report with the Annual Conference.
2) Purpose:
3) Membership:
   a) Eleven (11) members at large, the majority of whom shall be women;
   b) One member named by the Conference United Methodist Women;
   c) Any member of a related General Church Agency if not in this member at large number;
   d) The Chairperson shall be a woman;
   e) Ex-officio (voice and vote) two representatives elected by the Conference Council on Youth Ministries.
4) Organization:
5) Meetings:
6) Responsibilities:

h. Committee on Cooperative Ministry
1) Accountability: The Committee shall be accountable to the Conference Leadership Team in matters of program and budget and shall annually file a written report with the Annual Conference.
2) Purpose: To assist the conference and cabinet in fulfilling *The Book of Discipline of the United Methodist Church* requirements and the intent of the Cooperative Ministry Policy.
3) Membership:
   a) 5 to 9 members, one-half of which shall be members or pastors of a church which is part of a cooperative parish, on a multi-point charge or a part-time appointment.
   b) a Cabinet representative
4) Organization:
5) Meetings:
6) Responsibilities:
   a) develop tools, guidance and other training materials;
   b) recommend strategies to appropriate conference boards and agencies;
   c) work in concert with the conference and cabinet to integrate cooperative ministry with other initiatives and priorities.
   d) make as many resources available online as possible

i. Committee on Disability Concerns
1) Accountability: The Committee shall be accountable to the Conference Leadership Team in matters of program and budget and shall annually file a written report with the Annual Conference.
2) Purpose:
3) Membership:
   The committee shall include at least 10 members, representative of all six districts. The committee may be expanded to include additional members whenever this is needed to provide advocacy for persons with various disabilities. Members of the committee, including the chair, shall be nominated by the Committee on Nominations and elected by the Conference. The committee shall be accountable to the Leadership Team. The Committee will also have a representative on the Annual Conference Program Committee.
4) Organization:
5) Meetings:
6) Responsibilities:

j. Committee on Disaster Response Team
   1) Accountability: The Committee shall be accountable to the Conference Leadership Team in matters of program and budget and shall annually file a written report with the Annual Conference.
   2) Purpose: There shall be a Conference Disaster Response Team Committee whose purpose shall be:
      a) to work with the United Methodist Committee on Relief, and other organizations, in response to disasters within the bounds of the West Michigan Conference;
      b) to help provide beyond the boundaries of the Conference personnel and equipment as needed in response to emergency need;
      c) to assist local congregations in being trained and equipped to better handle emergencies within their own churches and communities
   3) Membership:
      a) A Conference Disaster Response Coordinator who shall be the Chairperson. The Coordinator shall be appointed by the Bishop in consultation with the Conference Nominating Committee and with UMCOR.
      b) Six District Coordinators selected by the respective District conferences.
      c) The Conference Volunteer In Mission Coordinator
      d) A representative from the Board of Global Missions
   4) Organization:
   5) Meetings:
   6) Responsibilities:

k. Committee on Hispanic/Latino Ministries
   1) Accountability. The Committee on Hispanic/Latino Ministry shall be accountable to the Conference Leadership Team in matters of program and budget and shall annually file a written report with the annual conference.
   2) Purpose: The committee:
      a) will relate to all conference agencies for the implementation of the National Plan for Hispanic Ministry as it may be adapted to meet the specific needs of the West Michigan Conference.
      b) will provide direction and leadership for Hispanic ministries of the conference
      c) shall establish governing policies for the committee and its staff.
   3) Membership:
      a) Nine members at large plus a chairperson shall be nominated by the Conference Committee on Nominations and elected by the annual conference. Terms shall be consistent with conference policy.
      b) The membership shall be composed of persons interested in Hispanic/Latino Ministries with special attention to representation from districts where there is a significant Hispanic population.
      c) Terms shall be consistent with conference policy.
      d) The committee may co-opt a maximum of four members.
         1) Terms shall be consistent with conference policy.
         2) Co-opted members may be asked to fill the following positions such as but not limited to:
            a) Training Coordinator.
            b) Grant application coordinator.
            c) Immigration advisor.
            e) ex-officio members
               1) District superintendent designated by the cabinet.
               2) Conference treasurer.
               3) Director of Connectional Ministries.
               4) Staff employed by the Conference Leadership Team and assigned to the Committee on Hispanic/Latino Ministry.

4) Organization:
   a) Chairperson, nominated by the Conference Committee on Nominations. in consultation with the Committee on Hispanic/Latino Ministry, and elected by the annual conference.
   b) Vice chairperson, secretary, and treasurer elected from the membership of the committee.
   c) Task forces, whose members may or may not be committee members, may be created to help the committee accomplish its work.
5) Meetings:
   a) The committee shall meet at least four times annually.
   b) Additional meetings may be held as needed to accomplish necessary work.
6) Responsibilities:
   a) Interpret and advocate for Hispanic ministries.
      1) Secure and share information about the National Plan for Hispanic Ministries and its resources with key conference leaders and focal leaders involved In Hispanic ministries.
      2) Promote the related conference Advance Special projects.
      3) Find stories that will illustrate various aspects of Hispanic Ministries/ National Plan being implemented and share these with local, conference, and national media as appropriate.
      4) Advocate appropriate responses to issues and concerns affecting Hispanics and Hispanic ministries. Secure information about the Plan for Hispanic Ministries and its resources and share it with key conference leaders and local leaders involved in Hispanic ministries.
   b) Planning
      1) Update the Hispanic population growth trends to develop or strengthen new or existing Hispanic ministries.
      2) Reexamine and adjust the conference plan on Hispanic ministries for both Hispanic and non-Hispanic congregations based on the assessment and review recommended above in 6.b.1.
   c) Training
      1) Provide training opportunities for lay missioner and pastor teams, (hired) Hispanic ministry coordinators, committee members, and conference and local leaders utilizing the developed curriculum resources.
      2) Train Hispanic and non-Hispanic local church leaders to develop Hispanic ministries or to assist them in strengthening and expanding Hispanic ministries utilizing developed resources as necessary.
      3) Identify and enlist Hispanic and non-Hispanic candidates interested in ordained ministry and in becoming lay missioners, lay pastors or Hispanic ministry coordinators and refer them to the appropriate conference agencies for follow-up.
   d) Securing and providing resources
      1) Secure and provide educational and evangelical resources for leaders and local congregations.
      2) Consult with the Conference Leadership Team in regard to the placement of the necessary personnel who may be hired by the Leadership Team in consultation with the Hispanic/Latino Ministries Committee.
      3) Request the Conference Leadership Team provide the necessary financial resources to support needed personnel for specific Hispanic/ Latino ministries.
   e) Monitoring, supporting, and evaluating
      1) Provide a support system for leaders involved in Hispanic ministries including networking, crisis management, recognition, and affirmation.

2) The committee shall annually monitor and evaluate the progress of each specific Hispanic ministry, including where sufficient and/or appropriate resources have been assigned.

l. Committee on New Church Establishment and Development
   1) Accountability: The Committee shall be accountable to the Conference Leadership Team in matters of program and budget and shall annually file a written report with the Annual Conference.
   2) Purpose:
   3) Membership:
      a) Twelve (12) members at-large;
      b) Three (3) of the above twelve (12) shall be or have been regular participants, members or pastors during the first ten years of a new church start.
      c) Ex-officio (voice and vote):
         1) one youth representative elected by the Conference Council on Youth Ministries.
         2) The Director of New Church Establishment.
   4) Organization:
   5) Meetings:
   6) Responsibilities:

m. Committee on Prison Ministry
   1) Accountability: The Committee shall be accountable to the Conference Leadership Team in matters of program and budget and shall annually file a written report with the Annual Conference.
   2) Purpose: To empower persons in local congregations to meet the needs of prisoners, their families and returning citizens
   3) Membership:
      a) Nine (9) members, including at least one from each District to be nominated by the Conference Nominating Committee and Leadership.
      b) Ex-officio (voice and vote) two youth representatives elected by the Conference Council on Youth Ministries.
   4) Organization: Chair, Recording Secretary, Staff representative and a member from each District
   5) Meetings: At least 6 times per year.
   6) Responsibilities: Training (i.e., mentor), Michigan legislative issues, updates on Prison and Jail work, and to fulfill the purpose as state above.

n. Committee on Racial Ethnic Local Church:
   1) Accountability: The committee shall be accountable to the Conference Leadership Team in matters of program and budget and shall annually file a written report with the Annual Conference.
   2) Purpose: To support and strengthen racial ethnic churches in the West Michigan Conference and build conference-wide support for special ministries in outreach, evangelism, and discipleship with diverse people and communities.
   3) Membership: The Racial Ethnic Local Church (RELC) Committee shall consist of eleven (11) members-at-large as nominated by the Committee of Nominations, including representatives from the RELC congregations. Ex-officio (voice and vote) one youth representative elective by the Conference Council on Youth Ministries.
   4) Organization:
      a) Chairperson
      b) Secretary and Treasurer
      c) Staff representatives
      d) A member from each district
   5) Meetings: Shall meet at least three (3) times a year.

6) Responsibilities:
- Keeping the vision of the ethnic local church concerns before the West Michigan Annual Conference.
- Providing guidance and resources to churches in the West Michigan Annual Conference as they minister with and to ethnic constituencies.
- Coordinating of West Michigan Annual Conference strategies related to ethnic local church concerns including general church emphases and initiatives.
- Providing a forum for dialogue among the ethnic local church constituencies, as well as with West Michigan Annual Conference agencies.
- Providing training for West Michigan Annual Conference and congregational leaders.
- Promoting and interpreting ethnic local church concerns to the West Michigan Annual Conference. This includes recommending funding for the ministries of the REL churches.
- Working with West Michigan Annual Conference to identify and nurture leaders, lay and clergy of ethnic communities.

o. Conference Council on Youth Ministries
1) Accountability: The council shall be accountable to the Conference Leadership Team in matters of program and budget and shall annually file a written report with the Annual Conference.
2) Purpose: Is to develop faithful and effective leaders within The United Methodist Church to positively influence faithful change.
3) Membership:
a) a Youth representative from each district;
b) a Conference Administrator;
c) an Annual Conference Liaison;
d) a Meeting Coordinator;
e) an Adult Workers with Youth Coordinator;
f) a Conference Staff representative;
g) a District Superintendent.
4) Organization:
5) Meetings:
6) Responsibilities:
a) Provide youth and youth ministry leaders with the skills and knowledge they need.
b) Provide connections to positively influence the West Michigan Conference and local congregations.
c) Administer the Youth Service Fund.
d) Sponsor an annual mission trip for young people (16-20) to Haiti.
e) Provide guidance and leadership to youth representatives attending the West Michigan Annual Conference.
f) Develop and administer a program for the continuing education of adult workers with youth (AWWY).

p. Michigan Area Haiti Task Force
1) Accountability: The Executive Committee shall be accountable to the Conference Leadership Team (CLT) in matters of program and budget and shall annually file a written report with both the West Michigan and Detroit annual conferences. The report should highlight the accomplishments of the stated program priorities and partner sites.
2) Purpose: The committee will facilitate the covenant relationship between the Michigan Area United Methodist conferences and the Haiti District of the Methodist Church in the Caribbean and the Americas (EMH), and the partnership with The United Methodist Committee on Relief (UMCOR), by:
a) Collaborating with our EMH covenant partner and UMCOR to establish Michigan Area program priorities for Haiti (Example: Haiti Hot Lunch) and a

list of approved partner sites (Example: EMH work sites [Jeremie, Baudin, etc.] or Advance partners, such as Grace Children's Hospital, HAPI, Haiti Solar Oven Project, Homes for Haitians, etc.).

b) Educating the Michigan Area on Haiti (history, culture, challenges, joys, faith and life) and on mission that helps without hurting (engaging with).
c) Promoting the priorities and partners within the covenant relationship.
d) Positively affirming our covenantal and partner relationships.
e) Working together with all partners in a supportive and mutual relationship.
f) Communicating opportunities to engage in an UMVIM team or other service that supports the covenant relationship.
g) Praying for one another regularly and providing a "safe" environment to share.

3) <u>Membership:</u>
Membership of Executive Committee:
a) A chair and co-chair who represent both conferences.
b) The North Central Jurisdictional UMCOR consultant. This person may serve in a 'dual' capacity of membership positions on the Executive Committee.
c) A member from each Conference Board of Global Ministries.
d) Two 'at-large' members from each Annual Conference, as selected by the current MAHTF Executive Committee.

Membership of "at-large" committee:
a) The Executive Committee.
b) 1 clergy or lay representative from each district of the West Michigan and Detroit Annual Conferences to be nominated by the respective Nominations' Committees with consideration of the individual's demonstrated interest in Haiti and willingness to support the covenant relationship to EMH. Care should be given to matters of inclusivity when nominating persons to the MAHTF.
c) Attendance by anyone with an involvement or interest in ministry with Haiti.

4) <u>Organization:</u>
The structure of the MAHTF shall consist of:
- an Executive Committee.
- a committee comprised of the Executive Committee plus "at-large" members and persons involved or interested in ministry with Haiti.

5) <u>Meetings:</u>
- The Executive Committee may be scheduled to meet 6 times per Annual Conference year (July 1 – June 30).
- The "at-large" committee may schedule an open meeting quarterly per Annual Conference year.

6) <u>Responsibilities:</u>

q. <u>Michigan Area Indian Workers Conference</u>
1) <u>Accountability:</u> The Conference shall be accountable to the Conference Leadership Team in matters of program and budget and shall annually file a written report with the Annual Conference.
2) <u>Purpose:</u>
3) <u>Membership:</u>
4) <u>Organization:</u>
5) <u>Meetings:</u>
6) <u>Responsibilities:</u>

r. <u>UMCOR/Hunger Committee</u>
1) <u>Accountability:</u> The Committee shall be accountable to the Conference Leadership Team in matters of program and budget and shall annually file a written report with the Annual Conference.
2) <u>Purpose:</u>

3) Membership:
   a) Chairperson nominated by Conference Nominating Committee.
   b) a representative of the Area Haiti Task Force
   c) Conference Disaster Response Team Coordinator
   d) No more than eight at large members named by the UMCOR/Hunger Committee, including but not limited to:
      1) A youth or young adult
      2) A United Methodist Woman
   e) Care shall be given to diversity and inclusivity in naming committee members.
4) Organization:
5) Meetings:
6) Responsibilities:

s. United Methodist Men:
There shall be a Conference United Methodist Men group as provided for in The Book of Discipline of The United Methodist Church.
1) Accountability: The organization shall be accountable to the Conference Leadership Team in matters of program and budget and shall annually file a written report with the Annual Conference.
2) Purpose:
3) Membership:
   a) The Conference Nominating Committee may nominate a man to be chairperson. One of those elected by a District Conference to head United Methodist Men work may be nominated as chairperson;
   b) The six District chairpersons of United Methodist Men, or persons selected by the several District conferences.
4) Organization:
5) Meetings:
6) Responsibilities:

t. United Methodist Women:
The organization of United Methodist Women as provided for in *The Book of Discipline of The United Methodist Church* shall comprise the Conference agency.

2) Communications and Records Ministries: Ministries of public relations, communication and promotion, and historical record keeping to help all know and share the programs of the Conference, Districts and congregations. There shall be the following organizational units:
   a. Communications Commission
   b. Commission on Archives and History

3) Communications Commission:
   a. Accountability: The Commission shall be accountable to the Conference Leadership Team in matters of program and budget and shall annually file a written report with the Annual Conference.
      1) Purpose:
      2) Membership:
         a) There shall be seven (7) members at large;
         b) One (1) representative for each District named by the district nominating committee.
         c) Ex-officio (voice but without vote): Conference Staff persons employed in communications or media tasks.
         d) Ex-officio (voice and vote) two youth representatives elected by the Conference Council on Youth Ministries.
      3) Organization:
      4) Meetings:
      5) Responsibilities:
   b. Commission on Archives and History:

1) Accountability: The Commission shall be accountable to the Conference Leadership Team in matters of program and budget and shall annually file a written report with the Annual Conference.
2) Purpose:
3) Membership:
   a) Seven (7) members at large;
   b) The Conference Historian, if one is named;
   c) The Commission may create a Historical Society as a Standing Committee.
   d) Ex-officio (voice and vote): Curator and Archivist
   e) Ex-officio (voice and vote) one youth elected by the Conference Council on Youth Ministries.
4) Organization:
5) Meetings:
6) Responsibilities

4) District Ministries (District Councils on Ministries or the equivalent): support, enablement, and cooperation with ministries essentially carried out for, with, on behalf of, and in local congregations, clusters of congregations, and districts.
Each District shall select/elect its own manner of organization as a District Council on Ministries/ Leadership Team to accomplish program ministries within the several Districts. One person from each District shall be designated to work with those from other Districts, as needed.

e. Finance and Property Ministries: administrative tasks of the Conference. There shall be the following organizational units.
1) Council on Finance and Administration
2) Conference Board of Trustees
3) Board of Pension and Health Benefits
4) Commission on Equitable Compensation
5) Council on Finance and Administration:
   a) Accountability: The Council is accountable to and will annually file a written report (including their funding) with the Annual Conference.
   b) Purpose:
   c) Membership:
      1. Fifteen (15 members at large. The majority of these 15 shall be laity. Of this number of 15 at least five (5) shall come from congregations of less than two hundred members;
      2. Ex-officio (voice and vote): any member of a related General Church Agency;
      3. Ex-officio (voice, but without vote): The Bishop (or Clergy Assistant to the Bishop), the Conference Treasurer, the Director of Connectional Ministries (or representative of the Conference Leadership Team), one District Superintendent.
      4. Ex-officio (voice and vote) one youth representative elected by the Conference Council on Youth Ministries.
      5. The Council shall elect from its membership, a President, a Vice- president, a Secretary, and other such officers, as it may deem necessary.
   d) Organization:
   e) Meetings:
   f) Responsibilities:
3) Conference Board of Trustees:
   a) Accountability: The Board is accountable to and will annually file a written report with the Annual Conference. It shall request funding through the Council on Finance and Administration.

b) Purpose:

c) Membership:
Twelve (12) members as provided for in the DISCIPLINE. The Conference Treasurer, Director of Connectional Ministry and one District Superintendent assigned by the Bishop, shall have voice but no vote.

d) Organization:

e) Meetings:

f) Responsibilities:

4) Board of Pension and Health Benefits:
There shall be organized a Board of Pension and Health Benefits as provided by The Book of Discipline of The United Methodist Church.

a) Accountability: The Board is accountable to and will annually file a written report with the Annual Conference. It shall request funding through the Council on Finance and Administration.

b) Purpose:

c) Membership:
1. At large, twelve (12) members, six (6) of whom shall be recommended by the Board itself prior to Annual Conference election.
2. Ex-officio and Staff (voice, but no vote): The Conference Treasurer who is designated as Conference Benefit Officer.
3. The Board is authorized to create ad hoc committees or task forces and appoint members who may not be members of the Board. The chairs of said ad hoc committees or task forces shall be from the membership of that Board.

d) Organization:

e) Meetings:

f) Responsibilities:

5) Commission on Equitable Compensation:

a) Accountability: The Commission is accountable to and will annually file a written report with the Annual Conference. It shall request funding through the Council on Finance and Administration.

b) Purpose:

c) Membership:
1. Twelve (12) members at large. In this number there shall be at least one layperson and one clergy person from congregations of fewer than two hundred members. Also in this number there shall be at least three (3) racial/ethnic representatives. Further, there shall be an equal number of laypersons and clergypersons in the total of ten.
2. Ex-officio (voice, but with vote): One (1) District Superintendent.
3. Ex-officio (voice, but without vote): either the Conference Treasurer or Assistant Treasurer.

d) Organization:

e) Meetings:

f) Responsibilities:

f. Human Resources Ministries personnel recruitment, support and guidance tasks of the Conference. There shall be the following organizational units:

- Abuse Prevention Team
- Area Committee on Episcopacy
- Board of Lay Ministries
- Board of Ordained Ministry
- Cabinet
- Committee on Leadership Development

- Conference Nominating Committee
- Conference Personnel Committee
- Joint Committee on Incapacity

1) Abuse Prevention Team
   a) Accountability: The Team is accountable to the Conference Leadership Team in matters of program and budget and shall annually file a written report with the Annual Conference.
   b) Purpose:
   c) Membership There shall be six (6) members at large nominated by CNC and elected by the Conference.
   d) Organization:
   e) Meetings:
   f) Responsibilities: The Abuse Prevention Team shall have the responsibility of implementing and overseeing the Abuse Prevention Policies of the Conference as enacted in June 1998 and/or changed in succeeding Annual Conference action.

2) Area Committee on Episcopacy:
   It shall be the policy of the Conference to participate with the Detroit Conference in an Area Committee on Episcopacy as provided in the DISCIPLINE.
   a) Accountability: The Committee is accountable to and will annually file a written report with the Annual Conference. It shall request funding through the Council on Finance and Administration.
   b) Purpose:
   c) Membership: Membership paralleling the Detroit Conference shall be nominated by The Committee on Nominations as follows:
      1. the Conference Lay Leader or Associate Conference Lay Leader;
      2. seven (7) persons elected at large; and,
      3. two (2) selected by the Bishop.
      Of these ten (10) persons at least four (4) shall be clergy. Representation of racial/ethnic persons and various ages shall be provided for in the membership. The lay and clergy members of the Jurisdictional Committee on the Episcopacy shall be ex-officio members with vote.
   d) Organization: The Committee shall elect its own officers.
   e) Meetings:
   f) Responsibilities:

3) Board of Lay Ministries:
   a) Accountability: The Board shall be accountable to the Conference Leadership Team in matters of program and budget and shall annually file a written report with the Annual Conference.
   b) Purpose:
   c) Membership:
      1. Two (2) members at-large, one of whom shall be a clergyperson;
      2. One (1) representative each, elected by the Conference United Methodist Women and the Conference United Methodist Men;
      3. The District Lay Leader from each District;
      4. The Conference Lay Leader.
      5. Associate Conference Lay Leaders.
      6. The Conference Director of Lay Speaking, and the Conference Coordinator of Scouting.
      7. The Conference Lay Leader or Associate Lay Leader shall be chairperson.
   d) Organization:
   e) Meetings:
   f) Responsibilities:

4) Board of Ordained Ministry:
   a) Accountability: The Board is accountable to and will annually file a written report with the Annual Conference. It shall request funding through the Council on Finance and Administration.
   b) Purpose:
   c) Membership:
      1. Forty-two members shall be nominated by the presiding bishop after consultation with the chairperson of the board, the executive committee, or a committee elected by the board of the previous quadrennium, and with the Cabinet;
      2. The membership shall fill the requirements in accordance with the current provisions of the DISCIPLINE.
   d) Organization:
   e) Meetings:
   f) Responsibilities:

5) Cabinet:
   The Cabinet's personnel responsibilities shall be those described in the DISCIPLINE.

6) Committee on Leadership Development (CLD):
   a) Accountability: The Committee shall be accountable to the Conference Leadership Team in matters of program and budget and shall annually file a written report with the Annual Conference.
   b) Purpose:
   c) Membership:
      1. eight (8) members at large;
      2. Ex-officio (with voice and vote): the President, or designee, of the Conference United Methodist Women and Men, the Conference Secretary, the Conference Lay Leader or Associate Conference Lay Leader, one (1) youth and a volunteer adult worker with youth (both to be named by the Conference Council on Youth Ministries); Ex-officio (voice but without vote): Director of Connectional Ministries, or designee.
      3. Members at large shall be nominated by the Cabinet (for four-year terms). As with all nominations before the Conference, additional nominations from the floor shall be accepted before voting. Each nominee shall have signed consent to serve statement, except oral consent will be sufficient for floor nominations.
      4. District Superintendents, persons employed by organizational units of the Conference (except for the Director of Connectional Ministries, see 2. above), and chairpersons of such units are not eligible to serve on CLD.
      5. In the event of a vacancy on CLD the Bishop will appoint a new member, subject to subsequent Conference election.
   d) Organization:
      1. CLD shall meet to organize at the earliest opportunity following election of its Chairperson and its membership. It may elect such officers as it deems necessary to carry on the business assigned to it. Such officers shall serve for a two-year term.
      2. Whenever possible, the clerical services CLD shall be provided through the facilities of the Conference Center. Other expenses shall be borne through a budget request for CLD of the Administrative section of the Conference budget.
   e) Meetings:
   f) Responsibilities:
      1. to educate, develop, and support leadership of the laity and clergy at all levels within the Conference.

2. to provide a program of leadership development for leadership of congregations, districts, and the Conference.
3. to care for adequate leadership development expertise.
4. to consult with and coordinate the leadership development being done in the Conference by groups such as districts, organizational units, local congregations, and Conference lay groups.
5. to evaluate the leadership development opportunities both within and outside the Church to discover the gaps and overlaps and where necessary encourage additional programming.
6. to distribute listings of current leadership development opportunities both within and outside the church-on the model of the continuing education opportunities for professionals in the Church which is distributed in the Conference Coordinated Mailing.
7. to maintain an up-to-date file of clergy and laity in present and past positions of leadership.
8. to maintain a record of leadership development opportunities completed by individuals. They shall make this record available to the various Nominating Committees of organizational units upon request. A system of recording Continuing Education Units (CEU's) might be developed.
9. to assist groups to do leadership development at their regular meetings or retreat settings.
10. to initiate and develop continuing leadership programs which shall include: clear descriptions of leadership positions; training; support; evaluation; exiting; working with and managing volunteers; group dynamics and effective leadership of a group; alternate ways of doing business in order to hold fewer face-to-face meetings with the attendance travel costs; learn how to write good program proposals; program planning and management; and research on future leadership positions and resources.

7) Conference Nomination Committee (CNC):

a) Accountability: The Committee is accountable to and will annually file a written report with the Annual Conference. It shall request funding through the Council on Finance and Administration.

b) Purpose:

c) Membership:

1. twelve (12) members at large;
2. Ex-officio (with voice and vote): the President, or designee, of the Conference United Methodist Women and Men, the Conference Secretary, the Conference Lay Leader or Associate Conference Lay Leader, two (2) youth (to be named by the Conference Council on Youth Ministries); Ex-officio (voice but without vote): Director of Connectional Ministries, or designee.
3. Members at large shall be nominated by the Cabinet (for four-year terms). As with all nominations before the Conference, additional nominations from the floor shall be accepted before voting. Each nominee shall have signed consent to serve statement, except oral consent will be sufficient for floor nominations.
4. District Superintendents, persons employed by organizational units of the Conference (except the Director of Connectional Ministries, see 2. above), and chairpersons of such units are not eligible to serve on CNC.
5. In the event of a vacancy on CNC the Bishop will appoint a new member, subject to subsequent Conference election.

d) Organization:

1. CNC shall meet to organize at the earliest opportunity following election of its Chairperson and its membership. It may elect such officers as it deems

necessary to carry on the business assigned to it. Such officers shall serve for a two-year term.

2. Whenever possible, the clerical services of CNC shall be provided through the facilities of the Conference Center. Other expenses shall be borne through a budget request for CNC of the Administrative section of the Conference budget.
3. Organizational units of the Conference shall prepare in a timely manner for CNC their nominations, including brief biographical sketches, for membership, etc. as provided for in this Plan of Organization.

e) Meetings:

f) Responsibilities:

1. to identify and recruit volunteer leadership for all Conference organizational units;
2. to nominate one person for each position that is to be elected by the Conference.
3. to monitor the creation and termination of task forces established by organizational units of the Conference; and to establish a networking system for the staffing of task forces that would provide lists of possible members to specific task forces
4. to prepare a slate of officers as described in the Plan of Organization.
5. to care for adequate District representation.

g) Report to the Conference:

1. CNC shall prepare a slate with one nominee for each position in the Conference to be elected by the Conference and present its first draft of nominations to the Cabinet for their consideration not later than 10 days prior to the Conference session. In preparing this slate, CNC is requested to be cognizant of all interests within the Annual Conference, such as theological diversity, urban/rural, large/small church, youth, young adults, other age categories, gender, and racial/ethnic inclusiveness. It is recommended that the Committee on Nominations seek to achieve in all its nominations the goal of 1/3 laymen, 1/3 laywomen and 1/3 clergy with racial/ethnic representation in each organizational unit. This applies in the nominations of chairpersons of organizational units, as well. Before completing nominating slates, CNC shall consult with the chairperson of each organizational unit for which nominations are being made.
2. There shall be the following exception in (1) above: For the nominations of Trustees for Albion and Adrian Colleges, CNC shall submit a name for each vacancy to be filled. Said names shall be submitted after consultation with the Board of Higher Education and Campus Ministry, and the nomination committee of the respective college pursuant to the DISCIPLINE, paragraph 732.4b(3).
3. The report shall be presented to the Conference at least one day before balloting, unless otherwise ordered by the Conference session, and shall be conducted as a regular election with acceptance by each nominee prior to placing his/her name in nomination.
4. In the nominations report that is presented to the Annual Conference, CNC shall by designation identify whether the nominees are lay or clergy.
5. There shall be the following exception in 1. above: For the nominations of members of the Board of Christian Camping (BCC), the BCC will consult with the Conference Nominating Committee as the BCC develops a slate of officers for approval and inclusion in the conference nominations report.

h) Replacement of members elected:

Any person named or elected to organizational units may be replaced at the subsequent Annual Conference if they have resigned or been inactive during the Conference year. The nominating procedure shall be the same as that of the original nomination. The organizational unit that has an inactive member shall notify the nominating unit originating the nomination. Effort shall first be made by the organizational unit to contact the inactive member to encourage either participation or resignation.

i) Nominations for General Church agencies:
The procedures for nominations to General Church agencies for the West Michigan Conference shall be as follows:
1. Immediately upon receipt of appropriate instructions, the Conference Secretary shall notify the Secretary of the General and Jurisdictional Conference Delegation of all General Church agencies for which nominees are required by the West Michigan Conference. The Delegation shall publicize through appropriate channels (Conference coordinated mailing, the "Michigan Area United Methodist Reporter", the "Michigan Christian Advocate", or other means) the General Church agencies for which nominees are required. Any United Methodist within the West Michigan Conference may make suggestions through the Secretary of the Delegation for any such nominations, including biographical information regarding such suggested nominees. CNC shall also make suggestions including biographical information for all such nominations through the Secretary of the Delegation. Any United Methodist within the West Michigan Conference may make suggestions through CNC for inclusion in its report.
2. Upon the recommendation from a committee composed of the Bishop and General and Jurisdictional Conference Delegation, and having allowed opportunity for nominations from the floor, the Annual Conference shall elect persons to be submitted to a jurisdictional pool used by the Jurisdictional Nominating Committee in selecting persons for election to General and Jurisdictional agencies. If, at the site of the Jurisdictional Conference, it becomes necessary for additional names to be submitted to the Jurisdictional Nominating Committee from the West Michigan Conference, the above committee is authorized to secure and submit such additional names as nominees of the West Michigan Conference.

8) Conference Personnel Committee:
a) Accountability: The committee is accountable to the Conference Leadership Team in matters of program and budget and shall annually file a written report with the Annual Conference.
b) Purpose: To hire, evaluate and support staff employed by the Conference Leadership Team.
c) Membership:
1. Nine (9) members at large.
2. Ex-officio (with voice and vote): the Bishop or Clergy Assistant to the Bishop; the Director of Connectional Ministries; one District Superintendent.
d) Organization: Chairperson, Secretary
e) Meetings: 2-4 meetings per year
f) Responsibilities: The Committee on Conference Personnel shall have the responsibility of establishing and coordinating equitable employment policies for the conference program staff employed by all organizational units of the Conference; providing for the hiring, guidance, and termination criteria for all such employees hired by the several agencies of the Conference, and ensuring the establishment of effective supervision. The Committee is responsible for the administration of the grievance process for said employees; its work is carried

out in consultation with the Director of Connectional Ministries to whom it provides guidance.

Further, our committee periodically reviews and updates the WMC Personnel Policy. We deal with grievances as outlined in this policy when they arise. This policy serves as a model for agencies and local congregations."

g. Other Conference Organizational Units

1) Units Under Annual Conference Fiscal and Governing Control.
Definition: The Annual Conference elects, meaning nominated by the Conference Nominating Committee and elected by the Annual Conference, 50% or more of the agency's governing Board, and provides 25% or more of the agency's budget.
 a) "Michigan Christian Advocate", linked to the Communications Commission;
 b) "Michigan Area Loan Fund linked to the Board of Global Ministries.

2) Units Under Annual Conference Fiscal Control. Definition: The Annual Conference elects less than 50% of the agency's governing Board, but provides 25% or more of the agency's budget.
 a) The School for Pastoral Ministry, linked to the Board of Ordained Ministry;
 b) The Area Historical Society linked to the Commission on Archives and History.

3) Units Under Conference Governing Control. Definition: The Annual Conference elects 50% or more of the agency's governing Board, but provides less than 25% of the agency's budget.

4) Units with Annual Conference Affiliation. Definition: The Annual Conference elects less than 50% of the agency's governing Board, and provides less than 25% of the agency's budget.
 a) Albion College, linked to the Board of Higher Education and Campus Ministry;
 b) Adrian College, linked to the Board of Higher Education and Campus Ministry;
 c) Methodist Children's Home Society, linked to the Board of Global Ministries;
 d) Michigan Commission/United Ministries in Higher Education, linked to the Board of Higher Education and Campus Ministry;
 e) Lake Louise Board, linked to the Board of Christian Camping;
 f) Michigan Council on Alcohol Problems linked to the Board of Church and Society.
 g) United Methodist Community House, linked to the UMW Women's Division
 h) Methodist Theological School in Ohio (MTSO), linked to the Board of Higher Education and Campus Ministry;

5) Units With Annual Conference Representative Affiliation. Definition: The Annual Conference has representation on the agency's governing Board, but such representation is completely determined by the agency.
 a) Clark Retirement Community linked to the Board of Global Ministries.
 b) Peoples Church, East Lansing, linked to the Lansing District;
 c) United Theological School in Ohio, linked to the Board of Higher Education and Campus Ministry;
 d) GarrettEvangelical Theological Seminary, linked to the Board of Higher Education and Campus Ministry;
 e) Center for Parish Development, linked to the Board of Global Ministries.

f) Bronson Health Care Group linked to the Board of Global Ministries.

g) United Methodist Foundation of Michigan:
There may be a United Methodist Foundation serving both annual conferences in the State of Michigan.

1. Accountability:
The foundation shall be accountable to the Detroit Annual Conference and the West Michigan Annual Conference.

2. Purpose:
To encourage the giving of gifts, conscientious investing and stewardship education for United Methodist churches in the Michigan Area.

3. Membership:
   a. There will be a board of directors with 12 directors elected at the Foundation's annual meeting. Six directors will be from the Detroit Annual Conference and six will be from the West Michigan Annual Conference. These directors shall be reported to each Annual Conference and their respective nominating committee.
   b. Directors are elected by the then-sitting board and serve three-year terms unless they are elected to fill an un-expired term. Directors may be reelected for a second full term, but no board director may serve for more than 9 consecutive years.
   c. Any vacancy occurring in the board of directors may be filled by a majority vote of the remaining directors present and voting at any regular or special meeting of the board. A director elected to fill a vacancy shall be elected for the un-expired term of his or her predecessor in office.
   d. Ex-officio without vote:
      (1) Area bishop (or designate);
      (2) Executive Director of Foundation;
      (3) Treasurers of each Michigan Annual Conference.

4. Organization:
   a. The officers of the Foundation shall be: chairperson, vice chairperson, secretary and treasurer. All officers, except the executive director, shall serve without compensation and be directors of the Foundation.
   b. There shall be an executive committee made up as follows: chairperson, vice chairperson, secretary, treasurer, stewardship committee chair, investment chair, finance/audit chair, personnel/management chair, marketing chair and the executive director.
   c. There shall be a 12-15 member advisory board in addition to the board of directors. The members of this board will be selected for specific skill needs for the work of the Foundation and will be invited to serve by the executive committee.
   d. There shall be five (5) standing committees: Investment, Stewardship, Finance/Audit, Marketing and Personnel/Management.
   e. The Foundation Board of Directors upon recommendation of the executive committee shall hire the executive director.

f. The Foundation shall meet at least twice annually with additional meetings scheduled and called by the chairperson and executive director. Special meetings may be called by the president or at least three (3) other directors of the board on three (3) days' notice to each director.

5. Responsibilities:
   a. Encourage the giving of gifts to United Methodist churches for the support of their ministries.
   b. Provide resources to United Methodist churches and their members regarding charitable giving and estate planning.
   c. Teach and encourage biblical stewardship principles to our churches and their members.
   d. Encourage and receive gifts, trusts and bequests of real and/or personal property on behalf of either the Detroit Annual Conference or the West Michigan Annual Conference.
   e. Offer responsible choices and opportunities for investing United Methodist financial assets.
   f. Ensure timely and accurate reporting to congregations on the status of funds held by the United Methodist Foundation of Michigan.

—WMC Photoss

XIV. RULES OF ORDER

I. RULES OF ORDER

RULE 1 – GOVERNANCE:

A. **PARLIAMENTARY RULES:**

The proceedings of the West Michigan Annual Conference of The United Methodist Church shall be governed by:

1. The acts of the General and Jurisdictional conferences, insofar as they apply to the organization and work of the Annual Conference.
2. The Rules of Order adopted by the West Michigan Annual Conference.
3. In all matters not established prior, parliamentary law as set forth in Roberts Rules of Order, Revised.
4. The operation of parliamentary rules governing the Conference may be suspended when 2/3 of the members present and voting, vote in favor of suspension.

B. **REFERENCE TO CONFERENCE AND DISCIPLINE:**

1. In all these Rules:
   a. The word Conference with the first letter capitalized shall mean the West Michigan Annual Conference.
   b. The word *"Discipline"* with the first letter capitalized shall mean the cuurent version of *Book of Discipline of The United Methodist Church.*

C. **COMMITTEE ON RULES:**

1. MEMBERSHIP – There shall be a standing committee on Conference Rules of Order composed of nine (9) members nominated by the Conference Committee on Nominations and elected by the Conference. It is recommended that the Committee include 1/3 laywomen, 1/3 laymen, 1/3 clergy. The Conference Facilitator, the Director of Connectional Ministries, and a representative designated by the Cabinet shall be member's ex-officio with voice, but without vote. This Committee shall serve from July 1 through June 30.
2. ORGANIZATION – Annually, following the Conference session, the Cabinet representative shall convene the committee for the purpose of electing such officers as the committee may decide are necessary. This shall be done by August 15th.
3. DUTIES AND RESPONSIBILITIES – During the year between Conference sessions the Committee shall:
   a. Be responsible for seeing that the Plan of Organization is in conformity with the Discipline.
   b. Receive recommendations from Conference organizational units, local churches, or individual church members within the Conference for changes in the Plan of Organization and/or the Rules of Order. The Committee may concur with these recommendations and report them to the Conference for action.
   c. General Conference Petitions
      1) Beginning the two (2) years preceding each General Conference the Committee would solicit petitions to General Conference from United Methodist organizations, churches, clergy and laypersons within the West Michigan Conference.
      2) The Committee may develop its own recommendations in the form of a petition to the General Conference.
      3) Consider petitions pertaining to General Conference matters which are referred from the Committee on Reference to this Committee instead of to a Legislative Committee or directly to the Conference.
      4) The report on the General Conference petitions shall be presented at the Conference session in the year before the General Conference. The report shall be mailed with the Pre-Conference Reports.
      5) Each petition received or developed by the Committee shall be included in the

report together with the recommendation of the Committee for concurrence or non-concurrence on each petition.

6) The Conference shall vote on the recommendations from the Committee with which the Committee concurs. All recommendations for non-concurrence shall be reported to the Conference but shall not be considered unless 1/5 (20%) of the Members of the Conference present and voting request consideration.
7) Each petition shall be debated and may be amended. The recommendation of the Committee shall be advisory only. The vote of the Conference shall be on each petition directly.
8) The Conference Secretary shall forward all petitions with which the Conference concurs to the General Conference Secretary in the manner and form required by the Discipline.
9) The Committee shall inform the petitioners who submitted petitions under this rule concerning the action of the Conference on their petition(s).
10) When considering and developing petitions to the General Conference, the Committee may consult with other persons, such as former General Conference delegates, persons knowledgeable about the general church (i.e., general agency members, etc.) and others who they feel can assist them in framing appropriate Annual Conference petitions to the General Conference.

D. CHANGES IN THE RULES OF ORDER:

1. These Rules of Order may be amended or changed by an affirmative vote of 2/3 of the members of the Conference present and voting.
   a. All petitions requesting changes in the Rules of Order shall be referred to the Committee on Rules of Order for its report at the opening session of Annual Conference recommending either concurrence or non-concurrence with the petition. The Committee's recommendation shall be advisory only. Each petition shall then be presented for action. If he/she elects, the petitioner shall have the opportunity to present and speak to the petition before discussion and debate as provided in Rule 12G.
   b. If the Committee recommends non-concurrence with a petition to amend or change the Rules of Order, the petitioner shall be notified as soon as possible in writing of this fact and the rationale for the non-concurrence recommendation.
   c. When the Conference is in session any proposed changes or amendments to the Rules of Order shall first be referred to the Committee and it shall report its recommendation to the Conference within twenty-four hours.
   d. The Committee may make any necessary changes to the Rules of Order to reflect the most recent provisions and paragraph numbers in the *Discipline.*

E. PUBLICATION:

The Rules of Order, as adopted and amended from time to time, shall be available on the Conference website in a format persons can download and/or print.

II OFFICERS OF THE CONFERENCE

RULE 2 – SECRETARY:

A. ELECTION OF CONFERENCE SECRETARY:

1. The Secretary of the Conference shall be nominated by the Conference Committee on Nominations, after consultation with the Bishop, and elected by the Conference.
2. In accordance with The Book of Discipline (¶603.7), the annual conference at the first session following the General Conference or jurisdictional conference shall elect a secretary to serve for the succeeding quadrennium. In the case of a vacancy in the interim of the sessions, the bishop, after consultation with the district superintendents, shall appoint a person to act until the next session of the annual conference.
3. The term of office shall begin on January 1 of the year following election and continue for four years.

B. DUTIES OF THE CONFERENCE SECRETARY:

1. Keep a fair and accurate record of the proceedings of the Conference.
2. Make a digital recording, whenever possible, with subject, time, and date of all business sessions. These recordings shall be kept on file for two years, and then transferred to the Conference Archive.
3. Preserve the Journals and papers of the Conference.
4. The Conference Secretary shall be the final editor of the Journal.
5. Have the record of the Conference sessions certified by himself/herself and the Conference President and published in the form of a Journal. This published journal shall be the official record of the Conference. Printed copies will be available for purchase.
6. Publish the names and addresses of Deaconesses, Diaconal Ministers, surviving spouses of clergy including Local Pastors, lay persons elected to Conference organizational units, persons on Honorable Location, retired Local Pastors, and clergy (including the clergy record of each) in the Journal. The name of the spouse shall be included in parentheses in the manner requested by the spouse.
7. Prepare a Pre-Conference Reports Booklet containing all reports required from official Conference organizational units that are listed in the previous year's Journal.
8. Provide forms for use by Conference members for writing their motions for presentation to the Conference Secretary.
9. By March 1 of the year for election of delegates to General and Jurisdictional conferences prepare and distribute via the Conference website a notification of the date for elections to all pastors under appointment, lay members of Conference and chairpersons of each district conference and request names of candidates for nomination as lay delegates.
10.

C. APPOINTMENT OF ASSISTANT SECRETARIES:

The Conference Secretary shall appoint such assistant secretaries with appropriate skills as deemed necessary for the Annual Conference and preparation of the Journal.

RULE 3 – FACILITATOR:

A. ELECTION OF CONFERENCE FACILITATOR:

1. The Conference Facilitator shall be nominated by the Conference Committee on Nominations and elected by the Conference.
2. The Facilitator shall be an impartial lay person with broad experience in the Church and able to communicate well.
3. The Facilitator shall serve from July 1 through June 30.

B. ASSISTANT FACILITATORS:

1. When deemed necessary, the Annual Conference Program Committee may appoint one or more assistant facilitators.
2. Assistant Facilitators shall serve for the duration of the Conference.
3. When the Assistant Facilitator(s) is not a member of the Conference, the expenses, including mileage, for attending the Conference shall be paid by the Conference Program Committee.

C. DUTIES OF THE CONFERENCE FACILITATOR(S):

1. The Facilitator shall occupy a specific location on the floor of the Conference. Assistant Facilitators shall be seated at specific locations in, or adjacent to, the floor of the Conference. These locations shall be announced to the Conference.
2. The Facilitator(s) shall assist any person who seeks assistance regarding the understanding and use of the Rules, procedures and resources of the Conference in session.
3. The Facilitator shall carry out such other duties as outlined in the "Rules of Order" and/or the "Plan of Organization."

RULE 4 – STATISTICIAN:

A. ELECTION OF CONFERENCE STATISTICIAN:

1. The Conference Statistician shall be nominated by the Conference Committee on Nominations, after consultation with the Bishop, and elected by the Conference.

The term of office shall begin on January 1 of the year following election and continue for four years.

B. **APPOINTMENT OF ASSISTANT STATISTICIANS:**

1. There shall be three assistant statisticians.
2. The Conference Statistician shall appoint such assistant statisticians with appropriate skills as deemed necessary for the task.

RULE 5 – TREASURER:

A. **ELECTION OF CONFERENCE TREASURER:**

1. The Conference Treasurer shall be nominated by the Conference Council on Finance and Administration, as ordered by the Discipline.
2. The election by the Conference shall occur at the first Conference session after the General Conference.

B. **SUPERVISION:**

The Conference Treasurer shall perform all duties of this office under the supervision of the Conference Council on Finance and Administration.

RULE 6 – CHANCELLOR:

The Chancellor shall be nominated by the Bishop and elected by the Conference. The term of office shall be at the discretion of the Bishop.

RULE 7 – LAY LEADER:

A. **ELECTION OF CONFERENCE LAY LEADER:**

1. The Conference Lay Leader shall be nominated by the Conference Committee on Nominations and elected by the Conference.
2. The term of office shall be (4) four years.
3. The tenure of this office shall be the same as the Conference organizational units.

B. **ELECTION OF ASSOCIATE CONFERENCE LAY LEADER(S)**

1. Associate Conference Lay Leader(s) shall be nominated by the Conference Committee on Nominations and elected by the Conference.
2. The tenure of this office shall be the same as the Conference organizational units.

III CONFERENCE MEMBERSHIP

RULE 8 – LAY MEMBERS AND CLERGY MEMBERS:

A. **ELECTION OF LAY MEMBERS:**

1. Lay Members and Reserve Lay Members shall be elected annually by the local church Charge conferences as described in the Discipline. Those elected shall serve at the Conference session immediately following their election. For churches with multiple clergy staff, the number of Lay Members elected shall be based on the clergy appointed to a church as of the close of the previous Annual Conference.
2. One young person between the ages of twelve (12) and seventeen (17) and one young person between the ages of eighteen (18) and thirty (30) from each District to be selected in such a manner as may be determined by the Annual Conference.
3. As soon as available each year and not later then March 1, the names, addresses, phone numbers and electronic mail addresses of all lay members to the next Annual Conference from local churches, District members at large and those serving under the provisions of the Constitution and Equalization of Lay Members formula (Rule 8-C) shall be posted on the Conference website. If all of this information is not available at the same time, the information that is will be posted and when additional information becomes available it will be added to the website.

B. **CLERGY MEMBERS:**

Clergy members of the Conference are as defined in ¶602.1 of the Discipline. [The clergy membership of an annual conference (¶370) shall consist of deacons and elders in full connection

(¶333), provisonal members (¶327), associate members, affiliate members (¶¶344.4, 586.4), and local pastors under full-time and part-time appointment to a pastoral charge (¶317), (see also ¶32).]

C. **EQUALIZATION OF LAY AND CLERGY MEMBERS**:

1. To equalize lay and clergy members for the Annual Conference session as required by the Constitution and Discipline of The United Methodist Church, the following procedure shall be used.
2. Lay Members of the Annual Conference are:
   a. Professing lay members elected by each charge of the conference.
   b. Those described in the Constitution and Book of Discipline (¶32, Article I and ¶602.4-2012); and,
   c. Additional lay persons selected as follows:
3. Additional Lay Members
   a. From the number of total clergy members reported in the previous year's Journal in the Disciplinary Question "What is the number of clergy members of the Annual Conference?" subtract the number of lay members determined in Item 2a&b above.
   b. This difference shall be the number of additional lay members to serve for the next Annual Conference as follows:
   c. These additional seats shall be filled by lay persons who are not members of the same Conference session in the preceding categories serving as of December 31 of the previous year in the following order:
      1) Members of general and jurisdictional boards, councils, and standing commissions or their divisions, departments, committees, units, and other sub-groups, who reside within the bounds of the West Michigan Conference;
      2) Chairpersons of West Michigan Conference boards;
      3) Treasurer of West Michigan Conference;
      4) Conference Facilitators;
      5) Members of the following agencies:
         - Conference Leadership Team (CLT);
         - Council on Finance and Administration (CFA);
         - Conference Program Committee;
         - Rules of Order Committee;
         - Committee on Journal
      6) Chairpersons of district leadership team or equivalent;
      7) Conference Missionary Secretary;
      8) Conference Secretary and all lay assistant secretaries;
      9) Conference Statistician;
      10) Conference Chancellor;
      11) Director of Communication
      12) Directors of West Michigan Conference campus ministries;
      13) Chairperson/coordinator of these other conference agencies, committees and groups:
         - Abuse Prevention Team
         - Archives and History
         - Christian Unity and Inter-Religious Concerns
         - Communications
         - Disability Concerns
         - Disaster Response Team
         - Episcopacy (vice chairperson if chairperson is not a member of West Michigan Conference)
         - Equitable Compensation
         - Hispanic/Latino Committee
         - Michigan Area Indian Workers Conference

- New Church Establishment and Development
- Nominations
- Leadership Development
- Older Adult Ministries
- Personnel
- Prison Ministry and Restorative Justice Concerns
- Racial/Ethnic Local Church
- Religion and Race
- Scouting
- Status and Role of Women
- UMCOR/Hunger

14) General and Jurisdictional Conference delegates and reserves elected for the last General and Jurisdictional conferences;
15) Conference Program Staff;
16) Associate Conference Lay Leaders;
17) Conference Council on Youth Ministries Coordinator
18) Conference Journal Editor

d. Where there is co-leadership in any group, both shall be included in the lay equalization formula.

e. District Lay Members: Any lay members remaining after providing for those above shall be divided equally among the six districts and each district conference shall elect the number of Lay Members allocated to that district. Each district conference shall also elect two alternate Lay Members to serve, in order of their election, if a regularly elected Lay Member is unable to serve.

1) The District Nominating Committee shall present the names of qualified lay persons to the District Conference.
2) In selecting their nominations the District Nominating Committee is requested to review all various interests within the district, theological diversity, urban and rural, large and small churches, youth, young adults, other age categories, women and ethnic communities.
3) Where there are Wesley Foundations and/or Wesley Fellowships, the district shall elect one Lay Member from those organizations, in consultation with those organizations, in their district as a part of their equalization number.
4) The Conference Committee on Rules of Order shall establish and implement a system of rotation so that from year to year, although the number of seats may not be evenly divisible by the number of districts, there shall be equitable representation from each district.

4. Expenses. Those persons who are seated because of their position of conference leadership shall have their expenses paid by the group on which they serve. The remaining persons elected by the district conferences shall have their expenses paid from funds made available by the Conference Council on Finance and Administration.

D. SEATING RESERVE LAY MEMBERS:

A Reserve Lay Member may be seated in the absence of the Lay Member from a Charge or District. This substitution may continue for a portion or for the entire Conference session. The Reserve Lay Member shall be responsible for notifying their District Superintendent in advance of assuming the seat.

E. LAY MEMBER'S REPORT TO THE LOCAL CHURCH:

The last person seated in the Conference session shall become the Lay Member from their Charge, and it shall be their duty to report the actions of the Conference to their Local Church(s) as soon as possible.

IV THE CONFERENCE SESSION

RULE 9 – PROGRAM COMMITTEE:

A. **THE CONFERENCE PROGRAM COMMITTEE:**

1. There shall be a standing committee on the Program of the Conference. This committee shall plan and arrange the entire program for the Conference Session.
2. The Membership of this Committee shall include:
   a. The Bishop
   b. The Clergy Assistant to the Bishop
   c. A District Superintendent selected by the Cabinet
   d. The host pastor
   e. The Conference Secretary
   f. The Conference Lay Leader or Associate Conference Lay Leader
   g. The Conference President of United Methodist Women
   h. The Conference President of United Methodist Men
   i. A youth representative of the Conference Youth Council
   j. The Director of Connectional Ministries
   k. The Director of Communications
   l. The Chairperson of the Committee on the Rules of Order
   m. The Conference Facilitator
   n. A representative designated by the host institution
   o. A representative from the Committee on Disability Concerns
   p. Six (6) members at large, one of whom shall be less than 30 years of age at the time of election. Three of the six shall be lay persons nominated by the Conference Committee on Nomiinations and elected by the Conference.
3. A chairperson, nominated by the Conference Committee on Nominations in consultation with the Bishop, shall be one of the six (6) members at large. The worship and childcare liaisons shall be selected by the Program Committee and have voice, but not vote, on the Program Committee.
4. The elected members are to be nominated by the Conference Committee on Nominations and elected by the Conference.

B. **PRINTED PROGRAM:**

1. A program shall be published in advance on the Conference website and printed for distribution at the Annual Conference and except for necessary changes approved by the Conference, it shall be the official program for the Conference session.
2. Only material that is approved by the Program Committee or is from an official United Methodist organization may be handed out at the doors to the bar of the Annual Conference.

RULE 10 – PRE-CONFERENCE PREPARATION:

A. The Conference Secretary shall prepare and post to the website Pre-Conference Reports containing all reports required from official Conference organizational units listed in the previous year's Journal.

B. The deadline for reports to be submitted to the Conference Secretary shall be set by the Conference Secretary.

C. The following shall be exempt from making Pre-Conference Reports: the District Superintendents, the Rules of Order Committee, the Conference Committee on Nominations, and the annual audits of the United Methodist Foundation and the Council on Finance and Administration.

D. All reports, resolutions or motions of substance which do not appear in the Pre-Conference Reports Booklet shall be presented to the Conference Committee on Reference.

E. All editorial changes or corrections in the Pre-Conference Reports shall be submitted to the Conference Secretary in writing at the time that organizational unit reports to the Conference.

F. The Pre-Conference Reports shall be posted on the Conference website in time for all Conference Members and others under appointment to access reports at least 60 days before the Conference convenes. The words "Not for Publication until Perfected and Acted Upon by the West Michigan

Conference of The United Methodist Church" shall be noted at the beginning of the document.

G. The design and implementation of thorough training for Conference members and alternate members, including an orientation session on each district and a briefing session immediately before the Conference begins, shall be the responsibility of the Conference Lay Leader and the Full Cabinet in consultation with the Annual Conference Program Committee Chair.

RULE 11 – EXECUTIVE AND CLERGY SESSIONS:

A. The Bishop shall convene an Executive Session when 2/3 of the Conference Members, present and voting, so order.

B. The Bishop may order or convene Clergy Sessions which are not Executive Sessions.

RULE 12 – PETITIONS TO ANNUAL CONFERENCE:

A. Petitions to initiate new business may be submitted by any local church, church organization, clergy or lay person within the West Michigan Annual Conference.

B. Petitions may be submitted by regular mail or electronic mail. A petition submitted by an individual clergy or lay person shall state the local church, or church organization, of which the petitioner is a member. All petitions shall include the petitioner's electronic mail address and telephone number(s) and are subject to verification of their validity.

C. A copy of each petition which requests funds from the Conference shall be submitted to the Council on Finance and Administration. The Council on Finance and Administration shall make its recommendation prior to the time the petition is considered at the Conference.

D. Deadlines shall be the following:

1. All petitions which are filed with the Director of Connectional Ministries by a date set by the Conference Secretary shall be posted to the Conference website with the Pre-Conference Reports at least 60 days prior to the Annual Conference. When several members of a church or church organization are listed as supporting the petition, only the name of the church or church organization and the number of persons listed will be printed in the legislative material. If an identical petition is filed by more than one individual or group, that petition shall be printed only once and the names and other identifying information of each church, church organization and/or individual(s) submitting the identical petition shall be printed below the petition.

2. **Response Petitions** – Additional petitions in response to any matter contained in either the Pre-Conference Reports or a petition may be filed with the Director of Connectional Ministries until 30 days prior to the opening of the Conference session. However, no petition containing new business which was not introduced in the Pre-Conference Reports or previously filed petitions shall be accepted. All response petitions shall be posted to the Conference website prior to the time the Conference session convenes.

3. No petitions filed within 30 days of the opening of the Conference session shall be accepted or considered except by suspension of the Rules or as Addenda (see Rule 22.D).

E. The original copy of each petition shall be kept on file until after the Conference has acted upon that petition.

F. Action on all petitions referred to a board or agency of the Annual Conference or where instructions are given to a board or agency of the Annual Conference shall be reported to the next Annual Conference in a manner to be established by the Conference Secretary by giving the name of the petition, action ordered, action taken.

G. When petitions are presented to the Conference for action, the petitioner or representative of the petitioner shall be given the opportunity to present the petition and speak to it for up to three minutes before other discussion or debate on the petition occurs, and shall also be available to answer questions about the petition. (This opportunity for a petitioner to speak will not apply to petitions which the Conference has approved by action on the Decision or Consent Calendar.)

RULE – 13 ATTENDANCE:

All Clergy and Lay Members shall attend all sessions of the Conference. Persons unable to attend shall report the reason to the Conference Secretary, and where appropriate to the District Superintendent, in writing.

RULE 14 – FLOOR OF THE CONFERENCE:

The limits of the floor of the Conference shall be fixed at the first business session. The Conference Program Committee shall consult with the Bishop or President and recommend limits. All Members must be seated within these limits in order to vote.

RULE 15 – IDENTIFICATION:

All vote counts shall be conducted by recognizing those eligible to vote on the question. The Conference Program Committee shall provide a color code system identifying Clergy Members, Lay Members, Visitors and any other, which may be determined. A guide for identification shall be published in the Conference Program.

RULE 16 – RETIRED LOCAL PASTORS:

Retired Local Pastors shall be granted seat and voice on the floor of the Annual Conference.

RULE 17 – ROLL CALL:

The Roll Call of the Conference shall be taken from the registration list of Clergy and Lay Members. No additional attendance checks shall be taken during the Conference.

RULE 18 – RECESS:

The Conference Program Committee shall provide a recess of not less than fifteen minutes somewhere in both the morning and afternoon business sessions.

RULE 19 – CORPORATE SESSION:

The Conference Program Committee shall designate a specific time for the Corporate Session to meet during the Conference. All recommendations for action at the Corporate Session shall be printed and distributed to members of the Conference at least 24 hours prior to their consideration.

RULE 20 – PREVIOUS DAY'S JOURNAL:

The previous day's Journal shall be posted at the main entrance(s) to the floor of the Conference by the opening of the day's session. Prior to the close of the day's business, the approval of the previous day's Journal shall be the order of the Day. The Conference Secretary shall be allowed to make any necessary corrections to the minutes of the closing day of Conference.

V. CONFERENCE PROCEDURE AND PARTICIPATION

RULE 21 – SUBMITTING REPORTS:

When a report is submitted to the Conference Secretary and printed in the Pre-Conference Reports it is before the Conference without further reading provided that:

A. Any portion of a report shall be read when it is ordered by 2/3 vote of the Conference.

B. A minority report from any Board, Agency or Committee shall be presented to the Conference immediately following the majority report and prior to debate, regardless of the number of people who endorse it, provided that 1/5 of the members of that Board, Agency, or Committee who are present and voting have agreed that the minority report presents an opinion which the Conference should hear. The signatories of the minority report shall select one of the signatories to present the minority report.

C. Materials in the Pre-Conference Reports shall be historical in nature only. Recommendations for legislative action shall be submitted separately to the Conference Secretary for inclusion in Decision Items publication and shall be referred to the Committee on Reference for processing.

RULE 22 – COMMITTEE ON REFERENCE:

A. **MEMBERSHIP:** There shall be a Committee on Reference composed of:

1. the Conference Lay Leader, or Associate Conference Lay Leader, who shall serve as Chairperson;
2. the Chairperson of the Conference Program Committee;
3. the Conference Facilitator;
4. the Director of Connectional Ministries; and
5. the Conference Secretary; and
6. the chair of the Rules of Order Committee.

B. **TERM OF OFFICE:**

The members of this Committee shall serve from the opening of the Conference session until the opening of the next regular session of the Conference.

C. **DUTIES AND RESPONSIBILITIES:**

1. Depending on the nature and amount of legislation, this Committee, in consultation with the Program Committee, shall decide if Legislative Committees will be employed.
2. If Legislative Committees are not used, legislative items will be referred directly to the Conference.
   a. Exceptions will include legislative items which have funding implications which will first be referred to the Conference Council on Finance and Administration, petitions to General Conference which will first be referred to the Committee on General Conference Petitions, items recommending changes in the Rules of Order which will first be referred to the Committee on Rules of Order, and items recommending changes in the "Plan of Organization" which will first be referred to the Rules of Order Committee. Legislative item pertaining to the Conference policy for health insurance program shall be referred to the Board of Pension and Health Benefits.
   b. The Reference Committee may place those items on a Decision Calendar which they deem would be acceptable to the Annual Conference without discussion. Any item on the Decision Calendar may be lifted at the written request of any member of the Annual Conference.
   c. The Reference Committee may report petitions as non-concurrence. Said petitions will not be before the Annual Conference unless so requested by 10% of the Annual Conference.
   d. The Reference Committee shall report out the petitions and may request the presence of a petitioner or the representative of an organization making a recommendation and/or petition for clarification.
3. If Legislative Committees are used, the following process shall be employed:
   a. Prior to the opening of the Conference session this Committee may assign the legislative recommendations in the Pre-Conference Reports, the properly filed petitions and any other business which will come before the Conference for action to a Legislative Committee.
   b. The Committee shall refer each petition or legislative item submitted to the Conference which has funding considerations to the Conference Council on Finance and Administration. The written recommendation of the Council on Finance and Administration shall be presented to both the Legislative Committee and the Conference at the times the proposal is being considered.
   c. Any legislation not considered by a Legislative Committee or considered, but not acted upon, shall be returned to the Conference for their consideration and action.
   d. Each amendment to legislation which is proposed by a Legislative Committee or by the Conference, which has funding considerations, shall be referred to the Council on Finance and Administration for their written recommendation prior to the final action by the current session of Conference.

e. Any petition which relates to General Conference shall be referred to the Committee on General Conference Petitions, and not to a Legislative Committee.

f. During the Conference session, any matter of substance not contained in the Pre-Conference Reports, the properly filed petitions and the response petitions shall be referred immediately to the Committee on Reference. The Committee shall report its recommendation to the Conference before the adjournment of the next business session.

D. ADDENDA TO REPORTS AND RECOMMENDATIONS:

1. Each addendum presented shall be referred to the Committee on Reference.
2. Addenda to reports and recommendations in the Pre-Conference Reports from the organizational units shall include an explanatory statement from the chairperson of the organizational unit stating the reason the material was not considered by that organizational unit in time for inclusion in its original Pre-Conference Report.
3. If the Committee on Reference determines that the material in the addendum could reasonably have been acted upon by the organizational unit and included in the Pre-Conference Reports the Committee may recommend that the proposed addendum not be considered by the Conference. When the Committee on Reference recommends non-consideration the Chairperson of the organizational unit submitting the addendum shall be advised promptly.
4. An addendum which is not recommended by the Committee on Reference to the Conference for action may not be considered unless the Conference in session suspends its rules for the specific purpose of consideration.
5. Addenda to Pre-Conference Reports shall be presented only when an organizational unit determines it is necessary to do so.

<u>RULE 23 – LEGISLATIVE COMMITTEES</u>:

A. LEGISLATIVE COMMITTEES:

The Conference may have Legislative Committees.

B. IF LEGISLATIVE COMMITTEES ARE USED THE FOLLOWING WILL APPLY:

1. The number of Legislative Committees shall be determined by the Committee on Reference.
2. Each Legislative Committee shall consist of Lay and Clergy Members of the Conference, plus part-time Local Pastors appointed at the current session of Conference.
3. Assignment of members to legislative committees:
   a. The assignment of Members to each of the Legislative Committees shall be the discretion of the Conference Program Committee
   b. Should the Pastor(s) and/or Lay Member(s) of the same local church be assigned to the same Legislative Committee, either the Pastor or Lay Member may request a change. The Chairperson of the Conference Program Committee or the Conference Facilitator shall reassign them to a different Committee.
   c. Any person with a handicapping condition may request a change. The Chairperson of the Conference Program Committee or the Conference Facilitator shall reassign them to a different Committee.
4. Leaders of Legislative Committees:
   a. The Conference Program Committee shall select from among the members of the Conference qualified persons to serve as officers such as are determined necessary by the Program Committee for each Legislative Committee.
   b. The Conference Program Committee shall provide orientation for all who will serve as Legislative Committee members prior to the Conference Session.
   c. All leaders of each Legislative Committee shall be members of that Committee with voice and vote.
5. The Privilege of Voice and Vote:
   a. The privilege of vote shall be granted to all Conference Members assigned to a Legislative Committee.

b. The privilege of voice in Legislative Committees shall be granted to the following:
   1) All Conference Members assigned to a Committee.
   2) Deaconesses, certified lay workers and registered visitors specifically assigned to a Committee.
   3) Retired Local Pastors.

c. The privilege of voice only during the discussion of a specific report or petition shall be granted to the following:
   1) Up to four representatives designated by the organizational unit whose report is being considered by the Committee. The representative of the organizational unit shall also have voice when any petition is being considered affecting the work of the unit.
   2) One petitioner or one representative of a petitioning church or organization for each petition being considered by a specific Legislative Committee. (If the petitioner cannot be present, they may designate an alternate in writing.)
   3) In case of identical or nearly identical petitions, only one person who is selected by the petitioners shall speak for the petitions.

6. DUTIES AND RESPONSIBILITIES:
   a. Each Legislative Committee shall study all matters referred to it and recommend each item by voting for concurrence, concurrence with amendment, or non-concurrence.
   b. The recommendations of all Legislative Committees shall be the property of the Conference.

7. REPORTING TO THE CONFERENCE:
   a. Each Legislative Committee shall report to the Conference.
   b. There shall be a Consent Calendar. All legislative items from all Legislative Committees reported to the Conference which meet the following criteria shall be included in the Consent Calendar and presented to the Conference as one item.
      1) All legislative items considered by Legislative Committees which received approval for concurrence, with or without amendment, by 90% of the Legislative Committee members present and voting shall be included in the Consent Calendar.
      2) Any legislative item included in the Consent Calendar may be removed from the Consent Calendar upon written request to the Conference Secretary by any Conference Member present.
      3) The budget of the West Michigan Annual Conference and legislative items which affect the Annual Conference budget may not be included on the Consent Calendar or on the Decision Calendar and must be brought to the full Conference for action. Conference Policies, Procedures and Rules regarding financial matters need to be considered by Legislative Committees and come before the Annual Conference only if they are changed.
   c. All recommendations for concurrence or concurrence by amendment by less than 90% of the Legislative Committee members present and voting shall automatically be before the Conference for action. Abstentions shall be counted as present, but not voting, and shall not be counted in the computation of votes.
   d. All recommendations for non-concurrence shall be reported to the Conference; however, these recommendations shall not be considered unless 10% of the members of the Conference vote for consideration.
   e. When the Legislative Committee reports to the Conference a representative of the organizational unit whose recommendation(s) and/or petition(s) is being considered shall be allowed to give a report for information not to exceed three minutes and may be present at a microphone to provide additional information should it be requested. The same consideration shall be given to a petitioner or their representative.
   f. All additions, corrections, and/or deletions regarding the list of Advance Specials as of the beginning of the Annual Conference shall be referred to the Executive Committee of the Conference Board of Global Ministries for their consideration and action. These

items shall be acted on in a timely fashion so as to enable them to be printed in the Journal.

g. This procedure for the consideration of legislative business shall apply to all matters including Pre-Conference Reports, addenda and petitions.

RULE 24 – AGENDA COMMITTEE:

A. MEMBERSHIP:

There shall be an Agenda Committee for the Conference with the following members:

1. Chairperson of Conference Program Committee, as Chairperson;
2. Chairperson of the Committee on Rules of Order;
3. Conference Facilitator;
4. Chairperson of the Committee on Reference;
5. A representative of the Conference Worship Committee;
6. The Director of Connectional Ministries.

B. DUTIES AND RESPONSIBILITIES:

1. Determine the order and time for the consideration of all legislative business which shall come before the Conference.
2. Advise, not later than the session immediately preceding, when specific matters will be considered by the Conference.
3. Coordinate and prioritize the entire agenda of the Conference to provide for the proper and timely consideration of all matters which require action by the Conference.
4. Consult with the Bishop, or President, the Conference Secretary, officers of Legislative Committees, representatives of organizational units and others as required in order to perform these responsibilities.

RULE 25 – MOTIONS AND RESOLUTIONS:

Each motion and/or resolution of substance (not procedure) which is introduced, by a member and/or a committee, shall be written in duplicate and presented to the Conference Secretary. The Secretary will provide the appropriate forms.

RULE 26 – SECURING THE FLOOR:

A. CONFERENCE MEMBER:

1. A Conference Member who desires to speak or present any matter to the conference shall raise the card provided while seated within the bar and wait to be recognized by the presiding bishop. When recognized, she/he shall proceed to the nearest microphone and first announce her/his name and local church or other conference relationship. Unless rising for a point of order or parliamentary inquiry, the member shall not speak until given the floor. Persons with handicapping conditions may be recognized through provided signs and then move to a microphone.
2. After being recognized by the President the speaker shall first identify himself/herself.
3. If the Member wishes to speak on a question of privilege, the Member shall state the request and wait until the President concurs it is a question of privilege.
4. A Member desiring a point of order shall stand from within the limits of the floor, call for the point of order, and wait to be recognized by the President. Upon recognition the Member shall move to the nearest microphone and speak.
5. Moments of courtesy may be accepted by the President without vote.

B. NON-MEMBER OF CONFERENCE:

A non-member shall be granted the privilege of the floor by consent of the Conference, the Conference Program Committee, or at the discretion of the President.

RULE 27 – LIMIT FOR SPEECHES:

A. No member shall speak more than once on the same subject until every member who chooses to speak has done so.

B. No member shall speak more than twice on the same subject or more than five minutes at one time unless an exception is granted by the Conference.

C. Addresses by non-members of the Conference shall be limited to fifteen minutes except for those persons scheduled by the Program Committee.

D. If the question is called and confirmed by the body, the maker of the legislation shall be allowed two (2) minutes for closing remarks.

RULE 28 – REFERRAL OR TABLING:

No motion, resolution, or report shall be referred or laid on the table until the mover or introducer has been allowed to speak on the question.

RULE 29 – VOTING:

All voting shall be by raising the card provided unless otherwise ordered by the Conference. A count may be ordered: a) by the President, or b) on the call of any Member, supported by 1/5 of the Members present and voting. A majority of those present and voting shall decide all questions unless otherwise directed by these Rules or the *Discipline*.

RULE 30 – COMMITTEE ON JOURNAL:

There shall be a Committee on the Journal.

A. **MEMBERSHIP:**
The membership shall consist of (6) six persons; (2) two clergy, (2) two laymen and (2) two laywomen, nominated by the Conference Committee on Nominations and elected by the Conference.

B. **DUTIES AND RESPONSIBILITIES:**
The Committee shall function under the direction of the Conference Secretary, and shall daily examine the proceedings of the Conference, establishing and reporting on the accuracy of such record, especially in regard to content as required by the Rules of Order.

C. **TERM OF OFFICE:**
The term of office shall be for four years.

RULE 31 – COMMITTEE ON MEMOIRS:

A. **MEMBERSHIP:**
There shall be a Committee on Memoirs comprised of (3) three persons, (1) one clergy, (1) one layman and (1) one laywoman, nominated by the Conference Committee on Nominations and elected by the Conference.

B. **DUTIES AND RESPONSIBILITIES:**

1. Keep a record of deaths of persons professionally related to the Conference, their spouses, and members of their immediate family living at home.
2. This record shall be made available for use in the Memorial Service at the Conference session and to the Conference Secretary for inclusion in the Memoirs section of the Journal.
3. Persons, whose deaths occur prior to the end of the Conference session, but after the preparation of materials for the Memorial Service, may be named in the service for that year, and, if possible, included in the Journal. Appropriate printed acknowledgment of such death may also be included in the materials for the Memorial Service the following year, but shall not be repeated in the Journal.
4. Deaths of persons in prior years about which information was not available at the time of the death shall be included in the Journal in the year in which the information is received.

VI. ELECTION OF DELEGATES AND PREPARATION FOR GENERAL AND JURISDICTIONAL CONFERENCES

RULE 32 – LAY AND CLERGY DELEGATES:

A. **ELIGIBILITY FOR ELECTION:**

1. Delegates shall be nominated and elected without regard to age, sex, race or any handicapping condition.

2. Lay persons must have been members of The United Methodist Church for at least two (2) years immediately prior to their election, and shall have been active participants in The United Methodist Church for at least four (4) years preceding their election. (Discipline article 36)
3. Lay delegates must be members of a United Methodist Church within the bounds of the West Michigan Conference at the time the General and Jurisdictional conferences are held.
4. The ordained clergy delegates to the General and Jurisdictional conferences shall be elected by and from the ministerial members in full connection with the West Michigan Conference (Discipline article 35)

B. PRE-CONFERENCE INFORMATION:

1. Notification that the election of delegates to the General and Jurisdictional Conference will occur at the next Conference session shall be distributed by the Conference Secretary.
2. This notification shall be e-mailed to each pastor under appointment, each lay member of Conference and the chairperson of each district conference posted to the Conference website before March 1.
3. In the same e-mailing and posting the Conference Secretary shall request that the name and a brief biographical sketch (100 words) of each potential delegate be submitted. Appropriate forms shall be enclosed, including space for the written consent of each nominee.
4. Nominations may be made by any local church council, charge conference, district conference, or any other organization within the West Michigan Conference, or by any lay person or clergy within the West Michigan Conference.
5. The names, biographical sketches and consent to serve shall be given to the Conference Secretary by April 1 of the year of the election. Copies of this material shall be posted to the Conference website and distributed at Annual Conference.

RULE 33 – ELECTION OF GENERAL & JURISDICTIONAL CONFERENCE DELEGATES:

A. DELEGATES:

1. The lay and clergy delegates to the General and Jurisdictional conferences shall be elected in accordance with the provisions of The Book of Discipline in effect at the time of election beginning with the 2016 General / Jurisdictional Conference elections.

B. TELLERS:

1. The Conference Secretary shall designate tellers from a list of names which shall have been submitted by the superintendents of the districts. A member of the Conference Secretary's staff shall serve as head of both groups of tellers.
2. The tellers will distribute all ballots, collect all ballots and be responsible for their count. The results shall be reported to the Conference Secretary and announced to the Conference by the bishop.

C. NOMINATIONS:

1. All clergy and lay persons whose biographical sketches have been submitted and posted to the Conference web site shall be considered as nominated. Additional clergy and lay persons may be nominated from the floor, provided written consent to serve if elected has been obtained prior to their nomination. No speeches may be made for a clergy or lay person nominated from the floor; however a printed biographical statement (100 words) may be distributed to the members of the Conference.

D. BALLOTING:

1. Ballots may be cast any time the Conference is in session.
2. The bishop shall announce the number of candidates which may be elected and the names and number of persons previously elected before each ballot is cast.
3. Each ballot shall be cast by distributing ballots, marking the ballots and standing within the limits of the Conference until ballots have been collected by the tellers.
4. On the first three ballots for General and Jurisdictional Conference delegates, respectively, the names of all those receiving three or more votes shall be read. On subsequent ballots only the names of persons receiving ten or more votes shall be read.

E. **INVALID BALLOTS:**

1. An individual's ballot shall be invalid if it contains more or less names (or identifying numbers) than the number of delegates to be elected on that ballot.
2. The intent of the voter shall be allowed regardless of mistakes in spelling.
3. If persons with the same name are mentioned and no initials are included that total ballot shall be invalid.

F. **ELECTIONS**

1. General Conference Delegates: – Balloting shall first occur for the number of lay and clergy General Conference delegates to be elected. A majority of all valid ballots cast shall be necessary for such elections.
2. Jurisdictional Conference Delegates: – The lay and clergy General Conference delegates shall be delegates to the Jurisdictional Conference. In addition, after balloting is completed for the General Conference delegates balloting shall continue for the remaining number of lay and clergy Jurisdictional Conference delegates to be elected. On each of the first six (6) ballots, a majority of all valid ballots cast shall be necessary for election. On the seventh ballot, the vote-getters in order of votes received shall be elected to complete the election of the Jurisdictional Conference delegates and reserve delegates.
3. Reserve Delegates:
   a. General Conference Reserve Delegates: –The delegates to the Jurisdictional Conference shall, in the order of their election, be the reserve delegates to the General Conference. The expenses of the first two persons, in order of election, serving as reserve delegates at the time of General Conference shall be paid by the Annual Conference using the same standards used by the General Conference.
   b. Jurisdictional Conference Reserve Delegates: – Persons receiving votes beyond those elected to the Jurisdictional Conference delegation as provided in Rule 33.F.2 shall, in the order of their election, be reserve delegates to the Jurisdictional Conference. The expenses of the first two persons, in order of election, serving as reserve delegates at the time of Jurisdictional Conference shall be paid by the Annual Conference using the same standards used by the Jurisdictional Conference.
4. Tie Votes: – If there is a tie on any ballot which results in an election of any delegate or reserve delegate, unless the persons tied agree between themselves their place within the delegation, the tie shall be resolved by drawing lots to determine the order of such persons within the delegation.

G. **VACANCIES**

If a vacancy occurs in the General or Jurisdictional Conference delegation by virtue of resignation, withdrawal, death or any other reason, all persons (lay or clergy) with votes below the person whose position is vacated will "move up" in the delegation, in order of their election.

RULE 34 – ORGANIZATION OF DELEGATION:

A. Following the election of the General and Jurisdictional Conference delegates the Bishop, or a person designated by him/her, shall convene the delegation, including the Reserve Delegates to Jurisdictional Conference, for the purpose of organizing the delegation. The convener shall preside until the chairperson is elected.

B. The delegation shall elect from its membership a chairperson, secretary and other officers as desired. Also, the delegation shall elect from its membership the persons to represent the Conference on each of the General and Jurisdictional Conference standing or legislative committees. It is recommended that the position of the Chairperson alternate between Lay and Clergy.

C. The delegation shall nominate and/or elect persons for General and Jurisdictional Boards, Councils, Commissions and Committees as required.

D. The method of selecting these officers and representatives shall be by written nomination and written ballot, unless a majority of the delegation present determines otherwise. A majority of the ballots cast shall be necessary for election, except for the election of members to the Jurisdictional

Committee on Episcopacy, which is mandated in the Discipline.

E. The delegation shall meet on call by the chairperson to consider the matters and issues related to General and Jurisdictional conferences, and to transact other business.

RULE 35 – NOMINATIONS FOR THE EPISCOPACY:

At the session immediately prior to the Jurisdictional Conference, the Conference may nominate candidates for election to the episcopacy as follows:

A. In the year that precedes any nomination for the episcopacy by the Annual Conference the newly elected Jurisdictional Conference Delegates shall conduct a thorough study of all known potential Episcopal nominees within the Jurisdiction. This study shall include interviews with such nominees when deemed appropriate. Results of this study, including any recommendations, shall be reported to the Annual Conference.

B. Nominations may be received from the floor.

C. The person making the nomination shall be limited to a three-minute speech for the nominee.

D. There shall be a 24-hour period between the nominations and the vote on the nominees.

E. To have the Annual Conference's recommendation, the nominee(s) shall have at least a majority vote of approval.

F. In the event of more nominations than vacancies, there shall be a written ballot. The number of names, as there are vacancies, receiving the highest vote shall be brought back to the floor. These shall then be voted on a second time. Those then receiving at least a majority vote of approval shall be the Annual Conference's recommendation.

RULE 36 – PETITIONS TO GENERAL CONFERENCE

A. Committee on General Conference Petitions

1. At the Annual Conference session two years prior to the next General Conference the Conference Nominating Committee shall nominate and the Conference shall elect a Committee on General Conference Petitions consisting of four (4) lay persons and four (4) clergy who have an interest in or knowledge of and experience in the general church and include:
   - One lay and one clergy delegate to a General Conference.
   - One member serving or having served on a General Agency.
   - One member of the Committee on Rules of Order
   - The Director of Connectional Ministries
2. No member of 1 the Committee may serve in more than one of the above categories.
3. The Director of Connectional Ministries shall convene the organizing meeting of the Committee at which it shall elect such leadership as it determines.
4. The Committee's term shall be for two years, ending at the conclusion of the annual conference at which General Conference petitions are considered.

B. Duties and Responsibilities

1. The Committee shall solicit petitions to General Conference from United Methodist organizations, churches, clergy and laypersons within the West Michigan Conference.
2. The Committee may also develop its own recommendations in the form of a petition to the General Conference.
3. Any other annual conference petitions pertaining to General Conference matters shall be considered by this committee.
4. When considering and developing petitions to the General Conference, it is recommended that the Committee consult with other persons, such as former General and Jurisdictional Conference delegates, persons knowledgeable about the general church (i.e. general agency members, staff, etc.) and others with experience and expertise who can assist them in their work.

C. Reporting to and Action by the Annual Conference

1. General Conference petitions shall be considered at the Annual Conference session the year prior to General Conference.
2. The Committee shall prepare a report on General Conference petitions together with its recommendation for concurrence, concurrence with amendment or non-concurrence on each

petition. This report shall be included in the pre-conference materials.

3. Each petition considered by the conference may be debated and may be amended.
4. The Conference shall vote on all petitions recommended by the Committee for concurrence or concurrence with amendment. All petitions recommended by the Committee for non-concurrence shall not be considered unless 20% of the members of the Conference present and voting request consideration.
5. Prior to annual conference the Committee shall inform each petitioner of its recommendation on her/his/their petition and following annual conference advise the petitioner of the conference action on her/his/their petition.

D. Forwarding Petitions to General Conference

By the deadline established by the General Conference Secretary, the Annual Conference Secretary shall forward all petitions approved by the Annual Conference to the General Conference in accordance with *The Book of Discipline* and related procedures.

RULE 37 – STATEMENT OF EFFECT:

The Rules of Order approved by the Conference in its most recent session shall supersede all previous Rules of the West Michigan Annual Conference.

— WMC Photos

— WMC Photos

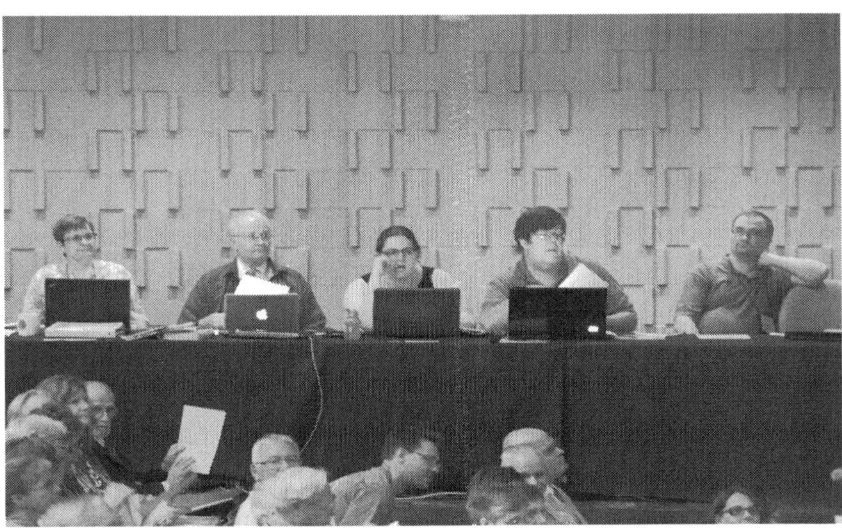

XV. ADDRESSES

A. MISSIONARIES SUPPORTED BY WEST MICHIGAN CONFERENCE

* New Projects for our support for 2012-2013

ACTIVE:

1. <u>In the Field:</u>

Robert Amundsen #773978/Pastor 3050-70
Pastor of Thousand Sticks UMC, Red Bird Mission
email: ramundsen08@gmail.com

Delbert Groves #12150Z
Director of Spiritual Growth at the New Life Center in Zambia
email: groves@newlifezambia.com

Sandy Groves #12151Z
Coordinator of ministries for women & children at New Life Center
email: groves@newlifezambia.com

Ellen Hoover #07990Z
Director of TESOL
(The English Speaking School of Lubumbashi)
email: jehoover@mwangaza.cd

Jeff Hoover #07989Z
Professor at University of Katanga, DR Congo
email: jehoover2002@yahoo.com

Dieudonne Karihano #3019569
Agriculturist in Mozambique
email: dkarihano@yahoo.com

Elma Jocson #13980Z
Surgeon waiting for re-assignment within the UMC medical health system
email: dokelma@yahoo.com

Darlene Logston #3021516
US-2 serving Primavera Foundation in Tucson, AZ
email: dlogston@umcmission.org

Sonya Luna #3019618
Hispanic Plan Missionary serving the Michigan Area
email: sluna@detroitconference.org

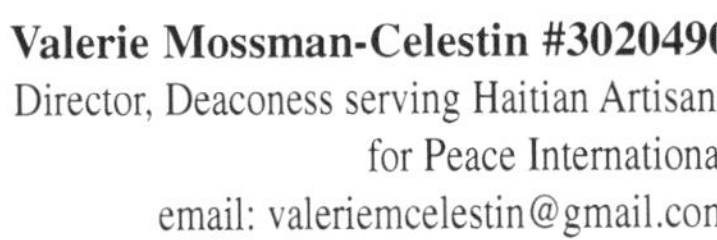

Valerie Mossman-Celestin #3020490
Director, Deaconess serving Haitian Artisans for Peace International
email: valeriemcelestin@gmail.com

Mbwizu Ndjungu #12909Z
Director United Methodist Initiative in Cameroon
email: ndjungunkemba@yahoo.com

Nkemba Ndjungu #12910Z
Director United Methodist Initiative in Cameroon
email: ndjungunkemba@yahoo.com

Stephanie Plotas #3021848
US2 from Battle Creek doing refugee ministry in Tucson AZ
email: splotas@umcmission.org

Kelly Schaefer #3021506
Mission Intern for Servant Hill Community in Wisconsin
email: kschaefer@umcmission.org

Helen Sheperd #11810Z
Hospice nurse at United Methodist Center in Mongolia
email: helensheperd@yahoo.com

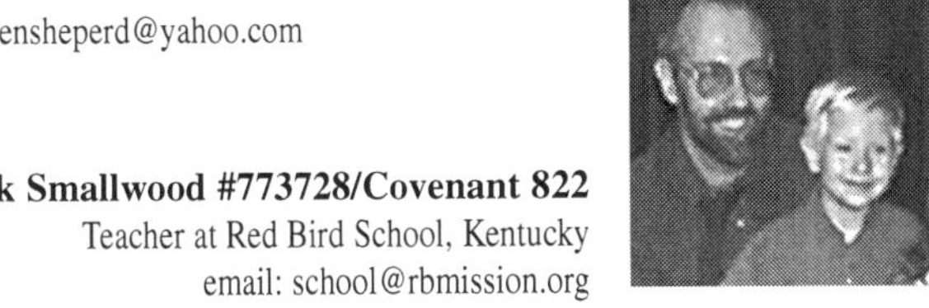

Mark Smallwood #773728/Covenant 822
Teacher at Red Bird School, Kentucky
email: school@rbmission.org

Rebecca Smallwood #773728/Covenant 822
Teacher at Red Bird School, Kentucky
email: school@rbmission.org

Ut To #14175Z
Leader of the United Methodist Initiative in Vietnam
email: utvanto@yahoo.com

Karen Vo-To #14174Z
Leader of the United Methodist Initiative in Vietnam
email: karenvoto@hotmail.com

Paul Webster #11865Z
Agricultural specialist in Mujila Falls, Zambia;
email: pwebster@wisconsinumc.org

2. Retired:

ANDERSON, Rev. Frank and Winona *(Belize, Trinidad, Jamaica)*
2050 S. Washington Rd., #1012, Holt MI 48842

BAUER, Dr. William and Rosemary *(India)*
2951 Quincy Lane, Lansing, MI 48910

BEAL, Kathleen *(Singapore, Korea)*
619 Appletree Dr., Holland, MI 49423
Dr. Philip Beal died 06-30-2009

CLOSSON, Nathalie *(Sierra Leone)*
died 02-02-2013

COLE, Betty *(Taiwan)*
P. O. Box 394, Pleasant Hill, TN 38578

COLE, Theodore *(Taiwan)*
died 03-04-2008

DORNON, Eleanor *(Japan)*
760 Plymouth Rd., Claremont, CA 91711
Ivan Dornon died 04-23-2008

ELLINGER, Lena Eschtruth *(Zaire)*
1400 N. Drake Rd., Apt. 191, Kalamazoo, MI 49006

ENRIGHT, Lorraine, *(Zaire)*
1919 Jackson Ln., Port Orange, FL 32127

FUKADA, Robert and Laura *(Japan)*
525 Mayflower Rd., Claremont, CA 91711

GISH, George and Yoko *(Japan)*
5-4-22 B-201 Minami Aoyama, Minato-Ku, Tokyo, Japan 107-0062

HENRY, Susie *(Bolivia)*
81 Hanover Rd., Reisterstown, MD 21136

HILLS, Larry and Laura *(Zaire)*
P. O. Box 402, Penney Farms, FL 32079

KEHRBERG, Norma *(Nepal)*
712 Ainapo St., Honolulu, HI 96825

LINN, Kennie and Evangeline *(India)*
P. O. Box 1000, Penney Farms, FL 32079

MADDOX, Charles and Patty *(Haiti)*
12801 Highway 431N, Central City KY 42330

MILLER, Ralph and Mary *(Mexico, Chile, Costa Rica)*
Apartado 130-4400, Ciudad Quesada, Costa Rica

RAHN, Rev. Robert and Janet *(Japan)*
1650 W. Glendale Ave. #4291, Phoenix AZ 85021

RICE, Shirleyann *(Malaysia)*
4120 Arlene Dr., Lansing MI, 49817

TOWNSEND, Theodore *(Alaska, India, Sierra Leone, Russia)*
Box 1018, Penney Farms, FL 32079
Rosemary Townsend Died 09-03-2012

VREELAND, Richard *(India, U.S.)*
182 Ameren Way, #752, Baldwin, MO 63021

WILLIAMS, Virginia *(Philippines, U.S.)*
7425 Montezuma Street, Austin TX 78744

B. DEACONESSES

1. Active:

MOSSMAN-CELESTIN, Valerie
300 Alten Ave., NE, Grand Rapids MI 49503

2. Retired:

CALDWELL, Janice
900 N. Cass Lake #124, Waterford MI 48328

HILL, Helene R.
Brooks-Howell Home, 266 Merrimon Ave., Asheville, NC 28801-1218

C. SURVIVING SPOUSES — MAILING ADDRESSES

Albery, Mary – 19355 Addison Drive, Southfield, MI 48075-2420 .... (248) 990-1447
Anderson, Virginia A – 4090 Tall Oaks Dr, Grand Ledge, MI 48837 .... (517) 627-7895
Baggs, Betty L – Timberline Lodge, 3770 Colwood Road, Caro, MI 48723 .... (989) 672-2525
Bates, Mardelle – 316 Emerald Dr, Charlotte, MI 48813 .... (517) 543-6669
Baumgart, Gloria – 3871 England Dr, Shelbyville, MI 49344 .... (269) 672-2152
Becker, Jeanne – 2985 Hillcrest Drive, New Era, MI 49446 .... (231) 861-5799
Beers, Helen – 553 Gidley Ave Apt H, Grand Haven, MI 49417-2358 .... (616) 844-4272
Benton, Katherine – 8530 Elkwood St., Byron Center, MI 49315 .... (616) 878-1405
Betts, Shirley – 501 King St. #114, Eaton Rapids, MI 48827 .... (517) 663-1626
Bintz, Ernestine – 1606 W Broadway, Mt Pleasant, MI 48858 .... (989) 773-0683
Boal, Linda – 320 W. Main St, Marquette, MI 49855 .... (231) 871-0781
Braun, Carol – 2730 Clyde Road, Ionia, MI 48846 .... (616) 527-0034
Breithaupt, Kathy – 18829 Lakewood Circle, Lake Ann, MI 49650 .... (231) 620-5508
Broyles, Brucilla – 2140 Robinson Road, Summit Township, MI 49203
Buker, Elaine M. – 10100 Hillview Dr. Apt.1213, Pensacola, FL 32514-5448 .... (850) 607-7743
Bullock, Bonnie – 196 Irving Park Drive, Battle Creek, MI 49017 .... (269) 965-2768
Burgess, Eula Jean – 422 Seaman Street, St Louis, MI 48880 .... (989) 681-4129
Burton-Collier, Linda J. – 2574 127th Ave, Allegan, MI 49010 .... (269) 793-7340
Cameron, Doris J – 1103 SW 11th Street, Boca Raton, FL 33486 .... (561) 395-5827
Cole, Susan – 25 Arrowhead Estates Ln, Chesterfield, MI 63017-1824 .... (636) 536-2585
Collins, Mary – PO Box 17, Northport, MI 49670 .... (231) 386-5169
Conn, Judith – 1738 E Front St, Traverse City, MI 49686 .... (231) 995-5294
Cook, Anne – 1013 Castle Drive, Weidman, MI 48893 .... (989) 644-5903
Crawford, Shirley – 3849 William Hume Dr, Zephyrhills, FL 33541 .... (813) 788-0534
Crotser, Doris Lee – 109 N. 2nd Street, Lawrence, MI 49064 .... (269) 674-4249
Crum, Grace – 2000 32nd St. SE, Grand Rapids, MI 49508 .... (616) 284-5445
Dahringer, Marjorie – 1056 S Hughes Rd, Howell, MI 48843
Daniels, Gail – 4282 Occidental Hwy., Adrian, MI 49221 .... (517) 266-9377
Dayringer, Joanne – 1551 Franklin St SE Apt 2020, Grand Rapids, MI 49506-3337 .... (616) 243-5045
Doherty, Joan – 7170 Davies Dr NE, Rockford, MI 49341 .... (616) 874-8095
Eddy, Ginger – 8020 Erie Ave, Chanhassen, MN 55317-9752 .... (952) 974-2092
Eidins, Irma – 518 E Chapin St, Cadillac, MI 49601 .... (231) 775-7642
Fassett, Mary Lou – 1551 Franklin SE Apt 2028, Grand Rapids, MI 49506 .... (616) 285-4795
Foldesi, Deb – 582 W Deerfield Road, Mt Pleasant, MI 48858 .... (989) 772-2548
Foltz, Meredyth – PO Box 399, Perrinton, MI 48871 .... (989) 236-5476
Francis, Donna – 1551 Franklin SE Apt 4001, Grand Rapids, MI 49506 .... (616) 245-7402
Frederick, Jody – 28450 Tiffin Dr, Chesterfield, MI 48047-6203 .... (586) 598-9887
Frick, Bonnie – 116 Wilmen Rd, Quincy, MI 49082 .... (517) 639-4496
Gierman, Adrianne – c/o Kristen Reed, 5324 Stanford Rd, Jacksonville, FL 32207
Gilroy, Grace – 39 Park Ave, Battle Creek, MI 49017 .... (269) 965-8830
Gladding, Irene – 15177 W Center Lake Dr, Tustin, MI 49688 .... (231) 829-3661
Glasgow, Joan M – 1351 Arch Road, Eaton Rapids, MI 48827 .... (517) 663-1612
Goodwin, Alice – 23708 Nilan Dr, Novi, MI 48375-3745 .... (313) 475-0727
Graham, Jean – 748 Clark Crossing, Grand Rapids, MI 49506 .... (616) 248-0639
Grauer, Patricia – 11442 East River Dr, DeWitt, MI 48820 .... (517) 669-3483
Griner, Beth – 6533 S. Betsie River Road, Interlochen, MI 49643-9508 .... (231) 276-9960
Hartmann, Alice – 2181 SW 2nd Ave, Ontario, OR 97914-1986 .... (541) 889-5198
Hippensteel, Johanna – 695 E Girard Road, Quincy, MI 49082 .... (517) 278-2118
Hollies, Charles – 1403 W. Broadway Ave. PMB 418, Apache Junction, AZ 85220 .... (517) 780-4503
Hoover, Ruth – 1101 W Michigan Ave, Jackson, MI 49202 .... (517) 784-5148
Hutchens, Gene – 1551 Franklin SE Apt 2027, Grand Rapids, MI 49506-3331 .... (616) 248-2815

Iseminger, Phyllis – 815 N Washington, Battle Creek, MI 49017 .... (269) 965-3407
Jacobs, Winifred – 427 Franklin St., PO Box 67, Grand Ledge, MI 48837 .... (517) 627-7407
Johns, Marlene – 3127 Heather Glynn Drive, Mulberry, FL 33860 .... (863) 425-9691
Summer: 6221 Honeymoon Dr, Lakeview, MI 48850
Johnson, Judy – 9459-32 Mission Gorge Rd, Santee, CA 92071 .... (619) 749-7859
Jones, Ruth – 540 Georgetown Dr. #36, Traverse City, MI 49684 .... (231) 947-1000
Jongeward, Elaine – 574 Belltower Ave, Deltona, FL 32725 .... (386) 574-0373
Karlzen, Martha Jane – PO Box 3, Charlotte, MI 48813 .... (517) 541-0653
Kirchenbauer, Mildred – Apt 2301, 1551 Franklin SE, Grand Rapids, MI 49506 .... (616) 245-4693
Kline, Tina – 28955 Pujol St Apt 10-B, Temecula, CA 92590-2837 .... (951) 506-0609
Kline-Hunt, Janet W – 7630 W St Andrews Circle, Portage, MI 49024-4402 .... (269) 373-1588
Lavengood, Lorraine A – 2537 Longmeadow St NW, Grand Rapids, MI 49504-2364 .... (616) 453-0687
Lowes, Carol – 27145 County Road 364, Mattawan, MI 49071-9558 .... (269) 668-6526
Lutz-Sempert, Joyce – 7651 W. Chelsea Ct, PO Box 5066, Homosassa Springs, FL 34447
Mann, Norma – 1551 Franklin SE Rm 4094, Grand Rapids, MI 49506-3310 .... (616) 245-6357
Mannino, Barbara – 8732 Huckleberry Lane, Lansing, MI 48917 .... (517) 449-3413
Matson, Jacqueline – 5792 Leisure South Dr SE, Kentwood, MI 49548 .... (616) 437-3022
Maurer, Edrye A. Eastman – 3639 Sweetgum Dr, Jackson, MI 49201-9029 .... (517) 962-2237
McConnell, Merwin (Mac) Hoyt – 110 Aspen Dr, Kerrville, TX 78028
Summer: 5047 N West Torch Lk Dr, Kewadin, MI 49648 .... (231) 264-9115
McDonald, Ramelle – c/o Carla Elliott, 4227 Huntington Dr, Jackson, MI 49203 .... (517) 782-4635
McLellan, Virginia – 4640 Shaw Road, Harrisville, MI 48740 .... (989) 724-6248
Meines, Noreen – 11279 Whispering Creek Dr, Allendale, MI 49401 .... (616) 895-5297
Miles, Louise K. – 5915 Cartago Dr, Lansing, MI 48911-6480 .... (989) 777-1248
Miller, Phyllis – 37644 Pinata Avenue, Zephyr Hills, FL 33541 .... (813) 788-1676
Minor, Eleanore – 5722 E Brenda Ln, Kalamazoo, MI 49004
Mohr, Phyllis – 4070 York Ln, Jackson, MI 49201
Moore, Tamara – 33250 Bernice Ave, Paw Paw, MI 49079-9504 .... (269) 657-6445
Mulder, Lydia – 2772 Pfeiffer Woods Drive, Grand Rapids, MI 49512 .... (616) 827-9457
Murphy, Patricia – 1892 Jasper Place, Ocala, FL 34472 .... (352) 694-1892
Myers, Beth – 262 Pennbrook, Battle Creek, MI 49017 .... (269) 274-9120
Myette, Ruth – 211 1/2 S. Spruce St, Traverse City, MI 49684 .... (231) 946-5993
Noordhof, Barbara – 14297 Leonard Rd, Spring Lake, MI 49456 .... (616) 935-9718
Page, Mildred – 8111 E Broadway Blvd Apt 307, Tucson, AZ 85710-3929 .... (520) 495-5880
Palmer Turner, Johncie – 1039 Crestwood Ln, Jackson, MI 49203 .... (517) 769-2329
Peters, Mary – 1119 McCullough St, Lansing, MI 48912 .... (517) 489-3795
Petersen, Elsie – Masonic Pathways, 1200 Wright Ave #233, Alma, MI 48801-1133 .... (989) 875-4665
Putnam, Amy – 1551 Franklin SE Apt. 3303, Grand Rapids, MI 49506-3331 .... (616) 475-0035
Regier, Hinako – 30 Seven Star Lane, Concord, MA 1742
Reinhart, Ruth – 9136 Flamingo Circle, N. Ft. Myers, FL 33903 .... (239) 652-9188
Summer: 309 Squires Dr, Lot #7, Litchfield, MI 49252 .... (517) 542-3910
Richards, Ruth – 733 Gilead Shores Dr, Bronson, MI 49028
Rothfuss, Jackie – 4404 Lake Street, PO Box 576, Bridgman, MI 49106-0576 .... (269) 465-5116
Sailor, Clara – 119 Broad St N, Battle Creek, MI 49017 .... (269) 963-2197
Salisbury, Marylin – 1551 Franklin SE #4004, Grand Rapids, MI 49506 .... (616) 246-6360
Schloop, Patricia – 1551 Franklin SE Apt 2022, Grand Rapids, MI 49506 .... (616) 246-1006
Scranton Bassett, Vivian – Apt. 3025, 1551 Franklin SE, Grand Rapids, MI 49506 .... (616) 247-0950
Shields, Ida – 6851 Goldenrod Ave NE, Rockford, MI 49341-9436 .... (616) 874-2113
Skinner, Bill – 460 S Edgar Rd, Mason, MI 48854-9744 .... (517) 676-1529
Smith, Beverly – 514 E Roselawn Dr, Logansport, IN 46947-2134 .... (269) 679-4646
Snow, Dorothy – 501 Leorie Street, North Muskegon, MI 49445 .... (231) 744-2659
Staser, Helen (Teddy) – 3440 Caroline #25, PO Box 1055, Penney Farms, FL 32079 .... (904) 529-8665
Stine, Jean – 9270 Jones Road, Bellevue, MI 49021 .... (269) 763-2706

Strait, Janet Sue – 1402 Suncrest Dr. NE, Grand Rapids, MI 49503 ..... (616) 245-1099
Taylor, Blanche – 1551 Franklin SE Apt 3063, Grand Rapids, MI 49506 ..... (616) 247-6654
Tennant, Jane – 801 W Middle Street, Apt 275, Chelsea, MI 48118 ..... (734) 475-6157
Tester, Lydia – 455 S. College Drive, Heston, KS 67062-8105
Vandlen, Gerry – 1551 Franklin St SE Apt 3027, Grand Rapids, MI 49506 ..... (616) 475-0125
Walker, Lorna – 2753 E. Waterview Dr., Avon Park, FL 33825-6015 ..... (863) 314-6502
Waterhouse, Elizabeth – McVeigh's TLC, 1015 S. Saint Johns St, Ithaca, MI 48847-1814.. (989) 763-5599
Weaver-Brown, Betty – 1421 Royal Oak, Portage, MI 49002 ..... (269) 327-2304
Whittern, Helen L – 640 Tiffin Street, PO Box 184, Hudson, MI 49247
Williams, Virginia – 36615 Cherry St, Newark, CA 94560
Wilson Allen, Mary Jane – 1835 12th Street, Manistee, MI 49660 ..... (231) 723-3731
Wood-Lozier, Bertie – 2050 S. Washington Rd. Apt 3024, Holt, MI 48842-8633 ..... (517) 694-7881
Yarlott, Irene – 2946 Creek Park Dr NE, Marietta, GA 30062 ..... (770) 321-5310
Yoh, Mary – 5026 Village Gardens Drive, Sarasota, FL 34234 ..... (616) 392-3942

D. ADDRESSES OF ELECTED LAYPERSONS

Adsmond, Dan – 225 W Osceola Ave, Reed City, MI 49677 ..... (231) 591-5867 (231) 832-5603
Aleshire, Sheila (Ray) – 2515 S Waverly Rd, Lansing, MI 48911 ..... (517) 393-5478
Anderson, Kathy – 12127 Edgerton Dr, Cedar Springs, MI 49319 ..... (616) 866-6800 (616) 696-1589
Anderson, Keith (Kim) – 775 133rd Ave, Wayland, MI 49348 ..... (616) 502-4935 (269) 792-9338
Apol, David (Marcia) – Front Apartment, 3246 Wayburn Ave SW, Grandville, MI 49418... (616) 292-6687
Armstrong, Beverly (Alan) – 9089 E. 7 Mile Rd., Luther, MI 49656-9576 ..... (231) 873-4185
Armstrong, Carole – 1216 Downer Ave, Lansing, MI 48912-4432 ..... (517) 485-9813
Asbury, Victor (Annette) – PO Box 80251, Lansing, MI 48908 ..... (517) 335-7759 (517) 580-3724
Baker, Christy – 605 W. Edgerton St., Howard City, MI 49329 ..... (231) 648-6126
Baker, James (Carole) – 2293 S Lincoln Road, Mt Pleasant, MI 48858 ..... (989) 773-7414
Baker, Mark (Ellen) – 1006 Hampshire Dr, St Johns, MI 48879-2404 ..... (989) 224-2415
Balderson, Sue – 68 Culbert Dr, Hastings, MI 49058 ..... (269) 945-2654 (269) 948-9029
Bank, Genie (Wayne) – 6651 Lakeshore Rd, Lexington, MI 48450 ..... (810) 359-7281
Baumer, Lois – 14420 Boichot Rd, Lansing, MI 48906 ..... (517) 485-8290
Belt, Michael (Cindy) – 918 Dykstra Rd, North Muskegon, MI 49445 ..... (231) 286-0797 (231) 747-9176
Bennett, David (Linda) – 2471 Veltema Dr, Holt, MI 48842 ..... (517) 694-0517
Berlin, Manzel – 2478 Grand Vista Court, Walker, MI 49534 ..... (816) 550-6172
Bina, Jean – 1460 10 Mile Rd NE, Comstock Park, MI 49321 ..... (616) 540-2802
Bixler, Anna & Dwight – 743 128th Ave, Shelbyville, MI 49344 ..... (269) 792-9948
Bloss, David (Susan) – 1150 Breton Rd SE, Grand Rapids, MI 49506 ..... (616) 977-3688 (616) 949-3610
Bosserd, Jim (Jane) – 3631 13 Mile Rd NW, Sparta, MI 49345 ..... (616) 887-7366 (616) 887-7805
Bradshaw, Roger – 120 S Division, Fremont, MI 49412 ..... (231) 924-6874
Brechting, Barbara – 5092 Southglow Ct SE, Kentwood, MI 49508-4714 ..... (616) 261-4814
Briggs, Lou Ellen – 234 Franklin, PO Box 425, Colon, MI 49040 ..... (269) 432-2673
Brooks, Jay (Barbara) – 1863 Eastbrook St. SE, Grand Rapids, MI 49508 .. (616) 243-6095 (616) 243-6079
Brooks, Kathie – 2410 Provincial House Dr, Lansing, MI 48910 ..... (517) 393-0074
Brown, Len – 118 Long Lake Rd, Marshall, MI 49068 ..... (269) 781-3715
Brown, Norvil – 9231 St. Ives Dr., Stanwood, MI 49346 ..... (231) 972-2918
Brubaker, Daniel – 523 Lincoln Lake Rd, Lowell, MI 49331-1358 ..... (517) 373-4925 (616) 897-6357
Brubaker, Tamara – 523 Lincoln Lake Rd, Lowell, MI 49331-1358 ..... (616) 460-3126
Bunn, Carol – 8560 N Arbogast Rd, Howard City, MI 49329 ..... (231) 937-4310 (231) 937-9189
Burkart, Sharon (Mark) – 1517 S Broadway St, Hastings, MI 49058 ..... (269) 660-8881
Burke, Arnold (Louella) – 2004 W Hansen Rd, Scottville, MI 49454 ..... (231) 845-1789

Burpee, Charles – 1621 Falcon Crest Dr NE, Grand Rapids, MI 49525-7012 .... (616) 752-2141 (616) 774-3612
Busley, Sus'ann (John) – 555 S Williamston Rd, Dansville, MI 48819 .... (517) 347-4173 ext.125 (517) 623-6239
Caballero, Stacy (Jose Luis) – 141 Kimball Ave, Battle Creek, MI 49014-5829 .... (269) 965-0285
Carr, Liz (Matt) – 2267 Sunset Bluff Dr, Holland, MI 49424 .... (317) 847-3661
Case, Jane – 113 West, PO Box 146, Napoleon, MI 49261 .... (517) 536-8781
Chappell, Shirley – 719 S Griffin, Grand Haven, MI 49417 .... (616) 846-4197
Cho, Koom – 12900 Chartreuse Dr, DeWitt, MI 48820 .... (517) 669-1275
Clark, Wendy (Al) – 4250 Summerwind Ave NE, Grand Rapids, MI 49525-9510 .... (616) 363-8500
Clement, Tom – 5223 Page Ave., Jackson, MI 49201 .... (517) 206-7380 (517) 764-1784
Cobb, Susan (Robert) – 9092 Deer Point Dr, Newaygo, MI 49337 .... (616) 784-4445 (616) 560-7023
Coffey, Judy (Tim) – 128 Forest Lawn Dr, Cadillac, MI 49601-9734 .... (231) 477-5486 (231) 775-6095
Coffman, Patsy (Dale) – 206 S Swegles St, St Johns, MI 48879 .... (989) 224-7692
Colthorp, Daniel – 5835 Demorrow Rd, Stevensville, MI 49127-1244 .... (269) 983-3929 (269) 428-8095
Cooper, Kathy (Curtis) – PO Box 1, Barryton, MI 49305-0001 .... (989) 382-9436
Costales, Jorge – 9841 Woodlawn, Portage, MI 49002 .... (269) 324-0697
Craig, Nancy – 1428 Safire Court, East Lansing, MI 48823 .... (517) 351-1391
Cutler, Blair – 623 Darby Lane, Kalamazoo, MI 49006
Dahlman, Laurie – 1228 Southern Ave, Kalamazoo, MI 49001-4339 .... (269) 343-1490
Damkoehler, Paula (Paul) – 141 W Front St, Ovid, MI 48866 .... (989) 307-5104
Darrow, Linda (Jon) – 633 N State Street, Alma, MI 48801 .... (989) 463-4078 (989) 763-8750
Davis, Carolyn & Daniel – 16655 Simmons, Cedar Springs, MI 49319 .... (616) 696-1939
Deemer, Julia – 16671 Fewins Road, Interlochen, MI 49643 .... (231) 275-7954
Dekker, David (Pearl) – 3209 Hillgate Circle, Lansing, MI 48912-5011 .... (517) 373-4082 (517) 324-4968
DeLany, Joseph & Mary-Jo – 3648 New Holland St., Hudsonville, MI 49426 .... (616) 797-0244
DeLany, Valerie – 3648 New Holland St, Hudsonville, MI 49426 .... (616) 797-0244
Depta, Linda (Daniel) – 358 Brittany Dr, Portage, MI 49024 .... (269) 373-7847 (269) 329-1858
Disegna, Wayne (Karen) – 6647 W. Jackson Rd., Ludington, MI 49431 .... (231) 843-6841
Donohue, William – 416 W Dill, DeWitt, MI 48820 .... (517) 881-7953
Dosca, Steve (Janeen) – 3883 Starchief St, Kalamazoo, MI 49048-6119 .... (269) 382-3487 (269) 345-5683
Doyal, Mark (Barb) – 525 University Dr, East Lansing, MI 48823-3046 .... (517) 336-0850 (517) 333-4203
Emmons, Susan (Allen) – 2226 Anderson Dr SE, Grand Rapids, MI 49506 .... (616) 245-9866
Erbes, Annette (Mark) – 1951 Heatherton Dr, Holt, MI 48842 .... (517) 649-8277
Everts, Sharon – 4918 W Blanchard Rd, Blanchard, MI 49310 .... (989) 866-2260
Falcon, Theresa – 7610 Ogemaw Tr, Mt Pleasant, MI 48858 .... (989) 773-5235
Fassett, Mary Lou – 1551 Franklin SE Apt 2028, Grand Rapids, MI 49506 .... (616) 285-4795
Fennell, Deborah – 3409 Rolfe Rd, Mason, MI 48854-9749 .... (517) 244-8707 (517) 676-1887
Floyd, Cynthia – 7640 Ogemaw Tr, Mt Pleasant, MI 48858 .... (989) 772-4930
Foreback, Laura – 804 First St, Lake Odessa, MI 48849 .... (517) 676-9449 (517) 896-4152
Francis, Merna (Aden) – 2924 N 33rd St, Galesburg, MI 49053 .... (269) 665-9430
Franklin, Susan – 2392 Fern Ct, Farwell, MI 48622 .... (989) 588-6378
Freeman, Shirley (Jim) – 2417 Winchell Ave, Kalamazoo, MI 49008 .... (269) 381-8208
Frey, Lauren – 26686 Southwestern, Redford, MI 48239 .... (734) 542-8390 (313) 937-2468
Fuller, Robert – 13307 Northland Dr, Cedar Springs, MI 49319 .... (616) 696-9856
Fyan, Benita (Rex) – 6460 Middle Lake Rd, Twin Lake, MI 49457 .... (231) 828-4029
Garbrecht, Bonnie (Allen) – 153 Garrison Ave, Battle Creek, MI 49017 .... (269) 964-9828
García, Naomi – 11 Fuller Ave SE, PO Box 6247, Grand Rapids, MI 49516-6247 .... (616) 459-4503
Gehman, William (Cynthia) – 4471 Foxtail Circle, Grand Ledge, MI 48837 .... (517) 626-6716
Gerke, Sarah – 291 W Burnham St, Battle Creek, MI 49015 .... (269) 966-8875

Gillette, Robert – 4091 12 Mile Road, Rockford, MI 49341 .... (616) 866-0934
Goerke, Meg – 2815 Topinabee Mail Rte Rd, Cheboygan, MI 49721 (231) 238-7764 ext.17 (231) 675-3461
Gombert, Dave (Pam) – 5074 Rum Creek Ct SE, Kentwood, MI 49508 .... (616) 698-1864
Gorman, Lisa – Lighthouse Ministries of Benton Harbor,
PO Box 1042 - 275 Pipestone, Benton Harbor, MI 49022 .... (269) 861-8749 (269) 277-9100
Graybill, Sue (Joe) – 4306 Indian Springs Dr SW, Grandville, MI 49418
Greenawalt, Lee – 1076 137th Ave, Wayland, MI 49348 .... (269) 792-2419
Grim, Steve – 571 Bertha Drive, Farwell, MI 48622 .... (989) 588-2652
Guy, Nichea Ver Veer (Greg) – 125 Baynton NE, Grand Rapids, MI 49503 (616) 456-7168 (616) 451-7058
Haas, Marcia (Tom) – 801 Plymouth SE, Grand Rapids, MI 49506 .... (616) 243-5760
Hahn, Mark – 305 E Hoffman Rd, St Louis, MI 48880 .... (989) 620-4316
Hall, Lawrence – 227 Fleming Dr, Alma, MI 48801 .... (989) 463-3007
Hall, Phoebe – 521 Selby St, PO Box 294, Hopkins, MI 49328-0294 .... (269) 793-7103
Ham, Nancy (Kenneth) – 1917 Maple Shade Dr, Williamston, MI 48895 .... (517) 655-2430 (517) 655-2754
Hammond, Philip (Kristin) – 3450 S 6th St, Kalamazoo, MI 49009 .... (269) 217-7331
Hansen, Susan (Randy) – 5181 Hancock St., Montague, MI 49437 .... (231) 894-4625
Harrison, Kristin – 7071 S. Center Highway, Traverse City, MI 49684
Hawkins, Joyce (Richard) – 3839 Eckert Road, Freeport, MI 49325 .... (616) 250-6256
Higginson, Carol – 1859 Southwood Avenue, Muskegon, MI 49441 .... (231) 759-0329
Hiler, Donald (Pat) – 3123 Waterford NE, Grand Rapids, MI 49505 .... (616) 363-6130
Hill, Charles "Chuck" – 521 W Orange St, Greenville, MI 48838 .... (616) 754-3848
Hills, Claire – 3510 Mineral Springs Trail, Mt Pleasant, MI 48858 .... (989) 317-0081
Hills, Michelle – 12300 W Michigan, Parma, MI 49269 .... (517) 780-7252 (517) 745-8455
Himes, Minette – 116 E Morrell St, Otsego, MI 49078 .... (269) 694-6474
Hoag, Dennis – 9430 E Bellevue, Eaton Rapids, MI 48827 .... (269) 449-1530
Hoekwater, Jane (Harris) – 4921 S Roosevelt Rd, Stevensville, MI 49127 .... (269) 235-9156
Hook, Jay – 2230 W Nemeskal Rd, Maple City, MI 49664 .... (231) 228-6250
Hudson, Nolan (Joan) – 6355 Bivens Rd, Nashville, MI 49073 .... (517) 852-1821
Huis, Shelia – 1202 Barber Rd, Hastings, MI 49058 .... (269) 945-9113
Huisingh, Rob (Debra) – 717 Fowler St, North Muskegon, MI 49445 .... (231) 744-6160
Huizing, John (Maureen) – 40 N. Plum Street, Hart, MI 49420 .... (231) 873-0418 (231) 873-0418
Hundley, Ruth (Pigeon) – 3035 Grenada Dr SE, Grand Rapids, MI 49546 .... (616) 427-3749
Hurlbut, Wynne – 36146 Cherry St, Gobles, MI 49055 .... (269) 628-2944
Huyck, Bridget (Clare) – 235 Dunham St, Sunfield, MI 48890 .... (517) 566-2066
Jackson, Phyllis (Andrew) – 978 Amber View Dr SW, Byron Center, MI 49315-9740 .... (616) 878-1284
John, Phyllis – 13735 Indian Rd, Kewadin, MI 49648 .... (231) 264-0527
Johnson, Michael – 84 E Kingman, Battle Creek, MI 49014 .... (269) 962-6401
Jones, Ruth – 540 Georgetown Dr. #36, Traverse City, MI 49684 .... (231) 947-1000
Jones, Vernon – 2370 Sepphire Lane, East Lansing, MI 48823 .... (517) 663-3585
Kaechele, Dave – 340 142nd Ave, Caledonia, MI 49316 .... (616) 891-1020
Keating, Katherine (James) – 3462 Algonquin Dr, Muskegon, MI 49441 .... (616) 234-4953 (616) 322-5436
Kinder, Glen – 640 Dart Road, Mason, MI 48854 .... (517) 676-5552
Knapp, Jane – 16998 E ON Ave, Climax, MI 49034 .... (269) 746-4915
Kozminski, Patti – 2568 Walker Woods Ct. NW, Grand Rapids, MI 49544 .... (616) 784-9105
Krahulik, Rachel – 8729 W St Joe Hwy, Lansing, MI 48917 .... (517) 627-8299
Krchmar, Judy – 3121 Snowglen Lane, Lansing, MI 48917-1732 .... (517) 214-2253 (517) 321-3765
Kroeze, Jenny – 640 Seminole Dr, Fremont, MI 49412 .... (888) 544-5388 (231) 924-4814
Kusterer, Betty – 68060 Territorial Rd, Watervilet, MI 49098 .... (269) 463-3336
Kyler, Inge – 8242 Stub Hwy, Eaton Rapids, MI 48827 .... (517) 646-9569
Lambrix, James (Deborah) – 1128 Idema Dr SE, Grand Rapids, MI 49506 .... (616) 949-4999

Lancaster, Lorraine (Dale) – 4722 Westgate Dr NW, Comstock Park, MI 49321 .... (616) 784-5662
Latimer, Amy – 305 N. Prospect St., St Johns, MI 48879 .... (989) 224-2293
Leavitt, Waltha Gaye – 8524 E. Colby Rd., Crystal, MI 48818 .... (989) 236-7330
LeBaron, Jim (Luann) – 13401 Peacock Rd, Laingsburg, MI 48848-9296 .... (517) 641-8042
Lee, Loretta (Steven) – 142 Greenwood Ave, Battle Creek, MI 49017 .... (269) 968-1987
Leppink, Ransom – PO Box 365, Lakeview, MI 48850 .... (989) 352-6430
Lester, Julie (Mark) – 1663 Grandeur Lane, St. Joseph, MI 49085 .... (269) 983-3929 (269) 429-5832
Lett, Steven (Diana) – 9417 W Scenic Lake Dr, Laingsburg, MI 48848-9749 .... (517) 372-4204
Loding, Jennifer (Jeff) – 13371 Morgan Mills Rd, Gowen, MI 49326 .... (616) 754-9565
Lott, Karen (Willlam) – 1310 Briarcliff SE, Grand Rapids, Mi 49546 .... (616) 676-2696
Luce, Linda – 104 N Fiske Rd, Coldwater, MI 49036 .... (517) 278-8443
Ludwick, Faith (Randy) – 664 W Chicago Rd, Bronson, MI 49028 .... (517) 369-6555 (517) 369-1507
Lundquist, C David – 5920 Wood Valley Road, Kalamazoo, MI 49009 .... (269) 352-0582
Lyon, Steve – 6030 Winterset, Lansing, MI 48911 .... (517) 335-0168 (517) 881-3555
MacGregor, Susan (James) – PO Box 914, Pentwater, MI 49449 .... (231) 869-4364
Maidens, Valerie – 1639 Black Bark Ln, Traverse City, MI 49686 .... (231) 534-8102 (231) 941-2360
Mallard, Mildred (Henry) – 18525 Division, Marshall, MI 49068 .... (269) 968-3503 (269) 781-4689
Marasigan, Sami – 541 Harp St SE, Grand Rapids, MI 49548 .... (616) 451-2879 (616) 532-3152
Marsh, Georgia (John) – 212 Chauncey Court, Marshall, MI 49068 .... (269) 781-2501
Mast, Sandy – PO Box 188, White Cloud, MI 49349 .... (231) 689-6330
Matchett, Timothy – 01362 Matchett Rd, Charlevoix, MI 49720 .... (231) 547-2154
McBride, Betty – 2970 138th Ave, Dorr, MI 49323-9533 .... (616) 813-7274
McCall, Sarah – 5506 Ridge Rd, Stevensville, MI 49127 .... (269) 429-5911 (269) 429-1322
McCartney, James – 1414 Safire Ct, East Lansing, MI 48823-6357 .... (517) 574-5262
McComb, Tom (Kerry) – 8460 W Price Rd, St Johns, MI 48879 .... (517) 230-7144 (517) 281-7577
McConnell, Kathy – 48482 Woodhenge Drive, Mattawan, MI 49071 .... (269) 668-2664
McDonald, Sharon (David) – 11380 South Shore Dr, Lake, MI 48632 .... (989) 773-6934 (989) 544-2490
McKenzie, Clarice – 396 Ford St., Bitely, MI 49309 .... (231) 745-3256
McNees, Zachary – 413 N Fancher Apt 3, Mt. Pleasant, MI 48858 .... (989) 773-6934 (269) 986-0108
McNeilly, Peggy – 13429 New Millpond Rd, Big Rapids, MI 49307 .... (231) 796-2056
Mentzer, Pat – 528 Middlebury Lane, Mason, MI 48854 .... (517) 676-9449 (517) 676-4232
Merchant, Michelle – 3181 Hill Rd NW, Rapid City, MI 49676 .... (231) 258-2820 (231) 564-0723
Meredith, Nora (Paul) – 1055 Flint Road, Coldwater, MI 49036 .... (517) 238-4654
Miller, Heather – 1568 Solon Street, Cedar Springs, MI 49319 .... (616) 696-4057
Mills, Joy – 1014 Barton Street, Otsego, MI 49078 .... (616) 233-5577 (269) 929-4954
Mills, Matt – 1014 Barton St, Otsego, MI 49078-1576 .... (269) 692-2801
Misener, Carmen – 2542 McCollum, Flint, MI 48504 .... (810) 234-5441
Mitchell, Joyce – 124 Boyd St, Fife Lake, MI 49633 .... (231) 879-5330
Morton, Carrie (David) – 4285 E Kirby Rd, Battle Creek, MI 49017 .... (269) 963-0231 (269) 964-7098
Mossman-Celestin, UM Deaconess, Valerie (Jacson) – 300 Alten Ave NE, Grand Rapids, MI 49503 .... (616) 459-6604
Murphy, Joy (Mike) – 2515 Union SE, Grand Rapids, MI 49507 .... (616) 245-5546
Nellist, Glenys – 1507 Lenox Dr SE, Grand Rapids, MI 49506 .... (269) 903-8549
Nordbrock, Mandana – 431 Timber Ridge Dr, Kalamazoo, MI 49006 .... (269) 372-7525 (269) 720-6152
Norton, Ken – 748 Bowers Rd, Bronson, MI 49028 .... (517) 369-1803
Nye, Mary Jo – 168 N. Wabash Avenue, Battle Creek, MI 49017-4753 .... (269) 565-0486
O'Neill, Denny (Kathy) – 4733 Cutter Parkway SE, Grand Rapids, MI 49546 .... (616) 949-9054
Oaster, Zach (Lindsay) – 4455 13 Mile Rd NE, Rockford, MI 49341 .... (616) 669-0730 (616) 856-2204
Olin, Denny (Melody) – 14432 Peninsula Dr, Traverse City, MI 49686 .... (231) 223-4141
Overmeyer, Diana – 8010 84th St., Caledonia, MI 49316 .... (616) 891-8482

ADDRESSES

Parks, Floyd L – 5880 Manorwood Dr, Kalamazoo, MI 49009-9110 .... (269) 375-2378
Perez, Joseph – 1330 Trenton, Adrian, MI 49221 .... (517) 263-1807
Phillips, Gayla – 1991 E. Gratiot County Line Road, St. Johns, MI 48879 .... (989) 838-2613
Pigeon, Leslie – 1854 Schanz Rd, Allegan, MI 49010 .... (269) 793-7769
Pigeon, Norm – 1854 Schanz Rd, Allegan, MI 49010 .... (269) 672-5255 (269) 793-7769
Polzin, Bill (Lisa) – 4241 4 Mile Rd NE, Grand Rapids, MI 49525-9794 .... (616) 554-8634 (616) 365-8178
Portillo, Ingrid – 4270 Nature Trail Dr SE #6-B, Kentwood, MI 49510 .... (616) 589-6598
Potes, Kelly (Toni) – 150 Ida Red, Sparta, MI 49345 .... (616) 887-7366 (616) 887-7288
Pratt, Jody (Gary) – 2984 5th St, Shelbyville, MI 49344 .... (616) 292-1220 (269) 792-0481
Proctor, Simmie (Louis) – 73486 8th Ave, South Haven, MI 49090 .... (269) 637-6053
Ramirez, Enrique (Nohemi) – 324 Griswold SE, Grand Rapids, MI 49507 .... (616) 560-4207
Rawson, Heidi – 200 E. Garfield Lot 230, Coldwater, MI 49036 .... (517) 617-9922
Reid, Helen – 3839 Alger Ave., White Cloud, MI 49349 .... (231) 689-0344
Rhodes, David – 606 Bjornson Lot A-3, Big Rapids, MI 49307 .... (231) 796-4185
Riggs, Betty – 699 Harbor Drive, Manistee, MI 49660 .... (231) 723-2414
Roberts, Mark – 6077 Wildwood Drive, Elwell, MI 48832 .... (989) 463-8531
Ryskamp, Fred – 1902 Sycamore Dr., Dorr, MI 49323-9302 .... (616) 681-2776
Salisbury, David – 10855 Thornberry Way, Zeeland, MI 49464-8686 .... (616) 772-2828
Scoggin, Bryon – 16498 S Red Bud Trail, Buchanan, MI 49107 .... (269) 695-0656
Searls Jr, James (Abby) – 53 East Central, Zeeland, MI 49464 .... (616) 405-2638 (616) 772-4306
Shelby, Pete – 1730 Probert Rd, Jackson, MI 49203
Shepard, Kathy – 7575 S Leaton Rd, Shepherd, MI 48883-9303 .... (989) 828-6486
Showerman, Joyce – 600 S Main St, Eaton Rapids, MI 48827-1426 .... (517) 663-3524 (517) 663-5284
Simmons, Eric (Carol Miskell) – 2528 Solar Way, Okemos, MI 48864 .... (517) 482-5750 (517) 337-6026
Singh, Vipin (Bernice) – 762 E Roosevelt, Battle Creek, MI 49017 .... (269) 830-3800
Skinner, Deborah (John) – 418 S Elizabeth, Mt Pleasant, MI 48858 .... (989) 773-2722 (989) 773-4340
Smith, Kevin – 418 Riverside DR, Lowell, MI 49331 .... (616) 421-8161
Smith, Richard – 2590 Graduate Way, Holt, MI 48842-9415 .... (517) 694-1833
Snyder, Steve (Sandy) – 108 Cypress Avenue, Holland, MI 49423-3024 .... (231) 777-5227 (616) 546-1966
Soles, Anne – 217 Old State Rd, PO Box 467, Pentwater, MI 49449 .... (231) 869-4059 (231) 869-7651
Spackman, Nona (Joseph) – 3806 Cornice Falls Dr Apt 6, Holt, MI 48842 .... (517) 694-8346
Spurlin-Hane, Julie (Paul) – 231 E South Ave, Hesperia, MI 49421 .... (231) 854-6132
Stange, Andrew (Sarah) – 118 S Mayhew St, New Buffalo, MI 49117 .... (269) 469-1250
Stickley, Mindy – 2742 144th Ave, Dorr, MI 49323 .... (616) 896-0913
Strader, Veroneze (Dick) – 178 Feld Drive, Battle Creek, MI 49037 .... (269) 963-6830
Strouse, Kathryn (Michael) – 220 N Main, PO Box 84, North Star, MI 48862-0084 .... (989) 875-2894
Swinger, Connie (Ted) – 255 Brown SW, Grand Rapids, MI 49507 .... (616) 452-3532
Tafolla, Linda – 100 N Broad St, Battle Creek, MI 49017 .... (269) 968-7399
Tate, Molly – 308 W Garfield, Charlevoix, MI 49720 .... (231) 330-6644
Tibbits, Gerry – 106 Hartwell Terrace, Mason, MI 48854-9281 .... (517) 596-3404
Tiburcio, Ivelisse – 3027 Union Ave SE, Wyoming, MI 49548 .... (616) 915-5166
Tiedt, Patrick – 9859 River Road, Evart, MI 49631 .... (231) 734-2932
Timmerman, Marj – 227 Fulton St E, Grand Rapids, MI 49503 .... (616) 451-2879 (616) 901-9224
Tobar, Lea (Felipi) – 2430 Highridge Ln SE, Grand Rapids, MI 49546-7536 .... (616) 940-0406
Trommater, William – 8896 E Wager Road, Lyons, MI 48851 .... (989) 855-2365
Troutman, Delberta – 108 Austin Dr, Hartford, MI 49057 .... (269) 308-3011
Tumonong, Prospero (Merrita) – 6247 Meadowlark Dr NE, Rockford, MI 49341
.... (616) 459-4503 (616) 866-5410
Uithoven, Betty – 9722 East ML Ave, Galesburg, MI 49053 .... (269) 665-9319
Urick, Walter (Karen) – 160 W Main St, PO Box 609, Hart, MI 49420 .... (231) 873-4279

VanderLaan, Clara – 6702 Waterview Dr, Grandville, MI 49418 .... (616) 457-1554
Veenstra, Charles – 41360 Fox Run, Novi, MI 48377 .... (248) 859-4626
Vinson, Mary Lou (Anthony) – 8315 W Cleveland Rd, Middleton, MI 48856 .... (989) 584-3324
Voigt, Lee (Robin) – 500 Washington Ave, Holland, MI 49423 .... (616) 395-5556
Voigts, Carol (Jack) – 12873 Cedar Creek Road, Wellston, MI 49689 .... (231) 848-4301
Vorbrich, Andrew (Sally) – 1914 Waite Ave, Kalamazoo, MI 49008 .... (269) 381-8844 (269) 343-1906
Waagner, Max (Pam) – 928 Sunburst Rd, Jackson, MI 49203 .... (517) 789-4473 (517) 787-2924
Waite, John (Josie) – 664 3 Mile Rd NE, Grand Rapids, MI 49505 .... (616) 977-9500 (616) 827-9536
Ward, John – 188 S Chester St, Pentwater, MI 49449 .... (231) 869-5900
Warnock, John (Mary Ann) – 1830 Linson Ct SE, Grand Rapids, MI 49546 .... (616) 942-8445
Weller, Ned – 95 Meadow Lane, Ithaca, MI 48847-1846 .... (989) 330-8559
Whaley, Ruth (David) – 4682 E Cleveland Rd, Ashley, MI 48806-9705 .... (989) 838-2579
White, Jim (Martha) – 2410 Emerald Lake Dr, East Lansing, MI 48823 .... (517) 347-7208 (517) 336-7785
Whittemore, Inge – 590 Wildview, Lowell, MI 49331 .... (616) 897-6525
Wieringa, Liam – 3818 Melody Lane, Hart, MI 49420 .... (231) 873-4766
Wilcox, Marsha (Gordon) – 9654 Bailey Drive, Lowell, MI 49331 .... (616) 897-8949
Williams, Caleb – 7146 Oakland Dr., Portage, MI 49024 .... (231) 313-9005
Williams, Donald (Sandy) – 5226 Forest View Court, Hudsonville, MI 49426 .... (616) 669-9086
Williams, John – 803 S Superior St Apt 301, Albion, MI 49224 .... (517) 629-6768
Williams, Molly – 2716 N 9th St, Kalamazoo, MI 49009 .... (269) 375-4867
Wiltse, David (Marjorie) – 7056 Northland Drive NE, Rockford, MI 49341-8838 .... (616) 866-1051
Witkowski, Laura (Matthew) – 1164 Treeway Dr NW, Sparta, MI 49345 .... (616) 459-4503
Woodard, Sue (Eddie) – 3815 Delano Dr, Eaton Rapids, MI 48827-9623 .... (517) 355-0284 (517) 628-2628
Worley, Bonnie – 2000 32nd St Apt 251, Grand Rapids, MI 49508 .... (616) 284-5543
Wright, Geraldine – 1513 E Gaylord St Apt C, Mt Pleasant, MI 48858 .... (989) 773-7580 (989) 772-0129
Yakes, Dan (Jeanne) – 409 Mill Pond Road, Whitehall, MI 49461 .... (231) 894-9279
Yalda, Christina – 1709 Hiawatha Dr SE, Grand Rapids, MI 49506 .... (616) 331-7135 (616) 246-0676
Yoder, Martha (Quenten) – 1441 Nicholas Ln, Charlotte, MI 48813-8786 .... (517) 765-2979
Yoder, Sue – 1126 Billings Ct SE Apt 1B, Grand Rapids, MI 49508-9789
Zimpfer, Judy (Gary) – PO Box 175, Alba, MI 49611-0175 .... (231) 584-2000 ext.124 (231) 584-3572
Zomer, Larry – 23450 2 Mile Rd, Reed City, MI 49667 .... (231) 832-4563

—WMC Photos

XVI. PASTORAL RECORD
of All Pastors

This Pastoral Record indicates appointments but is not necessarily a pension record. The date given following each appointment represents the initial year of that appointment, with changes occurring immediately following Annual Conference unless otherwise noted. Brackets around appointments indicate charges served prior to reception into the West Michigan Conference. (H) is the Home Address; (O) is an office address and (S) is a seasonal address.

This record is maintained by Kathy Hippensteel at the Conference Center. Correspondence should be directed to her by email, kathy@wmcumc.org, or at P.O. Box 6247, Grand Rapids, MI 49516-6247.

In this record R stands for year of reception into any former EUB Conference, any former Methodist Conference, or into our present United Methodist Conference or for reception into our West Michigan Conference from other conferences or denominations. D stands for year of ordination as Deacon; E for the year of ordination as Elder. The following key is used throughout the Pastoral Record:

DM = Diaconal Minister *(consecrated under provisions of 1992 or earlier Discipline)*
PM = Provisional Member *(ordained under provisions of 1992 or earlier Discipline)*
PD = Provisional Deacon FD = Deacon in full Connection
DP = Deacon from other denomination serving UM probation
OD = Deacon member of other annual conference
PE = Provisional Elder FE = Elder in full connection
EP = Elder/full minister from other denomination serving UM probation
OE = Elder member of other annual conference or other Methodist denomination
OF = Full member of other denomination
AF = Affiliated member AM = Associate Member
FL = Full Time Local Pastor SP = Student Local Pastor
PL = Part Time Local Pastor RP = Retired Provisional Member
RA = Retired Associate Member RLA = Retired Local Pastor under Appointment
RE = Retired Full Member SY = Supply Pastor
RL = Retired Local Pastor OR = Retired Member of Other Conference
RD = Retired Deacon LP = Other Local Pastor
OA = Associate member of other Annual Conference
OP = Provisional member of other Annual Conference
DSA = District Superintendent Assignment ++ = Ad Interim Appointment

PASTORAL RECORDS

***ADAMS, CRAIG L. (RE) (Robin) – (R-1973, D-1973, E-1977)**
In School 1973; Transferred from Detroit Conf, Muskegon: Wolf Lake 1975; Saugatuck/Ganges 1979; Horton Bay 1984; Ionia: Zion 1994: Weidman Sept 16, 1999; Carlisle 2006; Mt. Pleasant Trinity/Countryside/Leaton (LTFT 3/4) Dec 1, 2009; Retired 2010
(H) 5073 Rum Creek Ct SE, Grand Rapids, MI 49508 (616) 514-7474

***AINSLIE, PEGG (RE) – (R-1991, D-1975, E-1978)**
Nebraska Conf, Lexington 1977; Loup 1980; Noxen UMC, Noxen PA 1983; Windsor UMC, Windsor, NY 1988; Detroit Conf, Manchester 1989; Transferred from Detroit Conf, Okemos (Assoc) Nov 1, 1991; Lansing Central (Assoc) 1993; Retired 1997
(H) 2000 Pleasant Grove Rd, Lansing, MI 48910-2437 (517) 574-4175

ALLEN, CLIFFORD L. (FL) (Toni)
Ionia Zion (DSA) 2007; Ionia Zion, Nov. 10, 2007
(H) 620 N Rich St, Ionia, MI 48846 (616) 527-2025
Ionia Zion UMC: 423 W. Washington Street, Ionia MI 48846 (616) 527-1910

ALMEIDA, JANA LYNN (FE) (Gabriel) – (R-1996, D-1996, E-1999)
Vicksburg (Assoc) 1995; Grand Ledge (Assoc) 1997; Mt Pleasant Trinity/Countryside Oct 16, 1999; West Michigan Conf Staff (LTFT 1/2) 2004; Transitional Leave (para. 354.2c.2), Jan 1, 2010; Lincoln Road (LTFT 3/4) 2010
(H) 9437 W Lincoln Rd, Riverdale, MI 48877 (989) 466-2979
Lincoln Road UMC: 9479 W. Lincoln Rd, PO Box 100, Riverdale MI 48877 (989) 463-5704

***AMUNDSEN, WILLIAM J. (RE) (Catherine) – (R-1967, D-1967, E-1970)**
Edwardsburg 1969; Mesick/Harrietta 1972; Grand Rapids: Trinity (Assoc) 1979; Lowell May 1, 1982; Grand Ledge 1993; Retired 2003
(H) 735 Maycroft Rd, Lansing, MI 48917-2052 (517) 323-2445

***ANDERSON, FRANCIS F. (RE) (Winona) – (R-1958, D-1960, E-1962)**
[New Buffalo/Lakeside 1957] Marcellus 1958; Portage (Asst) 1961; Kalamazoo Chapel Hill Parish 1962; White Cloud Dec 9, 1962; Lansing Central (Assoc) 1966; Jackson Haven 1970: GBGM, World Division, Secondment to Methodist Church in the Caribbean and the Americas, Belize 1972; GBGMM, MCCA, Trinidad 1975: Napoleon Sept 1, 1978; GBGM, MCCA, Savanna-la-mar, Jamaica 1980; GBGM, MCCA, Duncans, Jamaica 1986; Detroit Conf, Hudson Nov 1, 1989; Retired 1991
(H) Great Lakes Christian Homes, 2050 S Washington Rd Apt 1012, Holt, MI 48842-8634 (517) 694-3084

***ANDREWS, J. LEON (RE) (Arlene) – (R-1951, D-1959, E-1962)**
Blanchard 1951; Riverdale 1955; Oshtemo 1960; Coloma 1962; Jackson Calvary 1968; Big Rapids First 1972; Grand Traverse District Superintendent, Aug 18, 1980; Grandville 1986; Marshall 1989; Retired 1992
(H) 741 Clark Crossing SE, Grand Rapids, MI 49506-3310 (616) 245-1589

ARTHUR, THOMAS F. (FE) (Sarah F.) – (R-2009, E-2012)
Lansing Sycamore Creek 2009
(H) 5058 Glendurgan Ct, Holt, MI 48842-9438 (517) 889-5540
Lansing Sycamore Creek UMC: 5127 Aurelius Rd Ste D, Lansing MI 48911 (517) 394-6100

AYOUB, GEORGE H. (FE) (Elizabeth) – (R-2014, D-1984, E-1987)
[Eastern Pennsylvania Conf., FE. Philadelphia Tacony 1984; Conf. Dir. of Camps & Conferences 12/17/88; Ex. Dir. of Camping Min., Luth. Outdoor Ret. Min. of MI 01/16/95] Appointed to Extension Ministries: Masonic Pathways Senior Living Services, St. Johns, Sept. 24, 1999; Transferred to West Michigan Conference / Appointed Executive Director of Camping Ministries March 1, 2014
(H) 6252 W Walker Rd, St Johns, MI 48879 (989) 224-2608
(O) West Michigan Conference – United Methodist Church, 11 Fuller Ave SE, PO Box 6247, Grand Rapids, MI 49516-6247 (616) 459-4503

BABB, MARK R. (FD) (Sue) – (D-1991, E-1993, FD-2002, R-2005)
[West Ohio Conf., Ebenezer (Student LP)1984; Second Creek/Edenton 1985; Red Lion 1988; Roundhead/Mt. Zion/Fletcher Chapel 1990; Hoytville 1993; Gibsonburg: Faith 1996; Incapacity Leave 1998;] Coldwater (Deacon) 2002; Transfered from West Ohio Conf., 2005; Coldwater (Deacon Full-Time) and Albion College (LTFT), Sept. 1, 2005; Coldwater (Deacon) (LTFT) and Albion College (LTFT), Jan. 1, 2006; Albion College (LTFT 1/2) 2006; St. Paul UCC, Waterloo, IL, Director of Music Ministries, Jan. 20, 2008; Transitional Leave Jun. 1, 2009; University of Phoenix, Associate Faculty (LTFT 1/2), Westminster Presbyterian Church, Choir Director (LTFT 1/4), Jackson First, Spiritual Formation Consultant (LTFT 1/4), June 1, 2010; University of Phoenix, Associate Faculty (LTFT 1/2), Federated Church of Grass Lake, Director of Music (LTFT 1/4), Jackson First, Spiritual Formation Consultant (LTFT 1/4), 2013
(H) 2440 Smiley Way, Jackson, MI 49203-3625 (517) 783-3803
(O) Federated Church of Grass Lake, 519 E Michigan Ave, Grass Lake, MI 49240 (517) 522-4480
Jackson First UMC: 275 W Michigan Ave, Jackson MI 49201 (517) 787-6460

BABB, SUSAN J. (FE) (Mark) – (D-1993, E-1995, R-2004)
[West Ohio Conf, Harveysburg/Oregonia (PTLP) 1988; Uniopolis/St. Johns (FTLP) 1990; Deshler First 1993; Gibsonburg Trinity 1996; West Unity 1999; Attending School 2001; Leave of Absence 2002] Transfered from West Ohio Conf; Jackson: First (Assoc.) Jan 16, 2004
(H) 2440 Smiley Way, Jackson, MI 49203 (517) 783-3803
Jackson First UMC: 275 W Michigan Ave, Jackson MI 49201 (517) 787-6460

***BABCOCK, WAYNE H. (RE) (Lois) – (R-1968, D-1972, E-1976)**
In School 1969; Bloomingdale/Townline Sept 1, 1969; In School 1971; Scottdale/Bridgman 1972; Marcellus/Wakelee Jan 1, 1975; Kingsley/Grant 1978; Webberville/Bell Oak 1983; Webberville Jan 16, 1987; Berrien Springs 1991; Kalamazoo Lawrence 1998; Retired January 1, 2003
(H) 32052 County Road 687, Bangor, MI 49013 (269) 427-2681

BAEK, SEUNG HO (ANDY) (FE) (Hehyoung) – (R-1997)

Transfer from Wisconsin Conf, Grand Rapids Michigan Suhbu Korean July 16, 1997; GBGM; New Church Ministry-Suhbu Korean Congregation 2001; Michigan Suhbu Korean UMC 2005 (Re-named "Church of All Nations" 2006); Church of All Nations/Oakdale 2006; Schoolcraft 2008; West Ohio Conf, Columbus Korean, Capitol Area North District (Para. 346.1) 2010; Union City/Athens (3/4 Time:1/4 Time) 2012

(H) 635 Walnut Lane, Union City, MI 49094 (517) 741-9041
Union City UMC: PO Box 95, Union City MI 49094-0095 (517) 741-7028
Athens UMC: 123 Clark St, PO Box 267, Athens MI 49011 (269) 729-9370

BAGLEY, DWAYNE E. (FE) (Michele) – (R-1998, D-1998, E-2001)

Webberville 1995; Albion 2002; Mason First 2009

(H) 616 Hall Blvd, Mason, MI 48854-1704 (517) 244-0456
Mason First UMC: 201 E Ash St, Mason MI 48854-1775 (517) 676-9449

***BAILEY, DEAN I. (RE) – (R-1958, D-1958, E-1960)**

[Leaton 1956]; Sanford 1960; Vicksburg 1966; Lowell 1969; Stevensville 1979; Traverse City Central 1987; Retired 2002; Alto/Bowne Center (LTFT 3/4) (DSA) 2002; Alto/Bowne Center (Ret.) (LTFT 45%) Jan. 1-June 30, 2014

(H) 3782 Murray Lake Ave, Lowell, MI 49331 (616) 691-8011

***BAILEY, PAUL F. (RE) (Lynn) – (R-1995, D-1962, E-1967)**

[Spencer, IA 1962; Monroe: E. Rainsinville 1963; Presby, Pique, OH 1964; Pontiac: NE Community (St. John's) 1966; Detroit West Outer Drive 1969; Honorable Location 1970; Transferred to West Michigan Conf, Associate Director, MICAP 1978; Honoarable Location 1979; Transferred to N. NY Conf, Waddington 1984; Transferred to Detroit Conf, Midland Homer 1988; Livingston Circuit Plainfield, Trinity Jan 1, 1990; Allen Park Trinity 1991;] Transferred from Detroit Conf, Potterville/West Benton 1995; Retired May 1, 2001; Ionia: Easton (DSA) April 13, 2003

(H) 2500 Breton Woods Dr SE Apt 1065, Grand Rapids, MI 49512-9156 (517) 930-3743
(S) 820 Trento, Venice, FL 34285

***BAILEY, ROBERT Q. (OR) (Rachel)**

[Free Methodist Church,Southern Michigan Conference, Retired Elder] Jackson Trinity (Ret.) (LTFT 1/2) 2014

(H) 375 Richard Street, PO Box 87, Spring Arbor, MI 49283 (517) 750-2821
Jackson Trinity UMC: 1508 Greenwood Ave, Jackson MI 49203-4048 (517) 782-7937

***BAILEY, THERON E. (RE) (Cheryl) – (R-1961, D-1961, E-1963)**

[Kewadin 1955; Union City 1957]; In School 1960; Ogdensburg/Wesley Foundation 1964; Hart/Mears 1966; Wyoming Wesley Park Dec 15, 1969; Sabbatical Sept 1, 1977; Empire Ad Interim Aug 1, 1978; Lansing First Sept 15, 1978; Conf Staff Program Coordination March 1, 1982; Grand Rapids St. Paul 1989; Retired 1994

(H) 3086 Slater Ave SE, Kentwood, MI 49512 (616) 956-5678

BAKER, MELANIE J. (FE) – (R-1984, D-1984, E-1987)

In School GETS 1984; Empire 1985; Leave of Absence 1988; North Adams/Jerome Oct 1, 1988; Battle Creek Birchwood 1995; Sabbatical Leave 2003; Lansing First 2004; Alma July 15, 2012; Leave of Absence 2013

(H) 3813 1/2 W Willow St, Lansing, MI 48917 (517) 204-5870

BAKER, PEGGY J. (FE) (Forrest) – (R-1999, D-1999, E-2003)

Comstock 1998; Harper Creek (New Church Start) 2006; Battle Creek Baseline/Bellevue 2011

(H) 523 Sherwood Rd, Bellevue, MI 49021 (269) 763-3201
Battle Creek Baseline UMC: 9617 E Baseline Rd, Battle Creek MI 49017 (269) 963-7710
Bellevue UMC: 122 W. Capital Ave., Bellevue MI 49021 (269) 763-9421

BALL, LYLE J. (PL) (Janet)

Chase Barton/Grant Center (DSA) 2010; Chase Barton/Grant Center (PTLP 1/2) Nov 1, 2010

(H) 6874 5 Mile Rd, Blanchard, MI 49310-9474 (231) 972-7335
Chase-Barton UMC: 6957 S Depot Street, PO Box 104, Chase MI 49623 (231) 832-5069
Grant Center UMC: 15260 21 Mile Road, Big Rapids MI 49307 (231) 796-8006

BALL, THOMAS E. (FE) (Kelly) – (R-1982, D-1982, E-1986)
In School Drew Theological School 1982; Girard/Ellis Corners 1984; Climax/Scotts Dec 1, 1988; Farwell 1994; Howard City: Heritage 2000; Cadillac 2007
(H) 114 Barbara St, Cadillac, MI 49601 (231) 775-1851
Cadillac UMC: 1020 E. Division St., PO Box 37, Cadillac MI 49601 (231) 775-5362

***BARNEY, JAMES W. (RE) (Marilyn) – (R-1972, D-1972, E-1975)**
[Milan/West Milan/Dummer, New Hampshire Conf 1974;] Transfered from New Hampshire Conf, Munith/Pleasant Lake 1979; Quincy 1983; Wayland 1987; Constantine Sept 15, 1991; Somerset Center 1998; Retired August 31, 2005
(H) 1713 Linden Trail, Kalamazoo, MI 49009 (269) 251-1187

***BARNEY, MARILYN B. (RE) (James) – (R-1985, D-1985, E-1990)**
In School, METHESCO 1985; Burnips/Monterey Center 1987; Three Rivers: Ninth Street/Jones Oct. 1, 1991; Hillside 1998; Retired 2008
(H) 1713 Linden Trail, Kalamazoo, MI 49009 (269) 251-1021

***BARRETT, WAYNE C. (RE) (Linda) – (R-1972, D-1972, E-1975)**
[Snow 1969]; Bloomingdale/Townline 1972; Muskegon Central (Assoc.) Nov 1, 1974; Grand Rapids Plainfield 1978; Plainfield/Director United Methodist Foundation Feb 1, 1982; Executive Director, United Methodist Foundation 1982 (Re-named "United Methodist Foundation of Michigan" 2006); Retired 2011
(H) 1517 Heathfield NE, Grand Rapids, MI 49505 (616) 458-9975

BARRY, B. GORDON (FE) (Susan) – (R-1982, D-1982, E-1985)
Remus/Halls Corner/Mecosta 1982; New Buffalo/Lakeside 1985; New Buffalo/Bridgman: Faith 1988; Lowell 1993; Stevensville 2003
(H) 5846 Ponderosa Dr, Stevensville, MI 49127 (269) 429-5749
Stevensville UMC: 5506 Ridge Rd., Stevensville MI 49127 (269) 429-5911

BARTELMAY, BRADLEY S. (FE) (Sherri Swanson) – (R-1996, D-1996, E-2002)
Stevensville (Assoc) 1990; New Buffalo/Bridgman: Faith 1993; New Buffalo: First, May 1, 2000 (Church Name Changed to Water's Edge UMC Jan 1, 2012)
(H) 19603 Oak Dr, New Buffalo, MI 49117 (269) 469-4488
Water's Edge UMC: 24 S. Whittaker, New Buffalo MI 49117 (269) 469-1250

***BARTHOLOMEW, JACK M. (RE) (Mildred) – (R-1975, D-1975, E-1979)**
[Quincy/Fisher Hill 1969-1974] In school 1975; Elk Rapids/Kewadin 1978; Hastings: Hope Feb. 16, 1983; Lansing: Calvary Feb. 15, 1986; Stanwood: Northland 1992; Retired 1995
(H) 1133 Yeomans St #96, Ionia, MI 48846 (616) 527-8852

BATTEN, LISA M. (FL) (Jim)
Wesley Foundation of Kalamazoo, Nov 15, 2009
(H) 225 E Jackson St, PO Box 282, Mendon, MI 49072-0282 (269) 496-7033
(O) Wesley Foundation of Kalamazoo, 2101 Wilbur Ave, Kalamazoo, MI 49006 (269) 344-4076

***BAUGHAN, EUGENE L. (RA) (Philis) – (R-1993, D-1979)**
Northeast Missaukee Parish 1974; Springport/Lee Center 1987; Brooks Corner/Sears 1991; Barnard/East Jordan/Norwood 1997; Retired 2002; Kewadin (Ret.) Nov. 1, 2009
(H) 400 Heartland Dr, Traverse City, MI 49684 (231) 943-0354
Kewadin UMC: PO Box 277, Kewadin MI 49648 (231) 264-9640

BEACHY, EMILY K. (PE) (W. Michael Beachy II) – (R-2012, PE-2012)
(Formerly Emily Slavicek) Girard Sept 1, 2010; Centreville 2014
(H) 304 E Market St, Centreville, MI 49032 (269) 467-7715
Centreville UMC: 305 E Main Street, Centreville MI 49032 (269) 467-8645

***BEACHY, WILLIAM M. (RE) (Barbara) – (R-2001)**
[West Ohio Conf; Monfort Heights UMC, Cincinnati, OH] Transfered from West Ohio Conf 2001; Lansing Trinity 2001; Retired 2014
(H) 230 E Knight St, Eaton Rapids, MI 48827 (517) 441-9456

BEALS, MARTHA SHEAGREN (PD) (Brian) – (R-2009)
Chaplain, Clark Retirement Community, Grand Rapids (Para 316.1) (1/4 Time), 2005; Chaplain, Clark Retirement Community and Grand Rapids First (Provisional Deacon), 2009; Leave of Absence Nov 20, 2009; Transitional Leave 2012; Leave of Absence 2013
(H) 2909 Woodcliff Circle SE, Grand Rapids, MI 49506 (616) 949-7349

BEAVAN, JOSEPH L. (FL) (Darcy)
Brooks Corners/Sears/Barryton Faith, Jan. 15, 2010; Rosebush 2014
(H) 3272 E Weidman Rd, Rosebush, MI 48878 (989) 433-5509
Rosebush UMC: 3805 School Street, PO Box 187, Rosebush MI 48878-0187 (989) 433-2957

BECK, ERIC S. (FE) (Heather) – (R-1979, D-1979, E-1983)
In School, 1979; Eaton Rapids (Assoc) Dec 1, 1980; Muskegon Unity 1983; Union City 1986; Kalamazoo Westwood Aug 1, 1995; Lake Odessa Central 2007; Jackson First 2012
(H) 1734 Malvern Dr, Jackson, MI 49203 (517) 962-2451
Jackson First UMC: 275 W Michigan Ave, Jackson MI 49201 (517) 787-6460

***BEKOFSKE, GARY L. (RE) (Nancy) – (R-1989, D-1972, E-1976)**
[Westfield, East Ohio Conf, 1972; Eastern Pennsylvania Conf: Morrisville 1975; Darby: Mt. Zion 1977; Philadelphia: Mount Pisgah/Providence 1980; Leave of Absence 1982; Philadelphia: Taylor Memorial Nov 1 1983; Philadelphia: Emmanuel 1984; Exec Sec for Emergency Response, Board of Global Ministries 1984] Transferred from Eastern Pennsylvania Conf 1989; Hillsdale June 1, 1989; Lansing: Grace 1996; Montague 2005; Muskegon: Central, Aug 16, 2009; Delton Faith 2010; Pentwater Centenary 2012; Retired 2014
(H) 733 W Elmwood Ave, Clawson, MI 48017 (248) 435-5027

BELL, DAVID S. (AF) (Ethel L.)
[East Ohio] Vice-President of Stewardship of the United Methodist Foundation of Michigan, Sept 1, 2007; President and Executive Director, United Methodist Foundation of Michigan 2011
(H) 5527 Timber Bend Drive, Brighton, MI 48116
(O) United Methodist Foundation of Michigan, 840 W Grand River Ave, Brighton, MI 48116 (810) 534-3001

***BENSEN, KENNETH W. (RE) (Sandra) – (R-1990, D-1990, E-1992)**
Lansing: Faith May 1, 1987; Retired 2003
(H) 502 W Calle Artistica, Green Valley, AZ 85614-6149 (520) 437-3971
(O) Habitat for Humanity of Michigan 618 S Creyts Ste C, Lansing, MI 48917

BENTLEY, TERRI L. (FL) (Tom)
Stevensville (Assoc) 2002; St Louis, Feb 1, 2008
(H) 116 N East St, St Louis, MI 48880-1721 (989) 681-2486
St Louis First UMC: 116 S. Franklin Street, St. Louis MI 48880 (989) 681-3320

BIGHAM-TSAI, KENNETHA J. (FE) (Kee C. Tsai) – (R-2006, E-2009)
East Lansing: University (Assoc.) 2006; Milwood 2011; Lansing District Superintendent 2013
(H) 6137 Horizon Dr, East Lansing, MI 48823
(O) Lansing District Office, 2111 University Park Dr Ste 500, Okemos, MI 48864-6907 (517) 347-4173

BILLS, WILLIAM C. (FE) (Julie) – (R-1990, D-1990, E-1993)
Burr Oak July 16, 1988; Marshall (Assoc.) 1991; Martin/Shelbyville 1994; Georgetown 2007
(H) 2032 Pinewood St, Jenison, MI 49428 (616) 719-3769
Georgetown UMC: 2766 Baldwin St, Jenison MI 49428 (616) 669-0730

***BISTAYI, JOSEPH J. (RE) (Cheryl) – (R-1970, D-1970, E-1973)**
[Ypsilanti: First (Assoc.) 1972; Dundee 1975;] Transferred from Detroit Conf., Portage: Chapel Hill Oct. 1, 1978; Battle Creek: Chapel Hill 1985; Conference Staff Person for Spiritual Formation 1993; Georgetown Aug.16,1999; Retired 2005
(H) 2336 Elliott SE, Grand Rapids, MI 49506 (616) 550-4374

BISTAYI, MATTHEW J. (PE) (Shellie) – (R-2007, PE-2007)
Brandywine: Trinity Jan. 1, 1999; Kalamazoo: First (Assoc) 2002; Bronson 2006; Allendale New Church Start 2009
(H) 10811 Lance Ave, Allendale, MI 49401 (616) 892-6240
Valley UMC: 5980 Lake Michigan Dr Ste B, Allendale MI 49401 (269) 501-8602

BITEMAN, DANIEL W. (FE) (Kellie Lynn) – (R-1988, D-1988, E-1996)
[Fife Lake/South Boardman, July 1, 1983; Chandler School of Theology; DeWitt Redeemer (Assoc) 1987;] Kalamazoo Lane Blvd 1988; Grawn 1996; Lawton St. Paul's 2006; Alden/Central Lake 2010
(H) 9022 Franklin, PO Box 157, Alden, MI 49612-0157 (231) 331-6762
Alden UMC: 9015 Helena, PO Box 130, Alden MI 49612-0130 (231) 331-4132
Central Lake UMC: PO Box 213, Central Lake MI 49622

BLACK, CARLETON R. (FL) (Barbara)
Ravenna (DSA) (1/2 Time) 2011; Ravenna (PTLP 3/4) Nov 12, 2011; Ravenna (Full-Time) 2012
(H) 3482 Lo Al Dr, Ravenna, MI 49451-9405 (231) 853-6111
Ravenna UMC: 12348 Stafford St, PO Box 191, Ravenna MI 49451 (231) 853-6688

***BLAKEY, DOROTHY M. (RD) – (Consecrated 1994, R-1997, FD-1997)**
Holland: First (LTFT 1/4) 1997; Retired 1999
(H) 5054 Maple Creek SE, Kentwood, MI 49508 (616) 455-8503

BLUNT, RICHARD W. (FE) (Natalie) – (R-1985, D-1985, E-1988)
[Eastern PA Conf.: Lumberville 1984-1986;] In school Princeton Theological Seminary 1985; Ogdensburg 1986; Manton 1993; Reed City Feb. 1, 1999; Lowell 2008; Okemos Community 2014
(H) 2441 S Wild Blossom Ct, East Lansing, MI 48823-7203 (517) 721-1301
Okemos Community Church: PO Box 680, Okemos MI 48805-0680 (517) 349-4220

***BOEHM, JAMES W. (RE) (Catheryn) – (R-1965, D-1966, E-1976)**
Gobles/Kendall Apr. 1, 1967-Sept. 1, 1969; Withdrew 1970; Readmitted 1973; Transferred from Detroit Conf., Newaygo 1975; Plainwell 1984; Kalamazoo District Superintendent 1989; Okemos Community 1996; Retired Sept. 1, 1998
(H) 73 N Eldridge Rd, PO Box 663, Beulah, MI 49617-0663 (231) 882-7074

***BOELENS, NANCY L. (RLA)**
[Detroit Conference, Middleburry UMC Sept. 1, 1996-June 30, 1998]; Bath/Gunnisonville 1998; Wayland 2003; Muskegon Unity/Sitka Nov. 1, 2006; Muskegon Unity 2008; Leave of Absence, Jan. 1, 2009; Retired April 12, 2009; Salem/Bradley Indian Mission UMCs (RLA 1/2), 2013
(H) 1875 Parkcrest Dr. S.W., Apt 2, Wyoming, MI 49519 (616) 914-9300
Salem Indian Mission of the UMC: 1875 Parkcrest Drive #2, Wyoming MI 49519
Bradley Indian Mission of the UMC: 1875 Parkcrest Drive #2, Wyoming MI 49519

***BOERSMA, GILBERT R. (RE) (Sara Jayne) – (R-1982, D-1982, E-1984)**
Frontier/Osseo 1982; Freeport/Middleville (Assoc) 1985; Muskegon Wolf Lake Jan 1, 1989; Pastoral Care Coordinator, Hospice of Oceana & Muskegon Counties Feb 1, 1995; In School, CPE Residency Program, Bronson Medical Center 1997; Chaplain, Hackley Hospital June 15, 1998; Manager, Spiritual Care Services, Hackley Hospital 2004; Transitional Leave, April 17, 2009; Muskegon Unity (LTFT 1/4) 2009; Retired Oct 31, 2011
(H) 3364 Davis Rd, Muskegon, MI 49441-4102 (231) 557-5640

BOLEY, JOHN W. (FE) (Diane) – (R-1991, D-1991, E-1994)
In School, Duke Divinity School 1991; Mancelona/Alba June 16, 1992; Lansing Central 1997; Mt. Pleasant First 2002; Kalamazoo First 2010; Kalamazoo District Superintendent 2014
(H) 2717 Frederick Ave, Kalamazoo, MI 49008 (269) 216-3012
(O) Kalamazoo District Office, 810 Rankin Ave Ste B, Kalamazoo, MI 49006 (269) 372-7525

BOLTZ, PEGGY ANN (FL)
Marcellus 1995; Shelby 2002; Lawton St. Paul's 2010; Oshtemo 2011-2013; Bellaire 2013
(H) 111 W Antrim St, Bellaire, MI 49615-9594 (231) 267-3133
Bellaire Community UMC: 401 N Bridge St, PO Box 235, Bellaire MI 49615-0235 (231) 533-8133

BONDARENKO, GARY D. (FE) (Lisa) – (R-1989, D-1989, E-1993)
Charlotte (Assoc.) July 16, 1988; Boyne City/Boyne Falls June 16, 1991; East Lansing: Aldersgate 2000; Wayland Nov. 15, 2006; Stanwood Northland 2014
(H) 18835 Fillmore Rd, Stanwood, MI 49346 (231) 823-2514
Stanwood Northland UMC: 6842 Northland Dr., PO Box 26, Stanwood MI 49346-0026 (231) 629-4590

BONGARD, CONNIE R. (FL) (Frank)
Leaton May 1, 1992; Mt. Pleasant: First (Assoc.) Aug. 1, 1994; Edmore: Faith 1997; Farwell Jan. 1, 2007
(H) 551 N Superior St, Farwell, MI 48622 (989) 588-9620
Farwell UMC: 281 E. Ohio Street, PO Box 709, Farwell MI 48622 (989) 588-2931

BOULDREY, SCOTT M. (FL) (Dawn)
[2010 Candidacy for OM or LM accepted by a DCOM in Another Conf (West Ohio Conf: Vanlue Christ 2003; Powell Memorial 2007)] Battle Creek Christ 2011; Battle Creek Christ (PTLP 3/4) and Battle Creek First (PTLP 1/4) 2014
(H) 15 Woodlawn Ave N, Battle Creek, MI 49037-1539 (269) 282-1490
Battle Creek Christ UMC: 65 Bedford Road N, Battle Creek MI 49037 (269) 965-3251
Battle Creek First UMC: 111 East Michigan Avenue, Battle Creek MI 49014-4012 (269) 963-5567

***BOURNS, CAROL LYNN (RP) – (R-1992, D-1992)**
North Evart/Sylvan (1/4 Time) Sept. 1, 1991; Leave of Absence Jan. 1, 1995; Incapacity Leave 1997; Retired 2007
(H) 144 W 4th St Apt 403, Clare, MI 48617 (989) 544-2719

BOUTELL, JAMES (TOMMY) THOMAS (PE) (Shelly) – (R-2010, PE-2010)
Olivet (PTLP) 2008; Marne 2010;
(H) 14861 Washington St, Marne, MI 49435 (616) 677-3991
Marne UMC: 14861 Washington, PO Box 85, Marne MI 49435 (616) 677-3957

***BOVEE, KEITH A. (RE) (Elnora) – (R-1956, D-1956, E-1958)**
[Frontier 1952; Centerville 1954]; Muskegon: Central (Assoc.) 1957; North Muskegon 1959; Lowell 1963; St. Johns First 1965; Voluntary Location 1968; Left Appointment 1974; Marne 1982; Ionia: First 1985; Shelby 1991; Retired 1994
(H) 751 Clark Crossing SE, Grand Rapids, MI 49506 (616) 206-4060

***BOWDEN, DIANNE M. (RE) (Jeff) – (R-2002, E-2005)**
In School; Nashville January 16, 2002; Muskegon Crestwood 2007; Incapacity Leave May 1, 2008; Retired 2013
(H) 2310 Avenal Ct, Murfreesboro, TN 37129-6612 (615) 410-3399

BOWMAN, JEFFREY J. (FL) (Cheryl)
Vermontville/Gresham 1995; White Cloud 2002; Muskegon Heights Temple 2012
(H) 1205 Yorkshire Dr, Muskegon, MI 49441-5358 (231) 798-9309
Muskegon Hts Temple UMC: 2500 Jefferson, Muskegon Heights MI 49444 (231) 733-1065

BOWMAN, LETISHA M. (FE) (Brian) – (R-2011, E-2014)
Saugatuck (DSA) 2005; Saugatuck (PTLP) 2007; Grand Rapids First (Assoc) 2011
(H) 3358 Oak Hollow Dr SE, Grand Rapids, MI 49546-2126 (616) 260-2994
Grand Rapids First UMC: 227 Fulton St E, Grand Rapids MI 49503-3236 (616) 451-2879

BREMER, KENNETH J. (FE) (Vicky) – (R-1990, D-1990, E-1995)
In School, Asbury Theological Seminary 1990; Holton June 1, 1992; St Johns: Pilgrim 2006; Rockford 2014
(H) 6821 Homestead Dr NE, Rockford, MI 49341 (616) 884-3051
Rockford UMC: 159 Maple St, Rockford MI 49341 (616) 866-9515

***BRICKER, J. MELVIN (RE) – (R-1966, D-1966, E-1968)**
Kalamazoo: First (Assoc.) 1966; Frankfort/Elberta 1971; Rockford 1980; Grandville 1989; Retired 1995
(H) 1216 Oakmont Dr #8, Walnut Creek, CA 94595 (925) 482-0555

BRILLHART, JAMES (BRAD) BRADLEY (FE) (Julia) – (R-1999, D-1999, E-2004)
Hesperia/Ferry 1999; Howard City Heritage 2007; Lowell 2014
(H) 640 Shepard Dr, Lowell, MI 49331 (616) 897-8267
Lowell UMC: 621 E Main St, Lowell MI 49331 (616) 897-5936

***BROMBEREK, PATRICIA L. (RE) (Glen Brown) – (R-2004, E-2009)**
Niles Grace 2002; Center Park 2004; Newaygo 2006; Newaygo Feb 1, 2011 (LTFT 3/4); Retired 2011
(H) 348 Lyon Lake Rd, Marshall, MI 49068 (269) 558-2030

BROMLEY, DENNIS B. (PE) (JoAnn) – (R-2000, D-2000, AM-2000, PE-2014)
[Epsilon/Levering (DSA) 1993]; Epsilon/Levering Nov 16, 1993; Epsilon/Levering/Pellston Sept 1, 1997; Clare 2003; Ludington United 2013
(H) 914 Seminole, Ludington, MI 49431 (231) 425-4386
Ludington United UMC: 5810 Bryant Road, Ludington MI 49431-1504 (231) 843-8340

BROOK, PATRICIA L. (FE) (Roger) – (R-2001, E-2004)
In School; DeWitt: Redeemer (Assoc.) 1999; Marne Feb. 1, 2002; Hillsdale 2010
(H) 1079 Markris Dr, Hillsdale, MI 49242 (517) 437-2392
Hillsdale First UMC: 45 N. Manning, Hillsdale MI 49242 (517) 437-3681

BROOKS, RONALD K. (FE) (Penny) – (R-1985, D-1985, E-1988)
In School, Iliff School of Theology 1985; Center Eaton/Brookfield 1985; Nashville 1988; Lawrence May 16, 1991; Lansing Mt Hope (Assoc.) 1998; Lansing Mt Hope 1999; Lawton St Paul 2000; Carson City 2006; Voluntary Leave of Absence 2008; Lansing Central 2009; Jackson Brookside 2013
(H) 217 Mohawk, Jackson, MI 49203 (517) 782-2706
Jackson Brookside UMC: 4000 Francis, Jackson MI 49203 (517) 782-5167

***BROWN, DALE DONALD (RE) (Esther) – (R-1959, D-1959, E-1962)**
[Stanwood 1951; Edmore 1954]; Comstock 1960; Evart 1961; Grandville 1964; St. Joseph Feb. 1, 1973; Battle Creek: First Jan. 16, 1983; Retired 1993
(H) 162 Lakewood Dr, East Leroy, MI 49051 (269) 979-9303

BROWN, KATHY E. (FE) – (R-1985, D-1985, E-1987)
Traverse City: Central (Assoc.) 1985; Litchfield 1990; Hastings: First Feb. 1, 2001; Plainwell 2010
(H) 714 E Gun River Dr, Plainwell, MI 49080 (269) 312-1378
Plainwell First UMC: 200 Park St., PO Box 85, Plainwell MI 49080 (269) 685-5113

***BROWN, LAWRENCE P. (RE) (Beverly) – (R-1988, D-1988, E-1992)**
In School, Asbury Theological Seminary 1988; Somerset Center/Moscow Plains 1989; Somerset Center Jan 1, 1993; Lakeview: Asbury/Belvidere 1996; New Life UMC Jan 1, 1998; Ionia First 2006; Retired 2014
(H) 118 Monroe St, South Haven, MI 49090

BROWN, MARY S. (FE) (Carl) – (R-1996, D-1994, E-1997)
Baldwin/Luther 1995 (para. 426.1); Transfered from Detroit Conf., Baldwin/Luther 1996; Bellaire Community Oct. 16, 1998; Traverse City Christ and Kewadin 2009; Grawn Nov. 1, 2009; Montague 2014
(H) 5181 Hancock St, Montague, MI 49437 (231) 357-4506
Montague UMC: 8555 Cook St, Montague MI 49437 (231) 894-5789

BROWNE, JENNIFER (FE) – (R-1998, E-1984; FE-2008)
Reed City (Assoc.) Jan 15, 1997; Transfered from United Church of Christ 1998; Appointment to Attend School (para. 416.6) Dec 1, 1998; Albion College, Assistant to the President (para. 335.1a)(LTFT 1/2) 2000; Leave of Absence March 1, 2003; Brighton First (Assoc.), Ann Arbor District, Detroit Conf, (para. 337.1) 2003; Grand Rapids First (Assoc.) 2006; East Lansing University 2011
(H) 3343 Glasgow Drive, Lansing, MI 48911 (517) 898-4575
East Lansing University UMC: 1120 S Harrison Rd, East Lansing MI 48823-5201 (517) 351-7030

***BRUBAKER, ELLEN A. (RE) (John Ross Thompson) – (R-1974, D-1974, E-1976)**
Transferred from Detroit Conf, Traverse City Central (Assoc) 1975; Traverse City Central (Assoc)/ Ogdensburg 1978; Belding 1981; Grand Rapids District Superintendent 1983; Grand Haven 1989; Grand Rapids Aldersgate 1992; Retired Dec 31, 2001
(H) 4114 Sawkaw Dr NE, Grand Rapids, MI 49525-1858 (616) 361-6539

BUCHNER, GREGORY L. (FE) (AnnMarie) – (R-2005, E-2008)
Three Oaks (DSA) 11/15/97 - 6/98; Wakelee (DSA)1998; Wakelee Nov. 16, 1999; Rosebush 2005; United Church of Ovid 2008; Mecosta New Hope 2013
(H) 3955 9 Mile Rd, Remus, MI 49340 (989) 967-8801
Mecosta New Hope UMC: 7296 9 Mile Road, Mecosta MI 49332-9722 (231) 972-2838

***BUCK, STEVEN J. (OR) (Susan)**
[Detroit Conf, Retired Elder]; Lansing Trinity (Ret.) 2014
(H) 4100 Mountain Glade Apt 5, Holt, MI 48842 (810) 444-7089
Lansing Trinity UMC: 7533 W St Joe Hwy, Lansing MI 48917-9647 (517) 627-8388

BUEGE, DONALD L. (FE) (Cynthia) – (R-1977, D-1977, E-1981)
In School, 1977; Vergennes/Lowell (Assoc.) 1979; Mesick/Harrietta Sept 1, 1980; Keeler/Silver Creek Jan 1, 1984; Evart/Avondale 1990; Avondale/N Evart/Sylvan (LTFT 1/4) 2000; Leslie/Felt Plains (LTFT 3/4) Jan 15, 2006; Fife Lake Parish 2014
(H) 124 Boyd St, Fife Lake, MI 49633 (231) 879-5330
East Boardman UMC: PO Box 69, South Boardman MI 49680 (231) 879-5330
Fife Lake UMC: PO Box 69, Fife Lake MI 49633 (231) 879-4270
South Boardman UMC: 5488 Dagle St, PO Box 112, South Boardman MI 49680 (231) 879-5330

***BUKER, ELAINE M. (RA) – (D-1985)**
[St. Paul (Assoc.), Parkersburg, WV 1976-1978]; Big Rapids: Third/Paris/Rodney Sept. 1, 1981; Mendon 1986; Portland 1992; Retired 1997
(H) 10100 Hillview Dr. Apt.1213, Pensacola, FL 32514-5448 (850) 607-7743

BUKOSKI, JERRY J. (PL) (Sandra)
Barry-Eaton Cooperative Ministry: Quimby (DSA) (1/4 time) 2013; Barry-Eaton Cooperative Ministry: Quimby (PTLP 1/4) 2014
(H) 1069 S Ionia Rd, Vermontville, MI 49096-8576 (517) 588-8415
Quimby UMC: PO Box 63, Hastings MI 49058 (269) 945-9392

BUNCH, BRIAN R. (FL) (Kendra)
[N Indiana Conf, Muncie District, Losantville UMC (DSA) 1991; Losantville UMC (Student LP) 1993; Losantville UMC (PTLP) 1995;] Brooks Corners and Sears 1997; Brooks Corners/Barryton-Chippewa Lake/Sears Mar 1, 2002; Northeast Missaukee Parish Aug 1, 2005; Delton Faith 2012
(H) 146 Bush St, Delton, MI 49046-9798 (269) 623-5335
Delton Faith UMC: 503 S Grove, PO Box 467, Delton MI 49046-0467 (269) 623-5400

***BURGESS, RAY W. (RE) (Martha) – (R-1961, D-1961, E-1965)**
[Detroit Conf.: Detroit Aldersgate (Assoc.) 1967; Flint: Flint Park 1968-Jan. 1, 1970;] Transferred from Detroit Conf Jan 1, 1970; Wesley Foundation Director, Ferris State College, Jan 1, 1970; Grand Rapids: South 1979; Sturgis 1988; Muskegon: Central 1993; Retired 2000
(H) 10915 Pioneer Trail, Boyne Falls, MI 49713-9217 (231) 549-3066
(S) 8701 S Kolb 7-232, Tucson, AZ 85706-9607 (520) 574-6692

BURSON, LINDA J. (FE) (Douglas Rose) – (R-1997, D-1987, E-1990)
Transferred from New York Conf, Homer/Lyon Lake 1997; Leave of Absence Jan 1, 2000; Conference Staff Aug 1, 2000; Leave of Absence July 1, 2008; Kalamazoo Sunnyside, Mar 1, 2009; Leave of Absence 2009
(H) 240 Cullom Way, Clarksville, TN 37043 (931) 358-3351

BURTON-KRIEGER, ERIC M. (PE) (Meagan) – (R-2012, PE-2012)
Serving Tennessee Conf, Brentwood (Assoc) 2012
(H) 1707 Hillside Ave, Nashville, TN 37203-4931
(O) Brentwood UMC, 309 Franklin Rd, Brentwood, TN 37027 (615) 373-3663

***BUWALDA, DENNIS G. (RE) (Carol) – (R-1968, D-1969, E-1970)**
Transferred from Indiana South Conf (EUB), Adamsville 1968; Berrien Springs Mar 15, 1975; North Muskegon Sept 1, 1978; Holt 1982; Lansing: Trinity 1989; Grand Traverse District Superintendent 1992; United Methodist Foundation 1999 (Re-Named "United Methodist Foundation of Michigan," 2006); Retired Apr 1, 2008; Interim Lansing District Superintendent Jan 1-July 1, 2009
(H) 5693 S Clinton Trail, Eaton Rapids, MI 48827 (517) 663-4418

CADARETTE, KATHRYN S. (FE) (David) – (R-1994, D-1994, E-1996)
(Formerly Kathryn Slaughter) Horton Bay 1994; Horton Bay/Greensky Hill Indian Mission Feb 1, 1998; Leave of Absence 2000; Harbor Springs/Alanson 2003; Reed City 2011
(H) 219 S State St, Reed City, MI 49677 (231) 675-2172
Reed City UMC: 503 S. Chestnut, Reed City MI 49677 (231) 832-9441

***CAIN, FREDERICK G. (OR) – (R-2013)**
[Indiana Conference, Retired Elder] Camden/Montgomery/Stokes Chapel (Ret.) (LTFT 1/2) 2013
(H) 201 S Main St, PO Box 155, Camden, MI 49232 (517) 797-5530
Camden UMC: 201 S Main St, PO Box 155, Camden MI 49232 (517) 368-5406
Montgomery UMC: 201 S Main St, PO Box 155, Camden MI 49232 (517) 269-4232
Stokes Chapel UMC: 201 S Main St, PO Box 155, Camden MI 49232 (517) 368-5406

CARTER, JANET S. (FD) – (R-2005, FD-2009)
(Formerly Janet Amon) Chaplain, Heartland Home Health Care & Hospice and Pine Rest Christian Mental Health Services, Grand Rapids (para. 331.1a), 2005; Chaplain, Pine Rest Christian Mental Health Services, Grand Rapids (para. 331.1a), Oct 23, 2006; Chaplain, Pine Rest Christian Mental Health Services & Grand Rapids First (Deacon), 2009
(H) 669 Braeside Dr, Byron Center, MI 49315 (616) 260-9604
(O) Pine Rest Christian Mental Health Services, 300 68th St SE, Grand Rapids, MI 49508 (616) 281-6363 ext.2117

CATELLIER, PATRICIA L. (FD) – (R-2010, PD-2010, FD-2014)
Chaplain, Borgess Medical Center, Kalamazoo (LTFT 1/2) (para. 344.1.d) 2010
(H) 5025 Coopers Landing Dr Apt 8, Kalamazoo, MI 49004-6605 (269) 382-0708
(O) Borgess Medical Center, 1521 Gull Road, Kalamazoo, MI 49048 (269) 226-7000

***CERMAK, JOHN E. (RE) (Adele) – (D-1957, E-1959)**
Battle Creek: Washington Heights Sept. 1953; N.E. Co. Conf. Myricks/Dighton 1956; Kalamazoo: Oakwood 1959; Okemos 1966; Sabbatical Sept. 1, 1974; Okemos 1975; Jackson: First 1987; Retired 1994
(H) 10540 N. Shore Dr, PO Box 839, Northport, MI 49670-0839 (231) 386-5204

CHALKER, MELANY A. (FE) (Darryl) – (R-2005, E-2008)
[Detroit Conf: Springville 2005 (Para. 346.1)] Concord 2006; Marshall 2013
(H) 762 N Kalamazoo Ave, Marshall, MI 49068-1071 (517) 403-8528
Marshall UMC: 721 Old US 27N, Marshall MI 49068-9609 (269) 781-5107

CHARNLEY, STEPHEN MG (FE) (Cynthia) – (D-1978, E-1982)
[Wisconsin Conf.: Hebron/Pleasant Valley/Siloam 1979; Kenosha: First (Assoc.) 1982]; transferred from Wisconsin Conf., Newaygo 1988; Gull Lake 1994; Greenville First 2008; Greenville First, Turk Lake/ Belding Cooperative Parish 2013; Kalamazoo First 2014
(H) 471 W South St #403, Kalamazoo, MI 49007 (269) 312-8633
Kalamazoo First UMC: 212 South Park Street, Kalamazoo MI 49007 (269) 381-6340

***CHARNLEY, VICTOR D. (RE) – (R-1978, D-1976, E-1976)**
[Grand Haven (Assoc.) 1978]; Received from American Baptist Church, Grand Haven (Assoc.) 1979; Battle Creek: Trinity 1984; Muskegon: Crestwood 1995; Mecosta: New Hope 2004; Retired 2013
(H) 1361 Overseas Highway Lot A13, Marathon, FL 33050

***CHARTER, JOHN T. (RA) (Murelann) – (D-1972)**
Battle Creek: Calvary 1972; Homer/Lyon Lake/Marengo 1973; Homer/Lyon Lake 1975; Mendon 1978; Niles: Grace 1981; Battle Creek: Christ Nov. 16, 1992; Retired 1999
(H) 6600 Constitution Blvd, Apt. 215, Portage, MI 49024 (269) 353-4014

***CHEYNE, DAVID A. (RE) – (R-1973, D-1973, E-1975)**
[Mulliken Sept. 4, 1972] 1973; Sand Lake/South Ensley 1975; Hersey/Grant Center 1977; Alden/Central Lake 1982; Webberville 1991; Hillside 1995; Three Oaks 1998; Baldwin/Luther Jan. 16, 1999; Pine River Parish: LeRoy/Ashton 1999; Sodus: Chapel Hill 2003; Retired 2005
(H) 5909 Bois Isle Dr #2C, Haslett, MI 48840 (517) 339-2514

CHO, BO RIN (FE) (Koom) – (R-2004, D-1990, E-1992 (Minnesota))
[Minnesota Conf: Ed: BA Seoul Theol Sem; MDiv GETS 1989; Adm: LP 1989; PM 1990; FM 1992; Ord: D 1990; E 1992; App: Gordonsville-Glenville 1989; Rochester Evangel (A) 1990; Mpls Minnesota Christ Korean 1995] Lansing Korean (para. 337.1.) March 1, 2004; transferred from Minnesota Conference 2013; Lansing Asbury 2014
(H) 2412 Post Oak Ln, Lansing, MI 48912 (517) 484-3306
Lansing Asbury UMC: 2200 Lake Lansing Rd, Lansing MI 48912-3614 (517) 484-5794

CHRISTMAN, CATHERINE M (FE) (Michael) – (R-2009, PE-2009, E-2014)
Nashville (PTLP) 2007; Nashville (FTLP) April 1, 2008; Nashville 2009; Detroit Conf, Midland First (Assoc) (para. 346.1) 2010; Detroit Conf, Vassar First 2013
(H) 706 Cork Pine Lane, Vassar, MI 48768 (989) 823-2131
(O) Vassar First UMC, 139 North Main St, Vassar, MI 48768 (989) 823-8811

CHU, WILLIAM W. (FE) (Julie Greyerbiehl) – (R-2005, E-2008)
Burr Oak (Student Local Pastor) 2001; Garrett-Evangelical Theological Seminary Coordinator of Educational Technologies 2003 (LP w/o Appointment); Elk Rapids/Kewadin/Williamsburg 2005; Elk Rapids/Kewadin/Williamsburg (Co-pastor) 2008; Coloma/Watervliet 2009; East Lansing University (Assoc.) (1/2 Time) / MSU Wesley Foundation, Director (1/2 Time) 2011
(H) 733 Orchard Dr, Williamston, MI 48895 (517) 992-5038
(O) Wesley Foundation - Michigan State University, 1118 S. Harrison, East Lansing, MI 48823 (517) 332-0861
East Lansing University UMC: 1120 S Harrison Rd, East Lansing MI 48823-5201 (517) 351-7030

CLAXTON, MELISSA J. (PE) (Edward L. Claxton II) – (R-2011, PE-2011)
North Parma (Student Local Pastor) 2009; Springport/North Parma 2010
(H) 223 S Union, Parma, MI 49269 (517) 531-4740
North Parma UMC: PO Box 25, Parma MI 49269 (517) 531-4619
Springport UMC: PO Box E, Springport MI 49284-1004 (517) 857-2777

***CLEGG JR, WILLIAM V. (RE) (Joni) – (R-1981, D-1981, E-1986)**
In School Asbury Theological Seminary 1981; Haslett Mission Jan 16, 1984; Haslett Aldersgate 1985; Wyoming Wesley Park 1994; Retired 2011; Parmelee (DSA) (LTFT 1/4) Nov. 11, 2012; Parmelee (Ret.) (LTFT 1/4) Jan. 1, 2014
(H) 4593 N Camrose Court, Wyoming, MI 49519 (616) 366-2486
Parmelee UMC: 9266 W Parmelee Rd, PO Box 237, Middleville MI 49333 (269) 795-8816

COBB, MARTIN T. (PE) (Jessica) – (R-2007, PE-2007)
Burr Oak 1999; Middleton/Maple Rapids/Christian Crossroads Cooperative Parish 2001; Old Mission Peninsula 2006; Litchfield/Quincy 2010; Fremont 2013
(H) 352 Butterfield, Fremont, MI 49412 (231) 924-2456
Fremont UMC: 351 Butterfield St., Fremont MI 49412 (231) 924-0030

COE, BUFFORD W. (FE) (Lisa) – (R-1994, D-1974, E-1978)
[Detroit Conf.: Dryden, Attica Jan. 1977; In school, Boston School of Theology 1983; Brockton, MA: Central (Assoc.) (para. 425.1) 1987; Redford: Aldersgate (Assoc.) 1990;] Transferred from Detroit Conf., Hastings: First 1994; Vicksburg Oct. 15, 2000
(H) 4104 Waterview Dr, Vicksburg, MI 49097 (269) 649-0602
Vicksburg UMC: 217 S. Main Street, Vicksburg MI 49097 (269) 649-2343

***COMER, MICHAEL P. (OR) (Anne) – (R-1982, D-1972, E-1975)**
[In school St. Paul's School of Theology 1972; North Central New York Conf.: Cuyler/Fabius 1974; In school G-ETS/Northwestern University 1978; Retired 2009] Pastoral Counselor, Samaritan Center of Battle Creek 1982; Pastoral Counselor (private practice) 1989; police psychologist, Michigan State Police, Mar. 17, 2002; Police Psychologist Michigan State Police and Psychologist with the Michigan Department of Natural Resources (Ret.) 2011-2013
(H) 5153 Oak Hills Dr, Eaton Rapids, MI 48827 (517) 663-1571

CONKLIN, JOHN (JACK) J. (PE) (Pattie) – (R-2008, AM-2008, PE-2014)
Mesick/Harrietta (DSA) 2001; Mesick/Harrietta Dec 1, 2001; Scottville 2009
(H) 301 W Maple Ave, Scottville, MI 49454 (231) 757-4781
Scottville UMC: 114 W State St, Scottville MI 49454 (231) 757-3567

***CONKLIN, MICHAEL T. (RE) (Deborah) – (R-1979, D-1979, E-1983)**
In School 1979; Pokagon 1981; Boyne City/Boyne Falls 1983; Centreville 1989; Coopersville Aug 1, 1997; Jackson: Calvary 1999; Lowell 2003; Courtland-Oakfield 2008; Middleville/Snow 2009; Retired 2012
(H) 125 Heather Ridge Road, Battle Creek, MI 49017 (616) 204-8125

COOK, ROBERT B. (FE) (Lisa Richey) – (R-2003, E-2006)
Grand Rapids Trinity (Assoc) 2001; Leave of Absence 2006; Muskegon Heights Temple Sept 1, 2006; Lansing Mt. Hope 2012
(H) 1707 Woodside Dr, East Lansing, MI 48823 (517) 449-4826
Lansing Mt Hope UMC: 501 E Mt Hope Ave, Lansing MI 48910-9136 (517) 482-1549

COOLEY, CAROL B. (AF)
[West Ohio Conf., Incapacity Leave]
(H) 2308 Gallatin Dr, Davison, MI 48423 (810) 743-7130

***COOMBS, KATHRYN M. (RE) (James) – (R-1977, D-1977, E-1983)**
Transferred from Iowa Conf, Quincy 1977; Leave of Absence 1979; Watervliet Dec 1, 1981; Ionia Zion/Easton Sept 16, 1984; Ionia Easton (LTFT 3/4) Nov 1, 1986; Leave of Absence 1990; Empire 1991; Elk Rapids/Kewadin 1998; Frankfort/Elberta 1999; Leave of Absence March 1, 2002; Retired 2002; Northport Indian Mission (DSA) 2003-2005; Traverse City Christ (DSA) 2010-2011
(H) 11127 Oviatt Rd, Honor, MI 49640-9592 (231) 326-5852

***COURTER, WILBUR (RE) – (R-1967, D-1967, E-1970)**
Comstock 1967; transferred from Detroit Conf. 1970; Alcoholism Program Coordinator, Kalamazoo Alcohol & Addiction Council Jan. 1, 1973; Kalamazoo County Health Dept., Office of Substance Abuse Services 1976; Kalamazoo County Juvenile Home Supt. 1982; West Side Family Mental Health Clinic, Kalamazoo 1985; Retired 1998
(H) 1367 N 26th St, Kalamazoo, MI 49048 (269) 382-4136

***CRABTREE, JANE A. (RA) (Jean) – (D-1994)**
North Evart/Sylvan, Jan. 16, 1988; Turk Lake 1990; Lake City 1996; Fennville/Pearl 2000; Family Leave 2002; Retired July 16, 2003; Olivet (DSA) July 1-Dec. 12, 2010
(H) 2538 N Mundy Ave, White Cloud, MI 49349 (231) 689-3415

***CRABTREE, JEAN ARTHUR (RA) (Jane) – (D-1962, E-1964)**
Stanwood Sept. 1955; Fenwick Circuit 1959; Howard City 1962; Newaygo 1967; Hartford 1972; Mesick/Harrietta 1979; Parma/North Parma Sept. 1, 1980; Barryton/Chippewa Lake 1984; Six Lakes/Millbrook 1990; Six Lakes (LTFT 3/4) 1993; Retired March 31, 1994; North Evart/Sylvan 1996; Fennville/Pearl (Assoc.) 2000; Avondale/North Evart/Sylvan (DSA) Nov. 5, 2006 - July 2007; Olivet (DSA) July 1-Dec. 12, 2010
(H) 2538 N Mundy Ave, White Cloud, MI 49349 (231) 689-3415

***CRAWFORD, DAVID L. (RE) (Kathryn) – (R-1950, D-1953, E-1954)**
[Portage (Asst.) April 12, 1949; Galien Oct. 1, 1950]; Galien/Dayton 1953; Comstock 1954; transferred to Western New York Conf. Buffalo: Central Park, Minister of Education & Administration, 1957; transferred from Western New York Conf., Cadillac: First 1960; Executive Sec. Board of Education 1965; Lansing: Christ 1969; Albion District Supt. 1977; Traverse City: Central 1981; Hartford 1987; Retired 1990
(H) Apt 2095, 1551 Franklin SE GR, Grand Rapids, MI 49506 (616) 475-5768

CROEL, ANDREW L. (FE) (Anne) – (R-2005, E-2008)
Dimondale/Grovenburg 2005; Carson City 2008; St. Johns Pilgrim 2014
(H) 2917 W Parks Rd, St. Johns, MI 48879 (989) 224-4423
St Johns Pilgrim UMC: 2965 W Parks Road, St. Johns MI 48879 (989) 224-6865

CULVER, GREGORY P. (FE) – (R-2000, D-2000, E-2006)
Muskegon: Central (Assoc.) 1998; Frankfort/Elberta 2002; Charlevoix 2010
(H) 1206 State St, Charlevoix, MI 49720 (231) 547-5168
Charlevoix UMC: 104 State St, Charlevoix MI 49720 (231) 547-2654

***CULVER, MARTIN H. (RLA) (Barbara)**
Keswick(DSA)1991; Keswick August 1, 1991; Ionia First 2000; Milwood 2006; Lane Blvd (DSA) March 18, 2007-March 25, 2008; Retired 2011; Center Park (RLA 1/4) 2011
(H) 511 Landsdowne Ave, Portage, MI 49002 (269) 615-1360
Center Park UMC: 18662 Moorepark Rd., Three Rivers MI 49093 (269) 279-9109

CUMMINGS, JEFFREY O. (PL) (Bridget)
Galien/Olive Branch (DSA) (3/4 Time) Jan 1, 2012; Galien/Olive Branch (PTLP 3/4) 2013
(H) 201 N Cleveland Ave, Galien, MI 49113 (269) 545-8074
Galien & Olive Branch UMCs: 208 N. Cleveland Ave., PO Box 266, Galien MI 49113 (269) 545-2275

CUMMINS, TERRI L. (FL)
Shelby 2010; Shelby/Claybanks 2014
(H) 89 E 4th St, Shelby, MI 49455-1137 (231) 861-4331
Shelby UMC: 68 E. Third St., Shelby MI 49455 (231) 861-2020
Claybanks UMC: 117 S Division, Whitehall MI 49461

CYPRET, CORI LYNN (PE) – (R-2012, PE-2012)
Coopersville 2012
(H) 422 Harrison St., Coopersville, MI 49404 (616) 384-3210
Coopersville UMC: 105 68th Ave N, Coopersville MI 49404-9704 (616) 997-9225

***DALTON, BILLIE R. (RE) (Georgia) – (R-1985, D-1985, E-1989)**
[Pompeii/Perrinton/Newark, Sept. 1965; Mt. Pleasant First (Assoc) 1970;] In School: Perkins School of Theology, SMU 1985; Lawton/Almena 1987; South Haven First 1995; Kalamazoo Sunnyside (LTFT 3/4) 2004; Kalamazoo Sunnyside (Full-Time) 2006; (LTFT 3/4) 2007; Battle Creek First, March 1, 2009; Retired Sept. 1, 2013; Battle Creek First (Ret.) (LTFT 1/2), Sept. 1, 2013-Mar. 4, 2014
(H) 32757 Walden Way, Paw Paw, MI 49079 (269) 964-4362

DAMKOEHLER, PAUL A. (FL) (Paula)
Webberville Jan 1, 2008; United Church of Ovid 2013
(H) 141 W Front St, Ovid, MI 48866-9601 (989) 307-5104
Ovid: United Church: 131 West Front Street, PO Box 106, Ovid MI 48866 (989) 834-5958

***DANIEL, REVA HAWKE (RE) (Jerry) – (R-1988, D-1987, E-1990)**
Pokagon (PTLP) 1984; Transferred from Detroit Conf, Three Rivers: Ninth Street/Jones 1988; Leslie/Felt Plains (FE) Oct. 1, 1991; Baldwin/Luther May 1, 1993; Jonesville/Allen 1995; West Mendon 1997; Hopkins/South Monterey 2001; Retired 2005
(H) 1140 138th Ave, Wayland, MI 49348 (616) 550-2645

DAVENPORT, THOMAS A. (FE) (Elyse Connors) – (R-2004, E-1991)
[Detroit Conf: Provisional 1987, Full Elder 1991, Wellsville, Blissfield: Emmanuel (Assoc) 1989; Pontiac St. James, Sept 1990; Manchester 1994; Protestant Chaplain, Syracuse University (Para. 335.1A), Jan 1, 1999] Director, WMU Wesley Foundation 2002; Bangor Simpson (WMC) 2007; Transferred from Detroit Conf 2011
(H) 1227 Grand Ave, Kalamazoo, MI 49006-3254 (269) 353-9711
Bangor Simpson UMC: 507 Joy St., Bangor MI 49013-1123 (269) 427-7725

DAVIS JR, CORNELIUS N. (FE) (Lela Brown-Davis) – (R-2002, E-2005)
Grand Rapids: Plainfield 1999; Lansing: Faith Connections (New Church Start) 2002; 1/4 Lansing: Faith Connections, 3/4 Lansing: New Church Start 2003; Faith UMC/South Lansing Ministries 2005; Kalamazoo District Superintendent 2008; serving in Detroit Conference, Southfield Hope 2014
(H) 29274 Glen Oaks Blvd W, Farmington Hills, MI 48334-2932 (248) 862-5086
(O) Southfield Hope UMC, 26275 Northwestern Hwy, Southfield, MI 48076 (248) 356-1020

DEBOW, MARTIN M. (FE) (Cynthia) – (R-1985, D-1985, E-1988)
In School Asbury 1985; Grovenburg 1986; Coopersville 1990; Robbins 1997; Lansing Asbury 2008; Eaton Rapids First 2014
(H) 702 State St, Eaton Rapids, MI 48823 (517) 663-8256
Eaton Rapids First UMC: 600 S Main St, Eaton Rapids MI 48827-1426 (517) 663-3524

DELONG, KIMBERLY A. (FD) (Cameron) – (R-2009, FD-2012)
Grand Rapids First (Deacon - Director of Education) (LTFT 1/2) 2009; Turk Lake/Belding (LTFT 1/2) Aug. 15, 2012; Greenville First, Turk Lake/Belding Cooperative Parish (Deacon) (LTFT 1/2) 2013
(H) 4934 Brownstone Dr NE, Rockford, MI 49341 (616) 866-3191
Greenville First UMC: 204 W. Cass Street, Greenville MI 48838 (616) 754-8532
Turk Lake UMC: 8900 W. Colby Road, Greenville MI 48838 (616) 754-3718
Belding UMC: 301 South Pleasant, Belding MI 48809 (616) 794-1244

***DEMOSS, LYNN A. (RE) (Kay) – (R-1961, D-1961, E-1963)**
Coleman/North Bradley 1963; Fremont 1966; Albion 1969; Muskegon: Central 1979; Grand Rapids: First April 16, 1988; Lansing: Central 1993; Retired 1997
(H) 2006 Mills Ave, North Muskegon, MI 49445 (231) 744-0336

DEMOSS, MARIEL KAY (FD) (Lynn) – (Consecrated 1985, R-1997, FD-1997)
Coordinator of Education and Lay Development, Kalamazoo First 1985; Editor-Publisher, Michigan Christian Advocate 1987; Editor/Publisher, Blodgett Press 1995; Mission to Area People, Coordinator of Volunteers, Muskegon Heights 1997; Editor/Publisher, Blodgett Press 1998; Editor/Publisher, Blodgett Press (LTFT 1/2) and Minister of Education, Muskegon Central (LTFT 1/2) Jan 1, 2003; Minister of Adult Education, Muskegon Central (LTFT 1/4) and Conference Secretary of Global Ministries (LTFT 1/4) (Para. 331.6) 2005; Minister of Discipleship, Muskegon Central (LTFT 1/2) July 1, 2009; Minister of Discipleship, Muskegon Central (LTFT 1/2) and Web Editor, West Michigan Conference, (LTFT 1/4) 2012; Minister of Discipleship, Muskegon Central (LTFT 1/4) and Michigan Area Communications Team (LTFT 1/2) 2013
(H) 2006 Mills Ave, North Muskegon, MI 49445 (231) 744-0336
(O) Muskegon Central UMC: 1011 Second Street, Muskegon MI 49440 (231) 722-6545

***DEPPE, ISABELL M. (RE) – (R-1990, D-1984, E-1992)**
Transferred from New York Conf., Center Eaton/Brookfield 1990; Lansing: Potter Park 1991-Dec. 31, 1997; Sabbatical Leave (para. 349), Jan. 1, 1998-June 30, 1998; Vicksburg 1998.; Involuntary Retired Sept. 2000
(H) 11492 Fordyce Rd, Farwell, MI 48622 (989) 588-3467

***DIBBET, JAMES A. (RE) (Gloria) – (R-2001, E-2004)**
St. Johns Salem/Greenbush/Lowe 1999; Sodus Chapel Hill 2005; Retired 2011
(H) 220 Whitetail Dr, Prudenville, MI 48651 (989) 400-2055

***DIMMICK JR, VANCE M. (RE) (Ann) – (R-1958, E-1966)**
Transferred from Central Pennsylvania Conf, Weidman 1977; Grand Rapids Northlawn 1984; Retired 1992; Snow (DSA) 2008-2009; Parmelee (LTFT 1/4) (DSA) Nov. 28, 2010-Nov. 5, 2012
(H) 944 Grindle Dr, Lowell, MI 49331 (616) 897-5326

DOBBS, DEANN J. (FE) – (R-2009, E-2012)
[Dansville/Vantown (DSA) Sept 1, 1994] Dansville/Vantown 1995; Country Chapel/Banfield 1996; Country Chapel Feb 14, 1999; Williamston: Crossroads Aug 1, 2002; Williamston: Crossroads (3/4 Time), Feb 1, 2007; Williamston: Crossroads (Full-Time), Nov 16, 2007; Reading 2008; Indian River 2012; Grand Rapids Genesis 2014
(H) 832 Firwood Dr, Middleville, MI 49333 (616) 916-2684
Grand Rapids Genesis UMC: 1601 Galbraith Ave SE Ste 304,
Grand Rapids MI 49546-6479 (616) 974-0400

DOBBS, WILLIAM D. (AF) (Janice) – (R-1973, D-1973, E-1978)
[West Mendon (DSA) 1972;] West Mendon 1973; Lansing Calvary 1978; Ludington United 1983; East Lansing University 1991; Holland First 1996; Central District Superintendent 2005 [Central District Renamed Heartland District 2009]; Clergy Assistant to the Bishop, MI Episcopal Area 2010; Transferred to Detroit Conference 2013
(H) PO Box 546, Mt Pleasant, MI 48804 (517) 898-9791
(O) Michigan Area Episcopal Office, MI Area Episcopal Office, 1011 Northcrest Road,
Lansing, MI 48906 (517) 347-4030

***DOUBBLESTEIN, WILLIAM H. (RE) (Karen) – (R-1978, D-1978, E-1982)**
[Grandville (Assoc.) 1974-Aug. 1977]; In School 1978; Galien/Olive Branch 1980; Springport/Lee Center Oct 16, 1983; Byron Center 1987; Dowagiac: First 2004; Retired 2006
(H) 3350 100th St, Byron Center, MI 49315 (616) 583-9047

DOUGLAS, SANDRA V. (FD) – (R-2008, FD-2011)
Benton Harbor Peace Temple (1/4 Time) (Deacon) and Executive Director, Harbor Harvest Urban Ministries, 2008; Executive Director, Harbor Harvest Urban Ministries (LTFT 3/4) and Washington Heights (Interim LTFT 1/4) 2009; Executive Director, Harbor Harvest Urban Ministries (LTFT 3/4) and Kalamazoo Westwood (LTFT 1/4) 2011; Kalamazoo Westwood (Deacon) (LTFT 1/4) Jan 1, 2012; Guardian Finance and Advocacy Services, Representative Payee (LTFT 3/4) (Para. 331.6) and Kalamazoo Westwood (Deacon) (LTFT 1/4) 2012
(H) 2021 March St, Kalamazoo, MI 49001-3957 (269) 369-8803
(O) Guardian Finance and Advocacy Services, 420 E Alcott St, Kalamazoo, MI 49001 (269) 344-0688 ext465
Kalamazoo Westwood UMC: 538 Nichols Road, Kalamazoo MI 49006-2994 (269) 344-7165

***DRYER, DAVID L. (RE) (Tudie) – (R-1963, D-1963, E-1966)**
Osseo Charge 1963; Mendon 1966; Pine River Parish April 1968; Dansville/Vantown 1974; Hesperia/Ferry 1980; Lake City 1985; Battle Creek: Trinity 1996; Retired 2006; Battle Creek Birchwood Jan 1-June 30, 2007
(H) 2150 Gethings Road, Battle Creek, MI 49015-9607 (269) 441-0456

***DUFFEY, PAULA JANE (RE) (Richard) – (R-1992, D-1992, E-1994)**
Howard City: Maple Hill (PTLP) Nov. 1, 1980-1988; Winn/Blanchard/Pine River/Coomer (FTLP) 1990; Blanchard/Pine River/Coomer (LTFT 3/4) 1994; Blanchard/Pine River/Coomer 1996; Lansing: Calvary 1998; Retired 2005
(H) 13599 Deaner Rd, Howard City, MI 49329 (231) 762-4473

***DUNCAN, DANIEL M. (RE) (Mary Whittaker) – (R-1986, D-1983, E-1988)**
Transferred from Detroit Conf, Snow/Vergennes 1986; Muskegon Central (Assoc) 1989; Fremont 1994; Grand Haven 2003; Retired 2014
(H) 909 Warren Place, Kalamazoo, MI 49006 (616) 502-5092

DYE, MONA J. (FL) (William)
Fountain (PTLP) Dec 1, 2007; Fountain/Free Soil (PTLP) 2009; Ashley/Bannister/Greenbush 2011
(H) 307 N Farr St, PO Box 7, Ashley, MI 48806 (989) 847-2305
Ashley UMC: PO Box 7, Ashley MI 48806 (989) 862-4392
Bannister UMC: 103 Hanvey St., Bannister MI 48807 (989) 862-4392
Greenbush UMC: PO Box 7, Ashley MI 48806 (989) 429-1892

DYE, WILLIAM F. (PL) (Mona)
Empire Feb 1, 2003; Bear Lake/Arcadia 2006; Fenwick/Palo/Vickeryville (PTLP 1/4) 2011; Pompeii/Perrinton/Middleton/North Star (PTLP 3/4) July 15, 2012
(H) 307 N Farr St, PO Box 7, Ashley, MI 48806 (989) 847-2305
Pompeii UMC: PO Box 125, Pompeii MI 48874 (989) 838-4159
Perrinton UMC: PO Box 125, Pompeii MI 48874 (989) 236-5398
Middleton & North Star UMCs: PO Box 125, Pompeii MI 48874

ECKERT, ROBERT W. (PL) (Mary)
Grand Rapids Olivet 2001; LP w/o Appointment, March 1, 2005; Wyoming Park (Assoc.) (PTLP 1/4), April 1, 2006; Church of All Nations (PTLP) 2008; LP w/o Appointment 2009; Courtland-Oakfield (PTLP 3/4) 2011
(H) 9777 Myers Lake Ave NE, Rockford, MI 49341-9508 (616) 291-7093
Courtland-Oakfield UMC: 10295 Myers Lake Ave NE, Rockford MI 49341-9511 (616) 866-4298

ELDERS, MARCIA L. (OF) (David)
[Reformed Church of America] Wyoming: South Wyoming (LTFT 1/4) 2003; Wyoming: South Wyoming (LTFT 1/2) Oct. 1, 2006; Wyoming: South Wyoming (LTFT 3/4) Jan. 1, 2009
(H) 3246 Wayburn Ave SW, Grandville, MI 49418-1913 (616) 292-6712
South Wyoming UMC: 2730 56th St SW, Wyoming MI 49418 (616) 532-0131

***ELDRED, ELDON K. (RE) (Rhea) – (R-1966, D-1966, E-1968)**
[Perrinton/Pompeii Charge 1963; In School, 1965]; N Georgia Conf, Senoia (Assoc.) 1966; Farwell Dec. 1967; Edmore 1969; Sparta 1973; Fremont Mar 1, 1979; Albion District Superintendent Mar 1, 1987; Grand Haven 1992; Retired 2003
(H) 130 Woodslee Court, Muskegon, MI 49444-7795 (616) 402-3169

***ELENBAAS, JOE D. (RE) (Mary) – (E-1988)**
[Minnesota Conf., Burnsville: River Hills UMC: Burnsville, MN;] Transfered from Minnesota Conf., Ludington: United 2000; Incapacity Leave Nov. 30, 2006; Retired 2010
(H) 7999 W Falmouth Rd, McBain, MI 49657 (231) 233-5193

***ELLINGER, JOHN W. (RE) (Sally) – (R-1968, D-1968, E-1971)**
[New York Conf.: Community, Poughkeepsie, NY 1970;] Transferred from New York Conf., Jackson First (Assoc.) Jan. 15, 1972; Kalamazoo: Sunnyside 1976; Lansing: Grace 1981; Albion: First 1985; Holland 1990; Lansing District Superintendent 1996; Traverse City: Central 2002; Retired 2007; Traverse City Christ (DSA) Dec. 1, 2009-June 1, 2010
(H) 1819 Timberlane Dr, Traverse City, MI 49686 (231) 631-9237

***ELLINWOOD, CHARLES R. (AF)**
[North Indiana Conference, Retired]
(H) 8924 Cherry Ave, PO Box 222, Kewadin, MI 49648-0222 (231) 264-8469

ELMORE, DAVID G. (OE) (Julie) – (R-2013)
[Alaska Missionary Conference - Pacific Northwest, Elder] Concord 2013
(H) 229 W Center St, PO Box 392, Concord, MI 49237 (517) 524-6111
Concord UMC: 119 S. Main St., PO Box 366, Concord MI 49237 (517) 524-6156

ELMORE, JULIE YODER (OE) (David G.) – (R-2013)
(Formerly Julie Yoder) [Alaska Missionary Conference - Pacific Northwest, FE] LP w/o Appointment 2002; transferred to Alaska Missionary Conf 2008; Litchfield/Quincy 2013
(H) 969 Adams St, Litchfield, MI 49252-9779 (517) 542-3775
Litchfield UMC: 160 Marshall St, PO Box 472, Litchfield MI 49252-0472 (517) 542-3366
Quincy UMC: 32 W. Chicago St., Quincy MI 49082 (517) 639-5035

ERBES, MARK R. (FE) (Annette) – (R-1996, D-1996, E-2000)
In School 1996; Faith Community (Assoc), Xenia OH, West Ohio Conf 1996 (Para. 426.1, Book of Discipline 1992); Mt Pleasant: First (Assoc) 1997; Constantine 2001; Muskegon Lake Harbor 2007; Holt 2014
(H) 1951 Heatherton Dr, Holt, MI 48842 (517) 649-8277
Holt UMC: PO Box 168, Holt MI 48842-0168 (517) 694-8168

***ERICKSON, RICHARD R. (RE) (Jayne) – (R-1969, D-1969, E-1973)**
In School 1969; Woodland 1972; Woodland/Welcome Corners 1975; Jackson First (Assoc) 1976; Manistee 1982; Director, Wesley Foundation, Michigan State University 1990; Retired 2006
(H) 819 Crown Blvd, East Lansing, MI 48823-1341 (517) 351-3241

***EVANS, THOMAS J. (RE) (Judy) – (R-1974, D-1974, E-1977)**
In school 1974; Comstock/Portage (Assoc.) 1976; Comstock Oct. 1, 1980; Leland/Kewsick 1984; Leland 1988; Eaton Rapids Feb. 1, 1994; Ludington 2007; Retired 2013
(H) 8630 Lake Drive, Springport, MI 49284

FANCHER, NANCY V. (PD) – (R-2013, PE-2013)
Peace (DSA) March 16, 2005; Peace (PTLP) Nov 15, 2005; LP w/o Appointment, March 31, 2006
(H) 1317 W Saginaw St, Lansing, MI 48915-1957 (517) 371-3311

FARMER-LEWIS, LINDA J. (OE) (Bill) – (R-2011)
[Transfer to Wisconsin Conf 2003; Kenosha First 2003] Leland (Para. 346.1) 2011; Lansing Central 2013
(H) 14 Hidden Ridge Trail, Jackson, MI 49203 (517) 783-9003
Lansing Central UMC: 215 N Capitol Ave, Lansing MI 48933-1372 (517) 485-9477

FARNUM, CHARLES D. (FE) (Kendall) – (R-1997, D-1997, E-2002)
Middleton/Maple Rapids 1997; Battle Creek: Maple 2001; Leave of Absence July 1-16, 2006; CMU Wesley Foundation (LTFT 1/2) and Mt. Pleasant First (Assoc) (LTFT 1/2) July 16, 2006; CMU Wesley Foundation (LTFT 3/4) 2007; CMU Wesley Foundation (Full-Time) Jan. 1, 2008; CMU Wesley Foundation (LTFT 1/4) Jan. 1, 2014
(H) 1160 Glen Ave, Mt Pleasant, MI 48858 (989) 545-1761
(O) Wesley Foundation - Central Michigan University, 1400 S Washington St, Mt Pleasant, MI 48858 (989) 545-1761

***FAUST, ELMER J. (RE) (Wilma) – (R-1966, D-1961, E-1963)**
[Eddyville/Kirkville Charge, So. Iowa Conf. 1954; Mich. Conf.: Blanchard Charge 1955; Ferry/Hesperia 1959]; Dunaway Church, Kentucky Conf. 1963; In school 1965; Empire/Leland 1966; Charlevoix/ Greensky Hill Indian Mission 1969; Delton Faith 1975; Retired 1990
(H) 640 S Grove, Delton, MI 49046 (269) 623-5520

FAY, BARBARA (AM) (Fred) – (R-2009, AM-2009)
Ganges (FTLP) 1997; LP w/o Appointment, 12-31-04; Plainwell (Assoc) (PTLP) 2007; Frankfort/Elberta 2010
(H) 320 Maple Street, Frankfort, MI 49635 (231) 352-4724
Frankfort UMC: 537 Crystal Ave, PO Box 1010, Frankfort MI 49635 (231) 352-7427
Elberta UMC: PO Box 405, Elberta MI 49628 (231) 352-4311

FEIGHNER, BRYCE E. (FE) (Eileen) – (R-2007, E-2013)
Kalamo (1/4 Time) 2004; Kalamo (LTFT 1/2), Jan 1, 2007; Kalamo (LTFT 1/4) and Quimby (LTFT 1/4) 2011; Barry-Eaton Cooperative Ministry: Gresham (LTFT 1/2) 2013
(H) 220 N Chester Rd, Charlotte, MI 48813-9547 (517) 541-9605
Gresham UMC: 4800 Lamie Highway, Charlotte MI 48813 (517) 652-1580

FERRIS-MCCANN, DONALD R. (FE) (Lisa) – (R-1983, D-1983, E-1986)
In school G-ETS 1983; Mason (Assoc.) 1984; Frankfort/Elberta April 1, 1989; Cassopolis 1993; Lake Odessa: Central 2000; Battle Creek First 2007; Incapacity Leave Feb. 1, 2009; Elsie (LTFT 3/4) 2013; Elsie/Salem May 1, 2014
(H) 156 W Main St, Elsie, MI 48831 (989) 862-5780
Elsie UMC: PO Box 189, Elsie MI 48831-0189 (989) 862-5239
Salem UMC: 2307 W Maple Rapids Rd, St. Johns MI 48879

***FIELD, RAYMOND D. (RE) – (R-1990, D-1980, E-1986)**
[Detroit Conf.: Norway Grace/Faithhorn 1983; Vernon/Bancroft 1985; West Mich. Conf.: Eagle (LTFT 1/4) 1988; Eagle (LTFT 1/2) 1989;] Transferred from Detroit Conf. 1990; Eagle (LTFT 1/4) 1990; Bath/Gunnisonville 1993; Hesperia/Ferry 1998; Hopkins/South Monterey 1999; Hersey 2001; Retired May 1, 2003
(H) 526 Togstad Glen, Madison, WI 53711-1425 (608) 238-8571

***FILBRANDT, HAROLD F. (RE) (Marian) – (R-1959, D-1959, E-1962)**
[Twelve Corners Church 1950; Lacota/Casco 1955]; Gobles/Kendall 1959; Frankfort Dec. 1964; Ludington: First 1967; Marshall 1974; St. Joseph: First Feb. 16, 1983; Holland April 1, 1987; Fremont 1990; Retired 1994; Glenn (Ret.) (LTFT 1/4) 2014
(H) 77020 County Road 380, South Haven, MI 49090 (269) 637-3087
Glenn UMC: PO Box 46, Glenn MI 49416 (269) 227-3930

***FINKBEINER, STANLEY A. (RA) (Betty) – (D-1974)**
Hopkins/South Monterey Feb. 1970; Kent City: Chapel Hill 1974; Edmore 1981; Portland Feb. 16, 1987; Grand Rapids: Northlawn 1992; Retired 1996
(H) 1551 Franklin St SE Apt 2017, Grand Rapids, MI 49506-3337 (616) 245-1006
(S) 529 Tina St, Inverness, FL 34452-4562 (352) 860-1397

***FISCHER, FREDERICK H. (RE) – (R-1958, E-1961)**
Suttons Bay (EUB) 1958; Howard City: Maple Hill (EUB) 1962; Berrien Springs/Arden (EUB) May 1965; Rosebush/Leaton Jan. 1, 1970; Leave of absence 1978; Williamston Center/Wheatfield; July 1, 1980; Elsie/Duplain 1985; Elsie Jan. 1, 1990; Retired 1996
(H) 3123 E. Grand River Rd., Williamston, MI 48895-9161 (517) 655-4896

***FISHER, JOHN W. (RE) (Corinne) – (R-1975, D-1975, E-1980)**
In school 1975; Niles: Wesley (Assoc.) 1977; Schoolcraft/Pleasant Valley 1978; Casco 1980; North Muskegon 1986; Kalamazoo: Sunnyside 1992; South Haven: First 2004; Retirement 2013; Oshtemo (Ret.) (LTFT 1/2) 2013
(H) 3506 East Shore Dr, Portage, MI 49002 (269) 327-3277
Oshtemo UMC: 6574 Stadium Dr, PO Box 12, Oshtemo MI 49077-0012 (269) 375-5656

FITZGERALD, ERIN B. (PE) (Joel) – (R-2012, PE-2012)
(Formerly Erin Brodhagen) Grand Rapids St. Paul's 2012
(H) 2716 Byron Center Rd SW, Wyoming, MI 49519 (616) 510-7941
Grand Rapids St Paul's UMC: 3334 Breton Rd. SE, Grand Rapids MI 49512-2798 (616) 949-0880

FITZGERALD, JOEL T. (FL) (Erin Lea)
Wyoming Park 2012
(H) 2716 Byron Center Ave SW, Wyoming, MI 49519-2118 (616) 848-9759
Wyoming Park UMC: 2244 Porter St. SW, Wyoming MI 49519 (616) 532-7624

***FLAGEL, DAVID L. (RE) (Rebecca) – (R-1975, D-1975, E-1977)**
In School 1975; North Adams/Jerome Sept 1, 1975; Coopersville 1980; Ionia Parish LeValley/Berlin Center March 1, 1989; Lake Odessa Lakewood 2003; Retired 2013
(H) 13566 Hill Country Drive SE, Lowell, MI 49331 (616) 821-7743

***FLEMING, GEORGE W. (RE) (Edna) – (R-1963, E-1965)**
Turk Lake (EUB)/Greenville (Assoc.) 1965; Sodus: Chapel Hill Aug. 1, 1975; Charlotte 1987; Retired 2002
(H) 793 68th St, South Haven, MI 49090 (269) 637-4406

FLESSNER, JODIE R. (FE) – (R-1993, D-1993, E-1997)
In School United 1993; Pompeii/Perrinton/North Star 1994; Pompeii/Perrinton/North Star/Christian Crossroads Cooperative Parish 2001; Pine River Parish: LeRoy/Ashton 2003; Caledonia 2012
(H) 260 Vine St, Caledonia, MI 49316 (616) 891-8167
Caledonia UMC: 250 Vine St, Caledonia MI 49316 (616) 891-8669

***FLORY, BARBARA J. (RE) (Robert) – (R-1989, D-1989, E-1992)**
In School Asbury Theological Seminary 1989; Concord Jan 1, 1990; Holt (Assoc.)/Alaiedon Township New Church Start 1998; Lansing Sycamore Creek 2000; New Church Development (LTFT 1/2) 2009; Retired 2011
(H) 4517 Weswilmar Dr, Holt, MI 48842 (517) 694-7114

***FLOYD, CAROLYN (RE) – (R-1992, D-1992, E-1995)**
West Mendon 1990-1997; Mancelona/Alba 1997; St. Johns: First 2000; Perry/Shaftsburg 2003; Retired 2008; Detroit Conference, Algonac Trinity and Marine City (Ret.) (LTFT 1/2) 2013; Algonac Trinity (Ret.) (LTFT 1/2) Feb. 1-July 1, 2014
(H) 3437 Gratiot Ave, Port Huron, MI 48060-2244 (810) 982-1629

FONS, VALERIE (FE) (Joseph Ervin) – (R-1998, D-1998, E-2002)
Bell Oak/Webberville 1995; Galien/Olive Branch 1999; Pokagon (LTFT 1/2) 2001; Family Leave 2003; Bread and Water, LLC and L.A.U.N.C.H., Wisconsin Conf (para. 344.1.d), Oct 1, 2009
(H) 1349 Main Rd, Washington Island, WI 54246-9010 (920) 847-2393
(O) Bread and Water, LLC and L.A.U.N.C.H. (Wisconsin), 1275 Main Rd, Washington Island, WI 54246 (920) 847-2400

FOSTER, RICHARD J. (FL) (Renee)
Williamston Crossroads (DSA) (1/4 Time) Aug. 1, 2012; Williamston Crossroads (PTLP 1/4) Nov. 10, 2012; M-52 Cooperative Ministry: Webberville (PTLP 3/4) and Williamston Crossroads (PTLP 1/4) 2013
(H) 120 E Beech St, Webberville, MI 48892-9702 (517) 521-3434
Webberville UMC: 4215 E Holt Rd, Webberville MI 48892-8208 (517) 521-3631
Williamston Crossroads UMC: 5491 N Zimmer Rd, Williamston MI 48895-9181 (517) 655-1466

***FOX, JAMES E. (RE) (Helen) – (R-1965, D-1965, E-1968)**
[Leaton Community 1961; Rosebush/Center 1962; Grand Rapids Epworth/Westgate 1964]; Lansing Trinity 1968; Shelby Nov 15, 1971; Wyoming Wesley Park Sept 1, 1977; Three River First May 1, 1985; Fennville/Pearl 1990; Hastings Hope 1992; Retired 1995; Woodland (DSA) July 22, 2008-2011
(H) 1112 N Hanover St, Hastings, MI 49058 (269) 945-0190

***FOX, THOMAS P. (RE) (Kathleen) – (R-1986, D-1986, E-1992)**
Mesick/Harrietta 1986; Reading 1992; Portage: Prairie (Full-Time) 1999; Portage: Prairie (LTFT 3/4), Jan 1, 2008; Homer/Lyon Lake 2008; Retired 2012
(H) 1626 Lake Dr Apt 189, Haslett, MI 48840

***FRANKE, RAE L. (RD) (Charles) – (Consecrated 1980, R-1998, FD-1998)**
Lansing: Trinity (Deacon) 1998; Voluntary Leave of Absence January 1, 2003; Retired January 1, 2004
(H) 2555 Amelia Lane, Lansing, MI 48917 (517) 322-0484

***FRENCH, LILLIAN T. (RE) (Michael) – (R-2002, E-2005)**
Attending School; Dimondale Nov 16, 1999; St. Louis 2002; Jackson Calvary Jan 1, 2008; Retired Sept 1, 2010
(H) 4151 Lancashire Dr, Jackson, MI 49203 (517) 990-0395

FREYSINGER, ROBERT J. (FE) (Marion Robin) – (R-1981, D-1981, E-1985)
In School METHESCO 1981; Center Eaton/Brookfield Oct 16, 1982; Kalamazoo Lane Blvd 1985; Napoleon 1988; Millville 2004; Millville (LTFT 3/4) and Stockbridge (LTFT 1/4) 2011; Kalkaska 2013
(H) 2301 Shawn Rd NW, Kalkaska, MI 49646 (231) 258-5995
Kalkaska UMC: 2525 Beebe Rd, Kalkaska MI 49646 (231) 258-2820

FRIEDRICK, PHILLIP J. (FE) (Gail) – (R-1984, D-1984, E-1988)
In School Perkins School of Theology 1984; Highland Park (Assoc), Dallas, TX 1984-1985; Galien/Olive Branch 1986; Battle Creek: Birchwood 1991; Alma 1995; North Muskegon Community July 15, 2012
(H) 2317 Marquard St, Muskegon, MI 49445 (231) 744-1443
North Muskegon Community UMC: 1614 Ruddiman, North Muskegon MI 49445 (231) 744-4491

***FRY, CHARLES EARL (RE) (Betty Jean) – (R-1951, D-1953, E-1955)**
[Scotts 1949]; Scotts/Climax 1951; Decatur 1953; Benton Harbor (Assoc.) Sept. 1956; Grand Rapids: Aldersgate 1959; Kalamazoo: Parchment 1964; Conf. Assoc. Program Director 1968; Battle Creek: First Jan. 15, 1973; Central District Supt. 1978; Grand Rapids: Trinity 1984; Retired 1989
(H) 4253 Embassy Dr SE, Grand Rapids, MI 49546 (616) 956-5653

***FRY, DONALD R. (RE) (Anna) – (R-1967, D-1967, E-1970)**
Waterloo Village/First 1969; Sonoma/Newton 1970; Ionia Parish 1971; Marne 1973; White Pigeon Nov 22, 1977; Marion/Cadillac South Community 1981; Newaygo 1994; Three Rivers First 2000; Ovid United 2006; Retired 2008; Dansville (DSA) (LTFT 1/4) 2008-2011
(H) 12283 Balsam Ave, Sand Lake, MI 49343-9606 (616) 577-3577

***FULLMER, CHARLES W. (RE) (Margaret) – (R-1956, D-1957, E-1959)**
Lyon Lake/Marengo Fall 1956; Lyon Lake 1957; Kalamazoo: First (Asst.) 1959; Grand Rapids: Valley 1962; Reed City 1966; Ionia: First 1970; Grandville 1977; Petoskey 1986; Chaplain, Clark Retirement Community March 1, 1994; Retired 1997; Amble (DSA) Aug. 1, 1999
(H) 733 Clark Crossing, Grand Rapids, MI 49506 (989) 352-7002
(S) 702 S Meridian #763, Apache Junction, AZ 85120

***GARROD, CHARLES F. (RE) – (R-1957, D-1957, E-1960)**
[Lawton/Porter 1955]; Kalamazoo: Simpson 1962; St. Louis Jan. 1, 1967; Grand Haven 1972; Grand Rapids: Trinity 1978; Central District Supt. 1984; Lansing: Asbury 1990; Grand Rapids District Supt. Oct. 1, 1992; Retired 1995
(H) Apt. 1020, 1551 Franklin Street SE, Grand Rapids, MI 49506-3337 (616) 456-6985

GOLDEN, DALE A. (FE) (Joleen) – (R-2005, E-2011)
Blanchard/Pine River/Coomer (DSA) 1998; Blanchard/Pine River/Coomer Nov 16, 1998; Breckenridge 2005-2013; Leave of Absence 2013; Florida-Southeast Conf, Homestead 2014
(H) 4331 Watkins Lane, Lakeland, FL 33813 (989) 330-1932
(O) Homestead UMC, 622 N Krome Ave, Homestead, FL 33030 (305) 248-4770

GORDON, BRENDA E. (FE) – (R-2000, D-2000, E-2007)
In School; Hinchman/Oronoko 2000; Empire 2006; Berrien Springs/Pokagon 2014
(H) 10 S 10th St, Niles, MI 49120 (231) 631-1055
Berrien Springs UMC: 310 West Mars, Berrien Springs MI 49103 (269) 471-7220
Pokagon UMC: 31393 Kansas St, Dowagiac MI 49047-9708 (269) 683-8515

GORDON, DIANE (FE) (Tom) – (R-2004, E-2007)
Ashley/Bannister 2003; Battle Creek Trinity 2006; Muskegon Central 2010; Mt. Pleasant First 2013
(H) 1109 Glenwood Dr, Mt. Pleasant, MI 48858 (231) 457-3744
Mt Pleasant First UMC: 400 S. Main Street, Mount Pleasant MI 48858 (989) 773-6934

***GORDON, LINDA R. (OR) (Bruce)**
[Illinois Great Rivers Conference, Retired AM 2011] Hinchman/Oronoko (Ret.) (LTFT 1/2) 2014
(H) 116 S Detroit St, Buchanan, MI 49107 (269) 815-6094
Hinchman & Oronoko UMCs: 8154 Church St, Berrien Springs MI 49103 (269) 471-5492

GORDY, SAMUEL C. (PL) (Elizabeth)
Morris Chapel (PTLP 1/4) March 11, 2012; Northwest (PTLP 1/4) 2013
(H) 35795 Riverview Dr, Paw Paw, MI 49079-9670 (269) 657-6410
Northwest UMC: 3140 N 3rd Street, Kalamazoo MI 49009 (269) 290-1312

GRAHAM, DONALD J. (FL) (Judy)
Ionia: Zion 2001; Colon/Burr Oak 2007; Martin/Shelbyville 2012; Muskegon Lakeside 2014
(H) 3951 Grand Haven Rd, Norton Shores, MI 49441 (269) 503-0354
Muskegon Lakeside UMC: 2160 Crozier Ave, Muskegon MI 49441 (231) 759-7850

GRANADA, LEMUEL O. (PL) (Colleen)
Fountain (DSA) 2002; Fountain Nov 15, 2002; Brethren Epworth 2003; Fountain 2005; LP w/o Appointment, Nov 30, 2007; Hersey (PTLP 1/4) July 29, 2012
(H) 351 2nd St, Manistee, MI 49660-1747 (231) 723-2763
Hersey UMC: 200 W. Second Street, PO Box 85, Hersey MI 49639 (231) 832-5168

***GRANT, JAMES C. (RE) – (R-1957, D-1958, E-1959)**
Alema/Glendale 1957; Dowagiac 1960; Grand Rapids: Second 1966; Kalamazoo: Oakwood 1972; Byron Center Mar. 1, 1975; Otsego 1985; Leave of absence March 6, 1992; Otsego Aug. 1, 1992; Marion/ Cadillac: South Community 1994; Retired June 23, 1999
(H) 1029 Wedgewood Drive, Plainwell, MI 49080 (269) 685-0079

***GRANT, RONALD B. (RE) (Carol) – (R-1973, D-1973, E-1976)**
In School 1973; Concord 1975; Director, Wesley Foundation, Western Michigan University 1982; Leave of Absence Aug 15, 1992; In School, Western Michigan University 1994; Limited Licensed Psychologist Feb 1, 1995; Retired Nov. 1, 2012
(H) 3716 Edinburgh Dr, Kalamazoo, MI 49006 (269) 375-0321

***GRAYBILL, JOSEPH M. (RE) (Sue) – (R-1982, E-1984)**
[Free Methodist Church: Student Chaplain, Spring Arbor College 1969; Parkway Heights Free Methodist, Detroit (Asst) 1970; Pikeville UMC, Pikeville, KY (Assoc.) 1972; Fairplain Free Methodist, Benton Harbor 1975; Dansville/Vantown 1980]; Transferred from Free Methodist Church, Dansville/Vantown 1982; Edmore Faith April 1, 1987; Leland 1997; Retired 2011
(H) 4306 Indian Springs Dr SW, Grandville, MI 49418 (231) 342-2222

GREENE, CYNTHIA S.L. (FE) – (R-1998, D-1993, E-1995)
[W North Carolina Conf, Shooting Creek UMC, Hayesville, NC, 1984; Cherry Street UMC, Kernersville, NC, 1986; Mindanao Conf, GBGM Missionary (Evangelism and Christian Education), Philippines, 1987; W Ohio Conf, Castine/Savona UMC, Castine, OH, 1991; Oregon-Idaho Conf, Cherry Park, Portand, Oregon, April 30, 1998] Transferred from Oregon-Idaho Conf: Lansing Trinity (Assoc) May 1, 1998; Byron Center 2003; Ithaca/Beebe 2010
(H) 601 N Union St, Ithaca, MI 48847 (989) 875-3086
Ithaca &Beebe UMCs: 327 E. Center Street, Ithaca MI 48847 (989) 875-4313

***GRETTENBERGER, GEORGE R. (RE) (Diane) – (R-1953, D-1954, E-1955)**
In school 1953; Middleville 1955; transferred to Argentina Annual Conf. 1959; transferred from Argentina Annual Conf. 1965; Lansing: Potter Park 1965; Cadillac Nov. 1967; Cadillac: United 1970; Mason 1980; Jackson: Calvary 1989; Retired 1992
(H) 1931 Osage Dr, Okemos, MI 48864 (517) 347-4604

GRETTENBERGER, LOUIS W. (FE) (Karen) – (R-1987, D-1987, E-1989)
Candler School of Theology; Manton 1987; Manton 1989; Traverse City: Christ 1993; Sparta 2009
(H) 1960 Skyview Dr, Sparta, MI 49345 (616) 887-0783
Sparta UMC: 54 E. Division St., Sparta MI 49345 (616) 887-8255

GREYERBIEHL, JULIE A. (FE) (Bill Chu) – (R-2009, E-2013)
Elk Rapids/Kewadin/Williamsburg (Assoc.) 2005; Elk Rapids/Kewadin/Williamsburg (Co-pastor) 2008; Silver Creek/Keeler 2009; Williamston 2011
(H) 733 Orchard Dr, Williamston, MI 48895 (517) 992-5038
Williamston UMC: 211 S Putnam St, Williamston MI 48895-1309 (517) 655-2430

***GRIENKE, A. RAY (RE) (Beverly) – (R-1969, D-1969, E-1971)**
Transferred from South Indiana Conf., Battle Creek: Sonoma/Newton 1971; Boyne City/Boyne Falls Jan. 15, 1974; Kent City: Chapel Hill 1981; Carson City 1985; Retired Aug. 16, 1999
(H) 1920 Wank Ave, St Joseph, MO 64507 (616) 676-0538

GRIFFIN JR, HERBERT L. (FE) (Ellainia) – (R-1991, D-1991, E-1993)
Battle Creek Washington Heights (Assoc) 1990; US Navy Chaplain 1993
(H) 11334 Village Ridge Rd, San Diego, CA 92131-3900 (858) 397-2532
(O) US Navy, ATTN: Regimental Chaplain, 1st Marine Regiment, 1st Marine Division, Camp Pendleton, CA 92055

***GROFF, KATHLEEN (OR) (Joseph) – (R-2011)**
[Detroit Conf, Retired Elder] Newaygo (Ret.) (LTFT 3/4) 2011; Newaygo (Ret.) (LTFT 45%) Jan. 1, 2014; Newaygo (Ret.) (LTFT 3/4) May 8, 2014
(H) 104 State Rd, PO Box 366, Newaygo, MI 49337 (231) 652-5272
Newaygo UMC: 101 W. State Road, PO Box 366, Newaygo MI 49337 (231) 652-6581

GUETSCHOW, KEVIN K. (FL) (Karen)
Kent City Chapel Hill 2010
(H) 14555 Fruit Ridge Ave, Kent City, MI 49330-9751 (616) 675-7241
Kent City Chapel Hill UMC: 14591 Fruit Ridge Ave NW, Kent City MI 49330 (616) 675-7184

***GYSEL, JAMES M. (RE) (Shari) – (R-1977, D-1977, E-1981)**
In School 1977; Quincy 1979; Lansing Central (Assoc.) 1983; Battle Creek Chapel Hill 1993; Retired 2011; Lee Center (Ret.) (LTFT 1/4) 2014
(H) 3239 Nighthawk Lane, Battle Creek, MI 49015 (269) 979-8192
Lee Center UMC: 22392 24 Mile Road, Olivet MI 49076-9533

HAAS, PATRICIA ANN (FE) – (R-2011, E-2014)
Pokagon (PTLP) 2003; Keswick 2011
(H) 3400 S. Center Hwy, Suttons Bay, MI 49682 (231) 271-4117
Keswick UMC: 3376 S Center Hwy, Suttons Bay MI 49682 (231) 271-3755

HAASE, DAVID L. (PL) (Linda)
Townline (DSA 1/4 Time) and Breedsville (DSA 1/4 Time) Jan 3, 2008; Townline (PTLP 1/4) and Breedsville (PTLP 1/4) 2008; Riverside (Pastor)(PTLP 1/4) and Coloma (Assoc) (PTLP 1/4) 2014
(H) 211 W Saint Joseph St, Watervliet, MI 49098-9214 (269) 463-3536
Coloma UMC: 144 South Church St, PO Box 670, Coloma MI 49038 (269) 468-6062
Riverside UMC: PO Box 152, Riverside MI 49084 (269) 849-1131

HAGAN, SUEANN K. (FL) (Lloyd)
Chase Barton/Grant Center Oct 16, 2003; Battle Creek Convis Union 2006
(H) 12040 N Drive North, Battle Creek, MI 49014-8417 (269) 964-2741
Battle Creek Convis Union UMC: 18990 12 Mile Rd, Battle Creek MI 49014-8496 (269) 965-3787

***HAGANS, GERALD F. (RE) (Susan) – (R-1983, D-1983, E-1986)**
In School United Theological Seminary 1983; Gordon/Pitsburg (West Ohio Conf) 1981-1984; Muskegon: Central (Assoc) 1984; Constantine 1989; Muskegon Heights: Temple August 1, 1991; Retired Sept 1, 2006; Sitka (Ret.) (LTFT 1/4) Nov 15, 2009
(H) 1249 Lakeshore Dr #305, Muskegon, MI 49441 (231) 744-1767
Sitka UMC: 9606 S. Dickinson Rd., Holton MI 49425 (231) 744-1767

***HAGANS, SUSAN J. (RE) (Gerald) – (R-1986, D-1986, E-1989)**
Muskegon Unity (LTFT) 1986; Muskegon Unity 1987; Holland First (Assoc) Nov 15, 1988; Muskegon Lake Harbor 1995; Grand Rapids District Superintendent 2000-2006; Retired 2006
(H) 1249 Lakeshore Dr #305, Muskegon, MI 49441 (231) 744-1767

HAGGARD, WILLIAM E. (FE) (Robin) – (R-1980, D-1980, E-1984)
In School 1980; Lake Ann 1982; Cedar Springs/East Nelson 1989; Traverse City Asbury 1995; Lansing Mt Hope 2002; Grand Rapids District Superintendent 2012
(H) 5576 W Grove Dr SE, Kentwood, MI 49512 (616) 430-9964
(O) Grand Rapids District Office, PO Box 6247, Grand Rapids, MI 49516-6247 (616) 459-4503

HAHN, ANITA K. (FE) (Kevin) – (R-1998, E-2001)
Whitehall/Claybanks 1998; New Life 2006; Grand Traverse District Superintendent 2011
(H) 4505 Stone Ridge Ct, Traverse City, MI 49684 (231) 421-8397
(O) Grand Traverse District Office, 1249 Three Mile Rd S, Traverse City, MI 49696 (231) 947-5281

HALL, NELSON L. (FL) (Sandy)
Baldwin/Luther (DSA) 1999; Baldwin/Luther Nov. 16, 1999; Wakelee 2005; Augusta Fellowship (PTLP 1/2) 2007; Gobles/Kendall 2013
(H) 31880 Jefferson Ave, Gobles, MI 49055-9659 (269) 628-9126
Gobles UMC: 210 E. Exchange St., PO Box 57, Gobles MI 49055 (269) 628-2263
Kendall UMC: PO Box 57, Gobles MI 49055 (269) 628-2263

HALLER, GARY (FE) (Laurie) – (R-1979, D-1979, E-1983)
In school 1979; Traverse City: Central (Assoc.)/Ogdensburg 1981; Traverse City: Central (Assoc.) Jan. 1, 1982; Pentwater: Centenary 1985; Grand Rapids: First (co-pastor) 1993; Detroit Conference, Birmingham First (Senior Pastor) 2013
(H) 1043 Chesterfield Ave, Birmingham, MI 48009 (248) 258-0903
(O) Birmingham: First UMC, 1589 W Maple, Birmingham, MI 48009 (248) 646-1200

HALLER, LAURIE A. (FE) (Gary) – (R-1987, E-1990)
Ogdensburg Jan 1, 1982; Ludington (Assoc) (Part-Time) 1985; Transfered from General Conference Mennonite Church 1987; Hart 1989; Grand Rapids: First (Co-Pastor) 1993; Grand Rapids District Superintendent 2006; Grand Rapids Aldersgate/Plainfield 2012; Detroit Conference, Birmingham First (Senior Pastor) 2013
(H) 1043 Chesterfield Ave, Birmingham, MI 48009 (248) 258-0903
(O) Birmingham: First UMC, 1589 W Maple, Birmingham, MI 48009 (248) 646-1200

***HAMLIN, FREDERICK G. (RE) (Joan) – (R-1982, D-1982, E-1987)**
Benton Harbor Grace 1978; In school GETS Sept. 1982; Watervliet Nov. 20, 1984; Byron Center 1985; Camden/Montgomery/Stokes Chapel 1987; Retired 1994; DSA: Saugatuck 1996-1998
(H) P O Box 458, Douglas, MI 49406 (269) 543-4790

***HAMLIN, JOAN K. (RE) (Fred) – (R-1984, D-1984, E-1987)**
In School, GETS, Sept. 1982; Bridgman (Part-Time) 1983; Burnips/Monterey Center 1985; Quincy 1987; Retired 1994; Saugatuck (DSA) 1996-1998
(H) PO Box 458, Douglas, MI 49406 (269) 543-4790

HANE, PAUL E. (FL) (Julie Spurlin-Hane)
North Adams/Jerome (DSA) 2002; North Adams/Jerome June 1, 2003; Hesperia/Ferry 2011
(H) 231 E South Ave, Hesperia, MI 49421-9105 (231) 854-6132
Hesperia & Ferry UMCs: 187 E. South Ave., Hesperia MI 49421 (231) 854-5345

***HANEY, CLAUDETTE I. KERNS (RE) – (R-1991, D-1991, E-1993)**
Harbor Springs/Alanson 1990; Homer/Lyon Lake April 16, 1993; Lawton/Almena 1995; Lawton 1996; Cassopolis 2000; Retired 2005
(H) 51 Las Yucas, Green Valley, AZ 85614 (520) 829-6002

***HANLON, JOYCE (RD) (Charles) – (Consecrated 1992, R-1997, FD-1997)**
Psychotherapist, Psychology Associates of Grand Rapids, P.C. 1992; Reflections Counseling & Consultation Services 1995; Retired 2001
(H) 7797 Teakwood, Jenison, MI 49428 (616) 457-2901

***HANSEN, LLOYD R. (RE) (Beth) – (R-1948, E-1952)**
Cloverdale (EUB) 1950; Galien (EUB) 1952; Capac (EUB) 1956; Three Rivers (EUB) 1959; Mendon (EUB) 1960; Benton Harbor First (EUB) 1963; Mt. Pleasant (EUB) 1964; without appointment 1967; Voluntary location 1969; readmitted 1973; Mindolo Ecumenical Foundation, Kitwe, Zambia, Africa, 1973; Scottville Feb. 1, 1976; Cedar Springs/East Nelson Nov. 1, 1980; West Mendon Aug. 1, 1983; Augusta 1987; Retired 1988; Alto/Bowne Center, Jan. 1-July 1, 1990; Snow Vergennes Nov. 1, 1990-June 1, 1991; Evangelical Seminary, Puerto Rico March 22, 1994-March 1995; Sand Lake/South Ensley Feb. 1, 2002-June 30, 2002
(H) 1516 Sherman SE #2, Grand Rapids, MI 49506-2761 (616) 776-1281

HANSEN, RANDALL R. (FE) (Susan) – (R-1993, E-1982)
[San Pablo/Chaplain of Instituto Crandon, Montevideo, Uruguay 1977; San Pablo/Valparaiso and San Jose de Carrasco Meth. Community Centers, Montevideo, Uruguay 1980; Albion First (Assoc) 1983; Mercedes, Uruguay 1985; Mercedes and Paysandu, Uruguay 1987; Mercedes, Uruguay 1990; Fennville/Pearl July 16, 1992;] Transferred from Uruguay Evangelical Methodist Conf, Fennville/Pearl 1993; Muskegon: Central 2000; Montague, Aug 16, 2009; Medical Leave 2014
(H) 5181 Hancock St, Montague, MI 49437 (231) 894-4625

***HANSEN, RONALD W. (RE) (Jan) – (R-1977, D-1977, E-1980)**
In School 1977; Fennville/Pearl 1978; Ovid Feb 1, 1984; Leave of Absence 1993; Hartford 1999; Retired 2011; Northwest (DSA) (LTFT 1/4) 2012-2013
(H) 7615 Andrea Lane, Portage, MI 49024 (269) 208-5410

HARPOLE, JASON E. (PL) (Sharla)
Breedsville (PTLP 1/4) 2014
(H) 205 Amos Ave, Portage, MI 49002 (269) 388-8312
Breedsville UMC: 113 W Main Street, PO Box 21, Breedsville MI 49027 (269) 359-1077

HARPOLE, PATRICIA A. (AM) (Everett) – (R-2004, D-2004)
(Formerly Patricia A. Myles) Brandywine Trinity 1993-April 17, 1994; LP w/o Appointment, Apr. 17, 1994; [Transferred to Ohio Conf., Redeemer UMC (Assoc.), Columbus, OH, Jan. 1999-June 2002;] Transferred from Ohio Conf., May 2002; Townline/Breedsville Nov. 1, 2002; Dowling: Country Chapel 2004; LifeSpring 2009; Indian River 2014
(H) 5954 Berry Lane, Indian River, MI 49749 (269) 806-2814
Indian River UMC: PO Box 457, Indian River MI 49749 (231) 238-7764

***HAUSERMANN, CARL L. (RE) (Marcia) – (R-1964, D-1964, E-1967)**
Galien 1964; Grand Rapids First (Assoc) 1967; Coloma/Riverside 1971; Ionia First 1977; Jackson Calvary 1983; Portage Chapel Hill 1989; Retired 2001
(H) 6070 Baywood Drive, Portage, MI 49024 (269) 323-7122

***HAYES, GEOFFREY L. (RE) (Pamela) – (R-1970, D-1970, E-1974)**
In School 1970; Grand Rapids: First (Assoc.) 1973; Lansing: Asbury 1978; Stevensville 1987; Surrender of Credentials March 23, 1994; Re-admitted 1998; Grand Rapids: Faith 1998; Retired 2009
(H) 112 Woodruff Ct, Cary, NC 27518 (919) 233-6950

***HAYES, STANLEY L. (RE) (Joyce) – (R-1963, D-1963, E-1965)**
[Leaton 1959; in school 1961]; Grand Traverse Larger Parish 1964; Kingsley Circuit 1965; East Jordan Oct. 15, 1966; Cedar Springs 1970; Cedar Springs/East Nelson 1972; Evart/Avondale Oct. 15, 1975; Fennville/Pearl Apr. 1, 1984; Breckenridge 1990; Grass Lake 1994; Retired 1999; Kalkaska (DSA) Oct. 1, 1999; Ogdensburg (DSA) 2002
(H) 316 N. Main St., PO Box 67, Fife Lake, MI 49633 (231) 879-3884

***HAYNES, LEONARD B. (RE) (Birute) – (R-1970, D-1970, E-1973)**
Riverside 1970; Kingscreek 1972; Pine Rest Christian Hospital 1975; Bethesda Hospital 1976; transferred from West Ohio Conf., Director of Pastoral Care, Chaplain, Bronson Methodist Hospital 1979; Leave of absence March 24, 1983-June 15, 1983; Hinchman/Oronoko 1983; Shepherd/Pleasant Valley 1986; Lansing: Calvary 1992; Leave of Absence March 1, 1998-June 30, 1998; Retired 1998
(H) 13630 W Meath Dr, Homer Glen, IL 60491-9137 (708) 828-7653

HAZLE, JUDITH A. (PL) (Stuart)
Shepardsville (CLM) (1/4 time) Aug 1, 2009; Shepardsville (PTLP 1/4 time) Nov 10, 2012
(H) 1795 W Centerline Rd, St Johns, MI 48879-9275 (989) 224-4260
Shepardsville UMC: 6990 East Winfield Road, Ovid MI 48866 (989) 834-5104

HEATON, LYLE D. (FE) (Sylvia) – (R-1978, D-1978, E-1982)
In School 1978; Barryton 1979; Barryton/Chippewa Lake 1980; Middleton/Maple Rapids 1984; Delta Mills 1990; Wacousta Community Jan 1, 1999; Lansing Christ 2013
(H) 4747 W Stoll Rd, Lansing, MI 48906-9384 (517) 580-5058
Lansing Christ UMC: 517 W Jolly Rd, Lansing MI 48910-6609 (517) 394-2727

HEFFELFINGER, CONSTANCE L. (FE) (Randy Wedeven) – (R-1976, D-1976, E-1980)
Transferred from East Ohio Conf., in school 1977; Fremont (Assoc.) 1978; Woodland/Welcome Corners 1981; Saugatuck/Ganges 1984; Saugatuck (LTFT 1/2) Jan. 1, 1990; Incapacity Leave Sept. 1, 1995
(H) 199 W 20th St, Holland, MI 49423-4180 (616) 393-0919

***HEIFNER, KEITH W. (RE) (Becky) – (R-1976, D-1971, E-1973)**
[Sullivan Grace, Sullivan MO 1971;] Maplewood 1977; Transferred from Missouri East Conf., Counselor, Samaritan Counseling Center, Battle Creek ad interim 1980; Staff Pastoral Counselor, Samaritan Counseling Center, Battle Creek 1981; Executive Director, Samaritan Center of South Central Michigan, Battle Creek 1986; Battle Creek Pastoral Counseling Jan. 1, 1990; Big Rapids: First 1993; Marshall 1996; Parma/North Parma 1999; Galesburg 2003; Retired 2006
(H) 3164 Brimstead Dr, Franklin, TN 37064-6224
(S) 4985 Sandra Bay Dr Unit 101, Naples, FL 34109

HEISLER, BENTON R. (FE) (Linda) – (R-1985, D-1985, E-1988)
In school METHESCO 1985; St. Joseph (Assoc.) 1986; Charlevoix/Greensky Hill Indian Mission Aug. 16, 1988; Lansing: Asbury Nov. 16, 1992; Mt. Pleasant: First 1997; Lansing District Superintendent 2002; West Michigan Conference Director of Connectional Ministries, Jan. 1, 2009
(H) 3579 Tricklewood Dr SE, Grand Rapids, MI 49546-7245 (616) 974-9152
(O) West Michigan Conference - United Methodist Church, 11 Fuller Ave SE, PO Box 6247, Grand Rapids, MI 49516-6247 (616) 459-4503

HELLER, VIRGINIA L. (FE) – (R-1996, D-1996, E-1999)
Muskegon Central (Assoc) 1996; Keeler/Silver Creek 1998; Battle Creek Baseline/Bellevue 2004; Portage Chapel Hill (Assoc) 2011; Leland 2013; South Haven 2014
(H) 12320 76th St, South Haven, MI 49090 (269) 637-4803
South Haven UMC: 429 Michigan, South Haven MI 49090-1333 (269) 637-2502

HERRELL, DEVON R. (FE) – (R-2005, E-2008)
Traverse Bay (Assoc.) 2005; Lake Ann, June 15, 2008; South Haven First 2013; Director of Wesley Foundation at Ferris State University 2014
(H) 14610 Tomahawk Ln, Big Rapids, MI 49307 (231) 649-2302
(O) Wesley Foundation - Ferris State University, 628 S Warren Ave, Big Rapids, MI 49307 (231) 796-8315

***HERTEL, WILLIAM A. (RE) (Janet) – (R-1963, D-1963, E-1966)**
[Allen 1961]; Niles (Assoc.) 1964; White Cloud/East Denver 1966; White Cloud 1968; Grand Rapids: St. Paul's 1969; Lake Odessa: Central 1974; Traverse City: Asbury Sept. 16, 1980; Lansing: Asbury 1987; Delton: Faith 1990; Retired 2001
(H) 2531 Vista Point Ct NW, Grand Rapids, MI 49534

HILLS, DAVID F. (FE) (Claire) – (R-1992, D-1992, E-1994)
Big Rapids Third/Paris/Rodney 1992; Climax/Scotts 1994; Coloma/Watervliet Aug 1, 1999; Delton Faith 2007; Heartland District Superintendent 2010
(H) 3510 Mineral Springs Trail, Mt Pleasant, MI 48858 (989) 317-0081
(O) Heartland District Office, 1400 S Washington Street Ste A, Mt. Pleasant, MI 48858 (989) 773-5140

***HINKLIN, ROBERT L. (RE) – (R-1963, E-1966)**
In-School (EUB) May 12, 1963; Jasper (EUB) 1966; Jasper/Weston 1968; Napoleon 1969; Grand Rapids: Plainfield/Epworth 1972; Georgetown Feb. 1, 1976; Lansing: Mt. Hope 1984; Portage: First March l, 1987; Grandville 1998; Retired 2001; Fennville/Pearl (DSA) 2002
(H) 231 Henley Dr, Naples, FL 34104 (239) 774-3053

HODGE, JAMES E. (FE) (Kathleen) – (R-1984, D-1984, E-1986)
Somerset Center/Moscow Plains 1984; Bangor: Simpson 1989; Bangor: Simpson/Breedsville 1990; Shelby 1994; Grandville (Assoc) 2001; Caledonia 2005; Vountary Leave of Absence 2012; Grand Rapids Aldersgate 2013
(H) 5160 Windcrest Ct SW, Wyoming, MI 49418 (616) 308-9925
Grand Rapids Aldersgate UMC: 4301 Ambrose Avenue NE, Grand Rapids MI 49525-6122 (616) 363-3446

***HODGE, LAWRENCE E. (RE) (Ruth) – (R-1964, D-1965, E-1966)**
[Bloomingdale/Townline July 1960; Keeler 1963]; Elk Lake Parish 1966; Muskegon: Central (Assoc.) Nov. 1968; Battle Creek: Birchwood 1971; Muskegon: Crestwood 1980; Hillside 1983; Ionia: First 1991; Retired 2000
(H) 9947 Huntington Rd, Battle Creek, MI 49017 (269) 969-9483

HOEKWATER, HARRIS J. (FE) (Jane) – (R-1980, D-1980, E-1985)
In School GETS 1980; Perry/Shaftsburg 1983; Sunfield Jan 15, 1992; Concord 1998; Pentwater Centenary 2006; St. Joseph First 2012
(H) 4921 S Roosevelt Rd, Stevensville, MI 49127 (269) 235-9156
St Joseph First UMC: 2950 Lakeview Ave., St. Joseph MI 49085 (269) 983-3929

HOFMANN, DANIEL B. (FE) (Mary) – (R-1993, D-1993, E-1996)
In School United 1993; West Ohio Conf: Ithaca, Arcanum, OH 1993 (LTFT 3/4) (para. 426.1); Ravenna 1994; Delton Faith 2001; Eaton Rapids First 2007; Leland 2014
(H) 4840 Golfview Dr, PO Box 1134, Leland, MI 49654-1134 (231) 994-2159
Leland UMC: 106 N 4th St, PO Box 602, Leland MI 49654 (231) 256-9161

***HOUK, RONALD A. (RE) (Anna Belle) – (R-1961, D-1961, E-1963)**
[Prairieville 1954; Kentucky Conf, Winchester Dunaway 1958]; Muskegon Central (Assoc) 1964; Shelby Jan 15, 1966; Eaton Rapids Oct 15, 1971; Lansing District Superintendent Jan 16, 1982; St. Joseph First 1987; Retired 1997; Crystal Valley/Walkerville (DSA) Nov 8, 1999; Fountain (DSA) July 1, 2004-June 30, 2005
(H) 4585 S Lakeshore Dr, Ludington, MI 49431 (231) 845-7510

***HUBLEY, LAURENCE E. (RE) – (R-1991)**
[Colon Nov. 1, 1985;] Transferred from Free Methodist, Hillside 1991; Hastings: Hope 1995; Muskegon: Wolf Lake 2000; Incapacity Leave 2001; Retired June 1, 2002
(H) 5625 Vintage Lane, Apt. 101, Kalamazoo, MI 49009 (269) 388-5282

HUGHES, ROBERT M. (FE) (Becky) – (R-2006, E-2009)
Union City 2004; Reading 2012; Leave of Absence July 13, 2014
(H) 361 Calhoun St, Union City, MI 49094 (517) 677-6381

***HULETT, JAMES R. (RE) (Linda) – (R-1964, D-1964, E-1967)**
[Gladwin Circuit (West Michigan) 1957; Noonan/Columbus, N Dakota Conf, 1960; In School, 1962]; Cando/Churchs Ferry 1965; Transferred from N Dakota Conf, Lake Odessa: Lakewood 1978; Sparta 1985; Vicksburg 1993; Retired 1998
(H) 674 Gardenview Ct SW, Byron Center, MI 49315-8346

HUNDLEY, ROBERT L. (FE) (Ruth (Pigeon) – (R-1982, D-1982, E-1989)
Center Eaton/Brookfield 1980; East Lansing University (Assoc.) Aug 1, 1982; Director of Pastoral Care, Michigan Capital Medical Center Sept 1, 1990; Lansing First 1996; Mason First 2000; Lansing District Superintendent 2009; Grand Rapids First 2013
(H) 3035 Grenada Dr SE, Grand Rapids, MI 49546 (616) 427-3749
Grand Rapids First UMC: 227 Fulton St E, Grand Rapids MI 49503-3236 (616) 451-2879

***HUSTON, JOSEPH D. (RE) – (R-1970, D-1970, E-1973)**
Camden Charge Sept 1, 1970; Concord 1972; Transferred to Detroit Conf, Metropolitan Detroit (Assoc) 1975; Transferred from Detroit Conf, Robbins/Grovenburg Oct 15, 1977; Grand Rapids St Paul's Feb 16, 1982; Holt 1989; Central District Superintendent 1999; Georgetown 2005; Lansing Central 2007; Retired 2009; Dimondale (1/4) and Grovenburg (Ret.) (1/4) 2009
(H) 6747 Creyts Rd, Dimondale, MI 48821 (517) 646-6530
Dimondale UMC: PO Box 387, Dimondale MI 48821-0387 (517) 646-0641
Grovenburg UMC: 1368 Grovenburg Rd, Holt MI 48842-8628 (517) 694-7683

HUTCHISON, BENJAMIN DAVID (OE) – (R-2014)
(Formerly Benjamin Bras) [Member of African Methodist Episcopal] Cassopolis (DSA) (1/2 time) Jan. 1, 2013; Cassopolis (para. 346.1) Jan. 1, 2014
(H) 61165 Quinnesec Road, Cassopolis, MI 49031 (269) 569-1586
Cassopolis UMC: 209 South Rowland Street, PO Box 175, Cassopolis MI 49031-0175 (269) 445-3107

HUVAERE, CATHI M. (FE) – (R-1996, D-1996, E-2002)
(Formerly Cathi Gowin) Marne 1993; Grand Rapids Aldersgate Feb 1, 2002; Grand Rapids St. Paul's 2005; Niles Wesley 2012
(H) 1502 Broadway, Niles, MI 49120 (616) 550-2570
Niles Wesley UMC: 302 Cedar Street, Niles MI 49120 (269) 683-7250

HUYCK, CLARE WALTER (FL) (Bridget)
Pompeii/Perrinton/North Star/Middleton (DSA) 2007; Pompeii/Perrinton/North Star/Middleton Nov 10, 2007; Sunfield/Sebewa Center 2012; Barry-Eaton Cooperative Ministry: Sunfield (PTLP 3/4) and Mulliken 2013 (PTLP 1/4)
(H) 235 Dunham St, Sunfield, MI 48890-9772 (517) 566-2066
Mulliken UMC: 400 Charlotte St, Mulliken MI 48861-9772 (517) 649-8382
Sunfield UMC: 227 Logan St, Sunfield MI 48890 (517) 566-8448

***HYNES, JAMES L. (RE) (Bernadine) – (R-1966, E-1968)**
Transferred from Detroit Conf., Wacousta 1986; Leave of Absence 1992; Nashville 1994; Retired 2000
(H) 4207 Embassy Dr SE, Grand Rapids, MI 49546 (616) 949-0979

IDSINGA, CYDNEY M. (FL)
Girard 2014
(H) 992 Marshall Rd, Coldwater, MI 49036 (517) 279-0123
Girard UMC: 990 Marshall Rd., Coldwater MI 49036 (517) 279-9418

***IRIS, RONALD LEWIS FIGGINS (AF)**
[Detroit Conference, Retired Elder] Crystal Valley/Walkerville (Ret.) (LTFT 1/4) Dec. 1, 2013
(H) 2774 W Victory Dr, Ludington, MI 49431 (231) 843-8352
Crystal Valley UMC: PO Box 125, Walkerville MI 49459 (231) 873-5422
Walkerville UMC: PO Box 125, Walkerville MI 49459 (231) 873-4236

IVANOV, MARY LETTA-BEMENT (FE) (Ivan) – (R-2001, E-2004)
Ravenna 2001; Cedar Springs 2008; Muskegon Lake Harbor 2014
(H) 1322 Clayton Ave, Muskegon, MI 49441 (231) 798-3951
Muskegon Lake Harbor UMC: 4861 Henry St, Muskegon MI 49441-4536 (231) 798-2181

***JACKSON, ANDREW (RE) (Phyllis) – (R-1997, D-1997, E-1999)**
Grand Rapids: St. Paul's (Assoc.) (Part-Time) Feb. 1, 1987; Carlisle (Part-Time) 1994; Carlisle (Full-Time) 1997; Retired 2006; Carlisle (Ret.) (LTFT 1/2) Dec. 1, 2009-2010; Alto/Bowne Center (Ret.) (LTFT 3/4) 2014
(H) 978 Amber View Dr SW, Byron Center, MI 49315-9740 (616) 878-1284
Alto UMC: 11365 64th St SE, PO Box 122, Alto MI 49302 (616) 868-7306
Bowne Center UMC: 3782 Murray Lake Ave, Lowell MI 49331

***JAQUETTE, DALE F. (RA) (Betty) – (D-1986)**
Pompeii/Perrinton/North Star Aug. 16, 1981; Reading April 16, 1990; Retired 1992
(H) 504 Palm Ave, Wildwood, FL 34785-9428 (352) 330-1670

***JAQUISH, JERRY L. (RE) (Joy) – (R-1981, D-1981, E-1984)**
Epsilon/Levering 1981; Leave of Absence 1987; White Cloud 1988; Manistee 2002; Retired 2012
(H) 956 N Thornapple Ave, PO Box 144, White Cloud, MI 49349 (231) 689-0079

***JENSEN, CURTIS E. (RE) (Anne) – (R-1970, D-1970, E-1975)**
In school 1971; Mt. Pleasant First (Assoc.) 1972; Mancelona/Alba 1975; Berrien Springs 1983; Buchanan: First 1987; Pentwater: Centenary January 16, 1996; Lake Odessa: Lakewood 2001; Hillsdale 2003; Retired 2010
(H) 915 Meadowbrook Dr., Mt Pleasant, MI 48858 (989) 317-3500

***JOHN SR, THOMAS H. (RLA) (Phyllis)**
Kewadin: Indian Mission 1998; Kewadin/Northport Indian Missions 2005; Retired 2012; Kewadin/ Northport Indian Missions 2012
(H) 13735 Indian Rd, Kewadin, MI 49648 (231) 264-0527
Kewadin Indian Mission UMC: PO Box 227, Kewadin MI 49648 (231) 632-4920
Northport Indian Mission UMC: PO Box 401, Northport MI 49670 (231) 941-2360

***JOHNSON, DEBORAH M. (RE) – (R-1979, D-1979, E-1983)**
In school 1979; Manton 1981; Marne 1985; Organizing Pastor, Hudsonville Sept. 1, 1990-1997; Lansing: Asbury 1997; Sturgis 2008; Retired July 8, 2014
(H) 22849 110th Ave, Tustin, MI 49688 (231) 825-2580

JOHNSON, JAN M. (FL) (James)
Mercy Health Partners, Chaplain (para. 344.1d) Nov. 13, 2010
(H) 1541 Fifth St, Muskegon, MI 49444-1849 (231) 343-8268
(O) Mercy Health Partners, 1500 E Sherman Blvd, PO Box 358, Muskegon, MI 49443 (231) 672-3629

JOHNSON, JANE ELLEN (FE) (Charles) – (R-2001, E-2005)
Farwell 2000; Lansing Grace January 1, 2007
(H) 2915 S Cambridge Rd, Lansing, MI 48911 (517) 484-0227
Lansing Grace UMC: 1900 Boston Blvd, Lansing MI 48910-2456 (517) 482-5750

JOHNSON, MARK G. (FE) (Johnie) – (R-1983, D-1983, E-1985)
Fenwick/Palo/Vickeryville March 16, 1982; Lawrence 1986; Kent City Chapel Hill May 1, 1991; Hillsdale 1996; Ionia Parrish LeValley/Berlin Center 2003; Bath/Gunnisonville 2007
(H) 13505 Webster Rd, Bath, MI 48808 (517) 898-6960
Bath UMC: PO Box 308, Bath MI 48808-0308 (517) 641-6551
Gunnisonville UMC: 2031 E Clark Rd, Bath MI 48808-9413 (517) 482-7987

JOHNSON, MELODY PIERCE HURLEY (OE) – (R-2002)
[Detroit Conf.] Chaplain, Porter Hills Presbyterian Retirement Community 2002
(H) 1211 Troon Ct SE, Grand Rapids, MI 49546 (616) 949-8185
(O) Porter Hills Presbyterian Retirement Community, 4450 Cascade Rd SE Ste 200, Grand Rapids, MI 49546-8330 (616) 949-4975

JOHNSON, NATHANIEL W. (FE) (Lisa) – (R-1991, D-1990, E-1993)
[North Indiana Conf: Orland/Nevada Mills 1988;] Transferred from North Indiana Conf, Belding 1991; Vergennes Sept 1, 1996; CPE, Bronson Methodist Hospital, Kalamazoo (Para. 326.1,3) 2010; Leave of Absence, Sept 6, 2011; Heartland Home Health Care & Hospice, Spiritual Care, Grand Rapids (Para. 344.1d), Oct 4, 2011; Chaplain, Heartland Home Health Care & Hospice (LTFT 3/4) Grand Rapids, and Chaplain, Spectrum United Memorial Hospital, Greenville (LTFT 1/4) (Para. 344.1d), July 9, 2012; Chaplain in Pediatrics/NICU at DeVos Childrens Hospital, Grand Rapids (full-time), Oct. 10, 2012; Chaplain, Helen DeVos Children's Hospital and Spectrum Health United Hospital, Grand Rapids 2014
(H) 2821 Boynton Ave NE, Ada, MI 49301 (616) 682-1210
(O) Helen DeVos Children's Hospital & Spectrum Health United Hospital, 100 Michigan St NE, Grand Rapids, MI 49503 (616) 391-3147

***JOHNSON, WILLIAM C. (RE) (Judy) – (R-1972, D-1972, E-1975)**
In School 1972; Jonesville/Allen 1974; Holland (Assoc) 1977; Grand Rapids: Aldersgate 1981; Marshall 1992; Wyoming Park 1996; Retired 2012
(H) 4390 Summerlane NE, Grand Rapids, MI 49525 (616) 361-0024

***JOHNSTON, DAVID L. (RE) (Ann Marie) – (R-1977, D-1975, E-1976)**
Bellevue/Kalamo 1977; DeWitt: Redeemer May 1, 1983; Lansing: Grace 1985; Jackson: Brookside 1992; Leave of Absence June 24, 2005; Retired 2009
(H) 122 Bingham Dr, Brooklyn, MI 48230-8926 (517) 784-1346

***JONES, MARGARET ZEE (RE) (John "Jack") – (R-2002, E-2005)**
In school 2002; Chaplain and Bereavement Coordinator, McLaren-Ingham Visiting Nurse and Hospice Services (para. 335.1 D) Sept. 1, 2002; Chaplain and Bereavement Coordinator, McLaren-Ingham Visiting Nurse and Hospice Services and Retired June 24, 2006 (para. 344.1.a.)
(H) 599 Pebblebrook Ln, East Lansing, MI 48823 (517) 351-0728

***JONES, ROBERT E. (RE) (Carol) – (R-1970, D-1970, E-1973)**
In School 1970; Frontier/Osseo 1971; Mendon Nov 15, 1973; Grand Rapids First (Assoc) 1978; Montague 1983; Lansing Christ 1992; Big Rapids First 1996; Scottville 2004; Retired 2009
(H) 5648 Nancy Dr SW, Wyoming, MI 49418-9788 (616) 719-3935

JOSLYN, MONA K. (FE) – (R-1998, D-1998, E-2001)
D.S. Assignment: Nottawa/Leonidas Oct. 1994; Waterloo First/Waterloo Village Aug. 1, 1997; Bronson 1998; Galesburg 2006; Gull Lake 2010
(H) 13091 M 89, Augusta, MI 49012 (269) 731-5829
Gull Lake UMC: 8640 Gull Rd, Richland MI 49083 (269) 629-5137

JUE, JENNIFER J. (FE) (Erik Wong) – (R-2007, E-2010)
Napoleon 2007; Detroit Conference, Wayne First 2013; Detroit Conference, Oxford 2014
(H) 91 Cross Timbers Dr, Oxford, MI 48371 (248) 628-1022
(O) Oxford UMC, 21 E Burdick St, Oxford, MI 48371 (248) 628-1289

***KADWELL JR, EMMETT H. (RE) (Mary) – (R-1973, D-1973, E-1978)**
In school 1973; Ashley/Bannister 1975; Empire Oct 1, 1978; Stanwood: Northland 1982; Lake Odessa Central 1992.; Niles: Wesley Jan 1, 2000; Reed City 2008; Retired 2011; Saugatuck (Ret.) (LTFT 1/4) Sept 1, 2011
(H) 2794 6th St, Shelbyville, MI 49344 (231) 912-0806
Saugatuck UMC: 250 Mason St., PO Box 647, Saugatuck MI 49453 (269) 857-2295

KALAJAINEN, BRADLEY P. (FE) (Colleen) – (R-1982, D-1982, E-1984)
Freeport/Middleville/Parmalee (Assoc.) Jan. 1, 1981; Freeport 1982; Grand Rapids: First (Assoc.) 1985; Grand Rapids: Cornerstone 1990
(H) 7810 Golf Meadows Dr SE, Caledonia, MI 49316-8462 (616) 891-8443
Grand Rapids Cornerstone UMC: 1675 84th St SE, Caledonia MI 49316 (616) 698-3170

KALAJAINEN, RODNEY J. (FE) (Janet) – (R-1979, D-1979, E-1981)
St Johns Parish 1978; Shepardsville/Price 1979; Mt Pleasant First (Assoc.) 1981; Battle Creek Birchwood 1984; DeWitt: Redeemer 1988
(H) 2155 Longwoods Dr, DeWitt, MI 48820 (517) 669-9140
DeWitt Redeemer UMC: 13980 Schavey Rd, DeWitt MI 48820-9013 (517) 669-3430

KASPER, JOHN G. (FE) (Deb) – (R-2005, E-2008)
[DS Assignment: Hersey Aug 1, 1994;] Hersey 1995; Galien/Olive Branch 2001; Dowagiac First 2006; Clare 2013
(H) 714 S Rainbow Dr, Clare, MI 48617 (989) 386-7683
Clare UMC: 105 E. Seventh Street, Clare MI 48617 (989) 386-2591

KATZMARK, PEGGY A. (FL)
Robbins 2014
(H) 827 S Waverly Rd, Eaton Rapids, MI 48827 (517) 663-8417
Robbins UMC: 6419 Bunker Rd, Eaton Rapids MI 48827-9108 (517) 663-5226

***KELLER, RON L. (RE) (Patricia) – (R-1959, D-1959, E-1962)**
[Battle Creek: Washington Hgts. Sept. 1, 1956; Northeast Ohio Conf., Republic 1958] 1959; Union City 1962; Battle Creek: Birchwood 1966; Rockford 1970; Conf. Staff Director 1973; Kalamazoo: Milwood Jan. 1, 1982; Muskegon: Central 1988; Battle Creek: First 1993; Retired 1998; Kalamazoo: First, Interim Pastor Jan. 1, 2000-July 1, 2000
(H) 2121 Magnolia Lane, Flint, MI 48532 (810) 820-7021

KENDALL, JAYME L. (FE) – (R-2004, E-2008)
Elsie 2004; Chaplain, Michigan Army National Guard (para. 344,1c), July 11, 2005; CPE, Covenant Counseling and Family Resource Center, Snellville, GA, June 1, 2007; Chaplain, Abbey Hospice, Social Circle, GA, Sept 1, 2008; Chaplain, United States Air Force, Kirtland Air Force Base (para. 344.1d) June 1, 2010
(H) 5103 Stormy Hls, San Antonio, TX 78247 (505) 319-7873
(O) United States Air Force, Kirtland Air Force Base Chapel, 1950 Second St SE, Kirtland Air Force Base, NM 87117-5606 (505) 846-5691

***KENDALL, O. JAY (RE) (Janis) – (R-1993, D-1984, E-1986)**
[Central Illinois Conf: Otterbein 1984; US Army Chaplain 1987;] Transferred from Central Illinois Conf, Northeast Missaukee Parish Sept 1, 1993; Leave of Absence 2005; Indian River (Assoc.) (LTFT 1/4) 2007; Retired Sept. 1, 2012
(H) 3300 M 68 Hwy, PO Box 2038, Indian River, MI 49749-2038 (231) 238-0816

***KERSTEN, ROBERT L. (RE) (Carol) – (D-1963, E-1968)**
Stanwood/Higbee Oct. 1960; Burr Oak 1962; Napoleon 1967; transferred to Detroit Conf., Mio 1969; Hillman/Spratt 1975; Ishpeming Wesley (Assoc.) 1978; Poseyville/Gordonville 1980; Kilmanagh 1982; transferred from Detroit Conf., Woodland/Welcome Corners 1987; Vermontville/Gresham 1991; Retired 1995
(H) 1618 Peggy Place, Lansing, MI 48910 (517) 394-2225

KEYTE, DONNA JEAN (PL) (Steven)
Lacota Sept. 1, 2003; Almena (PTLP 1/2), Jan. 1, 2006; Almena (PTLP 1/4), Jan. 1, 2007; Almena (PTLP 1/2), Jan. 1, 2008
(H) 7632 Sandyridge St, Portage, MI 49024-5028 (269) 329-1560
Almena UMC: 27503 County Rd 375, Paw Paw MI 49079 (269) 668-2811

KIDD, SEAN K. (FL) (Christine)
Pokagon (DSA) (1/2 time) 2011-2014; Martin/Shelbyville 2014
(H) 948 Lee St, PO Box 86, Martin, MI 49070 (269) 672-4132
Martin UMC: 969 E. Allegan, PO Box 154, Martin MI 49070 (269) 672-7097
Shelbyville UMC: PO Box 154, Martin MI 49070 (269) 672-5927

KILPATRICK, BRYAN KELLY (FL)
Brooks Corners/Barryton Faith/Sears 2014
(H) 5951 30th Ave, Sears, MI 49679 (231) 734-2733
Brooks Corners UMC: 5951 30th Avenue, Sears MI 49679 (231) 734-2733
Barryton Faith UMC: 5951 30th Ave., Sears MI 48679 (989) 382-5431
Sears UMC: 5951 30th Avenue, Sears MI 49679 (231) 734-2733

KINTIGH, BRUCE R. (FE) (Paula) – (R-1979, D-1979, E-1983)
In School 1979; Shepardsville/Price 1981; Kingsley/Grant 1988; Hart 1993; Battle Creek Christ Jan 1, 1999; Girard/Ellis Corners 2007 [Ellis Corners Closed 12-31-07]; Battle Creek Trinity 2010; Battle Creek Birchwood/Trinity (1/2 Time:1/2 Time) 2012
(H) 17102 11 Mile Rd, Battle Creek, MI 49014 (269) 223-7245
Battle Creek Birchwood UMC: 3003 Gethings Rd., Battle Creek MI 49015 (269) 963-2084
Battle Creek Trinity UMC: 10 W. Bidwell, Battle Creek MI 49015 (269) 962-4900

***KNAPP, DAVID G. (RE) (Jane) – (R-1976, D-1976, E-1980)**
In school 1976; Hopkins/South Monterey 1978; Adamsville Oct. 16, 1982; Jackson: First (Assoc.) 1986; Detroit Conf.: Waterman/Preston 1989; Transferred to Detroit Conf. 1990; Transferred from Detroit Conf., Grand Rapids: Pawating Magedwin and Salem/Bradley Indian Mission 1992; Benton Harbor: Peace Temple 1995; Climax/Scotts 2003; Retired 2009; Mendon/West Mendon (interim) (LTFT 1/4) Jan. 1-June 30, 2013
(H) 16998 E ON Ave, Climax, MI 49034-0125 (269) 746-4915

***KOHNS, NORMAN C. (RE) (Carole) – (R-1967, D-1967, E-1969)**
In School 1967; La Rue, TX 1968; Munising-Trenary 1969; Transferred from Detroit Conf, Grand Rapids Aldersgate Jan 1, 1974; Grand Rapids Aldersgate/Westgate 1977; Grand Rapids Aldersgate 1978; Kalamazoo Sunnyside 1981; In School Eden Theological Seminary, St. Louis, MO 1985; Resident Therapist, Care and Counseling, Eden Seminary, St. Louis, MO 1986; Samaritan Counseling Center of South Bend, IN 1988; Riverside/Scottdale Nov 16, 1992-1993; Director of Pastoral Counseling, Hospice of Greater Kalamazoo 1993; Caledonia 1996; Retired 2005
(H) 5845 Lyn Haven Dr SE, Kentwood, MI 49512 (616) 554-1244

KOUGHN, E. JEANNE (FE) – (R-2004)
Director, Wesley Foundation, Ferris State University 2003; [Transfer from Iowa Conf July 1, 2004]; Traverse Bay (Assoc) 2008; Hillside/Somerset Center 2009; Sturgis 2014
(H) 1332 Rolling Ridge Ln, Sturgis, MI 49091 (269) 651-6087
Sturgis UMC: 200 Pleasant Ave., Sturgis MI 49091 (269) 651-5990

***KRAKLAN, JACK GORDAN (RE) – (R-1959, E-1962)**
LaSalle/Zion (EUB) 1962; Ludington: St. Paul (EUB) 1967; Hart-Mears 1971; Traverse City: Emmanuel 1979; Colon 1983; Jonesville/Allen 1985; Leave of absence 1988; Retired 1991
(H) 200 W Edgewood Blvd Apt 254, Lansing, MI 48911 (810) 956-6877

KRAUS JR, JAMES W. (FD) (Lorie) – (Consecrated 1998, FD-2001)
Director of Music and Director of Leadership Development, St. Joseph: First 1998; St. Joseph: First (Deacon) 2001
(H) 2820 Willa Dr, St Joseph, MI 49085-2555 (269) 983-5798
St Joseph First UMC: 2950 Lakeview Ave., St. Joseph MI 49085 (269) 983-3929

***KUHN, RICHARD (RE) – (R-1959, D-1959, E-1961)**
Leland/Keswick Sept. 1, 1971; transferred from Minnesota Conf. 1972; Frankfort/Elberta 1980; Buchanan Faith/Morris Chapel 1982; St. Louis 1987; Retired 1998
(H) 10143 Lakeside Drive, Perrinton, MI 48871 (989) 682-4814

KURSCH, KATHLEEN S. (FE) – (R-1999, E-2003)
Waterloo First/Waterloo Village 1998; Grand Ledge: First (Assoc.) Feb. 1, 2000; Grand Ledge: First (Assoc.) (LTFT 1/2) / Delta Mills (LTFT 1/2) 2003; Grand Rapids: South Sept. 1, 2004; Shepherd 2007
(H) 175 North Dr, Shepherd, MI 48883 (989) 828-5700
Shepherd UMC: 107 W Wright Ave, PO Box 309, Shepherd MI 48883 (989) 828-5866

***LAFRANCE, SALLY J. (RE) (David) – (R-2000)**
[West Ohio conf., Bascom UMC: Bascom, OH;] Transfered from West Ohio conf., Climax/Scotts Oct. 1, 1999; Ogdensburg 2001; Twin Lake 2002; Retired Oct. 1, 2004
(H) 15132 Snowberry Ct, Spring Lake, MI 49456 (616) 850-2157

***LAIDLER, D. KEITH (RE) (Judy) – (R-1957, E-1961)**
[Coleman supply (EUB) 1956;] Coleman (EUB) 1957; in school 1958; Petoskey (EUB) 1961; Brown City (EUB) 1964; Buchanan: Faith 1968; Leighton 1972; St. Johns: First Oct. 15, 1977; Paw Paw 1984; Lake Odessa: Central 1989; Montague 1992; Retired 1997; Delta Mills (DSA) Jan. 1 - June 30, 1999; Delta Mills (DSA) 2005-2007
(H) 3335 Starboard Dr, Holland, MI 49424-5425 (616) 786-2774

LANCASTER, JANICE T. (FD) (Terry Tock) – (R-2010, PD-2010, FD-2013)
Holland Hospital, Psychiatric Nurse / Holland First (Assoc-Congregational Care) (LTFT 1/4 unpaid) 2010; Primary Appt-Emmanuel Hospice of Grand Rapids, Clinical Nurse / Secondary Appt-Northlawn (Assoc-Congregational Care) (LTFT 1/4 unpaid) Feb. 1, 2014
(H) 4722 Westgate Dr, Comstock Park, MI 49321 (616) 784-5662
(O) Emmanuel Hospice of Grand Rapids, 2161 Leonard St NW, Grand Rapids, MI 49504 (616) 719-0919
Grand Rapids Northlawn UMC: 1157 Northlawn NE, Grand Rapids MI 49505 (616) 361-8503

LANE, M. CHRISTOPHER (FE) (Jane Lippert) – (R-1986, D- 1982, E-1988)
[In school, Boston University School of Theology 1982; Oregon State Hospital (CPE) 1985;] transferred from Holston Conf., Winn/Blanchard/Pine River/Coomer 1986; Muskegon: Crestwood 1990; Grand Rapids: Genesis (co-pastor) 1995; Martin / Shelbyville 2007; Traverse City Central (Assoc.) 2009
(H) 10160 E Pickwick Ct, Traverse City, MI 49684 (231) 947-5594
Traverse City Central UMC: 222 Cass St., Traverse City MI 49684 (231) 946-5191

***LAWTON, GEORGE W. (RLA) (Beverly)**
Lakeside Sept. 1, 1999; Retired 2007; Lakeside (RLA 1/4) 2007
(H) 8000 Warren Woods Rd #79, Three Oaks, MI 49128-8519 (269) 469-8468
Lakeside UMC: PO Box 402, Union Pier MI 49129 (269) 469-8468

LAWTON, GREGORY W. (FD) – (R-2007, FD-2010)
Resolution Services Center of Central Michigan (1/2 Time) / Grand Ledge First (Deacon) (1/2 Time) 2007; Grand Ledge First (Deacon) (LTFT 1/2) and Interim Director of Campus Ministry, Wesley Foundation at MSU (LFT 1/2) Dec. 5, 2010; Interim Director of Campus Ministry, Grand Valley State University (LTFT 3/4) 2011; Director, Wesley Fellowship at Grand Valley State University (Full-Time) 2012
(H) 2603 Falcon Pointe Dr NW, Grand Rapids, MI 49534 (616) 805-5407
(O) Wesley Fellowship at Grand Valley State University, Wesley Fellowship @ GVSU, 4539 Luce St., Jenison, MI 49428 (616) 805-5407

***LEE, JANET A. (RD) (William) – (R-1986, FD-1997)**
[Detroit Conf: Southfield 1954; Royal Oak First 1957; Clawson 1961]; Transferred from Detroit Conf 1986, Consultant of Church Music and the Arts; Hillsdale First, Minister of Music and Arts, and Hillsdale Daily News, Religion and Lifestyles Editor, 1988; Retired 2002, Serving Hillsdale First, Minister of Music and Arts

(H) 4300 W Bacon Rd, Hillsdale, MI 49242 (517) 437-4949

***LEE, JUNG KEE (RE) (Eun Su) – (R-1998, D- , E-1991)**
[East Ohio Conf; Korean UMC: Youngstown, OH;] Transfered from East Ohio Conf; Lansing Korean 1998; Seoul Theological University January 1, 2004; Retired Feb. 28, 2013

***LESTER, BEN B. (RE) (Linda) – (R-1990, D-1990, E-1993)**
Howard City First/Amble/Coral 1988; Cedar Springs/East Nelson 1995; Hart 2003; Retired 2011

(H) 1575 Hess Lake Dr, Grant, MI 49327 (231) 834-8868

***LEWIS, EUGENE A. (RE) (Marilyn) – (R-1965, D-1965, E-1967)**
[Glenn-Pearl 1963]; Glenn/Pearl/Casco 1965; Hanover/Horton/Hillside Dec. 1, 1966; Belding/Orleans July 15, 1972; Grand Rapids: Faith 1977; Wacousta 1984; Clare 1986; Stevensville 1994; Retired 2003

(H) 25080 27 1/2 St, Gobles, MI 49055 (269) 628-1482

***LEWIS, KENDALL A. (RE) (Doris) – (R-1970, D-1970, E-1974)**
Transferred from Detroit Conf., Banfield/Briggs/Dowling-S. Maple Grove 1973; Country Chapel/ Banfield 1975; Marion/Cadillac South Community 1977; White Pigeon 1981; Mendon Jan. 1985; Big Rapids: Third/Paris/Rodney 1986; Retired 1990

(H) 179 Summer Street, Battle Creek, MI 49015 (269) 441-1921

LEYDORF-KECK, KATHRYN L. (PL) (Roger Keck)
Salem/Lowe/Maple Rapids (DSA) 2007; Salem/Lowe/Maple Rapids Nov. 10, 2007; Lowe/Maple Rapids (3/4 Time) May 1, 2014

(H) 10886 S Woodbridge Rd, Bannister, MI 48807 (517) 282-4446
Maple Rapids UMC: 330 Maple St, Maple Rapids MI 48853 (989) 224-8811
Lowe UMC: 5485 W Lowe Rd, St. Johns MI 48879 (989) 224-8811

LIM, SEOK NAM (FL)
Lansing Korean 2014

(H) (517) 669-1275
Lansing Korean UMC: 2400 E Lake Lansing Rd, East Lansing MI 48823-9712 (517) 333-3633

LINDEMAN, STEPHEN FREDERICK (PE) (Trish) – (R-2014, PE-2014)
Greenville First, Turk Lake/Belding Cooperative Parish (PTLP 1/4) 2013; Cedar Springs 2014

(H) 128 E Muskegon St, Cedar Springs, MI 49319 (616) 263-9542
Cedar Springs UMC: 140 S Main St, PO Box K, Cedar Springs MI 49319 (616) 696-1140

***LINDLAND, KENNETH A.O. (RE) (Agnes) – (R-1949, D-1951, E-1952, F-1952)**
Wolf Lake (summer) 1951; Wolf Lake 1952; Wolf Lake/Lake Harbor 1956; Lake Harbor Aug. 1957; Lake Harbor/Unity 1959; Muskegon: Unity/Twin Lake 1961; Wyoming: Wesley Park 1965; Grand Rapids: Oakdale/Westgate Dec. 1, 1969; Kalamazoo: Stockbridge 1973; Traverse City: Emmanuel 1977; Grass Lake 1979; Mulliken/Saranac Mission Sept. 1, 1983; Mulliken/Sebewa Center Nov. 16, 1984; Retired 1987

(H) 1551 Franklin SE Apt 2001, Grand Rapids, MI 49506 (616) 452-2148
(S) 11182-67 Morningside Dr, Boyne Falls, MI 49713 (951) 752-2441

LIPPERT, JANE R. (FE) (M Christopher L Lane) – (R-1984, D-1984, E-1988)
In School, Boston University School of Theology 1984; Oregon State Hospital (CPE) 1985; Riverdale Lincoln Road 1986; Muskegon: Unity (LTFT 1/2) 1990; Grand Rapids: Genesis (co-pastor) (LTFT 1/2) 1995; Leave of Absence 2007; Traverse Bay 2009

(H) 10160 E Pickwick Ct, Traverse City, MI 49684 (231) 947-5594
Traverse Bay UMC: 1200 Ramsdell St., Traverse City MI 49684-1451 (231) 946-5323

LISKE, JULIE (FD) – (R-1994, D-1994, E-1996, FD-2008)
(Formerly Julie Dix) Transferred from Detroit Conf, Portage Chapel Hill (Assoc.) 1994-Nov 30, 1997; Chaplain, Clark Retirement Community Dec 1, 1997; Wayland Aug 1, 2001; Leave of Absence 2003; Spectrum Health: Chaplain (para. 335.1d) (LTFT) 2004; Leave of Absence March 8, 2005; Kalamazoo First (Assoc.) 2006; Executive Director, Metropolitan Ministry of Greater Grand Rapids (LTFT 3/4), 2010; Executive Director, Metropolitan Ministry of Greater Grand Rapids (LTFT 3/4) and Grand Rapids Trinity UMC (Assoc.) (LTFT 1/4) Nov. 8, 2010
(H) 1857 Mayberry St SE, Grand Rapids, MI 49508 (616) 299-0115
(O) United Methodist Metropolitan Ministry of Greater Grand Rapids, 1100 Lake Drive SE, Grand Rapids, MI 49506 (616) 456-7133
Grand Rapids Trinity UMC: 1100 Lake Dr SE, Grand Rapids MI 49506-1538 (616) 456-7168

LITCHFIELD, CARL Q. (FE) (Geri) – (R-1985, D-1985, E-1988)
[Cheshire, West Ohio Conf., Jan 1, 1983-1986]; In school METHESCO 1985; Brooks Corners/Sears 1986; Woodland/Welcome Corners 1991; Boyne City/Boyne Falls 2000; Litchfield 2005; Bellaire Community 2009; Kingsley 2013
(H) PO Box 337, 449 N. Brownson St., Kingsley, MI 49649 (231) 263-5999
Kingsley UMC: PO Box 395, 113 W Blair Street, Kingsley MI 49649 (231) 263-5278

***LITCHFIELD, DAVID L. (RE) (Vera) – (R-1966, E-1969)**
Scottdale (EUB) 1966; W. Mendon Dec. 15, 1968; Mendon/W. Mendon 1969; Elsie/Duplain Nov. 15, 1970; Niles: Grace 1976; Bellaire Jan. 15, 1981; Kalamazoo: Oakwood/Oshtemo 1987; Keeler/Silver Creek 1992; Springport/Lee Center 1998; Battle Creek: Convis Union 2001; Retired 2006
(H) 103 Hubbard Dr, New Carlisle, IN 46552 (574) 654-2297

***LITCHFIELD, GERALDINE M. (RA) (Carl) – (R-2001, D-2001)**
Woodland/Welcome Corners (Assoc.) Jan. 1, 1993-1994; Brookfield (1/2 Time) 1995; Horton Bay/Greensky Hill Indian Mission 2000; leave of absence July 1-Aug. 31, 2005; Somerset Center Sept. 1, 2005; Quincy 2007; Williamsburg/Elk Rapids 2009; Retired 2014
(H) PO Box 337, 449 N. Brownson St., Kingsley, MI 49649 (231) 263-5999

LITCHFIELD, GLENN C. (FE) (Dorie) – (R-1981, D-1981, E-1985)
In School GETS 1981; Vermontville/Gresham 1983; Ashley/Bannister 1990; Kent City Chapel Hill 1996; Cassopolis 2005; Climax/Scotts 2009
(H) 331 Prairie Dr, Climax, MI 49034 (269) 746-8728
Climax UMC: 133 East Maple, PO Box 125, Climax MI 49034-0125 (269) 746-4023
Scotts UMC: 8458 Wallene, PO Box 112, Scotts MI 49088 (269) 626-9757

LOGSTON, JANE D. (FE) (Russell) – (R-1994, D-1988, E-1991)
[West Virginia Conf: CPE at Cabell/Huntington Hospital 1988; Matoaka 1989; Princeton First (Assoc.) 1992; Leave of Absence 1993;] Transferred from West Virginia Conf, Quincy 1994; Mason: First (Assoc.) 1996; Family Leave July 1, 1998; Newberry (Detroit Conf - para. 337.1) 2001; Lawrence 2003; Hinchman/Oronoko (LTFT 1/2) 2006; Berrien Springs/Hinchman/Oronoko 2012; Bear Lake/Arcadia 2014
(H) 12318 Smith St, PO Box 157, Bear Lake, MI 49614-0157 (231) 970-2048
Bear Lake UMC: 7861 Main St, PO Box 157, Bear Lake MI 49614-0157 (231) 864-3680
Arcadia UMC: 3378 Division, PO Box 72, Arcadia MI 49613 (231) 864-3680

LOGSTON, RUSSELL K. (FE) (Jane) – (R-1994, D-1986, E-1991)
[West Virginia Conf: Pleasant Valley 1984; Ceredo 1987; New Salem/Sandlick 1989;] Transferred from West Virginia Conf, Camden/Montgomery/Stokes Chapel 1994; Dansville/Vantown 1996; Constantine 1998; Family Leave 2001; Riverside (LTFT 1/4) Jan 1, 2005; Riverside (LTFT 1/2) Jan 1, 2006; Galien/Olive Branch 2006; Sodus Chapel Hill 2011; Empire 2014
(H) 10205 Aylsworth Rd, PO Box 261, Empire, MI 49630 (231) 326-6098
Empire UMC: 10050 W. Michigan St., PO Box 261, Empire MI 49630 (231) 326-5510

***LONGDEN, LEICESTER R. (RE) (Linda) – (R-1992, D-1973, E-1976)**
[Oregon-Idaho Conf: Salem Clear Lake 1973; Portland Rose City Park (Assoc) 1977; Leave of Absence 1981; Drew University Graduate School 1984; Para. 426.1 Book of Discipline: Chaplain to Drew University 1989;] Transferred from Oregon-Idaho Conf, Lansing Trinity 1992; Associate Professor of Evangelism & Discipleship, University of Dubuque Theological Seminary (Para. 335.1a) 2001; Retired 2013
(H) 10710 Shagbark Rd, Dubuque, IA 52003 (563) 583-9174
(O) Univ of Dubuque Theological Seminary 2000 University Ave, Dubuque, IA 52001-5099 (563) 589-3634

LOOMIS, SCOTT R. (FL) (Kimberly S.)
Pine River Parish (DSA) 2012; Pine River Parish Nov. 10, 2012
(H) 400 W Gilbert St, PO Box 234, LeRoy, MI 49655-0234 (231) 768-4512
Pine River Parish: LeRoy UMC: PO Box 38, LeRoy MI 49655-0038 (231) 768-4972
Pine River Parish: Ashton UMC: PO Box 38, LeRoy MI 49655-0038 (231) 832-8347

LORING, MARY K. (FL) (Mark)
Twin Lake (PTLP 1/2) 2010; Chaplain, Clark Retirement Community (PTLP 1/2) 2013; Coordinator of Pastoral Care, Clark Retirement Community (FTLP) June 1, 2014
(H) 3055 Deli Dr NE, Grand Rapids, MI 49525-3182 (616) 363-0480
(O) Clark Retirement Community, 1551 Franklin SE, Grand Rapids, MI 49506-3331 (616) 452-1568

***LOVER, JOHN D. (RE) (Grace) – (R-1994, D-1961, E-1963)**
[Detroit Conf: Wellsville 1959; NE Ohio Conf: Howard 1960; Detroit Conf: Livingston 1963; Britton Grace 1966; North Branch/Clifford 1969; Lexington/Bethel 1977; Nebraska Conf.: Benkelman/Max 1983; Monument Valley Parish 1984; Fall City Parish 1991; Sargent/Comstock 1993;] Transferred from Nebraska Conf., Indian River/Pellston 1994; Indian River Sept. 1, 1997; Retired 2000
(H) 725 Highland Terrace, Sheboygan, WI 53083 (920) 395-2055

***LOWLEY, PAUL E. (RE) (Marjan) – (R-1991)**
Transferred from Northern Illinois Conf. June 1, 1991, Ludington: United 1991; Retired 2000
(H) 9591 Trails End Rd, Petoskey, MI 49770-8625 (231) 347-9373

***LYMAN, CAROLE S. (RE) (Frank) – (R-1985, D-1985, E-1989)**
Muskegon Lake Harbor (Assoc. LTFT 1/2) Nov. 1, 1984; Muskegon: Lake Harbor (Assoc. LTFT 3/4) Jan. 1, 1991; Plainwell: First (Co-pastor) 1991; East Lansing: University (Co-pastor) 1996; Grand Rapids Trinity 2006; Retired 2010
(H) 29543 Seahorse Cove, Laguna Niguel, CA 92677 (616) 558-1924

***LYMAN JR, FRANK W. (RE) (Carole) – (R-1976, D-1976, E-1980)**
[Plymouth (Assoc.) 1978;] Transferred from Detroit Conf., Muskegon: Lake Harbor 1981; Plainwell: First (Co-pastor) 1991; East Lansing: University (Co-pastor) 1996; Grand Rapids Trinity 2006; Retired 2010
(H) 29543 Seahorse Cove, Laguna Niguel, CA 92677 (616) 558-1924

LYNCH, ROBERT K. (FE) (Leslie) – (R-1993, D-1977-Roman Catholic, E-1995)
Mason (Assoc) 1992; Paw Paw 1995; Kalamazoo: Milwood 1999; North Muskegon Community 2006; Allegan 2012
(H) 1310 South M 40, Allegan, MI 49010 (269) 673-2512
Allegan UMC: 409 Trowbridge St., Allegan MI 49010 (269) 673-4236

***LYONS, GARY V. (RE) – (D-1969, E-1975)**
Transferred from Detroit Conf., Vermontville/Gresham 1972; Chaplain, U.S. Navy April 5, 1976; Retired 1996
(H) 522 Albion Circle, Gallatin, TN 37066 (615) 230-9754

MANNING, SCOTT E. (FE) – (R-2007, E-2011)
Middleville/Freeport 2004; Middleville 2006; Constantine/White Pigeon 2009
(H) 265 White Pigeon St, Constantine, MI 49042 (269) 435-4885
Constantine UMC: 285 White Pigeon St., Constantine MI 49042 (269) 435-8151
White Pigeon UMC: PO Box 518, White Pigeon MI 49099 (269) 483-9054

***MARTIN, CHARLES WILLIAM (RE) – (R-1948, D-1950, E-1952)**
Newaygo 1951; Sanford 1956; Hartford 1960; Edmore 1965; Middleville/Freeport 1969; Clare Oct. 1, 1973; Wyoming Park 1979; South Haven 1984; Retired 1989
(H) 9034 W Chippewa Trail, Shelby, MI 49455-9415 (231) 861-4986

MARTIN, GREGORY J. (FE) – (R-1982, D-1982, E-1987)
In School Wesley Theological Seminary 1982; Leave of Absence 1984; Battle Creek: Baseline Oct 1, 1984; First Congregational United Church of Christ, Downers Grove, IL 1987; Reed City 1993; Albion Dec 1, 1998; Director, Wesley Foundation, University of Michigan (Para 335.1a) 2002; Grand Rapids Aldersgate 2006; Voluntary Leave of Absence (Para 354.2a) 2012
(H) 10601 Abigail St, Portage, MI 49002-7342 (616) 550-1709

***MATHIEU, PAMELA J. (RD) – (Consecrated 1977, R-1997, FD-1997)**
[New York Conf, Endicott, NY: First UMC 1972; Certified 1973-Wyoming Conf; Detroit Conf, Adrian First 1973; Paducah, KY: Broadway 1979; Howell First 1980; Monroe St Paul's 1990] Transferred from Detroit Conf, Director of Visitation and Adult Ministries, Lansing Mt Hope 1995; Transitional Leave, Dec 31, 2005; Incapacity Leave March 1, 2006; Retired 2012
(H) 2500 Lakeshore Blvd., Apt. A222, Ypsilanti, MI 48198

MAURER, EDRYE A. EASTMAN (FE) – (R-2003, E-2006)
In School 1999; Lake City 2000; Jackson: Calvary Sept. 1, 2010; Jackson: Calvary/Zion 2013
(H) 3639 Sweetgum Dr, Jackson, MI 49201-9029 (517) 962-2237
Jackson Calvary UMC: 925 Backus St, Jackson MI 49202 (517) 782-0543
Jackson Zion UMC: 7498 Cooper Rd, Jackson MI 49201 (517) 769-2570

***MAYO, ROBERT J. (RE) (Sharon) – (R-1980, D-1980, E-1983)**
[Saratoga/Mt Zion 1979]; Transferred from Northern Indiana Conf, Marcellus/Wakelee 1981; Hastings Hope April 1, 1986; Traverse City Emmanuel 1992; Grand Rapids St. Paul 1999; Grand Traverse District Superintendent 2005; Battle Creek Chapel Hill 2011; Retired June 30, 2013
(H) 4651 Springmont Dr SE, Kentwood, MI 49512 (616) 617-4704

***MAZUR, PAUL D. (RE) (Margaret) – (R-1968, D-1968, E-1971)**
[Frontier 1963; Girard 1966]; Baseline 1969; Hillside Sept. 15, 1972; Climax/Scotts Sept. 1, 1974; Carson City/Hubbardston 1978; Buchanan: First 1985; Frankfort/Elberta 1987; Coopersville April 1, 1989; Retired 1990
(H) 536 Harwood Ct, Eaton Rapids, MI 48827-1686 (517) 663-2687

MCBRIDE, DAVID L. (FE) (Bonnie) – (R-1985, D-1985, E-1987)
Holton/Sitka 1983; Holton Jan 1985; Marshall (Assoc.) 1988; Ithaca/Beebe 1991; Leighton 2006
(H) 4180 Second St, Caledonia, MI 49316 (616) 891-1646
Leighton UMC: 4180 Second St, Caledonia MI 49316-9627 (616) 891-8028

***MCCAW, KENNETH D. (RE) (Jeanne) – (R-1958, D-1960, E-1962)**
Transferred from Indiana Conf., Caledonia 1962; Muskegon Parish Dec. 1966; Grand Rapids: South 1969; Portage 1975; Kalamazoo District Supt. 1983; Conference Council Director 1989; Kalamazoo: First 1991; Medical Disability Jan. 1, 2000; Retired 2000
(H) 4211 Embassy Dr SE, Grand Rapids, MI 49546-2438 (616) 975-1875

MCCOY, J. PATRICK (FE) (Susan) – (R-1977, D-1977, E-1982)
In school 1977; Three Rivers: First/Ninth Street (Assoc.) Oct. 1, 1980; Resident Supervisory CPE, North Carolina Memorial Hosp., Chapel Hill, NC 1983; Director of Clinical Chaplaincy Iowa Methodist Medical Center, Des Moines, IA Oct. 15, 1985; Director of Chaplaincy, Dartmouth-Hitchcock Medical Center, Lebanon, NH Nov. 1, 1993
(H) 32 Sargent St, Norwich, VT 5055 (802) 649-3736
(O) Dartmouth-Hitchcock Medical Center, 1 Medical Center Dr, Lebanon, NH 03756-0001 (603) 650-7939

***MCCREEDY, ALLEN D. (RE) (Mina Ann) – (R-1965, D-1965, E-1970)**
Kalamazoo: Sunnyside 1967; Kalamazoo: Westwood 1973; Reed City 1977; Cadillac 1990; Retired 2000
(H) 2015 Kaylyn Dr, Cadillac, MI 49601-8210 (231) 775-8254

MCDERMONT, TREVOR J. (FL) (Susan)
Grand Rapids Church of All Nations (PTLP) 2009; Camden/Montgomery/Stokes Chapel (PTLP 3/4) 2010; Paw Paw 2013
(H) 52333 Ackley Terrace, Paw Paw, MI 49079-9567 (269) 657-4506
Paw Paw UMC: 420 W. Michigan Ave., Paw Paw MI 49079 (269) 657-7727

MCKENNEY, WAYNE E. (FL) (Sally)
D.S. Assignment: Chase Barton/Grant Center 1995; Chase Barton/Grant Center Nov. 16, 1995; Webberville August 1, 2002; Boyne City/Boyne Falls 2005; LifeSpring/Lawton St. Paul's 2014
LifeSpring UMC: 1560 S 8th Street, Oshtemo MI 49009 (269) 353-1303
Lawton St Paul's UMC: 63855 N. M-40, PO Box 456, Lawton MI 49065 (269) 624-1050

***MCNARY, SANDRA B. HOFFMAN (RE) (Charles) – (R-1994, D-1984, E-1988)**
[Tennessee Conf.: Mt. Carmel 1982; Bethesda: Wesley Chapel 1986;] Transferred from Tennessee Conf., Bangor: Simpson 1994-2007; Retired 2007
(H) 32054 CR 687, Bangor, MI 49013-9405 (269) 427-0766

***MCNAUGHTON, JOHN W. (RE) (Donna Lee) – (R-1971, D-1971, E-1974)**
In school 1971; transferred from Detroit Conf., Webberville/Bell Oak 1973; Kalamazoo: Oakwood 1979; Concord 1982; Grand Rapids: Plainfield 1984; Gobles-Kendall 1986; para. 426.1 Book of Discipline: Methodist Church, Blackheath Circuit, England 1987; Frankfort/Elberta 1993; Kalamazoo: Lane Blvd. 1996; Kalamazoo: Stockbridge/Lane Blvd. 1998; Kalamazoo: Stockbridge Ave. (LTFT 1/2) Jan. 16, 2000; Kalamazoo: Stockbridge Ave/Northwest May 1, 2000; Retired 2003; Bloomingdale (interim pastor) Dec. 8-31, 2008
(H) 2910 Bronson Blvd, Kalamazoo, MI 49008-2372 (269) 383-3433

MCPHERSON, ROB A. (FE) (Kristi) – (R-1997, E-2001)
Grandville (Assoc.) 1994; Ovid: United 1999; Buchanan First 2006
(H) 304 Pontiac Court, Buchanan, MI 49107-1273 (269) 695-3896
Buchanan First UMC: 132 S. Oak Street, Buchanan MI 49107 (269) 695-3282

***MCREYNOLDS, RUSSELL F. (RE) – (R-1991)**
[Detroit Conf, Flint Bethel 1973;] Transferred from Detroit Conf June 1, 1991, Washington Heights June 16, 1991; Kalamazoo District Superintendent 1996; Lansing Central 2002; Retired 2007; Lansing Faith & South Lansing Ministries (Ret.) 2008
(H) 1721 Dover Place, Lansing, MI 48910-1146 (517) 483-2727
Lansing Faith & South Lansing Ministries: 4301 S Waverly Rd, Lansing MI 48911-2560 (517) 882-0661

MEISTER, DAVID W. (FE) (Denise) – (R-1977, D-1977, E-1980)
Transferred from East Ohio Conf., Rosebush/Leaton 1978; Lakeview/Belvidere 1980; Litchfield 1985; Leave of Absence March 16, 1990; Haslett: Aldersgate 1994; Union City Aug. 1, 1995; Centreville Aug. 16, 1997; Buchanan: First 2003; Casco 2006
(H) 870 66th St, South Haven, MI 49090 (269) 227-3914
Casco UMC: 880 66th Street, South Haven MI 49090 (269) 227-3328

***MERCER, DOROTHY DOUGLAS (RD) (David) – (Consecrated 1987, R-1997, FD-1997)**
Director of Music, Grand Rapids: Faith 1987; Stanwood (LTFT 1/4) 1997; Retired March 1, 2003
(H) 8651 Mohawk Ct, Stanwood, MI 49346 (231) 972-7175

MESSNER, JOHN D. (FL) (Sally)
Marcellus/Wakelee (DSA) 2007; Marcellus/Wakelee Jan. 1, 2008
(H) 224 Davis St, Marcellus, MI 49067 (269) 646-7791
Marcellus UMC: 197 W Main St, PO Box 396, Marcellus MI 49067 (269) 646-5801
Wakelee UMC: 15921 Dutch Settlement, Marcellus MI 49067-9530 (269) 646-2049

METZGER, KIMBERLY A. (PE) (Gary A.) – (R-2008, PE-2008)
(Formerly Kimberly Tallent; Married 7/1/11) Dansville Aug 1, 2006; Dimondale/Grovenburg 2008; Country Chapel 2009; North Adams/Jerome/Osseo 2011; Leave of Absence Dec 19, 2011
(H) 4933 S Charlton Park Rd, Hastings, MI 49058 (269) 282-4622

MILAM, CHARLES (ED) EDWARD (FL) (Jennifer)

Big Rapids Third Ave/Paris/Rodney (DSA) 2011; Big Rapids Third Ave/Paris/Rodney, Nov 12, 2011; Carson City 2014

(H) 121 S Abbott St, Carson City, MI 48811 (989) 584-3366
Carson City UMC: 119 E Elm Street, PO Box 298, Carson City MI 48811 (989) 584-3797

***MILES, DAVID L. (RE) (Marilyn) – (R-1963, D-1963, E-1966)**

In school School of Theology at Claremont 1963; Transferred to Pacific Northwest Conf., Mt. Lake Terrace/Bothell, Washington (Assoc.) 1964; Asotin/Anatone, Washington 1965; Transferred from Pacific Northwest Conf. June 1, 1967; Battle Creek: First (Assoc.) 1967; Grand Haven (Assoc.) 1971; Elsie/Duplain 1976; Farwell 1983; Breckenridge 1994; Retired 1999

(H) 309 Fieldstone Dr, Hemlock, MI 48626 (989) 642-3075

***MILLER, CLYDE E. (RA) (Judith) – (R-1971, D-1964, E-1966)**

[South Indiana Conf.: Cynthiana 1960; Lyons 1963; Monroe City 1966; without appointment 1967-1971;] Evansville Asbury 1971; transferred from South Indiana Conf., Pentwater/Smith Corners 1973; Pentwater 1976; Pentwater/Smith Corners 1977; Dowagiac Dec. 1, 1979; Lansing: Christ April 16, 1983; Leave of absence Jan. 31, 1987; Retired 1987

(H) 1117 Park St, Pentwater, MI 49449 (231) 869-2151

MILLER, DARRYL L. (PL) (Shari Ann)

Sand Lake/South Ensley (DSA) (PTLP 1/2) Jan. 1, 2007; Sand Lake/South Ensley (PTLP 1/2) Dec. 1, 2007; Sand Lake/South Ensley (PTLP 1/4) 2011

(H) 1568 Solon, Cedar Springs, MI 49319-9438 (616) 696-4057
Sand Lake UMC: PO Box 97, Sand Lake MI 49343 (616) 636-5673
South Ensley UMC: PO Box 97, Sand Lake MI 49343 (616) 636-5659

MILLER, MARK D. (OE) – (R-2013)

[Detroit Conference, Elder] Muskegon Central 2013

(H) 1707 Ritter Dr, Norton Shores, MI 49441 (231) 766-8989
Muskegon Central UMC: 1011 Second Street, Muskegon MI 49440 (231) 722-6545

MILLER, TIMOTHY JAY (FE) (Deborah Reid-Miller) – (R-1992)

Transferred from Louisville Conf. June 1, 1992; Leave of Absence June 1, 1992; Hersey July 1, 1992; Barryton/Chippewa Lake (LTFT 3/4) 1994; Grand Rapids: Pawating Magedwin and Salem/Bradley Indian Missions 1995; Grand Rapids: Pa Wa Ting Ma Ged Win 1999; Incapacity Leave Jan. 1, 2002

(H) 3080 Waterchase Way SW Apt 110, Wyoming, MI 49519-5961 (616) 350-2909

***MINGER, DAVID H. (RE) – (R-1991, D-1991, E-1993)**

Nottawa (Part-Time) Oct 1, 1983; Athens Sept 1, 1987; Springport/Lee Center 1991; Portage Prairie 1995; Traverse City Emmanuel 1999; Ogdensburg (Re-Named Old Mission Peninsula UMC) Feb 1, 2003; Retired 2006; Pleasant Lake/Jackson Zion (DSA) 2008; Griffith (Ret.) (LTFT 1/4) 2013

(H) 806 Emmaus Rd, Eaton Rapids, MI 48827 (517) 256-5857
Griffith UMC: 9537 S Clinton Trail, Eaton Rapids MI 48827 (517) 663-6262

MINGER, STACY R. (FE) – (R-1988, D-1988, E-1991)

In School, Asbury Theological Seminary 1988; Girard/Ellis Corners 1989; In School, Asbury Theological Seminary 1994; Wayland 1995; To Attend School,University of Kentucky August 1, 2001; Asbury Theological Seminary, Associate Professor (para. 335.1b) 2004

(H) 406 Wabarto Way, Nicholasville, KY 40356-2812
(O) Asbury Theological Seminary, 204 N Lexington Ave, Wilmore, KY 40390 (859) 858-2000

***MINOR, DANIEL J. (RE) (Jolene) – (R-1968, D-1968, E-1970)**

Transferred from East Ohio Conf., East Jordan/Barnard/Norwood April 15, 1974; Shelby 1981; Parchment 1989; Retired 2011

(H) 719 Bayberry Ln, Otsego, MI 49078-1508 (269) 692-2119

MITCHELL, MARK E. (FL) (Joyce)

Howard City: First/Amble/Coral 1995; Howard City: Maple Hill/First/Coral (Assoc) Aug 1, 1999; Howard City: Heritage (Assoc) Aug 1, 1999; Homer/Lyon Lake 2000; Evart 2008; Fife Lake Parish 2012; Sodus Chapel Hill 2014

(H) 4033 Naomi Rd, Sodus, MI 49126 (269) 925-4528
Sodus Chapel Hill UMC: 4071 Naomi Road, Sodus MI 49126 (269) 927-3454

MITCHUM, JAMES P. (FE) (Michelle) – (R-1984, E-1986)
Charlotte (Assoc.) April 16, 1983; Robbins June 1, 1987; Petoskey 1997
(H) 900 Jennings, Petoskey, MI 49770 (231) 374-4747
Petoskey UMC: 1804 E. Mitchell Road, Petoskey MI 49770-9686 (231) 347-2733

MOLNER, HEATHER A. (PE) (Bert) – (R-2014, PE-2014)
(Formerly Heather McDougall) Silver Creek/Keeler 2011; Milwood 2013
(H) 6830 Cypress St, Portage, MI 49024-3208 (269) 459-6237
Kalamazoo Milwood UMC: 3919 Portage Road, Kalamazoo MI 49001 (269) 381-6720

MOMANY, CHRISTOPHER P. (FE) (Kimberly) – (R-1986, D-1986, E-1989)
In school Princeton Theological Seminary 1986; Mecosta: New Hope 1987; Pentwater: Centenary 1993; Chaplain & Director of Church Relations, Adrian College January 1, 1996
(H) 1325 University Ave, Adrian, MI 49221 (517) 265-8144
(O) Adrian College, Adrian College Valade Hall 133, 110 S Madison St, Adrian, MI 49221-2575 (517) 265-5161 ext4211

MONDRAGON, REY CARLOS BORJA (OE) – (R-2014)
[Detroit Conference, Elder] Hartford (para. 346.1) 2014
(H) 143 Paras Hill Dr, Hartford, MI 49057 (734) 645-8991
Hartford UMC: 425 East Main Street, Hartford MI 49057 (269) 621-4103

***MOORE, JOHN L. (RE) (Ellie) – (R-1981, E-1961 (Free Methodist), E-2007 (WMAC))**
[Transferred in from Free Methodist, 1981] Arden Nov. 1, 1980; Kalamazoo: Stockbridge March 16, 1988; Galesburg 1992; Retired 1995; Center Park 1995-1997; Union City (DSA) Aug. 17, 1997-2004; Portage First (Assoc.) (DSA) Oct. 1, 2006; Portage First (Assoc.) (DSA 3/4) and Kalamazoo Stockbridge Avenue (DSA 1/4) 2007; Portage First (Assoc.) (DSA 3/4) 2010; Portage First (Assoc.) (DSA 1/2) and Galesburg (DSA 1/2) 2012-2013; Trowbridge (Ret.) (LTFT 1/4) 2014
(H) 2924 Vanderbilt Ave, Portage, MI 49024 (269) 327-1243
Trowbridge UMC: 355 26th Street, Otsego MI 49078-9621 (269) 673-5502

MOORE, JOY JITTAUN (FE) – (R-1989, D-1989, E-1991)
Jackson: First (Assoc.) 1988; Battle Creek: Baseline 1990; Chaplain and Director of Church Relations, Adrian College Aug. 16, 1993; Battle Creek: Trinity 1995; Lansing: Trinity (assoc.) May 1, 1996; Asbury Theological Seminary, Director of Women's Ministries and Ethnic Concerns 1997; Director of Student Life 1998; Asbury Theological Seminary, Instructor of Preaching (para. 335.1a) Aug. 16, 2000; Asbury Theological Seminary, Professor of Preaching July 1, 2003; Greenville 2007; Duke Divinity School, Associate Dean for Lifelong Learning, 2008; Duke Divinity School, Associate Dean for Black Church Studies and Church Relations 2009; Fuller Theological Seminary, Associate Dean of African-American Church Studies and Assistant Professor of Preaching, Sept. 1, 2012 (para. 344.1a)
(H) 700 Locust St, Pasadena, CA 91101-1630
(O) Fuller Theological Seminary, 135 N Oakland Ave, Pasadena, CA 91182 (626) 584-5599

MOORE, RICHARD D. (FE) (Margo) – (R-1988, D-1988, E-1992)
In School Asbury Theological Seminary 1988; Howard City Maple Hill 1989; Howard City Maple Hill/First/Coral Aug 1, 1999; Howard City Heritage Aug 1, 1999; Hastings Hope 2000
(H) 121 W North St, Hastings, MI 49058 (269) 945-3397
Hastings Hope UMC: PO Box 410, Hastings MI 49058-0410 (269) 945-4995

MOORE-JUMONVILLE, ROBERT S. (FE) (Kimberly) – (R-2008)
[Transferred from Illinois Great Rivers Conf 2008] Spring Arbor Univ, Associate Professor of Religion 2007; Spring Arbor University and Pope 2010
(H) 21 Dickens Street, Spring Arbor, MI 49283 (517) 524-6818
(O) Spring Arbor University, Spring Arbor University, 106 East Main Street, Spring Arbor, MI 49283 (517) 750-6693
Pope UMC: 10401 Townley Rd, Springport MI 49284-0228 (517) 857-3655

MORRISON, DIANNE DOTEN (PL) (Richard)
Sturgis (Assoc) Jan 1, 1996; LP w/o Appointment Dec 31, 1997; Gull Lake (Assoc) 1998; Country Chapel Feb 1, 2001; Muskegon Crestwood 2004; Hesperia/Ferry (PTLP) 2007; Traverse City Christ (PTLP 1/4) 2011
(H) 7750 S West Bayshore Dr, Traverse City, MI 49684 (231) 944-5704
Traverse City Christ UMC: 1249 Three Mile Rd. S, Traverse City MI 49696 (231) 946-3048

MORRISON, REBECCA K. (FE) – (R-2003, E-2008)
In School; Potterville January 16, 2002; Big Rapids First 2011
(H) 14080 Wildwood Dr, Big Rapids, MI 49307-8782 (231) 796-5311
Big Rapids First UMC: 304 Elm Street, Big Rapids MI 49307 (231) 796-7771

***MORRISON, RICHARD A. (RE) (Dianne Doten) – (R-1967, D-1967, E-1969)**
In school 1967; Jackson First (Assoc.) 1969; Bainbridge Newhope 1971; Missioner, Alaska Missionary Conf 1972; Transferred to West Ohio Conf, North Broadway (Assoc.) 1975; Pastoral Counseling Services, Inc. (ABLC) 1981; Transferred from West Ohio Conf, Alden/Central Lake June 1, 1992; Sturgis 1995; Albion District Superintendent Jan 1, 1998; Muskegon Lake Harbor 2004; Hesperia/Ferry (DSA) 2007-2011; Retired 2007
(H) 7750 S West Bayshore Dr, Traverse City, MI 49684 (231) 944-5503

***MORSE, JOHN D. (RE) (Darleen) – (R-1971, D-1971, E-1975)**
In School 1971; Center Eaton/Brookfield 1973; Sunfield/Sebewa Center Feb 1, 1976; Frankfort/Elberta 1982; Traverse City: Christ 1987; Jackson: First (Assoc) 1993; Coopersville 1999; Retired 2012; Twin Lake (Ret.) (LTFT 1/2) 2013; Twin Lake (Ret.) (LTFT 45%) Jan. 1, 2014
(H) 14879 Cross Lane, Spring Lake, MI 49456 (616) 844-0841
Twin Lake UMC: 5940 S Main St, PO Box 352, Twin Lake MI 49457-0352 (231) 828-4083

MORT, JAMES J. (FE) (Janet) – (R-2007, E-2010)
Marion/Cadillac South Community, 2007
(H) 205 Flemming St, Marion, MI 49665 (231) 743-0062
Marion UMC: 216 W Main St, PO Box C, Marion MI 49665 (231) 743-2834
Cadillac South Community UMC: PO Box C, Marion MI 49665 (231) 775-3067

***MORTON, DAVID L. (RE) (Carrie) – (R-1959, E-1966)**
Gilead (EUB) 1961; Scottdale (EUB) 1963; Vicksburg (EUB) 1965; Hillsdale (Assoc) 1969; Kent City: Chapel Hill 1970; Delta Mills/Eagle Jan 15, 1974; Jackson: First (Assoc) 1982; Battle Creek: Maple 1986; Battle Creek Health System, Chaplain May 1, 1996; Retired 2001; Battle Creek First (Ret.) (LTFT 1/4), March 5-June 30, 2014
(H) 4285 E Kirby Rd, Battle Creek, MI 49017 (269) 964-7098

MULLIGAN, CHERYL A. (PD) – (R-2012, PD-2012)
Respiratory Therapist, Helen DeVos Pediatric Pulmonary Clinic, Grand Rapids (Full-Time) and Pastoral Care Minister at Genesis UMC (10 Hrs/Week Unpaid), 2012; Primary: Respiratory Therapist, Helen DeVos Pediatric Pulmonary Clinic, Grand Rapids (Full-Time) and (secondary) Lowell UMC Jan. 1, 2014
(H) 3170 Buttrick Ave SE, Ada, MI 49301-9216 (616) 340-7995
(O) Helen DeVos Pediatric Pulmonary Clinic, 35 Michigan St NE Ste 3003,
Grand Rapids, MI 49503 (616) 267-2200
Lowell UMC: 621 E Main St, Lowell MI 49331 (616) 897-5936

MURPHY, MARSHALL (PL) (Marian)
Battle Creek Washington Heights (PTLP 1/4) 2011; Battle Creek First (PTLP 1/2) and Washington Heights (PTLP 1/4) 2014
(H) 26 W Roosevelt, Battle Creek, MI 49037 (269) 223-7949
Battle Creek First UMC: 111 East Michigan Ave, Battle Creek MI 49014-4012 (269) 963-5567
Battle Creek Washington Heights UMC: 153 N Wood St, Battle Creek MI 49037 (269) 968-8773

NASH, KENNETH J. (FE) (Christine Frances) – (R-2000, E-2004)
[Kentucky Conf, Elkhorn and Stoner Creek UMCs: Kentucky]; Transfered from Kentucky Conf, Carson City 2000; Cornerstone (Assoc) 2006; Cornerstone (Assoc) (LTFT 1/4) 2011; Cornerstone (Assoc.) (Full-Time) 2012
(H) 6760 Airfield Ct SW, Byron Center, MI 49315 (616) 534-2074
Grand Rapids Cornerstone UMC: 1675 84th St SE, Caledonia MI 49316 (616) 698-3170

NEIHARDT, MICHAEL (FL)
Horton Bay (PTLP 1/4) 2013; Boyne City/Boyne Falls (3/4 time) / Horton Bay (1/4 time) 2014
(H) 2347 Shawn Rd., Kalkaska, MI 49646 (231) 258-6180
Boyne City UMC: 324 S. Park St., Boyne City MI 49712 (231) 582-9776
Boyne Falls UMC: 324 S Park St, Boyne City MI 49712 (231) 582-9776
Horton Bay UMC: 4961 Boyne City Rd, Boyne City MI 49712-9217 (231) 582-9262

NELLIST, DAVID (OE) (Glenys) – (R-2000)
[British Methodist Conference] Schoolcraft 2000; Gull Lake 2008; Grand Rapids: Trinity 2010
(H) 1507 Lenox Dr SE, Grand Rapids, MI 49506 (269) 903-8560
Grand Rapids Trinity UMC: 1100 Lake Dr SE, Grand Rapids MI 49506-1538 (616) 456-7168

***NELSON, DAVID B. (RE) (Jean Freeland) – (R-1961, D-1961, E-1964)**
[Mt. Pleasant: Wesley Foundation Director, Central Mich. Univ. 1959; Camden/Montgomery 1960]; Saugatuck/New Richmond 1962; Coopersville/Nunica Jan. 1965; Portage: Chapel Hill March 1968; Ithaca 1972; Ithaca/Beebe 1976; Lansing Faith Sept. 16, 1980; Hastings: First 1985; Plainwell 1989; Conference Council Director 1991; Retired 1998
(H) 84 N M 37 Hwy, Hastings, MI 49058-8273 (989) 297-0257

NELSON, FOREST (BERT) BERTRAN (OF) (Susan Garbarind)
[Presbyterian Church USA] Lyons-Muir Church (LTFT 3/4) (para. 346.2), January 1, 2005
(H) 1074 Olmstead Road, Muir, MI 48860 (616) 891-8918
Lyons-Muir Church: 1074 Olmstead Road, Muir MI 48860 (989) 855-2247

NGUYEN, DANIEL DUNG (FL) (Minh Ha Le)
[North Texas Conf: Vietnamese Living Faith UMC, Highland Village, TX 1-1-12] Grand Rapids Vietnamese 2012
(H) 497 Harp St. SE, Kentwood, MI 49548 (616) 288-3007
Grand Rapids Vietnamese UMC: 212 Bellevue St SE, Wyoming MI 49548 (616) 534-6262

NICHOLS, LAWRENCE A. (FL)
Waterloo First/Waterloo Village (DSA) 1978; Waterloo First/Waterloo Village 1979-1988; Jackson Zion Feb 1, 1994; Hersey 2003; Byron Center 2010
(H) 8650 Meadow Haven Dr SW, Byron Center, MI 49315-9243 (616) 878-9739
Byron Center UMC: 2490 Prescott SW, Byron Center MI 49315 (616) 878-1618

***NISWENDER, R. IVAN (RE) (Phyllis) – (R-1953, E-1958)**
Hersey (EUB) 1958; Hersey/Grant Center (EUB) 1960; Battle Creek: Calvary (EUB) 1962; Grand Rapids: Northlawn (EUB) 1966; Perry/Shaftsburg 1969; Honorable Location 1971; Trowbridge 1981; Readmitted 1989; Trowbridge (LTFT 3/4) 1989; Trowbridge 1993; Retired 1994
(H) 1425 Avalon Ct, Winona Lake, IN 46590 (574) 372-6344

NOGGLE, JAMES C. (PE) (Karen) – (R-1995, D-1995, AM-1995, PE-2014)
Nashville Parish: Peace and Quimby 1989; Millville March 1, 1993; Mecosta: New Hope 1997; Harrison: The Gathering (New Church Start) 2004; The Gathering (WMAC)/Wagarville/Wooden Shoe (DAC) 2009; Grand Rapids: Northlawn 2010; Lake Odessa Lakewood 2013
(H) 10290 N Polk Ave, Harrison, MI 48625 (269) 367-4161
Lake Odessa Lakewood UMC: 10265 E Brown Rd, Lake Odessa MI 48849-9207 (269) 367-4800

NYSTROM, ROBERT D. (FE) (Ronda) – (R-1989, D-1989, E-1992)
Hopkins/South Monterey 1989; Traverse City Central (Assoc) 1992; Bronson 1994; St Louis 1998; Dimondale & East Lansing Chapel Hill 2002; East Lansing Chapel Hill (LTFT 1/2) Jan 16, 2004; Webberville 2005; Battle Creek Birchwood 2007; Battle Creek Birchwood (LTFT 3/4) and Athens (LTFT 1/4) 2011; Three Rivers First (LTFT 1/2) 2012; Three Rivers First/Mendon 2013
(H) 1101 Elm St, Three Rivers, MI 49093 (269) 278-5565
Three Rivers First UMC: 215 N. Main, Three Rivers MI 49093 (269) 278-4722
Mendon UMC: PO Box 308, Mendon MI 49072-0308 (269) 496-4295

OLIN, MELODY LANE (FL) (Denny)
Blanchard-Pine River/Coomer/Winn (DSA) 2006; Blanchard-Pine River/Coomer/Winn (FTLP) Nov. 15, 2006; Old Mission Peninsula 2010
(H) 14432 Peninsula Dr, Traverse City, MI 49686 (231) 223-4141
Old Mission Peninsula UMC: 16426 Center Rd, Traverse City MI 49686-9775 (231) 223-4393

OLSEN, SUSAN D. (FE) (Robert) – (R-2008, E-2011)
Hesperia/Ferry (PTLP) Jan 1, 1998-July 1, 1998; Gobles/Kendall 1998-July 15, 2004; Mt Pleasant Trinity/Countryside/Leaton July 16, 2004; Welcome Corners/Freeport/Peace Aug 1, 2006
(H) 175 Cherry St, Freeport, MI 49325 (616) 765-3838
Welcome Corners UMC: 3185 N M-43 Hwy, Hastings MI 49058-7944 (269) 945-2654
Freeport UMC: PO Box 142, Freeport MI 49325-0142 (616) 765-5316
Peace UMC: 6043 E M-79 Hwy, Nashville MI 49073 (517) 852-1993

***ORR, KARIN K. (RE) – (R-2003, E-2006)**
Centreville 2003; Retired 2014
(H) 1135 La Salette Dr SE, Grand Rapids, MI 49546 (616) 901-4382

OSTEMA, DALE P. (FE) (Deborah) – (R-1987, D-1987, E-1990)
In School, METHESCO 1987; Baldwin: Covenant Community 1988; Charlevoix/Greensky Hill Feb 1, 1993; Charlevoix Feb 1, 1998; Cadillac 2000; Traverse City Central 2007
(H) 1713 Indian Woods Dr, Traverse City, MI 49686 (231) 933-4026
Traverse City Central UMC: 222 Cass St., Traverse City MI 49684 (231) 946-5191

OTIS, SCOTT K. (FE) (Carolyn) – (R-1988, D-1988, E-1991)
In School, METHESCO 1988; Lyons/Muir (Student Appointment) July 16, 1988; Lyons/Muir (Full-Time) Nov 16, 1988; Lyons/Muir/Ionia: Easton 1990; Mecosta: New Hope 1993; Portland 1997; Grand Rapids: Cornerstone (Assoc/New Church Start) 2003; Cross Wind Community (New Church Start) Oct 1, 2004
(H) 4380 Tracy Tr, Dorr, MI 49323 (616) 681-0302
CrossWind Community UMC: 1683 142nd Avenue, Dorr MI 49323 (616) 681-0302

PAHL, CRAIG A. (FL)
Jonesville/Allen 2000; Jonesville/Allen/Moscow Plains 2001; Jonesville/Allen/Moscow Plains, Full-Time 2004; Jonesville/Allen 2007; Barnard/East Jordan/Norwood 2014
(H) 305 Esterly, PO Box 238, East Jordan, MI 49727 (231) 536-7596
Barnard UMC: PO Box 878, East Jordan MI 49727-0878 (231) 547-5269
East Jordan UMC: PO Box 878, East Jordan MI 49727-0878 (231) 536-2161
Norwood UMC: PO Box 878, East Jordan MI 49727-0878

PALMER, DAVID (MIKE) MICHAEL (FL) (Darla)
Mt. Pleasant Trinity/Countryside/Leaton 2010
(H) 250 S Crawford Rd, Mt Pleasant, MI 48858-9053 (989) 772-3725
Mt Pleasant Trinity UMC: 202 S Elizabeth Street, Mt Pleasant MI 48858 (989) 772-5690
Countryside UMC: 202 S. Elizabeth Street, Mt Pleasant MI 48858 (989) 773-0359
Leaton UMC: 6890 E Beal City Road, Mt Pleasant MI 48858 (989) 773-3838

***PANSE, WADE S. (RE) (Patti) – (R-1978, D-1978, E-1980)**
Burr Oak 1978; Robbins March 1, 1982; Lansing: Mt Hope, May 1, 1987; Director of Alumni, Asbury Theological School, Oct 16, 1992; Mt. Pleasant: First 1995; St. Joseph: First 1997; Retired Jan 1, 2012
(H) 1218 Riverwood Terrace, St Joseph, MI 49085 (269) 982-2920

PAPARELLA, AMEE A. (PE) (James A.) – (R-2009, PE-2009)
(Formerly Amee Miller, married 5-21-11) Williamston 2009; Appointed to Attend School - Michigan State University (Para. 416.6) 2011; Director/Organizer for Women's Advocacy, General Board of Church and Society (Para. 344.1a) Aug. 27, 2012; Wacousta 2013
(H) 9590 Looking Glass Brook Dr, Grand Ledge, MI 48837 (517) 862-2599
Wacousta UMC: 9180 Herbison Rd, Eagle MI 48822-9718 (517) 626-6623

PARMALEE, CHAD M. (PE) (Roschenne) – (R-2014, PE-2014)
Jackson Brookside Sept 1, 2005; Battle Creek Chapel Hill 2013
(H) 192 Brentwood Dr, Battle Creek, MI 49015-4512 (269) 589-9872
Battle Creek Chapel Hill UMC: 157 Chapel Hill Drive, Battle Creek MI 49015-4631 (269) 963-0231

PARSONS, CYNTHIA M. (FE) (Jeff) – (R-1988, D-1988, E-1992)
(Formerly Cynthia Schaefer) In school METHESCO 1988; North East Missaukee Parish 1989; Williamsburg 1993; Kalamazoo First (Assoc.) 1997; Casco 2001; Berrien Springs (LTFT 1/2) 2006; Detroit Conference, Owendale/Gagetown (LTFT 3/4) (para. 346.1) 2012; Detroit Conference, Sebewaing: Trinity 2014
(H) 513 Washington, Sebewaing, MI 48759 (989) 883-2350
(O) Sebewaing Trinity UMC, 513 Washington, Sebewaing, MI 48759 (989) 883-3350

***PASSENGER, EDWARD L. (RE) (Sally) – (R-1959, D-1960, E-1962)**
[Wheeler 1958]; in school 1960; Northport/Leland/Northport Indian Mission 1962; Alden Sept. 15, 1965; Caledonia/Parmelee Dec. 1, 1966; Hart/Mears Dec. 1, 1969; Honorable Location June 1971; Chaplain, Ionia Temporary Correctional Facility 1987; Carson City Temporary Correctional Facility, Dec. 28, 1987; Retired 1999
(H) 526 Ferry St, Spring Lake, MI 49456-1212 (616) 566-8833

PATERA, NANCY J. (FL) (Greg)
Ionia Easton (PTLP 1/2) Jan. 1, 2007; Burnips/Monterey Center 2014
(H) 4290 Summer Creek Dr, Dorr, MI 49323 (616) 371-7051
Burnips & Monterey Center UMCs: PO Box 30, Burnips MI 49314 (616) 896-8410

***PATTERSON, PAUL E. (RE) (Beverly) – (R-1951, D-1952, E-1955)**
[Altoona: Mardorf (Central PA) 1948; Edwardsburg Oct. 1, 1950] In School, Garrett 1951; Edwardsburg 1951; Grand Rapids: First (Assoc.) 1955; Wacousta 1957; Cedar Springs 1958; Grand Rapids: South Sept. 7, 1960; Ludington: First 1964; Kalamazoo: Westwood 1967; Sparta 1968; Allegan 1973; Paw Paw 1979; Grand Rapids: Faith 1984; St. Johns: First 1987; Barryton/Chippewa Lake July 1-Oct. 1, 1990; Retired Oct. 1, 1990
(H) Clark Retirement Community, 1551 Franklin SE Apt. 4065,
Grand Rapids, MI 49506 (616) 616-243-2967

PAYNE, MARK R. (FE) (Nola) – (R-1994, D-1994, E-1997)
Rosebush 1992; Rosebush (LTFT 1/2) 1994; Rosebush (LTFT 3/4) Jan 1, 1995; Rosebush (LTFT 3/4) and Clare (Assoc-LTFT 1/4) 1995; Rosebush 1996; Life Spring (New Church Start) 2001; Robbins 2009; Hastings First 2014
(H) 935 N Taffee Dr, Hastings, MI 49058 (269) 945-2343
Hastings First UMC: 209 W Green St, Hastings MI 49058-2229 (269) 945-9574

***PAYNE, WILLIAM V. (RE) (Jayne) – (R-1960, D-1960, E-1962)**
[East Osceola Circuit 1951; Middle Branch Church 1954; Leave of absence 1955; Dowagiac 1957]; Decatur 1960; Edmore 1961; Paw Paw 1965; Hillsdale 1979; Sodus: Chapel Hill 1987; Retired 1996
(H) 8000 Warren Woods Rd Lot 64, Three Oaks, MI 49128 (269) 469-7643

PEBLEY, PATRICIA A. (FL) (Allen D.)
Jackson Trinity/Parma (PTLP 1/2) 2012; Hillside/Somerset Center 2014
(H) 6094 Folks Rd, Horton, MI 49246 (517) 563-8920
Hillside UMC: 6100 Folks Rd., Horton MI 49246 (517) 563-2835
Somerset Center UMC: 12095 E. Chicago Rd., PO Box 277, Somerset Center MI 49282 (517) 688-4330

***PEDERSEN, DOUGLAS L. (RE) (Darlene) – (R-1970, D-1970, E-1972)**
Center Park 1970; transferred from Minnesota Conf., St. Joseph (Assoc.) 1971; Saugatuck/Ganges Oct. 15, 1973; Turk Lake Aug. 15, 1975; Wyoming: Wesley Park (Assoc.) 1979; Wayland 1982; Grand Rapids: Faith 1987; Leland Feb. 16, 1994-1997; Williamsburg 1997; Traverse City: Emmanuel/Williamsburg Feb. 1, 2003; Traverse Bay/Williamsburg Jan. 2005 (Emmanuel merged with Asbury becoming Traverse Bay January 2005); Retired 2005
(H) 102 W Terrace Lane Commons, PO Box 314, Leland, MI 49654-0314 (231) 256-9088

PENNY III, KELLAS D. (FL) (Leanne)
[Oklahoma Conf, United Campus Ministry, Executive Director] Harrison: The Gathering (PTLP 1/2) 2013; Rivercrest New Church Start, Jan. 1, 2014
(H) 930 Elmdale, Grand Rapids, MI 49525 (616) 209-2828
Grand Rapids Rivercrest Church: 214 Spencer NE, Grand Rapids MI 49505 (580) 559-1207

***PERKINS, A. EDWARD (RE) (Shirley) – (R-1981, D-1967, E-1970)**
[Weston 1964; Indianola/Morral/Hepburn 1967; Saginaw: First (Assoc.) 1970; Lambertville 1972; Insight Inc., Hurley Hospital, Flint 1974; Director of Alcoholism Programs, Satellite Clinics, Ford Hospital, Detroit 1975; Honorable Location 1976; Bronson Dec. 1, 1980;] Transferred from Detroit Conf., Bronson 1981; Fremont April 1, 1987; Lansing District Supt. 1990; Grand Rapids: Trinity 1996; Retired 2006; Interim Conference Director Oct. 1-Dec. 31, 2008
(H) 3052 Bonita Dr SE, Grand Rapids, MI 49508 (616) 241-6622

PETERSON, GARY L. (FL) (Reba)
Olivet (DSA) 2006; Fennville/Pearl 2008
(H) 687 W Fennville St, Fennville, MI 49408-8404 (269) 561-2537
Fennville Pearl UMCs: 5849 124th Ave, PO Box 407, Fennville MI 49408 (269) 561-5048

***PETRO, SUSAN M. (RE) (John Geiser) – (R-1994, D-1994, E-1996)**
Gull Lake (Assoc) 1994-Dec 31, 1997; Gull Lake (Assoc) Dec 31, 1997; Portage: Chapel Hill (Assoc) Jan 1, 1998; Genesis 2007; Retired 2014
(H) 1881 Forest Lake Dr SE, Grand Rapids, MI 49546 (616) 550-6850

PETRUCCI, BARRY T. (FE) (Lesa) – (R-1984, D-1984, E-1988)
In School, Yale Divinity School 1984; Grandville (Assoc) 1986; Grand Rapids: Olivet 1989; Director, Grand Rapids Metro Ministries Jan 1, 1995; Portage: Chapel Hill 2001
(H) 5300 Bronson Blvd, Portage, MI 49024 (269) 276-0482
Portage Chapel Hill UMC: 7028 Oakland Dr., Portage MI 49024 (269) 327-6643

PHILLIPS, DANIEL J.W. (PL)
Barry-Eaton Cooperative Ministry: Kalamo (PTLP 1/4) 2013
(H) 947 Sever Dr, East Lansing, MI 48823 (810) 986-0240
Kalamo UMC: 1475 S Ionia Rd, Vermontville MI 49096

PIER-FITZGERALD, J. LYNN (FE) (Tom) – (R-1977, D-1977, E-1980)
In School 1977; East Lansing: Chapel Hill/Gunnisonville 1978; White Cloud (LTFT 1/2) May 16, 1984; Wyoming Park (Assoc LTFT 1/2) 1988; Leave of Absence 1989; Grand Rapids: Plainfield Aug 16, 1991; Grand Traverse District Superintendent 1999; Holland First 2005
(H) 83 West 18th St, Holland, MI 49423 (616) 393-6242
Holland First UMC: 57 West 10th St, Holland MI 49423 (616) 396-5205

PIER-FITZGERALD, THOMAS M. (FE) (Lynn) – (R-1977, D-1977, E-1980)
In School 1977; East Lansing University (Assoc.) 1978; East Lansing Chapel Hill/Gunnisonville 1982; White Cloud (LTFT 1/2) May 16, 1984; Grand Rapids South 1988; Sabbatical Leave July 1, 1998; Elk Rapids/Kewadin (LTFT 3/4) 1999; Grandville 2005
(H) 83 West 18th St, Holland, MI 49423 (616) 393-6242
Grandville UMC: 3140 S Wilson, Grandville MI 49418 (616) 538-3070

PINTO, MICHAEL A. (PL) (Susan)
Lacota (DSA) 2006; Lacota (PTLP 1/4) 2007
(H) 2321 Tamarack, Kalamazoo, MI 49006-1426 (269) 342-2747
Lacota UMC: 01160 CR 681, PO Box 7, Lacota MI 49063 (269) 253-4382

PLACE, STEVEN C. (FL) (Ilse)
LP w/o Appointment 2010; Church of All Nations, Jan 1, 2011
(H) 5669 Bentbrook St SE, Kentwood, MI 49508-6504 (616) 281-2355
Grand Rapids Mosaic UMC: 4275 Shaffer Ave SE, Kentwood MI 49512 (616) 554-4969

POHL, JON L. (FL) (Diane)
Avondale/North Evart/Sylvan (DSA) Jan 15, 2006; Ashley/Bannister/Greenbush 2006; Ludington St Paul 2011
(H) 3257 W Kinney Rd, Ludington, MI 49431-9780 (231) 843-8470
Ludington St Paul UMC: 3212 W. Kinney Rd., Ludington MI 49431 (231) 843-3275

***POHL, KEITH I. (RE) (Roberta) – (R-1958, D-1958, E-1960)**
Nashville 1958; Grand Rapids First (Asst.) 1961; Rockford 1964; Wesley Foundation Director, Michigan State Univ. Oct. 1966; Assoc. Editor Michigan Christian Advocate 1972; Editor Michigan Christian Advocate Oct. 1, 1973; Editor-Publisher Michigan Christian Advocate 1977; East Lansing: University Aug. 1, 1980; Editor Circuit Rider Sept. 1, 1986; Retired Dec. 31, 1993
(H) 665 N Aurelius Rd, Mason, MI 48854-9528 (517) 244-0389

***POHLY, GERALD A. (RE) (Eileen) – (R-1952, E-1957)**
Battle Creek: Calvary (EUB) 1956; Magnolia (EUB) 1961; Wyoming Park April 1969; Central District Supt. March 1, 1973; Grand Haven 1978; Grand Rapids: Trinity 1989; Retired 1996
(H) 2529 Grove Bluff SE, Grand Rapids, MI 49546 (616) 949-0757

POSNIK JR, RALPH A. (FL) (Karen)
Barnard/East Jordan/Norwood (DSA) May 15, 2009; Barnard/East Jordan/Norwood Nov. 15, 2009; Portage Prairie 2014
(H) 3310 Chicago Rd, Niles, MI 49120 (269) 695-9822
Portage Prairie UMC: 2450 Orange Road, Niles MI 49120 (269) 695-6708

POWERS, JON R. (FE) (Susan Speer-Powers) – (R-1972, D-1972, E-1975)
In school 1972; East Lansing: University (Assoc.) 1974; Portage: Chapel Hill 1978; Hillside Sept. 16, 1978; Chaplain and Director of Church Relations, Adrian College Aug. 16, 1981; University Chaplain, Ohio Wesleyan University Aug. 16, 1988
(H) 104 W Winter St, Delaware, OH 43015 (614) 369-1709
(O) Ohio Wesleyan University, 40 Rowland Ave, Delaware, OH 43015 (614) 368-3082

POWERS, NANCY G. (FE) (Paul) – (R-2006, E-2010)
Reading 2006; Battle Creek Sonoma/Newton 2008; Perry/Shaftsburg 2012
(H) 121 S Madison St, PO Box 142, Perry, MI 48872 (517) 625-3444
Perry UMC: PO Box 15, Perry MI 48872-0015
Shaftsburg UMC: PO Box 161, Shaftsburg MI 48882-0161 (517) 675-1567

PRATT, D. KAY (AM) (Merlin) – (R-2002, D-2002)
[South Indiana Conf: DS Assignment: Freetown 1987; DS Assignment: Newberry 1988; Vallonia 1989; St Paul 1991;] Transferred to West Michigan Conf, Country Chapel/Banfield (Co-Pastor - 1/4 Time) 1992-1996; Shepardsville/Price 1996; St Johns: Pilgrim (Assoc.) 2004; Leave of Absence 2006; [Detroit Conf] Denton: Faith Aug 15, 2008; Leave of Absence 2010; PAPA'S Ministries, Jamaica (para. 344.1.d) 2011
(H) 1857 South County Road 50 W, Brownstown, IN 47220 (876) 993-2680
(O) PAPA'S Ministries (Pastors and Priests Available for Service) / Methodist Resources Development Officer, 1857 South County Road 50 W, Brownstown, IN 47220 (876) 505-8256

PRATT, MERLIN H. (AM) (D Kay) – (R-1997, D-1997)
[Waterloo Village/First (DSA) (Part-Time) 1988-Feb 1, 1991;] Country Chapel/Banfield 1991-1996; Elsie 1996; St Johns Pilgrim 2003; LOA 2006; [Detroit Conf] Canton Cherry Hill Aug 15, 2008; LOA July 1, 2011; Port Antonio Circuit, Jamaica District of the Methodist Church in the Caribbean and The Americas (para. 344.1.d) Sept. 1, 2011
(H) 1857 South County Road 50 W, Brownstown, IN 47220 (876) 993-2680
(O) PAPA'S Ministries (Pastors and Priests Available for Service) / Methodist Resources Development Officer, 1857 South County Road 50 W, Brownstown, IN 47220 (876) 505-8256

PRENTISS, DEAN N. (FE) (Adrianne) – (R-1998, E-2000)
[transferred from Detroit Conference 2003] Mt Pleasant: Trinity/Countryside 1995; Williamston Sept 15, 1999; Big Rapids First 2008; Wyoming Wesley Park 2011
(H) 2664 Borglum Avenue NE, Grand Rapids, MI 49505 (616) 514-7124
Wesley Park UMC: 1150 32nd St SW, Wyoming MI 49509 (616) 534-4411

PRICE, DAVID A. (FL) (Mary)
Weidman (DSA) 2006; Weidman (full-time) Nov. 15, 2006; Dowagiac First 2013
(H) 504 Sunnyside Dr, Dowagiac, MI 49047-1162 (269) 782-2444
Dowagiac First UMC: 326 N Lowe, PO Box 393, Dowagiac MI 49047 (269) 782-5167

PRICE, WAYNE A. (FE) (Joy) – (R-2000)

[North Carolina conf., Appointed to attend school]; Transfered from North Carolina conf., Keswick 2000; Shepherd 2004; Kalamazoo Westwood 2007

(H) 1003 Greenway Terrace, Kalamazoo, MI 49006-2616 (269) 762-4787
Kalamazoo Westwood UMC: 538 Nichols Road, Kalamazoo MI 49006-2994 (269) 344-7165

PUCKETT, TIMOTHY R. (PL) (Esther)

Frontier (PTLP 1/4) 2011; Frontier/Osseo (PTLP 1/2) Jan 1, 2012 [Osseo UMC merged w/ North Adams UMC 4-6-14]; North Adams/Jerome (PTLP 1/4) 2014

(H) 10445 Folks Rd, Hanover, MI 49241-9777 (517) 936-5835
North Adams UMC: 228 E Main St, PO Box 62, North Adams MI 49262 (517) 287-5190
Jerome UMC: 8768 Jerome Rd N, Jerome MI 49249

***PUMFERY, ROBERT L. (RE) (Carole) – (R-1965, D-1965, E-1968)**

Camden/Montgomery 1965; transferred to Mindanao Conf. Jan. 5, 1969; transferred from Mindanao Conf., New Buffalo/Lakeside 1974; Muskegon Heights: Temple 1979; Allegan 1983; Three Rivers: First 1990; Ovid: United 1997; Retired 1999; Townline/Breedsville 1999 - October 31, 2002

(H) 21345 52nd St, Grand Junction, MI 49056 (269) 427-5513

QUERY, TODD J. (FD) – (R-2004, FD-2008)

[Transferred from Detroit Conf 2004] Holland First (Deacon) (Para 337.1) 2003; Serving in Virginia Conf, Williamsburg First UMC (Deacon)(Para 346.1) 2006; Transitional Leave Dec 31, 2012; Leave of Absence Jan 1, 2014

(H) 2620 Sir Thomas Way, Williamsburg, VA 23185 (757) 208-0207

***RADER, BLAINE B. (RE) (Sharon) – (R-1958, E-1964)**

Detroit: Grace (EUB) 1960; in school, Dayton First (Ohio) 1961; Detroit Conf., in school 1964; Chairperson and Associate Professor of Psychology, Adrian College 1966; Educational Coordinator Community Pastoral Counseling and Consultation Center, Lutheran General Hospital, Park Ridge, Illinois 1973; transferred to Northern Illinois Conf. 1975; transferred from Northern Illinois Conf., Executive Director, Samaritan Counseling Center, Battle Creek 1978; Comprehensive Psychological Service, Grand Rapids 1983; Clinical Director, Samaritan Counseling Center of Central Mich. Jan. 1, 1987; Clinical Director, Samaritan Counseling Center of Central Mich. (LTFT 1/2) and Pastoral Counselor, Pastoral Counseling and Consultation (LTFT 1/2) 1990; Leave of absence Sept. 1, 1992; Private practice of pastoral counseling Jan. 27, 1993; Executive Director, Samaritan Counseling Center of Southern Wisconsin Jan. 1, 1995; Wisconsin Conf., Good Shepherd UMC (para. 337.1) 1997.; Wisconsin Conf., Madison: Bethany UMC, (para. 337.1) 2001; Retired 2004

(H) 450 Davis St #362, Evanston, IL 60201 (312) 255-8544

RADTKE, CLIFFORD L. (FL) (Beverly)

Lawrence 2006

(H) 115 E James St, Lawrence, MI 49064-9415 (269) 674-8386
Lawrence UMC: 122 S Exchange St, PO Box 276, Lawrence MI 49064 (269) 674-8381

RAFFERTY, BRIAN F. (FE) (Andrea) – (R-1993, D-1993, E-1995)

Burr Oak 1991; Kingsley/Grant 1993; Grand Haven (Assoc)/West Olive Area New Church Start 1999; New Foundation Church 2002; Cedar Springs/East Nelson 2003; Cedar Springs 2004; Williamston Crossroads 2008-2010; Family Leave 2010

(H) 244 Church Hill Downs Blvd, Williamston, MI 48895-9053 (517) 648-8747

RAMIREZ, NOHEMI VIVAS DE (OE) (Enrique) – (R-2013)

[Rio Grande Conference, Elder] La Nueva Esperanza (LTFT 3/4) and WMC New Church Position (LTFT 1/4) (para. 346.1) 2013

(H) 324 Griswold SE, Grand Rapids, MI 49507 (616) 248-1770
Grand Rapids Iglesia Metodista Unida La Nueva Esperanza: 1005 Evergreen St. SE, Grand Rapids MI 49507 (616) 560-4207

RAMSEY, MICHAEL J. (PL) (Kathy)

Carlisle (PTLP 1/2) 2010; Carlisle (PTLP 3/4) Jan 1, 2011

(H) 8649 Shore Way Dr, Byron Center, MI 49315 (616) 878-9165
Carlisle UMC: 1084 76th St SW, Byron Center MI 49315 (616) 878-1836

***RANDELS, JEANNE M. (RE) (Paul Hartman) – (R-1982, D-1982, E-1984)**
Marshall (Assoc.) 1981; Grand Rapids Plainfield Feb 23, 1988; Albion Aug 16, 1991; Okemos Community Oct 16, 1998; Retired Jan. 1, 2014
(H) 3786 Yosemite Dr, Okemos, MI 48864-3837 (517) 349-3595

***RANDOLPH, BERNARD R. (RA) – (D-1956, E-1959)**
Sanford-Averill 1948; Mt. Pleasant/Deerfield Center 1952; Hesperia/East Denver 1954; Big Rapids Circuit 1959; Houghton Lake Parish 1964; Wayland 1966; Benton Harbor: Grace 1970; Ludington St. Paul 1971; Stanwood: Northland 1974; Whitehall/Claybanks March 1, 1975; Elk Rapids/Kewadin 1976; Retired 1978
(H) Royal View Retirement Community, 9100 Buchanan Rd #205, Mecosta, MI 49332
(S) 4918 14th St W Lot C5, Bradenton, FL 34207-2451

***REECE, WAYNE G. (RE) (Jo) – (R-1958, D-1958, E-1960)**
Transferred from North Indiana Conf. May 26, 1963; Field Worker Conf., Board of Education 1963; Bangor 1966; General Board of Education 1970; Board of Discipleship, Section of Curriculum Resources 1973; Board of Discipleship, Curriculum Resources Committee 1977; Kalamazoo: First (Assoc.) Feb. 15, 1979; Big Rapids: First 1985; Mason: First 1992; Retired 2000
(H) 12 McKendree Circle, Hermitage, TN 37076 (615) 818-0272

REESE, JEFFREY L. (FE) (Carin) – (R-2005, D-2005, E-2009)
[Red Bird Missionary conf., Red Bird Mission & Thousandsticks UMC: Red Bird, KY; 1991-1993] Edwardsburg Sept. 16, 1993; Edwardsburg/Adamsville Aug. 15, 1996-Nov. 30, 1997; Edwardsburg: Hope Dec. 1, 1997
(H) PO Box 444, Edwardsburg, MI 49112 (269) 358-6115
Edwardsburg Hope UMC: 69941 Elkhart Rd., PO Box 624, Edwardsburg MI 49112 (269) 663-5321

***REEVES, KENNETH C. (RE) (Susanne) – (R-1995, D-1978, E-1982)**
[Detroit Conf.: Britton: Grace, Wellsville 1979; LaPorte, Mapleton 1982; Port Sanilac, Forester, McGregor 1985; Erie 1991;] Transferred from Detroit Conf., Riverdale: Lincoln Road 1995-1997; Burnips/Monterey Center 1997; Marion/Cadillac: South Community 2004; Retired 2006; Marion/Cadillac: South Community (DSA) 2006-2007
(H) 201 James Drive, Roscommon, MI 48653 (989) 821-8504

REUM, BETH A. (PE) – (R-2011, PE-2011)
LP w/o Appointment 2002; Manton 2009; Silver Creek/Keeler 2013
(H) 53441 Garrett Rd, Dowagiac, MI 49047 (269) 782-2828
Silver Creek & Keeler UMCs: 31994 Middle Crossing Rd, Dowagiac MI 49047 (269) 782-7061

RICHIE, JAMES A. (FE) (Alice) – (R-2000, D-2000, E-2004)
[North Georgia Conf, Mt Zion UMC, 1994] Transfered from North Georgia Conf, Lansing New Church Start 2000; Battle Creek: Washington Heights 2002; Cassopolis 2009; Baldwin Covenant Community/Luther 2012
(H) 2386 W 44th St, Baldwin, MI 49304 (231) 745-2522
Baldwin Covenant Community UMC: 5330 S M-37, PO Box 250, Baldwin MI 49304 (231) 745-3232
Luther UMC: 315 State St, PO Box 175, Luther MI 49656 (231) 797-0073

***RICKARD, O'RYAN (RLA) – (R-2005, PE-2005, RL-2013)**
Morris Chapel 2003; Townline/Breedsville 2004; Salem/Greenbush/Lowe 2005; Salem/Lowe/Maple Rapids 2006; Coloma/Watervliet 2007; Portage Prairie/Arden 2009; PE Discontinued 2013; Retired LP 2013; Portage Prairie/Arden (RLA 3/4) 2013; Arden (RLA 1/4) 2014
(H) 6148 Avon St, Portage, MI 49024 (269) 235-1700
Arden UMC: 6891 M 139, Berrien Springs MI 49103 (269) 429-4931

RIEGLER, ANNE W. (PL) (Mike)
LP w/o Appointment 2007; Amble (PTLP 3/4) Aug. 15, 2009
(H) 320 S Maple St, Edmore, MI 48829-7300 (231) 631-0573
Amble UMC: PO Box 392, Howard City MI 49329

RIEGLER, MICHAEL A. (AM) (Anne) – (R-2012)
Big Rapids Third Avenue/Paris/Rodney, Sept 11, 2005; Edmore Faith 2011
(H) 320 S Maple St, Edmore, MI 48829
Edmore Faith UMC: 833 S First Street, Edmore MI 48829 (989) 427-5575

***RILEY, RICHARD M. (RE) (Janis) – (R-1975, D-1975, E-1979)**
In school 1975; Sturgis (Assoc.) 1977; Middleton/Maple Rapids 1980; Kalkaska 1984; Rockford 1993; Retired 2014
(H) 4305 Rezen Ct, Rockford, MI 49341 (616) 866-0522

ROBERTSON, JAMES C. (PL)
Townline (PTLP 1/4) 2014
(H) 55130 County Rd 384, Grand Junction, MI 49056 (269) 434-6499
Townline UMC: 41470 24th Ave., Bloomingdale MI 49026 (269) 521-4559

***ROBINSON, BEATRICE K. (RE) – (R-1990, D-1990, E-1992)**
Pokagon (Part-Time) 1988; Riverdale: Lincoln Road 1990; Holland: First (Assoc.) 1995; Jackson: Trinity 1998; Bath/Gunnisonville 2006; Retired 2007
(H) 706 Huntington Blvd, Albion, MI 49224 (517) 629-5881

***ROOSE, RANDALL E. (RA) (LaVonna) – (R-1987, E-1960)**
From Church of the Brethren; Weidman Jan. 1, 1986; Retired 1993; Leaton (DSA) Aug. 1, 1999
(H) 3380 S Genuine Road, Mt Pleasant, MI 48858 (989) 772-1001

***ROSA, MARVIN R. (RE) (Annette) – (R-1968, D-1968, E-1971)**
[Rosebush/Center 1964; Augusta/Hickory Corners 1967] 1968; Grand Rapids: Trinity (Assoc.) Feb. 15, 1972; Clare 1979; Grand Traverse District Supt. 1986; Big Rapids: First 1992; Leave of absence March 31, 1993 - July 1, 1995; Pastor without appointment 1995 (see Judicial Council ruling #782); Frankfort/Elberta 1996; Retired 1999
(H) 19558 Maple, PO Box 123, Lake Ann, MI 49650-0123 (231) 275-7557

***ROSS, EDWARD C. (RE) (Monika) – (R-1976, D-1976, E-1980)**
In School, 1976; Mt Pleasant First (Assoc) 1978; Gull Lake 1981; Jackson First 1994; Retired 2012; Lansing Christ (Interim) Jan 1-June 30, 2013; Waterloo Village (Ret.) (LTFT 1/4) 2013
(H) 5976 McCain Rd, Jackson, MI 49201-9329 (517) 750-3987
Waterloo Village UMC: 8110 Washington St, Grass Lake MI 49240-9241 (734) 475-1171

ROTH JR, ROBERT H. (FE) – (R-1979, D-1979, E-1982)
In school, Duke Divinity School 1979; Lansing Central (Assoc) May 22, 1980; Otsego 1983; Chaplain, Albion College 1985; Center Eaton/Brookfield (LTFT 3/4) 1988; Grand Ledge (Assoc LTFT 3/4) 1990; Grand Ledge (Assoc) 1991; Williamston 1994; Retired 1999; Ann Arbor First (Assoc) (LTFT 1/2) (para. 346.1) and Director, Wesley Foundation at University of Michigan (LTFT 1/2) (para. 344.1), 2009; Returned from Voluntary Retirement (para. 358.7) 2010; Director, Wesley Foundation at U of M (para. 344.1.d) 2014
(H) 2884 Sorrento, Ann Arbor, MI 48104 (734) 369-8068
(O) Wesley Foundation - University of Michigan, c/o First UMC, 120 S State Street, Ann Arbor, MI 48104 (734) 662-4536

***RUBINGH, LARRY W. (RE) (Linda) – (R-1981, D-1981, E-1987)**
Camden/Montgomery/Stokes Chapel May 1983; Stevensville (Assoc) 1987; Holton 1988; Battle Creek Convis Union Jan 1, 1992; Jackson Calvary 1997; Grass Lake 1999; Stockbridge/Munith 2007; Munith (LTFT 1/4) Oct 15, 2010; Incapacity Leave Sept 6, 2011; Retired 2012
(H) 2480 N Portage Rd, Jackson, MI 49201-8489 (517) 812-6636

***RUSSELL, DONALD A. (RE) – (R-1958, D-1958, E-1962)**
Transferred from Kentucky Conf., Aug. 15, 1960; Byron Center 1960; Byron Center/Market St. 1964; Lawton/Porter 1966; Watervliet 1971; Sabbatical 1975; Wellspring Mission Group, Church of the Savior, Washington, D.C. 1976; Honorable Location 1977; Readmitted, The Church of the Savior, Washington, D.C. 1980; Retired 1996
(H) 4651 County Rd 612 NE, Kalkaska, MI 49646 (231) 258-6728

***SANDERS, WILLIAM P. (RE) (Manila) – (R-1988, D-1980, E-1985)**
[In school Colgate Rochester Divinity School 1980; Detroit Conf., St. Timothy 1981, Inkster: Christ 1983; Franklin 1987;] Transferred from Detroit Conf., Bellevue/Kalamo 1988; Buchanan: First Feb. 2, 1996; Retired 2003; Detroit Conference, Fairgrove/Watrousville (Ret.) 2013
(H) 6116 Slocum St., Unionville, MI 48767 (989) 674-2421
(O) Fairgrove/Watrousville UMCs, 5116 W Center, PO Box 10, Fairgrove, MI 48733 (989) 683-6564

SAYLES, THERESA (LITTLE EAGLE) (FE) (Ed) – (R-2000, E-2006)
Grand Rapids: Oakdale/Pa Wa Ting Ma Ged Win 2003; Battle Creek Maple 2006; Portage Prairie 2008-2009; Incapacity Leave April 15, 2009
(H) 256 Nottingham Rd, Elkton, MD 21921

SCHLIMM, MATTHEW R. (FE) (Melanie) – (R-2002, E-2005)
[Minnesota conf., Cross Winds UMC: Maple Grove, MN;] (para. 337.1) 2002.; appointed to attend school - Duke University 2003; Assistant Professor of Old Testament, University of Dubuque Theological Seminary, Sept. 1, 2008
(H) 2130 Fairway Drive, Dubuque, IA 52001 (563) 557-1100
(O) University of Dubuque Theological Seminary, 2000 University Ave, Dubuque, IA 52001 (563) 589-3109

SCHNEIDER, TERRILL (AM) (Linda) – (R-2004, D-2004)
Scottdale June 1, 1995; Scottdale/Bridgman: Faith May 1, 2000
(H) 4276 Scottdale Rd, St Joseph, MI 49085-9366 (269) 556-9869
Scottdale UMC: 4276 Scottdale Rd., St. Joseph MI 49085-9366 (269) 429-7270
Bridgman Faith UMC: 9156 Red Arrow Hwy, PO Box 414, Bridgman MI 49106 (269) 465-3696

***SCHOENHERR, LEONARD R. (RE) (Janette) – (R-1987, D-1973, E-1975)**
Transferred from North Indiana Conf, Watervliet June 9, 1987; Coloma and Watervliet Feb 16, 1996; Marshall 1999; Retired June 30, 2013; Galesburg (Ret.) (LTFT 1/2) 2013; Galesburg (Ret.) (LTFT 1/4) Jan 1, 2014
(H) 4500 Mountain Ash Lane, Kalamazoo, MI 49004 (269) 903-2182
Galesburg UMC: 111 W Battle Creek St, PO Box 518, Galesburg MI 49053 (269) 665-7952

SCHROCK, JEFFREY J. (FL) (Kathi)
In School 1999; Marion/Cadillac South Community 2000; Sunfield/Sebewa Center 2004; NE Missaukee Parish 2012
(H) 7037 E Houghton Lake Rd, Merritt, MI 49667-9786 (231) 328-2039
NE Missaukee Parish: Merritt-Butterfield UMC: 428 S Merritt Rd, Merritt MI 49667 (231) 328-4598
Moorestown-Stittsville UMC: 4509 E Moorestown Rd, Lake City MI 49651 (231) 328-4598

SCOTT, JOHN A. (FE) (Rebecca) – (R-2001, D-2001, E-2004)
In School; Girard/Ellis Corners 2000; Girard/Ellis Corners/Quincy (Co-Pastor) Sept 1, 2003; New Church Start: Traverse City Windward 2007; New Life 2011
(H) 8544 M 46, Lakeview, MI 48850 (989) 352-6728
New Life UMC: 6584 M 46, Six Lakes MI 48886 (989) 352-7788

***SCOVEL, WARD N. (RE) (Mary) – (R-1976, D-1976, E-1980)**
In school 1976; Muskegon: Central (Assoc.) 1978; Battle Creek: Birchwood 1980; Wyoming Park 1984; Paw Paw 1989; Leave of absence 1995; Retired Mar. 1, 1998
(H) 112 Doncaster Ln, Bluffton, SC 29909-6002 (843) 705-3633

***SEAVER, HOWARD (RA) (Judy) – (R-2001, D-2001)**
[Fife Lake/Boardmans Parish (DSA) 1994] Fife Lake/Boardmans Parish Nov 16, 1994; Retired 2012
(H) 3932 Deater Dr NW, Rapid City, MI 49676 (231) 331-6867

SELLECK, DAVID A. (FE) (Anne) – (R-1972, D-1972, E-1975)
In School 1972; St. Joseph (Assoc) 1974; Constantine April 1, 1976; Stockbridge Sept 16, 1979; Hillsdale 1987; Leave of Absence Dec 1, 1988; Honorable Location 1993; Readmitted 2002; Muskegon: Lakeside 2002; Martin/Shelbyville 2009; Manistee 2012
(H) 819 Elm Street, Manistee, MI 49660 (231) 723-3304
Manistee UMC: 387 First St, Manistee MI 49660 (231) 723-6219

SELLECK, GERALD L. (FE) (Claudia) – (R-1977, D-1977, E-1981)
In school 1977; Somerset Center/Moscow Plains 1979; Kalamazoo: First (Assoc.) 1982; Courtland/Oakfield Dec. 1984; Hartford 1990; Manistee 1998; Leave of Absence 2002; Holton 2006
(H) 8670 Ward St, P.O. Box 39, Holton, MI 49425 (231) 821-0374
Holton UMC: 9530 Holton-Duck Lake Rd., Holton MI 49425 (231) 821-2323

***SELLECK, RICHARD A. (RE) (Eloise) – (R-1961, D-1961, E-1963)**
[Ogdensburg 1955]; in school 1961; Grand Rapids: Oakdale 1963; Rockford Oct. 1966; Muskegon Heights 1970; Kalamazoo District Supt. 1977; Conf. Staff Council Director 1983; Lansing: Christ March 1, 1987; Sand Lake/South Ensley 1992; Retired 1996
(H) 1024 Terrace, 1551 Franklin SE, Grand Rapids, MI 49506 (616) 248-7982

SHAFER, NOREEN S. (PL) (Todd)
Manton (PTLP 3/4) 2013
(H) 406 Sunnyside St, Mancelona, MI 49659-9771 (231) 587-9446
Manton UMC: PO Box B, Manton MI 49663-0902 (231) 824-3593

SHAFER, TODD W. (FL) (Noreen)
Mancelona/Alba (DSA) July 15, 2010; Mancelona/Alba Nov 1, 2010
(H) 406 Sunnyside St, Mancelona, MI 49659 (231) 587-9446
Mancelona & Allba UMCs: PO Box 301, Mancelona MI 49659 (231) 587-8461

SHALER, JOSEPH D. (FE) (Terri) – (R-2001, E-2003)
Otsego 2001
(H) 411 Walden Dr, Otsego, MI 49078-9652 (269) 806-9087
Otsego UMC: 223 E. Allegan St., PO Box 443, Otsego MI 49078-0443 (269) 694-2939

***SHAPLEY, JANE B. (RE) (Allen) – (R-1984, D-1984, E-1987)**
In school GETS 1984; Kalamazoo: First (Assoc.) 1985; Grand Rapids: Oakdale 1987; Retired 1996
(H) PO Box 345, Malahat, BC VOR 2LO CANADA (250) 743-1199

***SHEEN, BRIAN K. (RA) (Bonnie) – (R-1988)**
St. John: Pilgrim 1970; In school 1983; Leave of Absence Nov. 17, 1983; Lansing: Central Free Methodist (assoc.) 1985; Withdrew to unite with the Free Methodist Church 1987; Davidson Free Methodist 1990; Owosso Free Methodist 1993-1995; Received from Free Methodist 1998; Sunfield 1998; Retired 2004
(H) 3102 S DeWitt Rd, St Johns, MI 48879 (989) 224-6181

***SHROUT, LARRY R. (RE) (Sheila) – (R-1970, D-1970, E-1977)**
Transferred from Nebraska Conf., Colon 1980; St. Johns Pilgrim 1983; Retired 1998
(H) 237 W Slope Way, Canton, GA 30115 (770) 704-0711

SHUMAKER, ANTHONY C. (FL) (Linda)
Almena (DSA) 2002; Almena Dec 1, 2002; LP w/o Appointment 2003; Burnips/Monterery Center 2004; Trowbridge (PTLP 3/4) 2008; Middleville/Snow 2012
(H) 1497 120th Ave, Hopkins, MI 49328-9626 (269) 650-5112
Middleville UMC: 111 Church St, PO Box 400, Middleville MI 49333 (269) 795-9266
Snow UMC: 3189 Snow Ave. SE, Lowell MI 49331 (616) 897-9863

SIMMONS, GARY L. (PE) (BethAnn Perkins-Simmons) – (R-2014, PE-2014)
Mulliken (PTLP 1/4) and Woodland (PTLP 1/4) 2011; Barry-Eaton Cooperative Ministry: Nashville (PTLP 1/2) and Vermontville (PTLP 1/4) and Woodland (PTLP 1/4) 2013; Barry-Eaton Cooperative Ministry: Nashville (LTFT 1/2) and Vermontville (LTFT 1/4) and Woodland (LTFT 1/4) 2014
(H) 1137 DeGroff St, Grand Ledge, MI 48837-2150 (517) 622-2286
Nashville UMC: PO Box 370, Nashville MI 49073-0370 (517) 852-2043
Vermontville UMC: PO Box 186, Vermontville MI 49096-0186 (517) 726-0526
Woodland UMC: 203 N Main St, Woodland MI 48897-9638 (269) 367-4061

SIMON, MICHAEL J. (FL) (Beth)
Chase Barton/Grant Center (PTLP 1/2) 2006; The Gathering (WMAC)/Wagarville (DAC-Saginaw Bay District) (PTLP 1/2) 2010; Lake Ann 2013
(H) 6596 First St, Lake Ann, MI 49650-9549 (231) 349-1914
Lake Ann UMC: 6583 First St, Lake Ann MI 49650 (231) 275-7236

SKUTAR, CYNTHIA A. (FE) (Jerry Welborn) – (R-1987, D-1987, E-1990)
In school METHESCO 1987; Hersey 1988; Kalamazoo First (Assoc.) 1992; Three Rivers: First 1997; Muskegon: Lake Harbor 2000; Coldwater 2004; Mt. Pleasant: First 2010; Grand Ledge First 2013
(H) 912 E Scott St, Grand Ledge, MI 48837 (517) 627-7347
Grand Ledge First UMC: 411 Harrison St, Grand Ledge MI 48837-1575 (517) 627-3256

SLAGER, RONALD D. (PL) (Jo)
Kalamazoo Stockbridge Avenue (PTLP 1/4) 2010
(H) 6481 East S Ave, Scotts, MI 49088 (269) 327-8291
Kalamazoo Stockbridge Avenue UMC: 1009 E Stockbridge Ave, Kalamazoo MI 49001 (269) 385-8919

***SLATE, EDWARD H. (RE) (Patsy) – (R-1974, D-1974, E-1978)**
In School 1974; Whitehall/Claybanks 1976; Leave of Absence April 17, 1983; Comstock 1984; South Haven 1989; Stanwood: Northland 1995; Evart 2006; Niles Wesley 2008; Retired 2012; Buchanan Faith (Ret.) (LTFT 1/2) 2012
(H) 1358 Honeysuckle Ln, Niles, MI 49120 (269) 262-0011
Buchanan Faith UMC: 728 North Detroit Street, Buchanan MI 49107 (269) 695-3261

***SLATTERY, DENNIS (DEN) E. (RE) (Karen) – (R-1982, D-1982, E-1985)**
In School Anderson School of Theology 1982; Ravenna 1983; Climax/Scotts April 1, 1987; Army Chaplaincy, Fort Hood, TX Oct 1, 1988; Keeler/Silver Creek 1990; Marcellus/Wakelee 1992; Wakelee 1995; Ludington: St. Paul 1998; LeValley/Berlin Center 2007; Retired 2012; Grass Lake (Ret.) (LTFT 1/4) 2012
(H) 659 Church St, Grass Lake, MI 49240 (517) 522-8135
Grass Lake UMC: 449 E. Michigan Ave., Grass Lake MI 49240 (517) 522-8040

***SMALL, STEPHEN C. (RE) (Karen) – (R-2001, E-2004)**
Glenn Nov. 16, 1998; Center Park 2001; Brookfield Eaton 2004; Retired October 1, 2004; Riverside (DSA) 2009-2014
(H) 9658 Allen Court, South Haven, MI 49090 (269) 637-1692

***SMITH, BETTY A. (RE) (Bill Biergans) – (R-1990, D-1990, E-1992)**
Ludington United (Assoc.) 1990; Wacousta 1992; Coldwater 1998; Retired 2004; Potter Park (DSA) October 16, 2004-2005; Grand Ledge (Interim) Jan. 1-Mar. 31, 2013
(H) 1822 Willow Creek Dr, Lansing, MI 48917-7807 (517) 323-0278

***SMITH, CHARLES W. (RE) (Arlene) – (R-1971, D-1971, E-1976)**
In school 1971; Transferred from North Indiana Conf April 1, 1974; Centreville/Nottawa 1974; Centreville 1976; East Lansing Chapel Hill/Gunnisonville 1984; Shepardsville/Price 1988; Courtland/Oakfield 1996; Ravenna 2008; Retired 2011
(H) 341 Guy St, Cedar Springs, MI 49319 (616) 970-6269

SMITH, JEAN M. (AM) (Gary) – (R-2010, AM-2010)
Saugatuck (DSA) 2001; Saugatuck Dec 1, 2001; Saugatuck/Ganges Jan 16, 2005; Ganges/Glenn 2005; Lake City Sept 1, 2010
(H) 133 N Park St, Lake City, MI 49651 (231) 839-7542
Lake City UMC: PO Box - Drawer P, Lake City MI 49651 (231) 839-2123

***SMITH, ROBERT C. (RE) (Dorothy) – (R-1944, D-1945, E-1946)**
[St. Johns Parish 1940; Banfield/Dowling 1941] 1944; Middleville 1946; Ovid/Shepardsville 1951; Mt. Pleasant 1958; Jackson: First 1966; Grand Rapids District Supt. 1971; Conf. Staff Council Director 1977; Retired 1983; Consultant to UMCOR, General Board of Global Ministries 1983-Dec. 31, 1992
(H) 1551 Franklin St. SE, Grand Rapids, MI 49506 (616) 246-7199

SMITH, SCOTT B. (FL) (Stacy)
Weidman 2013
(H) 5765 Lindy Ln, Weidman, MI 48893-7726 (989) 644-3441
Weidman UMC: 3200 N. Woodruff Rd., PO Box 98, Weidman MI 48893 (989) 644-3148

***SMITH, WESLEY E. (RA) (Phyllis) – (R-1982, D-1981)**
[Burnips/Monterey Center 1977]; Hersey/Grant Center 1982; Disability leave Feb. 1, 1984; White Pigeon Jan. 1985; Disability leave Aug. 23, 1990; Retired 1996
(H) 1845 Boston SE Ste 308, Grand Rapids, MI 49506 (616) 805-0020

SMITH-JANG, BARBARA L. (FE) (Soo Chan) – (R-1993, D-1993, E-1996)
In school G-ETS 1993; Grand Ledge: First (Assoc.) 1994; Family Leave 1997; GBGM Missionary to Korea (para. 335.1b,c) 2000; Pastoral Counselor, Taejon Christian School, South Korea 2003
(H) Yeolmea Apt 802-901, Yusong-gu No-eun-dong 520-1, Taejon City, South Korea 305-325 (042) 471-7029
(O) Taejon Christian International School, 210-1 O-Jung Dong Daedeok-Gu, Daejeon, Republic of Korea 306-819 (042) 829-7029

SNOOK, EDWIN D. (FL) (Ellen)
Big Rapids: Third Ave/Paris/Rodney (DSA) 2002; Big Rapids: Third Ave/Paris/Rodney Dec 1, 2002; Elsie July 16, 2005; White Cloud 2012
(H) 718 E Pine Hill Ave, White Cloud, MI 49349-9146 (231) 689-6774
White Cloud UMC: 1125 Newell St., PO Box 188, White Cloud MI 49349 (231) 689-5911

***SODERHOLM, MARY L. (RA) (David) – (R-1986, D-1986)**
(Formerly Mary Schippers-DeMunter) Country Chapel/Banfield 1986; Snow/Vergennes 1991; Leave of absence April 1, 1995; Involuntary Retirement 1998; Woodland (DSA) 2004-2008
(H) 6407 Mikado St, Oscoda, MI 48750 (231) 450-0901

SORDEN, KAREN J. (FE) – (R-2007, E-2012)
Baldwin Covenant Community/Luther 2005; Lake Odessa Central 2012
(H) 455 Sixth Ave, Lake Odessa, MI 48849 (616) 374-8294
Lake Odessa Central UMC: PO Box 485, Lake Odessa MI 48849-0485 (616) 374-8861

SPACHMAN, DONALD E. (FE) (Shelly) – (R-1982, D-1982, E-1984)
Grawn 1982; Shepherd/Pleasant Valley 1992; Shepherd 1997; Keswick 2004; Hastings First 2010; Greenville First, Turk Lake/Belding Cooperative Parish 2014
(H) 405 W Grant St, Greenville, MI 48838 (616) 712-6024
Greenville First UMC: 204 W. Cass Street, Greenville MI 48838 (616) 754-8532
Turk Lake UMC: 8900 W. Colby Road, Greenville MI 48838 (616) 754-3718
Belding UMC: 301 South Pleasant, Belding MI 48809 (616) 794-1244

***SPACKMAN, JOSEPH L. (RE) (Nona) – (R-1985, D-1985, E-1989)**
[Mulliken Ad Interim 1982]; In school, United Theological Seminary 1985; Mulliken/Sebewa Center 1987; St. Johns: Parish: Salem/Greenbush/Lowe 1991; Allegan 1999; Paw Paw 2007; Retired 2013; Delta Mills (Ret.) (LTFT 1/4) 2013
(H) 3806 Cornice Falls Dr Apt 6, Holt, MI 48842 (517) 694-8346
Delta Mills UMC: 6809 Delta River Dr, Lansing MI 48906-9002 (517) 321-8100

***SPAHR, SANDRA LEE (RE) (Michael) – (R-2000, E-2003)**
[West Ohio Conf: Harpster (Student Pastor), July 15, 1996-June 31, 2000]; Newaygo 2000; Retired 2006; Jackson Trinity/Parma (DSA) 2006; Webberville (DSA) 2007-Dec 31, 2007; Rocky Mountain Conf, Monte Vista/Bowen (1/2 Time)(para. 358.6) 2010
(H) 3229 Northridge Dr, Pueblo, CO 81008 (719) 568-5858
(O) Monte Vista / Bowen UMCs, 215 Washington Street, Monte Vista, CO 81144 (719) 852-2853

***SPALENKA, GORDON E. (RE) (Nancy) – (R-1957, D-1958, E-1960)**
In school Garrett 1956-1960; Griffith (Assoc.), Griffith, IN 1957-1959; Holton/Twin Lake 1959; Lake Harbor 1961; Boyne City/Boyne Falls 1964; Ovid 1965; Leslie/Felt Plains 1969; Bronson/Snow Prairie Oct. 15, 1969; Arden 1972; Bear Lake/Arcadia/Pleasanton 1975; Mt. Pleasant: Trinity/Chippewa 1980; Centerville 1984; Bellaire 1987; Mulliken/Sebewa Center 1991; Retired 1993
(H) 2119 Waldron Street SW, Wyoming, MI 49519 (616) 249-0513

***SPRAGG, CAROLIN S. (RE) – (R-1991, D-1991, E-1994)**
(Formerly Carolin Salisbury) In School, G-ETS 1991; Parma/North Parma 1992; Paw Paw 1999; Fremont 2007; Retired 2013
(H) 1063 Gale Rd, Eaton Rapids, MI 48827 (269) 598-0266

***STARK, ROBERT W. (RE) (Mary) – (R-1998, D-1998, E-2002)**
[North Evart/Sylvan (DSA) Nov 1, 1990; Pine River Parish (DSA) 1991;] Pine River Parish LeRoy/Ashton/Luther August 1, 1991; Pine River Parish LeRoy/Ashton May 1, 1993; Girard/Ellis Corners 1996; Kalkaska 2000; Retired 2008; Grant (DSA) (LTFT 1/4) July-Nov. 2011
(H) 11649 E 14 1/2 Rd, Manton, MI 49663-8598 (231) 824-3294

STARKEY, NATHANIEL R. (FL) (Amy)
Williamsburg 2014
(H) 8401 Crisp Rd, Williamsburg, MI 49690 (586) 229-5767
Williamsburg UMC: PO Box 40, Williamsburg MI 49690 (231) 267-5792

***STEARS, ETHEL Z. (RE) (Robert Richards) – (R-1978, D-1978, E-1981)**
In school 1978; Springport/Lee Center 1979; Grand Rapids: Trinity (Assoc.) Sept. 16, 1983; Grand Rapids: Plainfield 1986; Director of Development, Clark Home Jan. 1988; Chaplain, M.J. Clark Memorial Home 1989; Sabbatical Jan. 15, 1994; Grand Rapids: St. Paul 1994; Retired 1999
(H) 46 Rivertop Drive, Lowell, MI 49331 (616) 897-0162

STEEN, KATHRYN M. (FE) – (R-1994, D-1994, E-1997)
Big Rapids: Third Ave./Paris/Rodney 1994; Mancelona/Alba 2000; appointed to attend school, CPE, Bronson Methodist Hospital 2007; Leave of Absence, Sept. 1, 2008; Chaplain, Munson Medical Center, Nov. 10, 2008
(H) 951 Hammond Place S, Traverse City, MI 49686 (231) 421-5138
(O) Munson Medical Center, 1105 Sixth Street, Traverse City, MI 49684 (231) 935-7163

STEP, GARY G. (FE) (Lori) – (R-2000, E-2003)
In School 1999; Indian River 2000; Conference Staff, Director of New Church Development and Congregational Transformation (Para. 344.1a) 2012
(H) 6666 Crown Point Drive, Hudsonville, MI 49426 (231) 420-2676
(O) West Michigan Conference - United Methodist Church, 11 Fuller Ave SE, PO Box 6247, Grand Rapids, MI 49516-6247 (616) 459-4503

STERNER, JOHN M. (PL)
[Retired Presbyterian Local Elder] Colon/Burr Oak (PTLP 3/4) 2012
(H) 403 Maple, PO Box 65, Colon, MI 49040 (269) 432-3754
Colon UMC: 224 N. Blackstone, PO Box 646, Colon MI 49040 (269) 432-2783
Burr Oak UMC: 105 S. Fourth St., PO Box 91, Burr Oak MI 49030 (269) 489-2985

STILWELL, JAMES W. (FL) (Pamela)
Grand Rapids Olivet, (DSA) March 1, 2005; Grand Rapids Olivet 1/4 Time June 1, 2005; Benton Harbor Peace Temple/Arden 2006; Benton Harbor Peace Temple 2009; Three Rivers Ninth Street/Schoolcraft Pleasant Valley 2009
(H) 700 9th St, Three Rivers, MI 49093-1206 (269) 279-9267
Three Rivers Ninth Street UMC: 700 Ninth St, Three Rivers MI 49093 (269) 273-2065
Schoolcraft Pleasant Valley UMC: 9300 West XY Ave, PO Box 517, Schoolcraft MI 49087-0517 (269) 679-5352

STODDARD, LINDA D. (FE) – (R-1970, D-1970, E-1973)
Oshtemo/Northwest 1972; Bainbridge New Hope/Scottdale Oct 15, 1976; Battle Creek Convis Union May 16, 1983; Leave of Absence Jan 1, 1992; Staff Chaplain, Battle Creek Health System, Para 335.1d (LTFT 1/4) 2000; Battle Creek Maple (LTFT 1/4) 2008
(H) 99 Mowerson Dr, Battle Creek, MI 49017 (269) 965-1671
Battle Creek Maple UMC: 342 Capital Ave. NE, Battle Creek MI 49017 (269) 964-1252

STOLL, MATTHEW T. (FE) (Amy) – (R-2003, E-2006)
Epsilon/New Hope 2003; Vergennes 2010
(H) 110 Tia Trail, Lowell, MI 49331 (616) 987-1887
Vergennes UMC: 10411 Bailey Dr. NE, Lowell MI 49331 (616) 897-6141

***STOVER, ROBERT P. (RE) (Kathleen) – (R-1975, D-1975, E-1977)**
In School 1975; Camden/Montgomery/Stokes Chapel 1976; Niles: Portage Prairie 1980; Portage Prairie 1982; Cedar Springs/East Nelson 1987; Ludington: St. Paul 1989; Grand Rapids: South 1998; Napoleon 2004; Allegan 2007; Retired 2012; Homer/Lyon Lake (Ret.) (LTFT 3/4) 2012
(H) 105 E Adams St, Homer, MI 49245 (517) 568-1126
Homer UMC: PO Box 175, Homer MI 49245-0175 (517) 568-4001
Lyon Lake UMC: PO Box 175, Homer MI 49245-0175 (269) 789-0017

STRANGE, MACK C. (OF) (Barbara)
[Southern Baptist Church] Grand Rapids South 2007
(H) 5103 Marlowe SE, Grand Rapids, MI 49508 (616) 532-9226
Grand Rapids South UMC: 4500 S. Division Ave., Grand Rapids MI 49548 (616) 534-8931

***STREEVY, MICHAEL P. (RE) – (R-1987, D-1987, E-1995)**
Elk Rapids/Kewadin April 1, 1987; Jonesville/Allen 1988; Battle Creek: Sonoma/Newton 1995; Galesburg Nov. 16, 1999; Parma/North Parma 2003; North Parma (LTFT 3/4), Nov. 1, 2005; Full-Time 2008; Litchfield/Quincy 2009; Retired 2010
(H) 9205 Ironwood Way, Highlands Ranch, CO 80129 (585) 943-4328

STULL-LIPPS, LINDA (LYNE) K. (PE) (David Lipps) – (R-2007, PE-2007)
Parma Jan 15, 2006; Center Park 2006; Potterville 2011
(H) 4115 Scenic View Ct, Potterville, MI 48876-8600 (517) 645-4526
Potterville UMC: PO Box 458, Potterville MI 48876-0458 (517) 645-7701

***SUMMERS, VERNE CARL (RE) (Dawn) – (R-1962, D-1955, E-1964)**
[Detroit Conf. Forester 1953]; Beaverton/Dale 1956; in school 1960; Elk Rapids 1963; Elk Rapids Parish 1965; Jackson: Brookside 1966; Charlotte Sept. 1, 1974; Okemos 1987; Mason 1989; Retired 1992
(H) 1175 W Herbison Rd, DeWitt, MI 48820-8307 (517) 669-2815

SUNDELL, RAYMOND R. (FE) (Jennifer) – (R-1993, D-1989, E-1992)
[Central Illinois Conf: Cowden/Lakewood 1987;] Transferred from Central Illinois Conf, Elk Rapids/Kewadin 1993; St Johns Pilgrim 1998; Fennville/Pearl 2003; Perry/Shaftsburg 2008; LeValley/Berlin Center 2012
(H) 1461 E David Hwy, Ionia, MI 48846-9674 (616) 527-9656
LeValley & Berlin Center UMC: 4018 Kelsey Highway, Ionia MI 48846 (616) 527-1480

SURGEON-RIDER, MELODYE (FE) – (R-1994, D-1994, E-2005)
In School G-ETS 1994; Family Leave 1996; Marcellus 2002; Jackson Trinity/Parma 2007; Evart 2012
(H) 8543 Seven Mile Rd, Evart, MI 49631 (231) 734-2003
Evart UMC: PO Box 425, Evart MI 49631 (231) 734-2130

SWANSON, SHERRI L. (FE) (Brad Bartelmay) – (R-1991, D-1987, E-1994)
[Iowa Conf.: In school GETS 1987; Recruitment, GETS 1989; Clinical Pastoral Education, Bronson Methodist Hospital 1990;] Transferred from Iowa Conf., Galien/Olive Branch 1991; Galien/Olive Branch (LTFT 3/4) 1993; Lakeside (LTFT 1/4) 1995; Three Oaks Sept. 1, 1999
(H) 19603 Oak Dr, New Buffalo, MI 49117 (269) 469-4488
Three Oaks UMC: 2 East Sycamore Street, Three Oaks MI 49128 (269) 756-2053

SWEET, MARY A. (FL) (Jeffrey)
Harbor Springs/Alanson 2011; Whitehall/Crestwood 2014
(H) 1220 Creston, Muskegon, MI 49442 (231) 881-7367
Whitehall UMC: 117 S. Division, Whitehall MI 49461 (231) 893-2315
Muskegon Crestwood UMC: 1220 Creston, Muskegon MI 49442 (231) 773-9696

SYKES, LORI J. (FE) (Gary) – (R-2007, E-2010)
St Johns First 2007; Lansing First July 15, 2012
(H) 3727 Delta River Dr, Lansing, MI 48906-3476 (517) 721-1676
Lansing First UMC: 3827 Delta River Dr, Lansing MI 48906-3477 (517) 321-5187

***SYNWOLT, ROYAL J. (RE) (Constance) – (R-1952, D-1952, E-1954)**
Coloma/Riverside Oct. 1951; Portage 1955; Lansing: Mt. Hope 1962; Muskegon: Central 1966; transferred to Detroit Conf., Conf. Staff Program Consultant 1971; Area Asst. to the Bishop Dec. 1976; transferred from Detroit Conf. 1983; Kalamazoo: First 1983; Retired 1991
(H) 11214 Morning Side Dr, Boyne Falls, MI 49713-9699 (231) 549-2547
(S) 870 NW Sarria Ct, Port St Lucie, FL 34986 (772) 873-0949

***TABER, HAROLD M. (RE) (Miriam) – (R-1950, D-1952, E-1955)**
[Springport Parish (Assoc.) 1949]; in school 1950; Shepherd/Pleasant Valley 1952; Shepherd/Indian Mission 1956; Wacousta 1958; Casnovia/Kent City 1960; Houghton Lake Parish 1962; Middleville 1964; Middleville/Freeport 1966; Jackson: Trinity 1969; Kalamazoo: Lane Blvd. 1972; Scottville 1975; Granted disability Jan. 25, 1976; Burr Oak 1977; Granted disability 1978; Retired 1980
(H) Clark Retirement Community, 1551 Franklin Ave SE Apt 4012, Grand Rapids, MI 49506 (616) 475-0717

***TEN HAVE, MILTON J. (RE) (Mary) – (R-1962, D-1962, E-1964)**
[Hastings Parish 1961] 1962; Climax July 28, 1963; Mesick/Brethren/Harrietta 1965; Evart 1967; Galesburg Jan. 15, 1970; Bellevue/Kalamo 1973; Harbor Springs/Alanson 1977; Riverdale/Elwell 1979; Munith/Pleasant Lake 1986; Retired 1990
(H) c/o Kathy Haraburda, 549 Beech Street, Clinton, IN 47842 (765) 832-1925

***TESTOLIN, ROY G. (RE) (Sandy) – (R-1990)**
Staff Pastoral Counselor (para. 337.1), Battle Creek: First 1990; Transferred from Wisconsin Conf 1999; Pastoral Counselor, Heritage Interfaith Counseling Center, Battle Creek 1999; Retired Nov. 1, 2013
(H) 232 Hawthorne Rd, Marshall, MI 49068-9638 (269) 781-9257
(O) Heritage Interfaith Counseling Center, 9 Heritage Oak Lane Ste 3, Battle Creek, MI 49015 (269) 979-5180

THOMAS, DEBORAH S. (OE) (Paul W.) – (R-2013)
[Detroit Conference, Elder] Alma 2013
(H) 627 Woodworth Ave, Alma, MI 48801 (989) 463-1485
Alma UMC: 501 Gratiot Ave, Alma MI 48801 (989) 463-4305

THOMAS, PAUL W. (FL) (Debbie)
Breckenridge 2013
(H) 627 Woodworth Ave, Alma, MI 48801-1746 (989) 463-1485
Breckenridge UMC: PO Box 248, Breckenridge MI 48615 (989) 842-3632

***THOMPSON, J. TODD (RE) (Jodi) – (R-1989, D-1989, E-1992)**
In school United Theological Seminary 1989; Alto/Bowne Center 1990; Muskegon: Wolf Lake/Unity 1995; Muskegon: Wolf Lake 1998; Charlevoix 2000; Retired 2010
(H) 4354 M-66 North, Charlevoix, MI 49720 (231) 675-2135

***THOMPSON, JOHN ROSS (RE) (Ellen Brubaker) – (R-1995, D-1966, E-1968)**
[Western Pennsylvania Conf: In School, Drew University 1966; Center 1968; St Paul's Oct 1980; Council Director 1990;] Transferred from Western Pennsylvania Conf, Grandville 1995; Conference Director 1998; East Lansing University 2006, Retired Dec. 31, 2010
(H) 4114 Sawkaw NE, Grand Rapids, MI 49525 (616) 361-6539

THOMPSON, MARK E. (FE) – (R-1988, D-1988, E-1990)
Riverside/Scottdale Jan. 1, 1987; Niles Grace Nov. 16, 1992; Bellevue/Kalamo 1996; Keeler/Silver Creek 2004; Grand Rapids Faith 2009
(H) 1018 Charlotte Ave NW, Grand Rapids, MI 49504-3770 (616) 453-4519
Grand Rapids Faith UMC: 2600 Seventh St. NW, Grand Rapids MI 49504 (616) 453-0693

***THOMPSON, R. JOHN (RE) (Sheryl) – (R-1998, D-1998, E-2003)**
Hudsonville 1997; Hudsonville/Holland: First (Assoc) 1998; Litchfield April 1, 2001; Kent City Chapel Hill 2005; Retired 2010; Unity (DSA) (LTFT 1/4) Nov. 1, 2011-2014
(H) 2418 Valleywood Ct, Muskegon, MI 49441 (231) 563-6417

***THOMPSON, RONALD J. (RE) (Hope) – (R-1961, D-1961, E-1963)**
[Detroit Conf., Waterford: Trinity 1961; Warren: Wesley 1967; Caro 1972;] transferred from Detroit Conf., DeWitt Oct. 15, 1975; Marshall April 5, 1983; Mt. Pleasant: First 1989; Retired 1995
(H) 1010 Tee Drive, Lake Isabella, MI 48893 (989) 644-3225

THURSTON-COX, HILLARY (OE) (Vaughn) – (R-2014)
[Free Methodist] Epsilon/New Hope/Harbor Springs/Alanson (Assoc.) 2014
(H) 8204 E Mitchell Rd, Petoskey, MI 49770 (231) 347-5382
Epsilon UMC: 8251 E. Mitchell Rd., Petoskey MI 49770 (231) 347-6608
New Hope UMC of Emmett County: 4516 N US 31, PO Box 72, Levering MI 49755 (231) 537-2000
Harbor Springs UMC: 343 East Main St., Harbor Springs MI 49740 (231) 526-2414
Alanson UMC: 343 E Main St, Harbor Springs MI 49740 (231) 548-5709

THURSTON-COX, VAUGHN (OE) – (R-2008)
[Free Methodist] Ferris State University Wesley Foundation Director, 2008; Epsilon/New Hope of Emmett County 2010; Epsilon/New Hope/Harbor Springs/Alanson 2014
(H) 8204 E Mitchell Rd, Petoskey, MI 49770-8831 (231) 347-5382
Epsilon UMC: 8251 E. Mitchell Rd., Petoskey MI 49770 (231) 347-6608
New Hope UMC of Emmett County: 4516 N US 31, PO Box 72, Levering MI 49755 (231) 537-2000
Harbor Springs UMC: 343 East Main St., Harbor Springs MI 49740 (231) 526-2414
Alanson UMC: 343 E Main St, Harbor Springs MI 49740 (231) 548-5709

TOMMY, DOMINIC A. (FE) (Comfort) – (R-2000, E-2003)
D.S. Assignment: Grand Rapids: First (Assoc.) 1997; Grand Rapids: First (Assoc.) (PTLP) Nov. 16, 1997-Apr. 13, 1999; Grand Rapids: Olivet (Assoc.) Apr. 16, 1999; Alto/Bowne Center 2000; Berrien Springs/Arden 2002; Stanwood: Northland 2006; Hopkins/South Monterey 2014
(H) 3226 Badger Ave SW, Wyoming, MI 49509 (616) 534-7626
Hopkins UMC: PO Box 356, Hopkins MI 49328 (269) 793-7323
South Monterey UMC: PO Box 356, Hopkins MI 49328 (269) 793-7323

***TORREY, WILLIAM JAMES (RE) (Eileen) – (R-1952, D-1953, E-1956)**
[Oshtemo 1951] 1952; Wayland 1956; Wacousta 1960; Battle Creek: Chapel Hill 1964; South Haven 1968; Ludington: United 1974; Jackson: Brookside Sept. 15, 1978; Portage: Chapel Hill 1985; Rockford 1989; Retired 1993; Portage: First (Assoc., LTFT) 1993-May 1996
(H) 28 Owl Brook Rd, Ashland, NH 3217 (603) 968-6348

***TOSHALIS, GERALD L. (RE) (Barbara) – (R-1968, D-1968, E-1973)**
In school 1968; Voluntary Location 1971; Readmitted, Grand Rapids Community Counseling - Personal Growth Ministry 1972; Director, Samaritan Health and Living Center 1979; San Diego: First (para. 426.1 Book of Discipline) 1990; Grand Rapids: Trinity (Assoc.) 1992; Grandville 2001; Grand Rapids Aldersgate (interim) 2005; Retired 2006
(H) 2225 Spencer Drive, Middleville, MI 49333 (269) 795-9799

TOWNLEY, ALICE FLEMING (FE) (Michael) – (R-1997, D-1997, E-2000)
Center Park 1997; Family Leave 2001; Williamston (3-6 Months Interim, para. 338.3b) July 15, 2008; Family Leave 2009; Okemos Presbyterian Church (Parish Assoc), Feb 1, 2010
(H) 1035 Prescott Dr, East Lansing, MI 48823-2445 (517) 324-5432
(O) Okemos Presbyterian Church, 2258 Bennett Rd, Okemos, MI 48823 (517) 507-5117

***TOWNSEND, RAYMOND J. (RE) (Joyce) – (R-1987, D-1987, E-1990)**
In School, METHESCO 1984-1988; Detroit Conf, Samaria/Lulu 1984-1988; Plainwell (Assoc.) 1988; Leighton 1991; Sparta 2006; Retired 2009
(H) 7178 Cornerstone Dr., Caledonia, MI 49316 (616) 204-3495

TREMAN, COLLEEN T. (FD) (Keith) – (Consecrated June 1984, R-1997, FD-1997)
Transferred from West Ohio Conf, Muskegon Central, Director of Christian Education, Sept 1, 1985; Muskegon Lakeside, Director of Christian Education Jan 1, 1990; Kalamazoo First, Coordinator of Children's Ministries July 1, 1990; Leave of Absence Jan 15, 1998; Sturgis (Deacon-LTFT 1/2) 1998-2008; Lansing Mt Hope (Deacon, Children's Coordinator) (LTFT 1/2) 2008
(H) 309 Grape St, Portland, MI 48875-1134 (517) 647-6460
Lansing Mt Hope UMC: 501 E Mt Hope Ave, Lansing MI 48910-9136 (517) 482-1549

TREMAN, KEITH R. (FE) (Colleen) – (R-1983, D-1983, E-1987)
In School GETS 1983; Whitehall/Claybanks 1985; Kalamazoo First (Assoc.) 1990; Sturgis Jan 15, 1998; Portland 2008
(H) 309 Grape St, Portland, MI 48875-1134 (517) 647-6460
Portland UMC: 310 E Bridge St, Portland MI 48875-1439 (517) 647-4649

TROWBRIDGE, SUSAN J. (FE) (Roger) – (R-1994, D-1987, E-1990)
[Newton, MA 1986; Detroit Conf, Flushing 1988-1991; Vermontville, MI: First Congregational 1992; DSA: Peace/Quimby April 1, 1993;] Transferred from Detroit Conf, Peace/Quimby (LTFT 3/4) 1994; Peace 1998; Leave of Absence, March 15, 2005; Munith and Stockbridge (LTFT 1/2) 2014
(H) 329 S Main, PO Box 151, Vermontville, MI 49096-0151 (517) 726-0541
Munith UMC: PO Box 189, Munith MI 49259-0189 (517) 596-2441
Stockbridge UMC: 219 E Elizabeth St, Stockbridge MI 49285-9666 (517) 851-7676

TUPPER, MICHAEL J. (FE) (Lori) – (R-1993, D-1983, E-1986)
[North Indiana Conf: Hammond Woodmar (Assoc.) 1983; South Bend Clay (Assoc.) 1991;] Transferred from North Indiana Conf, Casco April 16, 1993; Pentwater Centenary 2001; Appointed to Hope UMC, Red Bird Missionary Conf 2006 (para. 346.1); Parchment 2011
(H) 45554 West Street, Lawrence, MI 49064 (269) 303-3743
Parchment UMC: 225 Glendale Blvd, Parchment MI 49004 (269) 344-0125

***TURNER, ARTHUR R. (RE) (Johncie Palmer Turner) – (R-1968, D-1968, E-1972)**
Scottdale/Bridgman April 1, 1970; Manton/Fife Lake/East Boardman/South Boardman 1971; Lansing Potter Park 1976; Battle Creek Baseline 1981; Ashley/Bannister 1984; Handicapper Information Advocate, Handicapper Information Council & Patient Equipment Locker 1990; Honorable Location 1991; Ad-Interim, Morrice/Bennington/Pittsburg, Detroit Conf-Flint District, 1998; Morrice/Bennington/Pittsburg-Detroit Conf, (Para. 337.1, Begun June 2, 1999) 2002; Munith/Pleasant Lake 2004; Incapacity Leave, Nov 15, 2005; Retired 2006; North Adams/Jerome (DSA) Feb 1, 2012-2014
(H) 1039 Crestwood Ln, Jackson, MI 49203 (517) 769-2329

***TURNER, MOLLY C. (RE) – (R-1969, D-1969, E-1972)**
In School 1968; Manton/Fife Lake/East Boardman/South Boardman (Assoc) 1971; Lansing Mt Hope (Assoc) 1976; Vermontville/Gresham 1979; Breckenridge 1983; Central District Superintendent 1990; Area Assistant to the Bishop 1993; Grand Ledge First 2003; Retired 2012; Grand Ledge First (Interim July-Dec) 2012
(H) 1873 Hamilton Rd, Okemos, MI 48864-1812 (517) 214-6308

TUTHILL, TIMOTHY T. (FE) (Susan) – (R-1998, D-1998, E-2001)
Mason: First (Assoc) 1998; MSU Wesley Foundation 2006; Director of Pastoral Care, Clark Retirement Community 2010; Director of Life Enrichment, Clark Retirement Community Oct. 1, 2013
(H) 2139 Glen Echo Dr SE, Grand Rapids, MI 49546-5518 (616) 635-2669
(O) Clark Retirement Community, 1551 Franklin SE, Grand Rapids, MI 49506-3331 (616) 452-1568

***VALE, DIANE (DIA) E. (RE) (Marc) – (R-1973, D-1973, E-1977)**
In school 1973; Fife Lake/Boardmans Parish 1976; Lawton Oct. 15, 1977; The Institute for Advanced Pastoral Studies, Bloomfield Hills May 1, 1980; Sabbatical 1983; Weidman 1984; Leave of absence July 15, 1985; Retired 1990
(H) 17600 Garvey Road, Chelsea, MI 48118 (734) 475-9526

***VANDENBRINK, SANDRA KAY (RLA) (Noel Matthews)**
In Seminary, MTSO, 1993; 1993-95 Trinway-Dresden Charge, E Ohio Conf; 1995-1997 Barton-on-Humber Circuit, British Methodist Church; Hudsonville 2001; Salem/Bradley Indian Missions (PTLP 1/4 Interim) Jan 16, 2005; (PTLP 1/2) July 1, 2005; (PTLP 3/4) Jan 1, 2007; Retired 2013; Director, Senior Meals Program of Salem/Bradley Indian Mission UMCs (RLA 1/4) 2013
(H) 3933 Kerri Ct, Holland, MI 49424 (616) 738-9030
Salem Indian Mission of the UMC: 1875 Parkcrest Drive #2, Wyoming MI 49519
Bradley Indian Mission of the UMC: 1875 Parkcrest Drive #2, Wyoming MI 49519

VANDERBILT, HERBERT J. (PL) (Emmy)
East Nelson (PTLP 1/2) 2004
(H) 2204 Gee Dr, Lowell, MI 49331 (616) 897-8642
East Nelson UMC: 9024 18 Mile Rd NE, Cedar Springs MI 49319-9217 (616) 696-0661

VANDOP, JONATHAN D. (FE) (Darcie) – (R-2009, E-2014)
Rosebush 2008; Ionia First (FE) 2014
(H) 119 E Main St, Ionia, MI 48846 (616) 527-4654
Ionia First UMC: 105 E. Main Street, Ionia MI 48846 (616) 527-1860

***VANLENTE, CHARLES R. (RA) (Linda) – (D-1973)**

Ashton Charge Sept. 1963; Morris Chapel/Niles Dec. 1964-Sept. 1965; St. Johns: Salem Jan. 15, 1970; Howard City: Maple Hill 1972; Honorable Location Aug. 15, 1976; Holton/Sitka/Twin Lake Ad Interim 1978; Readmitted Holton/Sitka/Twin Lake 1982; Cassopolis 1983; Kalkaska 1993; Grand Rapids: Northlawn 1996; Retired 2010

(H) 2103 Shetland Dr NE, Grand Rapids, MI 49505 (616) 719-1833

VANLENTE, RONALD D. (FE) (Kathleen Logsdon) – (R-2012, D-1991, E-1998) (W North Carolina)

[Western North Carolina Conf] Coloma/Watervliet (LTFT 3/4) (Para. 346.1) 2011 [Watervliet UMC merged w/ Coloma UMC 6-26-11]; Coloma (full-time) Jan. 1, 2012; transferred from Western North Carolina Conference 2013

(H) 331 Tannery Dr, Coloma, MI 49038 (269) 468-4905
Coloma UMC: 144 South Church St, PO Box 670, Coloma MI 49038 (269) 468-6062

***VAUGHT, KENNETH R. (RE) (Helen) – (R-1952, E-1957)**

Transferred from Indiana South (EUB), Hastings Hope 1968; Battle Creek Christ Jan 16, 1983; Leighton 1986; Nashville June 1, 1991; Retired 1994; Quimby (DSA) 1998-2011

(H) 1641 S Broadway, Hastings, MI 49058 (269) 948-3972

VEILLEUX, CYNTHIA L. (PL)

Frontier/Osseo (DSA) Nov 1, 2010; Bronson (PTLP 3/4) 2011

(H) 330 E Corey St, Bronson, MI 49028-1504 (517) 858-1022
Bronson UMC: 312 E. Chicago St., Bronson MI 49028 (517) 369-6555

***VENTURA, OSCAR (RE) (Naomi) – (R-1996, D-1975, E-1978)**

[Puerto Rico Conf.: Cidra 1975, Ponce Palya 1980, Transfered to Wisconsin Conf.; Kenosha: First Hispanic Ministry 1986;] Transfered from Wisconsin Conf.; Grand Rapids: La Nueva Esperanza Sept. 1, 1996; Involuntary Leave of Absence Sept. 2002; Grand Rapids: Iglesia Metodista Unida La Nueva Esperanza, March 16, 2003; Retired 2009

(H) Apartado Postal 97, Calle Carlos Lassy #13, Barahona, Republica Dominicana 82000
(O) Apartado Postal #97, Barahona, Republica Dominicana

***VERNON, DOUGLAS W. (RE) (Jane) – (R-1967, E-1970)**

Niles Trinity 1969; Kalamazoo First (Assoc) 1971; Stockbridge Nov 1974; [Transfered to Detroit Conf, Birmingham: First (Assoc) Sept 1979; Mackinaw City Church of the Straits Nov 15, 1984; Detroit St Timothy's Jan 1, 1988; Northville First UMC 1991] Transfered from Detroit Conf, Kalamazoo First 2000; Retired 2010; Lawton St Paul's (DSA) (LTFT 1/4) 2011-2014

(H) 3643 Woodcliff Dr, Kalamazoo, MI 49008-2513 (269) 544-2683

VITTOZ, IRENE L. (PL) (Gary)

Brookfield Eaton (DSA), October 2004; Brookfield Eaton (PTLP) Nov 15, 2005; Brookfield Eaton (PTLP) and Pope (PTLP) 2008; Brookfield Eaton (PTLP 1/4) and Lee Center (PTLP 1/4) 2010; Brookfield Eaton (PTLP 1/4) 2014

(H) 5503 Long Hwy, Eaton Rapids, MI 48827-9016 (517) 543-5361
Brookfield Eaton UMC: 7681 Brookfield, PO Box 430, Charlotte MI 48813-0430 (517) 543-4225

***VUURENS, DONALD (RE) (Florence) – (R-1976, D-1976, E-1979)**

Received by transfer from Reformed Church of America 1976; Holton/Sitka/Twin Lake Oct. 15, 1975; Leighton Jan. 1, 1978; Bear Lake/Arcadia 1980; Milville Feb. 1, 1983; Adamsville 1986; Retired Oct. 16, 1995; DSA Crystal Valley/Walkerville 1996

(H) 2685 Forest Hills Drive, Muskegon, MI 49441-3441 (231) 828-4341

WAGNER, GLENN M. (FE) (Nancy) – (R-1992, D-1976, E-1982)

[Northern Illinois Conf: Freeport Faith (Assoc.) 1979; Harvard 1986;] Transferred from Northern Illinois Conf: North Muskegon Community 1992; Holt 2006; Grand Haven Church of the Dunes 2014

(H) 633 Hillock Ct, Grand Haven, MI 49417 (616) 842-3586
Grand Haven Church of the Dunes: 717 Sheldon Road, Grand Haven MI 49417-1860 (616) 842-7980

***WAGNER, LYNN W. (RE) – (R-1965, D-1965, E-1970)**
Hillsdale (Assoc.) 1966; Niles Wesley (Assoc.) 1969; Howard City Circuit Sept. 15, 1970; Evart Circuit March 1, 1971; Keeler/Silver Creek Oct. 15, 1973; Mulliken/Grand Ledge (Assoc.) 1975; Country Chapel/Banfield 1977; Nashville 1984; Middleville/Parmelee 1988; Battle Creek: Maple 1996; Lyons-Muir/Ionia: Easton 2001; Retired September 1, 2002
(H) 116 S Clinton St, Charlotte, MI 48813-1422 (517) 543-8186

WALES, GARY S. (FE) (Cynthia Kaye) – (R-1988, D-1988, E-1990)
Fife Lake/Boardman 1987; Trowbridge 1994; Kingsley 2008; Charlotte Lawrence Avenue 2013
(H) 1072 N Stonehill Dr, Charlotte, MI 48813 (517) 231-6775
Charlotte Lawrence Avenue UMC: PO Box 36, Charlotte MI 48813-0036 (517) 543-4670

***WALSWORTH, LOWELL F. (RE) (Jessica) – (R-1959, D-1959, E-1962)**
[Hastings Parish 1957]; Lyon Lake/Marengo 1959; in school 1961; Kalamazoo First (Assoc.) 1962; Bellevue/Kalamo 1966; Grand Rapids: First (Assoc.) 1971; Edwardsburg/Niles: Trinity 1973; Battle Creek: Trinity 1978; Vicksburg 1981; Sturgis 1993; Assoc. Professor of Communications, Olivet College 1995; Retired 2002
(H) 1412 E Hatch, Sturgis, MI 49091 (269) 659-4688

***WALWORTH JR, MAURICE E. (RE) (Sally) – (R-1993, D-1985, E-1989)**
[Central Texas Conf: Maypearl-Venus 1983; Dawson/Penelope 1985; Round Rock First (Senior Assoc & Business Mgr) 1987; Southwest Texas Conf: George West First 1989; Corpus Christi St. Peter's by-the-Sea July-Oct 1993;] Transferred from Southwest Texas Conf, Battle Creek Baseline Nov 1, 1993; Lansing Christ 1996; Jackson Calvary 2003; Retired 2006; Munith/Pleasant Lake (DSA) 2006; Pleasant Lake (DSA) 2007-Sept 30, 2007; Somerset Center (DSA) 2008-2009; Munith (DSA) Sept 6, 2011-2012
(H) 257 Lake Heights, PO Box 612, Grass Lake, MI 49240-0612 (517) 522-3936

WASNICH, KELLY M. (PL)
Leslie/Felt Plains (PTLP 1/2) 2014
(H) 401 E Ash St, Mason, MI 48854 (517) 604-6157
Leslie UMC: 401 S Main St, Leslie MI 49251-9402 (517) 589-9211
Felt Plains UMC: 401 S Main St, Leslie MI 49251-9402

***WEGNER, GLENN R. (RE) (Evelyn) – (R-1984, D-1975, E-1978)**
Transferred from Detroit Conf., Woodland/Welcome Corners 1984; Epsilon/Levering 1987; West Ohio Conf., Seaman Sept. 1, 1992 (para. 426.1 Book of Discipline); Battle Creek: Baseline 1996; Retired 2004
(H) 3788 Bass Road, Williamsburg, OH 45176 (269) 967-3850

WEILER, CARA BETH ANN (FD) (Matthew) – (R-2008, FD-2011)
Portage Chapel Hill (Deacon) (LTFT 1/4) Oct 1, 2007; Transferred from Northern Illinois Conf 2008; Kalamazoo Sunnyside (Deacon)(LTFT 1/4), Oct 1, 2009; Kalamazoo Sunnyside (Deacon) (LTFT 1/4) and Southwest Michigan Children's Trauma Assessment Center (LTFT 1/2) Nov 18, 2009
(H) 3279 Cardinal Hills Trail, Kalamazoo, MI 49004 (269) 323-9279
(O) Southwest Michigan Childen's Trauma Assessment Center, Unified Clinics - WMU, 1000 Oakland Drive, Kalamazoo, MI 49008 (269) 387-7073
Kalamazoo Sunnyside UMC: 2800 Gull Road, Kalamazoo MI 49048-1384 (269) 349-3047

WEILER, JOHN (MATT) MATTHEW (FE) (Cara) – (R-2009, E-2013)
Portage Chapel Hill (Assoc.) 2007; Portage Chapel Hill (Assoc.)(1/2 time) and Sunnyside (1/2 time) 2009; Sunnyside 2011
(H) 3279 Cardinal Hills Trail, Kalamazoo, MI 49004 (269) 762-5591
Kalamazoo Sunnyside UMC: 2800 Gull Road, Kalamazoo MI 49048-1384 (269) 349-3047

WEINBERGER, STEPHAN (FE) – (R-1985, E-1975, Presby. Church)
Indian River/Pellston July 1, 1984; St. Johns: First 1990; Lansing: First 2000; Oaks Correctional Facility 2004; Lansing: Calvary/Potter Park 2005; Lansing Calvary July 1, 2006; Lansing Calvary/Wheatfield Aug. 1, 2006; Mancelona/Alba 2007; Muskegon Lakeside/Crestwood 2010; Heritage 2014
(H) 18985 W Coral Rd, Howard City, MI 49329 (231) 937-4748
Heritage UMC: 19931 W. Kendaville Rd, Pierson MI 49339 (231) 937-4310

***WELSCH, P. KAY (AF)**
[Retired Elder, Wisconsin Conf] Turk Lake (DSA) (LTFT) July 16, 2005-2012
(H) 9440 Cutler Road, PO Box 318, Lakeview, MI 48850 (989) 352-1209

***WELSH, GERALD L. (RE) (Martha Gene) – (R-1957, D-1957, E-1960)**
[Sand Lake Circuit 1953; in school 1956]; Alma (Assoc.) Jan. 1960; Carson City 1961; Harbor Springs Sept. 1965; Stevensville 1968; Bellaire Oct. 15, 1969; Martin/Shelbyville 1976; Evart/Avondale 1984; Bronson 1990; Retired 1994
(H) 35 Roberts Court, Coopersville, MI 49404 (616) 837-7157

***WESSMAN, ROBERT L. (RE) (Leslie) – (R-1974, D-1974, E-1981)**
In school 1974; Mason (Assoc.) 1979; Caledonia 1984; Allegan 1990; Retired 1999
(H) 6476 Castle Ave, Holland, MI 49423-8988 (616) 335-8983

WHEAT, KAREN S. (FE) (Vincent) – (R-1972, D-1972, E-1975)
In School 1972; Niles: Wesley (Assoc) 1974; Gobles/Kendall Sept 15, 1976; Jackson: Trinity 1986; Battle Creek: First 1998; Charlotte: Lawrence Aveune 2002; Schoolcraft 2010
(H) 318 Willow Ct, Schoolcraft, MI 49087 (269) 679-4501
Schoolcraft UMC: 342 N Grand Ave, PO Box 336, Schoolcraft MI 49087 (269) 679-4845

WHEELER, JENNIFER J (PL)
Augusta (DSA) 2013; Augusta Fellowship (PTLP 1/4) Nov 9, 2013
(H) PO Box 137, Galesburg, MI 49053-0137 (231) 343-0388
Augusta Fellowship UMC: 103 N. Webster, PO Box 337, Augusta MI 49012 (269) 731-4222

***WHITLOCK, BOBBY DALE (RE) (Nancy Jo) – (R-1985, D-1977, E-1980)**
Transferred from Oklahoma Conf, Remus/Halls Corner/Mecosta Sept 16, 1985; Dansville/Vantown May 16, 1987; Caledonia 1990; Scottville Jan 6, 1996; Big Rapids First 2004; Robbins 2008; Retired 2009; Wolf Lake (DSA) (LTFT 1/2) 2011; Wolf Lake (Ret.) (LTFT 45%) Jan. 1 - Sept. 1, 2014
(H) 4512 S Quarterline, Muskegon, MI 49444 (231) 457-4705
Muskegon Wolf Lake UMC: 370 Vista Terrace, Muskegon MI 49442 (231) 788-3663

WICKS, JEREMY J. (FL) (Toinette)
Dansville (DSA) (1/4 Time) 2011; Dansville (PTLP 1/4) Nov 13, 2011; Dansville and Wheatfield (PTLP 1/2) 2012; M-52 Cooperative Ministry: Millville (1/2 Time) and Dansville (1/4 Time) and Wheatfield (1/4 Time) 2013; M-52 Cooperative Ministry: Millville (1/2 Time) and Dansville (1/4 Time) and New Church Start (1/4 Time) 2014
(H) 1956 N M 52, Stockbridge, MI 49285-9625 (517) 623-6594
Dansville UMC: PO Box 175, Dansville MI 48819-0175 (517) 851-7853
Millville UMC: 1932 N M-52, Stockbridge MI 49285-9625 (517) 851-7853
New Church Start:

WIELAND, RYAN B. (FE) (Stacey M.B.) – (R-2012, E-2010 (Iowa))
[Iowa Conf, Elder] Dowling Country Chapel (LTFT 3/4) 2011; Transferred from Iowa Conference 2013
(H) 3400 Lacey Rd, Dowling, MI 49050 (269) 758-3400
Country Chapel UMC: PO Box 26, Dowling MI 49050-0026 (269) 721-8077

WIERINGA, REBECCA L. (FE) (Jeremy Chad) – (R-2011, E-2014)
(Formerly Rebecca Farrester) Hart 2011
(H) 3818 Melody Lane, Hart, MI 49420 (231) 873-4766
Hart UMC: 308 S. State St., Hart MI 49420 (231) 873-3516

WIERMAN, COLLEEN A. (FL) (Brian)
Brethren Epworth (PTLP 1/4) 2011; Brethren Epworth/Grant (PTLP 1/2), Nov 27, 2011; Grawn (PTLP 1/2) and Grant (PTLP 1/4) and Kingsley (Assoc.) (PTLP 1/4), 2014
(H) 8658 Hency Rd, Kingsley, MI 49649 (231) 263-4145
Grant UMC: PO Box 454, Interlochen MI 49643 (231) 269-3981
Grawn UMC: 1260 S West Silver Lake Rd, Traverse City MI 49685 (231) 943-8353
Kingsley UMC: 113 W Blair Street, PO Box 395, Kingsley MI 49649 (231) 263-5278

WILLIAMS, BEVERLEY J. (FL) (Harry)
Mesick/Harrietta (DSA) 2012; Mesick/Harrietta Nov. 10, 2012
(H) 3851 N 15 Rd, Mesick, MI 49668-9757 (231) 885-1179
Mesick UMC: PO Box 337, Mesick MI 49668 (231) 885-1699
Harrietta UMC: 116 N. Davis Street, PO Box 13, Harrietta MI 49638 (231) 389-0267

WILLIAMS, CHARLES A. (FE) – (R-1995, D-1995, E-2000)
Mesick/Harrietta 1992-Feb 14, 1997; Belding Feb 15, 1997; Quincy Jan 1, 1999; Alden/Central Lake 2003; Keswick 2010; Leave of Absence 2011; Detroit Conference, Houghton: Grace 2013
(H) 807 Oak Grove Pkwy, Houghton, MI 49931 (906) 482-1751
(O) Houghton: Grace UMC, 201 Isle Royle, Houghton, MI 49931 (906) 482-2780

WILLIAMS, JEFFREY C. (FE) (Beverly) – (R-1987, D-1987, E-1991)
In School GETS 1987; Center Park Aug 1, 1989; Director, WMU Wesley Foundation Feb 16, 1993; New Church Start/Rockford (Assoc.) 2002; White Pines New Church Start 2004; White Pines and Courtland-Oakfield 2009; Hartford 2011; Wayland 2014
(H) 220 Church St, Wayland, MI 49348 (269) 944-9231
Wayland UMC: 200 Church St., Wayland MI 49348 (269) 792-2208

WILLIAMS, JEREMY PH (FE) (Tamara) – (R-1996, D-1996, E-2001)
Arden 1995; Berrien Springs/Arden 1998; Traverse City Asbury 2002; Traverse Bay Jan 2005 (Asbury & Emmanuel merged January 2005); Albion First 2009
(H) 11184 29 Mile Rd, Albion, MI 49224-9735 (517) 629-6531
Albion First UMC: 600 E. Michigan, Albion MI 49224 (517) 629-9425

***WILLIAMS, MYRON K. (RE) (Maudy) – (R-1953, E-1956)**
Ludington (EUB) 1956; Sodus/Chapel Hill (EUB) 1960; Vicksburg 1969; Holt 1972; Hastings: First 1982; Wyoming: Wesley Park 1985; Retired 1994
(H) 1743 S. Stebbins Rd., White Cloud, MI 49349 (231) 689-1689
(S) 5430 E. Arbor Ave, Mesa, AZ 85206 (480) 981-3713

***WILLIAMS, NOLAN R. (RA) (Sandra) – (D-1970)**
Coral/Amble 1966; Stanwood/Higbe 1967; Stanwood Northland 1971; Ionia Zion/Easton 1974; Ithaca/Beebe Oct 1, 1980; Niles Wesley 1991; Retired Jan 1, 2000
(H) 4231 Embassy Dr SE, Grand Rapids, MI 49546-2438 (616) 957-3222

***WILLIAMS, RICHARD K. (RE) (Susan) – (R-1969, D-1969, E-1972)**
In school 1969; Benton Harbor: Peace Temple (Assoc.) 1971; Constantine April 1, 1973; Honorable Location 1976; Galien/Olive Branch ad interim Feb. 1, 1977; Muskegon: Wolf Lake Oct. 1, 1979; Lansing: Trinity (Assoc.) Nov. 1, 1983; Hesperia/Ferry 1985; Leave of Absence Oct. 1, 1997; Retired 2001
(H) 444 Mary Ln, Fremont, MI 49412-1378 (231) 854-3005

WILLIAMS, TAMARA S. (FE) (Jeremy) – (R-1993, D-1987, E-1990)
[Baltimore-Washington Conf.: Chesapeake Charge (Cedar Grove/Oakland) 1988; Cedar Grove 1992;] Transferred from Baltimore-Washington Conf., Stevensville (Assoc.) 1993; Traverse City: Central (Assoc.) 2002; Albion District Superintendent 2009
(H) 11184 29 Mile Rd, Albion, MI 49224 (517) 629-6531
(O) Albion District Office, 600 E Michigan, Albion, MI 49224 (517) 629-8150

***WILSON, MARGARET HALLS (RE) (Benjamin) – (R-1984, D-1984, E-1989)**
In school METHESCO 1984; Alto/Bowne Center 1985; Portage Prairie 1989; Marshall (Assoc.) 1994; Otsego 1998; Evart 2000; Grawn 2006; Retired Nov. 1, 2009
(H) 441 Norweigan Trail, Harrison, MI 48625 (231) 743-0119

***WILSON, RICHARD D. (RE) – (R-1963, D-1963, E-1967)**
Muskegon: Unity/Twin Lakes 1965; Cadillac: Selma St./South Community Oct. 1966; Big Rapids Parish Nov. 1968; Howard City/Coral/Maple Hill March 1, 1971; Howard City: First/Coral 1972; Kalamazoo: Lane Blvd. 1975; Muskegon: Lakeside 1981; Buchanan: Faith/Morris Chapel 1987; Sodus: Chapel Hill 1996; Battle Creek: Sonoma/Newton 2003; Retired 2008
(H) 548 East Drive, Marshall, MI 49068 (269) 781-4082

***WINGEIER, DOUGLAS E. (RE)**
Transfered from Wisconsin conf., Retired 2000
(H) 266 Merrimon Ave, Asheville, NC 28801-1218 (828) 456-3857

***WOLFE, GREGORY R. (RE) (Sue) – (R-1973, D-1973, E-1975)**
Clinical Pastoral Education Program, Milledgeville State Hospital 1973; Potterville/West Benton 1974; Keeler/Silver Creek Oct. 16, 1978; Grass Lake Nov. 16, 1983; Clare 1994; Portland 2003; Kalkaska 2008; Retired 2013; Napoleon (Ret.) (LTFT 3/4) 2013
(H) 10014 Sunset Dr, Jackson, MI 49201-9850 (517) 536-4903
Napoleon UMC: PO Box 337, Napoleon MI 49261 (517) 536-8609

WOOD, GREGORY B. (FE) (Beverly) – (R-1980, D-1980, E-1984)
In school 1980; New Buffalo/Lakeside Feb. 1, 1982; Lansing :Trinity (Assoc.) 1985; Manistee 1990; Portage: First 1998
(H) 8731 Newhouse, Portage, MI 49024 (269) 327-0410
Portage First UMC: 8740 S Westnedge Ave, Portage MI 49002 (269) 327-6761

WORLEY, RONALD L. (PL) (Shelly)
Crystal Valley/Walkerville (PTLP 1/2) 2004; LP w/o Appointment, Dec. 1, 2013; Muskegon Unity (PTLP 1/4) 2014
(H) 76 W Muskegon St NW, PO Box 254, Kent City, MI 49330 (616) 485-4441
Muskegon Unity UMC: 1600 North Getty St, Muskegon MI 49445 (231) 744-1972

WRIGHT, CHRISTINA LYNN (FD) – (R-2009, FD-2012)
Cleveland Clinic, Advance Directives Coordinator, June 7, 2009; University of West Georgia to attend school (para. 326.1), Aug 1, 2009
(H) 717 Burns Rd #3114, Carrollton, GA 30117 (617) 875-6955

WRIGHT, TIMOTHY B. (FE) (Paula) – (R-2005, E-2008)
Horton Bay/Greensky Hill Indian Mission 2005; Grand Rapids Northlawn 2013
(H) 1141 Northlawn NE, Grand Rapids, MI 49505 (616) 361-2321
Grand Rapids Northlawn UMC: 1157 Northlawn NE, Grand Rapids MI 49505 (616) 361-8503

***YINGLING, DAVID W. (RE) – (R-1969, D-1969, E-1973)**
Transferred from East Ohio Conf., Kalamazoo: Milwood (Assoc.) 1972; Edmore 1976; Charlevoix/ Greensky Hill Indian Mission 1981; Battle Creek: Birchwood 1988; Retired 1991
(H) 2034 Willow Run Cir, Enon, OH 45323-9786 (937) 864-2166

***YOUELLS, RICHARD A. (RE) (Carol) – (R-1960, D-1960, E-1963)**
[Silver Creek 1958]; Bridgman 1963; Wesley Foundation Director, CMU 1965; Flint Wesley Foundation Director 1969; Potterville/West Benton/Dimondale 1970; South Haven 1974; Grand Rapids: Olivet Aug. 16, 1979; Muskegon Heights: Temple 1989; Grand Haven: Church of the Dunes (Assoc.) 1991; Retired 1995
(H) 740 Clark Crossing S.E., Grand Rapids, MI 49506 (616) 243-3759

YOUNG, MELANIE S. (FE) – (R-1993, D-1993, E-1995)
Weidman 1993; Muskegon: Central (Assoc.) 1994; Leave of Absence 1996; In school, CPE Residency Program, Rochester Methodist Hospital Sept. 1, 1996; Grovenburg 1997; Quincy 1998; Director, Wesley Foundation, Ferris State University Oct 1, 1998; Burr Oak (LTFT 1/2) 2003; Appointed to attend school 2006; Constantine 2007; Leave of Absence 2009; Pentwater Centenary 2014
(H) 124 S Rutledge St, Pentwater, MI 49449 (231) 869-6881
Pentwater Centenary UMC: 82 S Hancock, PO Box 111, Pentwater MI 49449 (231) 869-5900

YOUNG, STEVEN R. (FE) (Kathy) – (R-1982, D-1982, E-1985)
Turk Lake 1982; Muskegon Lakeside 1987; Sparta 1993; Ithaca/Beebe 2006; Coldwater 2010
(H) 20 Parsons Ct, Coldwater, MI 49036 (517) 278-2854
Coldwater UMC: 26 Marshall St, Coldwater MI 49036 (517) 279-8402

***ZACHMAN, LEE F. (RE) (Barbara) – (R-1977, D-1974, E-1981)**
Eaton Rapids (Assoc.) Jan 15, 1977; North Adams/Jerome 1980; Martin/Shelbyville 1984; Wyoming Park April 16, 1994; Middleville/Parmelee 1996; Parmelee (LTFT 1/2) 2004; Retired December 1, 2010
(H) 3645 Lakeshore Dr, Shelbyville, MI 49344 (269) 397-1243

ZIENERT, ELLEN K. (FE) (Mark Baker) – (R-2010, PE-2010, E-2013)
East Lansing Chapel Hill (DSA) 2005; East Lansing Chapel Hill (Part-Time) Nov 15, 2005; East Lansing Chapel Hill (LTFT 1/4) and Williamston: Crossroads (LTFT 1/4) 2010; St. Johns First July 15, 2012
(H) 1006 Hampshire Dr, St. Johns, MI 48879-2404 (989) 224-2415
St Johns First UMC: 200 E. State Street, St. Johns MI 48879 (989) 224-6859

XVII-A. CLERGY ON HONORABLE or ADMINISTRATIVE LOCATION

This Pastoral Record indicates appointments but is not necessarily a pension record. The date given following each appointment represents the initial year of that appointment, with changes occurring immediately following Annual Conference unless otherwise noted. Brackets around appointments indicate charges served prior to reception into the West Michigan Conference. (H) is the Home Address; (O) is an office address and (S) is a seasonal address.

This record is maintained by Kathy Hippensteel at the Conference Center. Correspondence should be directed to her by email, kathy@wmcumc.org, or at P.O. Box 6247, Grand Rapids, MI 49516-6247.

HL = Honorable Location AL = Administrative Location
RHL = Retired Honorable Location

***BENNER, DWIGHT M. (RHL) (Joan) – (R-1970, D-1970, E-1972)**
Transferred from Northern Illinois Conf Athens/East LeRoy/Fulton 1970; Portage (Assoc.) 1972; Grand Rapids Second 1974; Coloma/Riverside 1977; Evart Circuit Sept 1, 1981; Leave of Absence 1983; Honorable Location 1988 (Charge Conf: Birmingham First, Detroit Conf.); Retired 2009
(H) 21660 Meadow Ln, Franklin, MI 48025-4850 (248) 723-0676

***CARR, WILLIAM D. (RHL) (Carolyn) – (R-1982, D-1982, E-1986)**
In School METHESCO 1982; Belding 1983; Galien/Olive Branch Oct 16, 1983; Hamilton Grove (H), New Carlisle, IN, April 16, 1986; Leave of Absence Oct 15, 1988; Bear Lake/Arcadia 1989; Honorable Location 1993 (Charge Conf: Allegan); Retired March 1, 2003
(H) 3615 Bay View Dr, Allegan, MI 49010-8951 (269) 686-0290

CROSSMAN, THOMAS A. (HL) – (R-1983, D-1983, E-1986)
Leaton Aug 16, 1980-Aug 1981 (Local Pastor); In school Union Theological Seminary 1983; Mt Pleasant First (Assoc.) 1981; Leave of Absence June 30, 1986; Honorable Location 1991 (Charge Conf: Church of St. Paul and St. Andrew, New York, NY)
(H) 687 W 204th Street #6J, New York, NY 10034-1290 (212) 567-0437

DEMPSEY, BRUCE W. (HL) (Anne) – (R-1979, D-1979, E-1983)
In School 1979; Edwardsburg 1981; Muskegon Wolf Lake Nov 1, 1983; Leave of Absence Nov 1, 1988; Honorable Location 1993 (Charge Conf: Montague)
(H) 3950 Westbrook Dr, Muskegon, MI 49444-4165 (231) 557-0971

***DRAGGOO, DAVID L. (RHL) – (R-1962, D-1962, E-1966)**
Morris Chapel 1962; Sturgis (Assoc.) Nov 1964; Burr Oak 1967; Perry/Shaftsburg 1971; LOA 1981; Honorable Location 1986 (Charge Conf: Laingsburg, Detroit Conf.); Retired 2009
(H) 9637 Jason Rd, Laingsburg, MI 48848-9282 (517) 651-6846

HAINER, C. DAVID (HL) (Rhonda) – (R-1981, D-1981, E-1985)
In School GETS 1981; Bainbridge New Hope/Scottdale 1983; Belding Nov 1, 1983, Kent City Chapel Hill Oct 1, 1988; Leave of Absence March 1, 1991; Honorable Location 1996; (Charge Conf: Riverside, Moline, IL)
(H) 8249 Skipjack Dr, Indianapolis, IN 46236-9583 (616) 706-4496

HILL, VALERIE MARIE (AL) – (R-1979, D-1979, E-1983)
In School Perkins School of Theology 1979; Hinchman-Oronoko 1981; Bear Lake/Arcadia March 1, 1983; Frontier, Osseo 1985; Comstock 1989; Leave of Absence 1991; Springport/Lee Center 1996; Pine River Parish: LeRoy/Ashton (Interim)1998; Administrative Location 1999
(H) 11380 Heintzelman Ave NE, Rockford, MI 49341-9534 (616) 808-6100

***LEACH, JAMES E. (RHL) – (R-1954, D-1955, E-1957)**
Hopkins 1955; Kalamazoo First (Assoc.) 1956; Grand Rapids Second 1959; Executive Secretary, Michigan Conf Board of Education 1962; Big Rapids First 1965; Honorable Location 1972; Retired 1994 (Charge Conf: Memorial UMC, Lake Placid, FL)
(H) 3398 Crestwood Dr, Salt Lake City, UT 84109-3202

LONG, MICHAEL EDWARD (HL) (Jean) – (R-1983, D-1983, E-1986)
In School Asbury Theological Seminary 1983; Rosebush (LTFT 3/4) Clare (Assoc) (LTFT 1/4) 1984; Rosebush/Geneva Hope (Detroit Conf) 1990; Grawn 1992; Sommerset Center 1996; Honorable Location 1998 (Charge Conf: Traverse Bay)
(H) 1764 Linden Ave, Traverse City, MI 49686-4735 (231) 645-9584

MACARTHUR, TERRY L. (HL) – (R-1974, D-1974, E-1977)
In School, Sparta/Bloomfield, OH 1974; St Johns Salem/Greenbush/Lowe 1976; Three Oaks Oct 16, 1979; In School, Union Theological Seminary 1983; Leave of Absence 1984; Honorable Location June 15, 1985 (Charge Conf: Portage Chapel Hill)
(H) 17 Chemin Taverney, 1218 Grand Saconnex, Switzerland (+41) 227-9832 31

MCKINVEN-COPUS, CLINTON E. (HL) (Laurie) – (R-1984, D-1984, E-1987)
Transferred from Wisconsin Conf, Fife Lake/Boardman 1985; West Mendon 1987; Leslie/Felt Plains 1990; Leave of Absence Sept 16, 1991; Perry/Shaftsburg Feb 1, 1992; Grand Rapids Olivet Jan 1, 1995; SECOM (para. 335.1d) Jan 1, 2001; Leave of Absence Feb 15, 2005; Honorable Location 2007 (Charge Conf: Ludington United)
(H) 5480 S Lakeshore Dr, Ludington, MI 49431-9751 (231) 845-9414
(O) City of Manistee Housing Commission, 237 Sixth Ave, Manistee, MI 49660 (231) 723-6201 ext.102

***MCKINVEN-COPUS, LAURIE J. (RHL) (Clinton) – (R-1984, D-1984, E-1987)**
In School GETS 1984; Manton 1985; Nottawa/Leonidas (LTFT) 1987; Munith/Pleasant Lake 1990; Leave of Absence Sept 16, 1991; United Methodist Community House, Church and Community Liaison 1996; Honorable Location April 2, 2005 (Charge Conf: Ludington United); Retired 2013
(H) 5480 S Lakeshore Dr, Ludington, MI 49431-9751 (231) 845-9414

***MCNARY, CHARLES D. (RHL) (Sandra Hoffman McNary) – (R-1965, D-1965, E-1968)**
[Winn/Coomer/Millbrook 1961; Casnovia/Kent City 1964]; Kent City 1967; Bangor 1970; Honorable Location 1977; Retired 1995; Morris Chapel (DSA) 2002-2003 (Charge Conf: Bangor Simpson)
(H) 32054 County Road 687, Bangor, MI 49013-9405 (269) 427-0766

***MEREDITH, THURLAN E. (RHL) – (R-1966, D-1966, E-1969)**
[Gladwin Parish Jan 1960; Courtland/Oakfield Nov 1963] 1966; Martin/Shelbyville 1970; Grand Rapids Northlawn 1976; Lake Odessa Central 1984; Disability 1986; Leave of Absence 1988; Honorable Location 1993; Snow (ad interim) 1995 (Charge Conf: Grand Rapids Northlawn); Retired 2008
(H) 632 Hensel Ave NW #93, Comstock Park, MI 49321-8933 (616) 785-8494

MYERS, ALLEN C. (HL) (Janice Myers) – (R-1967, E-1970)
East Ohio Conf: Nashville, Ohio (UCC) 1970; In School University of Michigan 1970; Supernumerary 1975; Honorable Location 1977; Transferred from East Ohio Conf 1980; Honorable Location 1980 (Charge Conf: Grand Rapids Trinity)
(H) 2011 Orville St, SE, Grand Rapids, MI 49506-4535 (616) 452-5339

***OTTO, EDWARD F. (RHL) (Nancy) – (R-1968, D-1968, E-1970)**
Transferred from Wisconsin Conf, East Lansing: Chapel Hill/Gunnisonville 1969; Wacousta Dec 15, 1971; Honorable Location Oct 1, 1978 (Charge Conf: First UMC, Chicago, IL); Retired 2012
(H) 1335 S Prairie Ave Unit #405, Chicago, IL 60605-3121 (312) 945-3966

***SCHEIBNER, PAUL K. (RHL) (Elaine) – (R-1959, D-1959, E-1963)**
Preaching License 1958; Girard 1959; In school 1960; Concord 1962; Martin/Shelbyville 1965; Dansville/Vantown 1970; East Lansing Chapel Hill/Gunnisonville 1974; Leave of Absence 1978; Honorable Location 1983; Retired 1993
(H) 631 Nixon Blvd, Roscommon, MI 48653-8760 (989) 821-9723

***SCHROEDER, J. CHRIS (RHL) (Carolyn) – (R-1976, D-1976, E-1981)**
Alden/Central Lake 1976; Sunfield/Sebewa Center 1982; Sunfield Nov 16, 1984; Leave of Absence Jan 1, 1992; Honorable Location 1998; Retired 2011
(H) 1605 Woodcliff Ave SE, Grand Rapids, MI 49506 (616) 954-0776

***SILVERNAIL, WILBUR L. (RHL) – (R-1950, E-1955)**
Portage Prairie (EUB) 1955; Waterloo (EUB) 1960; Voluntary Location 1969; Honorable Location 1971; Retired 1993
(H) 3832 Perrine Rd, Rives Junction, MI 49277-9642 (517) 569-3715

***SMALL, DAVID E. (RHL) (Elaine Lewis-Small) – (R-1982, E-1982, E-1985)**
[Niles Trinity 1981]; Brandywine Trinity 1982; Morristown UMC, Northern New Jersey (para. 425.1); In School, Drew University 1988; Anderson and Asbury UMCs, Northern New Jersey Conf (para. 337.1) 1998; Honorable Location 1999; Pacific NW Conf: Nooksack Valley, Everson, WA (Ad Interim Appointment) 2008; (Charge Conf: Garden Street UMC, Bellingham, WA); Retired 2012
(H) 3 Sanwick Point Ct, Bellingham, WA 98229-7934 (360) 305-8442

***SPOOR, DALE D. (RHL) – (R-1961, D-1961, E-1964)**
[Kalamazoo Milwood (Assoc.) 1960]; Marcellus/Wakelee 1961; Hartford 1965; Wacousta 1967; Stockbridge Dec 15, 1971; Honorable Location Oct 1974; Retired 1993
(H) 3215 W Mt Hope Ave Apt 221, Lansing, MI 48911-1281 (517) 580-8638

***STEELE, PHILIP P. (RHL) (Nancy) – (R-1964, D-1964, E-1968)**
[Schoolcraft 1961; METHESCO 1963-66]; Wolf Lake/Sitka Summer 1964; Cooper UCC Summer 1965; Portage First (Assoc.) May 3, 1966; Coopersville March 1, 1968; Battle Creek Birchwood 1970; Honorable Location 1971 (Charge Conf: Kalamazoo Milwood); Retired 2006; Kalamazoo Lane Blvd (DSA), Oct 8, 2006-Jan 1, 2007
(H) 56881 Murray St, PO Box 85, Mattawan, MI 49071-0085 (269) 668-3973

***TOMLINSON, ROBERT E. (RHL) (Karan) – (R-1976, D-1974, E-1978)**
Pompeii/Perrinton 1974; Pompeii/Perrinton/North Star 1976; Mt. Pleasant Trinity/Chippewa Feb 1, 1977; Caledonia 1980; Augusta, Feb 16, 1984; Bangor Simpson 1987; Honorable Location 1989 (Charge Conf: Battle Creek: Chapel Hill); Retired 2001
(H) 36 Rockhampton Ridge, Battle Creek, MI 49014-8373 (269) 968-4930

TRAN, VINH Q. Q. (AL)
Vietnamese United Methodist Ministry of the Michigan Area Jan 1, 1986; Vietnamese United Methodist Ministry of the Michigan Area (1/2 Time) Grand Rapids: Vietnamese (1/2 Time) Sept 1, 1987; Grand Rapids Vietnamese 1995; Incapacity Leave Feb 1, 2004; Administrative Location (para. 362.4), March 22, 2005
(H) 2708 Colton Dr SE, Grand Rapids, MI 49506 (616) 940-4721

***VERMEULEN, BERTRAM W. (RHL) (Alice) – (R-1958, D-1958, E-1962)**
[Bloomingdale Charge 1954; Three Rivers Ninth St, 1957] 1958; Litchfield 1961; Lansing Mt. Hope (Assoc.) 1965; DeWitt Emmanuel 1967; Fremont Oct 15, 1969; Leave of Absence Jan 1, 1979; Honorable Location 1984; Retired 1998
(H) 1551 Franklin St SE Apt 3008, Grand Rapids, MI 49506-3356

***WELLFARE, ROBERT W. (RHL) (Barbara) – (R-1957, D-1957, E-1960)**
Sonoma/Newton Feb 1, 1958; Grand Rapids Trinity (Assoc.) 1960; Cedar Springs 1961; Wheeler 1962; Professor Olivet College 1966; Niles Portage Prairie/Trinity 1971; Niles Portage Prairie 1973; Honorable Location Oct 1974 (Charge Conf: University Carillon, Oveido, FL); Retired 2002
(H) 9784 W Marquette Est, Branch, MI 49402-9486 (231) 898-2047

WISDOM-LONG, MICHELLE M. (HL) (Richard Long) – (R-1998)
[North Georgia Conf (Elder), Kingswood UMC, Dunwoody, GA] Transfered from North Georgia Conf., Kalamazoo First (Assoc.) (para. 337.1) 1998; Family Leave 2000; Pleasant Valley (LTFT 1/4) 2001; Pleasant Valley (LTFT 1/2) Jan 1, 2007; Leave of Absence 2008; Kalamazoo First (Assoc.) (LTFT 1/2) 2010; Honorable Location 2011 (Charge Conf: Kalamazoo First)
(H) 6071 Thunder Bluff Rd, Kalamazoo, MI 49009-9127 (269) 372-0826

XXVII-B. DSA SERVICE RECORD

This DSA Service Record indicates assignments by District Superintendents to serve on a weekly basis. The date given following each assignment represents the initial year of that assignment, with changes occurring immediately following Annual Conference unless otherwise noted. Brackets around assignments indicate charges served prior to reception into the West Michigan Conference. (H) is the Home Address.This record is maintained by Kathy Hippensteel at the Conference Center. Correspondence should be directed to her by email, kathy@wmcumc.org, or at P.O. Box 6247, Grand Rapids, MI 49516-6247

DSA = District Superintendent Assignment

AHTI, RICHARD J. (DSA)
Wheatfield (DSA) (1/4 time) 2014
(H) 4461 Oaklawn Dr, Okemos, MI 48864-2921 (517) 349-1314
Wheatfield UMC: 520 E Holt Rd, Williamston, MI 48895-9463 (517) 851-7853

CADARETTE, DAVID (DSA) (Kathyrn)
Big Rapids Third Avenue/Paris/Rodney (DSA) 2014
(H) 219 S State St, Reed City, MI 49677 (231) 675-1624
Third Avenue / Paris UMCs: 226 N Third Ave, Big Rapids, MI 49307 (231) 796-4157
Rodney UMC: PO Box 14, Rodney, MI 49342 (231) 796-4157

COFFEY, JUDY (DSA) (Tim)
Epworth Brethren (DSA) (1/4 time) 2014
(H) 128 Forest Lawn Dr, Cadillac, MI 49601-9734 (231) 775-6095
Brethren Epworth UMC: 3939 High Bridge Rd, PO Box 177, Brethren, MI 49619 (231) 477-5486

ERSKINE, GERALD (DSA)
Fenwick/Palo/Vickeryville (DSA) 2014
(H) 10963 Sundog Trail, Perrinton, MI 48871 (989) 682-4779
Fenwick / Palo / Vickeryville UMCs: PO Box 241, Sheridan, MI 48884 (989) 291-5547

HARRINGTON, SALLY KAY (DSA)
[South German Methodist Conf, Retired FE] Galesburg (DSA) (LTFT 1/2), Nov 1, 2010-2012; Sonoma/Newton (DSA) (LTFT 1/2), 2012
(H) 4495 B Drive South, Battle Creek, MI 49015 (269) 917-2823
Battle Creek Sonoma UMC: 4790 Capital Ave SW, Battle Creek, MI 49015 (269) 979-1000
Battle Creek Newton UMC: 8804 F Drive South, Ceresco, MI 49033 (269) 979-2779

IDEN, ERIC (DSA)
Allen (DSA) 2014
(H) 300 Hanover St, Concord, MI 49237 (517) 945-2802
Allen UMC: 167 W Chicago Rd, PO Box 103, Allen, MI 49227 (517) 200-8416

MAY, THOREAU (DSA) (Karen May)
West Mendon (DSA) 2013
(H) 52952 Lakehead Dr, Mendon, MI 49072 (269) 496-8070
West Mendon UMC: 22994 Portage Lake Road, Mendon, MI 49072 (269) 496-7364

MAYS, JONATHAN D. (DSA)
Greensky Hill (DSA) (1/2 time) 2013
(H) 409 Prospect St, Charlevoix, MI 49720 (231) 459-8067
Greensky Hill UMC: 8484 Green Sky Hill Rd, Charlevoix, MI 49720-9686 (231) 547-2028

MILLER, ALEXANDER (SANDY) (DSA)
Nottawa (DSA 1/4 time) 2003
(H) 61616 Filmore Rd, Sturgis, MI 49091-9318 (269) 467-7134
Nottawa UMC: 25838 M-86, PO Box 27, Nottawa, MI 49075 (269) 467-7134

MORGAN, RUSSELL D. (CLM) (Karla Morgan)
Avondale/North Evart/Sylvan (CLM), July 8, 2007; Avondale/North Evart (CLM), Nov 9, 2009; Fenwick/Palo/Vickeryville (CLM) (1/4 Time), July 15, 2012; Blanchard-Pine River/Coomer/Winn UMCs (CLM/DSA) 2014
(H) 8135 Mill St, PO Box 366, Winn, MI 48896 (989) 824-0653
Blanchard-Pine River / Coomer UMCs: 7655 W. Blanchard Rd, Blanchard, MI 49310 (989) 561-2864
Winn UMC: 8187 S. Winn Road, Mt. Pleasant, MI 48858 (989) 866-2417

NADER, VINCENT JOHN (DSA)
Harrison: The Gathering (DSA) May 1, 2014; Harrison: The Gathering / Wagarville (Detroit Conference) (DSA) June 1, 2014
(H) 714 Foell Court, Gladwin, MI 48624 (248) 914-3221
Harrison: The Gathering: 426 N. First St. Suite 106, PO Box 904, Harrison, MI 48625 (989) 539-1445

NEWMAN, CAROL A. (DSA) (Budd)
[D.S. Assignment: Lawton/Almena (Assoc.) 1995;] Lawton/Almena (Assoc.) November 16, 1995; Almena/Northwest 1996; Almena 2000-2002; Bloomingdale (DSA) (1/4 time), Sept. 23, 2012
(H) 20584 Meadow Dr, Gobles, MI 49055 (269) 628-2414
Bloomingdale UMC: PO Box 9, Bloomingdale, MI 49026 (269) 521-3323

PEASE, CHRISTINE L. (DSA)
Pleasant Lake (DSA) (1/4 time) 2014
(H) 340 Pleasant St, Charlotte, MI 48813 (517) 543-5618
Pleasant Lake UMC: 4815 E Territorial Rd, PO Box 83, Pleasant Lake, MI 49272

RETZLOFF, GERRY (DSA)
Marengo (DSA 1/4 time) Jan. 1, 2010
(H) 29 Wolfe, Battle Creek, MI 49017 (269) 660-0141
Marengo UMC: 221 N. Chapel Hill Dr., Battle Creek, MI 49015

ROBERTS, RICHARD D. (DSA) (Lucinda)
Free Soil/Fountain (DSA) (1/4 time) 2013
(H) 2415 E Michigan St, Free Soil, MI 49411 (231) 233-8954
Free Soil UMC: PO Box 71, Freesoil, MI 49411
Fountain UMC: PO Box 173, Fountain, MI 49410 (231) 690-4591

SNODGRASS, II, ROBERT L. (DSA) (Kathe)
Morris Chapel (DSA) (1/4 time) 2014
(H) 16270 Lewis Rd, Vandalia, MI 49095 (574) 261-5139
Morris Chapel UMC: 1730 Holiday, Niles, MI 49120-8007 (269) 684-5194

SPERRY, DONNA JEAN (DSA) (George)
Ionia Easton (DSA) 2014
(H) 230 Churchill St., Ionia, MI 48846 (586) 255-6228
Ionia Easton UMC: 4970 Potters Rd, Ionia, MI 48846 (616) 527-6529

TOMASINO, ANTHONY J. (DSA) (Cordelia)
Niles: Grace (DSA) (1/4 time), Oct. 17, 2004
(H) 2729 Congress St, Niles, MI 49120 (269) 684-3454
Niles Grace UMC: 501 Grant Street, Niles, MI 49120-2955 (269) 683-8770

TUCKER, MARCIA A. (DSA)
Ganges (DSA) (1/4 time) 2014
(H) 6948 Colver, Fennville, MI 49408 (269) 857-4797
Ganges UMC: 2218 68th Street, PO Box 511, Fennville, MI 49408 (269) 543-3581

VANDERLAAN, KENNETH D. (DSA) (Dawn)
Mears (DSA) (1/4 Time) 1993; Mears (DSA) (1/2 time), Jan 1, 2009
(H) 5763 W 9th St, Mears, MI 49436-9569 (231) 742-0152
Mears UMC: 1990 N. Joy St., PO Box 100, Mears, MI 49436 (231) 873-0875

WARD, JENNIFER C. (DSA)
Jonesville (DSA) 2014
(H) 161 Waterman Ave, Coldwater, MI 49036 (269) 462-8225
Jonesville UMC: 203 Concord Rd., Jonesville, MI 49250 (517) 849-9565

WHITE-PIGEON, OWEN L. (DSA) (Carol White-Pigeon)
[Kewadin Indian Mission (DSA) 1993] Mt Pleasant Chippewa Indian 1994 (1/3 Time); Discontinued as a Local Pastor 2011; Mt Pleasant Chippewa Indian (DSA) 2011
(H) 3490 S Leaton Rd, Mt Pleasant, MI 48858 (989) 772-5521
Mt Pleasant Chippewa Indian UMC: 3490 S. Leaton, Mt Pleasant, MI 48858

XVIII. DIACONAL MINISTERS SERVICE RECORD

***CASE, JANE (DR) — (Consecrated June 1995)**
Organist, Napoleon UMC 1995; Retired 2011
PO Box 146, 113 West, Napoleon, MI 49261 (517) 536-8781

FLEGAL, DAPHNA (DM) — (Gary) (Consecrated June 1978)
Transferred from North Georgia Conf.; Director of Christian Education, Lansing First and East Lansing University, Dec. 1, 1987; Diaconal Minister of Program, Lansing First 1991; Editor of Children's Publications, General Board of Discipleship 1992
610 Burgundy Dr, Madison, TN 37115-3502 (615) 885-6621
PO Box 801, Nashville, TN 37202 (615) 749-6818

***FOSTER, MARGARET L (DR) — (Consecrated June 14, 1986)**
Staff Support, Dyslexia Resource Center; Retired 1999
660 Lake Dr, Altamonte Springs, FL 32701-5412 (517) 349-3122

***HILL, HELENE (DR) — (Consecrated June 16, 1978)**
(Coopersville Public Schools 1977); Coopersville Public Schools 1981; Retired 1986
266 Merrimon Ave, Apt D, Asheville, NC 28801-1218 (705) 255-8065

*Denotes retired person.
†Denotes mailing address when it is other than the home address

Jane Case

Margaret L. Foster

Helene R. Hill

XIX. RETIRED LOCAL PASTORS RECORD AND LOCAL PASTORS WITHOUT APPOINTMENT

This Pastoral Record indicates appointments but is not necessarily a pension record. The date given following each appointment represents the initial year of that appointment, with changes occurring immediately following Annual Conference unless otherwise noted. Brackets around appointments indicate charges served prior to reception into the West Michigan Conference. (H) is the Home Address; (O) is an office address and (S) is a seasonal address.

This record is maintained by Kathy Hippensteel at the Conference Center. Correspondence should be directed to her by email, kathy@wmcumc.org, or at P.O. Box 6247, Grand Rapids, MI 49516-6247.

RL = Retired Local Pastor LPNA = Local Pastor without Appointment
RLA = Retired Local Pastor under Appointment

***BERNTSEN, GAYLE SUE – see Zaagman (Berntsen), Gayle Sue**

***BAKER, SHEILA F. (RL) (Keith P)**
Riverside (DSA) 2004; Riverside December 1, 2004; Townline/Breedsville 2005; Northwest/Townline 2007; Northwest (PTLP 1/4) Jan. 3, 2008; Trowbridge (PTLP 1/2) 2012; Retired Feb. 2, 2014
(H) 27399 22nd Ave, Gobles, MI 49055-9224 (269) 628-4882

BALGENORTH, JACK E. (LPNA) (Anita)
LP w/o Appointment 2001; Jones 2009 (PTLP 1/4); Ganges/Glenn (PTLP 1/2) Sept 1, 2010; LP w/o Appointment 2014
(H) 5169 Heathrow Ave, Kalamazoo, MI 49009-7737 (269) 372-8001

***BEAN, REX (RL) (Margaret)**
Chase/Barton 1982; Retired 1987
(H) Clark Retirement Community, 1551 Franklin SE Apt 3020, Grand Rapids, MI 49506-3331 (616) 243-1618

***BENNETT, LEO (BUD) ELWOOD (RL) (Joyce) – (D-1959, E-1961)**
South Cadillac 1956; Alden/Kewadin 1961; Cedar Springs Sept. 15, 1965; Wayland 1970; Lawrence 1979; Hinchman/Oronoko 1986; Jackson: First (Assoc.) 1989; Retired 1993
(H) 630 Hastings Ave Apt 315, Holland, MI 49423 (616) 393-6122
(S) 1855 West Southern Ave #414, Apache Junction, AZ 85220

***BOELENS, NANCY L. (RLA)**
[Detroit Conference, Middleburry UMC Sept. 1, 1996-June 30, 1998]; Bath/Gunnisonville 1998; Wayland 2003; Muskegon Unity/Sitka Nov. 1, 2006; Muskegon Unity 2008; Leave of Absence, Jan. 1, 2009; Retired April 12, 2009; Salem/Bradley Indian Mission UMCs (RLA 1/2), 2013
(H) 1875 Parkcrest Dr. S.W., Apt 2, Wyoming, MI 49519 (616) 914-9300
Salem Indian Mission of the UMC: 3644 28th St, Hopkins, MI 49328
Bradley Indian Mission of the UMC: 695 128th Ave, Shelbyville, MI 49344

***BURTON-COLLIER, LINDA J. (RL) (Earl Collier) – (R-2005; PE-2005; FL-2010)**
White Pigeon (DSA) 2001; White Pigeon 2002; Hopkins/South Monterey 2005; Retired 2014
(H) 2574 127th Ave, Allegan, MI 49010 (269) 793-7340

***CABOT, ROBERTA W. (RL) (Sam)**
Muskegon Wolf Lake Nov 15, 2001; Muskegon Wolf Lake (PTLP) May 10, 2010; Arcadia/Bear Lake 2011; Retired 2014
(H) Kingdom Life Healing Ministries, 28 Caberfae Hwy, Manistee, MI 49660 (231) 557-0166

***CARLSON, DAVID GUNNAR (RL) (Normajean Carlson)**
Grass Lake (PTLP) 2007; Retired 2010
(H) 2185 Moon St, Muskegon, MI 49441 (231) 755-8168

***CARLSON, LINDA J. (RL) (Ted)**
Jackson: Calvary (Assoc.) (PTLP) 1993; Manton (FTLP) Feb 16, 1999; Retired 2009
(H) 1720 SE 72nd Ave, Portland, OR 97215-3510

***CHEYNE, PAULETTE G. (RL)**
[Bell Oak and Wheatfield (DSA) 1991;] Bell Oak/Wheatfield (PTLP 1/2) Sept 1, 1992; Bell Oak/Wheatfield (PTLP 3/4) Jan 1, 1995; Freeport/Middleville/Parmelee (Assoc.) June 1, 1995; Winn 1999; Blanchard-Pine River/Coomer/Winn 2005; Comstock 2006; East Lansing Aldersgate Nov 15, 2006; East Lansing Aldersgate/Delta Mills (FTLP) 2007; Retired Apr 1, 2008; Delta Mills (RLA 1/4) Apr 1, 2008-2013
(H) 3041 E Frost Rd, Williamston, MI 48895 (517) 896-3787

***COX, ESTHER (RL)**
Welcome Corners 1969-75; Quimby 1970-72; LP w/o Appointment 1975-1988; Retired 1988

***CULVER, MARTIN H. (RLA) (Barbara)**
Keswick(DSA)1991; Keswick August 1, 1991; Ionia First 2000; Milwood 2006; Lane Blvd (DSA) March 18, 2007-March 25, 2008; Retired 2011; Center Park (RLA 1/4) 2011
(H) 511 Landsdowne Ave, Portage, MI 49002 (269) 615-1360
Center Park UMC: 18662 Moorepark Rd., Three Rivers MI 49093 (269) 279-9109

***DELO, MERLIN (RL) (Juanita) – (D-1966, E-1968)**
Middleton/Sethton 1964; Hesperia/Ferry 1966-1978; East Jordan 1986; Retired 1997
(H) 2706 S Maple Island Rd, Fremont, MI 49412-9372 (231) 924-4182

***DOWNING-SIGLIN, JUDY K. (RL)**
[Gobles/Kendall (DSA) 1987;] Gobles/Kendall 1988; Marshall (Assoc.) 1998; Lyons/Muir/Ionia: Easton 1999; Retired 2001
(H) 5959 Barnhart Rd, Ludington, MI 49431-8601 (520) 625-4304
(S) 3620 W. Calle Cinco, Green Valley, AZ 85622 (520) 625-4304

***DUFFEY, RICHARD J. (RL) (Jane)**
Howard City: Maple Hill Nov 1, 1980-1988; Six Lakes 1994; New Life UMC (Co-Pastor) Jan 1, 1998-June 30, 1998; Grovenburg (PTLP)1998; Retired 2005
(H) 13599 Deaner Rd, Howard City, MI 49329 (231) 762-4473

***FLEMING, EDNA M. (RL) (George)**
Charlotte (Assoc.) 1995; LP w/o Appointment 2002; Retired 2011
(H) 793 68th St, South Haven, MI 49090 (269) 637-4406

***FRITZ, RICHARD A. (RL) (Marjean)**
Burnips/Monterey Center 2008; Retired 2014
(H) 589 Peterson, Muskegon, MI 49445

***GACKLER, JOYCE F. (RL) (Ken)**
Grand Rapids Plainfield (PTLP 1/2) June 1, 2005; Retired 2012
(H) 410 Johnson St, Caledonia, MI 49316 (616) 891-5682

***GASTIAN, SANDRA J. (RL)**
[Athens (DSA) 1991;] Athens Aug 1, 1991; Retired Jan 1, 2011
(H) 416 N 22nd St, Springfield, MI 49037 (269) 964-9050

***GAY, SUE J. (RL) (David)**
[Augusta (DSA) June 1, 1993;] Augusta (FTLP) 1994; Augusta (PTLP) January 1, 2005; Retired 2007
(H) 4222 NE 129 Pl, Portland, OR 97230

***GREENE, CARL E. (RL) (Deanna)**
Brethren Epworth (DSA) 2005; Brethren Epworth (PTLP) Nov 11, 2005; Brethren Epworth/Grant (PTLP) March 15, 2006; Retired 2011
(H) 3021 Glen Malier Drive, Beulah, MI 49617-9478 (231) 375-1006

HOTELLING, DALE A. (LPNA) (Beth)
Ogdensburg (DSA) 1995; Ogdensburg 1996; Kalamazoo First (Assoc.) July 16, 2000; LP w/o Appointment, July 1 - Dec 31, 2004; Conference Staff, Jan 1, 2005; Muskegon Crestwood 2008; LP w/o Appointment 2010; White Pines (PTLP 1/2) 2011; LP w/o Appointment Aug. 31, 2012
(H) 3256 Dorais Dr NE, Grand Rapids, MI 49525

***JOHN SR, THOMAS H. (RLA) (Phyllis John)**
Kewadin: Indian Mission 1998; Kewadin/Northport Indian Missions 2005; Retired 2012; Kewadin/Northport Indian Missions 2012
(H) 13735 Indian Rd, Kewadin, MI 49648 (231) 264-0527
Kewadin Indian Mission UMC: PO Box 227, Kewadin MI 49648 (231) 632-4920
Northport Indian Mission UMC: PO Box 401, Northport MI 49670 (231) 941-2360

***KEIM, J. ROBERT (RL) (Judi)**
Sturgis (Assoc) (PTLP 1/2) Dec 16, 1999; Retired Dec 31, 2011
(H) 427 Mortimer, Sturgis, MI 49091 (269) 467-7541

KINDEL, MONA L. (LPNA) (Marlin Kindel)
Mesick/Harrietta 2009; Elsie (PTLP 3/4) 2012; LP w/o Appointment 2013
(H) 210 N Garfield St, Maple Rapids, MI 48853 (231) 846-1854

***KORNOWSKI, SUZANNE P. (RL) (James Ferguson)**
Kalamazoo Oakwood/Oshtemo (DSA) 2000; Oshtemo (Part-Time) December 1, 2002; Oshtemo March 21, 2004; Retired 2011
(H) 252 Bobwhite Dr, Pensacola, FL 32514

LAIMON, JEANNE M. (LPNA) (John W.)
Wheatfield (DSA) 2007; Wheatfield (PTLP 1/4) Dec 1, 2007; Munith (PTLP 1/4) 2012; M-52 Cooperative Ministry: Munith (PTLP 1/4) and Pleasant Lake (PTLP 1/4) and Stockbridge (PTLP 1/4) and Waterloo First (PTLP 1/4) 2013; (Waterloo First Closed 02.16.2014); LP w/o Appointment 2014
(H) 6701 Hawkins Rd, Jackson, MI 49201-9579 (517) 769-6570

***LAWTON, GEORGE W. (RLA) (Beverly)**
Lakeside Sept. 1, 1999; Retired 2007; Lakeside (RLA 1/4) 2007
(H) 8000 Warren Woods Rd #79, Three Oaks, MI 49128-8519 (269) 469-8468
Lakeside UMC: PO Box 402, Union Pier MI 49129 (269) 469-8468

***MICHAEL, VERNON L. (RL) (Helen) – (D-1958, E-1961)**
Coleman/North Bradley 1954; Hart 1961; Byron Center/Market St. 1966; Niles: Trinity 1967; Schoolcraft/Pleasant Valley 1969; Coopersville 1970; Marne 1980; Granted disability 1982; Retired 1987
(H) 170 Grove, Coopersville, MI 49404 (616) 837-9508

MILLER, DEBORAH REID (LPNA) (Timothy)
Transferred from Louisville Conf, Chase Barton-Grant Center June 1, 1992; LP w/o Appointment 1995; Freeport Aug 16, 1999; Grand Rapids PaWaTingMaGedWin Feb 1, 2002; Benton Harbor Peace Temple 2003; LP W/O Appointment Nov 14, 2003
(H) 3080 Waterchase Way SW Apt 110, Wyoming, MI 49519-5961 (616) 350-2909

***NALETT, LARRY W. (RL) (Elaine)**
Eagle 1993; Fenwick/Palo/Vickeryville 1998; Retired Aug. 9, 2004
(H) 4504 S Lund Rd, Sheridan, MI 48884 (989) 261-3075

***NIELSEN, JUDITH A. (RL)**
Munith / Pleasant Lake 1998-2000; LP w/o Appointment 2000; Retired 2007
(H) 3024 Norwich Rd, Lansing, MI 48911 (517) 882-0608

***RICKARD, O'RYAN (RLA) – (R-2005; PE-2005; RL-2013)**
Morris Chapel 2003; Townline/Breedsville 2004; Salem/Greenbush/Lowe 2005; Salem/Lowe/Maple Rapids 2006; Coloma/Watervliet 2007; Portage Prairie/Arden 2009; PE Discontinued 2013; Retired LP 2013; Portage Prairie/Arden (RLA 3/4) 2013; Arden (RLA 1/4) 2014
(H) 6148 Avon St, Portage, MI 49024 (269) 235-1700
Arden UMC: 6891 M 139, Berrien Springs MI 49103 (269) 429-4931

***RITTER, JOHN F. (RL) (Delcina)**
Ashley/Bannister Oct. 16, 1978; Rosebush 1980; Edwardsburg March 1, 1984; Crystal Valley/Walkerville/Smith Corners 1988; Carlisle Sept. 1, 1990; Girard/Ellis Corners 1994; Turk Lake 1996; Retired Nov. 1, 2001
(H) 2490 E Levering Rd, Levering, MI 49755-9321 (231) 537-2777

***ROBINSON-FISHER, CAROLYN A. (RL) (Don)**
Wheatfield (1/4 Time) 1988; Middleton/Maple Rapids 1991; Millville 1997; Three Rivers Ninth Street/ Jones 1998; Battle Creek Christ 2007; Retired 2011
(H) 20908 Collier Rd, Battle Creek, MI 49037 (269) 589-6487

***SHATZ, CONNIE E. (RL) (Eugene Shatz)**
Belding (PTLP 1/4) 1999; Retired 2012
(H) 11448 Heintzelman NE, Rockford, MI 49341 (616) 754-8023

***SMITH, KATHLEEN (RL) (Dennis)**
Vermontville/Gresham 2002, Retired Dec. 31, 2012
(H) 7500 Bayne Rd, Woodland, MI 48897-9632

***STERNAMAN, JOHN R. (RL) (Linda)**
Riverside Dec. 1, 1997; Retired 2002
(H) 5792 Clymer Rd, Coloma, MI 49038-9394 (269) 468-6454

***STONE, DIANE E. (RL)**
Camden/Montgomery/Stokes Chapel (DSA) 1996-Nov 15, 1996; Camden/Montgomery/Stokes Chapel (Full-Time) Nov 16, 1996; Springport/Lee Center 2004 (PTLP); Retired 2010
(H) 234 S. Clemens Ave., Lansing, MI 48912-3006 (517) 775-0286

***TABOR, KENNETH E. (RL) (Eldonna)**
Free Soil/Fountain Nov. 1, 1999; Crystal Valley/Walkerville 2000; Ludington: United (Assoc.)(1/4 Time) 2004; Ludington: United (Assoc.)(Full-Time) Oct 1, 2006; Ludington: United (Assoc.)(PTLP) 2007; Retired 2010
(H) 1243 Blue Heron Dr, Ludington, MI 49431-1070 (231) 845-6101

***VANDENBRINK, SANDRA KAY (RLA) (Noel Matthews)**
In Seminary, MTSO, 1993; 1993-95 Trinway-Dresden Charge, E Ohio Conf; 1995-1997 Barton-on-Humber Circuit, British Methodist Church; Hudsonville 2001; Salem/Bradley Indian Missions (PTLP 1/4 Interim) Jan 16, 2005; (PTLP 1/2) July 1, 2005; (PTLP 3/4) Jan 1, 2007; Retired 2013; Director, Senior Meals Program of Salem/Bradley Indian Mission UMCs (RLA 1/4) 2013
(H) 3933 Kerri Ct, Holland, MI 49424 (616) 738-9030
Salem Indian Mission of the UMC: 3644 28th St, Hopkins, MI 49328
Bradley Indian Mission of the UMC: 695 128th Ave, Shelbyville, MI 49344

***WENDELL, DONALD R. (RL) (Violet)**
[D.S. Assignment: Moscow Plains Jan. 1, 1993;] Moscow Plains 1993; Nottawa Jan. 1, 1996; Jackson: Zion July 15, 2003; LP w/o Appointment, Mar. 15, 2006; Bloomingdale (1/4 time) 2006; Mt Pleasant Trinity/Countryside/Leaton November 30, 2008; Retired Nov. 1, 2009
(H) 137 W. Michigan Ave, Galesburg, MI 49053 (269) 200-5205

***WOOLUM, DONALD (RL)**
[Detroit Conf., Salem Grove 1987; Morrice/Benning/Pittsburg 1990; Mt. Bethel 1993]; Mulliken/ Sebewa Center 1997; Retired 2003
(H) 1104 Clark Rd, Lansing, MI 48917-2154 (517) 649-8689

***YOUNGS, DAVID L. (RL) (Doris)**
Bloomingdale/Townline March 14, 1976; Bloomingdale (Part-Time) 1978; Retired 2006; Breedsville 2007; Breedsville and Townline Jan 3-June, 2008
(H) 1108 Barton St, Otsego, MI 49078-1571 (269) 694-9125

***ZAAGMAN (BERNTSEN), GAYLE SUE (RL) (John Zaagman)**
(formerly Gayle Berntsen) Muskegon: Unity (DSA) Sept. 16, 1999; Muskegon: Unity Feb. 1, 2001; Reading Sept. 1, 2001; Whitehall/Claybanks 2006; Retired 2014
(H) 3662 Courtland Dr, Muskegon, MI 49441 (231) 780-3119

XX. PASTORAL PHOTOS

Craig L. Adams

Pegg Ainslie

Clifford L. Allen

Jayme L. Allen

Jana Lynn Almeida

William J. Amundsen

Francis F. Anderson

J. Leon Andrews

Thomas F. Arthur

George H. Ayoub

Mark R. Babb

Susan J. Babb

Wayne H. Babcock

Sueng Ho Baek

Dwayne E. Bagley

Dean I. Bailey

Paul F. Bailey

Theron E. Bailey

Melanie J. Baker-Streevy

Peggy J. Baker

Sheila F. Baker

Thomas E. Ball

James W. Barney

Marilyn B. Barney

Wayne C. Barrett

B. Gordon Barry

Bradley S. Bartelmay

Jack Bartholomew

Eugene L. Baughan

Emily K. Beachy

William H. Beachy

Martha Beals

Rex Bean

Joseph Beavan

Eric S. Beck

Gary L. Bekofske

David S. Bell

Leo E. Bennett

Kenneth W. Bensen

Terri L. Bentley

Kennetha J. Bigham-Tsai

William C. Bills

Joseph J. Bistayi

Daniel W. Biteman Jr.

Dorothy M. Blakey

Richard W. Blunt

James W. Boehm

Nancy L. Boelens

Gilbert R. Boersma

John W. Boley

Peggy A. Boltz

Gary D. Bondarenko

Connie R. Bongard

Carol L. Bourns

James T. Boutell

Keith A. Bovee

Dianne M. Bowden

Jeffrey J. Bowman

Letisha M. Bowman

Kenneth J. Bremer

J. Melvin Bricker

James B. Brillhart

Patricia L. Bromberek

Dennis B. Bromley

Patricia L. Brook

Ronald K. Brooks

Dale D. Brown

Kathy E. Brown

Lawrence P. Brown

Mary S. Brown

Jennifer Browne

Ellen A. Brubaker

Gregory L. Buchner

Donald L. Buege

Elaine M. Buker

Brian R. Bunch

Ray W. Burgess

Linda J. Burson

Linda J. Burton

Dennis G. Buwalda

Roberta W. Cabot

Kathryn S. Cadarette

David G. Carlson

Linda J. Carlson

Pat L. Catellier

John E. Cermak

Melany A. Chalker

Stephen MG Charnley

Victor D. Charnley

John T. Charter

David A. Cheyne

Paulette G. Cheyne

Catherine M. Christman

William W. Chu

Melissa Claxton

William V. Clegg Jr.

Martin T. Cobb

Bufford W. Coe

John J. Conklin

Michael T. Conklin

Robert Cook

Kathryn M. Coombs

Wilber E. Courter

Jane A. Crabtree

Jean A. Crabtree

David L. Crawford

Andrew Croel

Gregory P. Culver

Martin H. Culver

Terri Cummins

Billie R. Dalton

Paul A. Damkoehler

Reva H. Daniel

Thomas A. Davenport

Cornelius N. Davis

Martin M. DeBow

Merlin Delo

Kimberly A. DeLong

Lynn A. DeMoss

M. Kaye DeMoss

Isabell M. Deppe

James A. Dibbet

Vance M. Dimmick Jr.

DeAnn J. Dobbs

William D. Dobbs

William Doubblestein

Judy K. Downing

David L. Dryer

Paula J. Duffey

Richard J. Duffey

Daniel M. Duncan

Mona J. Dye

William F. Dye

Edrye A. Eastman-Maurer

Marcia L. Elders

Eldon K. Eldred

John W. Ellinger

Mark R. Erbes

Richard R. Erickson

Thomas J. Evans

Linda Farmer-Lewis

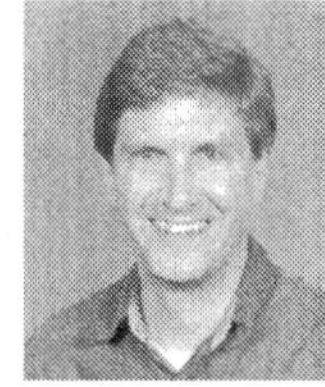
Charles D. Farnum

Elmer J. Faust

Barbara Jo Fay

Bryce E. Feighner

Donald R. Ferris

Raymond D. Field

Harold F. Filbrandt

Stanley A. Finkbeiner

Frederick H. Fischer

John W. Fisher

David L. Flagel

Edna M. Fleming

George W. Fleming

Jodie R. Flessner

Barbara J. Flory

Carolyn C. Floyd

Thomas P. Fox

Rea L. Franke

Lillian T. French

Robert J. Freysinger

Phillip J. Friedrick

Richard A. Fritz

Charles E. Fry

Donald R. Fry

Charles W. Fullmer

Joyce F. Gackler

Charles F. Garrod

Sandra J. Gastian

Sue J. Gay

Dale A. Golden

Brenda E. Gordon

Diane L. Gordon

Samuel Gordy

Donald J. Graham

Lemuel O. Granada

James C. Grant

Ronald B. Grant

Joseph M. Graybill

Carl E. Greene

George R. Grettenberger

Louis W. Grettenberger

Julie A. Greyerbiehl

A. Ray Grienke

Herbert L. Griffin Jr.

James M. Gysel

Patricia A. Haas

David L. Haase

Sueann K. Hagan

Gerald F. Hagans

Susan J. Hagans

William E. Haggard

Anita K. Hahn

Nelson L. Hall

Gary T. Haller

Laurie A. Haller

Fred G. Hamlin

Joan K. Hamlin

Paul E. Hane

Claudette I. Haney

Joyce N. Hanlon

Lloyd R. Hansen

Randall R. Hansen

Ronald W. Hansen

Patricia A. Harpole

Carl L. Hausermann

Geoffrey L. Hayes

Stanley L. Hayes

Leonard B. Haynes

Judy Hazle

Lyle D. Heaton

Constance L. Heffelfinger

Keith W. Heifner

Benton R. Heisler

Virginia L. Heller

Robert J. Henning

Devon R. Herrell

William A. Hertel

Valerie Hill

David F. Hills

Robert L. Hinklin

James E. Hodge

Lawrence E. Hodge

Harris J. Hoekwater

Daniel B. Hofmann

Ronald A. Houk

Laurence E. Hubley

Robert M. Hughes

James R. Hulett

Robert L. Hundley

Joseph D. Huston

Benjamin D. Hutchison

Cathi M. Huvaere

Clare W. Huyck

James L. Hynes

Ron Iris

Mary L. Ivanov

Andrew. Jackson

Dale F. Jaquette

Jerry L. Jaquish

Curtis E. Jensen

Thomas H. John Sr

Deborah M. Johnson

Jane E. Johnson

Mark G. Johnson

Nathaniel W. Johnson

William C. Johnson

David L. Johnston

Margaret Z. Jones

Robert E. Jones

Mona K. Joslyn

Jennifer J. Jue

Emmett H. Kadwell Jr.

Bradley P. Kalajainen

Rodney J. Kalajainen

John G. Kasper

J. Robert Keim

Ron L. Keller

O. Jay Kendall

Robert L. Kersten

Donna J. Keyte

Bruce R. Kintigh

David G. Knapp

Norman C. Kohns

Suzanne P. Kornowski

E. Jeanne Koughn

Jack G. Kraklan

James W. Kraus Jr.

Richard Kuhn

Kathleen S. Kursch

Sally J. LaFrance

D. Keith. Laidler

Janice "Jan" Lancaster

M. Christopher Lane

George W. Lawton

Gregory W. Lawton

Janet A. Lee

Jung Kee Lee

Ben B. Lester

Eugene A. Lewis

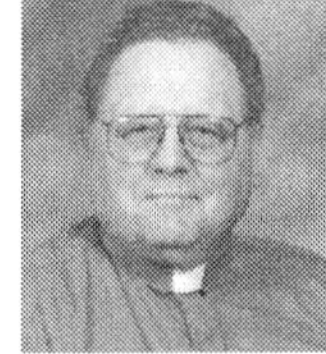
Kendall A. Lewis

Kathryn L. Leydorf

Steve Lindeman

Kenneth Lindland

Jane R. Lippert

Julie A. Liske

Carl Q. Litchfield

David L. Litchfield

Geraldine M. Litchfield

Glenn C. Litchfield

Jane D. Logston

Russell K. Logston

Leicester R. Longden

Mary Loring

John D. Lover

Paul E. Lowley

Frank W. Lyman Jr.

Carole S. Lyman

Robert K. Lynch

Scott E. Manning

C. William Martin

Gregory J. Martin

Pamela J. Mathieu

Robert J. Mayo

Paul D. Mazur

David L. McBride

Kenneth D. McCaw

J. Patrick McCoy

Allan D. McCreedy

Trevor McDermont

Wayne E. McKenney

Clinton McKinven-Copus

Laurie McKinven-Copus

Sandra B. McNary

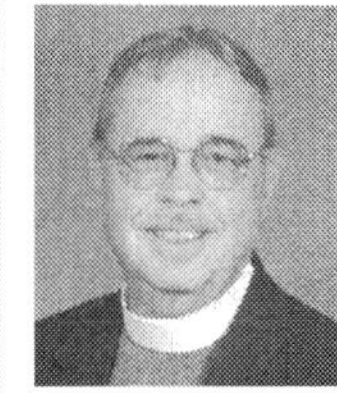
John W. McNaughton

Rob A. McPherson

Russell F. McReynolds

David W. Meister

Dorothy Mercer

Therlan E. Meredith

John D. Messner

Kimberly A. Metzger

Vernon L. Michael

Charles "Ed" Milam

David L. Miles

Darryl L. Miller

Timothy J. Miller

David H. Minger

Stacy R. Minger

Daniel J. Minor

Mark E. Mitchell

James P. Mitchum

Heather Molner

Christopher P. Momany

Joy Jittaun Moore

Richard D. Moore

Diane D. Morrison

Rebecca K. Morrison

Richard A. Morrison

John D. Morse

James J. Mort

David L. Morton

Larry W. Nalett

Kenneth J. Nash

David Nellist

David B. Nelson

Carol A. Newman

Lawrence A. Nichols

Judith A. Nielsen

R. Ivan Niswender

James C. Noggle

Robert D. Nystrom

Melody Lane Olin

Susan D. Olsen

Karin K. Orr

Sharyn K. Osmond

Dale P. Ostema

Scott K. Otis

Theresa Oyler-Sayles

Craig A. Pahl

Wade S. Panse

Amee A. Paparella

Chad M. Parmalee

Cynthia M. Parsons

Edward L. Passenger

Nancy J. Patera

Paul E. Patterson

Mark R. Payne

William V. Payne

Pat Pebley

Douglas L. Pedersen

A. Edward Perkins

Gary Peterson

Susan M. Petro

Barry T. Petrucci

J. Lynn Pier-Fitzgerald

Thomas Pier-Fitzgerald

Jon L. Pohl

Keith I. Pohl

Gerald A. Pohly

Ralph A. Posnik Jr.

Jon R. Powers

Nancy G. Powers

D. Kay Pratt

Merlin H. Pratt

Dean N. Prentiss

David Price

Wayne A. Price

Harvey K. Prochnau

Timothy R. Pucket

Robert L. Pumfery

Todd Query

Blaine B. Rader

Clifford L. Radtke

Brian F. Rafferty

Michael Ramsey

Jeanne M. Randels

Bernard R. Randolph

Wayne G. Reece

Jeffrey L. Reese

Kenneth C. Reeves

Beth Reum

James A. Richie

O'Ryan Rickard

Melodye S. Rider

Michael A. Riegler

Richard M. Riley

John F. Ritter

Carolyn Robinson-Fisher

Beatrice K. Robinson

Randall E. Roose

Marvin R. Rosa

Edward C. Ross

Robert H. Roth Jr.

Larry W. Rubingh

William P. Sanders

M. Schippers-DeMunter

Matthew R. Schlimm

Terry M. Schneider

Leonard R. Schoenherr

J. Chris Schroeder

John A. Scott

Ward N. Scovel Jr.

Howard Seaver

David A. Selleck

Gerald L. Selleck

Richard A. Selleck

Todd Shafer

Joseph D. Shaler

Jane B. Shapely

Connie E. Shatz

Brian K. Sheen

Larry R. Shrout

Anthony C. Shumaker

Gary L. Simmons

Michael J. Simon

Cynthia A. Skutar

Edward H. Slate

Den E. Slattery

David E. Small

Barbara L. Smith-Jang

Betty A. Smith

Charles W. Smith

Jean M. Smith

Kathleen Smith

Robert C. Smith

Wesley E. Smith

Edwin D. Snook

Karen J. Sorden

 Donald E. Spachman	 Joseph L. Spackman	 Sandra L. Spahr	 Gordon E. Spalenka	 Carolyn S. Spragg
 Robert W. Stark	 Ethel Z. Stears	 Kathryn M. Steen	 Gary G. Step	 John Sternaman
 James W. Stilwell	 Linda D. Stoddard	 Matthew Stoll	 Diane Stone	 Robert P. Stover
 Michael P. Streevy	 Lyne Stull-Lipps	 Verne C. Summers	 Raymond R. Sundell	 Sherri L. Swanson
 Lori J. Sykes	  Royal J. Synwolt	 Harold M. Taber	 Milton J. TenHave	 Paul Thomas
 J. Todd Thompson	 John Ross Thompson	 Mark E. Thompson	  R. John Thompson	 Ronald J. Thompson

Vaughn Thurston-Cox

Dominic A. Tommy

William J. Torrey

Gerald L. Toshalis

Alice F. Townley

Raymond J. Townsend

Vinh Q. Tran

Colleen Treman

Keith R. Treman

Susan J. Trowbridge

Michael J. Tupper

Arthur R. Turner

Molly C. Turner

Timothy T. Tuthill

Diane E. Vale

Charles R. Van Lente

Sandra K. VandenBrink

Jonathan D. VanDop

Kenneth R. Vaught

Cynthia L. Veilleux

Oscar Ventura

Douglas W. Vernon

Donald J. Vuurens

Glenn M. Wagner

Lynn W. Wagner

Gary S. Wales

Lowell F. Walsworth

Maurice E. Walworth Jr.

Glenn R. Wegner

Cara Weiler

J. Matt Weiler

Stephan Weinberger

Gerald L. Welsh

Robert L. Wessman

Karen S. Wheat

Jennifer Wheeler

Bobby D. Whitlock

Jeremy Wicks

Rebecca L. Wieringa

Colleen Wierman

Charles A. Williams

Jeffrey C. Williams

Jeremy PH Williams

Myron K. Williams

Nolan R. Williams

Richard K. Williams

Tamara S. Williams

Margaret H. Wilson

Richard D. Wilson

Douglas E. Wingeier

Michelle Wisdom-Long

Gregory R. Wolfe

Gregory B. Wood

Donald Woolum

Ronald L. Worley

Christina Lynn Wright

Timothy B. Wright

David W. Yingling

Richard A. Youells

Melanie S. Young

Steven R. Young

Gayle S. Zaagman

Lee F. Zachman

Ellen K. Zienert

—WMC Photos

to proclaim joy to a despairing world,
to initiate peace in the midst of violence—
to create a "little heaven below."

XXI–A. LOCAL CHURCH PASTORAL HISTORIES

In Church Pastoral Histories the dates given following each name indicate a pastoral change at the time of Annual Conference unless otherwise noted. These records begin with the pastor serving each church at the time of the 1968 EUB-Methodist merger. Questions and correspondence about Church Pastoral Histories should be directed to Kathy Hippensteel at the Conference Center, by email, kathy@wmcumc.org, or at P.O. Box 6247, Grand Rapids, MI 49516-6247.

Alanson UMC – *Grand Traverse District*
Phillip Howell 1968-1971; Philip Brown 1971-1977; Milton TenHave 1977-1979; Richard Matson 1979-1987; Catherine Kelsey 1987-1990; Claudette Haney 1990-April 1993; Birt A. Beers May 1993-1995; Lawrence R. Wood 1995-2003; Kathryn S. Cadarette 2003-2011; Mary A. Sweet 2011-2014; Vaughn Thurston-Cox 2014- ; [Epsilon/New Hope/Harbor Springs/Alanson became a 4-point charge 2014] Hillary Thurston-Cox (Assoc.) 2014-

Alba UMC – *Grand Traverse District*
M. Helen Jackson 1968-1972; George Gierman 1972-1975; Curtis Jensen 1975-1983; Timothy Graham 1983-1990; Gary Coates 1990-Aug. 1991; Pulpit Supply Sept.-Oct. 1991; Wayne Gorsline Nov. 1991-June 15, 1992; John W. Boley June 16, 1992-1997; Carolyn C. Floyd 1997-2000; Kathryn M. Steen 2000-2007; Stephan Weinberger 2007-2010; Zawdie K. Abiade July 1-July 4, 2010; Todd Shafer (DSA) July 15, 2010; Todd Shafer Nov. 1, 2010-

Albion First UMC – *Albion District*
Don Baker Jan. 1966-1969; Lynn A. DeMoss 1969-1979; David S. Evans 1979-1985; Randall R. Hansen (Assoc.) 1983-1985; John W. Ellinger 1985-1990; Dean L. Francis 1990-1991; Jeanne M. Randels Aug. 1991-Oct. 15, 1998; Gregory J. Martin Dec. 1, 1998-2002; Dwayne E. Bagley 2002-2009; Jeremy PH Williams 2009-

Alden UMC – *Grand Traverse District*
Leonard Yarlott 1968-1970; Paul Hartman 1970-1974; Daniel Miles 1974-1976; Chris Schroeder 1976-1982; David Cheyne 1982-1991; Wayne Gorsline (interim) July-Nov. 1991; Peter H. Shumar Nov. 1991-May 1992; Richard A. Morrison 1992-1995; Richard L. Matson 1995-2003; Charles A. Williams 2003-2010; Daniel W. Biteman 2010-

Allegan UMC – *Kalamazoo District*
Lester Clough 1968-1973; Paul Patterson 1973-1979; Clarence Hutchens 1979-1983; Robert L. Pumfery 1983-1990; Robert L. Wessman 1990-1999; Joseph L. Spackman 1999-2007; Robert P. Stover 2007-2012; Robert K. Lynch 2012-

Allen UMC – *Albion District*
Wayne Fleenor 1967-1970; Peter Kunnen 1970-1972; Morris Reinhart 1972-1974; William Johnson 1974-1977; Derryl Cook 1977-1978; M. John Palmer 1978-1982; Lloyd Walker 1982-1985; Jack Kraklan 1985-1988; Michael Baker-Streevy 1988-1995; Reva Hawke 1995-1997; Nelson Ray 1997-2000; Craig A. Pahl 2000-2014; [Jonesville/Allen became single charges 2014] Eric Iden (DSA) 2014-

Alma UMC – *Heartland District*
George Elliott 1967-Nov. 1975; Donald Scranton Dec. 1975-1981; Charles D. Grauer 1981-1989; David S. Yoh 1989-1995; Phillip J. Friedrick 1995-2012; Melanie J. Baker July 15, 2012-2013; Deborah S. Thomas 2013-

Almena UMC – *Kalamazoo District*
Raymond Carpenter 1966-1977; Philip Steele 1977-1980; C. Nesseth 1980-1981; Dean Francis 1981-1985; Beverly Gaska 1985-1987; Billie R. Dalton 1987-1995; Claudette K. Haney 1995-1996; Carol Newman (Assoc.) 1995-1996; Carol A. Newman 1996-2002; Anthony C. Shumaker 2002-2003; Cindy E. Holmquist 2003-Dec. 31, 2005; Donna J. Keyte Jan. 1, 2006-

Alto UMC – *Grand Rapids District*
Beulah Poe 1962-1971; Carter Miller 1971-1973; John Eversole 1973-1977; Keith Avery June-Oct. 1977; Albert Sprauge Oct. 1977-Jan. 1978; Herb Kinsey Jan. 1978-May 1979; Martin Fox May 1979-Oct. 1982; Herb Kinsey Oct. 1982-1983; Harold Diepert 1983-March 1985; Margaret Peterson 1985-1989; Jill Rose July-Dec. 1989; Lloyd Hansen Dec. 1989-1990; Todd Thompson 1990-1995; Bryan Schneider-Thomas 1995-2000; Dominic A. Tommy 2000-2002; Dean Irwin Bailey (DSA) 2002-2014; Andrew Jackson (Retired) 2014-

Amble UMC – *Heartland District*
Albert Rill 1968-Nov. 1971; Larry Dekema Jan. 1972-1975; Joseph Shaw 1975-1979; John Gurney 1979-Nov. 8, 1981; David England Oct. 1, 1982-1984; Ben Lester 1988-1995; Mark Mitchell (DSA) 1995-July 31, 1999; Charles W. Fullmer (DSA) Aug. 1, 1999-Oct. 31, 2001; Bryan Schneider-Thomas Nov. 1, 2001-2009; Anne W. Riegler Aug. 15, 2009-

Arcadia UMC – *Grand Traverse District*
Stephen Hubbell 1967-1969; Richard Matson 1969-1971; Ken Curtis 1971-March 1975; Raymond Roe April-June 1975; Gordon Spalenka 1975-1980; Donald Vuurens 1980-1983; Valerie Hill 1983-1985; John Backoff 1985-1989; William Carr 1989-1993; Pulpit Supply July-Nov. 1993; Arthur C. Murphy Dec. 1, 1993-1999; Mark D. Anderson Feb. 1, 2000-2006; William F. Dye 2006-2011; Robert W. Cabot 2011-2014; Jane D. Logston 2014-

Arden UMC – *Kalamazoo District*
Frederick Fischer 1965-1970; Harrison Harnden 1970-1972; Gordon Spalenka 1972-1975; Wayne Gorsline 1975-1980; John Moore 1980-1988; Jesse Schoebell 1988-1995; Jeremy P.H. Williams 1995-2002; Dominic A. Tommy 2002-2006; James W. Stilwell 2006-2009; [Portage Prairie/Arden two-point charge 2009] O'Ryan Rickard 2009- [Arden single-point charge 2014]

Ashley UMC – *Heartland District*
Wayne Sparks 1966-1970; William Cox 1970-1972; Marjorie Matthews June-Sept. 1972; Joseph Dudley Sept. 1972-1973; Miriam DeMint 1973-1975; Emmett Kadwell 1975-Oct. 1978; John Ritter Oct. 1978-1980; Mark Johnston 1980-1982; Donald McLellan 1982-1984; Arthur R. Turner 1984-1990; Glenn C. Litchfield 1990-1996; Robert J. Besemer Sept. 1, 1996-1999; Jana L. Jirak 1999-2003; Diane L. Gordon 2003-2006; Jon L. Pohl 2006-2011; Mona J. Dye 2011-

Athens UMC – *Albion District*
Garold L. Simison Sept. 1965-1969; James Gerhardt 1969-1970; Dwight Benner 1970-1972; John Bauer 1972-Jan. 1974; Gary Kintigh Feb. 1974-1977; Walter Rothfuss 1977-1978; Wendy S. Pratt 1978-Dec. 1979; Terry Howard Dec. 1979-1980; Richard Young Aug. 1980-1986; Robert G. Woodring 1986-1987; David Minger Sept. 1987-1991; Sandra J. Gastian 1991-Dec. 31, 2010; Allen Pebley (DSA) date?-2011; Robert D. Nystrom (1/4 time) 2011-2012; [Union City / Athens became two-point charge 2012] Seung Ho Baek (1/4 time) 2012-

Augusta Fellowship UMC – *Albion District*
Marvin Rosa 1967-Feb. 1972; Richard Cobb March 1972-1976; Matthew Walkotten Aug. 1976-Sept. 1977; Herbert Lowes Feb. 1978-Dec. 1983; Robert Tomlinson Feb. 1984-87; Lloyd Hansen 1987-1988; Nelson Ray 1988-May 1993; Sue Gay 1993-2007; Nelson Hall 2007-2013; Jennifer J. Wheeler 2013-

Avondale UMC – *Heartland District*
Edward R. Jones 1967-1969; Walter Easton 1969-1971; Daniel L. Reedy 1971-1972; H. Howard Fuller 1973-1975; Laurence Waterhouse June-Oct. 1975; Stanley Hayes Oct. 1975-March 1984; Gerald Welsh 1984-1990; Donald L. Buege 1990-Jan. 2006; Jon Pohl Jan. 15 - June 30, 2006; Jean A. Crabtree (DSA) Nov. 5, 2006--July 2007; Russell Morgan (DSA) July 8, 2007-2012; Kara Lynne Burns (CLM) July 22, 2012-

Baldwin Covenant Community UMC – *Grand Traverse District*
Rebecca Neal Niese 1984-1988; Dale Peter Ostema 1988-Jan. 1993; Reva Hawke May 1993-1995; Mary S. Brown 1995-Oct 15, 1998; David A. Cheyne Jan. 16, 1999-June 30, 1999; Nelson Hall 1999-2005; Karen J. Sorden 2005-2012; James A. Richie 2012-

Bangor Simpson UMC – *Kalamazoo District*

Wayne C. Reece Oct. 1966-1970; Charles D. McNary 1970-1977; Lawrence D. Higgins 1977-1981; Robert C. Carson 1981-1984; Morris J. Reinhart 1984-1987; Robert E. Tomlinson 1987-1989; James E. Hodge 1989-1994; Sandra B. Hoffman 1994-2007; Thomas A. Davenport 2007-

Bannister UMC – *Heartland District*

Wayne Sparks 1966-1970; William Cox 1970-1972; Marjorie Matthews June-Sept. 1972; Joseph Dudley Sept. 1972-1973; Miriam DeMint 1973-1975; Emmett Kadwell 1975-Oct. 1978; John Ritter Oct. 1978-1980; Mark Johnston 1980-1982; Donald McLellan 1982-1984; Arthur R. Turner 1984-1990; Glenn C. Litchfield 1990-1996; Robert J. Besemer Sept. 1, 1996-1999; Jana L. Jirak 1999-2003; Diane L. Gordon 2003-2006; Jon L. Pohl 2006-2011; Mona J. Dye 2011-

Barnard UMC – *Grand Traverse District*

Stanley Hayes 1967-1970; Lester Priest 1970-Jan. 1974; Daniel Minor April 1974-1981; Betty Burton 1981-1982; Glenn Britton 1982-1983; Supply pastor 1983-Aug. 1985; Robert Bellairs Aug. 1985-1996; Bernard W. Griner (DSA) 1996-1997; Eugene L. Baughan 1997-2002; D. Michael Maurer 2002-Nov. 10, 2008; Ralph Posnik (DSA) Nov. 23, 2008; Ralph Posnik Nov. 15, 2009-2014; Craig A. Pahl 2014-

Barryton Faith UMC – *Heartland District*

Thomas Tarrant 1967-March 1969; Isaac Sayers March 1969-1975; Altha Barnes 1975-1979; Lyle Heaton 1979-1984; Jean Crabtree 1984-1990; Pulpit Supply 1990-1991; Arthur C. Murphy 1991-Dec. 1, 1993; William W. Dornbush Jan. 1-June 30, 1994; Timothy J. Miller 1994-1995; Kevin Parkins 1995-1998; Robert E. Smith July 16, 1998-Feb. 1, 2001; James E. Cook (DSA) 2001-Feb. 28, 2002; Merged with Chippewa Lake Jan. 1, 2002 (See Barryton-Chippewa Lake for current listings); Brian R. Bunch Mar. 1, 2002-2005; Ronald DeGraw Aug. 1, 2005-Nov. 6, 2005; James L. Breithaupt Mar. 15, 2006-Oct. 19, 2009; Joseph Beavan Jan. 15, 2010-2014; Bryan K. Kilpatrick 2014-

Bath UMC – *Lansing District*

Alma Glotfelty 1968-1970; Tom Daggy 1970-1971; Clarence Keith 1971-1976; Dan Miles June-Dec. 1976; Tom Peters Feb. 1977-1993; Raymond D. Field 1993-1998; Nancy L. Besemer 1998-2003; Thomas L. Truby Oct. 15, 2003-2006; Beatrice K. Robinson 2006-2007; Mark G. Johnson 2007-

Battle Creek Baseline UMC – *Albion District*

Richard Budden 1966-1969; Paul Mazur 1969-Sept. 1972; Charles Grauer Sept.-Dec. 1972; Marvin Iseminger Jan. 1973-1977; Harold Diepert 1977-1978; Sharon Rader 1978-1981; Arthur Turner 1981-1984; Gregory J. Martin Sept. 1984-1987; Robert Woodring Sept. 1987-1990; Joy Jittaun Moore 1990-Aug. 15, 1993; Maurice E. Walworth, Jr. Nov. 1, 1993-1996; Glenn R. Wegner 1996-2004; Virginia L. Heller 2004-2011; Peggy J. Baker 2011-

Battle Creek Birchwood UMC – *Albion District*

Ron L. Keller 1966-1970; Philip P. Steele 1970-1971; Lawrence E. Hodge 1971-1980; Ward N. Scovel 1980-1984; Rodney J. Kalajainen 1984-1988; David W. Yingling 1988-1991; Phillip J. Friedrick 1991-1995; Melanie J. Baker-Streevy 1995-2003; Karen A. Tompkins 2003-Jan. 1, 2007; David Dryer Jan. 1-June 30, 2007; Robert D. Nystrom 2007-2011; Robert D. Nystrom (3/4 time) 2011-2012; [Battle Creek Birchwood / Trinity became two-point charge 2012] Bruce R. Kintigh (1/2 time) 2012-

Battle Creek Chapel Hill UMC – *Albion District*

Royce Robinson 1968-1973; William J. Richards 1973-May 1976; Heath T. Goodwin May 1976-1981; Donald Scranton 1981-1985; Joseph J. Bistayi 1985-1993; James M. Gysel 1993-2011; Robert J. Mayo 2011-2013; Chad M. Parmalee 2013-

Battle Creek Christ UMC – *Albion District*

Gaylord Howell 1966-1973; Chester Erickson 1973-1978; Morris Bauman 1973-Jan. 1983; Kenneth Vaught Jan. 1983-1986; B. James Varner 1986-July 1992; John Charter Nov. 1992-Jan. 1, 1999; Bruce R. Kintigh Jan. 1, 1999-2007; Carolyn A. Robinson-Fisher 2007-2011; Scott M. Bouldrey 2011-

Battle Creek Convis Union UMC – *Albion District*

Howard McDonald 1968-1973; Willard Gilroy 1973-1979; Dennis Paulson 1979-Apr. 1983; Linda D. Stoddard May 1983-Dec. 1991; Larry W. Rubingh Jan. 1992-1997; Lewis A. Buchner 1997-2001; David L. Litchfield 2001-2006; Sueann Hagan 2006-

Battle Creek First UMC – *Albion District*

John Tennant 1966-Jan. 1973; David Lee Miles (Assoc.) 1967-1971; Charles Fry Jan. 1973-1978; Howard Lyman 1978-1982; Neil Bintz July-Nov. 1982; Merle Broyles (interim) Nov. 1982-Jan. 1983; Dale Brown Jan. 1983-1993; Ron L. Keller 1993-1998; Karen S. Wheat 1998-2002; William P. Myers, Jr. 2002-Apr. 15, 2007; Donald R. Ferris 2007- ; Billie R. Dalton Mar. 1, 2009-Mar. 5, 2014; David L. Morton Mar. 5-June 30, 2014; Marshall Murphy 2014- ; Scott M. Bouldrey 2014-

Battle Creek Maple UMC – *Albion District*

Donald Sailor 1966-1972; Jack Baumgart 1972-1980; Curtis Strader 1980-1986; David L. Morton 1986-1996; Lynn W. Wagner 1996-2001; Charles D. Farnum 2001-2006; Theresa Little Eagle Sayles 2006-2008; Linda D. Stoddard 2008-

Battle Creek Newton UMC – *Albion District*

Howard Moore May 1968-1970; Ray Grienke 1970-Jan. 1974; Ray McBratnie Jan. 1974-1976; Kenneth Curtis 1976-1981; Harry Johnson 1981-1985; Gary Kintigh 1985-1993; Charles M. Shields 1993-1995; Michael Baker-Streevy 1995-Nov. 16, 1999; Charles Edward Rothy 2000-2003; Richard Duane Wilson 2003-2008; Nancy G. Powers 2008-2012; Sally Harrington (DSA) 2012-

Battle Creek Sonoma UMC – *Albion District*

Howard Moore May 1968-1970; Ray Grienke 1970-Jan. 1974; Ray McBratnie Jan. 1974-1976; Kenneth Curtis 1976-1981; Harry Johnson 1981-1985; Gary Kintigh 1985-1993; Charles M. Shields 1993-1995; Michael Baker-Streevy 1995-Nov. 16, 1999; Charles Edward Rothy 2000-2003; Richard Duane Wilson 2003-2008; Nancy G. Powers 2008-2012; Sally Harrington (DSA) 2012-

Battle Creek Trinity UMC – *Albion District*

Harold L. Mann 1968-1973; Wirth G. Tennant 1973-1978; Lowell Walsworth 1978-1981; Lloyd M. Schloop 1981-1984; Victor Charnley 1984-1995; Joy Jittaun Moore 1995-1996; David L. Dryer 1996-2006; Diane Gordon 2006-2010; Bruce R. Kintigh 2010-2012; [Battle Creek Birchwood / Trinity became two-point charge 2012] Bruce R. Kintigh 2012- (1/2 time);

Battle Creek Washington Heights UMC – *Albion District*

Donald Grant 1967-1972; John L. Thompkins Sept. 1972-1975; Pulpit Supply 1975-1976; Clifton Bullock 1976-Feb. 1991; Herbert Griffin (Assoc.) 1990-1993; Russell McReynolds 1991-1996; Howard (Rick) McKire 1996-Feb. 27, 1997; Curnell Graham 1997-2002; James A. Richie 2002-2009; Sandra V. Douglas (1/4 time) 2009-2011; Marshall Murphy 2011-

Bear Lake UMC – *Grand Traverse District*

Stephen Hubbell 1967-1969; Richard Matson 1969-1971; Ken Curtis 1971-March 1975; Raymond Roe April-June 1975; Gordon Spalenka 1975-1980; Donald Vuurens 1980-1983; Valerie Hill 1983-1985; John Backoff 1985-1989; William Carr 1989-1993; Pulpit Supply July-Nov. 1993; Arthur C. Murphy Dec. 1, 1993-1999; Mark D. Anderson Feb. 1, 2000-2006; William F. Dye 2006-2011; Roberta W. Cabot 2011-2014; Jane D. Logston 2014-

Beebe UMC – *Heartland District*

Wayne Sparks 1968-1970; Larry Uhrig 1970-1971; Ralph Kline 1971-Sept. 1974; Supply pastor Sept. 1974-1976; David Nelson 1976-Sept. 1980; Nolan Williams Oct. 1980-1991; David McBride 1991-2006; Steven R. Young 2006-2010; Cynthia Greene 2010-

Belding UMC – *Heartland District*

Ross E. Tracy 1966-1972; Eugene A. Lewis 1972-1977; Richard A. Strait 1977-1981; Ellen A. Brubaker 1981-1983; William D. Carr July-Oct. 1983; C. David Hainer Nov. 1983-Oct. 1988; Theodore F. Cole Oct. 1988-1991; Nathaniel W. Johnson 1991- Aug. 31, 1996; Charles A. Williams Feb. 15, 1997-Jan. 1, 1999; Connie Shatz 1999-2012; [Turk Lake / Belding became two-point charge 2012] Kimberly A. DeLong Aug. 15, 2012-2013; [Greenville First, Turk Lake/Belding Cooperative Parish 2013] Kimberly A. DeLong (Deacon) 2013- ; Stephen MG Charnley 2013-2014; Stephen F. Lindeman 2013-2014; Donald E. Spachman 2014-

Bellaire Community UMC – *Grand Traverse District*
James Lavengood Sept. 1965-Sept. 1969; Gerald Welsh Oct. 1969-1976; Alan Volkema 1976-1977; Garth Smith 1977-1981; David Litchfield 1981-1987; Gordon Spalenka 1987-1991; Richard A. Powell 1991-1998; D.S. Assignment 1998; Mary S. Brown Oct. 16, 1998-2009; Carl Q. Litchfield 2009-2013; Peggy A. Boltz 2013-

Bellevue UMC – *Albion District*
Lowell F. Walsworth 1966-1971; Laurence R. Grubaugh 1971-1973; Milton J. Tenhave 1973-1977; David L. Johnston 1977-May 1983; James William Schoettle May 1983-1988; William P. Sanders 1988-Feb. 1996; Mark E. Thompson 1996-2004; Virginia L. Heller 2004-2011; Peggy J. Baker 2011-

Berlin Center UMC – *Heartland District*
Luther Brokaw 1967-1971; Donald Fry 1971-1973; Lloyd Walker 1973-Aug. 1979; Willis Braun Aug. 16, 1979-Feb. 1989; David L. Flagel March 1989-2003; Mark G. Johnson 2003-2007; Dennis E. Slattery 2007-2012; Raymond R. Sundell 2012-

Berrien Springs UMC – *Kalamazoo District*
David Lutz, March 1967-1969; William A. Wurzel 1969-Feb. 1975; Dennis Buwalda March 1975-Sept. 1978; Gaylord Howell Sept. 1978-1983; Curtis Jensen 1983-1987; Edward & Priscilla Seward 1987-March 1990; Ross Bunce Jr. (Interim) 1990-1991; Wayne H. Babcock 1991-1998; Jeremy P.H. Williams 1998-2002; Dominic A. Tommy 2002-2006; Cynthia M. Parsons 2006-2012; [Berrien Springs/Hinchman/Oronoko became three-point charge 2012] Jane D. Logston (part-time) 2012-2014; [Berrien Springs/Pokagon became a 2-point charge 2014] Brenda E. Gordon 2014-

Big Rapids First UMC – *Heartland District*
James E. Leach 1965-1972; J. Leon Andrews 1972-1980; Richard Johns 1980-1985; Wayne G. Reece 1985-1992; Marvin R. Rosa 1992-March 31, 1993; Keith W. Heifner 1993-1996; Robert E. Jones 1996-2004; Bobby Dale Whitlock 2004-2008; Dean N. Prentiss 2008-2011; Rebecca K. Morrison 2011-

Blanchard-Pine River UMC – *Heartland District*
Harold E. Arman 1968-1969; Leslie D. Smith 1969-1977; James C. Sabo-Shuler 1977-1980; James W. Burgess 1980-1986; M. Christopher Lane 1986-1990; Paula Jane Duffey 1990-1998; Dale A. Golden 1998-2005; Paulette G. Cheyne 2005-2006; Melody Lane Olin (DSA) 2006; Melody Olin Nov. 15, 2006-2010; Lawrence Wonsey 2010-2014; Russell D. Morgan (CLM/DSA) 2014-

Bloomingdale UMC – *Kalamazoo District*
Wayne Babcock 1969-1971; Gerald Hudlund 1971-1972; Wayne Barrett 1972-1973; Pulpit supply 1973-1976; David L. Youngs 1976-2006; Donald R. Wendell 2006-Nov. 30, 2008; John W. McNaughton Dec. 8-31, 2008; Eugene B. Moore, Jan. 1, 2009, 2012; Carol A. Newman (DSA 1/4), Sept. 23, 2012-

Bowne Center UMC – *Grand Rapids District*
Beulah Poe 1962-1971; Carter Miller 1971-1973; John Eversole 1973-1977; Keith Avery June-Oct. 1977; Albert Sprauge Oct. 1977-Jan. 1978; Herb Kinsey Jan. 1978-May 1979; Martin Fox May 1979-Oct. 1982; Herb Kinsey Oct. 1982-1983; Harold Diepert 1983-March 1985; Margaret Peterson 1985-1989; Jill Rose July-Dec. 1989; Lloyd Hansen Dec. 1989-1990; Todd Thompson 1990-1995; Bryan Schneider-Thomas 1995-2000; Dominic A. Tommy 2000-2002; Dean Irwin Bailey (DSA) 2002-2014; Andrew Jackson (Retired) 2014-

Boyne City UMC – *Grand Traverse District*
R.J. McBratnie 1965-1970; Bruce Pierce 1970-Dec. 1973; Ray Grienke Jan. 15, 1974-1981; Forest Crum 1981-1983; Michael T. Conklin 1983-1989; John Backoff 1989-April 1991; Max Gladding (retired) April-June 1991; Gary D. Bondarenko 1991-2000; Carl Q. Litchfield 2000-2005; Wayne E. McKenney 2005-2014; [Boyne City/Boyne Falls/Horton Bay became a 3-point charge 2014] Michael Neihardt 2014-

Boyne Falls UMC – *Grand Traverse District*

R.J. McBratnie 1965-1970; Bruce Pierce 1970-Dec. 1973; Ray Grienke Jan. 15, 1974-1981; Forest Crum 1981-1983; Michael T. Conklin 1983-1989; John Backoff 1989-April 1991; Max Gladding (retired) April-June 1991; Gary D. Bondarenko 1991-2000; Carl Q. Litchfield 2000-2005; Wayne E. McKenney 2005-2014; [Boyne City/Boyne Falls/Horton Bay became a 3-point charge 2014] Michael Neihardt 2014-

Bradley Indian Mission of the UMC – *Grand Rapids District*

Lewis White Eagle Church 1972-1990; Pulpit Supply 1990-1992; David G. Knapp 1992-1995; Timothy J. Miller 1995-1999; John Pesblakal (DSA)1999-Aug. 31, 2001; Calvin Hill Sept. 1, 2001-2003; Wesley S. Rehberg (DSA) 2003-2005; Sandra VandenBrink, Jan. 16, 2005-2013; Sandra VandenBrink, (Retired) Director, Senior Meals Program 2013- ; Nancy L. Boelens (Retired) 2013-

Breckenridge UMC – *Heartland District*

Allen Wittrup 1966-1969; Gilbert Heaton 1969-1972; Birt Beers 1972-1977; Philip Brown 1977-1983; Molly Turner 1983-1990; Stanley Hayes 1990-1994; David L. Miles 1994-1999; Emilie Forward 1999-2005; Dale A. Golden 2005-2013; Paul W. Thomas 2013-

Breedsville UMC – *Kalamazoo District*

Lloyd Bronson 1967-1978; Lloyd Bronson 1978-1981; Charles McNary 1981-1991; James Hodge 1991-1992; Kenneth J. Littke 1992-1998; D.S. Assignment 1998; Jana Jirak Sept. 16, 1998-1999; Robert L. Pumfery 1999-October 31, 2002; Patricia Anne Harpole November 1, 2002-2004; O'Ryan Rickard 2004-2005; Sheila F. Baker 2005-2007; David L. Youngs 2007-2008; David L. Haase (DSA) (1/4 time) Jan. 3, 2008; David L. Haase (1/4 time) July 1, 2008-2014; Jason E. Harpole (1/4 time) 2014-

Brethren Epworth UMC – *Grand Traverse District*

Ward Pierce 1967-1971; Floyd Soper 1986-1993; Russell M. Garrigus (Ret) (DSA) 1993-2002; Lemuel O. Granada 2003-2005; Carl Greene (DSA) 2005; Carl Greene, Nov. 12, 2005-2011; Colleen A. Wierman (1/4 time) 2011-2014; [Brethren Epworth / Grant became single-point charges 2014] Judy Coffey (DSA) 2014-

Bridgman Faith UMC – *Kalamazoo District*

Walter Easton 1968-1969; David Lutz 1969-Jan. 1970; Arthur & Molly Turner April 1970-1971; Merritt Edner 1971-1972; Wayne Babcock 1972-Dec. 1974; Stanley Buck Jan. 1975-Dec. 1981; Daniel Graber Jan. 1982-1983; Joan Hamlin 1983-1985; Laura Truby 1985-Jan. 1987; Richard Bates March-Nov. 1987; Ross Bunce Nov. 1987-1988; B. Gordon Barry 1988-1993; Bradley S. Bartelmay 1993-May 1, 2000; Terrill M. Schneider May 1, 2000-

Bronson UMC – *Albion District*

Lloyd A. Phillips 1961-Oct. 1969; Gordon E. Spalenka Oct. 1969-1972; Charles W. Richards 1972-1977; Eldon C. Schram 1977-Oct. 1980; Paul Walter Oct.-Dec. 1980; A. Edward Perkins Dec. 1980-April 1987; Marilyn Barney April-May 1987; Milton John Palmer May 1987-1990; Gerald L. Welsh 1990-1994; Robert D. Nystrom 1994-1998; Mona Joslyn 1998-2006; Matthew Bistayi 2006-2009; Shane Chellis (DSA) 2009-2010; Shane Chellis (part-time) May 25, 2010-2011; Cindy Veilleux 2011-

Brookfield Eaton UMC – *Lansing District*

John H. King, Jr. 1967-1971; Miriam DeMint 1971-1973; John Morse 1973-March 1976; James Allred March 1976-Sept. 1979; Pulpit Supply Sept. 1979-1980; Robert Hundley 1980-1982; Pulpit Supply July-Oct. 1982; Robert Freysinger Oct. 1982-1985; Ronald Brooks 1985-1988; Robert Roth 1988-1990; Isabel Deppe 1990-1991; Charlene Minger 1991-1995; Geraldine M. Litchfield 1995-2000; Kevin E. Hale 2000-2004; Stephen C. Small 2004-Oct. 1, 2004; Irene Vittoz (DSA) Oct. 1, 2004; Irene Vittoz Nov. 15, 2005-

Brooks Corners UMC – *Heartland District*

Carter Miller 1968-March 1971; Lynn Wagner March 1971-Oct. 1973; Pulpit Supply Nov. 1973-1974; Darryl Cook 1974-May 1977; Kenneth Kline 1977-1986; Carl Q. Litchfield 1986-1991; Eugene L. Baughan 1991-1997; Brian R. Bunch 1997-2005; Ronald DeGraw Aug. 1, 2005-Nov. 6, 2005; James L. Breithaupt Mar. 15, 2006-Oct. 19, 2009; Joseph L. Beavan Jan. 15, 2010-2014; Bryan K. Kilpatrick 2014-

Buchanan Faith UMC – *Kalamazoo District*
D. Keith Laidler 1968-1972; Kenneth L. Snow 1972-1982; Richard C. Kuhn 1982-1987; Richard D. Wilson 1987-1996; Zawdie K. Abiade 1996-2002; Ralph K. Hawkins 2002-2004; Christopher A. Kruchkow 2004-Feb. 15, 2012; [Buchanan Faith UMC became single point charge 2012] Edward H. Slate (DSA) (1/2 time) 2012-

Buchanan First UMC – *Kalamazoo District*
C. Robert Carson 1966-1972; Ronald Entenman 1972-1979; Ward D. Pierce 1979-1985; Paul D. Mazur 1985-1987; Curtis E. Jensen 1987-Jan. 1996; William P. Sanders Feb. 2, 1996-2003; David W. Meister 2003-2006; Rob A. McPherson 2006-

Burnips UMC – *Kalamazoo District*
Ron Smith Oct. 1991-1997; Kenneth C. Reeves 1997-2004; Anthony Carrol Shumaker 2004-2008; Richard A. Fritz 2008-2014; Nancy J. Patera 2014-

Burr Oak UMC – *Albion District*
David Draggoo 1967-1971; P.T. Wachterhauser 1971-1974; Larry D. Higgins 1974-1977; Harold Tabor 1977-1978; Wade S. Panse 1978-March 1982; Dan Bennett 1982-1983; Timothy Boal 1983-1986; John Buker 1986-1988; William Bills 1988-1991; Brian Rafferty 1991-1993; Ruth A. Bonser 1993-1994; Emilie Forward 1994-1999; Martin Cobb 1999-2001; William Chu 2001-2003; Melanie S. Young (1/2 time) 2003-2006; Donald J. Graham 2007-2012; John Sterner 2012-

Byron Center UMC – *Grand Rapids District*
Max Gladding 1966-1975; James C. Grant 1975-1985; Fred Hamlin 1985-1987; William H. Doubblestein 1987-2004; Cynthia S.L. Greene 2004-2010; Lawrence A. Nichols 2010-

Cadillac South Community UMC – *Grand Traverse District*
Richard Wilson Nov. 1966-Nov. 1968; Richard Matson Dec. 1968-Oct. 1969; Edward Eidins Oct. 1969-1971; Robert R. Boyer 1971-1977; Kendall A. Lewis 1977-1981; Donald Fry 1981-1994; James C. Grant 1994-1999; Howard H. Harvey 1999-2000; Jeffrey Schrock 2000-2004; Kenneth C. Reeves 2004-2006; Kenneth C. Reeves (DSA) 2006-7; James J. Mort 2007-

Cadillac UMC – *Grand Traverse District*
George Grettenberger Nov. 1967-1980; Richard Wilson 1980-1990; Allen D. McCreedy 1990-2000; Dale P. Ostema 2000-2007; Thomas E. Ball 2007-

Caledonia UMC – *Grand Rapids District*
Edward D. Passenger 1966-1969; Robert Boyer 1969-1971; Lloyd Van Lente 1971-1976; Adam Chyrowski 1976-1980; Robert Tomlinson 1980-1984; Robert Wessman 1984-1990; Bobby Dale Whitlock 1990-Jan. 1996; Norman C. Kohns 1996-2005; James E. Hodge 2005-2012; Jodie R. Flessner 2012-

Camden UMC – *Albion District*
Karl L. Zeigler 1968-1969; John H. Gurney 1969-Aug. 1970; Joseph Huston Aug. 1970-1972; Richard Huskey 1972-1974; J. Brian Selleck 1974-Feb. 1976; Robert P. Stover March 1976-1980; Stephen Beech 1980-1983; Larry W. Rubingh 1983-1987; Frederick G. Hamlin 1987-1994; Russell K. Logston 1994-1996; Diane Stone Nov. 16, 1996-2004; Edward Mohr 2004-2010; Trevor McDermont 2010-2013; Frederick G. Cain (Retired) (part-time) 2013-

Carlisle UMC – *Grand Rapids District*
John Rothfuss 1968-1971; Curtis Cruff 1971-1975; Leonard Yarlott 1975-1979; Timothy Graham 1979-1983; John Buker 1983-1986; Larry Mannino 1986-1990; John Ritter 1990-1994; Andrew Jackson 1994-2006; Craig L Adams 2006-Dec. 1, 2009; Andrew Jackson (DSA) Dec. 1, 2009-2010; Mike Ramsey 2010-

Carson City UMC – *Heartland District*
Raymond D. Flessner 1970-1978; Paul D. Mazur 1978-1985; A. Ray Grienke 1985-Aug. 16, 1999; Richard A. Powell Aug. 16, 1999-Dec. 16, 1999; Robert E. Horton (DSA) Dec. 16, 1999-July 1, 2000; Kenneth J. Nash 2000-2006; Ronald K. Brooks 2006-2008; Andrew L. Croel 2008-2014; Charles Edward Milam 2014-

Casco UMC – *Kalamazoo District*

Lawrence Lee 1968-1970; O.I. Lundberg 1970-1971; Adam Chyrowski 1971-1977; Athel Lynch 1977-1979; Dan Graber 1979-1980; John Fisher 1980-1986; Theodore Cole 1986-Sept. 1988; Willard Gilroy Oct. 1988-April 15, 1993; Michael J. Tupper April 16, 1993-2001; Cynthia M. Parsons 2001-2006; David W. Meister 2006-

Cassopolis UMC – *Kalamazoo District*

Fred W. McNeil 1960-63; Joseph Wood 1966-1976; James G. Crosby 1976-1983; Charles Van Lente 1983-1993; Donald R. Ferris 1993-2000; Claudette Haney 2000-2005; Glenn Litchfield 2005-2009; James A. Richie 2009-2012; Dawn Laupp 2012-Dec, 31, 2012; Benjamin D. Hutchison Jan. 1, 2013-

Cedar Springs UMC – *Grand Rapids District*

Leo Bennett 1965-1970; Stanley Hayes 1970-Oct. 1975; Ralph Kallweit Jan. 1976-1980; Lloyd Hansen 1980-1983; Arthur Jackson 1983-1987; Robert Stover 1987-1989; William Haggard 1989-1995; Ben B. Lester 1995-2003; Brian F. Rafferty 2003-2008; Mary Letta-Bement Ivanov 2008-2014; Stephen F. Lindeman 204-

Center Park UMC – *Albion District*

Richard Darhing 1969-1970; Douglas Pederson 1970-1971; Luther Brokaw 1971-1975; Logan Weaver 1975-1978; Albert O'Rourke Sept. 1978-April 1982; Jesse Schwoebell 1982-1988; Dwight Stoner 1988-1989; Jeffrey Williams August 1989-Feb. 1993; Nelson Ray June 1993-1995; John L. Moore 1995-1997; Alice Fleming Townley 1997-2001; Stephen C. Small 2001-2004; Patricia L. Bromberek 2004-2006; Linda K. Stull-Lipps 2006-2011; Martin Culver 2011-

Central Lake UMC – *Grand Traverse District*

Leonard Yarlott 1967-1969; Paul Hartman 1970-1974; Daniel Miles 1974-1976; Chris Schroeder 1976-1982; David Cheyne 1982-1991; Celia Hastings, June-Nov. 1991; Peter H. Shumar Nov. 1991-May 1992; Richard A. Morrison June 1992-1995; Richard L. Matson 1995-2003; Charles A. Williams 2003-2010; Daniel W. Biteman 2010-

Centreville UMC – *Albion District*

Rudy A. Wittenbach 1967-1974; Charles W. Smith 1974-1984; Gordon E. Spalenka 1984-1987; Paul G. Donelson 1987-1989; Michael T. Conklin 1989-Aug. 1, 1997; David W. Meister Aug. 16, 1997-2003; Karin Orr 2003-2014; Emily K. Beachy 2014-

Charlevoix UMC – *Grand Traverse District*

Leona Winegarden 1965-1969; Elmer J. Faust 1969-1975; Austin Regier 1975-1981; David Yingling 1981-1988; Benton R. Heisler 1988-Nov. 15, 1992; Dale Peter Ostema Feb. 1, 1993-2000; J. Todd Thompson 2000-2010; Gregory P. Culver 2010-

Charlotte Lawrence Avenue UMC – *Lansing District*

Forrest E. Mohr 1966-1970; Lester Bailey 1970-1974; Verne Summers Sept. 1974-1987; James Mitchum (Assoc.) Apr. 1983-May 1987; George W. Fleming 1987-2002; Don Entenman (Assoc.) 1987-1988; Gary Bondarenko (Assoc.) 1988-1991; Edna Fleming (Assoc.) 1995-2002; Karen S. Wheat 2002-2010; Terry Fisher 2010-2013; Gary S. Wales 2013-

Chase-Barton UMC – *Heartland District*

Michael Nicholson 1988-Dec. 1991; Paul Patterson (ret.) Jan.-June 1992; Deborah R. Miller June 1, 1992-1995; Wayne McKinney (DSA) 1995-July 31, 2002; Timothy W. Doubblestein Sept. 1, 2002-Sept. 15, 2003; Sueann K. Hagan Oct. 16, 2003-2006; Michael J. Simon 2006-2010; Lyle J. Ball (DSA) 2010; Lyle J. Ball Nov. 1, 2010-

Clare UMC – *Heartland District*

Donald Winegar 1966-Sept. 1973; C. William Martin Oct. 1973-1979; Marvin R. Rosa 1979-1986; Eugene A. Lewis 1986-1994; Gregory R. Wolfe 1994-2003; Mark R. Payne (Assoc. 1/4 time) 1995-1996; Dennis B. Bromley 2003-2013; John G. Kasper 2013-

Claybanks UMC – *Grand Rapids District*
Charles Dunbar 1965-1971; Richard Matson 1971-1975; Bernard Randolph 1975-1976; Edward Slate 1976-1983; Steve Smith 1983-1985; Keith Treman 1985-1990; Kay B. Bosworth 1990-1998; Anita Hahn 1998-2006; Gayle Berntsen 2006-2014; [Claybanks realigned from Whitehall/Claybanks to Shelby/Claybanks 2014] Terri L. Cummins 2014-

Climax UMC – *Albion District*
Garth Smith 1965-1971; Pulpit Supply July-Nov. 1971; Wilbur Williams Nov. 1971-Aug. 1973; Paul Mazur Sept. 1973-1978; Pulpit Supply July-Dec. 1978; Donald Robinson Dec. 1978-Aug. 1979; James Allred Sept. 1979-Dec. 1986; Pulpit Supply Jan.-Apr. 1987; Dennis Slattery Apr. 1987-Oct. 1988; Pulpit Supply Oct.-Dec. 1988; Thomas E. Ball Dec. 1988-1994; David F. Hills 1994-Aug. 1, 1999; Sally J. LaFrance Oct. 1, 1999-2001; Thomas L. Truby 2001-March 1, 2003; David G. Knapp 2003-2009; Glenn C. Litchfield 2009-

Coldwater UMC – *Albion District*
Mark D. Graham 1968-Sept. 1974; Lester C. Bailey Sept. 1974-1982; James M. Morgan 1982-1988; Royce R. Robinson 1988-1989; Charles W. Richards 1989-1988; Betty A. Smith 1998-2004; Mark Babb (Deacon) 2002-2006; Cynthia Ann Skutar 2004-2010; Denise J. Downs (Assoc.) 2007-2008; Steven R. Young 2010-

Coloma UMC – *Kalamazoo District*
George W. Chaffee 1968-1971; Carl Hausermann 1971-1977; Elizabeth Perry Nord (Assoc.) 1976-1981; Dwight Benner 1977-Sept. 1981; Timothy Closson Jan. 1982-Oct. 1986; Laura C. Truby Jan. 1987-1991; Richard Rossiter 1992-Feb. 4, 1996; Leonard R. Schoenherr Feb. 16, 1996-1999; David F. Hills Aug. 1, 1999-2007; O'Ryan Rickard 2007-2009; William W. Chu 2009-2011; Ron Van Lente 2011- [Watervliet UMC merged w/ Coloma UMC 6-26-11]; David L. Haase (assoc.) 2014-

Colon UMC – *Albion District*
Leon Shaffer 1967-Nov. 1, 1973; Larry R. Sachau March 15, 1974-1979; Theodore Bennink 1979-1980; Larry R. Shrout 1980-1983; Jack Kraklan 1983-1985; Lawrence Hubley Nov. 1, 1985-1991; Raymond D. Flesner 1991-1999; Arthur C. Murphy 1999-Jan. 15, 2007; Donald J. Graham 2007-2012; John Sterner 2012-

Concord UMC – *Albion District*
Everett Love 1967-1969; Daniel Miles 1969-Dec. 1971; Pulpit Supply Jan.-June 1972; Joseph Huston 1972-1975; Ronald Grant 1975-1982; John McNaughton 1982-1984; Pulpit Supply 1984-1986; David Hansen 1986-1989; Ed Dahringer (interim) July-Dec. 1989; Barbara M. Flory Jan. 1990-1998; Harris J. Hoekwater 1998-2006; Melany A. Chalker 2006-2013; David Elmore 2013-

Constantine UMC – *Albion District*
Adam Chyrowski 1966-1971; Roger Wittrup 1971-April 1973; Richard Williams April 1973-April 1976; David Selleck April 1976-Sept. 1979; R. Paul Doherty Dec. 1979-1987; Walter Rothfuss 1987-1989; Gerald Hagans 1989-Aug. 1991. James W. Barney Sept. 1991-1998; Russell K. Logston 1998-2001; Mark R. Erbes 2001-2007; Melanie Young 2007-2009; Scott E. Manning [Constantine / White Pigeon became a two-point charge 2009]

Coomer UMC – *Heartland District*
Harold Armon 1968-1969; Lawrence Smith 1969-1970; Athel Lynch 1970-1973; Joseph Dudley 1973-1974; Kathy Nickerson 1974-1977; James Sabo-Schuler 1977-1980; James Burgess 1980-1986; M. Christopher Lane 1986-1990; Paula Jane Duffey 1990-1998; Dale A. Golden 1998-2005; Paulette G. Cheyne 2005-2006; Melody Lane Olin (DSA) 2006; Melody Olin Nov. 15, 2006-2010; Lawrence Wonsey 2010-2014; Russell D. Morgan (CLM/DSA) 2014-

Coopersville UMC – *Grand Rapids District*
Philip P. Steele 1968-1969; Vernon L. Michael 1970-1980; David L. Flagel 1980-1989; Paul D. Mazur 1989-1990; Martin M. DeBow 1990-1997; Michael T. Conklin Aug. 1, 1997-1999; John D. Morse 1999-2012; Cori Cypret 2012-

Country Chapel UMC – *Lansing District*

Marvin Iseminger 1968-1973; Kendall Lewis 1973-1977; Lynn Wagner 1977-1984; Carl Olson 1984-1985; James Cook 1985-1986; Mary Horn (Schippers) 1986-1991; Merlin Pratt 1991-1996; Kay Pratt (co-pastor) 1992-1996; DeAnn J. Dobbs 1996-Oct. 1, 2000; Dianne D. Morrison Feb. 1, 2001-2004; Patricia Anne Harpole 2004-2009; Kimberly A. Tallent 2009-2011; Ryan Wieland 2011-

Countryside UMC – *Heartland District*

George Rule 1968-1970; Joseph Dudley 1970-Sept. 1972; Daren C. Durey Oct. 1972-Jan. 1977; Robert E. Tomlinson Feb. 1977-1980; Gordon Spalenka 1980-1984; Janelle Gerken 1984-Jan. 1987; Michael J. Kent May 1987-Jan. 1991; James Cook 1991-1995; Dean Prentiss 1995-Sept. 14, 1999; Susan D. Olsen July 16, 2004-2006; Sharyn K. Osmond Aug. 1, 2006-Nov. 30, 2008; Donald R. Wendell Nov. 30, 2008-Nov. 1, 2009; Craig L. Adams Dec. 1, 2009-2010; David Michael Palmer 2010-

Courtland-Oakfield UMC – *Grand Rapids District*

T.E. Meredith 1968-1970; Richard E. Cobb 1970-March 1972; William J. Bildner 1972-1977; Wendell Stine 1977-1983; Forest H. Crum 1983-Sept. 1984; Gerald Selleck Dec. 1984-1990; Charles K. Stanley Nov. 1, 1990-1996; Charles W. Smith 1996-2008; Michael T. Conklin 2008-2009; Jeffrey C. Williams 2009-2011; Robert Eckert 2011-

CrossWind Community UMC – *Grand Rapids District*

[new church start 2004; chartered 2009] Scott K. Otis, Oct. 1, 2004-

Crystal Valley UMC – *Grand Traverse District*

Hubert Bengsten 1965-1974; Pulpit supply 1974-1975; Charles Bowman 1975-Jan. 1977; Harry Parker Feb. 1977-1980; Rebecca Neal Niese 1980-1984; Michael Nicholson 1984-1988; John Ritter 1988-Sept. 1990; Max Gladding Sept.-Oct. 1990; A. Ruth Bonser Oct. 1990-1993; Nancy Bugajski 1993-Oct. 1995; Donald J. Vuurens (DSA) 1996-1998; Steven J. Hale 1998-Nov. 8, 1999; Ronald A. Houk (DSA) Nov. 8, 1999-2000; Kenneth E. Tabor 2000-2004; Ronald L. Worley 2004--Nov. 30, 2013; Ronald Iris (Retired) Dec. 1, 2013-

Dansville UMC – *Lansing District*

Silas Foltz 1968-1970; Paul Schreibner 1970-1974; David Dryer 1974-1980; Joseph Graybill 1980-May 1987; Bobby Dale Whitlock 1987-May 1990; Clyde Miller (interim) May-Sept. 1990; Genevieve DeHoog Oct. 1990-1994; Pulpit Supply July-Aug. 1994; DeAnn J. Dobbs Sept. 1, 1994-1996; Russell K. Logston 1996-1998; DSA 1998-1999; Stephen F. Ezop 1999-June 30, 2002; Sharyn K. Osmond 2002-2006; Kimberly A. Tallent Aug. 1, 2006-2008; Donald R. Fry (DSA) (1/4 time) 2008-2011; Jeremy J. Wicks (1/4 time) 2011- [M-52 Cooperative Ministry 2013]

Delta Mills UMC – *Lansing District*

Donald H. Thomson 1963-1969; Bruce Pierce Aug. 1969-1970; Raymond J. McBratnie 1970-1973; Dave Morton 1973-1982; William Dornbush 1982-1986; Clarence W. Hutchens Nov. 1986-Jan. 1987; Janelle E.R. Gerkin Jan. 1987-1990; Lyle D. Heaton 1990-Jan. 1, 1999; D. Keith Laidler Jan. 1, 1999-June 30, 1999; Robert J. Besemer 1999-2002; Kathleen S. Kursch 2003-Aug. 31, 2004; Keith Laidler 2005-2007; Paulette G. Cheyne 2007-2013; Joseph L. Spackman (Retired) (1/4 time) 2013-

Delton Faith UMC – *Albion District*

Earl Champlin 1968-1971; Gordon Showers 1971-1975; Elmer Faust 1975-1990; William A. Hertel 1990-2001; Daniel B. Hofmann 2001-2007; David F. Hills 2007-2010; Gary L. Bekofske 2010-2012; Brian R. Bunch 2012-

DeWitt Redeemer UMC – *Lansing District*

Rodney J. Kalajainen 1988-; Patricia L. Brook (Assoc.) 1999-Jan. 31, 2002

Dimondale UMC – *Lansing District*

Tom Peters 1967-1970; Richard Youells 1970-1974; Thomas Weber 1974-Apr. 1978; John Ristow Apr. 1978-1979; Daryl Boyd 1979-May 1981; Heidi Joos 1981-1983; Glenn Herriman 1983-1985; Richard Powell 1985-1988; Bonnie Yost-McBain 1988-Nov. 1990; Donald D. Entenman 1991-Jan. 31, 1994; Joyce DeToni-Hill Feb. 16, 1994-Oct. 15, 1999; Lillian T. French Nov. 16, 1999-2002; Robert David Nystrom 2002-2004; Thomas Peters (DSA) 2004-2005; Andrew L. Croel 2005-2008; Kimberly A. Tallent 2008-2009; Joseph D. Huston (DSA) 2009-

Dowagiac First UMC – *Kalamazoo District*

John H. Ristow 1966-1978; Dale Benton 1979-1980; Clyde Miller 1980-1983; Claude Ridley 1983-1987; R. Paul Doherty 1987-2004; William H. Doubblestein 2004-2006; John K. Kasper 2006-2013; David A. Price 2013-

East Boardman UMC – *Grand Traverse District*

Gerald L. Hedlund 1966-1971; Arthur and Molly Turner (co-pastors) 1971-1976; Diane Vale 1976-Oct. 1977; Marion Nye Oct. 1977-1985; Clinton McKinven-Copus 1985-1987; Gary Wales 1987-1994; Howard Seaver 1994-2012; Mark E. Mitchell 2012-2014; Donald L. Buege 2014-

East Jordan UMC – *Grand Traverse District*

Stanley L. Hayes Nov. 1966-1970; Lester E. Priest 1970-Jan. 1974; Daniel J. Minor April 1974-1981; Phillip W. Simmons Sept. 1981-1984; Brian Secor 1984-1986; Merlin K. Delo 1986-1997, Eugene L. Baughan 1997-2002; D. Michael Maurer 2002-Nov. 10, 2008; Ralph Posnik (DSA) Nov. 23, 2008; Ralph Posnik Nov. 15, 2009-2014; Craig A. Pahl 2014-

East Lansing Peoples Church – *Lansing District*

East Lansing University UMC – *Lansing District*

Alden Burns 1966-1971; Arno Wallschlaeger (Assoc.) 1968-1977; Donn Doten 1971-1979; Jon Powers (Assoc.) 1974-1978; Tom Pier-Fitzgerald (Assoc.) 1978-1982; Keith Pohl 1980-1986; Robert Hundley (Assoc.) 1982-1990; Sharon Z. Rader 1986-1989; Gessel Berry, Jr. 1989-1991; William Dobbs 1991-1996; Marguerite M. Rivera (Assoc.) April 16, 1995-1996; Frank W. Lyman, Jr. & Carole S. Lyman (co-pastors) 1996-2006; John Ross Thompson 2006-Dec. 31, 2010; Kennetha Bigham-Tsai (Assoc.) 2006-2011; Jennifer Browne 2011- ; William W. Chu (Assoc.) 2011-

East Nelson UMC – *Grand Rapids District*

Leo Bennett 1965-1970; Stanley Hayes 1970-Oct. 1975; Ralph Kallweit Jan. 1976-1980; Lloyd Hansen 1980-1983; Arthur Jackson 1983-1987; Robert Stover 1987-1989;William Haggard 1989-1995; Ben B. Lester 1995-2003; Brian F. Rafferty 2003-2004; Herbert VanderBilt 2004-

Eaton Rapids First UMC – *Lansing District*

Ronald A. Houk Oct. 1971-Jan. 1982; Eric S. Beck (Assoc.) Dec. 1980-1983; Robert E. Betts Feb. 1982-1988; Larry W. Mannino (Assoc.) 1983-1986; Larry E. Irvine 1988-Oct. 15, 1993; Howard (Rick) McKire (Assoc.) Jan. 1993-; Thomas J. Evans Feb. 1, 1994-2007; Daniel B. Hofmann 2007-2014; Martin M. DeBow 2014-

Edmore Faith UMC – *Heartland District*

C. William Martin 1965-1969; Eldon Eldred 1969-1973; Howard McDonald 1973-1976; David Yingling 1976-1981; Stanley Finkbeiner 1981-Feb. 1987; Stephen Charnley (interim) Feb.-April 1987; Joseph Graybill April 1987-1997; Connie R. Bongard 1997-Jan. 1, 2007; Esther R. Barton (DSA) Jan. 1-June 30, 2007; Susan E. Poynter 2007-2011; Michael A. Riegler 2011-

Edwardsburg Hope UMC – *Kalamazoo District*

(Formerly Adamsville and Edwardsburg); Jeffrey L. Reese Dec. 1, 1997-

Elberta UMC – *Grand Traverse District*

Richard M. Wilson 1967-1971; John Melvin Bricker 1971-1980; Richard C. Kuhn 1980-1982; John D. Morse 1982-1987; Paul D. Mazur 1987-April 1989; Donald R. Ferris April 1989-1993; John W. McNaughton 1993-1996; Marvin R. Rosa 1996-1999; Kathryn M. Coombs 1999-2002; Gregory P. Culver 2002-2010; Barbara J. Fay 2010-

Elsie UMC – *Heartland District*

Gordon Showers 1965-1970; David Litchfield 1970-1976; David Miles 1976-1983; Joe Glover 1983-1985; Fred Fischer 1985-1996; Merlin Pratt 1996-2003; David C. Blair 2003-2004; Jayme L. Kendall 2004-2005; Edwin D. Snook July 16, 2005-2012; Mona Kindel (3/4 time) 2012-2013; Donald R. Ferris-McCann (3/4 time) 2013- [Elsie/Salem became a charge 5-1-14]

Empire UMC – *Grand Traverse District*

Elmer J. Faust 1966-1969; Edward R. Jones 1969-1971; Alvin Doten 1971-1976; Harry R. Johnson 1976-Sept. 1978; Emmett Kadwell Jr. Oct. 1978-1982; Andrew Weeks 1982-1985; Melanie Baker-Streevy 1985-1988; Kenneth Curtis 1988-1991; Kathryn M. Coombs 1991-1998; William (Will) McDonald 1998-Jan. 31, 2003; William F. Dye Feb. 1, 2003-2006; Brenda E. Gordon 2006-2014; Russell K. Logston 2014-

Epsilon UMC – *Grand Traverse District*

Norman Crotser 1968-1969; Seward Walton 1969-1976; John Gurney 1976-1979; Marvin Iseminger 1979-1981; Jerry Jaquish 1981-1987; Glenn Wegner 1987-Aug. 1992; John F. Greer Sept.-Nov. 1992; Dennis Bromley Jan. 1993-2003; Matthew Todd Stoll 2003-2010; Vaughn Thurston-Cox 2010- ; [Epsilon/New Hope/Harbor Springs/Alanson became a 4-point charge 2014] Hillary Thurston-Cox (Assoc.) 2014-

Evart UMC – *Heartland District*

Milton TenHave 1967-1970; Marjorie Matthews Feb.-Oct. 1970; Laurence Waterhouse Oct. 1970-Oct. 1975; Stanley Hayes Oct. 1975-March 1984; Gerald Welsh 1984-1990; Donald Buege 1990-2000; Margaret Halls Wilson 2000-2006; Edward H. Slate, 2006-2008; Mark Mitchell 2008-2012; Melodye Surgeon-Rider 2012-

Farwell UMC – *Heartland District*

Leroy Howe 1967-Dec. 1967; Eldon K. Eldred Dec. 1967-1969; George B. Rule 1969-Feb. 1970; Altha M. Barnes Feb. 15-June 1970; Miriam F. DeMint 1970-1971; Chester J. Erickson 1971-1974; John W. Bullock 1974-1978; Dwight J. Burton 1978-1983; David L. Miles 1983-1994; Thomas E. Ball 1994-2000; Jane Ellen Johnson 2000-Jan. 1, 2007; Connie R. Bongard Jan. 1, 2007-

Felt Plains UMC – *Lansing District*

William Wurzel 1966-1969; Gordon E. Spalenka June-Oct. 1969; Arthur A. Jackson Oct. 1969-1972; Wayne E. Sparks 1972-1975; James M. Morgan 1975-1982; Max J. Gladding 1982-1990; Clinton McKinven-Copus 1990-Oct. 1991; Reva Hawke Oct. 1991-April 1993; Derek DeToni-Hill 1993-Oct. 15, 1999; Janet Sweet-Richardson Nov. 1, 1999-2003; Carroll Arthur Fowler 2003-Jan. 1, 2006; Donald L. Buege Jan. 15, 2006-2014; Kelly M. Wasnich 2014-

Fennville UMC – *Kalamazoo District*

Lloyd R. VanLente 1968-1971; Matthew Walkotten 1971-1976; Miriam DeMint 1976-1978; Ronald Hansen 1978-1984; Stanley Hayes 1984-1990; James Fox 1990-1992; Randall R. Hansen 1992-2000; Jane A. Crabtree 2000-2002; Jean Crabtree (DSA) (Assoc.) 2000-2002; Robert L. Hinklin (DSA) 2002-2003; Raymond R. Sundell 2003-2008; Gary L. Peterson 2008-

Fenwick UMC – *Heartland District*

John H. Gurney 1970-1976; Norman Crotser 1976-Dec. 1978; Daniel R. Bennett 1979-March 1982; Mark G. Johnson March 1982-1986; James E. Cook 1986-1991; Howard H. Harvey 1991-1996; Patrick Glass 1996-1998; Larry W. Nalett 1998-Aug. 9, 2004; Charles E. Cerling Aug. 10, 2004-2009; Jolennda Cole (DSA) 2009-2010; Jolennda Cole 2010-2011; William F. Dye 2011-2012; Russell D. Morgan (CLM) July 15, 2012-2014; Gerald Erskine (DSA) 2014-

Ferry UMC – *Grand Rapids District*

Merlin Delo 1966-1978; William Bowers 1978-1980; David Dryer 1980-1984; Richard Williams 1984-Oct 1, 1997; Pulpit Supply Oct. 1, 1997 - Dec. 31, 1997; Susan Olsen Jan. 1, 1998-July 1, 1998; Raymond D. Field 1998-1999; James Bradley Brillhart 1999-2007; Dianne D. Morrison 2007-2011; Richard D. Morrison (DSA) 2007-2011; Paul E. Hane 2011-

Fife Lake UMC – *Grand Traverse District*

Gerald L. Hedlund 1966-1971; Arthur and Molly Turner (co-pastors) 1971-1976; Diane Vale 1976-Oct. 1977; Marion Nye Dec. 1977-1978; Pulpit Supply 1978-1979; Athel Lynch 1979-1981; Pulpit Supply 1981-1983; Daniel Biteman, Jr. 1983-1985; Clinton McKinven-Copus 1985-1987; Gary Wales 1987-1994; Howard Seaver 1994-2012; Mark E. Mitchell 2012-2014; Donald L. Buege 2014-

Fountain UMC – *Grand Traverse District*

Viola Norman 1967-1971; Robert Doner June-Dec. 1971; Lewis Buchner Jan. 1972-Aug. 1972; Russell Garrigus Sept. 1972-1993; Warren Wood (DSA) 1993-Nov. 1, 1999; Kenneth E. Tabor Nov. 1, 1999-2000; Janet Lynne O'Brien (DSA) 2001-Nov. 30, 2001; Jan O'Brien (part-time) Dec. 1, 2001-2002; Lemuel O. Granada 2002-2003; Lemuel Granada 2005-Nov. 30, 2007; Mona J. Dye (part-time) Dec. 1, 2007-2011; Joyce A. Theisen (DSA) 2011-2013; Richard D. Roberts (DSA) 2013-

Frankfort UMC – *Grand Traverse District*

Richard M. Wilson 1967-1971; John Melvin Bricker 1971-1980; Richard C. Kuhn 1980-1982; John D. Morse 1982-1987; Paul D. Mazur 1987-April 1989; Donald R. Ferris April 1989-1993; John W. McNaughton 1993-1996; Marvin R. Rosa 1996-1999; Kathryn M. Coombs 1999-2002; Gregory P. Culver 2002-2010; Barbara J. Fay 2010-

Free Soil UMC – *Grand Traverse District*

Viola Norman 1967-1971; Robert Doner June-Dec. 1971; Lewis Buchner Jan. 1972-Aug. 1972; Russell Garrigus Sept. 1972-1993; Warren Wood (DSA) 1993-Nov. 1, 1999; Kenneth E. Tabor Nov. 1, 1999-2000; Janet Lynne O'Brien (DSA) 2001-Nov. 30, 2001; Janet Lynne O'Brien (part-time) Dec. 1, 2001-2009; Mona Dye 2009-2011; Joyce A. Theisen (DSA) 2011-2013; Richard D. Roberts (DSA) 2013-

Freeport UMC – *Lansing District*

Harold M. Taber 1966-1969; Charles W. Martin 1969-Oct. 1973; Harold R. Simon Nov. 1973-Oct. 1976; Arthur D. Jackson Apr. 1977-1981; Bradley P. Kalajainen Jan. 1981-1985; Gilbert R. Boersma 1985-Jan. 1989; Janet K. Sweet 1989-1991; Carroll A. Fowler 1991-April 15, 1995; Paulette Cheyne June 1, 1995-1999; Richard A. Powell 1999-Aug. 15, 1999; Deborah R. Miller Aug. 16, 1999-Jan. 31, 2002; Paul Peterson (DSA) 2002-2004; Scott E. Manning 2004-2006; Susan D. Olsen 2006-

Fremont UMC – *Grand Rapids District*

Lynn DeMoss 1966-1969; Bertram Vermeulen 1969-1978; Constance Heffelfinger (Assoc.) 1978-1981; Eldon K. Eldred 1979-1987; A. Edward Perkins 1987-1990; Harold F. Filbrandt 1990-1994; Daniel M. Duncan 1994-2003; Lawrence R. Wood 2003-2007; Carolin S. Spragg 2007-2013; Martin T. Cobb 2013-

Frontier UMC – *Albion District*

Kenneth Karlzen 1966-1968; Charles D. Grauer 1968-1970; Daniel W. Harris 1970-1971; Robert E. Jones 1971-Nov. 15, 1973; Marion V. Nye Nov. 15, 1973-1976; Daniel R. Bennett Feb. 1, 1977-1979; Leonard J. Yarlott 1979-1982; Gilbert R. Boersma 1982-1985; Valerie M. Hill 1985-1989; Jerry L. Hippensteel 1989-1994; Susan Deason 1994-1998; Kathy L. Nitz 1998-Aug. 15, 1999; Donald Lee (DSA) 2002-2010; Cynthia Veilleux (DSA) Nov. 1, 2010-2011; Timothy R. Puckett (part-time) 2011-2014

Galesburg UMC – *Albion District*

Laurence R. Lowell 1968-1969; Pulpit Supply 1969-1970; Milton J. TenHave 1970-1973; Jack Scott 1973-1977; Allan Valkema 1977-1980; Larry Grubaugh 1980-1988; Rochelle Ray 1988-1992; John L. Moore 1992-1995; Charles M. Shields 1995-1997; Janet Sweet-Richardson 1997-Nov. 1, 1999; Michael Baker-Streevy Nov. 16, 1999-2003; Keith W. Heifner 2003-2006; Mona K. Joslyn 2006-2010; [Comstock UMC merged w/ Galesburg UMC 04-29-07]; Sally K. Harrington (DSA) Nov. 1, 2010-2012; John L. Moore (DSA) (1/2 time) 2012-2013; Leonard R. Schoenherr (Retired) 2013-

Galien UMC – *Kalamazoo District*

Lawrence Smith 1967-1969; Willard Gilroy 1969-1973; Arthur Beadle 1973-1976; Gordon Everett (interim) July-Nov. 1976; Richard Williams Dec. 1976-Oct. 1979; Paul Smith Nov. 1979-March 1980; Joseph Wood (interim) March-June 1980; William Doubblestein 1980-1983; William Carr 1983-April 1986; Joseph Wood (interim) April-June 1986; Phillip Friedrick 1986-1991; Sherri Swanson 1991-1995; Charlene A. Minger 1995-1999; Valerie Fons 1999-2001; John G. Kasper 2001-2006; Russell K. Logston 2006-2011; Jeffrey O. Cummings Jan. 1, 2012-

Ganges UMC – *Kalamazoo District*
Lloyd R. Van Lente Jan. 1966-1971; Matthew Walkoton 1971-1973; Douglas L. Pederson 1973-1975; Richard W. McLain 1975-1979; Craig L. Adams 1979-1984; Constance L. Heffelfinger 1984-Jan. 1990; Aurther D. Jackson Jan. 1990-Jan. 1991; Leonard Coon Jan.-June 1991; John Burgess 1991-1994; Marcia L. Elders 1994-1997; Barbara Jo Fay 1997-Dec.31, 2004; Jean M. Smith Jan. 16, 2005-Sept. 1, 2010; Jack E. Balgenorth Sept. 1, 2010-2014; [Ganges/Glenn became single charges 2014] Marcia A. Tucker (DSA) 2014-

Georgetown UMC – *Grand Rapids District*
Robert Hinklin Feb. 1, 1976-1984; John R. Smith 1984-Feb. 18, 1999; Joseph J. Bistayi Aug. 16,1999-2005; Joseph D. Huston 2005-2007; William C. Bills 2007-

Girard UMC – *Albion District*
C. Jack Scott 1968-1970; William E. Miles 1970-1971; Harold M. Deipert 1971-1973; Norman A. Charter 1973-1976; Densel G. Fuller 1976-1981; Jerry L. Hippensteel 1981-1984; Thomas E. Ball 1984-Nov. 1988; Stanley Fenner Dec. 1988-1989; Stacy R. Minger 1989-1994; John F. Ritter 1994-1996; Robert Stark 1996-2000; John Scott 2000-Sept. 1, 2003; John A. Scott & Rebecca Scott (CoPastors) Sept 2003-2007; Bruce R. Kintigh 2007-2010; Emily (Slavicek) Beachy Sept. 1, 2010-2014; Cydney Idsinga 2014-

Glenn UMC – *Kalamazoo District*
Lloyd Van Lente 1968-1969; Harold Arman 1969-1971; Arthur Beadle 1971-1973; Pulpit Supply 1973-1974; O. Bernard Strother 1974-1998; Stephen Small Nov. 16, 1998-2001; John R. Cantwell (DSA) 2002-2005; Jean A. Smith 2005-Sept. 1, 2010; Jack E. Balgenorth Sept. 1, 2010-2014; [Ganges/Glenn became single charges 2014] Harold F. Filbrandt (Retired) 2014-

Gobles UMC – *Kalamazoo District*
James Boehm 1967-1970; Allen Valkema 1970-1971; William Miles 1971-1974; Rudolph Wittenback 1974-1976; Karen S. Slager-Wheat 1976-1986; John McNaughton 1986-1987; Judy K. Downing 1987-1998; Susan Olsen 1998-2004; Mary Beth Rhine 2004-2010; Edward Mohr L. 2010-Sept. 11, 2012; Nelson L. Hall 2013-

Grand Haven Church of the Dunes – *Grand Rapids District*
Albert W. Frevert 1965-1972; David Miles (Assoc.) 1971-1976; Charles F. Garrod 1972-1978; Lawrence Wiliford (Assoc.) 1976-1978; Gerald A. Pohly 1978-1989; Victor Charnley (Assoc.) 1978-1984; Robert Gillette (Assoc.) 1984-1991; Ellen A. Brubaker 1989-1992; Richard Youells (Assoc.) 1991-1995; Eldon K. Eldred 1992-2003; Brian F. Rafferty (Assoc.) 1999-2003; Daniel M. Duncan 2003-2014; Glenn M. Wagner 2014-

Grand Ledge First UMC – *Lansing District*
H. James Birdsall 1967-1973; Royce R. Robinson 1973-1983; Philip L. Brown 1983-1989; Lynn E. Grimes 1989-1993; Robert H. Roth, Jr. (Assoc.) 1991-1994; William J. Amundsen 1993-2003; Barbara Smith Jang (Assoc.) 1994-1997; Jana L. Almeida (Assoc.) 1997-Oct. 15, 1999; Kathleen S. Kursch (Assoc.) Feb. 1, 2000-Aug. 31, 2004; Molly C. Turner 2003-2012; Molly Turner (DSA) July-Dec. 31, 2012; Gregory W. Lawton (Deacon) 2007-2011; Betty A. Smith (Interim) Jan. 1-Mar. 31, 2013; Terry A. Euper Apr. 1-June 30, 2013; Cynthia Skutar 2013-

Grand Rapids Aldersgate UMC – *Grand Rapids District*
Clinton Galloway 1967-Dec. 1973; Norman Kohns Jan. 1974-1981; William Johnson 1981-1992; Thomas B. Jones (Assoc.) 1990-Dec. 31, 1995; Ellen A. Brubaker 1992-Jan. 1, 2002; Cathi M. Gowin Feb. 1, 2002-2005; Gerald L. Toshalis 2005-2006; Gregory J. Martin 2006-2012; [Grand Rapids Aldersgate / Plainfield became two-point charge 2012] Laurie A. Haller 2012-2013; [became single-point charge 2013] James E. Hodge 2013-

Grand Rapids Cornerstone UMC – *Grand Rapids District*
[new church start 1990] Bradley P. Kalajainen 1990- ; Scott Keith Otis (Assoc.) 2003-Oct. 1, 2004; Kenneth J. Nash (Assoc.) 2006-

Grand Rapids Faith UMC – *Grand Rapids District*

Second UMC and Valley UMC merged in 1977 to become Faith UMC. Eugene Lewis 1977-1984; Paul Patterson 1984-1987; Douglas Pedersen 1987-Feb. 15, 1994; Kim L. Gladding 1994-1998; Geoffrey L. Hayes 1998-2009; Mark E. Thompson 2009-

Grand Rapids First UMC – *Grand Rapids District*

Donald B. Strobe 1964-1972; Carl L. Hausermann (Assoc.) 1967-1971; Lowell F. Walsworth (Assoc.) 1971-1973; John S. Jury 1972-Nov. 1974; Geoffrey L. Hayes (Assoc.) 1973-1978; William W. DesAutels Dec. 1974-1981; Robert E. Jones (Assoc.) 1978-1983; Robert C. Brubaker 1981-Nov. 1987; Darwin R. Salisbury (Assoc.) 1983-1985; Bradley P. Kalajainen (Assoc.) 1985-1990; Lynn A. DeMoss April 1988-1993; Joyce DeToni-Hill (Assoc.) 1990-1991; Derek DeToni-Hill (Assoc.) 1990-1993; Gary T. Haller (Co-pastor) 1993-2013; Laurie A. Haller (Co-pastor) 1993-2006; Dominic A. Tommy (Assoc.) 1997-1999; Jennifer Browne (Assoc.) 2006-2011; Kim DeLong (Deacon - Director of Education)(1/2 time) 2009-2012; Martha Beals (Deacon) (part-time) July 1-Nov. 20, 2009; Janet Carter (Deacon) (part-time) 2009- ; Letisha Bowman (Assoc.) 2011- ; Robert L. Hundley 2013-

Grand Rapids Genesis UMC – *Grand Rapids District*

[new church start 1995] M. Christopher Lane & Jane R. Lippert (co-pastors) 1995-2007; Susan M. Petro 2007-2014; DeAnn J. Dobbs 2014-

Grand Rapids Iglesia Metodista Unida La Nueva Esperanza – *Grand Rapids District*

Miguel A. Rivera 1983-1986; Francisco Diaz 1986-1991; Juan B. Falcon 1992-Sep. 1995; Oscar Ventura Sept. 1995-Sept. 2002; Isidro Carrera Sept. 2002-March 16, 2003; Oscar Ventura Sept. Mar. 16, 2003-2009; Jorge Rodriguez 2009-2013; Nohemi Ramirez 2013-

Grand Rapids Mosaic UMC – *Grand Rapids District*

[new church start 1997; "Michigan Suhbu Korean UMC" re-named "Church of All Nations", 2006; renamed "Mosaic UMC" 2012] Seung Ho Baek July 16, 1997-2008; Robert Eckert (part-time) 2008-2009; Trevor McDermont 2009-2010; Steven C. Place Jan. 1, 2011-

Grand Rapids Northlawn UMC – *Grand Rapids District*

Ivan Niswender 1966-1969; Leonard Putnam 1969-1973; Carlton Benson 1973-1976; Thurlan Meredith 1976-1984; Vance Dimmick, Jr. 1984-1992; Stanley Finkbeiner 1992-1996; Charles R. VanLente 1996-2010; James C. Noggle 2010-2013; Timothy B. Wright 2013- ; Janice T. Lancaster (Deacon) Feb. 1, 2014-

Grand Rapids Rivercrest Church – *Grand Rapids District*

Rivercrest new church start (formerly Plainfield UMC] Kellas D. Penny, III Jan. 1, 2014-

Grand Rapids South UMC – *Grand Rapids District*

Donald Cozadd 1967-1969; Kenneth McCaw 1969-1975; Clarence Hutchens 1975-1979; Ray Burgess 1979-1988; Thomas M. Pier-Fitzgerald 1988-1998; Robert P. Stover 1998-2004; Kathleen S. Kursch Sept. 1, 2004-2007; Mack Strange 2007-

Grand Rapids St Paul's UMC – *Grand Rapids District*

John S. Myette 1964-1969; William A. Hertell 1969-1974; Robert E. Betts 1974-1982; Edward Trimmer (Assoc.) 1981-1982; Joseph D. Huston 1982-1989; Andrew Jackson (Assoc. part-time) Sept. 1-1986-1994; Theron E. Bailey 1989-1994; Ethel Z. Stears 1994-1999; Robert J. Mayo 1999-2005; Cathi M. Huvaere (formerly Catherine M. Gowin) 2005-2012; Erin L. Fitzgerald 2012-

Grand Rapids Trinity UMC – *Grand Rapids District*

Donn P. Doten 1962-1971; Philip A. Carpenter (Assoc.) 1966-1972; Lawrence R. Taylor 1971-1978; Marvin R. Rosa (Assoc.) Feb. 1972-1979; Charles F. Garrod 1978-1984; William John Amundsen (Assoc.) 1979-1982; Edward A. Trimmer (Assoc.) 1982-1983; Ethel Stears (Assoc.) Sept. 1983-1986; Charles Fry 1984-1989; Timothy P. Boal (Assoc.) 1986-1992; Gerald A. Pohly 1989-1996; Gerald Toshalis (Assoc.) 1992-2001; A. Edward Perkins 1996-2006; Robert Cook (Assoc.) 2001-2006; Carole and Frank Lyman (Co-pastors) 2006-2010; David Nellist 2010- ; Julie Dix (Assoc.) Nov. 8, 2010-

Grand Rapids Vietnamese UMC – *Grand Rapids District*

Vinh Q. Tran Sept.1, 1987-2004; Cuong Nguyen 2004-2008; Sanh Van Tran 2008-2012; Dung Q. Nguyen 2012-

Grandville UMC – *Grand Rapids District*

Dale Brown 1964-Feb. 1973; L. George Babcock (Assoc.) 1967-1972; E. William Wiltse March 1973-1977; William H. Doubblestein (Assoc.) 1974-Aug. 1977; Charles Fullmer 1977-1986; Leon Andrews 1986-1989; Barry Petrucci (Assoc.) 1986-1989; Kim L. Gladding (Assoc.) 1989-1994; J. Melvin Bricker 1989-1995; Rob McPherson (Assoc.) 1994-1999; John Ross Thompson 1995-1998; Robert L. Hinklin 1998-2001; Cathy Rafferty (Assoc.) 1999-2001; Gerald L. Toshalis 2001-; James Edward Hodge (Assoc.) 2001-2005; Thomas M. Pier-Fitzgerald 2005-

Grant Center UMC – *Heartland District*

David A. Cheyne 1977-1982; Wesley E. Smith 1982-Feb.1984; Martin D. Fox May 1984-Sept. 1986; Nelson Ray Dec. 1986-1988; Michael Nicholson 1988-Dec. 1991; Paul Patterson (ret.) Jan.-June 1992; Deborah R. Miller June 1, 1992-1995; Wayne McKinney (DSA) 1995-July 31, 2002; Timothy W. Doubblestein Sept. 1, 2002-Sept. 15, 2003; Sueann K. Hagan Oct. 16, 2003-2006; Michael J. Simon 2006-2010; Lyle J. Ball (DSA) 2010; Lyle J. Ball Nov. 1, 2010-

Grant UMC – *Grand Traverse District*

Marion Nye 1966-1970; Silas H. Foltz 1970-1971; Lewis (Bud) Buckner 1972-1978; Wayne Babcock 1978-1983; Beverly Prestwood-Taylor 1983-1986; Beverly Prestwood Taylor (3/4 time) 1986-May 1988; Bruce Prestwood-Taylor (3/4 time) 1986-May 1988; Bruce Kintigh 1988-1993; Brian F. Rafferty 1993-1999; Craig South 1999-2002; James L. Breithaupt (1/4 time) 2002-2004; James L. Breithaupt (1/2 time) 2004-Mar. 15, 2006; Carl Greene, Mar. 15, 2006-2011; Robert W. Stark (DSA) 2011; Colleen A. Wierman (1/4 time) Nov. 27, 2011- [Brethren Epworth / Grant became single-point charges 2014]

Grass Lake UMC – *Albion District*

Kenneth Harris Dec. 1966-1969; Dale Culver 1969-Dec. 1972; Charles Grauer Jan. 1973-1976; Howard McDonald 1976-1979; Kenneth Lindland 1979-Sept. 1983; Gregory Wolfe Nov. 1983-1994; Stanley L. Hayes 1994-1999; Larry W. Rubingh 1999-2007; D. Gunnar Carlson 2007-2010; Esther Barton (DSA) 2010-2012; Dennis E. Slattery (DSA) (1/4 time) 2012-

Grawn UMC – *Grand Traverse District*

Carter Miller 1968-1969; Richard LaCicero 1969-Nov. 1970; Russell J. Lautner Nov. 1970-1982; Don Spachman 1982-1992; Michael E. Long 1992-1996; Daniel W. Biteman, Jr. 1996-2006; Margaret Halls Wilson 2006-Nov. 1, 2009; Mary S. Brown, Nov. 1, 2009-2014; Colleen A. Wierman (1/2 time) 2014-

Greenbush UMC – *Heartland District*

William Tate 1967-1969; Robert Boyer 1969-1970; Charles VanLente 1970-1972; Everett Love June-Dec. 1972; Norman Wood 1973-1976; Terry MacArthur 1976-Oct. 15, 1979; Robert Gillette Jan. 1980-1984; Merritt Bongard 1984-1991; Joseph Spackman 1991-1999; James Dibbet 1999-2005; O'Ryan Rickard 2005-2006; Jon L. Pohl 2006-2011; Mona J. Dye 2011-

Greensky Hill UMC – *Grand Traverse District*

Leona Winegarden 1965-1969; Elmer J. Faust 1969-1975; Austin Regier 1975-1981; David Yingling 1981-1988; Benton R. Heisler 1988-Nov. 15, 1992; Dale Peter Ostema Feb. 1, 1993-Feb. 1, 1998; Kathryn S. Slaughter Feb. 1, 1998-2000; Geraldine M. Litchfield 2000-2005; Timothy B. Wright 2005-2013; [became single-point charge 2013] Jonathan D. Mays (DSA) 2013-

Greenville First UMC – *Heartland District*

Darwin R. Salisbury 1964-March 1970; Howard A. Smith March 1970-1972; Harold A. Jayne 1972-Sept. 1977; Kenneth W. Karlzen Sept. 1977-March 1982; Harold L. Mann March 1982-1988; Laren J. Strait (Assoc.) 1980-; Harry R. Johnson 1988-2007; Joy Jittaun Moore 2007-2008; Stephen MG Charnley 2008-14; Stephen F. Lindeman 2013-14; Kimberly A. DeLong (Deacon) 2013- [Greenville First, Turk Lake/Belding Cooperative Parish 2013] Donald E. Spachman 2014-

Gresham UMC – *Lansing District*

David C. Haney 1967-1969; William R. Tate 1969-1972; Gary V. Lyons 1972-April 1976; Gerald A. Salisbury April 1976-1979; Molly C. Turner 1979-1983; Glenn C. Litchfield 1983-1990; Richard W. Young 1990-1991; Robert L. Kersten 1991-1995; Jeffrey J. Bowman 1995-2002; Kathleen Smith 2002-Dec. 31, 2012; [Vermontville/Gresham no longer two-point charge 2013] [Barry-Eaton Cooperative Ministry 2013] Bryce E. Feighner 2013-

Griffith UMC – *Albion District*
Lambert G. McClintic 1952-1995; Jack Fugate 1995-July 15, 2008; Charlene A. Minger (1/4 time) 2009-2013; David H. Minger (Retired) (1/4 time) 2013-

Grovenburg UMC – *Lansing District*
Maurice Glasgow 1966-1978; Paul Mergener (Assoc.) 1976-Oct. 1978; Joseph Huston Oct. 1978-Oct. 1981; Paul Wehner Oct. 1981-1986; Marty DeBow 1986-1990; Kyewoon Choi 1990-1997; Melanie S. Young 1997-1998; Richard J. Duffey 1998-2005; Andrew L. Croel 2005-2008; Kimberly A. Tallent 2008-2009; Joseph D. Huston (DSA) 2009-

Gull Lake UMC – *Kalamazoo District*
Keith Heifner Sept. 1980-1981; Edward C. Ross 1981-1994; Stephen M.G. Charnley 1994-2008; Susan M. Petro (Assoc.) 1994-Dec. 31, 1997; Dianne Doten Morrison (Assoc.) 1998-Feb. 1, 2001; David Nellist 2008-2010; Mona K. Joslyn 2010-

Gunnisonville UMC – *Lansing District*
Stephen Beach 1968-1969; Edward F. Otto 1969-Dec. 1972; Daniel Miles Dec. 1972-1974; Paul K. Scheibner 1974-1978; J. Lynn Pier-Fitzgerald 1978-May 1984; Thomas M. Pier-Fitzgerald (co-pastor) 1982-May 1984; Charles W. Smith May 1984-1988; Carl W. Staser 1988-Jan. 1991; Thomas Peters Jan. 1, 1991-1993; Raymond D. Field 1993-1998; Nancy L. Besemer 1998-2003; Thomas L. Truby Oct. 15, 2003-2006; Beatrice K. Robinson 2006-2007; Mark G. Johnson 2007-

Harbor Springs UMC – *Grand Traverse District*
Phillip Howell 1968-1971; Philip Brown 1971-1977; Milton TenHave 1977-1979; Richard Matson 1979-1987; Catherine Kelsey 1987-1990; Claudette Haney 1990-April 1993; Birt A. Beers May 1993-1995; Lawrence R. Wood 1995-2003; Kathryn S. Cadarette 2003-2011; Mary A. Sweet 2011-2014; Vaughn Thurston-Cox 2014- ; [Epsilon/New Hope/Harbor Springs/Alanson became a 4-point charge 2014] Hillary Thurston-Cox (Assoc.) 2014-

Harrietta UMC – *Grand Traverse District*
Ward Pierce 1967-1972; Bill Amundsen 1972-1979; Jean Crabtree 1979-Aug. 1980; Donald Buege Sept. 1980-Jan. 1984; Bruce Prestwood-Taylor Jan. 1984-1986; Thomas P. Fox 1986-1992; Charles A. Williams 1992-Feb 14, 1997; J. David Thompson Nov. 16, 1997-2001; John J. Conklin (DSA) 2001-Nov. 30, 2001; John J. Conklin Dec. 1, 2001-2009; Mona L. Kindel 2009-2012; Beverley Williams 2012-

Harrison: The Gathering – *Heartland District*
[new church start 2004; mission congregation 2009; became 3-point charge: The Gathering (WMAC) & Wagarville/Wooden Shoe UMCs (DAC-Saginaw District) 2009] James C. Noggle 2004-2010; Michael J. Simon 2010-2013; Kellas D. Penny (1/2 time) July 1-Dec.31, 2013; Vincent J. Nader May 1, 2014-

Hart UMC – *Grand Traverse District*
Theron Bailey 1966-Dec. 1969; Edward Passenger Dec. 1969-1971; Jack Kraklan 1971-1979; Lloyd Walker 1979-1982; Kenneth Snow 1982-1989; Laurie Haller 1989-1993; Bruce R. Kintigh 1993-Jan. 1, 1999; Harvey Prochnau Feb. 1, 1999-2003; Ben Bill Lester 2003-2011; Rebecca Farrester Wieringa 2011-

Hartford UMC – *Kalamazoo District*
Morris Reinhart 1967-1972; Jean Crabtree 1972-1979; John Hice 1979-1987; David L. Crawford 1987-1990; Gerald L. Selleck 1990-1998; Richard A. Powell 1998-1999; Ronald W. Hansen 1999-2011; Jeffrey C. Williams 2011-2014; Rey Mondragon 2014-

Hastings First UMC – *Lansing District*
Emeral Price 1967-March 1969; Stanley Buck April 1969-Dec. 1972; Sidney Short Jan. 1973-1982; Myron Williams 1982-May 1985; David Nelson 1985-1989; Philip L. Brown 1989-1994; Bufford W. Coe 1994-Oct. 15, 2000; Kathy E. Brown Feb. 1, 2001-2010; Donald E. Spachman 2010-2014; Mark R. Payne 2014-

Hastings Hope UMC – *Lansing District*
Kenneth Vaught 1968-January 1983; Jack Bartholomew February 1983-February1986; Robert Mayo April 1986-1992; James E. Fox 1992-1995; Laurence E. Hubley 1995-2000; Richard D. Moore 2000-

Heritage UMC – *Heartland District*
Richard D. Moore Aug. 1 1999-2000; Mark Mitchell (Assoc.) Aug. 1, 1999-2000; Thomas E. Ball 2000-2007; James Bradley Brillhart, 2007-2014; Stephan Weinberger 2014-

Hersey UMC – *Heartland District*
Otto Flachsmann 1964-1969; M.K. Matter 1969-1977; David A. Cheyne 1977-1982; Wesley E. Smith 1982-1984; Martin D. Fox 1984-Sept. 1986; Nelson Ray Dec. 1986-1988; Cynthia A. Skutar 1988-1992; Timothy J. Miller 1992-1994; Pulpit Supply July 1994; John G. Kasper Aug. 1, 1994-2001; Raymond D. Field 2001-2003; Lawrence A. Nichols 2003-2010; Mary Beth Rhine 2010-2012; Lemuel O. Granada (1/4 time) July 29, 2012-

Hesperia UMC – *Grand Rapids District*
Merlin Delo 1966-1978; William Bowers 1978-1980; David Dryer 1980-1984; Richard Williams 1984-Oct. 1, 1997; Pulpit Supply Oct. 1, 1997 - Dec. 31, 1997; Susan Olsen Jan. 1, 1998-July 1, 1998; Raymond D. Field 1998-1999; James Bradley Brillhart 1999-2007; Dianne D. Morrison 2007-2011; Richard D. Morrison (DSA) 2007-2011; Paul E. Hane 2011-

Hillsdale First UMC – *Albion District*
John Francis 1968-1971; David S. Evans 1971-1979; William V. Payne 1979-1987; David A. Selleck 1987-Dec. 1988; Hugh C. White (Interim) Dec. 1988-1989; Gary L. Bekofske 1989-1996; Mark G. Johnson 1996-2003; Curtis Eugene Jensen 2003-2010; Patricia L. Brook 2010-

Hillside UMC – *Albion District*
Eugene Lewis 1966-1972; Paul Mazur 1972-1974; Tom Jones 74-78; Jon Powers 78-81; Larry Wiliford 81-83; Lawrence Hodge 1983-1991; Laurence E. Hubley 1991-1995; David A. Cheyne 1995-1998; Marilyn B. Barney 1998-2008; Denise J. Downs 2008-2009; [Hillside/Somerset Center two-point charge 2009] E. Jeanne Koughns 2009-2014; Patricia A. Pebley 2014-

Hinchman UMC – *Kalamazoo District*
Robert Strauss 1968-1981; Valerie Hill 1981-March 1983; Leonard Haynes 1983-1986; Leo Bennett 1986-1989; Walter J. Rothfuss 1989-2000; Brenda Gordon 2000-2006; Jane D. Logston (part-time) 2006-14; [Berrien Springs / Hinchman / Oronoko became 3-point charge 2012] [Hinchman / Oronoko became 2-point charge 2014] Linda R. Gordon 2014-

Holland First UMC – *Grand Rapids District*
Hilding W. Kilgren 1963-1970; Paul E. Robinson (Assoc.) 1965-1972; Darwin R. Salisbury 1970-1977; Brent Phillips (Assoc.) 1972-1973; John L. Francis 1977-1987; William C. Johnson (Assoc.) 1977-1981; Heath T. Goodwin (part-time) 1981-1983; Robert S. Treat (part-time) 1983-1988; Harold F. Filbrandt 1987-1990; Susan J. Hagans (Assoc.) 1988-1995; John W. Ellinger 1990-1996; Beatrice K. Rose (Assoc.) 1995-1998; William E. Dobbs 1996-2005; R. John Thompson (Assoc.) 1998-Apr. 1, 2001; Karen A. Tompkins (Assoc.) 1998-2003; Todd J. Query (Deacon) 2003-2006; J. Lynn Pier-Fitzgerald 2005- ; Janice T. Lancaster (Assoc. Pastor of Congregational Care) 2010-Jan. 30, 2014

Holt UMC – *Lansing District*
Philip R. Glotfelty, Jr. 1964-1970; Douglas A. Smih 1970-1972; Myron K. Williams 1972-1982; Dennis Buwalda 1982-1989; Joseph D. Huston 1989-1999; Barbara J. Flory (Assoc.) 1998-2000; Lynn E. Grimes 1999-2006; Glenn M. Wagner 2006-2014; Mark R. Erbes 2014-

Holton UMC – *Grand Rapids District*
Ira J. Noordhof 1967-1975; Donald Vuurens 1975-Jan. 1978; Pulpit Supply Jan.-June 1978; Charles Van Lente 1978-1983; David McBride 1983-1988; Larry Rubingh 1988-Dec. 1991; Pulpit Supply Jan.-June 1992; Kenneth Bremer 1992-2006; Gerald Selleck 2006-

Homer UMC – *Albion District*
Ronald Wise 1968-1969; Orvel Lundberg 1969-1970; E. Lenton Sutcliffe 1970-1971; Daniel D. Corl 1971-1973; John T. Charter 1973-1978; Harold Deipert 1978-1983; Walter Rothfuss 1983-1987; Linda Farmer-Lewis Sept. 1987-Dec. 1992; Claudette Haney Apr. 16, 1993-1995; Nelson Ray 1995-1997; Linda J. Burson 1997-Jan. 1, 2000; Mark Mitchell 2000-2008; Thomas P. Fox 2008-2012; Robert P. Stover (DSA) 2012-

Hopkins UMC – *Kalamazoo District*

Glenn Britton 1968-Jan. 1970; Stanley Finkbeiner Feb. 1970-1974; Densel Fuller 1974-1976; Brent Phillips 1976-1978; David Knapp 1978-Oct. 15, 1982; Robert J. Stillson Nov. 1982-1989; Robert D. Nystrom 1989-1992; Marjory A. Berkompas 1992-June 13, 1996; David S. Yoh (DSA) 1996-1999; Raymond D. Field 1999-2001; Reva H. Daniel 2001-2005; Linda J. Burton 2005-2014; Dominic A. Tommy 2014-

Horton Bay UMC – *Grand Traverse District*

Seward Walton 1968-1976; John Gurney 1976-1978; Steve Tower 1978-1979; Carl Staser 1979-1980; Allen Valkema 1980-1982; Martin Fox 1982-1984; Craig Adams 1984-1994; Kathryn S. Slaughter 1994-2000; Geraldine M. Litchfield 2000-2005; Timothy B. Wright 2005-2013; [became single-point charge 2013] Michael R. Neihardt (1/4 time) 2013- ; [Boyne City/Boyne Falls/Horton Bay became a 3-point charge 2014]

Indian River UMC – *Grand Traverse District*

Gerald Janousek 1968-1970; Argle Leesler 1970-1972; Robert Elder 1972-1976; Morris Reinhart 1976-1984; Steve Weinberger 1984-1990; Larry Mannino 1990-1994; John D. Lover 1994-2000; Gary G. Step 2000-2012; O. Jay Kendall (Assoc.) 2007-Aug. 31, 2012; DeAnn J. Dobbs 2012-2014; Patricia A. Harpole 2014-

Ionia Easton UMC – *Heartland District*

George W. Chaffee 1971-1974; Nolan Williams 1974-Oct. 1980; Eldon Schram Oct. 1980-Sept. 1984; Kathryn M. Williams Sept. 1984-Nov. 1986; Kathryn M. Coombs Nov. 1986-1990; Scott K. Otis 1990-1993; David J. Blincoe 1993-Aug. 15, 1994; Supplied by Presbyterian Church Sept. 1994; Don Wells (Presbyterian) 1995-Jan. 6, 1999; Judy K. Downing 1999-2001; Lynn W. Wagner 2001-Sept. 1, 2002; Paul F. Bailey (DSA) April 13, 2003; Thomas R. Reaume Sept 1, 2004-Jan. 1, 2007; Nancy J. Patera, Jan. 1, 2007-2014; Donna Jean Sperry (DSA) 2014-

Ionia First UMC – *Heartland District*

Lester C. Bailey 1964-1970; Charles W. Fullmer 1970-1977; Carl L. Hausermann 1977-1983; John F. Sorensen 1983-1985; Keith A. Bovee 1985-1991; Lawrence E. Hodge 1991-2000; Martin H. Culver 2000-2006; Lawrence P. Brown 2006-2014; Jonathan D. Van Dop 2014-

Ionia Zion UMC – *Heartland District*

Chester Erickson 1967-1971; George Chaffee 1971-1974; Nolan Williams 1974-Oct. 1980; Eldon Schram Oct. 1980-1984; Kathryn Williams (Coombs) 1984-Sept. 1986; William Dornbush Nov. 1986-Dec. 31, 1993; Pulpit Supply Jan. 1- June 30, 1994; Craig L. Adams 1994-Sept. 15, 1999; Arlo Vandlen (DSA) Jan. 24, 2000-2001; Donald Graham 2001-2007; Cliff Allen (DSA) 2007; Cliff Allen, Nov. 10, 2007-

Ithaca UMC – *Heartland District*

John F. Sorensen 1967-1972; David B. Nelson, Jr. 1972-1980; Nolan R. Williams 1980-1991; David L. McBride 1991-2006; Steven R. Young 2006-2010; Cynthia Greene 2010-

Jackson Brookside UMC – *Albion District*

Verne Summers 1966-Aug. 1974; Verner Kilgren Sept. 1974-Sept. 15, 1978; William Torrey Sept. 15, 1978-1985; Richard Johns 1985-1992; David L. Johnston 1992-2005; Charles Campbell July 15, 2005-Sept 1, 2005; Chad M. Parmalee Sept 1, 2005-2013; Ronald K. Brooks 2013-

Jackson Calvary UMC – *Albion District*

J. Leon Andrews 1968-1972; Haven UMC merged with Calvary in 1972; Donald P. Sailor 1972-1977; Claude Ridley 1977-1983; Carl L. Hausermann 1983-1989; George R. Grettenberger 1989-1992; Timothy P. Boal 1992-1997; Linda J. Carlson (Assoc.) 1993-Feb. 16, 1999; Michael T. Conklin 1999-2003; Maurice E. Walworth, Jr. 2003-2006; Linda H. Hollies 2006-Aug. 18, 2007; Lillian T. French Jan. 1, 2008-Sept. 1, 2010; Edrye Maurer Sept. 1, 2010- [Jackson Calvary & Zion became two-point charge 2013]

Jackson First UMC – *Albion District*

Robert C. Smith 1966-1971; E. Lenten Sutcliffe (Assoc.) 1968-1971; Richard A. Morrison (Assoc.) 1969-1971; Merle D. Broyles 1971-1981; Wilbur A. Williams (Assoc.) 1971-1973; David C. Brown (Assoc.) 1971-1973; Ivon Gonsor (Assoc.) 1973-1974; George Chaffee (Assoc.) 1974-1984; John Ellinger (Assoc.) Jan. 1972-1976; Richard Erickson (Assoc.) 1976-1982; Larry Taylor 1981-1987; David Morton (Assoc.) 1982-1986; Ted Cole (Assoc.) 1984-1986; Linda Farmer-Lewis (Assoc.) 1986-1987; David Knapp (Assoc.) 1986-1989; Joy Moore 1988-1990; John Cermak 1987-1994; Leo E. Bennett (Assoc.) 1989-1993; Donette Bourke (Deacon) 1990- 2003; John D. Morse (Assoc.) 1993-1999; Edward C. Ross 1994-; Sanda Sanganza (Assoc.) 1999-2001; Charles Campbell (Assoc.) 2003-2007; Susan Babb (Assoc.) 2004- ; Mark Babb (Deacon-Spiritual Formation Consultant) June 1, 2010- ; Eric S. Beck 2012-

Jackson Trinity UMC – *Albion District*

(Jackson Trinity is a merged congregation of Greenwood Ave. UMC, Greenwood Park EUB and Francis Street EUB); James Crosby 1968-1969; Harold Kirkenbauer 1968-1969; Harold Taber 1969-1972; Dale Crawford 1972-1977; B. James Varner 1977-1986; Karen Slager Wheat 1986-1998; Beatrice K. Robinson 1998-2006; [Jackson Trinity / Parma became a charge 2006] Sandra L. Spahr (DSA) 2006-2007; Melodye Surgeon Rider 2007-2012; Patricia A. Pebley (1/2 time) 2012-2014; [Jackson Trinity became single-point charge 2014] Robert Q. Bailey (Retired) 2014-

Jackson Zion UMC – *Albion District*

Amos R. Bogart Jan. 1968-1969; Frederick W. Werth 1969-1971; Charles R. Campbell 1971-1981; D. David Ward 1981-Jan. 7, 1994; Lawrence A. Nichols Feb. 1, 1994-2003; Donald R. Wendell July 15, 2003-Mar. 15, 2006; William Lang (DSA), Oct. 1, 2006-2007; [Pleasant Lake & Jackson Zion became two-point charge 2008] David H. Minger (DSA) 2008-2013; [Jackson Calvary & Zion became two-point charge 2013] Edrye A. Eastman Maurer 2013-

Jerome UMC – *Albion District*

Kenneth W. Karlzen 1968-1971; Thomas R. Jones 1971-Aug. 1974; David Flagel Sept. 1975-1980; Lee F. Zachman 1980-1984; Donald McLellan 1984-Sept. 1988; Melanie Baker-Streevy Oct. 1988-1995; Rochelle Ray 1995-2000; Tim Doubblestein 2000-Aug. 31, 2002; Charles Richards Sept. 1-Dec. 31, 2002; Paul Hane Jan. 1, 2003-2011; Kimberly A. Metzger July 1-Dec. 19, 2011; Arthur R. Turner (DSA) Feb. 1, 2012-2014; Timothy R. Puckett 2014-

Jonesville UMC – *Albion District*

Densel Fuller 1968-1974; William Johnson 1974-1977; Derryl Cook 1977-1978; M. John Palmer 1978-1982; Lloyd Walker 1982-1985; Jack Kraklan 1985-1988; Michael Baker-Streevy 1988-1995; Reva Hawke 1995-1997; Nelson Ray 1997-2000; Craig Pahl 2000-2014; [Jonesville/Allen became single charges 2014] Jennifer Ward (DSA) 2014-

Kalamazoo First UMC – *Kalamazoo District*

James W. Wright 1964-1972; J. Melvin Bricker (Assoc.) 1966-1971; O. Lavern Merritt (Assoc.) 1968-1970; Ray R. Fassett (Assoc.) 1970-1974; Hoover Rupert 1972-1983; Douglas W. Vernon (Assoc.) 1971-1974; Marvin Zimmerman (Assoc.) 1974-1976; Donald Ludman (Assoc.) 1974-1978; William Richards (Assoc.) 1976-1979; Richard Beckett (Assoc.) 1977-1987; Mac Kelly (Assoc.) 1978-1982; Wayne Reece (Assoc.) 1979-1985; Gerald Selleck (Assoc.) 1982-1984; Royal Synwolt 1983-1991; Jane Shapley (Assoc.) 1985-1987; Dean Francis (Assoc.) 1985-1990; Richard Rossiter (Assoc.) 1987-1992; George Hartmann (Assoc.) 1987-1994; Keith Treman (Assoc.) 1990-1998; Kenneth McCaw 1991-Jan. 1, 2000; Cynthia A. Skutar (Assoc.) 1992-1997; Cynthia M. Schaefer (Assoc.) 1997-2001; Michelle Wisdom-Long (Assoc.) 1998-2000; Ron Keller (interim senior pastor) Jan. 1, 2000-July 1, 2000; Douglas W. Vernon 2000-2010; Dale A. Hotelling (Assoc.) July 16, 2000-2004; Matthew J. Bistayi (Assoc.) 2002-2006; Julie Dix (Assoc.) 2006-2010; John W. Boley 2010-2014; Michelle M. Wisdom-Long (Assoc.) 2010-2011; Stephen MG Charnley 2014-

Kalamazoo Milwood UMC – *Kalamazoo District*

Richard C. Miles 1966-1970; Heath T. Goodwin 1970-1971; Alden B. Burns 1971-Dec. 1981; John H. Hice (Assoc.) 1977-1979; Ron L. Keller Jan. 1982-1988; James M. Morgan 1988-1999; Robert K. Lynch 1999-2006; Martin H. Culver 2006-2011; Kennetha J. Bigham-Tsai 2011-2013; Heather A. McDougall 2013-

Kalamazoo Stockbridge Avenue UMC – *Kalamazoo District*
Lloyd Schloop 1968-1973; Kenneth O. Lindland 1973-1977; Charles W. Richards 1977-1986; Curtis Strader 1986-1988; John Moore 1988-1992; Dwight J. Burton 1992-1998; John W. McNaughton 1998-2003; Calvin Y. Hill 2003-2007; John L. Moore (DSA) 2007-2010; Ronald D. Slager 2010-

Kalamazoo Sunnyside UMC – *Kalamazoo District*
Allen D. McCreedy 1967-1973; Robert H. Conn 1973-1976; John W. Ellinger 1976-1981; Norman C. Kohns 1981-1985; Paul L. Hartman 1985-1992; John W. Fisher 1992-2004; Billie R. Dalton 2004-Feb. 28, 2009; Linda J. Burson, Mar. 1-July 1, 2009; John Matthew Weiler (1/2 time) 2009- ; Cara Weiler (deacon 1/4 time) Oct. 1, 2009-

Kalamazoo Westwood UMC – *Kalamazoo District*
A.R. Davis 1968-1973; Allen D. McCreedy 1973-1977; E. William Wiltse 1977-1980; Merged with Kalamazoo Simpson 1980; Jack H. Baumgart 1980-1984; Larry E. Irvine 1984-1988; Kenneth W. Karlzen 1988-July 31, 1995; Eric S. Beck Aug. 1, 1995-2007; Wayne A. Price 2007- ; Sandra Douglas (Deacon) (1/4 time) 2011-

Kalamo UMC – *Lansing District*
Lowell F. Walsworth 1966-1971; Laurence R. Grubaugh 1971-1973; Milton J. Tenhave 1973-1977; David L. Johnston 1977-May 1983; James William Schoettle May 1983-1988; William P. Sanders 1988-Feb. 1996; Mark E. Thompson 1996-2004; Bryce Feighner 2004-2013; [Barry-Eaton Cooperative Ministry 2013] Dan Phillips 2013-

Kalkaska UMC – *Grand Traverse District*
Richard M. Riley 1984-1993; Charles R. VanLente 1993-1996; Charles K. Stanley 1996-Oct. 1, 1999; Stanley Lee Hayes (DSA) Oct. 1, 1999-July 1, 2000; Robert W. Stark 2000-2008; Gregory R. Wolfe 2008-2013; Robert J. Freysinger 2013-

Keeler UMC – *Kalamazoo District*
Meredith Rupe 1968-Nov. 1970; Gary E. Gamble Nov. 1970-1973; Supply pastor June-Oct. 1973; Lynn W. Wagner Oct. 1973-1975; Daniel R. Barker 1975-Sept. 1978; Gregory R. Wolfe Oct. 1978-Nov. 1983; Donald L. Buege Jan. 1984-1990; Dennis E. Slattery 1990-1992; David L. Litchfield 1992-1998; Virginia L. Heller 1998-2004; Mark E. Thompson 2004-2009; Julie A. Greyerbiehl 2009-2011; Heather McDougall 2011-2013; Beth A. Reum 2013-

Kendall UMC – *Kalamazoo District*
James Boehm 1967-1970; Allen Valkema 1970-1971; William Miles 1971-1974; Rudolph Wittenback 1974-1976; Karen S. Slager-Wheat 1976-1986; John McNaughton 1986-1987; Judy K. Downing 1987-1998; Susan Olsen 1998-2004; Mary Beth Rhine 2004-2010; Edward Mohr L. 2010-Sept. 11, 2012; Nelson L. Hall 2013-

Kent City Chapel Hill UMC – *Grand Rapids District*
Charles McNary 1964-1970; David Morton 1970-Jan. 1974; Stanley Finkbeiner 1974-1981; Ray Grienke 1981-1985; Willard Gilroy 1985-Oct. 1988; David Hainer Oct. 1988-March 1991; Mark Johnson May 1991-1996; Glenn C. Litchfield 1996-2005; R. John Thompson 2005-2010; Kevin Guetschow 2010-

Keswick UMC – *Grand Traverse District*
Dale Crawford 1968-Oct. 1971; Richard Kuhn Oct. 1971-1980; John Myette 1980-1984; Tom Evans 1984-1988; Wayne Gorsline 1988-1991; Martin H. Culver 1991-1999; Wayne A. Price 2000-2004; Donald E. Spachman 2004-2010; Charles A. Williams 2010-2011; Patricia A. Haas 2011-

Kewadin Indian Mission UMC – *Grand Traverse District*
Harry John Sr. Jan. 1975-1993; Owen White-Pigeon (DSA) 1993-1994; Cletus Marshall 1994-Feb. 5, 1995; Pulpit Supply Feb. 6-June 1995; Delfred White-Crow (DSA) 1995-Nov. 15, 1997; Delfred White-Crow (part-time) Nov. 16, 1997-Apr. 16, 1998; DSA Apr. 16, 1998; Thomas H. John Jr 1998-

Kewadin UMC – *Grand Traverse District*

Glenn Loy 1968-Sept. 1970; Russell Lautner (Assoc.) 1968-Oct. 1970; Gordon Showers Oct. 1970-Nov. 1971; Robert Doner Dec. 1971-1976; Bernard Randolph 1976-1978; Jack Bartholomew 1978-Feb. 1983; Stephen Beach Feb. 1983-Nov. 1986; Michael Baker-Streevy Dec. 1986-1988; Charles M. Shields 1988-1993; Raymond R. Sundell 1993-1998; Kathryn M. Coombs 1998-1999; Janilyn McConnell (Deacon) 1998-2003; Thomas M. Pier-Fitzgerald 1999-2005; William W. Chu & Julie A. Greyerbiehl (Chu) 2005-2009; Mary S. Brown July 1-Nov. 1, 2009; Eugene L. Baughan (DSA) Nov. 1, 2009-

Kingsley UMC – *Grand Traverse District*

Marion Nye 1966-1970; Silas H. Foltz 1970-1971; Lewis (Bud) Buckner 1972-1978; Wayne Babcock 1978-1983; Beverly Prestwood-Taylor 1983-1986; Beverly Prestwood Taylor (3/4 time) 1986-May 1988; Bruce Prestwood-Taylor (3/4 time) 1986-May 1988; Bruce Kintigh 1988-1993; Brian F. Rafferty 1993-1999; Charlene A. Minger 1999-2008; Gary S. Wales 2008-2013; Carl Q. Litchfield 2013- ; Colleen A. Wierman (Assoc.) (1/4 time) 2014-

Lacota UMC – *Kalamazoo District*

Robert Victor 1966-1969; John Hagans 1969-1974; Pulpit Supply 1974-1977; Joseph Pratt 1977-1980; Carl C. Nisbet 1980-Aug. 31, 2003; Donna Jean Keyte Sept. 1, 2003-Jan. 1, 2006; Michael A. Pinto (DSA) 2006; Michael A. Pinto 2007-

Lake Ann UMC – *Grand Traverse District*

Carter Miller 1966-1969; Richard LoCicero 1969-1970; Russell J. Lautner Oct. 1970-1982; William E. Haggard 1982-1989; Charles J. Towersey 1989-Apr. 15, 2008; James L. Breithaupt (Assoc. 1/2 time) 2004-Mar. 15, 2006; Devon R. Herrell June 15, 2008-2013; Michael J. Simon 2013-

Lake City UMC – *Grand Traverse District*

J. William Schoettle 1965-Feb. 1970; Leonard J. Yarlott Feb. 1970-1972; Ward D. Pierce 1972-Aug. 1976; Ross Bunce Aug. 1976-1979; Willard Gilroy 1979-1985; David L. Dryer 1985-1996; Jane A. Crabtree 1996-2000; Edrye (Eastman-Sealey) Maurer 2000-Sept. 1, 2010; Jean M. Smith Sept. 1, 2010-

Lake Odessa Central UMC – *Lansing District*

Marvin F. Zimmerman 1967-1974; William A. Hertel 1974-Sept. 1980; Steve Keller 1980-1984; Thurlan E. Meredith 1984-1986; Charles W. Richards 1986-1989; D. Keith Laidler 1989-1992; Emmett H. Kadwell, Jr. 1992-Jan. 1, 2000; Charles M. Shields Feb. 1, 2000-July 1, 2000; Donald R. Ferris 2000-2007; Eric S. Beck 2007-2012; Karen J. Sorden 2012-

Lake Odessa Lakewood UMC – *Lansing District*

Wilbur A. Williams 1967-1971; Charles A. Dunbar 1971-1978; James R. Hulett 1978-1985; Ward D. Pierce 1985-2001; Curtis E. Jensen 2001-2003; David Lee Flagel 2003-2013; James C. Noggle 2013-

Lakeside UMC – *Kalamazoo District*

Robert Carson 1958-1964; Laurence R. Grubaugh 1964-1968; John Bullock 1968-1974; Robert Pumfery 1974-1979; Pulpit Supply 1979-1981; Charles Tooman 1981-1982; Gregory Wood 1982-1985; B. Gordon Barry 1985-1988; Steven Pearson 1988-1990; Ruth Haynes-Merrifield 1990-1995; Sherri L. Swanson 1995-Sept. 1, 1999; George W. Lawton Sept. 1, 1999-

Lansing Asbury UMC – *Lansing District*

Douglas A. Smith 1960-1970; John S. Myette 1970-1978; Geoffrey L. Hayes 1978-1987; William A. Hertel 1987-1990; Charles F. Garrod 1990-Oct. 1992; Benton R. Heisler Nov. 1992-1997; Deborah M. Johnson 1997-2008; Martin M. DeBow 2008-2014; Bo Rin Cho 2014-

Lansing Central UMC – *Lansing District*

Howard A. Lyman Feb. 1967-1978; Francis F. Anderson (Assoc.) 1966-1970; Peter H. Kunnen (Assoc.) 1968-1970; Robert E. Betts (Assoc.) 1970-1974; Charles Grauer (Assoc.) 1970-1972; Paul L. Hartman (Assoc.) 1974-Jan. 1980; Samuel H. Evans (Assoc.) 1975-1977; Lloyd VanLente (Assoc.) 1977-1982; Neil F. Bintz 1978-1982; Robert H. Roth, Jr. (Assoc.) May 1980-1983; Sidney A. Short 1982-1993; James M. Gysel (Assoc.) 1983-1993; Lynn A. DeMoss 1993-1997; Pegg Ainslie (Assoc.) 1993-1997; John W. Boley 1997-2002; Russell F. McReynolds 2002-2007; Joseph D. Huston 2007-2009; Ronald K. Brooks 2009-2013; Linda J. Farmer-Lewis 2013-

Lansing Christ UMC – *Lansing District*

Wilson Tennant 1966-1969; Meinte Schuurmans (Assoc) 1966-1980; David L. Crawford 1969-1977; Thomas L. Weber (Assoc) 1974-1978; Donald P. Sailor 1977-February 1983; Clyde E. Miller April 1983-March 1987; Eric Burrows (Assoc) 1983-1984; Philip Simmons (Assoc) 1984-1985; James J. Walker (Assoc) 1985-1989; Richard A. Selleck March 1987-1992; Rebecca N. Niese (Assoc) 1991-October 31, 1994; Robert E. Jones 1992-1996; Maurice E. Walworth, Jr. 1996-2003; Charles David Grauer 2003-Dec. 31, 2012; Edward C. Ross (Interim), Jan. 1-June 30, 2013; Lyle D. Heaton 2013-

Lansing Faith & South Lansing Ministries – *Lansing District*

J. Edward Cherryholmes Apr. 1964-Apr. 1969; Richard E. Johns Apr. 1969-1980; David B. Nelson Jr. 1980-1985; John Palmer 1985-May 1987; Kenneth W. Bensen May 1987-2003; James A. Richie (Assoc.) 2000-2002; Cornelius Davis (Assoc. 1/4 time) 2003-2008; (Lansing Faith merged with South Lansing Ministries 2005); Russell F. McReynolds (DSA) 2008-

Lansing First UMC – *Lansing District*

Francis C. Johannides 1968-1972; John F. Sorensen 1972-Sept. 1978; Theron E. Bailey Sept. 1978-March 1982; Kenneth W. Karlzen March 1982-1988; Mark D. Graham 1988-1996; Robert L. Hundley 1996-2000; Stephan Weinberger 2000-2004; Melanie J. Baker 2004-2012; Lori J. Sykes July 15, 2012-

Lansing Grace UMC – *Lansing District*

Clarence W. Hutchens 1967-1975; Paul F. Albery 1975-1981; John W. Ellinger 1981-1985; David L. Johnston 1985-1992; Richard E. Johns 1992-1996; Gary L. Bekofske 1996-2005; Timothy P. Boal 2005-2006; Jane Ellen Johnson Jan. 1, 2007-

Lansing Korean UMC – *Lansing District*

Young Ho Ahn 1984-Sept. 1985; Chung Soon Chang Sept. 1985-1988; Hyo Nam Hwang Oct. 1988-1998; Jung Kee Lee 1998-Dec. 31, 2003; Bo Rin Cho Mar. 1, 2004-2014; Seok Nam Lin 2014-

Lansing Mt Hope UMC – *Lansing District*

Donald Merrill 1967-Oct. 1975; George Elliott Nov. 1975-1979; Lloyd Phillips 1979-1984; Robert Hinklin 1984-Feb. 1987; Wade Panse May 1987-Oct. 1992; Paul C. Frederick Dec. 1992-1999; Pamela J. Mathieu (Deacon) 1995- Ronald K. Brooks (Assoc.) 1998-1999; Ronald K. Brooks 1999-2000; Linda H. Hollies 2000-2001; William Earl Haggard 2002-2012; Lansing Calvary UMC merged w/ Mt. Hope UMC 07-01-07]; Colleen Treman (Deacon, Children's Coordinator) 2008- ; Rob Cook 2012-

Lansing Sycamore Creek UMC – *Lansing District*

[new church start 2000] Barbara J. Flory 2000-2009; Thomas F. Arthur 2009-

Lansing Trinity UMC – *Lansing District*

James E. Fox 1968-1971; Gerald R. Bates 1971-1979; Larry Sachua 1979-1989; Richard Williams (Assoc.) 1983-1985; Gregory Wood (Assoc.) 1985-1990; Dennis Buwalda 1989-1992; Paul C. Frederick (Assoc.) 1990-Dec. 1992; Leicester Longden 1992-2001; Linda J. Farmer-Lewis (Assoc.) Jan. 1993-1994; Joy J. Moore (Assoc.) 1995-1997; Cynthia S.L. Green (Assoc.) May 1, 1998-2004; Rae L. Franke (Deacon) 1998-2003; William Beachy 2001-2014; Steve J. Buck 2014-

Lansing Vietnamese UMC – *Lansing District*

Vinh Q. Tran, Jan. 1, 1986 - 2004; Cuong M. Nguyen 2004-2008; Tho Van Phan (DSA) 2009-Oct. 15, 2009

Lawrence UMC – *Kalamazoo District*

Kenneth Snow 1967-1972; Norman Crotser 1972-1976; George Gierman 1976-1979; Leo Bennett 1979-1986; Mark Johnson 1986-Apr. 1991; Ronald K. Brooks May 1991-1998; Wayne H. Babcock 1998-Dec. 31, 2002; David S. Yoh (DSA) Jan. 1, 2003-July 1, 2003; Jane D. Logston 2003-2006; Clifford L. Radtke 2006-

Lawton St Paul's UMC – *Kalamazoo District*

Donald Russell 1968-1971; Roger Nielson 1971-1974; Al Sprague 1974-1977; Diane Vale 1977-1980; Jeff Edwards 1980-1981; Dean Francis 1981-1985; Beverly Gaska 1985-1987; Billie R. Dalton 1987-1995; Claudette I. Haney 1995-2000; Ronald K. Brooks 2000-2006; Daniel W. Biteman 2006-2010; Peggy A. Boltz 2010-2011; Douglas W. Vernon (DSA) (1/4 time) 2011-2014; [LifeSpring/Lawton St. Paul's became 2-point charge 2014] Wayne E. McKenney 2014-

Leaton UMC – *Heartland District*

Paul Peet 1968-1969; Fred Fischer 1969-1978; David Meister 1978-1979; Pulpit Supply 1979-1980; Thomas Crossman 1980-1981; Pulpit Supply 1981-Jan. 1984; Dale Barry Jan.-Aug. 1984; Tim Girkin Oct.-Nov. 1984; Byron Coleman Nov. 1984-Jan. 1992; Connie Bongard Jan. 1992-1994; Thomas R. Jones (retired) 1994-July 31, 1999; Randall E. Roose (DSA) Aug. 1, 1999-2004; Susan D. Olsen July 16, 2004-2006; Sharyn K. Osmond Aug. 1, 2006-Nov. 30, 2008; Donald R. Wendell Nov. 30, 2008-Nov. 1, 2009; Craig L. Adams Dec. 1, 2009--2010; David Michael Palmer 2010-

Lee Center UMC – *Albion District*

Lynn Chapel 1965-March 1971; Beulah Poe March 1971-1976; Robert Doner 1976-1978; Joel Campbell 1978-1979; Ethel Stears 1979-Sept. 16, 1983; William Doubblestein Oct. 16, 1983-1987; Eugene Baughan 1987-1991; David H. Minger 1991-1995; Wayne Willer 1995-1996; Valerie Hill 1996-1998; David L. Litchfield 1998-2001; David Blair 2001-2003; Diane E. Stone 2004-2010; Irene L. Vittoz 2010-2014 [Lee Center UMC became single-point charge 7-1-10]; James Gysel (Retired) 2014-

Leighton UMC – *Grand Rapids District*

James Sherwood 1965-1972; Keith Laidler 1972-1977; Curtis Cruff July-Dec. 1977; Donald Vuurens Jan. 1978-1980; Richard W. McClain 1980-1986; Kenneth Vaught 1986-May 31, 1991; Raymond Townsend 1991-2006; David L. McBride 2006-

Leland UMC – *Grand Traverse District*

Elmer J. Faust 1966-1969; Edward Jones 1969-1971; Richard Kuhn Nov. 1971-1980; John Myette 1980-1984; Tom Evans 1984-Jan. 31, 1994; Doug L. Pedersen Feb. 16, 1994-1997; Joseph M. Graybill 1997-2011; Linda J. Farmer-Lewis 2011-2013; Virginia L. Heller 2013-2014; Daniel B. Hofmann 2014-

Leslie UMC – *Lansing District*

William Wurzel 1966-1969; Gordon E. Spalenka June-Oct. 1969; Arthur A. Jackson Oct. 1969-1972; Wayne E. Sparks 1972-1975; James M. Morgan 1975-1982; Max J. Gladding 1982-1990; Clinton McKinven-Copus 1990-Oct. 1991; Reva Hawke Oct. 1991-April 1993; Derek DeToni-Hill 1993-Oct. 15, 1999; Janet Sweet-Richardson Nov. 1, 1999-2003; Carroll Arthur Fowler 2003-Jan. 1, 2006; Donald L. Buege Jan. 15, 2006-2014; Kelly M. Wasnich 2014-

LeValley UMC – *Heartland District*

Luther Brokaw 1967-1971; Donald Fry 1971-1973; Lloyd Walker 1973-Aug. 1979; Willis Braun Aug. 16, 1979-Feb. 1989; David L. Flagel March 1989-2003; Mark G. Johnson 2003-2007; Dennis E. Slattery 2007-2012; Raymond R. Sundell 2012-

LifeSpring UMC – *Kalamazoo District*

[new church start 2001] Mark R. Payne 2001-2009; Patricia A. Harpole 2009-2014; [LifeSpring/Lawton St. Paul's became 2-point charge 2014] Wayne E. McKenney 2014-

Lincoln Road UMC – *Heartland District*

John Buckner 1966-1972; Eldon Schram 1973-1977; Marvin Iseminger 1977-1979; Milton TenHave 1979-1986; Jane Lippert 1986-1990; Beatrice Rose 1990-1995; Kenneth C. Reeves 1995-1997; Lois M. Munn 1997-2000; Charles M. Shields 2000-2002; Nancy J. Bitterling 2002-2010; Jana Lynn Almeida 2010-

Litchfield UMC – *Albion District*

Dorr Garrett 1968-1970; Peter Kunnen 1970-1972; Morris Reinhart 1972-1976; Stephen Keller 1976-Dec. 1979; Paul Hartman Jan. 1980-1985; David Meister 1985-March 1990; Kathy Brown 1990-Feb. 1, 2001; R. John Thompson Apr. 1, 2001-2005; Carl Q. Litchfield 2005-2009; [Litchfield/Quincy two-point charge 2009] Michael P. Baker-Streevy 2009-2010; Martin T. Cobb 2010-2013; Julie Elmore 2013-

Lowe UMC – *Heartland District*

William Tate 1967-1969; Robert Boyer 1969-1970; Charles VanLente 1970-1972; Everett Love June-Dec. 1972; Harold McGuire 1973-1974; Terry MacArthur 1976-Oct. 15, 1979; Robert Gillette Jan. 1980-1984; Merritt Bongard 1984-1991; Joseph Spackman 1991-1999; James Dibbet 1999-2005; O'Ryan Rickard 2005-2007; Kathryn L. Leydorf (DSA) 2007; Kathryn L. Leydorf Nov. 10, 2007-[Salem/Maple Rapids/Lowe charge re-aligned 5-1-14 to Maple Rapids/Lowe charge]

Lowell UMC – *Grand Rapids District*

G. Robert Webber 1965-1969; Hartwell Gosney (Assoc.) 1968-Oct. 1972; Dean E. Bailey 1969-1979; Gerald R. Bates 1979-Apr. 1982; Donald L. Buege (Assoc.) 1979-Aug. 1980; Beulah P. Poe (Assoc.) Sept. 1980-1982; William J. Amundsen 1982-1993; B. Gordon Barry 1993-2003; Michael T. Conklin 2003-2008; Richard W. Blunt 2008-2014; Cheryl A. Mulligan (Deacon) Jan. 1, 2014- ; James Bradley Brillhart 2014-

Ludington St Paul UMC – *Grand Traverse District*

Jack Kraklan 1967-1971; Bernard Randolph 1971-1974; Forest Crum 1974-1981; Ray D. Flessner 1981-1989; Robert P. Stover 1989-1998; Dennis E. Slattery 1998-2007; Robert J. Henning 2007-2011; Jon L. Pohl 2011-

Ludington United UMC – *Grand Traverse District*

Harold F. Filbrandt 1967-1974; William J. Torrey 1974-1978; John F. Sorensen Sept. 15, 1978-1983; William D. Dobbs 1983-1991; Laurie A. Haller (Assoc.) 1985-1989; Paul E. Lowley 1991-2000; Betty A. Smith (Assoc.) 1990-1992; Joe D. Elenbaas 2000-Nov 30, 2006; Kenneth E. Tabor (Assoc.) 2004-2010; Thomas J. Evans 2007-2013; Dennis B. Bromley 2013-

Luther UMC – *Grand Traverse District*

David Dryer 1968-1974; Ilona Sabo-Schuler 1974-1977; Robert Boyer 1977-1979; Harold Simon 1979-1983; Mark Gaylord-Miles 1983-Dec. 1984; Pulpit Supply Jan.-June 1985; Douglas Kokx 1985-1991; Robert Stark 1991-April 1993; Reva Hawke May 1993-1995; Mary S. Brown 1995-Oct. 15, 1998; David A. Cheyne Jan. 16, 1999-June 30, 1999; Nelson Hall 1999-2005; Karen J. Sorden 2005-2012; James A. Richie 2012-

Lyon Lake UMC – *Albion District*

A. Ray Noland Sept. 1968-1973; John T. Charter 1973-1978; Harold Deipert 1978-1983; Walter Rothfuss1983-1987; Linda Farmer-Lewis Sept. 1987-Dec. 1992; Claudette Haney April 16, 1993-1995, Nelson Ray 1995-1997; Linda J. Burson 1997-Jan. 1, 2000; Mark Mitchell 2000-2008; Thomas P. Fox 2008-2012; Robert P. Stover (DSA) 2012-

Lyons-Muir Church – *Heartland District*

Richard Strait 1972-1977; George Matter 1977-1979; Howard McDonald 1979-1982; Byron Coleman 1982-1984; Bette Dobie 1984-1988; Scott Otis 1988-1993; David J. Blincoe 1993-Aug. 15, 1994; Supplied by Presbyterian Church Sept. 1994; Don Wells (Presbyterian) 1995-Jan. 6, 1999; Judy K. Downing 1999-2001; Lynn W. Wagner 2001-Sept. 1, 2002; Kathy Jean Clark Aug. 1, 2003-?Jan. 1,2005; Forrest B. Nelson Jan. 1, 2005-

Mancelona UMC – *Grand Traverse District*

M. Helen Jackson 1968-1972; George Gierman 1972-1975; Curtis Jensen 1975-1983; Timothy Graham 1983-1990; Gary Coates 1990-Aug. 1991; Pulpit Supply Sept.-Oct. 1991; Wayne Gorsline Nov. 1991-June 15, 1992; John W. Boley June 16, 1992-1997; Carolyn C. Floyd 1997-2000; Kathryn M. Steen 2000-2007; Stephan Weinberger 2007-2010; Zawdie K. Abiade July 1-July 4, 2010; Todd Shafer (DSA) July 15, 2010; Todd Shafer Nov. 1, 2010-

Manistee UMC – *Grand Traverse District*

Carleton A. Benson Sept. 1968-1971; Richard M. Wilson 1971-1980; Gilbert B. Heaton 1980-1982; Richard R. Erickson 1982-1990; Gregory B. Wood 1990-1998; Gerald L. Selleck 1998-2002; Jerry Lee Jaquish 2002-2012; David A. Selleck 2012-

Manton UMC – *Grand Traverse District*

Eduard Eidens 1967-1969; J. William Schoette 1969-1970; Leonard J. Yarlott 1970-1971; Arthur R. Turner 1971-1976; Molly C. Turner (Assoc.) 1971-1976; Norman Charter 1976-1977; J.T. Wood 1977-1981; Deborah Johnson 1981-1985; Laurie McKinven-Copus 1985-1987; Louis W. Grettenberger 1987-1993; Richard W. Blunt 1993-Feb. 1, 1999; Linda J. Carlson Feb. 16, 1999-2009; Beth A. Reum 2009-2013; Noreen S. Shafer 2013-

Maple Rapids UMC – *Heartland District*

William Tate 1967-1969; Robert Boyer 1969-Feb. 1970; Charles VanLente Feb. 1970-May 1972; Abe Caster May 1972-Jan. 1973; Eldon Schram Feb.-June 1973; J. Thomas Churn 1973-1979; Richard Whale 1979-1980; Richard Riley 1980-1984; Lyle Heaton 1984-1990; Tim Wohlford 1990-1991; Carolyn Robinson 1991-1997; Charles D. Farnum 1997-2001; Martin Cobb 2001-2006; O'Ryan Rickard 2006-2007; Kathryn L. Leydorf (DSA) 2007; Kathryn L. Leydorf Nov. 10, 2007- [Salem/Maple Rapids/Lowe charge re-aligned 5-1-14 to Maple Rapids/Lowe charge]

Marcellus UMC – *Kalamazoo District*

Ira Fett 1968-1969; Donald Ludman 1969-1974; Wayne Babcock 1975-1978; Derryl Cook 1978-1981; Robert Mayo 1981-1986; Kenneth I. Kline 1986-1992; Dennis E. Slattery 1992-1995; Peggy A. Boltz 1995-2002; Melodye Surgeon Rider 2002-2007; John D. Messner (DSA) 2007; John D. Messner Jan. 1, 2008-

Marengo UMC – *Albion District*

Stanley Fenner 1989-Aug. 8, 2000; Gerry Retzloff (DSA) Jan. 1, 2010-

Marion UMC – *Grand Traverse District*

Edward R. Jones 1967-1969; Walter S. Easton 1969-1971; Robert R. Boyer 1971-1977; Kendall A. Lewis 1977-1981; Donald R. Fry 1981-1994; James C. Grant 1994-1999; Howard H. Harvey 1999-2000; Jeffrey Schrock 2000-2004; Kenneth C. Reeves 2004-2006; Kenneth C. Reeves (DSA) 2006-7; James J. Mort 2007-

Marne UMC – *Grand Rapids District*

Kenneth E. Curtis 1967-1969; Don W. Eddy 1969-1971; Kenneth W. Karlzen 1971-1973; Donald Fry 1973-1977; Douglas Knight 1977-1980; Vernon Michael 1980-1982; Keith Bovee 1982-1985; Deborah M. Johnson 1985-1990; Timothy W. Graham 1990-1993; Cathi M. Gowin 1993-Jan. 31, 2002; Patricia L. Brook Feb. 1, 2002-2010; James Thomas Boutell 2010-

Marshall UMC – *Albion District*

Charles Manker 1968-1970; Ralph Witmer 1970-1974; Harold Filbrandt 1974-1983; Jeanne Randels (Assoc.) 1981-1988; Ronald Thompson 1983-1989; David McBride (Assoc.) 1988-1991; Leon Andrews 1989-1992; William Bills (Assoc.) 1991-1994; William Johnson 1992-1996; Margaret H. Peterson (Assoc.) 1994-1998 ; Keith W. Heifner 1996-1999; Judy K. Downing (Assoc.) 1998-1999; Leonard R. Schoenherr 1999-2013; Melany A. Chalker 2013-

Martin UMC – *Grand Rapids District*

Paul Scheibner 1965-1970; Thurlan Meridith 1970-1976; Gerald L. Welsh 1976-1984; Lee F. Zachman 1984-April 15, 1994; William C. Bills 1994-2007; Christopher L. Lane 2007-2009; David A. Selleck 2009-2012; Donald J. Graham 2012-2014; Sean K. Kidd 2014-

Mason First UMC – *Lansing District*

Keith L. Hayes 1966-1980; Robert L. Wessman (Assoc.) 1979-1984; George R. Grettenberger 1980-1989; Donald R. Ferris (Assoc.) 1984-1989; Verne C. Summers 1989-1992; Charles B. Hodges (Assoc.) 1989-March 1991; Wayne G. Reece 1992-2000; Robert K. Lynch (Assoc.) 1992-1995; Jane D. Logston (Assoc.) 1996-1998; Timothy Tuthill (Assoc.) 1998-2006; Robert L. Hundley 2000-2009; Dwayne E. Bagley 2009-

Mears UMC – *Grand Traverse District*
Kenneth L. Snow 1990-1993; Kenneth Vanderlaan (DSA) 1993-

Mecosta New Hope UMC – *Heartland District*
Gordon L. Terpening 1968-1971; Norman Charter 1971-1973; Pulpit Supply 1973-1974; Michael Nickerson 1974-1977; Ilona Sabo-Schuler 1977-1982; B. Gordon Barry 1982-1985; Pulpit Supply July-Oct. 1985; Bobby Dale Whitlock Oct. 1985-Apr. 1987; Pulpit Supply April-June 1987; Remus, Mecosta and Halls Corners merged to form New Hope in 1987; Christopher Momany 1987-1993; Scott K. Otis 1993-1997; James C. Noggle 1997-2004; Victor D. Charnley 2004-2013; Gregory L. Buchner 2013-

Mendon UMC – *Albion District*
Marcius Taber 1968-1969; David Litchfield 1969-1970; Harold Simon 1970-Nov. 1973; Robert Jones Nov. 1973-1978; John Charter 1978-1981; Ira Noordhoff 1981-Jan. 1985; Kendall Lewis Jan. 1985-1986; Elaine Buker 1986-1992; Rochelle Ray 1992-1995; Thomas L. Truby 1995-2001; Ward D. Pierce (DSA) 2001-Dec. 2, 2012 (died); David G. Knapp (interim) Jan. 1-June 30, 2013; [Three Rivers First / Mendon became two-point charge 2013] Robert D. Nystrom 2013-

Mesick UMC – *Grand Traverse District*
Ward Pierce 1967-1972; Bill Amundsen 1972-1979; Jean Crabtree 1979-Aug. 1980; Donald Buege Sept. 1980-Jan. 1984; Bruce Prestwood-Taylor Jan. 1984-1986; Thomas P. Fox 1986-1992; Charles A. Williams 1992-Feb. 14, 1997; J. David Thompson Nov. 16, 1997-2001; John J. Conklin (DSA) 2001-Nov. 30, 2001; John J. Conklin Dec. 1, 2001-2009; Mona L. Kindel 2009-2012; Beverley Williams 2012-

Middleton UMC – *Heartland District*
De Layne Hersey 1967-1969; Herald Cox Sept. 1969-Sept. 1971; Lloyd Hansen Sept. 1971-May 1972; Abe Caster May 1972-Jan. 1973; Eldon Schram Feb.-June 1973; J. Thomas Churn 1973-1979; Richard Whale 1979-1980; Richard Riley 1980-1984; Lyle Heaton 1984-1990; Tim Wohlford 1990-1991; Carolyn A. Robinson 1991-1997; Charles D. Farnum 1997-2001; Martin Cobb 2001-2006; William F. Foldesi 2006-Apr. 7, 2007; Clare Huyck (DSA) 2007; Clare Huyck Nov. 10, 2007-2012; William F. Dye July 15, 2012-

Middleville UMC – *Grand Rapids District*
Harold M. Taber 1964-1969; C. William Martin 1969-1973; Harold Simon Nov. 1973-Oct. 1976; Arthur Jackson April 1977-Aug. 1983; Bradley Kalajainen (Assoc.) Jan. 1981-1985; Carl Staser Oct. 1983-1988; Lynn W. Wagner 1988-1996; Lee F. Zachman 1996-2004; Scott E. Manning 2004-2009; [Middleville/Snow two-point charge 2009] Michael T. Conklin 2009-2012; Anthony C. Shumaker 2012-

Millville UMC – *Lansing District*
Daniel Harris 1965-1970; Dorr Garrett 1970-1973; Lester Priest Jan. 15, 1974-1980; Robert Stillson 1980-Nov. 15, 1982; Donald Vuurens Feb. 1983-1986; Richard Young 1986-1990; Jeffrey Wright 1990-Jan. 1993; James C. Noggle March 1993-1997; Carolyn A. Robinson 1997-1998; Richard A. Tester 1998-2004; Robert J. Freysinger 2004-2013; [M-52 Cooperative Ministry 2013] Jeremy J. Wicks (1/2 time) 2013-

Montague UMC – *Grand Rapids District*
Wirth G. Tennant 1965-1972; Gilbert B. Heaton 1972-1977; Birt A. Beers 1977-1983; Robert E. Jones, Jr. 1983-1992; D. Keith Laidler 1992-1997; Timothy P. Boal 1997-2005; Gary Bekofske 2005-2009; Randall R. Hansen 2009-2014; Mary S. Brown 2014-

Monterey Center UMC – *Kalamazoo District*
Ron Smith Oct. 1991-1997; Kenneth C. Reeves 1997-2004; Anthony Carrol Shumaker 2004-2008; Richard A. Fritz 2008-2014; Nancy J. Patera 2014-

Montgomery UMC – *Albion District*

Karl L. Zeigler 1968-1969; John H. Gurney 1969-Aug. 1970; Joseph Huston Aug. 1970-1972; Richard Huskey 1972-1974; J. Brian Selleck 1974-Feb. 1976; Robert P. Stover March 1976-1980; Stephen Beech 1980-1983; Larry W. Rubingh 1983-1987; Frederick G. Hamlin 1987-1994; Russell K. Logston 1994-1996; Diane Stone Nov. 16, 1996-2004; Edward Mohr 2004-2010; Trevor McDermont 2010-2013; Frederick G. Cain (Retired) (part-time) 2013-

Morris Chapel UMC – *Kalamazoo District*

Albert O'Rourke 1968-1970; Douglas Vernon 1970-1971; Pulpit Supply 1971-1972; Kenneth L. Snow 1972-1982; Richard C. Kuhn 1982-1987; Richard D. Wilson 1987-1996; Zawdie K. Abiade 1996-2002; Charles D. McNary (DSA) 2002-2003; O'Ryan Rickard 2003-2004; Christopher A. Kruchkow 2004-Feb. 15, 2012; [Morris Chapel UMC became single point charge 2012] Samuel Gordy (1/4 time) Mar. 11, 2012-2013; Rob Snodgrass (DSA) 2014-

Mt Pleasant Chippewa Indian UMC – *Heartland District*

Joseph Sprague 1974-1986, Maynard Hinman DSA 1986-1987, Joseph Sprague 1984-1986, Chris Cavender DSA 1990-12/1991, James Burgess Jan.1992-June1992, Joseph Sprague June 15,1992-1994, Carla Sineway 1/3 time 1994-11/1/03, Matthew Sprague 1/3 time 1994-11/15/95, Owen White-Pigeon 1/3 time 1994; Owen White-Pigeon (DSA) 2011-

Mt Pleasant First UMC – *Heartland District*

Paul Albery 1966-1970; Neil Bintz 1970-1978; Albert W. Frevert 1978-1989; Edward C. Ross (Assoc.) 1978-1981; Rodney J. Kalajainen (Assoc.) 1981-1984; Thomas Crossman (Assoc.) 1984-1986; Steven M. Smith (Assoc.) 1986-1991; Ronald J. Thompson 1989-1995; Janet K. Sweet (Assoc.) 1991-1994; Connie R. Bongard (Assoc.) Aug. 1, 1994-1997; Wade S. Panse 1995-1997; Benton R. Heisler 1997-2002; Mark R. Erbes (Assoc.) 1997-2001; Michelle LaMew (Assoc.) 2001-; John W. Boley 2002-2010; Charles D. Farnum (Assoc.) July 16, 2006-2007; Cynthia A. Skutar 2010-2013; Diane Gordon 2013-

Mt Pleasant Trinity UMC – *Heartland District*

G.B. Rule 1967-1969; J.A. Dudley 1969-1972; Daren C. Durey 1972-1977; Robert E. Tomlinson 1977-1980; Gordon E. Spalenka 1980-1984; Janelle E. Gerken 1984-1987; Michael J. Kent 1987-1991; James Cook 1991-1995; Dean Prentiss 1995-Sept. 14, 1999; Jana Lynn Almeida Oct. 16, 1999-2004; Susan D. Olsen July 16, 2004-2006; Sharyn K. Osmond Aug. 1, 2006-Nov. 30, 2008; Donald R. Wendell Nov. 30, 2008-Nov. 1, 2009; Craig L. Adams Dec. 1, 2009-2010; David Michael Palmer 2010-

Mulliken UMC – *Lansing District*

Everatt Love 1968-1972; David A. Cheyne 1972-1975; Lynn Wagner 1975-1977; John Eversole 1977-1982; Joseph Spackman 1982-1983; Ken Lindland 1983-1987; Joseph Spackman 1987-1991; Gordon Spalenka 1991-1993; Robert Besemer 1993-Aug. 31, 1996; Donald Woolum Sept. 16, 1996-2003; Judith Lee Scholten 2003-2011; Gary L. Simmons 2011-2013; [Barry-Eaton Cooperative Ministry 2013] Claire W. Huyck 2013-

Munith UMC – *Lansing District*

Frederick Werth 1967-1971; Bert L. Cole March 1972-1973; Larry Irvine 1973-1975; Thomas Adams 1976-1978; James Barney 1979-1983; Linda Farmer-Lewis 1983-1986; Milton TenHave 1986-1990; Laurie McKinven-Copus 1990-Sept. 1991; Robert Marston Oct. 1991-1998; Judith A. Nielson 1998-2000; Charles Cerling 2000-Aug. 9, 2004; Arthur R. Turner 2004-Nov. 15, 2005; Kenneth Karlzen (DSA) Dec. 2005-2006; Maurice Walworth (DSA) 2006-2007; Larry W. Rubingh 2007-Sept. 6, 2011; Maurice E. Walworth, Jr. (pulpit supply) Sept. 6, 2011-2012; Jeanne M. Laimon (1/4 time) 2012-2014 [M-52 Cooperative Ministry 2013-2014]; Susan J. Trowbridge 2014-

Muskegon Central UMC – *Grand Rapids District*

Royal J. Synwolt 1966-1971; Robert H. Jongeward 1971-1979; Lynn A. DeMoss 1979-1988; Ron L. Keller 1988-1993; Daniel M. Duncan (Assoc.) 1989-1994; Ray W. Burgess 1993-2000; Melanie S. Young (Assoc.) 1994-1996; Virginia L. Heller (Assoc.) 1996-1998; Gregory P. Culver (Assoc.) 1998-2002; Randall R. Hansen 2000-2009; M. Kay DeMoss (Deacon) 2003- ; Gary L. Bekofske 2009-2010; Diane Gordon 2010-2013; Mark D. Miller 2013-

Muskegon Crestwood UMC – *Grand Rapids District*
Carl B. Strange 1962-1969; John S. Myette 1969-1970; Phillip R. Glotfelty, Jr. 1970-1973; Kenneth W. Karlzen 1973-1977; David G. Showers 1977-1980; Lawrence E. Hodge 1980-1983; Birt A. Beers 1983-1990; M. Chris Lane 1990-1995; Victor D. Charnley 1995-2004; Dianne D. Morrison 2004-2007; Diane M Bowden 2007-2008; Dale Hotelling 2008-2010; Stephan Weinberger 2010-2014; [Crestwood realigned from Lakeside/Crestwood to Whitehall/Crestwood 2014] Mary A. Sweet 2014-

Muskegon Hts Temple UMC – *Grand Rapids District*
Verner Kilgren 1962-1970; Richard Selleck 1970-1977; Dale Crawford 1977-1979; Robert Pumfrey 1979-1983; Don Eddy 1983-1989; Richard Youells 1989-1991; Gerald F. Hagans 1991-Sept. 1, 2006; Robert B. Cook Sept. 1, 2006-2012; Jeffrey J. Bowman 2012-

Muskegon Lake Harbor UMC – *Grand Rapids District*
Wayne Speese 1964-1975; Harold Kirchenbauer Oct. 1975-1981; Frank Lyman 1981-1991; Carole Lyman (Assoc.) 1984-1991; Jack Stubbs 1991-1995; Susan J. Hagans 1995-2000; Cynthia Ann Skutar 2000-2004; Richard A. Morrison 2004-2007; Mark R. Erbes 2007-2014; Mary Letta-Bement Ivanov 2014-

Muskegon Lakeside UMC – *Grand Rapids District*
Robert Treat 1967-1981; Richard D. Wilson 1981-1987; Steven R. Young 1987-1993; William P. Myers, Jr. 1993-2002; David A. Selleck 2002-2009; Zawdie K. Abiade 2009-2010; Stephan Weinberger 2010-2014; [Lakeside became a single-point charge 2014] Donald J. Graham 2014-

Muskegon Unity UMC – *Grand Rapids District*
Kenneth McCaw Dec. 1966-1969; Austin Regier 1969-1975; Joseph Glover 1975-1983; Eric Beck 1983-1986; Susan Krill (Hagans) 1986-Nov. 1988; Ron Robotham Jan. 1989-1990; Jane Lippert 1990-1995; J. Todd Thompson 1995-1998; Kimberly A. DeLong 1998-Sept. 16, 1999; Gayle Berntsen Sept, 16, 1999-Sept. 1, 2001; James Meines Dec. 1, 2001-2005; Brian M. McLellan (DSA) 2005-Feb. 15, 2006; James Meines (DSA) Apr. 15, 2006-Oct. 31, 2006; Nancy L. (Besemer) Boelens Nov. 1, 2006-Dec. 31, 2008; Gilbert R. Boersma (1/4 time) 2009-Oct. 31, 2011; R. John Thompson (DSA) (1/4 time) Nov. 1, 2011-2014; Ronald L. Worley 2014

Muskegon Wolf Lake UMC – *Grand Rapids District*
Kenneth McCaw Nov. 1966-1969; Austin Reiger 1969-1975; Craig Adams 1975-Aug. 1979; Richard Williams Sept. 1979-Nov. 1983; Bruce Dempsey Nov. 1983-Nov. 1988; Gilbert Boersma Jan. 1989-Jan. 31, 1995; Pulpit Supply Feb.-June 1995; J. Todd Thompson 1995-2000; Laurence E. Hubley 2000-Nov. 15, 2001; Roberta W. Cabot Nov. 16, 2001-2011; Bobby Dale Whitlock (Retired) 2011-Sept. 1, 2014

Napoleon UMC – *Albion District*
Robert Kersten 1967-1969; Robert Hinklin 1969-1972; Douglas Smith 1972-1973; Marjorie Matthews 1973-Dec. 1975; J. Brian Selleck March 1976-Sept. 1978; Francis Anderson Sept. 1978-Sept. 1980; Wayne Gorsline Sept. 1980-1988; Robert J. Freysinger 1988-2004; Robert P. Stover 2004-2007; Jennifer Jue 2007-2013; Gregory R. Wolfe (Retired) 2013-

Nashville UMC – *Lansing District*
James Crosby 1969-1975; Leonard F. Putnam 1975-1984; Lynn Wagner 1984-1988; Ronald K. Brooks 1988-May 15, 1991; Kenneth Vaught June 1, 1991-1994; James L. Hynes 1994-2000; Gail C. Patterson 2000-Dec. 31, 2001; Dianne M. Bowden January 16, 2002-2007; Cathy M. Christman 2007-2010; Nancy J. Bitterling 2010-2013; Gary L. Simmons 2013- [Barry-Eaton Cooperative Ministry 2013]

NE Missaukee Parish: Merritt-Butterfield UMC – *Grand Traverse District*
Athel Lynch 1968-1970; Marion Nye 1970-1973; Eugene Baughan 1974-1987; Bernard Griner 1988-1989; Cynthia Schaefer 1989-1993; (Merritt and Butterfield merged on July 1, 1991.) Pulpit Supply July 1-Aug. 31, 1993; O. Jay Kendall Sept. 1, 1993-2005; Brian R Bunch, Aug. 1, 2005-2012; Jeffrey J. Schrock 2012-

NE Missaukee Parish: Moorestown-Stittsville UMC – *Grand Traverse District*
Athel Lynch 1968-1970; Marion Nye 1970-1973; Eugene Baughan 1974-1987; Bernard Griner 1988-1989; Cynthia Schaefer 1989-1993; Stittsville merged with Moorestown in 1993; O. Jay Kendall Sept. 1, 1993-2005; Brian R Bunch, Aug. 1, 2005-2012; Jeffrey J. Schrock 2012-

New Church Start – *Lansing District*
[M-52 Cooperative Ministry 2014] Jeremy J. Wicks 2014-

New Hope UMC of Emmett County – *Grand Traverse District*
Matthew Todd Stoll 2003-2010; Vaughn Thurston-Cox 2010- ; [Epsilon/New Hope/Harbor Springs/ Alanson became a 4-point charge 2014] Hillary Thurston-Cox (Assoc.) 2014-

New Life UMC – *Heartland District*
Lawrence P. Brown Jan. 1, 1998-2006; Richard J. Duffy (co-pastor) Jan. 1, 1998-June 30, 1998; Anita Hahn 2006-2011; John A. Scott 2011-

Newaygo UMC – *Grand Rapids District*
Jean Crabtree 1967-1972; Paul E. Robinson 1972-1975; James W. Boehm 1975-1984; John S. Myette 1984-1988; Stephen M.G. Charlney 1988-1994; Donald R. Fry 1994-1999; Sandra L. Spahr 2000-2006; Patricia L. Bromberek 2006-2011; Kathy Groff 2011-

Niles Grace UMC – *Kalamazoo District*
Leonard Putnam 1964-1969; Orin M. Bailey 1969-1971; Don Cozadd 1971-1976; David Litchfield 1976-1981; John Charter 1981-Nov. 1992; Mark E. Thompson Nov. 1992-1996; Glenn McNeil 1996-2000; Nancy J. Bitterling 2000-2002; Patricia L. Bromberek (SP-DSA) 2002-2004; Anthony Tomasino (DSA) Oct. 17, 2004-

Niles Wesley UMC – *Kalamazoo District*
Robert Trenery 1968-1974; Mark Graham 1974-1984; Lloyd Phillips 1984-1991; Nolan R. Williams 1991-Jan. 1, 2000; Emmett H. Kadwell, Jr. Jan. 1, 2000-2008; Edward H. Slate 2008-2012; Cathi M. Huvaere 2012-

North Adams UMC – *Albion District*
Kenneth W. Karlzen 1968-1971; Thomas R. Jones 1971-Aug. 1974; David Flagel Sept. 1975-1980; Lee F. Zachman 1980-1984; Donald McLellan 1984-Sept. 1988; Melanie Baker-Streevy Oct. 1988-1995; Rochelle Ray 1995-2000; Tim Doubblestein 2000-Aug. 31, 2002; Charles Richards Sept. 1-Dec. 31, 2002; Paul Hane Jan. 1, 2003-2011; Kimberly A. Metzger July 1-Dec. 19, 2011; Arthur R. Turner (DSA) Feb. 1, 2012-2014 [Osseo UMC merged w/ North Adams UMC 4-6-14] Timothy R. Puckett 2014-

North Evart UMC – *Heartland District*
Carter Miller 1968-March 1971; Lynn Wagner March. 1971-Oct. 1973; Pulpit Supply Nov. 1973-1974; Darryl Cook 1974-May 1977; Kenneth Kline 1977-1981; Pulpit Supply June-Aug. 1981; Dwight Benner Sept. 1981-1983; Purlin Wesseling Aug. 1983-1986; Frank Closson 1986-Jan. 1988; Jane Crabtree Jan. 1988-1990; Pulpit Supply July-Nov. 1991; Robert Stark Nov. 1990-Aug. 1991; Carol Lynn Bourns Sept. 1991-Dec. 31, 1994; Pulpit Supply Jan. 1995-1996; Jean Crabtree (DSA) 1996-2000; Donald L. Buege 2000-Jan. 2006; Jon Pohl Jan. 15 - June 30, 2006; Jean A. Crabtree (DSA) Nov. 5, 2006--July 2007; Russell Morgan (DSA) July 8, 2007-2012; Kara Lynne Burns (CLM) July 22, 2012-

North Muskegon Community UMC – *Grand Rapids District*
David S. Yoh 1968-Sept. 1978; Dennis Buwalda Sept. 1978-1982; Laurence L. Waterhouse 1982-1986; John W. Fisher 1986-1992; Glenn M. Wagner 1992-2006; Robert K. Lynch 2006-2012; Phillip J. Friedrick July 15, 2012-

North Parma UMC – *Albion District*
Edward Dahringer 1968-Sept. 1980; Jean Crabtree Nov. 1980-Jan. 1984; Jerry Hippensteel 1984-1989; Charlotte Lewis 1989-1992; Carolin S. Spragg 1992-1999; Keith W. Heifner 1999-2003; Michael P. Baker-Streevy 2003-2009; Melissa Claxton 2009- [North Parma / Springport became two-point charge 7-1-10]

North Star UMC – *Heartland District*
Robert E. Tomlinson 1974-Jan. 1977; Donald L. Warmouth Feb. 1977-1978; Glenn Britton 1978-1979; Lois H. Gremban 1979-1981; Dale F. Jaquette Aug. 1981-April 1990; T. Ried Martin 1990-1993; Karen E. Nesius 1993-1994; Jodie Flessner 1994-2003; William F. Foldesi Nov. 16, 2003-Apr. 7, 2007; Clare Huyck (DSA) 2007; Clare Huyck Nov. 10, 2007-2012; William F. Dye July 15, 2012-

Northport Indian Mission UMC – *Grand Traverse District*
Marshall Collins (DSA) 1991-2001; Kathryn Coombs (DSA) 2003-2005; Thomas H. John Jr. 2005-

Northwest UMC – *Kalamazoo District*
Ray Carpenter 1967-1972; Linda Stoddard 1972-1976; Dorcas Lohr 1976-1982; Pulpit supply 1982-1983; Alden B. Burns 1983-1996; Carol A. Newman 1996-2000; John W. McNaughton 2000-2003; Calvin Y. Hill 2003-2007; Sheila F. Baker 2007-2012; Ronald W. Hansen (DSA) (1/4 time) 2012-2013; Samuel C. Gordy (1/4 time) 2013-

Norwood UMC – *Grand Traverse District*
Stanley Hayes 1967-1970; Lester Priest 1970-Jan. 1974; Daniel Minor April 1974-1981; Betty Burton 1981-1982; Glenn Britton 1982-1983; Supply pastor 1983-Aug. 1985; Robert Bellairs Aug. 1985-1996; Bernard W. Griner (DSA) 1996-1997; Eugene L. Baughan 1997-2002; D. Michael Maurer 2002-Nov. 10, 2008; Ralph Posnik (DSA) Nov. 23, 2008; Ralph Posnik Nov. 15, 2009-2014; Craig A. Pahl 2014-

Nottawa UMC – *Albion District*
Rudy A. Wittebach 1967-1974; Charles W. Smith 1974-1976; Elanor Carpenter 1976-Nov. 1980; Carl Leth Nov. 1980-Oct. 1983; David H. Minger Oct. 1983-1987; Laurie J. McKinven-Copus 1987-1990; Emilie Forward 1990-1994; Pulpit Supply July-Sept. 1994; Mona Joslyn (DSA) Oct. 1994-1996; Donald R. Wendell Jan. 1996-July 15, 2003; Alexander Miller (DSA) 2003-

Okemos Community Church – *Lansing District*
John E. Cermak 1966-1987; Lynn E. Grimes (Assoc.) 1983-1986; Verne C. Summers 1987-1989; Richard C. Sneed (Assoc.) 1989-1991; Charles D. Grauer 1989-1996; Pegg Ainslie (Assoc.) 1991-1993; Joyce DeToni-Hill (Assoc.) 1993-Feb. 15, 1994; James W. Boehm 1996-Sept. 1, 1998; Jeanne M. Randels Oct. 16, 1998-Jan. 1, 2014; Richard W. Blunt 2014-

Old Mission Peninsula UMC – *Grand Traverse District*
Richard W. Blunt 1986-1993; Orin L. Daniels 1993-1995; Dale Hotelling 1995-July 16, 2000; Sally J. LaFrance 2001-2002; Stanley Lee Hayes (DSA) 2002-Jan. 31, 2003; David H. Minger Feb. 1, 2003-2006 (Church changed name from Ogdensburg to Old Mission Peninsula 2004); Martin Cobb 2006-2010; Melody Lane Olin 2010-

Olive Branch UMC – *Kalamazoo District*
Leslie Smith 1965-1969; Willard Gilroy 1969-1973; Arthur Beadle 1973-1976; Gordon Everett (interim) July-Nov. 1976; Richard Williams Dec. 1976-Oct. 1979; Paul Smith Nov. 1979-March 1980; Joseph Wood (interim) March-June 1980; William Doubblestein 1980-1983; William Carr 1983-April 1986; Joseph Wood (interim) April-June 1986; Phillip Friedrick 1986-1991; Sherri Swanson 1991-1995; Charlene A. Minger 1995-1999; Valerie Fons 1999-2001; John G. Kasper 2001-2006; Russell K. Logston 2006-2011; Jeffrey O. Cummings Jan. 1, 2012-

Oronoko UMC – *Kalamazoo District*
Robert Strauss 1968-1981; Valerie Hill 1981-March 1983; Leonard Haynes 1983-1986; Leo Bennett 1986-1989; Walter J. Rothfuss 1989-2000; Brenda Gordon 2000-2006; Jane D. Logston (part-time) 2006-14; [Berrien Springs/Hinchman/Oronoko became 3-point charge 2012] [Hinchman/Oronoko became 2-point charge 2014] Linda R. Gordon 2014-

Oshtemo UMC – *Kalamazoo District*
Jay Gunnett Apr. 1968-1971; Laurence Dekema 1971-Jan. 1972; Linda Stoddard 1972-Oct. 1976; Pulpit Supply Oct. 1976-1977; Dorcas Lohr 1977-1982; Kenneth H. Kline 1982-1987; David L. Litchfield 1987-1992; Lewis A. Buchner 1992-1997; Charles M. Shields 1997-Feb. 1, 2000; Suzanne Kornowski 2000-2011 (Kalamazoo: Oakwood merged with Oshtemo on October 27, 2002) Peggy Boltz 2011-2013; John W. Fisher (Retired) 2013-

Otsego UMC – *Kalamazoo District*
Birt Beers 1967-1972; Leonard Yarlott 1972-1975; J. William Schoettle 1975-1983; Robert H. Roth, Jr. 1983-1985; James C. Grant 1985-March 1992; Emerson Minor (interim) March-August 1992; James C. Grant 1992-1994; Philip L. Brown 1994-1998; Margaret H. Peterson 1998-2000; Joseph D. Shaler 2001-

Ovid: United Church – *Heartland District*

Claude B. Ridley, Jr. 1972-1977; Gilbert B. Heaton 1977-1980; Carl W. Staser 1980-Oct. 1983; Ronald W. Hansen Feb. 1, 1984-1993; Richard L. Matson 1993-1995; Steven D. Pearson 1995-1997; Robert L. Pumfery 1997-1999; Rob A. McPherson 1999-2006; Donald R. Fry 2006-2008; Gregory L. Buchner 2008-2013; Paul A. Damkoehler 2013-

Palo UMC – *Heartland District*

John H. Gurney 1970-1976; Norman Crotser 1976-Dec. 1978; Daniel R. Bennett 1979-March 1982; Mark G. Johnson March 1982-1986; James E. Cook 1986-1991; Howard H. Harvey 1991-1996; Patrick Glass 1996-1998; Larry W. Nalett 1998-Aug. 9, 2004; Charles E. Cerling Aug. 10, 2004-2009; Jolennda Cole (DSA) 2009-2010; Jolennda Cole 2010-2011; William F. Dye 2011-2012; Russell D. Morgan (CLM) July 15, 2012-2014; Gerald Erskine (DSA) 2014-

Parchment UMC – *Kalamazoo District*

Wayne Groat Feb. 1968-Feb. 1969; James W. Dempsey March 1969-1973; Gaylord D. Howell 1973-1978; David S. Yoh Sept. 1978-1989; Daniel J. Minor 1989-2011; Michael J. Tupper 2011-

Paris UMC – *Heartland District*

Richard Wilson 1968-1971; Lynn Chapel 1971-1979; John Buker 1979-1981; Elaine Buker 1981-1986; Kendall Lewis 1986-1990; J. Robert Collins 1990-Oct. 1991; David F. Hills 1992-1994; Kathryn M. Steen 1994-2000; Dawn A. Beamish Jan. 1, 2001-2002; Edwin D. Snook 2002-2005; Michael A. Riegler Sept. 11, 2005-2011; Ed Milam (DSA) July 1-Nov. 12, 2011; Ed Milam Nov. 12, 2011-2014; David J. Cadarette Sr. (DSA) 2014-

Parmelee UMC – *Grand Rapids District*

Edward D. Passenger 1966-1969; Robert Boyer 1969-1971; Lloyd Van Lente 1971-1976; Adam Chyrowski 1976-1980; Robert Tomlinson 1980-1981; Arthur Jackson 1981-Aug. 1983; Carl Staser Oct. 1983-1988; Lynn W. Wagner 1988-1996; Lee F. Zachman 1996-2004; Lee F. Zachman (1/2 time) 2004-Nov. 30, 2010; Vance Dimmick (DSA) (1/4 time) Nov. 28, 2010-Nov. 5, 2012; William V. Clegg, Jr (1/4 time) Nov. 11, 2012-

Paw Paw UMC – *Kalamazoo District*

William Payne 1965-1979; Paul Patterson 1979-1984; Keith Laidler 1984-1989; Ward N. Scovel 1989-1995; Robert K. Lynch 1995-1999; Carolin S. Spragg 1999-2007; Joseph L. Spackman 2007-2013; Trevor J. McDermont 2013-

Peace UMC – *Lansing District*

Robert E. Boyer 1968-1969; Marion R. Putnam 1969-Jan. 1970; E.F. Rhoades Feb.-July 1970; Michael Williams Aug. 1970-1971; William P. Reynders 1971-Feb. 1972; Thomas Churn March 1972-April 1973; Thomas Peters May 1973-Aug. 1976; Dale D. Spoor Sept. 1976-Dec. 1979; Steven Reid Jan. 1980-Jan. 1984; Mary Curtis March 1984-1989; James Noggle 1989-Feb. 1993; Susan A. Trowbridge March 1993-March 15, 2005; Nancy V. Fancher (DSA) March 16, 2005-March 31, 2006; Susan D. Olsen 2006-

Pearl UMC – *Kalamazoo District*

Ronald Wise 1968-1969; Harold Arman 1969-1971; Arthur Beadle 1971-1973; Matthew Walkotten 1973-1976; Miriam DeMint 1976-1978; Ronald Hansen 1978-1984; Stanley Hayes 1984-1990; James Fox 1990-1992; Randall R. Hansen 1992-2000; Jane A. Crabtree 2000-2002; Jean Crabtree (DSA) (Assoc.) 2000-2002; Robert L. Hinklin (DSA) 2002-; Raymond R. Sundell 2003-2008; Gary L. Peterson 2008-

Pentwater Centenary UMC – *Grand Traverse District*

W. Jackson 1967-1970; Glenn B. Britton 1970-1973; Clyde Miller 1973-1979; Charles M. Johnson 1979-1982; Milton John Palmer 1982-1985; Gary T. Haller 1985-1993; Christopher P. Momany 1993-Dec. 31, 1996; Curtis E. Jensen Jan. 16, 1996-2001; Michael J. Tupper 2001-2006; Harris J. Hoekwater 2006-2012; Gary L. Bekofske 2012-2014; Melanie S. Young 2014-

Perrinton UMC – *Heartland District*

Robert E. Tomlinson 1974-Jan. 1977; Donald L. Warmouth Feb. 1977-1978; Glenn Britton 1978-1979; Lois H. Gremban 1979-1981; Dale F. Jaquette Aug. 1981-April 1990; T. Ried Martin 1990-1993; Karen E. Nesius 1993-1994; Jodie Flessner 1994; William F. Foldesi Nov. 16, 2003-Apr. 7, 2007; Clare Huyck (DSA) 2007; Clare Huyck Nov. 10, 2007-2012; William F. Dye July 15, 2012-

Perry UMC – *Lansing District*

Karl W. Patow 1962-1969; Ivan Niswender 1969-1971; David Draggoo 1971-1981; Jeff Siker-Giesler 1981-1983; Harris Hoekwater 1983-Jan. 1992; Clinton McKinven-Copus Feb. 1992-Dec. 31, 1994; Pulpit Supply Jan. 1-April 15, 1995; Carroll A. Fowler April 16, 1995-2003; Carolyn C. Floyd 2003-2008; Raymond R. Sundell 2008-2012; Nancy G. Powers 2012-

Petoskey UMC – *Grand Traverse District*

Ralph P. Witmer 1964-Sept. 1970; Charles L. Manker Sept. 1970-Oct. 15, 1975; Donald H. Merrill Oct. 15, 1975-1986; Charles W. Fullmer 1986-April 30, 1994; Don W. Eddy March 1, 1994-Dec. 1996; James P. Mitchum 1997-

Pine River Parish: Ashton UMC – *Grand Traverse District*

David Dryer April 1968-1974; Ilona Sabo-Schuler 1974-1977; Robert Boyer 1977-1979; Harold R. Simon 1979-1983; Mark Gaylord-Miles 1983-Jan. 1985; Pulpit Supply Jan.-June 1985; Douglas Kokx 1985-1991; Robert W. Stark 1991-1996; Valerie M. Sisson Sept. 16, 1996-1998; Valerie M. Hill 1998-1999; David A. Cheyne 1999-2003; Jodie R. Flessner 2003-2012; Scott R. Loomis 2012-

Pine River Parish: LeRoy UMC – *Grand Traverse District*

David Dryer 1968-1974; Ilona Sabo-Schuler 1974-1977; Robert Boyer 1977-1979; Harold R. Simon 1979-1983 Mark Gaylord-Miles 1983-Jan. 1985; Pulpit Supply Jan.-June 1985; Douglas Kokx 1985-1991; Robert Stark 1991-1996; Valerie M. Sisson Sept. 16, 1996-1998; Valerie M. Hill 1998-1999; David A. Cheyne 1999-2003; Jodie R. Flessner 2003-2012; Scott R. Loomis 2012-

Plainwell First UMC – *Kalamazoo District*

Emerson B. Minor 1964-1984; James W. Boehm 1984-1989; Raymond Townsend (Assoc.) 1988-1991; David B. Nelson, Jr. 1989-1991; Frank W. Lyman, Jr. and Carole Strobe Lyman (co-pastors) 1991-1996; Charles D. Grauer 1996-2003; Cindy E. Holmquist (Assoc.) 2001-June 30, 2003; Harvey K. Prochnau 2003-2010; Barbara Jo Fay (Assoc.) 2007-2010; Kathy E. Brown 2010-

Pleasant Lake UMC – *Lansing District*

Frederick Werth 1967-1971; Bert L. Cole March 1972-1973; Larry Irvine 1973-1975; Thomas Adams 1976-1978; James Barney 1979-1983; Linda Farmer-Lewis 1983-1986; Milton TenHave 1986-1990; Laurie McKinven-Copus 1990-Sept. 1991; Robert Marston Oct. 1991-1998; Judith A. Nielson 1998-2000; Charles E. Cerling 2000-Aug. 9, 2004; Arthur R. Turner 2004-Nov. 15, 2005; Kenneth Karlzen (DSA) Dec. 2005-2006; Maurice Walworth (DSA) 2006-Sept. 30, 2007; Thomas Peters (DSA) Oct. 1, 2007-Apr. 23, 2008; [Pleasant Lake & Jackson Zion became two-point charge 2008] David H. Minger (DSA) 2008-2013; [Pleasant Lake became single-point charge 2013] [M-52 Cooperative Ministry 2013-2014] Jeanne M. Laimon (1/4 time) 2013-2014; Christine L. Pease (DSA) 2014-

Pokagon UMC – *Kalamazoo District*

Albert A. O'Rourke 1962-1974; Harold Deipert 1974-1977; Gary D. Kintigh 1977-1981; Michael Conklin 1981-1983; Theodore H. Bennink (retired, part-time) 1983-1984; Reva Hawke 1984-1988; Beatrice Rose 1988-1990; Claude Ridley (retired) May 1-Nov. 1, 1990; Theodore Bennink (retired) Nov. 1, 1990-April 30, 1991; Claude Ridley (retired May 1-Nov. 1, 1991; Richard Muessig (DSA) Nov. 1, 1991-April 30, 1992; Claude Ridley (retired) May 1-Aug. 30, 1992; Richard Muessig Sept. 1992-2001; Valerie Fons 2001-2003; Patrica Ann Haas 2003-2011; Sean K. Kidd (DSA) (1/2 time) 2011-2014; [Berrien Springs/Pokagon became a 2-point charge 2014] Brenda E. Gordon 2014-

Pompeii UMC – *Heartland District*

Robert E. Tomlinson 1974-Jan. 1977; Donald L. Warmouth Feb. 1977-1978; Glenn Britton 1978-1979; Lois H. Gremban 1979-1981; Dale F. Jaquette Aug. 1981-April 1990; T. Ried Martin 1990-1993; Karen E. Nesius 1993-1994; Jodie Flessner 1994-2003; William F. Foldesi Nov. 16, 2003-Apr. 7, 2007; Clare Huyck (DSA) 2007; Clare Huyck Nov. 10, 2007-2012; William F. Dye July 15, 2012-

Pope UMC – *Albion District*
Lambert G. McClintic 1952-1995; Jack Fugate 1995-July 15, 2008; Irene Vittoz (part-time) 2009-2010; Robert S. Moore-Jumonville 2010-

Portage Chapel Hill UMC – *Kalamazoo District*
David Nelson 1968-1972; Dow Chamberlain 1972-1978; Jon Powers July-August 1978; Joseph Bistayi Sept. 1978-1985; William Torrey 1985-1989; Carl Hausermann 1989-2001; Julie A. Liske (Assoc.) 1994-Nov. 30, 1997; Susan M. Petro (Assoc.) Jan. 1, 1998-2007; Barry Thayer Petrucci 2001- ; John M. Weiler (Assoc.) 2007-2011; Cara Weiler (deacon 1/4 time) Oct. 1, 2007-Oct. 1, 2009; Virginia L. Heller (Assoc.) 2011-2013

Portage First UMC – *Kalamazoo District*
Donald Scranton 1967-1970; Paul Albery 1970-1975; Kenneth McCaw 1975-1983; Logan Weaver (Assoc.) Oct. 1, 1980; Royce Robinson 1983-Dec. 1986; Robert Hinklin March 1987-1998; Logan Weaver (Pastor Emeritus, Assoc.) Jan. 1, 1988; William J. Torrey (Ret. Assoc.) 1993-1995; Gregory B. Wood 1998- ; John L. Moore (Ret. Assoc.) (DSA), Oct. 1, 2006-2013

Portage Prairie UMC – *Kalamazoo District*
Darrell Osborn 1968-1970; Robert Welfare 1970-1974; Robert Stillson 1974-1980; Robert Stover 1980-1987; Morris Reinhart 1987-1989; Margaret Peterson 1989-1994; Larry W. Mannino 1994-1995; David H. Minger 1995-1999; Thomas P. Fox 1999-2008; Theresa Little Eagle Sayles 2008-Apr. 15,2009; [Portage Prairie/Arden two-point charge 2009] O'Ryan Rickard 2009-2014; Ralph A. Posnik Jr 2014- [Portage Prairie single-point charge 2014]

Portland UMC – *Lansing District*
Raymond Norton 1967-1969; Donald Cozadd 1969-1971; Carlton Benson 1971-1973; Harold Homer 1973-1978; C. Dow Chamberlain 1978-Nov. 1985; David Evans (interim) Nov. 1985-Feb. 1986; Dale Crawford Feb.-Oct. 1986; David Evans (interim) Oct. 1986-Feb. 1987; Stanley Finkbiener 1987-1992; Elaine M. Buker 1992-1997; Scott K. Otis 1997-2003; Gregory Ryan Wolfe 2003-2008; Keith R. Treman 2008-

Potterville UMC – *Lansing District*
Thomas Peters 1967-1970; Richard Youells 1970-1974; Gregory Wolfe 1974-Oct. 1978; J. Thomas Churn Oct. 1978-1982; Austin Regier 1982-1987; Beverly Gaska 1987-Jan. 1991; Charles B. Hodges March 1991-March 1992; Milton J. TenHave (interim) March-July 1992; John Buker 1992-1995; Paul F. Bailey 1995-May 1, 2001; Rebecca K. Morrison Jan. 16, 2002-2011; Lyne Stull-Lipps 2011-

Quimby UMC – *Lansing District*
John Joldersma 1965-1970; Esther Cox 1970-1971; William P. Reynders 1971-Feb. 1972; Thomas Churn March 1972-April 1973; Thomas Peters May 1973-Aug. 1976; Dale D. Spoor Sept. 1976-Dec. 1979; Steven Reid Jan. 1980-Jan. 1984; Mary Curtis March 1984-1989; James Noggle 1989-Feb. 1993; Susan A. Trowbridge, March 1993-1998; Kenneth R. Vaught (DSA) 1998-2011; Bryce E. Feighner 2011-2013; [Barry-Eaton Cooperative Ministry 2013] Jerry Bukoski 2013-

Quincy UMC – *Albion District*
W. Ernest Combellack 1967-1969; Jack Bartholomew 1969-1974; Bruce Keegstra 1974-1977; Kay Williams 1977-1979; Jim Gysel 1979-1983; James Barney 1983-1987; Joan Hamlin 1987-1994; Jane D. Logston 1994-1996; John Knowlton 1996-1998; Melanie S. Young 1998-Oct. 1, 1998; Charles A. Williams Jan. 1, 1999-2003; John A. Scott & Rebecca Scott (CoPastors) Sept. 2003-2007; Geraldine M. Litchfield 2007-2009; [Litchfield/Quincy two-point charge 2009] Michael P. Baker-Streevy 2009-2010; Martin T. Cobb 2010-2013; Julie Elmore 2013-

Ravenna UMC – *Grand Rapids District*
Harry R. Johnson 1967-Dec. 1968; William Foster Dec. 1968-1973; William Bowers 1973-1978; Lewis Buchner 1978-1983; Dennis Slattery 1983-1987; Kenneth Curtis 1987-1988; Rick Powell 1988-1991; Pamela Kail 1991-1994; Daniel B. Hofmann 1994-2001; Mary Bement Ivanov 2001-2008; Charles W. Smith 2008-2011; Carleton R. Black (DSA) 2011; Carleton R. Black Nov. 12, 2011-

Reading UMC – *Albion District*

Harold Cox 1968-Sept. 1969; William Bowers Sept. 1969-1972; Eric Johnson 1972-1975; Dennis Paulson 1975-1979; Altha M. Barnes 1979-1983; Harold R. Simon 1983-March 1990; Dale F. Jaquette April 1990-1992; Thomas P. Fox 1992-1999; Kathy L. Nitz Aug. 16, 1999-July 31, 2001; Gayle Berntsen Sept. 1, 2001-2006; Nancy G. Powers 2006-2008; DeAnn J. Dobbs 2008-2012; Robert M. Hughes 2012-2014

Reed City UMC – *Heartland District*

Charles W. Fullmer 1966-1970; Forrest E. Mohr 1970-1977; Allen D. McCreedy 1977-1990; Richard L. Matson 1990-1993; Gregory J. Martin 1993-Dec. 1, 1998; Jennifer Browne (Assoc.) Jan. 15, 1997-Dec. 1, 1998; Richard W. Blunt Feb. 1, 1999-2008; Emmett H. Kadwell, Jr. 2008-2011; Kathryn S. Cadarette 2011-

Riverside UMC – *Kalamazoo District*

George Chaffee 1968-1971; Carl L. Hausermann 1971-1977; Elizabeth Perry Nord 1976-Oct. 1986; Mark Thompson Jan. 1987-Nov. 15, 1992; Norman C. Kohns Nov. 16, 1992-1993; Jackie Bralick 1993-Feb. 1, 1995; Pulpit Supply Feb.-April 1995; Alan D. Stover May 1, 1995-Sept. 25, 1997; John Sternaman Dec. 1, 1997-2002; Michael R. Bohms 2002-Dec. 31, 2003; Thomas Meyer (DSA) Feb. 1, 2004-June 30, 2004; Sheila F. Baker 2004-2005; Russell K. Logston 2005-2006; Walter G. Gerstung (DSA) July 1, 2006; David S. Yoh (DSA), Oct. 4, 2006-2009; Stephen C. Small (DSA) 2009-2014; David L. Haase 2014-

Robbins UMC – *Lansing District*

Maurice Glasgow 1966-1977; Joseph Huston 1977-1982; Wade Panse 1982-1987; James P. Mitchum 1987-1997; Martin M. DeBow 1997-2008; Bobby Dale Whitlock 2008-2009; Mark R. Payne 2009-2014; Peggy A. Katzmark 2014-

Rockford UMC – *Grand Rapids District*

Richard A. Selleck 1966-1970; Ron L. Keller 1970-1973; George A. Belknap 1973-1978; John S. Myette 1978-1980; J. Melvin Bricker 1980-1989; Leonard F. Putnam (Assoc. part-time) 1984-1994; William J. Torrey 1989-1993; Richard M. Riley 1993-2014; Jeffrey Charles Williams (Assoc.) 2002-2004; Kenneth J. Bremer 2014-

Rodney UMC – *Heartland District*

Richard Wilson 1968-1971; Lynn Chapel 1971-1979; John Buker 1979-1981; Elaine Buker 1981-1986; Kendall Lewis 1986-1990; J. Robert Collins 1990-Oct. 1991; David F. Hills 1992-1994; Kathryn M. Steen 1994-2000; Dawn A. Beamish Jan. 1, 2001-2002; Edwin D. Snook 2002-2005; Michael A. Riegler Sept. 11, 2005-2011; Ed Milam (DSA) July 1-Nov. 12, 2011; Ed Milam Nov. 12, 2011-2014; David J. Cadarette Sr. (DSA) 2014-

Rosebush UMC – *Heartland District*

Paul Peet 1968-1969; Fred Fischer 1969-1978; David Meister 1978-1980; John Ritter 1980-1984; Michael Long 1984-1992; Mark R. Payne 1992-2001; Brian Charles LaMew 2001-May 1, 2005; Gregory L. Buchner 2005-2008; Jonathan D. Van Dop 2008-2014; Joseph L. Beavan 2014-

Salem Indian Mission of the UMC – *Grand Rapids District*

Lewis White Eagle Church 1948-1990; Pulpit Supply 1990-1992; David G. Knapp 1992-1995; Timothy J. Miller 1995-1999; John Pesblakal (DSA)1999-Aug. 31, 2001; Calvin Hill Sept. 1, 2001-2003; Wesley S. Rehberg (DSA) 2003-2005; Sandra VandenBrink, Jan. 16, 2005-2013; Sandra VandenBrink, (Retired) Director, Senior Meals Program 2013- ; Nancy L. Boelens (Retired) 2013-

Salem UMC – *Heartland District*

William Tate 1967-1969; Robert Boyer 1969-1970; Charles VanLente 1970-1972; Everett Love June-Dec. 1972; Paul Jones 1973-1975; Douglas Jones 1975-1976; Terry MacArthur 1976-Oct. 15, 1979; Robert Gillette Jan. 1980-1984; Merritt Bongard 1984-1991; Joseph Spackman 1991-1999; James Dibbet 1999-2005; O'Ryan Rickard 2005-2007; Kathryn L. Leydorf (DSA) 2007; Kathryn L. Leydorf Nov. 10, 2007-2014; [Elsie/Salem became a charge 5-1-14] Donald R. Ferris-McCann May 1, 2014-

Sand Lake UMC – *Heartland District*

Jerry L. Hippensteel 1977-1981; Richard Strait 1981-1984; Richard Fairbrother 1984-1989; Mary Curtis 1989-91; Richard Sneed 1991-1992; Richard A. Selleck 1992-1996; Howard H. Harvey 1996-1999; Nathan D. Junius 1999-Feb. 1, 2002; Lloyd R. Hansen Feb. 1, 2002-June 30, 2002; Donald Turkelson (DSA)(part-time) 2002 - Nov. 30, 2007; Darryl Miller (DSA) (1/2 time) Jan. 1, 2007; Darryl Miller (part-time) Dec. 1, 2007-

Saugatuck UMC – *Grand Rapids District*

C. Dow Chamberlain 1967-1969; Harold Arman 1969-1971; Arthur Beadle 1971-1973; Douglas L. Pedersen Oct. 1973-Aug. 1975; Richard W. McClain Aug. 1975-1979; Craig L. Adams 1979-1984; Constance L. Heffelfinger 1984-1996; Fred & Joan Hamlin (DSA) 1996-1998; Karen A. Tompkins 1998-2001; Jean Smith (DSA) 2001; Jean Smith Dec. 1, 2001-2005; Letisha Bowman (DSA) 2005-2007; Letisha Bowman (part-time) 2007-2011; John Huenink July 1-Aug. 31, 2011; Emmett Kadwell (DSA) (1/4 time) Sept. 1, 2011-

Schoolcraft Pleasant Valley UMC – *Albion District*

Robert J. Stillson 1963-1969; Vern Michael 1969-1970; Roger Nielson 1970-1971; Lay Speakers 1971-1972; Dale Benton 1972-1978; John W. Fisher 1978-1980; Dale Crawford 1980-1983; Dwight J. Burton 1983-1992; Laura Truby 1992-1996; Ronald S. Scholte 1996-2000; Larry Reeves 2000; Michelle Wisdom-Long 2001-2008; [Schoolcraft Pleasant Valley / White Pigeon became a two-point charge 2008] Janet Luchs 2008-2009; [Three Rivers Ninth / Schoolcraft Pleasant Valley became a two-point charge 2009] James W. Stilwell 2009-

Schoolcraft UMC – *Kalamazoo District*

Robert J. Stillson 1963-1969; Vern Michael 1969-1970; Roger Nielson 1970-1971; Lay Speakers 1971-1972; Dale Benton 1972-1978; John W. Fisher 1978-1980; Dale Crawford 1980-1983; Dwight J. Burton 1983-1992; Laura C. Truby 1992-1998; Marilyn M. Sanders 1998-Jan. 16, 2000; Pete Love (DSA) 2000-; David Nellist 2000-2008; Seung Ho "Andy" Baek 2008-2010; Karen S. Wheat 2010-

Scottdale UMC – *Kalamazoo District*

David Litchfield 1966-1969; David Lutz 1969-1970; Arthur Turner 1970-1971; Merritt Edner 1971-1972; Wayne Babcock 1972-1975; Ross Bunce 1975-1977; Linda Stoddard 1977-1983; C. David Hainer 1983-1984; Elizabeth Perry Nord 1984-Oct. 1986; Mark Thompson Jan. 1987-Nov. 15, 1992; Norman C. Kohns Nov. 16, 1992-1993; Jackie Bralick 1993-Feb. 1, 1995; Pulpit Supply Feb.-May 1995; Terrill M. Schneider June 1, 1995-

Scotts UMC – *Albion District*

Garth Smith 1965-1971; Pulpit Supply July-Nov. 1971; Wilbur Williams Nov. 1971-Aug. 1973; Paul Mazur Sept. 1973-1978; Pulpit Supply July-Dec. 1978; Donald Robinson Dec. 1978-Aug. 1979; James Allred Sept. 1979-Dec. 1986; Pulpit Supply Jan.-Apr. 1987; Dennis Slattery Apr. 1987-Oct. 1988; Pulpit Supply Oct.-Dec. 1988; Thomas E. Ball Dec. 1988-1994; David F. Hills 1994-Aug. 1, 1999; Sally J. LaFrance Oct. 1, 1999-2001; Thomas L. Truby 2001-March 1, 2003; David G. Knapp 2003-2009; Glenn C. Litchfield 2009-

Scottville UMC – *Grand Traverse District*

Bernard Fetty 1964-Jan. 1970; J. William Schoettle Feb. 1970-1975; Harold Taber 1975-Jan. 1976; Lloyd R. Hansen Feb. 1976-Oct. 1980; William Mathae Nov. 1980-Dec. 1983; D. Hubert Lowes Jan. 1984-1993; Merritt F. Bongard 1993-Aug. 16, 1995; Pulpit Supply Aug. 1995-Jan. 1996; Bobbie Dale Whitlock Jan. 1996-2004; Robert Ellery Jones 2004-2009; John J. Conklin 2009-

Sears UMC – *Heartland District*

Dan Reedy 1968-1969; Carter Miller 1969-March 1971; Lynn Wagner March 1971-Oct. 1973; Eugene Baughn Oct. 1973-March 1974; Daryl Cook 1974-1977; Kenneth Kline 1977-1986; Carl Litchfield 1986-1991; Eugene L. Baughan 1991-1997; Brian R. Bunch 1997-2005; Ronald DeGraw Aug. 1, 2005-Nov. 6, 2005; James L. Breithaupt Mar. 15, 2006-Oct. 19, 2009; Joseph L. Beavan Jan. 15, 2010-2014; Bryan K. Kilpatrick 2014-

Sebewa Center UMC – *Lansing District*

Marjorie Matthews June-Sept. 1968; Robert D. Keith Sept. 1968-1971; Ralph Kallweit 1971-Jan. 1976; John Morse Feb. 1976-1982; Chris Schroeder 1982-Nov. 1984; Kenneth A.O. Lindland Nov. 1984-1987; Joseph L. Spackman 1987-1991; Gordon Spalenka 1991-1993; Robert Besemer 1993-Aug. 31, 1996; Donald Woolum Sept. 16, 1996-2003; Judith Lee Scholten 2003-2004; Jeffrey J. Schrock 2004-2012; Clare W. Huyck 2012-2013 [Sunfield/Sebewa Center no longer two-point charge 2013] [Barry-Eaton Cooperative Ministry 2013]

Shaftsburg UMC – *Lansing District*

Karl Patow 1962-1969; Ivan Niswender 1969-1971; David Draggoo 1971-1981; Jeff Siker-Geisler 1981-1983; Harris Hoekwater 1983-Jan. 1992; Clinton McKinven-Copus Feb. 1992-Dec. 31, 1994; Pulpit Supply Jan. 1-April 15, 1995; Carroll A. Fowler April 16, 1995-2003; Carolyn C. Floyd 2003-2008; Raymond R. Sundell 2008-2012; Nancy G. Powers 2012-

Shelby UMC – *Grand Rapids District*

Ronald Houk Jan. 1966-Oct. 1971; James Fox Nov. 1971-Aug. 1977; Robert Carson Sept. 1977-1981; Daniel Minor 1981-1989; Ray Flessner 1989-1991; Keith Bovee 1991-1994; James E. Hodge 1994-2001; Lewis A. Buchner 2001-Feb. 1, 2002; Peggy A. Boltz 2002-2010; Terri Cummins 2010- [Shelby became a two-point charge Shelby/Claybanks 2014]

Shelbyville UMC – *Grand Rapids District*

Paul Scheibner 1965-1970; Thurlan Meridith 1970-1976; Gerald L. Welsh 1976-1984; Lee F. Zachman 1984-April 15, 1994; William C. Bills 1994-2007; Christopher L. Lane 2007-2009; David A. Selleck 2009-2012; Donald J. Graham 2012-2014; Sean K. Kidd 2014-

Shepardsville UMC – *Heartland District*

Leroy Howe 1968-1969; Karl Ziegler 1969-1970; Roger Wittrup 1970-1971; Darold Boyd 1971-1978; Rodney Kalajainen 1979-1981; Bruce Kintigh 1981-1988; Charles Smith 1988-1996; D. Kay Pratt 1996-2004; Rob McPherson (Administrative Pastor) 2005; Gordon Schleicher (Administrative Pastor) 2006; Cheryll Warren (DSA) 2007; Cheryll Warren Nov. 10, 2007-June 30, 2009; Judy Hazle (DSA) Aug. 1, 2009-

Shepherd UMC – *Heartland District*

G. Albert Rill 1971-1976; Joseph Dudley 1976-Aug. 1979; Michael L. Selleck Aug. 1979-1986; Leonard B. Haynes 1986-1992; Donald E. Spachman 1992-2004; Wayne Allen Price 2004-2007; Kathleen S. Kursch 2007-

Silver Creek UMC – *Kalamazoo District*

Meredith Rupe 1968-Nov. 1970; Gary Gamble Nov. 1970-May 1973; Supply pastor June-Oct. 1973; Lynn Wagner Oct. 1973-1975; Daniel Barker 1975-Sept. 1978; Gregory Wolfe Oct. 1978-Nov. 1983; Donald Buege Jan. 1984-1990; Dennis Slattery 1990-1992; David L. Litchfield 1992-1988; Virginia L. Heller 1998-2004; Mark E. Thompson 2004-2009; Julie A. Greyerbiehl 2009-2011; Heather McDougall 2011-2013; Beth A. Reum 2013-

Sitka UMC – *Grand Rapids District*

Kenneth D. McCaw 1967-1968; Austin W. Regier 1969; Ira J. Noordhof 1971-1975; Donald J. Vuurens, Oct. 15, 1975-Dec. 31, 1977; Wayne Speese (Pulpit Supply) Jan. 1, 1978-June 1978; Charles R. VanLente 1978-1983; Steven D. Pearson 1983-1988; Kathryn B. Robotham 1988-1990; Michael A. Van Horn 1990-1991; Leonard Coon 1991-Nov. 1, 1999; Milton Stahl (interim) Nov. 1, 1999-July 1, 2000; Patrick Cameron 2000-Nov. 30, 2001; James Meines December 1, 2001-2005; Brian M. McLellan (DSA) 2005-Feb. 15, 2006; James Meines (DSA) Apr. 15, 2006-Oct. 31, 2006; Nancy L. (Besemer) Boelens Nov. 1, 2006-2008; Paul Lynn (part-time) 2008-Nov. 15, 2009; Gerald F. Hagans (DSA) (1/4 time) Nov. 15, 2009-

Snow UMC – *Grand Rapids District*

Ralph Tweedy 1967-1969; Wayne Barrett 1969-1972; Steven Beach 1972-1974; Ed Passenger 1974-1977; Allen Wittrup 1977-1985; Richard Strait 1985-1986; Dan Duncan 1986-1989; Tracey Taylor 1989-1990; Lloyd Hansen 1990-1991; Mary (Horn) Schippers 1991-March 31, 1995; Pulpit Supply April-June 1995; Thurland Meredith (ad interim) 1995-2008; Vance Dimmick (DSA) 2008-2009; [Middleville/Snow two-point charge 2009] Michael T. Conklin 2009-2012; Anthony C. Shumaker 2012-

Sodus Chapel Hill UMC – *Kalamazoo District*

Myron Kent Williams 1960-1969; B. James Varner 1969-1973; Leonard Putnam 1973-1975; George Fleming 1975-1987; William V. Payne 1987-1996; Richard D. Wilson 1996-2003; David A. Cheyne 2003-2005; James A. Dibbet 2005-2011; Russell K. Logston 2011-2014; Mark E. Mitchell 2014-

Somerset Center UMC – *Albion District*

Richard Stoddard 1968-1974; David Showers 1974-1976; Martin Fox 1976-1979; Gerald Selleck 1979-1982; Mark Kelly 1982-1983; Dr. Campbell 1983-1984; Jim Hodge 1984-1989; Lawrence P. Brown 1989-1996; Michael E. Long 1996-1998; James W. Barney 1998-2005; Geraldine M. Litchfield 2005-2007; Denise J. Downs 2007-2008; Maurice Walworth Jr. (DSA) 2008-2009; [Hillside/Somerset Center two-point charge 2009] E. Jeanne Koughns 2009-2014; Patricia A. Pebley 2014-

South Boardman UMC – *Grand Traverse District*

Gerald L. Hedlund 1966-1971; Arthur and Molly Turner (co-pastors) 1971-1976; Diane Vale 1976-Oct. 1977; Marion Nye Dec. 1977-1978; Pulpit Supply 1978-1979; Athel Lynch 1979-1981; Pulpit Supply 1981-1983; Daniel Biteman, Jr. 1983-1985; Clinton McKinven-Copus 1985-1987; Gary Wales 1987-1994; Howard Seaver 1994-2012; Mark E. Mitchell 2012-2014; Donald L. Buege 2014-

South Ensley UMC – *Heartland District*

Jerry L. Hippensteel 1977-1981; Richard Strait 1981-1984; Richard Fairbrother 1984-1989; Mary Curtis 1989-91; Richard Sneed 1991-1992; Richard A. Selleck 1992-1996; Howard H. Harvey 1996-1999; Nathan D. Junius 1999-Feb. 1, 2002; Lloyd R. Hansen Feb. 1, 2002-June 30, 2002; Donald Turkelson (DSA)(part-time) 2002-Nov. 30, 2007; Darryl Miller (DSA) (1/2 time) Jan. 1, 2007; Darryl Miller (part-time) Dec. 1, 2007-

South Haven UMC – *Kalamazoo District*

William Torrey 1968-1974; Richard Youells 1974-Aug. 15, 1979; Larry Irvine Sept. 16, 1979-1984; C. William Martin 1984-1989; Edward Slate 1989-1995; Billie R. Dalton 1995-2004; John W. Fisher 2004-2013; Devon R. Herrell 2013-2014; Virginia L. Heller 2014-

South Monterey UMC – *Kalamazoo District*

Glenn Britton 1968-Jan. 1970; Stanley Finkbeiner Feb. 1970-1974; Densel Fuller 1974-1976; Brent Phillips 1976-1978; David Knapp 1978-Oct. 15, 1982; Robert J. Stillson Nov. 1982-1989; Robert D. Nystrom 1989-1992; Marjory A. Berkompas 1992-June 13, 1996; David S. Yoh (DSA) 1996-1999; Raymond D. Field 1999-2001; Reva H. Daniel 2001-2005; Linda J. Burton 2005-2014; Dominic A. Tommy 2014-

South Wyoming UMC – *Grand Rapids District*

Walter Rothfus 1968-1971; Curtis Cruff 1971-1975; Leonard Yarlott 1975-1979; Edward Trimmer 1979-1981; Ben Chapman 1981-1982; Howard Harvey 1982-1988; John Myette 1988-March 15, 1991; Arthur D. Jackson March 15, 1991-Dec. 31, 1993; John Myette Jan. 1, 1994-1995; Lois M. Munn 1995-1997; Donald D. Entenman 1997-Sept. 30, 1997; Rhonda J. Prater Nov. 16, 1997-2003; Marcia L. Elders (part-time) 2003-

Sparta UMC – *Grand Rapids District*

Paul Patterson 1968-1973; Eldon K. Eldred 1973-April 1979; Ronald Entenman 1979-1985; James R. Hulett 1985-1993; Steven R. Young 1993-2006; Raymond J. Townsend 2006-2009; Louis W. Grettenberger 2009-

Springport UMC – *Albion District*
Lynn Chapel 1965-March 1971; Beulah Poe March 1971-1976; Robert Doner 1976-1978; Joel Campbell 1978-1979; Ethel Stears 1979-Sept. 16, 1983; William Doubblestein Oct. 16, 1983-1987; Eugene Baughan 1987-1991; David H. Minger 1991-1995; Wayne Willer 1995-1996; Valerie Hill 1996-1998; David L. Litchfield 1998-2001; David Blair 2001-2003; Diane E. Stone 2004-2010; Melissa Claxton 2010- [North Parma / Springport became two-point charge 7-1-10]

St Johns First UMC – *Heartland District*
Harold Homer 1968-1972; Francis Johannides 1972-1977; Keith Laidler 1977-1984; Mark Graham 1984-1987; Paul Patterson 1987-1990; Stephan Weinberger 1990-2000; Carolyn C. Floyd 2000-2003; Margery A. Schleicher 2003-2007; Lori J. Sykes 2007-2012; Ellen K. Zienert July 15, 2012-

St Johns Pilgrim UMC – *Heartland District*
Eugene Friesen 1966-1970; Brian K. Sheen 1970-1983; Larry R. Shrout 1983-1998; Raymond R. Sundell1998-2003; Merlin H. Pratt 2003-2006; D. Kay Pratt (Assoc.) 2004-2006; Price UMC merged with St Johns Pilgrim 2005; Kenneth J. Bremer 2006-2014; Andrew L. Croel 2014-

St Joseph First UMC – *Kalamazoo District*
Sidney A. Short Feb. 1968-Jan. 1973; Richard E. Johns (Assoc.) Apr. 1968-Apr. 1969; Gary Gamble (Assoc.) 1969-1971; Douglas L. Pedersen (Assoc.) 1971-Oct.1973; Dale D. Brown Feb. 1973-Dec. 1982; David A. Selleck (Assoc.) 1974-Mar. 1976; Harold F. Filbrandt Feb. 1983-Mar. 1987; Benton R. Heisler (Assoc.) 1986-Aug. 1988; Ronald A. Houk 1987-1997; Charles K. Stanley (Assoc.) Oct. 1988-Oct. 1990; Shelley L. Caulder (Assoc.) Dec. 1991-1996; Thomas C. Nikkel (Assoc.) 1996-2000; Wade S. Panse 1997-Jan. 1, 2012; James W. Kraus, Jr. (Deacon) 2001- ; Terry Euper (DSA) Jan. 1, 2012; Harris J. Hoekwater 2012-

St Louis First UMC – *Heartland District*
Harold L. Mann 1972-March 1982; Gerald R. Bates April 1982-1987; Richard C. Kuhn 1987-1998; Robert D. Nystrom 1998-2002; Lillian T. French 2002-Dec. 31, 2007; [Pleasant Valley UMC merged w/ St. Louis UMC 01-01-08] Terri L. Bentley Feb. 1, 2008-

Stanwood Northland UMC – *Heartland District*
Nolan Williams 1967-1974; Bernard Randolph 1974-March 1975; Max Gladding March 1975-1982; Emmett Kadwell 1982-1992; Jack Bartholomew 1992-1995; Edward H. Slate 1995-2006; Dominic A. Tommy 2006-2014; Gary D. Bondarenko 2014-

Stevensville UMC – *Kalamazoo District*
Gerald Welsh 1968-Oct. 1969; Lloyd Phillips Oct. 1969-1979; Dean Bailey 1979-1987; Steve Emery (Assoc.) 1981-1987; Geoffrey Hayes 1987-March 23, 1994; Larry Rubingh (Assoc.) 1987-1988; Jeffrey Wright (Assoc.) 1988-1990; Bradley Bartelmay (Assoc.) 1990-1993; Tamara S.M. Williams (Assoc.) 1993-2002; Eugene A. Lewis 1994-2003; Terri L. Bentley (Assoc.) 2002-Feb. 1, 2008; Beryl Gordon Barry 2003-

Stockbridge UMC – *Lansing District*
William Frayer 1965-1969; Raymond Norton 1969-1971; Dale Spoor 1971-Sept. 1974; Douglas Vernon Oct. 1974-Sept. 1979; David Selleck Oct. 1979-1987; Richard Matson 1987-1990; Birt Beers 1990-1993; Stuart L. Proctor 1993-Sept. 1995; Robert J. Henning 1996-2007; Larry W. Rubingh 2007-Oct. 15, 2010; Galen L. Goodwin (Retired Elder, Greater New Jersey Conf), Interim Pastor, Oct. 24, 2010-July 1, 2011; Robert J. Freysinger 2011-2013; [M-52 Cooperative Ministry 2013-2014] Jeanne M. Laimon (1/4 time) 2013-2014; Susan J. Trowbridge 2014-

Stokes Chapel UMC – *Albion District*
Karl L. Zeigler 1968-1969; John H. Gurney 1969-Aug. 1970; Joseph Huston Aug. 1970-1972; Richard Huskey 1972-1974; J. Brian Selleck 1974-Feb. 1976; Robert P. Stover March 1976-1980; Stephen Beech 1980-1983; Larry W. Rubingh 1983-1987; Frederick G. Hamlin 1987-1994; Russell K. Logston 1994-1996; Diane Stone Nov. 16, 1996-2004; Edward Mohr 2004-2010; Trevor McDermont 2010-2013; Frederick G. Cain (Retired) (part-time) 2013-

Sturgis UMC – *Albion District*

Charles B. Hahn 1966-1970; Hilding Kilgren 1970-1977; Miriam DeMint (Assoc.) 1969-1970; David Dunn (Assoc.) 1970-1973; Dennis Paulsen (Assoc.) 1973-1975; Edward Boase (Assoc.) 1975-1977; George Hartmann 1977-1987; Richard Riley (Assoc.) 1977-1980; Mark Graham 1987-1988; Susan Adsmond Fox July-Sept. 1987; Ray W. Burgess 1988-1993; Lowell F. Walsworth 1993-1995; Richard A. Morrison 1995-Jan. 1, 1998; Dianne Morrison (Assoc.) Jan. 1996-Jan. 1, 1998; Keith R. Treman Jan. 15, 1998-2008; Colleen T. Treman (Deacon) 1998-2008; J. Robert Keim (Assoc.) Dec. 16, 1999-Dec. 31, 2011; Deborah M. Johnson 2008-2014; E. Jeanne Koughn 2014-

Sunfield UMC – *Lansing District*

Marjorie S. Matthews June-Sept. 1968; Robert Keith Sept. 1968-1971; Ralph G. Kallweit 1971-Jan. 1976; John Morse Feb. 1976-1982; J. Chris Schroeder 1982-Jan. 1992; Harris J. Hoekwater Jan. 1992-1998; Brian K. Sheen 1998-2004; Jeffrey J. Schrock 2004-2012; Clare W. Huyck 2012- [Sunfield/ Sebewa Center no longer two-point charge 2013] [Barry-Eaton Cooperative Ministry 2013]

Third Avenue UMC – *Heartland District*

Richard D. Wilson 1968-1971; Lynn Chapel 1971-1979; John Buker 1979-Jan. 1981; Elaine Buker Jan. 1981-1986; Kendall Lewis 1986-1990; J. Robert Collins 1990-Oct. 1991; Albert Frevert (interim) Jan.-June 1992; David Hills 1992-1994; Kathryn M. Steen 1994-2000; Dawn A. Beamish Jan. 1, 2001-2002; Edwin D. Snook 2002-2005; Michael A. Riegler Sept. 11, 2005-2011; Ed Milam (DSA) July 1-Nov. 12, 2011; Ed Milam Nov. 12, 2011-2014; David J. Cadarette Sr. (DSA) 2014-

Three Oaks UMC – *Kalamazoo District*

Larry Waterhouse Apr. 1966-Oct. 1970; Meredith Rupe Nov. 1970-Nov. 1975; Larry Irvine Nov. 1975-Sept. 1979; Terry MacArthur Sept. 1979-1983; Ross Bunce 1983-1985; Lloyd Walker 1985-1988; Steven Pearson 1988-1995; Orin L. Daniels 1995-1998; David A. Cheyne 1998-Jan. 16, 1999; Sherri L. Swanson Sept. 1, 1999-

Three Rivers First UMC – *Albion District*

Richard H. Beckett 1968-1976; Charles D. Grauer 1976-1981; Raymond McBratnie (Assoc.) 1976-1980; James Patrick McCoy (Assoc.) Oct. 1980-1983; Frank B. Closson 1981-April 1985; John A. Backoff (Assoc.) 1983-1985; James E. Fox May 1985-1990; Robert L. Pumphery 1990-1997; Cynthia A. Skutar 1997-2000; Donald R. Fry 2000-2006; Maria L. Rutland Nov. 1, 2006-2012; Robert D. Nystrom (1/2 time) 2012- ; [Three Rivers First / Mendon became two-point charge 2013]

Three Rivers Ninth Street UMC – *Albion District*

Eugene Moore 1968-1972; Helen Jackson 1972-Jan. 1974; Albert A. O'Rourke Nov. 1974-1976; Charles Grauer 1976-1981; Raymond McBratnie (Assoc.) 1976-Aug. 1980; James Patrick McCoy (Assoc.) Oct. 1980-1983; Frank Closson 1981-April 1985; John A. Backoff (Assoc.) 1983-1985; Phillip Simmons 1985-1988; Reva Hawke 1988-Oct. 1991; Marilyn B. Barney Oct. 1991-1998; Carolyn A. Robinson 1998-2007; Thomas R. Reaume (part-time) 2007-2009; [Three Rivers Ninth / Schoolcraft Pleasant Valley became a two-point charge 2009] James W. Stilwell 2009-

Townline UMC – *Kalamazoo District*

John Gurney 1965-1969; Wayne Babcock 1969-1971; Gerald Hudlund 1971-1972; Wayne Barrett 1972-1974; Pulpit Supply 1974-1976; David Youngs 1976-1978; Lloyd Bronson 1978-1985; Dwight Stoner 1985-1988; Donald Williams 1988-1990; William Brady 1990-1991; Kenneth J. Littke 1991-1998; D.S. Assignment 1998; Jana Jirak Sept. 16, 1998-1999; Robert L. Pumfery 1999-October 31, 2002; Patricia Anne Harpole November 1, 2002-2004; O'Ryan Rickard 2004-2005; Sheila F. Baker 2005-Jan. 3, 2008; David L. Youngs Jan. 3, 2008 - June 2008; David L. Haase (DSA) (1/4 time) Jan. 3, 2008; David L. Haase (1/4 time) July 1, 2008-2014; James C. Robertson (1/4 time) 2014-

Traverse Bay UMC – *Grand Traverse District*

Traverse City Asbury & Emmanuel merged to become Traverse Bay UMC January 2005; [ASBURY: Dale E. Crawford 1967-Oct. 1971; Wilson Tennant Nov. 1971-May 1976; Richard E. Cobb 1976-Aug. 1980; Wirth G. Tennant (Assoc.) 1978-Sept. 1983; William A. Hertel Sept. 1980-1987; John H. Hice 1987-1995; William E. Haggard 1995-2002; Jeremy P.H. Williams 2002- ;] [EMMANUEL: George Belknap 1966-1973; B. James Varner 1973-1977; Kenneth A.O. Lindland 1977-1979; Jack Kraklan 1979-1983; Steven Averill 1983-April 1989; Lewis Buchner 1989-1992; Robert J. Mayo 1992-1999; David H. Minger 1999-Jan. 31, 2003; Douglas L. Pedersen Feb. 1, 2003- ;] Jeremy P.H. Williams 2002-2009; Douglas L. Pedersen Feb. 1, 2003-2005; Devon R. Herrell (Assoc.) 2005-2008; Jeanne E. Koughn (Assoc.) 2008-2009; Jane R. Lippert 2009-

Traverse City Central UMC – *Grand Traverse District*

William N. DesAutels 1968-Nov. 1974; Robert C. Brubaker Dec. 1974-1981; Ellen A. Brubaker (Assoc.) 1975-1981; Joanne Parshall (Assoc.) 1981-Sept. 1982; David L. Crawford 1981-1987; Gary T. Haller (Assoc.) 1981-1985; Kathy E. Brown (Assoc.) 1985-1990; Dean I. Bailey 1987- 2002; Steven R. Emery-Wright (Assoc.) Aug. 1990-May 1992; Robert D. Nystrom (Assoc.) 1992-1994; John W. Ellinger 2002-2007; Tamara S.M. Williams (Assoc.) 2002-2009; Dale Ostema 2007- ; Christopher M. Lane (Assoc.) 2009-

Traverse City Christ UMC – *Grand Traverse District*

John D. Morse 1987-1993; Louis W. Grettenberger 1993-2009; Mary S. Brown July 1-Nov. 1, 2009; Hal Ferris (DSA) Nov. 1-30, 2009; John W. Ellinger (DSA) Dec. 1, 2009-June 1, 2010; Kathryn M. Coombs (DSA) 2010-2011; Dianne Doten Morrison 2011-

Trowbridge UMC – *Kalamazoo District*

Henry Houseman 1962-1974; Leon Shaffer 1974-1981; R. Ivan Niswender 1981-1994; Gary S. Wales 1994-2008; Anthony C. Shumaker (part-time) 2008-2012; Sheila F. Baker (1/2 time) 2012-Feb. 2, 2014; John L. Moore (Retired) 2014-

Turk Lake UMC – *Heartland District*

George Fleming 1965-1975; Douglas Pedersen 1975-1979; Jim Hartman 1979-1982; Steven Young 1982-1987; Joyce DeToni-Hill 1987-1990; Jane Crabtree 1990-1996; John F. Ritter 1996-Nov. 1, 2001; Ronald W. DeGraw Nov. 1, 2001-2005; Kay Welsch (DSA) July 16, 2005-2012; [Turk Lake / Belding became two-point charge 2012] Kimberly A. DeLong Aug. 15, 2012-2013; [Greenville First, Turk Lake/Belding Cooperative Parish 2013] Kimberly A. DeLong (Deacon) 2013- ; Stephen MG Charnley 2013-14; Stephen F. Lindeman 2013-14; Donald E. Spachman 2014-

Twin Lake UMC – *Grand Rapids District*

Kenneth D. McCaw 1967-1968; Austin W. Regier 1969; Alma H. Glotfelty 1970; Ira J. Noordhof 1971-1975; Donald J. Vuurens, Oct. 15, 1975-Dec. 31, 1977; Wayne Speese (Pulpit Supply) Jan. 1, 1978-June 1978; Charles R. VanLente 1978-1983; Steven D. Pearson 1983-1988; Kathryn B. Robotham 1988-1990; Michael A. Van Horn 1990-1991; Leonard Coon 1991-Oct. 31, 1999; Milton Stahl (interim) Nov. 1, 1999-July 1, 2000; Patrick Cameron 2000-2002; Sally J. LaFrance 2002-Oct. 1, 2004; Paul R. Doherty (DSA) Nov. 1, 2004-2010; Mary Loring 2010-2013; John D. Morse (Retired) 2013-

Union City UMC – *Albion District*

Philip L. Brown 1966-1971; Walter J. Rothfuss 1971-1973; Larry Grubaugh 1973-1980; Adam Chyrowski 1980-1986; Eric S. Beck 1986-July 31, 1995; David W. Meister Aug. 1, 1995-Aug. 15, 1997; D.S. Assignment Aug. 16, 1997; John L. Moore (DSA) Aug. 17, 1997-2004; Robert M. Hughes 2004-2012; [Union City / Athens became two-point charge 2012] Seung Ho Baek (3/4 time) 2012-

Valley UMC – *Grand Rapids District*

[new church start 2009] Matthew Bistayi 2009- [chartered 9-22-2013]

Vergennes UMC – *Grand Rapids District*

William Vowell 1968-1969; Phillip Carpenter 1969-1977; Luren Strait 1978-1979; Donald Buege 1979-Sept. 1, 1980; Stanley Forkner Sept. 1, 1980-1986; Daniel Duncan 1986-1989; Tracy Taylor 1989-1990; Lloyd Hansen 1990-1991; Mary Schippers 1991-March 31, 1995; Pulpit Supply April-June 1995; David F. Stout 1995-1996; Nathaniel W. Johnson Sept. 1, 1996-2010; Matthew Stoll 2010-

Vermontville UMC – *Lansing District*

David C. Haney 1967-1969; William R. Tate 1969-1972; Gary V. Lyons 1972-April 1976; Gerald A. Salisbury April 1976-1979; Molly C. Turner 1979-1983; Glenn C. Litchfield 1983-1990; Richard W. Young 1990-1991; Robert L. Kersten 1991-1995; Jeffrey J. Bowman 1995-2002; Kathleen Smith 2002-Dec. 31, 2012; [Vermontville/Gresham no longer two-point charge 2013] [Barry-Eaton Cooperative Ministry 2013] Gary L. Simmons (1/4 time) 2013-

Vickeryville UMC – *Heartland District*

John H. Gurney 1970-1976; Norman Crotser 1976-Dec. 1978; Daniel R. Bennett 1979-March 1982; Mark G. Johnson March 1982-1986; James E. Cook 1986-1991; Howard H. Harvey 1991-1996; Patrick Glass 1996-1998; Larry W. Nalett 1998-Aug. 9, 2004; Charles E. Cerling Aug. 10, 2004-2009; Jolennda Cole (DSA) 2009-2010; Jolennda Cole 2010-2011; William F. Dye 2011-2012; Russell D. Morgan (CLM) July 15, 2012-2014; Gerald Erskine (DSA) 2014-

Vicksburg UMC – *Kalamazoo District*

Dean Bailey (Methodist) 1966-1969; David Morton (EUB) 1965-1969; Myron K. Williams 1969-1972; C. Robert Carson 1972-Oct. 1977; Francis C. Johannides Oct. 1977-1981; Lowell F. Walsworth; 1981-1993; Lawrence R. Wood (Assoc.) 1991-1995; James R. Hulett 1993-1997; Jana Lynn Almeida (Assoc.) 1995-1997; Isabell M. Deppe 1998-Sept. 2000; Bufford W. Coe, Oct. 15, 2000-

Wacousta UMC – *Lansing District*

Dale Spoor 1967-1971; Edward Otto 1971-1977; John R. Smith 1977-1984; Eugene Lewis 1984-1986; James Hynes 1986-1992; Betty A. Smith 1992-1998; D.S. Assignment 1998; Lyle D. Heaton Jan. 1, 1999-2013; Amee A. Paparella 2013-

Wakelee UMC – *Kalamazoo District*

Ira Fett 1968-1969; Donald Ludman 1969-1974; Wayne Babcock 1975-1978; Derryl Cook 1978-1981; Robert Mayo 1981-1986; Kenneth I. Kline 1986-1992; Dennis E. Slattery 1992-1998; Gregory L. Buchner (DSA) 1998-Nov. 16, 1999; Gregory L. Buchner Nov. 16, 1999-2005; Nelson L. Hall 2005-2007; John D. Messner (DSA) 2007; John D. Messner Jan. 1, 2008-

Walkerville UMC – *Grand Traverse District*

A. Ruth Bonser Oct. 1990-1993; Nancy Bugajski 1993-1996; Donald J. Vuurens (DSA) 1996-1998; Steven J. Hale 1998-Nov. 8, 1999; Ronald A. Houk (DSA) Nov. 8, 1999-2000; Kenneth E. Tabor 2000-2004; Ronald L. Worley 2004-Nov. 30, 2013; Ronald Iris (Retired) Dec. 1, 2013-

Water's Edge UMC – *Kalamazoo District*

John Bullock 1968-1974; Robert Pumfery 1974-1979; Joseph Beattie 1979-1980; Ken Vanderlaan 1980-1981; Charles Tooman 1981-Jan. 1982; Gregory B. Wood Feb. 1, 1982-1985; B. Gordon Barry 1985-1993; Bradley S. Bartelmay 1993- [1/1/12 New Buffalo First UMC renamed Water's Edge UMC]

Waterloo Village UMC – *Lansing District*

Wilbur Silvernail 1960-1969; Donald R. Fry 1969-1970; Altha M. Barnes 1970-1975; Richard M. Young 1975-1976; Glenn Kjellburg 1976-1978; Pulpit Supply 1978-1979; L. A. Nichols 1979-1988; Merlin Pratt 1988-1991; Wayne Willer 1991-1995; Pulpit Supply 1995; Kathleen A. Groff Dec. 1995-July 31, 1997; Mona Joslyn Aug. 1, 1997-1998; Kathleen S. Kursch 1998-Feb. 1, 2000; Georgiana M. Dack (1/4 time) Feb. 1, 2000-2013; [Waterloo Village/First no longer two-point charge 2013] Edward C. Ross (Retired) (1/4 time) 2013-

Wayland UMC – *Grand Rapids District*

H. Forest Crum, 1960-66; Bernard R. Randolph 1966-1970; Leo E. Bennett 1970-1979; Richard W. Barker 1979-1982; Douglas L. Pedersen 1982-1987; James W. Barney 1987-Sept. 1991; Wendell R. Stine Sept. 1991-1995; Stacy R. Minger 1995-Jul. 31, 2001; Julie A. Dix Aug. 1, 2001-2003; Nancy L. Besemer 2003-Nov. 1, 2006; Gary D. Bondarenko Nov. 15, 2006-2014; Jeffrey C. Williams 2014-

Webberville UMC – *Lansing District*

Gary Lyons 1968-1969; Milford Bowen 1969-1973; John McNaughton 1973-1979; Ross Bunce 1979-1983; Wayne Babcock 1983-1991; David Cheyne 1991-1995; Dwayne E. Bagley 1995-2002; Wayne E. McKenney Aug. 1, 2002-2005; Robert D. Nystrom 2005-2007; Sandra L. Spahr (DSA) 2007-Dec. 31, 2007; Paul A. Damkoehler, Jan. 1, 2008-2013; [M-52 Cooperative Ministry 2013] Richard J. Foster (3/4 time) 2013-

Weidman UMC – *Heartland District*

James Linton 1967-1969; Lawrence R. Smith 1969-1970; Athel J. Lynch 1970-1977; Vance M. Dimmick, Jr. 1977-1984; Diane E. Vale 1984-1985; Pulpit supply July 1985-Jan. 1986; Randall E. Roose Jan. 1986-1993; Melanie S. Young 1993-1994; Jerry L. Hippensteel 1994-March 26, 1995; Pulpit Supply April-June 1995; James H.K. Lawrence 1995-May 10, 1999; Craig L. Adams Sept. 16, 1999-2006; David Price (DSA) 2006-Nov. 15, 2006; David Price Nov. 15, 2006-2013; Scott B. Smith 2013-

Welcome Corners UMC – *Lansing District*

John Jodersma 1967-Nov. 1968; Stanley Finkbeiner Nov. 1968-1969; Esther Cox 1969-1975; Richard Erickson 1975-1976; Clinton Bradley-Galloway 1976-1981; Constance Heffelfinger 1981-1984; Glenn Wegner 1984-1987; Robert Kersten 1987-1991; Carl Q. Litchfield 1991-2000; Geraldine M. Litchfield (Assoc.) Jan. 1993-1994; Soo Han Yoon Aug. 1, 2000-Jan. 31, 2001; Robert E. Smith Feb. 1, 2001-Dec. 31, 2003; Robert E. Smith (part-time) Dec. 31, 2003-2006; Susan D. Olsen 2006-

Wesley Park UMC – *Grand Rapids District*

Kenneth Lindland 1968-Dec. 1969; Theron Bailey Dec. 1969-Sept. 1977; James E. Fox Sept. 1977-April 1985; (Griggs St. UMC merged with Wesley Park in Jan. 1979. Ward Pierce was pastor of Griggs St.)Ward Pierce Jan.-March 1979; Douglas Pedersen (Assoc.) 1979-1982; Myron K. Williams 1985-1994; William V. Clegg 1994-2011; Dean N. Prentiss 2011-

West Mendon UMC – *Albion District*

William Foster 1965-Dec. 1968; David Litchfield Dec. 15, 1968-1971; Harold Simon 1971-1973; William Dobbs 1973-1978; Frank Closson 1978-1981; Larry Higgins 1981-1983; Lloyd Hansen 1983-1987; Clinton McKinven-Copus 1987-1990; Carolyn Floyd 1990-1997; Reva Hawke 1997-2001; Ward D. Pierce (DSA) 2001-Dec. 2, 2012 (died); David G. Knapp (interim) Jan. 1, 2013-June 30, 2013; [West Mendon became single-point charge 2013] Thoreau May (DSA) 2013-

Wheatfield UMC – *Lansing District*

Eugene Tate Oct.-Dec. 1968; Dennis Ferris Dec. 1968-April 1969; Wayne Gorsline April 1969-1975; Millard Wilson 1975-1977; Marcel Elliott 1977-Jan. 1978; Thomas Butcher Jan. 1978-Oct. 1979; Dennis Demond Oct. 1979-1980; Fred Fischer 1980-1985; Susan Adsmand 1985-1987; David Wendland 1987-1988; Carolyn Hare Robinson 1988-1991; Paulette Cheyne 1991-1995; Valerie Fons 1995-1999; Stephen F. Ezop 1999-June 30, 2002; Sharyn K. Osmond 2002-2006; Stephan Weinberger Aug. 1, 2006-2007; Jeanne Laimon (DSA) 2007; Jeanne Laimon (1/4 time) Dec. 1, 2007-2012; Jeremy J. Wicks (1/4 time) 2012-2014 [M-52 Cooperative Ministry 2013-2014]; Richard J. Ahti (DSA) 2014-

White Cloud UMC – *Grand Rapids District*

William A. Hertel 1966-1969; Kenneth E. Curtis 1969-1971; Allan R. Valkema 1971-1976; Peter H. Kunnen 1976-Jan. 1984; Thomas and Lynn Pier-Fitzgerald (co-pastors) May 1984-1988; Jerry L. Jaquish 1988-2002, Jeffrey J. Bowman 2002-2012; Edwin D. Snook 2012-

White Pigeon UMC – *Albion District*

Lyle Chapman 1965-1969; Robert Stillson 1969-1975; Daniel Wolcott 1975-Sept. 1977; Donald Fry Nov. 1977-1981; Kendall Lewis 1981-Jan. 1985; Wesley Smith Jan. 1985-Sept. 1990; Charles Vizthum Nov. 1990-July 31, 1995; Mary Pieh 1996-1998; Patrick Glass 1998-Sept. 15, 2001; Linda J. Burton (DSA) 2001-2002; Linda J. Burton 2002-2005; Ronna L. Swartz 2005-2007; Janet L. Luchs (part-time) 2007-2009 [Schoolcraft Pleasant Valley / White Pigeon became a two-point charge 2008]; Scott E. Manning [Constantine / White Pigeon became a two-point charge 2009]

Whitehall UMC – *Grand Rapids District*

Charles Dunbar 1965-1971; Richard Matson 1971-1975; Bernard Randolph 1975-1976; Edward Slate 1976-1983; Steve Smith 1983-1985; Keith Treman 1985-1990; Kay B. Bosworth 1990-1998; Anita Hahn 1998-2006; Gayle Berntsen 2006-2014; [Whitehall realigned from Whitehall/Claybanks to Whitehall/Crestwood 2014] Mary A. Sweet 2014-

Williamsburg UMC – *Grand Traverse District*

Merritt F. Bongard 1991-1993; Cynthia W. Schaefer 1993-1997; Douglas L. Pedersen 1997-2005; William W. Chu & Julie A. Greyerbiehl (Chu) 2005-2009; Geraldine M. Litchfield 2009-2014 [Elk Rapids UMC merged w/ Williamsburg UMC 4-1-11] Nathaniel R. Starkey 2014-

Williamston Crossroads UMC – *Lansing District*

Williamston: Center and Bell Oak merged to become Williamston: Crossroads UMC June 14, 2000; Patricia A. Skinner June 14, 2000-2002; DeAnn J. Dobbs 2002-2008; Brian F. Rafferty 2008-2010; Ellen K. Zienert 2010-2012; Richard J. Foster (1/4 time) Aug. 1, 2012- [M-52 Cooperative Ministry 2013]

Williamston UMC – *Lansing District*

Ferris S. Woodruff 1966-1979; Harold A. Kirchenbauer 1969-Oct. 1975; Laurence L. Waterhouse Oct. 1975-1982; Ilona R. Sabo-Shuler 1982-1994; Robert H. Roth, Jr. 1994-1999; Dean Prentiss Sept. 15, 1999-2008; Alice Fleming Townley (3-6 months interim, para. 338.3b) July 15, 2008-2009; Amee Anne Miller 2009-2011; Julie A. Greyerbiehl 2011-

Winn UMC – *Heartland District*

Harold Arman 1968-1969; Lawrence Smith 1969-1970; Athel J. Lynch 1970-1973; Joseph A. Dudley 1973-1974; Kathy Nickerson 1974-1977; James C. Sabo-Schuler 1977-1980; James W. Burgess 1980-1986; M. Christopher Lane 1986-1990; Paula Jane Duffey 1990-1994; Philip Bacon 1994-1997; Ron Smith 1997-1999; Paulette Cheyne 1999-2006; Melody Lane Olin (DSA) 2006; Melody Olin Nov. 15, 2006-2010; Lawrence Wonsey 2010-2014; Russell D. Morgan (CLM/DSA) 2014-

Woodland UMC – *Lansing District*

Claude Ridley 1968-1972; Richard Erickson 1972-1976; Clinton Bradley-Galloway 1976-1981; Constance Hefflefinger 1981-1984; Glenn Wegner 1984-1987; Robert Kersten 1987-1991; Carl Litchfield 1991-2000; Geraldine M. Litchfield (Assoc.) Jan. 1993-1994; Soo Han Yoon Aug. 1, 2000-Jan. 31, 2001; Robert E. Smith Feb. 1, 2001-Dec. 31, 2003; Mary Schippers-DeMunter (DSA) 2004-2008; James E. Fox (DSA) July 22, 2008-2011; Gary L. Simmons (1/4 time) 2011- [Barry-Eaton Cooperative Ministry 2013

Wyoming Park UMC – *Grand Rapids District*

James W. Dempsey 1965-1969; Gerald A. Pohly 1969-Feb. 1973; John P. Hitchens (Assoc.) 1972-1985; Stanley H. Forkner March 1, 1973-1979; C. William Martin 1979-1984; Ward N. Scovel 1984-1989; Don Eddy 1989-Feb. 28, 1994; Lee F. Zachman April 16, 1994-1996; William C. Johnson 1996-2012; Robert Eckert (Assoc.) Apr. 1, 2006-2008; Joel T. Fitzgerald 2012-

DISCONTINUED CHURCHES

Congregations discontinued in accordance with ¶2548 of *The Book of Discipline, 2008.*

Benton Harbor Peace Temple UMC – *Kalamazoo District*

George Hartman 1966-1971; Carlos Page 1971-1989; Dow Chamberlain 1989-Nov. 30, 1993; Donald Entenman Feb. 1, 1994-1995; David G. Knapp 1995-2003; Deborah R. Miller 2003-Nov. 14, 2003; David S. Yoh (DSA) Nov. 15, 2003-2006; James W. Stilwell 2006-2009; Sandra V. Douglas (Deacon) (1/4 time) 2008-2009 [Benton Harbor: Peace Temple UMC discontinued 6-30-09]

Brandywine: Trinity UMC – *Kalamazoo District*

Vernon L. Michaels 1967-1969; Douglas Vernon 1969-1971; Robert Wellfare 1971-1973; Lowell F. Walsworth 1973-1978; Raymond D. Flessnor 1978-1981; David E. Small 1981-1987; Arthur C. Murphy Aug. 1987-1991; Edward A. Friesen 1991-1993; Patricia A. Myles 1993-Apr. 17, 1994; Richard L. Eslinger 1994-Nov. 1, 1998; Matthew Bistayi Jan. 1, 1999-2002; Allen J. Duyck 2002-Sept. 22, 2003; Carl Harrison Feb. 1, 2004-2008; Christopher A Kruchkow (DSA) 2008-2009 [Brandywine: Trinity UMC discontinued 8-30-08]

Eagle UMC – *Lansing District*

William Cox 1968-1970; Raymond J. McBratnie 1970-1974; David Morton 1974-1982; William Dornbush 1982-Nov. 1986; Janell E.R. Gerken Jan. 1987-1988; Raymond D. Field 1988-1993; Larry W. Nalott 1993-1998; Stephen F. Ezop 1998-1999; D. Michael Maurer Aug. 16, 1999-2002; Judith Lee Scholten 2003-2011 [Eagle UMC discontinued 10-15-11]

East Lansing Aldersgate UMC – *Lansing District*
William Clegg 1984-1994; David W. Meister 1994-July 31, 1995; Kenneth W. Karlzen Aug. 1, 1995-2000; Gary D. Bondarenko 2000-Nov. 15, 2006; Paulette G. Cheyne Nov. 15, 2006-Apr. 1, 2008 [East Lansing Aldersgate UMC discontinued 4-1-08]

East Lansing Chapel Hill UMC – *Lansing District*
Stephen Beach 1968-1969; Edward F. Otto 1969-Dec. 1972; Daniel Miles Dec. 1972-1974; Paul K. Scheibner 1974-1978; J. Lynn Pier-Fitzgerald 1978-May 1984; Thomas M. Pier-Fitzgerald (co-pastor) 1982-May 1984; Charles W. Smith May 1984-1988; Carl W. Staser 1988-Jan. 1991; Beverly E. Gaska Jan. 1991-July 31, 1995; D. Michael Maurer Aug. 1, 1995-2002; Robert David Nystrom 2002-Jan. 15, 2004; Robert David Nystrom (1/2 time) Jan. 16, 2004-2005; Ellen K. Zienert 2005-2012; [East Lansing Chapel Hill discontinued 6-24-12]

Ellis Corners UMC – *Albion District*
Logan Weaver 1968-1976; Densel G. Fuller 1976-1981; Jerry L. Hippensteel 1981-1984; Thomas E. Ball 1984-Nov. 1988; Stanley Fenner Dec. 1988-1989; Stacy R. Minger 1989-1994; John F. Ritter 1994-1996; Robert Stark 1996-2000; John Scott 2000-Sept. 1, 2003; John A. Scott & Rebecca Scott (CoPastors) Sept. 2003-2007; Bruce R. Kintigh 2007- ; [Ellis Corners UMC discontinued 12-31-07]

Grand Rapids Oakdale UMC – *Grand Rapids District*
Arthur Jackson 1966-Oct. 1969; Kenneth Lindland Dec. 1969-1973; Brent Phillips 1973-1976; Douglas Knight 1976-1978; Charles Dunbar 1978-1979; Ed Trimmer 1979-1982; Cathy Kelsey 1982-1987; Jane Shapley 1987-1996; Marguerite R. Bermann 1996-1999; Calvin Hill Aug. 16, 1999-2003; Theresa Little Eagle Oyler-Sayles 2003-2006; Andy Baek 2006-2008 [Oakdale UMC discontinued 6-30-08]

Grand Rapids Olivet UMC – *Grand Rapids District*
Grand Orin Bailey 1964-1969; Allen Wittrup 1969-1977; C. Jack Scott 1977-1979; Richard Youells Aug. 1979-1989; Barry T. Petrucci 1989-Dec. 31, 1994; Clinton McKinven-Copus Jan. 1, 1995-Jan. 1, 2001; Dominic A. Tommy (Assoc.) Apr. 16, 1999-2000.; Robert Eckert (DSA) 2001-2005; James Stilwell March 1, 2005-2006; Gary Peterson (DSA) 2006-2008; James Thomas Boutell (part-time) 2008-2010; Jean & Jane Crabtree (DSA) 2010- [discontinued 12-12-10]

Grand Rapids Plainfield UMC – *Grand Rapids District*
K.C. Downing 1967-1969; C. Dow Chamberlain 1969-1972; Don W. Eddy (Assoc.) 1971-1979; Robert L. Hinklin 1972-1976; Marvin F. Zimmerman 1976-1978; Wayne C. Barrett 1978-1982; Neal M. Kelly 1982-1984; John McNaughton 1984-1986; Ethel Z. Stears 1986-1988; Jeanne Randels 1988-1991; Lynn Pier-Fitzgerald 1991-1999; Neil Davis 1999-2002; Robert R. Cornelison 2002-2005; Joyce F. Gackler June 1, 2005-2012; [Grand Rapids Aldersgate / Plainfield became two-point charge 2012] Laurie A. Haller 2012-2013 [Plainfield UMC discontinued 06-30-13]

Hudsonville UMC – *Grand Rapids District*
Deborah Johnson Sept. 1990-1997; R. John Thompson 1997-Apr. 1, 2001; Sandra K. VandenBrink 2001-Jan. 1, 2005; [Hudsonville UMC discontinued 01-01-05]

Jones UMC – *Albion District*
Reva Hawke 1988-Oct. 1991; Marilyn B. Barney Oct. 1991-1998; Carolyn A. Robinson 1998-2007; Thomas R. Reaume (part-time) 2007-2009; Jack Balgenorth 2009-Sept. 1, 2010 [discontinued 9-1-10]

Kalamazoo Lane Blvd UMC – *Kalamazoo District*
Marion Burkett 1966-1969; James Lavengood 1969-1972; Harold Taber 1972-1975; Richard D. Wilson 1975-1981; Gary Kintigh 1981-1985; Robert Freysinger 1985-1988; Daniel Biteman 1988-1996; John W. McNaughton 1996-Jan. 16, 2000; James Dyke (DSA) 2000-2006; David S. Yoh (DSA), July 1, 2006-Oct. 4, 2006; Philip P. Steele (DSA), Oct. 8, 2006; Kevin E. Hale (DSA), Jan. 1, 2007; Martin H. Culver (DSA), Mar. 18, 2007-Mar. 25, 2008 [Lane Boulevard UMC discontinued 3-25-08]

Lansing Potter Park UMC – *Lansing District*

Ronald Entenman 1967-1972; Peter Kunnen 1972-1976; Arthur Turner 1976-1981; Clinton Bradley-Galloway 1981-1983; Lewis Buchner 1983-1986; Zawdie Abiade 1986-1988; Donald Entenman 1988-1991; Isabell Deppe 1991-Dec. 31, 1997; D. Michael Maurer (Pastor Interim, part time) Jan. 1, 1998-June 30, 1998; Grace Kathleen O'Connor 1998-2001; Lamarr V. Gibson 2001-2004; Betty A. Smith (DSA) October 16, 2004-2005; Stephan Weinberger 2005-2006; [Potter Park UMC discontinued 06-30-06]

Moscow Plains UMC – *Albion District*

Densel Fuller Feb. 1969-1974; David Showers 1974-1976; Martin Fox 1976-1979; Gerald Selleck 1979-1982; Mark Kelly 1982-1983; Dr. Campbell 1983-1984; Jim Hodge 1984-1989; Lawrence P. Brown 1989-Dec. 1992; Donald R. Wendell Jan 1, 1993-Dec. 31, 1995; Bernice Taylor-Alley (DSA) 1996-2001; Craig Pahl 2001-2007; [Moscow Plains UMC discontinued 06-30-07]

Outland – *Albion District*

[new church start 2006] Peggy J. Baker 2006-2011; Stacy Caballero 2011-Mar. 1, 2012 [Outland discontinued 2-29-12]

Parma UMC – *Albion District*

Edward Dahringer 1968-Sept. 1980; Jean Crabtree Nov. 1980-Jan. 1984; Jerry Hippensteel 1984-1989; Charlotte Lewis 1989-1992; Carolin S. Spragg 1992-1999; Keith W. Heifner 1999-2003; Michael P. Baker-Streevy 2003-Nov. 1, 2005; Lynn Stull-Lipps Jan. 15-June 30, 2006; [Jackson Trinity / Parma became a charge 2006] Sandra L. Spahr (DSA) 2006-2007; Melodye Surgeon Rider 2007-2012; Patricia A. Pebley (1/2 time) 2012-2014 [Parma UMC discontinued 05-28-14]

Pawating Magedwin UMC – *Grand Rapids District*

David G. Knapp 1992-1995; Timothy J. Miller 1995-Jan. 31, 2002; Deborah R. Miller Feb. 1, 2002-2003; Theresa Little Eagle Oyler-Sayles 2003-2006; [Pawating Magedwin UMC discontinued 07-01-06]

Sylvan UMC – *Heartland District*

Kenneth I. Kline 1977-1981; Pulpit Supply June-Aug. 1981; Dwight Benner Sept. 1981-1983; Purlin Wesseling Aug. 1983-1986; Frank Closson 1986-Jan. 1988; Jane Crabtree Jan. 1988-1990; Pulpit Supply July-Nov. 1991; Robert Stark Nov. 1990-Aug. 1991; Carol L. Bourns Sept. 1991-Dec. 31, 1994; Pulpit Supply Jan. 1995-1996; Jean Crabtree (DSA) 1996-2000; Donald L. Buege 2000-Jan. 2006; Jon Pohl Jan. 15 - June 30, 2006; Jean A. Crabtree (DSA) Nov. 5, 2006-July 2007; Russell Morgan (DSA) July 8, 2007-Nov. 9, 2009; Pat Robinson (DSA) Nov. 9, 2009 [Sylvan UMC became single-point charge Nov. 9, 2009] [discontinued 12-31-11]

Traverse City Windward – *Grand Traverse District*

[new church start 2007] John A. Scott 2007-2011; Rebecca Scott (Assoc.) Nov. 1, 2008-2010 [Windward new church start discontinued 5-15-11]

Waterloo First UMC – *Lansing District*

Wilbur Silvernail 1960-1969; Donald R. Fry 1969-1970; Altha M. Barnes 1970-1975; Richard M. Young 1975-1976; Glenn Kjellburg 1976-1978; Pulpit Supply 1978-1979; L. A. Nichols 1979-1988; Merlin Pratt 1988-1991; Wayne Willer 1991-1995; Pulpit Supply 1995; Kathleen A. Groff Dec. 1995-July 31, 1997; Mona Joslyn Aug. 1, 1997-1998; Kathleen S. Kursch 1998-Feb. 1, 2000; Georgiana M. Dack (1/4 time) Feb. 1, 2000-2013; [Waterloo Village/First no longer two-point charge 2013] [M-52 Cooperative Ministry 2013] Jeanne M. Laimon (1/4 time) 2013-2014 [Waterloo First UMC was discontinued 2-16-14]

White Pines UMC – *Grand Rapids District*

[new church start 2004] Jeffrey C. Williams 2004-2011; Dale A. Hotelling 2011-Aug. 31, 2012 [White Pines new church start discontinued 8-31-12]

MERGED CHURCHES

Comstock UMC – *Kalamazoo District*

Wilbur Courter 1967-Jan. 1973; David Dunn Jan. 1973-Dec. 1973; David Charter Feb. 1974-Feb. 1976; Thomas Evans 1976-1984; Edward Slate 1984-1989; Valerie Hill 1989-1991; Mary Curtis 1991-1998; Peggy J. Baker 1998-2006; Paulette G. Cheyne 2006-Nov. 15, 2006; [Comstock UMC merged w/ Galesburg UMC 04-29-07]

Elk Rapids UMC – *Grand Traverse District*

Lawrence Hodge 1966-Nov. 1968; Glen Loy Oct. 1968-Oct. 1970; A.J. Lynch (Assoc.) June-Oct. 1968; R.J. Lautner (Assoc.) 1968-Oct. 1970; Gordon Showers Oct. 1970-Oct. 1971; Robert Doner Dec. 1971-1976; Bernard Randolph 1976-1978; Jack Barthlomew 1978-Feb. 1983; Stephen Beach April 1983-Nov. 1986; Michael Baker-Streevy Dec. 1986-1988; Charles Shields 1988-1993; Raymond R. Sundell 1993-1998; Kathryn M. Coombs 1998-1999; Thomas M. Pier-Fitzgerald 1999-2005; William W. Chu & Julie A. Greyerbiehl (Chu) 2005-2009; Geraldine M. Litchfield 2009- [Elk Rapids UMC merged w/ Williamsburg UMC 4-1-11]

Lansing Calvary UMC – *Lansing District*

Morris Bauman 1965-1973; H. James Birdsall 1973-1978; William Dobbs 1978-1983; Dale Crawford 1983-Feb. 1986; Jack M. Bartholomew Feb. 1986-1992; Leonard B. Haynes 1992-1998; Paula Jane Duffey 1998-2005; Stephan Weinberger 2005-2007; [Lansing Calvary UMC merged w/ Mt. Hope UMC 07-01-07]

Osseo UMC – *Albion District*

William F. Bowers 1966-Sept. 15, 1969; Charles D. Grauer Sept. 15, 1969-1970; Daniel W. Harris 1970-1971; Robert E. Jones 1971-Nov. 15, 1973; Marion V. Nye Nov. 15, 1973-1976; Daniel R. Bennett Feb. 1, 1977-1979; Leonard J. Yarlott 1979-1982; Gilbert R. Boersma 1982-1985; Valerie M. Hill 1985-1989; Jerry L. Hippensteel 1989-1994; Susan Deason 1994-1998; Kathy L. Nitz 1998-Aug. 15, 1999; Clarence Able (DSA) 2001-2002; Donald E. Lee 2003-2010; Cynthia Veilleux (DSA) Nov. 1, 2010-2011; Kimberly A. Metzger July 1-Dec. 19, 2011; Timothy Puckett (part-time) Jan. 1, 2012- [Osseo UMC merged w/ North Adams UMC 4-6-14]

Pleasant Valley UMC – *Heartland District*

G. Albert Rill 1971-1976; Joseph Dudley 1976-Aug. 1979; Michael L. Selleck Aug. 1979-1986; Leonard B. Haynes 1986-1992; Donald E. Spachman 1992-1997; Doris Lyon 1997-Jan. 1, 2008 [Pleasant Valley UMC merged w/ St. Louis UMC 01-01-08]

Watervliet UMC – *Kalamazoo District*

Lawrence Grubaugh 1968-1971; Donald Russell 1971-1975; Joseph Wood 1975-1978; Lawrence Wiliford 1978-Sept. 1981; Katherine Williams (Coombs) Dec. 1981-Sept. 1984; Fred Hamlin Nov. 1984-1985; Kenneth Curtis 1985-May 1987; Len Schoenherr 1987-1999; David F. Hills Aug. 1, 1999-2007; O'Ryan Rickard 2007-2009; William W. Chu 2009-2011; Ron Van Lente 2011- [Watervliet UMC merged w/ Coloma UMC 6-26-11]

—WMC Photos

XXI–B. DISTRICT SUPERINTENDENTS HISTORY

Michigan Annual Conference Methodist Episcopal Church 1929-1939
Michigan Annual Conference of the Methodist Church 1940-1968
West Michigan Annual Conference of the United Methodist Church 1969-Present

Albion District

1929-1930 M.W. Duffey
1930-1934 Cecil E. Pollock
1935-1937 Albert H. Pellowe
1938-1942 Lloyd H. Nixon
1943-1948 Spencer B. Owens
1948-1954 William H. Helrigel
1955-1958 Richard C. Miles
1959-1963 Howard A. Lyman
1964-1968 Stanley Buck
1969-1970 Lawrence Taylor
1971-1976 John L. Francis
1977-1980 David L. Crawford
1981-1986 William W. DesAutels
1987-1991 Eldon K. Eldred
1992-1997 Paul L. Hartman
1998-2003 Richard A. Morrison
2003-2009 Jerome R. DeVine
2009-present Tamara S. Williams

Grand Rapids District

1929-1391 Clark S. Wheeler
1932-1934 Hugh Kennedy
1935-1940 L.L. Dewey
1941-1946 Edmond H. Babbitt
1947-1952 L. Winston Stone
1953-1958 Maurice D. McKean
1959-1964 Keith T. Avery
1965-1970 Carlos C. Page
1971-1976 Robert C. Smith
1977-1982 Darwin R. Salisbury
1983-1988 Ellen A. Brubaker
1989-1992 Sharon Z. Rader
(Elected Bishop July 15, 1992)
1992-1993 Ilona R. Sabo-Shuler
(Effective September 1, 1992)
1993-1994 Charles F. Garrod
1995-1999 John H. Hice
2000-2006 Susan J. Hagans
2006-2012 Laurie A. Haller
2012-present William E. Haggard

Grand Traverse District

1929-1930 J.O. Randall
1931-1935 Moses E. Reusch
1936-1937 Glenn M. Frye
1938-1942 Wm. H. Helrigel
1943-1948 Leslie J. Nevins
1949-1953 Russell R. King
1954-1959 William Blanding
1960-1964 Heath T. Goodwin
1965-1969 Howard A. Smith
1970-1975 Donald Scranton
1976-1980 Marjorie S. Matthews
(Elected Bishop July 17, 1980)
1981-1985 J. Leon Andrews
(Effective August 18, 1980)
1986-1991 Marvin R. Rosa
1991-1998 Dennis Buwalda
1998-2005 Lynn Pier-Fitzgerald
2005-2011 Robert J. Mayo
2011-present Anita K. Hahn

Big Rapids District

1929-1932 J.C. DeVinney
1933-1937 Victor W. Thrall
1938-1939 Stanley B. Niles
1939-1942 W. Maylan Jones
1943-1948 Byron A. Hahn
1949-1954 Clark H. Phillips
1955-1960 Leon Manning
1961-1962 Emeral E. Price
1963 changed to Central District

Central District

1963-1966 Emeral E. Price
1967-1972 E. William Wiltse
1973-1977 Gerald A. Pohly
1978-1983 Charles Fry
1984-1989 Charles F. Garrod
1990-1992 Molly C. Turner
1993-1998 Lynn E. Grimes
1998-2005 Joseph D. Huston
2005-2009 William D. Dobbs
2009 changed to Heartland District

Heartland District

2009-2010 William D. Dobbs
2010-present David F. Hills

Kalamazoo District

1929-1930 R.E. Meader
1931-1934 W.F. Kendrick
1935-1940 Henry W. Ellinger
1941-1946 Raymond B. Spurlock
1947-1952 Richard D. Wearne
1953-1954 Richard C. Miles
1955-1960 Harold R. Kinney
1961-1965 Charles B. Hahn
1966-1970 Robert H Jongeward
1971-1976 George O. Hartmann
1977-1982 Richard A. Selleck
1983-1988 Kenneth D. McCaw
1989-1995 James Boehm
1995-2001 Russell F. McReynolds
2001-2008 Zawdie K. Abiade
2008-2014 Cornelius (Neil) N. Davis
2014-present John W. Boley

Lansing District

1929-1930 Cecil E. Pollock
1931-1966 Lansing listed with Albion
1967-1971 Harold A. Jayne
1972-1977 Albert W. Frevert
1978-1981 Lawrence R. Taylor
1982-1986 Ronald A. Houk
1987-1989 Quincy D. Cooper
1990-1995 A. Edward Perkins
1996-2001 John W. Ellinger
2001-2009 Benton R. Heisler
1/1/09-6/30/09 Dennis G. Buwalda, *Interim*
2009-2013 Robert L. Hundley
2013-present Kennetha Bigham-Tsai

— WMC Photos

Report of 2013 Ministry Share Support — 5 Year History

Church	Current Pastor	2013 Apportioned	2013 Amt. Paid	2013 % Paid	2009	2010	2011	2012	2013
ALBION DISTRICT									
1010 Albion	Jeremy Williams	29,354.00	29,353.92	100%	100%	100%	100%	100%	100%
1020 Athens	Seung Ho (Andy) Baek	4,769.00	4,769.00	100%	100%	66%	100%	100%	100%
1030 Augusta	Jennifer Wheeler	7,247.00	2,900.00	40%	71%	80%	81%	39%	40%
BATTLE CREEK:									
1040 Baseline	Peggy Baker	12,057.00	12,057.00	100%	100%	100%	100%	100%	100%
1050 Birchwood	Bruce Kintigh	14,462.00	14,461.56	100%	92%	71%	92%	100%	100%
1060 Chapel Hill	Chad Parmalee	55,637.00	55,637.00	100%	100%	100%	100%	81%	100%
1070 Christ	Scott Bouldrey	21,254.00	7,915.57	37%	101%	100%	100%	75%	37%
1080 Convis Union	Sueann Hagan	12,183.00	12,183.00	100%	101%	100%	100%	100%	100%
1090 First	Bille Dalton	31,216.00	31,216.00	100%	86%	83%	100%	100%	100%
1100 Maple	Linda Stoddard	13,809.00	13,809.00	100%	75%	100%	100%	101%	100%
1110 Sonoma	Sally Harrington	4,845.00	4,228.62	87%	100%	100%	100%	100%	87%
1111 Newton	Sally Harrington	8,891.00	6,707.05	75%	100%	100%	100%	60%	75%
1120 Trinity	Bruce Kintigh	11,225.00	1,355.00	12%	100%	100%	9%	36%	12%
1130 Washington Heights	Marshall Murphy	6,830.00	6,830.00	100%	7%	48%	100%	100%	100%
1044 Bellevue	Peggy Baker	11,773.00	11,773.00	100%	100%	100%	100%	100%	100%
1140 Bronson	Cynthia Veilleux	11,533.00	11,533.00	100%	26%	67%	100%	100%	100%
1150 Burr Oak	John Sterner	5,339.00	5,339.04	100%	74%	71%	54%	76%	100%
1160 Camden	Frederick Cain	4,059.00	1,495.00	37%	9%	40%	112%	100%	37%
1161 Montgomery	Frederick Cain	3,059.00	3,601.32	118%	83%	100%	100%	100%	118%
1162 Stokes Chapel	Frederick Cain	4,017.00	4,017.00	100%	48%	100%	100%	100%	100%
1170 Center Park	Martin Culver	11,359.00	11,359.00	100%	100%	33%	100%	100%	100%
1180 Centreville	Karin Orr	19,561.00	19,560.96	100%	100%	100%	100%	100%	100%
1190 Climax	Glenn Litchfield	15,073.00	15,073.00	100%	100%	100%	86%	90%	100%
1191 Scotts	Glenn Litchfield	6,055.00	4,547.44	75%	100%	100%	60%	101%	75%
1200 Coldwater	Steven Young	37,783.00	37,783.00	100%	100%	100%	89%	100%	100%
1210 Colon	John Sterner	10,124.00	10,124.04	100%	100%	100%	100%	100%	100%
1220 Concord	David Elmore	21,954.00	13,647.50	62%	63%	54%	75%	100%	62%
1230 Constantine	Scott Manning	12,180.00	12,138.00	100%	100%	100%	100%	100%	100%
1084 Delton: Faith	Brian Bunch	17,122.00	7,798.56	46%	100%	100%	25%	47%	46%
1250 Frontier	Timothy Puckett	5,068.00	5,067.96	100%	103%	100%	100%	100%	100%
1251 Osseo	Timothy Puckett	3,174.00	3,174.00	100%	100%	100%	100%	100%	100%
1260 Galesburg	Leonard Schoenherr	11,167.00	11,167.00	100%	100%	100%	100%	100%	100%
1270 Girard	Emily Beachy	15,440.00	15,440.00	100%	36%	100%	86%	100%	100%
1271 Ellis Corners	DISCONTINUED				0%				
1280 Grass Lake	Den Slattery	14,687.00	14,687.04	100%	101%	48%	100%	100%	100%
1290 Hillsdale	Patricia Brook	17,468.00	17,470.00	100%	100%	100%	100%	100%	100%
1300 Hillside	E. Jeanne Koughn	15,523.00	15,523.00	100%	76%	34%	84%	73%	100%
1310 Homer	Robert Stover	6,906.00	6,906.00	100%	4%	1%	0%	70%	100%

Report of 2013 Ministry Share Support — 5 Year History

Church	Current Pastor	2013 Apportioned	2013 Amt. Paid	2013 % Paid	2009	2010	2011	2012	2013
1311 Lyon Lake	Robert Stover	6,561.00	6,560.55	100%	100%	100%	100%	100%	100%
JACKSON:									
1320 Brookside	Ronald Brooks	22,020.00	19,984.89	91%	100%	100%	80%	83%	91%
1330 Calvary	Edrye Maurer	24,930.00	4,436.00	18%	100%	100%	21%	43%	18%
1340 First	Eric Beck	84,965.00	84,964.92	100%	100%	100%	100%	100%	100%
1350 Trinity	Patricia Pebley	12,845.00	12,845.00	100%	50%	51%	56%	58%	100%
1360 Zion	Edrye Maurer	2,875.00	2,875.00	100%	50%	75%	78%	100%	100%
1365 Pleasant Lake	Moved to Lansing District	2,665.00	2,665.00	100%	100%	101%	100%	100%	100%
1370 Jonesville	Craig Pahl	13,122.00	2,020.00	15%	64%	20%	0%	36%	15%
1371 Allen	Craig Pahl	6,082.00	6,083.00	100%	45%	100%	100%	100%	100%
1380 Litchfield	Julie Elmore	14,133.00	9,911.96	70%	93%	100%	100%	51%	70%
1390 Marengo	Gerry Retzloff	1,365.00	-	0%	0%	0%	0%	0%	0%
1400 Marshall	Melany Chalker	62,754.00	62,754.00	100%	89%	100%	100%	100%	100%
1410 Mendon	Robert Nystrom	11,913.00	11,913.00	100%	100%	100%	100%	100%	100%
1415 Moscow Plains	DISCONTINUED				0%				
1430 Napoleon	Gregory Wolfe	14,822.00	7,411.16	50%	100%	100%	100%	100%	50%
1440 North Adams	Arthur Turner	6,052.00	6,061.60	100%	79%	100%	73%	100%	100%
1441 Jerome	Arthur Turner	4,353.00	4,353.48	100%	100%	100%	100%	100%	100%
1450 Nottawa	Sandy Miller	1,247.00	1,247.00	100%	100%	100%	100%	100%	100%
1460 Parma	Patricia Pebley	3,184.00	3,184.00	100%	100%	100%	100%	100%	100%
1461 North Parma	Melissa Claxton	9,737.00	9,737.00	100%	100%	100%	101%	100%	100%
1470 Pope	Robert Moore-Jumonville	2,514.00	2,514.00	100%	100%	100%	100%	100%	100%
1471 Griffith	David Minger	5,685.00	-	0%	100%	100%	100%	100%	0%
1480 Quincy	Julie Elmore	10,547.00	10,537.00	100%	100%	100%	100%	100%	100%
1490 Reading	Robert Hughes	14,631.00	14,631.00	100%	103%	100%	100%	100%	100%
1500 Somerset Center	E. Jeanne Koughn	6,785.00	6,785.00	100%	100%	100%	100%	100%	100%
1510 Springport	Melissa Claxton	6,715.00	6,715.00	100%	100%	110%	100%	100%	100%
1511 Lee Center	Irene Vittoz	5,709.00	5,712.50	100%	103%	100%	101%	100%	100%
1520 Sturgis	Deborah Johnson	41,292.00	41,292.00	100%	100%	100%	100%	100%	100%
THREE RIVERS:									
1530 First	Robert Nystrom	16,815.00	600.00	4%	16%	48%	7%	33%	4%
1540 Ninth Street	James Stilwell	6,024.00	6,024.00	100%	99%	100%	100%	100%	100%
1541 Jones	DISCONTINUED				100%				
1550 Union City	Seung Ho (Andy) Baek	18,242.00	18,242.00	100%	100%	100%	100%	100%	100%
1570 West Mendon	Thoreau May	11,625.00	11,625.00	100%	100%	100%	100%	100%	100%
1575 Pleasant Valley	James Stilwell	8,146.00	8,145.96	100%	100%	100%	100%	100%	100%
1580 White Pigeon	Scott Manning	5,182.00	5,182.30	100%	100%	100%	100%	100%	100%
ALBION DISTRICT TOTAL		979,740.00	859,660.90	88%	89%	89%	8600%	87%	88%

MINISTRY SHARE HISTORY

Report of 2013 Ministry Share Support — 5 Year History

Church	Current Pastor	2013 Apportioned	2013 Amt. Paid	2013 % Paid	2009	2010	2011	2012	2013
GRAND RAPIDS DISTRICT									
3010 Alto	Dean Bailey	7,440.00	7,440.00	100%	100%	103%	101%	100%	100%
3011 Bowne Center	Dean Bailey	7,383.00	7,383.00	100%	100%	100%	100%	100%	100%
3030 Byron Center	Lawrence Nichols	25,248.00	25,248.00	100%	27%	100%	100%	100%	100%
3040 Caledonia	Jodie Flessner	24,856.00	25,015.96	101%	100%	100%	100%	100%	101%
3050 Carlisle	Michael Ramsey	18,012.00	10,008.00	56%	25%	65%	73%	112%	56%
3060 Cedar Springs	Mary Ivanov	25,852.00	25,852.00	100%	100%	100%	100%	100%	100%
3061 East Nelson	Herb VanderBilt	12,647.00	12,647.00	100%	100%	100%	100%	101%	100%
3070 Coopersville	Cori Lynn Cypret	18,419.00	18,420.00	100%	74%	100%	100%	100%	100%
3080 Courtland-Oakfield	Robert Eckert	12,801.00	12,801.00	100%	100%	100%	100%	100%	100%
3100 Fremont	Martin Cobb	47,002.00	35,866.00	76%	100%	100%	100%	95%	76%
3110 Georgetown	William Bills	74,088.00	74,088.00	100%	100%	100%	100%	100%	100%
3120 Grand Haven	Daniel Duncan	71,111.00	71,111.00	100%	73%	100%	100%	100%	100%
GRAND RAPIDS:									
3130 Aldersgate	James Hodge	30,351.00	30,351.00	100%	99%	100%	100%	100%	100%
3145 Cornerstone	Bradley P. Kalajainen	234,160.00	234,159.84	100%	100%	101%	100%	100%	100%
3905 Crosswind	Scott Otis	10,451.00	10,451.00	100%			100%	100%	100%
3150 Faith	Mark Thompson	30,579.00	30,579.00	100%	100%	100%	100%	100%	100%
3160 First	Robert Hundley	170,963.00	171,463.01	100%	100%	100%	100%	100%	100%
3163 Genesis	Sue Petro	34,329.00	34,329.00	100%	100%	50%	56%	100%	100%
3165 La Nueva Esperanza	Nohemi Ramirez	5,484.00	-	0%	7%	7%	43%	0%	0%
3170 Northlawn	Tim Wright	28,140.00	28,313.66	101%	62%	63%	74%	76%	101%
3180 Oakdale	DISCONTINUED								
3190 Olivet	DISCONTINUED				94%	100%			
3200 Plainfield	DISCONTINUED	11,296.00	4,706.60	42%	24%	100%	100%	100%	42%
3210 St. Paul's	Erin Fitzgerald	35,567.00	35,567.00	100%	100%	100%	100%	100%	100%
3220 South	Mack Strange	20,379.00	20,379.00	100%	89%	100%	55%	83%	100%
3230 Trinity	David Nellist	85,486.00	85,485.96	100%	100%	100%	100%	100%	100%
3235 Vietnamese	Daniel Nguyen	4,967.00	5,727.00	115%	89%	92%	100%	100%	115%
3240 Grandville	Tom Pier-Fitzgerald	44,670.00	44,670.00	100%	100%	100%	100%	100%	100%
3250 Hesperia	Paul Hane	9,745.00	9,745.00	100%	100%	101%	84%	100%	100%
3251 Ferry	Paul Hane	6,741.00	6,741.10	100%	100%	100%	100%	100%	100%
3260 Holland	Lynn Pier-Fizgerald	78,923.00	78,923.00	100%	100%	100%	100%	100%	100%
3270 Holton	Gerald Selleck	28,417.00	28,417.00	100%	100%	100%	100%	100%	100%
3290 Kent City Chapel Hill	Kevin Guetschow	15,487.00	15,484.13	100%	93%	80%	84%	104%	100%
3300 Leighton	David McBride	29,185.00	21,068.00	72%	50%	78%	72%	77%	72%
3310 Lowell	Richard Blunt	42,072.00	27,668.00	66%	100%	100%	100%	100%	66%

Report of 2013 Ministry Share Support — 5 Year History

	Church	Current Pastor	2013 Apportioned	2013 Amt. Paid	2013 % Paid	2009	2010	2011	2012	2013
3320	Marne	James (Tommy) Boutell	15,586.00	11,912.40	76%	86%	100%	84%	69%	76%
3330	Martin	Donald Graham	19,281.00	19,281.00	100%	98%	73%	101%	100%	100%
3331	Shelbyville	Donald Graham	7,708.00	7,708.00	100%	100%	100%	100%	100%	100%
3340	Middleville	Anthony Shumaker	22,478.00	22,478.00	100%	100%	100%	100%	100%	100%
3341	Parmalee	William Clegg	5,979.00	5,979.00	100%	100%	100%	100%	100%	100%
3350	Montague	Randall Hansen	31,244.00	31,698.35	101%	71%	100%	100%	100%	101%
3538	Valley Church	Matt Bistayi	-	10,000.00						
	MUSKEGON:									
3360	Central	Mark Miller	57,312.00	57,311.88	100%	100%	100%	100%	100%	100%
3370	Crestwood	Stephan Weinberger	12,999.00	2,979.73	23%	10%	12%	25%	29%	23%
3380	Lake Harbor	Mark Erbes	43,331.00	43,331.00	100%	64%	100%	90%	100%	100%
3390	Lakeside	Stephan Weinberger	18,069.00	6,551.00	36%	100%	57%	30%	13%	36%
3400	Unity	R.John Thompson	5,580.00	5,580.00	100%	100%	100%	100%	78%	100%
3410	Wolf Lake	Bobby Whitlock	14,691.00	8,200.00	56%	19%	61%	10%	29%	56%
3420	Muskegon Hts Temple	Jeffrey Bowman	28,811.00	28,811.00	100%	100%	100%	100%	100%	100%
3430	Newaygo	Kathleen Groff	15,412.00	15,412.00	100%	100%	100%	100%	100%	100%
3440	North Muskegon	Phillip Friedrick	38,182.00	38,181.96	100%	100%	100%	100%	100%	100%
3460	Ravenna	Chaleton Black	14,343.00	12,693.90	89%	100%	42%	100%	100%	89%
3470	Rockford	Richard M. Riley	87,267.00	65,152.68	75%	100%	100%	100%	94%	75%
3480	Salem Indian Mission	Nancy Boelens	1,831.00	1,830.96	100%	100%	100%	100%	100%	100%
3481	Bradley Indian Mission	Nancy Boelens	2,666.00	2,666.00	100%	100%	100%	100%	100%	100%
3500	Saugatuck	Emmett Kadwll Jr.	7,178.00	7,178.00	100%	100%	100%	100%	100%	100%
3510	Shelby	Terri Cummins	15,414.00	8,930.00	58%	74%	100%	100%	100%	58%
3520	Snow	Anthony Shumaker	8,755.00	5,898.49	67%	74%	93%	52%	80%	67%
3530	Sparta	Louis Grettenberger	43,772.00	43,771.12	100%	100%	102%	100%	100%	100%
3535	Twin Lake	John Morse	11,528.00	6,029.00	52%	99%	100%	100%	82%	52%
3536	Sitka	Gerald Hagans	2,230.00	2,230.00	100%	100%	100%	100%	100%	100%
3540	Vergennes	Matthew Stoll	30,303.00	30,303.00	100%	92%	100%	100%	100%	100%
3550	Wayland	Gary Bondarenko	18,347.00	14,677.44	80%	50%	72%	80%	80%	80%
3560	White Cloud	Edwin Snook	24,629.00	22,522.60	91%	100%	100%	100%	100%	91%
3570	Whitehall	Gayle Bernsten	12,220.00	12,220.00	100%	94%	100%	100%	100%	100%
3571	Claybanks	Gayle Bernsten	6,001.00	6,001.00	100%	100%	100%	100%	100%	100%
	WYOMING:									
3141	South Wyoming	Marcia Elder	13,116.00	6,080.39	46%	100%	100%	100%	100%	46%
3580	Wesley Park	Dean Prentiss	66,010.00	66,010.00	100%	100%	100%	100%	100%	100%
3590	Wyoming Park	Joel Fitzgerald	24,323.00	5,684.16	23%	77%	100%	100%	49%	23%
	GRAND RAPIDS DISTRICT TOTAL		2,028,847.00	1,885,402.32	93%	90%	95%	94%	95%	93%

Report of 2013 Ministry Share Support — 5 Year History

Church	Current Pastor	2013 Apportioned	2013 Amt. Paid	2013 % Paid	2009	2010	2011	2012	2013
GRAND TRAVERSE DISTRICT									
4010 Alden	Daniel Biteman	9,991.00	10,200.00	102%	100%	100%	100%	100%	102%
4011 Central Lake	Daniel Biteman	4,122.00	2,576.29	63%	100%	100%	100%	100%	63%
4013 Baldwin Covenant Comm	James Richie	10,864.00	5,583.08	51%	102%	121%	100%	100%	51%
4014 Luther	James Richie	3,535.00	3,535.00	100%	100%	100%	100%	100%	100%
4015 Barnard	Ralph Posnik	3,806.00	-	0%	100%	100%	100%	100%	0%
4016 East Jordan	Ralph Posnik	10,715.00	10,715.04	100%	100%	100%	100%	100%	100%
4017 Norwood	Ralph Posnik	2,218.00	2,217.96	100%	100%	100%	100%	100%	100%
4020 Bear Lake	Roberta Cabot	14,799.00	14,799.00	100%	100%	42%	100%	75%	100%
4021 Arcadia	Roberta Cabot	2,606.00	1,125.00	43%	86%	62%	0%	40%	43%
4030 Bellaire	Peggy Boltz	22,031.00	22,031.00	100%	100%	100%	100%	100%	100%
4040 Boyne City	Wayne McKenney	10,438.00	1,961.50	19%	28%	16%	17%	15%	19%
4041 Boyne Falls	Wayne McKenney	4,425.00	884.00	20%	21%	38%	19%	0%	20%
4050 Epworth	Colleen Wierman	4,746.00	4,746.00	100%	100%	100%	100%	100%	100%
4060 Cadillac	Thomas Ball	40,690.00	37,626.45	92%	100%	100%	67%	56%	92%
4070 Charlevoix	Gregory Culver	15,108.00	12,598.00	83%	90%	88%	74%	55%	83%
4090 Crystal Valley	Ron Iris	4,350.00	4,350.00	100%	100%	100%	100%	100%	100%
4091 Walkerville	Ron Iris	3,457.00	3,457.00	100%	100%	100%	100%	100%	100%
4110 Elk Rapids	MERGED	-	-		22%	58%	0%	0%	
4111 Kewadin	Eugene Baughan	7,214.00	7,415.92	103%	100%	100%	100%	100%	103%
4120 Empire	Brenda Gordon	15,605.00	15,627.00	100%	100%	100%	100%	103%	100%
4131 New Hope Emmet Cty	Vaughn Thurston-Cox	8,296.00	8,295.96	100%	100%	171%	100%	100%	100%
4130 Epsilon	Vaughn Thurston-Cox	10,776.00	6,866.40	64%	99%	100%	101%	100%	64%
Fife Lake-Boardman Parish:									
4140 Fife Lake	Mark Mitchell	4,590.00	4,589.96	100%	99%	100%	100%	100%	100%
4142 South Boardman	Mark Mitchell	2,188.00	2,188.04	100%	100%	100%	100%	100%	100%
4143 East Boardman	Mark Mitchell	4,663.00	3,447.00	74%	94%	75%	75%	72%	74%
4150 Frankfort	Barbara Jo Fay	17,430.00	17,430.00	100%	28%	100%	100%	100%	100%
4151 Elberta	Barbara Jo Fay	4,464.00	4,464.00	100%	100%	100%	100%	100%	100%
4160 Free Soil	Richard Roberts	1,500.00	-	0%	41%	100%	8%	0%	0%
4161 Fountain	Richard Roberts	1,780.00	-	0%	100%	100%	100%	67%	0%
4165 Grawn	Mary Brown	12,563.00	1,182.97	9%	58%	83%	42%	58%	9%
4170 Harbor Springs	Mary Sweet	10,507.00	5,253.48	50%	100%	100%	58%	33%	50%
4171 Alanson	Marry Sweet	6,816.00	5,206.19	76%	100%	100%	100%	62%	76%
4180 Hart	Rebecca Wieringa	19,170.00	19,413.00	101%	70%	100%	100%	100%	101%
4190 Horton Bay	Michael Neihardt	7,330.00	3,000.00	41%	100%	100%	41%	0%	41%
4191 Greensky Hill Indian	Jonathan Mays	6,162.00	1,013.00	16%	100%	100%	97%	15%	16%
4200 Indian River	DeAnn Dobbs	35,169.00	35,169.00	100%	100%	100%	100%	100%	100%

Report of 2013 Ministry Share Support — 5 Year History

	Church	Current Pastor	2013 Apportioned	2013 Amt. Paid	2013 % Paid	2009	2010	2011	2012	2013
4205	Kalkaska	Robert Freysinger	29,051.00	4,841.84	17%	33%	25%	38%	22%	17%
4208	Keswick	Patricia Ann Haas	20,363.00	20,513.00	101%	100%	100%	100%	100%	101%
4210	Kewadin Indian	Thomas H John Sr	3,094.00	3,094.00	100%	104%	100%	100%	100%	100%
4220	Kingsley	Carl Litchfield	21,876.00	21,879.00	100%	100%	100%	100%	100%	100%
4221	Grant	Colleen Wierman	6,096.00	6,096.00	100%	100%	100%	100%	100%	100%
4230	Lake Ann	Michael Simon	15,684.00	2,800.00	18%	17%	17%	33%	27%	18%
4240	Lake City	Jean Smith	15,943.00	8,830.08	55%	100%	100%	80%	71%	55%
4250	Leland	Virginia Heller	35,557.00	36,056.96	101%	100%	100%	100%	100%	101%
	LUDINGTON:									
4270	St. Paul	Jon Pohl	21,250.00	17,124.00	81%	73%	67%	83%	91%	81%
4280	United	Dennis Bromley	46,939.00	46,938.96	100%	70%	100%	100%	100%	100%
4290	Mancelona	Todd Shafer	11,601.00	11,639.00	100%	21%	100%	100%	100%	100%
4291	Alba	Todd Shafer	3,830.00	3,830.00	100%	52%	53%	102%	100%	100%
4300	Manistee	David Selleck	41,984.00	36,054.02	86%	71%	71%	81%	71%	86%
4310	Manton	Noreen Shafer	15,974.00	15,974.00	100%	101%	100%	100%	100%	100%
4320	Marion	James Mort	7,014.00	2,209.50	32%	95%	67%	40%	33%	32%
4321	Cadillac South Comm	James Mort	5,284.00	3,708.80	70%	100%	100%	103%	100%	70%
4330	Mears	Ken VanderLaan	11,865.00	11,865.00	100%	92%	100%	100%	100%	100%
4340	Mesick	Beverely Williams	6,422.00	4,699.96	73%	103%	100%	100%	100%	73%
4341	Harrietta	Beverely Williams	7,112.00	7,112.00	100%	100%	100%	100%	100%	100%
	North East Missaukee Parish:									
4351	Merritt-Butterfield	Jeffrey Schrock	14,364.00	8,379.07	58%	99%	100%	100%	100%	58%
4352	Moorestown-Stittsville	Jeffrey Schrock	5,937.00	5,937.00	100%	100%	100%	100%	100%	100%
4360	Northport Indian	Thomas John Sr.	1,473.00	1,473.00	100%	92%	100%	100%	100%	100%
4370	Old Mission Peninsula	Melody Olin	14,907.00	14,928.00	100%	89%	100%	100%	100%	100%
4380	Pentwater	Gary Bekofske	20,227.00	20,299.98	100%	100%	100%	100%	100%	100%
4390	Petoskey	James P Mitchum	60,487.00	60,702.00	100%	100%	100%	100%	100%	100%
	Pine River Parish:									
4400	Ashton	Scott Loomis	4,596.00	4,596.00	100%	80%	100%	100%	100%	100%
4401	LeRoy	Scott Loomis	10,435.00	7,826.22	75%	100%	100%	100%	100%	75%
4410	Scottville	John (Jack) Conklin	18,711.00	13,756.39	74%	38%	50%	51%	19%	74%
	TRAVERSE CITY:									
4420	Traverse Bay	Jane Lippert	36,727.00	36,907.96	100%	58%	100%	100%	100%	100%
4430	Central	Dale Ostema	121,887.00	121,887.00	100%	100%	100%	100%	100%	100%
4435	Christ	Dianne Morrison	12,728.00	2,400.00	19%	17%	6%	13%	19%	19%
4440	Emmanuel	DISCONTINUED								
4450	Williamsburg	Geraldine Litchfield	11,362.00	11,362.00	100%	97%	100%	100%	100%	100%
	GRAND TRAVERSE DISTRICT TOTAL		1,004,904.00	854,687.98	85%	83%	92%	87%	83%	85%

MINISTRY SHARE HISTORY

Report of 2013 Ministry Share Support

5 Year History

No.	Church	Current Pastor	2013 Apportioned	2013 Amt. Paid	2013 % Paid	2009	2010	2011	2012	2013
	HEARTLAND DISTRICT									
2010	Alma	Deborah Thomas	27,692.00	265.00	1%	100%	100%	100%	50%	1%
2030	Ashlely	Mona Dye	5,205.00	5,205.00	100%	100%	100%	100%	100%	100%
2031	Bannister	Mona Dye	5,891.00	5,891.00	100%	100%	97%	101%	100%	100%
2040	Barryton Faith	Joseph Beavan	6,101.00	6,101.00	100%	100%		100%	100%	100%
	Chippewa Lake	DISCONTINUED								
2050	Belding	Stephen Lindman	6,904.00	1,727.05	25%	7%	51%	63%	32%	25%
	BIG RAPIDS:									
2060	First	Rebecca Morrison	31,368.00	31,370.00	100%	100%	100%	100%	100%	100%
2070	Third Avenue	Ed Milam	6,170.00	6,170.04	100%	100%	100%	100%	100%	100%
2071	Paris	Ed Milam	4,915.00	4,915.00	100%	100%	100%	100%	100%	100%
2072	Rodney	Ed Milam	1,868.00	1,836.00	98%	100%	100%	100%	100%	98%
2075	Blanchard-Pine River	Lawrence Wonsey	4,842.00	3,631.50	75%	25%	50%	100%	100%	75%
2076	Coomer	Lawrence Wonsey	2,203.00	2,203.00	100%	18%	100%	100%	100%	100%
2080	Breckenridge	Paul Thomas	15,338.00	8,359.43	55%	100%	100%	100%	100%	55%
2090	Brooks Corners	Joseph Beavan	8,889.00	8,889.00	100%	100%	100%	100%	100%	100%
2091	Sears	Joseph Beavan	1,872.00	1,872.00	100%	100%	100%	100%	100%	100%
2100	Carson City	Andrew Croel	22,579.00	17,779.00	79%	100%	72%	71%	50%	79%
2105	Chase Barton	Lyle Ball	6,117.00	6,117.00	100%	100%	100%	100%	100%	100%
2106	Grant Center	Lyle Ball	4,423.00	4,423.00	100%	100%	100%	100%	100%	100%
2110	Clare	John Kasper	32,293.00	32,292.96	100%	100%	100%	100%	100%	100%
2120	Edmore	Michael Riegler	18,525.00	18,525.01	100%	100%	100%	100%	100%	100%
2130	Elsie	Donald Ferris-McCann	18,462.00	7,692.50	42%	101%	101%	100%	100%	42%
	EVART:									
2140	Evart	Melodye Surgeon-Rider	17,942.00	13,457.00	75%	100%	100%	100%	100%	75%
2141	Avondale		1,136.00	1,136.00	100%	100%	100%	103%	100%	100%
2150	North Evart		506.00	506.00	100%	100%	100%	100%	100%	100%
2151	Sylvan	DISCONTINUED	-	-		100%	100%	100%	0%	
2160	Farwell	Connie Bongard	17,573.00	14,109.94	80%	100%	100%	100%	100%	80%
2170	Fenwick	Russell Morgan	2,196.00	2,196.00	100%	100%	100%	100%	100%	100%
2171	Palo	Russell Morgan	2,271.00	1,250.00	55%	22%	25%	32%	58%	55%
2172	Vickeryville	Russell Morgan	1,795.00	958.00	53%	3%	81%	80%	19%	53%
2180	Greenville	Stephen Charnley	32,029.00	18,299.96	57%	25%	55%	47%	65%	57%
2190	Hersey	Lemuel Granada	10,185.00	10,185.00	100%	100%	100%	100%	100%	100%
	HOWARD CITY:									
2200	First	MERGED								
2210	Heritage	James Bradley Brillhart	22,743.00	6,822.87	30%	100%	100%	100%	62%	30%
2201	Coral	MERGED								
2202	Amble	Anne Riegler	7,671.00	7,671.00	100%	100%	102%	100%	100%	100%
	Maple Hill	MERGED								
	IONIA:									
2220	First	Lawrence Brown	22,558.00	20,600.96	91%	100%	100%	100%	100%	91%
2230	Zion	Cliff Allen	17,197.00	7,260.55	42%	13%	25%	83%	100%	42%

Report of 2013 Ministry Share Support — 5 Year History

Church		Current Pastor	2013 Apportioned	2013 Amt. Paid	2013 % Paid	2009	2010	2011	2012	2013
	Ionia Parish:									
2240	LeValley	Raymond Sundell	16,391.00	16,391.04	100%	78%	66%	86%	100%	100%
2241	Berlin Center	Raymond Sundell	7,810.00	7,810.00	100%	100%	100%	81%	97%	100%
2250	Ithaca	Cynthia Greene	21,972.00	21,974.88	100%	87%	62%	100%	100%	100%
2251	Beebe	Cynthia Greene	1,918.00	1,918.00	100%	100%	100%	105%	100%	100%
2260	New Life UMC	John Scott	28,151.00	28,151.00	100%	100%	100%	100%	100%	100%
2270	Leaton	David (Mike) Palmer	5,770.00	5,770.00	100%	100%	100%	100%	100%	100%
2280	Lyons/Muir	Forest (Bert) Nelson	9,985.00	750.00	8%	16%	7%	8%	19%	8%
2281	Easton	Nancy Patera	7,929.00	7,929.00	100%	100%	100%	100%	100%	100%
2285	Mecosta: New Hope	Gregory Buchner	38,317.00	19,158.00	50%	100%	100%	100%	40%	50%
2290	Middleton	Bill Dye	2,795.00	2,795.00	100%	100%	100%	92%	100%	100%
2291	Maple Rapids	Kathryn Leydorf	6,794.00	6,794.00	100%	105%	100%	100%	100%	100%
	MT. PLEASANT:									
2310	Chippewa Indian	Owen White-Pigeon	6,569.00	-	0%	0%	0%	0%	0%	0%
2320	First	Diane Gordon	54,924.00	54,924.00	100%	100%	100%	100%	100%	100%
2330	Trinity	David (Mike) Palmer	5,028.00	3,900.00	78%	61%	13%	49%	74%	78%
2331	Countryside	David (Mike) Palmer	6,420.00	6,420.00	100%	100%	100%	100%	100%	100%
2350	Ovid	Paul Damkoehler	9,815.00	6,850.00	70%	29%	37%	43%	100%	70%
2355	Pleasant Valley	MERGED								
2360	Pompeii	Bill Dye	4,140.00	4,140.00	100%	100%	100%	100%	100%	100%
2361	Perrinton	Bill Dye	2,361.00	2,361.00	100%	25%	40%	25%	100%	100%
2362	North Star	Bill Dye	326.00	326.00	100%	23%	36%	52%	100%	100%
2370	Reed City	Kathryn Cadarette	27,459.00	27,467.00	100%	68%	82%	90%	99%	100%
2390	Riverdale: Lincoln Road	Jana Lynn Almeida	16,879.00	17,045.58	101%	101%	106%	103%	131%	101%
2400	Rosebush	Jonathan VanDop	13,237.00	13,237.00	100%	100%	100%	100%	100%	100%
2455	Sand Lake	Darryl Miller	2,455.00	2,460.00	100%	182%	71%	534%	67%	100%
2456	South Ensley	Darryl Miller	5,086.00	5,064.30	100%	100%	61%	100%	99%	100%
	ST. JOHNS:									
2410	First	Ellen Zienert	20,491.00	20,491.00	100%	100%	100%	85%	100%	100%
2420	Pilgrim	Kenneth Bremer	43,256.00	43,256.00	100%	100%	100%	100%	100%	100%
2430	Salem	Kathryn Leydorf	6,067.00	6,067.00	100%	100%	100%	102%	100%	100%
2431	Greenbush	Mona Dye	3,384.00	3,384.00	100%	100%	100%	100%	100%	100%
2432	Lowe	Kathryn Leydorf	9,218.00	9,218.00	100%	100%	100%	100%	100%	100%
2440	St. Louis	Terri Bentley	20,874.00	20,874.00	100%	100%	100%	100%	100%	100%
2450	Shepardsville	Judy Hazle	3,429.00	3,430.00	100%	58%	100%	57%	77%	100%
2451	Price	DISCONTINUED								
2460	Shepherd	Kathleen Kursh	18,852.00	18,852.00	100%	100%	100%	100%	100%	100%
2480	Stanwood: Northland	Dominic Tommy	19,174.00	19,174.00	100%	50%	79%	100%	100%	100%
2490	Turk Lake	Stephen Lindman	6,600.00	6,600.00	100%	54%	38%	12%	84%	100%
2500	Weidman	Scott Smith	16,167.00	16,167.00	100%	100%	100%	100%	100%	100%
2510	Winn	Lawrence Wonsey	5,369.00	5,369.00	100%	100%	100%	92%	83%	100%
	HEARTLAND DISTRICT TOTAL		862,871.00	716,235.57	83%	85%	88%	91%	90%	83%

Report of 2013 Ministry Share Support — 5 Year History

Church	Current Pastor	2013 Apportioned	2013 Amt. Paid	2013 % Paid	2009	2010	2011	2012	2013
KALAMAZOO DISTRICT									
5011 Hope Edwardsburg	Jeffery Reese	36,178.00	36,178.00	100%	100%	100%	100%	100%	100%
5020 Allegan	Robert Lynch	24,370.00	12,845.79	53%	40%	52%	0%	42%	53%
5040 Arden	O'Ryan Rickard	6,894.00	2,700.00	39%	28%	35%	32%	40%	39%
5060 Bangor: Simpson	Thomas Davenport	21,788.00	1,821.86	8%	100%	100%	33%	5%	8%
BENTON HARBOR:									
5090 Peace Temple	DISCONTINUED				2%				
5100 Berrien Springs	Jane Logston	9,839.00	4,816.19	49%	100%	49%	30%	35%	49%
5110 Bloomingdale	Carol Newman	3,455.00	1,872.00	54%	0%	104%	100%	18%	54%
5115 Brandywine: Trinity	DISCONTINUED								
BUCHANAN:									
5140 Faith	Edward Slate	16,277.00	3,806.25	23%	46%	34%	64%	20%	23%
5141 Morris Chapel	Samuel Gordy	4,325.00	4,325.00	100%	100%	60%	100%	100%	100%
5150 First	Rob McPherson	21,244.00	11,772.00	55%	69%	52%	38%	36%	55%
5130 Burnips	Richard Fritz	7,612.00	6,000.00	79%	75%	78%	78%	86%	79%
5131 Monterey Center	Richard Fritz	5,447.00	5,447.04	100%	100%	100%	100%	99%	100%
5160 Casco	David Meister	17,564.00	1,196.00	7%	13%	50%	10%	25%	7%
5170 Cassopolis	Benjamin Hutchison	12,538.00	3,000.00	24%	3%	100%	100%	10%	24%
5180 Coloma	Ron Van Lente	21,199.00	21,352.24	101%	100%	100%	100%	101%	101%
5190 Comstock	MERGED								
5200 Dowagiac	Dave Price	23,138.00	1,000.00	4%	15%	24%	5%	4%	4%
5210 Fennville	Gary Peterson	11,422.00	3,686.00	32%	13%	39%	26%	30%	32%
5211 Pearl	Gary Peterson	3,266.00	3,266.08	100%	100%	100%	101%	100%	100%
5220 Galien	Jeff Cummings	5,977.00	2,312.92	39%	23%	18%	58%	28%	39%
5221 Olive Branch	Jeff Cummings	6,920.00	6,920.00	100%	100%	100%	23%	100%	100%
5215 Ganges	Jack Balgenorth	5,716.00	1,904.00	33%	100%	71%	100%	23%	33%
5230 Glenn	Jack Balgenorth	3,616.00	1,800.00	50%	17%	62%	57%	0%	50%
5240 Gobles	Nelson Hall	8,985.00	8,985.00	100%	100%	100%	100%	100%	100%
5241 Kendall	Nelson Hall	5,813.00	5,813.00	100%	100%	100%	100%	100%	100%
5246 Gull Lake	Mona Joslyn	25,970.00	23,730.00	91%	48%	55%	34%	64%	91%
5250 Hartford	Jeff Williams	19,548.00	19,548.00	100%	100%	100%	100%	100%	100%
5260 Hinchman	Jane Logston	4,130.00	4,130.00	100%	100%	100%	100%	100%	100%
5261 Oronoko	Jane Logston	2,067.00	2,067.00	100%	100%	75%	35%	100%	100%
5272 Hopkins	Linda Burton-Collier	7,377.00	7,377.00	100%	100%	37%	53%	23%	100%
5273 South Monterey	Linda Burton-Collier	5,583.00	5,583.00	100%	100%	100%	100%	100%	100%
KALAMAZOO:									
5280 First	John Boley	118,605.00	118,605.00	100%	100%	100%	100%	100%	100%
5285 Lifespring	Patricia Harpole								
5290 Lane Boulevard	DISCONTINUED								
5300 Milwood	Heather McDougall	30,142.00	30,142.00	100%	68%	100%	100%	100%	100%
5311 Oshtemo	John Fisher	14,721.00	6,476.70	44%	75%	100%	85%	31%	44%
5320 Stockbridge	Ronald Slager	8,829.00	4,040.00	46%	100%	72%	27%	48%	46%

Report of 2013 Ministry Share Support

5 Year History

Church		Current Pastor	2013 Apportioned	2013 Amt. Paid	2013 % Paid	2009	2010	2011	2012	2013
5330	Sunnyside	John Matthew Weiler	18,372.00	18,372.00	100%	100%	100%	100%	100%	100%
5340	Westwood	Wayne Price	41,966.00	31,428.00	75%	54%	75%	100%	89%	75%
5350	Keeler	Beth Reum	4,789.00	1,778.00	37%	100%	100%	100%	100%	37%
5351	Silver Creek	Beth Reum	10,364.00	7,896.00	76%	100%	100%	100%	100%	76%
5360	Lacota	Michael Pinto	3,982.00	3,982.00	100%	100%	100%	100%	100%	100%
5365	Lakeside	George W Lawton	4,757.00	4,757.00	100%	100%	100%	100%	100%	100%
5370	Lawrence	Clifford Radtke	13,071.00	1,300.00	10%	42%	7%	8%	8%	10%
5380	Lawton: St. Paul's	Douglas Vernon	15,365.00	8,962.80	58%	0%	2%	7%	32%	58%
5381	Almena	Donna Keyte	10,095.00	10,095.00	100%	108%	102%	100%	100%	100%
5390	Marcellus	John Messner	8,112.00	8,112.00	100%	83%	100%	100%	100%	100%
5400	New Buffalo	Bradley S. Bartelmay	20,174.00	20,173.76	100%	100%	100%	100%	100%	100%
5402	Bridgman: Faith	Terrill Schneider	5,769.00	5,768.64	100%	101%	100%	100%	100%	100%
	NILES:									
5410	Grace	Anthony Tomasino	7,319.00	727.00	10%	100%	50%	44%	26%	10%
5430	Wesley	Cathi Huvaere	32,292.00	17,112.60	53%	100%	92%	76%	28%	53%
5440	Northwest	Samuel Gordy	3,872.00	3,872.00	100%	100%	100%	100%	100%	100%
5450	Otsego	Joseph Shaler	25,280.00	25,280.00	100%	100%	100%	100%	100%	100%
5460	Parchment	Michael Tupper	27,438.00	9,000.00	33%	53%	35%	26%	13%	33%
5470	Paw Paw	Trevor McDermont	22,066.00	6,238.00	28%	3%	101%	65%	15%	28%
5480	Plainwell	Kathy Brown	33,101.00	33,101.00	100%	100%	100%	100%	100%	100%
5485	Pleasant Valley	DISCONTINUED								
5490	Pokagon	Sean Kidd	10,520.00	10,520.20	100%	100%	100%	100%	99%	100%
	PORTAGE:									
5500	Chapel Hill	Barry Petrucci	90,030.00	90,030.00	100%	100%	100%	102%	84%	100%
5510	First	Gregory Wood	64,539.00	64,539.00	100%	100%	100%	100%	100%	100%
5512	Portage Prairie	O'Ryan Rickard	10,846.00	5,400.00	50%	33%	0%	0%	4%	50%
5515	Riverside	Stephen Small	6,131.00	6,131.04	100%	100%	100%	100%	100%	100%
5516	Scottdale	Terrill M. Schneider	7,109.00	7,109.00	100%	100%	100%	100%	100%	100%
5520	St. Joseph	Harris Hoekwater	77,160.00	77,160.12	100%	100%	100%	100%	100%	100%
5530	Schoolcraft	Karen Wheat	16,286.00	1,395.00	9%	83%	50%	13%	13%	9%
5540	Sodus: Chapel Hill	Russell Logston	20,786.00	7,682.00	37%	100%	100%	100%	57%	37%
5550	South Haven	Devon Herrell	23,354.00	-	0%	75%	67%	54%	13%	0%
5560	Stevensville	Gordon Barry	44,507.00	44,507.00	100%	100%	100%	100%	100%	100%
5580	Three Oaks	Sherri Swanson	15,447.00	15,447.00	100%	100%	100%	75%	100%	100%
5587	Townline	David Haase	3,381.00	3,381.00	100%	100%	101%	100%	100%	100%
5588	Breedsville	David Haase	2,737.00	2,750.00	100%	101%	100%	101%	102%	100%
5590	Trowbridge	Sheila Baker	13,905.00	13,905.00	100%	56%	69%	25%	100%	100%
5600	Vicksburg	Bufford Coe	41,694.00	20,847.00	50%	75%	100%	100%	100%	50%
5605	Wakelee	John Messner	8,977.00	9,725.65	108%	100%	100%	100%	100%	108%
5610	Watervliet	Merged w/Coloma	-	-		0%	0%	9%	0%	
	KALAMAZOO DISTRICT TOTAL		1,286,148.00	973,002.88	76%	79%	82%	77%	73%	76%

MINISTRY SHARE HISTORY

Report of 2013 Ministry Share Support — 5 Year History

Church	Current Pastor	2013 Apportioned	2013 Amt. Paid	2013 % Paid	2009	2010	2011	2012	2013
LANSING DISTRICT									
6010 Bath	Mark Johnson	7,923.00	7,262.41	92%	100%	100%	100%	100%	92%
6011 Gunnisonville	Mark Johnson	15,039.00	15,039.00	100%	100%	100%	100%	100%	100%
Bell Oak	DISCONTINUED								
6016 Wheatfield	Jeremy Wicks	5,029.00	5,029.00	100%	100%	101%	100%	100%	100%
6031 Brookfield	Irene Vittoz	5,835.00	5,835.00	100%	126%	99%	101%	100%	100%
6040 Charlotte: Lawrence Ave.	Gary Wales	35,603.00	1,100.00	3%	46%	75%	70%	77%	3%
6050 Country Chapel	Ryan Wieland	13,058.00	13,057.80	100%	100%	42%	100%	100%	100%
6060 Dansville	Jeremy Wicks	3,644.00	1,939.00	53%	29%	35%	100%	100%	53%
6070 Delta Mills	Joseph Spackman	5,600.00	5,600.00	100%	100%	100%	100%	101%	100%
6090 DeWitt: Redeemer	Rodney J Kalajainen	111,613.00	111,613.00	100%	100%	100%	100%	100%	100%
6100 Dimondale	Joseph Huston	10,579.00	2,000.00	19%	6%	101%	101%	100%	19%
6105 Eagle	DISCONTINUED	-	-		59%	64%	27%	0%	
EAST LANSING:									
6110 Chapel Hill	DISCONTINUED	-	-		100%	100%	100%	100%	
6130 University	Jennifer Browne	73,049.00	73,049.16	100%	100%	100%	100%	100%	100%
6140 Eaton Rapids	Daniel Hofmann	57,024.00	45,587.88	80%	100%	100%	100%	100%	80%
6145 Freeport	Susan Olsen	2,987.00	2,987.00	100%	100%	100%	100%	100%	100%
6150 Grand Ledge	Cynthia Skutar	45,969.00	45,969.00	100%	100%	100%	100%	100%	100%
6155 Grovenburg	Joseph Huston	8,321.00	5,200.60	62%	27%	41%	60%	82%	62%
6158 Haslett: Aldersgate	DISCONTINUED				0%				
HASTINGS:									
6160 First	Donald Spachman	31,017.00	31,017.00	100%	6%	25%	100%	100%	100%
6170 Hope	Richard Moore	18,326.00	18,326.04	100%	92%	100%	79%	100%	100%
6180 Holt	Glenn Wagner	55,867.00	55,867.00	100%	100%	100%	100%	100%	100%
6185 Kalamo	Dan Phillips	4,472.00	4,472.00	100%	100%	100%	100%	100%	100%
LAKE ODESSA:									
6190 Central	Karen Sorden	27,944.00	25,615.37	92%	100%	100%	100%	102%	92%
6200 Lakewood	James Noggle	36,570.00	25,821.70	71%	100%	75%	50%	58%	71%
LANSING:									
6210 Asbury	Martin DeBow	31,639.00	31,639.00	100%	100%	104%	100%	100%	100%
6220 Calvary	MERGED				0%				
6230 Central	Linda Farmer-Lewis	55,693.00	12,441.00	22%	1%	16%	12%	31%	22%
6240 Christ	Lyle D Heaton	26,082.00	17,387.82	67%	54%	62%	8%	29%	67%
6250 Faith	Russell McReynolds	12,211.00	12,216.00	100%	100%	129%	110%	100%	100%
6260 First	Lori Sykes	29,075.00	29,075.00	100%	100%	100%	91%	100%	100%

Report of 2013 Ministry Share Support — 5 Year History

Church		Current Pastor	2013 Apportioned	2013 Amt. Paid	2013 % Paid	2009	2010	2011	2012	2013
6270	Grace	Jane Ellen Johnson	27,237.00	27,237.00	100%	108%	102%	103%	100%	100%
6275	Korean	Bo Rin Cho	17,198.00	17,198.00	100%	92%	100%	100%	100%	100%
6280	Mt. Hope	Robert Cook	73,893.00	73,896.00	100%	100%	108%	91%	100%	100%
6300	Trinity	William Beachy	72,669.00	44,525.00	61%	74%	75%	14%	45%	61%
6310	Leslie	Donald Buege	10,043.00	10,043.00	100%	100%	25%	50%	100%	100%
6311	Felt Plains	Donald Buege	4,360.00	250.00	6%	100%	100%	25%	78%	6%
6320	Mason	Dwayne Bagley	53,516.00	53,520.00	100%	100%	100%	101%	100%	100%
6330	Millville	Jeremy Wicks	18,889.00	5,453.59	29%	29%	0%	14%	1%	29%
6340	Mulliken	Clare Huyck	5,979.00	-	0%	82%	71%	59%	62%	0%
6342	Sebewa Center	Clare Huyck	2,481.00	1,379.00	56%	7%	15%	8%	0%	56%
6335	Munith	Jeanne Laimon	6,556.00	6,556.00	100%	92%	100%	100%	100%	100%
6336	Pleasant Lake	Jeanne Laimon								
6350	Nashville	Gary Simmons	13,677.00	13,505.58	99%	52%	61%	100%	100%	100%
6360	Peace	Susan Olsen	4,781.00	3,173.41	66%	100%	100%	100%	100%	66%
6361	Quimby	Jerry Bukoski	2,385.00	2,186.25	92%	100%	105%	100%	100%	100%
6370	Okemos Community	Jeanne M Randels	72,453.00	47,000.00	65%	90%	63%	66%	72%	65%
6380	Perry	Nancy Powers	6,226.00	6,226.00	100%	100%	80%	66%	100%	100%
6381	Shaftsburg	Nancy Powers	8,027.00	8,027.00	100%	100%	100%	100%	100%	100%
6390	Portland	Keith Treman	37,436.00	37,436.00	100%	70%	80%	100%	80%	100%
6400	Potterville	Lyne Stull-Lipps	21,219.00	21,219.00	100%	100%	100%	100%	100%	100%
6410	Robbins	Mark Payne	26,489.00	916.87	3%	72%	43%	8%	7%	3%
6420	Stockbridge	Jeanne Laimon	11,947.00	7,012.56	59%	1%	45%	4%	42%	59%
6430	Sunfield	Clare Huyck	17,649.00	2,934.81	17%	20%	83%	9%	78%	17%
6435	Sycamore Creek	Thomas Arthur	18,923.00	18,923.00	100%	100%	100%	100%	100%	100%
6440	Vermontville	Gary Simmons	5,686.00	5,686.00	100%	100%	100%	84%	100%	100%
6441	Gresham	Bryce Feighner	6,402.00	6,408.00	100%	100%	100%	100%	100%	100%
6450	Wacousta	Amee Paperella	20,831.00	20,831.00	100%	100%	87%	50%	110%	100%
6460	Webberville	Richard Foster	19,458.00	19,464.00	100%	100%	100%	56%	100%	100%
6470	Williamston	Julie Greyerbiehl	20,085.00	20,085.00	100%	100%	100%	100%	100%	100%
6480	Crossroads	Richard Foster	10,423.00	10,427.58	100%	99%	100%	101%	100%	100%
6455	Waterloo Village	Edward Ross	3,615.00	3,615.00	100%	100%	52%	39%	100%	100%
6456	Waterloo First	Jeanne Laimon	2,372.00	1,383.66	58%	43%	52%	61%	100%	58%
6490	Woodland	Gary Simmons	6,513.00	6,513.00	100%	100%	100%	102%	100%	100%
6491	Welcome Corners	Susan Olsen	5,091.00	5,091.00	100%	100%	100%	100%	100%	100%
	LANSING DISTRICT TOTAL		1,364,678.00	1,113,269.09	82%	81%	82%	76%	84%	82%

MINISTRY SHARE HISTORY

WEST MICHIGAN CONFERENCE OF THE UNITED METHODIST CHURCH

REPORT ON THE FINANCIAL STATEMENTS
(with additional information)

YEAR ENDED DECEMBER, 2013
(with comparative totals for the year ended December 31, 2012)

CONTENTS

Maner Costerisan PC
2425 E. Grand River Ave.
Suite 1
Lansing, MI 48912-3291
T: 517 323 7500
F: 517 323 6346
www.manercpa.com

INDEPENDENT AUDITOR'S REPORT

To the Council of Finance and Administration of the
West Michigan Annual Conference of the United Methodist Church

Report on the Financial Statements

We have audited the accompanying financial statements of the Council of Finance and Administration of the West Michigan Annual Conference of the United Methodist Church which comprise the statements of assets, liabilities and net assets - modified cash basis as of December 31, 2013 and 2012, and the related statement of support, revenue and other receipts, expenses, other disbursements and changes in net assets - modified cash basis for the year ended December 31, 2013, and the related notes to the financial statements.

Management's Responsibility for the Financial Statements

Management is responsible for the preparation and fair presentation of these financial statements in accordance with the modified cash basis of accounting described in Note 1; this includes determining that the modified cash basis of accounting is an acceptable basis for the preparation of the financial statements in the circumstances. Management is also responsible for the design, implementation, and maintenance of internal control relevant to the preparation and fair presentation of financial statements that are free from material misstatement, whether due to fraud or error.

Auditor's Responsibility

Our responsibility is to express an opinion on these financial statements based on our audit. We conducted our audit in accordance with auditing standards generally accepted in the United States of America. Those standards require that we plan and perform the audit to obtain reasonable assurance about whether the financial statements are free from material misstatement.

An audit involves performing procedures to obtain audit evidence about the amounts and disclosures in the financial statements. The procedures selected depend on the auditor's judgment, including the assessment of the risks of material misstatement of the financial statements, whether due to fraud or error. In making those risk assessments, the auditor considers internal control relevant to the Entity's preparation and fair presentation of the financial statements in order to design audit procedures that are appropriate in the circumstances, but not for the purpose of expressing an opinion on the effectiveness of the Entity's internal control. Accordingly, we express no such opinion. An audit also includes evaluating the appropriateness of accounting policies used and the reasonableness of significant accounting estimates made by management, as well as evaluating the overall presentation of the financial statements.

We believe that the audit evidence we have obtained is sufficient and appropriate to provide a basis for our audit opinion.

Opinion

In our opinion, the financial statements referred to above present fairly, in all material respects, the assets, liabilities and net assets - modified cash basis of the Council of Finance and Administration of the West Michigan Annual Conference of the United Methodist Church as of December 31, 2013 and 2012, and its support, revenue and other receipts, expenses, other disbursements and changes in net assets - modified cash for the year ended December 31, 2013, in accordance with the basis of accounting as described in Note 1.

Other Matters

Report on Summarized Comparative Information

We have previously audited the Council of Finance and Administration of the West Michigan Annual Conference of the United Methodist Church's 2012 financial statements, and our report dated May 21, 2013, expressed an unmodified opinion on those audited financial statements. In our opinion, the summarized comparative information presented in the statement of support, revenue and other receipts, expenses, other disbursements and changes in net assets - modified cash basis for the year ended December 31, 2012 is consistent, in all material respects, with the audited financial statements from which it has been derived.

Basis of Accounting

We draw attention to Note 1 of the financial statements, which describes the basis of accounting. The financial statements are prepared on the modified cash basis of accounting, which is a basis of accounting other than accounting principles generally accepted in the United States of America. Our opinion is not modified with respect to that matter.

Report on Supplementary Information

Our audit was conducted for the purpose of forming an opinion on the financial statements as a whole. The supplementary information, as identified in the table of contents, is presented for purposes of additional analysis and is not a required part of the financial statements. Such information is the responsibility of management and was derived from and relates directly to the underlying accounting and other records used to prepare the financial statements. The information has been subjected to the auditing procedures applied in the audits of the financial statements and certain additional procedures, including comparing and reconciling such information directly to the underlying accounting and other records used to prepare the financial statements or to the financial statements themselves, and other additional procedures in accordance with auditing standards generally accepted in the United States of America. In our opinion, the information is fairly stated in all material respects in relation to the financial statements as a whole.

Maner Costerisan PC

May 21, 2014

COUNCIL OF FINANCE AND ADMINISTRATION OF THE WEST MICHIGAN ANNUAL CONFERENCE OF THE UNITED METHODIST CHURCH STATEMENTS OF ASSETS, LIABILITIES AND NET ASSETS - MODIFIED CASH BASIS DECEMBER 31, 2013 AND 2012

	2013	2012
ASSETS		
Cash and cash equivalents	$ 608,051	$ 525,189
Investments	21,035,149	18,897,036
Receipts in transit	613,065	772,292
Notes and loans receivable	531,169	620,601
Property and equipment - net	2,385,558	2,483,459
TOTAL ASSETS	$ 25,172,992	$ 23,298,577
LIABILITIES AND NET ASSETS		
LIABILITIES:		
Payroll withholding	$ -	$ 48,317
Assets held on behalf of others	903,754	919,652
Total liabilities	903,754	967,969
NET ASSETS:		
Unrestricted	23,011,778	21,165,256
Temporarily restricted	1,246,853	1,154,745
Permanently restricted	10,607	10,607
Total net assets	24,269,238	22,330,608
TOTAL LIABILITIES AND NET ASSETS	$ 25,172,992	$ 23,298,577

See notes to financial statements.

COUNCIL OF FINANCE AND ADMINISTRATION OF THE WEST MICHIGAN ANNUAL CONFERENCE OF THE UNITED METHODIST CHURCH STATEMENT OF SUPPORT, REVENUE AND OTHER RECEIPTS, EXPENSES, OTHER DISBURSEMENTS AND CHANGES IN NET ASSETS - MODIFIED CASH BASIS YEAR ENDED DECEMBER 31, 2013 (with comparative totals for the year ended December 31, 2012)

	2013				
	Unrestricted	Temporarily restricted	Permanently restricted	Total	2012
SUPPORT, REVENUE AND OTHER RECEIPTS:					
Support and revenue:					
Ministry shares	$ 5,801,511	$ 54,002	$ -	$ 5,855,513	$ 5,748,508
Special offerings	226,613	1,326,712	-	1,553,325	1,607,530
Investment income	2,939,568	143,472	-	3,083,040	2,243,271
Camp registration and rental fees	912,668	11,323	-	923,991	1,145,061
Other income	679,207	155,433	-	834,640	606,154
Net assets released from restrictions	1,598,834	(1,598,834)	-	-	-
Total support and revenue	12,158,401	92,108	-	12,250,509	11,350,524
Other receipts:					
CPP holiday refunds	-	-	-	-	459,432
Pension billings	2,035,843	-	-	2,035,843	2,103,597
Insurance billings	4,703,832	-	-	4,703,832	4,222,553
Total support, revenue and other receipts	18,898,076	92,108	-	18,990,184	18,136,106
EXPENSES AND OTHER DISBURSEMENTS:					
Expenses:					
Salaries	2,098,179	-	-	2,098,179	2,109,785
Health and life insurance	1,814,305	-	-	1,814,305	1,934,582
Pension and post-employment benefit expense	214,186	-	-	214,186	215,370
Other employee costs	254,275	-	-	254,275	282,520
Training and continuing education	69,461	-	-	69,461	53,651
Travel, meeting and moving expenses	395,965	-	-	395,965	349,877
Operating and administrative expenses	1,336,379	-	-	1,336,379	1,220,670
Parsonage and building expenditures	135,367	-	-	135,367	78,952
World Service	856,829	-	-	856,829	895,886
Programs and conference benevolence	2,786,010	-	-	2,786,010	2,917,842
Depreciation and amortization	140,750	-	-	140,750	167,999
Remittances to General Conference	868,808	-	-	868,808	900,351
Total expenses	10,970,514	-	-	10,970,514	11,127,485
Other disbursements:					
Remittances to Board of Pensions	2,614,815	-	-	2,614,815	2,626,545
Health and life insurance	3,466,225	-	-	3,466,225	3,406,605
Total expenses and other disbursements	17,051,554	-	-	17,051,554	17,160,635
Increase (decrease) in net assets	1,846,522	92,108	-	1,938,630	975,471
Net assets - beginning of year	21,165,256	1,154,745	10,607	22,330,608	21,355,137
Net assets - end of year	$ 23,011,778	$ 1,246,853	$ 10,607	$ 24,269,238	$ 22,330,608

See notes to financial statements.

COUNCIL OF FINANCE AND ADMINISTRATION OF THE WEST MICHIGAN ANNUAL CONFERENCE OF THE UNITED METHODIST CHURCH NOTES TO FINANCIAL STATEMENTS

NOTE 1 - SUMMARY OF SIGNIFICANT ACCOUNTING POLICIES

Basis of accounting - The books and records of the Council are maintained on the modified cash basis of accounting. Under this method, income is recognized when received and expenses are recorded at the time of payment except for the recognition of certain assets and liabilities related to the timing of local church contributions at year end, reimbursement of health insurance premiums, payroll deductions, investments, property and equipment, notes and loans receivable and assets held on behalf of others in an agency capacity. Additionally, certain amounts held on the Council's behalf at the General Board of Pensions and Health Benefits (GBOPHB) are not included in these financial statements and related cash flows attributable to local churches are reported as other receipts and disbursements. See Note 8.

Financial statement presentation - The statement of support, revenue and other receipts, expenses, other disbursements and changes in net assets - modified cash basis includes certain prior-year summarized comparative information in total but not by net asset class. Such information does not include sufficient detail to constitute a presentation in conformity with the modified cash basis of accounting. Accordingly, such information should be read in conjunction with the Council's prior-year statement of support, revenue, and other receipts, expenses, other disbursements and changes in net assets - modified cash basis from which the summarized information was derived.

The Council is required to report information regarding its financial position and activities according to three classes of net assets: unrestricted net assets, temporarily restricted net assets, and permanently restricted net assets. Donor-restricted support is reported as an increase in temporarily or permanently restricted net assets, depending on the nature of the restriction. When a restriction expires (that is, when a stipulated time restriction ends or purpose restriction is accomplished) temporarily restricted net assets are reclassified to unrestricted net assets and reported in the statement of activities as net assets released from restrictions.

- Unrestricted net assets represent funds available for current operations, support for local churches, various missions, educational programs, and youth summer camps.
- Temporarily restricted net assets consist of contributions or earnings which have been restricted by the donor.
- Permanently restricted net assets are gift instruments requiring the principal be maintained intact in perpetuity and only the income be used for purposes specified by the donor.

Fund accounting - to facilitate observance of limitations and restrictions placed on the use of available resources, the accounts are maintained in accordance with the principles of fund accounting. Funds are established according to the nature and purpose of resources available to the Council. The assets, liabilities, net assets and financial activity of the Council are recorded in the following self-balancing fund groups:

COUNCIL OF FINANCE AND ADMINISTRATION OF THE WEST MICHIGAN ANNUAL CONFERENCE OF THE UNITED METHODIST CHURCH NOTES TO FINANCIAL STATEMENTS

NOTE 1 - SUMMARY OF SIGNIFICANT ACCOUNTING POLICIES (Continued)

- Connectional Ministry and Administration fund - resources available for current operations in supervision and administration of the mission and ministry of the West Michigan Annual Conference of the United Methodist Church.
- World Service and Conference Benevolence fund - resources available for distribution to the United Methodist denominational programs and the West Michigan Annual Conference of the United Methodist Church program agencies.
- Six Lanes and Advanced Specials fund - resources to allow churches direct involvement in the causes promoted by the Council agencies. Member churches select individual causes to fund from a listing prepared by the Council.
- Ministerial Education and Black College fund - resources available for providing financial support for the recruitment and education of ordained ministers and to provide financial support to traditionally black colleges related to the Church.
- Camping and Outdoor Education fund - resources available for Council retreat centers and camping programs.
- Pension and Health Benefits and Life Insurance fund - resources available for support, relief, assistance and pensioning of clergy, lay workers for the various units of the Council and their families.
- Plant fund - property and equipment owned and used directly in the operation of the Council.
- Loan Program fund - resources used to assist local churches and camps in financing capital expenditures.
- New Church Development fund - resources available for new church development.
- Other funds - resources for designated purposes related to other programs the Council supports.

Functional allocation of expenses - The costs of the various programs and other activities have been summarized on a functional basis in Note 10. Accordingly, certain costs have been allocated between the programs and supporting services benefited.

Cash and cash equivalents includes all highly liquid investments purchased with an original maturity of three months or less.

COUNCIL OF FINANCE AND ADMINISTRATION OF THE WEST MICHIGAN ANNUAL CONFERENCE OF THE UNITED METHODIST CHURCH NOTES TO FINANCIAL STATEMENTS

NOTE 1 - SUMMARY OF SIGNIFICANT ACCOUNTING POLICIES (Concluded)

Investments are recorded at fair value and consist of various debt and equity securities. Unrealized gains and losses are recorded in the statement of support, revenue and other receipts, expenses, other disbursements and changes in net assets. Investments in money market funds are recorded at cost.

Receipts in transit include contributions collected by local ministries during the years ended December 31, 2013 and 2012, but not received by the Council until after year end.

Notes and loans receivable consists of outstanding principal for loans the Council provided to local churches to help finance capital expenditures.

Property and equipment is capitalized at cost. Donated assets are recorded at fair value at date of donation. Parsonages are recorded at original cost plus the cost of subsequent additions. Depreciation is computed over the estimated useful life of assets using the straight-line method. Additions to property and equipment over S1,000 are capitalized. Cost of maintenance and repairs are charged to expense when incurred. The useful lives adopted for the purpose of computing depreciation are:

Parsonages and improvements	30 to 40 years
Camp buildings and equipment	5 to 40 years
Council center furniture and equipment	5 to 7 years

Assets held on behalf of others includes cash held in an agency capacity.

NOTE 2 - ORGANIZATION, RISKS AND UNCERTAINTIES

The Council of Finance and Administration of the West Michigan Annual Conference of the United Methodist Church (the Council) is a Michigan Non-Profit Corporation. The purpose of the Council is to develop and administer a comprehensive and coordinated plan of fiscal and administrative policies, procedures, and management services for the annual conference. The member churches are located in the western half of the Lower Peninsula of Michigan. Using ministry shares and special offerings received from its member churches, the Council contributes to denominational ministries and provides support for various missions, educational programs and summer youth camps. The Council is exempt from income taxes under provisions of Section 501(c)(3) of the Internal Revenue Code.

COUNCIL OF FINANCE AND ADMINISTRATION OF THE WEST MICHIGAN ANNUAL CONFERENCE OF THE UNITED METHODIST CHURCH NOTES TO FINANCIAL STATEMENTS

NOTE 2 - ORGANIZATION, RISKS AND UNCERTAINTIES (Continued)

The Council is required to disclose significant concentrations of credit risk regardless of the degree of such risk. Financial instruments which potentially subject the organization to concentrations of significant credit risk consist of cash and cash equivalents, and investments. The Council places its cash with FDIC insured financial institutions and thereby limits the amount of credit exposure to any one financial institution. Credit risk with respect to investments is limited due to the wide variety of companies and industries. Although such investments and cash balances may exceed the federally insured limits at certain times during the year and at year-end they are, in the opinion of management, subject to minimal risk. The Council maintains a diversified investment portfolio which is subject to market risk.

Investments are disclosed in Notes 3 and 4 and consist largely of amounts invested in various funds by the United Methodist Foundation of Michigan (UMF) as well as the General Board of Pension and Health Benefits of the United Methodist Church (GBOPHB).

UMF Pooled Trust Fund - The Fund is available for exclusive investment by the Foundation arising from charitable contributions made through charitable remainder trusts, other charitable trusts, funds operating as charitable trusts, or gift annuity contracts. The primary investment objective of the Fund is to provide for long term capital growth. The Foundation also may consider investments in securities of other United Methodist organizations based primarily upon their religious affiliation and the desire of the Foundation to support their ministry. The Fund seeks to achieve its investment objectives by investing in a diversified portfolio of common stocks, bonds and money market instruments.

UMF Stock Fund - The Fund seeks to achieve long-term capital appreciation through investments in stocks and other securities, with primary emphasis on U.S. large capitalization companies and secondary emphasis on global and international equities and on U.S. small and middle capitalization companies. The Fund is subject to the general investment restrictions and the socially responsible investment criteria as adopted by the UMF Foundation.

UMF Bond Fund - The Fund's primary objective is to achieve a high level of current income, with capital appreciation as a secondary objective, by investing in investment-grade debt securities. The Fund invests in U.S. Treasury and agency securities, preferred shares and other fixed income securities rated as investment grade by a Nationally Recognized Statistical Rating Organization. The Fund is subject to the general investment restrictions and the socially responsible investment criteria as adopted by the UMF Foundation.

UMF Money Market Fund - The Fund's objective is to seek maximum current income consistent with liquidity and the maintenance of a portfolio of high quality short-term money market securities. The Fund attempts to achieve its objective by investing in a diversified portfolio of U.S. dollar denominated money market securities. These securities primarily consist of short term U.S. Government securities, U.S. Government agency securities, and securities issued by U.S. Government sponsored enterprises and U.S. Government instrumentalities, commercial paper and repurchase agreements.

COUNCIL OF FINANCE AND ADMINISTRATION OF THE WEST MICHIGAN ANNUAL CONFERENCE OF THE UNITED METHODIST CHURCH NOTES TO FINANCIAL STATEMENTS

NOTE 2 - ORGANIZATION, RISKS AND UNCERTAINTIES (Continued)

GBOPHB Short Term Investment Fund - The Fund seeks to maximize current income consistent with preservation of capital. The Fund seeks to achieve its investment objective through the exposure to short-term fixed income securities in the sweep account. The Fund exclusively holds cash and cash equivalents in the form of units of the sweep account. The sweep account holds U.S. government bonds, agency bonds, corporate bonds, securitized projects, dollar denominated international fixed income securities, commercial paper, certificates of deposit, and other similar types of investments. The performance objective of the Fund is to slightly outperform its performance benchmark, the Bank of America Merrill Lynch 3-Month Treasury Bill Index.

GBOPHB Fixed Income Fund - The Fund seeks to earn current income by investing in a broad mix of fixed-income instruments. The performance objective of the Fund is to outperform the performance benchmark (Barclays Capital U.S. Universal Index, excluding Mortgage-Backed Securities) by 0.50% (net of fees) over a market cycle (3 to 5 years). The Fund is primarily composed of a broad range of fixed-income instruments, such as U.S. and non-U.S. government bonds, agency bonds, corporate bonds, mortgage-backed securities and asset-backed securities.

GBOPHB Multiple Asset Fund - The Fund seeks to maximize long-term investment returns, including current income and capital appreciation, while reducing short-term risk by investing in a broad mix of investments. The performance objective of the Fund is to outperform the investment returns of its performance benchmark (45% Russell 3000 Index, 20% MSCI ACWI excluding USA IMI, 25% Barclays Capital U.S. Universal Index excluding Mortgage Backed Securities, and 10% Barclays Capital U.S. Government Inflation-Linked Bond Index) by 0.8% on average per year (net of fees) over an extended investment cycle (10 to 20 years).

GBOPHB U.S. Equity Fund - The Fund seeks to earn long-term capital appreciation from a broadly diversified portfolio comprised primarily of U.S. listed equities and equity index futures. The performance objective of the Fund is to outperform the investment returns of its performance benchmark, the Russell 3000 Index, over a market cycle (three to five years) by 0.75% on average per year.

The process of preparing financial statements requires the use of estimates and assumptions regarding certain types of assets, revenues, and expenditures. Such estimates primarily relate to unsettled transactions and events as of the date of the financial statements. Accordingly, upon settlement, actual results may differ from estimated amounts.

Tax positions are taken based on interpretation of federal, state and local income tax laws. Management periodically reviews and evaluates the status of uncertain tax positions and makes estimates of amounts, including interest and penalties, ultimately due or owed. No amounts have been identified, or recorded, as uncertain tax positions. Federal, state and local tax returns generally remain open for examination by the various taxing authorities for a period of three to four years.

COUNCIL OF FINANCE AND ADMINISTRATION OF THE WEST MICHIGAN ANNUAL CONFERENCE OF THE UNITED METHODIST CHURCH NOTES TO FINANCIAL STATEMENTS

NOTE 2 - ORGANIZATION, RISKS AND UNCERTAINTIES (Concluded)

The Council evaluates events and transactions that occur after year end for potential recognition or disclosure in the financial statements. As of the auditor's opinion date, which is the date the financial statements were available to be issued, there were no subsequent events which required recognition or disclosure.

NOTE 3 - INVESTMENTS

The Council transfers certain amounts to the United Methodist Foundation of Michigan (the Foundation). The Foundation was formed as a nonprofit organization by member churches of the West Michigan Annual Conference and Detroit Annual Conferences. It is governed and monitored by its own independent commission. The Foundation's primary purpose is to broaden the financial base of member churches by assisting in and receiving planned and deferred gifts, assisting in the set-up and marketing of endowment funds, and the generation of market-level returns on invested monies through the use of investment pools.

The Council also transfers funds to the General Board of Pension and Health Benefits (GBOPHB). The GBOPHB is a not-for-profit administrative agency of The United Methodist Church, responsible for the general supervision and administration of investments and benefit services according to the principles of The United Methodist Church.

COUNCIL OF FINANCE AND ADMINISTRATION OF THE WEST MICHIGAN ANNUAL CONFERENCE OF THE UNITED METHODIST CHURCH NOTES TO FINANCIAL STATEMENTS

NOTE 3 - INVESTMENTS (Continued)

Investments at December 31 consist of the following:

	2013	2012
Direct investments:		
Mutual funds:		
Basic materials	$ 68,050	$ 115,150
Financials	566,990	94,330
Other	-	45,491
Common stocks:		
Basic materials	846,549	732,039
Financials	1,298,571	1,212,450
Industrial goods	246,575	337,535
Health care	1,345,516	1,357,141
Technology	796,508	880,488
Consumer goods	595,392	527,032
Conglomerates	25,479	18,591
Services	366,278	542,504
REITs	1,337,968	1,806,602
Utilities	444,365	436,489
Transportation	98,940	56,550
Retail services	-	155,100
Food & beverages	88,532	63,837
Apparel & accessories	222,900	189,360
Preferred stock:		
Financials	-	51,200
Master limited partnerships	423,305	357,759
Corporate bonds	182,501	-
Money market	2,669,569	799,116
Pooled funds managed by the Foundation:		
UMF Pooled Trust Fund	869,159	785,615
UMF Stock Fund	831,929	240,154
UMF Bond Fund	405,675	188,232
UMF Money Market Fund	2,870	1,397
Pooled funds managed by the General Board of Pension and Health Benefits (GBOPHB):		
Short Term Investment Fund	270,553	53,742
Fixed Income Fund	1,540,796	1,656,774
U.S. Equity Fund	553,682	486,292
Multiple Asset Fund	4,936,497	5,706,066
	$ 21,035,149	$ 18,897,036

COUNCIL OF FINANCE AND ADMINISTRATION OF THE
WEST MICHIGAN ANNUAL CONFERENCE OF THE UNITED METHODIST CHURCH
NOTES TO FINANCIAL STATEMENTS

NOTE 3 - INVESTMENTS (Concluded)

Income from cash deposits and investments consist of the following at December 31:

	2013	2012
Interest and dividends	$ 348,063	$ 342,766
Interest received from financing	24,502	25,968
Realized gain on sale of investments	1,964,872	1,041,153
Change in unrealized appreciation	745,603	833,384
Total investment income	$ 3,083,040	$ 2,243,271

Investment related expenses of approximately $79,000 and $77,000 were incurred for the years ended December 31, 2013 and 2012.

NOTE 4 - FAIR VALUE MEASUREMENTS

Accounting standards establish a hierarchy that prioritizes the inputs to valuation techniques giving the highest priority to readily available unadjusted quoted prices in active markets for identical assets (Level 1 measurements) and the lowest priority to unobservable inputs (Level 3 measurements) when market prices are not readily available or reliable. The three levels of the hierarchy are described below:

Level 1: Quoted prices in active markets for identical securities.

Level 2: Prices determined using other significant observable inputs. Observable inputs are inputs that other market participants may use in pricing a security. These may include quoted prices for similar securities, interest rates, prepayment speeds, credit risk and others.

Level 3: Prices determined using significant unobservable inputs. In situations where quoted prices or observable inputs are unavailable or deemed less relevant (for example, when there is little or no market activity for an investment at the end of the period), unobservable inputs may be used. Unobservable inputs reflect the Council's own assumptions about the factors market participants would use in pricing an investment, and would be based on the best information available.

COUNCIL OF FINANCE AND ADMINISTRATION OF THE WEST MICHIGAN ANNUAL CONFERENCE OF THE UNITED METHODIST CHURCH NOTES TO FINANCIAL STATEMENTS

NOTE 4 - FAIR VALUE MEASUREMENTS (Continued)

From time to time, changes in valuation techniques may result in reclassification of an investment's assigned level within the hierarchy.

The asset or liability's fair value measurement level within the fair value hierarchy is based on the lowest level of any input that is significant to the fair value measurement. Valuation techniques used need to maximize the use of observable inputs and minimize the use of unobservable inputs.

Following is a description of the valuation methodologies used for assets measured at fair value. There have been no changes in the methodologies used at December 31, 2013 and 2012.

Common stocks, preferred stocks and corporate bonds: Valued at the closing price reported on the active market on which the individual securities traded.

Mutual funds and preferred stock funds: Valued at the net asset value ("NAV") of shares held by the Council at year end.

Pooled funds: Valued based upon the Councils allocable share of the underlying investments made and reported by the United Methodist Foundation and the General Board of Pension and Health Benefits to the Council.

The preceding methods described may produce a fair value calculation that may not be indicative of net realizable value or reflective of future fair values. Furthermore, although the Council believes its valuation methods are appropriate and consistent with other market participants, the use of different methodologies or assumptions to determine the fair value of certain financial instruments could result in a different fair value measurement at the reporting date.

**COUNCIL OF FINANCE AND ADMINISTRATION OF THE
WEST MICHIGAN ANNUAL CONFERENCE OF THE UNITED METHODIST CHURCH
NOTES TO FINANCIAL STATEMENTS**

NOTE 4 - FAIR VALUE MEASUREMENTS (Continued)

The following is a market value summary by the level of the inputs used in evaluating the Council's assets carried at fair value at December 31. The inputs or methodology used for valuing securities may not be an indication of the risk associated with investing in those securities.

	2013			
Description	Level 1:	Level 2:	Level 3:	Total
Direct investments:				
Mutual funds:				
Basic materials	$ 68,050	$ -	$ -	$ 68,050
Financials	566,990	-	-	566,990
Common stocks:				
Basic materials	846,549	-	-	846,549
Financials	1,298,571	-	-	1,298,571
Industrial goods	246,575	-	-	246,575
Health care	1,345,516	-	-	1,345,516
Technology	796,508	-	-	796,508
Consumer goods	595,392	-	-	595,392
Conglomerates	25,479	-	-	25,479
Services	366,278	-	-	366,278
REITs	1,337,968	-	-	1,337,968
Utilities	444,365	-	-	444,365
Transportation	98,940	-	-	98,940
Food & beverages	88,532	-	-	88,532
Apparel & accessories	222,900	-	-	222,900
Preferred stock:				
Master limited partnerships	423,305	-	-	423,305
Corporate bonds	-	182,501	-	182,501
Pooled funds held:				
UMF Foundation	-	-	2,109,633	2,109,633
GBOPHB	-	-	7,301,528	7,301,528
Total investments	$ 8,771,918	$ 182,501	$ 9,411,161	18,365,580
Money market funds at cost				2,669,569
Total				$21,035,149

COUNCIL OF FINANCE AND ADMINISTRATION OF THE WEST MICHIGAN ANNUAL CONFERENCE OF THE UNITED METHODIST CHURCH NOTES TO FINANCIAL STATEMENTS

NOTE 4 - FAIR VALUE MEASUREMENTS (Continued)

	2012			
Description	Level 1:	Level 2:	Level 3:	Total
Direct investments:				
Mutual funds:				
Basic materials	$ 115,150	$ -	$ -	$ 115,150
Financials	94,330	-	-	94,330
Other	45,491	-	-	45,491
Common stocks:				
Basic materials	732,039	-	-	732,039
Financials	1,212,450	-	-	1,212,450
Industrial goods	337,535	-	-	337,535
Health care	1,357,141	-	-	1,357,141
Technology	880,488	-	-	880,488
Consumer goods	527,032	-	-	527,032
Conglomerates	18,591	-	-	18,591
Services	542,504	-	-	542,504
REITs	1,806,602	-	-	1,806,602
Utilities	436,489	-	-	436,489
Transportation	56,550	-	-	56,550
Retail services	155,100	-	-	155,100
Food & beverages	63,837	-	-	63,837
Apparel & accessories	189,360	-	-	189,360
Preferred stock:				
Financials	51,200	-	-	51,200
Master limited partnerships	357,759	-	-	357,759
Pooled funds held:				
UMF Foundation	-	-	1,215,398	1,215,398
GBOPHB	-	-	7,902,874	7,902,874
Total investments	$ 8,979,648	$ -	$ 9,118,272	18,097,920
Money market funds at cost				799,116
Total				$ 18,897,036

Investments held at the General Board of Pension and Health Benefits as well as the Foundation include numerous securities that are combined with the investment portfolios of other church organizations. As such, they are considered Level 3 investments.

COUNCIL OF FINANCE AND ADMINISTRATION OF THE WEST MICHIGAN ANNUAL CONFERENCE OF THE UNITED METHODIST CHURCH NOTES TO FINANCIAL STATEMENTS

NOTE 4 - FAIR VALUE MEASUREMENTS (Concluded)

The following is a reconciliation of the beginning and ending balances for assets and liabilities measured at fair value on a recurring basis using significant unobservable inputs (Level 3):

	Funds held at the Foundation	Funds held at the GBOPHB	Total
Balance January 1, 2012	$ 1,173,407	$ 7,913,872	$ 9,087,279
Total unrealized gains or losses included in earnings	75,328	401,821	477,149
Purchases	36,823	6,353,869	6,390,692
Proceeds from sale	(70,159)	(6,766,688)	(6,836,847)
Balance December 31, 2012	1,215,399	7,902,874	9,118,273
Total unrealized gains or losses included in earnings	166,847	274,803	441,650
Purchases	805,737	3,864,008	4,669,745
Proceeds from sale	(78,350)	(4,740,157)	(4,818,507)
Balance December 31, 2013	$ 2,109,633	$ 7,301,528	$ 9,411,161

As of December 31, 2013:

	Funds held at the Foundation	Funds held at the GBOPHB	Total
The estimated amount of total gains and losses for the year included in earnings attributable to the change in unrealized gains or losses relating to assets still held at year end.	$ 166,847	$ 274,803	$ 441,650

Gains and losses (realized and unrealized) included in earnings for the year ended December 31, 2013, are reported in investment income (loss).

**COUNCIL OF FINANCE AND ADMINISTRATION OF THE
WEST MICHIGAN ANNUAL CONFERENCE OF THE UNITED METHODIST CHURCH
NOTES TO FINANCIAL STATEMENTS**

NOTE 5 - PROPERTY AND EQUIPMENT

Property and equipment consist of the following at December 31.

	2013	2012
Parsonages:		
District	$ 966,834	$ 1,043,202
Area	218,595	218,595
Camps:		
Land	198,000	198,000
Buildings	3,046,652	3,001,298
Vehicles	221,740	221,740
Equipment	192,530	182,749
Conference center furniture and equipment	576,225	570,235
District offices furniture, equipment and vehicles	135,635	120,909
Area office furniture and equipment	34,193	32,912
	5,590,404	5,589,640
Less accumulated depreciation	3,204,846	3,106,181
Net property and equipment	$ 2,385,558	$ 2,483,459
Depreciation and amortization expense	$ 140,750	$ 167,999
District parsonages:		
Lansing District Superintendent	$ -	$ 80,438
Grand Rapids District Superintendent	241,032	241,032
Grand Traverse Superintendent	259,730	255,660
Heartland District Superintendent	291,072	291,072
Kalamazoo District Superintendent	175,000	175,000
Total district parsonages	$ 966,834	$ 1,043,202
Area parsonages:		
15160 Duxbury Lane, DeWitt Township	$ 186,926	$ 186,926
Okemos office building	31,669	31,669
Total area parsonages	$ 218,595	$ 218,595

The area parsonages are owned jointly with the Detroit Annual Conference. The above amount represents the Council of Finance and Administration of the West Michigan Annual Conference's share, which approximates forty-two percent of the original cost basis of the property.

Land included in the parsonages listed above amounted to approximately $180,000 and $195,000 at December 31, 2013 and 2012, respectively.

COUNCIL OF FINANCE AND ADMINISTRATION OF THE WEST MICHIGAN ANNUAL CONFERENCE OF THE UNITED METHODIST CHURCH NOTES TO FINANCIAL STATEMENTS

NOTE 6 - FINANCING RECEIVABLES

Notes and loans receivable consist of the following, as of December 31.

	2013	2012
Note receivable from the Millville UMC, with monthly payments of $2,153, including interest of 3% maturing December 2020.	$ 159,816	$ 180,882
Note receivable from the Portage Chapel Hill UMC, with monthly payments of $615, including interest of 4.25% maturing December 2018.	32,671	38,522
Note receivable from the Climax/Scotts UMC, with monthly payments of $845, including interest of 3% maturing June 2019.	50,743	59,221
Note receivable from the Church of All Nations, with monthly payments of $636, including interest of 5% maturing April 2015.	9,831	16,786
Note receivable from the Reading UMC, with monthly payments of $382, including interest of 2.75% maturing December 2021.	23,223	31,647
Note receivable from the Scotts UMC, with monthly payments of $137, including interest of 3% maturing March 2021.	8,679	12,233
Note receivable from the Quincy UMC, with monthly payments of $241, including interest of 3% maturing November 2018.	14,276	17,425
Note receivable from the Valley UMC, with monthly payments of $971, including interest of 3% maturing November 2021.	127,915	135,604
Note receivable from the Courtland-Oakfield UMC, with monthly payments of $1,402, including interest of 3% maturing November 2021.	104,015	128,281
	$ 531,169	$ 620,601

COUNCIL OF FINANCE AND ADMINISTRATION OF THE WEST MICHIGAN ANNUAL CONFERENCE OF THE UNITED METHODIST CHURCH NOTES TO FINANCIAL STATEMENTS

NOTE 6 - FINANCING RECEIVABLES (Concluded)

Maturities of financing receivables at December 31 are as follows:

Years ending December 31,	
2013	$ 73,132
2014	70,351
2015	69,992
2016	72,195
2017	73,870
Thereafter	171,629
	$ 531,169

Notes receivable are carried at unpaid principal balances, less an allowance for doubtful collection. Management periodically evaluates the adequacy of the allowance based on past experience and potential adverse situations that may affect the borrower's ability to repay. It is management's policy to write off a loan only when they are deemed permanently uncollectible. As of December 31, 2013 and 2012, management believes that no allowance is necessary.

The classification of notes receivable regarding age and interest accrual status at December 31 are as follows:

	2013			2012		
	Principal	Interest	Total	Principal	Interest	Total
Current	$ 531,169	$ -	$ 531,169	$ 620,601	$ -	$ 620,601
Past due:						
30-59 days	-	-	-	-	-	-
60-89 days	-	-	-	-	-	-
≥ 90 days	-	-	-	-	-	-
Total past due	-	-	-	-	-	-
Total financing receivables	$ 531,169	$ -	$ 531,169	$ 620,601	$ -	$ 620,601

Past due interest has not been accrued under the modified cash basis of accounting.

COUNCIL OF FINANCE AND ADMINISTRATION OF THE WEST MICHIGAN ANNUAL CONFERENCE OF THE UNITED METHODIST CHURCH NOTES TO FINANCIAL STATEMENTS

NOTE 7 - LEASES

The Michigan Area Headquarters (the Headquarters), supported jointly by the Council of Finance and Administration of the West Michigan Annual Conference and the Detroit Annual Conference, leased office space in 2000. The Headquarters pays rent expense from its budget, but the Council of Finance and Administration of the West Michigan Annual Conference, Detroit Annual Conference and the Headquarters are jointly responsible for the lease. The lease expires in July 2014. The base monthly lease rate is $6,500 with annual escalation for cost of living.

NOTE 8 - PENSION AND OTHER POST-EMPLOYMENT BENEFITS

From 1982 through 2006, the Council contributed to the Ministerial Pension Plan (MPP Annuities) that was administered by the GBOPHB to fund clergy retirement benefits. The GBOPHB has taken the position that the Council is responsible for funding any shortfall in benefits. The Council's portion of the total estimated actuarial liability based on the most recent actuarial calculation as of January 1, 2013 was projected to be $41,285,541 in 2015. The Council's expected contribution for 2014 and 2015 was $0.

The Council participates in a voluntary multi-employer defined contribution pension plan that covers substantially all Council lay and clergy employees. The Council contributes between 9 and 12 percent of each participant's annual wages. Contributions made by the Council approximated $90,000 and $86,000 for each of the years ended December 31, 2013 and 2012, respectively.

Additionally, the Council participates in a defined benefit pension plan that is frozen (Pre-1982 Plan). The Plan is administered by the GBOPHB. The Council's plan assets exceeded the estimated actuarial plan liability based on the most recent actuarial calculation as of January 1, 2013 by $3,110,053 or 108% in 2015.

Effective January 1, 2007, the Council adopted the Clergy Retirement Security Program (CRSP-DB). This program is an amendment and restatement of the previous clergy pension program. Regular contributions made by the Council approximated $457,000 and $467,000 for the years ended December 31, 2013 and 2012, respectively. The Council was also required to make additional contributions of $1,903,954 and $1,909,487 for the years ended December 31, 2013 and 2012, respectively. The Council's expected contribution based on the most recent actuarial calculation as of January 1, 2012 was projected to be $1,410,002 for 2014. The Council's expected contribution based on the most recent actuarial calculation as of January 1, 2013 was projected to be $1,381,701 for 2015.

The Council's policy is to fund the majority of costs of qualified retirees' (clergy and lay employees) health care coverage. Such costs are expensed when paid and amounted to approximately $1,088,000 and $1,037,000 for the years ended December 31, 2013 and 2012, respectively. The projected unfunded post-employment medical benefits liability, based on the most recent actuarial calculation dated April 17, 2014 was projected to be $5,266,000 as of December 31, 2014.

COUNCIL OF FINANCE AND ADMINISTRATION OF THE WEST MICHIGAN ANNUAL CONFERENCE OF THE UNITED METHODIST CHURCH NOTES TO FINANCIAL STATEMENTS

NOTE 9 - RELATED PARTY TRANSACTIONS

The Council conducts essentially all transactions, other than purchases of goods and services and sales of certain property, with affiliated congregations. Certain administrative expenses are reimbursed by related organizations. The Council also processes payroll transactions for affiliated organizations at no charge. The value of these services has not been determined but is not considered significant to the financial statements.

NOTE 10 - FUNCTIONAL ALLOCATION OF EXPENSES

The functional allocation of the Council's expenses as they relate to programs and management and general are listed below.

	2013	2012
Programs:		
Connectional Ministry and Administration	$ 2,296,178	$ 2,376,126
World Service and Conference Benevolence	2,320,532	2,326,578
Six Lanes and Advanced Specials	1,438,969	1,424,403
Ministerial Education and Black College fund	415,373	404,032
Camping and Outdoor Education	596,324	759,978
Pension and Health Benefits and Life Insurance fund	1,358,341	1,518,768
New Church Development	456,510	398,956
Other funds	10,365	47,495
Total programs	8,892,592	9,256,336
Management and general	2,077,922	1,871,149
	$ 10,970,514	$ 11,127,485

Fundraising has not been segregated on the basis of immateriality.

COUNCIL OF FINANCE AND ADMINISTRATION OF THE WEST MICHIGAN ANNUAL CONFERENCE OF THE UNITED METHODIST CHURCH NOTES TO FINANCIAL STATEMENTS

NOTE 11 - RESTRICTED NET ASSETS

Temporarily restricted net assets are available for the following purposes at December 31:

	2013	2012
New Church Investment fund - restricted for development of new churches	$ 30,733	$ 24,271
Camp endowment - restricted for the upkeep and running of camps	857,074	774,800
Special Offerings - contributions designated by local churches	169,523	187,994
Ministerial training - designated for the training of clergy	189,523	167,680
	$ 1,246,853	$ 1,154,745

Net assets amounting to $1,598,834 and $1,588,550 were released from restrictions during the years ended December 31, 2013 and 2012, respectively, by incurring expenses satisfying their restricted purposes.

Permanently restricted net assets are available for the following purposes at December 31:

	2013	2012
Permanent endowment - restricted for world service	$ 10,607	$ 10,607

NOTE 12 - ENDOWMENTS

Endowments consist of funds established for a variety of purposes and may include both donor-restricted funds and funds internally designated to function as endowments. Restrictions are both permanent and temporary and assets associated with endowment funds are classified and reported based on the existence or absence of these restrictions.

The Council has interpreted the Uniform Prudent Management of Institutional Funds Act (UPMIFA) as permitting the preservation of the historical value of the original gift of the donor-restricted endowment funds absent explicit donor stipulations to the contrary. As a result, when directed by the gift instrument, the Council classifies as permanently restricted net assets (a) the original value of gifts donated to the permanent endowment, (b) the original value of subsequent gifts to the permanent endowment, and (c) accumulations to the permanent endowment made in accordance with the direction of the applicable donor gift instrument. The remaining portion of the donor-restricted endowment fund that is not classified in permanently restricted net assets is classified as temporarily restricted net assets until the restricted purpose has been accomplished. The Council considers the following factors in making a determination to appropriate or accumulate donor-restricted endowment funds.

COUNCIL OF FINANCE AND ADMINISTRATION OF THE WEST MICHIGAN ANNUAL CONFERENCE OF THE UNITED METHODIST CHURCH NOTES TO FINANCIAL STATEMENTS

NOTE 12 - ENDOWMENTS (Concluded)

1. The duration and preservation of the fund.
2. The purposes of the organization and the donor-restricted endowment fund.
3. General economic conditions.
4. The possible effect of inflation and deflation.
5. The expected total return from income and the appreciation of investments.
6. Other resources of the organization
7. The investment policies of the Council.

The Council's investment and spending practices for endowment assets attempt to provide a predictable stream of funding to programs supported while seeking to maintain the purchasing power of the endowment assets.

Investment earnings from donor-restricted endowment funds are classified as temporarily restricted income until explicit donor stipulations are satisfied. In the event that the fair value of donor-restricted endowment funds falls below the level required to be maintained in perpetuity, the resulting deficiency is recorded as a reduction of unrestricted net assets.

Changes in endowment net assets are as follows.

	Temporarily restricted	Permanently restricted	Total
Endowment net assets January 1, 2012	$ 750,788	$ 10,607	$ 761,395
Investment return:			
Investment income	24,230	-	24,230
Net appreciation (realized and unrealized)	44,829	-	44,829
Total investment return	69,059	-	69,059
Approved for expenditure	(45,047)	-	(45,047)
Endowment net assets December 31, 2012	774,800	10,607	785,407
Investment return:			
Investment income	19,077	-	19,077
Net appreciation (realized and unrealized)	109,685	-	109,685
Total investment return	128,762	-	128,762
Approved for expenditure	(46,488)	-	(46,488)
Endowment net assets December 31, 2013	$ 857,074	$ 10,607	$ 867,681

COUNCIL OF FINANCE AND ADMINISTRATION OF THE WEST MICHIGAN ANNUAL CONFERENCE OF THE UNITED METHODIST CHURCH NOTES TO FINANCIAL STATEMENTS

NOTE 13 - CONTINGENCIES

From time to time the Council is involved in various legal proceedings that have arisen in the ordinary course of business. Management does not believe that the outcome of these proceedings, either individually or in the aggregate, will have a material adverse effect on the Council's financial position or future results of operations.

Effective September 1, 2009 the Council became primarily self-insured, up to certain limits, for health claims through Professional Benefits Services. The plan includes all participating Council employees as well as affiliated congregation clergy. The Council has purchased stop-loss insurance, which will reimburse the Council for individual policies that exceed $100,000 annually. Claims are expensed as paid. The total claims expense under the program was approximately $3,800,000 and $3,700,000 for Council employees for the years ended December 31, 2013 and 2012, respectively. The Council is reimbursed for stop loss premiums and claims paid for affiliates covered under the Plan. The total amount of claims incurred but not reported attributable to the Council has not been determined, however, claims incurred in December estimated in the amount of $240,078 were paid in 2014.

NOTE 14 - COMMITMENT

In August 2013, the Michigan Area United Methodist Ministry Center entered into an $825,000 mortgage agreement, the proceeds of which to be used for the acquisition of office space to be leased by the Michigan Area Headquarters of the United Methodist Church. The Council has entered into an agreement with the Michigan Area Headquarters (the Headquarters) and the Detroit Annual Conference of the United Methodist Church to provide support to the Headquarters for the lease payments. Lease payments are to be sufficient to repay the underlying mortgage note for the office space in the original amount of $825,000 including accrued interest from August 15, 2013 through the completion date of the premises, and shall be based upon a fifteen year amortization schedule commencing upon completion of the premises and continue monthly for sixty months, including interest at 4.74% per annum. The Council's portion of the monthly payments based on an anticipated completion date of August 2014 are expected to be approximately $8,064.

COUNCIL OF FINANCE AND ADMINISTRATION OF THE
WEST MICHIGAN ANNUAL CONFERENCE OF THE UNITED METHODIST CHURCH
NOTES TO FINANCIAL STATEMENTS

NOTE 14 - COMMITMENT (Concluded)

The following anticipated maturity schedule for the Council commitment is based on an anticipated completion date of August 2014:

Year ending December 31,	Principal	Interest	Total Commitment
2014	$ 14,546	$ 25,775	$ 40,321
2015	79,622	17,148	96,770
2016	83,479	13,291	96,770
2017	87,523	9,247	96,770
2018	91,763	5,007	96,770
2019	55,568	881	56,449
	$ 412,501	$ 71,349	$ 483,850

SUPPLEMENTARY INFORMATION

COUNCIL OF FINANCE AND ADMINISTRATION OF THE
WEST MICHIGAN ANNUAL CONFERENCE OF THE UNITED METHODIST CHURCH
COMBINING STATEMENT OF SUPPORT, REVENUE AND OTHER RECEIPTS, EXPENSES, OTHER DISBURSEMENTS AND CHANGES IN NET ASSETS - MODIFIED CASH BASIS
YEAR ENDED DECEMBER 31, 2013
(with comparative totals for the year ended December 31, 2012)

	2013					
	Connectional Ministry and Administration fund	World Service and Conference Benevolence fund	Six Lanes and Advance Specials fund	Ministerial Education and Black College fund	Camping and Outdoor Education fund	Pension and Health Benefits and Life Insurance fund
SUPPORT, REVENUE AND OTHER RECEIPTS:						
Support and revenue:						
Ministry shares	$ 2,660,415	$ 2,370,721	$ -	$ 409,317	$ -	$ 47,741
Special offerings	-	-	-		-	-
Investment income	351,234	8,575	-	-	-	2,481,815
Camp registration and rental fees	152,168	11,859	-	-	747,541	-
Other income	252,240	68,577	-	7,143	225,698	31,939
Net assets released from restrictions	3,201	52,713	1,438,969	-	58,522	-
Total support and revenue	3,419,258	2,512,445	1,438,969	416,460	1,031,761	2,561,495
Other receipts:						
CPP holiday refunds	-	-	-	-	-	-
Pension billings	-	-	-	-	-	2,035,843
Insurance billings	164,308	-	-	-	-	4,539,524
Total support, revenue and other receipts	3,583,566	2,512,445	1,438,969	416,460	1,031,761	9,136,862
EXPENSES AND OTHER DISBURSEMENTS:						
Expenses:						
Salaries	996,062	523,392	-	-	318,555	-
Health and life insurance	252,920	96,954	-	-	35,256	1,356,728
Pension and post-employment benefit expense	131,997	35,637	-	-	12,809	-
Other employee costs	190,029	22,335	-	-	36,161	1,530
Training and continuing education	23,821	4,029	-	-	3,807	-
Travel, meeting and moving expenses	300,190	72,526	-	-	1,307	2,111
Operating and administrative expenses	528,398	59,450	-	-	367,646	267,715
Parsonage and building expenditures	37,575	-	-	-	93,132	-
World Service	-	856,829	-	-	-	-
Programs and conference benevolence	350,484	759,128	1,309,059	77,418	193,543	83
Depreciation and amortization	-	-	-	-	-	-
Remittances to General Conference	374,686	26,257	129,910	337,955	-	-
Total expenses	3,186,162	2,456,537	1,438,969	415,373	1,062,216	1,628,167
Other disbursements:						
Remittances to Board of Pensions	-	-	-	-	-	2,614,815
Health and life insurance	-	-	-	-	-	3,466,225
Total expenses and other disbursements	3,186,162	2,456,537	1,438,969	415,373	1,062,216	7,709,207
Increase (decrease) in net assets before transfers	397,404	55,908	-	1,087	(30,455)	1,427,655
Transfers	113,867	(15,929)	-	-	(25,134)	(105,262)
Increase (decrease) in net assets	511,271	39,979	-	1,087	(55,589)	1,322,393
Net assets - beginning of year	464,283	73,077	-	-	(445,157)	16,955,960
Net assets - end of year	$ 975,554	$ 113,056	$ -	$ 1,087	$ (500,746)	$ 18,278,353

2013								
Plant fund	Loan Program fund	New Church Development fund	Other Funds	Total unrestricted	Temporarily restricted	Permanently restricted	Totals	2012
$ -	$ -	$ 313,317	$ -	$ 5,801,511	$ 54,002	$ -	$ 5,855,513	$ 5,748,508
-	-	226,613	-	226,613	1,326,712	-	1,553,325	1,607,530
-	97,890	54	-	2,939,568	143,472	-	3,083,040	2,243,271
-	-	-	1,100	912,668	11,323	-	923,991	1,145,061
-	-	79,141	14,469	679,207	155,433	-	834,640	606,154
-	-	43	45,386	1,598,834	(1,598,834)	-	-	-
-	97,890	619,168	60,955	12,158,401	92,108	-	12,250,509	11,350,524
-	-	-	-	-	-	-	-	459,432
-	-	-	-	2,035,843	-	-	2,035,843	2,103,597
-	-	-	-	4,703,832	-	-	4,703,832	4,222,553
-	97,890	619,168	60,955	18,898,076	92,108	-	18,990,184	18,136,106
-	-	260,170	-	2,098,179	-	-	2,098,179	2,109,785
-	-	72,447	-	1,814,305	-	-	1,814,305	1,934,582
-	-	33,743	-	214,186	-	-	214,186	215,370
-	-	4,220	-	254,275	-	-	254,275	282,520
-	-	10,288	27,516	69,461	-	-	69,461	53,651
-	-	18,304	1,527	395,965	-	-	395,965	349,877
-	-	101,607	11,563	1,336,379	-	-	1,336,379	1,220,670
-	-	4,660	-	135,367	-	-	135,367	78,952
-	-	-	-	856,829	-	-	856,829	895,886
-	-	85,930	10,365	2,786,010	-	-	2,786,010	2,917,842
140,750	-	-	-	140,750	-	-	140,750	167,999
-	-	-	-	868,808	-	-	868,808	900,351
140,750	-	591,369	50,971	10,970,514	-	-	10,970,514	11,127,485
-	-	-	-	2,614,815	-	-	2,614,815	2,626,545
-	-	-	-	3,466,225	-	-	3,466,225	3,406,605
140,750	-	591,369	50,971	17,051,554	-	-	17,051,554	17,160,635
(140,750)	97,890	27,799	9,984	1,846,522	92,108	-	1,938,630	975,471
42,848	-	(11,590)	1,200	-	-	-	-	-
(97,902)	97,890	16,209	11,184	1,846,522	92,108	-	1,938,630	975,471
2,483,460	1,359,911	221,446	52,276	21,165,256	1,154,745	10,607	22,330,608	21,355,137
$ 2,385,558	$ 1,457,801	$ 237,655	$ 63,460	$ 23,011,778	$ 1,246,853	$ 10,607	$ 24,269,238	$ 22,330,608

West Michigan
Annual Conference

of The

United Methodist Church

The 46th Session

STATISTICIAN'S and
TREASURER'S REPORTS

January 1, 2013
through
December 31, 2013

THOMAS FOX, Statistician
PROSPERO TUMONONG, Treasurer

Table I – Statistical Report *January 1, 2013 through December 31, 2013*

2013 TABLE 1 MEMBERSHIP & PARTICIPATION	MEMBERSHIP LAST YR	PROFESSION OF FAITH	RESTORED BY AFFIRMATION	CORRECT BY ADDITION	RECVD FM OTHER UMC'S	RECVD FM NON-UMC	REMOVED BY CHARGE CONF	WITHDRAWN	CORRECT BY SUBTRACTION	TRANSFER TO OTHER UMC	TRANSFER TO NON-UMC	REMOVED BY DEATH	TOTAL PROFESSING MEMBERS	ASIAN	AFRICAN AMER/BLACK	HISPANIC/LATINO	NATIVE AMERICAN	PACIFIC ISLANDER	WHITE	Multi-Racial	FEMALE	MALE	AVG WORSHIP ATTENDANCE	BAPTIZED THIS YEAR (12 or Younger)	BAPTIZED THIS YEAR (13 or Older)	BAPTIZED NON-MEMBERS
CHURCH	1	2a	2b	2c	3	4	5a	5b	5c	6	7	8	9	9a	9b	9c	9d	9e	9f	9g	9h	9i	10	11a	11b	12
ALBION FIRST	275	0	1	0	0	0	16	3	0	0	0	5	252	0	0	0	0	0	250	2	124	128	93	0	0	15
ATHENS	34	0	0	0	1	0	0	0	0	0	0	1	34	0	0	0	0	0	34	0	19	15	30	1	0	30
AUGUSTA FELLOWSHIP	44	0	0	2	0	0	0	0	0	0	0	1	45	0	2	0	0	0	43	0	29	16	36	0	0	0
BASELINE	63	3	1	0	0	0	0	0	0	0	0	1	66	0	0	0	0	0	66	0	38	28	66	1	0	18
BELLEVUE	125	2	0	0	1	0	0	0	0	0	0	0	128	0	0	0	0	0	128	0	86	42	65	5	9	18
BIRCHWOOD	106	3	0	0	0	0	7	0	0	0	0	1	101	0	0	0	0	0	101	0	63	38	65	0	0	19
CHAPEL HILL	406	4	0	0	4	2	29	8	0	1	3	10	365	3	1	0	0	0	361	0	235	130	187	6	1	55
BATTLE CREEK CHRIST	122	3	0	5	0	0	17	0	0	0	0	7	106	0	2	1	1	0	102	0	48	58	63	2	1	4
CONVIS UNION	66	5	0	0	1	1	0	0	0	0	0	0	73	0	0	0	0	0	73	0	51	22	44	0	2	12
DELTON FAITH	166	4	0	0	4	0	0	0	0	1	0	6	167	0	0	0	0	0	167	0	108	59	107	0	0	0
BATTLE CREEK FIRST	264	2	0	0	2	0	10	2	0	0	0	6	250	0	4	0	0	0	245	1	154	96	123	1	1	1
BATTLE CREEK MAPLE	85	0	1	0	0	0	0	0	0	0	0	3	83	3	1	0	0	0	75	4	60	23	74	0	2	10
SONOMA	43	0	1	0	2	0	0	0	0	0	0	1	45	0	0	0	0	0	45	0	32	13	26	0	0	0
NEWTON	84	0	0	0	0	0	0	0	0	0	0	0	84	0	0	0	0	0	84	0	50	34	70	1	0	0
BATTLE CREEK TRINITY	83	1	0	0	0	0	0	0	0	0	0	7	77	2	0	0	0	0	75	0	44	33	45	0	0	0
WASHINGTON HEIGHTS	42	0	0	0	0	0	0	0	0	0	0	0	42	0	42	0	0	0	0	0	35	7	33	0	0	0
BRONSON FIRST	89	3	0	0	1	1	0	0	0	0	0	2	92	0	0	0	0	0	92	0	49	43	47	1	0	0
BURR OAK	47	4	0	0	1	0	0	0	2	0	0	0	50	0	0	0	0	0	48	2	33	17	28	0	1	2
CAMDEN	21	0	0	0	2	0	0	0	0	0	0	1	22	0	0	0	0	0	22	0	13	9	19	2	0	0
MONTGOMERY	29	0	0	0	0	0	0	0	0	0	0	0	29	0	0	0	0	0	29	0	15	14	20	0	0	0
STOKES CHAPEL	17	0	0	0	0	0	0	0	0	0	0	1	16	0	0	0	0	0	16	0	8	8	32	0	0	0
CENTER PARK	124	2	0	0	0	0	0	0	3	0	0	1	122	0	0	0	0	0	122	0	76	46	91	1	0	54
CENTREVILLE	207	4	0	0	3	2	0	0	0	2	0	1	213	0	2	0	0	0	211	0	119	94	100	3	1	74
CLIMAX	106	0	0	0	0	0	0	0	0	0	0	0	106	0	0	0	0	0	106	0	72	34	69	0	0	0
SCOTTS	43	0	0	0	0	0	0	0	0	0	0	0	43	0	0	0	0	0	43	0	30	13	34	0	0	0
COLDWATER	364	5	0	0	5	3	9	0	0	1	0	11	356	0	0	0	0	0	356	0	233	123	140	2	4	0
COLON	66	0	0	0	0	0	0	0	0	0	0	1	65	0	0	0	0	0	65	0	44	21	45	0	0	0
CONCORD	158	13	0	0	0	0	4	0	0	2	0	4	161	0	0	0	2	0	159	0	110	51	102	12	12	18
CONSTANTINE	156	0	0	0	0	0	0	0	0	0	0	0	156	0	0	0	0	0	156	0	98	58	54	0	0	36
FRONTIER	53	0	0	0	0	0	1	0	0	0	0	2	50	1	0	0	0	0	49	0	32	18	26	0	0	0
OSSEO	18	2	0	0	0	0	0	0	0	2	0	0	18	0	0	0	0	0	18	0	11	7	17	0	0	0
GALESBURG	140	6	3	0	1	1	10	0	52	0	1	1	87	0	0	0	2	0	85	0	59	28	67	1	2	10
GIRARD	103	0	0	0	1	0	0	0	0	0	0	2	102	0	0	0	0	0	102	0	59	43	79	1	0	0
GRASS LAKE	137	1	0	0	2	6	0	14	0	1	1	2	128	0	0	1	1	0	126	0	78	50	91	3	0	29
HILLSDALE	168	0	0	0	0	0	0	1	0	0	0	5	162	0	0	0	0	0	162	0	107	55	106	1	0	0
HILLSIDE	128	13	0	0	2	0	0	0	0	2	0	3	138	0	0	0	0	0	137	1	92	46	63	1	6	0
HOMER	53	1	0	0	0	2	0	1	0	0	0	0	55	0	0	0	0	0	55	0	37	18	38	2	2	4

2013 TABLE 1 MEMBERSHIP & PARTICIPATION

CHURCH	MEMBERSHIP LAST YR	PROFESSION OF FAITH	RESTORED BY AFFIRMATION	CORRECT BY ADDITION	RECVD FM OTHER UMC'S	RECVD FM NON-UMC	REMOVED BY CHARGE CONF	WITHDRAWN	CORRECT BY SUBTRACTION	TRANSFER TO OTHER UMC	TRANSFER TO NON-UMC	REMOVED BY DEATH	TOTAL PROFESSING MEMBERS	ASIAN	AFRICAN AMER/BLACK	HISPANIC/LATINO	NATIVE AMERICAN	PACIFIC ISLANDER	WHITE	Multi-Racial	FEMALE	MALE	AVG WORSHIP ATTENDANCE	BAPTIZED THIS YEAR (12 or Younger)	BAPTIZED THIS YEAR (13 or Older)	BAPTIZED NON-MEMBERS
	1	2a	2b	2c	3	4	5a	5b	5c	6	7	8	9	9a	9b	9c	9d	9e	9f	9g	9h	9i	10	11a	11b	12
LYON LAKE	45	4	0	0	2	0	0	0	0	0	0	0	51	0	0	0	0	0	51	0	28	23	47	0	0	10
BROOKSIDE	191	1	0	3	0	0	5	0	0	4	0	7	179	1	0	0	0	0	178	0	113	66	96	2	2	30
JACKSON CALVARY	146	2	2	0	2	0	2	1	0	2	0	6	141	0	3	0	0	0	138	0	100	41	68	2	0	27
JACKSON FIRST	866	7	0	3	4	1	0	3	0	6	0	16	856	3	3	0	0	0	849	1	522	334	271	0	0	0
TRINITY JACKSON	92	0	0	0	2	0	12	4	0	0	0	1	77	1	0	0	0	0	76	0	46	31	47	1	0	0
ZION JACKSON	17	0	0	0	0	0	0	0	0	0	0	0	17	0	0	0	0	0	17	0	13	4	21	0	0	14
JONESVILLE	144	0	0	0	0	0	0	0	0	0	0	3	141	0	0	0	0	0	141	0	89	52	99	0	0	0
ALLEN	49	1	0	0	0	0	0	0	0	0	0	3	47	0	1	0	0	0	46	0	28	19	50	0	0	10
LITCHFIELD	126	0	0	0	1	0	0	0	0	2	0	6	119	0	0	0	0	0	119	0	67	52	51	2	2	44
MARENGO	8	0	0	0	0	0	0	0	0	0	0	0	8	0	0	0	0	0	8	0	5	3	2	0	0	0
MARSHALL	591	0	0	0	0	1	0	14	0	4	0	8	566	0	0	1	0	0	565	0	290	276	308	6	11	12
MENDON	115	0	0	0	0	0	0	0	0	0	0	4	111	0	0	0	0	0	111	0	57	54	37	0	0	0
NAPOLEON	119	6	1	0	0	0	0	0	0	2	0	2	122	0	0	0	1	0	121	0	81	41	63	0	1	11
NORTH ADAMS	38	0	0	0	0	0	0	0	0	0	0	3	35	0	0	0	0	0	35	0	25	10	28	0	0	0
JEROME	29	0	0	0	0	0	2	1	0	0	0	0	26	0	0	0	0	0	26	0	17	9	22	0	0	0
NOTTAWA	11	0	0	0	0	0	0	0	0	0	0	0	11	0	0	0	0	0	11	0	8	3	10	2	0	0
PARMA	20	0	0	0	0	0	0	0	0	0	0	2	18	0	0	0	0	0	18	0	15	3	15	0	0	0
NORTH PARMA	86	3	0	0	0	0	0	0	4	0	2	0	83	1	0	0	0	0	82	0	47	36	45	2	1	20
POPE	27	0	0	0	0	0	0	0	0	0	0	0	27	0	0	0	0	0	27	0	18	9	28	0	0	0
GRIFFITH	55	0	0	0	0	0	0	0	0	0	0	2	53	0	0	0	0	0	53	0	36	17	37	0	0	0
QUINCY	78	0	0	0	0	0	0	0	0	6	0	1	71	0	0	0	0	0	71	0	48	23	61	0	1	0
READING	117	0	0	0	0	0	0	0	0	1	0	2	114	0	0	0	0	0	114	0	77	37	76	2	0	26
SOMERSET CENTER	56	0	0	0	0	0	0	0	0	1	0	3	52	0	0	0	0	0	52	0	36	16	25	0	0	1
SPRINGPORT	48	3	0	0	0	0	0	0	0	0	0	2	49	0	0	0	0	0	49	0	34	15	52	1	1	0
LEE CENTER	53	0	0	0	0	0	0	0	0	0	0	0	53	0	0	0	0	0	53	0	27	26	30	1	0	10
STURGIS	419	11	0	0	3	0	0	0	0	0	0	6	427	0	0	0	0	0	427	0	262	165	171	1	4	87
THREE RIVERS FIRST	180	0	0	0	0	0	0	2	0	4	0	5	169	1	1	0	0	0	166	1	110	59	60	0	0	50
THREE RIVERS NINTH STREET	48	1	0	0	0	0	0	0	0	0	0	0	49	0	0	0	0	0	49	0	37	12	30	0	0	0
UNION CITY	108	2	1	0	0	0	0	0	0	4	0	4	103	2	0	0	0	0	101	0	60	43	60	3	0	15
WEST MENDON	107	0	0	0	0	0	0	0	0	0	0	0	107	0	4	3	0	0	100	0	60	47	75	0	1	15
SCHOOLCRAFT PLEASANT VALLEY	64	2	0	4	0	0	0	0	0	0	0	1	69	0	0	0	0	0	69	0	40	29	43	0	0	20
WHITE PIGEON	60	3	0	0	0	0	0	0	0	0	0	1	62	0	0	0	0	0	62	0	43	19	30	0	0	0
ALBION DISTRICT	8,348	127	11	17	47	20	124	54	61	48	7	174	8,102	18	66	6	7	0	7,993	12	4,990	3,112	4,453	72	68	811
LAST YEAR	8,687	153	14	23	49	16	131	109	70	48	8	185	8,391	21	64	6	6	0	8,281	13	5,263	3,128	4,651	124		787
INC/(DEC)	(339)	(26)	(3)	(6)	(2)	4	(7)	(55)	(9)	0	(1)	(11)	(289)	(3)	2	0	1	0	(288)	(1)	(273)	(16)	(261)	(52)	68	24

STATISTICAL INFO

2013 TABLE 1 MEMBERSHIP & PARTICIPATION	OTHER CONSTITUENTS	ENROLLED IN CONFIRMATION CLASS	CHILDREN IN CHRISTIAN FORMATION GROUPS	YOUTH IN CHRISTIAN FORMATION GROUPS	YOUNG ADULTS IN CHRISTIAN FORMATION	OTHER ADULTS IN CHRISTIAN FORMATION	TOTAL PERSONS IN CHRISTIAN FORMATION	AVG SUNDAY SCHOOL ATTENDANCE	VACATION BIBLE SCHOOL PARTICIPANTS	NUMBER OF SUNDAY SCHOOL CLASSES	NUMBER OF CLASSES OUTSIDE SUNDAY SCHOOL	SHORT TERM CLASSES	UM MEN MEMBERS	PAID TO UMM PROJECTS	UMW MEMBERS	PAID TO UMW LOCAL PROJECTS	VIM TEAMS SENT OUT	PERSONS IN VIM TEAMS	PERSONS IN MISSIONS	PERSONS SERVED IN DAYCARE AND/OR EDUCATION	PERSONS SERVED IN OUTREACH, JUSTICE, MERCY
CHURCH	13	14	15	16	17	18	19	20	21	22	23	24	25a	25b	26a	26b	27a	27b	28	29	30
ALBION FIRST	47	0	12	8	0	25	45	12	145	3	2	0	0	0	50	2,371	0	0	0	0	345
ATHENS	70	0	5	0	0	9	14	5	0	1	1	0	0	0	12	250	0	0	0	0	75
AUGUSTA FELLOWSHIP	15	0	2	2	0	0	4	2	15	1	1	0	0	0	0	0	0	0	15	0	200
BASELINE	49	0	23	2	1	47	73	34	75	6	2	9	0	0	0	0	0	0	4	0	9
BELLEVUE	97	1	3	0	2	54	59	7	76	1	2	9	20	1,316	23	1,755	0	0	3	0	1,277
BIRCHWOOD	28	1	0	0	0	16	16	0	0	0	3	3	0	0	0	0	0	0	0	0	100
CHAPEL HILL	186	0	10	6	0	170	186	30	53	2	3	10	0	0	0	0	2	22	43	40	125
BATTLE CREEK CHRIST	37	0	6	0	0	60	66	15	0	3	7	1	23	960	21	6,940	0	1	4	7	382
CONVIS UNION	52	1	1	1	0	15	17	9	0	0	0	3	0	0	14	620	0	0	0	0	250
DELTON FAITH	79	0	11	4	0	64	79	61	0	8	1	2	0	0	0	0	3	14	26	0	208
BATTLE CREEK FIRST	40	0	15	15	0	70	100	40	45	3	6	2	0	0	0	0	15	8	10	39	5,500
BATTLE CREEK MAPLE	60	0	11	5	8	26	50	28	0	4	2	2	0	0	0	0	0	0	0	0	2,500
SONOMA	12	0	0	0	0	0	0	0	0	0	0	3	0	0	0	0	0	0	2	0	15
NEWTON	91	1	6	0	0	25	31	3	33	1	1	3	0	0	6	1,420	0	0	0	0	435
BATTLE CREEK TRINITY	38	0	0	0	0	8	8	30	0	6	2	2	0	0	0	0	0	0	0	0	0
WASHINGTON HEIGHTS	0	0	10	0	0	10	20	7	0	2	2	0	0	0	6	320	0	0	5	0	5
BRONSON FIRST	23	0	8	0	0	24	32	6	39	2	1	2	0	0	8	216	0	2	16	538	300
BURR OAK	0	0	0	0	0	9	9	0	0	0	0	0	0	0	0	0	0	0	0	0	0
CAMDEN	0	5	0	0	0	0	0	3	0	1	0	0	0	0	5	170	0	0	0	0	0
MONTGOMERY	12	0	1	0	0	2	3	1	0	0	0	0	0	0	6	6,237	0	0	0	0	100
STOKES CHAPEL	0	0	1	1	0	20	22	14	0	3	1	0	0	0	14	1,008	0	0	0	0	100
CENTER PARK	82	0	0	10	0	25	35	28	20	6	2	0	0	0	0	0	0	0	0	0	0
CENTREVILLE	83	0	35	5	5	69	114	55	75	5	1	1	0	0	0	0	0	0	30	30	4,500
CLIMAX	76	0	0	0	0	8	8	42	0	4	2	2	0	0	27	0	0	0	0	15	0
SCOTTS	30	0	5	0	0	6	11	11	0	3	3	1	0	0	25	0	0	0	0	15	14
COLDWATER	70	0	63	11	2	165	241	30	25	5	6	13	24	425	89	7,744	0	0	170	0	10,870
COLON	0	0	0	0	0	9	9	0	0	0	1	0	0	0	0	0	0	0	0	0	0
CONCORD	118	0	27	38	13	159	237	49	141	5	15	2	40	2,422	24	2,270	1	4	0	0	7,090
CONSTANTINE	36	0	0	0	0	4	4	5	44	1	0	3	0	0	0	0	0	0	0	0	200
FRONTIER	18	0	0	0	0	9	9	0	0	0	0	2	0	0	9	284	0	0	14	0	1,839
OSSEO	11	0	0	0	0	7	7	0	0	0	2	2	0	0	0	0	0	0	6	0	501
GALESBURG	42	0	11	5	0	42	58	16	0	4	9	2	8	450	9	1,250	0	0	22	0	1,740
GIRARD	44	0	4	15	0	26	45	20	0	4	0	0	0	539	0	1,443	0	0	0	0	0
GRASS LAKE	0	0	13	6	0	18	37	17	35	3	2	0	10	264	5	150	0	0	0	0	350
HILLSDALE	76	0	6	6	3	20	35	1	0	1	4	0	0	0	0	0	0	0	0	6	100
HILLSIDE	95	0	4	7	2	5	18	11	43	18	0	0	7	3,897	15	2,504	0	0	0	0	100
HOMER	0	2	10	0	0	9	19	16	45	2	2	4	0	0	0	600	0	0	0	0	0

2013 TABLE 1 MEMBERSHIP & PARTICIPATION	OTHER CONSTITUENTS	ENROLLED IN CONFIRMATION CLASS	CHILDREN IN CHRISTIAN FORMATION GROUPS	YOUTH IN CHRISTIAN FORMATION GROUPS	YOUNG ADULTS IN CHRISTIAN FORMATION	OTHER ADULTS IN CHRISTIAN FORMATION	TOTAL PERSONS IN CHRISTIAN FORMATION	AVG SUNDAY SCHOOL ATTENDANCE	VACATION BIBLE SCHOOL PARTICIPANTS	NUMBER OF SUNDAY SCHOOL CLASSES	NUMBER OF CLASSES OUTSIDE SUNDAY SCHOOL	SHORT TERM CLASSES	UM MEN MEMBERS	PAID TO UMM PROJECTS	UMW MEMBERS	PAID TO UMW LOCAL PROJECTS	VIM TEAMS SENT OUT	PERSONS IN VIM TEAMS	PERSONS IN MISSIONS	PERSONS SERVED IN DAYCARE AND/OR EDUCATION	PERSONS SERVED IN OUTREACH, JUSTICE, MERCY
CHURCH	13	14	15	16	17	18	19	20	21	22	23	24	25a	25b	26a	26b	27a	27b	28	29	30
LYON LAKE	12	4	2	0	0	12	14	6	0	0	0	4	0	0	0	0	0	0	0	0	0
BROOKSIDE	46	0	9	20	0	70	99	28	20	2	1	1	0	0	0	0	0	0	0	0	324
JACKSON CALVARY	60	0	1	0	0	87	88	18	0	2	3	2	0	0	12	487	0	0	7	3	150
JACKSON FIRST	282	7	15	18	20	58	111	24	0	5	30	3	0	0	55	1,440	0	0	10	0	0
TRINITY JACKSON	0	0	4	7	0	25	36	25	15	4	3	0	10	4,250	0	0	0	0	0	30	632
ZION JACKSON	23	0	0	0	0	0	0	5	0	1	0	0	4	100	14	534	0	0	0	0	0
JONESVILLE	50	0	10	30	12	8	60	16	35	8	3	2	0	0	0	0	0	0	12	0	270
ALLEN	18	0	0	7	0	10	17	6	5	1	1	0	0	0	28	500	0	0	0	0	75
LITCHFIELD	88	0	45	9	0	19	73	8	22	2	2	2	0	0	26	0	0	0	20	54	275
MARENGO	0	0	0	0	0	0	0	0	0	0	0	0	0	0	0	0	0	0	0	0	0
MARSHALL	175	16	69	92	69	92	322	68	109	9	3	4	0	0	0	0	0	0	638	0	3,165
MENDON	0	0	5	5	0	8	18	5	0	3	1	2	4	0	0	0	0	0	3	0	50
NAPOLEON	41	0	7	1	2	23	33	18	80	2	3	1	0	0	12	1,893	0	0	0	80	230
NORTH ADAMS	10	0	0	0	0	9	9	9	25	1	0	1	0	0	5	2,726	0	0	0	0	400
JEROME	0	0	0	0	0	0	0	0	20	0	0	5	0	0	10	592	0	0	0	0	16
NOTTAWA	40	0	6	1	0	7	14	14	0	2	1	1	0	0	0	0	0	0	0	0	35
PARMA	9	0	2	0	0	4	6	2	0	0	0	1	0	0	0	0	0	0	0	0	40
NORTH PARMA	17	0	6	40	0	21	67	22	21	4	3	1	8	0	34	1,677	0	0	0	0	2,072
POPE	64	0	1	0	0	0	1	0	0	3	0	0	0	0	7	0	0	0	0	0	0
GRIFFITH	33	0	8	0	0	0	8	9	0	2	1	0	0	0	17	960	0	0	0	0	0
QUINCY	25	1	9	3	0	30	42	40	0	4	2	2	0	0	0	0	0	0	0	0	1,285
READING	151	0	21	5	0	15	41	20	50	3	4	0	5	0	50	3,000	0	0	0	60	1,000
SOMERSET CENTER	0	0	0	0	0	0	0	0	0	0	0	0	0	0	14	500	0	0	0	0	0
SPRINGPORT	0	0	14	6	0	8	28	12	46	1	1	2	0	0	0	0	1	15	15	0	252
LEE CENTER	50	0	0	2	2	12	16	7	36	1	0	2	0	0	0	0	0	0	0	0	50
STURGIS	30	6	15	35	8	100	158	75	20	5	8	10	0	0	0	0	1	29	8	0	90
THREE RIVERS FIRST	57	0	12	6	0	20	38	8	0	12	20	50	0	0	30	3,000	0	2	0	0	6
THREE RIVERS NINTH STREET	19	0	9	0	0	6	15	0	0	0	0	0	0	0	13	593	0	0	0	0	300
UNION CITY	54	0	6	5	5	27	43	30	50	4	4	1	0	0	57	12,233	0	0	0	0	500
WEST MENDON	51	0	0	0	0	0	0	15	120	2	0	1	16	0	10	0	0	0	0	0	0
SCHOOLCRAFT PLEASANT VALLEY	0	0	5	2	0	15	22	15	0	1	2	1	0	0	0	0	0	0	0	0	0
WHITE PIGEON	34	7	0	0	0	17	17	4	0	1	0	3	0	0	15	542	0	0	3	0	160
ALBION DISTRICT	3,156	52	584	441	154	1,938	3,117	1,117	1,583	193	182	185	179	14,623	777	68,229	23	97	1,086	917	50,607
LAST YEAR	3,105	56	780	502	128	1,998	3,408	1,229	1,792	187	154	170	210	19,796	811	93,912	8	94	291	716	68,143
INC/(DEC)	51	(4)	(196)	(61)	26	(60)	(291)	(112)	(209)	6	28	15	(31)	(5,173)	(34)	(25,683)	15	3	795	201	(17,536)

STATISTICAL INFO

2013 TABLE 1 MEMBERSHIP & PARTICIPATION	MEMBERSHIP LAST YR	PROFESSION OF FAITH	RESTORED BY AFFIRMATION	CORRECT BY ADDITION	RECVD FM OTHER UMC'S	RECVD FM NON-UMC	REMOVED BY CHARGE CONF	WITHDRAWN	CORRECT BY SUBTRACTION	TRANSFER TO OTHER UMC	TRANSFER TO NON-UMC	REMOVED BY DEATH	TOTAL PROFESSING MEMBERS	ASIAN	AFRICAN AMER/BLACK	HISPANIC/LATINO	NATIVE AMERICAN	PACIFIC ISLANDER	WHITE	Multi-Racial	FEMALE	MALE	AVG WORSHIP ATTENDANCE	BAPTIZED THIS YEAR (12 or Younger)	BAPTIZED THIS YEAR (13 or Older)	BAPTIZED NON-MEMBERS
CHURCH	1	2a	2b	2c	3	4	5a	5b	5c	6	7	8	9	9a	9b	9c	9d	9e	9f	9g	9h	9i	10	11a	11b	12
ALTO	68	2	0	0	3	3	1	0	0	0	0	0	75	0	0	0	0	0	72	3	46	29	50	0	1	13
BOWNE CENTER	86	0	0	0	1	1	0	0	0	0	0	0	88	0	0	0	0	0	88	0	53	35	50	0	0	20
BYRON CENTER	175	0	0	0	0	0	9	0	0	0	0	1	165	0	0	0	0	0	165	0	98	67	97	0	0	0
CALEDONIA	183	3	0	0	1	0	0	5	0	5	1	3	173	0	0	0	0	0	173	0	102	71	101	2	0	0
CARLISLE	119	0	0	2	0	0	0	4	0	0	0	2	115	0	1	0	0	0	114	0	68	47	80	0	0	4
CEDAR SPRINGS	158	3	0	0	3	2	2	1	0	0	0	2	161	0	0	0	0	0	161	0	100	61	139	6	2	46
EAST NELSON	96	0	0	3	7	0	0	0	0	0	0	1	105	0	0	0	0	0	105	0	66	39	90	1	2	2
COOPERSVILLE	116	13	0	0	1	1	0	0	0	0	0	3	128	1	0	0	0	0	127	0	88	40	107	3	2	52
COURTLAND-OAKFIELD	89	3	0	0	1	0	0	0	0	0	0	0	93	0	0	0	0	0	93	0	54	39	81	1	0	0
FREMONT	437	0	0	0	1	0	9	8	0	9	0	7	405	2	0	1	0	0	401	1	231	174	133	0	0	134
GEORGETOWN	528	11	1	0	3	10	16	9	0	5	0	5	518	3	2	0	0	4	509	0	297	221	287	6	0	97
GRAND HAVEN CHURCH OF THE DUNES	675	0	11	0	6	2	0	2	5	1	0	16	670	0	0	0	0	1	667	2	399	271	299	6	0	31
ALDERSGATE	184	5	0	5	0	0	0	0	0	2	3	0	189	0	5	2	0	0	182	0	113	76	82	0	1	30
SOUTH WYOMING	111	1	0	0	1	2	0	0	0	2	0	3	110	0	5	0	0	0	105	0	73	37	95	4	0	47
CORNERSTONE	1,446	125	5	0	11	9	19	6	0	0	10	4	1,557	8	13	10	5	3	1,508	10	822	735	1,751	73	37	89
FAITH GRAND RAPIDS	243	0	0	0	0	1	0	0	0	0	1	6	237	1	0	1	2	0	232	1	133	104	140	1	1	53
FIRST GRAND RAPIDS	971	13	0	0	4	2	13	9	5	7	0	12	944	4	9	4	0	2	924	1	540	404	496	15	6	186
GENESIS	201	7	0	0	10	5	3	1	0	1	2	1	215	7	2	3	0	0	203	0	126	89	156	8	2	25
LA NUEVA ESPERANZA	95	7	0	0	0	0	0	0	0	0	0	0	102	0	0	93	0	0	9	0	56	46	72	0	0	0
NORTHLAWN	192	0	0	0	5	0	0	0	6	0	0	4	187	0	0	1	0	0	181	5	130	57	103	0	0	0
PLAINFIELD	63	0	0	0	0	0	63	0	0	0	0	0	0	0	0	0	0	0	0	0	0	0	15	0	0	0
SAINT PAULS GRAND RAPIDS	241	1	0	0	4	0	2	4	0	8	1	0	231	3	4	0	0	0	221	3	140	91	106	3	0	22
SOUTH GRAND RAPIDS	129	1	7	0	0	0	0	0	0	0	0	8	129	0	2	3	0	0	124	0	74	55	80	0	0	0
TRINITY GRAND RAPIDS	563	7	0	0	6	1	11	2	0	2	1	16	545	5	6	6	1	1	526	0	309	236	212	8	1	115
VIETNAMESE GRAND RAPIDS	150	5	5	0	5	0	0	5	30	0	0	0	130	126	0	0	0	0	4	0	78	52	120	6	2	8
GRANDVILLE	273	1	0	0	2	0	2	0	0	2	1	7	264	1	0	0	0	0	263	0	178	86	150	2	0	0
HESPERIA	77	6	0	0	1	0	0	0	0	1	1	1	81	0	0	1	0	0	80	0	56	25	61	3	0	64
FERRY	43	0	0	0	0	0	0	0	0	0	0	2	41	0	0	0	0	0	41	0	26	15	36	0	0	14
HOLLAND	634	7	0	0	11	8	8	4	0	3	2	16	627	4	1	5	0	0	616	1	360	267	293	4	1	54
HOLTON	210	11	0	11	2	0	5	0	4	0	0	4	221	0	0	0	0	0	221	0	135	86	211	1	5	4
KENT CITY CHAPEL HILL	113	0	0	0	0	0	0	0	2	0	0	2	109	0	0	0	0	0	109	0	59	50	68	3	0	22
LEIGHTON	148	21	1	0	0	5	8	4	0	0	1	7	155	0	0	0	0	0	154	1	84	71	154	1	4	51
LOWELL	349	12	3	0	0	3	14	0	0	6	0	5	342	3	0	4	1	0	332	2	237	105	163	7	0	63
MARNE	72	4	0	0	0	3	0	3	0	0	1	1	74	0	0	0	0	0	74	0	42	32	103	3	2	1
MARTIN	163	3	0	0	0	0	1	0	0	3	0	4	158	0	0	0	0	0	158	0	85	73	103	6	1	1
SHELBYVILLE	62	4	0	0	2	0	0	0	0	0	0	1	67	0	0	0	0	0	67	0	31	36	63	0	1	0
MIDDLEVILLE	196	6	1	0	0	0	33	0	0	0	0	4	166	0	0	0	0	0	166	0	95	71	122	0	0	22

2013 TABLE 1 MEMBERSHIP & PARTICIPATION

CHURCH	MEMBERSHIP LAST YR	PROFESSION OF FAITH	RESTORED BY AFFIRMATION	CORRECT BY ADDITION	RECVD FM OTHER UMC'S	RECVD FM NON-UMC	REMOVED BY CHARGE CONF	WITHDRAWN	CORRECT BY SUBTRACTION	TRANSFER TO OTHER UMC	TRANSFER TO NON-UMC	REMOVED BY DEATH	TOTAL PROFESSING MEMBERS	ASIAN	AFRICAN AMER/BLACK	HISPANIC/LATINO	NATIVE AMERICAN	PACIFIC ISLANDER	WHITE	Multi-Racial	FEMALE	MALE	AVG WORSHIP ATTENDANCE	BAPTIZED THIS YEAR (12 or Younger)	BAPTIZED THIS YEAR (13 or Older)	BAPTIZED NON-MEMBERS
	1	2a	2b	2c	3	4	5a	5b	5c	6	7	8	9	9a	9b	9c	9d	9e	9f	9g	9h	9i	10	11a	11b	12
PARMELEE	53	3	0	0	0	1	0	0	0	0	0	2	55	0	0	0	0	0	55	0	37	18	33	0	0	0
MONTAGUE	305	0	0	0	0	0	0	0	0	0	0	3	302	2	1	0	1	0	298	0	238	64	96	0	0	0
CENTRAL MUSKEGON	321	7	2	0	0	2	0	0	0	1	0	6	325	2	2	1	0	0	316	4	199	126	117	1	0	1
CRESTWOOD	143	2	0	0	0	0	2	2	6	1	0	2	132	0	3	1	1	0	127	0	71	61	62	0	3	5
LAKE HARBOR	395	8	2	0	4	2	8	7	0	2	0	6	388	1	2	0	0	0	385	0	230	158	176	6	0	42
LAKESIDE	109	0	2	0	0	0	5	4	3	0	0	0	99	0	0	0	1	0	98	0	66	33	62	0	0	0
UNITY	36	0	0	0	0	0	0	0	0	0	0	0	36	0	0	0	0	0	36	0	27	9	25	0	0	6
WOLF LAKE	107	0	0	0	0	0	0	6	0	0	0	4	97	0	0	0	0	0	97	0	59	38	61	0	4	3
MUSKEGON HEIGHTS TEMPLE	137	4	0	0	0	1	0	1	0	0	0	1	140	0	16	8	0	0	116	0	82	58	77	0	0	4
NEWAYGO	95	1	2	0	0	0	0	0	0	0	0	0	98	0	0	0	0	0	98	0	71	27	73	0	0	22
NORTH MUSKEGON COMMUNITY	351	0	0	0	6	0	0	0	0	1	0	8	348	0	0	0	0	0	348	0	199	149	172	5	3	8
RAVENNA	98	5	0	0	0	0	0	0	0	0	0	5	98	1	0	0	0	0	97	0	67	31	65	0	0	0
ROCKFORD	571	16	2	0	8	4	25	8	0	7	3	5	553	0	0	0	0	1	552	0	299	254	338	4	0	0
SALEM INDIAN MISSION	42	0	0	0	0	0	0	0	12	0	0	2	28	0	0	0	23	0	5	0	26	2	20	0	0	15
BRADLEY INDIAN MISSION	28	0	0	0	0	0	0	0	0	0	0	0	28	0	0	0	19	0	9	0	12	16	36	0	0	6
SAUGATUCK	58	0	0	0	0	0	0	0	0	0	0	1	57	0	0	0	2	0	55	0	35	22	36	0	0	2
SHELBY	124	3	0	0	0	0	4	0	0	1	4	6	112	0	0	3	0	0	109	0	66	46	70	1	1	0
SNOW	59	0	0	0	0	0	0	0	0	0	0	2	57	0	0	0	0	0	57	0	30	27	32	0	0	8
SPARTA	251	19	2	0	1	3	9	1	0	1	0	6	259	0	0	2	0	5	252	0	157	102	209	8	2	8
TWIN LAKE	80	0	0	0	0	0	0	0	0	0	0	0	80	0	0	0	0	0	80	0	50	30	50	0	0	0
SITKA	19	0	0	0	2	0	0	1	0	0	0	0	20	0	0	0	0	0	20	0	13	7	25	0	0	0
VALLEY CHURCH ALLENDALE NEW CHUR	70	0	0	0	0	0	0	0	0	0	0	0	70	0	0	0	0	0	70	0	35	35	70	0	0	0
VERGENNES	129	0	0	0	0	0	0	0	0	0	0	1	128	0	0	0	0	0	128	0	73	55	92	2	0	2
WAYLAND	145	7	0	0	1	0	0	0	0	4	0	4	145	2	0	0	0	0	143	0	86	59	60	0	0	89
WHITE CLOUD	137	2	0	5	0	0	0	0	0	0	0	0	144	0	0	0	1	0	143	0	88	56	105	2	2	38
WHITEHALL	79	0	0	0	3	1	0	0	0	2	0	3	78	0	0	0	0	0	78	0	40	38	60	1	0	1
CLAYBANKS	56	0	0	0	2	3	0	0	0	1	0	2	58	0	0	0	0	0	58	0	40	18	58	0	1	0
WESLEY PARK	305	7	0	0	2	2	1	17	0	0	2	10	286	0	10	10	0	1	264	1	194	92	218	18	2	17
WYOMING PARK	142	0	2	144	0	2	0	4	142	0	3	2	139	0	1	0	3	1	134	0	85	54	104	123	0	0
CROSSWIND COMMUNITY	91	11	0	0	0	2	0	10	8	0	0	0	86	0	2	1	0	0	83	0	48	38	148	16	3	16
GRAND RAPIDS DISTRICT	14,195	377	48	170	120	81	273	128	223	78	37	229	14,023	176	87	160	60	19	13,486	35	8,307	5,716	9,219	360	92	1,563
LAST YEAR	14,290	345	58	159	127	120	285	152	193	90	52	202	14,125	195	96	156	73	20	13,557	28	8,454	5,671	9,355	341		1,643
INC/(DEC)	(95)	32	(10)	11	(7)	(39)	(12)	(24)	30	(12)	(15)	27	(102)	(19)	(9)	4	(13)	(1)	(71)	7	(147)	45	(136)	19	92	(80)

2013 TABLE 1 MEMBERSHIP & PARTICIPATION

CHURCH	OTHER CONSTITUENTS	ENROLLED IN CONFIRMATION CLASS	CHILDREN IN CHRISTIAN FORMATION GROUPS	YOUTH IN CHRISTIAN FORMATION GROUPS	YOUNG ADULTS IN CHRISTIAN FORMATION	OTHER ADULTS IN CHRISTIAN FORMATION	TOTAL PERSONS IN CHRISTIAN FORMATION	AVG SUNDAY SCHOOL ATTENDANCE	VACATION BIBLE SCHOOL PARTICIPANTS	NUMBER OF SUNDAY SCHOOL CLASSES	NUMBER OF CLASSES OUTSIDE SUNDAY SCHOOL	SHORT TERM CLASSES	UM MEN MEMBERS	PAID TO UMM PROJECTS	UMW MEMBERS	PAID TO UMW LOCAL PROJECTS	VIM TEAMS SENT OUT	PERSONS IN VIM TEAMS	PERSONS IN MISSIONS	PERSONS SERVED IN DAYCARE AND/OR EDUCATION	PERSONS SERVED IN OUTREACH, JUSTICE, MERCY
	13	14	15	16	17	18	19	20	21	22	23	24	25a	25b	26a	26b	27a	27b	28	29	30
ALTO	53	2	8	0	0	25	33	3	0	2	0	3	0	0	18	1,364	0	0	0	0	158
BOWNE CENTER	60	0	26	0	0	5	31	0	0	4	0	0	0	0	0	600	0	0	0	0	310
BYRON CENTER	0	0	32	16	0	34	82	44	34	6	3	0	0	0	0	0	0	0	4	0	0
CALEDONIA	108	0	7	6	4	64	81	50	10	3	0	1	0	0	10	7,000	0	0	12	0	400
CARLISLE	56	0	0	0	0	16	16	0	24	0	1	0	0	0	0	0	0	0	0	0	0
CEDAR SPRINGS	230	0	65	20	15	120	220	35	65	6	5	1	10	868	25	1,432	1	3	150	40	375
EAST NELSON	0	0	8	9	0	10	27	18	30	18	0	0	0	0	0	0	0	0	0	0	0
COOPERSVILLE	164	14	20	22	2	38	82	27	0	5	10	0	0	0	0	0	0	0	63	0	496
COURTLAND-OAKFIELD	20	0	10	6	0	20	36	0	8	1	2	1	0	0	20	0	0	0	0	0	0
FREMONT	179	0	56	8	16	149	229	65	0	24	37	50	0	0	61	2,300	0	0	0	30	5,924
GEORGETOWN	258	0	69	33	40	352	494	171	99	14	19	12	10	0	74	1,334	0	2	125	127	1,000
GRAND HAVEN CHURCH OF THE DUNES	96	7	36	23	8	78	145	62	62	9	5	5	35	1,564	100	4,402	1	3	11	88	120
ALDERSGATE	30	2	70	15	24	50	159	35	29	6	1	1	0	0	0	0	0	0	40	50	0
SOUTH WYOMING	50	0	0	20	0	15	35	45	30	0	0	2	0	0	27	642	0	0	0	0	110
CORNERSTONE	2,400	92	525	500	30	1,948	3,003	447	450	33	110	58	0	0	0	0	1	7	547	0	1,487
FAITH GRAND RAPIDS	72	4	0	0	0	10	10	32	65	7	4	1	15	0	0	0	0	0	28	0	0
FIRST GRAND RAPIDS	122	13	191	68	44	415	718	126	70	13	5	25	0	0	90	5,405	2	30	325	523	850
GENESIS	98	0	0	0	0	0	0	41	106	7	1	19	0	0	0	0	1	3	0	0	0
LA NUEVA ESPERANZA	0	0	14	12	0	21	47	15	0	0	0	0	0	0	0	0	0	0	0	0	80
NORTHLAWN	75	0	6	6	6	27	45	25	8	4	5	2	0	0	0	8,500	0	0	0	0	0
PLAINFIELD	0	0	0	0	0	0	0	0	0	0	0	0	0	0	0	0	0	0	0	0	0
SAINT PAULS GRAND RAPIDS	45	0	8	12	0	81	101	27	0	3	4	1	15	2,085	32	126	0	0	13	370	550
SOUTH GRAND RAPIDS	0	0	21	5	17	23	66	22	74	4	4	4	15	665	24	0	0	0	40	41	1,100
TRINITY GRAND RAPIDS	105	0	200	100	50	175	525	100	50	10	35	2	0	2,540	200	0	0	0	0	300	0
VIETNAMESE GRAND RAPIDS	80	0	25	25	22	0	72	72	0	5	1	0	30	0	40	200	0	1	10	0	0
GRANDVILLE	58	0	25	0	0	20	45	30	75	3	1	0	0	0	50	0	0	0	75	0	0
HESPERIA	50	0	7	0	0	12	19	12	34	2	0	1	0	0	26	1,881	0	0	0	0	5,562
FERRY	12	0	0	0	0	12	12	0	0	0	1	0	0	0	0	0	0	0	0	0	5,565
HOLLAND	83	7	80	46	0	96	222	102	70	12	9	4	0	0	83	13,870	0	0	0	75	163
HOLTON	65	18	100	20	2	62	184	30	100	4	3	1	0	0	14	1,000	2	10	10	0	400
KENT CITY CHAPEL HILL	12	0	18	0	0	40	58	20	0	2	3	4	0	0	0	0	0	0	0	0	0
LEIGHTON	56	0	72	34	5	120	231	75	80	11	7	5	0	0	0	0	0	0	120	0	1,591
LOWELL	163	5	50	30	8	0	88	24	65	3	1	5	0	0	92	1,650	0	0	0	0	607
MARNE	0	0	0	6	9	0	15	10	52	0	0	0	0	0	10	350	0	0	3	0	0
MARTIN	28	0	8	4	0	45	57	20	60	3	3	2	0	0	5	619	0	0	12	4	600
SHELBYVILLE	23	0	20	5	0	20	45	14	18	1	1	2	0	0	16	2,216	0	0	5	0	15
MIDDLEVILLE	75	2	0	12	20	32	64	21	38	5	5	4	16	3,275	40	4,239	0	0	3	0	325

2013 TABLE 1 MEMBERSHIP & PARTICIPATION

CHURCH	OTHER CONSTITUENTS	ENROLLED IN CONFIRMATION CLASS	CHILDREN IN CHRISTIAN FORMATION GROUPS	YOUTH IN CHRISTIAN FORMATION GROUPS	YOUNG ADULTS IN CHRISTIAN FORMATION	OTHER ADULTS IN CHRISTIAN FORMATION	TOTAL PERSONS IN CHRISTIAN FORMATION	AVG SUNDAY SCHOOL ATTENDANCE	VACATION BIBLE SCHOOL PARTICIPANTS	NUMBER OF SUNDAY SCHOOL CLASSES	NUMBER OF CLASSES OUTSIDE SUNDAY SCHOOL	SHORT TERM CLASSES	UM MEN MEMBERS	PAID TO UMM PROJECTS	UMW MEMBERS	PAID TO UMW LOCAL PROJECTS	VIM TEAMS SENT OUT	PERSONS IN VIM TEAMS	PERSONS IN MISSIONS	PERSONS SERVED IN DAYCARE AND/OR EDUCATION	PERSONS SERVED IN OUTREACH, JUSTICE, MERCY
	13	14	15	16	17	18	19	20	21	22	23	24	25a	25b	26a	26b	27a	27b	28	29	30
PARMELEE	0	0	0	0	0	0	0	0	0	0	0	0	0	0	0	0	0	0	0	0	0
MONTAGUE	0	0	20	25	10	36	91	10	50	5	2	2	0	0	43	0	0	0	0	0	80
CENTRAL MUSKEGON	75	0	10	3	0	30	43	35	15	2	4	1	0	1,300	77	1,200	0	0	0	28	1,000
CRESTWOOD	37	0	11	6	0	6	23	7	0	0	1	3	0	0	27	2,200	0	0	7	0	8,500
LAKE HARBOR	27	6	35	26	8	65	134	52	100	11	7	0	10	473	31	3,900	0	0	50	0	0
LAKESIDE	101	0	0	0	0	0	0	0	0	0	0	0	0	0	0	0	1	2	0	0	500
UNITY	6	0	0	0	0	0	0	0	0	0	0	0	0	0	15	0	0	0	0	0	0
WOLF LAKE	0	0	52	29	2	18	101	30	120	2	2	0	0	0	0	3,808	0	0	0	1	2,339
MUSKEGON HEIGHTS TEMPLE	55	4	15	7	4	54	80	12	0	3	1	5	10	182	15	917	0	0	32	80	8,200
NEWAYGO	141	2	0	0	0	50	50	28	12	3	1	0	0	0	36	2,697	0	0	0	9	0
NORTH MUSKEGON COMMUNITY	70	0	38	42	19	116	215	30	114	3	11	10	12	931	42	2,286	1	18	0	0	525
RAVENNA	40	0	12	12	0	46	70	8	40	2	4	2	0	0	0	0	0	0	5	0	0
ROCKFORD	0	5	103	41	15	190	349	80	87	5	24	13	0	0	0	0	0	0	68	0	650
SALEM INDIAN MISSION	20	0	7	10	0	12	29	0	0	0	0	0	0	0	0	0	0	0	0	0	90
BRADLEY INDIAN MISSION	8	0	6	0	1	2	9	4	0	0	0	0	0	0	0	0	0	0	0	0	100
SAUGATUCK	0	0	0	0	0	13	13	13	0	0	0	0	0	0	10	0	0	0	0	0	0
SHELBY	0	0	20	7	0	12	39	17	60	4	4	2	10	2,000	40	9,000	0	0	10	0	700
SNOW	15	0	0	0	0	0	0	8	0	2	0	0	0	0	9	0	0	0	0	0	0
SPARTA	138	9	40	50	5	136	231	42	73	5	19	3	30	0	62	928	0	0	135	0	1,000
TWIN LAKE	0	0	0	0	0	0	0	0	0	0	0	0	0	0	0	0	0	0	0	0	0
SITKA	12	0	9	4	0	9	22	13	0	2	0	1	0	0	0	0	0	0	0	0	50
VALLEY CHURCH ALLENDALE NEW CHUR	0	0	28	12	0	0	40	0	0	0	0	0	0	0	0	0	0	0	0	0	0
VERGENNES	116	0	47	14	0	22	83	31	78	7	11	5	0	0	0	0	0	0	96	0	0
WAYLAND	71	7	11	12	3	11	37	15	89	3	1	3	0	0	0	0	0	0	1	7	134
WHITE CLOUD	97	0	2	38	3	45	88	25	0	4	5	0	0	0	36	2,715	0	0	0	0	0
WHITEHALL	15	0	14	7	0	10	31	10	14	2	2	0	0	0	0	0	0	0	0	0	350
CLAYBANKS	21	0	20	2	0	6	28	16	25	5	0	1	0	0	12	1,033	0	0	0	0	100
WESLEY PARK	62	0	0	0	0	0	0	0	0	0	0	0	0	0	0	0	0	0	0	0	0
WYOMING PARK	123	0	29	3	21	31	84	60	43	8	2	0	0	0	0	0	0	0	10	0	100
CROSSWIND COMMUNITY	285	0	60	16	0	0	76	60	260	4	4	0	0	0	0	0	0	0	0	0	20,000
GRAND RAPIDS DISTRICT	6,461	199	2,366	1,429	413	5,055	9,263	2,426	2,986	312	391	267	218	15,883	1,512	89,814	10	79	2,010	1,773	72,206
LAST YEAR	6,654	208	2,404	1,493	373	4,287	8,557	2,697	3,320	313	359	238	237	12,272	1,654	87,163	9	108	861	4,036	68,143
INC/(DEC)	(193)	(9)	(38)	(64)	40	768	706	(271)	(334)	(1)	32	29	(19)	3,611	(142)	2,651	1	(29)	1,149	(2,263)	4,063

2013 TABLE 1 MEMBERSHIP & PARTICIPATION	MEMBERSHIP LAST YR	PROFESSION OF FAITH	RESTORED BY AFFIRMATION	CORRECT BY ADDITION	RECVD FM OTHER UMC'S	RECVD FM NON-UMC	REMOVED BY CHARGE CONF	WITHDRAWN	CORRECT BY SUBTRACTION	TRANSFER TO OTHER UMC	TRANSFER TO NON-UMC	REMOVED BY DEATH	TOTAL PROFESSING MEMBERS	ASIAN	AFRICAN AMER/BLACK	HISPANIC/LATINO	NATIVE AMERICAN	PACIFIC ISLANDER	WHITE	Multi-Racial	FEMALE	MALE	AVG WORSHIP ATTENDANCE	BAPTIZED THIS YEAR (12 or Younger)	BAPTIZED THIS YEAR (13 or Older)	BAPTIZED NON-MEMBERS
CHURCH	1	2a	2b	2c	3	4	5a	5b	5c	6	7	8	9	9a	9b	9c	9d	9e	9f	9g	9h	9i	10	11a	11b	12
ALDEN	69	0	0	4	0	0	0	2	0	0	0	4	67	0	0	0	0	0	67	0	44	23	59	0	0	7
CENTRAL LAKE	31	0	0	0	0	0	0	0	0	0	0	0	31	0	0	0	0	0	31	0	20	11	17	0	0	0
BALDWIN COVENANT COMMUNITY	53	3	0	9	1	1	10	1	0	0	1	1	54	0	1	0	0	0	53	0	36	18	54	0	1	0
LUTHER	23	5	0	0	0	0	0	0	0	0	0	0	28	0	0	0	0	0	28	0	15	13	32	0	1	0
BARNARD	62	0	0	0	0	0	0	0	12	0	0	0	50	0	0	0	0	0	50	0	31	19	40	0	0	1
EAST JORDAN	131	0	0	0	0	0	0	0	0	0	0	3	128	0	0	1	0	0	127	0	86	42	61	1	0	52
NORWOOD	10	0	0	2	0	0	0	0	0	0	0	0	12	0	0	0	1	0	11	0	8	4	14	0	0	0
BEAR LAKE	120	0	0	0	1	0	0	0	0	0	0	5	116	0	0	1	0	0	115	0	76	40	79	2	0	17
ARCADIA	27	0	0	0	0	0	0	0	9	0	0	1	17	0	0	0	0	0	17	0	12	5	15	0	0	0
BELLAIRE COMMUNITY	208	17	0	0	0	0	1	0	0	0	0	4	220	0	0	0	0	0	220	0	141	79	128	1	0	0
BOYNE CITY	79	0	0	0	0	0	6	1	0	0	0	5	67	0	0	0	0	0	67	0	42	25	42	0	0	25
BOYNE FALLS	32	3	0	0	1	0	1	0	0	0	0	0	35	0	0	0	0	0	35	0	23	12	26	5	2	3
BRETHREN EPWORTH	46	0	1	1	0	0	0	0	0	0	0	0	48	0	0	0	1	0	47	0	34	14	35	0	0	0
CADILLAC	459	4	0	0	6	2	0	1	0	2	0	7	461	0	0	0	0	0	461	0	261	200	186	8	1	167
CHARLEVOIX	113	0	0	0	0	0	6	0	8	0	0	2	97	0	0	0	0	0	97	0	77	20	46	1	0	0
CRYSTAL VALLEY	46	0	0	0	0	0	0	8	0	0	0	1	37	0	0	0	0	0	37	0	28	9	20	0	0	5
WALKERVILLE	16	1	0	1	0	0	0	0	0	0	0	0	18	0	0	0	0	0	18	0	12	6	29	0	0	8
KEWADIN	49	1	0	0	3	0	0	0	0	0	0	4	49	0	0	0	0	0	49	0	27	22	49	1	0	1
EMPIRE	94	0	0	0	0	0	0	0	0	0	0	1	93	0	0	0	1	0	92	0	57	36	65	0	0	12
EPSILON	69	0	0	0	0	0	0	2	0	0	0	0	67	0	0	0	0	0	67	0	40	27	55	0	0	0
NEW HOPE	92	2	0	0	0	0	0	0	0	0	0	1	93	0	0	0	0	0	92	1	63	30	52	0	0	0
FIFE LAKE	47	0	1	0	2	0	0	0	0	3	0	3	44	0	0	0	0	0	44	0	26	18	44	1	0	0
SOUTH BOARDMAN	6	0	0	0	0	0	0	0	0	0	0	0	6	0	0	0	0	0	6	0	4	2	12	0	0	15
EAST BOARDMAN	40	0	0	0	0	0	0	0	0	0	0	1	39	0	0	0	0	0	39	0	21	18	38	0	0	4
FRANKFORT	115	4	0	0	1	0	0	0	3	1	0	2	114	0	0	0	0	0	114	0	82	32	86	0	0	29
ELBERTA	32	3	0	0	0	0	1	0	1	1	0	1	31	0	0	0	0	0	31	0	21	10	27	0	0	19
FREESOIL-FOUNTAIN	16	0	0	0	0	0	0	0	0	2	0	0	14	0	2	0	0	0	12	0	11	3	8	2	0	0
FOUNTAIN	12	0	0	0	0	0	0	0	0	0	0	0	12	0	0	0	0	0	12	0	9	3	6	0	0	0
GRAWN	167	0	0	0	0	0	36	14	0	1	0	6	110	0	1	0	0	0	109	0	66	44	70	0	0	0
HARBOR SPRINGS	71	0	0	0	2	0	0	2	0	0	0	2	69	0	0	0	0	0	69	0	47	22	44	1	0	0
ALANSON	39	0	0	0	0	0	0	0	0	0	0	1	38	0	0	0	0	0	38	0	24	14	38	0	0	0
HART	124	0	0	0	0	0	0	0	8	0	1	0	115	0	0	0	0	0	115	0	76	39	120	0	0	47
HORTON BAY	43	0	0	0	0	0	0	0	3	0	0	0	40	0	0	0	0	0	40	0	24	16	34	3	0	0
GREENSKY HILL	77	8	0	0	1	1	0	0	0	0	0	2	85	0	0	1	35	0	49	0	55	30	64	0	0	14
INDIAN RIVER	296	19	0	0	7	2	0	4	6	0	2	1	311	0	2	0	5	0	302	2	186	125	283	2	1	1
KALKASKA	266	0	0	0	0	0	0	0	0	0	0	0	266	0	0	0	0	0	266	0	166	100	147	0	0	0
KESWICK	65	3	0	3	0	0	0	0	0	0	0	0	71	0	0	1	2	0	68	0	37	34	62	2	0	0

2013 TABLE 1 MEMBERSHIP & PARTICIPATION

CHURCH	MEMBERSHIP LAST YR	PROFESSION OF FAITH	RESTORED BY AFFIRMATION	CORRECT BY ADDITION	RECVD FM OTHER UMC'S	RECVD FM NON-UMC	REMOVED BY CHARGE CONF	WITHDRAWN	CORRECT BY SUBTRACTION	TRANSFER TO OTHER UMC	TRANSFER TO NON-UMC	REMOVED BY DEATH	TOTAL PROFESSING MEMBERS	ASIAN	AFRICAN AMER/BLACK	HISPANIC/LATINO	NATIVE AMERICAN	PACIFIC ISLANDER	WHITE	Multi-Racial	FEMALE	MALE	AVG WORSHIP ATTENDANCE	BAPTIZED THIS YEAR (12 or Younger)	BAPTIZED THIS YEAR (13 or Older)	BAPTIZED NON-MEMBERS
	1	2a	2b	2c	3	4	5a	5b	5c	6	7	8	9	9a	9b	9c	9d	9e	9f	9g	9h	9i	10	11a	11b	12
KEWADIN INDIAN MISSION	30	0	0	0	0	0	0	0	0	0	0	0	30	0	0	0	30	0	0	0	15	15	15	0	0	0
KINGSLEY	127	0	0	9	0	0	1	0	0	0	0	4	131	0	0	0	0	0	131	0	86	45	150	0	0	75
GRANT	60	11	0	0	1	0	0	0	0	0	0	2	70	0	0	0	0	0	70	0	45	25	68	0	0	2
LAKE ANN	146	10	0	0	0	0	0	3	0	0	2	1	150	0	1	0	1	0	146	2	85	65	146	0	0	5
LAKE CITY	166	6	0	0	8	2	0	0	0	0	0	2	180	0	0	0	0	0	180	0	109	71	80	1	1	43
LELAND	331	0	0	0	2	2	1	0	21	1	2	2	308	0	1	0	0	0	307	0	190	118	190	3	0	1
LUDINGTON ST PAUL	146	2	0	0	0	1	0	0	0	5	0	4	140	0	0	0	0	0	140	0	82	58	86	0	0	20
LUDINGTON UNITED	430	6	1	0	5	5	0	1	0	2	2	12	430	0	0	0	1	0	429	0	277	153	235	2	1	70
MANCELONA	94	0	0	0	1	0	0	10	1	0	0	1	83	0	0	0	0	0	83	0	58	25	64	0	0	0
ALBA	35	0	0	0	0	0	0	0	1	0	0	0	34	0	0	0	0	0	34	0	24	10	17	0	0	0
MANISTEE	317	8	0	0	0	1	0	1	0	1	0	7	317	0	0	0	0	1	316	0	179	138	180	0	2	56
MANTON	126	6	4	0	0	1	0	0	0	2	1	4	130	0	0	0	0	0	129	1	84	46	101	4	0	4
MARION	108	0	0	0	0	0	0	0	0	2	0	1	105	0	0	0	0	0	105	0	66	39	46	4	0	17
CADILLAC SOUTH COMMUNITY	42	0	0	0	0	0	0	0	0	0	0	2	40	0	0	0	0	0	40	0	21	19	32	4	1	1
MEARS	91	3	0	0	4	0	0	0	0	0	3	4	91	0	0	0	0	0	91	0	48	43	110	2	0	0
MESICK	67	1	0	0	0	0	0	0	0	0	0	1	67	0	0	0	0	0	67	0	45	22	42	0	1	1
HARRIETTA	70	0	0	0	0	0	0	0	0	0	0	2	68	0	0	0	2	0	66	0	41	27	54	3	0	0
MERRITT-BUTTERFIELD	87	2	0	3	2	0	0	28	0	0	0	4	62	0	0	0	0	0	62	0	42	20	62	0	0	0
MOORESTOWN-STITTSVILLE	47	0	0	0	0	0	0	0	0	0	0	0	47	0	0	0	0	0	0	0	0	0	42	0	0	0
NORTHPORT INDIAN MISSION	29	2	0	0	0	0	0	0	0	0	0	0	31	0	0	0	29	0	2	0	16	15	25	3	2	0
OLD MISSION PENINSULA	96	2	0	0	3	0	0	0	3	0	0	0	98	0	0	0	2	0	95	1	60	38	51	0	0	0
PENTWATER CENTENARY	157	2	0	0	3	2	0	0	0	0	0	9	155	0	0	0	0	0	155	0	94	61	104	0	0	0
PETOSKEY	541	7	0	0	5	0	4	1	0	6	2	7	533	3	2	0	5	3	520	0	315	218	215	3	3	81
ASHTON	48	0	0	0	1	0	0	0	0	0	0	2	47	0	0	0	0	0	47	0	31	16	31	3	0	19
LEROY	94	2	0	0	0	0	0	0	0	0	0	3	93	0	0	0	0	0	91	2	61	32	51	0	0	37
SCOTTVILLE	146	3	1	0	0	0	13	1	3	0	0	3	130	0	0	0	0	0	130	0	90	40	90	2	1	13
TRAVERSE BAY	256	4	0	0	0	0	0	0	4	4	2	8	242	0	0	0	1	0	241	0	155	87	163	9	1	0
CENTRAL TRAVERSE CITY	1,041	26	2	4	40	0	8	14	0	7	0	24	1,060	1	0	1	0	0	1,058	0	620	440	498	14	2	14
CHRIST TRAVERSE CITY	49	0	0	0	0	0	8	8	0	2	0	1	30	0	0	0	0	0	30	0	17	13	40	0	0	0
WILLIAMSBURG	0	5	0	78	0	0	0	1	0	1	0	3	78	0	0	0	0	0	78	0	50	28	51	3	0	0
GRAND TRAVERSE DISTRICT	8,222	181	10	114	100	20	96	103	83	43	18	171	8,133	4	10	5	116	4	7,938	9	4,994	3,092	5,226	90	21	886
LAST YEAR	8,374	185	20	16	73	38	68	50	77	47	24	140	8,300	6	12	4	112	4	8,151	11	5,107	3,193	5,400	143		1,042
INC/(DEC)	(152)	(4)	(10)	98	27	(18)	28	53	6	(4)	(6)	31	(167)	(2)	(2)	1	4	0	(213)	(2)	(113)	(101)	(174)	(53)	21	(156)

STATISTICAL INFO

2013 TABLE 1 MEMBERSHIP & PARTICIPATION

CHURCH	OTHER CONSTITUENTS	ENROLLED IN CONFIRMATION CLASS	CHILDREN IN CHRISTIAN FORMATION GROUPS	YOUTH IN CHRISTIAN FORMATION GROUPS	YOUNG ADULTS IN CHRISTIAN FORMATION	OTHER ADULTS IN CHRISTIAN FORMATION	TOTAL PERSONS IN CHRISTIAN FORMATION	AVG SUNDAY SCHOOL ATTENDANCE	VACATION BIBLE SCHOOL PARTICIPANTS	NUMBER OF SUNDAY SCHOOL CLASSES	NUMBER OF CLASSES OUTSIDE SUNDAY SCHOOL	SHORT TERM CLASSES	UM MEN MEMBERS	PAID TO UMM PROJECTS	UMW MEMBERS	PAID TO UMW LOCAL PROJECTS	VIM TEAMS SENT OUT	PERSONS IN VIM TEAMS	PERSONS IN MISSIONS	PERSONS SERVED IN DAYCARE AND/OR EDUCATION	PERSONS SERVED IN OUTREACH, JUSTICE, MERCY
	13	14	15	16	17	18	19	20	21	22	23	24	25a	25b	26a	26b	27a	27b	28	29	30
ALDEN	26	0	0	0	0	8	8	3	50	0	2	1	0	0	25	3,679	1	11	11	6	30
CENTRAL LAKE	0	0	0	0	0	0	0	0	0	0	0	0	0	0	0	0	0	0	0	0	0
BALDWIN COVENANT COMMUNITY	18	7	12	8	16	12	48	8	0	2	4	1	0	0	0	0	0	0	0	0	14
LUTHER	14	0	24	5	1	12	42	0	0	0	2	0	0	0	1	0	0	0	1	0	0
BARNARD	26	0	2	0	0	14	16	7	0	1	0	1	0	0	21	1,418	0	0	0	0	0
EAST JORDAN	69	1	0	0	0	0	0	6	4	1	3	1	0	0	5	1,600	0	0	44	0	3,000
NORWOOD	7	0	0	0	0	0	0	0	0	0	0	0	0	0	0	0	0	0	0	0	0
BEAR LAKE	32	1	35	6	0	36	77	5	51	2	5	0	0	0	0	0	0	0	0	0	175
ARCADIA	0	0	0	0	0	0	0	0	0	0	1	0	0	0	13	600	0	0	0	0	0
BELLAIRE COMMUNITY	110	0	6	0	0	66	72	3	84	2	4	0	0	0	0	0	0	0	0	0	0
BOYNE CITY	55	0	11	5	0	28	44	5	6	2	2	4	0	0	0	0	0	0	0	0	41
BOYNE FALLS	31	0	9	15	2	24	50	5	4	1	2	4	0	0	10	0	0	0	0	0	243
BRETHREN EPWORTH	29	0	20	2	0	10	32	6	60	0	1	1	0	0	0	0	0	0	20	0	150
CADILLAC	159	0	0	31	2	35	68	39	0	5	2	2	16	800	100	3,100	0	0	0	144	500
CHARLEVOIX	27	0	10	0	0	0	10	17	0	2	2	2	0	0	26	1,000	0	0	15	12	100
CRYSTAL VALLEY	27	0	0	10	0	0	10	6	0	0	0	0	0	0	17	1,000	0	0	6	0	500
WALKERVILLE	15	3	4	6	1	7	18	7	36	2	1	0	0	0	0	0	0	0	21	10	50
KEWADIN	30	0	0	0	0	0	0	6	6	1	0	0	0	0	10	2,693	0	0	0	0	0
EMPIRE	100	0	5	0	0	30	35	13	30	2	4	1	0	0	57	1,100	0	0	0	0	360
EPSILON	45	0	5	4	2	10	21	14	0	3	3	0	0	0	20	1,600	0	0	0	0	0
NEW HOPE	70	0	0	3	0	12	15	5	18	0	0	0	0	0	0	0	0	0	0	0	0
FIFE LAKE	24	0	0	0	0	15	15	0	20	0	2	0	0	0	13	150	0	0	0	0	12
SOUTH BOARDMAN	15	0	0	0	0	5	5	5	0	1	0	0	0	0	0	0	0	0	0	0	0
EAST BOARDMAN	20	0	9	2	0	12	23	10	69	2	1	1	0	0	0	0	0	0	0	0	41
FRANKFORT	5	0	0	0	0	0	0	13	0	2	0	5	0	0	64	2,165	0	0	89	0	324
ELBERTA	4	0	0	0	0	0	0	0	0	0	0	5	0	0	0	0	0	0	28	0	100
FREESOIL-FOUNTAIN	0	0	0	15	1	0	16	0	13	0	0	0	0	0	0	0	0	0	0	0	250
FOUNTAIN	0	0	0	0	0	0	0	0	0	0	0	0	0	0	0	0	0	0	0	0	0
GRAWN	0	4	8	0	0	20	28	0	12	2	1	3	0	0	0	0	0	0	0	20	0
HARBOR SPRINGS	71	0	0	5	2	16	23	2	0	1	2	1	0	0	14	740	0	0	7	6	0
ALANSON	38	0	0	3	1	4	8	7	9	0	0	1	0	0	0	0	0	0	0	40	96
HART	157	0	40	15	2	50	107	35	35	7	5	1	20	3,000	33	3,245	0	0	15	0	90
HORTON BAY	0	0	8	0	0	10	18	12	0	0	0	0	0	0	12	300	0	0	0	0	0
GREENSKY HILL	70	0	20	0	0	20	40	10	39	1	2	0	24	0	10	3,500	0	0	0	0	0
INDIAN RIVER	349	14	40	21	0	90	151	41	0	7	3	10	25	2,195	44	4,929	0	0	0	0	0
KALKASKA	0	0	0	0	0	0	0	0	0	0	0	0	0	0	0	0	0	0	0	0	0
KESWICK	73	0	10	2	0	22	34	28	0	3	2	2	0	0	0	0	0	0	2	0	0

2013 TABLE 1 MEMBERSHIP & PARTICIPATION

CHURCH	OTHER CONSTITUENTS	ENROLLED IN CONFIRMATION CLASS	CHILDREN IN CHRISTIAN FORMATION GROUPS	YOUTH IN CHRISTIAN FORMATION GROUPS	YOUNG ADULTS IN CHRISTIAN FORMATION	OTHER ADULTS IN CHRISTIAN FORMATION	TOTAL PERSONS IN CHRISTIAN FORMATION	AVG SUNDAY SCHOOL ATTENDANCE	VACATION BIBLE SCHOOL PARTICIPANTS	NUMBER OF SUNDAY SCHOOL CLASSES	NUMBER OF CLASSES OUTSIDE SUNDAY SCHOOL	SHORT TERM CLASSES	UM MEN MEMBERS	PAID TO UMM PROJECTS	UMW MEMBERS	PAID TO UMW LOCAL PROJECTS	VIM TEAMS SENT OUT	PERSONS IN VIM TEAMS	PERSONS IN MISSIONS	PERSONS SERVED IN DAYCARE AND/OR EDUCATION	PERSONS SERVED IN OUTREACH, JUSTICE, MERCY
	13	14	15	16	17	18	19	20	21	22	23	24	25a	25b	26a	26b	27a	27b	28	29	30
KEWADIN INDIAN MISSION	0	0	0	0	0	0	0	0	20	0	0	0	0	0	0	0	0	0	0	0	120
KINGSLEY	55	0	20	12	12	20	64	35	125	4	3	0	0	0	0	0	0	0	8	0	120
GRANT	34	0	16	8	0	15	39	15	0	2	3	1	0	0	15	0	0	0	0	0	100
LAKE ANN	115	0	17	12	17	115	161	33	56	3	5	2	16	400	40	1,728	1	8	0	45	500
LAKE CITY	85	0	10	3	0	45	58	17	0	4	0	0	0	0	44	4,079	0	0	0	25	80
LELAND	325	0	15	15	1	108	139	30	120	5	7	3	0	0	0	0	0	0	20	0	0
LUDINGTON ST PAUL	48	4	0	0	0	0	0	0	25	0	1	6	0	0	22	612	0	0	9	0	240
LUDINGTON UNITED	353	0	64	42	17	95	218	46	160	8	8	2	0	0	112	4,294	2	12	120	0	1,000
MANCELONA	113	0	11	0	0	71	82	14	0	1	0	5	0	0	25	1,989	0	0	0	0	100
ALBA	51	0	6	6	0	12	24	0	16	0	0	0	0	0	0	0	0	0	0	0	0
MANISTEE	64	0	63	18	5	158	244	30	170	7	3	6	0	0	63	1,640	0	0	100	25	350
MANTON	50	0	0	0	0	0	0	11	25	2	0	2	0	0	13	742	1	10	8	0	300
MARION	29	0	0	8	0	0	8	14	6	0	0	2	0	0	11	754	0	0	0	0	0
CADILLAC SOUTH COMMUNITY	0	0	0	0	0	4	4	6	0	1	0	1	0	0	0	0	0	0	0	0	0
MEARS	41	0	8	3	0	0	11	4	0	0	0	0	22	1,100	20	1,125	0	0	0	0	0
MESICK	0	0	7	1	0	0	8	5	24	1	8	4	0	0	0	0	0	0	0	0	95
HARRIETTA	0	0	0	3	0	0	3	4	7	0	4	0	0	0	0	0	0	0	0	0	5
MERRITT-BUTTERFIELD	57	0	0	7	0	2	9	27	0	2	1	0	0	0	0	0	0	0	0	0	0
MOORESTOWN-STITTSVILLE	0	0	0	0	6	12	18	0	14	0	4	0	0	0	0	0	0	1	0	0	0
NORTHPORT INDIAN MISSION	0	0	20	0	0	10	30	0	0	1	1	0	0	0	0	0	0	0	0	0	120
OLD MISSION PENINSULA	42	0	12	4	0	15	31	12	20	1	2	1	0	0	0	0	0	0	0	0	0
PENTWATER CENTENARY	0	0	23	0	0	28	51	15	0	4	0	0	21	0	37	1,290	0	0	0	0	520
PETOSKEY	202	7	38	15	3	62	118	42	90	8	10	8	0	0	68	3,020	2	2	30	120	750
ASHTON	62	0	0	0	0	16	16	0	0	0	1	1	0	0	0	0	0	0	0	0	120
LEROY	169	0	13	14	0	13	40	4	0	1	1	1	0	0	0	0	0	0	0	0	300
SCOTTVILLE	35	0	10	8	0	25	43	8	0	1	1	3	5	998	90	2,687	1	5	30	35	225
TRAVERSE BAY	105	0	0	0	0	8	8	24	82	7	0	5	0	0	52	1,925	1	5	0	0	0
CENTRAL TRAVERSE CITY	0	4	53	73	10	429	565	50	111	8	10	9	50	1,424	90	10,081	0	0	100	0	200
CHRIST TRAVERSE CITY	28	0	0	0	6	12	18	15	36	3	4	2	0	0	0	0	0	1	6	0	100
WILLIAMSBURG	137	0	0	0	0	28	28	0	0	0	0	1	0	0	0	0	0	0	0	0	24
GRAND TRAVERSE DISTRICT	3,916	45	684	410	107	1,871	3,072	779	1,653	126	133	112	199	9,917	1,197	68,785	9	55	690	488	11,445
LAST YEAR	4,485	76	676	452	126	1,972	3,226	873	1,624	146	101	127	172	9,519	1,170	74,119	10	71	129	547	7,201
INC/(DEC)	(569)	(31)	8	(42)	(19)	(101)	(154)	(94)	29	(20)	32	(15)	27	398	27	(5,334)	(1)	(16)	561	(59)	4,244

STATISTICAL INFO

2013 TABLE 1 MEMBERSHIP & PARTICIPATION	MEMBERSHIP LAST YR	PROFESSION OF FAITH	RESTORED BY AFFIRMATION	CORRECT BY ADDITION	RECV'D FM OTHER UMC'S	RECV'D FM NON-UMC	REMOVED BY CHARGE CONF	WITHDRAWN	CORRECT BY SUBTRACTION	TRANSFER TO OTHER UMC	TRANSFER TO NON-UMC	REMOVED BY DEATH	TOTAL PROFESSING MEMBERS	ASIAN	AFRICAN AMER/BLACK	HISPANIC/LATINO	NATIVE AMERICAN	PACIFIC ISLANDER	WHITE	Multi-Racial	FEMALE	MALE	AVG WORSHIP ATTENDANCE	BAPTIZED THIS YEAR (12 or Younger)	BAPTIZED THIS YEAR (13 or Older)	BAPTIZED NON-MEMBERS
CHURCH	1	2a	2b	2c	3	4	5a	5b	5c	6	7	8	9	9a	9b	9c	9d	9e	9f	9g	9h	9i	10	11a	11b	12
ALMA	239	2	0	0	2	3	0	0	1	2	0	5	238	0	0	0	0	0	238	0	143	95	104	1	1	2
ASHLEY	39	0	0	0	0	0	0	2	0	1	0	0	36	0	0	0	0	0	36	0	23	13	24	0	0	0
BANNISTER	38	4	2	0	0	0	1	0	0	0	0	1	42	0	0	0	0	0	42	0	27	15	27	1	0	1
BARRYTON FAITH	45	2	0	0	0	0	0	0	0	0	2	4	41	0	0	0	1	0	40	0	24	17	45	0	0	0
BELDING	47	0	0	0	0	0	0	0	0	0	0	1	46	0	0	0	0	0	46	0	35	11	30	0	0	1
BIG RAPIDS FIRST	314	11	0	0	2	0	2	3	0	5	0	2	315	1	0	2	1	0	311	0	175	140	164	5	2	35
THIRD AVENUE	61	1	0	0	0	0	3	0	0	2	0	3	54	0	2	0	0	0	52	0	34	20	57	0	0	0
PARIS	42	0	0	1	0	0	5	0	0	0	0	1	37	0	0	0	0	1	36	0	23	14	32	0	0	0
RODNEY	20	0	0	0	0	0	2	0	0	0	0	0	18	0	0	0	0	0	18	0	11	7	19	0	0	1
BLANCHARD-PINE RIVER	42	0	0	0	0	0	0	0	0	0	0	0	42	0	0	0	3	0	39	0	24	18	27	0	0	0
COOMER	35	0	0	0	0	0	0	0	0	0	0	0	35	0	0	0	0	0	35	0	24	11	18	0	0	0
BRECKENRIDGE	166	0	0	0	0	0	2	0	0	1	1	9	153	0	0	0	0	0	153	0	88	65	62	6	6	15
BROOKS CORNERS	33	0	0	0	0	0	0	0	0	0	2	4	27	0	0	0	0	0	27	0	14	13	28	0	0	0
SEARS	11	0	0	0	0	0	0	0	0	0	0	0	11	0	0	0	0	0	11	0	7	4	12	0	0	0
CARSON CITY	281	6	0	0	1	0	0	0	0	1	0	4	283	0	0	0	0	0	283	0	160	123	126	6	2	6
CHASE BARTON	31	0	0	0	0	0	0	2	0	0	0	1	28	0	0	0	0	0	28	0	18	10	24	0	0	0
GRANT CENTER	36	0	0	0	0	0	0	0	0	0	0	2	34	0	0	0	0	0	34	0	25	9	32	1	0	28
CLARE	342	3	0	0	6	0	2	2	0	6	0	4	337	0	0	0	0	0	337	0	208	129	177	1	2	7
EDMORE FAITH	183	0	0	0	0	0	0	0	0	0	0	2	181	0	0	0	0	0	181	0	117	64	98	0	0	5
ELSIE	207	3	0	0	0	0	0	0	3	0	2	8	197	0	0	0	0	0	197	0	122	75	80	0	1	0
EVART	95	0	0	0	0	0	0	0	0	3	0	4	88	0	0	0	0	0	88	0	68	20	62	0	0	0
AVONDALE	8	0	0	0	0	0	0	0	2	0	0	1	5	0	0	0	0	0	5	0	3	2	12	0	0	0
NORTH EVART	7	0	0	0	0	0	7	0	0	0	0	0	0	0	0	0	0	0	0	0	0	0	10	0	0	0
FARWELL	139	3	0	1	1	0	0	0	0	0	0	3	141	0	0	0	0	0	141	0	102	39	117	6	2	0
FENWICK	17	0	0	0	0	0	1	0	0	0	0	0	16	0	0	0	0	0	16	0	8	8	20	1	2	8
PALO	20	3	0	0	1	0	4	0	0	0	0	1	19	0	0	0	0	0	19	0	9	10	16	0	3	0
VICKERYVILLE	20	1	0	0	0	0	3	0	0	0	0	2	16	0	0	0	0	0	16	0	10	6	10	0	0	0
GREENVILLE	714	22	1	0	7	0	0	0	3	7	0	15	719	2	0	5	2	0	710	0	395	324	226	1	1	200
HERSEY	74	0	0	0	0	3	2	1	0	0	0	0	74	0	0	0	0	0	74	0	50	24	46	2	0	30
AMBLE	56	1	0	0	0	2	0	0	0	0	0	0	59	0	0	0	0	0	59	0	33	26	32	1	0	0
HERITAGE	241	11	0	0	2	0	0	0	0	0	0	4	250	0	1	0	0	0	244	5	144	106	122	6	1	78
FIRST IONIA	186	0	0	0	4	0	0	0	0	0	0	4	186	0	0	0	0	0	186	0	111	75	105	2	3	30
ZION IONIA	116	4	0	0	0	0	0	0	3	0	0	3	114	0	0	0	0	0	114	0	72	42	98	2	0	2
LEVALLEY	162	1	1	0	2	0	0	0	0	0	1	6	159	2	0	0	0	0	157	0	89	70	76	3	0	50
BERLIN CENTER	57	1	0	0	0	0	0	0	0	0	0	1	57	0	0	0	0	0	57	0	33	24	37	0	1	19
ITHACA	200	13	0	0	0	0	0	0	0	0	8	2	203	0	0	0	0	0	203	0	118	85	108	0	3	0
BEEBE	12	0	0	0	0	0	0	0	0	0	0	1	11	0	0	0	0	0	11	0	7	4	19	0	0	0

2013 TABLE 1 MEMBERSHIP & PARTICIPATION	MEMBERSHIP LAST YR	PROFESSION OF FAITH	RESTORED BY AFFIRMATION	CORRECT BY ADDITION	RECVD FM OTHER UMC'S	RECVD FM NON-UMC	REMOVED BY CHARGE CONF	WITHDRAWN	CORRECT BY SUBTRACTION	TRANSFER TO OTHER UMC	TRANSFER TO NON-UMC	REMOVED BY DEATH	TOTAL PROFESSING MEMBERS	ASIAN	AFRICAN AMER/BLACK	HISPANIC/LATINO	NATIVE AMERICAN	PACIFIC ISLANDER	WHITE	Multi-Racial	FEMALE	MALE	AVG WORSHIP ATTENDANCE	BAPTIZED THIS YEAR (12 or Younger)	BAPTIZED THIS YEAR (13 or Older)	BAPTIZED NON-MEMBERS
CHURCH	1	2a	2b	2c	3	4	5a	5b	5c	6	7	8	9	9a	9b	9c	9d	9e	9f	9g	9h	9i	10	11a	11b	12
LAKEVIEW NEW LIFE	249	5	0	0	2	2	0	9	0	3	3	2	241	0	1	2	1	0	235	2	150	91	136	6	16	16
LEATON	53	0	0	1	0	0	0	0	0	0	0	1	53	0	0	0	1	0	52	0	34	19	27	0	0	0
LYONS-MUIR	74	5	0	0	0	0	2	0	0	0	0	0	77	0	0	0	0	0	77	0	47	30	51	4	0	3
EASTON	81	2	0	0	3	0	0	0	0	0	0	0	86	0	0	0	0	0	86	0	63	23	54	2	2	0
MECOSTA NEW HOPE	537	3	0	0	5	0	0	2	15	0	6	6	516	1	6	0	0	0	509	0	288	228	212	2	0	74
MIDDLETON	23	0	0	0	0	0	0	0	10	0	0	1	12	0	1	0	1	0	10	0	7	5	14	0	0	0
MAPLE RAPIDS	56	2	0	0	0	0	0	0	0	0	0	2	56	0	0	0	0	0	56	0	39	17	29	0	0	0
CHIPPEWA INDIAN CHURCH																										
FIRST MT PLEASANT	380	0	1	0	1	0	0	0	0	1	0	5	376	7	1	7	0	0	361	0	248	128	213	4	0	0
TRINITY MOUNT PLEASANT	39	2	0	0	0	0	0	0	0	0	0	0	41	0	0	0	0	0	41	0	25	16	23	0	0	0
COUNTRYSIDE	47	0	0	0	0	0	0	0	0	0	0	0	47	0	0	0	1	0	46	0	32	15	30	0	1	0
OVID UNITED CHURCH	105	0	0	0	0	0	0	1	0	1	0	3	100	0	0	0	0	0	100	0	64	36	89	2	0	2
POMPEII	33	0	0	1	0	0	0	0	0	2	0	0	32	0	0	0	0	0	32	0	20	12	24	0	0	0
PERRINTON	15	0	0	0	0	0	0	0	0	0	0	0	15	0	0	0	0	0	15	0	11	4	18	0	0	0
NORTH STAR	5	0	0	0	0	0	0	0	0	0	0	0	5	0	0	0	0	0	5	0	4	1	6	0	0	0
REED CITY	376	5	0	0	4	0	50	1	0	1	0	8	325	3	0	0	0	0	322	0	187	138	139	3	0	30
RIVERDALE LINCOLN ROAD	127	7	1	0	2	0	0	0	0	0	0	4	133	0	1	2	0	0	130	0	85	48	76	3	3	7
ROSEBUSH	75	2	0	0	0	0	1	0	0	0	0	5	71	0	0	0	0	0	71	0	49	22	68	1	1	1
FIRST SAINT JOHNS	183	2	0	0	1	0	12	1	0	2	0	7	164	0	0	1	0	0	163	0	103	61	65	0	2	26
PILGRIM	219	1	0	0	2	0	8	4	0	0	0	3	207	0	0	0	0	1	206	0	116	91	217	0	0	113
SALEM	35	0	0	0	0	0	0	0	0	0	0	0	35	0	0	0	0	0	35	0	22	13	30	0	0	0
GREENBUSH	23	0	0	0	0	0	0	0	0	0	0	3	20	0	0	0	0	0	20	0	11	9	10	0	0	0
LOWE	51	2	0	0	1	0	0	0	0	0	0	1	53	0	0	0	0	0	53	0	34	19	43	1	0	0
SAINT LOUIS	226	5	0	0	0	0	5	0	0	0	0	5	221	0	0	2	0	0	219	0	134	87	107	1	4	47
SHEPARDSVILLE	35	0	0	0	0	0	0	0	0	0	0	1	34	0	0	0	0	0	34	0	20	14	30	0	0	0
SAND LAKE	18	0	0	0	0	3	0	0	0	0	0	1	20	0	0	0	0	0	20	0	14	6	33	0	0	0
SOUTH ENSLEY	34	2	0	0	0	0	0	0	0	0	0	1	35	0	0	0	0	0	33	2	24	11	40	0	0	0
SHEPHERD	148	0	0	0	0	0	0	0	1	1	0	2	144	0	0	1	0	0	143	0	89	55	64	1	0	0
STANWOOD NORTHLAND	153	0	0	0	0	0	3	0	0	0	0	2	148	0	2	0	0	0	144	2	100	48	78	0	0	0
TURK LAKE	75	0	0	0	0	0	1	0	3	0	0	4	67	0	0	0	0	0	67	0	50	17	30	0	0	25
WEIDMAN	206	5	0	0	0	0	0	6	0	3	3	0	199	0	0	0	1	0	198	0	124	75	103	0	0	0
WINN	44	0	0	0	0	0	0	0	0	0	0	0	44	0	0	0	0	0	44	0	30	14	24	0	0	0
HEARTLAND DISTRICT	8,061	142	6	4	49	13	116	34	41	42	28	165	7,849	16	15	22	12	2	7,771	11	4,778	3,071	4,385	75	59	862
LAST YEAR	8,310	178	2	7	35	19	134	76	81	42	18	139	8,061	12	14	21	12	2	7,989	11	4,887	3,174	4,681	178		869
INC/(DEC)	(249)	(36)	4	(3)	14	(6)	(18)	(42)	(40)	0	10	26	(212)	4	1	1	0	0	(218)	0	(109)	(103)	(296)	(103)	59	(7)

STATISTICAL INFO

STATISTICAL INFO

2013 TABLE 1 MEMBERSHIP & PARTICIPATION

CHURCH	OTHER CONSTITUENTS	ENROLLED IN CONFIRMATION CLASS	CHILDREN IN CHRISTIAN FORMATION GROUPS	YOUTH IN CHRISTIAN FORMATION GROUPS	YOUNG ADULTS IN CHRISTIAN FORMATION	OTHER ADULTS IN CHRISTIAN FORMATION	TOTAL PERSONS IN CHRISTIAN FORMATION	AVG SUNDAY SCHOOL ATTENDANCE	VACATION BIBLE SCHOOL PARTICIPANTS	NUMBER OF SUNDAY SCHOOL CLASSES	NUMBER OF CLASSES OUTSIDE SUNDAY SCHOOL	SHORT TERM CLASSES	UM MEN MEMBERS	PAID TO UMM PROJECTS	UMW MEMBERS	PAID TO UMW LOCAL PROJECTS	VIM TEAMS SENT OUT	PERSONS IN VIM TEAMS	PERSONS IN MISSIONS	PERSONS SERVED IN DAYCARE AND/OR EDUCATION	PERSONS SERVED IN OUTREACH, JUSTICE, MERCY
	13	14	15	16	17	18	19	20	21	22	23	24	25a	25b	26a	26b	27a	27b	28	29	30
ALMA	0	0	9	6	0	30	45	9	0	5	2	2	40	400	40	3,900	0	2	0	0	0
ASHLEY	13	0	24	0	0	10	34	10	24	1	1	3	0	0	11	280	0	0	0	22	100
BANNISTER	16	1	5	2	0	0	7	10	5	1	1	1	0	0	15	705	0	0	0	0	270
BARRYTON FAITH	0	0	0	0	0	15	15	6	5	0	0	0	0	0	15	1,053	0	0	0	0	0
BELDING	23	0	3	4	0	0	7	2	50	0	0	1	0	0	8	3,280	0	1	6	0	500
BIG RAPIDS FIRST	184	4	12	10	7	51	80	35	57	3	6	1	0	0	1	0	1	5	62	0	1,000
THIRD AVENUE	0	0	21	7	0	16	44	14	55	1	1	0	8	0	0	0	0	0	0	0	1,025
PARIS	0	0	0	0	0	0	0	3	4	0	0	0	0	50	0	0	0	0	0	0	260
RODNEY	10	0	0	0	0	0	0	0	2	0	0	0	3	100	0	0	0	0	0	0	286
BLANCHARD-PINE RIVER	0	0	6	2	0	6	14	3	40	4	0	0	0	0	0	0	0	0	0	0	150
COOMER	0	0	0	0	0	0	0	0	0	0	0	0	0	0	0	856	0	0	0	0	0
BRECKENRIDGE	25	0	6	0	0	13	19	6	0	6	1	1	0	0	10	3,255	0	0	18	0	1,019
BROOKS CORNERS	70	0	0	0	0	0	0	18	6	2	0	0	0	0	0	0	0	0	0	0	500
SEARS	15	0	0	0	0	7	7	0	0	0	1	0	0	0	0	0	0	0	0	0	0
CARSON CITY	120	0	66	8	0	89	163	44	86	5	5	4	0	0	35	3,133	0	0	0	0	0
CHASE BARTON	0	0	4	27	0	0	31	4	32	1	2	0	0	0	0	0	0	0	0	0	52
GRANT CENTER	23	0	5	0	0	26	31	7	0	2	3	0	0	0	15	0	0	0	0	0	260
CLARE	65	0	42	30	0	116	188	70	45	10	9	0	0	3,030	30	1,200	0	2	0	34	0
EDMORE FAITH	37	0	10	2	0	23	35	25	46	3	2	0	4	0	14	0	0	0	0	0	354
ELSIE	197	0	12	0	0	25	37	27	50	3	1	1	0	0	10	2,953	0	0	25	0	245
EVART	0	0	3	8	0	20	31	17	35	3	1	1	0	0	0	0	0	0	0	0	40
AVONDALE	0	0	0	0	0	0	0	0	0	0	0	0	0	0	0	0	0	0	0	0	0
NORTH EVART	4	0	0	0	0	0	0	0	0	0	0	0	0	0	0	0	0	0	0	0	0
FARWELL	0	0	68	6	7	40	121	33	60	4	4	2	0	0	20	3,200	0	0	1	10	725
FENWICK	26	0	5	0	0	1	6	5	0	1	0	0	0	0	8	540	0	0	0	0	20
PALO	8	0	5	0	0	12	17	17	0	2	0	0	0	0	0	0	0	0	0	0	9
VICKERYVILLE	11	0	0	0	0	5	5	5	0	1	0	0	0	0	0	0	0	0	0	0	11
GREENVILLE	82	8	12	14	0	34	60	45	25	7	5	6	0	0	65	4,858	0	0	36	72	74
HERSEY	37	0	15	15	0	0	30	25	10	5	0	0	0	0	0	0	0	0	0	0	0
AMBLE	29	0	4	1	0	12	17	7	0	4	1	2	0	0	0	600	0	0	0	0	85
HERITAGE	35	0	75	14	4	97	190	0	50	0	13	4	0	0	0	0	0	0	2	0	140
FIRST IONIA	50	0	20	15	6	12	53	20	60	3	1	3	0	0	48	2,000	0	0	0	0	35
ZION IONIA	63	0	10	0	0	53	63	63	8	8	12	1	0	0	1	0	0	0	0	0	815
LEVALLEY	200	0	20	17	0	30	67	29	65	4	5	6	0	0	20	2,220	0	0	0	50	80
BERLIN CENTER	60	0	4	5	0	25	34	5	65	3	2	2	0	0	15	1,810	0	0	0	0	200
ITHACA	0	0	31	20	0	0	51	31	31	6	8	21	0	235	0	978	0	1	0	26	345
BEEBE	0	0	0	0	0	0	0	0	0	0	3	0	0	0	0	0	0	0	0	0	0

2013 TABLE 1 MEMBERSHIP & PARTICIPATION	OTHER CONSTITUENTS	ENROLLED IN CONFIRMATION CLASS	CHILDREN IN CHRISTIAN FORMATION GROUPS	YOUTH IN CHRISTIAN FORMATION GROUPS	YOUNG ADULTS IN CHRISTIAN FORMATION	OTHER ADULTS IN CHRISTIAN FORMATION	TOTAL PERSONS IN CHRISTIAN FORMATION	AVG SUNDAY SCHOOL ATTENDANCE	VACATION BIBLE SCHOOL PARTICIPANTS	NUMBER OF SUNDAY SCHOOL CLASSES	NUMBER OF CLASSES OUTSIDE SUNDAY SCHOOL	SHORT TERM CLASSES	UM MEN MEMBERS	PAID TO UMM PROJECTS	UMW MEMBERS	PAID TO UMW LOCAL PROJECTS	VIM TEAMS SENT OUT	PERSONS IN VIM TEAMS	PERSONS IN MISSIONS	PERSONS SERVED IN DAYCARE AND/OR EDUCATION	PERSONS SERVED IN OUTREACH, JUSTICE, MERCY
CHURCH	13	14	15	16	17	18	19	20	21	22	23	24	25a	25b	26a	26b	27a	27b	28	29	30
LAKEVIEW NEW LIFE	110	12	52	13	12	64	141	34	15	6	1	0	15	3,008	50	1,425	0	0	1	0	500
LEATON	4	0	0	0	0	15	15	10	0	1	1	0	7	0	9	744	0	0	0	0	0
LYONS-MUIR	16	0	5	0	0	30	35	35	0	10	5	1	0	0	0	100	0	0	0	100	110
EASTON	0	0	0	0	0	0	0	0	0	10	15	0	0	0	16	850	0	0	0	0	45
MECOSTA NEW HOPE	50	3	20	45	6	530	601	9	60	2	30	5	15	3,986	60	4,775	0	4	20	0	3,310
MIDDLETON	6	0	0	0	0	0	0	0	0	0	0	0	0	0	0	0	0	0	0	0	0
MAPLE RAPIDS	23	0	0	0	0	0	0	6	50	2	0	0	0	0	8	1,050	0	0	0	0	0
CHIPPEWA INDIAN CHURCH																					
FIRST MT PLEASANT	223	0	35	23	11	50	119	43	50	6	6	0	0	0	73	660	0	0	0	12	0
TRINITY MOUNT PLEASANT	0	0	0	0	0	17	17	7	0	1	3	2	0	0	0	0	0	0	0	0	0
COUNTRYSIDE	0	8	11	0	0	11	22	0	0	3	0	0	0	0	11	1,492	1	0	0	0	0
OVID UNITED CHURCH	0	0	23	10	0	20	53	13	120	5	15	6	10	150	70	3,300	0	0	0	0	100
POMPEII	0	0	0	5	0	7	12	2	17	0	0	0	0	0	21	1,802	0	0	0	0	0
PERRINTON	0	0	20	5	0	5	30	3	2	0	0	0	0	0	20	2,273	0	0	0	0	6
NORTH STAR	0	0	0	0	0	0	0	0	0	0	0	0	0	0	0	0	0	0	0	0	0
REED CITY	158	0	33	12	0	20	65	24	70	3	10	2	0	0	50	10,986	0	0	7	0	30
RIVERDALE LINCOLN ROAD	59	0	32	21	0	8	61	15	5,312	2	3	4	10	425	18	931	1	9	54	0	129
ROSEBUSH	80	0	12	6	0	20	38	12	20	3	3	0	0	0	10	320	0	0	0	0	75
FIRST SAINT JOHNS	77	0	8	2	3	50	63	16	4	6	2	7	0	0	30	1,000	0	0	15	42	112
PILGRIM	86	0	49	34	11	122	216	115	135	12	7	3	0	0	0	0	2	23	50	0	175
SALEM	10	0	0	0	0	0	0	4	10	2	0	0	0	0	12	0	0	0	0	0	0
GREENBUSH	4	0	0	0	0	8	8	8	0	1	1	1	0	0	7	1,023	0	0	0	0	5
LOWE	0	0	0	0	0	0	0	0	0	1	0	0	0	0	0	0	0	0	0	0	0
SAINT LOUIS	78	5	0	0	0	0	0	25	52	2	0	2	10	2,595	48	2,370	0	0	12	0	150
SHEPARDSVILLE	30	0	1	0	0	12	13	1	30	1	1	1	0	0	9	2,500	0	0	0	0	200
SAND LAKE	0	0	11	9	0	18	38	15	20	2	1	4	0	0	9	3,468	0	0	46	25	1,291
SOUTH ENSLEY	0	7	10	0	0	9	19	9	30	1	1	2	0	0	10	100	0	0	36	0	900
SHEPHERD	34	0	4	2	0	44	50	0	33	2	4	3	0	0	22	718	0	0	0	25	25
STANWOOD NORTHLAND	0	0	14	3	0	12	29	17	15	3	2	0	0	0	25	2,000	0	0	0	25	1,700
TURK LAKE	25	0	0	0	0	0	0	0	15	0	0	2	6	0	10	50	0	0	5	0	40
WEIDMAN	0	0	11	0	0	50	61	11	35	3	2	6	6	570	25	4,109	0	0	0	0	469
WINN	0	0	5	2	0	7	14	0	0	0	0	1	0	0	0	0	0	0	0	0	85
HEARTLAND DISTRICT	2,476	48	853	405	67	1,897	3,222	1,029	7,011	188	203	114	134	14,549	1,004	84,867	5	47	396	443	18,057
LAST YEAR	2,700	64	895	420	85	2,087	3,487	1,088	2,117	179	231	117	152	14,879	1,078	83,724	2	7	149	297	12,901
INC/(DEC)	(224)	(16)	(42)	(15)	(18)	(190)	(265)	(59)	4,894	9	(28)	(3)	(18)	(330)	(74)	1,143	3	40	247	146	5,156

STATISTICAL INFO

2013 TABLE 1 MEMBERSHIP & PARTICIPATION	MEMBERSHIP LAST YR	PROFESSION OF FAITH	RESTORED BY AFFIRMATION	CORRECT BY ADDITION	RECVD FM OTHER UMC'S	RECVD FM NON-UMC	REMOVED BY CHARGE CONF	WITHDRAWN	CORRECT BY SUBTRACTION	TRANSFER TO OTHER UMC	TRANSFER TO NON-UMC	REMOVED BY DEATH	TOTAL PROFESSING MEMBERS	ASIAN	AFRICAN AMER/BLACK	HISPANIC/LATINO	NATIVE AMERICAN	PACIFIC ISLANDER	WHITE	Multi-Racial	FEMALE	MALE	AVG WORSHIP ATTENDANCE	BAPTIZED THIS YEAR (12 or Younger)	BAPTIZED THIS YEAR (13 or Older)	BAPTIZED NON-MEMBERS
CHURCH	1	2a	2b	2c	3	4	5a	5b	5c	6	7	8	9	9a	9b	9c	9d	9e	9f	9g	9h	9i	10	11a	11b	12
EDWARDSBURG HOPE	548	8	0	1	1	3	0	0	0	0	0	10	551	0	0	0	0	2	548	1	329	222	252	5	8	28
ALLEGAN	293	15	2	0	2	0	0	0	0	0	0	3	309	1	0	2	0	0	306	0	184	125	152	2	2	43
ARDEN	22	0	0	0	0	0	0	0	0	0	0	0	22	0	0	0	0	0	22	0	16	6	16	0	0	0
BANGOR SIMPSON	169	5	0	1	0	0	0	0	0	1	0	5	169	1	0	1	0	0	167	0	102	67	85	1	1	14
BERRIEN SPRINGS	53	0	0	0	0	0	3	0	0	0	0	1	49	0	0	0	0	0	49	0	40	9	25	0	0	0
BLOOMINGDALE	24	0	0	0	0	0	0	3	0	0	0	1	20	0	0	0	1	0	19	0	14	6	25	1	0	0
BURNIPS	47	0	0	3	0	0	0	0	0	0	0	1	49	0	0	0	0	0	49	0	28	21	48	0	0	15
MONTEREY CENTER	46	0	0	0	0	0	0	0	0	0	0	1	45	0	0	0	0	0	45	0	30	15	33	0	0	10
BUCHANAN FAITH	114	5	0	0	14	2	0	0	0	0	0	1	134	0	1	0	0	0	133	0	77	57	90	6	5	40
MORRIS CHAPEL	19	0	0	0	0	0	0	0	0	0	0	0	19	0	0	0	0	0	19	0	12	7	20	0	0	0
BUCHANAN FIRST	196	3	0	0	0	0	0	0	0	2	1	3	193	0	0	0	0	0	192	1	125	68	84	0	0	26
CASCO	188	11	0	0	1	0	2	0	0	0	0	2	196	0	0	0	0	0	196	0	108	88	115	2	3	79
CASSOPOLIS	93	5	0	1	2	0	0	0	0	1	0	2	98	0	2	0	0	0	96	0	57	41	76	3	1	0
COLOMA	199	4	0	0	0	0	9	0	0	0	0	4	190	0	0	0	0	1	187	2	127	63	96	1	2	24
DOWAGIAC FIRST	224	8	0	0	1	0	9	1	5	7	0	6	205	0	0	0	0	0	205	0	137	68	115	7	1	35
FENNVILLE	84	0	0	0	0	0	0	0	0	1	0	2	81	0	0	1	0	0	80	0	49	32	60	5	2	29
PEARL	33	0	0	0	0	0	0	0	0	0	0	0	33	0	0	0	0	0	33	0	24	9	30	2	0	8
GANGES	86	0	0	0	0	0	0	0	0	0	1	3	82	0	2	0	0	0	80	0	46	36	22	2	0	28
GALIEN	56	0	0	0	0	0	0	0	0	0	0	0	56	0	0	0	0	0	56	0	42	14	20	2	0	0
OLIVE BRANCH	73	0	0	0	0	0	0	0	0	0	0	0	73	0	0	0	0	0	73	0	47	26	40	0	0	0
GLENN	20	0	0	0	0	0	0	0	0	0	0	0	20	0	0	0	0	0	20	0	16	4	16	0	0	0
GOBLES	71	11	0	0	0	0	0	2	0	0	3	1	76	0	0	0	0	0	76	0	50	26	39	0	5	0
KENDALL	36	2	0	0	1	0	0	1	1	2	0	2	33	0	0	0	0	0	33	0	23	10	20	0	0	0
GULL LAKE	349	7	0	2	3	0	19	2	0	3	0	3	334	0	0	0	0	0	334	0	184	150	145	4	0	71
HARTFORD	222	1	0	0	0	1	0	0	0	1	0	6	217	3	2	3	0	0	209	0	131	86	131	2	0	53
HINCHMAN	69	0	0	0	0	0	0	0	0	0	0	0	69	0	0	0	0	0	69	0	41	28	15	0	0	0
ORONOKO	26	0	0	0	0	0	0	0	0	0	0	1	25	0	0	0	0	0	25	0	15	10	12	0	0	0
HOPKINS	71	2	0	0	0	0	0	2	2	1	0	0	68	0	0	0	0	0	68	0	41	27	40	1	0	15
SOUTH MONTEREY	35	2	0	0	0	0	0	0	0	0	0	0	37	0	0	0	0	0	37	0	19	18	19	0	0	6
FIRST KALAMAZOO	812	20	0	2	2	2	0	1	0	5	4	23	805	4	7	6	2	1	778	7	473	332	302	8	1	171
LIFESPRING	81	2	0	0	2	0	0	2	0	0	0	0	83	1	0	0	0	0	79	3	45	38	99	2	1	0
MILWOOD	224	1	0	67	0	2	73	4	0	2	4	11	200	1	1	0	0	0	198	0	127	73	107	1	1	60
OSHTEMO	113	1	0	0	6	2	1	0	0	1	0	4	116	0	0	0	0	0	116	0	71	45	90	1	0	1
STOCKBRIDGE AVENUE	69	0	0	0	0	0	0	0	0	0	0	0	69	0	4	4	0	1	60	0	40	29	40	0	0	0
SUNNYSIDE	106	5	0	0	4	0	6	2	0	2	0	3	102	2	2	0	0	0	98	0	67	35	70	0	0	12
WESTWOOD	350	15	0	3	3	2	28	80	0	0	0	3	262	1	7	2	0	0	252	0	165	97	203	5	5	62
KEELER	35	3	0	0	0	0	0	0	0	0	0	2	36	0	0	0	2	0	34	0	25	11	28	1	3	1

2013 TABLE 1 MEMBERSHIP & PARTICIPATION	MEMBERSHIP LAST YR	PROFESSION OF FAITH	RESTORED BY AFFIRMATION	CORRECT BY ADDITION	RECVD FM OTHER UMC'S	RECVD FM NON-UMC	REMOVED BY CHARGE CONF	WITHDRAWN	CORRECT BY SUBTRACTION	TRANSFER TO OTHER UMC	TRANSFER TO NON-UMC	REMOVED BY DEATH	TOTAL PROFESSING MEMBERS	ASIAN	AFRICAN AMER/BLACK	HISPANIC/LATINO	NATIVE AMERICAN	PACIFIC ISLANDER	WHITE	Multi-Racial	FEMALE	MALE	AVG WORSHIP ATTENDANCE	BAPTIZED THIS YEAR (12 or Younger)	BAPTIZED THIS YEAR (13 or Older)	BAPTIZED NON-MEMBERS
CHURCH	1	2a	2b	2c	3	4	5a	5b	5c	6	7	8	9	9a	9b	9c	9d	9e	9f	9g	9h	9i	10	11a	11b	12
SILVER CREEK	100	1	0	0	0	0	0	0	0	0	0	1	100	0	0	0	0	0	99	1	58	42	55	1	0	0
LACOTA	28	0	0	0	0	0	0	0	0	0	0	0	28	0	0	0	0	0	28	0	15	13	25	0	0	0
LAKESIDE	35	1	0	0	0	0	0	0	0	0	0	0	36	0	0	0	0	0	36	0	25	11	18	1	1	0
LAWRENCE	135	2	0	0	0	0	0	3	7	0	0	2	125	0	0	0	0	0	125	0	88	37	84	7	2	7
LAWTON ST PAULS	122	4	4	0	1	0	32	0	0	1	0	4	94	0	0	0	0	0	94	0	54	40	85	0	0	0
ALMENA	104	2	0	0	0	0	1	2	3	0	2	2	96	0	0	0	0	0	96	0	64	32	77	4	3	7
MARCELLUS	87	0	0	0	0	0	0	0	0	0	0	0	87	0	2	0	0	0	85	0	52	35	50	0	0	0
WATERS EDGE	171	7	0	0	0	2	0	2	0	0	0	4	174	1	0	0	0	0	173	0	111	63	126	2	0	1
BRIDGMAN FAITH	55	0	0	0	0	0	0	0	7	2	0	2	44	0	0	0	0	0	44	0	25	19	17	0	0	3
NILES GRACE	75	5	1	0	0	0	0	0	5	0	0	0	76	0	1	0	0	0	75	0	49	27	36	0	0	0
NILES WESLEY	335	0	0	0	5	0	0	23	0	15	4	10	288	0	0	0	2	0	286	0	177	111	80	2	0	2
NORTHWEST	24	0	0	0	0	0	0	0	0	2	0	0	22	0	0	0	0	0	22	0	12	10	27	1	0	1
OTSEGO	315	9	2	0	7	1	7	2	41	0	0	7	277	0	6	0	0	0	263	8	170	107	248	4	10	4
PARCHMENT	280	9	0	0	0	2	0	0	0	2	0	5	284	6	0	0	0	0	278	0	196	88	107	3	3	30
PAW PAW	197	0	0	13	5	0	0	0	0	0	0	3	212	0	0	0	0	0	212	0	130	82	68	5	1	0
PLAINWELL FIRST	242	1	0	0	3	0	4	4	0	0	2	4	232	0	0	0	0	0	232	0	140	92	147	2	0	80
POKAGON	108	0	0	0	0	0	0	0	0	0	0	0	108	0	0	0	0	0	108	0	70	38	71	0	0	3
PORTAGE CHAPEL HILL	566	17	2	1	7	2	20	8	0	5	2	4	556	2	0	0	0	0	553	1	330	226	311	13	2	168
PORTAGE FIRST	390	2	0	1	2	0	0	0	0	3	0	4	388	0	0	0	0	0	388	0	247	141	308	4	0	69
PORTAGE PRAIRIE	144	1	0	0	4	0	0	0	0	0	0	2	147	0	0	0	0	0	147	0	75	72	69	0	0	0
RIVERSIDE	68	0	0	0	0	0	0	0	0	0	0	0	68	0	0	0	0	1	66	1	42	26	38	0	0	0
SCOTTDALE	71	1	0	0	2	0	0	0	5	0	0	6	63	0	0	0	0	0	63	0	43	20	40	0	1	11
SAINT JOSEPH FIRST	514	5	2	0	6	0	5	8	1	5	0	12	496	2	0	3	0	0	486	5	285	211	295	5	3	12
SCHOOLCRAFT	240	1	0	0	0	0	0	0	0	0	0	1	240	0	0	0	0	0	237	3	137	103	87	2	0	2
SODUS CHAPEL HILL	205	4	0	0	0	0	0	0	0	1	0	3	205	0	0	0	0	0	205	0	131	74	96	0	0	53
SOUTH HAVEN FIRST	234	0	2	0	0	0	0	0	0	0	0	2	234	0	3	4	0	0	227	0	140	94	100	0	0	0
STEVENSVILLE	495	17	0	0	4	0	19	3	0	4	0	5	485	3	9	0	2	0	471	0	280	205	233	10	2	8
THREE OAKS	147	9	2	0	0	0	1	1	0	2	0	3	151	1	3	0	0	0	146	1	96	55	82	1	2	23
TOWNLINE	35	0	0	0	0	0	0	0	0	0	0	0	35	0	1	0	0	0	34	0	25	10	35	0	0	0
BREEDSVILLE	18	0	0	0	0	0	0	0	0	0	0	0	18	0	0	0	0	0	18	0	12	6	24	0	0	0
TROWBRIDGE	62	3	0	0	1	1	0	0	3	3	0	2	59	0	0	0	0	0	59	0	38	21	69	1	3	0
VICKSBURG	328	8	0	0	4	4	2	0	0	1	2	4	335	0	0	0	0	0	334	1	195	140	153	2	3	79
WAKELEE	85	0	0	0	0	0	0	0	0	0	0	0	85	0	0	0	0	0	85	0	74	11	60	0	0	0
KALAMAZOO DISTRICT	11,271	245	17	95	93	26	241	156	80	75	25	196	10,974	29	53	26	9	6	10,816	35	6,713	4,261	6,101	134	77	1,394
LAST YEAR	11,579	328	26	119	89	47	318	101	169	69	48	212	11,271	32	48	30	12	8	11,108	33	6,911	4,360	6,128	177		1,376
INC/(DEC)	(308)	(83)	(9)	(24)	4	(21)	(77)	55	(89)	6	(23)	(16)	(297)	(3)	5	(4)	(3)	(2)	(292)	2	(198)	(99)	(27)	(43)	77	18

STATISTICAL INFO

2013 TABLE 1 MEMBERSHIP & PARTICIPATION	OTHER CONSTITUENTS	ENROLLED IN CONFIRMATION CLASS	CHILDREN IN CHRISTIAN FORMATION GROUPS	YOUTH IN CHRISTIAN FORMATION GROUPS	YOUNG ADULTS IN CHRISTIAN FORMATION	OTHER ADULTS IN CHRISTIAN FORMATION	TOTAL PERSONS IN CHRISTIAN FORMATION	AVG SUNDAY SCHOOL ATTENDANCE	VACATION BIBLE SCHOOL PARTICIPANTS	NUMBER OF SUNDAY SCHOOL CLASSES	NUMBER OF CLASSES OUTSIDE SUNDAY SCHOOL	SHORT TERM CLASSES	UM MEN MEMBERS	PAID TO UMM PROJECTS	UMW MEMBERS	PAID TO UMW LOCAL PROJECTS	VIM TEAMS SENT OUT	PERSONS IN VIM TEAMS	PERSONS IN MISSIONS	PERSONS SERVED IN DAYCARE AND/OR EDUCATION	PERSONS SERVED IN OUTREACH, JUSTICE, MERCY
CHURCH	13	14	15	16	17	18	19	20	21	22	23	24	25a	25b	26a	26b	27a	27b	28	29	30
EDWARDSBURG HOPE	96	0	44	15	16	61	136	80	150	9	6	6	0	0	18	0	0	0	18	0	248
ALLEGAN	100	6	32	15	6	30	83	32	100	8	2	2	10	0	72	4,856	0	0	0	0	1,400
ARDEN	15	0	0	0	0	0	0	0	0	0	0	0	0	0	0	0	0	0	0	0	0
BANGOR SIMPSON	16	5	24	7	4	30	65	25	0	4	3	2	0	650	20	1,983	0	0	16	0	490
BERRIEN SPRINGS	20	0	0	0	0	10	10	20	0	2	0	0	0	0	20	0	0	0	0	10,328	10,328
BLOOMINGDALE	22	0	24	5	0	0	29	15	3	4	2	0	0	0	0	0	0	0	0	24	200
BURNIPS	40	0	8	10	0	8	26	6	80	1	1	0	0	0	0	750	0	0	14	0	54
MONTEREY CENTER	35	0	5	1	0	9	15	12	24	2	1	0	0	0	0	0	0	0	3	0	17
BUCHANAN FAITH	23	0	0	0	0	3	3	18	0	3	0	2	0	0	9	670	0	0	7	0	550
MORRIS CHAPEL	16	0	0	0	0	0	0	0	0	0	0	0	0	0	0	0	0	0	0	0	0
BUCHANAN FIRST	84	0	20	3	2	65	90	21	66	6	5	0	0	0	8	2,400	0	0	0	0	150
CASCO	221	10	21	16	10	62	109	25	80	4	4	3	28	1,040	32	5,150	0	0	56	25	280
CASSOPOLIS	58	0	0	8	0	2	10	15	0	3	0	3	0	0	0	0	0	0	2	0	85
COLOMA	33	0	4	12	0	19	35	14	30	0	0	46	0	0	0	0	0	0	59	0	1,762
DOWAGIAC FIRST	50	0	6	0	0	24	30	20	0	2	3	3	6	100	45	2,100	0	3	2	0	1,625
FENNVILLE	40	0	15	25	0	10	50	15	90	5	1	2	0	0	24	900	0	0	0	0	700
PEARL	8	0	5	0	0	0	5	5	0	1	0	0	0	0	0	0	0	0	0	0	30
GANGES	28	0	0	0	0	6	6	8	0	2	1	1	0	0	30	1,200	0	0	0	0	0
GALIEN	5	0	5	0	0	4	9	3	4	1	1	0	0	0	0	0	0	0	0	0	45
OLIVE BRANCH	0	0	0	0	0	0	0	5	12	1	0	0	0	0	0	0	0	0	0	0	0
GLENN	28	0	0	0	0	0	0	1	0	0	0	0	0	0	0	1,675	0	0	0	0	0
GOBLES	1	0	0	0	0	12	12	12	0	1	0	0	0	820	15	1,500	0	0	0	0	0
KENDALL	20	0	0	0	0	7	7	4	0	0	1	0	3	339	5	1,300	0	0	0	0	234
GULL LAKE	22	6	65	21	0	41	127	22	42	3	2	2	0	0	0	0	0	0	70	0	0
HARTFORD	85	0	36	29	0	37	102	27	45	7	6	0	0	0	12	4,323	1	2	32	0	903
HINCHMAN	16	0	0	0	0	0	0	0	0	0	0	0	0	0	0	0	0	0	0	2	0
ORONOKO	25	0	0	0	0	0	0	0	0	0	0	0	0	0	0	0	0	0	0	0	0
HOPKINS	17	6	9	6	0	20	35	8	8	2	2	0	0	0	11	1,196	0	0	0	26	259
SOUTH MONTEREY	2	1	0	1	0	1	2	0	0	0	2	0	0	0	0	0	0	0	0	0	266
FIRST KALAMAZOO	152	6	79	40	16	340	475	120	0	5	5	28	0	0	116	5,766	0	0	150	2,300	10,000
LIFESPRING	161	0	6	11	8	36	61	22	31	3	3	9	0	0	0	0	1	10	99	135	1,050
MILWOOD	100	3	18	7	1	48	74	8	46	1	6	1	0	0	26	4,000	0	0	1	28	700
OSHTEMO	80	0	7	0	0	18	25	25	0	3	1	1	0	0	18	1,170	0	0	0	0	75
STOCKBRIDGE AVENUE	0	0	4	16	0	0	20	3	0	20	0	12	0	0	18	3,133	0	0	0	0	0
SUNNYSIDE	35	0	7	0	10	45	62	7	0	1	2	3	0	0	22	2,452	1	2	250	0	12,940
WESTWOOD	83	0	32	22	25	160	239	75	44	4	2	18	0	0	40	867	0	0	60	0	775
KEELER	26	3	0	0	0	6	6	0	0	0	1	2	0	0	5	157	0	0	0	0	600

2013 TABLE 1 MEMBERSHIP & PARTICIPATION	OTHER CONSTITUENTS	ENROLLED IN CONFIRMATION CLASS	CHILDREN IN CHRISTIAN FORMATION GROUPS	YOUTH IN CHRISTIAN FORMATION GROUPS	YOUNG ADULTS IN CHRISTIAN FORMATION	OTHER ADULTS IN CHRISTIAN FORMATION	TOTAL PERSONS IN CHRISTIAN FORMATION	AVG SUNDAY SCHOOL ATTENDANCE	VACATION BIBLE SCHOOL PARTICIPANTS	NUMBER OF SUNDAY SCHOOL CLASSES	NUMBER OF CLASSES OUTSIDE SUNDAY SCHOOL	SHORT TERM CLASSES	UM MEN MEMBERS	PAID TO UMM PROJECTS	UMW MEMBERS	PAID TO UMW LOCAL PROJECTS	VIM TEAMS SENT OUT	PERSONS IN VIM TEAMS	PERSONS IN MISSIONS	PERSONS SERVED IN DAYCARE AND/OR EDUCATION	PERSONS SERVED IN OUTREACH, JUSTICE, MERCY
CHURCH	13	14	15	16	17	18	19	20	21	22	23	24	25a	25b	26a	26b	27a	27b	28	29	30
SILVER CREEK	0	0	0	0	0	14	14	0	0	0	0	2	0	0	8	1,223	0	0	0	0	600
LACOTA	0	0	0	0	0	12	12	12	0	2	0	0	0	0	0	0	0	0	0	0	0
LAKESIDE	12	0	0	0	0	0	0	0	0	0	0	0	0	0	0	0	0	0	0	0	0
LAWRENCE	13	8	50	13	0	15	78	0	50	3	2	0	0	0	13	1,250	0	0	0	0	0
LAWTON ST PAULS	0	0	0	5	0	10	15	12	100	4	2	3	0	0	18	0	0	0	5	0	150
ALMENA	69	0	0	7	0	18	25	40	0	5	1	4	10	261	0	0	0	0	0	0	761
MARCELLUS	0	0	44	8	0	24	76	0	24	1	5	4	0	0	8	0	0	0	0	188	72
WATERS EDGE	137	6	17	8	0	48	73	14	0	4	0	14	0	0	25	270	2	9	69	0	2,680
BRIDGMAN FAITH	6	0	0	0	0	0	0	0	0	0	0	0	0	0	0	0	0	0	0	0	20
NILES GRACE	0	0	0	0	0	0	0	13	0	1	0	0	0	0	0	0	0	0	0	0	22
NILES WESLEY	94	0	18	7	0	28	53	25	30	0	0	2	0	0	25	1,193	0	0	0	0	843
NORTHWEST	12	0	0	0	0	9	9	0	0	0	1	1	0	0	0	0	0	0	2	0	0
OTSEGO	181	0	74	31	0	44	149	101	125	6	2	2	8	0	25	6,120	0	0	0	0	2,100
PARCHMENT	74	2	4	9	0	30	43	29	0	5	0	2	14	2,850	50	4,102	0	0	0	15	500
PAW PAW	39	3	6	12	0	18	36	20	6	3	0	0	13	2,300	20	1,700	0	0	20	130	200
PLAINWELL FIRST	78	0	20	10	14	55	99	21	7	5	4	4	0	0	0	0	0	0	0	0	145
POKAGON	0	0	11	9	4	32	56	22	27	5	3	2	0	0	19	0	0	0	0	0	190
PORTAGE CHAPEL HILL	297	24	344	74	11	494	923	122	138	18	21	13	18	0	48	1,035	0	0	63	351	18,362
PORTAGE FIRST	252	0	68	29	0	256	353	73	0	11	22	0	0	0	0	0	0	0	0	0	0
PORTAGE PRAIRIE	25	0	0	0	0	0	0	33	20	4	0	0	0	0	0	0	0	0	0	0	20
RIVERSIDE	27	0	0	5	0	0	5	4	0	0	0	0	0	0	0	0	0	0	0	0	0
SCOTTDALE	23	0	0	0	0	12	12	10	0	2	1	1	0	0	27	3,004	0	0	0	0	250
SAINT JOSEPH FIRST	275	4	51	56	12	84	203	79	67	10	11	7	0	0	0	0	0	0	23	150	780
SCHOOLCRAFT	36	0	6	8	0	73	87	0	55	5	5	1	20	20	0	1,242	0	0	0	31	705
SODUS CHAPEL HILL	85	5	60	16	0	40	116	25	45	6	1	0	0	0	0	0	0	0	1	0	0
SOUTH HAVEN FIRST	330	0	5	8	12	20	45	20	25	6	2	3	24	4,000	22	0	0	0	0	0	100
STEVENSVILLE	245	4	42	24	14	230	310	64	58	7	2	8	0	0	93	8,639	0	0	0	80	0
THREE OAKS	56	4	22	10	0	34	66	13	12	5	2	1	0	0	0	0	1	5	20	0	100
TOWNLINE	48	0	0	0	0	0	0	0	45	1	2	0	0	0	0	0	0	0	0	0	200
BREEDSVILLE	40	0	0	0	0	0	0	0	0	1	2	2	0	0	0	0	0	0	0	0	1,500
TROWBRIDGE	44	4	7	0	0	10	17	17	18	2	1	1	0	0	0	0	0	0	0	0	38
VICKSBURG	100	5	26	53	5	202	286	51	85	9	9	5	0	0	119	4,905	0	0	96	127	1,364
WAKELEE	0	0	12	8	0	20	40	20	52	4	2	2	0	0	0	0	0	0	0	0	75
KALAMAZOO DISTRICT	4,361	115	1,363	680	170	2,946	5,159	1,513	1,844	243	166	230	154	12,380	1,086	82,231	6	31	1,138	13,940	77,543
LAST YEAR	4,425	124	1,433	674	166	2,895	5,168	1,691	1,914	253	122	194	154	10,389	1,057	89,853	3	37	504	3,659	87,756
INC/(DEC)	(64)	(9)	(70)	6	4	51	(9)	(178)	(70)	(10)	44	36	0	1,991	29	(7,622)	3	(6)	634	10,281	(10,213)

STATISTICAL INFO

STATISTICAL INFO

2013 TABLE 1 MEMBERSHIP & PARTICIPATION

CHURCH	MEMBERSHIP LAST YR	PROFESSION OF FAITH	RESTORED BY AFFIRMATION	CORRECT BY ADDITION	RECVD FM OTHER UMC'S	RECVD FM NON-UMC	REMOVED BY CHARGE CONF	WITHDRAWN	CORRECT BY SUBTRACTION	TRANSFER TO OTHER UMC	TRANSFER TO NON-UMC	REMOVED BY DEATH	TOTAL PROFESSING MEMBERS	ASIAN	AFRICAN AMER/BLACK	HISPANIC/LATINO	NATIVE AMERICAN	PACIFIC ISLANDER	WHITE	Multi-Racial	FEMALE	MALE	AVG WORSHIP ATTENDANCE	BAPTIZED THIS YEAR (12 or Younger)	BAPTIZED THIS YEAR (13 or Older)	BAPTIZED NON-MEMBERS
	1	2a	2b	2c	3	4	5a	5b	5c	6	7	8	9	9a	9b	9c	9d	9e	9f	9g	9h	9i	10	11a	11b	12
BATH	77	12	0	0	1	0	0	0	0	1	0	1	88	0	0	0	0	0	88	0	56	32	44	0	6	9
GUNNISONVILLE	64	5	0	0	1	0	0	0	0	1	0	2	67	0	0	0	0	0	67	0	45	22	62	0	0	17
WHEATFIELD	54	1	0	0	0	0	0	0	1	0	0	3	51	0	0	0	0	0	51	0	27	24	25	0	0	0
BROOKFIELD	25	4	0	0	2	0	0	0	0	0	0	0	31	0	0	1	0	0	30	0	20	11	35	2	3	2
CHARLOTTE LAWRENCE AVENUE	495	7	4	0	0	0	0	2	0	4	0	15	485	0	1	0	0	0	484	0	312	173	150	4	0	4
COUNTRY CHAPEL	120	4	2	0	2	3	0	0	0	0	0	4	127	0	0	3	0	0	124	0	78	49	78	1	0	8
DANSVILLE	24	0	0	0	0	0	0	0	1	1	0	1	21	0	0	0	0	0	21	0	15	6	10	0	0	0
DELTA MILLS	63	0	0	0	2	0	0	0	0	0	0	3	62	0	0	0	0	0	62	0	42	20	36	0	0	0
DEWITT REDEEMER	789	12	0	0	5	18	20	0	0	1	0	4	799	2	4	6	4	2	781	0	430	369	488	17	4	52
DIMONDALE	58	6	0	0	0	0	0	0	0	0	0	5	59	0	0	0	0	0	59	0	39	20	37	1	0	0
UNIVERSITY EAST LANSING	488	11	0	1	19	2	16	3	0	4	0	4	494	7	22	0	0	0	465	0	286	208	263	2	4	109
EATON RAPIDS FIRST	435	7	0	0	6	3	5	0	0	1	2	6	437	1	0	0	0	0	436	0	275	162	221	6	3	0
FREEPORT	12	0	0	0	0	0	0	0	0	0	0	1	11	0	0	0	0	0	11	0	8	3	9	0	0	8
GRAND LEDGE FIRST	510	10	0	0	0	0	0	2	0	7	0	13	498	1	5	9	1	0	482	0	306	192	210	4	1	116
GROVENBURG	44	0	0	0	0	0	0	0	0	0	0	3	41	0	0	0	0	0	41	0	26	15	28	1	1	0
HASTINGS FIRST	326	1	0	0	0	0	0	0	0	1	0	8	318	1	0	0	1	0	316	0	198	120	149	5	0	60
HASTINGS HOPE	148	0	0	0	0	0	0	0	0	0	1	0	147	0	0	0	0	0	147	0	103	44	85	0	0	0
HOLT	437	5	0	0	6	0	21	0	0	2	0	4	421	1	3	0	0	2	413	2	245	176	277	4	1	170
KALAMO	83	0	0	0	0	0	0	0	0	0	0	0	83	0	0	0	0	0	83	0	58	25	40	2	0	0
LAKE ODESSA CENTRAL	241	0	1	1	0	0	0	10	0	5	0	5	223	0	0	0	0	1	222	0	130	93	94	2	1	16
LAKE ODESSA LAKEWOOD	272	7	0	0	0	0	0	2	1	2	0	1	273	2	0	0	0	0	271	0	156	117	240	3	2	39
ASBURY LANSING	207	0	0	0	3	0	18	0	0	0	0	9	183	0	2	0	0	1	174	6	111	72	95	2	0	2
CENTRAL LANSING	362	0	0	0	6	0	21	1	0	4	1	11	330	1	16	3	1	0	301	8	192	138	111	2	0	2
CHRIST LANSING	136	4	1	0	0	0	2	0	3	1	0	4	131	0	3	2	1	2	123	0	86	45	79	0	0	5
FAITH/SOUTH LANSING	97	2	0	0	0	0	0	0	0	1	0	2	96	3	27	9	0	0	57	0	53	43	45	3	1	24
FIRST LANSING	222	0	0	0	4	0	7	10	5	1	0	7	196	0	14	0	0	3	178	1	135	61	90	0	0	15
GRACE LANSING	191	6	0	6	0	0	1	0	0	0	0	7	195	0	1	1	1	0	188	4	124	71	102	5	2	2
KOREAN LANSING	104	5	4	0	2	17	0	5	0	3	46	0	78	78	0	0	0	0	0	0	45	33	70	3	5	0
MOUNT HOPE	353	10	1	3	8	3	0	2	0	0	0	7	369	0	24	1	0	0	344	0	214	155	237	6	3	0
TRINITY LANSING	408	38	0	9	3	0	0	8	0	10	4	2	434	0	5	3	0	0	426	0	261	173	265	9	18	7
LESLIE	90	0	0	0	0	2	0	1	0	1	1	4	85	0	0	0	0	0	85	0	54	31	42	1	0	0
FELT PLAINS	18	0	0	0	0	0	0	0	0	0	0	0	18	0	0	0	0	0	18	0	10	8	17	0	0	0
MASON FIRST	467	0	0	0	4	0	4	0	0	0	1	10	456	0	3	0	0	0	452	1	257	199	196	9	3	152
MILLVILLE	108	7	2	0	1	0	0	0	5	0	1	0	112	0	0	0	0	0	112	0	70	42	77	1	1	0
MUNITH	30	3	0	0	1	0	0	0	0	0	0	0	34	0	0	0	0	0	34	0	19	15	33	0	0	0
PLEASANT LAKE	43	0	0	0	0	0	0	0	0	0	0	2	41	0	0	0	0	0	41	0	28	13	9	0	0	0
MULLIKEN	33	0	0	0	0	0	0	0	0	0	0	2	31	0	0	0	0	0	31	0	24	7	31	0	0	0

2013 TABLE 1 MEMBERSHIP & PARTICIPATION	MEMBERSHIP LAST YR	PROFESSION OF FAITH	RESTORED BY AFFIRMATION	CORRECT BY ADDITION	RECVD FM OTHER UMC'S	RECVD FM NON-UMC	REMOVED BY CHARGE CONF	WITHDRAWN	CORRECT BY SUBTRACTION	TRANSFER TO OTHER UMC	TRANSFER TO NON-UMC	REMOVED BY DEATH	TOTAL PROFESSING MEMBERS	ASIAN	AFRICAN AMER/BLACK	HISPANIC/LATINO	NATIVE AMERICAN	PACIFIC ISLANDER	WHITE	Multi-Racial	FEMALE	MALE	AVG WORSHIP ATTENDANCE	BAPTIZED THIS YEAR (12 or Younger)	BAPTIZED THIS YEAR (13 or Older)	BAPTIZED NON-MEMBERS
CHURCH	1	2a	2b	2c	3	4	5a	5b	5c	6	7	8	9	9a	9b	9c	9d	9e	9f	9g	9h	9i	10	11a	11b	12
SEBEWA CENTER	18	0	0	0	0	0	0	0	0	0	0	0	18	0	0	0	0	0	18	0	12	6	8	0	0	[illegible]
NASHVILLE	133	6	0	0	0	0	0	0	0	0	0	4	135	2	0	2	0	0	131	0	73	62	62	0	1	1[illegible]
PEACE	32	0	0	0	0	0	0	0	0	0	0	0	32	0	0	0	0	0	32	0	20	12	19	0	0	[illegible]
QUIMBY	25	0	0	0	0	0	0	0	0	0	0	0	25	0	0	0	0	0	25	0	15	10	24	0	0	[illegible]
OKEMOS	647	17	1	0	6	0	8	0	0	0	0	5	658	5	2	0	0	0	651	0	373	285	167	1	8	[illegible]
PERRY	40	1	0	3	2	0	0	0	1	0	0	4	41	0	0	0	0	0	41	0	25	16	30	1	0	[illegible]
SHAFTSBURG	61	0	0	0	0	0	0	0	4	0	0	4	53	0	0	0	0	0	53	0	31	22	41	0	0	2
PORTLAND	342	7	3	0	7	0	0	0	0	3	5	7	344	3	0	0	0	0	341	0	212	132	176	3	0	[illegible]
POTTERVILLE	155	2	1	0	4	1	1	0	0	2	0	3	157	0	0	3	0	0	154	0	108	49	100	2	1	2[illegible]
ROBBINS	221	5	0	0	2	0	11	0	10	1	1	4	201	0	0	0	1	0	200	0	128	73	103	3	6	[illegible]
STOCKBRIDGE	197	0	0	0	0	0	0	164	0	0	0	0	33	0	0	0	0	0	33	0	23	10	27	0	0	[illegible]
SUNFIELD	80	0	0	0	2	0	0	0	0	1	3	6	72	0	0	0	0	0	72	0	46	26	62	0	0	[illegible]
SYCAMORE CREEK	126	11	0	0	1	0	7	2	0	2	0	0	127	1	1	2	0	0	123	0	79	48	160	3	5	[illegible]
VERMONTVILLE	62	3	0	0	0	0	0	0	0	0	0	0	65	0	0	1	0	0	64	0	37	28	32	2	2	3[illegible]
GRESHAM	48	4	0	0	1	0	0	0	0	0	0	0	53	0	0	0	0	0	53	0	38	15	40	1	0	4[illegible]
WACOUSTA	226	3	0	0	0	0	0	0	0	0	0	0	229	0	0	0	0	0	228	1	133	96	95	5	0	3[illegible]
WATERLOO VILLAGE	33	0	0	16	0	0	0	0	0	0	0	0	49	0	0	0	0	0	49	0	35	14	28	0	0	[illegible]
WATERLOO FIRST	43	0	0	0	0	0	0	36	0	0	0	0	7	0	0	0	0	0	7	0	5	2	10	0	0	[illegible]
WEBBERVILLE	114	0	0	0	0	0	0	2	0	0	0	3	109	0	0	0	0	0	109	0	66	43	75	0	0	[illegible]
WILLIAMSTON	141	6	1	0	4	0	6	1	0	0	0	1	144	0	0	0	0	0	139	5	78	66	70	3	2	[illegible]
WILLIAMSTON CROSSROADS	48	3	0	0	0	0	0	0	8	1	0	3	39	0	0	0	0	0	39	0	26	13	56	3	0	[illegible]
WOODLAND	51	0	0	0	0	0	0	0	0	0	0	0	51	0	0	1	0	0	50	0	35	16	30	0	0	
WELCOME CORNERS	30	0	0	0	0	0	0	0	0	0	0	1	29	1	0	0	0	0	28	0	19	10	22	0	0	[illegible]
LANSING DISTRICT	10,507	235	21	39	105	49	148	251	39	61	66	195	10,196	109	133	47	10	11	9,858	28	6,155	4,041	5,517	122	84	1,01[illegible]
LAST YEAR	10,700	232	10	30	93	67	199	91	51	69	50	176	10,496	143	140	47	9	11	10,123	23	6,385	4,111	5,857	223		1,4[illegible]
INC/(DEC)	(193)	3	11	9	12	(18)	(51)	160	(12)	(8)	16	19	(300)	(34)	(7)	0	1	0	(265)	5	(230)	(70)	(340)	(101)	84	(39[illegible]

STATISTICAL INFO

2013 TABLE 1 MEMBERSHIP & PARTICIPATION	OTHER CONSTITUENTS	ENROLLED IN CONFIRMATION CLASS	CHILDREN IN CHRISTIAN FORMATION GROUPS	YOUTH IN CHRISTIAN FORMATION GROUPS	YOUNG ADULTS IN CHRISTIAN FORMATION	OTHER ADULTS IN CHRISTIAN FORMATION	TOTAL PERSONS IN CHRISTIAN FORMATION	AVG SUNDAY SCHOOL ATTENDANCE	VACATION BIBLE SCHOOL PARTICIPANTS	NUMBER OF SUNDAY SCHOOL CLASSES	NUMBER OF CLASSES OUTSIDE SUNDAY SCHOOL	SHORT TERM CLASSES	UM MEN MEMBERS	PAID TO UMM PROJECTS	UMW MEMBERS	PAID TO UMW LOCAL PROJECTS	VIM TEAMS SENT OUT	PERSONS IN VIM TEAMS	PERSONS IN MISSIONS	PERSONS SERVED IN DAYCARE AND/OR EDUCATION	PERSONS SERVED IN OUTREACH, JUSTICE, MERCY
CHURCH	13	14	15	16	17	18	19	20	21	22	23	24	25a	25b	26a	26b	27a	27b	28	29	30
BATH	61	10	40	15	3	30	88	0	60	0	0	2	0	0	17	425	0	0	10	0	0
GUNNISONVILLE	55	0	6	4	0	13	23	2	0	1	1	0	0	0	0	0	1	5	5	0	0
WHEATFIELD	17	0	0	0	0	0	0	2	0	0	0	0	0	0	0	0	0	0	0	0	0
BROOKFIELD	49	0	5	0	0	10	15	2	10	1	2	2	0	0	7	540	0	0	0	0	0
CHARLOTTE LAWRENCE AVENUE	0	7	27	7	3	3	40	62	18	7	0	0	8	0	0	500	0	0	1	5	60
COUNTRY CHAPEL	63	0	30	12	0	30	72	23	33	3	3	0	0	0	0	0	0	0	0	0	450
DANSVILLE	0	0	0	2	0	1	3	0	50	0	0	0	0	0	0	0	0	0	0	0	0
DELTA MILLS	0	0	3	0	0	8	11	3	0	3	8	11	0	0	18	485	0	0	0	0	22
DEWITT REDEEMER	1,158	6	238	162	112	244	756	215	221	18	22	6	0	0	0	0	0	0	117	275	3,500
DIMONDALE	29	0	5	0	0	5	10	5	0	0	0	0	8	0	0	0	0	0	0	0	0
UNIVERSITY EAST LANSING	47	0	53	39	50	150	292	40	81	6	7	6	44	750	35	4,935	1	12	200	30	200
EATON RAPIDS FIRST	420	4	41	15	0	85	141	63	151	7	7	2	14	0	46	3,375	1	14	115	112	252
FREEPORT	8	0	0	0	0	0	0	0	0	0	1	0	0	0	0	0	0	0	7	0	243
GRAND LEDGE FIRST	104	10	45	25	5	123	198	35	25	8	3	4	25	1,536	20	3,434	1	12	143	0	1,615
GROVENBURG	5	0	0	0	0	3	3	0	0	0	1	0	1	0	0	0	0	0	5	0	0
HASTINGS FIRST	167	0	24	12	6	77	119	34	32	3	4	5	0	0	14	1,500	0	0	20	0	1,855
HASTINGS HOPE	80	0	30	32	0	47	109	42	0	7	6	0	0	0	0	0	0	0	0	41	0
HOLT	300	1	46	42	5	247	340	48	52	7	10	22	0	364	75	5,354	0	0	19	121	131
KALAMO	190	0	0	0	0	0	0	5	0	0	0	0	0	0	10	0	0	0	0	0	100
LAKE ODESSA CENTRAL	52	0	7	10	0	29	46	37	0	7	1	5	0	0	42	1,175	0	0	10	15	500
LAKE ODESSA LAKEWOOD	202	7	257	158	10	117	542	70	95	12	9	2	0	0	0	0	1	9	16	25	600
ASBURY LANSING	0	0	7	11	0	44	62	12	11	1	3	2	0	0	67	2,500	2	11	0	0	0
CENTRAL LANSING	62	0	15	4	9	80	108	90	0	4	4	0	0	0	65	2,300	0	2	0	0	1,500
CHRIST LANSING	10	0	6	0	6	24	36	10	3	2	2	3	0	0	40	1,075	0	0	1	0	60
FAITH/SOUTH LANSING	10	2	8	10	7	25	50	15	10	4	3	2	0	0	0	0	0	0	10	0	2,100
FIRST LANSING	30	0	5	13	1	24	43	21	0	2	1	4	0	0	30	1,800	0	1	0	0	0
GRACE LANSING	101	0	18	12	12	26	68	25	10	3	4	2	8	500	20	2,999	0	0	3	0	275
KOREAN LANSING	0	2	17	5	25	22	69	35	0	3	6	0	6	0	14	1,500	0	0	5	0	0
MOUNT HOPE	103	0	65	29	12	234	340	130	45	16	3	13	0	0	42	3,965	0	0	100	75	292
TRINITY LANSING	354	25	99	100	2	124	325	50	129	9	14	4	0	0	0	0	0	0	0	100	275
LESLIE	0	1	0	1	0	6	7	5	0	1	0	0	0	0	0	0	0	0	0	0	0
FELT PLAINS	0	0	0	0	0	5	5	4	0	0	0	0	0	0	0	0	0	0	0	0	0
MASON FIRST	388	12	50	36	5	136	227	74	145	7	9	4	21	800	97	8,633	3	25	75	22	260
MILLVILLE	0	0	12	5	3	15	35	35	50	0	4	2	0	0	25	0	0	0	10	0	0
MUNITH	21	0	3	0	0	13	16	3	0	0	0	0	0	0	0	0	0	0	0	0	0
PLEASANT LAKE	0	0	0	0	0	0	0	0	0	0	0	0	0	0	12	471	0	0	0	0	0
MULLIKEN	0	0	0	0	0	0	0	5	0	1	1	0	0	0	0	0	0	0	0	0	170

2013 TABLE 1 MEMBERSHIP & PARTICIPATION	OTHER CONSTITUENTS	ENROLLED IN CONFIRMATION CLASS	CHILDREN IN CHRISTIAN FORMATION GROUPS	YOUTH IN CHRISTIAN FORMATION GROUPS	YOUNG ADULTS IN CHRISTIAN FORMATION	OTHER ADULTS IN CHRISTIAN FORMATION	TOTAL PERSONS IN CHRISTIAN FORMATION	AVG SUNDAY SCHOOL ATTENDANCE	VACATION BIBLE SCHOOL PARTICIPANTS	NUMBER OF SUNDAY SCHOOL CLASSES	NUMBER OF CLASSES OUTSIDE SUNDAY SCHOOL	SHORT TERM CLASSES	UM MEN MEMBERS	PAID TO UMM PROJECTS	UMW MEMBERS	PAID TO UMW LOCAL PROJECTS	VIM TEAMS SENT OUT	PERSONS IN VIM TEAMS	PERSONS IN MISSIONS	PERSONS SERVED IN DAYCARE AND/OR EDUCATION	PERSONS SERVED IN OUTREACH, JUSTICE, MERCY
CHURCH	13	14	15	16	17	18	19	20	21	22	23	24	25a	25b	26a	26b	27a	27b	28	29	30
SEBEWA CENTER	0	0	0	0	0	0	0	0	0	0	0	0	0	0	0	0	0	0	0	0	0
NASHVILLE	19	6	11	28	0	50	89	21	36	4	5	3	10	0	8	400	0	0	0	0	0
PEACE	30	0	0	0	1	3	4	0	0	0	1	0	0	0	18	334	1	5	20	0	150
QUIMBY	16	0	8	0	0	0	8	4	12	1	0	0	0	0	13	100	0	0	1	0	0
OKEMOS	61	10	49	54	0	14	117	50	82	7	3	2	0	0	22	12,476	0	1	30	0	0
PERRY	22	0	9	1	0	15	25	20	30	3	1	3	0	0	8	1,075	0	0	24	0	53
SHAFTSBURG	44	0	12	7	0	23	42	27	25	4	1	3	0	0	0	0	0	0	37	0	57
PORTLAND	105	7	40	25	10	20	95	33	125	7	5	3	0	0	20	1,970	0	0	0	70	100
POTTERVILLE	0	0	12	18	0	40	70	4	87	2	5	0	0	0	22	300	0	0	0	0	240
ROBBINS	38	5	0	0	0	13	13	60	0	0	0	0	0	0	0	0	0	0	15	0	43
STOCKBRIDGE	0	0	0	5	0	13	18	0	0	1	0	0	0	0	13	1,000	0	0	0	0	100
SUNFIELD	55	0	15	10	10	24	59	30	0	4	1	1	0	0	0	0	0	0	0	0	250
SYCAMORE CREEK	90	11	40	20	0	75	135	39	0	4	11	3	0	0	0	0	1	1	40	0	50
VERMONTVILLE	10	0	11	5	0	4	20	5	20	1	1	0	0	0	9	0	0	0	5	0	100
GRESHAM	17	0	0	0	0	0	0	10	0	0	0	0	0	0	12	2,634	0	0	0	0	0
WACOUSTA	50	0	13	15	0	0	28	10	0	2	0	4	0	0	17	200	0	0	0	0	100
WATERLOO VILLAGE	38	0	12	7	0	10	29	0	27	0	0	1	0	0	8	554	0	0	0	0	140
WATERLOO FIRST	0	0	0	0	0	0	0	0	0	0	0	0	0	0	0	0	0	0	0	0	0
WEBBERVILLE	0	0	8	16	0	54	78	26	40	6	4	1	19	4,492	33	2,150	0	0	30	0	17
WILLIAMSTON	35	0	12	9	0	0	21	9	25	1	2	1	0	0	0	0	0	0	50	0	425
WILLIAMSTON CROSSROADS	85	3	8	3	0	16	27	20	38	4	0	1	0	0	24	1,200	0	0	0	0	150
WOODLAND	16	0	0	0		10	10								12				4	0	0
WELCOME CORNERS	11	0	0	0	0	5	5	0	0	0	1	2	0	0	22	2,400	0	0	0	0	0
LANSING DISTRICT	4,828	129	1,422	984	297	2,389	5,092	1,570	1,778	194	180	131	164	8,442	957	73,759	12	98	1,128	891	16,435
LAST YEAR	4,723	132	1,465	896	277	2,324	4,962	1,739	1,840	216	156	161	170	8,431	1,032	70,636	16	82	591	1,054	14,013
INC/(DEC)	105	(3)	(43)	88	20	65	130	(169)	(62)	(22)	24	(30)	(6)	11	(75)	3,123	(4)	16	537	(163)	2,422

2013 TABLE 1 MEMBERSHIP & PARTICIPATION

	MEMBERSHIP LAST YR	PROFESSION OF FAITH	RESTORED BY AFFIRMATION	CORRECT BY ADDITION	RECVD FM OTHER UMC'S	RECVD FM NON-UMC	REMOVED BY CHARGE CONF	WITHDRAWN	CORRECT BY SUBTRACTION	TRANSFER TO OTHER UMC	TRANSFER TO NON-UMC	REMOVED BY DEATH	TOTAL PROFESSING MEMBERS	ASIAN	AFRICAN AMER/BLACK	HISPANIC/LATINO	NATIVE AMERICAN	PACIFIC ISLANDER	WHITE	Multi-Racial	FEMALE	MALE	AVG WORSHIP ATTENDANCE	BAPTIZED THIS YEAR (12 or Younger)	BAPTIZED THIS YEAR (13 or Older)	BAPTIZED NON-MEMBERS
CHURCH	1	2a	2b	2c	3	4	5a	5b	5c	6	7	8	9	9a	9b	9c	9d	9e	9f	9g	9h	9i	10	11a	11b	12
ALBION	8,348	127	11	17	47	20	124	54	61	48	7	174	8,102	18	66	6	7	0	7,993	12	4,990	3,112	5,517	72	68	811
HEARTLAND	8,061	142	6	4	49	13	116	34	41	42	28	165	7,849	16	15	22	12	2	7,771	11	4,778	3,071	6,101	75	59	862
GRAND RAPIDS	14,195	377	48	170	120	81	273	128	223	78	37	229	14,023	176	87	160	60	19	13,486	35	8,307	5,716	5,226	360	92	1,563
GRAND TRAVERSE	8,222	181	10	114	100	20	96	103	83	43	18	171	8,133	4	10	5	116	4	7,938	9	4,994	3,092	6,101	90	21	886
KALAMAZOO	11,271	245	17	95	93	26	241	156	80	75	25	196	10,974	29	53	26	9	6	10,816	35	6,713	4,261	5,517	134	77	1,394
LANSING	10,507	235	21	39	105	49	148	251	39	61	66	195	10,196	109	133	47	10	11	9,858	28	6,155	4,041	5,517	122	84	1,013
CONFERENCE	60,604	1,307	113	439	514	209	998	726	527	347	181	1,130	59,277	352	364	266	214	42	57,862	130	35,937	23,293	33,979	853	401	6,529
LAST YEAR	61,940	1,421	130	354	466	307	1,135	579	641	365	200	1,054	60,644	409	374	264	224	45	59,209	119	37,007	23,637	36,072	1,186	0	7,128
INCREASE(DECREASE)	(1,336)	(114)	(17)	85	48	(98)	(137)	147	(114)	(18)	(19)	76	(1,367)	(57)	(10)	2	(10)	(3)	(1,347)	11	(1,070)	(344)	(2,093)	(333)	401	(599)

2013 TABLE 1 MEMBERSHIP & PARTICIPATION	OTHER CONSTITUENTS	ENROLLED IN CONFIRMATION CLASS	CHILDREN IN CHRISTIAN FORMATION GROUPS	YOUTH IN CHRISTIAN FORMATION GROUPS	YOUNG ADULTS IN CHRISTIAN FORMATION	OTHER ADULTS IN CHRISTIAN FORMATION	TOTAL PERSONS IN CHRISTIAN FORMATION	AVG SUNDAY SCHOOL ATTENDANCE	VACATION BIBLE SCHOOL PARTICIPANTS	NUMBER OF SUNDAY SCHOOL CLASSES	NUMBER OF CLASSES OUTSIDE SUNDAY SCHOOL	SHORT TERM CLASSES	UM MEN MEMBERS	PAID TO UMM PROJECTS	UMW MEMBERS	PAID TO UMW LOCAL PROJECTS	VIM TEAMS SENT OUT	PERSONS IN VIM TEAMS	PERSONS IN MISSIONS	PERSONS SERVED IN DAYCARE AND/OR EDUCATION	PERSONS SERVED IN OUTREACH, JUSTICE, MERCY
CHURCH	13	14	15	16	17	18	19	20	21	22	23	24	25a	25b	26a	26b	27a	27b	28	29	30
ALBION	3,156	52	584	441	154	1,938	3,117	1,117	1,583	193	182	185	179	14,623	777	68,229	23	97	1,086	917	50,607
HEARTLAND	2,476	48	853	405	67	1,897	3,222	1,029	7,011	188	203	114	134	14,549	1,004	84,867	5	47	396	443	18,057
GRAND RAPIDS	6,461	199	2,366	1,429	413	5,055	9,263	2,426	2,986	312	391	267	218	15,883	1,512	89,814	10	79	2,010	1,773	72,206
GRAND TRAVERSE	3,916	45	684	410	107	1,871	3,072	779	1,653	126	133	112	199	9,917	1,197	68,785	9	55	690	488	11,445
KALAMAZOO	4,361	115	1,363	680	170	2,946	5,159	1,513	1,844	243	166	230	154	12,380	1,086	82,231	6	31	1,138	13,940	77,543
LANSING	4,828	129	1,422	984	297	2,389	5,092	1,570	1,778	194	180	131	164	8,442	957	73,759	12	98	1,128	891	16,435
CONFERENCE	25,198	588	7,272	4,349	1,208	16,096	28,925	8,434	16,855	1,256	1,255	1,039	1,048	75,794	6,533	467,685	65	407	6,448	18,452	246,293
LAST YEAR	26,092	660	7,653	4,437	1,155	15,563	28,808	9,317	12,607	1,294	1,123	1,007	1,095	75,286	6,802	499,407	48	399	2,525	10,309	258,157
INCREASE(DECREASE)	(894)	(72)	(381)	(88)	53	533	117	(883)	4,248	(38)	132	32	(47)	508	(269)	(31,722)	17	8	3,923	8,143	(11,864)

STATISTICAL INFO

Table II – Statistical Report *January 1, 2013 through December 31, 2013*

2013 TABLE 2 ASSETS & EXPENSES	LAND, BLDG & EQUIP	OTHER ASSETS	MORTGAGES	OTHER DEBTS	TOTAL APPORTIONED	MINISTRY SHARES PAID	DISTRICT APPORTIONEMENT	DISTRICT APPORTIONEMENT PAID	ADVANCE SPECIALS	WORLD SERVICE SPECIALS	YOUTH SERVICE FUND	CONFERENCE BENEVOLENCES	TOTAL CONFERENCE SPECIAL SUNDAYS	UMC CAUSES PAID DIRECTLY	NON-UMC CAUSES PAID DIRECTLY	HUMAN RELATIONS SUNDAY	ONE GREAT HOUR OF SHARING	PEACE W/ JUSTICE SUNDAY
Church	31	32	33	34	35a	35b	36a	36b	37	38	40	40b	42	43	44	45a	45b	45c
ALBION FIRST	1,547,000	500,000	0	0	26,592	26,592	2,537	2,537	5,026		20	102	273	0	0	129	276	
ATHENS	383,614	130,386	0	0	4,440	4,440	293	293	198		2			406	857			
AUGUSTA FELLOWSHIP	650,000	30,000	0	0	6,765	2,778	414	105	884		4			0	523			
BASELINE	1,690,000	158,243	0	0	11,423	11,423	544	544	1,330		2			1,284	3,141		293	94
BELLEVUE	2,200,000	153,043	0	0	10,561	10,561	1,131	1,131	2,210		0			0	457		223	
BIRCHWOOD	1,000,000	80,445	0	0	13,370	13,370	975	975	895		14	43	234	0	354	105	15	10
CHAPEL HILL	4,555,000	214,805	0	0	51,246	51,246	3,927	3,927	12,771		70	3,376		0	51,682	64	2,383	43
BATTLE CREEK CHRIST	200,000	100,000	0	0	20,012	7,456	1,080	396	50		0			1,253	23,274			
CONVIS UNION	1,825,000	0	0	0	11,519	11,519	561	561	760		14			0	5,711			30
DELTON FAITH	945,000	223,455	0	0	15,327	7,415	1,657	318	2,242		8			0	52,444			
BATTLE CREEK FIRST	4,842,000	15,000	127,000	0	28,756	28,756	2,209	2,209	1,270		30			1,000	0		50	
BATTLE CREEK MAPLE	2,892,000	53,160	23,589	0	12,873	12,873	837	837	1,538		0			732	2,550	74	192	151
SONOMA	345,000	19,200	0	0	4,436	3,884	371	312	778		4			0	768			
NEWTON	465,000	24,000	0	0	8,089	5,520	734	501	109		4	148	31	0	450			
BATTLE CREEK TRINITY	822,000	100,084	0	0	10,386	1,212	751	55	96		8			0	431	30	22	
WASHINGTON HEIGHTS	1,093,000	10,000	0	27,000	6,419	6,419	362	362			0	175		400	600			
BRONSON FIRST	2,083,750	12,000	0	0	10,657	10,657	794	794	1,761		0		167	2,147	1,704	121	519	
BURR OAK	300,000	2,500	0	0	4,887	4,887	414	414	525		0			0	709	0		
CAMDEN	590,000	0	0	0	3,865	1,301	164	164	284		0			0	0		14	
MONTGOMERY	540,000	20,000	0	0	2,788	3,281	250	293	455		0	(538)		0	954		20	
STOKES CHAPEL	360,000	35,208	0	0	3,833	3,833	155	155	302		0	(335)		186	728	70	85	
CENTER PARK	2,216,000	5,000	0	0	10,296	10,296	984	984	3,780		0			257	1,727		320	
CENTREVILLE	810,000	175,000	0	0	17,660	17,660	1,735	1,735	2,645		30			0	12,727	0	413	56
CLIMAX	1,041,854	145,266			14,050	14,050	915	915	2,032		0	152	75				100	12
SCOTTS	860,667	14,165			5,641	4,133	371	371	871		0	298	213			0	50	68
COLDWATER	6,171,000	645,770	0	0	34,211	34,211	3,305	3,305	4,226		4		132	0	10,190	20	50	40
COLON	700,000	142,453	0	0	9,469	9,469	570	570	789		12			0	0	0	140	46
CONCORD	1,945,000	45,533	360,290	0	20,021	12,443	1,519	946			161	1,670		12,157	16,908	93	99	
CONSTANTINE	1,130,000				10,777	10,739	1,320	1,316	833		0							20
FRONTIER	343,000	0	0	0	4,601	4,601	432	432	101		0			200	650	36		
OSSEO	310,000	0	0	0	2,978	2,978	173	173	40		0			210	840	30		
GALESBURG	380,000	238,397	0	0	9,883	9,883	1,208	1,208	614		0	114		0	1,009			
GIRARD	950,000	1,000,000	0	0	14,377	14,377	932	932			20	3		0	0	95	154	
GRASS LAKE	1,912,000	51,300	0	0	13,213	13,213	1,372	1,372			0			2,760	14,931			
HILLSDALE	5,155,039	10,222,727	0	0	15,858	15,861	1,476	1,476	9,902		12	1,000	660	2,500	18,536			
HILLSIDE	375,000	134,490	0	0	14,229	14,229	1,165	1,165	1,276		20	325	31	673	1,193		271	
HOMER	2,150,000	9,800	0	0	6,398	6,398	457	457	945		2	262	319	0	1,669		100	
LYON LAKE	1,200,000	97,800	0	0	6,126	6,126	388	388	1,920		0	590	283	0	1,040		85	25
BROOKSIDE	2,675,000	59,346	0	0	20,183	18,319	1,666	1,513	2,217		15	125	625	1,221	11,582	0	450	125
JACKSON CALVARY	5,000,000	218,410	0	8,200	23,447	3,112	1,303	1,303	2,348		0		374	0	4,436	0	388	
JACKSON FIRST	4,404,819	2,574,669	0	0	76,870	76,870	7,482	7,482	4,374		22			1,100	6,766	0	849	21
TRINITY JACKSON	1,910,000	72,041	0	0	11,789	11,789	941	941	397		24			0	9,174		308	

2013 TABLE 2 ASSETS & EXPENSES	LAND, BLDG & EQUIP	OTHER ASSETS	MORTGAGES	OTHER DEBTS	TOTAL APPORTIONED	MINISTRY SHARES PAID	DISTRICT APPORTIONEMENT	DISTRICT APPORTIONEMENT PAID	ADVANCE SPECIALS	WORLD SERVICE SPECIALS	YOUTH SERVICE FUND	CONFERENCE BENEVOLENCES	TOTAL CONFERENCE SPECIAL SUNDAYS	UMC CAUSES PAID DIRECTLY	NON-UMC CAUSES PAID DIRECTLY	HUMAN RELATIONS SUNDAY	ONE GREAT HOUR OF SHARING	PEACE W/ JUSTICE SUNDAY
Church	31	32	33	34	35a	35b	36a	36b	37	38	40	40b	42	43	44	45a	45b	45c
ZION JACKSON	250,000	19,488	0	15,672	2,693	2,693	147	147	655		14		30	0	1,919	10	117	10
JONESVILLE	1,000,000	0	0	0	11,747	1,811	1,225	187	562		9			0	9,396			
ALLEN	574,000	0	0	0	5,604	5,605	423	423	1,588		12			500	2,479			
LITCHFIELD	1,676,000	77,600	0	0	13,033	8,812	992	992	1,067		8		50	0	0	0	117	55
MARENGO	100,000				1,286	0	69	0			0							
MARSHALL	10,345,500	434,033	703,392	3,104	57,027	57,027	5,092	5,092	298		196		438	10,731	46,961	0	193	39
MENDON	999,999	55,000	0	0	10,812	10,812	1,010	1,010	753		8			0	16,360		6	
NAPOLEON	1,586,000	50,085	50,918	0	13,678	6,842	1,027	514	1,653		6			0	2,472	14		30
NORTH ADAMS	170,000	13,030	0	0	5,655	5,665	354	354	1,316		0			0	5,074	47	70	17
JEROME	89,000	28,824	0	0	4,016	4,016	302	302	2,202		4		53	0	1,030	0	102	39
NOTTAWA	40,000	0	0	0	1,130	1,130	104	104			4	70		0	408			
PARMA	513,300	11,525	0	0	2,980	2,980	181	181	45		0			1,487	0	46	83	
NORTH PARMA	500,000	74,462	0	0	8,879	8,879	734	734	1,308		56			0	5,063			
POPE	557,000				2,247	2,247	250	250	200		0		100			0	270	20
GRIFFITH	640,000	10,000	335,845	0	5,170	0	475	0	349		0	56		0	0	0	280	21
QUINCY	600,000	124,863	14,276	0	9,760	9,760	690	690	1,533		12			0	5,995		151	
READING	1,603,200	50,000	20,000	0	13,537	13,537	984	984	1,340		6			0	10,000		50	83
SOMERSET CENTER	450,000	440,418	0	0	6,245	5,791	492	456	310		0			0	0		45	
SPRINGPORT	450,000	37,000	0	0	6,212	6,212	449	449	908		6	316	184	2,921	6,505			
LEE CENTER	125,000	6,000	0	0	5,197	5,198	466	468	2,200		7	200		0	4,694		100	100
STURGIS	6,130,000	489,982	0	0	36,909	36,909	4,039	4,039	1,353		60			6,350	16,631	0	392	159
THREE RIVERS FIRST	3,435,000	0	0	21,619	14,877	531	1,812	65	151		0			0	1,001			
THREE RIVERS NINTH STREET	769,000	41,386	0	0	5,558	5,558	423	423	120		0	15		0	2,418	0	47	
UNION CITY	1,664,000	398,156	0	0	17,169	17,169	941	941	2,943		0	654	285	0	904	0	514	15
WEST MENDON	1,015,000	0	0	0	10,611	10,611	932	932	1,727		0			0	0	16		
SCHOOLCRAFT PLEASANT VALLEY	642,000	20,259	0	0	7,473	7,473	604	604	1,708		12		544	413	2,498			
WHITE PIGEON	1,627,336	22,966	0	0	4,633	4,633	509	509			4			0	1,022			
ALBION DISTRICT	108,519,078	20,138,773	1,635,310	75,595	894,459	782,081	74,600	66,717	99,083	0	926	8,821	5,101	50,888	403,545	1,000	10,406	1,329
LAST YEAR	99,487,781	19,406,503	1,865,315	43,756	887,496	757,194	48,896	43,611	106,672	0	2,164	9,635	6,429	33,657	359,542	2,377	10,642	1,875
INC/(DEC)	9,031,297	732,270	(230,005)	31,839	6,963	24,887	25,704	23,106	(7,589)	0	(1,238)	(814)	(1,328)	17,231	44,003	(1,377)	(236)	(546)

2013 TABLE 2 ASSETS & EXPENSES	NATIVE AMERICAN MINISTRIES SUNDAY	WORLD COMMUNION SUNDAY	UM STUDENT SUNDAY	CLERGY PENSION	CLERGY HEALTH CARE	PASTOR COMPENSATION	ASSOCIATE PASTOR COMPENSATION	CLERGY HOUSING	ACOUNTABLE REIMBURSEMENTS	NON-ACCOUNTABLE REIMBURSEMENTS	DEACONS SALARY & BENEFITS	DIACONAL MINISTERS SALARY & BENEFITS	OTHER LAY STAFF SALARY & BENEFITS	PROGRAM EXPENSES	OPERATING EXPENSES	LOAN PAYMENTS	CAPITAL IMPROVEMENTS	TOTAL EXPENSES COL 35b + 36b THRU 59
Church	45d	45e	45f	46	47	48	49	50	51	52	53	54	55	56	57	58	59	60
ALBION FIRST	10	203		0	0	49,676	0	4,642	2,051	0	0	0	52,314	6,686	58,815	172,840	14,792	396,984
ATHENS				0	2,457	6,483	0	1,900	2,087	0	0	0	0	2,764	14,848	0	0	36,735
AUGUSTA FELLOWSHIP				1,357	2,063	15,048	0	4,182	310	0	0	0	3,841	743	11,399	0	718	43,955
BASELINE	319	111	14	4,416	1,500	23,484	0	1,766	2,406	3,800	0	0	14,448	8,331	15,532	0	2,359	96,597
BELLEVUE	94	139		4,416	1,500	23,484	0	1,766	2,406	3,800	0	0	14,697	4,363	18,560	0	4,168	93,975
BIRCHWOOD	35			2,648	1,500	21,000	0	1,925	0	0	0	0	14,908	1,052	17,686	0	11,748	88,517
CHAPEL HILL	143	131	76	10,325	20,003	49,371	0	14,461	408	0	0	0	121,623	45,405	52,615	0	175,015	615,138
BATTLE CREEK CHRIST				6,540	16,782	43,598	0	6,644	0	0	0	0	12,845	2,442	37,971	0	0	159,251
CONVIS UNION		84		7,198	6,600	38,389	0	0	2,281	0	0	0	3,672	1,725	14,082	0	17,369	109,995
DELTON FAITH				7,241	17,378	38,616	0	4,815	2,318	0	0	0	12,782	2,993	29,300	0	9,987	187,857
BATTLE CREEK FIRST		140		7,000	0	28,343	0	6,064	3,000	0	0	0	88,965	1	57,502	0	0	224,330
BATTLE CREEK MAPLE	199	123	56	0	375	10,580	0	9,136	0	2,040	0	0	20,333	2,730	34,729	22,000	3,722	124,970
SONOMA				1,716	5,766	6,221	0	1,926	629	0	0	0	0	2,235	19,941	0	0	44,180
NEWTON				2,270	8,966	17,601	0	3,419	1,850	0	0	0	2,510	3,110	17,500	0	2,550	66,539
BATTLE CREEK TRINITY			3	2,648	1,500	21,000	0	0	0	0	0	0	10,032	1,974	15,642	0	6,982	61,635
WASHINGTON HEIGHTS				0	600	10,000	0	7,000	4,900	0	0	0	13,700	600	25,000	3,000	48,000	120,756
BRONSON FIRST	182	143		5,403	18,105	25,152	0	4,284	572	0	0	0	15,346	3,555	18,632	0	87,803	197,047
BURR OAK		58		0	3,000	8,100	0	1,480	855	0	0	0	1,741	824	10,329	0	2,087	35,009
CAMDEN		10		0	3,250	7,640	0	0	0	0	0	0	0	480	21,032	0	0	34,175
MONTGOMERY				851	1,190	9,627	0	2,928	1,333	0	0	0	0	177	5,298	0	0	25,869
STOKES CHAPEL				743	2,990	8,956	0	2,258	1,914	0	0	0	0	481	8,949	0	78,265	109,580
CENTER PARK				0	0	6,260	0	12,000	1,382	0	0	0	11,493	2,407	32,058	0	10,880	93,844
CENTREVILLE	65	67	40	6,553	16,128	43,686	0	1,000	0	1,000	0	0	30,338	10,196	69,446	0	28,323	242,108
CLIMAX	178		40			29,200												46,754
SCOTTS	85	66	40			17,150												23,345
COLDWATER	20	165	50	11,246	16,128	60,230	0	7,878	5,553	0	0	0	45,136	23,949	64,021	0	0	286,554
COLON	27	128	82	5,562	7,428	18,900	0	0	0	0	0	0	9,979	4,574	18,305	0	19,500	95,511
CONCORD	156			8,218	12,873	43,000	0	3,449	1,149	0	0	0	49,977	21,924	23,013	40,277	0	248,513
CONSTANTINE		47				30,582												43,537
FRONTIER	30			1,591	188	3,060	0	10,200	1,505	0	0	0	0	2,393	11,421	0	0	36,408
OSSEO				796	0	1,530	0	5,100	900	0	0	0	950	130	7,641	0	0	21,318
GALESBURG	69	72		0	750	18,750	0	6,250	360	0	0	0	29,061	2,098	27,830	0	49,810	147,878
GIRARD		33		7,072	16,128	37,277	0	3,262	1,722	0	0	0	18,653	3,876	19,132	0	0	122,736
GRASS LAKE				0	7,791	12,000	0	4,405	11,463	0	0	0	15,585	60	28,866	0	13,015	125,461
HILLSDALE			100	14,605	4,500	45,630	0	5,000	11,263	0	0	0	160,639	26,774	152,391	0	17,039	487,888
HILLSIDE		20		5,982	13,096	31,904	0	6,279	1,975	0	0	0	31,606	3,761	23,343	0	1,587	138,736
HOMER		90	35	716	1,725	13,000	0	2,658	0	5,417	0	0	5,662	2,892	16,594	9,470	5,689	74,100
LYON LAKE	55	40	41	716	1,725	13,000	0	2,658	5,417	0	0	0	1,997	1,495	12,560	0	5,895	56,056
BROOKSIDE	125		125	8,777	12,361	44,960	0	4,845	1,560	0	0	0	36,939	3,591	72,139	0	0	221,614
JACKSON CALVARY		35		8,176	17,128	43,607	0	5,111	1,016	0	0	0	54,292	593	53,850	0	0	195,769
JACKSON FIRST	67	70	20	19,139	23,452	60,000	39,938	13,395	5,825	4,500	0	0	245,407	15,309	137,597	0	7,831	670,034
TRINITY JACKSON		80		12,845	6,184	14,300	0	4,147	1,116	0	0	0	11,003	100	29,874	0	0	102,282

2013 TABLE 2 ASSETS & EXPENSES	NATIVE AMERICAN MINISTRIES SUNDAY	WORLD COMMUNION SUNDAY	UM STUDENT SUNDAY	CLERGY PENSION	CLERGY HEALTH CARE	PASTOR COMPENSATION	ASSOCIATE PASTOR COMPENSATION	CLERGY HOUSING	ACOUNTABLE REIMBURSEMENTS	NON-ACCOUNTABLE REIMBURSEMENTS	DEACONS SALARY & BENEFITS	DIACONAL MINISTERS SALARY & BENEFITS	OTHER LAY STAFF SALARY & BENEFITS	PROGRAM EXPENSES	OPERATING EXPENSES	LOAN PAYMENTS	CAPITAL IMPROVEMENTS	TOTAL EXPENSES COL 35b + 36b THRU 59
Church	45d	45e	45f	46	47	48	49	50	51	52	53	54	55	56	57	58	59	60
ZION JACKSON	50	50	10	0	0	7,540	0	0	0	0	0	0	0	865	12,815	2,483	24,470	53,878
JONESVILLE				5,212	10,752	25,045	0	9,999	3,624	0	0	0	15,415	2,791	17,840	0	850	103,493
ALLEN				2,606	5,376	12,523	0	5,000	1,812	0	0	0	4,682	270	10,152	0	7,642	60,670
LITCHFIELD	9	110	57	4,355	6,423	20,101	0	2,036	3,470	0	0	0	18,745	4,340	21,466	0	0	92,213
MARENGO																		0
MARSHALL		67	126	10,384	10,314	55,380	0	4,138	4,490	0	0	0	184,868	84,061	102,054	73,554	11,083	661,494
MENDON	110	10		1,665	3,261	13,880	0	1,805	7,166	0	0	0	21,763	2,291	21,530	0	12,674	115,104
NAPOLEON	33	39		5,132	9,191	37,271	0	0	2,222	0	0	0	4,610	5,619	18,993	14,833	5,380	114,854
NORTH ADAMS	17			0	375	7,800	0	3,000	115	0	0	0	0	720	10,608	9,873	7,585	52,636
JEROME	50			0	375	7,800	0	3,064	0	0	0	0	0	1,177	5,662	0	1,947	27,823
NOTTAWA				0	0	4,800	0	0	0	0	0	0	0	250	1,834	0	6,190	14,790
PARMA		27		480	480	3,200	0	747	362	0	0	0	0	454	8,333	0	0	18,905
NORTH PARMA				4,316	9,288	21,997	0	9,557	95	0	0	0	2,600	5,151	7,304	0	73,021	149,369
POPE	20	20	20			8,484												11,631
GRIFFITH	23	39		0	0	10,980	0	0	0	0	0	0	1,500	2,781	31,031	32,376	0	79,436
QUINCY				4,337	6,441	25,363	0	2,508	2,355	200	0	0	21,020	15,022	19,145	3,380	7,101	125,013
READING				7,367	9,333	42,750	0	4,506	3,282	0	0	0	11,172	3,266	15,547	12,335	2,000	137,558
SOMERSET CENTER	20		5	0	4,032	10,634	0	1,716	50	400	0	0	4,536	1	21,261	0	4,390	53,647
SPRINGPORT				8,843	8,843	16,126	0	2,206	1,018	0	0	0	2,600	217	11,773	0	818	69,945
LEE CENTER	100	100		1,064	0	7,000	0	0	441	0	0	0	0	900	3,959	0	0	26,531
STURGIS	334	380	262	12,065	17,459	64,561	0	5,014	3,185	0	0	0	75,925	52,866	208,233	0	68,600	574,777
THREE RIVERS FIRST				10,883	17,050	37,738	0	4,168	2,893	0	0	0	19,999	13,569	30,203	0	9,126	147,377
THREE RIVERS NINTH STREET		51		2,757	8,064	17,698	0	2,532	0	0	0	0	2,517	396	9,538	0	0	52,134
UNION CITY	114	10	43	6,934	8,615	38,448	0	2,348	2,715	0	0	0	17,419	3,140	17,387	0	12,243	132,841
WEST MENDON	26		20	0	0	23,175	0	0	10,750	0	0	0	14,070	5,000	34,000	0	0	100,327
SCHOOLCRAFT PLEASANT VALLEY				3,374	7,763	17,699	0	2,566	1,320	0	0	0	4,680	300	5,923	0	1,314	58,191
WHITE PIGEON				2,328	4,838	12,161	0	871	539	0	0	0	0	2,507	13,336	0	42,259	85,007
ALBION DISTRICT	2,765	2,958	1,265	270,868	421,383	1,600,549	39,938	246,014	133,430	21,157	0	0	1,590,595	426,747	1,965,370	396,421	923,827	9,473,184
LAST YEAR	2,201	2,688	1,307	282,604	447,206	1,644,521	41,440	273,935	128,839	17,286	18,450	0	1,556,626	372,007	1,954,192	286,941	681,708	9,200,945
INC/(DEC)	564	270	(42)	(11,736)	(25,823)	(43,972)	(1,502)	(27,921)	4,591	3,871	(18,450)	0	33,969	54,740	11,178	109,480	242,119	272,239

STATISTICAL INFO

STATISTICAL INFO

2013 TABLE 2 ASSETS & EXPENSES	LAND, BLDG & EQUIP	OTHER ASSETS	MORTGAGES	OTHER DEBTS	TOTAL APPORTIONED	MINISTRY SHARES PAID	DISTRICT APPORTIONEMENT	DISTRICT APPORTIONEMENT PAID	ADVANCE SPECIALS	WORLD SERVICE SPECIALS	YOUTH SERVICE FUND	CONFERENCE BENEVOLENCES	TOTAL CONFERENCE SPECIAL SUNDAYS	UMC CAUSES PAID DIRECTLY	NON-UMC CAUSES PAID DIRECTLY	HUMAN RELATIONS SUNDAY	ONE GREAT HOUR OF SHARING	PEACE W/ JUSTICE SUNDAY
Church	31	32	33	34	35a	35b	36a	36b	37	38	40	40b	42	43	44	45a	45b	45c
ALTO	1 200 000	70 000	351 500	0	6 497	6 497	891	891	1 239		2	252		0	5 770		40	
BOWNE CENTER	730 000	169 000	46 836	0	6 223	6 223	1 112	1 112	3 136		0	10		0	950			
BYRON CENTER	985 000	166 393	223 843	0	22 722	22 722	2 327	2 327	603		24	461		138	2 553			
CALEDONIA	700 000	370 000	0	0	22 225	22 369	2 444	2 460	2 951		16	200		0	2 879		90	
CARLISLE	850 000	90 000	58 243	0	16 334	9 072	1 552	864	877		0	663	25	2 351	3 191	15	20	15
CEDAR SPRINGS	3 167 000	86 331	0	0	23 511	23 511	2 120	2 120	13 794		40	134	786	0	27 181	0	643	107
EAST NELSON	807 000	0	0	0	11 374	11 374	1 176	1 176	1 551		10	40	20	0	4 287	0	175	75
COOPERSVILLE	470 000	75 000	351 593	0	16 490	16 491	1 798	1 798	947		4			1 021	1 258		245	
COURTLAND-OAKFIELD	650 000	0	101 673	0	11 658	11 658	1 047	1 047	5 165		6	1 000	1 500	0	4 167	0	131	43
FREMONT	3 827 201	0	0	0	40 910	31 216	5 715	4 362	6 639		47	983	100	0	4 726		185	
GEORGETOWN	3 000 000	281 648	0	0	63 569	63 569	9 920	9 920	14 291		110	9 200	2 300	0	12 960	0	135	15
GRAND HAVEN CHURCH OF THE DUNES	5 275 500	687 000	276 298	10 000	62 038	62 038	8 560	8 560	20 893		36	1 800		500	10 221		1 192	
ALDERSGATE	1 895 000	120 868	0	0	26 698	26 698	3 418	3 418	2 671		30	2 660	117	0	0	0	476	303
SOUTH WYOMING	1 750 000	73 177	0	0	11 199	4 023	1 831	1 971	219		0			1 963	3 484		157	
CORNERSTONE	13 310 888	1 327 324	4 101 324	61 407	206 003	206 003	25 499	25 499	25 855		1 074	10 000		153 000	140 978	0	305	573
FAITH GRAND RAPIDS	2 900 000	240 000	0	0	25 859	25 859	4 521	4 521	1 395		0	1 105		0	0	0	100	20
FIRST GRAND RAPIDS	31 498 005	4 705 008	30 000	0	151 630	152 130	17 971	17 971	13 904		196	1 500	4 000	3 200	61 419	0	500	500
GENESIS	2 700 000	0	1 137 323	0	30 415	30 415	3 680	3 680	921		0	32		0	16 808		100	
LA NUEVA ESPERANZA	0	0	0	0	3 776	0	1 663	0			0			0	0			
NORTHLAWN	2 500 000	0	440 000	0	24 143	24 292	3 811	3 834	632		0			0	0			
PLAINFIELD	3 450 000	110 304	0	0	9 984	4 160	1 233	515	180		1			0	25			
SAINT PAULS GRAND RAPIDS	1 325 000	433 710	0	0	30 259	30 259	5 045	5 045	4 161		30	2 367	88	395	2 012	0	578	
SOUTH GRAND RAPIDS	1 170 241	33 157	0	0	17 906	17 906	2 315	2 315	464		20			0	11 333	0	715	77
TRINITY GRAND RAPIDS	5 730 000	460 615	0	0	74 117	74 117	10 555	10 555	5 794	250	244			25 238	1 612		2 033	150
VIETNAMESE GRAND RAPIDS	200 000	90 000	0	0	2 688	3 099	2 242	2 585	1 286		18			1 200	750			
GRANDVILLE	4 000 000	0	0	0	39 057	39 057	5 305	5 305	7 236		8	7 697		500	3 231		862	
HESPERIA	387 200	170 000	0	0	8 536	8 536	1 137	1 137	376		6		70	2 327	3 643		321	
FERRY	154 000	0	0	0	6 100	6 100	594	594	728		0		213	0	9 808		78	
HOLLAND	9 940 000	920 000	0	7 384	69 546	69 546	8 780	8 780	7 408		62	2 844		11 032	5 829		2 168	472
HOLTON	2 001 438	7 370	0	0	24 750	24 750	3 437	3 437	1 983		40	400		1 000	1 200	0	603	80
KENT CITY CHAPEL HILL	1 385 000	0	0	0	13 880	13 878	1 500	1 500	312		0			0	3 220			
LEIGHTON	3 936 550	198 325	0	0	26 965	18 848	1 953	1 953	565		60			0	11 485			
LOWELL	4 310 000	103 254	0	0	37 231	26 460	4 435	1 152	7 706		0	600		0	1 850	0	385	176
MARNE	640 000	43 000	0	0	14 528	11 103	930	710	463	94	12			0	0		124	
MARTIN	1 100 000	125 000	0	0	16 930	16 930	2 211	2 211	1 242		10		354	383	9 765	0	190	86
SHELBYVILLE	575 000	37 000	0	0	6 911	6 911	724	724	574		20		87	0	692	0	94	38
MIDDLEVILLE	1 125 000	136 824	632 430	0	19 432	19 432	2 883	2 883	1 676		14	200	200	0	13 487			
PARMELEE	196 900	42 239	0	0	5 254	5 254	685	685	370		0			0	0			
MONTAGUE	3 704 000	41 662	0	0	25 786	26 206	5 214	5 248	2 207		46	767	1 076	0	1 495	0	210	178
CENTRAL MUSKEGON	875 049	2 567 600	0	0	51 409	51 409	5 484	5 484	11 054		24	1 745	248	0	9 812		316	
CRESTWOOD	2 300 000	144 001	112 863	0	10 489	2 196	2 421	776	169	2	1			2 013	300			
LAKE HARBOR	3 186 000	166 407	175 931	0	36 073	36 073	6 941	6 941	2 090		40			0	5 373	0	225	96

2013 TABLE 2 ASSETS & EXPENSES	LAND, BLDG & EQUIP	OTHER ASSETS	MORTGAGES	OTHER DEBTS	TOTAL APPORTIONED	MINISTRY SHARES PAID	DISTRICT APPORTIONEMENT	DISTRICT APPORTIONEMENT PAID	ADVANCE SPECIALS	WORLD SERVICE SPECIALS	YOUTH SERVICE FUND	CONFERENCE BENEVOLENCES	TOTAL CONFERENCE SPECIAL SUNDAYS	UMC CAUSES PAID DIRECTLY	NON-UMC CAUSES PAID DIRECTLY	HUMAN RELATIONS SUNDAY	ONE GREAT HOUR OF SHARING	PEACE W/ JUSTICE SUNDAY
Church	31	32	33	34	35a	35b	36a	36b	37	38	40	40b	42	43	44	45a	45b	45c
LAKESIDE	1,847,000	50,000	0	0	15,487	5,092	2,455	1,424	2,316	0	2	2		0	5,168			
UNITY	501,200	6,750			4,932	4,932	610	610	577		0						34	
WOLF LAKE	1,175,000	0	0	0	12,497	6,976	2,098	1,171			0			0	3,808			
MUSKEGON HEIGHTS TEMPLE	366,500	90,717	0	0	26,306	23,499	2,303	2,058	956		0			0	15,453	0	158	
NEWAYGO	1,063,403	122,220	0	0	14,089	14,089	1,215	1,215	570		0	0	166	0	0	0	88	61
NORTH MUSKEGON COMMUNITY	1,003,000	32,400	0	0	31,816	31,816	6,061	6,061	7,734		60	500	289	5,294	7,109	0	81	
RAVENNA	110,000	5,000	0	0	12,696	11,236	1,525	1,349	1,153		21	363	145	983	3,546		263	144
ROCKFORD	5,535,000	98,091	1,082,963	0	79,014	53,793	7,538	6,122	5,770		119	3,740	841	40,581	11,120	0	232	
SALEM INDIAN MISSION	244,000	1,039	0	0	1,258	1,258	543	543	5		20			0	198			
BRADLEY INDIAN MISSION	364,000	0	0	0	2,285	2,285	363	363			0	408		0	0			
SAUGATUCK	455,000	129,646	0	0	6,430	6,430	699	699	2,510		0			0	2,000	0	250	100
SHELBY	1,740,000	2,000	178,441	0	13,681	7,727	1,602	1,072	1,516		26	1,709	108	500	10,700	0	338	115
SNOW	450,000	0	0	0	7,576	5,104	1,121	755	575		0	40	80	0	250	0	226	40
SPARTA	1,200,000	187,385	0	0	39,987	39,987	3,336	3,336	2,699		142		346	51	10,638	0	145	35
TWIN LAKE	925,000	60,141			10,132	5,298	1,304	682	1,500		7							
SITKA	421,300	5,600	0	0	1,853	1,853	355	355			8			0	0			
VALLEY CHURCH ALLENDALE NEW CHURC	160,000	50,000	127,916	0	0	10,000								0	0			
VERGENNES	382,329	77,537	0	0	28,421	28,421	1,641	1,641	3,578		22			0	16,113			
WAYLAND	2,488,561	0	0	0	16,293	13,033	1,887	1,510	1,319		34	169		0	886			
WHITE CLOUD	2,664,000	163,000	51,136	0	22,550	20,622	1,862	1,703	848		40	425	125	0	0		372	
WHITEHALL	1,670,000	15,000	0	0	10,769	10,769	1,354	1,354			14			0	0			
CLAYBANKS	747,000	35,769	0	0	4,975	4,975	982	982	50		6			0	721		7	
WESLEY PARK	4,125,000	117,447	854,934	0	58,656	58,656	6,837	6,837	3,373		66	121	100	0	10,068	0	340	130
WYOMING PARK	3,000,000	31,000	457,162	0	21,400	2,761	2,746	2,746	8,194		12	1,843		0	55	65	147	42
CROSSWIND COMMUNITY	400,000	7,996	360,674	0	9,732	9,732	621	621			24	300		0	1,355			
GRAND RAPIDS DISTRICT	162,944,265	15,580,955	11,153,083	78,791	1,783,940	1,648,734	228,138	213,275	220,970	346	2,874	56,280	13,384	253,670	498,942	80	16,077	3,671
LAST YEAR	159,851,185	14,325,076	11,817,289	234,589	1,661,625	1,563,043	227,235	217,097	239,452	2,228	4,242	146,098	15,993	153,902	529,087	3,203	16,139	4,916
INC/(DEC)	3,093,080	1,255,879	(664,206)	(155,798)	122,315	85,691	903	(3,822)	(18,482)	(1,882)	(1,368)	(89,818)	(2,609)	99,768	(30,145)	(3,123)	(62)	(1,245)

STATISTICAL INFO

2013 TABLE 2 ASSETS & EXPENSES	NATIVE AMERICAN MINISTRIES SUNDAY	WORLD COMMUNION SUNDAY	UM STUDENT SUNDAY	CLERGY PENSION	CLERGY HEALTH CARE	PASTOR COMPENSATION	ASSOCIATE PASTOR COMPENSATION	CLERGY HOUSING	ACOUNTABLE REIMBURSEMENTS	NON-ACCOUNTABLE REIMBURSEMENTS	DEACONS SALARY & BENEFITS	DIACONAL MINISTERS SALARY & BENEFITS	OTHER LAY STAFF SALARY & BENEFITS	PROGRAM EXPENSES	OPERATING EXPENSES	LOAN PAYMENTS	CAPITAL IMPROVEMENTS	TOTAL EXPENSES COL 35b + 36b THRU 59
Church	45d	45e	45f	46	47	48	49	50	51	52	53	54	55	56	57	58	59	60
ALTO				0	1,875	17,340	0	6,450	0	0	0	0	1,782	2,234	21,300	44,280	12,341	122,293
BOWNE CENTER				0	2,000	17,340	0	6,450	0	0	0	0	5,944	1,131	9,328	16,235	347	70,206
BYRON CENTER				7,112	17,628	38,000	0	5,149	760	0	0	0	20,965	4,367	46,586	50,083	8,406	227,884
CALEDONIA	12	58	15	8,906	16,128	47,500	0	0	4,188	0	0	0	46,898	6,972	36,365	0	14,724	212,731
CARLISLE	15	20	15	3,390	16,878	2,447	0	25,000	2,389	0	0	0	22,072	2,008	36,646	7,500	0	135,473
CEDAR SPRINGS	175	92	73	8,822	4,500	47,048	0	9,835	2,683	0	0	0	29,511	9,816	45,831	0	12,411	239,113
EAST NELSON	30			0	0	19,946	0	0	3,882	0	0	0	20,386	8,572	32,379	0	0	103,903
COOPERSVILLE				10,091	14,909	38,203	0	4,469	424	0	0	0	16,835	4,197	21,084	34,934	0	166,910
COURTLAND-OAKFIELD	78	33	34	0	0	28,380	0	0	1,364	0	0	0	15,830	9,978	26,223	22,721	13,329	142,687
FREMONT		45		6,104	16,128	46,801	0	9,536	2,676	0	0	0	102,651	11,275	56,020	0	17,062	315,556
GEORGETOWN	20	130	62	13,388	16,128	62,253	0	17,000	4,077	0	0	0	211,438	22,444	70,642	0	88,539	618,621
GRAND HAVEN CHURCH OF THE DUNES				11,663	20,531	62,200	0	4,207	4,814	0	0	0	167,223	33,980	120,762	172,636	4,300	707,556
ALDERSGATE	75	145	25	10,350	7,120	48,375	0	11,250	2,557	0	0	0	42,103	3,644	50,932	0	0	212,949
SOUTH WYOMING				5,160	16,128	23,000	0	20,000	1,342	0	0	0	10,375	410	22,465	0	0	110,697
CORNERSTONE	356	505	310	41,532	22,031	94,013	77,866	47,193	11,647	0	0	0	1,020,226	172,470	773,620	436,869	981,653	4,243,578
FAITH GRAND RAPIDS		10		9,128	16,128	48,683	0	2,773	4,733	0	0	0	42,216	3,357	41,738	0	0	201,766
FIRST GRAND RAPIDS	500	1,000	500	29,491	15,910	92,251	39,861	44,500	13,195	7,147	0	0	645,825	73,083	257,540	0	93,247	1,569,370
GENESIS				12,240	3,000	49,600	0	22,000	1,508	5,273	0	0	80,320	10,210	68,773	109,892	7,100	421,872
LA NUEVA ESPERANZA				0	15,480	10,800	0	7,159	0	0	0	0	0	2,560	21,395	0	0	57,394
NORTHLAWN				10,835	11,904	42,500	0	3,980	5,935	0	0	0	28,066	5,700	25,000	129,579	9,600	301,857
PLAINFIELD				603	750	7,997	0	1,413	352	0	0	0	9,719	1,849	19,326	0	0	46,890
SAINT PAULS GRAND RAPIDS	88			7,015	10,926	35,052	0	12,000	3,686	0	0	0	61,321	5,415	34,557	0	14,426	229,421
SOUTH GRAND RAPIDS		82		7,875	4,500	42,000	0	11,877	3,682	0	0	0	30,936	24,352	28,493	0	0	186,627
TRINITY GRAND RAPIDS				13,602	17,628	58,350	12,731	24,750	11,624	0	0	0	196,039	34,413	128,953	0	3,612	621,695
VIETNAMESE GRAND RAPIDS				8,629	16,128	33,536	0	14,000	1,800	0	0	0	0	22,000	15,700	0	0	120,731
GRANDVILLE				9,635	11,064	53,734	0	11,022	3,680	0	0	0	85,919	3,239	71,678	0	0	313,867
HESPERIA	131	126		4,343	11,282	23,165	0	3,967	811	0	0	0	8,491	1,683	12,743	0	0	83,158
FERRY	200	0		2,443	6,347	13,030	0	1,507	456	0	0	0	5,188	1,160	8,799	0	340	56,991
HOLLAND	342	435		12,004	9,537	69,974	0	10,500	5,924	0	0	3,665	210,050	21,091	136,689	33,612	5,578	627,542
HOLTON	196	80		8,636	17,628	50,177	0	3,743	4,500	0	0	0	32,738	17,608	49,783	0	11,428	230,010
KENT CITY CHAPEL HILL				7,850	16,128	33,868	0	0	3,556	0	0	0	18,697	4,046	19,189	0	18,992	141,236
LEIGHTON				12,489	16,128	60,906	0	0	2,823	0	0	0	37,085	13,813	55,567	0	10,912	242,634
LOWELL	152	254		13,799	15,628	56,485	0	5,518	0	0	0	0	84,972	14,824	57,862	10,065	18,128	316,016
MARNE		25		7,016	3,000	37,422	0	3,430	1,583	1,433	0	0	27,192	2,500	21,228	0	78,209	195,544
MARTIN	129	40	99	4,777	12,165	22,961	0	4,980	2,580	0	0	0	22,955	3,098	24,609	0	4,439	134,003
SHELBYVILLE	10	17		0	5,224	9,840	0	1,776	0	0	0	0	8,101	3,418	6,404	0	3,586	47,516
MIDDLEVILLE				5,175	11,037	24,102	0	10,400	4,580	0	0	0	31,051	5,374	33,147	74,439	8,816	246,013
PARMELEE				0	0	18,200	0	0	0	0	0	0	0	1,527	11,204	0	0	37,240
MONTAGUE	263	390	286	10,850	16,963	58,120	0	7,130	6,319	0	0	0	35,988	2,033	43,962	0	7,851	227,588
CENTRAL MUSKEGON	340	477	185	12,653	18,359	47,750	0	4,801	4,820	2,806	12,985	0	131,737	18,454	99,295	74,987	32,140	541,881
CRESTWOOD				0	10,529	18,924	0	4,745	2,168	0	0	0	7,765	1,283	22,586	1,258	18,000	92,715
LAKE HARBOR	381	152	278	11,284	19,004	60,180	0	6,478	507	0	0	0	68,000	5,410	35,888	28,765	35,751	322,916

2013 TABLE 2 ASSETS & EXPENSES	NATIVE AMERICAN MINISTRIES SUNDAY	WORLD COMMUNION SUNDAY	UM STUDENT SUNDAY	CLERGY PENSION	CLERGY HEALTH CARE	PASTOR COMPENSATION	ASSOCIATE PASTOR COMPENSATION	CLERGY HOUSING	ACOUNTABLE REIMBURSEMENTS	NON-ACCOUNTABLE REIMBURSEMENTS	DEACONS SALARY & BENEFITS	DIACONAL MINISTERS , SALARY & BENEFITS	OTHER LAY STAFF SALARY & BENEFITS	PROGRAM EXPENSES	OPERATING EXPENSES	LOAN PAYMENTS	CAPITAL IMPROVEMENTS	TOTAL EXPENSES COL 35b + 36b THRU 59
Church	45d	45e	45f	46	47	48	49	50	51	52	53	54	55	56	57	58	59	60
LAKESIDE				5,322	10,577	28,385	0	3,168	4,231	0	0	0	45,310	3,862	30,599	0	5,209	150,667
UNITY						12,180												18,333
WOLF LAKE				5,880	2,500	21,125	0	1,114	1,962	0	0	0	22,642	7,101	45,536	0	3,660	123,475
MUSKEGON HEIGHTS TEMPLE	250		75	8,625	17,218	46,000	0	8,660	2,957	0	0	0	56,392	6,583	37,881	0	6,616	233,381
NEWAYGO	70	71	150	273	1,125	35,000	0	0	0	0	0	0	23,888	1,966	43,062	0	0	121,794
NORTH MUSKEGON COMMUNITY	191	82	202	12,735	18,869	59,921	0	7,172	0	5,680	0	0	49,104	8,675	41,706	3,225	0	266,506
RAVENNA	206	143		6,343	14,066	33,786	0	4,810	2,897	0	0	0	9,006	4,649	17,246	0	14,657	127,012
ROCKFORD	388	387	357	14,201	19,715	72,746	0	21,400	3,814	0	0	0	204,329	22,884	93,557	62,829	0	638,925
SALEM INDIAN MISSION				0	187	6,000	0	300	0	806	0	0	1,300	852	7,389	0	0	18,858
BRADLEY INDIAN MISSION				0	0	6,000	0	0	0	0	0	0	0	50	4,684	0	0	13,790
SAUGATUCK	100	100		0	0	18,100	0	17,800	467	0	0	0	9,486	7,687	9,932	0	0	75,661
SHELBY		91		0	4,060	33,850	0	5,237	4,035	0	0	0	21,279	1,565	23,236	38,205	18,077	173,446
SNOW	40			2,678	5,645	12,600	0	5,250	1,645	0	0	0	5,487	510	15,606	0	0	56,531
SPARTA	40	97	27	28,410	21,531	64,500	0	10,873	1,624	0	0	0	108,196	59,702	52,030	0	14,570	418,979
TWIN LAKE						10,000												17,487
SITKA				0	375	7,760	0	0	0	0	0	0	0	2,925	5,453	0	0	18,729
VALLEY CHURCH ALLENDALE NEW CHURC				0	0	45,000	0	0	0	0	0	0	0	0	0	0	0	55,000
VERGENNES				9,383	16,128	41,938	0	20,808	2,796	0	0	0	55,065	6,953	22,039	0	10,275	235,160
WAYLAND				7,735	156,280	42,370	0	4,161	3,060	0	0	0	18,361	7,007	15,983	0	0	271,908
WHITE CLOUD	221	85	20	7,425	17,902	35,326	0	4,855	856	2,500	0	0	15,525	14,013	38,353	18,635	0	179,851
WHITEHALL				4,211	11,612	20,755	0	3,483	0	0	0	0	12,738	1,441	19,262	0	0	85,639
CLAYBANKS				2,693	6,875	14,404	0	2,155	34	0	0	0	0	4,044	13,049	0	2,294	52,289
WESLEY PARK	205	100	129	10,314	18,332	55,280	0	18,540	1,487	0	0	0	127,038	11,516	57,583	125,731	28,653	534,599
WYOMING PARK		14		6,419	9,270	33,203	0	10,000	2,465	0	0	0	26,032	2,459	32,075	66,437	3,000	207,239
CROSSWIND COMMUNITY				11,895	16,128	54,802	0	24,500	2,741	0	0	0	29,015	12,420	19,445	34,361	0	217,339
GRAND RAPIDS DISTRICT	5,204	5,286	2,842	493,432	852,756	2,483,484	130,458	565,274	170,696	25,645	12,985	3,665	4,484,803	785,862	3,366,997	1,597,278	1,642,278	19,557,248
LAST YEAR	3,846	5,105	4,055	470,812	655,727	2,455,989	85,518	757,966	208,388	26,579	26,611	3,665	4,470,708	835,099	3,324,329	2,322,053	1,182,584	19,734,434
INC/(DEC)	1,358	181	(1,213)	22,620	197,029	27,495	44,940	(192,692)	(37,692)	(934)	(13,626)	0	14,095	(49,237)	42,668	(724,775)	459,694	(177,186)

2013 TABLE 2 ASSETS & EXPENSES

Church	LAND, BLDG & EQUIP	OTHER ASSETS	MORTGAGES	OTHER DEBTS	TOTAL APPORTIONED	MINISTRY SHARES PAID	DISTRICT APPORTIONEMENT	DISTRICT APPORTIONEMENT PAID	ADVANCE SPECIALS	WORLD SERVICE SPECIALS	YOUTH SERVICE FUND	CONFERENCE BENEVOLENCES	TOTAL CONFERENCE SPECIAL SUNDAYS	UMC CAUSES PAID DIRECTLY	NON-UMC CAUSES PAID DIRECTLY	HUMAN RELATIONS SUNDAY	ONE GREAT HOUR OF SHARING	PEACE W/ JUSTICE SUNDAY
	31	32	33	34	35a	35b	36a	36b	37	38	40	40b	42	43	44	45a	45b	45c
ALDEN	1,150,000	312,747			9,369	9,369	536	536	1,348		14	1,078	671			0	121	
CENTRAL LAKE	666,700	0			3,871	2,419	221	138	95		0					0	65	79
BALDWIN COVENANT COMMUNITY	585,000	0	0	0	10,400	5,201	378	190	453		3			0	5,200			
LUTHER	242,000	0	0	0	3,344	3,344	165	165	300		0			185	0		142	
BARNARD	465,000	0	0	0	3,327	0	443	0			0			0	1,052			
EAST JORDAN	750,000	90,000	0	0	9,648	9,648	993	993	3,406		0			200	5,301	0	128	40
NORWOOD	282,000	0	0	0	2,131	2,131	71	71			0			645	2,108	0	50	
BEAR LAKE	900,000	500,000	0	0	13,837	13,837	856	856	1,121		0	100	100	0	5,250			
ARCADIA	160,000	0	0	0	2,396	1,047	192	60	357		0			0	790			
BELLAIRE COMMUNITY	200,000	204,956	0	0	20,389	20,389	1,485	1,485			0			0	3,467		100	
BOYNE CITY	1,120,000	21,000	0	0	9,719	1,379	628	89	403		2		47	0	4,881		47	
BOYNE FALLS	270,000	7,000	0	0	4,144	573	229	229	213		20	37		0	443		100	
BRETHREN EPWORTH	600,000	8,950	0	0	4,388	4,388	320	320	310		4		100	0	2,116		50	
CADILLAC	2,357,000	91,200	15,190	0	36,989	32,085	3,327	2,381	11,573		24	475		2,682	10,108	0	676	1
CHARLEVOIX	2,452,330	22,160	0	0	14,135	7,484	864	766	967		0			0	2,025		118	
CRYSTAL VALLEY	318,500	141,548	0	0	3,991	3,991	328	328	515		0	180	54	0	0			
WALKERVILLE	410,000	50,820	0	0	3,316	3,316	115	115			0	100		0	1,663			
KEWADIN	861,500	60,220	0	0	6,784	6,219	378	346	2,956		0	265	374	0	0		215	
EMPIRE	926,000	0	0	0	14,796	14,818	693	693	2,385		2	1,000	66	200	2,341	0	308	1
EPSILON	450,000	30,000	0	0	10,203	6,501	485	308	836		6	80	206	0	4,626			
NEW HOPE	820,000	25,000	0	0	7,574	7,574	664	664	200		0			0	9,631			
FIFE LAKE	795,000	0	0	0	4,222	4,222	336	336	1,056		0		61	421	1,633	0	82	
SOUTH BOARDMAN	70,000	0	0	0	2,086	2,086	86	86			0			0	2,467			
EAST BOARDMAN	435,000	0	0	0	4,337	3,390	285	25	484		6	473		0	1,319		133	
FRANKFORT	1,545,000	464,875	0	0	16,510	16,510	793	793	2,954		0	1,407	429	0	11,219	0	150	55
ELBERTA	473,000	15,435	0	0	4,231	4,231	200	200	25		0			0	1,533	0	20	
FREESOIL-FOUNTAIN	670,000	5,000	0	0	1,404	0	79	0			0			0	0			
FOUNTAIN	150,000	0	0	0	1,681	0	86	0			0			0	0			
GRAWN	750,000	0	0	0	11,179	868	1,278	77	345		1			0	0	0		
HARBOR SPRINGS	2,557,000	139,670	0	7,125	9,907	4,955	514	257	789		5			150	360		77	
ALANSON	480,000	21,000	0	0	6,465	4,938	293	223	1,046		6			0	792		131	
HART	1,190,000	100,000	0	3,500	18,236	18,236	764	764			30			838	226	51	76	6
HORTON BAY	878,000	0	0	0	6,969	2,853	307	125	864		0	60		0	0			
GREENSKY HILL	400,000	85,000	0	0	5,597	921	522	86	2,274		0			0	0			
INDIAN RIVER	1,397,119	0	265,670	0	32,694	32,694	2,170	2,170			54			0	7,994			
KALKASKA	2,719,000				26,945	4,491	1,899	316	1,666		0							
KESWICK	915,777	0	186,854	0	19,729	19,729	478	478	1,025		4			0	0	8	20	5
KEWADIN INDIAN MISSION	625,000	18,000	0	0	2,872	2,633	200	183			0			0	450			
KINGSLEY	409,000	0	0	0	20,758	15,569	928	697	218		23			0	0			
GRANT	500,000	79,000	0	0	5,658	5,658	386	386	1,567		8			0	186			
LAKE ANN	1,893,472	12,053	309,891	85,000	14,500	2,786	1,042	14	2,250		0			2,600	4,435			
LAKE CITY	700,000	0	215,000	0	14,600	8,012	1,221	695	2,540		12	410	536	0	4,183	0	26	89

2013 TABLE 2 ASSETS & EXPENSES	LAND, BLDG & EQUIP	OTHER ASSETS	MORTGAGES	OTHER DEBTS	TOTAL APPORTIONED	MINISTRY SHARES PAID	DISTRICT APPORTIONEMENT	DISTRICT APPORTIONEMENT PAID	ADVANCE SPECIALS	WORLD SERVICE SPECIALS	YOUTH SERVICE FUND	CONFERENCE BENEVOLENCES	TOTAL CONFERENCE SPECIAL SUNDAYS	UMC CAUSES PAID DIRECTLY	NON-UMC CAUSES PAID DIRECTLY	HUMAN RELATIONS SUNDAY	ONE GREAT HOUR OF SHARING	PEACE W/ JUSTICE SUNDAY
Church	31	32	33	34	35a	35b	36a	36b	37	38	40	40b	42	43	44	45a	45b	45c
LELAND	2,463,000	563,897	182,037	0	32,853	32,853	2,413	2,413	15,272		38			0	19,312	0	230	
LUDINGTON ST PAUL	1,575,000	40,000	0	0	20,024	16,079	1,072	861	4,510		0			2,711	7,010		140	
LUDINGTON UNITED	4,360,000	208,000	1,000,000	0	43,418	43,418	3,063	3,063	3,564		124		15	51,600	12,800		567	2
MANCELONA	250,000	80,000	0	0	10,774	10,774	742	742	2,147		2			0	5,568			
ALBA	110,000	0	0	0	3,512	3,512	285	285	273		6			0	0			
MANISTEE	1,210,000	136,187	0	0	39,281	20,142	2,235	1,118			83			1,687	2,115			
MANTON	1,295,000	83,109	0	0	14,924	14,924	935	935	3,494		0	100	389	0	2,726		149	36
MARION	799,000	80,447	0	0	6,181	1,946	785	247	1,651		0	400	100	0	1,352			
CADILLAC SOUTH COMMUNITY	743,000	0	0	0	4,931	3,462	315	221	529		0			0	1,174			
MEARS	840,000	0	0	0	11,136	11,136	635	635			8			4,000	14,000			
MESICK	225,000	19,000	0	0	5,856	3,846	507	333	145		9			0	0			
HARRIETTA	500,000	2,000	0	0	6,565	6,565	493	493	220		4			0	0			
MERRITT-BUTTERFIELD	1,200,300	28,780	0	0	13,644	7,959	607	354			5			0	1,239			
MOORESTOWN-STITTSVILLE	425,000	31,270	0	0	5,552	5,552	336	336			6			0	10,424			
NORTHPORT INDIAN MISSION	390,000	15,000	0	0	1,271	1,165	192	175			0			0	3,419			
OLD MISSION PENINSULA	751,000	23,133	0	0	14,123	14,142	671	672	658		4		103	0	4,202			
PENTWATER CENTENARY	1,833,898	0	0	0	18,946	18,946	1,121	1,121	11,035		15	600	1,629	12,988	3,257	77	308	310
PETOSKEY	575,000	450,949	498,024	359	56,038	56,038	3,984	3,984	3,128		34	230		1,939	11,594	0	333	84
ASHTON	644,000	5,928	0	0	4,241	4,241	320	320	10		2			75	320	21		
LEROY	845,000	12,585	0	0	9,737	7,302	599	449	96		18			0	0	6	70	69
SCOTTVILLE	2,324,000	447,500	56,000	0	17,591	12,933	985	724	730		0		212	0	21,590			
TRAVERSE BAY	950,000	40,000	0	0	34,584	34,584	1,877	1,877	9,158		0	3,153	176	0	0			
CENTRAL TRAVERSE CITY	3,869,329	771,792	0	0	113,483	113,483	7,411	7,411	25,197		120	2,979	1,300	0	20,015		538	
CHRIST TRAVERSE CITY	1,100,000	100,000	446,428	0	12,276	2,315	358	68	449		0			0	0			
WILLIAMSBURG	459,000	414,740	0	0	10,673	10,673	607	607	383		0	138	154	0	1,162			
GRAND TRAVERSE DISTRICT	65,274,925	6,059,951	3,175,094	95,984	936,945	768,485	59,786	48,088	129,190	0	702	13,265	6,722	82,921	241,078	163	5,170	777
LAST YEAR	64,071,411	5,680,829	3,090,161	103,388	871,549	761,254	59,860	51,720	169,278	225	2,610	13,951	5,925	43,148	274,222	1,570	6,456	782
INC/(DEC)	1,203,514	379,122	84,933	(7,404)	65,396	7,231	(74)	(3,632)	(40,088)	(225)	(1,908)	(686)	797	39,773	(33,144)	(1,407)	(1,286)	(5)

STATISTICAL INFO

STATISTICAL INFO

2013 TABLE 2 ASSETS & EXPENSES	NATIVE AMERICAN MINISTRIES SUNDAY	WORLD COMMUNION SUNDAY	UM STUDENT SUNDAY	CLERGY PENSION	CLERGY HEALTH CARE	PASTOR COMPENSATION	ASSOCIATE PASTOR COMPENSATION	CLERGY HOUSING	ACOUNTABLE REIMBURSEMENTS	NON-ACCOUNTABLE REIMBURSEMENTS	DEACONS SALARY & BENEFITS	DIACONAL MINISTERS SALARY & BENEFITS	OTHER LAY STAFF SALARY & BENEFITS	PROGRAM EXPENSES	OPERATING EXPENSES	LOAN PAYMENTS	CAPITAL IMPROVEMENTS	TOTAL EXPENSES COL 35b + 36b THRU 59
Church	45d	45e	45f	46	47	48	49	50	51	52	53	54	55	56	57	58	59	60
ALDEN	100					32,250												45,487
CENTRAL LAKE	39					10,750												13,585
BALDWIN COVENANT COMMUNITY				0	16,125	42,961	0	4,800	5,000	0	0	0	0	14,400	16,430	0	0	110,763
LUTHER				0	0	1,874	0	5,317	0	0	0	0	0	150	8,591	0	0	20,068
BARNARD				1,812	1,135	7,843	0	863	1,135	0	0	0	3,973	776	4,208	0	2,209	25,006
EAST JORDAN	66	103	88	4,147	3,200	22,112	0	2,432	0	5,504	0	0	18,073	2,203	13,649	0	0	91,293
NORWOOD	50	200	150	689	864	4,595	0	505	532	133	0	0	0	1,402	6,885	0	3,234	24,244
BEAR LAKE				6,000	15,522	24,502	0	3,111	3,991	0	0	0	22,641	4,396	23,056	0	0	124,483
ARCADIA				802	3,880	6,126	0	0	1,000	0	0	0	3,202	1,043	6,051	0	0	24,358
BELLAIRE COMMUNITY				0	13,922	40,311	0	4,855	3,595	0	0	0	26,774	5,641	32,531	0	4,625	157,695
BOYNE CITY	5	28		6,927	0	31,337	0	3,488	5,357	0	0	0	22,776	4,370	16,280	0	5,522	102,938
BOYNE FALLS	100	71		1,954	0	8,839	0	984	1,511	0	0	0	6,227	618	5,480	2,409	13,808	43,616
BRETHREN EPWORTH		50	50	1,112	6,989	2,398	0	4,367	4,920	0	0	0	2,300	2,471	8,887	0	0	40,832
CADILLAC	171	204		12,026	16,128	68,738	0	7,129	8,344	0	0	0	82,408	15,311	63,361	12,000	21,754	367,579
CHARLEVOIX			52	8,200	3,000	44,370	0	0	1,000	0	0	0	19,500	2,010	15,000	0	5,000	109,492
CRYSTAL VALLEY		94		936	340	2,937	0	5,633	1,059	0	0	0	1,680	3,256	7,218	0	3,693	31,914
WALKERVILLE				1,044	349	3,276	0	6,283	1,909	0	0	0	0	1,061	15,209	0	19,737	54,062
KEWADIN				0	0	20,000	0	0	0	0	0	0	17,060	107	16,502	0	0	64,044
EMPIRE	125	110	107	9,060	16,128	43,184	0	2,067	1,440	0	0	0	19,020	5,618	27,835	0	0	146,508
EPSILON				4,158	8,814	20,471	0	2,830	0	0	0	0	4,800	2,127	12,541	0	894	69,198
NEW HOPE				4,811	8,863	20,533	0	2,888	4,070	0	0	0	0	1,210	17,389	0	856	78,689
FIFE LAKE		108		4,150	8,909	20,839	0	1,769	2,945	0	0	0	0	1,326	9,671	0	0	57,528
SOUTH BOARDMAN				537	1,153	2,697	0	229	381	0	0	0	0	71	2,975	0	0	12,682
EAST BOARDMAN				6,941	7,566	17,697	0	1,502	2,501	0	0	0	0	1,229	11,037	0	8,055	62,358
FRANKFORT	14	72	70	6,135	2,400	33,720	0	9,128	3,248	0	0	0	37,063	7,869	42,554	0	25,900	201,690
ELBERTA	5	5		0	0	7,853	0	3,706	900	0	0	0	8,055	658	7,639	0	1,125	35,955
FREESOIL-FOUNTAIN				0	0	8,760	0	0	0	0	0	0	0	1,500	11,218	0	0	21,478
FOUNTAIN				0	0	5,120	0	0	0	0	0	0	0	1	1	0	0	5,122
GRAWN				8,494	4,500	45,299	0	4,742	5,514	0	0	0	0	1,794	18,784	0	1,263	91,681
HARBOR SPRINGS		29		5,712	10,483	21,928	0	9,750	1,079	0	0	0	14,844	3,439	25,703	0	0	99,560
ALANSON				3,076	5,645	11,808	0	5,250	581	0	0	0	10,607	1,246	10,154	0	0	55,503
HART	76	78		6,809	16,980	32,983	0	6,887	9,886	0	0	0	37,270	7,903	26,717	5,500	23,538	194,854
HORTON BAY				970	0	10,440	0	2,026	587	0	0	0	3,396	956	15,579	0	0	37,856
GREENSKY HILL				2,533	16,980	20,392	0	664	3,168	0	0	0	0	8,185	20,652	0	0	75,855
INDIAN RIVER				9,000	16,128	48,003	0	0	6,064	0	0	0	68,534	8,319	52,334	48,768	2,686	302,748
KALKASKA						49,000												55,473
KESWICK		60		7,449	17,128	36,000	0	7,683	2,722	0	0	0	5,540	1,425	24,258	27,323	596	151,453
KEWADIN INDIAN MISSION				1,125	1,919	24,366	0	4,400	0	190	0	0	0	1,966	12,934	0	1,025	51,191
KINGSLEY				13,151	12,346	49,970	0	5,938	1,027	0	0	0	30,248	4,390	19,045	0	11,386	164,008
GRANT				58	9,677	2,314	0	8,251	3,470	0	0	0	2,400	7,679	21,356	0	10,453	73,463
LAKE ANN				5,973	17,121	40,077	0	999	0	0	0	0	15,266	3,263	38,258	40,082	1,908	175,032
LAKE CITY	89	23	63	3,000	17,628	39,536	0	3,833	2,020	0	0	0	10,439	2,839	18,736	40,601	4,923	160,233

2013 TABLE 2 ASSETS & EXPENSES	NATIVE AMERICAN MINISTRIES SUNDAY	WORLD COMMUNION SUNDAY	UM STUDENT SUNDAY	CLERGY PENSION	CLERGY HEALTH CARE	PASTOR COMPENSATION	ASSOCIATE PASTOR COMPENSATION	CLERGY HOUSING	ACOUNTABLE REIMBURSEMENTS	NON-ACCOUNTABLE REIMBURSEMENTS	DEACONS SALARY & BENEFITS	DIACONAL MINISTERS SALARY & BENEFITS	OTHER LAY STAFF SALARY & BENEFITS	PROGRAM EXPENSES	OPERATING EXPENSES	LOAN PAYMENTS	CAPITAL IMPROVEMENTS	TOTAL EXPENSES COL 35b + 36b THRU 59
Church	45d	45e	45f	46	47	48	49	50	51	52	53	54	55	56	57	58	59	60
LELAND		50	3	0	17,150	53,050	0	0	686	0	0	0	94,912	21,100	54,873	11,917	0	323,859
LUDINGTON ST PAUL	5			1,500	26,001	39,999	0	8,299	373	0	0	0	15,827	5,005	26,414	0	15,799	170,533
LUDINGTON UNITED			10	12,206	16,254	61,517	0	6,254	625	1,000	0	0	71,336	25,279	90,724	130,140	8,006	538,504
MANCELONA	348			6,213	8,992	24,332	0	4,950	4,432	0	0	0	5,485	8,973	22,771	0	2,434	108,163
ALBA				2,663	3,854	10,428	0	2,121	1,899	0	0	0	1,149	322	5,053	0	500	32,065
MANISTEE				9,606	20,155	50,000	0	0	5,785	0	0	0	82,739	12,779	53,667	0	33,353	293,229
MANTON	56	107		5,880	13,409	31,532	0	3,449	2,862	0	0	0	8,243	880	18,796	0	0	107,967
MARION				5,918	1,950	26,482	0	2,259	0	0	0	0	3,590	1,900	9,644	0	578	58,017
CADILLAC SOUTH COMMUNITY				2,674	1,050	14,259	0	4,768	0	0	0	0	1,500	2,143	10,622	0	2,046	44,448
MEARS				0	0	34,000	0	0	6,500	0	0	0	7,200	15,000	25,000	0	0	117,479
MESICK				0	0	16,768	0	2,936	2,700	0	0	0	0	3,344	9,308	0	1,010	40,399
HARRIETTA				0	0	16,768	0	4,178	2,759	0	0	0	0	6,924	17,944	0	5,745	61,600
MERRITT-BUTTERFIELD				4,584	10,322	24,448	0	3,255	1,838	0	0	0	8,905	2,260	21,184	0	0	86,353
MOORESTOWN-STITTSVILLE				2,579	5,806	13,752	0	804	1,616	0	0	0	0	1,301	5,115	0	0	47,291
NORTHPORT INDIAN MISSION				375	896	11,847	0	765	0	0	0	0	0	6,000	11,062	0	412	36,116
OLD MISSION PENINSULA		60		0	16,128	35,197	0	5,300	3,656	0	0	0	4,467	1,516	20,578	0	11,635	118,318
PENTWATER CENTENARY	288	252	139	7,967	20,208	52,420	0	6,167	60	575	0	0	15,745	23,193	45,261	0	4,684	227,245
PETOSKEY	181	61	35	14,262	15,628	68,289	0	8,773	3,754	0	0	0	135,277	21,995	69,583	81,129	12,429	508,760
ASHTON	46	15		2,186	5,645	11,691	0	0	1,886	0	0	0	1,320	50	6,279	0	4,381	38,488
LEROY	47	46	42	6,263	17,628	21,478	0	2,410	3,720	0	0	0	4,053	1,618	13,700	0	0	79,015
SCOTTVILLE				13,384	16,128	36,846	0	5,870	2,194	0	0	0	5,302	2,351	23,104	10,000	2,659	154,027
TRAVERSE BAY				10,562	8,342	53,831	0	3,834	3,806	0	0	0	99,413	10,011	47,033	0	0	285,780
CENTRAL TRAVERSE CITY				24,435	29,921	74,912	54,397	20,000	7,099	0	0	0	373,520	54,716	159,480	3,651	234,934	1,208,108
CHRIST TRAVERSE CITY				0	2,200	14,538	0	0	56	0	0	0	6,240	760	31,000	48,875	0	106,501
WILLIAMSBURG		11	10	0	0	41,700	0	11,028	4,347	0	0	0	16,182	1,080	25,923	0	16,113	129,511
GRAND TRAVERSE DISTRICT	1,811	1,837	819	282,048	539,489	1,828,293	54,397	241,729	153,609	7,402	0	0	1,456,501	364,728	1,530,826	462,395	530,908	8,753,353
LAST YEAR	1,462	2,028	806	293,268	541,871	1,857,172	65,478	329,077	145,016	8,813	0	4,908	1,400,064	393,358	1,608,109	607,130	499,261	9,088,962
INC/(DEC)	349	(191)	13	(11,220)	(2,382)	(28,879)	(11,081)	(87,348)	8,593	(1,411)	0	(4,908)	56,437	(28,630)	(77,283)	(144,735)	31,647	(335,609)

STATISTICAL INFO

2013 TABLE 2 ASSETS & EXPENSES

Church	LAND, BLDG & EQUIP	OTHER ASSETS	MORTGAGES	OTHER DEBTS	TOTAL APPORTIONED	MINISTRY SHARES PAID	DISTRICT APPORTIONEMENT	DISTRICT APPORTIONEMENT PAID	ADVANCE SPECIALS	WORLD SERVICE SPECIALS	YOUTH SERVICE FUND	CONFERENCE BENEVOLENCES	TOTAL CONFERENCE SPECIAL SUNDAYS	UMC CAUSES PAID DIRECTLY	NON-UMC CAUSES PAID DIRECTLY	HUMAN RELATIONS SUNDAY	ONE GREAT HOUR OF SHARING	PEACE W/ JUSTICE SUNDAY
	31	32	33	34	35a	35b	36a	36b	37	38	40	40b	42	43	44	45a	45b	45c
ALMA	4,146,000	436,502	79,570	0	26,213	0	1,231	0	1,395		0	0		0	5,188		0	
ASHLEY	125,000	26,000	0	0	4,960	4,960	200	200	707		4	35	35	614	727		12	
BANNISTER	325,000	0	0	0	5,647	5,647	197	197	1,190		0			0	0	20	80	
BARRYTON FAITH	300,000	255,800	0	0	5,811	5,811	226	226	42		16			0	495			
BELDING	1,146,000	21,544	8,308	0	6,591	1,608	246	70	633		5	20		0	5,100			
BIG RAPIDS FIRST	590,000	285,405	0	0	29,245	29,247	1,860	1,860	1,962		20	3,600		43,224	11,024	86	549	180
THIRD AVENUE	175,000	25,125	0	0	5,825	5,825	297	297	43		0	300		0	3,125			
PARIS	150,000	0	0	0	4,690	4,690	186	186	138		0	600		750	1,873			
RODNEY	120,000	10,000	0	0	1,776	1,776	77	45	70		0			0	1,135			
BLANCHARD-PINE RIVER	225,000				4,576	3,433	226	169			2							
COOMER	271,000	23,753	0	0	2,000	2,000	186	186			0			0	855			
BRECKENRIDGE	2,113,500	100,000	0	0	14,401	7,422	817	817	937		0		252	0	0	32	62	46
BROOKS CORNERS	500,000	500,000	0	0	8,660	8,660	157	157	1,334		0	1,006		0	14,467			
SEARS	50,000	9,000	0	0	1,791	1,791	66	66			0			0	0			
CARSON CITY	1,240,350	0	456,468	0	20,934	16,134	1,411	1,411	1,410		60		50	0	6,270	31	928	
CHASE BARTON	770,000	0	0	0	5,881	5,881	171	171			16			0	2,292			
GRANT CENTER	637,000	0	0	0	4,208	4,208	180	180			0			150	6,216			
CLARE	2,617,250	377,886	0	0	30,241	30,241	1,740	1,740	12,869		60	500	152	21,388	29,360		918	
EDMORE FAITH	1,381,500	157,136	0	0	17,501	17,501	866	866	3,350		12	2,701		0	5,440	0	285	15
ELSIE	1,028,500	90,000	0	0	17,272	7,197	1,046	437			0			0	0			
EVART	400,000	60,306	0	0	17,296	8,326	486	486	1,828		16			0	0	0		4
AVONDALE	94,200	5,739	0	0	1,087	1,087	40	40	77		0			0	184			
NORTH EVART	45,000	0	0	0	465	465	37	37	96		0			0	0			
FARWELL	320,000	65,000	124,480	0	16,662	13,199	760	760	822		12		82	0	605	0	100	110
FENWICK	682,000	12,176	0	0	2,082	2,082	97	97	174		0	37	86	0	248	8	80	11
PALO	456,000	20,062	0	0	2,136	1,226	117	3	98		0	23	31	0	93		6	3
VICKERYVILLE	486,000	5,043	0	0	1,675	838	106	106	61		0		30	0	275	0	17	7
GREENVILLE	3,623,000	142,565	1,847,626	0	28,265	16,150	3,471	1,983	3,499		43	400	600	0	5,975	150	503	150
HERSEY	500,000	0	0	0	9,708	9,708	386	386	326		10			150	3,461			
AMBLE	300,000	100,000	0	0	7,324	7,324	286	286	945		0	45		1,235	7,358	0	202	
HERITAGE	211,000	52,383	194,372	6,350	21,332	6,400	1,206	361			8			0	3,321		250	
FIRST IONIA	1,200,000	250,000	0	0	21,414	19,629	926	774	3,312		37	365		0	0			
ZION IONIA	750,000	150,000	0	0	16,463	6,956	537	225			25			0	250			
LEVALLEY	331,800	106,270	0	0	15,382	15,382	851	851	4,024		30	400	351	2,250	21,818		455	
BERLIN CENTER	125,500	28,871	0	0	7,443	7,443	297	297	150		8			8,507	19,386			
ITHACA	315,000	0	0	0	20,813	19,079	966	886	1,598		18	302	323	0	3,125		100	
BEEBE	345,500	3,266	0	0	1,826	1,826	77	77	134		0			0	0			
LAKEVIEW NEW LIFE	2,600,000	10,548	0	0	26,649	26,649	1,220	1,220	2,245		60			0	7,684			
LEATON	1,078,000	38,500	0	0	5,473	5,473	251	251	2,047		0	500	100	185	4,510	50	79	
LYONS-MUIR	500,000	500,000	0	0	9,535	717	371	28	151		0			0	8,000			
EASTON	1,218,000	7,082	0	0	7,450	7,450	417	417			0			0	600			
MECOSTA NEW HOPE	2,080,500	1,500	205,835	258,383	35,253	17,628	2,671	1,338	300		48			300	0			

2013 TABLE 2 ASSETS & EXPENSES

Church	LAND, BLDG & EQUIP	OTHER ASSETS	MORTGAGES	OTHER DEBTS	TOTAL APPORTIONED	MINISTRY SHARES PAID	DISTRICT APPORTIONEMENT	DISTRICT APPORTIONEMENT PAID	ADVANCE SPECIALS	WORLD SERVICE SPECIALS	YOUTH SERVICE FUND	CONFERENCE BENEVOLENCES	TOTAL CONFERENCE SPECIAL SUNDAYS	UMC CAUSES PAID DIRECTLY	NON-UMC CAUSES PAID DIRECTLY	HUMAN RELATIONS SUNDAY	ONE GREAT HOUR OF SHARING	PEACE W/ JUSTICE SUNDAY
	31	32	33	34	35a	35b	36a	36b	37	38	40	40b	42	43	44	45a	45b	45c
MIDDLETON	543,000	62,868	0	0	2,662	2,662	111	111			0			0	0		62	
MAPLE RAPIDS	405,000	40,000	0	0	6,454	6,454	286	286	40		0	10		0	0			
CHIPPEWA INDIAN CHURCH					6,515	0					0							
FIRST MT PLEASANT	3,720,000	310,000	0	0	52,033	52,033	2,426	2,426	9,031		32	3,265		2,041	15,090		1,105	
TRINITY MOUNT PLEASANT	550,000	0	22,000	0	4,802	3,724	186	145			0			0	1,346			
COUNTRYSIDE	450,000	39,000	22,000	0	6,123	6,123	246	246	234		0			0	778		65	50
OVID UNITED CHURCH	2,046,000	30,000	0	79,000	9,215	6,250	511	511	443		12			0	6,943		107	
POMPEII	1,025,000	4,000	0	0	3,941	3,941	166	166	100		0			0	706	0	61	39
PERRINTON	350,000	1,500	0	0	2,259	2,259	77	77	85		6		7	0	383	10	47	12
NORTH STAR	62,000	5,750	0	0	303	303	20	20			0			0	0	0		
REED CITY	2,960,157	100,000	0	0	25,318	25,326	1,906	1,906	3,653		24	1,186	10	4,000	2,000	0	51	55
RIVERDALE LINCOLN ROAD	915,000	45,483	0	0	16,126	16,286	611	619	4,479		8		1,090	866	4,746	0	368	105
ROSEBUSH	850,000	75,000	139,478	0	12,741	12,741	380	380	30	10	10			0	0			
FIRST SAINT JOHNS	2,829,713	528,554	0	1,638	19,370	19,370	946	946	2,915		14	632	70	3,296	3,714	0	513	73
PILGRIM	2,150,000	195,677	0	0	41,763	41,763	1,066	1,066	2,497		80	1,500		0	28,450	64	368	
SALEM	512,000	80,000	0	0	5,841	5,841	177	177	561		0	273		0	0			5
GREENBUSH	125,000	9,259	0	0	3,235	3,235	120	120	130		2		23	0	617	0	20	
LOWE	400,000	0	0	0	8,887	8,887	257	257			0			0	3,000			
SAINT LOUIS	3,000,000	39,018	0	0	19,466	19,466	1,246	1,246	4,947		0	900	600	5,961	15,777	0	200	100
SHEPARDSVILLE	666,000	0	0	0	3,222	3,223	166	166			14			3,430	1,722			
SAND LAKE	23,000	0	0	0	2,328	2,332	100	100	0		8	0		112	1,070			
SOUTH ENSLEY	41,000	0	0	0	4,866	4,847	180	180	950		0	2,200		0	4,722			
SHEPHERD	451,000	0	0	0	17,827	17,827	877	877	2,754		0	874	1,200	0	0		700	
STANWOOD NORTHLAND	1,600,000	120,000	0	0	18,134	16,305	877	877	2,099		12	500	250	0	7,187	0	50	50
TURK LAKE	1,394,000	0	0	0	6,158	6,158	377	377	2,250		14		536	0	0	10	35	36
WEIDMAN	900,000	0	0	0	14,926	14,926	1,117	1,117	2,920		0	360	440	8,539	900			
WINN	320,950	1,789	0	0	5,092	2,547	231	117			2			0	4,360			
HEARTLAND DISTRICT	63,861,420	5,565,360	3,100,137	345,371	813,563	663,898	41,625	34,706	88,085	10	748	22,534	6,318	106,998	283,971	461	8,378	1,051
LAST YEAR	62,375,659	5,312,038	3,343,233	365,665	776,317	703,718	39,019	35,632	108,771	0	3,256	28,238	5,821	91,573	357,389	2,156	8,399	1,024
INC/(DEC)	1,485,761	253,322	(243,096)	(20,294)	37,246	(39,820)	2,606	(926)	(20,686)	10	(2,508)	(5,704)	497	15,425	(73,418)	(1,695)	(21)	27

STATISTICAL INFO

2013 TABLE 2 ASSETS & EXPENSES	NATIVE AMERICAN MINISTRIES SUNDAY	WORLD COMMUNION SUNDAY	UM STUDENT SUNDAY	CLERGY PENSION	CLERGY HEALTH CARE	PASTOR COMPENSATION	ASSOCIATE PASTOR COMPENSATION	CLERGY HOUSING	ACOUNTABLE REIMBURSEMENTS	NON-ACCOUNTABLE REIMBURSEMENTS	DEACONS SALARY & BENEFITS	DIACONAL MINISTERS SALARY & BENEFITS	OTHER LAY STAFF SALARY & BENEFITS	PROGRAM EXPENSES	OPERATING EXPENSES	LOAN PAYMENTS	CAPITAL IMPROVEMENTS	TOTAL EXPENSES COL 35b + 36b THRU 59
Church	45d	45e	45f	46	47	48	49	50	51	52	53	54	55	56	57	58	59	60
ALMA		200		8,493	11,252	53,550	0	5,357	1,312	240	0	0	46,070	16,782	39,341	25,870	9,308	224,358
ASHLEY				2,353	4,766	12,551	0	2,358	1,112	0	0	0	2,260	411	3,577	0	1,242	37,924
BANNISTER				2,485	3,511	13,255	0	3,339	2,125	0	0	0	1,405	1,046	5,453	0	0	39,753
BARRYTON FAITH				2,190	5,504	12,229	0	1,440	2,771	0	0	0	3,096	840	4,315	0	10,783	49,758
BELDING				0	0	3,050	1,000	8,736	441	0	0	0	1,539	250	11,618	3,480	6,757	44,307
BIG RAPIDS FIRST	216	107	117	9,243	17,628	48,328	0	4,435	5,112	0	0	0	69,733	22,381	51,003	0	34,767	354,822
THIRD AVENUE				2,961	7,516	15,113	0	2,796	1,771	0	0	0	0	1,326	7,389	0	0	48,462
PARIS				2,508	6,924	13,308	0	2,352	1,500	0	0	0	0	1,495	3,912	0	0	40,236
RODNEY				896	2,274	4,778	0	846	536	0	0	0	0	450	2,450	0	0	15,256
BLANCHARD-PINE RIVER						17,284												20,888
COOMER				0	0	3,329	0	1,200	0	0	0	0	2,184	172	4,493	0	0	14,419
BRECKENRIDGE	16	51	31	8,610	6,282	36,267	0	2,163	2,292	0	0	0	13,094	1,017	27,164	0	0	106,555
BROOKS CORNERS				2,696	6,766	15,031	0	1,770	3,406	0	0	0	1,810	1,856	14,684	0	0	73,643
SEARS				963	2,422	5,382	0	634	1,219	0	0	0	218	1,500	305	0	2,600	17,100
CARSON CITY		57		9,288	16,128	41,538	0	6,721	1,640	0	0	0	37,207	2,812	36,380	66,333	5,043	249,441
CHASE BARTON				1,572	500	13,108	0	0	2,818	0	0	0	1,200	1,375	27,049	0	0	55,982
GRANT CENTER				1,572	500	13,108	0	0	2,818	0	0	0	3,215	2,816	6,913	0	0	41,696
CLARE		421		9,703	17,628	53,502	0	8,430	2,776	0	0	0	75,289	8,980	58,190	0	2,047	334,194
EDMORE FAITH	31	51	50	7,442	9,375	40,014	0	4,690	3,720	0	0	0	18,614	1,890	16,652	0	0	132,699
ELSIE				5,263	13,729	29,250	0	0	0	0	0	0	15,882	2,200	31,908	0	28,727	134,593
EVART	28	2		8,018	15,622	44,406	0	5,575	4,089	0	0	0	22,676	6,083	25,933	0	0	143,092
AVONDALE				20	32	3,630	0	0	0	0	0	0	0	63	2,818	0	0	7,951
NORTH EVART				3,000	0	3,960	0	0	0	0	0	0	100	1	3,500	0	0	11,159
FARWELL	60	65		2,000	16,128	47,375	0	5,484	0	5,895	0	0	11,233	3,738	17,888	10,944	0	136,500
FENWICK	7	9	10	0	0	4,000	0	1,483	917	0	0	0	0	176	8,125	0	383	17,933
PALO			6	0	0	4,000	0	1,483	917	0	0	0	0	91	8,351	0	184	16,515
VICKERYVILLE				0	0	4,000	0	1,483	917	0	0	0	0	20	4,973	0	0	12,727
GREENVILLE	150	150	150	10,388	16,128	56,650	3,358	14,727	0	1,011	0	0	62,493	3,365	65,182	220,565	58,063	541,833
HERSEY				0	0	17,800	0	4,996	325	0	0	0	4,060	3,527	14,547	0	8,058	67,354
AMBLE	110	55		4,962	9,240	24,804	0	0	3,172	300	0	0	2,479	535	6,790	0	7,275	77,117
HERITAGE				8,866	17,467	48,234	0	7,549	4,998	0	0	0	13,945	6,079	45,436	23,190	4,649	190,753
FIRST IONIA				12,000	15,258	46,135	0	2,000	0	0	0	0	38,978	2,500	38,775	0	7,500	187,263
ZION IONIA				8,412	3,000	36,868	0	6,432	3,426	880	0	0	17,030	2,205	21,534	0	4,439	111,682
LEVALLEY				6,187	14,423	33,000	0	8,400	4,563	0	0	0	19,781	4,835	31,006	0	45,127	212,883
BERLIN CENTER	250			0	2,063	11,000	0	962	1,569	0	0	0	12,180	2,416	10,259	0	3,631	80,111
ITHACA				8,687	17,628	42,281	0	0	7,333	0	0	0	38,535	6,883	26,924	0	0	173,702
BEEBE				0	0	5,257	0	0	0	0	0	0	1,600	3,528	4,098	0	14,873	31,393
LAKEVIEW NEW LIFE				10,005	3,000	44,160	0	6,810	6,185	8,870	0	0	66,238	7,834	48,967	0	20,113	260,040
LEATON		68	13	0	0	15,683	0	3,720	1,667	0	300	0	3,957	468	16,143	0	2,173	57,387
LYONS-MUIR				5,000	9,969	5,866	0	24,997	700	1,010	0	0	7,720	1,260	12,895	0	0	78,313
EASTON				5,812	3,000	11,998	0	10,000	3,033	0	0	0	5,866	846	17,277	0	9,072	75,371
MECOSTA NEW HOPE				11,692	17,002	54,310	0	12,919	5,029	0	0	0	51,270	44,594	50,122	48,219	2,738	317,509

2013 TABLE 2 ASSETS & EXPENSES

2013 TABLE 2 ASSETS & EXPENSES	NATIVE AMERICAN MINISTRIES SUNDAY	WORLD COMMUNION SUNDAY	UM STUDENT SUNDAY	CLERGY PENSION	CLERGY HEALTH CARE	PASTOR COMPENSATION	ASSOCIATE PASTOR COMPENSATION	CLERGY HOUSING	ACOUNTABLE REIMBURSEMENTS	NON-ACCOUNTABLE REIMBURSEMENTS	DEACONS SALARY & BENEFITS	DIACONAL MINISTERS SALARY & BENEFITS	OTHER LAY STAFF SALARY & BENEFITS	PROGRAM EXPENSES	OPERATING EXPENSES	LOAN PAYMENTS	CAPITAL IMPROVEMENTS	TOTAL EXPENSES COL 35b + 36b THRU 59
Church	45d	45e	45f	46	47	48	49	50	51	52	53	54	55	56	57	58	59	60
MIDDLETON				0	2,262	8,032	0	828	0	0	0	0	0	200	5,000	0	0	19,157
MAPLE RAPIDS	12	38		2,200	1,517	11,739	0	3,733	2,500	0	0	0	2,166	550	8,000	0	0	39,245
CHIPPEWA INDIAN CHURCH																		0
FIRST MT PLEASANT				12,601	16,128	59,470	0	3,825	2,855	0	0	0	135,013	56,740	100,026	0	26,998	498,679
TRINITY MOUNT PLEASANT				3,276	0	11,022	0	2,107	0	1,738	0	0	0	1,700	15,100	2,940	0	43,098
COUNTRYSIDE			95	3,626	0	11,022	0	2,107	201	1,738	0	0	1,300	4,422	21,954	2,940	3,674	60,575
OVID UNITED CHURCH				7,842	16,128	43,132	0	5,098	2,653	0	0	0	29,096	9,906	23,320	10,773	11,499	173,713
POMPEII	56		52	2,422	3,419	12,409	0	0	0	0	0	0	0	4,530	1,421	0	3,874	33,196
PERRINTON	11	20		0	2,233	7,294	0	3,376	0	0	0	0	0	4,593	4,164	0	0	24,577
NORTH STAR		26		0	0	2,120	0	0	0	0	0	0	0	50	2,000	0	0	4,519
REED CITY	260	145	127	15,988	17,628	52,670	0	5,578	0	0	0	0	59,328	3,751	36,600	0	0	230,286
RIVERDALE LINCOLN ROAD	220	70	107	0	3,000	36,518	0	0	0	0	0	0	18,098	8,351	40,761	0	16,756	152,448
ROSEBUSH				8,766	6,282	36,532	0	4,156	0	0	0	0	8,046	4,920	15,700	30,056	23,276	150,905
FIRST SAINT JOHNS	136	35	70	7,535	4,000	40,185	0	5,663	3,559	0	0	0	53,264	2,490	24,607	3,356	55,871	232,314
PILGRIM	20	155		10,345	17,628	54,198	0	3,058	2,869	0	0	0	62,416	38,248	47,897	0	11,109	323,731
SALEM	5	55		2,264	1,251	11,739	0	0	0	0	0	0	2,267	3,630	19,000	0	0	47,068
GREENBUSH		10		3,638	2,492	6,704	0	1,199	0	0	0	0	481	434	6,323	0	0	25,428
LOWE				2,200	1,517	11,739	0	3,733	5,036	0	0	0	2,013	4,239	7,233	0	0	49,854
SAINT LOUIS	100	200	100	9,255	6,180	29,957	0	4,250	3,435	0	0	0	25,207	3,609	41,313	0	16,264	189,067
SHEPARDSVILLE				0	500	4,800	0	0	205	0	0	0	4,500	4,172	12,563	0	2,630	37,925
SAND LAKE				0	0	6,060	0	0	0	0	0	0	500	1,193	9,947	0	0	21,322
SOUTH ENSLEY				0	0	6,432	0	5,762	131	0	0	0	4,315	8,184	9,922	0	0	47,645
SHEPHERD				7,875	15,593	42,000	0	4,500	3,800	0	0	0	10,400	3,281	36,374	0	0	148,055
STANWOOD NORTHLAND	100	50	50	12,634	3,280	45,277	0	4,557	3,509	3,600	0	0	14,748	13,543	22,400	0	16,310	167,388
TURK LAKE	57	21	15	0	1,740	3,020	0	12,064	703	0	0	0	3,350	2,738	13,453	0	0	46,577
WEIDMAN				7,234	17,617	16,737	0	4,373	877	1,553	0	0	17,306	4,176	16,927	0	2,856	118,858
WINN				1,471	7,096	7,605	0	2,400	1,320	250	0	0	6,963	2,671	19,210	0	0	56,012
HEARTLAND DISTRICT	1,845	2,061	993	304,459	440,156	1,587,805	4,358	258,644	119,862	27,085	300	0	1,133,734	362,967	1,395,554	448,666	480,669	7,786,316
LAST YEAR	1,249	1,974	774	289,558	452,207	1,610,160	0	240,297	124,996	14,479	0	350	1,081,512	324,793	1,409,963	475,617	590,039	7,963,945
INC/(DEC)	596	87	219	14,901	(12,051)	(22,355)	4,358	18,347	(5,134)	12,606	300	(350)	52,222	38,174	(14,409)	(26,951)	(109,370)	(177,629)

STATISTICAL INFO

2013 TABLE 2 ASSETS & EXPENSES	LAND, BLDG & EQUIP	OTHER ASSETS	MORTGAGES	OTHER DEBTS	TOTAL APPORTIONED	MINISTRY SHARES PAID	DISTRICT APPORTIONEMENT	DISTRICT APPORTIONEMENT PAID	ADVANCE SPECIALS	WORLD SERVICE SPECIALS	YOUTH SERVICE FUND	CONFERENCE BENEVOLENCES	TOTAL CONFERENCE SPECIAL SUNDAYS	UMC CAUSES PAID DIRECTLY	NON-UMC CAUSES PAID DIRECTLY	HUMAN RELATIONS SUNDAY	ONE GREAT HOUR OF SHARING	PEACE W/ JUSTICE SUNDAY
Church	31	32	33	34	35a	35b	36a	36b	37	38	40	40b	42	43	44	45a	45b	45c
EDWARDSBURG HOPE	1,390,000	144,182	475,228	4,552	31,953	31,953	3,944	3,944	3,079		36		269	4,125	19,585	0	604	90
ALLEGAN	2,580,000	145,000	0	0	21,912	11,798	2,264	996	9,343		6	522	525	0	0	0	239	32
ARDEN	557,900	0	0	0	6,677	2,700	166	0	360	50	0			0	0		15	
BANGOR SIMPSON	1,947,000	55,000	484,499	0	20,280	1,696	1,328	111	60		2			0	4,260			
BERRIEN SPRINGS	2,067,000	158,000	0	0	9,377	4,354	390	390	612		0			0	291			
BLOOMINGDALE	383,000	9,000	0	0	3,217	1,744	203	110			5			0	400			
BURNIPS	900,000	0	0	0	7,167	5,650	360	284	1,586		24			0	480			
MONTEREY CENTER	475,000	0	0	0	5,067	5,067	337	337	1,036		4			0	879			
BUCHANAN FAITH	2,634,500	0	0	0	15,238	3,643	922	144	1,260		0			0	5,118	5	111	
MORRIS CHAPEL	355,000	0	0	0	4,143	4,143	150	150	322		0			0	0		84	
BUCHANAN FIRST	2,319,000	92,000	21,595	0	19,570	10,646	1,500	1,126	564		0			2,958	1,643		463	
CASCO	3,257,000	102,977	0	0	16,126	1,196	1,290	0	3,881		0			0	723		344	80
CASSOPOLIS	50,000	138,152	0	0	11,711	2,819	727	156			2			0	0			
Coloma	975,000	194,808	0	0										300	2,623			
DOWAGIAC FIRST	997,000	175,000	0	0	21,112	1,000	1,830	0	1,224		0			366	718		30	
FENNVILLE	1,438,000	0	0	0	10,655	3,517	645	0	980		40			303	4,735	0	192	
PEARL	268,812	1,500	0	0	2,995	2,995	248	248	202		0	25	25	300	100		25	
GANGES	500,000	41,000	0	0	5,010	1,669	652	217	570		5	50	50	0	1,000	0		
GALIEN	604,400	0	0	0	5,507	2,208	428	86			0	100		0	944	0	43	
OLIVE BRANCH	528,000	0	0	0	6,346	6,346	525	525	680		0		102	0	4,157	75	187	128
GLENN	827,820	4,824	0	0	3,238	1,612	353	175	246		0			0	0			
GOBLES	350,000	20,000	0	0	8,396	8,396	525	525	222		0	365		100	0	0	108	30
KENDALL	204,000	42,000	0	0	5,517	5,517	254	254	294		0	293	54	138	999	0	65	5
GULL LAKE	1,280,000	39,426	467,261	0	22,253	22,253	3,510	1,270	5,880		36	853	200	0	3,160	50	748	50
HARTFORD	2,219,000	171,308	0	0	17,728	17,728	1,672	1,672	2,745		12	3,096	220	999	12,608		441	
HINCHMAN	200,000	14,000	0	0	3,585	3,585	517	517			0			1,525	400			
ORONOKO	170,000	50,000	0	0	1,865	1,865	188	188	25		0			218	1,125			
HOPKINS	3,670,000	75,000	0	0	6,752	6,752	563	563	775		10			232	94			
SOUTH MONTEREY	191,000	50,000	0	0	5,266	5,266	277	277	3,497		0	50	268	50	313			
FIRST KALAMAZOO	20,000,000	1,150,478	0	1,350,000	111,290	111,290	6,360	6,360	8,233		100	14,511	170	18,120	28,782	0	2,325	458
LIFESPRING	650,000	125,000	508,594	0					148					335	487			
MILWOOD	2,380,000	0	797,660	0	27,625	27,625	2,295	2,295			10	2,879		222	6,121			
OSHTEMO	1,693,000	27,200	0	0	13,760	6,056	855	376	1,770		0	24		971	536	0	156	33
STOCKBRIDGE AVENUE	100,000	0	0	0	8,166	3,690	600	350			0			41,814	0			
SUNNYSIDE	1,385,000	162,147	0	0	17,275	17,275	960	960	2,682		4	111	100	1,358	1,056	0	442	94
WESTWOOD	2,875,500	728,168	0	0	38,902	29,148	2,729	2,040	7,215		24	325	573	11,275	13,898	0	363	109
KEELER	360,000	0	0	0	4,478	1,467	277	277	863		0		115	42	820		12	19
SILVER CREEK	540,000	160,000	0	0	9,549	7,095	742	742	1,167		0	409	187	0	3,484	0	189	
LACOTA	336,500	30,100	0	0	3,743	3,743	210	210			0			0	2,503			
LAKESIDE	270,000	56,606	0	0	4,461	4,461	262	262	2,736		0	200	880	700	700	0	339	23
LAWRENCE	780,000	0	0	0	11,996	1,193	983	98			0			0	5,472			
LAWTON ST PAULS	1,784,000	84,833	387,753	0	14,302	8,343	953	556	556		0	196		459	733		55	55

2013 TABLE 2 ASSETS & EXPENSES	LAND, BLDG & EQUIP	OTHER ASSETS	MORTGAGES	OTHER DEBTS	TOTAL APPORTIONED	MINISTRY SHARES PAID	DISTRICT APPORTIONEMENT	DISTRICT APPORTIONEMENT PAID	ADVANCE SPECIALS	WORLD SERVICE SPECIALS	YOUTH SERVICE FUND	CONFERENCE BENEVOLENCES	TOTAL CONFERENCE SPECIAL SUNDAYS	UMC CAUSES PAID DIRECTLY	NON-UMC CAUSES PAID DIRECTLY	HUMAN RELATIONS SUNDAY	ONE GREAT HOUR OF SHARING	PEACE W/ JUSTICE SUNDAY
Church	31	32	33	34	35a	35b	36a	36b	37	38	40	40b	42	43	44	45a	45b	45c
ALMENA	1,113,800	96,532	0	0	9,219	9,219	787	787	3,821		18	328	463	3,279	3,958		146	
MARCELLUS	620,000				7,387	7,387	652	652	1,201		16		196				50	
WATERS EDGE	923,241	0	114,663	0	18,740	18,740	1,260	1,260	4,344		30	138	985	8,752	8,580	0	142	206
BRIDGMAN FAITH	349,000	0	0	0	5,300	5,300	428	428	2,249		0	160	524	0	620	0	302	116
NILES GRACE	2,145,000	66,000	0	0	6,810	682	457	45			0			142	795	5	95	30
NILES WESLEY	3,430,000	370,040	0	0	29,377	16,428	2,663	625	4,017		6		300	0	900		100	
NORTHWEST	350,000	347,068	0	0	3,619	3,619	225	225	235		0	90		0	543			
OTSEGO	2,600,000	136,140	185,000	0	22,730	22,730	2,295	2,295	410		80			0	5,200			
PARCHMENT	3,428,000	351,427	702,556	0	25,099	7,500	2,122	1,500	901		0			1,471	627		224	45
PAW PAW	3,725,480	10,850	12,000	0	20,229	4,401	1,666	1,666	2,682		16			0	5,600	0	389	80
PLAINWELL FIRST	4,715,800	110,000	737,010	0	30,863	30,863	1,957	1,957	3,057		44	150	357	230	8,780	0	319	70
POKAGON	400,000				9,618	9,618	810	810	3,119		18	582	234			0	667	12
PORTAGE CHAPEL HILL	4,457,000	138,746	714,335	40,755	85,168	85,168	4,080	4,080	11,561		128	30		17,512	605	0	3,819	273
PORTAGE FIRST	4,640,500	186,203	0	0	61,295	61,295	2,729	2,729	7,207		44			2,650	15,942		137	
PORTAGE PRAIRIE	1,859,246	0	0	0	9,700	4,830	1,072	534	4,281		0	300		3,029	1,939			
RIVERSIDE	375,000	79,000			5,568	5,568	510	510			10							
SCOTTDALE	800,000	0	0	3,415	6,503	6,503	556	556	837		0	1,519		0	0			
SAINT JOSEPH FIRST	5,431,155	464,262	0	0	72,498	72,498	3,953	3,953	5,967		152		395	13,308	17,476	0	746	10
SCHOOLCRAFT	1,491,000	61,957	109,033	0	14,397	945	1,754	350	1,703		24	670		0	12,140		200	
SODUS CHAPEL HILL	266,000	265,066	0	0	18,969	5,865	1,605	1,605	16,353		66	2,779	731	7,025	10,076	17	41	14
SOUTH HAVEN FIRST	837,229	0	0	0	21,389	0	1,785	0			0			0	42,038			
STEVENSVILLE	2,630,000	285,120	28,784	37,971	40,400	40,400	3,727	3,727	19,501		70	1,472	1,080	400	0	0	247	209
THREE OAKS	243,000	173,753	0	0	14,147	14,147	1,163	1,163	365		28	205	130	400	2,615	0	185	52
TOWNLINE	415,000	54,716	0	0	3,072	3,072	285	285	268		0		73	0	1,157	0	35	31
BREEDSVILLE	324,000	31,052	0	0	2,582	2,582	135	135	138		13	48	53	50	50	0	21	
TROWBRIDGE	1,400,000	35,000	0	0	13,315	13,315	488	488	204		0			463	5,833			
VICKSBURG	2,661,501	755,050	843,047	0	38,727	19,365	2,572	1,286	6,517	81	49	100	100	1,000	4,279	0	286	45
WAKELEE	589,000				8,260	8,948	638	692	632		17	(749)						
KALAMAZOO DISTRICT	118,712,384	8,265,691	6,589,018	1,436,693	1,169,191	880,492	85,368	63,134	166,383	131	1,149	31,831	9,359	146,621	280,700	152	15,731	2,399
LAST YEAR	113,499,820	7,730,287	6,720,527	2,176,733	1,207,759	927,672	81,543	59,971	198,081	0	1,950	26,141	9,464	71,060	309,734	2,867	15,273	2,458
INC/(DEC)	5,212,564	535,404	(131,509)	(740,040)	(38,568)	(47,180)	3,825	3,163	(31,698)	131	(801)	5,690	(105)	75,561	(29,034)	(2,715)	458	(59)

STATISTICAL INFO

STATISTICAL INFO

2013 TABLE 2 ASSETS & EXPENSES	NATIVE AMERICAN MINISTRIES SUNDAY	WORLD COMMUNION SUNDAY	UM STUDENT SUNDAY	CLERGY PENSION	CLERGY HEALTH CARE	PASTOR COMPENSATION	ASSOCIATE PASTOR COMPENSATION	CLERGY HOUSING	ACOUNTABLE REIMBURSEMENTS	NON-ACCOUNTABLE REIMBURSEMENTS	DEACONS SALARY & BENEFITS	DIACONAL MINISTERS SALARY & BENEFITS	OTHER LAY STAFF SALARY & BENEFITS	PROGRAM EXPENSES	OPERATING EXPENSES	LOAN PAYMENTS	CAPITAL IMPROVEMENTS	TOTAL EXPENSES COL 35b + 36b THRU 59
Church	45d	45e	45f	46	47	48	49	50	51	52	53	54	55	56	57	58	59	60
EDWARDSBURG HOPE	77	129	40	8,652	19,886	44,145	0	6,967	5,480	0	0	0	63,568	24,087	47,828	83,949	18,370	386,863
ALLEGAN	40	452	80	9,904	18,708	54,142	0	5,000	8,000	0	0	0	52,000	20,000	42,000	0	44,732	278,519
ARDEN				0	0	12,444	0	0	0	0	0	0	6,638	2,206	20,248	0	0	44,661
BANGOR SIMPSON		82		8,510	16,254	43,230	0	13,500	0	0	0	0	8,800	906	17,049	58,566	0	173,026
BERRIEN SPRINGS				4,131	5,811	25,313	0	0	302	556	0	0	8,696	1,477	5,287	0	30,659	87,879
BLOOMINGDALE				0	0	8,248	0	0	725	0	0	0	0	105	20,529	0	0	31,866
BURNIPS				6,002	0	18,810	0	1,620	1,960	0	0	0	4,865	3,726	10,891	0	7,812	63,710
MONTEREY CENTER				4,910	0	16,032	0	1,620	1,601	0	0	0	4,355	1,013	13,953	0	383	51,190
BUCHANAN FAITH		32		374	2,502	15,738	0	8,000	2,000	0	0	0	0	1,736	27,367	0	7,063	75,093
MORRIS CHAPEL				792	188	5,192	0	0	0	0	0	0	0	1,300	17,150	0	0	29,321
BUCHANAN FIRST				8,278	16,128	44,148	0	3,271	3,190	0	0	0	30,164	2,608	31,020	5,434	0	161,641
CASCO	28	30	10	8,433	16,128	44,917	0	8,135	7,746	525	0	0	23,691	10,231	32,123	10,071	0	168,292
CASSOPOLIS				0	2,417	25,901	0	6,476	5,028	0	0	0	19,531	3,618	42,598	0	0	108,546
Coloma				7,847	16,378	43,184	0	6,491	6,362	0	0	0	45,331	24,999	24,698	0	10,306	188,519
DOWAGIAC FIRST				9,322	16,163	41,719	0	4,945	1,304	0	0	0	34,928	25	25,709	27,395	9,219	174,067
FENNVILLE		115		6,380	12,902	27,626	0	2,990	1,703	0	0	0	14,617	3,164	17,393	0	1,190	97,847
PEARL		25		1,595	3,226	6,907	0	747	426	0	0	0	4,198	100	4,230	0	2,201	27,575
GANGES				0	0	8,160	0	3,600	600	240	0	0	6,675	479	27,596	0	4,916	55,827
GALIEN	16		25	2,259	8,790	12,576	0	1,969	821	0	0	0	3,416	5	6,248	0	0	39,506
OLIVE BRANCH	119	104	104	2,259	8,790	12,576	0	1,969	821	0	0	0	3,416	417	6,675	0	0	49,450
GLENN	71			0	0	12,600	0	0	0	0	0	0	0	1	3,000	0	0	17,705
GOBLES	42	30	10	2,061	2,569	16,544	0	1,517	1,826	0	0	0	1,448	3,237	25,410	0	0	64,440
KENDALL	5	10	5	555	999	8,555	3,229	941	1,018	0	0	0	1,541	1,122	11,511	0	12,729	49,839
GULL LAKE	50	50		9,157	17,628	48,800	0	4,168	0	2,023	0	0	69,744	14,808	34,122	45,275	1,173	281,498
HARTFORD	200	106		8,813	4,500	47,000	0	3,073	2,326	0	0	0	34,112	12,754	29,767	0	24,497	206,669
HINCHMAN				2,165	2,056	9,536	0	0	1,165	0	0	0	0	4,566	4,676	0	0	30,191
ORONOKO				2,149	2,047	9,548	0	0	1,165	100	0	150	0	173	6,425	0	0	25,178
HOPKINS		50		3,190	2,700	24,714	0	0	244	0	0	0	6,789	1,439	10,319	0	0	57,871
SOUTH MONTEREY		242		3,190	1,800	16,476	0	0	188	0	0	0	1,066	748	5,086	0	0	38,517
FIRST KALAMAZOO	274	450	356	10,636	14,400	70,300	64,525	40,624	1,290	0	0	0	299,316	141,752	158,482	249,739	59,592	1,302,085
LIFESPRING				0	16,128	38,784	0	18,000	1,001	0	0	0	914	652	19,073	44,538	0	140,060
MILWOOD				8,465	12,001	45,672	0	6,863	4,315	0	0	0	39,548	6,668	45,496	100,289	0	308,469
OSHTEMO	130	11	15	4,050	8,951	33,708	0	15,000	3,181	0	0	0	15,005	2,131	26,740	0	10,525	129,369
STOCKBRIDGE AVENUE				0	0	11,111	0	0	3,704	0	0	0	8,608	927	24,680	0	0	94,884
SUNNYSIDE	28	50	39	1,056	16,980	39,050	0	18,660	2,787	0	5,000	0	24,561	3,573	85,050	0	18,508	239,424
WESTWOOD	133	100	161	9,844	18,128	52,500	0	8,734	2,506	0	2,000	0	86,671	17,755	75,901	0	39,431	378,834
KEELER	31	20		2,240	4,581	10,556	0	3,062	785	0	0	0	2,812	564	9,234	0	109	37,609
SILVER CREEK		25	62	4,900	19,236	24,260	0	4,000	0	0	0	0	17,800	139	9,429	0	4,000	97,124
LACOTA				0	0	8,000	0	0	0	0	0	0	0	579	11,001	0	1,373	27,409
LAKESIDE	28	25		0	7,989	1,440	0	6,600	1,311	0	0	0	4,370	912	6,844	0	0	39,820
LAWRENCE				5,736	13,484	38,281	0	3,665	1,260	0	0	0	1,555	5,957	23,149	0	0	99,850
LAWTON ST PAULS	35			0	375	16,000	0	0	3,364	0	0	0	13,413	7,792	18,085	43,545	9,129	122,691

2013 TABLE 2 ASSETS & EXPENSES	NATIVE AMERICAN MINISTRIES SUNDAY	WORLD COMMUNION SUNDAY	UM STUDENT SUNDAY	CLERGY PENSION	CLERGY HEALTH CARE	PASTOR COMPENSATION	ASSOCIATE PASTOR COMPENSATION	CLERGY HOUSING	ACOUNTABLE REIMBURSEMENTS	NON-ACCOUNTABLE REIMBURSEMENTS	DEACONS SALARY & BENEFITS	DIACONAL MINISTERS SALARY & BENEFITS	OTHER LAY STAFF SALARY & BENEFITS	PROGRAM EXPENSES	OPERATING EXPENSES	LOAN PAYMENTS	CAPITAL IMPROVEMENTS	TOTAL EXPENSES COL 35b + 36b THRU 59
Church	45d	45e	45f	46	47	48	49	50	51	52	53	54	55	56	57	58	59	60
ALMENA				3,090	3,750	8,000	0	17,750	3,222	0	0	0	5,510	12,502	16,573	0	5,756	98,171
MARCELLUS						17,698												27,200
WATERS EDGE	166	211	144	13,195	14,700	56,875	0	3,500	2,907	0	0	0	46,051	27,676	56,011	96,052	27,198	387,863
BRIDGMAN FAITH	73	107	115	0	0	19,660	0	1,282	479	0	0	0	0	293	13,954	0	0	45,662
NILES GRACE	8			0	0	13,000	6,500	0	0	0	0	0	20,910	1,322	13,150	0	0	56,684
NILES WESLEY				9,188	17,378	49,000	0	1,849	2,504	0	0	0	35,670	5,934	33,871	0	38,534	216,304
NORTHWEST		96		765	375	10,400	0	3,751	343	0	0	0	0	369	4,874	0	19,163	44,848
OTSEGO				8,978	16,128	41,880	0	10,384	10,715	0	0	0	40,293	16,324	44,333	27,960	44,922	292,632
PARCHMENT	115			9,269	16,128	47,930	0	14,789	2,366	0	0	0	29,863	5,252	34,471	67,236	0	239,687
PAW PAW	25	408		8,295	9,564	31,269	0	5,158	1,345	0	0	0	44,259	466	32,437	5,000	0	153,060
PLAINWELL FIRST	81	220	45	10,113	17,255	54,000	0	2,878	2,190	0	0	0	53,622	15,972	84,929	90,943	5,338	383,413
POKAGON	2	62	15			14,552												29,691
PORTAGE CHAPEL HILL		481		15,653	26,909	63,556	23,028	25,043	10,631	0	4,992	4,052	134,336	38,186	238,800	102,386	28,002	839,231
PORTAGE FIRST				12,448	16,128	64,129	7,250	8,609	5,870	0	0	0	225,015	20,424	96,968	0	229,606	776,451
PORTAGE PRAIRIE				4,751	1,208	28,159	0	2,951	0	245	0	0	16,283	460	22,084	0	0	91,054
RIVERSIDE						7,250												13,338
SCOTTDALE				3,600	0	19,660	0	310	396	0	0	0	2,856	447	17,062	0	0	53,746
SAINT JOSEPH FIRST	51	53	50	13,434	16,128	61,296	0	18,264	1,548	0	74,096	0	209,712	30,529	72,617	0	41,321	653,604
SCHOOLCRAFT	135	45		8,330	17,902	39,377	0	8,537	2,414	0	0	0	25,668	12	16,300	12,672	15,069	162,493
SODUS CHAPEL HILL	31	47	56	10,256	11,498	45,100	0	3,630	2,318	0	0	0	21,656	10,615	31,322	0	55,502	236,603
SOUTH HAVEN FIRST				9,540	12,522	37,370	0	6,022	5,248	5,000	0	0	37,749	8,431	80,848	99,400	0	344,168
STEVENSVILLE	333	470	582	13,701	5,400	65,224	0	3,725	7,750	0	0	0	78,607	17,441	79,473	36,783	18,555	395,150
THREE OAKS	88	23	56	7,939	10,152	42,338	0	2,400	4,677	0	0	0	19,752	1,990	15,801	0	0	124,506
TOWNLINE	18	24	21	0	0	4,991	0	2,730	6,095	0	0	0	0	2,359	8,959	0	0	30,118
BREEDSVILLE	35	32	14	562	2,802	3,003	0	1,593	2,245	0	0	0	0	5,379	4,940	0	2,999	26,694
TROWBRIDGE				0	3,750	17,614	0	4,000	3,750	0	0	0	1,605	750	9,456	0	13,460	74,688
VICKSBURG		65		12,199	16,129	65,783	0	5,432	4,237	0	0	0	88,080	6,354	76,677	102,363	0	410,427
WAKELEE						17,698												27,238
KALAMAZOO DISTRICT	2,468	4,482	2,005	343,161	566,629	2,041,255	104,532	366,794	164,755	8,689	86,088	4,202	2,101,659	559,938	2,189,982	1,309,596	863,341	12,317,658
LAST YEAR	2,693	3,415	1,928	357,860	584,443	2,083,302	114,780	374,388	170,707	7,272	70,324	0	2,194,456	451,081	2,170,944	1,561,638	1,127,138	12,901,040
INC/(DEC)	(225)	1,067	77	(14,699)	(17,814)	(42,047)	(10,248)	(7,594)	(5,952)	1,417	15,764	4,202	(92,797)	108,857	19,038	(252,042)	(263,797)	(583,382)

STATISTICAL INFO

STATISTICAL INFO

2013 TABLE 2 ASSETS & EXPENSES	LAND, BLDG & EQUIP	OTHER ASSETS	MORTGAGES	OTHER DEBTS	TOTAL APPORTIONED	MINISTRY SHARES PAID	DISTRICT APPORTIONEMENT	DISTRICT APPORTIONEMENT PAID	ADVANCE SPECIALS	WORLD SERVICE SPECIALS	YOUTH SERVICE FUND	CONFERENCE BENEVOLENCES	TOTAL CONFERENCE SPECIAL SUNDAYS	UMC CAUSES PAID DIRECTLY	NON-UMC CAUSES PAID DIRECTLY	HUMAN RELATIONS SUNDAY	ONE GREAT HOUR OF SHARING	PEACE W/ JUSTICE SUNDAY
Church	31	32	33	34	35a	35b	36a	36b	37	38	40	40b	42	43	44	45a	45b	45c
BATH	908,000	102,920	64,712	0	7,170	6,573	664	609	623		33			0	9,328		260	
GUNNISONVILLE	550,000	335,620	0	0	14,338	14,338	591	591	1,454		4		371	903	8,333		674	
WHEATFIELD	235,000	0	0	0	4,499	4,499	497	497	545		0	230		0	3,279	5	80	100
BROOKFIELD	50,000	94,175	0	0	5,563	5,533	231	231	2,462		0	100	363	0	5,043		360	
CHARLOTTE LAWRENCE AVENUE	350,000	1,000,000	0	0	30,735	1,100	4,633	0	6,819		0		370	0	7,500	100	100	
COUNTRY CHAPEL	1,160,500	0	0	0	11,854	11,854	1,106	1,106	765		10	163		0	4,875			
DANSVILLE	420,000	0	0	10,791	3,358	1,653	239	239			22			0	881		45	
DELTA MILLS	275,000	132,816	0	0	4,982	4,972	581	581	1,182		0	84	100	913	2,752		100	
DEWITT REDEEMER	4,425,860	0	1,369,794	0	103,393	103,393	7,147	7,147	3,695		308			0	180,586			
DIMONDALE	1,126,000	0	15,280	0	9,971	1,884	534	101	290		0			0	4,726	11	185	
UNIVERSITY EAST LANSING	3,743,200	250,879	817,599	0	67,923	67,923	4,587	4,587	8,171		36	4,945	403	3,281	2,952	15	2,405	10
EATON RAPIDS FIRST	6,657,000	110,000	35,000	1,315	52,342	39,247	4,255	3,201	7,570		30	2,247	500	0	19,875		545	
FREEPORT	813,000	11,948	0	0	2,846	2,846	120	120	360		0	0		100	2,560		70	
GRAND LEDGE FIRST	4,206,000	495,069	11,078	0	40,951	40,951	4,615	4,615	4,645		100	619		0	20,017	573	660	100
GROVENBURG	200,000	25,000	136,028	0	7,856	4,910	405	254	44		1	560		0	417		73	
HASTINGS FIRST	6,111,000	557,000	0	0	27,846	27,846	2,957	2,957	3,098		8	266		0	18,208	0	80	189
HASTINGS HOPE	1,631,704	0	304,428	0	16,711	16,711	1,399	1,399	467		92			0	0		19	16
HOLT	4,561,202	242,639	0	0	51,373	51,373	4,034	4,034	2,553		80		179	16,986	16,513	168	1,081	193
KALAMO	90,000	22,000	0	0	3,690	3,690	755	755	296		0			0	0			
LAKE ODESSA CENTRAL	2,846,000	405,591	0	0	25,421	23,303	2,285	2,095	4,568		46	253	360	0	42,067	0	737	36
LAKE ODESSA LAKEWOOD	1,942,383	11,630	766,801	0	33,607	23,553	2,578	2,020	2,993		75	850	700	0	26		500	
ASBURY LANSING	4,001,010	575,264	0	0	29,437	26,984	1,962	1,800	5,660		20	1,584	145	910	2,545	30	277	10
CENTRAL LANSING	860,000	2,000,000	33,556	0	51,884	11,602	3,417	753	5,303		2	1,685	360	0	0	110	1,060	155
CHRIST LANSING	1,500,000	10,000	0	0	24,502	16,335	1,399	933	671		0			5,926	0	25	166	30
FAITH/SOUTH LANSING MINISTRIES	1,560,000	55,000	128,700	0	11,247	11,251	865	865			16		200	8,232	3,301	100	100	100
FIRST LANSING	4,216,000	0	29,928	0	26,704	26,704	2,145	2,145	1,549		28	656	208	0	381	15	350	115
GRACE LANSING	2,121,263	440,713	48,742	0	25,141	25,141	1,860	1,860	3,440		50	2,550	650	0	7,550		750	
KOREAN LANSING	350,000	100,000	140,000	0	15,902	15,902	1,152	1,152			26	(17,198)		0	0			
MOUNT HOPE	3,442,900	603,918	0	0	70,062	70,065	3,269	3,269	47,236		44	439		0	12,242	0		
TRINITY LANSING	7,588,687	613,300	2,712,086	0	68,083	41,715	3,822	2,342			159			0	0			
LESLIE	1,422,000	35,000	0	0	9,146	9,146	829	829	529		0			0	1,724		625	
FELT PLAINS	665,000	0	0	0	4,163	239	166	10	185		0			0	3,089			
MASON FIRST	5,025,000	955,257	1,352,758	11,340	48,731	48,731	4,338	4,338	6,898		86	700		13,312	10,526	0	530	55
MILLVILLE	1,491,000	0	150,351	0	17,764	5,337	994	103	1,885		0	13		140	3,639	0	3	
MUNITH	975,000	54,517	0	0	6,187	6,187	323	323	70		0			0	1,417			
PLEASANT LAKE	120,000	91,639	0	0	2,276	2,276	371	371	339		0		49	47	0	7	49	55
MULLIKEN	200,000	61,665	0	0	5,634	0	303	0			0			500	700			
SEBEWA CENTER	30,000	0	0	0	2,298	1,278	166	92	150		0			0	0			
NASHVILLE	654,000	62,000	0	4,416	12,391	12,220	1,178	1,178	1,074		16	(3,019)	171	0	1,146	0	168	116
PEACE	440,000	0	0	0	4,445	2,899	303	221	1,438		0	651	141	0	875	0	86	7
QUIMBY	68,000	0	0	0	2,203	2,019	166	153			0			0	0			
OKEMOS	5,500,000	603,073	0	0	65,807	40,354	6,051	6,051	8,399		108			0	22,676			

2013 TABLE 2 ASSETS & EXPENSES	LAND, BLDG & EQUIP	OTHER ASSETS	MORTGAGES	OTHER DEBTS	TOTAL APPORTIONED	MINISTRY SHARES PAID	DISTRICT APPORTIONEMENT	DISTRICT APPORTIONEMENT PAID	ADVANCE SPECIALS	WORLD SERVICE SPECIALS	YOUTH SERVICE FUND	CONFERENCE BENEVOLENCES	TOTAL CONFERENCE SPECIAL SUNDAYS	UMC CAUSES PAID DIRECTLY	NON-UMC CAUSES PAID DIRECTLY	HUMAN RELATIONS SUNDAY	ONE GREAT HOUR OF SHARING	PEACE W/ JUSTICE SUNDAY
Church	31	32	33	34	35a	35b	36a	36b	37	38	40	40b	42	43	44	45a	45b	45c
PERRY	1,157,000	123,000	0	0	5,845	5,845	330	330	469		8			0	814		28	25
SHAFTSBURG	811,000	20,000	78,618	0	7,460	7,460	506	506	727		6		48	0	400		149	154
PORTLAND	2,470,700	95,000	86,470	0	33,992	33,992	3,122	3,122	825		70	100		6,360	9,436			
POTTERVILLE	1,900,000	0	0	0	19,635	17,999	1,399	1,282	1,015		37			327	834		159	
ROBBINS	1,500,000	160,000	0	0	24,141	835	2,127	73	4,718		1	626	709	490	6,108		745	
STOCKBRIDGE	900,000	210,000	0	0	10,047	6,515	1,814	476	98		3			276	100		14	
SUNFIELD	1,185,000	0	0	0	16,782	2,341	727	116			239			0	12,823			
SYCAMORE CREEK	160,000	75,000	0	0	17,416	17,416	1,372	1,372	130		6			0	5,905			
VERMONTVILLE	374,000	18,000	0	0	5,104	5,104	544	544	378		0	204	208	0	537	0	110	
GRESHAM	125,000	17,000	0	0	5,943	5,947	415	415	466		0			0	139	125	118	
WACOUSTA	864,560	230,000	90,031	0	18,529	18,529	2,145	2,145	1,047		20	50		0	3,601		333	
WATERLOO VILLAGE	511,227	16,000	19,528	0	3,278	3,278	313	313			0			1,443	1,060	25	56	30
WATERLOO FIRST	145,500	0	0	0	1,934	1,128	424	247			0			0	0			
WEBBERVILLE	2,000,000	28,010	219,304	0	18,282	18,287	1,041	1,041	812		0	3,540	247	1,173	2,731		189	
WILLIAMSTON	2,800,000	254,373	0	0	18,244	18,244	1,694	1,694	6,243		12			0	8,820			
WILLIAMSTON CROSSROADS	1,813,700	70,000	0	0	9,754	9,758	591	591	400		6			0	4,000			
WOODLAND	84,000	16,000	0	0	5,999	5,999	470	470	112		0			0	1,843		150	
WELCOME CORNERS	455,000	11,250	0	0	4,761	4,761	295	295	5,673		0	113		0	500		80	
LANSING DISTRICT	103,788,396	11,402,266	8,610,792	27,862	1,257,582	1,017,975	98,621	80,959	160,539	0	1,808	3,011	6,482	61,319	481,400	1,309	14,269	1,496
LAST YEAR	103,055,287	11,082,080	9,148,061	49,447	1,264,743	938,772	98,570	83,771	236,054	350	2,293	16,078	6,863	59,491	463,524	3,019	14,926	1,657
INC/(DEC)	733,109	320,186	(537,269)	(21,585)	(7,161)	79,203	51	(2,812)	(75,515)	(350)	(485)	(13,067)	(381)	1,828	17,876	(1,710)	(657)	(161)

STATISTICAL INFO

2013 TABLE 2 ASSETS & EXPENSES

Church	NATIVE AMERICAN MINISTRIES SUNDAY	WORLD COMMUNION SUNDAY	UM STUDENT SUNDAY	CLERGY PENSION	CLERGY HEALTH CARE	PASTOR COMPENSATION	ASSOCIATE PASTOR COMPENSATION	CLERGY HOUSING	ACOUNTABLE REIMBURSEMENTS	NON-ACCOUNTABLE REIMBURSEMENTS	DEACONS SALARY & BENEFITS	DIACONAL MINISTERS SALARY & BENEFITS	OTHER LAY STAFF SALARY & BENEFITS	PROGRAM EXPENSES	OPERATING EXPENSES	LOAN PAYMENTS	CAPITAL IMPROVEMENTS	TOTAL EXPENSES COL 35b + 36b THRU 59
	45d	45e	45f	46	47	48	49	50	51	52	53	54	55	56	57	58	59	60
BATH				5,161	3,610	23,800	0	1,773	2,150	0	0	0	3,139	5,006	14,822	7,073	2,578	86,538
GUNNISONVILLE	266			5,442	3,752	26,351	0	5,740	2,634	0	0	0	7,921	12,846	30,436	0	0	122,056
WHEATFIELD	130	50	70	1,629	2,613	10,937	0	2,676	1,892	0	0	0	5,290	2,747	7,410	0	182	44,861
BROOKFIELD				0	0	5,004	0	12,000	2,459	527	0	0	2,768	4,038	7,473	0	3,529	51,890
CHARLOTTE LAWRENCE AVENUE	100	100		13,799	16,128	53,000	0	3,500	1,841	1,861	0	0	93,538	15,415	54,927	0	7,553	277,751
COUNTRY CHAPEL				7,088	3,000	33,000	0	3,512	1,103	0	0	0	9,735	4,907	23,905	0	228,913	333,936
DANSVILLE		15		1,757	2,356	10,937	0	3,552	1,626	0	0	0	0	1	12,052	0	0	35,136
DELTA MILLS				0	3,044	12,164	0	7,721	250	0	0	0	6,500	5,975	9,107	0	12,412	67,857
DEWITT REDEEMER				15,302	16,128	81,115	0	21,200	8,610	0	0	0	450,997	53,952	152,392	126,578	57,584	1,278,987
DIMONDALE	42	50	15	0	2,465	7,123	0	2,062	1,635	0	0	0	14,381	2,607	18,766	7,500	6,459	70,302
UNIVERSITY EAST LANSING	428	357	250	17,464	19,272	60,000	17,031	23,750	5,857	0	0	0	204,160	16,161	98,659	154,403	20,754	733,274
EATON RAPIDS FIRST				14,754	20,208	48,837	0	3,914	2,651	0	0	0	184,702	170,826	84,119	60,344	23,363	686,933
FREEPORT				1,680	3,226	8,961	0	1,200	1,300	0	0	0	0	8,543	9,454	0	0	40,420
GRAND LEDGE FIRST	180			8,412	8,064	64,252	0	4,211	3,843	0	0	0	107,333	15,012	76,488	927	93,871	454,873
GROVENBURG				0	720	6,476	0	1,661	4,284	0	0	0	4,239	878	10,093	18,439	0	53,049
HASTINGS FIRST	107			10,103	16,128	45,008	0	3,603	1,200	0	0	0	59,850	13,956	51,365	0	70,643	324,614
HASTINGS HOPE	65	50	12	10,247	16,128	49,985	0	4,625	3,675	0	0	0	13,733	7,042	42,563	70,019	0	236,848
HOLT	453	234	35	13,041	18,531	61,850	0	7,290	2,715	438	0	0	171,209	74,237	82,504	0	6,050	531,747
KALAMO				696	0	10,500	0	8,000	595	0	0	0	3,460	1,846	4,996	0	0	34,834
LAKE ODESSA CENTRAL	45	130	95	8,250	13,606	44,000	0	4,548	5,141	0	0	0	38,413	6,565	39,960	17,326	1,045	252,589
LAKE ODESSA LAKEWOOD				12,271	15,133	56,455	0	4,570	4,185	0	0	0	121,474	30,902	86,720	81,456	5,264	449,147
ASBURY LANSING		35	37	13,441	19,708	46,809	0	4,771	4,063	0	0	0	60,824	11,282	33,018	0	35,732	269,685
CENTRAL LANSING	213	127	65	5,000	10,854	50,850	0	6,350	0	0	0	0	144,579	5,539	146,534	4,201	18,000	413,342
CHRIST LANSING	56		15	15,352	2,245	43,895	0	9,500	0	0	0	0	70,636	6,770	56,783	0	0	229,338
FAITH/SOUTH LANSING MINISTRIES	100	100	100	0	0	33,600	0	33,600	0	0	0	0	6,530	1,645	35,485	28,180	6,926	170,431
FIRST LANSING	116	80	35	8,438	17,628	45,000	0	5,000	3,674	0	0	0	38,922	37,916	52,002	4,070	13,239	258,271
GRACE LANSING				12,056	19,008	51,500	0	4,604	4,800	0	0	0	61,124	2,596	37,940	7,435	17,420	260,474
KOREAN LANSING				8,810	17,282	42,338	0	17,000	2,250	0	0	0	0	847	20,795	12,413	0	121,617
MOUNT HOPE				17,022	15,634	50,049	0	20,000	1,480	0	37,103	0	188,062	102,136	72,680	0	6,000	643,461
TRINITY LANSING				11,018	18,386	49,200	0	29,999	4,500	0	0	0	218,066	22,455	125,393	81,360	0	604,593
LESLIE				630	2,450	10,833	0	13,192	4,094	0	0	0	9,546	2,392	15,100	0	0	71,090
FELT PLAINS				1,355	1,050	4,643	0	5,654	1,757	0	0	0	968	63	12,751	0	0	31,764
MASON FIRST	21	52	25	11,524	1,841	61,464	0	0	3,999	0	0	0	148,156	15,940	71,282	144,799	17,459	561,738
MILLVILLE	3	8	3	6,112	9,636	27,601	0	4,289	1,706	0	0	0	15,674	2,002	26,790	28,357	16,278	149,579
MUNITH				0	0	10,460	0	11,146	1,105	0	0	0	3,084	5,146	10,521	0	0	49,459
PLEASANT LAKE	22		30	0	0	5,605	0	1,865	73	0	0	0	0	812	5,652	0	0	17,252
MULLIKEN				2,050	4,620	8,999	0	0	0	0	0	0	0	1,255	10,051	0	0	28,175
SEBEWA CENTER				0	0	2,850	0	0	0	0	0	0	0	100	100	0	0	4,570
NASHVILLE	94	95	50	11,435	9,921	22,667	0	0	1,852	3,000	6,000	0	4,442	981	18,311	11,191	11,191	114,300
PEACE	14	12	20	3,465	5,645	15,681	0	2,100	1,925	0	0	0	0	571	3,335	0	380	39,466
QUIMBY				579	143	9,750	0	4,500	0	0	0	0	0	645	6,931	0	0	24,720
OKEMOS				13,129	19,031	61,136	0	30,000	3,914	0	0	0	201,916	29,956	73,457	0	73,264	583,391

2013 TABLE 2 ASSETS & EXPENSES	NATIVE AMERICAN MINISTRIES SUNDAY	WORLD COMMUNION SUNDAY	UM STUDENT SUNDAY	CLERGY PENSION	CLERGY HEALTH CARE	PASTOR COMPENSATION	ASSOCIATE PASTOR COMPENSATION	CLERGY HOUSING	ACOUNTABLE REIMBURSEMENTS	NON-ACCOUNTABLE REIMBURSEMENTS	DEACONS SALARY & BENEFITS	DIACONAL MINISTERS SALARY & BENEFITS	OTHER LAY STAFF SALARY & BENEFITS	PROGRAM EXPENSES	OPERATING EXPENSES	LOAN PAYMENTS	CAPITAL IMPROVEMENTS	TOTAL EXPENSES COL 36b + 36b THRU 59
Church	45d	45e	45f	46	47	48	49	50	51	52	53	54	55	56	57	58	59	60
PERRY	32	30	26	3,717	8,064	19,823	0	2,475	824	0	0	0	4,586	496	7,494	0	388	55,474
SHAFTSBURG	171	110	30	4,026	10,412	19,908	0	5,796	317	0	0	0	2,547	3,235	11,425	22,285	29,883	119,595
PORTLAND				12,281	18,870	57,500	0	6,853	4,500	0	0	0	49,093	32,144	65,670	6,000	29,470	336,286
POTTERVILLE				7,433	16,128	39,644	0	4,270	2,970	0	0	0	23,515	2,389	20,754	0	15,094	153,850
ROBBINS	5			11,156	16,128	48,500	0	5,421	605	0	0	0	32,996	3,948	32,494	0	12,639	178,197
STOCKBRIDGE		10	2	2,704	5,095	11,014	0	4,301	0	0	0	0	11,991	1,364	10,133	0	0	54,096
SUNFIELD				8,162	16,128	35,065	0	5,819	2,154	0	0	0	19,755	7,605	18,579	0	4,488	133,274
SYCAMORE CREEK				9,000	17,902	40,000	0	5,694	2,517	0	0	0	78,487	2,143	48,894	0	1,386	230,852
VERMONTVILLE	100	88		1,362	2,016	9,000	0	6,000	541	0	3,075	0	0	5,514	9,933	0	0	44,714
GRESHAM	123	89		3,786	750	20,000	1,050	16,000	409	0	0	0	1,475	675	8,519	0	0	60,086
WACOUSTA		344		9,665	4,989	40,534	0	5,730	3,000	0	0	0	18,274	5,984	25,050	40,304	17,730	197,329
WATERLOO VILLAGE	48	59		0	0	12,000	0	10,237	253	0	0	0	0	505	16,669	4,904	731	51,611
WATERLOO FIRST				0	2,289	2,550	0	1,445	0	0	0	0	0	52	256	0	0	7,967
WEBBERVILLE		16	19	6,047	14,112	40,313	0	13,435	4,172	0	0	0	12,137	2,108	32,821	33,462	34,482	221,144
WILLIAMSTON				3,519	11,064	39,750	0	11,464	2,747	0	0	0	31,315	5,900	32,962	0	21,357	195,091
WILLIAMSTON CROSSROADS				4,000	3,000	4,500	0	8,000	1,000	0	0	0	15,900	6,900	12,200	0	8,000	78,255
WOODLAND				1,321	6,048	7,192	0	6,000	1,559	0	2,970	0	0	1,047	12,296	0	0	47,007
WELCOME CORNERS	92			8,348	7,641	20,250	0	1,098	1,782	0	0	0	0	279	10,929	0	2,030	63,871
LANSING DISTRICT	3,026	2,241	934	385,039	519,830	1,842,228	18,081	454,716	130,188	5,826	49,148	0	2,977,442	786,798	2,130,200	973,026	933,767	13,043,057
LAST YEAR	1,471	1,885	960	376,228	489,088	1,820,941	22,500	506,846	135,395	11,256	35,769	0	2,916,550	752,067	2,093,218	913,827	759,803	12,664,602
INC/(DEC)	1,555	356	(26)	8,811	30,742	21,287	(4,419)	(52,130)	(5,207)	(5,430)	13,379	0	60,892	34,731	36,982	59,199	173,964	378,455

STATISTICAL INFO

2013 TABLE 2 ASSETS & EXPENSES	LAND, BLDG & EQUIP	OTHER ASSETS	MORTGAGES	OTHER DEBTS	TOTAL APPORTIONED	MINISTRY SHARES PAID	DISTRICT APPORTIONEMENT	DISTRICT APPORTIONEMENT PAID	ADVANCE SPECIALS	WORLD SERVICE SPECIALS	YOUTH SERVICE FUND	CONFERENCE BENEVOLENCES	TOTAL CONFERENCE SPECIAL SUNDAYS	UMC CAUSES PAID DIRECTLY	NON-UMC CAUSES PAID DIRECTLY	HUMAN RELATIONS SUNDAY	ONE GREAT HOUR OF SHARING	PEACE W/ JUSTICE SUNDAY
Church	31	32	33	34	35a	35b	36a	36b	37	38	40	40b	42	43	44	45a	45b	45c
ALBION DISTRICT	108,519,078	20,138,773	1,635,310	75,595	894,459	782,081	74,600	66,717	99,083	0	926	8,821	5,101	50,888	403,545	1,000	10,406	1,329
HEARTLAND DISTRICT	63,861,420	5,565,360	3,100,137	345,371	813,563	663,898	41,625	34,706	88,085	10	748	22,534	6,318	106,998	283,971	461	8,378	1,051
GRAND RAPIDS DISTRICT	162,944,265	15,580,955	11,153,083	78,791	1,783,940	1,648,734	228,138	213,275	220,970	346	2,874	56,280	13,384	253,670	498,942	80	16,077	3,671
GRAND TRAVERSE DISTRICT	65,274,925	6,059,951	3,175,094	95,984	936,945	768,485	59,786	48,088	129,190	0	702	13,265	6,722	82,921	241,078	163	5,170	777
KALAMAZOO DISTRICT	118,712,384	8,265,691	6,589,018	1,436,693	1,169,191	880,492	85,368	63,134	166,383	131	1,149	31,831	9,359	146,621	280,700	152	15,731	2,399
LANSING DISTRICT	103,788,396	11,402,266	8,610,792	27,862	1,257,582	1,017,975	98,621	80,959	160,539	0	1,808	3,011	6,482	61,319	481,400	1,309	14,269	1,496
CONFERENCE	623,100,468	67,012,996	34,263,434	2,060,296	6,855,680	5,761,665	588,138	506,879	864,250	487	8,207	135,742	47,366	702,417	2,189,636	3,165	70,031	10,723
LAST YEAR	602,341,143	63,536,813	35,984,586	2,973,578	6,669,489	5,651,653	555,123	491,802	1,058,308	2,803	16,515	240,141	50,495	452,831	2,293,498	15,192	71,835	12,712
INCREASE(DECREASE)	20,759,325	3,476,183	(1,721,152)	(913,282)	186,191	110,012	33,015	15,077	(194,058)	(2,316)	(8,308)	(104,399)	(3,129)	249,586	(103,862)	(12,027)	(1,804)	(1,989)

2013 TABLE 2 ASSETS & EXPENSES	NATIVE AMERICAN MINISTRIES SUNDAY	WORLD COMMUNION SUNDAY	UM STUDENT SUNDAY	CLERGY PENSION	CLERGY HEALTH CARE	PASTOR COMPENSATION	ASSOCIATE PASTOR COMPENSATION	CLERGY HOUSING	ACOUNTABLE REIMBURSEMENTS	NON-ACCOUNTABLE REIMBURSEMENTS	DEACONS SALARY & BENEFITS	DIACONAL MINISTERS SALARY & BENEFITS	OTHER LAY STAFF SALARY & BENEFITS	PROGRAM EXPENSES	OPERATING EXPENSES	LOAN PAYMENTS	CAPITAL IMPROVEMENTS	TOTAL EXPENSES COL 36b + 36b THRU 59
Church	45d	45e	45f	46	47	48	49	50	51	52	53	54	55	56	57	58	59	60
ALBION DISTRICT	2,765	2,958	1,265	270,868	421,383	1,600,549	39,938	246,014	133,430	21,157	0	0	1,590,595	426,747	1,965,370	396,421	923,827	9,473,184
HEARTLAND DISTRICT	1,845	2,061	993	304,459	440,156	1,587,805	4,358	258,644	119,862	27,085	300	0	1,133,734	362,967	1,395,554	448,666	480,669	7,786,316
GRAND RAPIDS DISTRICT	5,204	5,286	2,842	493,432	852,756	2,483,484	130,458	565,274	170,696	25,645	12,985	3,665	4,484,803	785,862	3,366,997	1,597,278	1,642,278	19,557,248
GRAND TRAVERSE DISTRICT	1,811	1,837	819	282,048	539,489	1,828,293	54,397	241,729	153,609	7,402	0	0	1,456,501	364,728	1,530,826	462,395	530,908	8,753,353
KALAMAZOO DISTRICT	2,468	4,482	2,005	343,161	566,629	2,041,255	104,532	366,794	164,755	8,689	86,088	4,202	2,101,659	559,938	2,189,982	1,309,596	863,341	12,317,658
LANSING DISTRICT	3,026	2,241	934	385,039	519,830	1,842,228	18,081	454,716	130,188	5,826	49,148	0	2,977,442	786,798	2,130,200	973,026	933,767	13,043,057
CONFERENCE	17,119	18,865	8,858	2,079,007	3,340,243	11,383,614	351,764	2,133,171	872,540	95,804	148,521	7,867	13,744,734	3,287,040	12,578,929	5,187,382	5,374,790	70,930,816
LAST YEAR	12,922	17,095	9,830	2,070,330	3,170,542	11,472,085	329,716	2,482,509	913,341	85,685	151,154	8,923	13,619,916	3,128,405	12,560,755	6,167,206	4,840,533	71,553,928
INCREASE(DECREASE)	4,197	1,770	(972)	8,677	169,701	(88,471)	22,048	(349,338)	(40,801)	10,119	(2,633)	(1,056)	124,818	158,635	18,174	(979,824)	534,257	(623,112)

Table III – Statistical Report *January 1, 2013 through December 31, 2013*

TABLE 3 2013 CHURCH INCOME			RECEIPTS FOR CHURCH ANNUAL BUDGET							
		NUMBER OF HOUSEHOLD GIVING TO CHURCH	RECEIVED FROM PLEDGES	RECEIVED FROM IDENTIFIED NON-PLEDGES	RECEIVED FROM UNIDENTIFED GIVERS	INTEREST & DIVIDENDS	PROCEEDS FROM SALE OF CHURCH ASSETS	RECEIPTS FROM BLDG USE, FEES, RENTALS	FUNDRAISERS & OTHER SOURCES	TOTAL INCOME FOR ANNUAL BUDGETMINISTRY SHARES BASE (LINES 62a to 62g)
Church	Pastor	61	62a	62b	62c	62d	62e	62f	62g	62
ALBION FIRST	Jeremy Williams	103	152,092	32,053	0	366	2,199	14,865	3,264	204,839
ATHENS	Seung Ho (Andy) Baek	34	0	27,901	1,068	6	0	0	4,418	33,393
AUGUSTA FELLOWSHIP	Jennifer Wheeler	25	0	39,462	2,728	27	0	1,375	1,393	44,985
BASELINE	Peggy J Baker	46	60,941	19,833	4,657	211	0	200	0	85,842
BELLEVUE	Peggy J Baker	75	51,743	38,685	2,519	0	0	521	0	93,468
BIRCHWOOD	Bruce R Kintigh	51	92,949	0	1,400	0	2,239	1,913	701	99,202
CHAPEL HILL	Chad M Parmalee	204	324,062	27,377	2,523	945	0	2,519	7,919	365,345
BATTLE CREEK CHRIST	Scott M Bouldrey	82	100,617	0	2,176	4,396	0	2,818	2,079	112,086
CONVIS UNION	Sueann K Hagan	35	0	91,479	1,874	9	0	5	0	93,367
DELTON FAITH	Brian R Bunch	90	0	112,984	2,799	12	0	1,424	0	117,219
BATTLE CREEK FIRST	Billie R Dalton	150	188,971	25,202	3,819	53	0	5,400	2,500	225,945
BATTLE CREEK MAPLE	Linda D Stoddard	60	0	86,470	3,161	0	0	2,284	3,729	95,644
SONOMA	Sally K Harrington	14	0	22,917	2,317	0	0	0	2,451	27,685
NEWTON	Sally K Harrington	60	24,500	43,850	2,500	1	0	0	11,400	82,251
BATTLE CREEK TRINITY	Bruce R Kintigh	42	0	50,347	0	671	501	100	10,185	61,804
WASHINGTON HEIGHTS	Marshall Murphy	24	53,000	0	0	0	0	450	0	53,450
BRONSON FIRST	Cynthia Veilleux	40	0	78,195	3,334	0	0	0	0	81,529
BURR OAK	John Sterner	22	0	25,547	1,704	187	0	6,000	2,126	35,564
CAMDEN	Frederick Gerald Cain	21	18,478	3,825	468	0	0	425	6,206	29,402
MONTGOMERY	Frederick Gerald Cain	20	0	14,510	6,217	647	0	75	4,400	25,849
STOKES CHAPEL	Frederick Gerald Cain	14	25,342	6,687	3,630	904	0	0	260	36,823
CENTER PARK	Martin H Culver	45	60,125	20,901	4,973	0	0	7,906	3,036	96,941
CENTREVILLE	Karin K Orr	84	118,677	55,379	4,600	0	0	3,690	4,723	187,069
CLIMAX	Glenn C Litchfield	48	115,321							115,321
SCOTTS	Glenn C Litchfield	1	46,304							46,304
COLDWATER	Steven R Young	180	143,033	70,915	0	0	3,776	2,274	42,561	262,559
COLON	John Sterner	52	0	69,873	0	5	2,572	747	67	73,264
CONCORD	David G Elmore	74	115,287	34,016	0	57	4,111	1,960	0	155,431
CONSTANTINE	Scott Ernest Manning	35	90,871							90,871
FRONTIER	Timothy Puckett	29	0	22,488	3,531	6	0	4,600	2,522	33,147
OSSEO	Timothy Puckett	14	0	14,448	292	0	0	6,250	500	21,490
GALESBURG	Leonard R Schoenherr	43	0	75,032	2,718	656	0	400	2,627	81,433
GIRARD	Emily Beachy	40	0	112,528	6,640	0	0	0	0	119,168
GRASS LAKE	Dennis E Slattery	86	69,783	40,887	7,200	0	0	663	0	118,533
HILLSDALE	Patricia L Brook	85	26,882	67,284	4,151	4,690	0	(300)	3,912	106,619
HILLSIDE	E Jeanne Koughn	87	83,781	29,344	2,443	277	0	890	2,871	119,606
HOMER	Robert P Stover	20	0	56,920	0	0	0	200	900	58,020
LYON LAKE	Robert P Stover	18	0	47,232	0	0	0	7,950	0	55,182

TABLE 3 2013 CHURCH INCOME

		RECEIPTS FOR CHURCH ANNUAL BUDGET								
		NUMBER OF HOUSEHOLD GIVING TO CHURCH	RECEIVED FROM PLEDGES	RECEIVED FROM IDENTIFIED NON-PLEDGES	RECEIVED FROM UNIDENTIFED GIVERS	INTEREST & DIVIDENDS	PROCEEDS FROM SALE OF CHURCH ASSETS	RECEIPTS FROM BLDG USE, FEES, RENTALS	FUNDRAISERS & OTHER SOURCES	TOTAL INCOME FOR ANNUAL BUDGETMINISTRY SHARES BASE (LINES 62a to 62g)
Church	Pastor	61	62a	62b	62c	62d	62e	62f	62g	62
BROOKSIDE	Ronald K Brooks	87	142,920	20,093	3,819	8	0	1,165	0	168,005
JACKSON CALVARY	Edrye A Eastman Maurer	87	105,332	47,771	2,611	14	0	9,657	8,018	173,403
JACKSON FIRST	Eric S Beck	413	527,871	80,475	6,566	35	0	4,855	0	619,802
TRINITY JACKSON	Patricia Pebley	42	87,233	0	637	20	0	1,486	0	89,376
ZION JACKSON	Edrye A Eastman Maurer	18	0	16,617	2,277	20	0	4,350	0	23,264
JONESVILLE	Craig A Pahl	85	0	86,074	3,626	6	0	340	0	90,046
ALLEN	Craig A Pahl	35	0	42,712	2,416	0	0	0	4,739	49,867
LITCHFIELD	Julie Elmore	50	44,570	33,589	0	1,943	0	1,370	0	81,472
MARENGO	Gerry Retzloff	1			10,555					10,617
MARSHALL	Melany A Chalker	386	324,606	124,558	0	270	5,564	0	2,264	457,262
MENDON	Robert D Nystrom	28	67,100	0	4,693	13	0	270	0	72,076
NAPOLEON	Gregory Ryan Wolfe	65	72,750	22,974	3,197	1,462	0	607	1,009	101,999
NORTH ADAMS	Arthur R Turner	24	0	29,419	3,514	2	0	1,254	2,962	37,151
JEROME	Arthur R Turner	25	0	23,114	2,457	0	0	1,099	370	27,040
NOTTAWA	Alexander Miller	11	0	10,352	159	0	0	0	0	10,511
PARMA	Patricia Pebley	14	13,910	0	458	3	0	1,650	0	16,021
NORTH PARMA	Melissa Claxton	37	0	61,356	2,556	47	0	0	0	63,959
POPE	Robert S Moore-Jumonville	33	20,449		3,096					23,545
GRIFFITH	David H Minger	47	0	18,618	3,413	0	0	300	6,881	29,212
QUINCY	Julie Elmore	62	0	60,603	6,333	1	0	550	0	67,487
READING	Robert M Hughes	75	125,000	4,300	1,900	320	200	1,500	1,400	134,620
SOMERSET CENTER	E Jeanne Koughn	21	14,915	31,203	970	0	0	0	0	47,088
SPRINGPORT	Melissa Claxton	31	0	44,782	3,352	0	0	458	0	48,592
LEE CENTER	Irene L Vittoz	20	0	36,184	0	0	0	0	4,539	40,723
STURGIS	Deborah M Johnson	226	231,997	50,303	0	20	149	2,081	1,959	286,509
THREE RIVERS FIRST	Robert D Nystrom	63	0	141,064	3,340	0	0	0	250	144,654
THREE RIVERS NINTH STREET	James W Stilwell	30	0	32,823	5,053	977	0	0	9,579	48,432
UNION CITY	Seung (Andy) Ho Baek	45	95,475	20,212	3,998	0	0	0	157	119,842
WEST MENDON	Thoreau D May	51	0	88,448	2,291	0	0	0	0	90,739
SCHOOLCRAFT PLEASANT VALLEY	James W Stilwell	28	0	46,057	7,199	3	0	100	220	53,579
WHITE PIGEON	Scott Ernest Manning	45	0	46,686	720	17	0	0	0	47,423
ALBION DISTRICT	TAMARA WILLIAMS	4,338	3,836,887	2,684,958	176,648	19,307	21,311	110,696	171,097	7,020,965
LAST YEAR		4,464	3,884,498	2,626,169	215,674	13,243	6,721	91,194	135,829	6,973,328
INC/(DEC)		(126)	(47,611)	58,789	(39,026)	6,064	14,590	19,502	35,268	47,637

TABLE 3 2013 CHURCH INCOME	CAPITAL CAMPAIGNS & OTHER DESIGNATED PROJECTS					CONNECTIONAL & OTHER SOURCES			
	CAPITAL CAMPAIGNS & OTHER DESIGNATED PROJECTS	MEMORIALS, BEQUESTS, ENDOWMENTS	OTHER SOURCES & SUPPORT OF PROJECTS	SPECIAL OFFERINGS FOR MISSION	TOTAL 68.a TO 68.d	EQUITABLE COMPENSATION SUPPORT	ADVANCE SPECIALS RECEIVED	GRANTS FROM OTHER SOURCES	TOTAL 69.a TO 69.c
Church	63a	63b	63c	63d	63	64a	64b	64c	64
ALBION FIRST	106,482	1,092	0	8,036	115,610	0	0	0	0
ATHENS	760	720	0	1,149	2,629	0	0	0	0
AUGUSTA FELLOWSHIP	571	880	0	1,239	2,690	0	0	0	0
BASELINE	0	1,110	1,473	2,161	4,744	0	0	1,076	1,076
BELLEVUE	3,768	95	6,825	4,641	15,329	0	0	2,697	2,697
BIRCHWOOD	0	705	0	112	817	0	0	0	0
CHAPEL HILL	10,521	28,852	16,333	65,631	121,337	0	0	0	0
BATTLE CREEK CHRIST	0	3,945	2,012	163	6,120	0	0	0	0
CONVIS UNION	0	100	1,802	0	1,902	0	0	0	0
DELTON FAITH	0	3,962	0	55,244	59,206	3,324	0	0	3,324
BATTLE CREEK FIRST	0	1,500	0	1,377	2,877	0	0	1,000	1,000
BATTLE CREEK MAPLE	0	6,187	0	1,175	7,262	0	0	0	0
SONOMA	0	3,169	1,533	763	5,465	0	0	0	0
NEWTON	0	1,390	14,960	1,098	17,448	0	0	0	0
BATTLE CREEK TRINITY	0	1,326	0	358	1,684	0	0	0	0
WASHINGTON HEIGHTS	10,000	35	500	500	11,035	3,000	12,500	0	15,500
BRONSON FIRST	0	2,703	1,655	3,111	7,469	0	0	0	0
BURR OAK	0	430	0	734	1,164	0	0	0	0
CAMDEN	0	0	0	0	0	0	0	0	0
MONTGOMERY	0	660	142	993	1,795	0	0	0	0
STOKES CHAPEL	21,220	630	0	907	22,757	0	0	0	0
CENTER PARK	7,245	1,290	0	4,269	12,804	0	6,000	0	6,000
CENTREVILLE	8,903	4,663	0	11,556	25,122	0	0	0	0
CLIMAX	0	0	0	9,125	9,125	0	0	0	0
SCOTTS	0	0	0	1	1	0	0	0	0
COLDWATER	0	18,341	3,991	31,144	53,476	0	0	0	0
COLON	10,145	25	2,550	3,007	15,727	0	0	0	0
CONCORD	40,277	4,620	13,931	2,160	60,988	0	0	4,400	4,400
CONSTANTINE	14,635	1,623	2,026	4,228	22,512	3,000	54	0	3,054
FRONTIER	0	240	0	109	349	0	0	695	695
OSSEO	0	0	0	147	147	0	0	0	0
GALESBURG	0	25,056	3,068	6,493	34,617	0	0	0	0
GIRARD	0	2,560	0	284	2,844	0	0	0	0
GRASS LAKE	576	19,513	0	7,897	27,986	0	0	0	0
HILLSDALE	0	1,568,032	0	2,899	1,570,931	0	0	0	0
HILLSIDE	3,735	2,975	0	2,139	8,849	0	0	3,157	3,157
HOMER	0	1,450	4,829	3,200	9,479	0	0	0	0
LYON LAKE	0	3,425	0	2,894	6,319	0	0	0	0

TABLE 3 2013 CHURCH INCOME	CAPITAL CAMPAIGNS & OTHER DESIGNATED PROJECTS					CONNECTIONAL & OTHER SOURCES			
	CAPITAL CAMPAIGNS & OTHER DESIGNATED PROJECTS	MEMORIALS, BEQUESTS, ENDOWMENTS	OTHER SOURCES & SUPPORT OF PROJECTS	SPECIAL OFFERINGS FOR MISSION	TOTAL 68.a TO 68.d	EQUITABLE COMPENSATION SUPPORT	ADVANCE SPECIALS RECEIVED	GRANTS FROM OTHER SOURCES	TOTAL 69.a TO 69.c
Church	63a	63b	63c	63d	63	64a	64b	64c	64
BROOKSIDE	0	7,503	0	17,540	25,043	0	0	0	0
JACKSON CALVARY	0	1,440	0	3,898	5,338	0	0	3,958	3,958
JACKSON FIRST	0	1,627	0	5,902	7,529	0	0	0	0
TRINITY JACKSON	1,802	2,646	1,827	6,162	12,437	0	0	0	0
ZION JACKSON	0	0	9,871	746	10,617	0	0	0	0
JONESVILLE	4,727	1,169	0	487	6,383	0	0	0	0
ALLEN	1,370	14,351	0	586	16,307	0	0	0	0
LITCHFIELD	0	2,460	0	31,362	33,822	0	0	0	0
MARENGO									
MARSHALL	73,939	5,010	81,455	746	161,150	0	0	0	0
MENDON	0	0	0	1,082	1,082	0	0	0	0
NAPOLEON	5,205	80	14,478	2,553	22,316	0	0	0	0
NORTH ADAMS	0	2,140	0	1,967	4,107	0	0	0	0
JEROME	0	610	295	1,706	2,611	0	0	0	0
NOTTAWA	2,200	0	0	797	2,997	0	0	0	0
PARMA	0	1,470	2,786	219	4,475	0	0	0	0
NORTH PARMA	13,040	2,330	0	12,061	27,431	0	0	0	0
POPE			200		200				
GRIFFITH	18,992	650	1,657	2,230	23,529	0	0	0	0
QUINCY	3,787	24,629	13,627	7,442	49,485	0	0	0	0
READING	10,670	1,370	3,130	783	15,953	0	0	123	123
SOMERSET CENTER	0	915	298	110	1,323	0	0	0	0
SPRINGPORT	4,638	615	1,242	10,024	16,519	0	0	817	817
LEE CENTER	0	130	0	2,800	2,930	0	0	0	0
STURGIS	15,212	7,360	0	3,055	25,627	0	0	0	0
THREE RIVERS FIRST	0	21,118	14,000	1,328	36,446	0	0	0	0
THREE RIVERS NINTH STREET	0	19,964	0	3,242	23,206	1,360	0	0	1,360
UNION CITY	3,896	2,355	0	6,181	12,432	0	0	0	0
WEST MENDON	0	690	0	6,034	6,724	0	0	0	0
SCHOOLCRAFT PLEASANT VALLEY	0	755	0	10,398	11,153	2,720	0	0	2,720
WHITE PIGEON	11,000	25,000	3,874	0	39,874	0	0	0	0
ALBION DISTRICT	409,316	1,861,691	226,370	382,385	2,879,762	13,404	18,554	17,923	49,881
LAST YEAR	500,907	525,900	222,641	378,199	1,627,647	22,673	32,984	23,191	78,848
INC/(DEC)	(91,591)	1,335,791	3,729	4,186	1,252,115	(9,269)	(14,430)	(5,268)	(28,967)

STATISTICAL INFO

STATISTICAL INFO

TABLE 3 2013 CHURCH INCOME		RECEIPTS FOR CHURCH ANNUAL BUDGET								
		NUMBER OF HOUSEHOLD GIVING TO CHURCH	RECEIVED FROM PLEDGES	RECEIVED FROM IDENTIFIED NON-PLEDGES	RECEIVED FROM UNIDENTIFED GIVERS	INTEREST & DIVIDENDS	PROCEEDS FROM SALE OF CHURCH ASSETS	RECEIPTS FROM BLDG USE, FEES, RENTALS	FUNDRAISERS & OTHER SOURCES	TOTAL INCOME FOR ANNUAL BUDGETMINISTRY SHARES BASE (LINES 62a to 62g)
Church	Pastor	61	62a	62b	62c	62d	62e	62f	62g	62
ALTO	Dean Irwin Bailey	37	0	46,017	3,538	0	0	375	0	49,930
BOWNE CENTER	Dean Irwin Bailey	49	0	53,000	2,331	1	584	2,450	0	58,366
BYRON CENTER	Lawrence A Nichols	760	0	164,769	1,274	61	0	345	4,383	170,832
CALEDONIA	Jodie R Flessner	120	123,838	69,433	2,972	51	0	200	1,068	197,562
CARLISLE	Michael Ramsey	73	64,419	30,489	5,430	32	0	350	0	100,720
CEDAR SPRINGS	Mary Letta-Bement Ivanov	140	0	188,111	3,836	44	0	1,085	0	193,076
EAST NELSON	Herbert J VanderBilt	63	0	107,820	13,559	301	0	0	0	121,680
COOPERSVILLE	Cori Lynn Cypret	53	121,892	0	3,329	0	0	0	0	125,221
COURTLAND-OAKFIELD	Robert Eckert	62	88,423	19,821	10,329	8	0	550	0	119,131
FREMONT	Martin T Cobb	167	221,495	72,096	13,614	5,135	0	500	0	312,840
GEORGETOWN	William C Bills	262	287,080	151,149	5,239	3,463	0	3,578	2,009	452,518
GRAND HAVEN CHURCH OF THE D	Daniel M Duncan	328	374,189	116,573	22,067	0	0	3,505	16,773	533,107
ALDERSGATE	James E Hodge	113	172,526	260,730	1,800	69	0	7,720	5,613	448,458
SOUTH WYOMING	Marcia L Elders	75	75,732	14,557	0	4	0	5,032	2,704	98,029
CORNERSTONE	Bradley P Kalajainen	1,319	0	2,358,973	82,469	1,926	0	10,198	0	2,453,566
FAITH GRAND RAPIDS	Mark E Thompson	152	167,101	19,530	1,295	10,000	0	0	2,803	200,729
FIRST GRAND RAPIDS	Robert L Hundley	336	1,038,842	34,193	10,750	619	0	0	107,620	1,192,024
GENESIS	Susan M Petro	143	188,455	60,431	9,802	5,244	0	500	23,343	287,775
LA NUEVA ESPERANZA	Nohemi V Ramirez	15	14,744	0	3,259	0	0	0	2,979	20,982
NORTHLAWN	Timothy B Wright	81	164,660	0	2,798	0	0	0	0	167,458
PLAINFIELD	Laurie Haller	15	10,953	5,815	704	2,697	0	10,890	1,405	32,464
SAINT PAULS GRAND RAPIDS	Erin Fitzgerald	107	197,274	18,718	2,417	1,506	0	5,837	334	226,086
SOUTH GRAND RAPIDS	Mack C Strange	94	81,343	53,286	0	0	2,883	8,742	2,801	149,055
TRINITY GRAND RAPIDS	David Nellist	175	518,124	63,925	7,427	89	0	24,741	1,599	615,905
VIETNAMESE GRAND RAPIDS	Daniel Nguyen	30	0	40,000	0	0	0	0	0	40,000
GRANDVILLE	Thomas M Pier-Fitzgerald	177	189,224	87,552	3,328	426	350	2,215	0	283,095
HESPERIA	Paul E Hane	62	0	61,190	13,638	0	0	0	954	75,782
FERRY	Paul E Hane	35	0	50,636	4,962	0	0	0	0	55,598
HOLLAND	J Lynn Pier-Fitzgerald	303	460,276	62,205	8,397	0	0	3,735	19,474	554,087
HOLTON	Gerald L Selleck	162	0	195,237	32,178	0	0	600	0	228,015
KENT CITY CHAPEL HILL	Kevin Guetschow	66	0	109,169	0	0	4,614	0	0	113,783
LEIGHTON	David L McBride	113	146,922	74,300	7,672	28	0	1,860	0	230,782
LOWELL	Richard W Blunt	175	239,736	35,006	6,784	1,971	0	1,818	0	285,315
MARNE	James Thomas Boutell	45	0	104,000	900	0	0	0	0	104,900
MARTIN	Donald J Graham	75	0	121,262	2,612	0	0	1,630	0	125,504
SHELBYVILLE	Donald J Graham	38	0	56,595	290	101	0	50	0	57,036
MIDDLEVILLE	Anthony C Shumaker	75	185,706	25,959	4,855	41	0	0	0	216,561
PARMELEE	William V Clegg	27	0	40,836	0	0	0	0	0	40,836

2013 TABLE 3 CHURCH INCOME			RECEIPTS FOR CHURCH ANNUAL BUDGET							
		NUMBER OF HOUSEHOLD GIVING TO CHURCH	RECEIVED FROM PLEDGES	RECEIVED FROM IDENTIFIED NON-PLEDGES	RECEIVED FROM UNIDENTIFED GIVERS	INTEREST & DIVIDENDS	PROCEEDS FROM SALE OF CHURCH ASSETS	RECEIPTS FROM BLDG USE, FEES, RENTALS	FUNDRAISERS & OTHER SOURCES	TOTAL INCOME FOR ANNUAL BUDGETMINISTRY SHARES BASE (LINES 62a to 62g)
Church	Pastor	61	62a	62b	62c	62d	62e	62f	62g	62
MONTAGUE	Randall R Hansen	181	199,991	3,520	2,688	2	0	351	0	206,552
CENTRAL MUSKEGON	Mark D Miller	208	283,789	67,822	0	61,592	4,465	3,665	1,840	423,173
CRESTWOOD	Stephan Weinberger	43	73,674	0	202	3,050	0	239	6,247	83,412
LAKE HARBOR	Mark R Erbes	200	235,996	33,438	2,889	188	0	1,265	20,123	293,899
LAKESIDE	Stephan Weinberger	69	65,691	42,263	0	13,815	2,951	691	1,201	126,612
UNITY	R John Thompson	30		33,341	2,665	46		4,238	183	40,474
WOLF LAKE	Bobby Dale Whitlock	48	73,235	0	2,183	0	59,006	235	553	135,212
MUSKEGON HEIGHTS TEMPLE	Jeffrey J Bowman	101	147,343	41,008	2,040	0	0	0	25,544	215,935
NEWAYGO	Kathleen A Groff	80	80,195	24,806	1,728	1,035	0	655	197	108,616
NORTH MUSKEGON COMMUNITY	Phillip J Friedrick	155	244,502	0	0	9	0	0	0	244,511
RAVENNA	Carleton Black	65	0	101,219	1,332	0	0	355	0	102,906
ROCKFORD	Richard M Riley	400	630,838	0	0	733	0	10,101	0	641,672
SALEM INDIAN MISSION	Nancy L Boelens	8	4,777	2,400	702	0	0	0	379	8,258
BRADLEY INDIAN MISSION	Nancy L Boelens	9	0	12,197	0	0	0	0	754	12,951
SAUGATUCK	Emmett H Kadwell	61	48,959	0	2,021	4	0	200	0	51,184
SHELBY	Terri Cummins	58	70,786	5,735	3,335	4	0	903	0	80,763
SNOW	Anthony C Shumaker	20	0	49,671	0	0	0	0	0	49,671
SPARTA	Louis W Grettenberger	123	196,112	73,869	3,385	682	5,710	4,438	0	284,196
TWIN LAKE	John D Morse	38		63,261	6,660			649		70,569
SITKA	Gerald F Hagans	13	0	13,978	0	2	0	0	0	13,980
VALLEY CHURCH ALLENDALE NEW	Matthew J Bistayi	2								72,615
VERGENNES	Matthew Todd Stoll	94	183,774	34,037	3,963	60	0	1,280	11,649	234,763
WAYLAND	Gary D Bondarenko	59	74,860	33,007	1,480	0	0	868	3,841	114,056
WHITE CLOUD	Edwin D Snook	107	112,075	40,066	4,584	0	0	3,250	0	159,975
WHITEHALL	Gayle S Berntsen	40	0	81,912	2,958	5	0	2,140	2,955	89,970
CLAYBANKS	Gayle S Berntsen	39	0	39,682	9,319	208	0	50	0	49,259
WESLEY PARK	Dean N Prentiss	189	0	349,660	8,366	37	0	3,423	7,743	369,229
WYOMING PARK	Joel Thomas Fitzgerald	45	106,622	22,699	0	82	1,088	8,500	109	139,100
CROSSWIND COMMUNITY	Scott Keith Otis	68	158,896	49,093	6,378	0	0	0	0	214,367
GRAND RAPIDS DISTRICT	WILLIAM HAGGARD	8,675	8,125,069	6,192,067	364,733	115,371	81,651	146,002	279,180	15,376,688
LAST YEAR		7,600	9,320,547	4,834,534	459,155	73,919	10,000	283,889	208,427	14,663,594
INC/(DEC)		1,075	(1,195,478)	1,357,533	(94,422)	41,452	71,651	(137,887)	70,753	713,094

STATISTICAL INFO

TABLE 3 2013 CHURCH INCOME	CAPITAL CAMPAIGNS & OTHER DESIGNATED PROJECTS					CONNECTIONAL & OTHER SOURCES			
	CAPITAL CAMPAIGNS & OTHER DESIGNATED PROJECTS	MEMORIALS, BEQUESTS, ENDOWMENTS	OTHER SOURCES & SUPPORT OF PROJECTS	SPECIAL OFFERINGS FOR MISSION	TOTAL 68.a TO 68.d	EQUITABLE COMPENSATION SUPPORT	ADVANCE SPECIALS RECEIVED	GRANTS FROM OTHER SOURCES	TOTAL 69.a TO 69.c
Church	63a	63b	63c	63d	63	64a	64b	64c	64
ALTO	53,713	1,270	0	0	54,983	0	0	0	0
BOWNE CENTER	0	0	0	0	0	0	0	0	0
BYRON CENTER	46,458	0	0	8,886	55,344	0	0	0	0
CALEDONIA	32,552	1,516	0	5,926	39,994	0	0	0	0
CARLISLE	0	19,300	5,159	7,201	31,660	0	0	0	0
CEDAR SPRINGS	880	325	30,166	13,542	44,913	0	0	1,400	1,400
EAST NELSON	0	0	0	2,617	2,617	0	0	0	0
COOPERSVILLE	36,890	0	31,612	6,483	74,985	0	0	0	0
COURTLAND-OAKFIELD	23,882	1,300	0	9,521	34,703	0	0	0	0
FREMONT	0	0	1,076	33,824	34,900	0	0	0	0
GEORGETOWN	102,601	3,475	0	3,268	109,344	0	0	0	0
GRAND HAVEN CHURCH OF THE D	290,895	9,907	0	56,530	357,332	0	0	0	0
ALDERSGATE	11,700	10,894	12,360	7,214	42,168	0	0	1,500	1,500
SOUTH WYOMING	0	1,195	0	5,447	6,642	0	0	0	0
CORNERSTONE	681,783	585	60,809	3,946	747,123	0	0	60,000	60,000
FAITH GRAND RAPIDS	6,875	1,250	0	3,805	11,930	0	0	0	0
FIRST GRAND RAPIDS	819,823	497,049	0	22,886	1,339,758	0	0	162,916	162,916
GENESIS	0	0	0	19,756	19,756	0	1,500	0	1,500
LA NUEVA ESPERANZA	0	0	0	6,020	6,020	0	17,307	13,500	30,807
NORTHLAWN	87,306	104,221	0	1,000	192,527	4,000	0	0	4,000
PLAINFIELD	0	1,804	0	15	1,819	0	1,000	0	1,000
SAINT PAULS GRAND RAPIDS	15,715	50	0	12,111	27,876	0	0	0	0
SOUTH GRAND RAPIDS	1,039	1,375	0	2,222	4,636	0	0	0	0
TRINITY GRAND RAPIDS	9,988	58,084	17,129	22,106	107,307	0	0	0	0
VIETNAMESE GRAND RAPIDS	0	0	0	1,950	1,950	17,000	30,580	0	47,580
GRANDVILLE	0	6,195	91,180	0	97,375	0	0	0	0
HESPERIA	0	205	0	3,351	3,556	0	0	0	0
FERRY	0	0	0	563	563	0	0	0	0
HOLLAND	34,928	15,570	0	32,897	83,395	0	0	0	0
HOLTON	6,671	647	0	1,177	8,495	0	0	0	0
KENT CITY CHAPEL HILL	13,907	355	4,688	3,370	22,320	0	0	0	0
LEIGHTON	0	29,245	0	5,325	34,570	0	0	0	0
LOWELL	152,021	2,120	8,073	2,720	164,934	0	0	7,855	7,855
MARNE	0	0	0	0	0	0	0	0	0
MARTIN	4,946	4,819	0	12,319	22,084	0	0	0	0
SHELBYVILLE	0	1,875	771	691	3,337	0	0	0	0
MIDDLEVILLE	0	11,840	9,102	6,549	27,491	0	0	0	0
PARMELEE	0	610	0	0	610	0	0	0	0

2013 TABLE 3 CHURCH INCOME	CAPITAL CAMPAIGNS & OTHER DESIGNATED PROJECTS					CONNECTIONAL & OTHER SOURCES			
	CAPITAL CAMPAIGNS & OTHER DESIGNATED PROJECTS	MEMORIALS, BEQUESTS, ENDOWMENTS	OTHER SOURCES & SUPPORT OF PROJECTS	SPECIAL OFFERINGS FOR MISSION	TOTAL 68.a TO 68.d	EQUITABLE COMPENSATION SUPPORT	ADVANCE SPECIALS RECEIVED	GRANTS FROM OTHER SOURCES	TOTAL 69.a TO 69.c
Church	63a	63b	63c	63d	63	64a	64b	64c	64
MONTAGUE	7,659	1,446	0	9,579	18,684	0	0	500	500
CENTRAL MUSKEGON	17,668	30,529	0	27,911	76,108	0	0	0	0
CRESTWOOD	106,574	250	1,500	1,232	109,556	0	0	0	0
LAKE HARBOR	15,047	27,198	13,680	8,755	64,680	0	0	0	0
LAKESIDE	0	45	5,653	1,869	7,567	500	0	0	500
UNITY	6,663	464	0	0	7,127				
WOLF LAKE	0	55,098	0	0	55,098	0	0	0	0
MUSKEGON HEIGHTS TEMPLE	0	1,010	8,377	630	10,017	0	0	0	0
NEWAYGO	0	0	0	6,678	6,678	0	0	0	0
NORTH MUSKEGON COMMUNITY	0	14,480	0	8,525	23,005	0	0	0	0
RAVENNA	18,105	6,220	4,416	2,447	31,188	0	0	0	0
ROCKFORD	129,918	9,743	0	6,687	146,348	0	0	0	0
SALEM INDIAN MISSION	0	0	0	0	0	8,000	3,100	2,500	13,600
BRADLEY INDIAN MISSION	0	0	0	1	1	0	0	0	0
SAUGATUCK	23,146	0	0	3,698	26,844	0	0	0	0
SHELBY	0	3,265	50,838	14,030	68,133	2,400	0	0	2,400
SNOW	0	1,089	0	6,098	7,187	0	0	0	0
SPARTA	23,847	5,145	310	17,498	46,800	0	0	0	0
TWIN LAKE									
SITKA	200	0	2,795	0	2,995	0	0	0	0
VALLEY CHURCH ALLENDALE NEW									
VERGENNES	6,005	2,180	5,000	6,516	19,701	0	0	0	0
WAYLAND	0	89,859	0	1,659	91,518	0	0	0	0
WHITE CLOUD	0	1,556	10,778	2,274	14,608	0	0	0	0
WHITEHALL	0	0	0	0	0	0	1,600	0	1,600
CLAYBANKS	0	1,755	2,342	1,044	5,141	0	0	0	0
WESLEY PARK	101,304	7,312	11,351	6,042	126,009	0	0	0	0
WYOMING PARK	54,075	175	2,348	3,800	60,398	0	0	0	0
CROSSWIND COMMUNITY	4,423	0	0	1,628	6,051	0	0	0	0
GRAND RAPIDS DISTRICT	2,949,207	1,045,900	391,513	463,839	4,850,459	31,900	55,087	250,171	337,158
LAST YEAR	1,597,872	516,493	427,878	491,817	3,034,060	58,248	84,143	81,775	224,166
INC/(DEC)	1,351,335	529,407	(36,365)	(27,978)	1,816,399	(26,348)	(29,056)	168,396	112,992

STATISTICAL INFO

STATISTICAL INFO

TABLE 3 2013 CHURCH INCOME

		RECEIPTS FOR CHURCH ANNUAL BUDGET								
		NUMBER OF HOUSEHOLD GIVING TO CHURCH	RECEIVED FROM PLEDGES	RECEIVED FROM IDENTIFIED NON-PLEDGES	RECEIVED FROM UNIDENTIFED GIVERS	INTEREST & DIVIDENDS	PROCEEDS FROM SALE OF CHURCH ASSETS	RECEIPTS FROM BLDG USE FEES, RENTALS	FUNDRAISERS & OTHER SOURCES	TOTAL INCOME FOR ANNUAL BUDGETMINISTRY SHARES BASE (LINES 62a to 62g)
Church	Pastor	61	62a	62b	62c	62d	62e	62f	62g	62
ALDEN	Daniel W Biteman	43	33,151	18,004	5,860	15		1,045	1,796	59,872
CENTRAL LAKE	Daniel W Biteman	1		31,772						31,772
BALDWIN COVENANT COMMUNITY	James A Richie	36	51,337	5,005	17,349	0	0	0	0	73,691
LUTHER	James A Richie	18	13,070	5,505	6,041	83	0	0	1,880	26,579
BARNARD	Ralph Posnik	40	0	15,666	10,019	129	0	100	0	25,914
EAST JORDAN	Ralph Posnik	68	0	86,731	2,904	24	0	0	0	89,659
NORWOOD	Ralph Posnik	8	0	13,802	2,028	0	0	0	296	16,126
BEAR LAKE	Roberta W Cabot	73	0	104,893	4,838	8,260	500	837	1,244	120,572
ARCADIA	Roberta W Cabot	10	22,423	2,127	0	0	0	0	1,755	26,305
BELLAIRE COMMUNITY	Peggy A Boltz	157	0	159,532	0	650	0	0	0	160,182
BOYNE CITY	Wayne E McKenney	56	0	76,445	0	22	2,116	100	4,623	83,306
BOYNE FALLS	Wayne E McKenney	16	0	25,423	0	0	3,352	150	2,297	31,222
BRETHREN EPWORTH	Colleen Wierman	48	0	21,230	7,443	0	0	0	5,307	33,980
CADILLAC	Thomas Eric Ball	346	247,135	9,400	0	57	22,247	4,325	21,355	304,519
CHARLEVOIX	Gregory P Culver	50	0	96,207	1,353	0	0	0	5,249	102,809
CRYSTAL VALLEY	Ronald L F Iris	19	0	16,300	0	0	0	0	0	16,300
WALKERVILLE	Ronald L F Iris	21	0	30,300	0	0	0	0	0	30,300
KEWADIN	Eugene L Baughan	60	0	51,846	3,175	0	0	350	0	55,371
EMPIRE	Brenda E Gordon	79	0	119,976	3,723	0	0	91	4,055	127,845
EPSILON	Vaughn W Thurston-Cox	26	0	56,254	6,383	0	0	0	0	62,637
NEW HOPE	Vaughn W Thurston-Cox	32	0	58,353	3,742	12	0	0	0	62,107
FIFE LAKE	Mark E Mitchell	40	0	0	55,677	0	0	450	671	56,798
SOUTH BOARDMAN	Mark E Mitchell	5	0	12,996	0	0	0	0	0	12,996
EAST BOARDMAN	Mark E Mitchell	21	0	0	41,892	0	0	0	5,309	47,201
FRANKFORT	Barbara Jo Fay	107	102,126	43,301	2,897	2,516	0	125	3,345	154,310
ELBERTA	Barbara Jo Fay	39	13,027	18,758	1,086	107	0	0	366	33,344
FREESOIL-FOUNTAIN	Richard Roberts	16	0	200	8,673	0	0	0	700	9,573
FOUNTAIN	Richard Roberts	12	0	1,102	0	0	0	0	9,198	10,300
GRAWN	Mary S Brown	62	68,255	0	16,675	3	0	1,435	1,964	88,332
HARBOR SPRINGS	Mary Sweet	118	34,411	28,016	2,780	68	0	1,576	12,664	79,515
ALANSON	Mary Sweet	42	0	43,177	6,111	0	0	0	976	50,264
HART	Rebecca F Wieringa	78	130,530	13,463	7,915	11	0	575	500	152,994
HORTON BAY	Michael R Neihardt	18	0	43,021	3,200	105	0	0	0	46,326
GREENSKY HILL	Jonathan D Mays	60	0	40,347	9,742	883	0	100	6,072	57,144
INDIAN RIVER	DeAnn J Dobbs	170	0	146,716	15,745	26	0	1,625	0	164,112
KALKASKA	Robert J Freysinger	1	221,156							221,156
KESWICK	Patricia Ann Haas	47	82,180	58,505	2,256	48	0	3,620	1,321	147,930
KEWADIN INDIAN MISSION	Thomas H John	35	6,219	4,274	0	0	0	415	869	11,777

2013 TABLE 3 CHURCH INCOME		RECEIPTS FOR CHURCH ANNUAL BUDGET								
		NUMBER OF HOUSEHOLD GIVING TO CHURCH	RECEIVED FROM PLEDGES	RECEIVED FROM IDENTIFIED NON-PLEDGES	RECEIVED FROM UNIDENTIFED GIVERS	INTEREST & DIVIDENDS	PROCEEDS FROM SALE OF CHURCH ASSETS	RECEIPTS FROM BLDG USE, FEES, RENTALS	FUNDRAISERS & OTHER SOURCES	TOTAL INCOME FOR ANNUAL BUDGETMINISTRY SHARES BASE (LINES 62a to 62g)
Church	Pastor	61	62a	62b	62c	62d	62e	62f	62g	62
KINGSLEY	Carl Q Litchfield	75	0	157,805	17,540	57	0	0	0	175,402
GRANT	Colleen Wierman	30	0	36,469	6,458	0	0	0	851	43,778
LAKE ANN	Michael J Simon	85	0	161,069	9,315	32	0	1,310	7,430	179,156
LAKE CITY	Jean M Smith	63	82,682	12,260	2,805	0	0	3,668	8,186	109,601
LELAND	Virginia L Heller	242	218,904	96,217	6,646	169	0	10,300	12,993	345,229
LUDINGTON ST PAUL	Jon L Pohl	94	0	158,536	0	257	0	0	0	158,793
LUDINGTON UNITED	Dennis B Bromley	364	302,242	12,474	11,023	284	0	7,066	0	333,089
MANCELONA	Todd W Shafer	90	0	81,041	4,836	6,461	0	0	1,452	93,790
ALBA	Todd W Shafer	20	0	26,045	2,467	0	0	0	2,014	30,526
MANISTEE	David A Selleck	159	173,657	94,154	7,305	37	0	453	0	275,606
MANTON	Noreen Shafer	62	0	93,330	5,026	0	0	566	33,172	132,094
MARION	James J Mort	45	0	42,812	8,391	2,304	0	485	220	54,212
CADILLAC SOUTH COMMUNITY	James J Mort	20	0	34,486	4,063	69	0	115	285	39,018
MEARS	Kenneth D Vanderlaan	62	0	85,136	4,000	0	0	450	2,200	91,786
MESICK	Beverley Williams	43	0	35,110	2,652	667	0	300	853	39,582
HARRIETTA	Beverley Williams	69	0	40,999	4,000	41	0	300	3,641	48,981
MERRITT-BUTTERFIELD	Jeffrey J Schrock	57	0	56,890	22,187	0	0	0	0	79,077
MOORESTOWN-STITTSVILLE	Jeffrey J Schrock	44	0	28,083	0	0	5,700	0	0	33,783
NORTHPORT INDIAN MISSION	Thomas H John	31	5,408	2,624	0	0	0	0	1,850	9,882
OLD MISSION PENINSULA	Melody Lane Olin	44	0	97,522	3,107	65	0	912	85,142	186,748
PENTWATER CENTENARY	Gary L Bekofske	149	105,123	49,740	4,515	20	0	1,855	0	161,253
PETOSKEY	James P Mitchum	222	303,573	46,429	7,143	149	0	15,822	2,488	375,604
ASHTON	Scott Loomis	38	0	31,462	0	11	0	200	3,780	35,453
LEROY	Scott Loomis	31	0	65,097	2,750	0	0	550	2,547	70,944
SCOTTVILLE	John Joseph Conklin	102	82,576	40,169	4,965	5,385	0	5,631	0	138,726
TRAVERSE BAY	Jane R L Lippert	140	185,603	92,802	0	0	0	3,780	0	282,185
CENTRAL TRAVERSE CITY	Dale P Ostema	359	720,943	157,465	28,767	0	0	10,229	14,599	932,003
CHRIST TRAVERSE CITY	Dianne D Morrison	28	60,440	0	0	0	0	38,000	4,700	103,140
WILLIAMSBURG	Geraldine M Litchfield	35	0	64,919	3,709	3	0	1,230	5,534	75,395
GRAND TRAVERSE DIST	ANITA HAHN	4,881	3,266,171	3,359,793	423,177	29,030	33,915	120,141	287,749	7,519,977
LAST YEAR		4,598	3,417,813	3,131,953	506,506	30,766	1,445	117,573	148,210	7,354,266
INC/(DEC)		283	(151,642)	227,840	(83,329)	(1,736)	32,470	2,568	139,539	165,711

STATISTICAL INFO

2013 TABLE 3 CHURCH INCOME	CAPITAL CAMPAIGNS & OTHER DESIGNATED PROJECTS					CONNECTIONAL & OTHER SOURCES			
	CAPITAL CAMPAIGNS & OTHER DESIGNATED PROJECTS	MEMORIALS, BEQUESTS, ENDOWMENTS	OTHER SOURCES & SUPPORT OF PROJECTS	SPECIAL OFFERINGS FOR MISSION	TOTAL 68.a TO 68.d	EQUITABLE COMPENSATION SUPPORT	ADVANCE SPECIALS RECEIVED	GRANTS FROM OTHER SOURCES	TOTAL 69.a TO 69.c
Church	63a	63b	63c	63d	63	64a	64b	64c	64
ALDEN	1	19,889	3,240	6,043	29,173	0	0	0	0
CENTRAL LAKE	0	0	0	1	1	0	0	0	0
BALDWIN COVENANT COMMUNITY	0	2,600	4,800	0	7,400	32,643	0	0	32,643
LUTHER	0	575	1,664	442	2,681	0	0	0	0
BARNARD	0	480	2,906	2,306	5,692	0	0	0	0
EAST JORDAN	9,781	803	0	8,611	19,195	0	0	0	0
NORWOOD	0	0	0	0	0	0	0	0	0
BEAR LAKE	16,010	3,795	0	1,754	21,559	0	0	0	0
ARCADIA	0	500	0	0	500	0	0	0	0
BELLAIRE COMMUNITY	1,795	0	7,200	10,610	19,605	0	0	0	0
BOYNE CITY	5,300	2,088	0	6,020	13,408	0	0	0	0
BOYNE FALLS	12,400	0	0	1,767	14,167	0	0	0	0
BRETHREN EPWORTH	0	370	6,648	0	7,018	0	0	0	0
CADILLAC	25,438	4,501	13,531	27,595	71,065	0	384	0	384
CHARLEVOIX	0	861	0	4,219	5,080	0	0	0	0
CRYSTAL VALLEY	0	0	0	979	979	0	0	0	0
WALKERVILLE	0	0	0	1,944	1,944	0	0	0	0
KEWADIN	0	0	0	1,929	1,929	0	0	0	0
EMPIRE	0	705	6,941	5,294	12,940	0	0	0	0
EPSILON	0	0	5,273	531	5,804	0	0	500	500
NEW HOPE	4,756	1,171	2,778	10,636	19,341	0	0	0	0
FIFE LAKE	0	1,380	0	2,261	3,641	0	0	0	0
SOUTH BOARDMAN	194	1,157	0	0	1,351	0	0	0	0
EAST BOARDMAN	5,639	505	6,934	967	14,045	0	0	0	0
FRANKFORT	0	20,540	20,863	22,368	63,771	0	0	0	0
ELBERTA	467	3,115	4,834	7,514	15,930	0	0	0	0
FREESOIL-FOUNTAIN	0	0	0	0	0	0	8,889	0	8,889
FOUNTAIN		0	0	0	0	0	0	0	0
GRAWN	3,179	2,061	2,030	3,592	10,862	0	0	0	0
HARBOR SPRINGS	1,118	2,250	921	1,429	5,718	0	0	0	0
ALANSON	0	3,085	0	2,975	6,060	0	0	0	0
HART	23,418	7,219	29,820	0	60,457	0	0	300	300
HORTON BAY	0	200	5,412	2,087	7,699	0	0	0	0
GREENSKY HILL	0	0	0	4,075	4,075	12,745	1,518	0	14,263
INDIAN RIVER	12,930	8,967	88,090	3,800	113,787	0	0	0	0
KALKASKA									
KESWICK	0	993	0	1,243	2,236	0	0	0	0
KEWADIN INDIAN MISSION	0	0	0	975	975	12,500	22,499	0	34,999

TABLE 3 2013 CHURCH INCOME	CAPITAL CAMPAIGNS & OTHER DESIGNATED PROJECTS					CONNECTIONAL & OTHER SOURCES			
	CAPITAL CAMPAIGNS & OTHER DESIGNATED PROJECTS	MEMORIALS, BEQUESTS, ENDOWMENTS	OTHER SOURCES & SUPPORT OF PROJECTS	SPECIAL OFFERINGS FOR MISSION	TOTAL 68.a TO 68.d	EQUITABLE COMPENSATION SUPPORT	ADVANCE SPECIALS RECEIVED	GRANTS FROM OTHER SOURCES	TOTAL 69.a TO 69.c
Church	63a	63b	63c	63d	63	64a	64b	64c	64
KINGSLEY	0	540	7,193	5,330	13,063	0	0	0	0
GRANT	0	5,435	0	1,591	7,026	0	0	1,000	1,000
LAKE ANN	930	200	0	3,084	4,214	0	0	0	0
LAKE CITY	0	2,959	0	8,794	11,753	0	0	0	0
LELAND	0	1,050	0	15,232	16,282	0	0	0	0
LUDINGTON ST PAUL	0	3,830	0	2,749	6,579	0	0	0	0
LUDINGTON UNITED	113,999	4,520	20,563	43,132	182,214	0	0	0	0
MANCELONA	2,000	4,706	6,844	9,076	22,626	0	0	0	0
ALBA	0	0	0	273	273	0	0	0	0
MANISTEE	26,070	2,584	1,850	3,216	33,720	0	0	0	0
MANTON	0	25,116	0	4,330	29,446	0	0	0	0
MARION	0	200	7,787	0	7,987	0	0	0	0
CADILLAC SOUTH COMMUNITY	0	690	540	1,587	2,817	0	0	0	0
MEARS	0	540	0	4,000	4,540	0	0	0	0
MESICK	0	1,005	1,958	344	3,307	0	0	0	0
HARRIETTA	1,264	6,910	0	1,115	9,289	0	0	0	0
MERRITT-BUTTERFIELD	0	105	2,020	1,239	3,364	0	0	0	0
MOORESTOWN-STITTSVILLE	0	0	0	8,812	8,812	0	0	0	0
NORTHPORT INDIAN MISSION	0	0	0	2,263	2,263	0	16,568	2,400	18,968
OLD MISSION PENINSULA	500	0	11,500	7,170	19,170	0	0	0	0
PENTWATER CENTENARY	0	8,525	13,045	14,705	36,275	0	0	0	0
PETOSKEY	73,796	56,244	0	51,050	181,090	0	0	0	0
ASHTON	0	3,986	0	159	4,145	0	0	0	0
LEROY	0	1,625	0	496	2,121	0	0	0	0
SCOTTVILLE	9,181	3,891	5,645	2,358	21,075	0	0	0	0
TRAVERSE BAY	84,158	5,308	0	0	89,466	0	0	0	0
CENTRAL TRAVERSE CITY	227,305	34,717	0	55,621	317,643	0	0	0	0
CHRIST TRAVERSE CITY	0	0	0	0	0	0	0	0	0
WILLIAMSBURG	0	0	0	0	0	0	0	0	0
GRAND TRAVERSE DIST	661,629	264,496	292,830	391,693	1,610,648	57,888	49,858	4,200	111,946
LAST YEAR	517,604	282,463	238,774	408,378	1,447,219	53,389	30,887	24,807	109,083
INC/(DEC)	144,025	(17,967)	54,056	(16,685)	163,429	4,499	18,971	(20,607)	2,863

STATISTICAL INFO

TABLE 3 2013 CHURCH INCOME

		RECEIPTS FOR CHURCH ANNUAL BUDGET								
		NUMBER OF HOUSEHOLD GIVING TO CHURCH	RECEIVED FROM PLEDGES	RECEIVED FROM IDENTIFIED NON-PLEDGES	RECEIVED FROM UNIDENTIFED GIVERS	INTEREST & DIVIDENDS	PROCEEDS FROM SALE OF CHURCH ASSETS	RECEIPTS FROM BLDG USE, FEES, RENTALS	FUNDRAISERS & OTHER SOURCES	TOTAL INCOME FOR ANNUAL BUDGETMINISTRY SHARES BASE (LINES 62a to 62g)
Church	Pastor	61	62a	62b	62c	62d	62e	62f	62g	62
ALMA	Deborah S Thomas	140	158,767	0	2,552	109	0	0	0	161,428
ASHLEY	Mona Joann Dye	30	0	40,609	0	98	0	0	1,655	42,362
BANNISTER	Mona Joann Dye	33	0	36,272	2,854	0	0	275	3,911	43,312
BARRYTON FAITH	Joseph L Beavan	23	37,987	0	0	3	5,264	0	0	43,254
BELDING	Stephen M G Charnley	26	0	29,334	2,247	0	0	7,647	0	39,228
BIG RAPIDS FIRST	Rebecca K Morrison	152	199,341	103,828	6,200	0	0	1,527	0	310,896
THIRD AVENUE	Charles Ed Milam	85	0	29,402	0	50	11,160	1,180	0	41,792
PARIS	Charles Ed Milam	32	0	31,905	5,657	87	0	240	0	37,889
RODNEY	Charles Ed Milam	17	0	0	13,227	0	0	0	1,179	14,406
BLANCHARD-PINE RIVER	Lawrence Wonsey	11	29,407					490	5,259	35,156
COOMER	Lawrence Wonsey	12	2,600	10,180	3,380	56	0	350	1,080	17,646
BRECKENRIDGE	Paul W Thomas	67	44,626	56,158	4,278	2,261	1,950	2,250	3,514	115,037
BROOKS CORNERS	Joseph L Beavan	23	0	64,304	1,299	0	0	0	0	65,603
SEARS	Joseph L Beavan	11	0	10,787	6,892	0	0	0	0	17,679
CARSON CITY	Andrew L Croel	102	147,200	0	5,700	0	0	2,575	0	155,475
CHASE BARTON	Lyle J Ball	12	0	37,306	0	20	1,350	6,850	0	45,526
GRANT CENTER	Lyle J Ball	14	0	14,563	15,817	0	0	0	0	30,380
CLARE	John G Kasper	203	0	252,543	8,812	134	0	509	0	261,998
EDMORE FAITH	Michael A Riegler	73	0	116,407	4,172	1,400	0	110	9,392	131,481
ELSIE	Donald R Ferris-McCann	48	0	98,200	4,580	2,381	0	1,626	0	106,787
EVART	Melodye Surgeon Rider	52	133,109	2,335	4,954	0	0	5,966	0	146,364
AVONDALE	Kara Lynne Burns	11	0	4,603	5,588	298	0	0	0	10,489
NORTH EVART	Kara Lynne Burns	4	0	6,000	1,000	0	0	50	0	7,050
FARWELL	Connie R Bongard	74	0	107,601	8,601	1,158	0	6,418	13,650	137,428
FENWICK	Russell Morgan	19	0	11,187	4,569	0	0	25	0	15,781
PALO	Russell Morgan	13	0	9,692	2,401	10	0	0	232	12,335
VICKERYVILLE	Russell Morgan	12	0	8,450	1,332	0	0	0	0	9,782
GREENVILLE	Stephen M G Charnley	207	70,287	135,598	7,442	0	0	595	7,587	221,509
HERSEY	Lemuel O Granada	50	0	59,798	1,455	73	0	595	692	62,613
AMBLE	Anne W Riegler	44	0	60,053	750	221	0	0	0	61,024
HERITAGE	James Bradley Brillhart	120	0	143,439	6,857	56	0	2,526	9,412	162,290
FIRST IONIA	Lawrence P Brown	85	78,500	75,000	3,700	5,695	0	1,100	0	163,995
ZION IONIA	Clifford L Allen	41	74,128	0	23,476	28	0	0	853	98,485
LEVALLEY	Raymond R Sundell	59	0	118,632	6,416	2,548	0	1,375	0	128,971
BERLIN CENTER	Raymond R Sundell	58	0	51,897	0	52	0	200	0	52,149
ITHACA	Cynthia S L Greene	94	136,305	12,000	15,197		0	0	0	163,501
BEEBE	Cynthia S L Greene	12	0	0	14,107	0	0	0	0	14,107
LAKEVIEW NEW LIFE	John Allen Scott	140	136,065	79,230	7,624	103	0	3,905	1,278	228,205

2013 TABLE 3 CHURCH INCOME

Church	Pastor	NUMBER OF HOUSEHOLD GIVING TO CHURCH	RECEIPTS FOR CHURCH ANNUAL BUDGET: RECEIVED FROM PLEDGES	RECEIVED FROM IDENTIFIED NON-PLEDGES	RECEIVED FROM UNIDENTIFED GIVERS	INTEREST & DIVIDENDS	PROCEEDS FROM SALE OF CHURCH ASSETS	RECEIPTS FROM BLDG USE, FEES, RENTALS	FUNDRAISERS & OTHER SOURCES	TOTAL INCOME FOR ANNUAL BUDGETMINISTRY SHARES BASE (LINES 62a to 62g)
		61	62a	62b	62c	62d	62e	62f	62g	62
LEATON	D Michael Palmer	21	0	46,831	2,565	95	0	610	0	50,101
LYONS-MUIR	Forest Bert Nelson	35	68,642	2,244	510	0	0	0	3,330	74,726
EASTON	Nancy J Patera	80	53,510	0	3,791	0	0	700	3,512	61,513
MECOSTA NEW HOPE	Gregory L Buchner	115	0	233,790	7,174	46	0	2,575	6,555	250,140
MIDDLETON	William F Dye	9	0	18,518	735	429	0	0	9,271	28,953
MAPLE RAPIDS	Kathryn L Leydorf-Keck	32	0	47,088	1,705	500	0	0	0	49,293
CHIPPEWA INDIAN	Owen L White-Pigeon									0
FIRST MT PLEASANT	Diane L Gordon	198	390,104	0	9,193	48	0	1,300	0	400,645
TRINITY MOUNT PLEASANT	D Michael Palmer	16	0	35,415	4,256	40	0	0	392	40,103
COUNTRYSIDE	D Michael Palmer	20	0	38,707	1,400	95	0	0	4,927	45,129
OVID UNITED CHURCH	Paul A Damkoehler	1,020	65,755	65,755	0	0	6,274	2,483	2,405	142,672
POMPEII	William F Dye	17	0	32,811	0	0	0	0	1,505	34,316
PERRINTON	William F Dye	19	3,273	10,034	3,149	54	0	0	2,885	19,395
NORTH STAR	William F Dye	7	2,000	500	0	10	0	0	0	2,510
REED CITY	Kathryn S Cadarette	155	122,894	87,901	4,423	0	0	2,110	0	217,328
RIVERDALE LINCOLN ROAD	Jana Lynn Almeida	58	0	127,607	4,159	79	0	905	1,145	133,895
ROSEBUSH	Jonathan D Van Dop	68	63,186	31,592	6,848	12	0	200	0	101,838
FIRST SAINT JOHNS	Ellen K Zienert	93	96,093	58,859	911	2,567	0	736	2,331	161,497
PILGRIM	Kenneth J Bremer	158	0	301,558	6,879	158	0	8,875	0	317,470
SALEM	Kathryn L Leydorf-Keck	14	0	27,570	3,919	74	0	25	0	31,588
GREENBUSH	Mona Joann Dye	16	0	16,958	354	0	0	100	4,422	21,834
LOWE	Kathryn L Leydorf-Keck	46	0	70,627	4,176	209	0	0	999	76,011
SAINT LOUIS	Terri L Bentley	95	129,321	15,030	1,888	26	0	735	0	147,000
SHEPARDSVILLE	Judith Hazle	22	0	26,475	2,144	0	0	130	804	29,553
SAND LAKE	Darryl L Miller	25	0	0	17,950	0	0	810	0	18,760
SOUTH ENSLEY	Darryl L Miller	50	0	0	37,842	0	0	0	0	37.842
SHEPHERD	Kathleen S Kursch	62	134,262	0	4,968	11	0	3,541	939	143.721
STANWOOD NORTHLAND	Dominic A Tommy	70	0	120,792	2,833	446	0	0	802	124.873
TURK LAKE	Stephen M G Charnley	30	0	39,950	2,719	0	0	0	2,126	44,795
WEIDMAN	Scott B Smith	112	0	121,598	0	5	7,554	1,812	0	130,969
WINN	Lawrence Wonsey	20	0	29,861	0	36	0	0	15,168	45,065
HEARTLAND DISTRICT	DAVID HILLS	4,892	2,377,362	3,425,384	339,627	21,781	33,552	76,031	123,212	6,396,948
LAST YEAR		4,222	2,487,001	3,255,384	437,069	21,680	21,600	62,312	116,629	6,401,674
INC/(DEC)		670	(109,639)	170,000	(97,442)	101	11,952	13,719	6,583	(4,726)

TABLE 3 2013 CHURCH INCOME		RECEIPTS FOR CHURCH ANNUAL BUDGET								
		NUMBER OF HOUSEHOLD GIVING TO CHURCH	RECEIVED FROM PLEDGES	RECEIVED FROM IDENTIFIED NON-PLEDGES	RECEIVED FROM UNIDENTIFED GIVERS	INTEREST & DIVIDENDS	PROCEEDS FROM SALE OF CHURCH ASSETS	RECEIPTS FROM BLDG USE, FEES, RENTALS	FUNDRAISERS & OTHER SOURCES	TOTAL INCOME FOR ANNUAL BUDGETMINISTRY SHARES BASE (LINES 62a to 62g)
Church	Pastor	61	62a	62b	62c	62d	62e	62f	62g	62
ALTO	Dean Irwin Bailey	37	0	46,017	3,538	0	0	375	0	49,930
BOWNE CENTER	Dean Irwin Bailey	49	0	53,000	2,331	1	584	2,450	0	58,366
BYRON CENTER	Lawrence A Nichols	760	0	164,769	1,274	61	0	345	4,383	170,832
CALEDONIA	Jodie R Flessner	120	123,838	69,433	2,972	51	0	200	1,068	197,562
CARLISLE	Michael Ramsey	73	64,419	30,489	5,430	32	0	350	0	100,720
CEDAR SPRINGS	Mary Letta-Bement Ivanov	140	0	188,111	3,836	44	0	1,085	0	193,076
EAST NELSON	Herbert J VanderBilt	63	0	107,820	13,559	301	0	0	0	121,680
COOPERSVILLE	Cori Lynn Cypret	53	121,892	0	3,329	0	0	0	0	125,221
COURTLAND-OAKFIELD	Robert Eckert	62	88,423	19,821	10,329	8	0	550	0	119,131
FREMONT	Martin T Cobb	167	221,495	72,096	13,614	5,135	0	500	0	312,840
GEORGETOWN	William C Bills	262	287,080	151,149	5,239	3,463	0	3,578	2,009	452,518
GRAND HAVEN CHURCH OF THE D	Daniel M Duncan	328	374,189	116,573	22,067	0	0	3,505	16,773	533,107
ALDERSGATE	James E Hodge	113	172,526	260,730	1,800	69	0	7,720	5,613	448,458
SOUTH WYOMING	Marcia L Elders	75	75,732	14,557	0	4	0	5,032	2,704	98,029
CORNERSTONE	Bradley P Kalajainen	1,319	0	2,358,973	82,469	1,926	0	10,198	0	2,453,566
FAITH GRAND RAPIDS	Mark E Thompson	152	167,101	19,530	1,295	10,000	0	0	2,803	200,729
FIRST GRAND RAPIDS	Robert L Hundley	336	1,038,842	34,193	10,750	619	0	0	107,620	1,192,024
GENESIS	Susan M Petro	143	188,455	60,431	9,802	5,244	0	500	23,343	287,775
LA NUEVA ESPERANZA	Nohemi V Ramirez	15	14,744	0	3,259	0	0	0	2,979	20,982
NORTHLAWN	Timothy B Wright	81	164,660	0	2,798	0	0	0	0	167,458
PLAINFIELD	Laurie Haller	15	10,953	5,815	704	2,697	0	10,890	1,405	32,464
SAINT PAULS GRAND RAPIDS	Erin Fitzgerald	107	197,274	18,718	2,417	1,506	0	5,837	334	226,086
SOUTH GRAND RAPIDS	Mack C Strange	94	81,343	53,286	0	0	2,883	8,742	2,801	149,055
TRINITY GRAND RAPIDS	David Nellist	175	518,124	63,925	7,427	89	0	24,741	1,599	615,905
VIETNAMESE GRAND RAPIDS	Daniel Nguyen	30	0	40,000	0	0	0	0	0	40,000
GRANDVILLE	Thomas M Pier-Fitzgerald	177	189,224	87,552	3,328	426	350	2,215	0	283,095
HESPERIA	Paul E Hane	62	0	61,190	13,638	0	0	0	954	75,782
FERRY	Paul E Hane	35	0	50,636	4,962	0	0	0	0	55,598
HOLLAND	J Lynn Pier-Fitzgerald	303	460,276	62,205	8,397	0	0	3,735	19,474	554,087
HOLTON	Gerald L Selleck	162	0	195,237	32,178	0	0	600	0	228,015
KENT CITY CHAPEL HILL	Kevin Guetschow	66	0	109,169	0	0	4,614	0	0	113,783
LEIGHTON	David L McBride	113	146,922	74,300	7,672	28	0	1,860	0	230,782
LOWELL	Richard W Blunt	175	239,736	35,006	6,784	1,971	0	1,818	0	285,315
MARNE	James Thomas Boutell	45	0	104,000	900	0	0	0	0	104,900
MARTIN	Donald J Graham	75	0	121,262	2,612	0	0	1,630	0	125,504
SHELBYVILLE	Donald J Graham	38	0	56,595	290	101	0	50	0	57,036
MIDDLEVILLE	Anthony C Shumaker	75	185,706	25,959	4,855	41	0	0	0	216,561
PARMELEE	William V Clegg	27	0	40,836	0	0	0	0	0	40,836

2013 TABLE 3 CHURCH INCOME		RECEIPTS FOR CHURCH ANNUAL BUDGET								
		NUMBER OF HOUSEHOLD GIVING TO CHURCH	RECEIVED FROM PLEDGES	RECEIVED FROM IDENTIFIED NON-PLEDGES	RECEIVED FROM UNIDENTIFED GIVERS	INTEREST & DIVIDENDS	PROCEEDS FROM SALE OF CHURCH ASSETS	RECEIPTS FROM BLDG USE, FEES, RENTALS	FUNDRAISERS & OTHER SOURCES	TOTAL INCOME FOR ANNUAL BUDGETMINISTRY SHARES BASE (LINES 62a to 62g)
Church	Pastor	61	62a	62b	62c	62d	62e	62f	62g	62
MONTAGUE	Randall R Hansen	181	199,991	3,520	2,688	2	0	351	0	206,552
CENTRAL MUSKEGON	Mark D Miller	208	283,789	67,822	0	61,592	4,465	3,665	1,840	423,173
CRESTWOOD	Stephan Weinberger	43	73,674	0	202	3,050	0	239	6,247	83,412
LAKE HARBOR	Mark R Erbes	200	235,996	33,438	2,889	188	0	1,265	20,123	293,899
LAKESIDE	Stephan Weinberger	69	65,691	42,263	0	13,815	2,951	691	1,201	126,612
UNITY	R John Thompson	30		33,341	2,665	46		4,238	183	40,474
WOLF LAKE	Bobby Dale Whitlock	48	73,235	0	2,183	0	59,006	235	553	135,212
MUSKEGON HEIGHTS TEMPLE	Jeffrey J Bowman	101	147,343	41,008	2,040	0	0	0	25,544	215,935
NEWAYGO	Kathleen A Groff	80	80,195	24,806	1,728	1,035	0	655	197	108,616
NORTH MUSKEGON COMMUNITY	Phillip J Friedrick	155	244,502	0	0	9	0	0	0	244,511
RAVENNA	Carleton Black	65	0	101,219	1,332	0	0	355	0	102,906
ROCKFORD	Richard M Riley	400	630,838	0	0	733	0	10,101	0	641,672
SALEM INDIAN MISSION	Nancy L Boelens	8	4,777	2,400	702	0	0	0	379	8,258
BRADLEY INDIAN MISSION	Nancy L Boelens	9	0	12,197	0	0	0	0	754	12,951
SAUGATUCK	Emmett H Kadwell	61	48,959	0	2,021	4	0	200	0	51,184
SHELBY	Terri Cummins	58	70,786	5,735	3,335	4	0	903	0	80,763
SNOW	Anthony C Shumaker	20	0	49,671	0	0	0	0	0	49,671
SPARTA	Louis W Grettenberger	123	196,112	73,869	3,385	682	5,710	4,438	0	284,196
TWIN LAKE	John D Morse	38		63,261	6,660			649		70,569
SITKA	Gerald F Hagans	13	0	13,978	0	2	0	0	0	13,980
VALLEY CHURCH ALLENDALE NEW	Matthew J Bistayi	2								72,615
VERGENNES	Matthew Todd Stoll	94	183,774	34,037	3,963	60	0	1,280	11,649	234,763
WAYLAND	Gary D Bondarenko	59	74,860	33,007	1,480	0	0	868	3,841	114,056
WHITE CLOUD	Edwin D Snook	107	112,075	40,066	4,584	0	0	3,250	0	159,975
WHITEHALL	Gayle S Berntsen	40	0	81,912	2,958	5	0	2,140	2,955	89,970
CLAYBANKS	Gayle S Berntsen	39	0	39,682	9,319	208	0	50	0	49,259
WESLEY PARK	Dean N Prentiss	189	0	349,660	8,366	37	0	3,423	7,743	369,229
WYOMING PARK	Joel Thomas Fitzgerald	45	106,622	22,699	0	82	1,088	8,500	109	139,100
CROSSWIND COMMUNITY	Scott Keith Otis	68	158,896	49,093	6,378	0	0	0	0	214,367
GRAND RAPIDS DISTRICT	WILLIAM HAGGARD	8,675	8,125,069	6,192,067	364,733	115,371	81,651	146,002	279,180	15,376,688
LAST YEAR		7,600	9,320,547	4,834,534	459,155	73,919	10,000	283,889	208,427	14,663,594
INC/(DEC)		1,075	(1,195,478)	1,357,533	(94,422)	41,452	71,651	(137,887)	70,753	713,094

STATISTICAL INFO

STATISTICAL INFO

TABLE 3 2013 CHURCH INCOME		RECEIPTS FOR CHURCH ANNUAL BUDGET								
		NUMBER OF HOUSEHOLD GIVING TO CHURCH	RECEIVED FROM PLEDGES	RECEIVED FROM IDENTIFIED NON-PLEDGES	RECEIVED FROM UNIDENTIFED GIVERS	INTEREST & DIVIDENDS	PROCEEDS FROM SALE OF CHURCH ASSETS	RECEIPTS FROM BLDG USE, FEES, RENTALS	FUNDRAISERS & OTHER SOURCES	TOTAL INCOME FOR ANNUAL BUDGETMINISTRY SHARES BASE (LINES 62a to 62g)
Church	Pastor	61	62a	62b	62c	62d	62e	62f	62g	62
EDWARDSBURG HOPE	Jeffrey L Reese	222	0	242,397	5,675	122	0	467	3,880	252,541
ALLEGAN	Robert K Lynch	135	170,000	20,000	250	0	0	3,960	0	194,210
ARDEN	O'Ryan Rickard	19	0	29,365	42	0	0	12,001	0	41,408
BANGOR SIMPSON	Thomas A Davenport	36	84,045	31,720	8,259	0	0	11,350	375	135,749
BERRIEN SPRINGS	Jane D Logston	26	42,464	13,961	1,745	35	0	15,580	939	74,724
BLOOMINGDALE	Carol A Newman	15	0	18,835	2,576	0	0	0	0	21,411
BURNIPS	Richard A Fritz	66	0	48,705	4,920	11	0	4,272	6,030	63,938
MONTEREY CENTER	Richard A Fritz	19	0	35,191	350	37	0	423	3,787	39,788
BUCHANAN FAITH	Edward H Slate	65	77,782	25,927	4,667	463	0	0	0	108,839
MORRIS CHAPEL	Samuel C Gordy	15	0	9,255	16,351	3,334	0	0	0	28,940
BUCHANAN FIRST	Rob A McPherson	131	97,577	41,771	3,282	0	0	0	400	143,030
CASCO	David W Meister	120	0	117,743	4,317	0	0	2,088	205	124,353
CASSOPOLIS	Benjamin D Hutchison	62	0	88,795	6,259	0	0	260	0	95,314
Coloma	Ronald D Van Lente	99	131,315	37,931	2,771	0	0	6,650	0	178,667
DOWAGIAC FIRST	David Price	132	146,194	66	5,087	51	0	2,200	2,669	156,267
FENNVILLE	Gary L Peterson	50	0	72,394	2,316	0	0	568	0	75,278
PEARL	Gary L Peterson	20	0	0	27,369	0	0	0	35	27,404
GANGES	Jack E Balgenorth	14	25,000	500	500	0	0	0	3,500	29,500
GALIEN	Jeffrey O Cummings	23	38,641	0	0	0	0	60	3,658	42,359
OLIVE BRANCH	Jeffrey O Cummings	32	42,687	1,604	1,706	0	0	0	0	45,997
GLENN	Jack E Balgenorth	16	0	15,435	4,552	0	0	0	0	19,987
GOBLES	Nelson L Hall	44	58,355	0	1,791	0	0	100	0	60,246
KENDALL	Nelson L Hall	15	0	33,151	1,572	53	0	293	4,754	39,823
GULL LAKE	Mona K Joslyn	149	141,492	56,363	3,177	106	0	1,282	0	202,420
HARTFORD	Jeffrey C Williams	105	0	118,972	5,885	10	130	11,850	2,035	138,882
HINCHMAN	Jane D Logston	12	0	22,759	694	62	0	187	3,906	27,608
ORONOKO	Jane D Logston	8	0	12,649	2,549	4	0	50	0	15,252
HOPKINS	Linda J Burton-Collier	29	0	60,926	4,004	0	0	0	0	64,930
SOUTH MONTEREY	Linda J Burton-Collier	17	0	43,678	0	0	0	0	0	43,678
LIFESPRING	Patricia Anne Harpole	32	128,802	0	3,438	0	0	0	814	133,054
FIRST KALAMAZOO	John W Boley	470	756,565	54,871	9,341	20,702	0	20,449	31,399	893,327
MILWOOD	Heather A McDougall	144	159,219	15,111	2,861	0	0	8,080	21,262	206,533
OSHTEMO	John W Fisher	85	0	91,547	2,854	14	0	1,271	896	96,582
STOCKBRIDGE AVENUE	Ronald D Slager	59	41,814	0	0	0	0	0	0	41,814
SUNNYSIDE	John Matthew Weiler	63	113,934	12,479	3,826	3,504	0	180	15,588	149,511
WESTWOOD	Wayne A Price	165	290,607	20,505	5,129	38	0	1,484	0	317,763
KEELER	Beth A Reum	19	0	20,984	2,175	52	0	5,750	10,055	39,016
SILVER CREEK	Beth A Reum	32	10	69,578	4,897	0	0	400	0	74,885

2013 TABLE 3 CHURCH INCOME		RECEIPTS FOR CHURCH ANNUAL BUDGET								
		NUMBER OF HOUSEHOLD GIVING TO CHURCH	RECEIVED FROM PLEDGES	RECEIVED FROM IDENTIFIED NON-PLEDGES	RECEIVED FROM UNIDENTIFED GIVERS	INTEREST & DIVIDENDS	PROCEEDS FROM SALE OF CHURCH ASSETS	RECEIPTS FROM BLDG USE, FEES, RENTALS	FUNDRAISERS & OTHER SOURCES	TOTAL INCOME FOR ANNUAL BUDGETMINISTRY SHARES BASE (LINES 62a to 62g)
Church	Pastor	61	62a	62b	62c	62d	62e	62f	62g	62
LACOTA	Michael A Pinto	18	0	31,281	0	0	0	0	0	31,281
LAKESIDE	George W Lawton	19	19,370	0	2,592	53	0	3,250	3,292	28,557
LAWRENCE	Clifford L Radtke	50	0	75,732	4,450	81	0	700	13,142	94,105
LAWTON ST PAULS	Douglas W Vernon	64	64,737	20,920	4,467	90	0	500	3,438	94,152
ALMENA	Donna Jean Keyte	75	0	75,904	2,132	0	350	1,235	264	79,885
MARCELLUS	John D Messner	65		57,487	3,024	119				60,631
WATERS EDGE	Bradley S Bartelmay	98	171,451	28,692	5,350	86	0	2,400	4,303	212,282
BRIDGMAN FAITH	Terrill M Schneider	34	0	37,727	2,000	0	0	0	0	39,727
NILES GRACE	Anthony J Tomasino	42	28,819	0	1,615	2	0	500	279	31,215
NILES WESLEY	Catherine M Huvaere	55	107,361	57,552	2,636	86	0	150	12,737	180,522
NORTHWEST	Samuel C Gordy	29	0	25,365	0	56	0	0	0	25,421
OTSEGO	Joseph D Shaler	196	37,496	136,201	14,299	232	0	555	3,941	192,724
PARCHMENT	Michael J Tupper	130	110,552	65,829	1,722	71	100	525	1,373	180,172
PAW PAW	Trevor McDermont	73	119,418	0	3,236	0	0	3,375	1,951	127,980
PLAINWELL FIRST	Kathy E Brown	129	213,081	0	3,503	0	0	735	0	217,319
POKAGON	Sean K Kidd	43		71,285	7,121			535		78,941
PORTAGE CHAPEL HILL	Barry T Petrucci	304	596,182	506	8,507	3	0	5,347	65,785	676,330
PORTAGE FIRST	Gregory B Wood	225	0	459,969	1,021	236	0	31,289	382	492,897
PORTAGE PRAIRIE	O'Ryan Rickard	47	42,770	38,924	0	72	0	150	0	81,916
RIVERSIDE	Stephen C Small	35		44,697	1,000					45,697
SCOTTDALE	Terrill M Schneider	56	0	41,876	4,185	0	0	455	5,980	52,496
SAINT JOSEPH FIRST	Harris John Hoekwater	299	401,204	92,976	9,140	720	0	14,757	15,169	533,966
SCHOOLCRAFT	Karen Sue Wheat	38	0	83,619	2,363	0	0	1,323	16,129	103,434
SODUS CHAPEL HILL	Russell K Logston	131	81,329	48,553	4,697	932	3,500	1,095	7,477	147,583
SOUTH HAVEN FIRST	Devon R Herrell	105	0	179,356	0	27	0	0	0	179,383
STEVENSVILLE	B Gordon Barry	219	242,074	69,659	10,528	135	0	1,430	6,200	330,026
THREE OAKS	Sherri L Swanson	82	98,242	24,238	4,489	0	0	50	0	127,019
TOWNLINE	David L Haase	21	0	20,577	8,031	0	0	0	0	28,608
BREEDSVILLE	David L Haase	13	0	15,126	6,766	50	0	0	1,514	23,456
TROWBRIDGE	Sheila F Baker	42	0	52,563	19,897	10	0	0	0	72,470
VICKSBURG	Bufford W Coe	142	170,385	133,458	4,915	325	0	7,815	7,824	324,722
WAKELEE	John D Messner	58		63,953	1,715	12			2,050	67,730
KALAMAZOO DISTRICT	CORNELIUS DAVIS	5,702	5,050,974	3,539,193	302,589	31,997	4,080	189,426	289,417	9,407,675
LAST YEAR		6,208	5,433,316	3,174,067	334,078	52,246	14,328	186,688	212,962	9,407,685
INC/(DEC)		(506)	(382,342)	365,126	(31,489)	(20,249)	(10,248)	2,738	76,455	(10)

STATISTICAL INFO

TABLE 3 2013 CHURCH INCOME	CAPITAL CAMPAIGNS & OTHER DESIGNATED PROJECTS					CONNECTIONAL & OTHER SOURCES			
	CAPITAL CAMPAIGNS & OTHER DESIGNATED PROJECTS	MEMORIALS, BEQUESTS, ENDOWMENTS	OTHER SOURCES & SUPPORT OF PROJECTS	SPECIAL OFFERINGS FOR MISSION	TOTAL 68.a TO 68 d	EQUITABLE COMPENSATION SUPPORT	ADVANCE SPECIALS RECEIVED	GRANTS FROM OTHER SOURCES	TOTAL 69.a TO 69.c
Church	63a	63b	63c	63d	63	64a	64b	64c	64
EDWARDSBURG HOPE	87,482	1,472	7,765	31,651	128,370	0	500	0	500
ALLEGAN	25,000	8,000	8,000	10,000	51,000	0	0	0	0
ARDEN	0	395	0	873	1,268	0	0	0	0
BANGOR SIMPSON	60,778	509	0	376	61,663	0	0	0	0
BERRIEN SPRINGS	9,110	100	7,248	1,980	18,438	0	0	0	0
BLOOMINGDALE	0	0	0	0	0	0	0	0	0
BURNIPS	0	460	0	0	460	0	0	0	0
MONTEREY CENTER	0	0	0	0	0	0	0	0	0
BUCHANAN FAITH	0	1,885	3,515	5,149	10,549	0	0	0	0
MORRIS CHAPEL	0	135	0	0	135	0	0	0	0
BUCHANAN FIRST	9,721	2,390	3,420	2,308	17,839	0	0	0	0
CASCO	0	8,572	723	4,373	13,668	0	0	0	0
CASSOPOLIS	14,498	8,352	1,056	3,527	27,433	0	0	0	0
Coloma	1,525	1,385	119,106	18,421	140,437	0	0	0	0
DOWAGIAC FIRST	4,369	1,598	0	4,216	10,183	5,000	0	0	5,000
FENNVILLE	1,796	1,595	2,696	5,106	11,193	0	0	0	0
PEARL	0	0	1,800	375	2,175	0	0	0	0
GANGES	0	2,585	962	1,729	5,276	0	0	0	0
GALIEN	1,360	1,045	0	405	2,810	0	0	0	0
OLIVE BRANCH	0	0	0	100	100	0	0	0	0
GLENN	0	0	0	0	0	0	0	0	0
GOBLES	0	590	0	932	1,522	0	0	0	0
KENDALL	0	2,413	1,945	426	4,784	0	0	0	0
GULL LAKE	4,150	0	0	7,509	11,659	0	0	0	0
HARTFORD	5,475	13,990	4,472	21,651	45,588	0	0	0	0
HINCHMAN	0	0	3,780	0	3,780	0	0	0	0
ORONOKO	0	250	4,496	1,514	6,260	0	0	0	0
HOPKINS	0	0	0	830	830	0	0	0	0
SOUTH MONTEREY	0	0	0	4,594	4,594	0	0	0	0
LIFESPRING	0	0	0	783	783	0	8,399	3,200	11,599
FIRST KALAMAZOO	243,543	14,957	52,692	46,762	357,954	0	0	0	0
MILWOOD	80,234	6,382	13,021	0	99,637	0	0	0	0
OSHTEMO	3,779	220	11,213	3,826	19,038	1,600	0	0	1,600
STOCKBRIDGE AVENUE	0	0	0	175	175	0	0	0	0
SUNNYSIDE	0	15,893	0	1,546	17,439	10,000	9,900	1,255	21,155
WESTWOOD	0	480	28,307	53,862	82,649	0	0	0	0
KEELER	1,254	2,310	5,000	944	9,508	780	0	0	780
SILVER CREEK	3,846	7,140	0	2,132	13,118	2,000	0	0	2,000

TABLE 3 2013 CHURCH INCOME	CAPITAL CAMPAIGNS & OTHER DESIGNATED PROJECTS					CONNECTIONAL & OTHER SOURCES			
	CAPITAL CAMPAIGNS & OTHER DESIGNATED PROJECTS	MEMORIALS, BEQUESTS, ENDOWMENTS	OTHER SOURCES & SUPPORT OF PROJECTS	SPECIAL OFFERINGS FOR MISSION	TOTAL 68.a TO 68.d	EQUITABLE COMPENSATION SUPPORT	ADVANCE SPECIALS RECEIVED	GRANTS FROM OTHER SOURCES	TOTAL 69.a TO 69.c
Church	63a	63b	63c	63d	63	64a	64b	64c	64
LACOTA	0	0	0	0	0	0	0	0	0
LAKESIDE	0	0	0	7,178	7,178	0	0	0	0
LAWRENCE	0	50	7,343	1,346	8,739	0	0	0	0
LAWTON ST PAULS	23,501	300	495	7,446	31,742	0	0	0	0
ALMENA	4,284	2,220	9,504	8,145	24,153	0	0	0	0
MARCELLUS									
WATERS EDGE	38,185	0	10,737	8,752	57,674	0	0	141,000	141,000
BRIDGMAN FAITH	0	0	1,524	4,223	5,747	0	0	0	0
NILES GRACE	0	504	0	0	504	0	0	0	0
NILES WESLEY	0	33,489	0	2,618	36,107	0	0	0	0
NORTHWEST	0	0	0	473	473	0	0	0	0
OTSEGO	25,434	0	0	0	25,434	0	0	0	0
PARCHMENT	0	18,624	0	8,731	27,355	0	0	0	0
PAW PAW	0	796	0	603	1,399	0	0	0	0
PLAINWELL FIRST	90,943	980	1,485	6,242	99,650	0	0	1,000	1,000
POKAGON									
PORTAGE CHAPEL HILL	0	7,689	27,644	12,928	48,261	0	0	0	0
PORTAGE FIRST	0	1,200	2,423	7,233	10,856	0	0	0	0
PORTAGE PRAIRIE	5,525	5,500	0	1,643	12,668	0	0	0	0
RIVERSIDE									
SCOTTDALE	0	2,925	384	1,136	4,445	0	0	0	0
SAINT JOSEPH FIRST	49,997	5,424	0	18,430	73,851	0	0	0	0
SCHOOLCRAFT	10,925	26,899	0	19,240	57,064	0	0	0	0
SODUS CHAPEL HILL	0	63,046	0	0	63,046	0	0	0	0
SOUTH HAVEN FIRST	53,350	0	58,926	0	112,276	0	0	0	0
STEVENSVILLE	39,328	28,350	0	23,286	90,964	0	0	0	0
THREE OAKS	0	3,615	0	4,025	7,640	0	0	0	0
TOWNLINE	0	150	3,574	1,588	5,312	0	0	0	0
BREEDSVILLE	0	2,257	2,570	874	5,701	0	0	0	0
TROWBRIDGE	0	1,211	0	0	1,211	0	0	0	0
VICKSBURG	79,017	1,120	0	15,811	95,948	0	0	0	0
WAKELEE	1,785	0	0	6,619	8,404				
KALAMAZOO DISTRICT	980,194	311,452	407,826	406,645	2,106,117	19,380	18,799	146,455	184,634
LAST YEAR	1,478,708	342,168	229,244	519,520	2,569,640	20,156	3,677	7,100	30,933
INC/(DEC)	(498,514)	(30,716)	178,582	(112,875)	(463,523)	(776)	15,122	139,355	153,701

STATISTICAL INFO

STATISTICAL INFO

TABLE 3 2013 CHURCH INCOME

		RECEIPTS FOR CHURCH ANNUAL BUDGET								
		NUMBER OF HOUSEHOLD GIVING TO CHURCH	RECEIVED FROM PLEDGES	RECEIVED FROM IDENTIFIED NON-PLEDGES	RECEIVED FROM UNIDENTIFED GIVERS	INTEREST & DIVIDENDS	PROCEEDS FROM SALE OF CHURCH ASSETS	RECEIPTS FROM BLDG USE FEES, RENTALS	FUNDRAISERS & OTHER SOURCES	TOTAL INCOME FOR ANNUAL BUDGETMINISTRY SHARES BASE (LINES 62a to 62g)
Church	Pastor	61	62a	62b	62c	62d	62e	62f	62g	62
BATH	Mark Gregory Johnson	64	0	51,843	2,688	0	4,500	360	100	59,491
GUNNISONVILLE	Mark Gregory Johnson	0	46,157	35,773	2,834	0	0	0	0	84,764
WHEATFIELD	Jeremy J Wicks	30	0	36,051	2,986	0	0	0	0	39,037
BROOKFIELD	Irene L Vittoz	44	0	33,823	4,669	0	0	0	0	38,492
CHARLOTTE LAWRENCE AVENUE	Gary S Wales	250	173,079	58,420	5,959	200	800	4,885	5,298	248,641
COUNTRY CHAPEL	Ryan B Wieland	61	42,222	49,928	0	3,902	0	253	1,062	97,367
DANSVILLE	Jeremy J Wicks	6	0	19,243	0	0	0	8,400	2,416	30,059
DELTA MILLS	Joseph L Spackman	38	0	38,670	3,031	50	0	290	1,187	43,228
DEWITT REDEEMER	Rodney J Kalajainen	565	713,023	174,065	8,635	3,800	0	4,458	0	903,981
DIMONDALE	Joseph D Huston	38	43,348	11,147	7,430	0	0	0	0	61,925
UNIVERSITY EAST LANSING	Jennifer Browne	228	479,485	49,245	4,636	731	0	3,390	22,153	559,640
EATON RAPIDS FIRST	Daniel B Hofmann	236	235,587	145,030	15,010	833	0	3,018	0	399,478
FREEPORT	Susan D Olsen	7	0	15,160	2,294	121	0	0	0	17,575
GRAND LEDGE FIRST	Cynthia A Skutar	233	264,875	43,025	4,298	92	0	2,020	1,000	315,310
GROVENBURG	Joseph D Huston	30	46,260	6,359	1,314	2	0	680	2,357	56,972
HASTINGS FIRST	Donald E Spachman	183	0	229,540	0	25	4,595	2,595	16,925	253,680
HASTINGS HOPE	Richard D Moore	46	0	133,568	0	0	0	0	0	133,568
HOLT	Glenn M Wagner	331	328,503	3,039	481	60	0	12,135	1,060	345,278
KALAMO	Daniel Phillips	31	0	0	31,307	14	0	0	0	31,321
LAKE ODESSA CENTRAL	Karen J Sorden	81	147,379	49,969	2,413	1	0	0	0	199,762
LAKE ODESSA LAKEWOOD	James C Noggle	184	0	235,439	15,487	81	0	1,998	0	253,005
ASBURY LANSING	Martin M DeBow	108	162,856	48,545	3,156	12	0	428	25,527	240,524
CENTRAL LANSING	Linda J Farmer-Lewis	95	229,903	53,054	2,952	21	0	52,000	9,196	347,126
CHRIST LANSING	Lyle D Heaton	32	166,991	2,464	1,038	21	0	0	10,687	181,201
FAITH/SOUTH LANSING MINISTRIES	Russell F McReynolds	41	50,607	4,981	5,626	0	0	11,603	7,706	80,523
FIRST LANSING	Lori J Sykes	115	157,436	36,916	1,634	0	0	0	9,913	205,899
GRACE LANSING	Jane Ellen Johnson	74	162,173	38,451	4,401	0	0	2,000	0	207,025
KOREAN LANSING	Bo Rin Cho	22	43,407	16,989	9,156	0	0	28,151	3,080	100,783
MOUNT HOPE	Robert B Cook	190	476,638	48,086	5,706	7,692	16,644	3,180	0	557,946
TRINITY LANSING	William M Beachy	274	298,584	197,381	9,113	0	0	0	0	505,078
LESLIE	Donald Lee Buege	56	0	72,695	1,711	0	0	25	1,319	75,750
FELT PLAINS	Donald Lee Buege	16	0	24,133	1,692	0	0	0	2,818	28,643
MASON FIRST	Dwayne E Bagley	205	265,907	119,697	4,156	30	0	19,090	0	408,880
MILLVILLE	Jeremy J Wicks	65	0	98,153	0	0	0	0	0	98,153
MUNITH	Jeanne Laimon	24	0	45,665	2,456	326	0	250	5,783	54,480
PLEASANT LAKE	Jeanne Laimon	9	0	13,815	1,264	279	0	0	0	15,358
MULLIKEN	Clare W Huyck	23	0	23,458	2,447	0	0	0	5,004	30,909
SEBEWA CENTER	Clare W Huyck	7	0	12,871	0	0	0	0	3,844	16,715

2013 TABLE 3 CHURCH INCOME		RECEIPTS FOR CHURCH ANNUAL BUDGET								
		NUMBER OF HOUSEHOLD GIVING TO CHURCH	RECEIVED FROM PLEDGES	RECEIVED FROM IDENTIFIED NON-PLEDGES	RECEIVED FROM UNIDENTIFED GIVERS	INTEREST & DIVIDENDS	PROCEEDS FROM SALE OF CHURCH ASSETS	RECEIPTS FROM BLDG USE, FEES, RENTALS	FUNDRAISERS & OTHER SOURCES	TOTAL INCOME FOR ANNUAL BUDGETMINISTRY SHARES BASE (LINES 62a to 62g)
Church	Pastor	61	62a	62b	62c	62d	62e	62f	62g	62
NASHVILLE	Gary L Simmons	38	0	92,734	0	11	0	0	2,674	95,419
PEACE	Susan D Olsen	22	0	30,850	2,188	7	0	300	40	33,385
QUIMBY	Jerry Bukoski	16	0	20,008	8,146	0	0	0	0	28,154
OKEMOS	Jeanne E M Randels	170	468,826	0	17,608	320	0	4,153	0	490,907
PERRY	Nancy G Powers	24	0	49,552	663	1	155	100	0	50,471
SHAFTSBURG	Nancy G Powers	41	0	59,220	4,176	4	0	0	2,032	65,432
PORTLAND	Keith R Treman	184	175,978	84,579	3,367	298	0	545	11,502	276,269
POTTERVILLE	Linda K Stull-Lipps	89	0	147,187	2,093	16	0	3,746	1,095	154,137
ROBBINS	Mark R Payne	69	150,654	0	0	34	0	695	0	151,383
STOCKBRIDGE	Jeanne Laimon	24	54,483	0	0	0	0	0	0	54,483
SUNFIELD	Clare W Huyck	74	0	94,804	0	7	5,233	0	0	100,044
SYCAMORE CREEK	Thomas F Arthur	94	230,444	7,369	3,750	67	0	0	0	241,630
VERMONTVILLE	Gary L Simmons	34	0	35,462	0	40	2,308	1,591	4,104	43,505
GRESHAM	Bryce E Feighner	39	0	38,375	7,218	35	0	75	0	45,703
WACOUSTA	Amme Anne Paparella	46	124,381	8,321	4,265	0	0	1,722	0	138,689
WATERLOO VILLAGE	Edward C Ross	38	0	24,906	2,012	180	0	225	3,390	30,713
WATERLOO FIRST	Jeanne Laimon	15	0	8,314	0	0	0	0	2,868	11,182
WEBBERVILLE	Richard J Foster	69	89,908	32,651	0	425	6,818	11,885	4,058	145,745
WILLIAMSTON	Julie A Greyerbiehl	72	75,792	41,548	2,256	415	0	215	3,172	123,398
WILLIAMSTON CROSSROADS	Richard J Foster	50	0	78,271	1,800	6	0	150	5,560	85,787
WOODLAND	Gary L Simmons	24	0	38,510	2,030	17	0	1,500	0	42,057
WELCOME CORNERS	Susan D Olsen	26	0	32,004	3,182	0	0	578	4,534	40,298
LANSING DISTRICT	KENNETHA BIGHAM-TSAI	5,300	5,904,886	3,201,356	236,734	20,176	41,053	188,689	183,464	9,776,358
LAST YEAR		5,335	5,981,545	3,396,392	267,047	37,992	22,065	182,694	172,430	10,060,165
INC/(DEC)		(35)	(76,659)	(195,036)	(30,313)	(17,816)	18,988	5,995	11,034	(283,807)

STATISTICAL INFO

TABLE 3 2013 CHURCH INCOME	CAPITAL CAMPAIGNS & OTHER DESIGNATED PROJECTS					CONNECTIONAL & OTHER SOURCES			
	CAPITAL CAMPAIGNS & OTHER DESIGNATED PROJECTS	MEMORIALS, BEQUESTS, ENDOWMENTS	OTHER SOURCES & SUPPORT OF PROJECTS	SPECIAL OFFERINGS FOR MISSION	TOTAL 68.a TO 68.d	EQUITABLE COMPENSATION SUPPORT	ADVANCE SPECIALS RECEIVED	GRANTS FROM OTHER SOURCES	TOTAL 69.a TO 69.c
Church	63a	63b	63c	63d	63	64a	64b	64c	64
BATH	3,053	425	0	8,583	12,061	0	0	0	0
GUNNISONVILLE	10,921	1,395	0	8,794	21,110	0	0	0	0
WHEATFIELD	0	0	0	2,063	2,063	0	0	0	0
BROOKFIELD	0	0	0	0	0	0	0	0	0
CHARLOTTE LAWRENCE AVENUE	18,965	9,165	0	185	28,315	0	0	0	0
COUNTRY CHAPEL	22,450	2,330	0	1,258	26,038	0	0	0	0
DANSVILLE	0	125	0	810	935	0	0	0	0
DELTA MILLS	0	455	2,100	954	3,509	0	0	0	0
DEWITT REDEEMER	129,361	3,226	30,062	152,392	315,041	0	0	10,000	10,000
DIMONDALE	5,950	1,980	0	8,618	16,548	0	0	0	0
UNIVERSITY EAST LANSING	159,053	5,423	26,942	28,070	219,488	0	0	0	0
EATON RAPIDS FIRST	134,379	26,055	0	60,953	221,387	0	0	180,386	180,386
FREEPORT	0	25	840	7,060	7,925	0	0	440	440
GRAND LEDGE FIRST	0	13,844	0	26,994	40,838	0	0	0	0
GROVENBURG	0	355	0	122	477	0	0	0	0
HASTINGS FIRST	75,640	17,087	0	3,838	96,565	0	0	0	0
HASTINGS HOPE	0	0	0	141	141	0	0	0	0
HOLT	23,508	1,822	51,029	3,626	79,985	0	0	0	0
KALAMO	0	0	0	0	0	0	0	0	0
LAKE ODESSA CENTRAL	0	50,231	0	62,717	112,948	0	0	0	0
LAKE ODESSA LAKEWOOD	2,752	2,165	0	42,883	47,800	0	0	0	0
ASBURY LANSING	16,301	4,293	8,600	190	29,384	0	0	0	0
CENTRAL LANSING	0	6,853	21,846	5,421	34,120	0	0	0	0
CHRIST LANSING	0	9,988	5,000	10,776	25,764	0	12,000	0	12,000
FAITH/SOUTH LANSING MINISTRIES	0	5,828	0	0	5,828	0	42,656	0	42,656
FIRST LANSING	1,065	5,770	1,004	4,872	12,711	0	0	0	0
GRACE LANSING	0	596	0	18,074	18,670	1,200	0	0	1,200
KOREAN LANSING	0	0	0	0	0	0	1,140	0	1,140
MOUNT HOPE	0	16,078	0	92,413	108,491	0	0	0	0
TRINITY LANSING	359,940	0	0	0	359,940	0	0	0	0
LESLIE	1,805	0	0	1,955	3,760	0	0	0	0
FELT PLAINS	0	2,500	0	652	3,152	0	0	0	0
MASON FIRST	18,906	6,040	0	8,243	33,189	0	0	0	0
MILLVILLE	16,278	2,080	0	3,641	21,999	0	0	0	0
MUNITH	0	41,243	0	10,721	51,964	0	0	0	0
PLEASANT LAKE	0	85	0	602	687	0	0	0	0
MULLIKEN	1,916	0	0	3,006	4,922	0	0	0	0
SEBEWA CENTER	0	0	0	210	210	0	0	0	0

2013 TABLE 3 CHURCH INCOME	CAPITAL CAMPAIGNS & OTHER DESIGNATED PROJECTS					CONNECTIONAL & OTHER SOURCES			
	CAPITAL CAMPAIGNS & OTHER DESIGNATED PROJECTS	MEMORIALS, BEQUESTS, ENDOWMENTS	OTHER SOURCES & SUPPORT OF PROJECTS	SPECIAL OFFERINGS FOR MISSION	TOTAL 68.a TO 68.d	EQUITABLE COMPENSATION SUPPORT	ADVANCE SPECIALS RECEIVED	GRANTS FROM OTHER SOURCES	TOTAL 69.a TO 69.c
Church	63a	63b	63c	63d	63	64a	64b	64c	64
NASHVILLE	11,191	980	5,488	3,082	20,741	0	0	0	0
PEACE	0	0	1,749	2,404	4,153	0	0	0	0
QUIMBY	0	0	0	0	0	0	0	0	0
OKEMOS	37,373	9,829	0	0	47,202	0	0	0	0
PERRY	0	1,260	3,960	2,505	7,725	0	0	0	0
SHAFTSBURG	0	2,640	36,787	3,906	43,333	0	0	0	0
PORTLAND	25,938	1,315	0	0	27,253	0	0	0	0
POTTERVILLE	0	4,905	0	19,712	24,617	0	0	0	0
ROBBINS	6,555	2,405	14,466	6,862	30,288	0	0	0	0
STOCKBRIDGE	0	4,270	0	227	4,497	0	0	0	0
SUNFIELD	2,529	5,929	0	0	8,458	0	0	0	0
SYCAMORE CREEK	67,544	200	0	19,167	86,911	0	0	0	0
VERMONTVILLE	162	0	0	1,134	1,296	0	0	0	0
GRESHAM	0	5,086	0	598	5,684	0	0	0	0
WACOUSTA	4,570	1,295	3,620	9,052	18,537	0	0	0	0
WATERLOO VILLAGE	0	6,000	2,368	193	8,561	0	0	0	0
WATERLOO FIRST	0	0	0	0	0	0	0	0	0
WEBBERVILLE	33,202	1,100	11,399	2,707	48,408	0	0	0	0
WILLIAMSTON	10,571	60	0	4,776	15,407	0	6,250	3,750	10,000
WILLIAMSTON CROSSROADS	0	1,000	3,500	1,000	5,500	0	0	0	0
WOODLAND	660	0	0	656	1,316	0	0	0	0
WELCOME CORNERS	0	325	0	6,336	6,661	0	0	0	0
LANSING DISTRICT	1,202,538	286,061	230,760	665,154	2,384,513	1,200	62,046	194,576	257,822
LAST YEAR	815,254	372,775	305,939	567,366	2,061,334	0	73,322	169,160	242,482
INC/(DEC)	387,284	(86,714)	(75,179)	97,788	323,179	1,200	(11,276)	25,416	15,340

STATISTICAL INFO

2013 TABLE 3 CHURCH INCOME

		RECEIPTS FOR CHURCH ANNUAL BUDGET									
		NUMBER OF HOUSEHOLD GIVING TO CHURCH	RECEIVED FROM PLEDGES	RECEIVED FROM IDENTIFIED NON-PLEDGES	RECEIVED FROM UNIDENTIFED GIVERS	INTEREST & DIVIDENDS	PROCEEDS FROM SALE OF CHURCH ASSETS	RECEIPTS FROM BLDG USE, FEES, RENTALS	FUNDRAISERS & OTHER SOURCES	**TOTAL INCOME FOR ANNUAL BUDGETMINISTRY SHARES BASE (LINES 62a to 62g)**	CAPITAL CAMPAIGNS & OTHER DESIGNATED PROJECTS
Church	Pastor	61	62a	62b	62c	62d	62e	62f	62g	62	63a
ALBION	TAMARA WILLIAMS	4,338	3,836,887	2,684,958	176,648	19,307	21,311	110,696	171,097	7,020,965	409,316
CENTRAL	DAVID HILLS	4,892	2,377,362	3,425,384	339,627	21,781	33,552	76,031	123,212	6,396,948	419,523
GRAND RAPIDS	WILLIAM HAGGARD	8,675	8,125,069	6,192,067	364,733	115,371	81,651	146,002	279,180	15,376,688	2,949,207
GRAND TRAVERSE	ANITA HAHN	4,881	3,266,171	3,359,793	423,177	29,030	33,915	120,141	287,749	7,519,977	661,629
KALAMAZOO	CORNELIUS DAVIS	5,702	5,050,974	3,539,193	302,589	31,997	4,080	189,426	289,417	9,407,675	980,194
LANSING	KENNETHA BIGHAM-TSAI	5,300	5,904,886	3,201,356	236,734	20,176	41,053	188,689	183,464	9,776,358	1,202,538
CONFERENCE	DEBORAH L. KIESEY	33,788	28,561,349	22,402,750	1,843,506	237,663	215,562	830,985	1,334,119	55,498,611	6,622,407
LAST YEAR		32,427	30,524,720	20,418,499	2,219,529	229,846	76,159	924,350	994,487	54,860,712	5,303,534
INCREASE(DECREASE)		1,361	(1,963,371)	1,984,251	(376,023)	7,817	139,403	(93,365)	339,632	637,899	1,318,873

TABLE 3 2013 CHURCH INCOME

	CAPITAL CAMPAIGNS & OTHER DESIGNATED PROJECTS				CONNECTIONAL & OTHER SOURCES			
	MEMORIALS, BEQUESTS, ENDOWMENTS	OTHER SOURCES & SUPPORT OF PROJECTS	SPECIAL OFFERINGS FOR MISSION	TOTAL 68.a TO 68.d	EQUITABLE COMPENSATION SUPPORT	ADVANCE SPECIALS RECEIVED	GRANTS FROM OTHER SOURCES	TOTAL 69.a TO 69.c
Church	63b	63c	63d	63	64a	64b	64c	64
ALBION	1,861,691	226,370	382,385	2,879,762	13,404	18,554	17,923	49,881
CENTRAL	299,298	153,740	404,234	1,276,795	3,395	7,311	3,208	13,914
GRAND RAPIDS	1,045,900	391,513	463,839	4,850,459	31,900	55,087	250,171	337,158
GRAND TRAVERSE	264,496	292,830	391,693	1,610,648	57,888	49,858	4,200	111,946
KALAMAZOO	311,452	407,826	406,645	2,106,117	19,380	18,799	146,455	184,634
LANSING	286,061	230,760	665,154	2,384,513	1,200	62,046	194,576	257,822
CONFERENCE	4,068,898	1,703,039	2,713,950	15,108,294	127,167	211,655	616,533	955,355
LAST YEAR	2,306,387	1,495,323	2,729,879	11,835,123	168,030	234,912	309,583	712,525
INCREASE(DECREASE)	1,762,511	207,716	(15,929)	3,273,171	(40,863)	(23,257)	306,950	242,830

STATISTICAL INFO

XXIV. ORDINAND PHOTOS

Ordained Provisional Elders

Dennis B. Bromley

John J. Conklin

Stephen Lindeman

Heather Ann Molner

James C. Noggle

Chad M. Parmalee

Ordained Deacon

Patricia L. Catellier

Ordained Elders in Full Connection

Letisha M. Bowman

Cathy M. Christman

Patricia Ann Haas

Jonathan D, Van Dop

Rebecca L. Wieringa

ROADS TO CAMPSITES

It is the policy of the camping programs of the West Michigan Conference of the United Methodist Church to include and welcome persons of all races, economic levels and ethnic backgrounds.

ABOUT OUR CAMPS:

1. Albright, located just outside of Reed City, has a variety of options for accomodations. There are swimming, trails, and many other activity areas.

2. Crystal Springs, located just south of Dowagiac, offers cabin style accomodations. There is swimming available in the pool and a new dining hall to serve the campers.

3. Lake Michigan, located on the shore of Lake Michigan just south of Pentwater, takes in sand dunes, woods, water and trails.

4. Lake Louise is located north of Gaylord and is situated on the shore of beautiful Lake Louise. Camping here is in rustic cabins.

5. Lakeview, located midway between Six Lakes and Lakeview, is situated on Townline Lake. Trails and shore front facilities provide many options for activities.

6. Wesley Woods, located north of Battle Creek, provides beautiful lakeside enjoyment. Campers stay in cabins equipped with bunks. Swimming in the pool, games, and waterfront activities provide recreation for all.

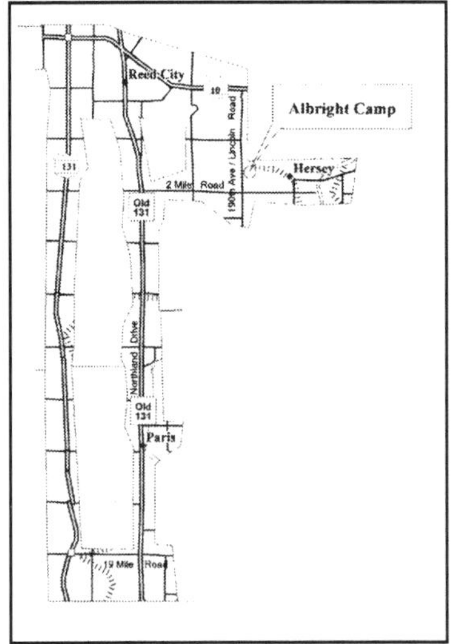

◄ Albright Camp

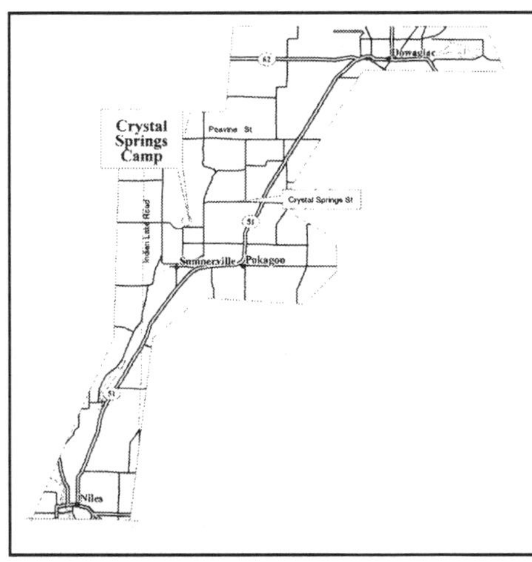

Crystal Springs Camp ►

MAPS

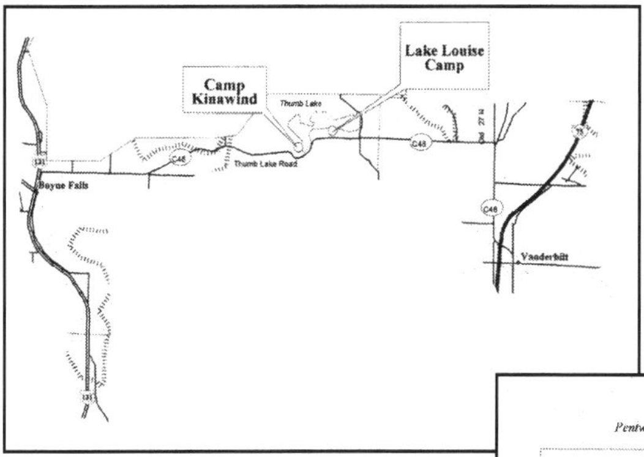

◄ Lake Louise Camp

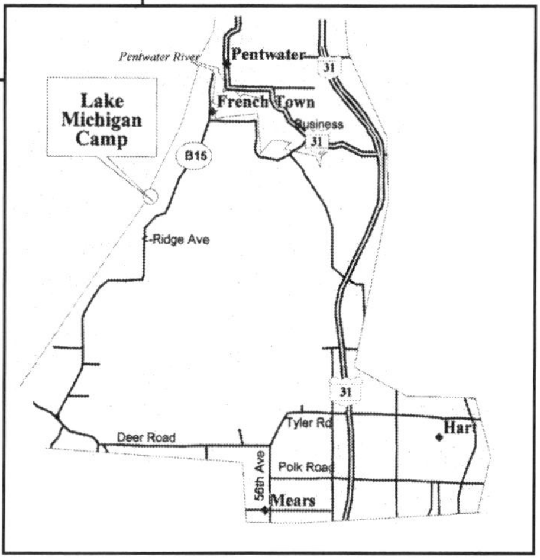

Lake Michigan Camp ►

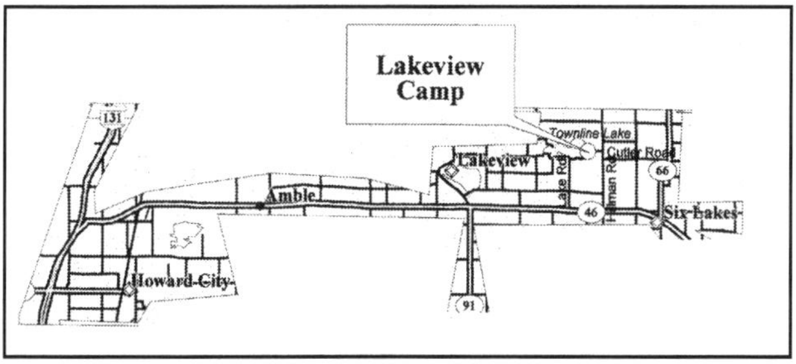

◄ Lakeview Camp

MAPS

Wesley Woods Camp ►

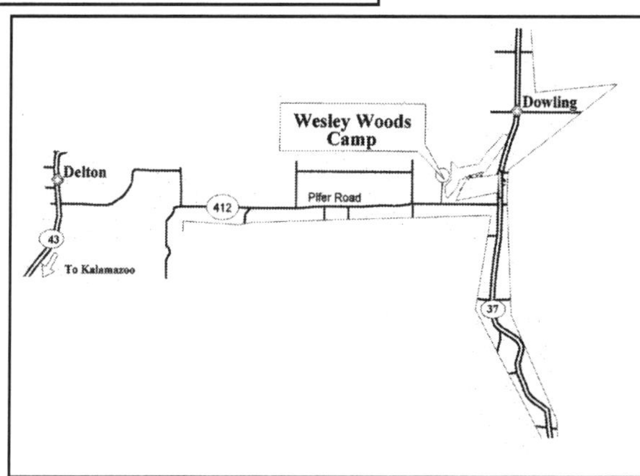

ALBION DISTRICT

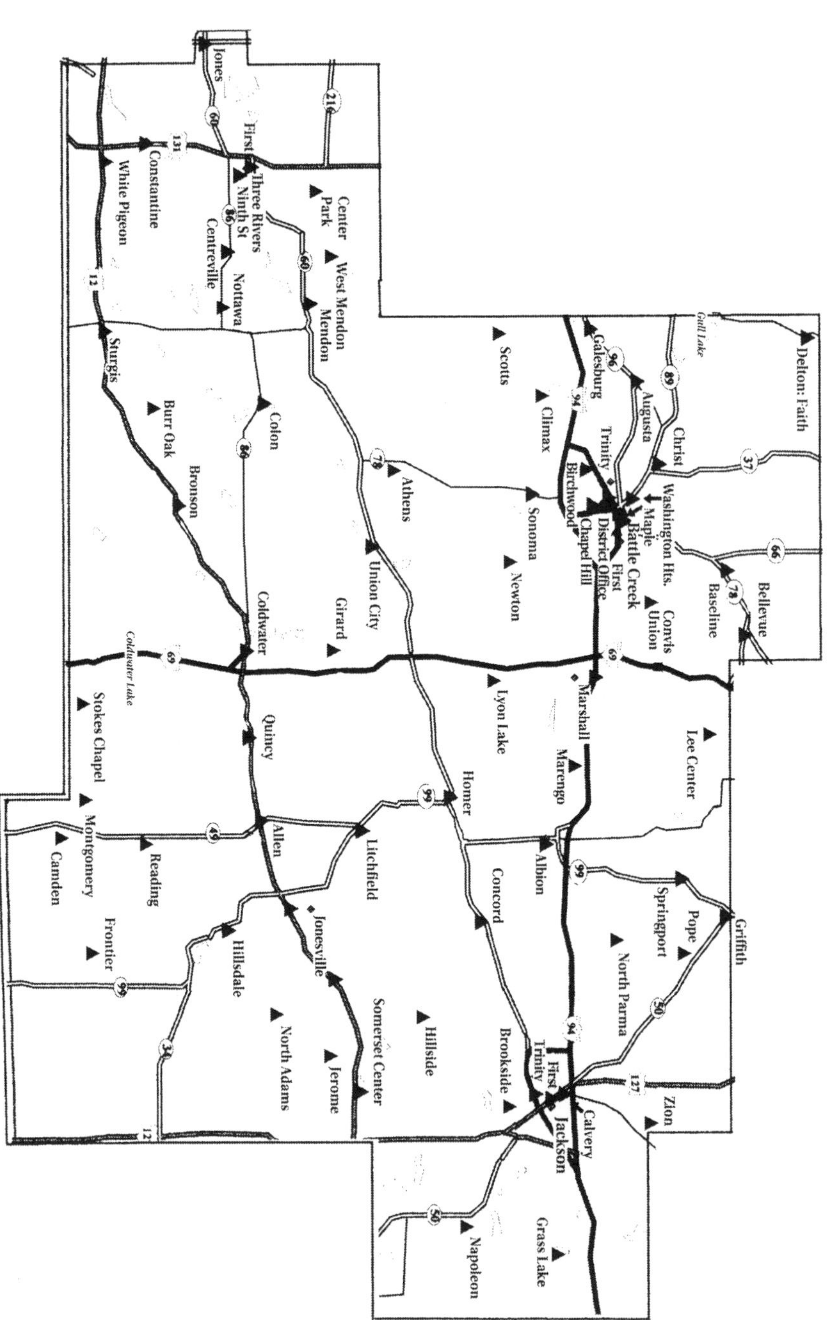

MAPS

HEARTLAND DISTRICT

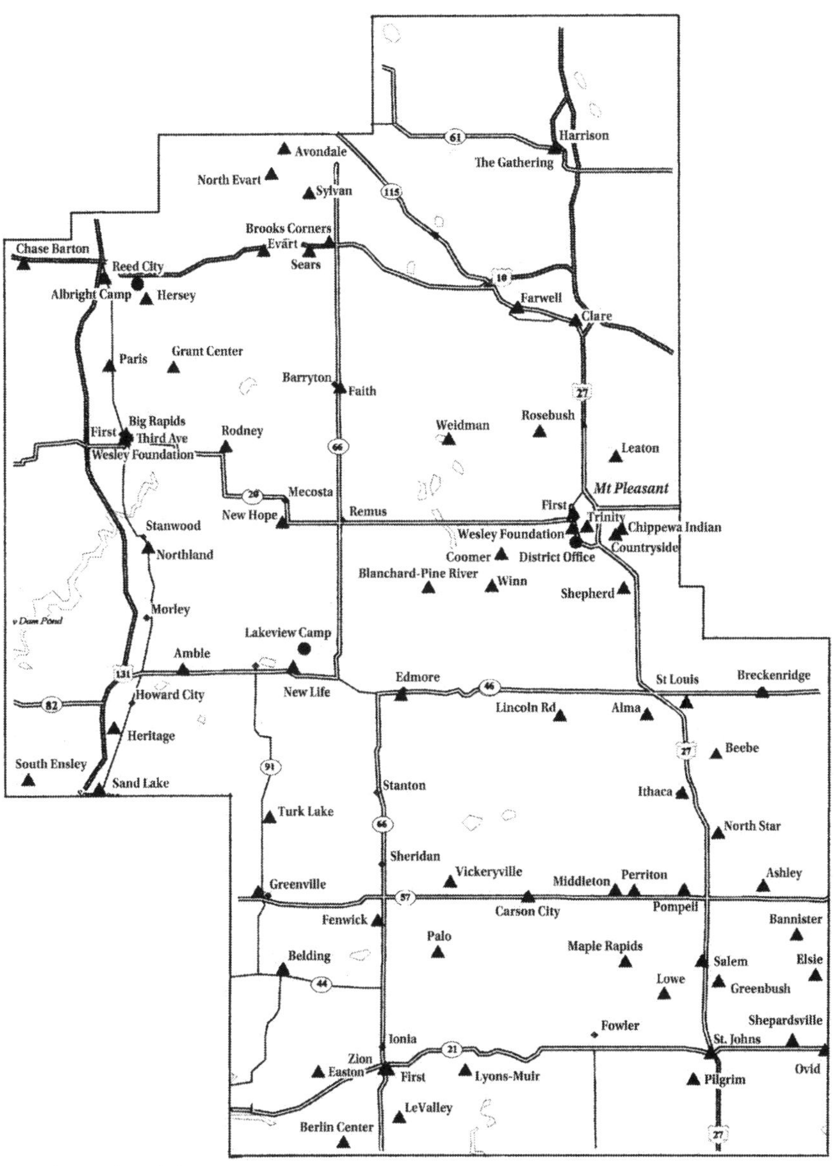

GRAND RAPIDS DISTRICT

GRAND RAPIDS URBAN DETAILS

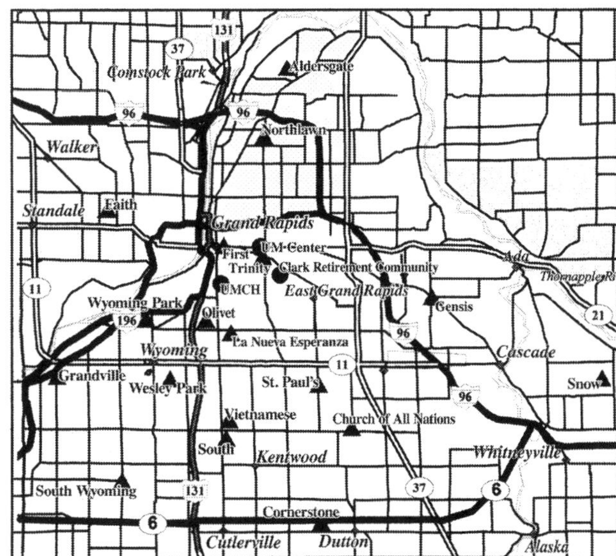

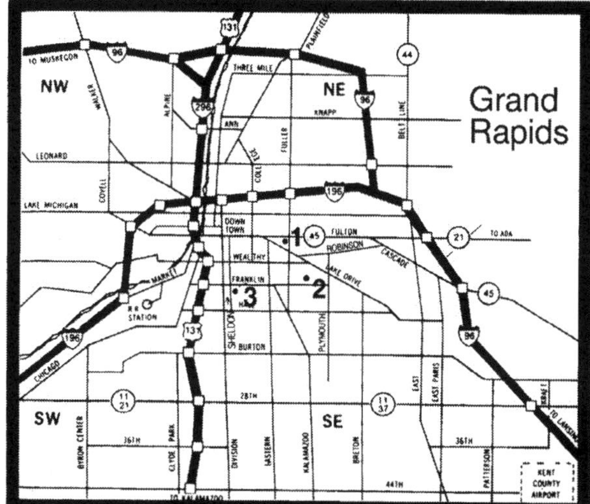

1 WEST MICHIGAN CONFERENCE CENTER, 11 Fuller Avenue, SE, Grand Rapids, MI 49506 (616) 459-4503

From North or South—Take 131 to I-196 east to Fuller Avenue exit; turn right (south) onto Fuller; go one block past Fulton. The Center is on the corner of Baldwin and Fuller.

From East—Take I-96 to Cascade Road West exit; Cascade merges with Fulton; take Fulton to Fuller; turn left onto Fuller and go one block south, to the corner of Fuller and Baldwin.

From West—Take I-196 east to Fuller Avenue exit; turn right (south) onto Fuller; go one block past Fulton. The Center is on the corner of Baldwim and Fuller.

2 CLARK RETIREMENT COMMUNITY, 1551 Franklin Se, Grand Rapids, MI 49506-331 (616) 452-1568 From North or South—Take 131 to I-196 east to Fuller Avenue exit; go south on Fuller to Franklin Street; turn left.

From East—Take I-96 to Cascade Road West exit; take Cascade Rd. west to Robinson Rd.; turn left and take Robinson Rd. to Plymouth; turn left and take Plymouth to Franklin; turn right.

From West—Take I-196 east to Fuller Avenue exit; go south on Fuller to Franklin Street; turn left.

3 UNITED METHODIST COMMUNITY HOUSE, 904 Sheldon SE, Grand Rapids, MI 49507 (616) 452-3226 From North or Soount—Take 131 to Hall Street exit; go east on Hall to Sheldon (a one way street going north).

From East or West—Take I-196 to 131; go south on 131 to Hall Street exit; go east on Hall to Sheldon (a one way street going north).

GRAND TRAVERSE DISTRICT – NORTH

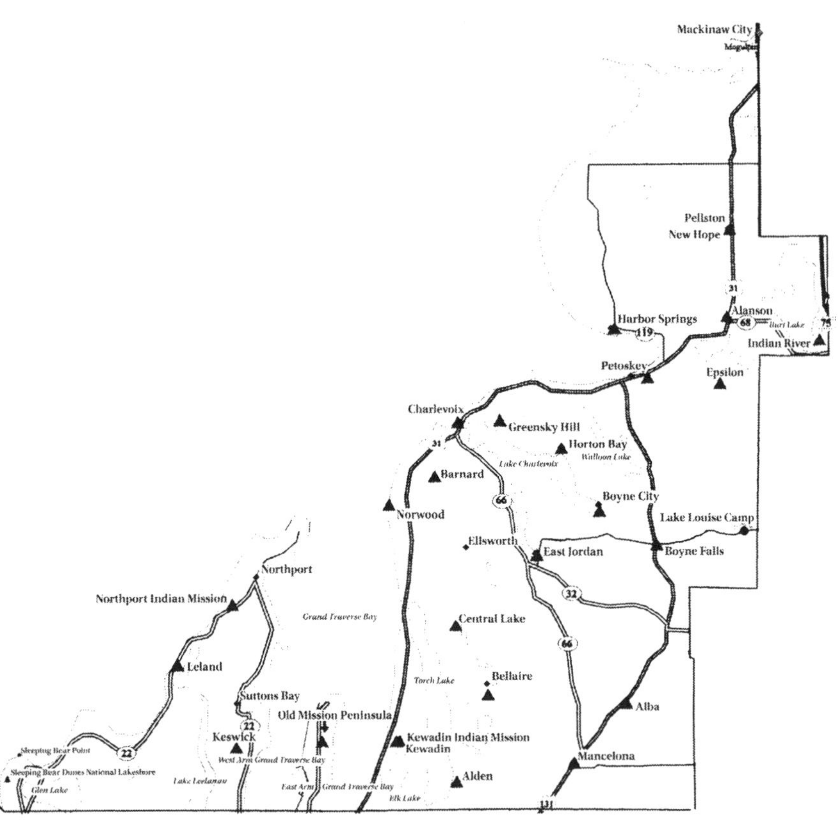

MAPS

GRAND TRAVERSE DISTRICT – SOUTH

KALAMAZOO DISTRICT

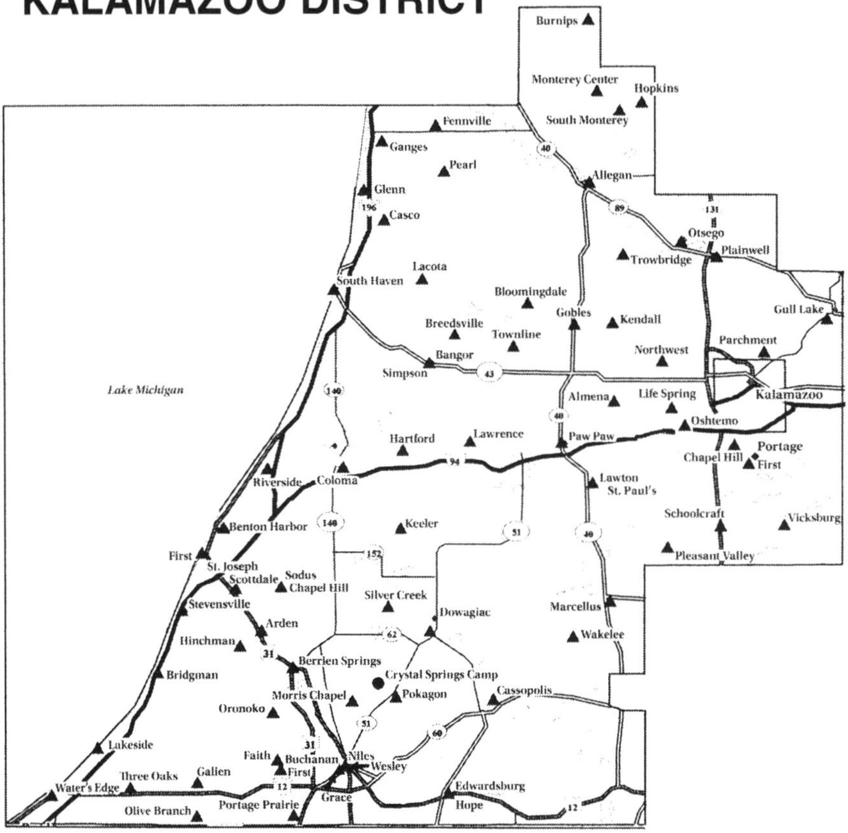

KALAMAZOO CITY DETAIL

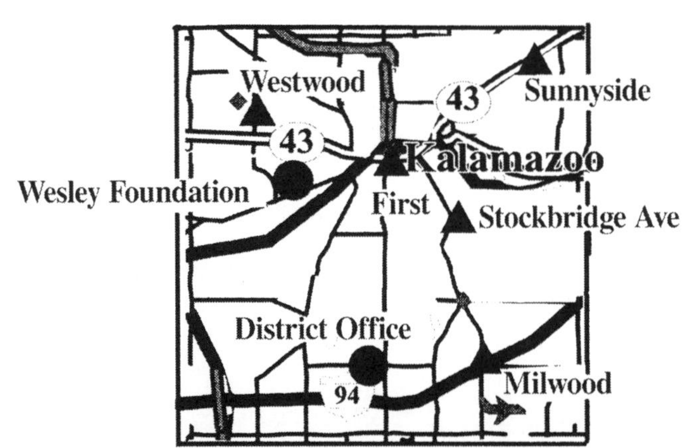

MAPS

LANSING DISTRICT

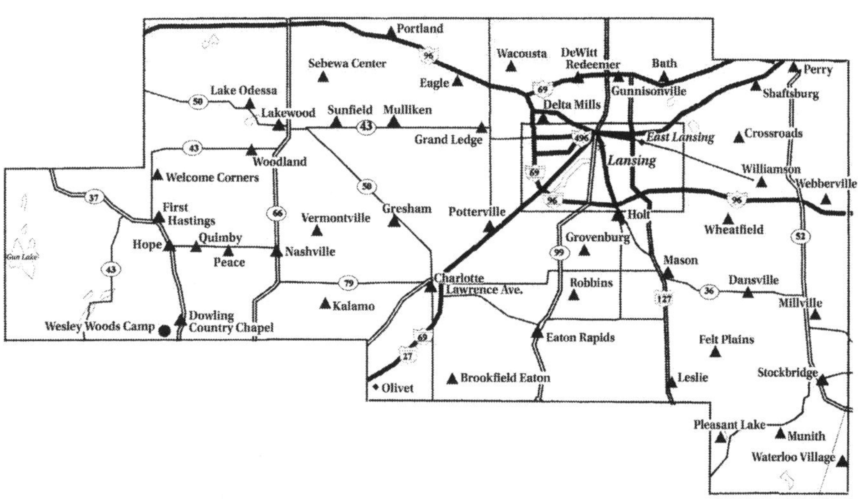

LANSING AREA DETAIL

XXVI. INDEX

A

B

INDEX

C

D

E

F

G

H

I

J

K

L

M

N

O

P

R

S

T

U

W

Y

Made in the USA
Charleston, SC
25 November 2014